Essays in Transportation Economics and Policy

Essays in Transportation Economics and Policy

A Handbook in Honor of John R. Meyer

José A. Gómez-Ibáñez
William B. Tye
Clifford Winston
Editors

BROOKINGS INSTITUTION PRESS
Washington, D.C.

Copyright © 1999
THE BROOKINGS INSTITUTION
1775 Massachusetts Avenue, N.W., Washington, D.C. 20036

All rights reserved

Library of Congress Cataloging-in-Publication data

Essays in transportation economics and policy : a handbook in honor of John R. Meyer / edited by José A. Gómez-Ibáñez, William B. Tye, and Clifford Winston.
    p. cm.
    Includes bibliographical references and index.
    ISBN 0-8157-3182-5 (acid-free paper)
    ISBN 0-8157-3181-7 (pbk. : acid-free paper)
    1. Transportation and state. 2. Transportation. 3. Meyer, John Robert. I. Meyer, John Robert. II. Gómez-Ibáñez, José A., 1948– III. Tye, W. B. (William B.) IV. Winston, Clifford, 1952–
    HE193 .E85   1998
    388—dc21   98-40260
                                                       CIP

9 8 7 6 5 4 3 2 1

The paper used in this publication meets minimum requirements of the American National Standard for Information Sciences—Permanence of Paper for Printed Library Materials: ANSI Z39.48-1984.

Editing by Martha V. Gottron

Research verification by Jennifer Eichberger

Typeset in Adobe Garamond

Composition by Cynthia Stock, Silver Spring, Maryland

Printed by R.R. Donnelly & Sons, Harrisonburg, Virginia

Contents

JOSÉ A. GÓMEZ-IBÁÑEZ
WILLIAM B. TYE
CLIFFORD WINSTON

1 The Legacy of John R. Meyer

This volume honors John R. Meyer, who transformed and led the field of transportation economics and policy from the 1950s through the 1990s. He enriched the field with new methods and ideas. Before John Meyer, scholarship in transportation policy was dominated by the analysis of institutions, legal constraints, and history. Meyer helped to introduce modern microeconomic analysis and statistical methods to the subject and thereby clarified many long-standing policy debates. But he also understood the importance of the traditional perspectives and incorporated them into his more modern approach. The result was studies that integrated the latest in statistical and economic techniques with a deep appreciation of institutions and politics. It is thus not surprising that his studies often changed the way policymakers and economists thought about problems, and his conclusions about and recommendations for changes in public policy were frequently adopted and stood the test of time.

John Meyer also changed the field by training several generations of transportation researchers and practitioners. He served as the mentor to many doctoral students and junior faculty during his tenures as a professor in Harvard's Department of Economics (1955–68), Yale's Department of Economics (1968–73), the Harvard Business School (1973–83), and Harvard's Kennedy School of Government (since 1983) and as president

1

of the National Bureau of Economic Research (1967–77). He was extraordinarily generous to his students and colleagues, both in offering them the opportunity to work with him and in promoting their research throughout their careers. His collaborative style is reflected in the fact that all of his twenty-one books are coauthored, usually with junior faculty and current or former students. He would gather around him a team of faculty and doctoral students to work on each book, but he inevitably did more than his share, generating the intellectual framework and key insights and drafting and redrafting the manuscript. By example and direction, he taught dozens of young scholars how to do research and set a standard of generosity in giving credit and coauthorship to his collaborators.

The practical value of Meyer's ideas are reflected in the fact that many public agencies and private companies sought him out as an advisor or board member. For example in the railroads, arguably Meyer's first love among transportation industries, he served as economic advisor to the senior management of the Canadian Pacific (1974–81); as a member of the board of directors of Conrail, the government corporation created to take over the bankrupt Penn Central Railroad (1976–78); and as vice chairman (1981–83) and board member (since 1978) of the Union Pacific. He also served on the boards of other large corporations and as advisor to the United States Department of Transportation, the World Bank, and other institutions.

John Meyer's Scholarship

John Meyer began his academic career in the 1950s when modern statistical techniques were just beginning to be applied to economic issues, and several of his earliest books were pioneering applications of statistics to problems outside transportation. In two influential books Meyer and his coauthors examined the determinants of business investment decisions and the business cycle, and in a third they made some of the first applications of modern econometric techniques to history, including an analysis of the economics of slavery before the U.S. Civil War.[1]

Meyer established his reputation in transportation with two books that transformed the study of intercity and urban transportation. In *The Economics of Competition in the Transportation Industries*, published in 1959, he and his coauthors advanced the then-radical proposition that many of

1. Meyer and Kuh (1957); Meyer and Glauber (1964); Conrad and Meyer (1964).

the problems in the intercity freight and passenger systems could be traced to an excess of government regulation. To see what might happen if government controls over prices and entry to these industries were relaxed, they applied modern statistical costing techniques to railroads, trucking, airlines, and other modes to determine the most economical mode of transport for different types of trips. This exercise suggested, among other things, that the railroads should be carrying more freight and fewer passengers than they were and that "piggy-back" service with truck trailers on railroad flatcars had great potential. Meyer and his coauthors also used modern industrial organization theory to analyze the potential for sustaining competition in various transportation industries. Their conclusion—that there was much to gain and little to fear from relaxing regulation in many sectors of transportation—would establish an agenda for a generation of scholars and ultimately help lead to the deregulation of the airline, railroad, and trucking industries in the late 1970s and early 1980s.

The Urban Transportation Problem, published in 1965, appeared when rapid suburban growth, central city decline, and increasing highway congestion were becoming topics of national concern. Many policymakers and opinion leaders were proposing some form of reinvigorated public transportation as the solution. Meyer and his coauthors examined this question systematically by looking first at the trends in land use and travel patterns and then at the comparative costs of different modes—auto, bus, and rail transit—in serving different types of urban commuting corridors. Their analysis quantified the extent to which businesses and residences were suburbanizing and the implications for traffic flows. In a pathbreaking chapter, they showed how racial discrimination in housing markets caused longer trips for minority households than for white households and how minority households were unlikely to be well served by suburban extensions of rail transit systems. The cost analysis showed that autos or buses were cheaper than rail transit in the lower-density travel corridors that were becoming more common with suburbanization. They concluded that eliminating subsidies to all types of travelers—motorists as well as public transit—would be better than to engage in a system of countervailing subsidies. Many of the dangers they warned of would be confirmed by subsequent experience and research.

John Meyer's influence in the training of transportation economists and professionals was strengthened in 1971, with the publication of a two-volume series on *Techniques of Transport Planning*. The first volume summarized succinctly the state of the art in costing, pricing, and demand forecasting for transportation and immediately became the standard text for doctoral students in the field. The second volume described an innovative effort to marry travel demand forecasting models and regional economic models to design an optimal transportation investment program for the country of Colombia.

In the subsequent decades, Meyer, his students, and his colleagues would continue to work on the themes of regulation, the comparative advantages of different modes, and the relationships among transportation, land use, and economic development. Their analyses evolved as new concerns were brought to the fore and research methods improved. Meyer still dominated the field in that none could match the depth of his insights, the breadth of his experience, or his energy for research. But increasingly transportation policy and economics attracted other strong scholars, some trained by Meyer and others drawn to the field by the intellectual excitement that he had created.

In urban transportation, Meyer's research agenda broadened as concerns about air pollution, safety, and energy conservation emerged or intensified in the 1970s. After Congress passed the landmark Clean Air Act of 1970, John Meyer was asked to chair a committee of the National Academy of Sciences to see whether the law's stringent and controversial automobile emissions standards were sensible. The committee was staffed in part by Meyer's doctoral students and colleagues, and its report, released in 1974, confirmed that tailpipe emissions standards were more cost-effective than other methods of reducing automobile pollution. It also suggested that the standards might be refined in various ways.[2] In 1981 Meyer drew together this and other research he and his colleagues had been doing to publish *Autos, Transit, and Cities*, an updated examination of the role of the automobile and public transportation in cities that became another standard text in graduate transportation courses.

As the situation in the U.S. railroad industry deteriorated sharply in the early 1970s, the Council of Economic Advisers asked Meyer to prepare a detailed assessment of the industry's condition and prospects. That report, completed in 1973, documented the desperate financial condition of the industry and the degree to which regulatory constraints, low labor productivity, and shortsighted management were handicapping its recovery.[3] Soon afterward Meyer began to serve on the boards of major railroads,

2. National Academy of Sciences (1974).
3. Task Force on Railroad Productivity (1973).

which constrained his freedom to write on railroad topics. But his report was influential in shaping the deregulation legislation of 1974 and 1980, and its recommendations for effective railroad strategies proved remarkably prescient during the industry's turnaround in the 1980s.

When the U.S. airline industry was deregulated in 1978, Meyer assembled one of his usual teams to analyze the consequences. Their first book, *Airline Deregulation: The Early Experience,* published in 1981, provided some of the first empirical evidence of the effects of deregulation on airline fares, service, and profits. A second, *Deregulation and the New Airline Entrepreneurs,* published in 1984, examined the competitive strategies of the new entrants and the incumbent airlines and speculated that competition could be maintained, although not at the intense levels of the early years. In a third volume, *Deregulation and the Future of Intercity Passenger Travel,* published in 1987, Meyer and his colleagues summarized their largely favorable conclusions about airline deregulation but also stepped back to analyze the costs and demand for the different intercity modes and speculate about their futures. They concluded that air and auto would continue to dominate the intercity passenger market in the United States, notwithstanding emerging new rail technologies such as the high-speed trains of France and Japan.

John Meyer had long worked abroad, particularly in developing countries as an advisor to the World Bank and others. When the developing world and the former communist countries began to increase the role of markets and reduce the role of government in providing transportation services in the late 1980s, Meyer was called on to advise and analyze the developments. In 1993 he and a colleague published *Going Private: The International Experience with Transport Privatization,* which examined the experiences of the developing countries, the United States, and Europe with the private provision of urban public transport, high performance highways, and airports and drew conclusions about the circumstances in which privatization would be both economically advantageous and politically acceptable. After advising the European Bank for Reconstruction and Development and the World Bank on restructuring the transport systems in the former Soviet Union and China, respectively, Meyer and a colleague summarized their thinking in 1996 in *Moving to Market: Restructuring Transport in the Former Soviet Union.*

In sum, John Meyer produced a prodigious body of scholarship, starting with the seminal books on intercity and urban transportation and continuing for nearly the next forty years to cover virtually every major development in transportation policy. This accomplishment is even more impressive in that he also continued to contribute to other fields, such as urban and regional economics, telecommunications policy, and corporate governance.[4]

The Plan of the Volume

This book is intended to serve as an introduction to transportation economics and policy for graduate students, advanced undergraduates, and other professionals interested in the field. It is designed to provide an updated version of John Meyer's classic *Techniques of Transport Planning* but with added emphasis on policy developments and analysis. The essays were first presented in draft form at a conference held at Harvard University on September 5 and 6, 1997, that was organized by Meyer's students, colleagues, and friends to mark his assumption of emeritus status in the University. The conference was supported generously by the Union Pacific Corporation and by Harvard University.

The book has four main sections. The first covers the basic analytic methods used in transportation economics and policy analysis: demand (chapter 2), costing (chapter 3), pricing (chapter 4), and project evaluation (chapter 5). The presentation assumes prior exposure to elementary microeconomics and statistics. An understanding of calculus is helpful but not essential.

The second section focuses on the automobile, as both the mainstay of the American transportation system and the source of some of its most serious difficulties. It begins with an examination of traffic congestion and possible remedies (chapter 6) and continues with analyses of progress in reducing air pollution (chapter 7) and energy consumption (chapter 8). It concludes with an assessment of the possibilities and limitations of policies to force improvements in automotive technology (chapter 9) and a discussion of the trends and prospects for auto ownership and road provision in developing countries (chapter 10).

Section three covers key issues in urban transportation: the past and future prospects for urban public transportation (chapter 11), the relation-

---

4. For example, in the closely related field of urban and regional economics see Kain and Meyer (1971), Kraft, Meyer, and Valette (1971), and Meyer and Quigley (1977); in telecommunications see Meyer and others (1980); in corporate governance see Farrar and Mayer (1970), Bos, Bergson, and Meyer (1984), and Meyer and Gustafson (1988).

ship between transportation and land use (chapter 12), and the effects of transportation accessibility on the employment of the poor (chapter 13). The final section concerns regulation and deregulation. It opens with an analysis of the effects deregulation has had on the U.S. airline, railroad, and trucking industries (chapter 14). This is followed by a more detailed discussion of how the railroad industry revived during the 1980s (chapter 15). The section concludes with an examination of the regulation of common carrier safety (chapter 16).

References: Books by John R. Meyer

Bos, Dieter, Abram Bergson, and John R. Meyer, eds. 1984. *Entrepreneurship: The Bonn-Harvard Schumpeter Centennial.* New York: Springer-Verlag.

Conrad, Alfred H., and John R. Meyer. 1964. *The Economics of Slavery and Other Studies in Econometric History.* Chicago: Aldine Publishing.

Farrar, Donald, and John R. Meyer. 1970. *Managerial Economics.* Prentice-Hall.

Gómez-Ibáñez, José A., and John R. Meyer. 1993. *Going Private: The International Experience with Transport Privatization.* Brookings.

Kain, John F., and John R. Meyer, eds. 1971. *Essays in Regional Economics.* Harvard University Press.

Kraft, Gerald, John R. Meyer, and Jean-Paul Valette. 1971. *The Role of Transportation in Regional Economic Development; A Charles River Associates Research Study.* Lexington, Mass: Heath-Lexington Books.

Meyer, John R., Robert W. Wilson, M. Alan Baughcum, Ellen Burton, and Louis Caouette. 1980. *The Economics of Competition in the Telecommunications Industries.* Cambridge, Mass: Oelgeschlager, Gunn and Hain.

Meyer, John R., and Robert R. Glauber. 1964. *Investment Decisions, Economic Forecasting and Public Policy.* Boston: Division of Research, Graduate School of Business Administration, Harvard University.

Meyer, John R., and James M. Gustafson, eds. 1988. *The U.S. Business Corporation: An Institution in Transition.* Ballinger.

Meyer, John R., and José A. Gómez-Ibáñez. 1981. *Autos, Transit, and Cities.* Harvard University Press.

Meyer, John R., John F. Kain, and Martin Wohl. 1965. *The Urban Transportation Problem.* Harvard University Press.

Meyer, John R., and Edwin Kuh. 1957. *The Investment Decision: An Empirical Study.* Harvard University Press.

Meyer, John R., and Clinton V. Oster, Jr., with Ivor P. Morgan, Benjamin A. Berman, and Diana Strassman. 1981. *Airline Deregulation: The Early Experience.* Boston: Auburn House.

Meyer, John R., and Clinton V. Oster, Jr., with Marni Clippinger, Andrew McKay, Don H. Pickrell, John S. Strong, and C. Kurt Zorn. 1984. *Deregulation and the New Airline Entrepreneurs.* MIT Press.

Meyer, John R., and Clinton V. Oster, Jr., with John S. Strong, José A. Gómez-Ibáñez, Don

H. Pickrell, Marni Clippinger, and Ivor P. Morgan. 1987. *Deregulation and the Future of Intercity Passenger Travel.* MIT Press.

Meyer, John R., Merton J. Peck, John R. Stenason, and Charles Zwick. 1959. *The Economics of Competition in the Transportation Industries.* Harvard University Press.

Meyer, John R., and John M. Quigley, eds, with contributions by Christopher H. Gadsden and others. 1977. *Local Public Finance and the Fiscal Squeeze: A Case Study.* Ballinger.

Meyer, John R., ed. 1971. *Techniques of Transport Planning.* Vol 1: John R. Meyer and Mahlon R. Straszheim, *Pricing and Project Evaluation.* Vol 2: David T. Kresge and Paul O. Roberts, *Systems Analysis and Simulation Models.* Brookings, Transport Research Program.

National Academy of Sciences. 1974. *Committee on the Costs and Benefits of Automobile Emission Control: Final Report.* National Academy Press.

Strong, John S., and John R. Meyer, with Clell G. Harral and Graham Smith. 1996. *Moving to Market: Restructuring Transport in the Former Soviet Union.* Harvard Institute of International Development. Harvard University Press.

Task Force on Railroad Productivity (John R. Meyer, chairman). 1973. *Improving Railroad Productivity: Final Report of the Task Force on Railroad Productivity.* Report to the Council of Economic Advisors and the National Commission on Productivity. Washington, D.C.

PART I

Techniques of Transportation Analysis

KENNETH A. SMALL
CLIFFORD WINSTON

2

The Demand for Transportation: Models and Applications

A distinguishing feature of transportation is that it is valued primarily as an input to many other activities. Firms ship products to distribution centers and retail outlets; businesses send their employees to meet with customers, suppliers, regulators, and coworkers; ordinary people travel to work and for leisure pursuits. Because of the variety of functions that transportation facilitates, researchers have developed a wide assortment of models to analyze transportation users' behavior.

These transportation demand models must account for the special features of transportation markets. First, transportation encompasses many interrelated decisions such as mode, destination, shipment characteristics, vehicle ownership, and residential and industrial location. The models must therefore account for the mutual effects of these decisions upon each other and for their differing time horizons. Second, transportation consists of a large number of distinct services differentiated by location and time. Understanding the spatial and temporal details of these transportation decisions is essential for facility planning and management.

The authors are grateful to David Brownstone, Charles Lave, Fred Mannering, and Kenneth Train for helpful comments.

A third feature is that travelers and shippers are sensitive to service quality. Thus demand models must incorporate quality indicators, some of which—travel time, service frequency, and route coverage, for example—are readily measurable, whereas others—comfort, crowding, reliability—are somewhat amorphous. The models must also control for demographic or socioeconomic factors because users differ in the values they place on the quality attributes. And because service quality often depends upon usage in congested or crowded conditions, the relationship between travel environment and transportation decisions is two-way and requires iterative calculations between demand models and facility performance models.

This chapter describes how transportation demand is analyzed and what has been learned from doing so. We first present a selection of the most important transportation demand models, with an emphasis on disaggregate models because they have generally been the most successful in capturing essential features of travel behavior.[1] We then show how the models have enriched the substantive knowledge of the demand for transportation and discuss how they have been used to address important transportation policy issues.

The traditional modeling structure for transportation demand distinguishes four decisions: how often to travel, to what destination, what mode of transportation to use, and what route to take. These decisions apply to both passenger and freight transportation and are known as trip generation, trip distribution, mode choice, and trip assignment.[2] More recent work has taken up several collateral decisions such as vehicle ownership and time of day of travel. Land use decisions, which interact with transportation decisions in a two-way causality, are dealt with in chapter 12.

Trip generation and distribution are closely related to land use and have received more attention from other disciplines than from economics.[3] For example, models from regional science project the trip-making potential from various types of land uses such as housing, shopping centers, or office buildings. Models of trip distribution typically use the travel distance or time between locations to convert these total trips into a set of origin-destination flows. The analysis of route choice relies heavily upon computerized networks and is often highly mathematical; usually it makes relatively simple assumptions about the economic forces behind travel

1. Other surveys of transportation demand models may be found in Oum, Waters, and Yong (1992); Small (1992); and Ortúzar and Willumsen (1994).
2. For clear expositions, see Meyer and Straszheim (1971: ch. 7) or Beesley and Kemp (1987).
3. See Ortúzar and Willumsen (1994: ch. 4–5) for a good review.

choices, while using a sophisticated framework of uncertainty, random influences, and dynamic considerations.[4]

Economists have primarily, though not exclusively, focused on mode choice. Mode choice is particularly sensitive to economic variables, and economic techniques are appropriate for illuminating its basic and subtle determinants. We therefore give mode choice the lion's share of attention in this chapter, but as we show, the techniques developed to analyze mode choice are broadly applicable to other travel behavior.

Aggregate Demand Models

Aggregate models rely on data describing the behavior of large groups of travelers or shippers. The most satisfactory ones have been based on standard microeconomic demand theory, which assumes that travelers maximize utility and that firms minimize costs.[5] The best models use flexible functional forms and impose the parametric restrictions implied by economic theory.

A neoclassical aggregate freight demand model can be derived, for example, by assuming that shippers are firms whose production techniques and transportation decisions are jointly chosen to minimize a cost function $C(Q,w,x,p)$, where Q is the firm's output, w is a set of factor prices relating to its production, x is a set of potential shipment characteristics, and p is a set of transportation prices. If it is assumed that the cost function is of a particular form known as translog,[6] then the expenditure share on a given mode is a linear function of the logarithms of the variables in the cost function.[7] Furthermore, specific restrictions on the parameters of the cost function itself are imposed by the theoretical conditions for cost-minimizing behavior. The parameters can be estimated from data on the expendi-

---

4. Boyce and Ran (1996).

5. See Oum and Gillen (1983) on maximizing utility; Oum (1979) and Friedlaender and Spady (1980) on minimizing cost.

6. A translog function is a linear combination of all possible first- and second-order terms in the logarithms of independent variables. For example, a first-order term might be $\beta_Q \ln Q$ while a second-order term might be $\beta_{QQ} (\ln Q)^2$ or $\beta_{Qx} (\ln Q)(\ln x)$ if x is just a single characteristic. This form can closely approximate an arbitrary function when the variables are close to a particular set of values chosen in advance, such as the average values in the sample.

7. The derivation makes use of Shepherd's Lemma, which states that a small increase in the price of an input increases cost by an amount equal to the use of that input. See Oum (1979) or Friedlaender and Spady (1980).

ture shares alone or on expenditure shares and total costs, in either case using multiple-equations methods in standard regression packages.

Many of the earlier aggregate models explained mode shares over a cross-section of specific geographic units such as city pairs or mileage blocks.[8] An alternative is the *direct demand* model, in which the total use of a given type of transportation is expressed as a function of its own characteristics and those of competing types, without worrying about where the function comes from. The advantage of this approach is that it automatically combines trip generation, distribution, and mode choice decisions. For example, Domencich and Kraft estimate equations to explain the total number of urban trips between a given origin and destination by a given mode for a given purpose.[9] Explanatory variables include demographic and land-use characteristics of the origin and of the destination and travel times and costs both for the mode in question and for competing modes. This type of approach is still in use, as illustrated by Wardman's estimation of the demand for intercity rail travel in Great Britain.[10]

Direct demand models are also used in time series. For example, Gaudry uses monthly data from Montreal's public transit system to explain how its ridership depends on average real income, weather, transit strikes, special tourist attractions, and other factors as well as on fares and service times for both transit and car.[11] Voith uses a combined time-series and cross-sectional approach to estimate how commuter rail ridership in Philadelphia varies with the characteristics of the route, some of which changed during the period covered by the data.[12]

Disaggregate Demand Models

Although aggregate models have a firm theoretical grounding and are easy to estimate, several advantages can be reaped by using data on individual decisionmakers such as firms and travelers.[13] First, the number of observations is much larger, leading to more precise estimates of parameters. Second, it is feasible to use a richer empirical specification, thus bet-

8. For examples, see Perle (1964) and Quandt and Baumol (1966).
9. Domencich and Kraft (1970).
10. Wardman (1997).
11. Gaudry (1975).
12. Voith (1997).
13. Domencich and McFadden (1975).

ter capturing the variation in characteristics of the decisionmaker and accounting for a more complete set of service quality attributes. Third, disaggregate models are well grounded in a microeconomic theory of individual or firm behavior that does not require the unrealistic assumption of identical decisionmakers. Fourth, disaggregate models are explicit about the source of random disturbances, which has improved their statistical properties.

Disaggregate models also use the actual values of variables facing each decisionmaker, rather than average values that may obscure a significant amount of information. The advantage of using actual values is illustrated by the importance of shipment size and trip distance in mode choice for surface freight. Small shipments and those going short distances tend overwhelmingly to use truck. Thus an aggregate model that uses average values for these variables may include many shipments where truck and rail do not seriously compete against each other. As a result the model may overstate the sensitivity of demand to price and service quality in some markets and understate it in others.

In this section and the next we present several of the most useful disaggregate demand models, each in the context of an important transportation application.[14] This section presents the underlying framework and three widely used disaggregate models. The next section describes more technically advanced models that enable researchers to analyze simultaneous choices, taste variation, and varied sources of unobserved influences.

The Random Utility Framework

The common starting point for virtually all disaggregate models in current use is a utility function with a random component.[15] We describe it in the context of mode choice, but the same approach is used to analyze the choice among any finite set of alternatives.

Suppose the decisionmaker chooses among J alternative modes such as auto, bus, and air for intercity passenger travel. The chosen mode is assumed to maximize the decisionmaker's utility, which for mode j is:

$$(2\text{-}1) \qquad U_j = V(X_j, S; \beta) + \varepsilon_j$$

14. Ben-Akiva and Lerman (1985), Train (1986), and Ortúzar and Willumson (1994: ch 7–8) provide more extensive treatments of disaggregate transportation demand models, with emphasis on transportation applications.

15. McFadden (1973). An exception is the Poisson model for analyzing trip generation at a disaggregate level, as exemplified by Terza and Wilson (1990).

where X_j denotes a set of modal attributes, S denotes characteristics of the decisionmaker, β denotes unknown parameters, and ε_j is an unobserved ("random") utility component representing other influences on the decisionmaker, including idiosyncratic preferences for mode j. The modal attributes X_j may contain an indicator (known as a "dummy variable") for mode j; in that case its coefficient (one of the parameters in vector β) represents an average preference for mode j, while ε_j represents a deviation from that average preference. The function V is called the "systematic" utility because the same functional form applies to all decisionmakers, unlike the random component that varies across decisionmakers.[16]

Because utility is partly random, choices can be predicted only as probabilities. The probability that the decisionmaker will choose mode i is:

$$(2\text{-}2) \qquad\qquad \begin{aligned} P_i &= \text{Prob } [U_i > U_j \text{ for all } j \neq i] \\ &= \text{Prob } [V_j + \varepsilon_j < V_i + \varepsilon_i \text{ for all } j \neq i] \\ &= \text{Prob } [\varepsilon_j - \varepsilon_i < V_i - V_j \text{ for all } j \neq i] \end{aligned}$$

where V_j is shorthand for $V(X_j, S; \beta)$. Thus the choice probability depends not only on the systematic utility differences $V_i - V_j$, but also on how the random utility differences $(\varepsilon_j - \varepsilon_i)$ are distributed across the population. Most of the models in subsequent sections differ only in their assumptions about this latter distribution.

The model is estimated by finding the values for unknown parameters that yield predicted choice probabilities matching actual choices as closely as possible. A common algorithm is the following: choose a trial set of parameters, calculate the logarithms of the probabilities of the observed choice for all members of the sample, add them, then repeat using new parameter values until this sum is made as large as possible. This method yields *maximum likelihood* parameter estimates.

The process is usually simplified by assuming that the utility function $V(X_j, S; \beta)$ is linear in parameters β. But utility can be a flexible function of the variables X_j, containing ratios, quadratic terms, logarithms, or other transformations and combinations.[17]

16. V is also called the "conditional indirect" utility because it reflects the result of the decisionmaker's optimization of other choices, such as consumption of other goods or purchase of other inputs, conditional on the attributes X_j.

17. Gaudry and Wills (1978) argue that better fits to the data can be attained by using even more flexible functions, known as Box-Cox transformations, which are nonlinear in parameters. One of several studies using Box-Cox transformations is that of Mandel, Gaudry, and Rothengatter (1994), who analyze rail travel in Germany.

Once the model is estimated, the decisionmakers who are relevant for the particular scenario at hand must still be described. The most common way to accomplish this is *sample enumeration*. Based on information about the actual population of interest, the analyst chooses a representative sample of individual decisionmakers, possibly but not necessarily the same as the sample on which the disaggregate model is estimated. Each member of the enumeration sample is assumed to represent a population segment of actual decisionmakers, all with the same observed characteristics as that sample member. The predicted probability of each choice is then used to estimate the fraction of that population segment making that choice.

Binary Probit and the Value of Travel Time

The simplest choice model involves just two alternatives. Consider the mode choice for an urban work trip. Let's call auto "alternative 1" and bus "alternative 2." Then there is only one utility difference, namely $\varepsilon_2 - \varepsilon_1$, in equation 2-2. A reasonable assumption is that this utility difference follows a bell curve, that is, it is normally distributed across the population. This assumption leads to the *probit* choice probability:

$$(2\text{-}3) \qquad\qquad P_1 = \Phi(V_1 - V_2)$$

where P_1 is the probability of choosing auto and Φ is the cumulative standard normal distribution function.[18] This choice model is simple to estimate and was used early on by Thomas Lisco and by Charles Lave to measure the value of time in urban commuting.[19]

Lave analyzed a sample, taken in the mid-1960s, of 280 urban commuters in the Chicago area choosing between automobile and transit. The estimated systematic utility function is:

$$V = -2.08D^T - 0.00759w \cdot t - 0.0186c - 0.0254(Inc \cdot Dist \cdot D^T)$$
$$+ 0.0255(Age \cdot D^T) - 0.057(Female \cdot D^T)$$

where D^T is an *alternative-specific dummy variable* equal to 1 for transit and 0 for auto. It enters the model independently (in the first term) and also

18. That is, $\Phi(x) = \dfrac{1}{\sqrt{2\pi}} \displaystyle\int_{-\infty}^{x} \exp(-t^2/2)dt$.

19. Lisco (1967); Lave (1969).

interacts with the traveler's income (*Inc*), trip distance (*Dist*), age, and a dummy variable indicating whether the traveler is female. The traveler's wage rate is denoted by *w*, travel time by *t*, and travel cost by *c*. Note that D^T, *t*, and *c* all vary from one mode to the other, whereas *w*, *Inc*, *Dist*, *Age*, and *Female* do not. Lave's more detailed results show that all estimated parameters are statistically significant except the last. The model indicates that travelers are less likely to take transit if their income or trip distance increases, but more likely to take transit as they become older.

This utility function is linear in travel time and cost. The value of travel time (*VOT*), defined as the marginal rate of substitution between time and cost, is just the ratio of the time and cost coefficients of that linear relation:[20]

$$VOT = \frac{-0.00759w}{-0.0186} = 0.41w.$$

Lave's finding, which is representative of other estimates in the literature, is that time is valued at 41 percent of the average wage rate. Note that the variables in this model were specified so that *VOT* is proportional to the wage rate. This approach is consistent with models of time allocation, which suggest that a person's trade-off between travel time and money is strongly related to his or her possibilities for earning money in the labor market.[21]

What if there are more than two alternatives? Although the probit model can be extended for this situation, it becomes much more difficult to estimate. The reason is that the right-hand side of equation 2-3 becomes a more complicated function, known as multidimensional cumulative normal, which can be computed only by using difficult numerical approximations. Thus when Lave wanted to consider other modes, such as rapid rail and commuter rail, he had to examine each pair separately, although he recognized that this approach could lead to inconsistencies. Fortunately, researchers have subsequently developed other models that can estimate many alternatives simultaneously, as we now describe.

---

20. More generally, the value of time is defined as $VOT = (\partial V/\partial t)/(\partial V/\partial c)$, where ∂ denotes a partial derivative.

21. Becker (1965); Bruzelius (1979). See Small (1992: 36–45) for further discussion and for a review of empirical findings on the value of time.

Multinomial Logit and Urban Mode Choice

When there are more than two alternatives, the key to obtaining a computationally convenient choice model is to have an easily calculated expression for the choice probability. McFadden derives such a model by assuming that each of the random utilities follows the extreme value distribution, which is almost indistinguishable from the normal distribution in practice.[22] The resulting choice probability is:

$$P_i = \frac{e^{V_i}}{\sum_{j=1}^{J} e^{V_j}} .$$

(2-4)

This model is known as *multinomial logit*, or just logit.[23]

The computational complexity of multinomial logit is not affected by whether J, the number of alternatives, is 3 or 300. But this simple structure does not come without a cost. Multinomial logit has a property called *independence from irrelevant alternatives* (IIA): the ratio of the probabilities of any two alternatives i and j depends on the corresponding systematic utilities V_i and V_j, but not on the systematic utilities for any other alternatives. This property implies, for example, that adding a new alternative mode k will not affect the relative proportions of people using existing modes; thus its patronage will be drawn proportionally from all these modes rather than preferentially from one or two close substitutes. The IIA assumption can be tested statistically, and if it is rejected, one can use alternative models, as discussed later.[24]

McFadden, Talvitie, and associates present a multinomial logit model of mode choice for urban work trips.[25] This model is estimated from data

22. McFadden (1973). The extreme value distribution is defined by $\text{Prob}[\varepsilon_i < x] = \exp(-e^{-\mu x})$, where $\exp(\cdot)$ and $e^{\cdot}$ both denote the exponential function, and μ is a scale parameter conventionally normalized to 1.

23. A few authors still reserve the term "multinomial logit" for a version of the model in which the coefficients, rather than the variables, depend on the alternative being considered—that is, the strict utility in equation 2-1 is written as $V(X, S; \beta_j)$ instead of $V(X_j, S; \beta)$. These authors use the term "conditional logit" for the model as we have defined it. As noted by Maddala (1983: 42), these are just two ways of writing the same model, so the distinction matters only for the terminology used to describe results and data structure.

24. Statistical tests are presented in Hausman and McFadden (1984), Small and Hsiao (1985), McFadden (1987), and Small (1994).

25. McFadden, Talvitie, and associates (1977:121–23).

generated by San Francisco Bay Area commuters choosing among four modes: auto driving alone; bus with walk access; bus with auto access; and carpool (two or more occupants). (The survey was undertaken shortly before the area's rapid rail system was opened.) Mode choice is explained by three observed attributes: round-trip variable cost c (in cents, including parking, tolls, gasoline, and maintenance); in-vehicle travel time t (in minutes); and out-of-vehicle travel time t^0 (in minutes, including walk, wait, and transfer times). Unobserved attributes for mode j are captured by the mode-specific dummy D^j, which, like D^T in the previous section, is defined as 1 for mode j and 0 for the other modes. (Because only utility differences affect mode choice, one of these mode-specific dummies—D^2 in this case—is omitted, thus defining a "base mode" to which the others are compared.) One socioeconomic characteristic, the traveler's after-tax wage rate w (in cents per minute), is also included in the model. The estimated utility function is:

$$V = -0.0412c/w \quad -0.0201t \quad -0.0531t^0 \quad -0.89D^1 \quad -1.78D^3 \quad -2.15D^4$$
$$(0.0054) \qquad (0.0072) \qquad (0.0070) \qquad (0.26) \qquad (0.24) \qquad (0.25)$$

with the standard errors of the parameter estimates shown in parentheses.

As expected, higher travel cost or greater in-vehicle or out-of-vehicle time for a given mode decreases the probability that commuters will select that mode. The negative mode-specific constants (the coefficients of D^1, D^3, and D^4) show that a traveler facing equal times and costs on all four modes would prefer bus with walk access (mode 2, the base mode). The especially large negative constants for bus with auto access (mode 3) and carpool (mode 4) may reflect unmeasured inconvenience associated with getting from the car to the bus stop and with arranging carpools. These are examples of service quality attributes that would be difficult to measure directly.

Once again, the model is specified so that the ratio of each of the time coefficients to the cost coefficient is proportional to the after-tax wage rate. The estimated parameters indicate that travelers value their in-vehicle and out-of-vehicle travel time at 49 percent and 129 percent, respectively, of their wage rate.[26] This much higher value of out-of-vehicle time relative to in-vehicle time indicates that travelers dislike the time they must spend getting to, transferring to, or waiting for a mode. An important conse-

26. Since $(-0.0201)/(-0.0412/w) = 0.49w$, and $(-0.0531)/(-0.0412/w) = 1.29w$.

quence of this finding, which has been verified by other studies, is that auto's low out-of-vehicle time gives it a significant competitive advantage over other modes.

Nested Logit and Vacation Travel Choice

In most transportation settings, mode choices are made jointly with other travel-related decisions. For example, a commuter may simultaneously choose what mode to use and how many cars to own. A freight shipper may simultaneously select a shipping mode and shipment size. If the two choices depend on each other in important ways, it is an error to pretend that one is exogenous while analyzing the other. For example, the number of automobiles owned by a household has a powerful influence on urban mode choice when it is included as an explanatory variable; but including it without accounting for the reverse causation (mode choice affecting auto ownership) will cause the influence of auto ownership to be overstated and the influence of other factors to be understated. This is why auto ownership is omitted as a variable in both of the studies just reviewed.

Joint choice models are designed to account for simultaneous decisions. Here we treat joint choices where both choices are discrete in nature. The earliest models identified and combined all possible combinations of two or more discrete choices, and used logit to estimate the choice among the combined alternatives.[27] But if a decisionmaker has idiosyncratic preferences for an entire class of outcomes—for example, all those involving not owning a car—then the random utilities for all those outcomes would be correlated with each other, and the probabilities would violate the IIA assumption.

McFadden developed the theoretical foundations for a widely used generalization of multinomial logit, called *nested logit*, that allows for such idiosyncratic preferences.[28] This model explicitly structures the joint choice process in terms of groups of possible outcomes. Random utilities are allowed to be correlated within groups but are assumed to be independent across groups. The model therefore allows for more flexible substitution patterns than logit and does not have to obey the IIA restriction.

---

27. For example, Ben-Akiva and Lerman (1974) estimate logit models of the joint choice of automobile ownership and work-trip mode. Lerman (1981) adds to those two choices two more: residential location, and housing type, both treated as discrete.

28. McFadden (1978). See also Train (1986: ch. 4).

Figure 2-1. *Preference Tree for Intercity Vacation Travel*

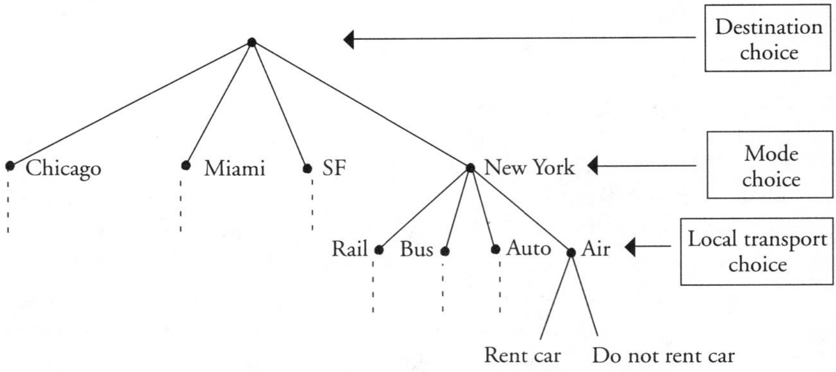

Source: Morrison and Winston (1985). See text for explanation.

Morrison and Winston estimate a nested logit model of intercity vacation travel.[29] The authors assume that vacation travelers simultaneously make three choices: where to travel, how to get there, and whether to rent a car at the destination. The structure of these choices is indicated by figure 2-1, in which each of the dashed lines indicates an additional branch of the tree analogous to the one shown for the same level node. (A node is a decision point, represented by a dot.) This diagram is not intended to indicate a sequential decision process, but rather to show the pattern of similarities within a simultaneous decision process. The diagram indicates that the traveler views all the various ways of getting to New York, for example, as more similar to each other than, say, all the places one can go by air. The two possible choices for air travel to New York—with or without renting a car—are even more similar to each other and thus appear as branches attached at the lowest level of the tree.

The random error components are assumed to follow an extreme value distribution, as in logit; but those components representing branches connecting to a common node are positively correlated with each other, while others are independent. This assumption produces the pattern of similarity suggested by the tree diagram and results in a convenient form for the choice probabilities: conditional on choosing any particular node, the choice

29. Morrison and Winston (1985).

probability for the next lower decision on the diagram is given by a logit probability. For example, conditional on New York as a destination, the choice among travel modes has the multinomial logit form of equation 2-4. In that case the utility V_j of each travel mode j (for example, air) is a combination of traits of that mode (for example, airline prices to New York) and a summary index of the convenience of local transportation (for example, the ease of getting around New York upon arriving there by air). That index, known as an "inclusive value," is constructed from the systematic utilities of the lower-level decision of whether to rent a car, a decision that in turn reflects factors such as rental car prices at airports in the New York area.

The model was estimated on a sample of 1,893 households making vacation trips in 1977. Here just one part of the results is described, namely, the estimated utility function for the top decision level, destination choice. Choice of destination is explained by round-trip distance to the destination (*dist*—measured in thousands of miles); a dummy variable (D^{plan}) equal to 1 if the traveler planned the trip more than a month in advance and 0 otherwise; two characteristics of the destination—mean temperature at the destination during the month of travel (*temp*), and a dummy variable for whether public transit is available there (D^{pt}); and the "inclusive value" index (I_d) for mode choices at that destination.[30] The estimated destination utility is:

$$V_d = -0.364(1-D^{plan}){\cdot}dist_d + 0.270D^{plan}{\cdot}dist_d + 0.019temp_d + 0.309D_d^{pt} + 0.519I_d$$
$$\quad\;\;(0.088) \qquad\qquad (0.075) \qquad\qquad (0.003) \qquad (0.058) \qquad (0.069)$$

where again standard errors of the parameter estimates are shown in parentheses. The first two estimated parameters indicate that travelers prefer closer destinations if they do not plan their travel far in advance and farther des-

---

30. The inclusive value for the mode choices available to destination d is defined as:

$$I_d = \ln\textstyle\sum_i \exp(V_{i|d} + \theta J_{i|d})$$

where $V_{i|d}$ is the systematic utility pertaining to using mode i to travel to destination d; $J_{i|d} = \ln\sum_\delta \exp(V_{\delta|i,d})$ is the inclusive value of the two alternative forms of local transportation (denoted $\delta = 1$ or 2) when mode i is used to travel to destination d; $V_{\delta|i,d}$ is the systematic utility of either of these two forms of local transportation; and θ is a parameter related to the correlation between the random utilities of the two forms of local transportation.

tinations if they do plan far in advance. Travelers on average prefer destinations that are warm and that have public transit.

The coefficient of inclusive value is positive, indicating that travelers' choice of where to spend their vacation is interconnected with their choice of mode to get there. For example, if air fares to San Francisco fall and those to other destinations do not, San Francisco is more likely to be selected as a destination—in addition to air becoming a more likely mode of travel. The coefficient of inclusive value is also less than 1 by a statistically significant amount, which together with its being positive, means that the nested logit structure is consistent with utility-maximizing behavior and fits better than a pure joint logit.[31]

Nested logit is not used only for joint choices; it is suitable for any set of discrete choices where alternatives are grouped by decisionmakers. In fact, nested logit is just one of a class of models, known as *generalized extreme value* (GEV) models, having logit as a special case.[32] The random utility components in all GEV models have the extreme value distribution, just like in logit, but they have a correlation pattern that varies from model to model. For example, the alternatives may have a natural ordering, as in the choice among several departure-time intervals for a work trip, with nearby intervals viewed as more similar to each other than to other intervals.[33] Nesting structures can be developed in which the groups overlap; for example in choosing among car types, all sports cars might form one group and all foreign cars another.[34] And ordered structures can be embedded within nesting structures, thus providing additional flexibility.[35]

Advanced Disaggregate Demand Models

As computational capabilities increase, researchers are frequently turning to advanced techniques that can handle more sophisticated model structures. We describe three such techniques in this section, again with applications. Nontechnical readers may wish to omit this section.

---

31. McFadden (1978); Train (1986: ch 4, n.1).
32. McFadden (1981).
33. Small (1987).
34. Chu (1981).
35. Small (1994); Bhat (1998).

Joint Discrete and Continuous Choices

Earlier we introduced a nested logit model in which two discrete choices are made simultaneously. Another kind of joint choice occurs when a continuous choice, such as how many miles per year a household chooses to drive an automobile, is made simultaneously with a discrete choice, such as the type of vehicle to own. This kind of structure has proven extremely useful in transportation demand studies. It requires some additional theoretical and econometric modeling, however, to account for the interrelationship between the two decisions.[36]

The basic theoretical framework for discrete-continuous models was pioneered by Dubin and McFadden.[37] They specify a random utility function that forms the basis for the discrete choice, then use Roy's identity to derive the continuous choice.[38] Thus both choices are consistent with utility-maximizing behavior. Mannering and Winston use this framework to estimate a model of vehicle type choice and utilization.[39] Other researchers have estimated discrete-continuous choice models of freight mode and shipment size.[40]

The primary wrinkle for analyzing this type of model is that the continuous part, which may look like an ordinary regression equation, contains a selection bias. This bias occurs because the regression equation is conditional on a particular outcome of the (interrelated) discrete choice. Take the example of a household choosing whether to own a car and, if so, how much to use it. The equation to explain utilization contains, of course, a random error term. But it will be estimated only for those people who choose to own a car and are thus more likely to have idiosyncratic reasons to use their car a lot. Consequently, the sample on which the utilization equation is estimated is self-selected to contain people likely to have relatively high utilization. Suppose the utilization equation were estimated on that sample without correcting for this bias, then used to analyze road-building policies that encourage more people to buy cars. It would

---

36. Mannering and Hensher (1987).

37. Dubin and McFadden (1984).

38. Roy's identity expresses an ordinary demand function in terms of the partial derivatives of an indirect utility function with respect to price and income.

39. Mannering and Winston (1985). Another study of automobile ownership and utilization is by Train (1986: ch. 8), who derives his model by using simple approximations to functional form rather than relying on strict utility-maximizing behavior.

40. Chiang, Roberts, and Ben-Akiva (1981); McFadden, Winston, and Boersch-Supan (1985).

overpredict the usage by the new car owners. Simple corrections are available to eliminate this type of bias.[41]

Multinomial Probit and Freight Mode Choice

A probit framework developed by Hausman and Wise offers another way, besides nested logit, to incorporate complex correlation patterns among alternatives.[42] At the same time it can capture taste variation across a population of transportation users. It does so by means of random coefficients: each variable enters the systematic utility not through a single coefficient, but through one that varies across the population. (For example, some travelers may greatly prefer warmer vacation destinations, as in the Morrison-Winston model discussed earlier, while others may care less or not at all.) Thus the Hausman-Wise model extends equation 2-1 in two ways. First, the random terms are distributed in accordance with a multivariate normal distribution with an arbitrary correlation pattern. Second, the unknown parameters vary randomly across the population, also following a multivariate normal distribution.

One application of multinomial probit with random coefficients has been to understand mode choice for freight shipments. Typically the decision is made by a physical distribution manager, who may have a particular attitude toward the uncertainties associated with long transit times and with variability in delivery time.[43] Because the manager's attitude may depend on his job security and personal characteristics, which are not easily observable, it is natural to model it as a random coefficient. Indeed, surveys of American and French freight managers provide evidence for substantial variability in their concern for shipment time.[44]

A study by Winston specifies the distribution manager's utility function to include not only transit time but uncertainty in transit time, both with random coefficients.[45] For some products, the results indicate clear variation across managers; for others, they do not. An example of the first situation is (formerly) regulated agricultural products, which tend to be low value per weight. Shippers of these products have the choice of rail,

---

41. Two classic treatments are Heckman (1978) and Lee (1979). Train (1986: ch. 5) provides a readable textbook presentation.

42. Hausman and Wise (1978).

43. See, for example, Daughety and Inaba (1978) and Daughety (1979).

44. Gellman Research Associates (1977); Wynter (1995).

45. Winston (1981a).

common-carrier truck, or private truck. The estimated utility function depends on three modal attributes: freight charges (*cost*) in thousands of dollars; mean transit time (*time*) in days; and the standard deviation of transit time (σ). The utility of certain modes relative to others also depends on characteristics of the shipment itself; more precisely, shipment size (*size*, in thousands of pounds), value-to-weight ratio (*value*, in dollars per thousand pounds), and distance from the nearest rail siding (*dist*, in miles) are all hypothesized to affect choice of rail relative to the others, whereas total annual sales by the shipper (*sales*, in billions of dollars per year) is hypothesized to affect the feasibility of private trucking. The estimated utility function for the average shipper is:

$$V = -3.09cost - 2.44time - 12.7\sigma + 11.5(\sigma/time) + 0.536D^r{\cdot}size$$
$$+ 0.035D^r{\cdot}value - 35.4D^r{\cdot}dist - 0.17D^p{\cdot}sales$$

where D^r and D^p are dummy variables for rail and for private trucking, respectively. The coefficients shown here are only averages because the actual coefficients are assumed to vary randomly across the population of shippers, with standard deviations that are estimated along with these average values.

The coefficient estimates indicate that these agricultural shippers are, on average, responsive to freight charges, transit time, and uncertainty in transit time (they are averse to such uncertainty, but less so for shorter shipments). They are also more likely to use rail for larger shipments and if they are located close to a rail siding. The coefficients for these five variables are statistically significant and the coefficients for *value* and *sales* are statistically insignificant.

This model suggests that transit time and its uncertainty are important considerations to shippers. The market elasticity of demand for common-carrier trucking is −0.32 with respect to cost, −0.59 with respect to transit time, and −0.18 with respect to the standard deviation of transit time. The demand for rail is somewhat less sensitive to transit time but more sensitive to its uncertainty.

Finally, the fact that these agricultural shippers are revealed to vary in their evaluations of these factors means some markets are relatively "captive," consisting of shippers who will not readily change their preferred mode, while others have shippers who are quite sensitive to price and service quality. Other commodities showing similar variation in shipper evaluation of price and service quality are chemicals, metals, machinery, and stone, clay, and glass products. Each of these industries contains some products that are quite standardized and heavy and others that are specialized, suggesting that rational considerations rather than personality quirks may account for the variation among shippers.

Mixed Logit and the Demand for Electric Vehicles

The Hausman-Wise model is not the only way to account for taste variation. Researchers have estimated logit models of automobile purchase with random coefficients to analyze how regulation and market forces affect vehicle fuel economy.[46] Others have estimated logit models that allow the value of time for intercity travel to vary randomly across the population, even for people with the same wage or income.[47]

Recent breakthroughs in computational methods have made it possible to consider even more general models of taste variation within the extended logit family. The approach is nicely illustrated by a study by Brownstone and Train of the potential market for passenger vehicles powered by fuels other than gasoline.[48] The study combines random coefficients with a very flexible error structure for the random-utility components.

The combination is accomplished by adding another random term η_j to the random utility function, equation 2-1, and allowing its distribution to depend quite generally on characteristics z_j of choice j. These characteristics could be the same as those in the systematic utility function, in which case this new random term captures the effect of random variation in coefficients across consumers. Or z_j could just be indicators of where alternative j fits into a tree structure, in which case the model is nested logit or some other type of generalized extreme value model. More generally, z_j could include both types of variables. The other random term, ε_j, is distributed the same way as in multinomial logit. This type of model is called *mixed logit*.

Mixed logit has become a viable force in travel demand because of the development of Monte Carlo methods for calculating the choice probabilities.[49] The basic idea is simple. If the "new" utility terms, η_j, were

---

46. Boyd and Mellman (1980); Cardell and Dunbar (1980).

47. Ben-Akiva, Bolduc, and Bradley (1993).

48. Brownstone and Train (forthcoming).

49. Such methods are known as "simulation"; see Stern (1997) for a general review, and Hajivassiliou and Ruud (1994) for applications to discrete choice.

known, the choice probability would just be multinomial logit, which is easy to calculate. The values of η_j are unknown, but the model does postulate a distribution for them. So a random number generator is used to choose a possible value for each η_j. Given these values, each of the choice probabilities P_i is calculated. Then another set of random numbers is drawn, and each P_i is recalculated. By repeating this procedure many times and averaging the results, a good approximation to P_i is obtained.

The Brownstone-Train study also illustrates the use of *stated preference* data in travel demand; these data reflect individuals' preferences in hypothetical situations. (This type of data is discussed in the next section.) In this application, stated preferences are used to forecast consumers' willingness to purchase cars not now available on the market. The model postulates vehicle choice among four fuel types—gasoline, natural gas, methanol, and electricity—as well as among several different body types and sizes. Respondents were asked to choose among hypothetical vehicles with specified characteristics; by varying these characteristics systematically (one of the luxuries of a stated preference survey), the researcher can find out how much weight people place on each.

To illustrate the two kinds of flexibility possible in mixed logit, we provide a partial listing of Brownstone and Train's estimation results as follows:

$$V = -0.264[price/\ln(income)] + 0.517range + (1.43 + 7.45\phi_1)size + (1.70$$
$$+ 5.99\phi_2)luggage + 2.46\phi_3 nonelectric + 1.07\phi_4 noncompressed + (other\ terms)$$

where *income* and vehicle *price* are in thousands of dollars; the *range* between refueling (or recharging) is in hundreds of miles; *size* is an index representing conventional vehicle classifications; *luggage* is luggage space (as a fraction of that typical of a comparably sized gasoline vehicle); *nonelectric* is a dummy variable for cars not running on electricity; and *noncompressed* is a dummy for cars not using natural gas. Among the *other terms* are additional vehicle performance measures, indicators for vehicle classification (such as station wagon or sports car), and several indicators of pure preference for or against any of the three nonconventional fuels. All parameters shown above are estimated with enough precision to pass tests of statistical significance easily.

The terms involving ϕ_1 and ϕ_2 represent the random coefficients. The first indicates that the coefficient of *size* varies according to a bell curve (normal distribution) with mean 1.43 and standard deviation 7.45. The second indicates that the coefficient of *luggage* has mean 1.70 and standard deviation 5.99. These estimates indicate a very wide variation in people's evaluation of these characteristics.[50]

The terms involving ϕ_3 and ϕ_4 represent correlation in random preferences across the four fuel types. The corresponding variables are specified in such a way as to produce an overlapping nested structure: the three nonelectric vehicle types are viewed as somewhat similar (for example, all rely on fossil fuels), and so are the three vehicle types using fuels that are not compressed (for example, the fuel distribution system could perhaps be serviced by a home mechanic). Different people may evaluate these facets of the various fuels quite differently; accordingly, these terms in the systematic utility function measure the degree of similarity, not the average direction, of preferences among fuels. Thus the coefficient $2.46\phi_3$ on *nonelectric* indicates neither a positive nor a negative preference on average (such a preference is contained in some of the *other terms*), but rather a random positive or negative preference that tends to affect all three nonelectric vehicles similarly. A comparable statement can be made about the coefficient $1.07\phi_4$. Note that methanol and gasoline share both sets of idiosyncratic preferences, so are especially close substitutes; whereas electric and natural gas vehicles share neither set and so are especially distant substitutes.

The practical value of using random coefficients is illustrated by policy simulations conducted by Brownstone and Train. Suppose we start with the current population of mostly gasoline-powered vehicles and introduce a small electric car into the market. Because people have idiosyncratic preferences for size (the term involving ϕ_1), this car will draw buyers disproportionately from owners of other small vehicles, rather than uniformly from all owners as the logit model would predict. Because smaller gasoline vehicles emit less pollution than some larger vehicles such as trucks and vans, the predicted impact of electric vehicles on air quality will be smaller using this model than using a standard logit model. Now suppose that sometime later a large methanol car is also introduced into the market. The mixed

---

50. For example, the average person in the sample, with *luggage* coefficient 1.70, would sacrifice $(0.517/1.70) = 30$ percent of typical luggage space for a 100 mile increase in range; but someone whose *size* coefficient is one standard deviation above the mean, or $1.70 + 5.99 = 7.69$, would sacrifice only $(0.517/7.69) = 6.7$ percent of luggage space for the same range increase. Many people (those for whom $1.70 + 5.99\phi_2 < 0$) actually prefer *less* luggage space, presumably because it would allow more interior room for the same size of vehicle. Similarly, many people prefer larger to smaller cars.

logit model predicts more switching from large than from small cars, for the same reason just stated; it also predicts more switching from gasoline than from electric cars, because gasoline and methanol are closer substitutes than are electric and methanol according to the correlation structure just described. Then the methanol car in this instance will have a *greater* impact on air quality than the logit model would predict. These substitution patterns are intuitive and important in developing strategies to introduce new fuel types, yet they would be missed by many conventional demand models.

Concluding Observations About Disaggregate Models

One cannot help but be impressed by the steady technical progress in disaggregate transportation demand modeling, progress that has enabled researchers to address questions involving complex substitution patterns, taste variation, and interrelated travel decisions. These complex demand structures are becoming easier to estimate. Most econometric software packages now have standard routines to estimate multinomial and nested logit models, and there are specialized programs to estimate mixed logit and multinomial probit models based on simulation estimators.

Despite these advances, complex models run the risk of asking the data to say more than they can. Their flexibility is useful only if it can be disentangled from randomness and data errors. A similar risk exists with very flexible functional forms for the systematic utility. Ultimately the ability to distinguish subtle effects is limited by the size, accuracy, range of variation, and other properties of the data set. In the following section, we examine more closely the nature of transportation demand data.

Transportation Demand Data

Virtually all travel demand analysis uses survey data. It is hard to overemphasize the importance of collecting reliable data, and there is a large body of experience on ways to do so. We leave to other writers the task of reviewing practical methods of data collection.[51] In this section, we discuss instead the structure of the data sets that are needed for various purposes. Issues include measuring the transportation environment facing decision-

---

51. See, for example, Ampt, Richardson, and Meyburg (1992) and Richardson (forthcoming).

makers, using hypothetical questions to elicit preferences, and using data collected at more than one point in time.

Measuring the Transportation Environment

Most transportation demand models include one or more "generic" variables, that is, variables such as travel time or cost that have the same meaning but different values for different alternatives. In the case of disaggregate models, one must know the value a generic variable takes for each individual in the sample, and for each of the possible modes. For example, to explain urban mode choices, Lave, in the study described earlier, needed to know what times and costs members of his sample faced using either auto or transit.

One way of meeting this requirement is to use values reported by the user. Doing so, however, has severe weaknesses. People are likely to have poor knowledge of the attributes of travel options they do not use. Even worse, the values they report may be biased to justify the choice they made. For example, people choosing to drive may believe bus service is very poor and so overstate the travel times by bus, while those who use transit exaggerate the severity of traffic congestion facing solo drivers. Such systematic misreporting would cause serious bias in the estimated model.[52] Furthermore, because a variable constructed this way appears very powerful in the model, the analyst may be delighted with it—not realizing that the causation runs at least partly in the opposite direction from that assumed by the model.

A better way to meet the data requirements of disaggregate models is to obtain objective estimates of the values of the variables. For example, McFadden, Talvitie, and associates' urban demand model, described earlier, used travel times and costs from computer-based network models of the highway and bus route systems, and Morrison and Winston's intercity demand model used travel times and costs from published airline, bus, and railroad guides.

---

52. MVA Consultancy and others (1987) find such bias to be severe in a study of the Tyne River crossing in England. Some would argue that these perceived values are what determine people's actual behavior, so should be used in the model. But that does not eliminate the bias. Perceived values can be accounted for without biasing the results by estimating a joint model of perception formation and mode choice, with each influencing the other. Mannering and Winston (1987) provide an example of this type of model in the context of seat-belt use and the perceived effectiveness of seat belts.

Stated Preference Data

Almost all of the empirical models presented in this paper have been estimated with data describing travelers' and shippers' preferences as revealed in actual decisionmaking. These data are said to portray *revealed preferences*. Another way to study decisionmaking is to ask respondents about hypothetical scenarios, in which case the preferences displayed are called *stated preferences*. Stated preference analysis is especially useful when people cannot reveal their preferences because an alternative is not available on the market, as in the case of Brownstone and Train's analysis of the demand for vehicles using alternative fuels, and Hensher and Bradley's study of the potential demand for high-speed rail in Australia.[53] Stated preference analysis is also useful when one wants to set up specialized decisionmaking situations that rarely occur in practice, as in Calfee and Winston's study of commuters' willingness to pay congestion tolls to save travel time given hypothetical scenarios of how the toll revenue will be disbursed.[54]

Stated preference data have some additional advantages. From a statistical point of view, explanatory variables generated from revealed preferences may not have a great deal of variation. If everyone faces the same bus fare, their choices cannot reveal what the effects of changing the bus fare would be. By contrast, when collecting stated preference data, the values for the explanatory variables can be varied widely and independently of each other, creating more opportunity to observe how decisionmakers respond to them. Another advantage of stated preferences is that people can rank several alternatives rather than just state their first choice, and thus provide additional information that can be used to improve precision of estimates.[55]

Nevertheless, many researchers are rightly cautious about believing people's responses concerning situations about which they have little experience. People may make implicit assumptions not intended by the researcher, or they may attempt to influence policy or demonstrate a particular set of values. Extensive experimentation has taught survey designers how to minimize such biases, but some danger remains.[56]

---

53. Brownstone and Train (forthcoming); Hensher and Bradley (1993).

54. Calfee and Winston (1998).

55. Beggs, Cardell, and Hausman (1981).

56. For surveys of this work see MVA Consultancy and others (1987), Bradley and Kroes (1992), and Hensher (1994). For a discussion of practical issues of data collection, especially in a developing nation, see Ortúzar and Garrido (1994).

An ideal solution in some situations may be to combine revealed and stated preference data to reap the advantages of both. An illustrative example is provided by Ben-Akiva and Morikawa, who examine survey data from the Netherlands.[57] They measure the effects of price and service quality on the use of rail service from Nijmegen, a city near the German border, to the capital region, a trip of about two hours. A principal objective of their analysis is to estimate travelers' value of travel time in this market. This example illustrates the type of applied study often encountered by local planning agencies, as well as a case where limited variation in the travel environment hampers inference.

Each respondent first provided revealed preference (RP) data based on an actual recent trip by either car or train. The same respondent was then given descriptions of two hypothetical trips, one by car and one by train, and asked about his or her preference. These stated preference (SP) data were designed to independently vary a few key modal characteristics: cost, time, number of transfers, and a comfort indicator.

Results of estimating a binary probit model of the choice between rail or car, based on the RP data, are presented in the first column of table 2-1. The coefficient of line-haul time is statistically negligible because it exhibited little variation across the sample. The rail constant indicates that, other things equal, people taking work trips strongly prefer rail (utility increment 1.74), while people taking nonwork trips prefer rail somewhat less strongly (utility increment 1.74 − 0.90 = 0.84). Transfers have a marked deterrent effect.

The second column shows results using the SP data. Two modifications have been made to the original model. First, the SP model includes an "inertia" variable equal to 1 for choosing the same mode as was used on the actual trip (known from the RP data) and to 0 for choosing the other mode. Second, people were not actually asked to choose one mode or the other, but rather to rate the strength of their likelihood of either choice: "definitely choose rail," "probably choose rail," "not sure," and so forth. Thus each answer is in one of five categories, which can be ordered from most likely to choose car (category 1) to most likely to choose rail (category 5). The utility in this case can be estimated using an *ordered probit* model, which assumes that the higher the systematic utility for rail relative to car,

57. Ben-Akiva and Morikawa (1990).

Table 2-1. *Choice of Rail or Car for Intercity Trips in the Netherlands*

Variables	RP model	SP model	Combined model Common coefficients	RP only	SP only
Rail constant	1.74	−0.97	. . .	1.61	−2.96
	(0.32)	(0.12)		(0.29)	(0.86)
Cost per person	−0.0257	−0.0072	−0.0240	. . .	. . .
	(0.0058)	(0.0014)	(0.0049)		
Line-haul time	0.0005	−0.0032	−0.0046	. . .	. . .
	(0.0035)	(0.0012)	(0.0024)		
Terminal time	−0.0263	−0.0066	−0.0250	. . .	. . .
	(0.0060)	(0.0021)	(0.0053)		
Number of transfers	−0.344	−0.053	−0.245	. . .	. . .
	(0.133)	(0.032)	(0.090)		
Nonwork dummy	−0.90	−0.02	. . .	−0.90	−0.13
	(0.23)	(0.08)		(0.22)	(0.26)
Inertia dummy	. . .	1.49	. . .	. . .	4.84
		(0.02)			(1.16)
Thresholds:					
μ_3	. . .	0.080	. . .	. . .	0.080
		(0.010)			(0.010)
μ_4	. . .	0.478	. . .	. . .	0.476
		(0.022)			(0.022)
Relative dispersion:					
σ_{RP}/σ_{SP}	. . .	. . .	0.294	. . .	. . .
			(0.069)		

Source: Ben-Akiva and Morikawa (1990: tables 1, 2, 4). Standard errors are in parentheses. See text for explanation of variables.

the more likely the respondent will select a category that strongly indicates choosing rail.[58]

The results in the second column of the table show that the line-haul time coefficient is now statistically significant, in fact quite large—it implies

58. Greene (1993, section 21.7.2) provides a good textbook treatment of this model. The probability of choosing category i (ranging from 1 to 5) is $P_i = \Phi(\mu_i - \beta X) - \Phi(\mu_{i-1} - \beta X)$, where $\Phi(\cdot)$ is the cumulative standard normal distribution function, βX is the systematic utility difference between rail and car, $\mu_1 - \mu_4$ are parameters to be estimated, $\mu_0 = -\infty$, and $\mu_5 = \infty$. If the model contains a constant term in βX, as this one does, one of the μ_js can be normalized to an arbitrary value. Because of the symmetry in the categories, the authors in this case can normalize two of the μ_js, which they do by assuming $\mu_2 = -\mu_3$ and $\mu_1 = -\mu_4$. See Johnson (1990) for a discussion of other models for ordered data.

a value of time of 0.45 guilders a minute, or about $13 an hour. The SP data also indicate far less tendency to favor rail for work trips, given identical trip characteristics, than do the RP data.[59]

The authors next present a model combining the RP and SP data. To do so they make three assumptions. First, the RP data are assumed to reflect actual behavior. Second, the SP data are assumed to be biased (relative to actual behavior) only in their portrayal of absolute modal preference and the influence of trip purpose. This bias is accounted for by postulating that the SP data are generated from a preference structure with its own separate values for the rail constant and for the nonwork dummy coefficient. Finally, the random error in the SP model is assumed to have a standard deviation σ_{SP} different from that for the RP model, σ_{RP}, thus allowing for either greater or less dispersion in people's preferences when answering hypothetical questions than when making actual choices.

The combined estimates are shown in the last three columns of the table.[60] They confirm that respondents answering the hypothetical (SP) questions were far less likely to favor rail than they did in actual (RP) situations. Furthermore, people exhibited much more dispersion in their random preferences when answering SP questions. The combined model yields a value of time of roughly $4.20 an hour, which appears more plausible than the value obtained from either data set alone.

Ortúzar and Iacobelli also combine RP and SP data in their study of intercity travel in Chile.[61] They find that the SP responses show less variance than the RP responses, just the opposite of the Ben-Akiva–Morikawa study, perhaps indicating that people felt more certain of their responses in this application. Recent work by Brownstone, Bunch, and Train uses the combined RP-SP methodology to better control for response bias in the SP questions used for the study of alternative fuels described earlier.[62] Generally, when RP and SP data are combined to estimate the demand for an alternative not yet available in the market, the RP data help measure the degree of dispersion in random utility and the utility constants relating to

59. From table 2-1, second column, people who actually use rail show only a mild tendency to favor rail in the hypothetical scenarios (utility increment = 1.49 − 0.97 = 0.52), while those who actually use car show a distinct tendency in the opposite direction (rail utility increment = − 0.97).

60. These estimates are obtained using a maximum likelihood routine written specifically for this model; however, Bradley and Daly (1997) show how the estimates can be obtained from standard nested-logit software by some clever manipulations of the data and tree structure.

61. Ortúzar and Iacobelli (1998).

62. Brownstone, Bunch, and Train (1998).

existing alternatives, while the SP data help refine the estimates of trade-offs and provide the only estimates of the utility constant(s) for the new alternative(s).

Panel Data

Thus far our discussion has focused on studies that use data from a single cross-sectional sample. Use of these data assumes that respondents have had time to adjust to their current situation or, if not, that the effects of incomplete adjustment vary randomly across the population. Cross-sectional studies are therefore appropriate for understanding long-run behavior.

Sometimes the analyst also needs to know the transitional dynamics that people follow when things change. These dynamics can be analyzed by following the behavior of the same individuals over time. Data collected this way are called *panel data.*

By capturing dynamic behavior at the individual level, panel data permit a more detailed understanding of the factors governing people's changing behavior, including response lags and learning by experience.[63] Observed persistence in behavior can arise from two very different causes, however. One is true behavioral inertia (adjustment lags), caused by impediments to changing behavior; this condition is also known as "state dependence" because behavior at any one time depends on the state in which one has been placed by past decisions. The other cause of persistent behavior is idiosyncratic factors that make one person regularly lean toward one choice and another person toward another; this situation is called "unobserved heterogeneity" because the persistence in behavior arises from factors that are unknown to the analyst and that vary across the population.

Panel data pose special estimation problems that arise from respondents' attrition as the survey evolves. Statistical techniques designed to minimize "nonrespondent" and "attrition" biases are available.[64]

Mannering and Winston use the National Family Opinion panel to estimate the effect of consumers' previous experience with a particular brand of automobile on their future automobile purchases—that is, the extent of their brand loyalty.[65] Each member of the panel kept records of his or her entire vehicle ownership history. The authors used these data to estimate

---

63. Raimond and Hensher (1997).
64. Heckman (1981a, b); Pendyala and Kitamura (1997).
65. Mannering and Winston (1991).

multinomial logit models of vehicle-type choice before and after 1980, specifying the number of previous General Motors (GM), Ford, Chrysler, Nissan, Honda, and Toyota purchases as explanatory variables. Their main finding was that brand loyalty toward American cars, particularly those manufactured by GM, had fallen substantially since 1980, while brand loyalty toward Japanese cars had risen. For example, before 1980 a previous GM purchase increased the probability that a consumer's next purchase would be a GM car by 6.3 percentage points, but after 1980 the increase was only 3.1 percentage points. In contrast, the effect of previous Toyota ownership on Toyota purchase probability increased, from 7 percentage points before 1980 to 14.3 percentage points after 1980.

Did the propensity for repeat purchases of a brand of car arise from true brand loyalty (state dependence) or persistent idiosyncratic factors (unobserved heterogeneity)? Mannering and Winston tested this question statistically and concluded that brand loyalty was the dominant factor.[66] This finding has implications both for manufacturers' marketing strategies and for government policies toward motor vehicle imports.

One of the most extensive panel data sets is the Dutch Mobility Panel, a stratified random survey of households in the Netherlands.[67] It has been used for many studies, well illustrated by Kitamura and Bunch's study of the number of cars owned by a household.[68] In one of their models, state dependence is measured by including, among the explanatory variables for car ownership at time t, measures of car ownership at an earlier time $t-1$ (about six months earlier). Heterogeneity is measured by assuming that random utility has two components: one that varies only by individual, and another that varies each time the individual is observed. The first component represents persistent idiosyncratic factors (unobserved heterogeneity). Kitamura and Bunch's results indicate a great deal of inertia in the system, but very little heterogeneity. The implication is that as incomes, fuel prices, or other factors affecting car ownership change, people will adjust only partially over a period of six months, but that eventually they will adjust because few have strong idiosyncrasies favoring a particular car

---

66. The authors found that their estimates of brand loyalty were not sensitive to omitted variables or to the use of models conditional on particular purchases (such as American brands), but they were sensitive to the temporal ordering of vehicle purchases. For example, if a consumer bought a GM car in 1970 and 1978, but then a Ford in 1980, then the effects of the previous GM purchases were insignificant because of the break in loyalty in 1980.

67. Van Wissen and Meurs (1989); Meurs and Ridder (1997).

68. Kitamura and Bunch (1990).

ownership level. Unfortunately, this finding was not very robust to variations in the assumed model structure, so it remains tentative.

Illustrative Empirical Findings

What do these models reveal about transportation behavior? Here we summarize some basic findings about travelers' and shippers' behavior by presenting two kinds of estimates: price and service elasticities of demand; and decisionmakers' values of travel time.

Elasticities

Demand responsiveness is often summarized in terms of demand elasticities, defined as the percentage change in the use of a particular transportation service resulting from a 1 percent change in an attribute such as price, trip time, or frequency of service offerings. Because travel demand results from several related decisions, as described earlier, it is sometimes helpful to decompose this elasticity into identifiable decision components. For example, the demand for rail freight service from Houston to Los Angeles reflects the effects of Houston-LA rail tariffs on the number and size of shipments originating in Houston, the proportion of them destined for Los Angeles, and the proportion of those sent by rail. Thus the total price elasticity for this service is the sum of a trip generation elasticity, a destination diversion elasticity, and a modal diversion elasticity. The latter is usually the largest.

In table 2-2 we present some estimates of demand elasticities, with respect to both price and service quality, for several major forms of transportation. Those derived from a translog cost function are long-run total elasticities because the cost function accounts for all three decision components and allows for choice of capital equipment. Those derived from a vehicle utilization model are short-run total elasticities; they again account for all three decision components but constrain the household's number of vehicles to be constant. The other elasticities shown are based on mode choice only, so they are modal diversion elasticities.

Elasticity estimates in freight transportation vary widely by commodity group. The table indicates the range of variation and, in some cases, the commodity groups with the smallest and largest elasticities. It is interesting that service-time elasticities can be as large as price elasticities, particularly in the case of perishable commodities.

Duh,

Table 2-2. *Transportation Price and Service Time Elasticities*

Market, model, elasticity type	Elasticity estimates			
Freight	*Rail*	*Truck*		
Aggregate mode split model[a]				
Price	−0.25 to −0.35	−0.25 to −0.35		
Transit time	−0.3 to −0.7	−0.3 to −0.7		
Aggregate model from translog cost function[b,c]				
Price	−0.37 to −1.16[d]	−0.58 to −1.81[e]		
Disaggregate mode choice model[b,f]				
Price	−0.08 to −2.68	−0.04 to −2.97		
Transit time	−0.07 to −2.33	−0.15 to −0.69		
Urban passenger[g]	*Auto*	*Bus*	*Rail*	
Price	−0.47	−0.58	−0.86	
In-vehicle time	−0.22	−0.60	−0.60	
Intercity passenger[h]	*Auto*	*Bus*	*Rail*	*Air*
Price	−0.45	−0.69	−1.20	−0.38
Travel time	−0.39	−2.11	−1.58	−0.43
Automobile utilization[i]	One-vehicle household	Two-vehicle household		
Short-run operating cost	−0.228	−0.059		
Long-run operating cost	−0.279	−0.099		

a. Levin (1978).

b. These estimates vary by commodity group; we report the largest and smallest.

c. Friedlaender and Spady (1981).

d. The first value applies to mineral products; the second value to petroleum products.

e. The first value applies to petroleum products; the second value to mineral products.

f. Winston (1981a).

g. McFadden (1974), multinomial logit mode choice model for work trips in the San Francisco Bay Area.

h. Morrison and Winston (1985), multinomial logit mode choice model for vacation trips in the United States.

i. Mannering and Winston (1985).

For urban passenger travel, price and in-vehicle-time elasticities are less than 1 in absolute value. Public policies that increase automobile costs or reduce transit in-vehicle times only modestly are therefore likely to have small effects on automobile usage and transit ridership, respectively. This conclusion is consistent with comprehensive studies of urban transportation policy such as those by Meyer, Kain, and Wohl and by Winston and

Shirley.[69] It also means that transit revenues can be increased by raising fares, a fact that is well known by transit managers though sometimes contested by user groups.

For intercity trips, a low travel-time elasticity also characterizes the auto and air modes, probably because these modes have highly captive markets—air has a large share of long-distance intercity trips, while auto has a large share of short-distance intercity trips. In contrast, intercity bus and rail travel are highly elastic with respect to travel time; thus these modes could significantly increase their market shares if service times could be improved. Intercity bus and air travel are price inelastic (elasticity less than 1 in absolute value), suggesting that either competition or regulation (during the period the model was estimated) was working to prevent carriers from charging monopoly fares. Rail service, in contrast, is price elastic, which is consistent with the possibility that Amtrak, the national carrier for rail passengers, was acting like a monopolist and that lower prices would generate substantial new passenger traffic.

Utilization of a given automobile tends to be cost-inelastic, indicating that even large increases in fuel prices or other costs will not reduce annual automobile travel very much. This is especially true for two-vehicle households because they can respond to an increase in fuel costs by shifting some driving to their most fuel-efficient vehicle. The low cost-elasticity of automobile utilization is consistent with studies showing that the consumer response to higher gasoline prices during the 1970s and early 1980s was primarily to purchase smaller cars rather than to drive cars less.

Values of Travel Time

We have previously shown how the parameters of transportation demand models can be used to calculate the value of travel time. In the case of passenger travel, this value depends on the utility or disutility that a decisionmaker attaches to time spent in a particular mode, as well as the opportunity cost of time used in travel.[70] Thus a high value of time could arise from a high opportunity cost of time or from great disutility of time spent on a particular mode.

In the case of freight, the value of time arises from the opportunity cost of having goods tied up in transit, which can reflect perishability, risk of

69. Meyer, Kain, and Wohl (1965); Winston and Shirley (1998).
70. Johnson (1966); Oort (1969).

Table 2-3. *Estimates of Value of Time by Transportation Mode*

Transportation mode	Estimate of value of time			
Freight[a]	Rail	Truck		
(As percentage of daily shipment value)				
Total transit time	6–21	8–18		
Urban work trips[b]	Auto	Bus		
(As percentage of after tax wage rate)				
In-vehicle time	140	76		
Walk access time	...	273		
Transfer wait time	...	195		
Intercity passenger[c]	Auto	Bus[d]	Rail[e]	Air
(As percentage of pretax wage rate)				
Total travel time	6	79–87	54–69	149

a. Winston (1979). The lower value in each range applies to primary and fabricated metals; the higher value applies to perishable agriculture products.

b. Calculated from McFadden, Talvitie, and associates (1977:116)

c. Morrison and Winston (1985). Estimates for vacation trips.

d. The lower value applies to low-income travelers, the higher value to high-income travelers.

e. The lower value applies to high-income travelers, the higher value to low-income travelers—just the reverse of bus. (But recall these are percentages of wage rates, so value of time generally still rises with income.)

theft, and capital carrying costs. If the value of transit time per day is expressed as a percentage of the shipment's value, it can be interpreted as a daily discount rate.

Table 2-3 presents illustrative estimates. For freight, shippers of perishable agricultural goods naturally have a very high value of time. The opposite is true of shippers of low-value manufactured products, such as primary and fabricated metals, that are not subject to spoilage or damage.

The value-of-time estimates for urban transportation are drawn from the study of commuting in the San Francisco Bay Area described earlier, but use a more elaborate specification of the systematic utility function. One surprising finding is that the value of in-vehicle time is higher for auto than for transit. Time spent in an automobile involves more privacy but also more effort (for the driver, at least), and apparently the latter is dominant—a result that may have changed with the subsequent spread of air conditioning, hi-fidelity sound, and cellular telephones in automobiles. Other studies of urban commuters in major industrialized cities have found values of in-vehicle time in the range of 20 to 100 percent of the pretax wage rate, leading Small to conclude that a typical value is 50 percent, with walking and waiting time valued two to three times higher.[71]

The value of time for intercity vacation trips probably reflects differing degrees of urgency and enjoyment of the trip by people using different modes. Auto travelers may enjoy side trips that take extra time, thus accounting for auto's low value of time. (This may be the one exception to the principle that travel is a derived demand rather than desired for its own sake.) Air travelers, in contrast, want to cover long distances quickly and do not derive much pleasure from time spent on the airplane, thus they have a very high value of time.[72] Rail and bus travelers fall in between.

Practical Applications

The parameter estimates, implied values of time, and elasticities obtained from transportation demand models are critical inputs into public policy on issues such as congestion relief, infrastructure investment, and industry regulation. They are also used to assist urban planning and to forecast the demand for new travel options. Most of these issues are covered in detail in other chapters in this volume, so here we provide only a brief overview.

Welfare Measures and Public Policy Issues

Evaluations of public policies often involve calculating their effects on economic welfare. A simple but important example is the efficiency loss that occurs when prices deviate from marginal costs. The usual measure of that loss accounts both for profits to firms (producer surplus) and for the value of consumption to travelers (consumer surplus). It is approximately $\frac{1}{2}\Delta P\Delta Q$, where ΔP is the price deviation and ΔQ is the resulting change in quantity. Expressed in elasticity form, the measure is:

$$(2\text{-}5) \qquad \Delta W = \tfrac{1}{2}RE_p(\Delta P/P)^2$$

---

71. Small (1992: 43–44).
72. Brand and others (1992: table 2) similarly report a much higher value of time for air than for auto in the case of nonbusiness travel.

where $R = PQ$ is revenue and E_p is the absolute value of the price elasticity of demand.[73] The more elastic the demand, the greater the distortion resulting from pricing at other than marginal cost and the greater the resulting loss of efficiency.

A more general measure involves the *compensating variation*, which measures the amount of money consumers would have to be given after a policy change to make them as well off as they were before the change. Under certain conditions it is identical to consumer surplus (the area under the demand curve and above the current price). In the case of a logit model of demand, the compensating variation can be expressed as:

(2-6)
$$CV = -\frac{1}{\mu}\left[\ln\sum_j \exp(\beta X_j)\right]_{X^0}^{X^1}$$

where β denotes the set of coefficients estimated from the demand model, X_j denotes the corresponding set of explanatory variables for alternative j, μ is a conversion factor (related to the price coefficient) to put the results in monetary units, and the notation X^0 and X^1 indicates that the expression in square brackets is to be evaluated at the initial and final values of the variables and the difference taken.[74] This expression permits evaluation of complex policies so long as their effects on the variables X can be accurately predicted.

We now turn to some examples of welfare calculations, beginning with urban transportation. Mohring estimates the welfare effects of several urban highway investments, using consumer surplus measures analogous to those leading to equation 2-5.[75] Kraus, Mohring, and Pinfold use similar techniques to evaluate the cost of nonoptimal pricing and investment policies on urban expressways.[76] Small uses a logit model of commuting mode choice to estimate compensating variations from alternative highway pricing strategies and from high-occupancy-vehicle lanes.[77] Because these policies affect the price and service times of the various modes, their welfare effects can be calculated from equation 2-6. In a related paper, Small uses the same equation to identify population subgroups that would gain, and

73. Equation 2-5 is the area on a demand diagram known as a "Harberger triangle," after Harberger (1964).

74. See Williams (1977) and Small and Rosen (1981).

75. Mohring (1965).

76. Kraus, Mohring, and Pinfold (1976).

77. Small (1983a).

those that would lose, from congestion pricing.[78] Winston and Shirley use an aggregate urban mode choice model to estimate compensating variations from charging optimal congestion tolls, imposing marginal-cost transit fares, and optimizing transit frequency. They conclude that an efficient urban transportation policy calls for more automobile travel spread more evenly throughout the day.[79]

For intercity transportation, one of the most significant issues has been the effects of industry regulation on the welfare of travelers, shippers, and carriers. Levin and Winston each use freight demand models to calculate the net welfare loss from freight transportation regulation, using equation 2-5.[80] Other studies have considered the welfare effects of the subsequent deregulation of airlines and surface freight transportation, using equation 2-6 (see Morrison and Winston's chapter in this volume).

An important response by many carriers to deregulation has been to merge with another carrier. Mergers confer costs on travelers if they enable the merged firm to raise prices, but they also confer benefits if they enable the merged firm to improve service. Transportation demand models have been used to estimate the potential benefits from improved service due to mergers of airlines and of railroads.[81]

Introducing New Travel Options

One of the common tasks asked of a travel demand analyst is to forecast the demand for a new transportation option. Examples include rapid rail urban transit, high-speed intercity rail, supersonic air transport, and even the space shuttle. More mundane examples include door-to-door demand-responsive transit service for elderly or handicapped populations, shared-ride taxi service, and airport shuttles.

Overall, the models have not been very successful on this score. Probably this is because the new travel options have unique characteristics that cannot be included in existing models, either because they lie outside current experience (such as three-hour transatlantic travel times) or because they are hard to measure (such as the fear that shared-ride taxis will pick up unsavory passengers). For example, Train investigated the ability of mode

78. Small (1983b).
79. Winston and Shirley (1998).
80. Levin (1978, 1981); Winston (1981b).
81. See Carlton, Landes, and Posner (1980) on airline mergers; Harris and Winston (1983) on railroad mergers.

choice models like those described earlier, calibrated on bus and auto modes, to predict patronage for the new Bay Area Rapid Transit (BART) service introduced to the San Francisco region in 1973. He found the models tended to overpredict BART use, perhaps because they failed to account fully for the difficulties of accessing a rail station.[82]

One of the hopes for stated preference data is that they will enable researchers to better account for novel characteristics of proposed alternative transportation arrangements. For example, Brand and others propose a way to forecast the demand for high-speed intercity rail service, using both revealed preference and stated preference data.[83] First, a direct demand model (based on revealed preference data) is estimated for existing modes. Then, based on stated preference surveys, the diversion from each existing mode is predicted. Finally, induced trip generation is estimated by assuming that the number of trips will be affected by the new service by the same amount as it would be by an equivalent upgraded existing service, based on conventional revealed preference models. This procedure allows for a flexible substitution pattern between the existing modes and the new one and also combines revealed preference and stated preference data in much the same spirit as the methods discussed earlier. We are not aware of any before-and-after studies of predictions using these methods.

Forecasts of the demand for new facilities are often necessary before an investment proceeds. But as noted in chapter 5, the record of such forecasts is dismal, especially in the case of urban rail transit. Although some of this failure can be blamed on deficiencies in the demand models, much of it probably indicates deeper problems in the way funding decisions are made for public projects. Too many people have strong incentives to misrepresent the viability of a project that will bring large amounts of money to an area.[84]

Assessment

How well do models of transportation demand meet their objectives? We have lauded the technical progress in demand modeling on the grounds that it has enabled analysts to address new questions. But has it produced correct answers?

82. Train (1978).
83. Brand and others (1992).
84. This problem is aptly reviewed by Wachs (1986, 1990).

If the objective is to predict the use of a particular transportation service at some date in the future, one is justified in taking a cynical view. Forecasts for new travel options, whether conventional or exotic, have often been far from the mark. In large part that is because models are asked to do what is impossible: predict accurate values for each of the many uncertainties in economic conditions, technology, administrative capabilities, logistical innovations, and other factors affecting demand. As argued in chapter 5, it is better to view projections as an exercise in understanding alternative possibilities than as forecasts of what is going to happen. In this respect, the ability of current demand models to elucidate the effects of numerous exogenous and policy variables makes them valuable aids in evaluating transportation investments and policies.

From a planning perspective, one indicator of how much trust can be placed in model outputs is their transferability across space and time. To what extent do models fit on data from St. Louis in 1985 help transportation analysts to understand urban travel in Denver in 1998? This type of question has been studied quite extensively.[85] The answer seems to be that the "generic" parts of disaggregate demand models—those that explain the response of decisionmakers to measurable traits that have similar meanings in many situations—transfer quite well, so long as the range of conditions in the new location is not too different from that in the old. Thus, for example, the relationship between value of time and income seems to be fairly general. In contrast, factors reflecting nongeneric influences do not transfer well. These include preferences for unmeasurable characteristics, as captured in mode-specific constants, and idiosyncratic preferences, as measured by the variance of error terms (or, when that variance is normalized, by the scale of all the other coefficients).

These observations have led to some well-defined strategies for transferring a model from one location or time period to another. One is simply to adjust the alternative-specific constants in order to predict the correct aggregate shares for the various alternatives in the new area.[86] Another is to collect a small survey sample in the new location in order to reestimate the alternative-specific constants and the overall scale of the utility function, the latter because it measures the strength of idiosyncratic preferences. A third strategy is to combine data sets, or to use special "Bayesian" tech-

85. Koppelman and Rose (1985).
86. Koppelman and Wilmot (1982).

niques on the new data set, in order to reestimate some parameters while giving weight to the original estimates of other parameters.[87]

One may also ask how well existing models account for transportation as a derived demand, arising from the desire to undertake varying activities distributed over time and space. For the most part, they do so only indirectly. Attempts to model activities directly have led to only modest gains in practice. For example, Kim and Mannering show how the duration of a shopping trip depends on the time of day, vehicle occupancy, gender, trip distance, and whether it is part of a work trip.[88] Unfortunately most of these variables are themselves determined simultaneously within an interrelated system of decisions, including activity duration; so researchers are still a long way from being able to derive the demand for transportation from first principles. It remains to be seen whether the current effort to build such models, as part of a microsimulation strategy of demand modeling, will have more success.[89]

Another example of limited but successful research into the fundamental determinants of travel behavior is the literature on how telecommunications have affected travel. Many people have asserted that the ability to transmit data cheaply, including video images in real time, will make much travel obsolete. Yet the telecommunications revolution goes back at least to Alexander Graham Bell and no noticeable drop in travel has occurred. The issue is really whether telecommunications and travel are substitutes or complements. There is much evidence for the latter: apparently, people take advantage of their greater ability to contact others by forming wider networks that are accompanied by even more travel to cement those relationships. Of course, the nature of that travel is considerably affected.[90]

Because transportation demand is derived from activity patterns, people care about the time of day they travel and the predictability of their travel arrangements. We have seen an example of the latter in the influence of transit-time reliability on freight mode choice. It is at least as important in urban transportation. Driving on a congested highway may be a great choice most of the time, but not when the occasional delay would result in missing an important meeting. As a result, the choices of mode, route, and time of day may be sensitive to the time pattern of congestion and to system

87. Ben-Akiva and Bolduc (1987).

88. Kim and Mannering (1997).

89. Wachs (1996) describes this research effort. Axhausen and Gärling (1992) and Miller and Salvini (forthcoming) review the state of the art of activity modeling.

90. For a thorough review, see Mokhtarian and Salomon (forthcoming).

reliability. Small, among others, has estimated models of time-of-day choice, which have begun to be integrated into standard modeling practice.[91] Reliability has been harder to handle because good measures of it are scarce, but some progress has been made.[92]

Conclusion

Practical experience suggests that transportation demand models have contributed accurate and informative evidence to public policy debates. In assessing policy issues as diverse as urban pricing and investment, taxation of heavy trucks, and regulation of intercity transportation, demand models have been the basis for welfare estimates in accord with the beliefs of informed observers using other methods. In some cases, such as congestion pricing, the demand models have enabled researchers to highlight certain political pitfalls in advance by identifying how various groups of travelers are affected. In others, such as airline deregulation, they have helped deflect spurious interpretations of events by demonstrating how things might have gone in the absence of deregulation.

Confidence in transportation demand models has stimulated the search for further technical advances and has encouraged applications to public policy and planning. Many of the contributions in these areas will be apparent to readers of other chapters in this volume. Additional contributions will undoubtedly appear in the handbook produced by the next generation of transportation researchers.

References

Abdel-Aty, Mohamed A., Ryuichi Kitamura, and Paul P. Jovanis. 1995. "Investigating Effect of Travel Time Variability on Route Choice Using Repeated-Measurement Stated Preference Data." *Transportation Research Record* 1493: 39–45.
Ampt, Elizabeth S., Anthony J. Richardson, and Arnim H. Meyburg, eds. 1992. *Selected Readings in Transport Survey Methodology*. Melbourne: Eucalyptus Press.

91. Small (1982); Bates and others (1996).
92. See, for example, Mahmassani, Caplice, and Walton (1990); Abdel-Aty, Kitamura, and Jovanis (1995); Calfee and Winston (1998); and Noland and others (1998).

Axhausen, Kay W., and Tommy Gärling. 1992. "Activity-Based Approaches to Travel Analysis: Conceptual Frameworks, Models, and Research Problems." *Transport Reviews* 12 (4): 323–41.

Bates, John, and others. 1996. "The London Congestion Charging Research Programme: 4. The Transport Models." *Traffic Engineering and Control* 37 (May): 334–39.

Becker, Gary S. 1965. "A Theory of the Allocation of Time." *Economic Journal* 75 (September): 493–517.

Beesley, Michael E., and Michael A. Kemp. 1987. "Urban Transportation." In *Handbook of Regional and Urban Economics, Volume II: Urban Economics,* edited by Edwin S. Mills. Amsterdam: North-Holland.

Beggs, S., S. Cardell, and J. Hausman 1981. "Assessing the Potential Demand for Electric Cars." *Journal of Econometrics* 16 (January): 1–19.

Ben-Akiva, Moshe, and Denis Bolduc. 1987. "Approaches to Model Transferability and Updating: The Combined Transfer Estimator." *Transportation Research Record* 1139:1–7.

Ben-Akiva, Moshe, Denis Bolduc, and Mark Bradley. 1993. "Estimation of Travel Choice Models with Randomly Distributed Values of Time." *Transportation Research Record* 1413: 88–97.

Ben-Akiva, Moshe, and Steven R. Lerman. 1974. "Some Estimation Results of a Simultaneous Model of Auto Ownership and Mode Choice to Work." *Transportation* 3 (November): 357–76.

————. 1985. *Discrete Choice Analysis: Theory and Application to Travel Demand.* MIT Press.

Ben-Akiva, Moshe, and Takayuki Morikawa. 1990. "Estimation of Travel Demand Models from Multiple Data Sources." In *Transportation and Traffic Theory,* edited by Masaki Koshi. New York: Elsevier.

Bhat, Chandra R. 1998. "Analysis of Travel Mode and Departure Time Choice for Urban Shopping Trips." *Transportation Research* 32B (August): 361–71.

Boyce, David E., and Bin Ran. 1996. *Modeling Dynamic Transportation Networks: An Intelligent Transportation System Oriented Approach.* New York: Springer-Verlag.

Boyd, J. Hayden, and Robert E. Mellman. 1980. "The Effect of Fuel Economy Standards on the U.S. Automotive Market: An Hedonic Demand Analysis." *Transportation Research* 14A (October–December): 367–78.

Bradley, M.A., and A.J. Daly. 1997. "Estimation of Logit Choice Models Using Mixed Stated-Preference and Revealed-Preference Information." In *Understanding Travel Behaviour in an Era of Change,* edited by Peter Stopher and Martin Lee-Gosselin. Oxford, U.K.: Elsevier Science Ltd.

Bradley, M.A., and E.P. Kroes. 1992. "Forecasting Issues in Stated Preference Survey Research." In Ampt, Richardson, and Meyburg (1992).

Brand, Daniel, and others. 1992. "Forecasting High-Speed Rail Ridership." *Transportation Research Record* 1341: 12–18.

Brownstone, David, David S. Bunch, and Kenneth Train. 1998. "Joint Mixed Logit Models of Stated and Revealed Preferences for Alternative-Fuel Vehicles." Working paper. University of California at Irvine, Department of Economics.

Brownstone, David, and Kenneth Train. Forthcoming. "Forecasting New Product Penetration with Flexible Substitution Patterns." *Journal of Econometrics.*

Bruzelius, Nils. 1979. *The Value of Travel Time.* London: Croom Helm.

Calfee, John, and Clifford Winston. 1998. "The Value of Automobile Travel Time: Implications for Congestion Policy." *Journal of Public Economics* 69 (July): 83–102.

Cardell, N. Scott, and Frederick C. Dunbar. 1980. "Measuring the Societal Impacts of Automobile Downsizing." *Transportation Research* 14A (October-December): 423–34.

Carlton, Dennis, William Landes, and Richard Posner. 1980. "Benefits of Airline Mergers." *Bell Journal of Economics* 11 (Autumn): 65–83.

Chiang, Yu-Sheng, Paul Roberts, and Moshe Ben-Akiva. 1981. "A Short-Run Freight Demand Model: The Joint Choice of Mode and Shipment Size." Paper presented at the 60th meeting of the Transportation Research Board, Washington, D.C.

Chu, Chaussie. 1981. "Structural Issues and Sources of Bias in Residential Location and Travel Mode Choice Models." Ph.D. dissertation, Northwestern University. Ann Arbor, Michigan: University Microfilms.

Daughety, Andrew F. 1979. "Freight Transport Demand Revisited: A Microeconomic View of Multimodal Multicharacteristic Service Uncertainty and the Demand for Freight Transport." *Transportation Research* 13B: 281–88.

Daughety, Andrew F., and Fred S. Inaba. 1978. "Empirical Aspects of Service-Differentiated Transport Demand." In *Motor Carrier Economic Regulation: Proceedings of a Workshop*, National Academy of Sciences, 329–49. Washington, D.C.: National Academy Press

Domencich, Thomas A., and Gerald Kraft. 1970. *Free Transit*. Lexington, Mass.: Heath Lexington Books.

Domencich, Thomas A., and Daniel McFadden. 1975. *Urban Travel Demand: A Behavioral Analysis*. Amsterdam: North Holland.

Dubin, Jeffrey, and Daniel McFadden. 1984. "An Econometric Analysis of Residential Electric Appliance Holdings and Consumption." *Econometrica* 52 (March): 345–62.

Friedlaender, Ann F., and Richard Spady. 1980. "A Derived Demand Function for Freight Transportation." *Review of Economics and Statistics* 62 (August): 432–41.

———. 1981. *Freight Transport Regulation*. MIT Press.

Gaudry, Marc. 1975. "An Aggregate Time-Series Analysis of Urban Transit Demand: The Montreal Case." *Transportation Research* 9 (August): 249–58.

——— and Michael J. Wills. 1978. "Estimating the Functional Form of Travel Demand Models." *Transportation Research* 12 (August): 257–89.

Gellman Research Associates. 1977. "An Annotated Bibliography of Shipper Attitude Studies." Paper prepared for the Association of American Railroads, Washington, D.C. June.

Golob, Thomas F., Ryuichi Kitamura, and Lyn Long, eds. 1997. *Panels for Transportation Planning: Methods and Applications*. Boston: Kluwer Academic Publishers.

Greene, William H. 1993. *Econometric Analysis*. Macmillan.

Hajivassiliou, Vassilis, and Paul Ruud. 1994. "Classical Estimation Methods for LDV Models Using Simulation." In *Handbook of Econometrics, Volume IV*, edited by Robert Engle and Daniel L. McFadden. New York: North-Holland.

Harberger, Arnold C. 1964. "Taxation, Resource Allocation, and Welfare." In *The Role of Direct and Indirect Taxes in the Federal Revenue System*, edited by John Due. Brookings.

Harris, Robert G., and Clifford Winston. 1983. "Potential Benefits of Railroad Mergers." *Review of Economics and Statistics* 65 (February): 32–40.

Hausman, Jerry A., and Daniel L. McFadden. 1984. "Specification Tests for the Multinomial Logit Model." *Econometrica* 52 (September): 1219–40.

Hausman, Jerry A., and David Wise. 1978. "A Conditional Probit Model for Qualitative Choice." *Econometrica* 46 (March): 403–26.

Heckman, James J. 1978. "Dummy Endogenous Variables in a Simultaneous Equation System." *Econometrica* 46 (July): 931–59.

———. 1981a. "Statistical Models for Discrete Panel Data." In Manski and McFadden (1981).

———. 1981b. "The Incidental Parameters Problem and the Problem of Initial Conditions in Estimating a Discrete Time-Discrete Data Stochastic Process." In Manski and McFadden (1981).

Hensher, David. 1994. "Stated Preference Analysis of Travel Choices: The State of Practice." *Transportation* 21 (May): 107–33.

Hensher, David, and Mark Bradley. 1993. "Using Stated Response Choice Data to Enrich Revealed Preference Discrete Choice Models." *Marketing Letters* 4 (April): 139–52.

Johnson, Lester W. 1990. "Discrete Choice Analysis with Ordered Alternatives." In *Spatial Choices and Processes,* edited by Manfred M. Fischer, Peter Nijkamp, and Yorgos Y. Papageorgiou. Amsterdam: North-Holland.

Johnson, M. Bruce. 1966. "Travel Time and the Price of Leisure." *Western Economic Journal* 4 (Spring): 135–45.

Kim, Soon-Gwan, and Fred L. Mannering. 1997. "Panel Data and Activity Duration Models: Econometric Alternatives and Application." In Golub, Kitamura, and Long (1997).

Kitamura, Ryuichi, and David S. Bunch. 1990. "Heterogeneity and State Dependence in Household Car Ownership: A Panel Analysis Using Ordered-Response Probit Models with Error Components." In *Transportation and Traffic Theory,* edited by M. Koshi. Amsterdam: Elsevier.

Koppelman, Frank S., and Geoffrey Rose. 1985. "Geographic Transfer of Travel Choice Models: Evaluation and Procedures." In *Optimization and Discrete Choice in Urban Systems,* vol. 247 of *Lecture Notes in Economics and Mathematical Systems,* edited by Bruce G. Hutchinson, Peter Nijkamp, and Michael Batty. Heidelberg: Springer-Verlag.

Koppelman, Frank S., and Chester G. Wilmot. 1982. "Transferability Analysis of Disaggregate Choice Models." *Transportation Research Record* 895:18–24.

Kraus, Marvin, Herbert Mohring, and Thomas Pinfold. 1976. "The Welfare Costs of Nonoptimum Pricing and Investment Policies for Freeway Transportation." *American Economic Review* 66 (September): 532–47.

Lave, Charles A. 1969. "A Behavioral Approach to Modal Split Forecasting." *Transportation Research* 3 (December): 463–80.

Lee, Lung-Fei. 1979. "Identification and Estimation in Binary Choice Models with Limited (Censored) Dependent Variables." *Econometrica* 47 (July): 977–96.

Lerman, Steven R. 1981. "Location, Housing, Automobile Ownership, and Mode to Work: A Joint Choice Model." *Transportation Research Record* 610: 6–11.

Levin, Richard C. 1978. "Allocation in Surface Freight Transportation: Does Rate Regulation Matter?" *Bell Journal of Economics* 9 (Spring): 18–45.

———.1981. "Railroad Rates, Profitability, and Welfare Under Deregulation." *Bell Journal of Economics* 12 (Spring): 1–26.

Lisco, Thomas E. 1967. "The Value of Commuters' Travel Time: A Study in Urban Transportation." Ph.D. dissertation, University of Chicago. Ann Arbor, Michigan: University Microfilms.

MVA Consultancy, Institute for Transport Studies of the University of Leeds, and Transport Studies Unit of the University of Oxford. 1987. *The Value of Travel Time Savings*. Newbury, England: Policy Journals.

Maddala, G.S. 1983. *Limited-Dependent and Qualitative Variables in Econometrics*. Cambridge University Press.

Mahmassani, Hani S., ed. Forthcoming. *Proceedings of the International Association for Travel Behaviour Research, Eighth Meeting*. Pergamon.

Mahmassani, Hani S., Christopher G. Caplice, and C. Michael Walton. 1990. "Characteristics of Urban Commuter Behavior: Switching Propensity and Use of Information." *Transportation Research Record* 1285: 57–69.

Mandel, Benedikt, Marc Gaudry, and Werner Rothengatter. 1994. "Linear or Nonlinear Utility Functions in Logit Models? The Impact on German High Speed Rail Demand Forecasts." *Transportation Research* 28B (April): 91–101.

Mannering, Fred, and David A. Hensher. 1987. "Discrete/Continuous Econometric Models and Their Application to Transport Analysis." *Transport Reviews* 7 (July-September): 227–44.

Mannering, Fred, and Clifford Winston. 1985. "A Dynamic Empirical Analysis of Household Vehicle Ownership and Utilization." *Rand Journal of Economics* 16 (Summer): 215–36.

———. 1987. "Recent Automobile Occupant Safety Proposals." In *Blind Intersection? Policy and the Automobile Industry*, edited by Clifford Winston and associates. Brookings.

———. 1991. "Brand Loyalty and the Decline of American Automobile Firms." *Brookings Papers on Economic Activity: Microeconomics*: 67–114.

Manski, Charles F., and Daniel L. McFadden, eds. 1981. *Structural Analysis of Discrete Data with Econometric Applications*. MIT Press.

McFadden, Daniel L. 1973. "Conditional Logit Analysis of Qualitative Choice Behavior." In *Frontiers in Econometrics*, edited by Paul Zarembka, 105–42. New York: Academic Press.

———. 1974. "The Measurement of Urban Travel Demand." *Journal of Public Economics* 3 (April): 303–28.

———. 1978. "Modelling the Choice of Residential Location." In *Spatial Interaction Theory and Planning Models*, edited by A. Karlquist and others, 75–96. Amsterdam: North-Holland Press.

———. 1981. "Econometric Models of Probabilistic Choice." In Manski and McFadden (1981).

———. 1987. "Specification Tests for the Multinomial Logit Model." *Journal of Econometrics* 34 (January): 62–82.

McFadden, Daniel L., Antii P. Talvitie, and associates. 1977. *Demand Model Estimation and Validation*. Special Report UCB-ITS-SR-77-9. Urban Travel Demand Forecasting Project, Phase I Final Report Series, Vol. V. University of California Institute of Transportation Studies, Berkeley.

McFadden, Daniel L., Clifford Winston, and Axel Boersch-Supan. 1985. "Joint Estimation of Freight Transportation Decisions Under Nonrandom Sampling." In *Analytical Studies in Transport Economics*, edited by Andrew F. Daughety, 137–57. Cambridge University Press.

Meurs, Henk, and Geert Ridder. 1997. "Attrition and Response Effects in the Dutch National Mobility Panel." In Golob, Kitamura, and Long (1997).

Meyer, John R., John F. Kain, and Martin Wohl. 1965. *The Urban Transportation Problem.* Harvard University Press.

Meyer, John R., and Mahlon R. Straszheim. 1971. *Techniques of Transport Planning,* Vol. I: *Pricing and Project Evaluation.* Brookings.

Miller, Eric J., and Paul A. Salvini. Forthcoming. "Activity-Based Travel Behavior Modeling in a Microsimulation Framework." In Mahmassani (forthcoming).

Mohring, Herbert. 1965. "Urban Highway Investments." In *Measuring Benefits of Government Investment,* edited by Robert Dorfman. Brookings.

Mokhtarian, Patricia L., and Ilan Salomon. Forthcoming. "Emerging Travel Patterns: Do Telecommunications Make a Difference?" In Mahmassani (forthcoming).

Morrison, Steven A., and Clifford Winston. 1985. "An Econometric Analysis of the Demand for Intercity Transportation." *Research in Transportation Economics* 2: 213–37.

Noland, Robert B., and others. 1998. "Simulating Travel Reliability." *Regional Science and Urban Economics* 28 (September): 535–64.

Oort, C. J. 1969. "The Evaluation of Travel Time." *Journal of Transport Economics and Policy* 3 (September): 279–86.

Ortúzar, Juan de Dios, and Rodrigo A. Garrido. 1994. "A Practical Assessment of Stated Preference Methods." *Transportation* 21 (August): 289–305.

Ortúzar, Juan de Dios, and Andrés Iacobelli. 1998. "Mixed Modelling of Interurban Trips by Coach and Train." *Transportation Research* 32A (June): 345–57.

Ortúzar, Juan de Dios, and Luis G. Willumsen. 1994. *Modelling Transport.* New York: Wiley.

Oum, Tae Hoon. 1979. "A Cross Sectional Study of Freight Transport Demand and Rail-Truck Competition in Canada." *Bell Journal of Economics* 10 (Autumn): 463–82.

Oum, Tae Hoon, and David Gillen. 1983. "The Structure of Inter-City Travel Demands in Canada: Theory, Tests and Empirical Results." *Transportation Research* 17B: 175–91.

Oum, Tae Hoon, W.G. Waters, II, and Jong Say Yong. 1992. "Concepts of Price Elasticities of Transport Demand and Recent Empirical Estimates." *Journal of Transport Economics and Policy* 26 (May): 139–54.

Pendyala, Ram M., and Ryuichi Kitamura. 1997. "Weighting Methods for Attrition in Choice-Based Panels." In Golob, Kitamura, and Long (1997).

Perle, Eugene. 1964. *The Demand for Transportation: Regional and Commodity Studies in the United States.* University of Chicago, Department of Geography.

Quandt, Richard, and William Baumol. 1966. "The Demand for Abstract Transport Modes: Theory and Measurement." *Journal of Regional Science* 6: 13–26.

Raimond, Timothy, and David A. Hensher. 1997. "A Review of Empirical Studies and Applications." In Golob, Kitamura, and Long (1997).

Richardson, Tony. Forthcoming. "Current Issues in Travel and Activity Surveys." In Mahmassani (forthcoming).

Small, Kenneth A. 1982. "The Scheduling of Consumer Activities: Work Trips." *American Economic Review* 72 (June): 467–79.

———. 1983a. "Bus Priority and Congestion Pricing on Urban Expressways." *Research in Transportation Economics* 1: 27–74.

———. 1983b. "The Incidence of Congestion Tolls on Urban Highways." *Journal of Urban Economics* 13 (January): 90–111.

————. 1987. "A Discrete Choice Model for Ordered Alternatives." *Econometrica* 55 (March): 409–24.

————. 1992. *Urban Transportation Economics.* Chur, Switzerland: Harwood Publishers.

————. 1994. "Approximate Generalized Extreme Value Models of Discrete Choice." *Journal of Econometrics* 62 (June): 351–82.

Small, Kenneth A., and Cheng Hsiao. 1985. "Multinomial Logit Specification Tests." *International Economic Review* 26 (October): 619–27.

Small, Kenneth A., and Harvey Rosen. 1981. "Applied Welfare Economics with Discrete Choice Models." *Econometrica* 49 (January): 105–30.

Stern, Steven. 1997. "Simulation-Based Estimation." *Journal of Economic Literature* 35 (December): 2006–39.

Terza, Joseph V., and Paul W. Wilson. 1990. "Analyzing Frequencies of Several Types of Events: A Mixed Multinomial-Poisson Approach." *Review of Economics and Statistics* 72 (February): 108–15.

Train, Kenneth. 1978. "A Validation Test of a Disaggregate Mode Choice Model." *Transportation Research* 12A: 167–74.

————. 1986. *Qualitative Choice Analysis: Theory, Econometrics, and an Application to Automobile Demand.* MIT Press.

Van Wissen, L.J.G., and H.J. Meurs. 1989. "The Dutch Mobility Panel: Experiences and Evaluation." *Transportation* 16 (May): 99–119.

Voith, Richard. 1997. "Fares, Service Levels, and Demographics: What Determines Commuter Rail Ridership in the Long Run?" *Journal of Urban Economics* 41 (March): 176–97.

Wachs, Martin. 1986. "Technique vs. Advocacy in Forecasting: A Study of Rail Rapid Transit." *Urban Resources* 4 (Fall): 23–30.

————. 1990. "Ethics and Advocacy in Forecasting for Public Policy." *Business and Professional Ethics Journal* 9 (Spring/Summer): 141–57.

Wachs, Martin, ed. 1996. "Special Issue: A New Generation of Travel Demand Models." *Transportation* 23 (August): 213–352.

Wardman, M. 1997. "Inter-Urban Rail Demand, Elasticities, and Competition in Great Britain: Evidence from Direct Demand Models." *Transportation Research* 33E (March): 15–28.

Williams, Huw C.W.L. 1977. "On the Formation of Travel Demand Models and Economic Evaluation Measures of User Benefit." *Environment and Planning* 9A (March): 285–344.

Winston, Clifford. 1979. "A Disaggregated Qualitative Mode Choice Model for Intercity Freight Transportation." Working paper SL 7904. University of California at Berkeley, Department of Economics.

————.1981a. "A Disaggregate Model of the Demand for Intercity Freight Transportation." *Econometrica* 49 (July): 981–1006.

————. 1981b. "The Welfare Effects of ICC Rate Regulation Revisited." *Bell Journal of Economics* 12 (Spring): 232–44.

Winston, Clifford, and Chad Shirley. 1998. *Alternate Route: Toward Efficient Urban Transportation.* Brookings.

Wynter, Laura M. 1995. "Stated Preference Survey for Calculating Values of Time of Road Freight Transport in France." *Transportation Research Record* 1477: 1–6.

RONALD R. BRAEUTIGAM

3 | *Learning about Transport Costs*

For many reasons the study of costs has long been of central interest in the transportation industry. Before the wave of regulatory reform began to sweep across the face of American industry in the 1970s, much of the motor carrier, railroad, pipeline, and airline industries was heavily regulated. Under regulatory agencies such as the Interstate Commerce Commission, the Federal Power Commission, and the Federal Energy Regulatory Commission, information about transport costs played a central role in determining rates.

During the 1970s policymakers began to reexamine public policy toward the transportation sector. Studies of costs, including economies of scale, were central in public policy debates as researchers sought to find out whether transportation markets were structurally more like natural monopolies or like markets that could sustain healthy competition. Then, as regulatory reform led to increased reliance on competition, the locus of decisionmaking about rates shifted from the regulatory agencies to the managers of transportation enterprises. Managers have required information on costs to make good business decisions about the types of transport services they will offer and the prices they will charge for those services.

The author would like to thank Mark Manuszak for his invaluable research assistance in this work.

This chapter examines the progress made during the past few decades in understanding transport costs. Specifically, the chapter focuses on the costs incurred by carriers in providing railroad, motor carrier, airline, or other transportation services. Many other types of costs are not addressed here, such as congestion costs, pollution costs and other externalities, and other costs to users of transport services, such as the value of time in travel. Progress in understanding has come on three fronts. First, there have been significant advances in the theoretical understanding of costs. For example, early cost studies did not recognize the proper role of factor prices in a cost function. Researchers such as McFadden and Nerlove showed the importance in empirical work of specifying cost functions that are consistent with production theory, including not only a proper treatment of factor prices, but also variables that might contribute to a change in technology over time.[1] Although these principles are now part of the material covered in standard graduate and even undergraduate courses in microeconomics, they helped define a renaissance in empirical studies of costs and production functions.

Second, improvements in empirical techniques have made it possible to learn more than ever about the underlying structure of technology in an industry. Early cost studies were often based on simple functional forms that embodied very strong assumptions about the nature of technology. They also were highly aggregated, effectively treating transportation firms as single product enterprises, and they often paid little attention to the quality of service provided. Empirical work in the past two decades has been advanced by the introduction of more flexible functional forms that contain as special cases many of the more specialized functional forms used by early investigators. Researchers have also improved techniques for studying the costs of multiproduct firms, allowing at least some degree of disaggregation of products.

Finally, as regulatory reform has been implemented, researchers have asked new kinds of questions about technology. For example, in the past regulators often studied costs to determine whether a firm's revenues would cover its costs or to measure the extent to which total costs could be divided into fixed and variable costs. Over time researchers have learned the importance of incorporating features of the transportation network into cost studies, for example, by distinguishing economies of size from econo-

---

1. McFadden (1978); Nerlove (1963). For a recent, concise treatment of various production and cost concepts, see Panzar (1989).

mies of density. As regulatory reform became a real possibility, researchers began to ask whether it was likely to lead to an industry structure compatible with competition.

To understand the evolution of transportation cost studies, it is useful to begin with a brief discussion of the kinds of cost studies that the Interstate Commerce Commission (ICC) commonly used before regulatory reform. Because issues of rail rate making were important even before the turn of the century, much of the early effort to measure transport costs focused on the railroad industry. Several academic researchers succeeded in pointing out the limitations of regulatory costing procedures and inspired a generation of improved studies. From that beginning point, I follow the flow of the literature through a series of improvements in the use of theory and empirical techniques.

After discussing several studies that have made important methodological contributions to the literature, I summarize findings from several of them about the major characteristics of selected transport modes, including economies of scale, density, size, and scope. At the outset, however, I note that this chapter is not intended to provide a comprehensive survey of transportation cost studies, an effort well beyond the scope of this paper and also one that has been attempted elsewhere, including the recent excellent survey by Oum and Waters.[2]

Early Studies of Rail Costs

It is not surprising that the early literature on transport costs primarily features studies of one of the oldest modern modes, the railroads. Beginning more than a century ago, policymakers recognized that certain features of the railroad industry made measuring the costs of rail services difficult. Among these features were the following:

—Railroads typically produced more than one type of freight service, and historically many railroads also provided substantial amounts of passenger service.

—Some of the costs of a typical railroad could be directly and unambiguously attributed to the production of individual services, whereas other costs were shared in the production of two or more services. The shared costs (or common costs) for a railroad were thought to represent a signifi-

2. Oum and Waters (1993).

cant portion of the total costs, including large fixed-cost items such as way and structure.

—Because of the large fixed common costs, a railroad would not be able to break even financially if all services were priced at marginal cost. In such a case at least some rail rates would have to exceed marginal cost if the firm were to remain financially viable.

These industry characteristics led to questions that perplexed generations of ICC railroad regulators. Given the presence of large common costs, what procedure should regulators use to determine the costs for individual services? And, given measures of costs, how should rail prices be set?

From the 1930s until the 1980s, the ICC measured costs and determined rates using fully distributed (or fully allocated) costs (FDC).[3] Under this approach, each service was typically assigned those costs that could directly and unambiguously be attributed to that service. For example, costs clearly attributable to passenger services (such as the costs of passenger cars) were assigned to passenger services. Similarly, costs clearly attributable to freight services (such as the costs of freight cars) were assigned to freight services. In addition to the directly attributable costs, each service was also assigned a portion of the common costs. The assignment of the common costs to the various services was made so that all of the common costs were allocated somewhere.

Under the FDC approach, once the costs were allocated, each service had a set of costs that were to be covered by the revenues from that service. Thus, a larger allocation of common costs to a given service meant that the service was expected to generate correspondingly larger revenues if the firm was to cover all of its costs.

The ICC's use of the FDC approach thus obscured the true nature of economic costs. Freight costs included not only the costs clearly associated with freight operations, but also some arbitrarily allocated portion of the common costs of the enterprise. In addition, the representation of costs was further masked by a very strong assumption about the relationship between allocated costs and the volume of traffic. For example, once the total allocated costs were determined for freight service, the ICC then speci-

---

3. The ICC employed "Rail Form A" as a basis for allocating common costs and distinguishing between fixed and variable costs starting in the 1930s. The FDC approach was confirmed in a major lengthy proceeding, ICC Docket 34013 *Rules to Govern the Assembly and Presenting of Cost Evidence,* Interstate Commerce Commission, Washington, D.C. (1962–70)

fied a linear relationship between the total allocated costs, C, and the volume of service, y:

$$(3\text{-}1) \qquad\qquad C = F + my,$$

where F represents fixed costs (that is, costs not sensitive to the volume of traffic), m is a constant marginal cost (and thus also equal to the average variable cost), and y is the level of output (measured in ton-miles). The cost function represented by equation 1 is said to be "affine."[4]

Several scholars, including John Meyer, offered important economic evaluations of the ICC's costing procedures.[5] They explained why the structure in equation 3-1 imposed very strong assumptions about the nature of the underlying technology of the industry and why the ICC's procedure was inadequate, even misleading, as a vehicle for analyzing costs. They also offered ideas about ways to improve the costing system.

Some of the main conclusions from this large literature are summarized as follows:

—The allocated cost relationship shown in equation 1 is not really a standard economic cost function at all, because it includes an arbitrary allocation of common costs to the service whose costs are being measured. It makes little economic sense to treat the allocated costs as a cost actually incurred in the provision of a service.

Economists have strongly objected to the use of cost allocation schemes for many decades, even before the phrase "fully distributed costs" pervaded regulatory proceedings. In 1891 F. W. Taussig wrote that "attempts have indeed been made at various times . . . to apportion the expenses, and assign to each item of traffic the sum which it costs. . . . Yet surely, the division is purely arbitrary." J. M. Clark wrote in 1923 that such a practice "offers great opportunities for the development of arbitrary and fictitious notions of cost, through the necessity of apportioning items somehow, even if there is no satisfactorily scientific basis on which to do it."[6]

Authors such as Meyer and his colleagues contributed an important insight that would be used by scholars in future years: One should avoid improper inferences that might result from the application of regression

---

4. An affine function in mathematics is a function with an intercept and a constant slope.
5. Meyer (1958). See also Meyer and others (1959), Borts (1960), Meyer and Kraft (1969), Friedlaender (1969), and Griliches (1972).
6. Taussig (1891: 450); J.M. Clark (1923: 14).

analyses to data containing arbitrary cost allocations. Instead, one might regress total costs on all outputs, avoiding cost allocations to individual services altogether.

—The characterization of output as a single, aggregated variable is overly simplistic. For example, if output is ton-miles of "freight," the structure in equation 3-1 assumes that it costs the firm the same amount to haul one ton of a commodity a hundred miles as it does to haul a hundred tons one mile. The structure also does not differentiate costs according to the type of commodity being hauled, the size of the network being served, or the density of the traffic movements along links in the network.[7]

—As Friedlaender noted, "various means of prorating the common or joint costs can be used, but all of them have an arbitrary element and hence are dangerous to use in prescribing rates."[8] And the ICC did use fully distributed costs for rate-making purposes. Because revenues were to be sufficient to cover the costs for the enterprise as a whole, the ICC required that the average rate for a type of traffic (such as freight traffic) be approximately equal to the average (allocated) cost. The ICC defined a "percent variable" to represent the percentage of total costs that were variable. If PV denotes the percent variable, then with the affine cost structure illustrated in figure 3-1, the percent variable also measures the ratio of marginal cost to average cost, as shown in equation 3-2.

$$(3\text{-}2) \quad PV = \frac{variable\ cost}{total\ cost} = \frac{my}{F + my} = \frac{m}{(F + my)/y} = \frac{marginal\ cost}{average\ cost}$$

For example, if the percent variable were 0.8, then variable costs represented about 80 percent of the fully distributed costs. Under extraordinary circumstances the ICC might allow the rate for a particular movement to go below the average allocated (fully distributed) cost but no lower than 80 percent of the FDC costs.

One of the difficulties with the ICC approach was that it applied the same percent variable figure (0.8) to all railroads, whether large or small. As equation 3-2 indicates, however, the percentage of total costs that are variable depends on the size of the firm. This is illustrated in figure 3-1. For

---

7. For more on the early literature that recognized the importance of incorporating network measures such as track miles and route miles in cost functions, see Keeler (1974) and Harris (1977).

8. Friedlaender (1969: 133). For more on the problems of fully distributed costs, see Braeutigam (1980) and Zajac (1978).

Figure 3-1. *Average and Marginal Cost with the Affine Cost Structure* $C = F + my$ *for Three Sizes of Railroads*

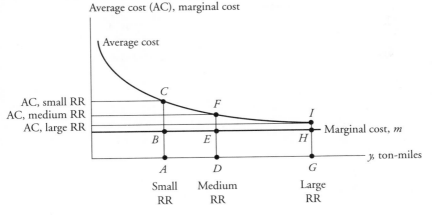

Source: Author's calculations. See text for explanation.

a small railroad, the percent variable, PV, is the ratio of marginal cost to average cost, which is the ratio of the length of segment AB to the length of the segment AC (written here as $AB{:}AC$). For a medium-size railroad, the PV is the ratio $DE{:}DF$, and for a large railroad, it is the ratio $GH{:}GI$. Obviously these ratios increase as the size of the railroad increases. Using ICC data on fully distributed costs and outputs, Griliches showed that, although medium-size railroads did have a PV of about 0.8, the PV ranged from about 0.63 for small railroads to about 0.95 for large railroads.[9] Borts found a similar range of PV for small, medium-size, and large railroads in the East, South, and West, concluding that there were economies of scale (in the sense of falling average allocated costs) everywhere except perhaps for the very large railroads in the East.[10]

It is not surprising that the costing procedures of the ICC led to substantial inefficiencies in railroad pricing before the industry was largely deregulated in the 1980s. In part these inefficiencies arose from measures of costs that were often misleading or simply incorrect, for reasons described earlier. In addition, as Friedlaender and many other authors have noted, economic inefficiencies are bound to arise when regulators base rates on costs alone (however well measured) while ignoring demand elasticities.

9. Griliches (1972).
10. Borts (1960).

Studies of Production Functions

In principal one could study production functions directly to examine questions such as whether there are economies of scale. In fact, several such studies have been done historically. One of the early studies in transportation was Cookenboo, who in 1955 examined a simple production function for a cross section of oil pipeline firms and found the following production relationship between the inputs in the pipeline process (the size of the pipeline and the pumping horsepower) and the volume of oil moved through the pipeline: $T = AH^{0.37}D^{1.73}$, where T represents pipeline throughput (volume), H the horsepower in the pumping facilities, and D the pipeline diameter; A is a constant.[11] An example of a Cobb-Douglas production function, this equation suggests that if both inputs are increased by 1 percent, the volume moved through the system will increase by 2.1 percent. (The sum of the exponents, 2.1, is referred to as the degree of economies of scale.) Because output increases by a larger proportion than the increase in inputs, this production function indicates that there will be economies of scale (increasing returns to scale) in oil pipeline transport.

Because the per unit cost of horsepower H and diameter D is roughly constant, oil pipelines exhibit declining average costs. If H and D are increased by 1 percent, total costs will increase by about 1 percent. Yet output T will increase by about 2.1 percent. Hence, economies of scale also translate into decreasing average costs for the production process.

Many engineering design studies also suggest substantial economies of scale in oil pipeline operations. For example, Wolbert wrote:

> There is no dispute that pipelines have substantial economies of scale. The basic reason is that as pipeline diameters are increased, *pipe costs* (up to existing mill facilities) increase somewhat less than proportionately, *construction costs* increase linearly, but *capacity* increases exponentially. . . . The *cost of pipe* for a 20-inch line is only 4.33 times that of a 4-inch line, yet the capacity of the larger line is 48 times that of the smaller line. . . . One 36-inch line is equal in capacity to seventeen 12-inch lines, but its *construction cost* is less than 3.5 times that of the one 12-inch line. . . . The per barrel cost of operating a 36-inch line is about 1/3 the cost of operating a 12-inch line.[12]

---

11. Cookenboo (1955).
12. Wolbert (1979: 99–100).

Studies of production functions have also been carried out for other modes and have been formulated to study firms that produce more than one type of transport service. For example, Klein analyzed data drawn from a cross section of seventy-eight railroads in the United States for two years, 1929 and 1936.[13] He estimated a production function of the following form: $(y_1)^r(y_1)^s = AK^aL^bF^e$, where y_1 is passenger miles, y_2 is ton-miles of freight, K measures capital input, L measures labor, and F measures fuel; r, s, A, a, b, and e are constants. He concluded that there were modestly increasing returns to scale in the industry ($a + b + e > 1$, but only slightly so).

In a later study using the same data set, Hasenkamp estimated a railroad production function with constant elasticity of substitution among inputs and constant elasticity of transformation among outputs.[14] The production function was $[b_1(y_1)^r + b_2(y_2)^r]^{s/r} = (a_1K^t + a_2L^t + a_3F^t)^{u/t}$, where the inputs and outputs are as defined earlier and the as, bs, r, s, t, and u are constants.

Hasenkamp found evidence of modestly increasing returns to scale, as did Klein. In addition, Hasenkamp's functional form enabled him to estimate the shape of the production transformation curve for the two outputs. He found that the production transformation curve was convex toward the origin, as illustrated in figure 3-2. He characterized this finding as providing evidence of economies of specialization in railroading. As the shape of the production transformation curve suggests, for a given amount of the three inputs, the typical railroad can produce a relatively large amount of freight service if it specializes in freight service, or it can produce a relatively large amount of passenger service if it specializes in passenger service. The total amount of freight and passenger services it can produce will be relatively limited, however, if the railroad produces both types of services (and therefore does not specialize).

These findings of economies of specialization foreshadowed several events observed in the railroad industry in recent years. In the United States freight railroads have largely abandoned passenger services, electing to specialize in freight services. In many other countries around the world, railroads have been reorganized so that separate entities provide freight operations and passenger services.

13. Klein (1974).
14. Hasenkamp (1976).

Figure 3-2. *Economies of Specialization for Railroads*

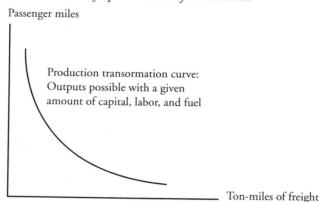

Source: Author's calculations. See text for explanation.

Proper Cost Functions

As noted earlier, empirical studies of costs greatly benefited from advances in the theory showing the connection between production functions and cost functions.[15] Marc Nerlove's study of the costs of generating electric power moved the state of the art in cost studies to a new level. He demonstrated the theoretical and empirical relationship between a Cobb-Douglas production function and its associated (dual) long-run cost function.

Nerlove was interested in whether there were economies of scale in electric power generation. He might have examined a *production* function of the form $y = AK^aL^bF^e$, where y measures the amount of electricity produced, K measures capital input, L measures labor, and F measures fuel, and where A, a, b, and e are constants. Had he done so, he would have concluded that there were economies of scale if $a + b + e > 1$, because doubling all inputs would more than double output. Similarly, he would have found constant returns to scale if $a + b + e = 1$, and decreasing returns to scale if $a + b + e < 1$.

Instead of estimating a production function, Nerlove studied the long-

15. For two landmark papers, see McFadden (1978) and Nerlove (1963).

run *cost* function that is associated with ("dual to") the Cobb-Douglas production function. He assumed that each electricity company tried to minimize its total expenditures in producing any observed level of electricity. If a firm has to pay a wage rate P_L for each unit of labor it employs, a rental price of P_K for each unit of capital it hires, and a factor price P_F for each unit of fuel it uses, then the total expenditures for the firm will be $E = P_K K + P_L L + P_F F$. If the firm minimizes its expenditures as it produces any observed level of output with the production function $y = AK^a L^b F^e$, then the total cost of producing y will be

$$(3\text{-}3) \qquad C = By^{1/(a + b + e)}(P_K)^{a/(a + b + e)}(P_L)^{b/(a + b + e)}(P_F)^{e/(a + b + e)},$$

where B itself is a combination of the constants in the production function.

Nerlove thus recognized that one could study the *cost* function to determine whether there were economies of scale. The easiest way to do that was to take the logarithms of the cost function shown in equation 3-3, leading to

$$(3\text{-}4) \qquad \ln C = d_0 + d_1 \ln y + d_2 \ln P_K + d_3 \ln P_L + d_4 \ln P_F,$$

where $d_0 = \ln B$, $d_1 = 1/(a + b + e)$, $d_2 = a/(a + b + e)$, $d_3 = b/(a + b + e)$, and $d_4 = e/(a + b + e) = (1 - d_2 - d_3)$. The coefficient d_1 is the elasticity of cost with respect to output. It shows the percentage change in total cost that will be incurred if the level of output is increased by 1 percent. For example, if the cost elasticity with respect to output is less than one $[1/(a + b + e) < 1]$, then average cost will be declining as output increases and there will be economies of scale $(a + b + e > 1)$.

Among other things, Nerlove's work showed that cost functions depend on more than total costs and output; a properly specified long-run cost function should include the prices of factors of production. Note that equations 3-3 and 3-4 do indeed depend on the factor prices P_K, P_L, and P_F.[16]

---

16. Moreover, the fact that the coefficients on the factor prices must sum to unity $(d_2 + d_3 + d_4 = 1)$ shows that cost functions must be "linear homogenous" in factor prices. For example, if the level of output is held constant and all factor prices double, then total costs must double. The linear homogeneity of a cost function in factor prices must hold for any cost function, including the more complex ones discussed later. In practice economists often impose constraints that guarantee that a cost function is "proper" (that is, consistent with the theory of costs). These restrictions should improve the efficiency of the estimation. Researchers normally treat such restrictions as hypotheses that are "main-

Today students in standard microeconomics courses (even at the undergraduate level) are taught that cost functions should include factor prices, but the inclusion of factor prices in empirical studies of costs was not common at the time Nerlove published his paper. In some studies authors omitted factor prices from the estimation on the grounds that they did not vary across the sample (for example, wage rates might be unionized and therefore the same for all firms). As Nerlove's work indicated, this would be valid only if *all* factor prices are invariant across the sample.[17]

Characterizing Outputs

Before going further, it is useful to think about the nature of the outputs of a transportation firm. As noted earlier, decades ago scholars such as Meyer, Griliches, and Borts pointed out that grossly aggregated measures of outputs such as ton miles and passenger miles failed to capture adequately the complexity of the services provided by the typical transportation enterprise. For example, suppose a firm's costs rise by 4 percent when the number of ton miles increases by 5 percent. One might ask how the increases in volume and cost were generated. Was it because the firm increased its traffic volume along one route, two routes, or on all routes proportionately? Or did the firm increase the number of routes it served? The aggregation of outputs can lead to overestimates or underestimates of the degrees of any economies of scale and obscure their sources.

Firms often haul many types of commodities with different service attributes and operate over a network with a variety of origins and destinations. Treating the movement of each commodity from each origin to each destination as a separate product would be desirable. There would

---

tained" rather than as hypotheses to be tested. One must keep in mind that imposing conditions of properness does not guarantee that a particular functional form is appropriate for studying a given technology. The estimation of a poorly chosen function form, even if it is "proper," may yield little insight about the nature of the underlying technology.

17. In early research some investigators chose to estimate cost functions instead of production functions because it is often reasonable to assume that *prices* of factors (which are right-hand side variables in a cost function) are exogenous variables. In a production function, however, the *levels* of factors are right-hand side variables, and it is not generally reasonable to assume that these variables are exogenous. Although the more sophisticated estimating procedures needed to deal with endogenous right-hand side variables are available today in virtually all econometrics packages, the procedures were not routine in the days of early empirical studies.

be so many outputs, however, that estimating a cost function would be impossible.

Because the amount of data and number of observations limit the ability to handle disaggregated outputs econometrically, researchers often take a pragmatic approach to disaggregation. As is shown later, those studying the costs of railroads, airlines, or buses may analyze passenger and freight outputs separately. Other authors have attempted to incorporate features of the network served into the cost function, often with simple characterizations such as the number of points served. A few researchers have shown that in some circumstances it may be possible to use spatially disaggregated flows, for example by keeping track of origins and destinations, to improve the understanding of costs.[18] This approach will clearly be more feasible when the number of origins and destinations is not large.

In cost studies researchers sometimes do attempt to recognize the various attributes of transport services, including service quality and other characteristics. In general this approach can also generate the need for a very large amount of data, especially if the number of attributes being measured is very large. For example, suppose y_i represents service i, and q_i represents a vector of attributes of this service. If there are m inputs (each with its own factor price) and n outputs, then a cost function for the firm would be symbolized by $C(y_1, y_2, ..., y_n, q_1, q_2, ..., q_n, w_1, w_2, ..., w_m)$. The actual form estimated could be very complicated, because any rather general functional form will involve terms that interact each argument of the cost function with every other argument.

One possible way to approach the problem just described is to study a "hedonic" cost function, as Spady and Friedlaender did.[19] A hedonic cost function is a compromise between a full multiproduct cost function and a simple cost function with only a single aggregate measure of output. Rather than trying to estimate a cost function with a very large number of outputs (including an output for movements from each origin to each destination), they specified costs as a function of aggregate ton miles and "hedonic" variables (measured by q_i), such as the average length of haul, the average size of a shipment, and the percentage of movements in less-than-truck-load (LTL) lots. They created a hedonic measure of output $\emptyset(y, q_1, q_2, ..., q_n)$, expressing the hedonic cost function as $C[\emptyset(y, q_1, q_2, ..., q_n), w_1, w_2, ..., w_m]$. From the viewpoint of estimation, this function imposes several re-

---

18. See, for example, Jara-Diaz (1988) and Jara-Diaz, Donoso, and Araneda (1992).
19. Spady and Friedlaender (1978).

strictions; for example, the hedonic measure for output $\emptyset(y, q)$ does not involve terms that interact y and q with factor prices. As a result, fewer parameters will be unknown, making it possible for the investigator to estimate a cost function when it would not otherwise be possible to do so because of a small sample size. Since 1978 several researchers have estimated hedonic cost functions.[20]

The introduction of network characteristics with hedonic measures has led to some important changes in results concerning economies of scale in the motor carrier industry. Spady and Friedlaender pointed out that many of the older studies found evidence of increasing returns to scale, primarily because they were misspecified in fundamental ways, including the failure to include factor prices and to include the attributes of services being produced. Spady and Friedlaender agreed that larger motor carriers *did* have lower average costs under regulation, but they concluded that the lower costs did not stem from economies of scale. Rather, regulation allowed larger firms to operate with longer hauls and more desirable route structures. When Spady and Friedlaender controlled for these attributes of service using their hedonic indexes, the estimates of returns to scale were constant. In other words, Spady and Friedlaender showed that lower average costs observed for larger firms were attributable to regulatory rules rather than to the nature of the technology of the motor carrier industry.[21]

In an especially innovative theoretical paper published in 1985, Spady suggested that it may be possible to capture important aspects of flows over a network with an "indexed quadratic" cost function.[22] He showed that if the cost of production along each link of the network is quadratic, there is a natural way of aggregating the flows in the network to construct a multiproduct cost function that is econometrically parsimonious. That multiproduct cost function is a true aggregate of the production processes in the various links of the network. To estimate this aggregate cost function, the investigator needs only to aggregate production data for the network and estimates of the first and second moments of the distribution of the traffic and technological characteristics over the individual links in the network. With the estimated multiproduct cost function, it is possible to derive meaningful inferences about the costs associated with movements

20. For examples of studies using hedonic measures, see Friedlaender and Spady (1981), Wang-Chiang and Friedlaender (1984), and Gillen, Oum, and Tretheway (1990).
21. Spady and Friedlaender (1978).
22. Spady (1985).

along any specific link of the network. At this writing, the author is not aware of an actual application of this promising technique in the transport sector.

It is worth observing that, before deregulation, outputs were typically treated as exogenous variables in the studies of costs. Nerlove first offered the justification for such an assumption in empirical cost studies of regulated industries in his pioneering work on returns to scale in the supply of electricity. The usual argument is that level of output can be regarded as exogenous if price is regulated and carriers are obligated to serve any customers requesting service at the regulated price (this condition of service is often referred to as the "common carrier obligation").[23] Following deregulation, however, firms have been able to set the prices of their services, and thus the levels of outputs can no longer be regarded as exogenous. Empirical studies must thus take into account the endogeneity of output with a technique such as instrumental variables.

Flexible Functional Forms

Although the Cobb-Douglas cost function examined by Nerlove is consistent with the theory of production and costs, it has some rather restrictive properties. For example, the elasticity of total cost with respect to output is a constant, no matter whether the firm is small or large. If this elasticity is less than unity, then there will be economies of scale for all outputs, and the average cost schedule will be declining for all outputs as well.[24]

In addition the elasticity of cost with respect to each factor price is constant. For example, in equation 3-4, d_3 represents the elasticity of cost with respect to the wage rate; with the Cobb-Douglas form the total cost

23. One must be cautious in using this approach to justify the treatment of the level of output as exogenous. Even if price is regulated and a firm is obligated to serve all customers who want service, the level of output may still be endogenous. For example, a firm might be able to affect the demand for its service by altering the quality of service, even if price is regulated. In the days of heavy price regulation of the airline industry, firms often vigorously competed on quality of service.

24. Nerlove recognized this problem in his work. One approach he took was to break the 145 electric utilities in his sample into five groups of 29 firms, with the smallest 29 firms in the first group, the next smallest 29 firms in the second group, and so on. He then estimated a separate Cobb-Douglas cost structure for each group and found that the elasticities of cost with respect to output increased to about unity (the average cost schedule flattened out) for the group of the largest utilities.

will always increase by d_3 percent every time the wage rate increases by 1 percent. Moreover, under the Cobb-Douglas cost structure, the share of expenditures on each factor of production is a constant, regardless of the relative factor prices or the level of output. For example, the share of total costs spent on labor is always d_3. Similarly, the shares of total costs spent on capital and fuel are always d_2 and d_4 respectively.[25] Finally, the elasticity of substitution of one factor for another is always unity under a Cobb-Douglas cost structure.[26]

Beginning in the 1970s one of the major innovations in cost studies was the introduction of less restrictive forms of proper cost functions that were suitable for empirical work. These so-called *flexible form* cost functions include among others the generalized Leontief function and the translog function.[27]

Because the translog function has proven to be the one most often employed in cost studies of several transportation modes, it is the focus of the following discussion. The long-run translog cost function for m outputs and n inputs is written as follows:

$$\ln C = a_0 + \sum_{i=1}^{m} a_i \ln y_i + \sum_{i=1}^{n} b_i \ln w_i + \frac{1}{2}\sum_{i=1}^{m} \sum_{j=1}^{m} a_{ij} \ln y_i \ln y_j$$

(3-5)

$$+ \frac{1}{2}\sum_{i=1}^{n} \sum_{j=1}^{n} b_{ij} \ln w_i \ln w_j + \sum_{i=1}^{m} \sum_{j=1}^{n} g_{ij} \ln y_i \ln w_j$$

where C is total cost, y_i is the level of output i, w_j is the price of input j.

In virtually all applications, the translog structure is estimated with a procedure first used in a well-known paper by Christensen and Greene.[28] These authors imposed a set of restrictions on the parameters that guaran-

25. From equation 3-4 and Shephard's lemma $(\partial C/\partial P_L = L)$, it follows that $d_3 = (\partial C/\partial P_L)(P_L/C) = P_L L/C$; in other words, d_3 is the "factor share of labor," the share of total costs spent on labor. Note that because the sum of the factor shares must always sum to unity, it can be seen once again why $d_2 + d_3 + d_4 = 1$ if the Cobb-Douglas cost function shown in equation 3-4 is proper.

26. For a demonstration of this, see Silberberg (1990).

27. See Diewert (1971) for the generalized Leontief function and Christensen, Jorgenson, and Lau (1971, 1973) for the translog function. Although I do not focus on the generalized Diewert form here, note that the basic form with constant returns to scale is $C = y \sum_i \sum_j \beta_{ij}(w_i)^{0.5}(w_j)^{0.5}$, where C is total cost, y is output, and w_i is the factor price of the ith factor. For this cost structure, the factors will be employed in fixed proportions, regardless of the factor prices. If x_i denotes the level of factor i employed, then $x_i/x_j = \beta_{ij}/\beta_{jj}$, so that the ratio of the inputs is independent of the level of output and the factor prices.

28. Christensen and Greene (1976).

tee that the cost function is linear homogenous in factor prices ($\sum_i b_i = 1$ and $\sum_j g_{ij} = 0$ for all i, and $\sum_i b_{ij} = 0$ for all j), so that it is a proper cost function. In addition, the coefficients are strained to be symmetric ($a_{ij} = a_{ji}$ for all i and j and $b_{ij} = b_{ji}$ for all i and j), so that the function is well behaved in its second derivatives. Finally, investigators often have factor share data (that is, data showing what percentage of total costs is expended on each factor). Where such data are available, factor share equations are typically estimated simultaneously with the cost function to improve the precision of the estimates.[29]

The Cobb-Douglas cost function is a special case of the translog cost function shown in equation 3-5. Note that if all of the terms containing a_{ij}, b_{ij}, and g_{ij} are set equal to zero, the remaining cost function is just

$$\ln C = a_0 + \sum_{i=1}^{m} a_i \ln y_i + \sum_{i=1}^{n} b_i \ln w_i \, ,$$

which is a Cobb-Douglas cost function with m outputs. The additional second-order terms in the translog allow the cost elasticities for output and for all of the factor prices to vary (instead of remain constant, as was the case with the Cobb-Douglas function) as output and factor prices change. For example, estimates of the extent of economies of scale are allowed to vary depending on the operating point at which they are measured. This is the sense in which the translog function is "flexible."[30]

What can be done if the sample includes zero values for some observations? For example, suppose that some railroads have positive amounts of freight and passenger traffic, while others specialize only in freight (with no observed passenger traffic). In that case the translog specification is problematic, because the logarithm of zero is negative infinity.

This problem can be addressed, however, using what is known as the Box-Cox transformation.[31] If data on y_i are sometimes zero, then instead of

---

29. For example, the factor share equation for the factor whose price is w_i would be $\partial \ln C / \partial \ln w_i = \partial C / \partial w_i \cdot w_i / C = w_i x_i / C = s_i$. The share of total cost spent on factor x_i. Then the factor share equation for factor i would be $s_i = a_i + \sum_{j=1}^{n} b_{ij} \ln y_j + \sum_{j=1}^{n} g_{ij} \ln y_j$.

30. Of course, no function is perfectly flexible, and there is a tension between having forms that are both flexible and proper over a large region of operations. For discussions of flexibility, see, for example, Guilkey, Lovell, and Sickles (1983) and Diewert and Wales (1987).

31. For a nice discussion of the translog with a Box-Cox transformation (sometimes called the "generalized" translog), see Caves, Christensen, and Tretheway (1980). This article also contains an application of the technique to the railroad industry.

entering data as $\ln y_i$, with the Box-Cox transformation the data are entered as $[(y_i)^\lambda - 1]/\lambda$, where λ is a parameter to be estimated in the regression. Now the number of parameters to estimate is the same as in a standard translog, except that for the additional parameter λ. It turns out that there are two polar cases of interest for λ. If $\lambda = 1$, then $[(y_i)^\lambda - 1]/\lambda$ is just y_i, in which case the Box-Cox transformation of y_i is y_i itself. Also, if $\lambda = 0$, then it can be shown that $\lim_{\lambda \to 0} [(y_i)^\lambda - 1]/\lambda = \ln y_i$. So the Box-Cox transformation includes as special cases the representations of y_i that are linear ($\lambda = 1$) and the natural logarithm ($\lambda = 0$), but has a less obvious interpretation for other values of λ.

There also are other ways of dealing with data sets that include observations with zero values for outputs. One such form is the quadratic-CES (constant elasticity of substitution) form introduced by Röller. If y is a vector of outputs and w a vector of factor prices, then the quadratic-CES function is of the form $C(y, w) = h(y)g(w)$, where h is a quadratic (or perhaps modified quadratic) function of outputs homogenous in factor prices and g is a function of prices written with a CES.[32]

Economies of Size and Density in Networks

As noted earlier, one of the features of the transportation industry that creates a challenge in the effort to characterize whether economies of scale exist is that services are often provided over a network, which raises the issue of what it means to increase output. Output might be increased by moving a higher volume of traffic over a given network, which would increase the density of traffic movements over existing links in the network. Output might also be increased by expanding the size of the network served, even though the density of movements along links of the network might not vary at all.

The basic distinction between size and density is illustrated in figure 3-3. Suppose at some initial operating point a firm provides service over the network illustrated in figure 3-3a. The firm serves four different points (nodes) in the network (points A, B, C and D), denoted by $N = 4$. The amount of traffic (measured in ton-miles) over each link is indicated in the figure, and the total amount over the network is 120 ton-miles ($y = 120$).

---

32. Röller (1990:202–10). If the function of outputs is purely quadratic, it will be $h = a_0 + \sum_{i=1}^{m} a_i \ln y_i$ $+ \frac{1}{2} \sum_{i=1}^{m} \sum_{j=1}^{m} a_{ij} \ln y_i \ln y_j$. It might also be modified to be of a form such as $h = a_0 + \sum_{i=1}^{m} a_i \ln y_i + \frac{1}{2} \sum_{i=1}^{m} \sum_{j=1}^{m} a_{ij} (\ln y_i \ln y_j)^\gamma$, where γ is an additional parameter to be estimated. The CES function g is of the form $[\sum_i b_i (w_i)^r]^{1/r}$. Note that this cost function is linear homogenous in factor prices.

Now suppose the amount of traffic is increased by 25 percent, so that $y = 150$ for the network as a whole. How might this increase in traffic affect operations in the network? To be sure, traffic might be distributed over the network in an infinite number of ways so that the total amount is $y = 150$. One way is illustrated in figure 3-3b. Here the network configuration remains as it was in figure 3-3a; the increased output has occurred by increasing the traffic volume (the density of traffic) along each link by 25 percent. In other words, the *size* of the network is unchanged, but the *density* of traffic movements has increased.

Another way of increasing the number of ton-miles is illustrated in figure 3-3c. Here the size of the network has been increased by adding another node (*E*) and a link to serve that node. There are now five nodes (*N* = 5), so the number of *nodes* has been increased by 25 percent, but the volume of traffic over the existing links has not been increased (the density of traffic is unchanged). In other words, the *size* of the network is increased, but the *density* of traffic movements is unchanged. This is the type of output expansion usually envisioned in studies of economies of scale.

Caves, Christensen, and Swanson suggested a way to distinguish between economies of size and economies of density in empirical work.[33] For a long-run cost function in which total cost C depends on a set of n outputs ($y_1, y_2, ..., y_n$) and the number of points (nodes) in the network, N, the degree of economies of density S_D is measured by

$$S_D = 1 / \sum_{i=1}^{n} e_{y_i}^c$$

where $e_{y_i}^c$ is the elasticity of total cost with respect to output i. S_D is therefore a measure of economies of scale when traffic volume is increased, but the number of nodes (the size of the network) is held fixed. Economies of density, constant returns to density, or diseconomies of density would be observed as S_D respectively is greater than, equal to, or less than 1.

The degree of economies of size S_S is measured by

$$S_S = 1 / (\sum_{i=1}^{n} e_{y_i}^c + e_N^c),$$

where, in addition to the terms already defined, e_N^c is the elasticity of total cost with respect to the number of nodes, N. S_S is therefore a measure of economies of scale (size) when output *and the size of the network* are in-

---

33. Caves, Christensen, and Swanson (1981).

Figure 3-3. *Economies of Size and Density*

a. Initial operation

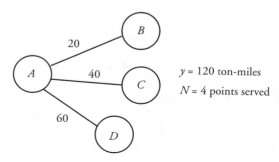

y = 120 ton-miles
N = 4 points served

b. Size of network held constant, density increased 25 percent

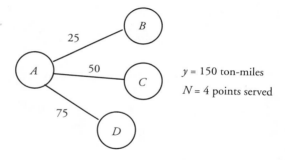

y = 150 ton-miles
N = 4 points served

c. Size of network increased 25 percent, density held constant

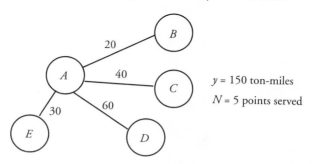

y = 150 ton-miles
N = 5 points served

Source: Author's calculations. See text for explanation.

creased. Economies of scale, constant returns to scale, or diseconomies of scale occur as S_S respectively is greater than, equal to, or less than 1.

Both firms and public policymakers may be interested in economies of size and economies of density. As discussed later, most recent cost studies of railroads, motor carriers, and airlines suggest that there are no significant economies of size. Studies often find economies of density for railroads and airlines, however. Economies of density are important to firms because they may be able to reduce costs by routing traffic to take advantage of these economies where they exist. Policymakers may ask how economies of density will affect the likelihood of effective competition.

Although an extensive discussion of the importance of economies of size and density in public policy is well beyond the scope of this chapter, neither one precludes the possibility that some form of competition can be successful in a market. For example, even if a railroad operates with significant economies of density in a market, its ability to raise prices will be limited if competition from motor carriers, pipelines, or water carriers is significant along that route. Similarly, an airline may operate with economies of density in a city-pair market and may even be the only carrier serving that market. Its ability to raise prices will be limited, however, if entry and exit by other potential carriers is relatively easy in that market.[34]

Economies of density are often also important in debates surrounding proposed mergers. Suppose two railroads wish to merge. Some parties (including shippers and other railroads) may object on the grounds that the merger will somehow lead to reduced competition and possibly higher rail tariffs. The railroads seeking to merge often attempt to demonstrate that reorganizing operations to take advantage of economies of density within the merged enterprise will result in cost savings. Policymakers must weigh such arguments in deciding whether to bless or challenge a merger.

An Illustration of Economies of Density and Size

Because cost studies may be new to many students, it may be helpful to examine an actual cost study to illustrate some of the principles discussed here. The illustration comes from work on airline costs by Caves, Christensen, and Tretheway, who carried out a study of the long-run costs of a cross section of airlines identified in table 3-1, using annual data from

34. For more on the policy alternatives that exist when firms have market power, see Braeutigam (1989) and Baumol, Panzar, and Willig (1982).

Table 3-1. *Illustration of Long-Run Cost Function*

$\ln C =$ constant $+ 0.836 \ln Y + 0.131 \ln N - 0.135 \ln D - 0.277 \ln G + 0.356 \ln w + 0.166 \ln f + 0.478 \ln r +$ time and firm dummies below:

	output	# points	stage length	load factor	wage rate	fuel price	cost of capital, material
coefficient	0.836	0.131	−0.135	−0.277	0.356	0.166	0.478
(s.e.)	(0.066)	(0.064)	(0.054)	(0.143)	(0.005)	(0.003)	(0.002)

Time (base, 1977)

1970	0.141	(0.038)
1971	0.140	(0.036)
1972	0.089	(0.032)
1973	0.091	(0.031)
1974	0.078	(0.030)
1975	0.076	(0.030)
1976	0.041	(0.028)
1978	−0.053	(0.031)
1979	−0.086	(0.035)
1980	−0.021	(0.035)
1981	0.015	(0.037)

Firm (base, Delta)

American	0.140	(0.049)	Western	−0.114	(0.085)
Braniff	−0.053	(0.073)	Air West	−0.026	(0.135)
Continental	−0.115	(0.083)	Frontier	−0.169	(0.129)
Eastern	0.092	(0.042)	North Central	−0.037	(0.137)
National	−0.077	(0.095)	Ozark	−0.074	(0.149)
Northeast	−0.095	(0.153)	Piedmont	−0.062	(0.143)
Northwest	−0.144	(0.060)	Republic premerger	0.029	(0.109)
Pan Am premerger	0.002	(0.101)	Republic postmerger	0.036	(0.109)
Pan Am postmerger	0.003	(0.090)	Southern	−0.081	(0.157)
TWA	0.133	(0.059)	Texas International	−0.134	(0.158)
United	0.081	(0.054)	U.S. Air	0.006	(0.092)

Source: Caves, Christensen and Tretheway (1983).

1970 to 1981. The table shows estimates of the cost function, which involves first-order terms of natural logarithms but no second-order terms. Thus the relationship shown in the table is a Cobb-Douglas cost function rather than a translog function.[35]

In the cost function, C denotes total cost, y is the number of passenger miles, N is the number of points in the network, D is the average stage length in the network (the average distance between takeoff and landing for airplanes on the system), G is the load factor (the ratio of occupied seats to total seats), w is the wage rate, f is the fuel price, and r is the firm's factor price of capital and material.

In addition, the authors used a set of dummy variables to capture year-specific effects, with the base year being 1977. A positive coefficient for a given year (for example, the coefficient 0.141 in 1970) indicates that the cost function is higher in that year than in the base year of 1977. The time dummies can be used to measure whether costs are falling over time as technical change takes place in an industry. A general decline in the coefficients of the time dummies over time indicates that technical change has led to reduced costs over time. They authors also included a set of dummy variables to reflect firm-specific effects, with the base firm being Delta. What kinds of empirical findings might be generated by this cost study?[36]

Finding 1: How will increases in factor prices affect total costs?

The point estimates indicate that the elasticity of total cost with respect to the wage rate is 0.356 (the coefficient on ln$w$), which means that as the wage rate increases by 1 percent, the total cost will increase by an estimated 0.356 of 1 percent. Similarly, the point estimates indicate that the elasticities of total cost with respect to the price of fuel and the price of capital and materials are respectively 0.166 and 0.478. So, for example, as the fuel price increases by 1 percent, the total cost will increase by an estimated 0.166 of 1 percent.[37]

---

35. Caves, Christensen, and Tretheway (1983, 1984). The authors examined the issues discussed here with a more flexible form, the translog cost function. The full set of results is not presented here.

36. The following discussion focuses on the conclusions that can be drawn by examining the point estimates. No attempt is made here to discuss the use of standard errors to construct confidence intervals for tests of hypotheses, because that effort is well beyond the scope of this chapter.

37. Note also that the cost function is proper in the sense that it is linear homogenous in factor prices; the coefficients on ln$w$, ln$f$, and ln$r$ all sum to unity. Thus, if all factor prices rise by 1 percent, total costs will also rise by 1 percent.

Finding 2: What does the cost study indicate about the share of total costs expended on the various factors of production?

Because this is a Cobb-Douglas cost function, the elasticity of cost with respect to the wage rate is also the estimate of the share of total costs expended on labor. Thus, labor costs make up about 35.6 percent of the total long-run cost for the typical airline. Similarly, fuel costs make up about 16.6 percent of total costs, and expenditures on capital and material are about 47.8 percent of total costs.

Finding 3: What does the study indicate about economies of density?

To examine economies of density, one would ask what happens if *y* (passenger miles) is increased by 1 percent, while the size of the network *N* remains fixed. This exercise is the one illustrated in figure 3-3b. In that case, the point estimate would indicate that costs would go up by 0.836 percent. Thus, the elasticity of cost with respect to output (there is only one output in this example) is 0.836, suggesting that total costs rise less rapidly than traffic volume when the network size is fixed (and density of traffic therefore increases over the given network). The degree of economies of density is $S_D = 1/0.836 = 1.196$. Because $S_D > 1$, the finding is consistent with economies of density.

Finding 4: What does the study indicate about economies of size?

To examine economies of size, one would ask what happens if y (passenger miles) and the size of the network N are each increased by 1 percent. This exercise is the one illustrated in figure 3-3c. Again, the elasticity of cost is 0.836 with respect to output and an additional 0.131 with respect to the number of nodes. The point estimates thus indicate that costs would go up by (0.836 + 0.131) percent, or by about 0.967 percent. The degree of economies of size is $S_S = 1/(0.836 + 0.131) = 1/0.967$. This number is very close to 1.0, suggesting that total costs rise by about the same percentage as traffic volume when the network size is also increased proportionately, and that returns to size are approximately constant.[38]

One of the substantive implications of this finding is that firms of all sizes can compete in the airline industry. Considered together, the answers to findings 3 and 4 suggest that costs per passenger mile are reduced not by operating a bigger network, but by increasing the density of traffic over the network.

---

38. Here especially one must resist the temptation to construct a confidence interval on the sum of coefficients with the data given in the table. To construct a confidence interval on the sum of coefficients, one would need to know the covariance of the estimates as well as the variances.

Finding 5: Is there evidence of cost-reducing technical change over time?
An examination of the estimates of the coefficients of the time dummies reveals that the magnitudes have generally fallen over time, at least up to 1980. This decline suggests productivity growth in the airline industry during the sample period.

In addition to these kinds of questions, one might also ask whether the results of such a study are sensible given what is known about an industry. This question helps assess the validity of the study. For example, in moving a given number of passenger miles over a network, one would expect total costs to be lower when the load factor is higher. A higher load factor would mean that the firm is making fewer flights to move the passengers or that it is using aircraft better suited to the volume of traffic. The negative coefficient on the load factor (–0.277) suggests that this is indeed the case.

Costs should also be lower when the stage length is greater. A longer stage length means fewer takeoffs and landings per passenger mile, and takeoffs and landings require extra fuel, operating time, and expenses on the ground. The coefficient on stage length is negative (–0.135), again confirming expectations.

Taken together, the findings from a study such as this one can help researchers understand much about the way the industry operates. Airlines do attempt to choose their routes (through entry, exit, and in some cases the creation of hub-and-spoke networks) and pricing strategies (in industry parlance, "yield management") to take advantage of economies of density. The study also reveals that the firms with the lowest costs are not necessarily the biggest airlines. For example, the coefficients on the firm-specific dummies for United and American are larger than the coefficients on the firm-specific dummies for many of the other smaller airlines. Thus, the study suggests that a firm need not be large to compete in this industry.

In attempting to assess whether there are economies of scale in transportation industries, it turns out that it matters whether the output is increased through increases in size or in density. For example, empirical research has often suggested that the railroad industry may experience significant increasing returns to density but constant or only slightly increasing returns to size (table 3-2).[39] As Keeler observes, the findings of economies of density in the railroad sector no doubt reflect the fact that "a relatively large part of the network is of the low density sort."[40] Economies of density

---

39. Such findings include, among others, Keeler (1974), Harmatuck (1979), Caves and others (1985), and Friedlaender and others (1993).
40. Keeler (1983: 53).

Table 3-2. *Selected Cost Studies of Railroads*

Study	Functional form	Data	Selected focus or conclusions[a]
Keeler (1974).	Cobb-Douglas (loglinear)	Panel of 51 firms, 1968–70	CRS, economies of density
Brown, Caves, and Christensen (1979).	Translog	Cross section, 67 firms, 1936	IRS
Caves and others (1985).	Translog	Panel, 43 firms, 1951–75	IRS for some carriers, CRS for large carriers, economies of density
Harmatuck (1979).	Translog	40 firms, 1968-70	Economies of density
Caves, Christensen, and Swanson (1981).	Translog	U.S. railroads, 1955–74.	Economies of density but less strong evidence of economies of scale, productivity growth
Braeutigam, Daughety, and Turnquist (1982).	Translog	One large RR, monthly, 1969–77	Economies of density, speed of service is important explanatory variable
De Borger (1992).	Translog with Box-Cox (nests translog and generalized Leontief)	Time series, 1 firm, 1950–86	Slight IRS or CRS, productivity growth < 2% per year.
Friedlaender, and others (1993).	Translog	Panel, 1974–86	Slight IRS, economies of density
Friedlaender and Spady (1981).	Translog	26 firms, annual, 1968–70	Economies of density, no economies of size
Kim (1987).	Translog with Box-Cox	56 Class I railroads in 1963	Slight IRS, diseconomies of scope between freight and pass.
Magura and Braeutigam (1997).	Semiparametric	Annual, 1958–1990	Mixture of cost complementarities, anticomplementarities
Filippini and Maggi (1992).	Translog, total and variable cost functions	48 Swiss private railroads, 1985–88	Economies of density

Source: See text for explanation.
a. CRS = constant returns to scale; IRS = increasing returns to scale.

have resulted in part from historical regulatory rules that made it difficult for railroads to abandon lines with low traffic volumes. They also exist because the railroad network itself may not have been developed to rationalize traffic in the most cost efficient manner. Since deregulation railroads have tried to realize some of the economies of density by abandoning track, seeking mergers to combine traffic and thus increase density, and tailoring contracts to shipper needs to stimulate volumes. Tables 3-3, 3-4, and 3-5 show similar findings in the trucking sector, airline industry, and various other modes, respectively.[41]

Economies of Scope, Cost Complementarities, and Anticomplementarities

In addition to studying costs to discover information about economies of scale, including economies of density and size, researchers may want to learn how the production of a combination of two or more outputs affects total cost. Under common carrier regulation, regulatory rules often specified the types of services a firm could offer. After deregulation firms were able to make decisions about the number of services they provided. Should a firm diversify into more services? Or should it specialize in the provision of fewer services? For those kinds of business decisions, firms needed to know whether a single firm providing a combination of services would encounter cost advantages or disadvantages.[42]

Suppose that the firm (for example, a railroad or an airline) produces two types of services: freight service, measured by y_1; and passenger service, measured by y_2. Further suppose that the total cost of production is $C(y_1, y_2)$.[43] Researchers might ask how an increase in the level of one service (y_1) will affect the marginal cost of producing the second service (y_2).

Mathematically the marginal cost of service 1 is just the partial derivative of C with respect to y_1, $\partial C/\partial y_1$. To find out how an increase in y_2 will affect the marginal cost of service 1, then one would examine the derivative of the marginal cost of service 1 with respect to the level of service 2; in

41. In the trucking sector, see Friedlaender and Spady (1981) and Winston and others (1990). In the airline industry, see Caves, Christensen, and Tretheway (1983), Gillen, Oum, and Tretheway (1990), and Keeler and Formby (1994).

42. The conceptual work on multiproduct cost functions by Baumol, Panzar, and Willig (1982) motivated much of the empirical research found in the literature on economies of scale and scope.

43. Here reference to the factor prices is suppressed to simplify the notation.

Table 3-3. *Selected Cost Studies of Motor Carriers*

Study	Functional form	Data	Selected focus or conclusions[a]
Spady and Friedlaender (1978).	Translog, hedonic	168 firms, 1972	CRS (or even DRS) when quality of service variables included
Harmatuck (1991).	Translog with Box-Cox	Panel of 17 large firms, 1974–83.	Mixed evidence on economies of scope
Koenker (1977).	Cobb-Douglas(loglinear)	Panel, 25 firms, 1948–72	U-shaped average cost schedule
Wang Chiang and Friedlaender (1984).	Translog, hedonic	105 large carriers, 1976	CRS
Grimm, Corsi, and Jarrell (1989).	Translog	1977, 1984–86	CRS, economies of load size, but not length of haul economies
Winston and others (1990).	Cobb-Douglas (loglinear)	1984, 1985	LTL: CRS, economies of density, load size, TL: slight IRS
Thomas and Callan (1992).	Translog	1984, specialized carriers	CRS, measure of shipment composition is important explanatory variable
Ying (1990).	Translog	61 firms, Class I and II carriers, 1975–84.	Slight DRS, tendency toward CRS after deregulation
Friedlaender and Spady (1981).	Translog, hedonic	26 firms, 1968–70	Economies of density, no economies of size
Allen and Liu (1995).	Translog	Panel of LTL firms, 1985–89	IRS in LTL after controlling for service quality
Daughety and Nelson (1988).	Translog	Panel, 1953–88	Cost functions in 1950s and 1982 more similar to one another than to cost functions in 1968 and 1978.
Harmatuck (1992).	Translog	9 LTL firms, 1974–88	IRS in all variations of specification
Daughety, Nelson, and Vigdor (1985).	Translog	85 general freight carriers, 1974–79	Slight DRS

Source: See text for explanation.

a. CRS = constant returns to scale; IRS = increasing returns to scale; DRS = decreasing returns to scale.

Table 3-4. *Selected Cost Studies of Airlines*

Study	Functional form	Data	Selected focus or conclusions[a]
Caves, Christensen, and Tretheway (1984).	Translog	Panel,1970–81	CRS or slight IRS
Gillen, Oum, and Tretheway (1990).	Translog, hedonic	Cross section, Canada, 1964–81.	Constant returns to size, increasing returns to density, some cost complementarity between scheduled and charter services. Trunk carriers more productive than regional carriers
Caves, Christensen, and Tretheway (1983).	Translog	Panel of local service and trunk carriers, 1970–81	Economies of density, but not economies of size
Keeler and Formby (1994).	Translog	Panel	CRS, cost anticomplementarities between passenger and freight, economies of density
Kumbhakar (1990).	Generalized McFadden	U.S. carriers, 1970–84	Economies of density, increasing returns to size, low productivity growth
Oum and Zhang (1991).	Variable costs recognizing asymmetry of fixed factor price	Canadian carriers, 1964–81.	IRS
McShan and Windle (1989).	Translog	Panel of carriers, 1977–84	Costs reduced by 0.1 percent for every one percent increase in hubbing

Source: See text for explanation.

a. CRS = constant returns to scale; IRS = increasing returns to scale.

Table 3-5. *Selected Other Cost Studies*

Study	Model/sector	Functional form	Data	Selected focus or conclusions[a]
Savage (1994).	Urban rail	Translog	13 heavy rail, 134 light rail systems, 1985–91	Economies of size for light rail, diseconomies of size for heavy rail, economies of density (light and heavy),
Gillen and Oum (1984).	Canadian motor coach, intercity	Translog	17 intercity bus firms	U-shaped re average cost curves, no economies of scope between passenger, charter, freight
Obeng (1984).	Urban bus	Translog	62 bus systems, 1982	DRS
Kumbhakar and Bhattacharyya (1996).	Publicly owned passenger bus companies in India	Translog, variable cost	31 firms, 1983–87	Main source of total factor productivity is from scale economies
Sickles and Streitwieser (1992).	Natural gas transmission	Translog	Gas transmission firms, 1978–85	IRS, little change in productivity over the sample period

Source: See text for explanation.

a. DRS = decreasing returns to scale; IRS = increasing returns to scale.

other words one would examine $\partial/\partial y_2(\partial C/\partial y_1) = \partial^2 C/\partial y_2 y_1$. If the marginal cost of service 1 falls as the amount of service 2 rises, then $\partial^2 C/\partial y_2 y_1 < 0$. At least in the neighborhood of the observations of interest, this condition demonstrates a kind of cost synergy from offering the two services together. In economic parlance, a condition in which $\partial^2 C/\partial y_2 y_1 < 0$ is referred to as one in which there are cost complementarities between service 1 and 2. If the opposite condition holds (that is, if $\partial^2 C/\partial y_2 y_1 > 0$), then there are cost anticomplementarities between the two services. At least locally (in the neighborhood of the observations), the marginal cost of one service increases when the level of the other service increases.

Cost complementarities and anticomplementarities are "local" concepts because they describe how the cost function behaves in the neighborhood of an observation or set of observations. At times, however, investigators may be interested in learning whether it is less costly to have the two products provided by the same entity at all. In that case the researcher will want to know whether there are economies or diseconomies of scope. The firm is said to operate with *economies of scope* in producing the outputs (y_1, y_2) if $C(y_1, y_2) < C(0, y_2) + C(y_1, 0)$, in which case it is less costly to produce the observed set of outputs with one firm than it is with two firms, each specializing in the production of only one service. If the inequality is reversed, then there are *diseconomies of scope*, and it will be less costly to produce the observed set of outputs with two firms, one producing only y_1 and the other producing only y_2.

Because an examination of economies of scope requires information about the nature of costs along the axes of output (where one of the outputs is zero), it is obvious that a cost function must be capable of evaluating costs when the level of an output is zero. The translog function cannot do this (because the logarithm of zero is negative infinity). Thus the translog function is not appropriate for examining economies of scope. (It may, however, still be a reasonable choice when examining cost complementarities.) In studying economies of scope, one might choose a generalized translog (that is, a translog with a Box-Cox transformation for outputs), or some other form such as Röller's quadratic-CES form.

Several studies have shed light on cost complementarities and economies of scope. For example, studies of railroads by Kim and by Magura and Braeutigam have found no evidence of cost complementarities and possibly cost anticomplementarities in freight and passenger rail services.[44] Evi-

44. Kim (1987); Magura and Braeutigam (1997).

dence of possible cost anticomplementarities would support Hasenkamp's conclusion about the shape of the production transformation curve for rail and passenger services, suggesting that there may be economies of specialization for these two types of services.[45] In other words, there may be no cost disadvantages realized from dividing passenger and freight services into separate operating entities. During the 1990s passenger and freight operations have been given to separate operating entities in England and in Germany; in the United States Amtrak has specialized in intercity passenger operations, while most other railroads specialize in intercity freight.

Harmatuck's 1991 study of seventeen large trucking firms found evidence of diseconomies of scope in the production of truckload and less-than-truckload services, suggesting that there may be cost savings from separate operations of these two types of services. In their study of the airline industry, Gillen, Oum, and Tretheway found some cost complementarity between scheduled and charter services, while Keeler and Formby found evidence of cost anticomplementarities in the provision of airline passenger and freight services. And in their study of the Canadian motor coach industry, Gillen and Oum found no economies of scope among passenger, charter, and freight bus services.[46]

Short-Run Costs

The discussion of cost studies to this point has focused on long-run costs. In economics the long run refers to a time period that is long enough for a firm to adjust *all* of its inputs to their optimal (cost-minimizing) levels as it produces any observed set of outputs. In the long run all factors of production are therefore variable. In that case, as indicated earlier, the firm's total cost function will depend on the levels of outputs produced and on *all* of the factor prices.

Often, however, a firm—especially one in a capital-intensive industry such as railroads or pipelines—may be interested in its costs in the short

---

45. Hasenkamp (1976).

46. Gillen, Oum, and Tretheway (1990); Keeler and Formby (1994); Gillen and Oum (1984). This chapter has focused on costs of providing transport services by carriers. Other types of cost studies, shed light on economies of scale and scope, however. For example, Small, Winston, and Evans (1989) examined costs of providing roads and found product-specific economies of scale in road durability and capacity but diseconomies of scope in the joint provision of roads for cars and trucks. Overall, the technology of providing roads is characterized by approximately constant returns to scale.

run. Perhaps the level of some factor or factors of production must be regarded as fixed when the firm plans its output. A factor might be fixed for any of several reasons. The firm may make its production decisions with a monthly or quarterly production horizon, but varying some factor may take a time much longer than that of the planning horizon. For example, although the firm may be able to adjust the amount of rail in place or the pipeline in the ground during a ten-year period, it may simply not be able to do so over a month's or even a year's planning horizon. In that case, many important operating decisions, including those about production levels and pricing, may need to be based on short-run costs.

Researchers will also be interested in short-run cost functions when the observations for cost studies are generated over time periods that are clearly consistent with the short run. For example, using quarterly data from the railroad industry to estimate directly a long-run cost function would be inappropriate because of the fixed nature of most railroad capital over a three-month horizon; in such a case a long-run function would be misspecified. Instead, a researcher would want to estimate a short-run cost function and then use that function to learn about the nature of costs in the short and long run.

When at least one factor of production is fixed, the firm is said to be operating in the short run. In the short run the total costs will be composed of *fixed costs,* that is, costs associated with the factors that cannot be varied during the planning horizon, and *variable costs,* that is, costs that can be varied with output. Because the firm cannot affect its fixed costs in the short run, it will try to minimize its variable costs of producing any observed output. The amount of the variable costs will depend on the amounts of outputs produced, the factor prices of the variable factors (that is, the inputs than can be adjusted in the short run), and the levels of the factors that are fixed.

To illustrate the idea of the variable cost function, suppose a firm has a plant size (a level of capital, K) that must be regarded as fixed, but that the firm can vary the amount of labor and fuel in the short run. Then the variable costs will depend on the amounts of outputs produced, the *level* of the fixed factor, capital, and the *prices* of variable factors, labor (P_L) and fuel (P_F). The variable cost function is then $V(y_1, y_2, ..., y_n, P_L, P_F, K)$, and the short-run total cost will be $C = rK + V(y_1, y_2, ..., y_n, P_L, P_F, K)$, where r is the factor price of capital, and $(y_1, y_2, ..., y_n)$ denote the levels of the n outputs.

If the firm is operating in a short-run situation, then an empirical study of short-run total costs should focus on the variable cost function. Further, if one is interested in investigating the difference between economies of size and economies of density, one can introduce into the variable cost function a measure of the size of the network, N, as was done in the long-run cost function earlier. In that case the variable cost function studied empirically would be $V(y_1, y_2, ..., y_n, N, P_L, P_F, K)$.[47]

Caves, Christensen, and Swanson have shown how to calculate the degree of economies of density (S_D) and the degree of economies of size (S_S) with the variable cost function.[48] In the formulas that follow, e_k denotes the elasticity of variable cost with respect to the level of the fixed factor (capital in the example), e_{y_i} is the elasticity of variable cost with respect to output i, and e_N is the elasticity of variable cost with respect to the number of nodes N.

$$S_D = (1 - e_k^v)/\sum_{i=1}^{n} e_{y_i}^v \text{ and } S_S = (1 - e_k^v)/(\sum_{i=1}^{n} e_{y_i}^v + e_N^v)$$

If $S_D > 1$, then there will be economies of density. If $S_S > 1$, then there will be economies of size.[49]

General Observations and Conclusions

Researchers have come a long way from the days of the heavy-handed costing systems of the Interstate Commerce Commission. Over the years advances in the theory of production and costs and in the empirical techniques available for studying costs have enabled economists to learn a good deal about the nature of the costs and technologies of the various transport modes.

Although there are marked differences in the types of conclusions that can be drawn from the vast literature on transport cost studies, an examination of tables 3-2, 3-3, 3-4, and 3-5 does reveal some general similarities within studies of a mode. For example, for railroads reasonably consistent evidence shows fairly strong economies of density and suggests constant

47. One might investigate a variable cost function using a loglinear form or a translog form (these are not written out here, but they involve the logarithm of V on the left-hand side and logarithms of the arguments of V on the right-hand side.

48. Caves, Christensen, and Swanson (1981).

49. For a given set of outputs, the short-run measure of economies of scale (whether density or size) may differ from the long-run measure, if the production structure is not homothetic. For more on this point, see Braeutigam and Daugherty (1983).

returns to size, especially for large railroads. These findings suggest that measures that increase traffic density (either by increasing the flow of traffic over existing lines or by eliminating lines that carry only very light amounts of traffic) may well reduce railroad costs. At the same time these studies suggest that the cost advantages from increasing the number of links served in the network are not great.

Evidence on economies of specialization is limited but growing. Hasenkamp's conclusions that there were economies of specialization in the U.S. railroad industry in the 1920s and 1930s has led some researchers to examine cost complementarities.[50] At this writing the author is unaware of any study that has found any clear evidence of cost complementarities, and the limited work that has been done suggests the possibility of anticomplementarities between freight and passenger services.

The movement toward separating passenger and freight operations in many countries should make research about cost complementarities and economies of scope of interest to policymakers for years to come. The obvious problem for researchers is that the operating data for an integrated firm (one providing both passenger and freight services) often yields little information about the behavior of the cost function "along the output axes" where specialized enterprises might operate. Policymakers are often more interested in the global issue addressed by economies of scope: Will the separation of a railroad into two separate entities, one specializing in passenger operations and the other in freight, reduce or increase the costs of rail operations? Thus, the data may support studies of cost complementarities but may be less suitable for studies designed to inquire about economies of scope.

For motor carriers most (but not all) evidence seems to point to constant returns to scale. There is some evidence that the less-than-truckload sector may operate with some increasing returns to scale, generated by economies of density.[51] Most cost studies of the trucking industry therefore reflect a technological structure that is conducive to an industry that would be (and is) highly competitive without regulation of prices and entry.

A student new to the transportation industry might ask whether the cost evidence always so strongly pointed to an inherently competitive industry structure, especially given the heavy regulation of prices and entry in the industry before the Motor Carrier Act of 1980. In this paper I have

50. Hasenkamp (1976).
51. See, for example, Winston and others (1990) and Allen and Liu (1995).

not reviewed cost studies of the motor carrier industry undertaken before 1977. Some of the studies before 1977 did suggest increasing returns to scale, but these earlier studies often failed to include factor prices and to control for the attributes of services being produced. When Spady and Friedlaender incorporated factor prices and included hedonic measures of quality of service, they found evidence of constant returns to scale.[52]

In the airline industry the evidence indicates that there are economies of density and that returns to size may be constant or slightly increasing. Economies of density are not surprising because average costs decline when a plane is filled and because larger planes typically can move traffic at a lower average cost. More recently research has yielded some insights about possible complementarities of costs in the airline industry. Gillen, Oum, and Tretheway have concluded that there may be some cost complementarity between scheduled and chartered services, while Keeler and Formby have observed that there may be cost anticomplementarities between freight and passenger services.[53]

The studies of economies of size and density suggest why the success of competition in this industry depends on the ease of entry and exit into airline markets. If there are economies of density, there may not be room for competition "within" the market (and indeed many city-pair markets are served by only one or two carriers). Rather competition must often be "for" the market.[54] Research on transportation cost functions has been strongly influenced by the regulatory environment that transportation firms have faced. As transportation firms adjust to regulatory reform, researchers are confronted with new methodological and substantive challenges, including the need to find still better ways of disaggregating outputs and of incorporating attributes of transport services and the structure of transportation networks in cost functions. In a less regulated setting cost studies must also properly treat variables that are endogenous, including output, service quality, and operating characteristics. Better, more flexible functional forms in parametric studies are also needed. Future studies will also no doubt benefit from the use of nonparametric analysis to characterize the

52. Spady and Friedlaender (1978).

53. Gillen, Oum, and Tretheway (1990); Keeler and Formby (1994).

54. There is a body of literature addressing the "contestability" of markets, that is, how easy it is to have vigorous competition "for" the market. A discussion of the arguments debating how contestable airline markets are is well beyond the scope of this article. For a description of contestable markets, see Baumol, Panzar, and Willig (1982).

shapes of cost surfaces that may not easily lend themselves to parametric analysis, even with highly flexible forms.

Studies of costs will continue to be important as new technologies and services emerge and as regulatory reform and privatization take place around the world. Both businesses and policymakers must understand costs as they evaluate substantive issues such as the potential savings from mergers and intermodal operations, the economic costs and benefits of providing access to a transportation network, the sources and measurement of productivity growth and technical change, and the effects of regulatory reform. A proper understanding of costs will be central to the making of sound business decisions and the design of enlightened public policy.

References

Allen, W. Bruce, and D. Liu. 1995. "Service Quality and Motor Carrier Costs: An Empirical Analysis." *Review of Economics and Statistics* 77 (3, August): 499–510.

Baumol, William J., John C. Panzar, and Robert D. Willig. 1982. *Contestable Markets and the Theory of Industry Structure*. Harcourt, Brace, Jovanovich.

Borts, George. 1960. "The Estimation of Rail Cost Functions." *Econometrica* 28 (January): 108–31.

Braeutigam, Ronald R. 1980. "An Analysis of Fully Distributed Cost Pricing in Regulated Industries." *Bell Journal of Economics* 11 (Spring): 182–96.

———. 1989. "Optimal Policies for Natural Monopolies." In *Handbook of Industrial Organization,* edited by Richard Schmalensee and Robert D. Willig. Vol. 2, 1289–1346. New York: Elsevier Science Publishing Co.

Braeutigam, Ronald R., and Andrew F. Daughety. 1983. "On the Estimation of Returns to Scale Using Variable Cost Functions." *Economic Letters* 11(1–2): 25–31.

Braeutigam, Ronald R., Andrew F. Daughety, and M. Turnquist. 1982. "The Estimation of a Hybrid Cost Function for a Railroad Firm." *Review of Economics and Statistics* 64 (August): 394–404.

Brown, R. S., Douglas W. Caves, and Laurits R. Christensen. 1979. "Modelling the Structure of Cost and Production for Multi-Product Firms." *Southern Economic Journal* 46 (July): 256–73.

Caves, Douglas W., Laurits R. Christensen, and Joseph A. Swanson. 1981. "Productivity Growth, Scale Economies, and Capacity Utilization in U.S. Railroads, 1955–1974." *American Economic Review* 75 (5, December): 994–1002.

Caves, Douglas W., Laurits R. Christensen, and Michael W. Tretheway. 1980. "Flexible Cost Functions for Multiproduct Firms." *Review of Economics and Statistics* 62 (August): 477–81.

———. 1983. "The Structure of Airline Costs and Prospects for the U.S. Airline Industry under Deregulation." SSRI Workshop Series Paper 8313. University of Wisconsin, Madison.

————. 1984. "Economies of Density vs. Economies of Scale: Why Truck and Local Service Airline Costs Differ." *Rand Journal of Economics* 15 (4, Winter): 471–89.

Caves, Douglas W., and others. 1985. "Network Effects and the Measurement of Returns to Scale and Density for U.S. Rrailroads." In *Analytical Studies in Transport Economics,* edited by Andrew F. Daughety, 97–120. Cambridge University Press.

Christensen, Laurits R., and W. Greene. 1976. "Economies of Scale in U.S. Electric Power Generation." *Journal of Political Economy* 84 (August): 655–76.

Christensen, Laurits R., Dale W. Jorgenson, and Lawrence J. Lau. 1971. "Conjugate Duality and the Transcendental Production Function." *Econometrica* 39 (July): 255.

————. 1973. "Transcendental Logarithmic Production Frontiers." *Review of Economics and Statistics* 55 (February): 28–45.

Clark, John Maurice. 1923. *Studies in the Economics of Overhead Costs.* University of Chicago Press.

Cookenboo, Leslie, Jr. 1955. *Crude Oil Pipelines and Competition in the Oil Industry.* Harvard University Press.

Daughety, Andrew F., and Forrest D. Nelson. 1988. "An Econometric Analysis of Changes in the Cost and Production Structure of the Trucking Industry, 1953–82." *Review of Economics and Statistics* 70 (1, February): 67–75.

Daughety, Andrew F., Forrest D. Nelson, and William R. Vigdor. 1985. "An Econometric Analysis of the Cost and Production Structure of the Trucking Industry." In *Analytical Studies in Transport Economics,* edited by Andrew F. Daughety, 65–95. Cambridge University Press.

De Borger, B. 1992. "Estimating a Multiple-Output Generalized Box-Cox Cost Function: Cost Structure and Productivity Growth in Belgian Railroad Operations, 1950–86." *European Economic Review* 36 (7, October): 1379–98.

Diewert, W. Erwin. 1971. "An Application of the Shephard Duality Theorem: A Generalized Leontief Production Function." *Journal of Political Economy* 79 (May–June): 481–507.

Diewert, W. Erwin, and Terence J. Wales. 1987. "Flexible Functional Forms and Global Curvature Conditions." *Econometrica* 55 (1, January): 43–68.

Filippini, M., and R. Maggi. 1992. "Efficiency and Ownership in the Case of the Swiss Private Railways." *International Journal of Transport Economics* 19 (3, October): 307–27.

Friedlaender, Ann F. 1969. *The Dilemma of Freight Transport Regulation.* Brookings.

Friedlaender, Ann F., and others. 1993. "Rail Costs and Capital Adjustments in a Quasi-Regulated Environment." *Journal of Transport Economics and Policy* 27 (2, May):131–52.

Friedlaender, Ann F., and Richard H. Spady. 1981. *Freight Transport Regulation: Equity, Efficiency, and Competition in the Rail and Trucking Industries.* MIT Press.

Gillen, David W., and Tae Hoon Oum. 1984. "A Study of the Cost Structures of the Canadian Intercity Motor Coach Industry." *Canadian Journal of Economics* 17 (May): 369–85.

Gillen, David W., Tae Hoon Oum, and Michael Tretheway. 1990. "Airline Cost Structure and Policy Implications: A Multi-product Approach for Canadian Airlines." *Journal of Transport Economics and Policy* 24 (1, January): 9–34.

Griliches, Zvi. 1972. "Cost Allocation in Railroad Regulation." *Bell Journal of Economics and Management Science* 3 (Spring): 26–41.

Grimm, Curtis M., Thomas M. Corsi, and Judith L. Jarrell. 1989. "U.S. Motor Carrier Cost Structure under Deregulation." *Logistics and Transportation Review* 25 (3, September): 231–49,

Guilkey, David K., C. Lovell, and Robin C. Sickles. 1983. "A Comparison of the Performance of Three Flexible Functional Forms." *International Economic Review* 24 (3, October): 591–616.

Harmatuck, Ronald J. 1979. "A Policy-Sensitive Railway Cost Function." *Logistics and Transportation Review* 15 (2, May): 277–315.

———. 1991. "Economies of Scale and Scope in the Motor Carrier Industry: An Analysis of the Cost Functions for 17 Large LTL Common Motor Carriers." *Journal of Transport Economics and Policy* 25 (2, May): 135–51.

———. 1992. "Motor Carrier Cost Function Comparisons." *Transportation Journal* 31 (4, Summer): 31–46.

Harris, Robert G. 1977. "Economies of Density in the Railroad Freight Industry." *Bell Journal of Economics* 8 (Autumn): 556–64.

Hasenkamp, George. 1976. "A Study of Multiple-Output Production Functions: Klein's Railroad Study Revisited." *Journal of Econometrics* 4 (August): 253–62.

Jara-Diaz, Sergio R. 1982. "The Estimation of Transport Cost Functions: A Methodological Review." *Transport Review* 2 (3): 257–78.

——— 1988. "Multioutput Analysis of Trucking Operations Using Spatially Dissaggregated Flows." *Transportation Research* 22B (3, May): 159–71.

Jara-Diaz, Sergio R., Pedro P. Donoso, and Jorge A. Araneda. 1992. "Estimation of Marginal Transport Costs: The Flow Aggregation Function Approach." *Journal of Transport Economics and Policy* 26 (1, January): 35–48.

Keeler, James P., and John P. Formby. 1994. "Cost Economics and Consolidation in the U.S. Airline Industry." *International Journal of Transport Economics* 21 (1, February): 21–45.

Keeler, Theodore E. 1974. "Railroad Costs, Returns to Scale, and Excess Capacity." *Review of Economics and Statistics* 56 (May): 201–8.

———. 1983. *Railroads, Freight, and Public Policy.* Brookings.

Kim, H. 1987. "Economies of Scale and Scope in Multiproduct Firms: Evidence from U.S. Railroads." *Applied Economics* 19 (6, June): 733–41.

Klein, Lawrence R. 1974. *A Textbook of Econometrics.* Prentice-Hall.

Koenker, Roger. 1977. "Optimal Scale and the Size Distribution of American Trucking Firms." *Journal of Transport Economics and Policy* 11 (1, January): 54–67.

Kumbhakar, Subal C. 1990. "A Reexamination of Returns to Scale, Density, and Technical Progress in U. S. Airlines." *Southern Economic Journal* 57 (2, October): 428–42.

Kumbhakar, Subal C., and Arunava Bhattacharyya. 1996. "Productivity Growth in Passenger-Bus Transportation: A Heteroskedastic Error Component Model with Unbalanced Panel Data." *Empirical Economics* 21 (4): 557–73.

Magura, M., and Ronald R. Braeutigam. 1997. "A Semiparametric Analysis of the Variable Cost Strucutre of the Deutsche Bundesbahn." Working Paper, Northwestern University, Department of Economics.

McFadden, Daniel. 1978. "Cost, Revenue, and Profit Functions." In *Production Economics: A Dual Approach to Theory and Applications,* edited by Melvin Fuss and Daniel McFadden. Vol. 1. New York: Elsevier North-Holland.

McShan, S., and R. Windle. 1989. "The Implications of Hub-and-Spoke Routing for Airline Costs and Competitiveness." *Logistics and Transportation Review* 25 (3, September): 209–30.

Meyer, John R. 1958. "Some Methodological Aspects of Statistical Costing as Illustrated by the Determination of Rail Passenger Costs." *American Economic Review* 48 (2, May): 209–22.

Meyer, John R., and Gerald Kraft. 1961. "The Evaluation of Satistical Costing Techniques as Applied in the Transportation Industry." *American Economic Review* 51 (2, May): 313–34.

Meyer, John R, and others. 1959. *The Economics of Competition in the Transportation Industries.* Harvard University Press.

Nerlove, Marc. 1963. "Returns to Scale in Electricity Supply." In *Measurement in Economics: Studies in Mathematical Economics and Econometrics in Memory of Yehuda Grunfeld,* edited by Carl F. Christ and others, 167–98. Stanford University Press.

Obeng, Kofi. 1984. "The Economics of Bus Transit Operations." *Logistics and Transportation Review* 20 (1, March): 45–65.

Oum, Tae Hoon, and William G. Waters, II. 1993. "A Survey of Recent Developments in Transportation Cost Function Research." *Logistics and Transportation Review* 32 (4): 423–60.

Oum, Tae Hoon, and Yimin Zhang. 1991. "Utilisation of Quasi-Fixed Inputs and Estimation of Cost Functions: An Application to Airline Costs." *Journal of Transport Economics and Policy* 25 (2, May): 121–34.

Panzar, John C. 1989. "Determinants of Firm Industry and Structure." In *Handbook of Industrial Organization,* edited by Richard C. Schmalensee and Robert D. Willig. Vol 1. Amsterdam: North-Holland.

Röller, Lars Hendrick. 1990. "Proper Quadratic Cost Functions with an Application to the Bell System." *Review of Economics and Statistics* 72 (May): 202–10.

Savage, Ian. 1994. "Scale Economies in Rail Transit Systems." Working paper. Northwestern University, Department of Economics.

Sickles, Robin C., and Streitwieser, Mary L. 1992. "The Structure of Technology, Substitution, and Productivity in the Interstate Natural Gas Transmission Industry under the NGPA of 1978." Working paper CES 92-9. U. S. Department of Commerce, Center for Economic Studies, Washington, D.C.

Silberberg, Eugene. 1990. *The Structure of Economics: A Mathematical Analysis.* 2d ed. McGraw-Hill.

Small, Kenneth, Clifford Winston, and Carol A.. Evans. 1989. *Road Work.* Brookings.

Spady, Richard H. 1985. "Using Indexed Quadratic Cost Functions to Model Network Technologies." In *Analytical Studies in Transport Economics,* edited by Andrew F. Daughety, 121–35. Cambridge University Press.

Spady, Richard H., and Ann F. Friedlaender. 1978. "Hedonic Cost Functions for the Regulated Trucking Industry." *Bell Journal of Economics* 9 (Spring): 154–79.

Taussig, Frank W. 1891. "A Contribution to the Theory of Railway Rates." *Quarterly Journal of Economics* 5 (July): 438–65.

Thomas, Janet M., and Seth J. Callan. 1992. "Cost Analysis of Specialized Motor Carriers: An Investigation of Aggregation and Specification Bias." *Logistics and Transportation Review* 28 (3, September): 217–30.

Wang-Chiang, Judy S., and Ann F. Friedlaender. 1984. "Output Aggregation, Network Effects, and the Measurement of Trucking Technology." *Review of Economics and Statistics* 66 (2, May): 267–76.

Winston, Clifford. 1985. "Conceptual Developments in the Economics of Transportation: An Interpretative Survey." *Journal of Economic Literature* 23 (March): 57–94.

Winston, Clifford, and others. 1990. *The Economic Effects of Surface Freight Deregulation.* Brookings.

Wolbert, George S., Jr. 1979. *U. S. Oil Pipelines.* Washington, D.C.: American Petroleum Institute.

Ying, John S. 1990. "The Inefficiency of Regulating a Competitive Industry: Productivity Gains in Trucking Following Reform." *Review of Economics and Statistics* 72 (2, May): 191–201.

Zajac, Edward E. 1978. *Fairness or Efficiency: An Introduction to Public Utility Pricing.* Cambridge, Mass.: Ballinger.

JOSÉ A. GÓMEZ-IBÁÑEZ

4 *Pricing*

Pricing is a central tool for resource allocation in the view of economists, who usually recommend that prices be set at marginal cost. Marginal cost is the increase in total cost that occurs from producing one more unit of output or service. Charging transport users their marginal cost ensures that they will make an extra trip or shipment only when the value to them of doing so is at least as great as the cost of providing it.

The public sector is often involved in providing transportation services; in the United States, the government typically provides the infrastructure—the highways, airports, and waterways—while the private sector operates the motor vehicles, aircraft, and ships that use the facilities. Although the public sector often provides transportation services, it seldom prices those services at marginal cost. For example, the primary fee for public highway use in the United States is the motor fuel tax, which effectively charges motorists about the same amount per vehicle mile no matter when or where they travel. As a result, motorists using an expensive urban expressway in rush hour may pay less than marginal cost, whereas motorists using a less expensive intercity road in an off-peak hour may pay more.

The author would like to thank John R. Meyer and Kenneth A. Small for helpful comments on earlier drafts and to absolve them of responsibility for errors that may remain.

By contrast, private sector transportation companies—such as railroads, trucking firms, and airlines—are more likely to charge their customers close to their marginal costs.[1] This is particularly likely where the firms operate in reasonably competitive markets, because competition drives prices down toward costs. Prices will deviate from marginal costs when carriers enjoy uncontested markets or monopoly power for a prolonged period of time and when the public sector regulates carriers' prices. Prices will deviate from *social* marginal costs when they do not reflect the costs of carriers' contributions to air or noise pollution.

The pervasive involvement of public agencies in transportation and the failure of these agencies to apply marginal cost pricing principles is caused in part by several peculiar characteristics of transportation. These characteristics are not unique to transportation—some are found in other capital-intensive network utilities, such as electricity and telephones. But they make both marginal cost pricing and private provision seem more complex and controversial in transportation than in many other industries.

First, different transportation users often share the same services or facilities. Autos, trucks, buses, and taxis share the roads; commercial jets and private planes often use the same runways; business and pleasure travelers occupy the same row in a plane; and passengers and freight are transported over the same railroad track. Joint use allows transportation firms to reduce the average cost per user by increasing the utilization of expensive facilities and equipment. But joint use can also make it difficult to allocate costs among the different types of users or to determine the marginal costs of each type. This ambiguity leads to claims that prices are discriminatory or inherently arbitrary and to calls for public regulation to ensure a fair allocation of costs and protect the more vulnerable classes of users.

Second, transportation facilities and services often exhibit economies of scale and large sunk costs. Firms with these characteristics have marginal costs that are lower than their average costs, so that pricing at marginal cost does not generate enough revenue for the firm to be financially self-sufficient.[2] The most obvious solution—a subsidy from government to balance the firm's budget—often leads to a public takeover, because public subsi-

1. Ignoring, for the moment, the possibility that they do not pay the marginal cost of the public infrastructure facilities they use as inputs.

2. Economies of scale are defined as situations in which the average cost declines as volume increases. Average cost can decline with volume only if the cost of providing an additional unit of output (that is, themarginal cost) is less than the average cost. Similarly, sunk costs are defned as costs that are not affected by volume. Thus sunk costs are not a part of marginal costs, and average costs that include sunk costs will be greater than marginal costs.

dies are usually more acceptable when accompanied by public ownership. The alternative solution often advocated by economists involves complex pricing schemes designed to raise more revenue than marginal cost pricing can but to leave usage about the same. The complexity of these schemes often makes them difficult to administer, however, or vulnerable to charges of unfairness.

Finally, transportation often raises equity concerns that seem to conflict with both marginal cost pricing and private provision. Transportation is not as central to ensuring equality of opportunity as are other services, notably education and health. But transportation provides access to those services, as well as to jobs and information. Equity concerns are often reflected in policies to ensure a basic level of transportation service to all communities or households. In the United States, for example, first-class mail is delivered to every address in the country every week day for the same price per letter, no matter how remote the location. This policy results in some correspondents paying more than marginal cost and others less, and in a system of cross-subsidies that a private mail firm would not voluntarily endure. But it also helps ensure that rural communities are better integrated into the economic, social, and political life of the nation.

The characteristics that complicate transport pricing and drive transport activities into the public sector are real, but they are also often exaggerated. This observation is one of John Meyer's insights, and it is the general theme of this chapter. Interest groups seeking to justify low prices, cross-subsidies and other policies have incentives to overstate the difficulties in allocating costs or the degree to which marginal costs fall short of average costs. But in many situations complex subsidy schemes or pricing regimes are not necessary. Marginal cost pricing—or a reasonably accurate approximation of it—is often practical to implement and consistent with cost recovery. Moreover, empirical research indicates that marginal cost pricing results in substantial net benefits to society. These conclusions may also imply that the private sector could supply some of the transportation services currently provided by the public sector, although that is a topic beyond the scope of this chapter.

To make the case that marginal cost pricing is both beneficial and practical, this chapter first outlines the basic pricing rules or guidelines that transport economists have developed over the years. The remainder of the chapter illustrates how these rules apply in practice using urban public transit fares, highway infrastructure finance, and price discrimination in air travel and postal services as examples.

Pricing Rules and Concepts

Transport economists assume that the goal of pricing is to maximize net social benefits of providing a transport service; net social benefits are usually defined as the difference between the willingness of consumers to pay for the service and the costs of producing it:

Net social benefits = consumer willingness to pay – production cost.

This formulation involves a number of strong assumptions, most notably that:

—The distribution of income is either just or not an appropriate concern for the pricing of this service.

—The consumer is the best judge of his or her own welfare.

—Unless specified, there are no externalities of production and consumption.

—All other goods that are close substitutes or complements are appropriately priced. [3]

Pricing a Simple Service

Accepting these assumptions for the moment, the net social benefits, *NSB*, for a transport service can be written as

$$(4\text{-}1) \qquad NSB = \int_0^Q P(X)dX - Q \cdot AC(Q) \, ,$$

where $P(X)$ is the inverse demand curve, X is a variable of integration, Q is the volume of trips carried, and AC is the average cost function. The first term on the right-hand side is consumer willingness to pay for the quantity of trips provided (as measured by the area under the demand curve), and the second term is the total cost.

The optimal price can be derived by setting the first derivative of equation 4-1 with respect to Q at zero and rearranging to yield

$$(4\text{-}2) \qquad P = AC + Q \cdot (dAC/dQ).$$

---

3. This list is adapted from Turvey (1971: 15).

The right-hand side of equation 4-2 is the marginal cost of producing an extra trip, so this is the familiar rule that price should be set at marginal cost.[4] Note the marginal cost has two components—an average cost per user, plus the change in the average cost from serving an additional user.

Whether a transport service that prices at marginal cost will be financially self-supporting depends on whether the service exhibits economies or diseconomies of scale. If neither is present—that is, if average costs are not affected by volume—then dAC/dQ is zero, so marginal cost (and price) equals average cost, and total revenues will exactly equal total costs. With economies of scale, dAC/dQ is negative and the service will operate at a loss; with diseconomies of scale, dAC/dQ is positive and the service will generate surpluses.

Separate Infrastructure and Operations

Ever since the famous studies of bridges in the 1840s by the French engineer Dupuit, transport economists have been concerned with the special case in which one enterprise provides the infrastructure and another enterprise the vehicles that operate on it.[5] It does not matter whether the infrastructure firm is a public enterprise and the users private, as is often the case in the United States, or whether both are private, as on the private toll roads common to many developing countries. In either situation, the net social benefit can be rewritten as

$$(4\text{-}3) \qquad NSB = \int_0^Q P(X)dX - Q \cdot UC(Q/L) - L \cdot CC(L),$$

where $P(X)$ is again the inverse demand curve and Q the number of trips carried. UC is the average cost to a user of operating a vehicle on the facility, CC is the average amortized cost to provide a unit of facility capacity, and L is the number of units of capacity.[6] CC is solely a function of L, which can be thought of as the number of lanes on a highway or runways at

---

4. The second-order conditions for a maximum require that the second derivative of equation 4-1 with respect to Q be negative. The second-order conditions are met if the slope of the marginal cost curve is greater than the slope of the demand curve, which is usually the case because the demand curve is always falling and the marginal cost curve is either rising or flat.

5. Dupuit (1844).

6. This simplified presentation is an adaptation of Winston (1985). Although I speak of this facility as a durable investment, I do not represent time formally. To do so would greatly complicate the equations and not contribute to the essential insights.

an airport.[7] UC is a function of the ratio of Q to L because average user costs presumably rise the more congested the facility becomes and fall the more generous the facility's capacity.

The optimal price is derived again by setting the first derivative of equation 4-3 with respect to Q at zero and rearranging:

$$(4\text{-}4) \qquad P = UC + Q \cdot (\partial UC / \partial Q).$$

The optimal price is the marginal cost imposed by a facility user. As before, it has two components: the average user cost, plus the change in average cost from serving an additional user. Neither component includes the cost of the facility, which seems to leave facility providers with no source of revenue to finance their investment. But that is not so, as I shall show in a moment.

The optimal level of investment in the facility can be derived by setting the first derivative of equation 4-3 with respect to L at zero and rearranging to yield

$$(4\text{-}5) \qquad CC + L \cdot (dCC / dL) = - Q \cdot (\partial UC / \partial L).$$

The left-hand side is the marginal cost of adding an additional unit of capacity to the facility, while the right-hand side is the savings in user costs from that additional unit. Thus equation 4-5 says that facility providers should expand the capacity to the point where the marginal cost of extra capacity to them just equals the marginal savings it brings for users.

Congestion Externalities and Tolls

Ever since Pigou and Knight raised the issue in the 1920s, transport economists also have been concerned about congestion when a facility is used by many different firms or individuals.[8] Congestion and average user costs increase as traffic volumes increase on a transportation facility. Motorists spend more time and burn more fuel on a congested highway, for example, and airlines and their passengers endure expensive delays as the airspace or runways of a major airport become crowded. If the facility users

---

7. Usually some facility costs are a function of Q as well—for example, the pavement damage caused by the passage of vehicles. I return to this issue in a later section on highway pricing.

8. Pigou (1920); Knight (1924).

are from different firms or households, then they will consider only the average cost of a trip in deciding whether to travel and not the delays and other costs that their decision imposes on other facility users. These delays imposed on others are externalities, and the failure of individual users to consider them leads to excessive use and congestion of the facility.

The remedy that Pigou and Knight proposed and that Vickery and others refined is to charge the facility users a congestion toll equal to the delays and other costs they impose on others.[9] One can show formally that the optimal toll, T, would be

(4-6) $$T = Q \cdot (\partial UC / \partial Q).$$

Referring back to equation 4, one can see that the toll closes the gap between the users' average cost, UC, and the optimal price for facility use.

A major contribution of Mohring and Harwitz was to show that the revenues from the congestion toll will just cover the costs of the facility provider so long as there are no economies or diseconomies of scale in facility capacity and the facility provider is investing optimally.[10] Toll revenues will fall short of the facility provider's costs if there are economies of scale in capacity and will exceed costs if there are diseconomies of scale in capacity.

The role of the congestion toll in financing facility costs can be better understood by recognizing that there are two ways to accommodate an additional trip: by imposing extra congestion on other users, which costs

---

9. Vickery (1963).

10. To demonstrate the Mohring and Harwitz result with this notation, one can take advantage of the fact that $\partial UC / \partial L = -Q/L \cdot (\partial UC / \partial Q)$ and substitute into equation 4-6:

(4-6') $$T = -L \cdot (\partial UC / \partial L).$$

Assuming that the facility provider is following the optimal investment rule (equation 4-5), then one can substitute for $\partial UC / \partial L$ and rearrange to obtain

(4-6'') $$T = [L/Q] \cdot [CC + L \cdot (dCC/dL)].$$

If there are neither economies nor diseconomies of scale in the provision of the facility, then $dCC/dL = 0$, so

(4-6''') $$T = L \cdot CC / Q,$$

which means that the congestion toll receipts ($Q \cdot T$) will just cover the facility provider's costs ($L \cdot CC$). By similar reasoning one can show that toll receipts will fall short of the facility costs if there are economies of scale in facility provision and will exceed facility costs if there are diseconomies of scale. For the original demonstration, see Mohring and Harwitz (1962: 81–86).

$Q \cdot (\partial UC/\partial Q)$; or by expanding the capacity of the facility so that the trip can be accommodated without added congestion, at a cost of $(L/Q) \cdot [CC + L \cdot (dCC/dL)]$. The optimal investment rule, shown in equation 4-5, says that one should exploit both methods to the point that their marginal costs are equal.[11] If the cost of congestion is greater, then it would be cheaper to accommodate more traffic by expanding the facility; if the cost of expanding the facility is greater, it would be cheaper to tolerate more congestion. Only when the two costs are equal is the facility the right size with the optimal level of congestion. But one would not charge a facility user both the congestion toll and the marginal cost of physically expanding the facility—that would be double charging because the user will incur one cost or another, not both. And if the investment in the facility is optimized, it does not matter which is charged because the two are equal.

As a practical matter, pricing is more fungible than capacity expansion; thus it would be the natural instrument for policymakers to use to optimize infrastructure use. Unfortunately, policymakers often find raising prices politically more controversial than spending more money on infrastructure capacity, so Americans frequently enjoy more capacity and lower prices than would be optimal.

Many of these complications disappear when the same enterprise operates all the vehicles using the facility, as sometimes happens in transportation. Railroads are the prime example; they traditionally own their tracks and all the trains that run on them. In such cases there is no congestion externality because the delays of adding an extra train to the schedule are internal to the company and its customers. The railroad does have to worry about the optimal mix of inputs—train sets, train crews, track infrastructure, and so forth—but that becomes a standard exercise in finding the cost-minimizing input mix and plant size for a firm. And the basic marginal cost rule in equation 4-2 applies for pricing the railroad's services.

Budget Constraints and Ramsey Pricing

Enterprises are frequently subject to budget constraints that conflict with marginal cost pricing. Governments are often reluctant to provide

---

11. To see this more clearly, one can take advantage of the fact that $\partial UC/\partial L = -Q/L \cdot (\partial UC/\partial Q)$, substitute into equation 4-5, and rearrange to obtain

(4-5')
$$[L/Q] \cdot [CC + L \cdot (dCC/dL)] = Q \cdot (\partial UC/\partial Q).$$

enterprises the subsidies that marginal cost pricing can require because raising taxes is politically difficult or causes economic distortions. For example, studies of industrialized economies typically show that taxes impose costs of 20 cents or more per dollar raised.[12] And governments often believe that subsidies undermine the incentives of managers to control costs and remain technically efficient.

Budgetary problems are especially common in transportation because transportation services often exhibit economies of scale so that marginal cost pricing does not generate enough revenues to cover costs.[13] As explained in the chapter on costs, the relevant economies are usually at the level of the traffic corridor, rather than at the level of the firm, and thus more accurately should be called economies of traffic density. The most commonly mentioned source of economies of scale or density is in the investment in the right-of-way. With a railroad, for example, the minimum size roadbed may serve quite a wide range of trains every day, so that as traffic increases in the corridor, average costs fall because roadbed costs are spread over the growing traffic volumes.

Transport and utility economists usually recommend inverse elasticity pricing in situations where marginal cost pricing would not generate enough revenue to meet budget constraints. Inverse elasticity pricing is often called Ramsey pricing after the economist who developed the first formal statement of the rule in the 1920s.[14] The basic idea is to charge those customers with the least price elastic demand (those whose desire for the service is least sensitive to price) the largest markups over marginal cost and thereby minimize the reduction in consumption that occurs from charging prices that are higher than marginal cost. In the extreme case where one group of customers has a perfectly price inelastic demand, for example, those customers could be charged whatever was necessary to bring the firm's budget into balance while the remaining customers could be charged marginal cost. If the cross-price elasticities of demand between different customers are zero, Ramsey's formula for prices to minimize distortions is

$$(4\text{-}7) \qquad (P_i - MC_i)/P_i = k/E_i,$$

12. See the discussion on project evaluation in chapter 5 of this volume or Browning (1987).

13. This whole discussion ignores the fact that government accounting practices may count costs differently than an economist would. Such discrepancies can be important, as described by Turvey (1971).

14. Ramsey (1927). Other seminal works on inverse elasticity pricing are Hotelling (1938) and the survey by Baumol and Bradford (1970).

where P_i is the price charged customer i, MC_i is the marginal cost of serving customer i, E_i is the absolute value of the price elasticity of demand of customer i, and k is a constant determined by the amount of revenue that must be raised to meet the budget target. Under this formula, the percentage markup over marginal cost for each customer, $(P_i - MC_i)/P_i$, is inversely proportional to the customer's demand elasticity, E_i; in other words, the lower the price elasticity of demand, the greater the percentage markup.[15]

Ramsey pricing is widely acknowledged to have serious limitations. It is often difficult to estimate the elasticities of demand for different customer groups, for example, and Ramsey pricing often sows the seeds of its own long-run destruction by creating strong incentives for customers paying high markup prices to find alternative services or sources. In the process, these customers will effectively change their demand elasticities, which requires a new set of Ramsey prices to be calculated. Worse, the number of customers with inelastic demand will decline, making it harder to charge some customers more than marginal cost without significantly reducing demand. Despite its limitations, Ramsey pricing is very appealing and often attempted in transportation.

Joint Costs, Economies of Scope, and Peak-Load Pricing

A related set of pricing complications occurs because transportation firms often use the same facilities, equipment, and labor to produce different services. In technical terms, they are multiproduct firms. This practice is common in transportation because it allows firms to improve the utilization of costly facilities and crews. An airline can increase aircraft and crew utilization, for example, by serving both the Caribbean and Europe because the demand for Caribbean travel peaks in the winter whereas the demand for European travel peaks in the summer. Similarly, a highway authority can usually accommodate light trucks more cheaply by modifying a highway intended for autos rather than by building a special purpose facility.

---

15. This formula applies if there is no cross-elasticity of demand between different customer groups. If there is, then the formula is:

$$(P_i - MC_i)/P_i = (k/E_i) - \sum_{j \text{ not} = i} \{[(P_j - MC_j)/P_j] \cdot E_{ij} \cdot [(P_i \cdot Q_i)/(P_j \cdot Q_j)]\},$$

where E_{ij} is the cross-elasticity of demand for j with respect to the price charged customer i.

Pricing in multiproduct firms can be confusing because it is not always clear how to allocate costs between products. Many costs can be uniquely attributed to particular products, but some are what economists call "joint." Joint costs occur when the provision of one service or product makes possible the provision of another service or product at little or no extra expense. The classic examples in economics texts are sheep and cotton. Raising sheep produces both wool and mutton, while growing cotton produces both fiber for cloth and seeds that can be used for oil. The wool and mutton and the fiber and oil are joint products of the same activities. The costs of raising the sheep or growing the cotton plants are joint costs, in that the provision of one product (wool or fiber) makes the other product (mutton or oil) available at little extra cost.

Joint costs are also embodied in the concept of economies of scope. Economies of scope are analogous to economies of scale except that they occur when the range of products produced increases rather than when the volume of any one product increases. There are economies of scope in two products if one firm can produce both products together more cheaply than two separate firms can each produce one of the products. Conversely, there are diseconomies of scope if production by one firm is more costly than production separately. Economies of scope are joint costs.[16]

In principle, joint costs should be allocated to the product whose demand is dominant. Consumers of cotton fiber should bear the joint costs of growing the cotton plant, for example, if the number of plants demanded for fiber exceeds the number demanded for oil, even when the fiber consumers are charged the entire cost of growing the plant, while the oil consumers are charged only the extra cost of pressing its seeds.

Problems can arise when the assignment of joint costs shifts the dominant demand. Suppose the demand for plants for fiber is less than the demand for plants for oil when fiber consumers are charged the joint costs, and vice versa. In that case the solution is to assign the joint costs to each product so their demand for the joint facility is the same. Fiber and oil consumers both would bear the cost of the cotton plant in the proportions

---

16. Mathematically, economies of scope are said to exist if the cost of producing two outputs jointly is less than the costs of producing them separately, that is, if $C(Q_1,Q_2) < C(Q_1,O) + C(O,Q_2)$, where Q_1 is the level of output of product one, Q_2 is the output of product two, and C is the total cost function. Joint costs can be defined as the savings from producing jointly, or $C(Q_1,0) + C(O,Q_2) - C(Q_1,Q_2)$. A natural measure of the degree of economies of scope is the ratio of the joint costs to total costs, or $[C(Q_1,0) + C(O,Q_2)] / C(Q_1,Q_2)$. For a more complete discussion, see Bailey and Friedlaender (1982).

that would make their demands for the number of plants equal. In a sense this allocation turns out to be a form of Ramsey pricing, because each product's contribution toward the joint cost is inversely related to its elasticity of demand. [17]

A very common example of joint costs in transportation and other utilities is peak and off-peak services. A highway, telephone, or electricity system that is designed to serve demand during peak hours of use, for example, automatically provides capacity for off-peak use. The costs of that capacity are joint costs. Peaking does not occur just by time of day, of course, but often by season or (in the case of transport) direction of travel as well. As with the cotton plant, the costs of the joint capacity are normally assigned to the peak users. If the number of lanes on a highway is determined by peak-hour, rather than off-peak, traffic volumes, for example, then the joint costs of those highway lanes are attributable to peak-hour motorists. If this allocation causes the peak to shift to other hours, then the solution, as with cotton, is to assign each time period just that degree of responsibility for the joint costs that makes the volumes equal in all time periods.

Second-Best Pricing

The pricing rules developed so far assume that all the complements, substitutes, and inputs to the transportation service are also priced at marginal cost. In the 1950s, however, two British economists demonstrated that pricing a good or service at marginal cost might not be optimal if at least one potential substitute, complement, or input is not priced at its marginal cost.[18] Economists since have developed rules for the optimal price in such a "second-best" environment.[19] If the mispriced goods are supplements or complements but not inputs to the good in question, which I will call good i, then the optimal price for good i is

$$(4\text{-}8) \qquad P_i - MC_i = -\sum_{j \,\text{not}\,=\,i} [(E_{ij} / E_i) \cdot (Q_j / Q_i) \cdot (P_j - MC_j)],$$

---

17. This solution was first developed by the famous French economist Marcel Boiteux (1960). For very readable explanations, see Mohring, (1976:59–64), or Farrar and Meyer (1970: 13–17).

18. Lipsey and Lancaster (1956). For an early exposition that is far clearer than Lipsey and Lancaster's original, see Green (1961).

19. The first-best environment would be one in which all other goods and services were priced at marginal cost.

where P_i, MC_i, and Q_i are the price, marginal cost, and quantity of good i; E_{ij} is the cross-price elasticity of demand for good j with respect to the price of good i; and E_i is the own price elasticity of demand for good i.[20] If the other goods are priced below marginal cost, for example, this formula requires that good i be priced below marginal cost if the other goods are all substitutes for it, but priced above marginal cost if the other goods are all complements to it. If the other mispriced goods are a mix of substitutes and complements, however, then one needs a great deal of information about the direct and cross-price elasticities of demand to determine whether good i should be priced above or below its marginal cost.

Although second-best situations are common in transportation and most other sectors of the economy, the complexity of second-best pricing rules has discouraged their application. In practice most economists assume it is safe to ignore second-best issues unless the mispriced goods are close substitutes or complements to the good being priced. Moreover, many economists believe that second-best pricing discourages the laudable quest of applying first-best rules more widely.

Urban Transit Fares and Subsidies

Many pricing issues are illustrated by the debate over public transit fares in industrialized countries. Public transit is usually defined to include buses, streetcars, and subways or metros. In most developing countries these services are provided by private companies that are expected to recover their costs out of the farebox. Private transit companies were the rule in much of Europe and North America as well until around the 1950s, when declining ridership forced transit operators to contract services and raise fares and eventually led the public sector to take over most firms. Over the years the financial performance of these firms deteriorated further; fares now cover less than half of operating expenses and make no contribution to capital expenses in most U.S. and many European cities. Taxpayers subsidize the balance of the costs.

The Vicious Cycle

Of the various arguments often used to justify low fares and high subsidies for transit, the least convincing to economists is that fare increases

20. Adapted from Turvey (1971: 24).

would set off a self-defeating cycle of decline. According to this argument, a fare increase reduces ridership, which, in turn, further increases the deficit and forces another fare increase. But this vicious cycle depends on transit demand being very sensitive to price. If the absolute value of the price elasticity is less than 1, then the fare increase should increase total revenues and reduce, rather than add, to the deficit.[21] Most estimates show that the price elasticity of demand for transit is around −0.4, well below the levels required.[22]

Economies of Scale

A second and more plausible argument for low fares is that transit is characterized by economies of scale, so that marginal cost is below average cost. Econometric studies of bus and rail transit firms generally show little evidence of scale economies, but they do not include rail capital costs or passenger time, which is where scale economies are often alleged.[23]

As noted earlier, right-of-way costs are often thought to be a source of scale economies for transport services that enjoy an exclusive right-of-way, such as a metro, some streetcar lines, or buses on an exclusive busway. The reasoning is that the same tunnel and tracks that carry ten trains or buses an hour could just as easily carry twenty, so that right-of-way cost per passenger declines rapidly with traffic volumes.

Economies of scale in the right-of-way are not likely to be large enough to justify large subsidies to transit, however, for three reasons. First, right-of-way costs are only a portion of total transit costs, so the resulting economies in total costs may be modest. For example, a statistical analysis of the costs of forty-nine rail transit systems in Europe estimated that marginal cost is 68 percent of average cost for underground rail and 86 percent of average cost for streetcars if train frequency is allowed to vary with passenger volume but the infrastructure remains unchanged.[24] This implies that marginal cost pricing should recover between 68 and 86 percent of total costs on these systems if infrastructure costs are fixed. Second, the gap

---

21. This also assumes that there are no cost savings from reduced traffic. If there are cost savings, then the absolute value of the price elasticity could be greater than 1 without stimulating the vicious cycle.

22. See the discussion of elasticities in chapter 3 on costs and the review of transit elasticity estimates in Goodwin (1992).

23. For a review of recent studies, see Small (1992: 56–57).

24. Wunsch (1996: 184).

between marginal and average costs should be even smaller if the infrastructure is allowed to adjust, because the investment in the right-of-way is more sensitive to passenger volumes than simple reasoning suggests. A very low volume streetcar line might need double tracks only at stations, for example, not along its entire length. As traffic volumes increased, passing sidings could be built at critical points until, gradually, a full two-track system was in place. The weight of the rail and the quality of the ballast and ties could be increased to reduce maintenance costs, and the power distribution system and signals upgraded. Finally, to the extent that certain transit technologies do exhibit strong economies in the right-of-way, they often do so in situations where they are dominated by alternative technologies. At the modest volumes where a subway or rail transit line might exhibit strong economies of scale, for example, a busway might actually be more cost effective. Similarly, at volumes where the busway exhibits strong economies, a bus on regular streets or expressways might be cheaper. In general, economies of scale in the right-of-way are diminished by the rich technological options available both within and among modes of transportation.

Mohring has demonstrated that passenger waiting times are another potential source of scale economies if they are included in system costs.[25] If a transit operator adjusts the schedule so that the vehicles on a route are fully loaded, then an extra passenger will force the operator to increase the schedule frequency slightly. The added frequency will improve service for the rest of the passengers by reducing the amount of time they have to spend at a stop or station waiting for a vehicle to arrive. This source of economies obviously applies to buses operating on city streets as well as to transit on exclusive rights-of-way. Indeed it applies to any type of scheduled service, such as airlines or liner shipping.

Transit operators may respond to the economies in waiting times by increasing vehicle size rather than schedule frequency, which would eliminate the savings to passengers. But if the firm shifts to larger vehicles, it presumably does so because they offer cost advantages, so that the firm is simply capturing the economies of traffic volumes, not eliminating them. Indeed, some research suggests that bus operators may have gone too far in increasing bus size in the United States and Europe and that smaller vehicles and higher frequencies would minimize the combined costs of operators and passengers.[26]

25. Mohring (1972).
26. This is suggested both by theoretical models and by the shift to minibuses after Britain deregulated its urban bus industry. See White, Turner, and Mbara (1992) and Gómez-Ibáñez and Meyer (1993).

Waiting times as a source of scale economies may be of limited practical significance, however. Although empirical research shows that travelers value reductions in waiting time highly, it is unclear whether increases in schedule frequency always translate into meaningful reductions in waiting time or schedule convenience. [27] In the case of a bus route, for example, added frequency may be most important when buses are scheduled ten to twenty minutes apart. At higher frequencies the gain from an added passenger may be too small to notice, especially since buses tend to bunch up on congested streets. At lower frequencies passengers probably learn the schedule and arrive at a stop to meet a specific bus, so a slight increase in frequency would likely not reduce waiting times, but only make the schedule a bit more convenient.

Traffic Congestion and Second-Best Pricing

Another argument used to justify low transit prices is that the theory of the second best applies to urban transportation. Urban motorists impose substantial congestion and pollution costs on others, particularly in the rush hours of major metropolitan areas. In the United States and many other countries, motor fuel taxes and other road use taxes and fees are not high enough to offset these external costs, so peak-hour driving is priced below marginal social costs. If it is impossible to create a "first-best" environment for transit by increasing the price of auto use, then it may be desirable to price transit below marginal cost to compensate.

Strictly speaking, before presuming that transit should be priced below marginal cost, one should consider what other goods and services besides autos are priced at other than marginal cost and whether they are substitutes or complements to transit. In practice, most analysts assume that mispricing in other sectors can be safely ignored because transit and auto use are not very sensitive to the prices of most other goods. Given that transit and auto use are substitutes, the formula for second-best pricing in equation 4-8 holds that transit should be priced below marginal cost. How much below marginal costs depends on three factors: the ratio of the cross- to direct price elasticities of demand, the extent of auto mispricing, and the ratio of auto to transit use.

27. This is true not just in urban transit but in most other transport modes. For example, Morrison and Winston (1986: table 3-3) estimate that the value air passengers place on reductions in waiting times when transferring between flights is 23 percent of their wage rate for pleasure travelers and 144 percent of their wage rate for business travelers.

Surprisingly few scholars have estimated the optimal second-best price for transit given the practical importance of this argument. One of the few studies was done by Glaister and Lewis in 1978 for London bus and rail transit fares. Their study assumed that cars had external congestion costs of £0.21 per passenger mile in the peak and that buses caused external costs of £0.05 per passenger mile in the peak. [28] They considered two cases in calculating the marginal costs of transit: one in which only the operating and external costs were considered; and a second in which capacity costs were also included and assigned to the peak. The results, summarized in table 4-1, show that the optimal transit fares would be only one-third to two-thirds of the estimated marginal costs. In the first case, the second-best strategy called for reducing transit fares below existing levels, especially for rail, resulting in a massive shift from auto and bus to rail use. In the second case, however, the second-best strategy called for raising transit fares above existing levels in the peak and for a significant shift away from peak rail use to cars, buses, and off-peak rail. In short, Glaister and Lewis's results suggest that if both capacity and operating expenses are considered, transit fares should not be as heavily subsidized as they were in London and more commuters should be traveling by car and bus and fewer on rail. [29]

Second-best strategies are even less likely to call for substantial transit subsidies in cities that are less congested and more auto-oriented than London. Glaister and Lewis's assumed external cost of £0.21 per auto passenger mile in 1978 would translate to $0.92 per passenger mile in 1997 dollars, much higher than available estimates for most cities and hours of the day. [30] Moreover, they assumed that the sensitivity of auto use to transit fares—as measured by the cross-elasticity of auto use to transit price—was much greater in London than is typical in most cities in industrialized countries. In many medium-size metropolitan areas in the United States and Europe, for example, the cross-elasticity of auto use to transit price is thought to be practically zero, which would imply that there should be no

28. The external congestion cost of the cars was assumed to decline linearly from £0.21 to £0.07 per passenger mile as traffic volumes declined by half; see Glaister and Lewis (1978: 350).

29. Glaister and Lewis (1978) also tested an intermediate case in which peak rail marginal costs were assumed to be only £0.10 per passenger mile. Even in that case car traffic was predicted to increase under the optimal second-best strategies.

30. The conversion was calculated using exchange rates and gross domestic product deflators reported by the International Monetary Fund (various years). For comparisons with auto externalities in U.S. cities, see, for example, Mohring's estimates of external congestion costs in this volume or the survey of external cost estimates in Gómez-Ibáñez (1997).

Table 4-1. *Estimates of Second-Best Transit Fares for the London Metropolitan Area*

		Bus		Transit	
Scenario	Car	Peak	Off-peak	Peak	Off-peak
Costs and fares (in pence per passenger mile)					
Existing					
External costs	21.0	5.0	0.0	0.0	0.0
Fare	—	4.3	4.3	4.3	4.3
Case 1[a]					
Marginal cost	—	11.0	6.0	2.0	1.0
Optimal fare	—	3.4	3.1	0.3	0.5
Case 2[b]					
Marginal cost	—	14.0	6.0	30.0	1.0
Optimal fare	—	5.2	2.1	20.4	0.4
Traffic volumes (in millions of passenger hours)					
Existing	1.46	0.70	0.18	1.76	0.22
Case 1	1.25	0.51	0.13	3.53	0.86
Case 2	1.59	0.79	0.17	1.08	1.20

Source: Glaister and Lewis (1978: 352).

a. Case 1 includes only operating and external costs, no capacity costs.

b. Case 2 includes capacity costs, which are assigned to the peak period.

reduction in transit fares to compensate for auto mispricing.[31] A study of Manchester, Merseyside, West Midlands (Birmingham), and West and South Yorkshire metropolitan areas in Britain, for example, found that second-best considerations had little effect on optimal transit fares because congestion levels and cross-elasticities of demand were lower than in London.[32] Similarly, in a recent study of transit policy in the United States, Winston and Shirley estimate that raising rail and bus fares to marginal costs in 1990 would have generated approximately $2.5 billion a year in net ben-

31. Glaister and Lewis (1978) assume that the elasticity of peak auto use is 0.025 with respect to bus fares and 0.056 with respect to rail fares, based on an earlier study in London by Lewis (1978). There are very few other studies of the elasticity of auto use with respect to transit prices to compare this estimate with, but one estimate suggests that it was effectively zero in Boston in the 1960s; see Kraft (1973).

32. Dodgson and Topham (1987).

efits. Although they did not estimate the optimal second-best fare, their results suggest that it was much closer to marginal costs than it was to the prevailing fares.[33]

Equity Considerations

A final argument often advanced for reducing transit fares below marginal costs is to help the poor or disadvantaged. Transit riders are often poorer on average than auto users, and poor households are less likely to own a car or may have only one car to share among several family members. Moreover, transport typically accounts for 19 percent of household expenditures and is needed to get to jobs, education, health care, and other basic services.[34]

The reason that economists often assume away equity concerns in pricing is not that they believe the distribution of opportunity or income is just, but that they are painfully aware of the limitations of pricing as a mechanism for redistribution. For example, economists often argue that it is less efficient to help poor people by reducing the price of a good or service they use than by giving them the equivalent in cash. This is even more true if the price reductions must be offered to all customers rather than only to the poor, so that much of the subsidy goes to people who are less in need.

Urban transit is a case in point. Many of the benefits of low fares go to people who are not poor, and the poor who do benefit might prefer alternatives. For example, in the largest and densest U.S. metropolitan areas, the average household income of urban public transit users is similar to the average household income of all metropolitan residents because transit patronage is dominated by commuters to the central business district, many of whom are highly paid. In the smaller and lower-density metropolitan areas, by contrast, most public transit riders are poor. The low densities usually make it expensive to provide convenient transit service; many riders might prefer to receive the subsidy in cash or in the form of a transportation voucher that could be used to buy a car, taxi rides, or other services besides conventional transit.

---

33. These estimates assume service frequency is not optimized as well. With optimized service, the net benefits are $6.1 billion for bus and $1.3 billion for rail; see Winston and Shirley (1998: table 4-1)

34. As measured in upublished data from the U.S. Bureau of Labor Statistics consumer expenditure survey, 1984–95.

In theory one could target transit subsidies more efficiently by giving discount fares or transportation vouchers only to the poor. But such policies are seldom adopted because focusing benefits more narrowly also reduces political support. Providing a cash grant instead of subsidizing transit eliminates support from transit managers, workers, and equipment suppliers, for example, while limiting fare reductions to poor riders reduces support from other users.

The danger of this line of reasoning is that it applies to some degree to just about every good and service, not just transit. If for each industry, in turn, it is decided there must be some other more efficient and politically palatable way of helping the poor, then nothing gets done. Economists thus often effectively abandon redistributional goals even when they believe in them

Related Issues and Applications

If it is sometimes difficult to make an affirmative case for low transit fares, the disadvantages of low fares also have become increasingly obvious. One is that raising taxes to finance transit subsidies imposes distortions and efficiency losses in the economy. A second is that most of the subsidies are apparently absorbed in higher wages for transit workers and reduced productivity rather than passed on to riders in the form of lower fares or improved service. Cities in Britain and the United States have demonstrated that this problem can be reduced by having private firms bid competitively for contracts to provide subsidized transit services.[35]

Many of the arguments made about urban transit fares apply to intercity rail passenger and freight tariffs as well. Railroads exhibit economies of density much like transit, so marginal cost may be below average cost. Airports and intercity highways are often congested and underpriced, so that second-best considerations might dictate pricing rail below marginal cost. In combination, these suggest that rail tariffs should be below marginal costs and well below average costs, and thus that railroads might need to be subsidized.[36] But as in the case of transit, the economies of scale in railroads are modest given the technological opportunities within and among modes and the extent of mispricing on competing modes, and the cross-

---

35. See the review in Gómez-Ibáñez and Meyer (1993).
36. For an interesting formal application of this to railroad pricing in Sweden, see Nilsson (1992).

elasticities of demand are low in many situations.[37] In short, subsidies to intercity rail may be justified, but probably only in selected situations.

Charging for Highway Infrastructure

The debates over how to price highway infrastructure illustrate several other pricing issues. The practical problems of collecting congestion tolls on urban roads are a central concern, but they are the subject of a separate chapter and so will not be dealt with extensively here. Air pollution caused by motor vehicles is also dealt with elsewhere and will be ignored here. Instead, I focus on two other topics: the treatment of sunk costs; and the allocation of financial responsibility between automobiles and trucks.

Recovering Long-Run Marginal and Sunk Costs

As explained earlier, Mohring and Harwitz showed that the revenues from marginal cost pricing will be sufficient to recover facility costs as long as there are no scale economies or diseconomies in the facility and the investment in the facility is optimal. In that case the congestion toll, which is the optimal price, is just equal to the average cost of accommodating another vehicle by expanding the facility.

Many highway planners and economists have questioned whether Mohring and Harwitz's observation applies to the real world. The primary objection is not to the assumption about scale economies—most highway facilities exhibit only slight, if any, economies from traffic volume.[38] Rather, the objection is to the assumption that the level of investment in the facility is optimal for current traffic levels.

Investment might not be optimal for at least two reasons. First, highways and many other types of transport infrastructure are usually durable and immobile and require long lead times to plan and build. As a result, highway authorities may be caught with more capacity than they need if traffic falls unexpectedly; conversely, they may have a serious shortfall if traffic grows rapidly and it takes years to get environmental and other per-

37. For an assessment of the degree to which different freight modes pay their marginal cost in the United States, see Transportation Research Board (1996).

38. For a concise review of the evidence, see the discussion of returns to scale in Small, Winston, and Evans (1989:100–01).

missions to expand the highway. Second, capacity may be "lumpy," in that there may appear to be economies to building capacity in large increments. A four-lane bridge may cost only about 50 percent more to build than a two-lane bridge, for example, so if one anticipates the eventual need for four lanes, building them immediately may be cheaper than building one two-lane bridge now and a second two-lane bridge later.[39]

The problem of pricing with nonoptimal investment is often described in the economics literature as a conflict between pricing at short-run or long-run marginal cost. In the simple analytic models presented at the beginning of the chapter, the short-run marginal cost is the cost of accommodating an extra vehicle by tolerating more congestion on the facility; the long-run marginal cost is the cost of accommodating the extra vehicle by physically expanding the facility so that congestion does not increase. If the highway authority is following the optimal pricing and investment policy, then short-run and long-run marginal costs will be equal to each other and to the highway toll. And if there are neither economies nor diseconomies of scale, long-run marginal cost will also be equal to long-run average cost, and toll revenues will cover the authority's costs. If highway investment is not optimal for current traffic volumes, however, then short-run marginal cost will be less than long-run marginal cost where there is excess capacity but greater where there is a capacity shortage. And because economists usually recommend short-run marginal cost as the appropriate marginal cost for pricing, toll revenues will therefore either fall short of or exceed the highway authority's costs.

This problem of short- and long-run marginal cost is also closely related to the problem of recovering sunk costs. Once a highway authority has invested in a facility, much of the cost is often regarded as sunk. Not all of the investment will be sunk even in the short run—there may be alternative uses for the land in the right-of-way, for example, and the asphalt might be dug up and recycled on another road. And in the long run many of the sunk investments will need to be renewed if the highway authority is going to continue to operate the road. But in the short run many of the highway authority's costs are sunk and thus should not be included in marginal costs.

---

39. An often-ignored cost of building a four-lane bridge is that the investment in the four-lane bridge will be underutilized for a longer period than the investment in a two-lane bridge. Thus the decision to build four lanes immediately is more attractive if traffic is expected to grow quickly and/or the discount rate is low.

The likelihood that capacity investments will not be optimal for current traffic levels is of enormous practical significance for highway policy. It implies, for example, that optimal prices on a facility will fluctuate widely during its lifetime. When a bridge first opens, the optimal price will be close to zero because the facility, presumably built to accommodate some future year's traffic, will be uncongested. As traffic builds up, congestion and the optimal toll will grow as well. But when traffic reaches the point where the bridge is widened or a second span added, the optimal toll will fall to zero again. Most toll roads and bridges do not vary their tolls as traffic develops and thus overcharge in the early years and undercharge later.

The mismatch between capacity and current traffic levels also undermines the common practice of earmarking fuel taxes, tolls, and other user charges for road construction and maintenance. For many years the World Bank opposed proposals by developing countries to create such road funds, largely on the grounds that the appropriate road user charge was the short-run marginal cost and that there was no a priori reason to expect that revenues would cover costs. [40] Indeed, in many developing countries the Bank also assumed that the short-run marginal cost was often well below the long-run marginal cost because rural and intercity roads seemed to be relatively uncongested. This assumption implied that the revenues from optimal road user charges would fall short of investment costs and that the national highway authorities would need support from general tax revenues.

Aligning capacity with traffic levels may not be as difficult as it seems, however, for two reasons. First, congestion is more prevalent than commonly thought, especially on lightly traveled facilities. On a two-lane rural road, for example, trucks can cause significant congestion if cars behind them cannot pass safely for miles. Often rural roads in developing countries are less than two full lanes wide, so vehicles coming from opposite directions must slow and pull onto the shoulder as they pass, another form of congestion.

Second, capacity is often less lumpy than it appears, which makes it easier to adjust investment levels especially if traffic is growing. Bridges and tunnels are something of exceptions, in that the minimum increment of capacity is usually a lane and it can be cheaper to add several lanes at once than one at a time. But with a normal highway, capacity can often be augmented gradually, for example, by selectively eliminating the steepest grades

---

40. The most influential statement of the World Bank position was by the economist Alan A. Walters; see Walters (1968).

and the tightest curves or by incrementally widening pavements and improving sight distances for passing. And when an entire highway route is considered as a whole, the lumpiness of the capacity at the bridges or tunnels along the way is less significant.

Even where capacity is poorly matched to current traffic volumes there may be reasons for charging the long-run, rather than the short-run, marginal cost. Economists usually recommend the short-run measure because it ensures that the existing facilities are efficiently utilized. But this argument is concerned with static or short-run efficiency, and dynamic or long-run considerations may sometimes conflict.

One such circumstance is where short-run marginal cost pricing prevents efficient highway investment. The World Bank eventually softened its opposition to road funds and the earmarking of fuel taxes, for example, because many governments in developing countries found it politically difficult to use scarce general tax revenues for roads, and so road maintenance and investment were seriously neglected. In theory one could have both optimal pricing and optimal investment, but in practice the two could not exist side by side. The Bank decided that the short-run efficiency losses from compromising a bit on pricing were smaller than the long-run efficiency gains from ensuring more adequate investment.[41]

A second circumstance is where price stability is important to customers. Customers may be making long-lived investments on the basis of current prices and may not understand (or may not believe) that prices are going to change over time. If manufacturers are deciding where to locate plants on the basis of current highway tolls or truck tariffs, for example, then pricing at long-run rather than short-run marginal costs would provide them with the correct long-run price signals in making these investments. Traffic would be too low or high in the short term, but this distortion might be more than offset by ensuring correct long-run investments by customers.[42]

---

41. See World Bank (1996) or Gwilliam (1997).

42. Another circumstance favoring stable prices is where prices are regulated by public authorities or commissions. Public regulators may find it politically difficult to adjust prices frequently in line with short-run marginal cost, especially if that cost fluctuates greatly with variations in demand or as new capacity is brought on line or old capacity is retired. Prices set close to long-run marginal cost are likely to be more stable and create less controversy. Finally, price stability may be important for customer goodwill even where prices are not regulated. Firms that raise prices greatly during capacity shortages may gain a reputation as unreliable suppliers or price gougers and may lose business in the long run. Some freight railroads in the United States believe that long-run pricing is the best policy, for example, because their long-term relationships with major manufacturers that locate plants on their rail lines would be damaged by frequent price shifts.

This is not to deny that there will be many cases where the receipts from optimal highway user charges bear little relation to highway authority costs. But optimal pricing may not require wildly fluctuating prices or prevent governments from having highway users pay the costs of building and maintaining the highway systems they use, even in rural areas.

Allocating Costs between Cars and Trucks

The discussion so far has treated all highway users as homogeneous when, in fact, a highway serves many different types of vehicles. The long-standing debate about whether autos and trucks pay their fair shares for highways illustrates some of the potential for confusion in pricing caused by the possibility of joint costs or economies of scope.

To understand this debate, one must use a slightly more complex description of highway costs and services. Think of a highway as producing two types of services: the basic capacity to carry traffic, which is what I have been discussing so far; and pavement durability and smoothness. The traffic-carrying capacity of a highway is determined by the number of lanes, lane width, grades, curves, and other factors. Highway engineers measure the demands that different vehicle types place on basic capacity relative to those of a standard passenger car. The number of passenger car equivalents, or PCEs, of capacity needed by a heavy truck varies according to terrain and other factors. A heavy truck on a level road might require only 1.2 PCEs of capacity, for example, whereas one on rolling terrain might require 4 PCEs because of the truck's lower horsepower-to-weight ratio.

A highway's pavement durability is determined by the type of pavement, its thickness, and the stresses it has been subject to since construction. Highway engineers measure the demands that different vehicle types place on pavement durability in terms of the damage caused by the passage of a reference axle weighing 18,000 pounds, approximately the weight of the axles on many heavy trucks. Pavement damage increases at the third or fourth power of axle weight. Thus the typical 1,000 pound axle on a passenger car produces only about 0.0001 equivalent standard axle loads, or ESAL, of damage. The number of ESALs a pavement can withstand before it needs to be resurfaced or rebuilt is a power function of the pavement thickness. Consequently, there are significant economies of scale in providing pavement durability because, for example, a pavement that is eleven inches thick is twice as durable as one that is nine inches thick, yet costs only a fraction more to build.

Since the 1950s, when the federal government began its massive program to construct the Interstate and Defense Highway System, the U.S. Congress has periodically asked the Federal Highway Administration to estimate the responsibilities of different vehicle types for highway costs. These studies are used as guidance in debates over how to set the various fuel taxes and vehicle registration fees that help finance the construction and maintenance of the highway system. Beginning with its first cost allocation report issued in stages between 1961 and 1965, the Federal Highway Administration developed what it called the "incremental" or "cost-occasioned" approach to allocating highway expenditures.[43] This approach has been refined in several important ways since, but it remains the fundamental model for all subsequent reports including the latest (1997) and is widely imitated in state and foreign studies.

The essential idea is to define a base highway system designed as if all traffic were passenger cars or light trucks. Any incremental increases in pavement or bridge strength, lane widths, or grading needed to accommodate vehicles that are larger or heavier or have lower horsepower-to-weight ratios are considered to be "occasioned" by those vehicles and assigned to them. Given the economies of pavement durability, most durability costs are in the base system rather than in the increments. In its first report, the highway administration assigned all but the last few inches of thickness to the base system, so that only about 36 percent of total costs were uniquely occasioned by particular vehicle types.[44] The 1982 report increased uniquely occasioned costs to about 50 percent by allocating new pavement costs to vehicle types according to the number of vehicle miles traveled weighted by the average ESALs per vehicle mile for each type, a practice retained in the latest report.[45] In essence, these studies estimated that half of all highway costs were joint costs between autos and trucks. And the studies argued that there was no objective basis to allocate these costs—that it was purely a question of equity.[46]

43. For a history of the early studies, see Congressional Budget Office (1978:59–73).

44. The results of cost allocation studies are often reported in ways that make it difficult to determine the perentage of total costs that are not uniquely occasioned by a class. This estimate is based on a calculation by the Congressional Budget Office (1978: 72) that 64.1 percent of total costs were allocated to the base vehicle, the automobile, in the first study. For the original reports, see U.S. Bureau of Public Roads (1961, 1965).

45. In the latest report, for example, the base system accounts for between 16 and 80 percent of new pavement costs depending upon the type of road and location; the average cost, which is not given, appears to be between 30 and 40 percent. See U.S. Department of Transportation (1997: V-6).

46. Early studies were more explicit about this; see, for example, U.S. Department of Transportation (1982: I-2 –I-3).

This methodology provoked a long, intense, and fruitless controversy about how to define the base system and who should pay for it. Critics of the Federal Highway Administration argued that it was arbitrary to pick autos as the base vehicle. As one put it,

> The trouble with this argument is its asymmetry: If trucks were considered to be the basic vehicles instead of cars—that is, if roads were assumed to be built primarily for trucks—then trucks would be assigned almost all the costs of pavement, since the incremental cost of improving an all-truck road to carry cars as well would be virtually nil. And it is not unreasonable to consider trucks as the basic vehicles.[47]

Truckers defended the Federal Highway Administration by arguing that the use of cars as the base vehicle reflected historical reality: early roads were designed primarily for autos, and the designs were upgraded over the years to accommodate heavier vehicles. To be safe, the truckers also argued that the base vehicle might be considered a fire truck or garbage truck, instead of a car, because most communities would not go without those services. In that case, the costs of strengthening pavements for commercial trucks would be even smaller, because fire and garbage trucks have very heavy axles.[48]

This debate overlooked the fundamental flaw in the Federal Highway Administration's approach, which was to focus primarily on pavement durability and ignore the basic traffic-carrying capacity of the highway system. In essence, the agency worried solely about who was responsible for the thickness of the pavement and neglected the question of who was responsible for how many lanes wide the pavement had to be.

The responsibilities of autos and trucks finally were sorted out systematically in a study of optimal highway pricing and investment policies by Small, Winston, and Evans. Not surprisingly, they found that the optimal highway user charge per vehicle mile traveled should have two components: one for pavement damage, based on a vehicle's ESAL value; and the second for congestion or basic capacity, based on its PCE value. They also found U.S. highway pricing and investment policies deficient in several respects. Actual user charges for trucks were more a function of total weight than axle weight, so that trucks carrying very heavy loads on few axles were

47. U.S. Congressional Budget Office (1979: 56).
48. Urban Institute and Sydec, Inc. (1990).

seriously undercharged. If rates were based on ESALs, truckers would have strong incentives to switch to vehicles that distributed weight over more axles, which would slightly increase truck capital and maintenance costs but greatly reduce pavement damage. Furthermore, the pavements were not built as strongly as they should have been, and the increase in the initial investments required to build them thicker now would be more than re- paid by reduced lifetime maintenance costs. The net gains to the economy as a whole from optimal highway pricing and investment would be close to $8 billion a year (in 1982 dollars), equivalent to half the annual highway maintenance expenditures.[49]

Equally interesting, Small and his colleagues also found few joint costs, so marginal cost pricing would generate roughly the revenues the highway agencies needed. They estimated the economies of scale in providing pave- ment durability and traffic volume separately, and then the economies of scope of providing durability and traffic volumes jointly in one facility. They found that the substantial returns to scale in pavement durability were offset by diseconomies of scope so that returns were nearly constant over all. As they explained:

> The wider the road is made in order to accommodate more cars, the greater the cost of any additional thickness required to handle a heavy vehicle, be- cause all the lanes must be built to the same thickness. These diseconomies of scope counteract the scale economies in the separate production of loadings and volume and the resulting deficits under marginal cost pricing.[50]

Their result implies that highway authorities would find it cheaper to re- strict trucks to certain lanes on jointly used highways, or even to build separate roads for cars and trucks in some circumstances.

In recent years the federal highway cost allocation procedure has evolved to more closely mimic the pricing scheme recommended by Small and his colleagues. The latest version allocates most pavement costs by ESAL- weighted vehicle miles traveled and the base system by PCE-weighted ve- hicle miles traveled, for example. But the government still rejects an explicit marginal cost framework, in part out of an exaggerated concern that rev-

49. Comparing the estimated annual savings to maintenance expenditures in 1985; see Small, Winston, and Evans (1989: 2, 72).

50. Small, Winston, and Evans (1989: 102). For a description of measures of economies of scale in multiproduct firms, see Bailey and Friedlaender (1982).

enues might not cover agency costs.[51] As a result, many of the potential efficiency gains from correctly pricing highway infrastructure are lost.

Other Applications

The issues in highway pricing described here apply to every other form of transportation infrastructure. Airports, waterways, and railroads all involve durable, immobile, and lumpy investments that often require long lead times to plan and construct. As a result, the basic capacity of the facility is not always optimal for current traffic levels, and many costs may appear sunk in the short run. As in the case of highways, however, congestion may be higher, capacity less lumpy, and sunk costs smaller than they first appear, with the result that short-run marginal cost may not be so different from long-run marginal cost and marginal cost pricing not so inconsistent with long-run cost recovery.

Similarly, these other forms of infrastructure also serve several different types of traffic simultaneously, with the resulting confusion about how to assign costs and whether some costs are joint. Airports often serve general as well as commercial aviation, a railroad may provide many different types of passenger and freight services on the same line, while the locks and dams of a waterway often serve barges and pleasure craft as well as provide flood control and irrigation. But again joint costs and the resulting complications may be smaller when one investigates economies of scale and scope carefully.[52]

Price Discrimination in Private and Regulated Enterprises

A final illustration of pricing issues is the debate over whether transportation carriers engage in price discrimination and, if so, whether it is desirable. Price discrimination occurs when different customers are charged different prices for the same service or when customers who use different

---

51. Another frequent argument is that marginal cost varies by location and time of day, while federal user charges do not; see, for example, U.S. Department of Transportation (1982: I-2) and U.S. Department of Transportation (1997: 24–28).

52. For example, there may be diseconomies of scope to providing freight and passenger service on the same railroad line because providing both the smooth rail and super-elevation needed by a passenger train and the heavy track needed for freight service on the same line is expensive; see Kim (1987), as cited in Small, Winston, and Evans (1989).

services are charged different markups over the marginal costs. Transportation has a long history of allegations of price discrimination, beginning with the railroads in the nineteenth century and continuing with the airlines in the twentieth.

Profit-Maximizing Prices and Competition

To this point I have been concerned with pricing rules that maximize net social benefits rather than the profits of an individual firm. To understand price discrimination, however, it is helpful first to review the rules for prices that maximize profits and how they are affected by competition.

The simplest case is where the firm charges all customers the same price. The goal is to maximize profits, π, which is the difference between total revenues and total costs. Using the same notation as before,

$$(4\text{-}9) \qquad \pi = Q \cdot P(Q) - Q \cdot AC(Q).$$

To get the profit-maximizing quantity, set the first derivative of equation 4-9 with respect to Q at zero, yielding

$$(4\text{-}10) \qquad P + Q \cdot (dP/dQ) = AC + Q \cdot (dAC/dQ).$$

This is the familiar rule that profit maximization occurs where marginal revenue (on the left-hand side) equals marginal cost (on the right-hand side). Rearranging slightly, the profit-maximizing price is

$$(4\text{-}11) \qquad P = AC + Q \cdot (dAC/dQ) - Q \cdot (dP/dQ).$$

Referring back to the socially optimal price in equation 4-2, one can see that the profit-maximizing price in equation 4-11 is higher by the amount $-Q \cdot (dP/dQ)$. (This term is positive or zero because dP/dQ is either negative or zero.) If the firm is in a perfectly competitive industry, however, then its output is too small to affect market price noticeably, so $dP/dQ = 0$, and the profit-maximizing price becomes the same as the socially optimal price. In short, in a perfectly competitive market, a firm will be forced to price at the social optimum: marginal cost. But in an imperfectly competitive market, a firm will set the price above marginal cost, and the less sensitive demand is to price, the more above marginal cost it will charge.[53]

53. The less sensitive quantity is to price, the larger dQ/dP is in absolute terms.

Similar rules apply if the firm is able to charge different prices to different customers. If the price charged one customer does not affect the quantity consumed by the others, then the pricing rule in equation 4-11 applies to each individual customer, and the less sensitive the customer is to price, the more he will pay relative to others. But perfect competition makes price discrimination impossible, because competitors will undercut any firm charging more than marginal cost. Thus price discrimination is a sign that competition is imperfect—in a perfectly competitive market, by contrast, the prices all firms charge all customers should converge on a single price.

Economists are somewhat more tolerant of the appearance of price discrimination in transportation than in other industries. In the first place, appearances can be deceiving—transportation costs are complex, and the differences in price may be based on differences in costs. Second, transportation is sometimes characterized by economies of scale or scope, and where this is the case, the firm must charge some customers above marginal cost if it is to avoid either bankruptcy or public subsidy. Ramsey pricing is the theoretically preferred form of price discrimination in such cases, because it minimizes the social losses that result if the firm must be financially self-sufficient. But if Ramsey pricing is not possible, a little profit-maximizing price discrimination may be an acceptable compromise.

Airline Pricing

The United States has relied on market competition to discipline airline fares since 1978, when government controls on fares and on entry and exit from routes were substantially eliminated. As explained in chapter 14, the experience has been largely successful: average fares are lower, service quality is better by most measures, and air travel is up. Although average fares are down, the variation in fares paid has increased significantly. Only about 10 percent of passengers now pay the standard coach fare, and carriers often offer twenty different fares on a route with some discounts as steep as 70 percent off coach.[54] Passengers using discount fares often pay half as much, or less, than the full-fare passengers in the seats next to them, although they often must make their reservation two weeks in advance or stay over on a Saturday in order to qualify for the lower fare.

---

54. For a description of the variation in airline fares, see Borenstein and Rose (1994) and Morrison and Winston (1995).

Whether this situation constitutes price discrimination is difficult to tell. On the one hand, some of the variation is clearly based on differences in airline costs. The demand for air travel peaks at certain seasons of the year, days of the week, and hours of the day, and peak capacity is costly to provide. It makes sense that airlines would offer discount fares to fill seats on off-peak flights. Similarly, travelers can often get reservations at the last minute if they are willing to pay the full fare, but it is expensive for the airlines to provide this convenience. To do so, the airlines must hold some empty seats for full-fare passengers up until the last minute instead of releasing them to travelers looking for discount fares. As a result, a higher proportion of the seats reserved for full fares depart empty, while the seats reserved for discount fares are often sold out. On the other hand, some of the restrictions placed on discount fares have no obvious basis in cost, which suggests that price discrimination must be involved to some degree. Requirements that travelers stay over a Saturday night serve no obvious purpose, for example, except to separate less price sensitive business travelers from the more price sensitive leisure travelers.

Data on how airline prices vary across routes support the view that both cost differences and discrimination are involved. Morrison and Winston found that the variation in fares offered is somewhat smaller on routes served by a larger number of carriers, for example, which is consistent with the hypothesis that imperfect competition contributes to the variation in fares.[55] But even on routes served by several carriers, the variation in fares is still high, which suggests that much of the variation is based on real cost differences rather than on discrimination.

It would be impossible to determine exactly how much price variation is based on cost and how much on discrimination without a very detailed understanding of airline costs and demand. The airlines have developed sophisticated "yield management" systems that analyze historical data on traffic and fares to help predict the profitability of alternative schedules and fares for each route. Once the schedule is set for a quarter, these systems monitor bookings in real time and modify the numbers of seats reserved for different fare classifications. Even with these systems the airlines are probably not exactly sure how profitable different fares are. And given the overall success of airline deregulation, most economists are understandably leery of trying to second-guess the airlines by reinstating government

---

55. This result holds for the period after 1986, as explained in Morrison and Winston (1995:17–19).

controls over fares. The more sensible strategy seems to be to try to reduce the remaining barriers to competition in the industry so that increased competition will keep price discrimination under control.

Ramsey Pricing at the Postal Service

If price discrimination is not always easy to detect, it is also not easy to do well. Many of the difficulties are illustrated by the experiences of governments in trying to create Ramsey pricing schemes to prevent the deficits that marginal cost pricing might cause for transport services with large economies of scale or scope. Several industries could serve as examples, but the U.S. Postal Service is an interesting case in point.

The U.S. Postal Service is owned by the government, but since 1970 it has been required by law to operate as a for-profit business and to recover its costs from the fees it charges. The Postal Service is also obligated to charge the same price for a domestic first-class letter regardless of how far or where in the country it is going and to deliver mail six days a week to every address in the United States. In return for these obligations, Congress has given it the exclusive right to deliver to mail boxes at individual homes and businesses. Partly because of this monopoly, its rates are regulated by a special government board.

The Postal Service has long argued that its commitment to provide delivery to every address every weekday means that the marginal cost of carrying an additional letter or package to any particular address is much less than the average cost. To recover its total costs, the Postal Service traditionally charges first-class letters a higher markup over marginal costs than third-class bulk mail (such as advertising circulars or magazines) or packages, reasoning that individual letters are less price sensitive than bulk mail and packages. The Postal Service explains these practices as Ramsey pricing and during the 1970s developed an elaborate series of cost and demand studies to further refine and defend its rates before its new regulatory board.[56]

The proceedings before the board demonstrated that the social gains from getting the Ramsey pricing exactly right are not always large. Tye estimated, for example, that for every dollar of revenue burden shifted from the more price-elastic third-class bulk mail to less price-elastic first-class letters, the gain in net social benefits for Postal Service customers was only

---

56. Tye (1983a).

4.4 cents.[57] The dollar shift in rates would be much more visible and politically controversial than the 4.4 cent net gain it brought, so it would be difficult to generate political support for proposed rate changes.

Even more troubling, the proceedings also showed that the Ramsey pricing formula is very sensitive to the direct- and cross-price elasticities assumed and that these elasticities are seldom known with great precision. A change in the estimated direct price elasticity for one class of mail from −0.5 to −0.3 could justify doubling the markup over marginal cost charged to that class. Despite an extensive statistical analysis, the standard errors of the estimated elasticities were often very high, so that very different markups over marginal cost among mail classes were based on statistically insignificant differences in the estimated elasticities.[58]

The large markups proposed for some mail classes also raised fears that they would be difficult to sustain in the long run. Price discrimination contains the seeds of its own destruction because it establishes strong incentives for competitors and customers to find new ways around it. This is especially true in the long run, when there is more time to develop new methods to steal the highly marked-up traffic. In the early twentieth century, for example, the railroads' practice of charging much higher markups on shipments of manufactured commodities than on shipments of bulk and agricultural commodities is thought to have encouraged the development of trucking. The high rail rates made the infant trucking industry profitable despite the poor quality of early roads and trucks. Similarly, high markups on first-class mail and packages probably would encourage the further development of alternative delivery systems such as United Parcel Service, Federal Express, the facsimile machine, and electronic mail.

In the end, legal challenges forced the Postal Service to reconsider whether the marginal costs of individual mail classes were as low as they seemed and thereby reduced the amount of revenue that had to be generated through Ramsey schemes.[59]

57. Tye (1983b: 250, 260).

58. Tye (1983b: 248, 255). For a similar example from the U.S. railroad industry, see Tye and Leonard (1983).

59. The law governing the Postal Service establishes several criteria for postal rates, but the essential idea is that rates should be based as much as possible on costs: "each class of mail or type of mail service [should] bear the direct and indirect costs attributable to that class or type plus that portion of all other costs of the Postal Service reasonably assignable to such class or type." See the Postal Reorganization Act as quoted in Tye (1983: 66).

Conclusions

In summary, many of the complications that make marginal cost pricing seem difficult in transportation are often exaggerated or can be solved with a little common sense. In this regard, John Meyer might have offered four basic tips.

First, beware of arguments that marginal costs are very different from average costs. It is true that transportation firms often exhibit economies of scale or scope or have facilities that are too small or large for current traffic. These characteristics often make marginal costs seem very small, because they imply that fixed, sunk, and joint costs are large and should be excluded. But it is also true that a transport firm or its customers often have strong incentives to understate marginal costs because in so doing they may justify government subsidies to the firm or provide its managers and regulators more discretion in deciding what different customers should pay. Very low estimates of marginal cost also may result from innocent misunderstandings of transport technology or of the rules of cost measurement or allocation. In short, when told that marginal cost is very different from average cost, one's first reaction should be to try to find the source of the error in the cost estimate rather than to design an elaborate subsidy or Ramsey pricing scheme to accommodate the difference.

Second, when determining price, it is important not to focus too narrowly on certain aspects of economic efficiency and ignore others. The conventional prescription for short-run marginal cost pricing is designed to optimize the efficient use of existing facilities, for example, which is an important goal. But, as the World Bank discovered with roads, short-run marginal cost pricing may conflict with the efficient allocation of resources in the long run if it generates too little revenue for maintenance and investment and if governments are simply unable or unwilling to supplement the road budget out of general tax receipts. Similarly, Ramsey pricing promises the efficiencies of marginal cost pricing while satisfying budget constraints. As the Postal Service and others have learned, however, the information requirements and transactions costs of implementing Ramsey pricing can be daunting. Another example is second-best pricing, which is designed to improve global resource allocation by compensating for mispricings in other sectors. But, as the example of urban transit illustrates, the net gains may be small or even negative if second-best pricing requires subsidies and the subsidies in turn encourage the transit firms to become technically inefficient. In sum, it is important to design a pricing regime that encourages the efficient use of existing facilities and resources, but it is also important not to overlook either the incentives it establishes for long-run and technical efficiency or the transactions and information costs it requires.

Third, marginal cost pricing—or some rough-and-ready approximation of it—is often more practical than it first seems, even in an industry as complicated as transportation. The problems of cost recovery are probably not as serious as often alleged if marginal cost is usually fairly close to average cost. The benefits of complex Ramsey or second-best pricing schemes are probably smaller than supposed, especially if the information and transaction costs and the potential for technical or investment inefficiencies are considered. In many transportation enterprises, it may be possible to design pricing regimes that closely approximate marginal cost, are consistent with cost recovery, are not overly complex to administer, and generate almost as many (or more) benefits than a regime based on a very strict and narrow interpretation of marginal cost.

Finally, empirical research shows the net benefits from bringing prices into line with marginal cost can be substantial. Estimates cited earlier suggest gains of $2.5 billion a year in 1990 dollars for urban transit, for example, and $8 billion a year in 1982 dollars for intercity highways. The gains for urban highways, airports, waterways, and other transportation facilities and services are probably comparable.

References

Bailey, Elizabeth E., and Ann F. Friedlaender. 1982. "Market Structure and Multiproduct Industries." *Journal of Economic Literature* 20 (September): 1024–48.

Baumol, William J., and David F. Bradford. 1970. "Optimal Departures from Marginal Cost Pricing." *American Economic Review* 60 (June): 265–83.

Boiteux, Marcel. 1960. "Peak Load Pricing." *Journal of Business* 33 (April): 157–79.

Borenstein, Severin, and Nancy L. Rose. 1994. "Competition and Price Dispersion in the U.S. Airline Industry." *Journal of Political Economy* 102 (4, August): 653–83.

Browning, Edgar K. 1987. "On the Marginal Welfare Cost of Taxation." *American Economic Review* 77 (March): 11–23.

Dodgson, J. S., and N. Topham. 1987. "Benefit Cost Rules for Urban Transit Subsidies: An Integration of Allocation, Distributional, and Public Finance Issues." *Journal of Transport Economics and Policy* 21 (January): 57–71.

Dupuit, Jules. 1844. "On the Measurement of the Utility of Public Works." Reprinted in *Transport: Selected Readings,* edited by Dennis Munby. Penguin, 1968.

Farrar, Donald E., and John R. Meyer. 1970. *Managerial Economics.* Prentice Hall.

Glaister, Stephen, and David Lewis. 1978. "An Integrated Fares Policy for Transport in London." *Journal of Public Economics* 9 (3, June): 341–55.

Gómez-Ibáñez, José A. 1997. "Estimating Whether Transport Users Pay Their Way: The State of the Art." In *The Full Costs and Benefits of Transportation: Contributions to Theory, Method, and Measurement,* edited by David Greene, Donald W. Jones, and Mark A. Delucchi. Berlin: Springer-Verlag.

Gómez-Ibáñez, José A., and John R. Meyer. 1993. *Going Private: The International Experience with Transport Privatization.* Brookings.

Goodwin, P. B. 1992. "A Review of New Demand Elasticities with Special Reference to Short and Long Run Effects of Price Changes." *Journal of Transport Economics and Policy* 26 (May): 155–69.

Green, H. A. John. 1961. "The Social Optimum in the Presence of Monopoly and Taxation." *Review of Economic Studies* 29 (October): 66–78.

Gwilliam, Ken M. 1997. "Sustainable Transport and Economic Development." *Journal of Transport Economics and Policy* 31 (September): 325–30.

Hotelling, H. 1938. "The General Welfare in Relation to the Problems of Taxation and of Railway and Utility Rates." *Econometrica* 6 (July): 242–69.

International Monetary Fund. Annual. *International Financial Statistics.* Washington, D.C.

Kim, H. Youn. 1987. "Economies of Scale and Scope in Multiproduct Firms: Evidence from U.S. Railroads." *Applied Economics* 19 (6, June): 733–41.

Knight, F. H. 1924. "Some Fallacies in the Interpretation of Social Cost." *Quarterly Journal of Economics* 38 (August): 582–606.

Kraft, Gerald. 1973. "Free Transit Revisited." *Public Policy* 21 (Winter): 79–105.

Lewis, David L. 1978. "Esimating the Influence of Public Policy on Road Traffic Levels in Greater London: A Rejoinder." *Journal of Transport Economics and Policy* 12 (1, January): 99–102.

Lipsey, Richard G., and K. Kelvin Lancaster. 1956. "The General Theory of the Second Best." *Review of Economic Studies* 24:11–32.

Mohring, Herbert. 1972. "Optimization and Scale Economies in Urban Bus Transportation." *American Economic Review* 62 (September): 591–604.

———. 1976 *Transportation Economics.* Cambridge, Mass.: Ballinger.

Mohring, Herbert, and Mitchell Harwitz. 1962. *Highway Benefits: An Analytical Framework.* Northwestern University Press.

Morrison, Steven A., and Clifford Winston. 1986. *The Economic Effects of Airline Deregulation.* Brookings.

———. 1995. *The Evolution of the Airline Industry.* Brookings.

Nilsson, Jan-Eric. 1992. "Second-Best Problems in Railway Infrastructure Pricing and Investment." *Journal of Transport Economics and Policy* 26 (September): 245–59.

Pigou, A.C. 1920. *The Economics of Welfare.* Macmillan.

Ramsey, E. P. A. 1927. "A Contribution to the Theory of Taxation." *Economic Journal* 37 (March): 47–61.

Small, Kenneth A. 1992. *Urban Transportation Economics.* Vol. 57 of *Fundamentals of Pure and Applied Science.* Chur, Switzerland: Harwood.

Small, Kenneth A., Clifford Winston, and Carol A. Evans. 1989. *Road Work: A New Highway Pricing and Investment Policy.* Brookings.

Transportation Research Board. 1996. *Paying Our Way: Estimating the Marginal Social Costs of Freight Transportation.* Special Report 246. Washington, D.C.

Turvey, Ralph. 1971. *Economic Analysis and Public Enterprises.* Totowa, N.J.: Rowman and Littlefield.

Tye, William B. 1983a. "The Postal Service: Economics Made Simplistic." *Journal of Policy Analysis and Management* 3 (Fall): 62–73.

———. 1983b. "Ironies to the Application of the Inverse Elasticity Rule to the Pricing of U.S. Postal Services." *Logistics and Transportation Review* 19 (October): 245–60.

Tye, William B., and Herman B. Leonard. 1983. "On the Problems of Applying Ramsey Pricing to the Railroad Industry with Uncertain Demand Elasticities." *Transportation Research* 17A (6, November): 439–50.

Urban Institute and Sydec, Inc. 1990. *Rationalization of Procedures for Highway Cost Allocation.* Report prepared fot the Trucking Research Institute. Washington, D.C. October.

U.S. Bureau of Public Roads. 1961. *Final Report of the Highway Cost Allocation Study.* House documents 54 and 77, 87th Cong., 1st Sess.

———. 1965. *Supplementary Report of the Highway Cost Allocation Study.* House document 124, 89th Cong., 1st Sess.

U.S. Congressional Budget Office. 1978. *Who Pays for Highways: Is a New Study of Highway Cost Allocation Needed?* Technical analysis paper. September.

———. 1979. *Guidelines for a Study of Highway Cost Allocation.* Washington, D.C. February.

U.S. Department of Transportation. 1982. *Final Report of the Federal Highway Cost Allocation Study.* Washington, D.C.

———. 1997. *1997 Federal Highway Cost Allocation Study.* Washington, D.C.

Vickery, William. 1963. "Pricing in Urban and Suburban Transport." *American Economic Review* 53 (May, *Papers and Proceedings*): 452–65.

Walters, Alan A. 1968. *The Economics of Road User Charges.* World Bank Staff Occasional Paper 5. Johns Hopkins University Press.

White, P. R., R. P. Turner, and T. C. Mbara. 1992. "Cost Benefit Analysis of Urban Minibus Operations." *Transportation* 19 (1): 59–74.

Winston, Clifford. 1985. "Conceptual Developments in the Economics of Transportation: An Interpretive Survey." *Journal of Economic Literature* 23 (1, March): 57–94.

Winston, Clifford, and Chad Shirley. 1998. *Alternative Route: Toward Efficient Urban Transportation.* Brookings.

World Bank. 1996. *Sustainable Transport: Priorities for Policy Reform.* Development in Practice series. Washington, D.C.

Wunsch, Pierre. 1996. "Cost and Productivity of Major Urban Transit Systems in Europe." *Journal of Transport Economics and Policy* 30 (2, May): 171–86.

KENNETH A. SMALL

5 | *Project Evaluation*

POLICYMAKING in the transportation arena often requires evaluating a proposed discrete change,
whether it be a physical investment or a new set of operating rules. Some
proposals, such as the rail tunnel under the English channel, are one-time
capital investments with long-lasting effects. Others, such as congestion
pricing proposed for the Netherlands, require major behavioral and political groundwork.

The optimization framework that proves useful in so much transportation analysis is inadequate to evaluate such all-or-nothing decisions. In an
optimization model, important aspects of a problem are represented by a
few variables that can be chosen to maximize some objective. For example,
Robert Strotz shows how highway capacity can be chosen to minimize
total travel costs in the presence of traffic congestion.[1] But often the change
is too sharp a break from existing practice, or the objectives too numerous,
to represent the problem this way. Perhaps a given highway improvement
not only expands capacity to handle peak traffic flows, but also speeds off-

The author is grateful for useful comments by Richard Arnott, Alberto Barreix, Arthur DeVany,
Don Fullerton, Amihai Glazer, Odd Larsen, Gabriel Roth, Donald Shoup, and participants at the
symposium in honor of John Meyer.
    1. Strotz (1965).

peak travel, reduces accidents, and imposes noise on residential neighborhoods. Perhaps the required capital expenditures occur in a complex time pattern, and the safety effects depend on future but uncertain demographic shifts. One would like a method for analyzing the merits of such a package of changes and for comparing it with alternative packages.

Such a method is called *project evaluation*. Performed skillfully, it identifies key consequences of a proposed project and provides quantitative information about them. Much of this information may be noncommensurable; that is, the consequences may not all be measured in the same units and hence the analyst may not be able to determine the extent to which they offset each other. For example, a tax-financed improvement in airway control equipment might improve safety but magnify existing income inequalities, leaving unanswered the question of how these effects should be weighed.

Thus, project evaluation is typically embedded in a larger decision-making process. John Meyer and Mahlon Straszheim argue, in their classic work on transportation planning, that project evaluation and pricing should be viewed as parts of a single integrated planning procedure.[2] They suggest a formal procedure that includes choosing among alternate objectives, such as maximizing profits or maximizing use of a facility. The procedure also involves identifying any constraints on optimal pricing, such as whether different prices can be charged to different consumers; such constraints are crucial because pricing distinctions can make a major difference in the social benefits achievable from a given facility design (see chapter 4).

The Role of Cost-Benefit Analysis

This chapter mainly considers one important part of the project evaluation toolkit, called *cost-benefit analysis*.[3] Cost-benefit analysis makes numerous and varied effects commensurable by quantifying them in terms of monetary equivalents. Methods are available to estimate the monetary value of travel-time savings, for example, or of new trips on an improved facility, and to compare costs and benefits occurring at widely different points in time. Furthermore, costs and benefits can sometimes be traced to particu-

---

2. Meyer and Straszheim (1971: ch. 14, esp. 232–36).
3. For just a few of the extensive reviews of cost-benefit methodology, see Prest and Turvey (1965), Mishan (1969), Boardman and others (1996), and the collected articles in Layard and Glaister (1994).

lar income, ethnic, or occupational groups, so the analyst may be able to describe the effect on the distribution of real incomes (that is, on standards of living). The usual form of assessment is based on adding up all the costs and benefits, to whomever they accrue. This method has an intuitive appeal as a commonsense approach to pursuing the social good. But its simplicity is misleading, for at least two objections can be levied against it.

First, only if *all* the relevant effects of a project can be measured as monetary equivalents, and only if decisionmakers are fully agreed on those measurements, can decisions on projects be reduced to a technical exercise. Many economists assume these two conditions are met, but others argue persuasively that the value of cost-benefit analysis is not to replace policymakers' subjective judgments, but rather to improve their understanding of the ramifications of alternative decisions.[4] János Kornai goes so far as to claim that it is "unnatural" to try to reduce all factors affecting a decision to a single dimension:

> A physician would never think of expressing the general state of health of a patient by one single scalar indicator. He knows that good lungs are not a substitute for bad kidneys. . . . Why cannot the economist also shift . . . to that way of thinking?[5]

Second, on what basis can projects that create "losers" be justified just because their aggregate benefits exceed their costs? Only in the highly artificial "representative individual" model, where everyone is identical and all are identically affected by the project, does positive aggregate net benefit imply an unambiguous improvement. Much theoretical literature has been devoted to this case, in particular to a variety of "index number" problems that arise in measuring benefits.[6] But the representative individual model is

---

4. Nash (1993).

5. Kornai (1979:88).

6. See, for example, Samuelson (1947), Hausman (1981), and McKenzie and Pearce (1982). The "index number" problem arises because the conversion factor between a travel improvement and money depends on the traveler's precise economic situation, which includes the travel conditions being changed by the project itself. Depending on how one imagines the continuous adjustment from the original state to the new one, one may assign any of several monetary measures such as *compensating variation* (amount the traveler could be paid after the change to be equally as well off as before), *equivalent variation* (amount the traveler could be paid before the change to be equally as well off as after), or change in *consumers' surplus* (the amount by which the area under a consumers' demand curve exceeds consumers' payments for the commodity). In practice, these measures seldom differ by much, so I ignore those differences here; see Willig (1976).

fundamentally inappropriate here. The need for cost-benefit analysis arises precisely because a real-world project creates conflicts of interest, in which people's different situations and preferences cause them to be affected differently. Otherwise all that would be needed is complete information, and the result would be a unanimous decision.

Both objections to cost-benefit analysis suggest that project evaluation is inherently political. Decisions about public investments are made in a political process, and the value of any particular evaluation technique, such as cost-benefit analysis, depends on how it informs that process. Thus, answers to the two objections must recognize this political element. Consider the first objection: Even though not all benefits and costs can be quantified in monetary terms, quantifying as many as possible at least helps to discipline debate by providing an easily understood point of comparison for other factors. Similarly, for the second objection: Although there will be losers, the analysis calls attention to situations where a project benefits one interest group at a high cost to others. Cost-benefit analysis is not a substitute for political decisions, but it makes their implications more transparent.

The point about identifying decisions that benefit one interest group at a high cost to others can be stated more formally. Cost-benefit analysis can identify those projects that are *potential Pareto improvements*, that is, projects for which the winners could in principle compensate losers so as to obtain unanimous consent.[7] For example, an airport expansion may bring so many benefits to users that they could easily "buy off" those residents harmed by the noise, if only there were a mechanism for doing so. Noise remediation programs, such as paying for double-glazed windows, are attempts to approximate such a mechanism. In practice no such mechanism can be perfect because it is impossible to measure precisely each person's benefits and costs. Nevertheless, a rule requiring that the sum of everyone's net benefits from a project be positive can at least limit the range of accepted projects to those that are potential Pareto improvements.

Thus it seems plausible that consistent application of a cost-benefit criterion would make most people better off, given "a rough randomness in distribution" of effects,[8] and would normally lead to "a strong probability that almost all would be better off after the lapse of a sufficient length of

---

7. This rationale is explicitly stated in the document setting out current U.S. government policy on project evaluation: see OMB (1992: sec. 10).
8. Hotelling (1938: 259).

time."[9] The reason is that no one knows what projects will come up for evaluation in the future, or who the winners and losers from such projects will be, so applying the same criterion to all decisions should over the long haul result in roughly equal treatment for everyone. (At least, this applies in the absence of systematic exploitation by a politically entrenched group.) At bottom, this is a "constitutional" rationale along the lines of James Buchanan and Gordon Tullock, who argue that rational individuals would analyze a proposed decision rule "in terms of the results it will produce, not on a single issue, but on the whole set of issues extending over a period," that is, they would view the rule as though it were embodied in a constitution.[10] The same idea appears in the literature on contract and nuisance law and also in political science, where it has been shown that under certain conditions all members of a legislature will favor a constitutional rule limiting the scope of pork-barrel projects.[11] Requiring projects to pass a cost-benefit test would be one such rule.

By identifying winners and losers, it becomes possible to take them into account in future policy decisions so that the kind of "rough randomness in distribution" just described is more likely to occur. Perhaps for this reason most analysts now prefer using cost-benefit analysis to identify and measure important distributional effects rather than assigning explicit "distributional weights" on costs and benefits to specific groups, as formerly recommended by the World Bank.[12] There is an important caveat to estimating distributional effects, however: markets adjust to new situations in complex ways, causing costs and benefits to shift from one party to another in a manner that is often far from transparent. This is especially true of transportation projects, which interact strongly with land markets and other locationally specific activities.[13]

Ideally, one should use a general equilibrium model of the entire economy to measure all relevant effects of a project. In practice, such an approach would go beyond the bounds of what can be said with confidence about a project's effects and would create new debates about techni-

9. Hicks(1941:111).

10. Buchanan and Tullock (1962: 121). Leonard and Zeckhauser (1986) express a similar view. See also Mishan (1969) and Buchanan (1975).

11. See Kronman (1980) on contract and nuisance law; see Weingast, Shepsle, and Johnsen (1981) on pork-barrel projects.

12. Jenkins (1997). OMB (1992: sec. 10) mandates that important distributional effects be analyzed and discussed.

13. Boyd (1976).

cal matters far removed from the project under consideration. So usually it is better to take a humbler view, measuring effects that are relatively well understood and leaving more far-reaching considerations, such as improved macroeconomic performance, to other forums.

Even so, applying cost-benefit analysis raises many methodological issues, some especially significant for transportation. For example, transportation projects often are intended to save people time or improve safety. They also may have significant environmental effects. How are such factors to be evaluated? This question is discussed in the next two sections.

Willingness to Pay: The Basic Concept

The starting point for measuring costs and benefits is *willingness to pay*: the amount of money each individual would be willing to pay for the change in his or her circumstances. (If it is negative, the change is a negative benefit or, equivalently, a cost.) The idea is that if the person did pay that amount, he or she would be indifferent to the change. This powerful concept provides a consistent principle for dealing with a wide variety of measurement issues that might at first seem disjointed and intractable.

The concept need not be restricted to those people most directly affected by a project. Expanding air traffic creates transportation services that users are willing to pay for, the direct effect; but it also creates noise that nearby residents are willing to pay to avoid. Reduced congestion on one road changes the amount of congestion on other roads, thereby creating positive or negative willingness to pay on the part of users throughout the network. A rail station in a previously isolated community may reduce unemployment there, creating additional benefits in reduced alcoholism or crime for which people who never use the station nevertheless have a measurable willingness to pay. Care, however, must be taken to limit the analysis to effects that are realistic and causally related to the project in question, as discussed in a later section.

The use of willingness to pay is what makes cost-benefit analysis consistent with the hypothetical compensation criterion described earlier. If the sum of everyone's willingness to pay for an entire project, including its financial elements, is positive, then it is a potential Pareto improvement.[14]

---

14. Strictly speaking, this statement is true only if the hypothetical payment is made *after* the change, in which case the willingness to pay equals the *compensating variation* (see footnote 6).

Willingness to pay is grounded in an acceptance of consumer sovereignty, so it does not apply to goods subject to per se social or moral judgment. It nonetheless can readily be applied to cases of externalities (spillover effects) by simply including those effects in the list of things for which willingness to pay is estimated. Thus, for example, air pollution can be included in benefits and costs by measuring people's willingness to pay to avoid all its adverse effects. But if society places extra value on the social interactions fostered by public transit, perhaps to promote social cohesion, that value will not be captured by the sum of individual willingness to pay for transit trips. (It would be captured if one also could separately measure and include individual willingness to pay for the better social milieu that is posited to result from more social interaction.)

The height of the demand curve for a conventional good, such as trips from home to shopping center by bus, measures the willingness to pay for an additional unit of that good at the margin. Therefore willingness to pay for a price reduction is correctly measured by the change in *consumers' surplus*, which is the area under the demand curve and above a horizontal line indicating the current price. This equivalence applies whether the demand curve results from continuous adjustments by each individual or from discrete adjustments as individuals switch from one category of trip-making to another.[15] Similarly, willingness to pay by suppliers is measured by the change in *producers' surplus*, which is the area above the supply curve and below the price line.

The use of consumers' and producers' surplus can easily be extended to quality improvements. For example, suppose the demand for bus trips is a function of the "full price" of a trip, including travel time (valued at individuals' willingness to pay for travel-time savings). This demand schedule might look like that in figure 5-1. Now suppose the waiting time for a bus is reduced, lowering the full price from C_0 to C_1. There are Q_0 existing users, each willing to pay (C_0-C_1) for the improvement; their aggregate benefit is therefore measured by the rectangle C_0AFC_1. There are Q_1-Q_0 new users, some willing to pay almost the full cost reduction (C_0-C_1) and others barely willing to pay anything (because even at the lower cost they are nearly indifferent between taking the bus and whatever is their next best option); adding all of them together, the aggregate benefit to new users

15. Small and Rosen (1981) give a formal demonstration. See also Domencich and McFadden (1975:94–99).

Figure 5-1. *Benefits to Existing and New Users*

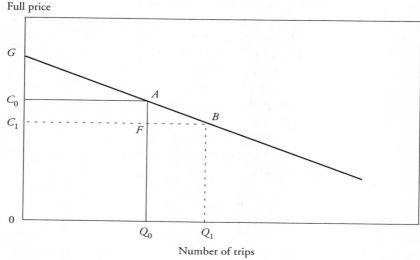

Source: Author's representation.

is the triangular area ABF.[16] The combined willingness to pay by existing and new users is therefore the trapezoidal area $C_0 ABC_1$. This area is also the change in consumers' surplus, which increased from area GAC_0 to area GBC_1. (Hence it would be double-counting to add the change in consumers' surplus to the value of time savings or other improvements.)[17]

If the demand curve is approximately linear between A and B, as in figure 5-1, then area ABF is approximately half the number of new users multiplied by the reduction in full price. This approximation, known as the "rule of one-half," greatly simplifies the estimation of benefits to new users because one need not estimate the entire demand curve, but only the number of *new* users and the cost savings to *existing* users.

16. It does not matter whether these new users are making new trips or are diverted from other routes, modes, or times of day—except that if they are diverted, it may be necessary to account for changes in other markets to the extent they are not priced at marginal cost. An example is accounting for costs or benefits caused by changes in unpriced congestion on other parts of a road network.

17. The analysis readily extends to the case where the "full price" depends on the number of trips through economies of scale or congestion effects; see, for example, Mackie, Toner, and Coombe (1996). More generally, it has been shown that under reasonable conditions, the increase in conventional consumers' surplus resulting from a quality improvement that raises the demand curve correctly measures willingness to pay for the improvement; see Bradford and Hildebrandt (1977).

One quirk in interpretation bears mention. Should the benefits to new users, area *ABF*, be considered part of the travel-time savings? In many discussions they are, because they arise from the reduced travel time made possible by the project. But new users did not use the bus before the improvement, so this area does not measure the difference between the time they spent traveling before and the time spent after the change. Indeed, some new users may now spend *more* time traveling than before, for example if they switched from auto travel. Nevertheless the benefits are real, representing value placed by these travelers on some characteristics of the bus mode, such as convenience, low cost, or opportunity to read while traveling. If one were to try to account for actual changes in travel time for new users, one would also have to measure and value each of these characteristics directly, which is virtually impossible; fortunately the indirect measure embodied in area *ABF* is just what is wanted.

What if the model used to measure the demand curve in figure 5-1 implies values of time that differ from those mandated by a government agency for use in cost-benefit analysis? For example, Transport Canada assigns to all adult nonbusiness travel a uniform value of time equal to 50 percent of the national average wage rate;[18] but the demand model used to analyze a particular Canadian project might imply some other value of time. It is relatively easy to "correct" the rectangle C_0AFC_1 by decomposing C_0-C_1 into its money component and its time component; but there is no obvious correction to the triangle ABF because line AB is inconsistent with the official value of time. Often the triangle is much smaller than the rectangle, so it does not matter much. Where it does matter, one solution is to reestimate the underlying demand model while forcing the coefficients to bear a relationship to each other consistent with the official value of time.[19] The resulting demand model may not fit the data as well, but in a crude way it takes into account additional information embodied in the earlier choice of the official value of time.

Willingness to pay also deals realistically with risk, even risk of events, such as injuries or deaths, often believed not amenable to monetary evaluation.[20] Most projects affect people's health or safety in an anonymous way, as when increased air pollution causes small increases in each person's risk

---

18. Transport Canada (1994: 47).
19. Small (1983) provides an example of fitting demand models to imply a specified value of time (models C and D, pp. 43–46).
20. Schelling (1968); Mishan (1971).

of getting lung cancer. Thus one does not ask Suzanne Citizen how much she would pay to avoid getting lung cancer. One instead asks (or estimates indirectly) how much she and others are willing to pay to avoid small measurable risks, for example by moving to less polluted but more expensive neighborhoods, by installing smoke detectors, or by ordering air bags for their cars. This kind of investigation has proven tractable, as described later.

Willingness to pay remains an appropriate measure of benefits and costs even when markets are not free. For example, people may be willing to pay more than the quoted price for fuel that is subject to price controls or for imports that are restricted by quotas. Similarly, if a resource such as labor or capital would otherwise be underemployed, willingness to pay may be less than the market price. Considerable literature exists on how to compute willingness to pay in such situations; often, it can be done by valuing an affected resource at a *shadow price* rather than a market price, the difference being estimated from an analysis of the market imperfection.[21] A warning is in order, however, when considering underemployed labor: macroeconomic policies may offset any job-creating or job-destroying effects of the project being evaluated because macroeconomic policies are aimed at other goals such as price stability, foreign exchange rates, or trade balances.

As already noted, transportation is closely tied to a host of other markets through their dependence on the physical presence of people or goods. Better transportation to a particular location can dramatically increase the prices of housing, retail goods, or land at that location, and it may decrease the wages offered to workers there. These changes create benefits or costs that are measured as changes in consumers' and producers' surplus in the associated markets. If these associated markets are competitive, such price changes provide offsetting benefits and costs to the various parties involved: the retailer's improved revenues are its shoppers' higher costs, while the landlord's gains are the tenant's losses. For this reason, a simple partial equilibrium analysis is often sufficient for estimating total benefits and costs— but is entirely inadequate for estimating their distribution across the population. I return in a later section to the question of when adjustments in other markets engender new costs or benefits as opposed to simply transferring costs or benefits from one party to another.

Finally, willingness to pay provides a way to compare costs and ben-

---

21. For a rigorous and elegant general treatment of shadow prices, see Drèze and Stern (1990). For a classic practical treatment, see Little (1950).

efits at different times. Numerous financial markets enable one to look at people's preferences concerning the trade-off between current and future consumption. This trade-off is especially important to transportation projects because so many of them require up-front capital expenditures in return for benefits extending far into the future. This issue, too, is discussed later.

Issues in Benefit Measurement

Using the willingness-to-pay principle, I turn to issues that come up frequently in transportation evaluations. This section examines three important categories of benefits: travel-time savings, safety improvements, and environmental improvements. This listing is roughly in order of their quantitative importance as components of measurable benefits from transportation projects.

Travel-Time Savings

Typically the dominant component of benefits from a transportation project is travel-time savings—or more broadly, benefits to existing and new users resulting from reductions in the travel time required for any particular type of trip. Air travel, surface freight shipping, and urban commuting all are examples of transportation activities in which time is thought to be an important element, with costs of lost time estimated to run into many billions of dollars and competitive outcomes depending closely on the ability to shave time off certain movements. Time savings may occur from a number of sources: a new high-speed rail service, a new highway through previously undeveloped land, congestion relief from expanding capacity, an operational improvement such as improved rail switching facilities, or an upgraded line-haul facility to permit higher speeds.

An extensive empirical literature, based on demand models like those discussed in chapter 2, has established that people and firms make reasonably predictable trade-offs between travel time and other factors when making travel choices. These studies are the basis for estimating the willingness to pay for travel-time savings, a quantity known as the "value of time." For example, one review concluded that the value of time for the journey to work averages about 50 percent of the before-tax wage rate, with a range across different industrialized cities from perhaps 20 to 100 percent.[22] Values have also been established for other types of trips and for freight.[23]

Unfortunately for the analyst, there is also ample evidence that the value of time varies widely among population subgroups and probably depends critically on individual circumstances. For example, people are willing to pay more on average to avoid time walking to a bus stop or waiting there for the bus than they are willing to pay to avoid spending the same amount of time riding on the bus. They will pay more to avoid time spent driving if it is in congested conditions. There is some evidence that people value increments of time more highly on medium-length trips than on short or long trips.[24] Probably the degree of comfort plays a key role in all these examples, as exemplified by the suggestive recent finding of a quite low value of time for regular long-distance automobile commuters, who probably have adapted their cars and schedules to reduce the boredom of driving.[25] Self-selection may also play a role in this last example: those with lower values of time are more likely to drive long distances regularly.

These variations should not be surprising, as time is not fungible: time saved in one circumstance cannot automatically be used in another. Ignoring such variations can result in poor decisions. For example, some evaluations of rapid rail systems have failed to account fully for the reluctance of people to make extra transfers or to walk longer distances to transit stops.

Some analysts overstate the specificity of the situation facing a person, however. For example, although many people have fixed work hours in the short run, they may have a choice among jobs with different work hours and therefore may in the long run be able to use travel-time savings to work longer hours. More generally, the constant turnover in jobs, residential locations, family status, habits, and other circumstances guarantees that a particular travel-time saving—such as thirty seconds from installation of a new traffic signal—will soon be incorporated into the routine of life and will not long be identified as a particular block of time to be reallocated. For this reason, there is no merit in claims that small time savings lack

22. Small (1992:43–45).

23. Waters (1996); Hensher (1989); MVA Consultancy and others (1987); Morrison and Winston (1986); and Winston (1981).

24. On medium versus short trips, see Ben-Akiva and Lerman (1985); their result is for work trips and may indicate that people appreciate some transition time between home and work. On medium versus long trips, see MVA Consultancy and others (1987).

25. Calfee and Winston (1998).

value because people cannot do anything productive in short time segments.[26] Rather, observed variations in the marginal valuation of different lengths of time savings are probably due to the variation in value of time with individual trip length or with total amount of time spent traveling.

Predicting the travel-time savings from many projects is complicated by offsetting behavioral shifts as a result of changes in unpriced congestion. Suppose a particular measure relieves congestion. After it is adopted, the system will tend to reequilibrate as people previously deterred by congestion, constituting what is known as the *latent demand* for the facility, take advantage of the improved conditions. In extreme cases, latent demand may be so great that congestion reverts to its former level.[27] More commonly, latent demand undoes some but not all of the expected congestion relief.

These behavioral shifts, if not fully accounted for, create two offsetting sources of error in estimating benefits from such a project. On the one hand, the amount of travel-time savings to existing users (area C_0AFC_1 in figure 5-1) will be overestimated because the reduction in full price, C_0-C_1, will be overstated. On the other hand, the benefits to new users (area ABF) will be underestimated or perhaps ignored entirely if those new users are not anticipated. Two examples illustrate the problem.

In the first example, the source of latent demand is people previously traveling at other times of day. This can be examined using a bottleneck model pioneered by William Vickrey.[28] Commuters face a cost β for each minute early they arrive at their destination, and a cost γ for each minute they are late; these costs are known as *schedule delay costs*. The equilibrium time pattern of trips involves maximum congestion at the times that people most desire to travel, with less congestion at other times, thereby serving as an inducement for some people to suffer the schedule delay costs. Now suppose the analyst incorrectly thinks that the observed trip pattern will not change in response to an expansion in capacity. It turns out that this analyst will overestimate the marginal benefits of expansion if the harmonic

---

26. An example of this fallacy is the strong dependence of value of time on "amount of time saved" in the summary recommendations of the influential manual published by American Association of State Highway and Transportation Officials (1978). As Waters (1992) has pointed out, such dependence would make project evaluation inconsistent because the evaluation of a project would depend critically on whether it was considered as a single project or as the cumulation of many small projects.

27. Examples are given by Pigou (1920) and Downs (1962).

28. Vickrey (1969); Arnott, de Palma, and Lindsey (1990).

mean of β and γ is less than the value of travel time.[29] The reason is that the low cost of schedule delay results in a lot of time-of-day shifting, undermining the hoped-for reduction in congestion. In the opposite case, where schedule delay costs are high so time-of-day shifts are small, the forecast of congestion reduction is pretty accurate, but the analyst neglects savings in schedule delay costs, so the benefits of capacity expansion are underestimated.

The second example is land use distortions. In a typical model of urban residential location, failure to price highway congestion causes the city to be inefficiently decentralized. Expansion of highway capacity tends to exacerbate this effect by encouraging residential relocations that create longer trips and hence new traffic. For this reason, congestion will not be reduced by as much as would otherwise be predicted. Again, there are offsetting benefits to the people who now can exercise their preferences for larger lots in outlying residential areas. In this case, however, it has been shown that at least for fixed workplace locations, the net effect of ignoring the land use changes is to overestimate benefits of capacity expansion.[30]

One important source of latent demand for a given route is traffic diverted from other routes. This can often be analyzed by a network model. If congestion is prevalent, it is important to measure accurately how congestion levels change throughout the network and to take into account the resulting costs and benefits.

Safety Improvements

Safety ranks high in public perceptions of transportation problems. Airline crashes or train derailments make national headlines, while local car wrecks are a routine of the evening news. Much effort and expense has gone into largely successful efforts to reduce safety hazards in transportation. Some of this effort is market-driven, while some is government-mandated. How can one evaluate the case for public policy intervention on behalf of safety, or the safety effects of intermodal substitutions that may occur because of other policies?

As I indicated earlier, changes in the risk of injuries, fatal or otherwise, can be evaluated based on the willingness-to-pay principle. Everyone makes

---

29. Small (1992: 137). The harmonic mean of β and γ is defined as $[2(\beta^{-1} + \gamma^{-1})]^{-1}$.

30. Arnott (1979). Empirical estimates suggest that the U.S. urban interstate highway system was overbuilt as a result of this effect; see Wheaton (1978).

decisions every day that implicitly place values on additional risks incurred; by making such valuations explicit, public decisions can be made more consistent with private ones. Empirically, the most reliable method to value risk of death appears to be comparing wages for jobs that are similar in all respects except occupational risk. Reviews of the numerous studies of this type suggest that on average, people in high-income nations in the early 1990s were willing to pay US$3 to $7 for each reduction of one in a million in the risk of death.[31] Taking the mid-range value of $5 and looking at a million such people, their aggregate willingness to pay for a risk reduction of that amount is then $5 million, and one life is expected to be saved. This result is summarized in the convenient but easily misunderstood statement that the *value of life* is $5 million.

Valuations of risk of death may deviate from this amount for specific types of situations; for example, evidence suggests that people are more reluctant to undertake risks over which they have no control, so the value of life for train accidents may be higher than that for car accidents. Willingness to pay for risk reduction appears to be approximately proportional to income. Whether it also depends on age or life expectancy is an open question.[32]

Many governmental agencies use a "value of life" that is considerably below the range suggested by the labor market studies: Transport Canada, for example, uses 1.5 million 1991 Canadian dollars, or about US$1.3 million.[33] Even this figure is far higher than the average person's personal wealth or the discounted sum of future earnings. But this poses no contradiction. No one is paying to avoid a sure death; rather, people are paying to lower the probabilities slightly. Using discounted future earnings to value risk of death is an older technique that is now discredited because it does not apply the willingness-to-pay principle and because it attempts to value the full transition between life and death rather than the small changes in risk that people actually face as a result of public policies.

Risks of serious injuries or illnesses can be evaluated in a similar way. A recent study suggests that the willingness to pay to reduce the risk of a typical serious (but nonfatal) traffic injury is about 10 percent of the willingness to pay to reduce the risk of a traffic fatality.[34] Because nonfatal

31. Viscusi (1993:1930); Kahn (1986).
32. Viscusi (1993).
33. Transport Canada (1994), converted to US$ using the 1991 exchange rate of US$1 = CA$1.146.
34. Jones-Lee, Loomes, and Philips (1995). See also Viscusi (1993).

injuries are much more numerous than fatal ones, this finding adds significantly to estimates of the total costs of accidents, which are quite high—comparable, for example, to total travel-time costs in the case of a typical urban commuting trip by automobile.[35]

Several additional conceptual issues complicate the empirical estimation of safety benefits. One is whether an individual's willingness to pay to avoid injury or death should be supplemented by the value of further benefits to relatives, insurance companies, or governments. All have an emotional or financial interest in the injured person's well-being; the question is whether the estimated willingness to pay already takes their interests into account. Assuming that labor market studies have been used to measure willingness to pay, one needs to know whether the individual's trade-off between wages and safety fully accounts for willingness to pay by all parties.

First, consider family members or other loved ones. If emotional bonds are mutual and fully recognized, my willingness to pay for safety already accounts for my family's concern for me. Furthermore, if it is my welfare as opposed to theirs that is my family's concern, then their altruism extends to both sides of the trade-off I am making—safety against other consumption—so does not necessarily affect the marginal rate of trade-off of one for the other.[36] So there is not much case for adding benefits accruing to family and friends.

Next, consider the effects of life, health, and disability insurance. If the differential job risks an individual faces are reflected in differential insurance rates, then part of the observed wage premium for safety implicitly pays for the insurance company's extra costs; in that case no additional amount need be added to the measured willingness to pay. If no such differential insurance rates exist, perhaps because of the insurance companies' inability to monitor these risk differentials, then the costs paid by insurance should be added to the willingness-to-pay measure.

Finally, consider government-borne costs of medical treatment or living expenses. It is unlikely that an individual would demand a wage premium to cover such costs, so they need to be added explicitly.

Another conceptual issue is related to the prediction, rather than the valuation, of the reduction in injuries or deaths. Just as programs designed to relieve congestion release latent demand for the congested facility, programs designed to improve safety may result in offsetting behavior that

---

35. Small (1992: 75–85).
36. Bergstrom (1982).

reduces safety. That is because the safety improvement reduces the marginal risk of related behavior, such as driving fast. Air bags, antilock brakes, and straightened roads are therefore likely to result in partially offsetting changes such as driving faster, talking on mobile telephones, or failing to fasten safety belts.[37] These behavioral adjustments not only offset part of the direct safety impacts, but may even cause a safety program to backfire by raising the danger to third parties such as bicyclists and pedestrians.

Such behavioral changes may or may not be considered when the effects of a project are predicted. If they are, then this offsetting behavior may provide some additional benefits that should in principle be valued and included in the evaluation—for example, the enjoyment of high-speed telephone conversations or the value of time saved by not putting on seat belts.[38]

An odd situation exists if the offsetting behavioral changes are not included in the forecast of a project's effects: the predictions of safety effects are wrong, yet the estimated benefits may be fairly accurate. The reason is that the benefits from reduced injuries are overstated, because some of those reductions will not actually occur due to offsetting behavior, but the benefits from that offsetting behavior are ignored. For example, suppose an analysis of antilock brakes ignores the fact that people with antilock brakes are more willing to drive when it is raining. Then not as many lives will be saved as thought, but people are receiving value from going on rainy days to events they would otherwise miss. In theory, these two errors in forecasting benefits fully offset each other provided the behavioral changes are small, involve no externalities, and are deemed socially valid goals for the individual.[39] In practice most people are likely to view some behavioral changes, such as more aggressive driving, as inappropriate for inclusion as benefits; so on balance the social benefits of safety improvements are probably somewhat overstated if offsetting behavior is ignored. Society may be happy about the people with antilock brakes who can get to church on rainy days, but not about those who use their newfound confidence to terrorize slower drivers.

37. See Peltzman (1975). Most empirical studies find that these behavioral changes occur but only partially offset the original safety improvement; see Chirinko and Harper (1993), and Peterson, Hoffer, and Millner (1995).

38. For a more thorough analysis of the time putting on seat belts and how it affects cost-benefit analysis, see Mannering and Winston (1987).

39. This statement is based on a version of the envelope theorem, which implies that if a person is optimizing both before and after a change in an external parameter, the first-order behavioral readjustments cause no additional changes to utility.

As with value of time, the value of reducing accident risk seems to vary with circumstance, as suggested by the earlier observation that people prefer risks they think they can control. This is a legitimate basis for differentiating values of different kinds of risks. It is important to distinguish true preferences from misperceptions, however. If people appear to place an unusually high or low value on a particular risk because they are misinformed about it, a case can be made for overriding those apparent preferences by using more accurate information available to the decisionmaker.[40] It is sometimes more feasible to promote cost-effectiveness in safety investments by using technical information at the project-evaluation stage than by launching public education campaigns concerning the actual risks.

Environmental Improvements

It is well recognized that transportation activities often damage the environment. These effects are frequently debated as part of a proposed policy, whether it be building a new airport or raising the gasoline tax. Furthermore, some very expensive policies are proposed explicitly on environmental grounds: electric cars, for example, and certain rail transit systems. How can such policies be evaluated? How does one know how much environmental protection is enough?

In theory, environmental effects can be evaluated using the principles already outlined. People are willing to pay for a better environment. Accounting for these effects, however, raises measurement issues that are even more difficult than those related to safety. Not only must the analyst deal with health effects and offsetting behavior, but in addition environmental effects are more varied, more diffusely distributed, and perhaps more prone to raising moral issues than are safety issues. Space precludes resolving these difficulties here, and I limit the discussion to the question: Is quantifying environmental benefits and costs in monetary terms, as part of project evaluation, worth the effort?

The primary argument for such quantification is that environmental and other benefits (and costs) can then be brought into a single comprehensive framework. If the quantitative estimates are credible, a unified frame-

---

40. For a discussion of whether people misperceive the probabilities associated with various risks, see Calfee and Winston (1993). A related issue is whether such misperceptions bias the empirical estimates of "value of life"; one reason for preferring labor market studies for such estimates, as described earlier, is that people are likely to be well informed about the nature of their jobs.

work should promote better decisions by forcing decisionmakers to make realistic trade-offs between environmental considerations and other costs and benefits. For example, several estimates imply that the air pollution costs of motor vehicles are significant compared with the costs of potential emission-control options, but rather small in relation to the implied value that people place on auto travel.[41] If these results hold up to further refinement, they suggest both a direction and a limitation on policy toward air pollution: namely, that further emission control policies are probably warranted, but that air pollution alone cannot justify sweeping measures to reduce motor vehicle traffic.

The primary argument against quantifying environmental effects in monetary terms is that doing so adds considerable uncertainty to the resulting evaluation, while lending an unwarranted aura of precision and completeness. For example, the above-mentioned research on air pollution is mainly on conventional pollutants accumulating in the lower atmosphere; extending the estimates to destruction of the stratospheric ozone layer or to global warming from greenhouse gases is highly speculative because those impacts occur over very long time scales, the scientific modeling process is uncertain, and the potential for technological change that might ameliorate adverse effects is unknown. Simply adding such estimates to others might erode confidence in the entire cost-benefit analysis.

In some cases, the uncertainty in benefits can be reduced by accepting as binding a political decision to hold harmful effects at specified levels. For example, a greenhouse gas treaty might stipulate levels of carbon dioxide emissions that countries may not exceed. Then the benefit of reducing one source can be measured as the marginal control cost at another source. Such political decisions may in fact be revised from time to time, however, violating the assumption that the decision was binding.

My own view is that in the case of "ordinary" (lower-atmosphere) air pollution, the methodology is sufficiently advanced to justify incorporating monetary estimates of its effects into cost-benefit analysis. The same is probably true of noise.[42] (Results should, of course, be shown disaggregated whenever possible so that one may conduct a sensitivity analysis by calculating how results are affected by alternative assumptions.) Other environmental effects—such as global warming, wildlife disruption, loss of biodiversity, and damage from urban water runoff—are too uncertain to

41. Small and Kazimi (1995); McCubbin and Delucchi (1996); Delucchi (1997: 45–46).
42. Delucchi and Hsu (1996).

warrant adding them to other benefits and costs, although quantification is still useful for purposes of prioritizing further research.

Issues Raised by Longevity of Decisions

Transportation investments are notable for their length of life. Frequently, large up-front capital requirements will yield benefits, as well as incur maintenance costs, many years into the future. For example, the "Big Dig" in Boston, involving a complex of highway connections around and across Boston Harbor, will cost an estimated $12 billion before most of its benefits are realized. Land clearance, rail trackage, port facilities, and tunnels are all examples of projects involving heavy and irreversible capital expenditures. Therefore, it becomes crucial to develop a clear understanding of the trade-offs between present costs and future benefits.

In this section I consider three issues raised by having to weigh the future against the present. First is forecasting capital cost and usage. Second is the choice of an interest rate. Third is the question whether conventional discounting procedures properly account for unborn generations of people when decisions have very long lifetimes.

Projections of Capital Costs and Travel Demand

Obviously, sound evaluation of a project depends on accurately predicting its effects. The stakes are especially high for the durable investments typical of transportation projects. Mistakes can result in disruptive bankruptcies or in burdensome taxpayer obligations for future bond payments on unproductive investments. For many transportation projects, the most important factors are the up-front capital expenditures, the future operating costs, and the future demand for travel on the facility. All are estimated from projections.

The record for such projections is not very encouraging. Don Pickrell demonstrates that in the project evaluations used at the decision point for ten rail transit systems recently built in the United States, capital costs were underestimated in all but one case. Furthermore, of those eight to nine cases where operating cost and ridership forecasts could be firmly determined, operating costs were underestimated in all but one case and ridership was overestimated in every case.[43] The errors were very large: in the

43. Pickrell (1989: table S-1).

median case, capital and operating costs were underestimated by one-third and ridership was overestimated by a factor of three. As a result of these errors, average cost per rail passenger turned out to exceed the forecast in every case by at least 188 percent, and in three cases by more than 700 percent!

Even for toll highways, where the use of private bond financing exerts more discipline on the initial projections, ten of fourteen recently examined U.S. projects experienced toll revenues well below projections.[44] The same bias was found in a review of seven large Danish highway bridge and tunnel projects.[45] Given that capital projects are heavily promoted by interested parties, it is difficult to avoid the conclusion that these errors are strategic.[46] In most cases, taxpayers will be left footing the bill for cost overruns, revenue shortfalls, or the carrying costs for capital expenditures that turned out to have few benefits.

A comparison of three cost-benefit studies of a new toll road near Vancouver, British Columbia, illustrates how dependent the results can be on travel forecasts.[47] The road, known as the Coquihalla Highway, connects the Vancouver region with popular resort areas to the northeast. It opened in phases between May 1986 and October 1990, and the three studies were conducted in mid 1986, late 1987, and early 1993. From the latest study it appears that the first two drastically underestimated both actual construction costs and actual traffic. Perhaps because these were academic studies, and so presumably without strategic bias, these two errors had offsetting rather than cumulative influences on the cost-benefit analysis; still, their sheer magnitudes are humbling.

A reasonable conclusion is that the real value of forecasting and analyzing the future is to learn about the factors affecting success rather than to predict success definitively. To paraphrase Kenneth Boulding, predictions are useful so long as no one believes them. At a minimum, sensitivity analyses should be conducted using alternate values of crucial parameters. More generally, the burden of proof should be placed on the proponents of a costly project to show that a favorable evaluation is robust to reasonable variations in crucial forecasts.

44. Muller (1996).
45. Skamris and Flyvbjerg (1996).
46. For a well-documented example, see Kain (1990).
47. Boardman, Mallery, and Vining (1994).

Discounting the Future

The principle of willingness to pay says that costs and benefits occurring in the future are valued less than those occurring today. This may be attributed to people's impatience or, equivalently, to the productive possibilities for investing their money. In either view, the traditional way of accounting for the difference is to divide t-year-later quantities by $(1+ r)^t$, where r is a *discount rate* closely related to the interest rate on financial assets. Presuming the costs and benefits occurring in later years are measured in real (that is, inflation-adjusted) money units, then the discount rate should also be real, meaning it is approximately the nominal rate less the rate of inflation.[48]

As already noted, many transportation projects require large initial investments and create benefits extending far into the future. The evaluation of these projects turns out to be critically dependent on the discount rate used. If a single stable market interest rate prevailed throughout the economy, the choice would be simple. In reality, numerous departures from perfectly competitive markets result in wedges between the interest rates faced by various economic actors. Among the most important wedges are those resulting from corporate and personal income taxes and from the incompleteness of capital markets, the latter arising in turn from the inability of lenders to monitor and enforce repayment agreements perfectly.

A simplified picture suffices to lay out the main issues. Suppose consumers can shift consumption from one time period to another by increasing or reducing their holdings of a risk-free government bond with real after-tax interest rate r_c, often taken to be 4 percent. (This value is somewhat higher than the typical after-tax rate on government bonds, in part to account for the fact that many consumers are net debtors rather than lenders in financial markets.) Then they would adjust their planned consumption paths until their *marginal rate of time preference in consumption*, defined as consumers' willingness to pay to accelerate consumption benefits from later to earlier years, is equal to r_c. Investment, on the other hand, is undertaken by private firms and earns a real net social rate of return (also called

---

48. More precisely, if n is a nominal discount rate (such as the market interest rate on government bonds) and π is the expected rate of inflation, the corresponding real discount rate r is defined by the equation $(1 + r)(1 + \pi) = 1 + n$. If π is small, this yields the approximation $1 + r \approx (1 + n)(1 - \pi) \approx 1 + n - \pi$, or $r \approx n - \pi$.

the value of marginal product of capital), which may be called r_i. A careful estimate made for the year 1989 gives the value of r_i as 9.6 percent.[49]

One approach to choosing the discount rate r for cost-benefit analysis is simply to take a weighted average of these two rates, r_c and r_i. The weights would reflect the proportions of the project's financial flows that are believed to be drawn from consumption and investment, respectively. If these proportions are about equal, for example, then using the above values for r_c and r_i yields an interest rate of 6.8 percent.

The weighted average interest rate is a reasonably simple and plausible procedure, but it is somewhat arbitrary because the flows determining the weights should themselves be discounted. A theoretically more rigorous approach, discussed in the appendix, overcomes this problem by converting each expenditure or benefit to an equivalent flow of consumption, taking account of any investment consequences it has. The equivalent consumption flows are then discounted at the marginal rate of time preference, r_c. This approach is known as the *shadow price of capital* because to every capital expenditure, it applies a multiplier indicating how much consumption must be given up because of that expenditure. A reasonable value for this multiplier is 1.5, based on U.S. conditions in 1989 (see appendix).

If an economy is open to foreign capital, internal conditions are less important because capital for transportation projects is likely to be drawn, directly or indirectly, from foreign sources. In the case of a small country with a very open economy, the opportunity cost of capital is close to the market interest rate on international loans, and this rate can be used for most discounting purposes.

Market interest rates also incorporate various degrees of risk. Loans to firms or nations with doubtful repayment prospects command a higher rate than other loans. It can be argued, however, that considering the risk of the project explicitly through some form of sensitivity analysis (as described later) is better than trying to account for risk through adjustments to the interest rate. This argument is especially valid when the risks for

---

49. This is based on the average nominal after-tax rate of return on AAA corporate bonds of 9.26 percent. Adjusting upward by a factor $(1 - 0.38)^{-1}$ (assuming an average marginal corporate tax rate, federal plus state, of 38 percent), gives a pretax nominal return of $n = 14.9$ percent; a downward adjustment is then made for inflation of $\pi = 4.8$ percent per year according to the formula $(1 + r_i)(1 + \pi) = 1 + n$, an example of the general formula presented in footnote 48. This calculation is in Boardman and others (1996: 172).

various projects under consideration are not highly correlated and are shared across the society at large.

The methods discussed here require considerable judgment on the part of the analyst. In practice, there are reasons to constrain the exercise of such judgment, for example to foster uniformity. As a result, government manuals often specify the real discount rate r to be used, unless there is a demonstrable reason that it should be different for the project in question. In the United States, that rate is specified by the Office of Management and Budget (OMB); it was 10 percent for many years but was changed to 7 percent in 1992. The rate is also specified to be 7 percent for Australian road projects, while Transport Canada mandates 10 percent.[50] In all these cases, sensitivity analysis is recommended to show how much the results are affected by assuming different discount rates. Note that the discount rates mandated by the U.S. and Australian governments are virtually identical to the figure derived earlier using the weighted-average method.

The Far Distant Future

The use of discounting has important and controversial implications for evaluating policies affecting distant generations. Examples of such policies include those related to nuclear waste disposal, global warming, species preservation, and soil conservation. Increasingly, transportation activities are being linked to such long-lived effects. Electricity use in some nations increases the use of nuclear power stations; new rural or suburban roads destroy wildlife habitat; extensive paving increases water runoff resulting in damage to adjacent soils and watersheds. Of particular concern today is a long-term accumulation of carbon dioxide in the atmosphere from burning fossil fuels, which probably will have a global warming effect causing changes in weather patterns and possibly in sea levels.[51] Because motor vehicle transportation consumes such large amounts of fossil fuel, whose combustion produces carbon dioxide, the manner in which such future costs are accounted for has major implications for transportation policy decisions.

Using conventional discounting, adverse future consequences that occur in the distant future have very small weight in a cost-benefit compari-

50. OMB (1992: sec. 8); Austroads (1996: 10); Transport Canada (1994: 66).
51. See Schmalensee (1993) and the accompanying symposium articles. See also Cline (1992) and Intergovernmental Panel on Climate Change (1996).

son. For example, imagine a climate disaster occurring in 150 years that causes damage of $10 trillion in constant 1998 dollars (more than today's U.S. annual gross domestic product). It has a discounted cost today of only $391 million using OMB's discount rate of 7 percent.[52] Many analysts question whether the marginal rate of time preference applying to private individuals can be extrapolated to distant unborn generations and advocate imposing explicit social preferences for maintaining future viability of human life with living standards deemed acceptable. Others, noting that living standards have increased steadily over much of the world's history, suggest that future generations will be richer than we are and so do not need our altruistic concern.

A more rigorous theoretical approach suggests that both arguments are partly right. The applicable principle comes from the theory of long-run growth with finite resources.[53] Suppose the welfare of future generations is given equal weight to that of today's consumers in an intertemporal social welfare function. The consumption path that maximizes social welfare then has the property that consumption is forever increasing, but at a growth rate that gradually approaches zero. Consumption at any time t is valued less than consumption at an earlier time, by a factor derived from a discount rate equal to the marginal productivity of capital. (In the version sketched here, this preference for earlier consumption results from people setting their marginal rate of time preference, r_c, exactly equal to the marginal rate of return on investment, r_i, thus ignoring the tax wedges discussed in the previous subsection.)

So far this looks like the case for conventional discounting. But not quite. In this scenario, the marginal productivity of invested capital r_i is not constant, but instead declines gradually to zero as the capital stock continues to expand indefinitely. So costs saved today can be invested in capital that in turn accumulates, but it accumulates at a gradually diminishing rate. Future benefits or costs should therefore still be discounted, but the discounting method must account for this saturation effect.

Suppose, for example, that when the $10 trillion disaster occurs 150 years hence, capital's annual rate of return has decreased from its value of 7 percent today to 3.5 percent, because of the increased capital intensity of the economy. Suppose also that the two rates r_c and r_i are equal at every point in time (as they are in the theory just described) because of market

---

52. Calculated from $\$10 \times 10^{12} / (1.07)^{150}$.
53. Dasgupta (1994: 363–69).

adjustments. Then the disaster has a discounted cost of about $4.75 billion—twelve times as large as that computed at a constant interest rate of 7 percent.[54] This is still a very heavy discount, and one could argue that it should be heavier still because new technologies seem to enhance the productivity of new capital and thereby prevent the posited decline in capital's rate of return.

Whatever the discount rates used, the discounting approach assumes—in the climate example—that if the considerable expense of restricting greenhouse gas emissions is undertaken today, society will to some extent reduce capital investment, which would have yielded net returns accumulating far into the future. Hence by not taking action now, the current generation can confer on future generations a much larger capital stock, which they can use to prevent or cope with climate changes. Is such an assumption realistic? Can the distant future be legitimately modeled as an extension of today's world of economic interrelationships? Again, it is the political system that will decide how these questions should be answered for purposes of guiding social decisions. The technical analysis described here simply demonstrates the consequences of alternative assumptions about future productivity of capital and shows that ultimately the question of discounting is not one of moral imperative but of predicting the future course of the economy.

External Costs, External Benefits, and Transfers

Recently the role of "external effects" has come to be recognized as crucial to transportation policy. Individual travelers or firms making transportation decisions impose significant effects on others, from congestion to noise to better business opportunities. How should these external effects be treated in project evaluation?

If every market affected by a transportation project could be accurately modeled, all costs and benefits would be accounted for by measuring the changes in the associated consumers' and producers' surpluses. In practice, it is more common to measure the primary effects in the transportation market itself and to consider ancillary changes separately. These ancillary changes can be divided into two categories.

---

54. Calculated as $10 \times 10^{12} / [(1.07 - \delta)(1.07 - 2\delta)(1.07 - 3\delta) \ldots (1.07 - 150\delta)]$, where $\delta = (.070 - .035)/150$ is the amount the discount rate is assumed to decline each year over the 150-year period.

First are *technological externalities*—direct effects on other parties that are outside the market system. The formal definition is that activities of one party appear as arguments in the utility or production function of another. Many technological externalities are negative, for example, air pollution (affecting people's welfare) or airport runway congestion (affecting airlines' production functions). Others are positive, such as the deterrent effect of passing traffic on street crime.

Second are *pecuniary externalities*—effects on other parties caused by changes in the prices at which they can engage in transactions. In competitive markets, pecuniary externalities are transfers of benefits from one party to another.[55] If a new subway improves accessibility to a particular street corner, stores located there may raise their prices, while office firms located there may be able to attract workers at lower wages. Landowners, in turn, raise rents, and if the land is sold, it will be at a higher price. Thus the original benefit, measured as reduced travel cost (including value of time), does not stay with the shoppers or workers who travel to that location but rather is transferred to landowners. If markets are fully competitive, if none of these activities creates technological externalities, and if the project is too small to alter aggregate market supplies, then the "lucky" shoppers and workers whose travel costs were reduced in the first instance will, in the end, find themselves exactly as well off as before: the retail store and the office firm will still just be able to make a competitive return after paying higher lease rents, while the existing landowner will end up with a transferred benefit exactly equal to the originally measured travel benefit. That is, landowners' increased rent is a measure of the subway's benefits, not an added benefit.

If markets are not competitive, however, or if the ancillary markets have technological externalities, then additional benefits or costs are created. This is an example of the more general proposition that pecuniary externalities have real effects where competition is imperfect.[56] Let us examine this possibility more closely.

Considerable interest has centered on alleged positive effects called "external benefits." It is well known that transportation improvements spur local business and thereby boost incomes. On close examination, however, most of these benefits turn out to be just transfers, either transfers of ben-

---

55. The extent of such transfers depends on the relative elasticities of supply and demand in these ancillary markets, as nicely explained by Boyd (1976). For further discussion, see Meyer and Straszheim (1971:199–202).

56. See, for example, Krugman (1991).

efits from travelers to other businesses or transfers of activity from one location to another. Thus including them as additional benefits is double-counting.

A more interesting example is benefits of "industrial reorganization." Often a transportation improvement makes possible a reorganization of production to take advantage of the increased ease of shipping intermediate goods. Plants or warehouses may be consolidated, inventories may be reduced, divisions of an enterprise may become more specialized—in each case because additional transportation can now be profitably substituted for other inputs to the production process. These look like important benefits, and they are: Herbert Mohring and Harold Williamson show that in plausible examples for the United States, they can easily exceed 10 percent of the total benefits of a transportation improvement. Mohring and Williamson also show, however, that these industrial reorganization benefits are fully captured in the demand curve for transportation and hence are transfers rather than new benefits. The reasoning is identical to my earlier discussion of benefits to new and existing users, illustrated in figure 5-1. The benefits of industrial reorganization are simply benefits attributable to new ways of using the transportation system, made newly profitable by the improvement. Thus, if quantity Q in the figure is interpreted as use of a transportation system by a firm, these new uses are represented by the quantity of trips Q_1-Q_0, and the benefits of industrial reorganization are equal to area ABF.[57]

Mohring and Williamson's demonstration assumes that the cost savings from transportation are internalized within a monopoly firm. If they are not, some of the "industrial reorganization" benefits leak out to the firm's customers. For a competitive industry, however, Sergio Jara-Díaz shows that the benefits are still captured by the demand curve for transportation.[58]

So when do pecuniary externalities create genuinely new external benefits? One case is when positive technological externalities among firms are strengthened by improved transportation. An important example is external economies of agglomeration, which are advantages that firms confer on each other through proximity. Such advantages include information sharing, ability of suppliers to reap scale economies, access to venture capital, access to local public goods, and access to a common pool of specialized labor to help buffer unexpected expansion or contraction. Such advantages

57. Mohring and Williamson (1969: esp. figure 2b and p. 256).
58. Jara-Díaz (1986).

have been extensively analyzed as part of the understanding of the sources of urban agglomeration.[59] If a transportation improvement facilitates the development of an urban agglomeration that depends on such economies, it may confer benefits beyond those measured by private demand curves for transportation—provided the agglomeration is really new and not just relocated from elsewhere.

Another situation in which external benefits are genuine is when the transportation improvement reduces monopoly power. Jara-Díaz carefully examines this case, which illustrates the more general advantage of opening trade between regions.[60] He considers two regions, each initially with a monopoly firm supplying the same good. If transportation costs between the regions are lowered, it becomes possible for the firm in one region to attract customers from the other by lowering its price. The resulting increased competition reduces prices throughout and thereby reduces the deadweight loss associated with monopoly pricing. As an example, suppose the demand curve in each region is linear and the firms are identical with constant marginal cost; Jara-Díaz shows that the total benefit from the transportation improvement is then half again as large as it would be measured in the usual way. Thus, at least theoretically, external benefits can be considerable.

Both technological and pecuniary sources of external benefits are likely to be largest when a transportation improvement opens up a new area for development, thereby tapping new sources of agglomeration economies and bringing previously isolated regional economies into a wider and more competitive economic system.[61] Thus they are likely to be important for less developed nations. By contrast, external benefits are probably small in large urban agglomerations in which competition is already strong and agglomeration economies are already fully realized.

Finally, what about the much-noted effects of public infrastructure on productivity?[62] The same principles apply. It is no news that a transportation improvement results in higher productivity—that is one of the main effects of the transportation-cost savings made possible by the improvement. Thus, higher productivity could be solely a reflection of direct travel benefits or a transfer of such benefits. If the higher productivity is also part

59. See, for example, Hoover (1948); Vernon (1960); Chinitz (1961); Eberts and McMillen (forthcoming); and Anas, Arnott, and Small (1998).

60. Jara-Díaz (1986).

61. For an early exposition of this view, see Margolis (1957).

62. Excellent reviews include Winston and Bosworth (1992) and Gramlich (1994).

of a process of taking advantage of agglomeration economies, or if it results in increased competition among formerly monopolistic suppliers, then some portion of it may represent external benefits that should be added to conventional benefit measures. More definitive statements will be possible only when the microeconomic underpinnings of productivity improvements are better understood.

Tax Distortions and the Marginal Cost of Public Funds

Most cost-benefit analyses proceed as though raising revenue to fund the project under consideration were just a matter of instructing citizens to turn the money over, with no other effects on the economy. This would be true of the "lump-sum" taxation of traditional welfare economics. Real taxes, however, are based on citizens' economic decisions and therefore have the potential to alter those decisions. What effect does this potential for distortion have on project evaluation?

A convenient metric for the distortionary effect is the "marginal cost of public funds" (MCF): the total reduction in people's welfare, expressed in dollars, required to raise $1 of revenue for public use (not counting the benefits from spending that money). In comparing costs and benefits of a project, any costs funded by raising taxes should then be multiplied by the MCF that is appropriate for that tax source.

The trouble is, the MCF varies widely according to the way tax revenues are raised, and it is also quite sensitive to assumptions about economic behavior. One study from the 1980s found that if all U.S. income tax rates were raised proportionally, the MCF would be between 1.21 and 1.74—that is, it would cost consumers between $1.21 and $1.74 to raise $1.00 of new revenue in this way.[63] The range represents alternate assumptions about the elasticity of labor supply and the extent to which project benefits substitute for private consumption.[64] A less progressive tax increase,

---

63. Browning (1987). The figures quoted are for the two rows in table 2 labeled $dm/dt = 1.39$, which is Browning's estimated ratio between the marginal and average tax rates (p. 19); and for the three columns labeled $m = 0.43$, indicating a 43 percent marginal tax rate, Browning's preferred estimate (p. 21).

64. The compensated labor supply elasticity was assumed alternately to be 0.2, 0.3, or 0.4. Project benefits were assumed alternately to have no effect on labor supply or to have the same effect as would a cash transfer. The former case would apply if the project benefits are in the form of a public good that is mathematically separable from private goods in consumers' utility functions, whereas the latter case would apply if the project benefits are a perfect substitute for private goods. For clarification of this distinction, see Ballard and Fullerton (1992) and Ahmed and Croushore (1996).

representing increases in sales, excise, or Social Security payroll taxes, is estimated to have an MCF of only 1.12 to 1.32; whereas a highly progressive increase, obtained by increasing marginal tax rates while holding inframarginal rates constant, costs $1.31 to as much as $2.60 for every $1.00 of revenue raised.[65] Some analysts argue for even higher values of the MCF by taking into account behavioral distortion other than labor supply—for example, increasing the consumption of tax-deductible items.[66]

Clearly, these alternate assumptions about the MCF can make a great deal of difference to the viability of any project financed by public funds. One could argue, however, that progressive taxation is in place to meet well-understood social objectives and that any changes in the degree of progressivity caused by financing a transportation project will be factored into overall political decisions about income distribution. This argument parallels that made earlier for macroeconomic effects. Thus treating a given project as having no effect on the overall progressivity of the tax system usually makes sense. One way to accomplish that is to assume that a tax proportional to income is added to the existing tax structure. That case leads to an MCF of 1.15 to 1.30 where benefits are separable and 1.18 to 1.44 where benefits substitute for private goods, again accounting just for labor supply. [67] Thus a value of 1.25 seems reasonable as a rough approximation for common use.

Conclusion: Project Evaluation as a Public Choice Process

This chapter covers many of the technical issues needed to provide sound evaluations of transportation projects. But in the end, project evaluation is performed for decisionmakers, not technicians. As noted in the introduction, the need for formal tools such as cost-benefit analysis arises because proposed projects create conflicting interests. How then can the tools best be used to promote good decisions?

A pessimistic view would be that project evaluation is inevitably corrupted by the interests of those who sponsor it or conduct it. Certainly,

65. The "less progressive" example is from Browning's (1987) two rows labeled dm/dt = 0.8 (table 2), while the "highly progressive" example is from the rows labeled dm/dt = 2.0; see Browning's discussion on p. 19. In both cases I continue to use his intermediate estimate of the marginal tax rate (m = 0.43); the range is even wider if that parameter is varied as well.

66. Feldstein (1997).

67. This case is Browning's two rows labeled dm/dt = 1.0 (table 2); again, I use his middle three columns.

ample evidence supports such a view. I noted earlier the systematic forecasting errors that seem to favor transit and highway projects being promoted by interested parties, whether private or public. Another example is the use for many years of unrealistically low discount rates for evaluating inland waterway and irrigation projects in the United States.[68]

But just as accounting rules curtail the tendency of corporations to manipulate financial statistics in their favor, professional standards for project evaluation limit the extent of deception that can pass for objective analysis. Don Pickrell suggests several ways to narrow the range of discretion for manipulating the results of project evaluations: require peer review of evaluations; limit the time horizon that can be considered; require more detailed engineering support of cost estimates; and require specified types of sensitivity analysis.[69]

Furthermore, formal project evaluation promotes understanding of the multiple effects of a project:

> [C]ost-benefit analysis . . . has accustomed preparers of decisions . . . to examine each project within comprehensive social interrelationships . . . [and] to examine thoroughly the whole series of expectable direct and indirect effects. . . . [It] develops in those who practice it "conditioned reflexes" to such complexity of analysis.[70]

One justification of the recent interest in legislation requiring cost-benefit analysis of major regulatory actions is to create some new "conditioned reflexes" so that decisionmakers consider the complex direct and indirect effects of a regulation.

Yet another benefit of formal project evaluation is that it can force explicit consideration of alternatives to a project being proposed. For example, proposed rail rapid transit systems are sometimes required to be compared with alternative bus systems. A more dramatic example would be to require highway improvements to be weighed against pricing alternatives.

One danger of formal project evaluation is that interest groups may use the results to convey a false sense of certainty to their positions. Even decisionmakers acting in good faith may mistake professionalism for precision. An important antidote to this tendency is to explore the sensitivity of

---

68. Krutilla and Eckstein (1958).
69. Pickrell (1992).
70. Kornai (1979: 95).

results with respect to important parameters. Even better is to compute the probability distributions of key results, such as net benefits, given assumptions about the joint probability distribution of key parameters. Such a process, known as "risk analysis," can make use of Monte Carlo simulation. Parameter values are drawn randomly from their assumed distribution and results recalculated; the process is then repeated many times so that the frequency distribution of calculated results approximates their true probability distribution, thereby faithfully representing the effects of the inherent uncertainty in the analysis. It is important to account for any anticipated correlations among uncertain parameters, for example the correlation between projected employment and average income, so that the results are not distorted by what are highly unlikely combinations of parameter values.[71]

David Lewis suggests going a step further and embedding the entire evaluation process in a public decisionmaking format that includes interactive sensitivity analysis and open discussion of the merits of assumptions used. Called "risk analysis process," this proposal is in the spirit of more open public involvement in decisionmaking. It combines the technical steps of cost-benefit analysis with educational and consensus-building tools. Lewis's version emphasizes the graphical presentation of probability distributions of results under alternative assumptions about the uncertainty in model inputs. At a minimum, it is hoped that this procedure will reduce the scope for technical argument among the various stakeholders in a decision. In favorable circumstances, Lewis reports, it leads to a surprising degree of consensus.[72] The risk analysis process can make the role of cost-benefit analysis in decisionmaking more explicit and can result in analysts adapting their technical tools to make them more transparent.

There is a danger that the risk analysis itself could exacerbate the false sense of certainty by suggesting that technical procedures such as Monte Carlo simulation can account for every source of uncertainty. The most sophisticated analysis possible may fail to account for problems such as administrative incompetence, deliberate political sabotage, unknown geological features, or new inventions that make a project prematurely obsolete. Indeed, it has been argued recently that for developing nations, these

---

71. Savvides (1994). For a fuller discussion of risk analysis in transportation project evaluation, see Meyer and Straszheim (1971: ch. 13). Monte Carlo analysis is recommended by Transport Canada (1994).
72. Lewis (1997); U.S. Federal Highway Administration (1996).

kinds of factors, affecting the gross performance of the project, are more important to project success than many of the technical factors of concern to methodologists—including technical factors that are highlighted in the evaluation methodology of the World Bank.[73] Similarly, formal analysis will often miss significant benefits by failing to foresee the many ramifications of a change. This may especially be a limitation in evaluating research and development projects. Could anyone in the 1890s have predicted the ramifications of inventing the automobile?

Yet another danger of formal evaluation is that it may assume an unrealistically simple structure for the rest of the economy. For example, many public projects that are subjected to cost-benefit analysis will displace private investments. Often the analysis assumes, explicitly or implicitly, that those private investments would take place under conditions of "perfect competition," so that the marginal social values of resources are measured by their prices. But private markets often embody strategic interactions that are far from the classical competitive model. The airline industry is illustrative. As noted by John Meyer and Mahlon Straszheim, and more recently by Gabriel Roth, a criterion of profit maximization may sometimes allocate resources between private and public sectors better than a criterion of net social benefits.[74] It is wise to scrutinize cost-benefit analyses when markets deviate strongly from perfect competition.

Finally, like it or not, project evaluation exists within a political context. The inevitable conceptual difficulties should be made transparent rather than hidden. Far from making the analysis the sole province of experts, these difficulties are the grist for political debate. The job of experts is to describe the effects of particular assumptions accurately and to develop frameworks for presenting data that clarify relationships. The best method of presentation is one that makes it possible to understand and justify political decisions that are in the interests of the citizenry at large, while embarrassing those who would make decisions favoring only narrow interest groups.

Appendix: Calculation of the Shadow Price of Capital

The problem with using the weighted average of interest rates r_c and r_i, applying respectively to private consumption and private investment, is

---

73. Jenkins (1997).
74. Meyer and Straszheim (1971: 202); Roth (1996: sec. 5.3).

that the benefit or expenditure flows needed to obtain the weights should themselves be discounted. Suppose a project displaces $1 million of private investment at its inception, incurs maintenance costs of $50,000 a year (constant dollars) over its fifty-year life, and also creates benefits in the form of additional consumption starting at $100,000 a year and rising thereafter at 1 percent a year until the end of its life. Without discounting these future benefits and costs, one cannot say what proportion of the project's effects should be assigned to consumption and what proportion to investment. But without knowing those proportions, one does not know at what interest rate to do the discounting. Thus, the definition of the weighted average is circular.

This circularity can be eliminated by multiplying each public investment expenditure by a *shadow price of capital*, which measures capital's contributions to future consumption.[75] The shadow price of capital takes into account distortions in market prices due to taxes or other factors and thereby bridges some of the gaps between various observed market interest rates.

The logic is like that of other shadow prices. Consider, for example, how shadow wages are used to account for distortions in market wages caused by labor taxation. Suppose labor is diverted from a competitive private labor market into tax-free employment for an international organization; then its opportunity cost is the value of its marginal product in private employment, which is equal to the market wage rate plus any payroll tax paid by private employers. Similarly, suppose capital is diverted from private investment where it would earn a competitive private net rate of return (that is, the after-tax rate of return). Then its social opportunity cost—the marginal contribution to production it would have made in the private sector—is the net private return plus any income or other taxes it would have generated.[76] What makes capital more complicated than other factors of production is that the taxes are paid in a stream over many years rather than at the time of the initial investment.

The shadow price of capital has been estimated to be 1.5, with a range from about 1.2 to 2.0, for the United States in 1989. The calculation goes

---

75. This approach was pioneered by Bradford (1975) and refined by Mendelsohn (1981). For a good review, see Lind (1986).

76. Vickrey (1962) makes this point specifically for urban land taken for road improvements, which if left in private hands would generate revenues from corporate and private income taxes, property taxes, and perhaps sales taxes. The point applies equally well to all forms of capital.

as follows. Each dollar of investment displaced by the proposed project is assumed to provide an infinite stream of gross returns at annual rate w when expressed as a fraction of the investment. In each year some portion of the return is consumed; the rest is reinvested, creating a similar set of future effects. One possible assumption is that a fraction s of the gross return is reinvested, where s is the average savings rate in the economy. If all rates of return are constant in time and if annual depreciation is a constant fraction δ of the capital stock, then these assumption imply that each dollar of investment in year zero has value V calculated from the following effects that it produces in year one:

—The original capital depreciates to a fraction $1 - \delta$ of its initial value;

—The gross return results in new investment equal to sw; and

—The gross return results in consumption equal to $(1 - s)w$.

The first two items are new capital, so they have value V per dollar as measured from year one; the third item is consumption, valued in year one at one dollar per dollar. Hence the year-one value of the effects of the original dollar of investment are $(1 - \delta + sw)V + (1 - s)w$. Discounting these by $(1 + r_c)^{-1}$ gives the original shadow price V. Thus V is the solution to the equation:

$$V = [(1 - \delta + sw)V + (1 - s)w] / (1 + r_c),$$

which gives the following formula for the shadow price of capital:[77]

$$V = (w - sw) / (r_c + \delta - sw).$$

This value is greater than one, assuming the rate of time preference r_c is less than the net private return $r_i / w - \delta$.

Using a rough estimate of 10 percent for the depreciation rate δ, and 15 percent for the savings rate s,[78] along with the earlier estimates $r_c = 0.04$ and $w - \delta = 0.096$, the formula above gives 1.51 for the shadow price of capital. In other words, each item in the cost-benefit calculation that reduces or adds to capital investment is multiplied by 1.51; all future costs and benefits are then discounted at 4 percent. Recalculating for r_c between 2 and 6 percent and $w - \delta$ between 8.6 and 10.6 percent, V takes values ranging from 1.20 to 1.97.

77. This equation is given by Lyon (1990). I have simplified the derivation by using the recursion approach, which attributes value V to investment in year one. Lyon also gives the subsequent alternative formula involving s_r.

78. As suggested by Boardman and others (1996: 172).

Different formulas result from alternative assumptions about savings behavior. For example, if it is assumed that a fixed fraction s_r is saved from the *net* return $r_i = w - \delta$, a similar argument results in the following shadow price of capital: $V = (r - s_r r) / (r_c - s_r r)$.

References

Ahmed, Shaghil, and Dean Croushore. 1996. "The Marginal Cost of Funds with Nonseparable Public Spending." *Public Finance Quarterly* 24 (April): 216–36.

American Association of State Highway and Transportation Officials. 1978. *A Manual on User Benefit Analysis of Highway and Bus-Transit Improvements, 1977.* Washington, D.C.

Anas, Alex, Richard Arnott, and Kenneth A. Small. 1998. "Urban Spatial Structure." *Journal of Economic Literature* (September): 1426–64.

Arnott, Richard J. 1979. "Unpriced Transport Congestion." *Journal of Economic Theory* 21(October): 294–316.

Arnott, Richard J., André de Palma, and Robin Lindsey. 1990. "Economics of a Bottleneck." *Journal of Urban Economics* 27 (January): 111–30.

Austroads. 1996. *Benefit Cost Analysis Manual.* AP-42/96: ARRB Transport Research. Sydney.

Ballard, Charles L., and Don Fullerton. 1992. "Distortionary Taxes and the Provision of Public Goods." *Journal of Economic Perspectives* 6 (Summer): 117–31.

Ben-Akiva, Moshe, and Steven R. Lerman. 1985. *Discrete Choice Analysis: Theory and Application to Travel Demand.* Vol. 9 in series on transportation studies. MIT Press.

Bergstrom, Theodore C. 1982. "When Is a Man's Life Worth More than His Human Capital?" In *The Value of Life and Safety: Proceedings of a Conference Held by the "Geneva Association,"* edited by Michael W. Jones-Lee, 3–26. Amsterdam: North-Holland.

Boardman, Anthony E., Wendy L. Mallery, and Aidan R. Vining. 1994. "Learning from *Ex Ante/Ex Post* Cost-Benefit Comparisons: The Coquihalla Highway Example." *Socio-Economic Planning Sciences* 28 (June): 69–84.

Boardman, Anthony E., and others. 1996. *Cost-Benefit Analysis: Concepts and Practice.* Prentice Hall.

Boyd, J. Hayden. 1976. "Benefits and Costs of Urban Transportation: He Who Is Inelastic Receiveth and Other Parables." *Transportation Research Forum: Proceedings of the Annual Meeting* 17:290–7.

Bradford, David F. 1975. "Constraints on Government Investment Opportunities and the Choice of Discount Rate." *American Economic Review* 65 (December): 887–99.

Bradford, David F., and Gregory G. Hildebrandt. 1977. "Observable Public Good Preferences." *Journal of Public Economics* 8 (October):111–31.

Browning, Edgar K. 1987. "On the Marginal Welfare Cost of Taxation." *American Economic Review* 77 (March): 11–23.

Buchanan, James M. 1975. "A Contractarian Paradigm for Applying Economic Theory." *American Economic Review* 65 (May, *Papers and Proceedings*): 225–30.

Buchanan, James M., and Gordon Tullock. 1962. *The Calculus of Consent: Logical Foundations of Constitutional Democracy.* University of Michigan Press.

Calfee, John E., and Clifford Winston. 1993. "The Consumer Welfare Effects of Liability for Pain and Suffering: An Exploratory Analysis." *Brookings Papers on Economic Activity: Microeconomics*: 133–96.

———. 1998. "The Value of Automobile Travel Time: Implications for Congestion Policy." *Journal of Public Economics* 69 (July): 83–102

Chinitz, Benjamin. 1961. "Contrasts in Agglomeration: New York and Pittsburgh." *American Economic Review* 51 (May, *Papers and Proceedings*): 279–89.

Chirinko, Robert S., and Edward P. Harper, Jr. 1993. "Buckle Up or Slow Down? New Estimates of Offsetting Behavior and Their Implications for Automobile Safety Regulation." *Journal of Policy Analysis and Management* 12 (Spring): 270–96.

Cline, William R. 1992. *The Economics of Global Warming.* Washington, D.C. Institute for International Economics.

Dasgupta, Partha. 1994. "Exhaustible Resources: Resource Depletion, Research and Development, and the Social Rate of Discount." In Layard and Glaister, 349–72.

Delucchi, Mark A. 1997. *The Annualized Social Cost of Motor Vehicle Use in the U.S., 1990–1991: Summary of Theory, Data, Methods, and Results.* Report 1 in the series *The Annualized Social Cost of Motor-Vehicle Use in the United States, Based on 1990–1991 Data.* UCD-ITS-RR-96-3 (1). University of California at Davis, Institute of Transportation Studies. June.

Delucchi, Mark A., and Shi-Ling Hsu. 1996. *The External Damage Cost of Direct Noise from Motor Vehicles: Details by Urbanized Area.* Report 14 in the series *The Annualized Social Cost of Motor-Vehicle Use in the United States, Based on 1990–1991 Data.* Report UCD-ITS-RR-96-3 (14). University of California at Davis, Institute of Transportation Studies. December.

Domencich, Thomas A., and Daniel McFadden. 1975. *Urban Travel Demand: A Behavioral Analysis.* Vol. 93 of *Contributions to Economic Analysis.* Amsterdam: North-Holland.

Downs, Anthony. 1962. "The Law of Peak-Hour Expressway Congestion." *Traffic Quarterly* 16 (July): 393–409.

Dréze, Jean, and Nicholas Stern. 1990. "Policy Reform, Shadow Prices, and Market Prices." *Journal of Public Economics* 42 (June): 1–45.

Eberts, Randall W., and Daniel P. McMillen. Forthcoming. "Agglomeration Economies and Urban Public Infrastructure." In *Handbook of Regional and Urban Economics.* Vol. 3: *Applied Urban Economics,* edited by Paul Cheshire and Edwin S. Mills. Amsterdam: Elsevier.

Feldstein, Martin. 1997. "How Big Should Government Be?" *National Tax Journal* 50 (June): 197–213.

Gramlich, Edward M. 1994. "Infrastructure Investment: A Review Essay." *Journal of Economic Literature* 32 (September): 1176–96.

Hausman, Jerry A. 1981. "Exact Consumer's Surplus and Deadweight Loss." *American Economic Review* 71 (September): 662–76.

Hensher, David A. 1989. "Behavioural and Resource Values of Travel Time Savings: A Bicentennial Update." *Australian Road Research* 19 (September): 223–29.

Hicks, John R. 1941. "The Rehabilitation of Consumers' Surplus." *Review of Economic Studies* 8 (February): 108–16.

Hoover, Edgar M. 1948. *The Location of Economic Activity.* McGraw-Hill.

Hotelling, Harold. 1938. "The General Welfare in Relation to Problems of Taxation and of Railway and Utility Rates." *Econometrica* 6 (July): 242–69.

Intergovernmental Panel on Climate Change. 1996. *Climate Change 1995: The IPCC Second Assessment Report*. Cambridge University Press.

Jara-Díaz, Sergio R. 1986. "On the Relation Between Users' Benefits and the Economic Effects of Transportation Activities." *Journal of Regional Science* 26 (May): 379–91.

Jenkins, Glenn P. 1997. "Project Analysis and the World Bank." *American Economic Review* 87 (May, *Papers and Proceedings*): 38–42.

Jones-Lee, Michael W., Graham Loomes, and P. R. Philips. 1995. "Valuing the Prevention of Non-Fatal Road Injuries: Contingent Valuation vs. Standard Gambles." *Oxford Economic Papers* 47 (October): 676–95.

Kain, John F. 1990. "Deception in Dallas: Strategic Misrepresentation in Rail Transit Promotion and Evaluation." *Journal of the American Planning Association* 56 (Spring): 184–96.

Khan, Shulamit. 1986. "Economic Estimates of the Value of Life." *IEEE Technology and Society Magazine* 5 (June): 24–31.

Kornai, János. 1979. "Appraisal of Project Appraisal." In *Economics and Human Welfare: Essays in Honor of Tibor Scitovsky*, edited by Michael J. Boskin, 75–99. New York: Academic Press.

Kronman, Anthony T. 1980. "Wealth Maximization as a Normative Principle." *Journal of Legal Studies* 9 (March): 227–42.

Krugman, Paul. 1991. *Geography and Trade*. MIT Press.

Krutilla, John V., and Otto Eckstein for Resources for the Future. 1958. *Multiple Purpose River Development: Studies in Applied Economic Analysis*. Johns Hopkins Press.

Layard, Richard, and Stephen Glaister, eds. 1994. *Cost-Benefit Analysis*. Cambridge University Press.

Leonard, Herman B., and Richard J. Zeckhauser. 1986. "Cost-Benefit Analysis Applied to Risks: Its Philosophy and Legitimacy." In *Values at Risk*, edited by Douglas MacLean. Totowa, N.J.: Rowman & Allanheld.

Lewis, David. 1997. "Handling Uncertainty in Project Evaluations." Paper presented at the annual meeting of the Transportation Research Board, Washington, D.C. January 12–16.

Lind, Robert C. 1986. "The Shadow Price of Capital: Implications for the Opportunity Cost of Public Programs, the Burden of the Debt, and Tax Reform." In *Social Choice and Public Decision Making: Essays in Honor of Kenneth J. Arrow*. Vol. 1, edited by Walter P. Heller, Ross M. Starr, and David A. Starrett, 189–212. Cambridge University Press.

Little, Ian Michael David. 1950. *A Critique of Welfare Economics*. Oxford: Clarendon Press.

Lyon, Randolph M. 1990. "Federal Discount Policy, the Shadow Price of Capital, and Challenges for Reform." *Journal of Environmental Economics and Management* 18 (March, part 2): S29–S50, appendix 1.

McCubbin, Donald R., and Mark A. Delucchi. 1996. *The Social Cost of the Health Effects of Motor-Vehicle Air Pollution*. Report 11 in the series *The Annualized Social Cost of Motor Vehicle Use in the United States, Based on 1990–1991 Data*. Report UCD-ITS-RR-96-3 (11). University of California at Davis, Institute of Transportation Studies. August.

McKenzie, G. W., and T. F. Pearce. 1982. "Welfare Measurement: A Synthesis." *American Economic Review* 72 (September): 669–82.

Mackie, Peter, Jeremy Toner, and Denvil Coombe. 1996. "A Critical Comment on the COBACHECK Method of Estimating the Effects of Induced Traffic on the Economic Benefits of Road Schemes." *Traffic Engineering and Control* 37 (September): 500–2.

Mannering, Fred, and Clifford Winston. 1987. "U.S. Automobile Market Demand." In *Blind Intersection? Policy and the Automobile Industry,* edited by Clifford Winston and associates, 36–60. Brookings.

Margolis, Julius. 1957. "Secondary Benefits, External Economies, and the Justification of Public Investment." *Review of Economics and Statistics* 39: 284–91.

Mendelsohn, Robert. 1981. "The Choice of Discount Rates for Public Projects." *American Economic Review* 71 (March): 239–41.

Meyer, John R., and Mahlon R. Straszheim. 1971. *Techniques of Transport Planning.* Vol. 1: *Pricing and Project Evaluation.* Brookings.

Mishan, E. J. 1969. *Welfare Economics: An Assessment.* Amsterdam: North Holland.

————. 1971. "Evaluation of Life and Limb: A Theoretical Approach." *Journal of Political Economy* 79 (July/August): 687–705.

Mohring, Herbert, and Harold F. Williamson, Jr. 1969. "Scale and 'Industrial Reorganisation' Economies of Transport Improvements." *Journal of Transport Economics and Policy* 3 (September): 251–71.

Morrison, Steven, and Clifford Winston. 1986. *The Economic Effects of Airline Deregulation.* Brookings.

Muller, Robert H. 1996. "Examining Toll Road Feasibility Studies." *Public Works Financing* (June): 16–20.

MVA Consultancy, Institute for Transport Studies of the University of Leeds, and Transport Studies Unit of Oxford University. 1987. *The Value of Travel Time Savings: A Report of Research Undertaken for the Department of Transport.* Newbury, U.K.: Policy Journals.

Nash, Christopher A. 1993. "Cost-Benefit Analysis of Transport Projects." In *Efficiency in the Public Sector: The Theory and Practice of Cost-Benefit Analysis,* edited by Alan Williams and Emilio Giardina, 83–105. Aldershot, U.K.: Edward Elgar.

OMB (U.S. Office of Management and Budget). 1992. *Guidelines and Discount Rates for Benefit-Cost Analysis of Federal Programs.* Circular A-94, rev. Washington, D. C. October 29.

Peltzman, Sam. 1975. "The Effects of Automobile Safety Regulation." *Journal of Political Economy* 83 (August): 677–725.

Peterson, Steven, George Hoffer, and Edward Millner. 1995. "Are Drivers of Air-Bag-Equipped Cars More Aggressive? A Test of the Offsetting Behavior Hypothesis." *Journal of Law and Economics* 38 (October): 251–64.

Pickrell, Don H. 1989. *Urban Rail Transit Projects: Forecast Versus Actual Ridership and Costs.* Cambridge: U.S. Department of Transportation, Transportation Systems Center. October.

————. 1992. "A Desire Named Streetcar: Fantasy and Fact in Rail Transit Planning." *Journal of the American Planning Association* 58 (Spring): 158–76.

Pigou, Arthur C. 1920. *The Economics of Welfare.* London: Macmillan.

Prest, A. R., and R. Turvey. 1965. "Cost-Benefit Analysis: A Survey." *Economic Journal* 75 (December): 683–735.

Roth, Gabriel. 1996. *Roads in a Market Economy.* Aldershot, U.K.: Avebury Technical.

Samuelson, Paul A. 1947. *Foundations of Economic Analysis.* Harvard University Press.

Savvides, Savvakis. 1994. "Risk Analysis in Investment Appraisal." *Project Appraisal* 9 (March): 3–18.

Schelling, Thomas C. 1968. "The Life You Save May Be Your Own." In *Problems in Public Expenditure Analysis,* edited by Samuel B. Chase, 127–76. Brookings.

Schmalensee, Richard. 1993. "Symposium on Global Climate Change." *Journal of Economic Perspectives* 7 (Fall): 3–10.

Skamris, Mette K., and Bent Flyvbjerg. 1996. "Accuracy of Traffic Forecasts and Cost Estimates on Large Transportation Projects." *Transportation Research Record* (1518): 65–69.

Small, Kenneth A. 1983. "Bus Priority and Congestion Pricing." In *Research in Transportation Economics.* Vol. I, edited by Theodore R. Keeler, 27–74. Greenwich, Conn.: JAI Press.

———. 1992. *Urban Transportation Economics.* Vol. 51 of *Fundamentals of Pure and Applied Economics.* Chur, Switzerland: Harwood Academic Publishers.

Small, Kenneth A., and Camilla Kazimi. 1995. "On the Costs of Air Pollution from Motor Vehicles." *Journal of Transport Economics and Policy* 29 (January): 7–32.

Small, Kenneth A., and Harvey S. Rosen. 1981. "Applied Welfare Economics with Discrete Choice Models." *Econometrica* 49 (January): 105–30.

Strotz, Robert H. 1965. "Urban Transportation Parables." In *The Public Economy of Urban Communities,* edited by Julius Margolis. Washington, D.C.: Resources for the Future, 127–69.

Transport Canada. 1994. *Guide to Benefit-Cost Analysis in Transport Canada.* Ottawa. September.

U.S. Federal Highway Administration. 1996. *Exploring the Application of Benefit/Cost Methodologies to Transportation Infrastructure Decision Making.* No. 16 of *Searching for Solutions: A Policy Discussion Series.* Washington, D.C. July.

Vernon, Raymond. 1960. *Metropolis 1985: An Interpretation of the Findings of the New York Metropolitan Region Study .* Harvard University Press.

Vickrey, William S. 1962. "General and Specific Financing of Urban Services." In *Public Expenditure Decisions in the Urban Community,* edited by Howard G. Schaller, 62–90. Washington, D.C.: Resources for the Future.

———. 1969. "Congestion Theory and Transport Investment." *Amercan Economic Review* 59 (May, *Papers and Proceedings*):251–60.

Viscusi, V. Kip. 1993. "The Value of Risks to Life and Health." *Journal of Economic Literature* 31 (December): 1912–46.

Waters, W. G., II. 1992. *The Value of Time Savings for the Economic Evaluation of Highway Investments in British Columbia.* Research report for Planning Services Branch, British Columbia Ministry of Transportation and Highways. University of British Columbia, Centre for Transportation Studies, Vancouver. March.

———. 1996. "Values of Travel Time Savings in Road Transport Project Evaluation." In *Proceedings of the World Conference on Transport Research, Transport Policy.* Vol. 3 of *World Transport Research,* 213–23. New York: Elsevier.

Weingast, Barry R., Kenneth A. Shepsle, and Christopher Johnsen. 1981. "The Political Economy of Benefits and Costs: A Neoclassical Approach to Distributive Politics." *Journal of Political Economy* 89 (August): 642–64.

Wheaton, William C. 1978. "Price-Induced Distortions in Urban Highway Investment." *Bell Journal of Economics* 9 (Autumn): 622–32.

Willig, Robert D. 1976. "Consumer's Surplus Without Apology." *American Economic Review* 66 (September): 589–97.

Winston, Clifford. 1981. "A Disaggregate Model of the Demand for Intercity Freight Transportation." *Econometrica* 49 (July): 981–1006.

Winston, Clifford, and Barry Bosworth. 1992. "Public Infrastructure." In *Setting Domestic Priorities: What Can Government Do?,* edited by Henry J. Aaron and Charles L. Schultze. Brookings.

PART II

The Automobile in Society

HERBERT MOHRING

6 Congestion

T HE USERS of road and other transportation networks
not only experience congestion, they create it. In
deciding how and when to travel, most travelers take into account the congestion they expect to experience; few consider the costs their trips impose
on others by adding to congestion. Charging tolls equal to the costs travelers impose on each other—a concept first seen in the economics literature
in the 1920s—could both optimize the use of existing transportation facilities in the short run and provide information vital to optimizing the
characteristics of these facilities in the long run.[1]

This chapter's first section documents this claim. Although its discussion applies to any congestible facility, the remainder of the chapter deals
almost entirely with congestion on urban roads and the costs and benefits
of its antidotes. It describes and compares the techniques currently used in
North America to cope with urban traffic congestion and then reviews the
world's very limited experience with using tolls to force road users to reflect

The author is indebted to the editors and others for helpful comments, particularly David Anderson, Richard Arnott, and Robin Lindsay. Anderson is the brains behind this paper. Without his remarkable capacity to make complicated computer packages sing, our congestion-toll estimates would
have been impossible.
1. Pigou (1920); Knight (1924).

181

in their travel decisions the costs their road use imposes on others. These costs are then quantified, as are the effects, benefits, and costs of using congestion pricing to optimize the road network of the Twin Cities Metropolitan Area, perhaps the *least* congested of the United States' major urban areas. Finally the chapter discusses important unsolved problems associated with congestion pricing as well as issues that have been at least partially solved in the literature but that are swept under the rug here.

The Theory of Congestion Pricing

In general terms, "congestion" arises when buyers supply some of the variable inputs—most commonly their own time or that of commodities they own—required to produce a good or service and when the quantity of these inputs required for a unit of output, the quality of the product, or both depend on the rate at which purchases are made. Defined this way, congestion occurs in many economic activities. The wait for service in a department store is typically substantially longer during the week before Christmas than in late January. The greater is the attendance at a movie performance, the smaller are the odds of finding a seat with an unencumbered view of the screen. And, of course, in driving on urban roads, more congestion means both more time-consuming and—for most—more unpleasant trips.

The technology of road congestion can be developed by exploiting a variant of the commonly cited rule of safe road behavior that drivers should stay 2–3 seconds behind the vehicles they follow. Suppose that all drivers stay 1.8 seconds behind the vehicles in front of them. As roads become more crowded, the distance between vehicles must diminish. The speed required to stay 1.8 seconds behind must therefore also diminish. Each traveler who joins a traffic stream reduces the average distance between the vehicles in it, thereby imposing a cost on them by slowing them down. In deciding whether to make a trip, most travelers take into account the costs congestion will impose on them. Few take into account the costs their decision to travel will impose on others by slowing them down. It is this unrecognized external cost, or externality, that underlies economists' espousal of congestion pricing.

If all travelers follow the 1.8-seconds rule, relationships would occur between the *instantaneous* ratio of actual traffic volumes to capacity (about 2,000 vehicles per lane-hour on an expressway) and the average and marginal travel times per mile suggested by the *AVC* and *SRMC* curves in figure 6-1. (For proofs, see appendix.) Curve *AVC* depicts the travel-time cost that the occupants of the average vehicle would incur; curve *SRMC* includes this time cost *plus* the costs these occupants impose on all other vehicles in the traffic stream by adding to congestion. *AVC* illustrates a commonly observed phenomenon of urban expressway travel: At speeds above about 30 miles per hour (mph), *reduced* speeds are associated with *increased* traffic flows. In the top, backward-bending portion of *AVC*, however, *reduced* speeds accompany *lower* traffic flows. Some of the world's most congested cities—Bangkok, Athens, Rome, Jakarta—seem to be in this unpleasant state most of the time.

To help understand the economics of road and other types of congestion, it is useful to make explicit the very close parallel between road operation depicted in figure 6-1 and, in figure 6-2, the operation of the competitive business firms with which microeconomics textbooks deal. For both roads and business firms, the curve labeled *AVC* depicts average variable production costs—mainly travel time for trips in figure 6-1, and labor, raw materials, fuel, and the like for *X*s in figure 6-2.[2] Both production processes reflect the economist's "law of diminishing marginal productivity": each additional trip or unit of *X* requires successively larger doses of variable inputs as the road and *X*-producing capital equipment are used more intensively; holding capital inputs fixed, as output rates increase, the short-run *marginal* costs of *X*s and trips increase more rapidly than do their *average* variable costs.

In figures 6-1 and 6-2, output declines when variable inputs are used at rates greater than those necessary to maximize the output that the stock of fixed capital equipment can produce. Although no business firm would voluntarily use such input combinations, all urban freeway users have participated in such inefficiency during peak periods. In heavy but free-flowing traffic, something—an accident, for example, or unusually heavy entry at some interchange—forces some drivers to slam on their brakes. Their abrupt slowdowns force those who follow to slam on *their* brakes. The resulting chain reaction abruptly converts a traffic stream averaging 50 mph into one in which all travel in lockstep at 10–20 mph.

---

2. The total costs of travel include not just what travelers would willingly pay to save travel time, but also vehicle operating costs, road damage imposed by heavy vehicles, and the environmental damage that results from noise and vehicles' chemical emissions. For expositional succinctness, however, I treat time as the only cost of travel.

Figure 6-1. *Urban Road Equilibria with and without Congestion Pricing*

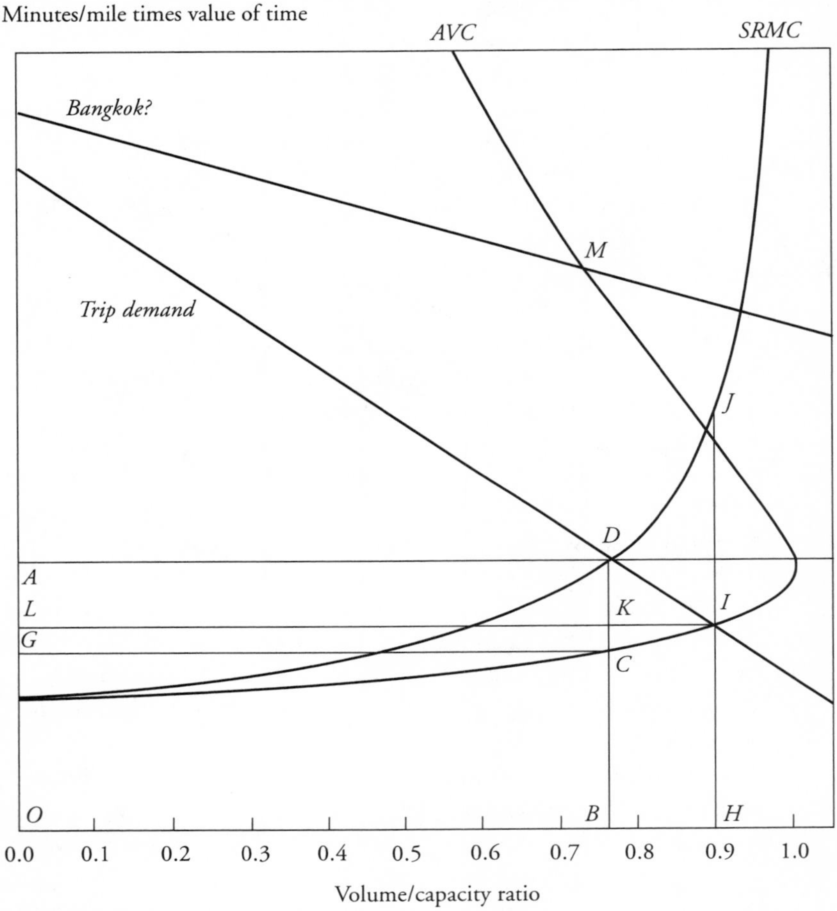
Minutes/mile times value of time
AVC
SRMC
Bangkok?
M
Trip demand
J
D
A
L
G
K
I
C
O
B
H
0.0
0.1
0.2
0.3
0.4
0.5
0.6
0.7
0.8
0.9
1.0
Volume/capacity ratio

Source: Authors' calculations.

For the *X* producer, if the competitive market price of an *X* is *OA*, the firm would produce *OB Xs* a week, the rate at which its short-run marginal cost equals the market price. Doing so would generate total revenues of *OADB*. These revenues would cover the firm's *total* variable costs, *OGCB*, leaving *ADCG* as a reward to the firm's bond- and stockholders for supplying its fixed capital equipment. If *ADCG* exceeds the costs of financing and maintaining the firm's fixed capital, it and other firms would gain from

Figure 6-2. *Equilibrium of Competitive X-Producing Firm*

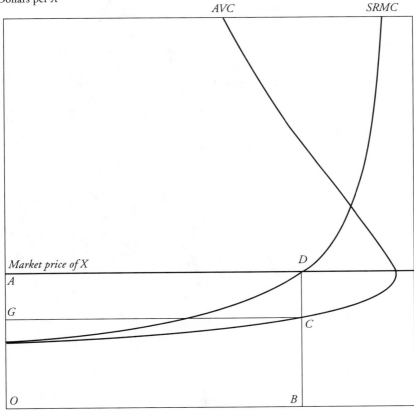

Dollars per X

Xs per week (thousands)

Source: Authors' calculations.

expanding capacity. If they do, both the market price and weekly returns per unit of output will fall until, in long-run equilibrium, the weekly counterpart of *ADCG* just covers weekly capital costs.

To introduce the customer side of the urban trip market, suppose that a household's members get utility from consuming a general-purpose commodity, stuff (*S*), conveniently priced at $1 a unit, and from what happens at the ends of the *T* trips a week, each costing $*F* (for "fare") and requiring *t* minutes. Travel itself is unpleasant, however. The household spends its income on stuff and on trips so as to maximize its utility, a function $U = U(S, T, tT)$. It turns out that this household would treat the price of a trip as the actual dollar outlay, F, for the trip plus Vt, the cost the household attaches to the time the trip requires (see appendix). V (measured in dollars per hour) is the rate at which the household would be willing to sacrifice stuff to save travel time, its "value of travel time" for short.

Accepting the notion that it is the "full price" of a trip, $F + Vt$, that affects travel decisions, ignoring vehicle operating and accident costs, and multiplying travel time per trip on the vertical dimension of figure 6-1 by the average travel-time value for the population, V_{av}, converts the dimensions of the axis from minutes per mile to dollars per mile, which can be used to discuss the short- and long-run optimizing behavior of a benevolent highway authority that desires to maximize the social contribution of a road. With no tolls, the trip-demand schedule in figure 6-1 would result in a travel rate of OH. At this rate, supply equals demand, that is, the trip demand schedule intersects the schedule of costs travelers bear directly. At this rate of travel, by adding to the level of congestion, each traveler imposes a cost of IJ on all other travelers. Thus, IJ is the "gap" between the full cost to society of a trip and the cost each individual traveler bears directly.

Associated with gap IJ is a deadweight loss of DIJ an hour for trips that are valued at less than their aggregate social costs.[3] Imposing a toll of DC per trip would force off the road the BH trips that account for this loss. This toll would not only eliminate the deadweight loss, DIJ, but would also generate revenues of $ADCG$. The eliminated BH trips, however, had an aggregate net value of DKI to those who took them. In addition, tolls would increase by DK, the *full* price of a trip for the average traveler, for a total of $LKDA$ for all of those who continue to travel despite the increased cost of trips.[4] That tolls would eliminate the deadweight losses from unpriced congestion and lower the time costs of still-made trips guarantees that increased toll revenues would exceed consumer losses. Hence, in principle, a compensation system for losers could be found that would not only leave them better off, but also provide funds for the highway authority to per-

---

3. The deadweight loss is the amount by which the cost of producing a group of commodities (*BH* trips in this case) exceeds the value their consumers attach to them.

4. The line labeled "Bangkok?" in figure 6-1 suggests that congestion tolls could lead both to more travel at lower price in extremely congested metropolitan areas—truly a win-win situation. But drawing a line on a diagram does not guarantee that the equilibrium it suggests could actually exist; see the last section of this paper.

form good works. Sadly to say, finding a practice to satisfy this principle is not easy.

Similarities between the results of interpreting figure 6-2 for a profit-maximizing producer of Xs and figure 6-1 for an optimizing road authority extend to the relationship in long-run equilibrium between capital costs and quasi-rents. Suppose that the road-services production function is subject to constant returns to scale so that doubling both fixed and variable inputs would precisely double total output. Suppose also that the road authority has no influence on the prices it pays for inputs. Then, the appendix shows, an optimally designed and priced road would generate revenues equal to its capital costs, just as would happen in a competitive market in long-run equilibrium.

Are roads subject to constant returns? For rural roads, geometric reasoning of the sort introduced and quantified by Meyer, Kain, and Wohl clearly justifies a "no" answer.[5] For the typical rural expressway, the road surface area accounts for less than half of the total outlays for rights-of-way and earth-moving; a 50 percent increase in capacity results in much less than a 50 percent increase in costs. The issue is less clear for urban freeways. Several scholars including me have used questionable economic reasoning to conclude that urban freeways are subject to sharply diminishing returns.[6] More reasonable approaches lead to estimates of increasing returns of such modest proportions that increasing tolls above marginal costs by enough to cover total costs would produce only small welfare losses.[7]

Battling Congestion

Major urban areas in North America currently employ five techniques to ameliorate peak-period traffic congestion.[8] First, bus operations are heavily

---

5. Meyer, Kain, and Wohl (1965).
6. See, for example, Mohring (1975) and Walters (1968).
7. Keeler and Small (1977); Kraus (1981).
8. A sixth technique, parking controls, is an underused congestion-reducing tool. Many cities temporarily increase peak-period arterial-road capacity by prohibiting parking. To discourage peak-period auto commuting to central business districts, surcharges on parking rates in those districts have been implemented in a few cities. Singapore accompanied its institution in 1975 of peak-period tolls on cars entering its central area with sharp increases in parking charges. These rate increases played a major role in the subsequent substantial reduction in central area traffic. For a valuable discussion of parking policy strengths and weaknesses, see Verhoef, Nijkamp, and Reitfeld (1995).

subsidized in many areas, and buses together with other high-occupancy vehicles (HOVs) such as car pools are given preferential access to road capacity by allowing them on city street and expressway HOV lanes reserved expressly for them. Second, vehicles are metered onto freeways in many areas to reduce traffic volumes, thereby reducing the chances that traffic conditions will shift into the backward-bending portion of figure 6-1's *AVC* curve. Third, in Washington, Ottawa, and perhaps other company towns, office opening and closing hours are staggered. Fourth, in all areas, road construction continues albeit at a rate that will result in steadily increasing congestion unless successfully accompanied by other traffic-reducing measures. Finally, congestion pricing is actually employed on a stretch of privately operated toll road in California's Orange County and on Interstate 15 in San Diego. In San Diego congestion pricing is in the form of high-occupancy/toll, or HOT, lanes, where drivers of single-occupancy vehicles (SOVs) are allowed to buy underutilized space on HOV lanes. Several areas have announced plans to permit HOT lanes, but not all of them will actually come into being.

Subsidies

I once argued that producing bus trips involves what are today termed "economies of density."[9] True, maintaining and operating a fleet of half-a-dozen or so buses exhausts those scale economies that exist. An increase in the demand for service along any given route, however, induces additional service, which, in turn, reduces the time interval between buses and thus passenger waiting time and the full prices of their trips.[10] If serving additional passengers had no effect on the time a bus spends boarding and discharging passengers, the optimal service frequency on a route would

---

9. Mohring (1972).

10. In estimating the time required for bus trips, it is common to assume that, on average, travelers wait half the headway (that is, half the interval between scheduled arrivals) on the bus routes they use. It is as if the only wait of relevance is that for a bus to come and as if, not knowing route schedules, travelers walk to a stop and wait. But bus schedules are published and usually followed, albeit with some randomness. Particularly on infrequently served routes, a strong incentive exists to limit waits at origin stops by studying schedules. But waits at other than origins are often, perhaps usually, also relevant. Many trips require transfers at intermediate points. There waits equal to half the headway seem plausible. Also, many trips, particularly during peak periods, involve scheduled arrival times. If work begins at 9 a.m. and the boss forbids being late, a half-hour headway with arrival at 8:35 a.m. and 9:05 a.m. involves a twenty-five minute wait at destination. To estimate accurately the waiting time component of a mass transit trip requires detailed knowledge of the trip's characteristics.

be proportional to the square root of that route's demand for service. These density economies justify substantial bus subsidies, I estimated. In addition, the structure of existing taxes on automobile use heavily subsidizes peak-period auto travel. Second-best pricing considerations therefore dictate subsidies in addition to those justified by density economies. (For a discussion on second-best pricing, see chapter 4.)

HOV Lanes

Providing a reserved lane with a volume-to-capacity ratio lower than that on the remainder of a road allows its users to travel faster. The greater the disparity between speeds on the reserved and regular lanes, the greater the incentive for regular-lane travelers to shift to HOVs. Because road space per traveler is lower for HOVs, such shifts reduce the road's overall average volume-to-capacity ratio and, hence, increases the average speed of travel on it.

To explore the benefits of reserved lanes, I developed highly simplified but still very complicated models of the commuting choices travelers with different values of travel time would make between buses and automobiles under alternative pricing, subsidy, and lane-restriction policies.[11] The first paper, published in 1979, restricted attention to service with the fifty-five-passenger fume belchers that have long provided the bulk of mass transit service in the United States. I drew four conclusions in this study. First, if marginal-cost prices could be imposed on congested roads, preferential access for HOVs would have essentially no effect on aggregate travel costs. Second, under prevailing traffic and pricing conditions, preferential access has much to commend it. Although marginal-cost pricing could do appreciably better, reserved bus lanes could substantially reduce peak-period travel costs. Third, under the road-use conditions for which preferential access would yield substantial relief from congestion, road expansion would also yield significant net benefits. Fourth, if pouring concrete is part of the long-run best answer, then whether fifty-five-passenger buses are an efficient mode of urban travel is open to serious doubt.

Subsequently, Alan Walters argued that my having restricted attention to fifty-five-passenger buses was excessively parochial; were competitive free enterprise allowed to do the job, it would produce more frequent service

11. Mohring (1979, 1983).

with smaller buses operated by lower-wage drivers.[12] He buttressed his logic with several examples from the United Kingdom of successful competition by unsubsidized operators of minibuses with what had been monopoly service by heavily subsidized large buses.

Walters's paper induced me to incorporate into my mode-choice models minibuses whose operators received wages comparable to those of taxi drivers rather than the much higher pay that bus drivers currently receive from most publicly operated bus systems. My conclusion: incorporating minibuses into the analysis significantly altered my conclusions about bus scale economies but had little effect on my preferential access results. If the practice of grossly underpricing auto travel in urban areas is accepted as immutable, the superiority of minibuses over standard buses is substantially greater than would be the case under a marginal-cost-pricing regime. But, just as with standard buses, optimization of a minibus system in the absence of auto tolls would call for substantial subsidies. Furthermore, with both bus types, reserved bus lanes and, inferentially, other techniques for giving HOVs preferential access to road capacity can yield very substantial reductions in peak-period travel costs when constraints exist on auto tolls.

Ramp Metering

Turbulence around freeway entrance and exit ramps is a major source of the "incidents" that abruptly shift traffic-flow patterns from the lower to the upper branch of the *AVC* curve in figure 6-1. Some claim that accidents and other traffic incidents account for about 50 percent of all highway congestion.[13] Metering access to freeways reduces incident frequency in two ways. First, the queues at access ramps that normally develop with metering discourage short freeway trips. Second, metering reduces variations in expressway entry rates, thereby reducing turbulence and eliminating short-run surges in entry that could momentarily exceed freeway capacity, thereby triggering lockstep congestion. Metering expands effective freeway capacity, thereby increasing the speeds at which any given traffic volume flows. In large measure, however, it does so by substituting traveler delays in entry-ramp queues for some of the delays travelers would experience on expressways in the absence of metering. Metering is heavily used and works

12. Walters (1982).
13. Schrank, Turner, and Lomax (1993).

well in the Twin Cities of Minneapolis and St. Paul, where congestion is modest. Its usefulness in heavily congested areas is limited, however. There, the degree to which entry must be restricted to keep freeways flowing freely is so great that queues quickly grow to lengths that interfere with traffic on surface arterials. For this reason, ramp meters must be turned off in Chicago at the peaks of peak periods to prevent arterial gridlock.

Staggered Business Hours

Business firms value operating hours that coincide with those of the firms with which they deal. Yet the benefits of common hours come at a cost that individual firms probably do not take fully into account. Each firm recognizes that choosing common hours is associated with congested commuting. In deciding when to open and close, however, few consider the costs their choices impose on other firms and their employees by adding to this congestion. The U.S. and Canadian governments play so large a role in their capital cities that, long ago, they internalized the effects of their working-hour decisions by staggering work hours.[14] Do other company towns do so?

Road Expansion

Pouring concrete may well be part of an optimal policy for dealing with urban traffic congestion even with congestion pricing. But instituting congestion pricing would definitely reduce the pressures to build. Congestion pricing would provide a powerful incentive to shift travel away from the peaks of peak periods. It would therefore not only speed travel, but also reduce pressure to expand road capacity.

Congestion Pricing's Effects on Other Congestion-Reducing Techniques

How does congestion pricing fit in with the remaining currently used congestion-fighting techniques discussed above? Society employs two basic instruments to induce socially desirable behavior: Bribe people to do good; charge them for doing bad. Economists have long recognized the

---

14. Safavian and McLean (1975) provide a comprehensive empirical survey of staggered work hours, flextime, and compressed work-week programs.

greater efficiency of the latter tool; setting the price equal to marginal cost is, after all, essential for a Pareto-optimal organization of economic activity.

That economies of density exist in providing mass-transit services implies that subsidies for mass transit would be required even if marginal-cost prices prevailed in all markets. Now, however, mass transit subsidies primarily serve as bribes to lure travelers—particularly peak-period travelers—out of automobiles. These bribes have not been very successful; mass transit accounts for considerably less than 10 percent of peak-period travel in all but a few of the largest urban areas in North American. The problem: the convenience of auto travel is so great that, at its current heavily subsidized price, luring a substantial share of peak-period travelers from their autos would require negative fares of appreciable magnitude.[15] By reducing or, if extensively enough employed, eliminating peak-period auto subsidies, congestion pricing would level the mass transit–auto playing field. Charging (near) marginal-cost prices for both modes rather than heavily subsidizing both would significantly reduce peak-period travel. By shifting travel from auto to mass transit, congestion pricing would result in increased service frequency, hence shorter waits for service, hence lower *full* prices for mass transit.

HOV lanes are just as much subsidies to mass transit as are cash grants that permit lower fares and more frequent service. The two differ only in the currency used: HOV lanes subsidize with valuable travel-time savings; conventional subsidies use valuable money. Just as congestion pricing would reduce the optimal size of cash grants to mass transit, so too would pricing reduce the optimal size of time-saving grants. In a regime of full marginal-cost congestion pricing, HOV lanes would serve no useful purpose.

Not so with ramp metering. Metering currently improves traffic flow by both reducing and making more uniform the rates at which vehicles enter freeways. Both effects reduce the frequency with which traffic streams enter the backward-bending portion of figure 6-1's *AVC* schedule. With congestion pricing, money rather than time-consuming waits in queues would reduce average expressway entry rates. But even with congestion pricing, using meters to reduce very short-run variations in entry rates would improve traffic flows.

By forcing employees to recognize the full costs of their commuting decisions, congestion pricing would provide them with a much greater

---

15. Moses and Williamson (1963).

incentive than currently exists to lobby for changes in working hours. Their doing so could force firms to internalize the full costs of their working-hour decisions just as national governments have in Washington and Ottawa.

The Modest History of Congestion Pricing

What economists today term congestion pricing first entered the economics literature in the early 1920s in a famed dispute between two giants of the profession, A. C. Pigou and Frank Knight. Pigou wrote,

> Suppose there are two roads ABD and ACD both leading from A to D. If left to itself, traffic would be so distributed that the trouble involved in driving a "representative" cart along each of the two roads would be equal. But, in some circumstances, it would be possible, by shifting a few carts from route B to route C, greatly to lessen the trouble of driving those still left on B, while only slightly increasing the trouble of driving along C. In these circumstances a rightly chosen measure of differential taxation against road B would create an "artificial" situation superior to the "natural" one. But the measure of differentiation must be rightly chosen.[16]

Knight responded, in effect, that the resource misallocation Pigou addressed resulted from the absence of property rights in fixed assets, roads in this case, and that Pigou's "'artificial' situation" effectively replicates a world in which road services are provided by self-seeking individuals who buy and sell in competitive markets.[17]

Serious, extended discussion of congestion pricing in the economics literature began in the late 1950s.[18] The British Ministry of Transport undertook an extended study of the subject during the early 1960s that resulted in the seminal *Smeed Report,* which has profoundly affected thinking about congestion by economists and engineers.[19] It seems safe to assert that most professional economists regard congestion pricing as a tool whose time arrived long ago. Yet the world possesses few operating urban conges-

16. Pigou (1920: 193–4).
17. Knight (1924).
18. Works by Beckmann, McGuire, and Winsten (1956), Walters (1961), and Vickrey (1963) are particularly notable.
19. Ministry of Transport (1964).

tion-pricing schemes. Clearly, economists have not been overwhelmingly successful in communicating the virtues of congestion pricing.

"Road pricing" evokes visions of toll booths at every street corner or expressway interchange. Particularly for the short trips that predominate in urban areas, manual toll collection, where it is used, absorbs a large fraction of toll revenues and slows travel appreciably. Fortunately, alternatives to manual collection are already in use. More advanced techniques are in fairly advanced stages of development.

The world's first congestion-pricing system, Singapore's "Area Licensing Scheme" (ALS), was introduced in 1975. To cross legally a cordon line around Singapore's central business district during the peak period on weekday mornings, most vehicles were required to display on their windshields a license that cost about US$1 a day or $20 a month. Only trucks and vehicles with more than three passengers were not required to display licenses. The truck exemption was soon withdrawn; the HOV exemption ended in 1989. Monitors stationed at each of the twenty-one entry points to the central area wrote down the license numbers (they now use zoom cameras) of noncomplying vehicles. Their owners were mailed traffic tickets fining them US$18 for a first offense; several tickets could result in vehicle confiscation.

Singapore's ALS was, in some respects, incredibly successful. Its planners aimed at a 25 percent reduction in central area morning traffic; they achieved a 75 percent reduction in private vehicle travel and a 50 percent reduction in all vehicles entering the cordoned area. Indeed, if anything, Singapore overdid it: Congestion just outside the cordon line was so great that, despite free flow within it, travel times per bus or auto trip to central area destinations did not change.

At first blush, the extreme effectiveness of Singapore's program is puzzling. The country's living standards are and were high; gross domestic product per capita was about a third of that in the United States in 1975. Taxes on auto ownership were and are among the world's highest; only the most affluent Singaporeans owned private passenger vehicles. That a $1 charge could induce 75 percent of high-income Singaporeans to abandon auto commuting with fewer than four occupants is puzzling. A partial explanation: at the same time that the ALS was implemented, average parking charges in the central area were doubled and uniform hourly parking charges were changed to rates that varied with location and duration of stay. The effect of these changes on the full price of auto commuting is imperfectly known.

Singapore's ALS satisfies several of the road-pricing desiderata that the *Smeed Report* and subsequent writers have identified: The system is simple and understandable. Prices are stable and easily ascertained before a journey. Payment in advance is possible. The "equipment"—paper licenses and human observers—is reliable and, at least in Singapore, largely free from fraud and evasion. Visitors and occasional users can easily be equipped at low cost.

But the ALS did and does have shortcomings: Charges are not closely related to a traveler's use of road services; all that matters for charging is whether a vehicle crosses the cordon line during the morning peak (and, since 1989, the afternoon peak, plus, at a lower fee, the interval between). How far or in what level of congestion a vehicle travels within the central area or in reaching it is irrelevant. Only limited temporal and spatial variations in charges are possible; colors, shapes, and sizes of licenses can be varied to identify different time periods and areas, but reliable identification by human monitors dictates using only a few combinations.

Had it been instituted, the all-electronic system that Hong Kong tested during the early 1980s promised to improve on several of the Singapore ALS's limitations—those on spatial and temporal price variations, in particular. In the trial system, passage over inductive loops embedded beneath road surfaces triggered US$60 transponders mounted under vehicles to send identification codes to a central computer. There, a charge appropriate to the time and location of the code's transmission would have been added to the monthly road-use bills vehicle owners would have received. Sadly for the progress of congestion pricing, the then newly instituted, popularly elected district councils objected so vigorously to these pricing proposals that the colonial government effectively withdrew them. Most prominent among the objections was that the system could be used to identify the movements of vehicle operators and therefore invade their privacy—a concern heightened by Hong Kong's then impending takeover by the Peoples' Republic of China.

Stickers (as in Singapore), read-only tags (as in Hong Kong), and bar-code identification panels are already widely used for enforcement and automatic toll collection. The simplicity and low cost of read-only tags makes it easy to provide for visitors and occasional users. More complex and costly read-write units can store and process on-vehicle information received from a roadside communication device. Such devices could end worries of users that tolls would allow governments to keep track of their whereabouts. The higher production and installation costs of these devices would limit their availability to occasional users and visitors, however.

Apart from Singapore's ALS, I am aware of only six operating systems that might reasonably be labeled "congestion pricing." A few more are in various stages of planning and development. Others, like the system in Hong Kong, were seriously proposed but ultimately rejected. Those in operation include Singapore-like cordon-line tolls on vehicles entering the central business districts of Norway's three largest cities, only one of which varies its toll with congestion levels. The only other congestion-pricing scheme presently in operation in Europe involves a toll road connecting Paris with English Channel resort areas. Recreational travelers returning to Paris heavily congested the southbound side of this road during late afternoons on summer Sundays. The toll-road authority changed the Sunday toll from the approximate equivalent of US$6 a trip regardless of time of day to approximately US$8 during the peak travel period and US$4 during the remainder of the day. The change spread the flow of traffic much more uniformly through the day. It thereby greatly reduced peak-period congestion without appreciably affecting toll revenues.

Two congestion-pricing systems are currently operating in the United States, both in California. A recent state law allowed California's Department of Transportation (Caltrans) to contract with the California Private Transportation Company (CPTC) to construct and operate for thirty-five years four toll lanes in ten miles of the median of State Route 91, the primary link between Orange and Riverside counties south and east of Los Angeles. CPTC's prices are not regulated, but the company is subject to a rate-of-return constraint. These lanes function, in part, as a HOV facility; vehicles with more than two occupants travel free unless low profits require fees. In addition, vehicles with fewer than three occupants may pay to use the facility if equipped with smart cards, which cost about $30 to produce. The toll structure was designed to attract travelers with $13-an-hour or greater travel-time values; tolls initially varied between 25¢ in the early morning hours and $2.50 during peak periods. As demand increases, tolls are adjusted to prevent appreciable congestion in the restricted lanes; the peak-period toll is now $2.75. CPTC estimated that tolls would cover its operating costs and yield a 17–20 percent return on its $88 million investment. It does not release financial results. A few months after opening, it indicated that transponder subscriptions had substantially exceeded initial expectations. In early 1998, however, a reduced fee schedule was imposed on vehicles with more than two passengers.

In 1988 reversible HOV lanes were opened in the median strip of Interstate Highway 15 in San Diego. These lanes carried fewer travelers per lane than did the expressway's general purpose lanes. The California Legislature approved the San Diego Association of Governments' (SANDAG) request to sell some of this excess capacity to SOVs, a practice now termed converting HOV lanes into HOT lanes. Before opening the HOV lanes to SOVs, on what it announced to be a trial basis, SANDAG offered at $50— first-come, first-served—the maximum number of monthly Singapore-type licenses that, it estimated, would maintain "level-of-service-A speeds." The supply was exhausted in less than a day. Conclusion: the price was too low. Announcing a price increase resulted in vehement, initially successful opposition from recipients of first-month licenses. Californians take property rights in below-market prices for government-provided services very seriously.

SANDAG aims ultimately to control SOV access to HOV lanes electronically. Real-time monitoring of available capacity would allow real-time specification of tolls designed to maximize HOV-lane use subject to a service level constraint. Although CPTC's equipment can make and announce instantaneous toll changes on SR91, it has chosen not to use this facility. Accidents and randomness in travel patterns are inevitable. This being the case, maintaining a fixed service level requires variable prices; with fixed prices, variable service is inevitable. When, in its preopening marketing research, CPTC offered focus groups a choice between exactly predictable service and exactly predictable prices, the latter was the overwhelming choice.

Alas, congestion pricing proposals are more often vanquished than victorious. To cite just one example, for at least a decade, California highway authorities lamented heavy peak-period congestion on the San Francisco–Oakland Bay Bridge at its effective round-trip toll of $1. Stop-and-go driving at its entry points contributes significantly to air pollution and wastes enormous amounts of travel time. Bay Area residents consistently rank transportation as their most important problem. The area's five counties have each voted 1 percent sales taxes to fund transportation improvements. The California legislature passed a measure in 1988 calling for an areawide vote on whether to raise tolls on all area bridges by $1 to finance a variety of bridge and approach improvements and to devote 90 percent of bridge tolls to transit improvements. Nearly three-fourths of the voters endorsed this proposal.

The Intermodal Surface Transportation Efficiency Act of 1991 provided a further incentive to employ pricing solutions to Bay Area bridge congestion. The federal law authorized grants to communities for congestion-pricing demonstrations. Of the few communities that applied, most were interested in introducing HOT lanes on freeways, projects that at the time the U.S. Department of Transportation regarded as either immoral or insufficiently ambitious. The one application that was approved in the first round was to the Bay Area's Metropolitan Transportation Commission (MTC) and Caltrans to introduce congestion pricing on the Oakland-Bay Bridge. They devoted the grant's first-year funds to a study aimed at demonstrating what is probably impossible to demonstrate: that, regardless of what is done with toll revenues, pricing would benefit *all* bridge users. The pricing plan that the MTC and CalTrans ultimately decided upon required action by the state legislature to change bridge tolls. No legislator would sponsor such a measure. The Bay Bridge round-trip toll is still $1.

Why have congestion-pricing proposals had such few successes? The demand schedule labeled "Bangkok?" in figure 6-1 suggests the possibility that congestion pricing could result in more trips at lower *full* prices and toll revenues to boot; truly a win-win situation. But there is serious doubt that a stable "Bangkok?" equilibrium could exist. From a road-use equilibrium at a point like *I* in figure 6-1, the speed-increasing effects of congestion tolls would result in the toll imposed on each user exceeding its cost to the user. The immediate effect of congestion tolls, however, would be to make most of those who pay them worse off. To claim the contrary—taxing you will make you better off regardless of what is done with the revenue—is the Laffer curve upside-down. Contemporary citizens dislike taxes and distrust governments. Unless (a) urban travelers can be persuaded that Bangkok-type equilibrium prevails during peak periods or (b) losers can somehow be reimbursed from toll revenues in a fashion that does not distort their travel behavior appreciably away from the with-toll optimum or (c) a detailed toll-revenue-expenditure program can be found that a substantial majority agrees justifies paying tolls, congestion-pricing packages will continue to be a very hard sell.

Benefits and Costs of Congestion Pricing in the Twin Cities

The Twin Cities Metropolitan Area employs most of the congestion-reducing techniques just described. Metering entry at freeway access ramps during peak periods is almost universal. HOV use is encouraged by

Table 6-1. *1990 Peak Hour Travel Conditions*

Conditions	a.m. Peak	p.m. Peak
Trips	518,100	678,100
Vehicle miles	5,071,600	5,590,200
Travel time (hours)	152,000	164,200
Travel-time cost (dollars)	1,900,000	2,052,500
Total gap (dollars)	1,049,500	949,600
Gap/travel-time cost (percent)	55.2	46.3

Source: Author's calculations, based on the 1990 Travel Behavior Inventory.

allowing them to bypass queues of SOVs at a growing number of entry ramps and by giving them reserved "diamond lanes" on two freeways and heavily subsidized parking at the Minneapolis central business district end of one expressway. However, widespread opposition to publicly provided "Lexus lanes" has postponed—perhaps permanently—plans to convert one HOV lane into a HOT lane.

How would this system's performance compare to that of collecting from each vehicle—HOV or SOV—an amount equal to the costs it imposes on all other vehicles by adding to the level of congestion? David Anderson, a former advisee of mine, and I searched for answers to this question by working with packages of computer programs that transportation planners use to predict traffic patterns on road networks. Our analysis relies on data from the 1990 Travel Behavior Inventory (TBI) of the Twin Cities area, a survey in June–November 1990 of 9,746 households, which took a total of approximately 98,000 daily trips. Survey trip data were expanded using cordon-line counts and Census of Population data to reflect private vehicle travel in the entire metropolitan area on the average 1990 weekday. The results reported here deal mainly with those trips that were on the road at some point during the morning peak travel hour, 6:45–7:45 a.m. Each trip studied originated in one of the 1,200 traffic-analysis zones into which planners have divided the metropolitan area and terminated in one of the other zones; congestion is generally not significant for intrazonal trips. Table 6-1 contains data on 1990 peak-hour travel conditions. It suggests that the average peak-hour trip imposes costs on other travelers equal to roughly half of the cost directly experienced by those taking the average trip.

The network studied is composed of the 20,336 road links on each of which more than 1,000 trips were taken on an average weekday. These "coded" links connect 7,363 intersections, or "nodes." Examples of links include several-block stretches of an arterial or collector street and, on expressways, an access ramp, HOV lane, or one-way segment between two interchanges. TBI surveys obtain origin and destination addresses for each trip but not the route taken. The parts of the traffic-analysis programs on which Anderson and I rely most intensively rest on the assumption that each traveler selects that route—a series of links—for each trip that minimizes the trip's "impedance." *Average* travel time is the usual measure of impedance, but a variety of other measures could be used, *marginal* travel time, in particular. The analysis programs "load" trips onto the network using an iterative process that reaches an equilibrium in which no traveler is able to find a route with less impedance.

Peak-period travel does not take place at a constant rate but, rather, gradually increases to a peak, then decreases. Someone traveling at the peak of the peak period is more likely to experience the backward-bending portion of curve *AVC* in figure 6-1 than is someone who travels at the beginning or end of the peak. Still, both peak-of-the-peak and fringe-of-the-peak travelers almost always get where they are going; peak-of-the-peak trips just take longer. For this reason and because the computer packages cannot handle figure 6-1's backward-bending cost curves, Anderson and I work with a monotonically increasing relationship between traffic volume and travel time per trip. The difficulties of working with continuously changing traffic flows force us to suppose trips to be distributed uniformly through the periods under analysis.

The usual default measure of travel time for some link, call it link i, is what the manual for one computer package terms "the historic standard Bureau of Public Roads capacity restraint formula." Using it, the time required to traverse link i, t_i, is

$$(6\text{-}1) \qquad t_i = t_{i0}[1 + 0.15(T_i/K_i)^4],$$

where T_i is the rate at which vehicles travel on link i, K_i is a measure of the link's capacity, and t_{i0} is the time required to traverse link i when no other trips are being taken on it. This relationship underlies the cost curves in figure 6-3. If equation 6-1 gives travel time per trip on link i, the total travel time, τ_i, expended by those who travel on it during an hour can be found by multiplying equation 6-1 through by T_i:

$$(6\text{-}2) \qquad \tau_i = T_i t_i = T_i t_{i0}[1 + 0.15(T_i/K_i)^4].$$

Marginal travel time—the change in total travel time when an additional traveler is added to the traffic stream—can therefore be written

$$(6\text{-}3) \qquad \partial \tau / \partial T_i = t_{i0} \, [1 + 0.75(T_i/K_i)^4].$$

Travel time is assumed to be the only cost of trips that travelers bear directly; sensitivity analyses indicate that incorporating vehicle operating costs would not appreciably affect the results reported here. The difference between equations 6-3 and 6-1—marginal travel time *minus* average travel time on link *i*—multiplied by the average value of travel time is the cost an additional traveler imposes on all other travelers by adding to congestion on the link.

Most of the foregoing discussion implicitly assumes three things: that travelers know with certainty the time required for regularly taken trips; that this time does not vary from day to day; and that their travel time values are independent of their trips' purposes, the congestion levels experienced, and the mode of transport—car or mass transit. In fact, trip durations vary with weather and traffic conditions. The day-to-day variance of durations increases with the average level of congestion. Evidence is strong that time spent walking and waiting is more costly than time in transit, that commuting time is more costly than time spent in other travel activities, and that travelers differ in their relative valuations of auto and mass-transit travel times.

Two recent studies, one by Calfee and Winston, the other by Small and others, examine these multidimensional aspects of travel time.[20] Both studies conclude that congested travel time is more costly than uncongested travel time. Both find that, as fractions of income, the average value of travel time decreases (and its standard deviation increases) with increases in income. Small and others also incorporate "scheduling variables" into their analysis. These are the probability of being late and the averages of time early (when early) and time late (when late). Including travel time variability in models that incorporate these scheduling variables adds nothing to their predictive abilities.

The inferences I draw from these studies are that well-off travelers enjoy or find productive driving their climate-controlled BMWs with state-of-the-art stereo systems and cellular phones but dislike the scheduling problems that the uncertain durations of congested trips impose. Un-

---

20. Calfee and Winston (1998); Small and others (1997).

fortunately, the TBI provides no information from which travel time variability can be inferred; the cost of travel time must be treated as one-dimensional.

Since the 1960s some thirty to forty studies that estimate unidimensional values of travel time have appeared in the economics literature. Unlike the multidimensional studies by Calfee and Winston and Small and others, these estimates of average community-wide values of travel time tend to be greater fractions of average wages in high- than in low-wage communities. Studies that differentiate among income groups tend to find ratios of time values to income that increase with income. These conclusions are broadly consistent with Lisco, who found that at mid-1960s price levels, a sample of suburban Chicago commuters valued travel time at $2.50 to $2.70 an hour on average.[21] He also found that, given equal commuting times, these commuters were willing to pay $1.50 to $2.50 extra to ride in their cars rather than to use mass transit. Lisco was unable to estimate directly the way in which values of time and comfort vary with income. He regarded as the "most plausible" way to allocate the income effect between comfort and time a procedure that gave a zero value of time to households with no income. This allocation resulted in a travel-time value that, as a fraction of income, increased roughly linearly from zero at zero income to about 50 percent at an annual income of about $35,000 (translated into present-day price levels). Above that income amount, the ratio of time value to income held steady at about 50 percent.

These findings have led me to assign travel-time values equal to 50 percent of income to households with annual incomes greater than $35,000. Those with yearly incomes less than $35,000 are assigned values of travel time as a fraction of income, V/I, that increases linearly from zero at zero income to 50 percent at income of $35,000. This procedure implies that someone who earns $40,000 by working 2,000 hours a year at $20 an hour is willing, on average, to pay $10 to save an hour of travel time. Those who earn $17,500 a year—$8.75 an hour—are, on average, willing to pay only a quarter of their hourly income—$2.19—to save an hour of travel time. Applying the Lisco income/travel-time relationship to the TBI menu of trips yields a morning peak-hour average of about $12.50 per private-passenger-vehicle hour. The results reported in figure 6-3 and tables 6-2 and 6-3 apply this $12.50 value to each trip. The travel-time value associated with each trip taker's income is used in the calculations underlying the

21. Lisco (1967).

Table 6-2. *Distribution of Current Gaps between Traveler-Borne Costs and Marginal Costs of Travel During the Morning Peak Hour on the Twin Cities Road Network*

	All coded road links			Expressways only		
Gap/mile (cents)	Miles of road	Vehicle miles	Aggregate gaps (dollars)	Miles of expressway	Vehicle miles	Aggregate gaps (dollars)
0–2.5	7,644	1,742,600	8,900	298	433,400	3,300
2.5–5.0	400	399,200	14,700	53	165,800	6,300
5.0–25	892	1,364,100	185,100	154	718,000	102,100
25–50	348	709,100	255,300	64	364,600	131,800
More than 50	392	939,700	992,700	74	473,700	376,700
Total	9,676	5,154,700	1,456,700	643	2,155,500	620,200

Source: Author's calculations.

remaining tables. Multiplying $12.50 by the difference for link i between equations 6-3 and 6-1—marginal travel time *minus* average travel time—gives what I term the "gap" for that link:

$$Gap = \$12.50 \cdot t_{i0} \cdot 0.6 \cdot (T_i/K_i)^4 = \$7.50 \cdot t_{i0} \cdot (T_i/K_i)$$

If the number of trips taken were independent of the price charged for them, the gap would be close to the appropriate congestion toll for link i. "Close," not "equal": the existing equilibrium is one in which the same *average* travel time prevails along all routes used between each origin-destination (OD) pair. Equality of *average* travel time among the routes used for an OD pair does not guarantee equality of *marginal* travel times. By yielding equal *marginal* travel costs along the routes used between each OD pair, congestion pricing would reduce aggregate travel costs even with a completely inelastic travel demand.

But imposing tolls would almost certainly lead to reduced travel and, hence, reduced congestion. Therefore, I use "toll" to refer only to monetary charges exacted from travelers, and "gap" to refer to $12.50 times the difference between equations 6-3 and 6-1 for roads on which vehicle congestion tolls are not imposed. To emphasize, the gap on link i is the cost a link i traveler imposes on other link i travelers *when congestion tolls are not charged on link* i.

Table 6-2 summarizes morning peak-hour gaps in the Twin Cities. On 7,644 miles of the 9,676-mile coded road network and 298 of the 643 miles of expressway, the congestion cost each vehicle imposes on all others amounts to less than 2.5¢ a vehicle mile—roughly the price fuel taxes impose. At the opposite extreme, on 392 miles of all coded links and 74 miles of expressway, gaps between directly borne and marginal costs of a vehicle mile exceed 50¢. The aggregate daily gap is nearly $1.5 million on the entire network and more than $600,000 on its expressway component.

Imposing Tolls on All Congested Roads

Figure 6-3 summarizes on one very crowded page the results of our work, which ignores income-group differences in travel behavior. If, during the morning peak hour, the occupants of each vehicle on the road network value their travel time at $12.50 an hour, the average time cost drivers incur directly is 37¢ a vehicle mile, whereas the "gap" between these directly experienced costs and the full marginal costs of their trips averages 26¢ a vehicle mile. Thus, on average, drivers' directly experienced time costs account for nearly 60 percent of the full costs to society of their morning peak-hour trips. On the most congested ten-mile stretch of freeway, the gap is 62¢ a vehicle mile, and on a few scattered road links, it exceeds $5 a mile.

Suppose that the full-price elasticity of demand is –1.0—that is, that a 1 percent increase in the full price of trips leads to a 1 percent reduction in the rate at which they are taken—and that advanced electronics could collect tolls from vehicle operators without delays or, for the moment, capital or operating costs.[22] It would then be efficient to impose marginal-cost tolls on all congested roads whether they be freeways, arterials, or collectors. With "congested" defined as experiencing congestion-delay costs greater than the 2.5¢ a mile or so that fuel taxes impose on auto travelers, about 2,000 of a total of about 9,700 miles of road in the Twin Cities are "congested" during the morning peak hour. Putting tolls on all of these roads would reduce traffic volumes by about 12 percent on average and by about 25 percent on the most heavily congested stretches of freeway. On these heavily congested stretches, congestion tolls would average about 21¢ a vehicle mile. On the average road, tolls would be about 9¢ a mile.

As figure 6-3 suggests, the direct effect of congestion tolls would be to make the average road user worse off. Almost all would pay more for the

22. At first glance, an elasticity of –1 may seem high; elasticities reported in the literature range roughly between –0.1 and –0.6. But these are dollar-cost elasticities, not full-price elasticities. Applying a general principle, (full-price elasticity) times (dollar-cost)/(full price) = (dollar-cost elasticity). Recent surveys of elasticity values include Goodwin (1992) and Oum, Waters, and Yong (1992).

Figure 6-3. *Morning Peak-Hour Congestion Costs, Tolls, and Traffic Reductions: Full-price Elasticity = −1, All Congested Roads Tolled*
Dollars per mile

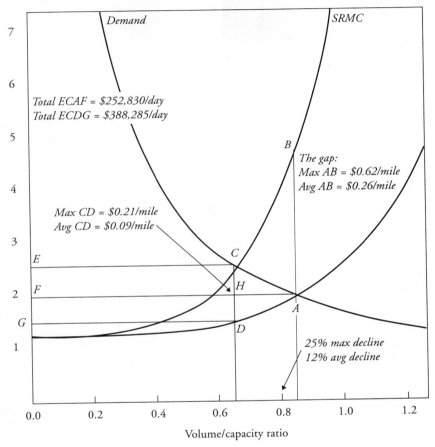

Source: Authors' calculations.

trips they continue to take and would no longer take some trips that formerly yielded net benefits. Although all travelers would benefit from faster trips, toll payments would exceed the value of these time savings for most. Only two small groups would gain from congestion pricing regardless of how toll revenues are used: current mass transit users, and high-income auto travelers. Mass transit users would benefit from the more frequent service generated by toll-induced diversion of travelers from auto to bus and, at least on freeways, from faster travel times. On the most congested roads, auto users with incomes greater than about $80,000 a year would gain more from travel-time savings than they would lose in the tolls they pay. On less congested roads, only travelers with incomes well into the six-figure range would gain more in time savings than they lose in tolls.

For the morning peak hour, total toll collections (area $ECDG$ in figure 6-3) would be about $390,000 each weekday. Collections for an entire day would be about $1.5 million. Tolls would impose costs (area $ECAF$) of about $250,000 on those who forgo trips (area CHA) and those who continue to travel despite the tolls (area $ECHF$). This latter area equals the difference between the tolls continuing travelers pay and the value of the time they save. Thus, during the morning peak hour, congestion pricing would generate $1.54 of revenue for each dollar of cost borne by travelers ($390,000 divided by $250,000). Informal reports from California's SR91 tollway indicate collection costs on its very simple system to be less than 10 percent of its revenues. Other estimates of electronic toll-collection costs are higher but still only a modest fraction of toll revenues. In principle, anyway, a scheme for redistributing this loot that would make everyone better off should be possible. Sadly to say, such a scheme has yet to be devised.

Table 6-3 summarizes the effects of tolls on travel rates and costs, on revenue and efficiency gains, and on consumer-surplus losses. Note that tolls would produce efficiency gains even if demand is completely inelastic. They would do so by reducing or eliminating differences in the marginal costs of travel along the routes used in equilibrium to travel between each origin-destination pair. Note also that imposing tolls only on expressways at 25 percent of the difference between the marginal and average costs of trips on them would cut surplus losses by 85–91 percent but would generate efficiency gains equal to 25–30 percent of those from placing tolls on all congested roads.

Imposing Tolls Only on Limited Access Roads

That even electronic toll collection is costly implies that putting tolls on lightly congested roads would be inefficient. Indeed, at current congestion levels, transactions costs may be so great that placing tolls only on limited access roads would be optimal. On them, only exit and access ramps must be monitored. Also, because most of the capital costs of monitoring

Table 6-3. *Present and Toll Equilibria for Morning Peak Hour on the Twin Cities Road Network*

(dollars unless otherwise specified)

Conditions	No tolls	Elasticity		
		0.0	*–0.5*	*–1.0*
Tolls on all roads				
Trips (number)	518,100	518,100	478,100	460,000
Travel time cost	1,900,000	1,833,800	1,600,000	1,498,800
Toll revenue	. . .	672,800	406,800	323,500
Lost surplus	. . .	620,300	313,100	218,600
Efficiency gains	. . .	52,400	93,600	104,900
Tolls on expressways[a] *only*				
Trips (number)	. . .	518,100	513,400	510,500
Travel time cost	. . .	1,882,500	1,846,300	1,825,000
Toll revenue	. . .	69,800	66,100	63,700
Lost surplus	. . .	55,500	39,400	31,700
Efficiency gains	. . .	14,300	26,700	32,000

Source: Author's calculations.

a. When tolls are imposed only on expressways, link tolls equal 25 percent of the difference between average and marginal trip costs.

are independent of traffic levels, the more heavily traveled a road, the greater would be its gross returns per dollar of monitoring costs. Limited access roads are more heavily traveled than most other roads; in the Twin Cities, they account for less than 7 percent of total roadway mileage but 42 percent of peak-hour vehicle miles.

If congestion pricing is applied just to part of a network, charging users of the tolled portion close to the costs they impose on each other would excessively divert traffic to the untolled portion. In the Twin Cities, tolling just freeways at the full cost users impose on each other would divert so much traffic to untolled arterials that the aggregate resource costs of travel on the entire network would be substantially greater than with no tolls.

The literature on Ramsey-rule pricing provides the principles needed to construct constrained-optimal tolls for a subset of a network's congested roads.[23] Programming these principles has been difficult. Thus far, Ander-

23. For discussion of Ramsey-rule pricing, see chapter 4.

son and I have restricted attention to setting charges on each tolled link equal to the same fraction of the difference between that link's marginal and average congestion costs. In the Twin Cities, aggregate benefits do not vary greatly for fractions in the 20 to 40 percent range. With inelastic demand, imposing tolls on each expressway link at one-fourth of the difference between marginal and directly borne travel costs (again, the "gap" for short) turns out to be optimal for the morning peak hour and nearly optimal for the afternoon peak. A 25 percent fraction yields significant efficiency gains regardless of the elasticity of demand. Daily gains are approximately $25,000 with totally inelastic demand and increase with demand elasticity. During the morning peak, gains for all demand elasticities tested equal about 30 percent of those when tolls are placed on all roads. These gains mainly result from the more efficient route choice that pricing induces; total travel falls by less than 1 percent with a –0.5 demand elasticity.

The bottom half of table 6-3 summarizes these results. They suggest that imposing tolls only on limited access roads would be more acceptable politically than putting tolls on all congested roads. A toll equal to 25 percent of the gap yields consumer losses and toll revenues that are respectively about 9–15 percent and 10–20 percent of those when all roads are tolled. The average toll would be only 3.5¢ per freeway mile driven. Toll revenue is insensitive to the elasticity of demand; for elasticities in the 0 to –1 range, weekly revenue would range between $60,000 and $70,000 for the morning peak period, and between $55,000 and $62,000 for the afternoon peak.

Taking Value-of-Time Differences into Account

One of the computer packages Anderson and I use, Emme/2, allows different income groups to respond differently to any given menu of tolls. The iterative process involved in finding an equilibrium distribution of trips is time consuming. Although the 1990 Travel Behavior Inventory distinguished eight income classes, we have thus far collapsed them into four groups. Even then, finding an equilibrium takes about two days on a reasonably fast Pentium computer. Table 6-4 gives some details on these income groups and on their travel patterns.

Tables 6-5, 6-6, and 6-7 give different perspectives on the effects on these groups of placing tolls on all roads as well as only on freeways. Note from table 6-5 that, with totally inelastic peak-hour travel, low income travelers would have the worst of all worlds. Seeking uncongested routes to

Table 6-4. *Data on Morning Peak-Hour Travel on the Twin Cities Road Network, by Income Group*

Income bracket	Average annual household income ($)	Fraction of all households (%)	Travel-time value ($/hour)	Number of trips	Time cost ($)
Less than $35,000	25,900	36.8	5.40	104,900	161,800
$35,000–55,000	44,900	28.8	11.25	213,400	724,500
$55,000–75,000	65,000	16.2	16.25	117,400	584,700
More than $75,000	87,520	18.2	21.88	82,300	563,700
Total	. . .	100.0	12.88	518,000	2,034,700

Source: Author's calculations.

Table 6-5. *Morning Peak-Hour Travel on the Twin Cities Road Network by Four Income Groups and Their Responses to Tolls*
(dollars unless otherwise specified)

Time-value group	Number of trips taken	Time cost	Tolls paid	Total time + toll costs
With no tolls				
Low	104,994	161,819	. . .	. . .
Medium-low	213,391	724,475	. . .	. . .
Medium-high	117,429	584,690	. . .	. . .
High	82,262	563,737	. . .	. . .
All	518,076	2,034,721	. . .	. . .
All roads tolled, inelastic demand				
Low	104,994	178,351	138,395	316,746
Medium-low	213,391	703,560	384,710	1,088,270
Medium-high	117,429	545,124	241,240	786,364
High	82,262	521,735	175,551	697,286
All	518,076	1,944,770	939,896	2,884,666
All roads tolled, −1 full-price elasticity of demand				
Low	80,375	117,227	44,956	162,183
Medium-low	185,544	554,982	171,162	726,144
Medium-high	107,720	463,613	121,520	585,133
High	78,511	467,996	96,203	564,199
All	452,150	1,603,818	433,841	2,037,659

Source: Author's calculations.

Table 6-6. *Effects of Tolls on the Four Income Classes during the Morning Peak on the Twin Cities Road Network*

(dollars)

Income group	Elasticity: 0			Elasticity: −1		
	Time cost	Toll	Lost surplus	Time cost	Toll	Lost surplus
Aggregate effects with tolls on all roads						
Low	178,400	138,400	150,900	117,200	45,000	54,000
Medium-low	703,600	384,700	363,800	555,000	171,200	124,000
Medium-high	545,100	241,200	201,700	463,600	121,500	58,400
High	521,700	175,600	133,500	468,000	96,200	27,200
Per trip effects with tolls on all roads						
Low	. . .	1.32	1.44	. . .	0.56	0.52
Medium-low	. . .	1.80	1.70	. . .	0.92	0.58
Medium-high	. . .	2.05	1.72	. . .	1.13	0.50
High	. . .	2.13	1.62	. . .	1.23	0.33
Aggregate effects with tolls only on expressways[a]						
Low	168,500	8,100	14,700	156,700	7,300	9,300
Medium-low	718,700	45,800	40,000	694,300	40,000	18,200
Medium-high	571,600	36,000	23,000	559,300	33,500	5,800
High	548,600	27,200	12,100	542,000	25,800	0
Per trip effects with tolls only on expressways[a]						
Low	. . .	0.08	0.14	. . .	0.07	0.09
Medium-low	. . .	0.21	0.19	. . .	0.19	0.09
Medium-high	. . .	0.31	0.20	. . .	0.29	0.05
High	. . .	0.33	0.15	. . .	0.31	0.00

Source: Author's calculations.
a. Tolls set at 25 percent of "gap."

avoid tolls would make their trips so circuitous that they would be burdened not only by tolls, but also by spending more time on the road than they would in the absence of tolls; their time plus money costs of travel would almost double. In the inelastic demand case, congestion pricing would increase their travel costs by 96 percent, compared with 24 percent for the high-income group and 42 percent for all travelers. With a −1.0 full-price elasticity of demand, their surplus loss would equal 34 percent of the total costs of their trips before the toll was paid. The corresponding fractions are 5 percent for the high-income group and 13 percent for all travelers.

Table 6-7. *Effect of Tolls, by Income Group, During the Morning Peak on the Time and Distance Traveled on the Twin Cities Road Network and on Aggregate Differences between Marginal and Average Congestion Costs*

Time-value group	Time spent traveling (hours)		Vehicle miles traveled		Aggregate marginal less average costs ($)	
	Expressway	Other	Expressway	Other	Expressway	Other
With no tolls						
Low	10,700	19,500	423,000	572,000	118,100	135,500
Medium-low	23,600	41,300	919,000	1,214,000	282,800	330,500
Medium-high	14,300	21,900	512,000	636,000	179,300	190,500
High	10,700	15,200	420,000	437,000	132,400	134,200
All	59,300	97,900	2,274,000	2,859,000	712,600	790,700
Tolls on all roads, −1 full-price elasticity of demand						
Low	4,400	17,300	208,000	552,000	12,400	32,600
Medium-low	15,500	34,100	711,000	1,111,000	70,700	100,500
Medium-high	11,300	17,500	512,000	567,000	59,100	62,400
High	9,200	12,400	420,000	397,000	48,600	47,600
All	40,400	81,300	1,851,000	2,627,000	190,700	243,100
Tolls only on expressways,ᵃ −1 full-price elasticity of demand						
Low	5,600	23,200	245,000	684,000	29,000	157,000
Medium-low	19,600	42,400	819,000	1,245,000	160,000	342,900
Medium-high	14,100	20,600	576,000	600,000	134,000	187,900
High	11,200	13,900	460,000	402,000	103,300	125,500
All	50,500	100,100	2,100,000	2,931,000	426,300	812,300

Source: Author's calculations
a. Tolls on each expressway link equal 25 percent of the difference between marginal and average trip costs.

Table 6-6 indicates that travel-time savings partially compensate the three higher-income groups for the tolls they pay; for them, tolls paid are appreciably greater than lost surpluses. For the lowest-income group, however, tolls are less than lost surplus, even with elastic demands; increased circuity increases both the dollar and the time costs of their trips.

Obviously, imposing tolls only on freeways would shift traffic from them to surface roads. Perhaps surprisingly, marginal-cost congestion pricing on all congested roads would also reduce freeway traffic by more than it would reduce arterial traffic. Putting tolls on all congested roads would reduce expressway vehicle miles by 19 percent and nonexpressway vehicle miles by 8 percent in the elastic demand case. With tolls only on freeways and set at 25 percent of the difference between marginal and average congestion costs, expressway vehicle miles would decline by 8 percent, while arterial travel would increase by 3 percent.

Unresolved Issues

In a nutshell, introducing congestion pricing to an urban road network would substantially increase the efficiency with which it operates. But many problems must be solved to ensure that congestion pricing could make (almost) everyone better off.

Income Distributional Problems

Unless figure 6-1's Bangkok equilibrium prevails, the immediate effect of road pricing would be to make worse off most of those who pay tolls and those who no longer use the road network because of the tolls. This welfare effect would be regressive; damages—both proportional and absolute— would be inversely related to the incomes of those affected. Its efficiency benefits imply that the toll revenue raised by congestion pricing would exceed the money value of the costs imposed on affected travelers. In principle, then, it should be possible to compensate losers *and* to have some resources left over for public purposes. Putting this principle into practice is much easier said than done, however. Unless those who pay tolls are very stupid, returning tolls to them would destroy the incentive effects of pricing. Returning toll revenues to each member of a group to which toll payers belong regardless of their actual travel behavior would be better, but finding such a group is not easy. Item: less than 20 percent of Twin Cities households have one or more members who travel during the morning peak hour. Returning average toll collections per toll-paying household to all households and all of the other compensation schemes that I have examined would require much more cash than congestion tolls would provide.

Are All Peak-Period Congestion Equilibria of the Non-Bangkok Type?

In Bangkok (and Athens and Mexico City and. . .) traffic seems chronically either at a dead stop or in the lockstep pattern that characterizes "hypercongestion"—the backward bending part of figure 6-1's *AVC* curve. Without worrying about stability issues, some researchers have pointed out that a system in equilibrium at *M* in figure 6-1, where the Bangkok demand schedule intersects the *AVC* curve, would be the best of all possible worlds. Shifting from a price-equals-average-cost equilibrium to a price-equals-marginal-cost equilibrium would result not only in more trips at a lower price, but also in more government revenue to boot!

Conventional economic analysis regards equilibria at points like *M* as unstable. Suppose that a road is momentarily at point *M* and that a sudden surge of traffic reduces speed. Trips demanded would then fall, causing a further reduction in speed and so forth. Demand would quickly fall to zero. Equilibrium at *M* followed by a shock that slightly increases speed would have the reverse effect—an increase in speed followed by an increase in demand and so on. In a recent manuscript, Chu and Small show that although it is frequently seen, the hypercongested portion of the *AVC* schedule is unsuitable as a supply curve for equilibrium analysis because hypercongestion occurs as a response to transient demand fluctuations. They also provide tractable models for handling such fluctuations both for one-dimensional expressways and two-dimensional street networks. In brief, they show that, sadly, congestion pricing is not a magic potion that will make everyone better off regardless of the uses to which toll revenues are put.

The Cost of Travel Time

Some thirty to forty published studies contain estimates of the amounts travelers would willingly pay to save travel time. These estimates differ substantially. In distinguishing between distaste for expected travel time and variability in travel time, Calfee and Winston and Small and others conclude that travel-time values are modest fractions of income and that these fractions diminish with increases in income.[24] Reductions in the variability of travel time, however, are valued at fractions of income that increase with income. Most studies have not distinguished between values of expected travel time and values of travel-time variability. Studies that take into account only expected travel time have generally derived travel-time values that are larger fractions of income and that increase with income levels. Optimal congestion tolls, revenues, and benefits from road expan-

24. Calfee and Winston (1998); Small and others (1997).

sion would be much smaller with multidimensional time values than with time values based solely on expected travel times.

Sadly to say, little is known about what travelers are willing to pay to save travel time. The little that is known applies almost entirely to the values wage earners attach to choosing between auto and mass transit for commuting journeys. What wage earners are willing to pay to save time on nonwork trips is virtually a mystery, as is the relationship between the incomes of income-earning members of households and the amounts that non-income-earning members are willing to pay to save travel time. Such information is essential in planning optimal road networks and prices for their use.

The Daily Ebb and Flow of Urban Travel

Contrary to the assumption of much urban transport research, including Anderson's and my Twin Cities analyses, weekday urban travel does not vary discontinuously between steady flows at respectively high and low levels during peak and off-peak periods. Rather it gradually builds from a very low level early in the day to a morning peak, declines to a moderate mid-day level and then builds against to an afternoon peak, from which it gradually declines to the low level of early morning hours. When capacity is added to a traffic network, congestion at the peaks of peak periods changes little; the capacity increment primarily affects duration of the peak, not its severity.

In one of many seminal papers, William Vickrey tells a simple parable that accounts for these phenomena.[25] Vickrey supposes a population whose members each place the same nonnegative values on different travel-related activities: one value (v_1) on time at home, a second (v_2) on travel to work, and other values on time at work before it begins (v_3) and after it begins (v_4), where $v_4 > v_1 > v_3 > v_2$. Vickrey assumes that the times at which travelers' jobs begin are uniformly distributed between 8 a.m. and 9 a.m. He assumes travel time to be independent of the rate at which trips are taken—indeed, zero to avoid algebraic clutter—except at a constriction in the road, a bottleneck, with capacity so limited that everyone cannot arrive at work exactly on time. In such an environment, all commuters will adjust their departure times to maximize the total values they attach to their morning activities. If, as Vickrey assumes, all commuters attach the same values to each of these activities, in equilibrium, all would end up with the same

25. Vickrey (1969).

aggregate activity values. Time in a queue waiting to pass through the bottle-neck brings about this equality. Some leave home very early and spend little or no time in the queue but much time at their places of employment before the workday begins. Others arrange to arrive at work just on time but pay for their promptness with long waits in the queue. Still others arrive late, thereby losing highly valued work time, but are rewarded with long stays at home and short waits in the bottleneck queue.

Vickrey's parable has probably generated more subsequent research than any other single entry in his voluminous bibliography. Two collections have particularly intrigued me: Several papers by Arnott, dePalma, and Lindsey have, inter alia, introduced stochastic elements, heterogeneous commuters, discontinuously changing tolls, elastic demands, and networks into the picture.[26] Henderson has relaxed in a variety of ways Vickrey's didactically brilliant assumptions that delays occur only at bottlenecks and that home-to-bottleneck and bottleneck-to-work trips are instantaneous.[27]

Despite the voluminous effort that many have devoted to extending Vickrey's parable, many unanswered questions remain before his insight can be employed to optimize the design and pricing of urban transportation networks. A small sample: What is the best way to incorporate flow congestion into models aimed at pricing implementation? Vickrey assumed respective values of time at home, in transit, and at work before and after it begins to be 2¢, 0, 1¢, and 4¢ a minute. How do these actual values differ among commuters and travel modes? Operating from company towns, as they do, the U.S. and Canadian governments long ago internalized the costs of peak-period congestion by staggering the starting times of work at their capital-city agencies. Congestion pricing should have a qualitatively similar effect on other urban areas. What would this effect be?

Appendix: Proofs of Propositions about Traveler Behavior and the Optimal Design and Pricing of Roads

Traveler Behavior and the "Full Price" of Travel

Suppose that a household derives utility from consuming s units a week of a general purpose commodity, stuff, conveniently priced at $1 a unit. It

26. Arnott, de Palma, and Lindsay (1995).
27. Henderson (1985).

also derives utility from what happens There during each of the b trips per week it takes from Here to There and back. However, it incurs disutility from the time, $\tau = bt$, it spends traveling where t is the number of hours required for a tirp.

The household's problem, then, is to maximize its utility, $u(s,b,\tau)$, subject to its budget constraint, $I = s + Fb$, where F is the round-trip fare. Setting up the Lagrangian expression and differentiating with respect to s and b yields

(6-A1) $$z_s = u_s - \lambda = 0 \text{ and}$$

(6-A2) $$z_b = u_b + u_\tau t - \lambda F = 0$$

as first-order conditions for utility maximization where subscripts refer to partial derivatives. The ratio of the marginal *dis*utility of travel time to the marginal utility of dollars, u_τ / u_s has the dimension dollars per hour. It therefore seems reasonable to call this ratio $-V$, the money cost the household attaches to its travel time. Dividing equation 6-A2 by equation 6-A1 and rearranging terms then yields

(6-A3) $$u_b / u_s = F + Vt.$$

This relationship says that the household will equate the ratio of the marginal utility of bus trips to that of dollars with the fare plus the time cost of a trip, an expression that is commonly referred to in the economics literature as the "full price" of a trip.

The Optimal Relationship between
Congestion Tolls and Capacity Costs

If producing trips on a highway involves constant returns to scale, travel time per trip can be written as a function of the volume-capacity ratio, N/K, and the hourly cost of capacity can be written as $P_K K$, where P_K is the hourly price of a unit of capacity—depreciation, maintenance, and the interest that the funds invested in capacity could have earned if invested elsewhere. Ignoring vehicle operating costs for simplicity and denoting the average value to vehicle occupants of an hour's travel time by V, the total *variable* costs of the trips taken during an hour can be written

(6-A4) $$VC = Variable\ Costs = VNT = VNf(N/K).$$

The short-run marginal cost of a trip is

(6-A5) $\quad \partial VC/\partial N = Vf(N/K) + VNf'[\partial(N/K)/\partial N] = Vf(N/K) + Vf'N/K.$

The first term on the right of equation 6-A5 is the average time cost per trip; the second is the difference between the trip's average and marginal time costs—the cost each vehicle in the traffic stream imposes on the occupants of all other vehicles in the stream by slowing their trips. To set the price of a trip equal to its marginal cost, a toll equal to this latter amount must be charged each of the N travelers. If this were done, total toll collections would be $Vf'N^2/K$.

A plausible highway-authority objective is to select that capacity level for a highway that would minimize the *total* costs of travel on it—the time and other costs that users incur directly *plus* the cost to the authority of providing the highway's services, $P_K K$. More capacity means faster trips, but greater highway capital costs. The total cost of N trips an hour on a highway is

(6-A6) $\qquad\qquad$ *Total Costs* $= VNf(N/K) + P_K K.$

Differentiating with respect to K, setting the result equal to zero, and rearranging terms yields

(6-A7) $\qquad\qquad\qquad -Vf'N^2/K^2 + P_K = 0$

as the condition that must be satisfied by the cost-minimizing capacity level. In words, this equation says that the last dollar per hour spent to expand capacity should yield hourly user-cost savings of a dollar.

Multiplying equation 6-A7 through by K and rearranging terms yields

(6-A8) $\qquad\qquad\qquad Vf'N^2/K = P_K K.$

The right-hand side of equation 6-A8 is the hourly cost of the road's capacity. Again, from equation 6-A5, total toll collections would be $Vf'N^2/K$. But this is the left-hand side of 6-A8, the total hourly cost of the highway. Thus, given constant returns to scale, an optimally priced road that has been designed to minimize the sum of user and provider costs would generate toll revenues just sufficient to cover its provider's costs. Given constant returns to scale, optimally designed and priced roads would be exactly self-supporting.

Figure 6-1's Relationship between Travel Time per Mile and the Volume/Capacity Ratio on a Road

The relationship developed here was first suggested by Greenshields.[28] Sweeping under the rug worries about how to differentiate between drivers on any given road who would prefer to travel at 40 mph and those who would like to travel at 85 mph, a relationship commonly used by civil engineers is

Flow (in vehicles per hour) = Speed (in miles per hour)
× Density (in vehicles per mile)

Driving instruction manuals say that, for safety, the relationship between speed and density should be linear: "Stay two seconds behind the car in front of you." Suppose that the speed-density relationship *is* linear, that S^* and D^* are respectively the speed at which vehicles would travel if no one else is on the road and the density at which the road becomes a parking lot. We can then write

$$S = a + bD.$$

Using $S = S^*$ when $D = 0$ and $D = D^*$ when $S = 0$ to solve for a and b gives

(6-A9) $\qquad S = S^* - D\, S^* / D^*$ or $S / S^* = 1 - D / D^*.$

Flow on this road is maximized when $S = S^*/2$, $D = D^*/2$ and hence maximum flow is $F_{max} = D^* S^* / 4$. From equation 6-A9,

(6-A10) $\qquad F = SD^*(1 - S/S^*) = N$ and

$$F/F_{max} = 4SD^* (1 - S/S^*)/(S^*D^*) = 4S(1 - S/S^*)/S^* = F/K.$$

The traveler input for trips is time = 1/speed, not speed itself. Therefore, rewrite (6-A3) as

$$F/F_{max} \equiv N/K = 4t^*(1 - t^*/t)/t.$$

28. Greenshields (1935).

Solving for the roots of this quadratic yields

(6-A11) $t = 2t^*[1 \pm (1 - N/K)^{1/2}]/(N/K).$

In the root of equation 6-A11 that involves the lower travel time, total travel time is

$$tN = 2t^*[1 - (1 - N/K)^{1/2}]K.$$

Differentiating with respect to N gives

$$dtN/dN = t^*/(1 - N/K)^{1/2}$$

as marginal travel time per mile. Suppose that travelers all stay 1.8 seconds behind the vehicles in front of them.

$$[(60 \text{ sec/min}) \cdot (60 \text{ min/hr})]/(1.8 \text{ sec/veh}) = 2,000 \text{ veh/hr}$$

is the capacity of each road lane. At 30 mph, a vehicle travels 44 feet in a second or 79.2 feet in 1.8 seconds. If all vehicles in a traffic stream that pass a given point during some hour are evenly spaced and travel at 30 mph, they will be spread over a 30-mile stretch of road.

$$[(30 \text{ mi}) \cdot (5,280 \text{ ft/mi})]/(79.2 \text{ ft/veh}) = 2,000 \text{ veh/hr.}$$

So, if each vehicle stays 1.8 seconds behind the front of the vehicle in front of it, at capacity, they travel at 30 mph.

References

Arnott, Richard, Andre de Palma, and Robin Lindsay. 1995. "Recent Developments in the Bottleneck Model." Working Papers in Economics 305. Boston College.

Beckmann, Martin J., C. B. McGuire, and Christopher B. Winsten. 1956. *Studies in the Economics of Transportation.* Yale University Press.

Calfee, John E., and Clifford M. Winston. 1998. "The Value of Automobile Travel Time: Implications for Congestion Policy." *Journal of Public Economics* 69 (July): 83–102.

Chu, Xuehao, and Kenneth A. Small. 1996. "Hypercongestion." Working paper. University of California at Irvine, Department of Economics. December.

De Meza, David, and J. R. Gould. 1987. "Free Access versus Private Property in a Resource: Income Distributions Compared." *Journal of Political Economy* 95 (December): 1317–25.

Goodwin, P. B. 1992. "A Review of News Demand Elasticities with Special Reference to Short and Long Run Effects of Price Changes." *Journal of Transport Economics and Policy* 26 (May): 155–69.

Greenshields, Bruce D. 1935. "A Study of Traffic Capacity." *Proceedings of the Annual Meeting: Highway Research Board.* 14 (Part 1): 448–77.

Henderson, J. Vernon. 1985. *Economic Theory and the Cities,* 2d ed. Orlando: Academic Press.

Keeler, Theodore E., and Kenneth A. Small. 1977. "Optimal Peak Load Pricing, Investment, and Service Levels on Urban Expressways." *Journal of Political Economy* 85 (February): 1–25.

Knight, Frank H. 1924. "Some Fallacies in Interpretation of Social Costs." *Quarterly Journal of Economics* 38 (August): 582–606.

Kraus, Marvin. 1981. "Scale Economies Analysis for Urban Highway Networks." *Journal of Urban Economics* 9 (January): 1–22.

Lisco, Thomas. 1967. "The Value of Commuters' Travel Time: A Study in Urban Transportation." Ph.D. diss. University of Chicago, Department of Economics.

Meyer, John R., John F. Kain, and Martin Wohl. 1965. *The Urban Transportation Problem.* Harvard University Press.

Mohring, Herbert. 1972. "Optimization and Scale Economies in Urban Bus Transportation." *American Economic Review* 62 (September): 591–604.

———. 1976. *Transportation Economics.* Cambridge, Mass.: Ballinger.

———. 1979. "The Benefits of Reserved Bus Lanes, Mass Transit Subsidies, and Marginal Cost Pricing in Alleviating Traffic Congestion." In *Current Issues in Urban Economics,* edited by Peter Mieszkowski and Mahlon Strazheim, 165–95. Johns Hopkins University Press.

———. 1983. "Minibuses in Urban Transportation." *Journal of Urban Economics* 14 (November): 293–317.

Moses, Leon N., and Harold F. Williamson, Jr. 1963. "Value of Time, Choice of Mode, and the Subsidy Issue in Urban Transportation." *Journal of Political Economy* 71 (June): 247–64.

Oum, Tae Hoon, William. G. Waters, and Jong-Say Yong. 1992. "Concepts of Price Elasticities of Transport Demand and Recent Empirical Estimates." *Journal of Transport Economics and Policy* 26 (May): 135–54.

Pigou, Arthur C. 1920. *The Economics of Welfare.* London: Macmillan.

Safavian, Reza, and Keith G. McLean. 1975. "Variable Work Hours: Who Benefits?" *Traffic Engineering* 45 (March): 17–25.

Schrank, David L., Shawn M. Turner, and Timothy J. Lomax. 1993. "Estimates of Urban Roadway Congestion—1990." U.S. Department of Transportation Report FHWA/TX-90/1131-5. Texas A&M University, Texas Transportation Institute, College Station, Texas.

Small, Kenneth A., and others. 1997. "Valuation of Travel-Time Savings and Predictability in Congested Conditions for Highway User-Cost Estimation." Draft report for the National Cooperative Highway Research Program, Project 2-18(2), FY 1993. Washington, D.C.

Transportation Research Board. 1980. *Alternative Work Schedules: Impacts on Transportation.* National Cooperative Highway Research Program Synthesis of Highway Practice 73. Washington, D.C.

United Kingdom. Ministry of Transport. 1964. *Road Pricing: The Economic and Technical Possibilities.* London: Her Majesty's Stationary Office.

Verhoef, E. T., P. Nijkamp, and P. Reitfeld. 1995. "The Economics of Regulatory Parking Policies: The (Im)possibilities of Parking Policies in Traffic Regulation." *Transportation Research* 29A (March): 141–56.

Vickrey, William. 1963. "Pricing in Urban and Suburban Transportation." *American Economic Review* 53 (May, *Papers and Proceedings*): 452–65.

———. 1969. "Congestion Theory and Transport Investment." *American Economic Review* 59 (May, *Papers and Proceedings*): 251–60.

Walters, Alan A. 1961. "The Theory and Measurement of Private and Social Cost of Highway Congestion." *Econometrica* 29 (October): 676–99.

———. 1968. *The Economics of Road Use Charges.* World Bank Staff Occasional Paper 5. Johns Hopkins University Press.

———. 1982. "Externalities in Urban Buses." *Journal of Urban Economics* 11 (January): 60–72.

ARNOLD M. HOWITT
ALAN ALTSHULER

7 | The Politics of Controlling Auto Air Pollution

For more than thirty years, the United States has sought to improve regional air quality by regulating transportation-related emissions. Initiated under the Motor Vehicle Air Pollution Control Act of 1965 and expanded by three major revisions of the Clean Air Act (1970, 1977, and 1990), this regulatory program has employed three different approaches: (1) national technology mandates intended to make cars run cleaner by requiring auto manufacturers to develop effective vehicle emission control systems and oil companies to market less-polluting fuels; (2) mandates on state governments to curb motorists' auto use and keep their vehicle emission control systems in working order; and (3) requirements that transportation infrastructure investments be consistent with state commitments to meet national air quality standards.

These policies have achieved important successes. Although total vehicle mileage more than doubled between 1970 and 1995, emissions of all auto-related pollutants declined; on a vehicle-mile basis, they declined even

The authors wish to thank Mary Graham, David Harrison, David Luberoff, and James Shrouds for thoughtful comments on earlier drafts of this paper. They also appreciate research assistance provided by James Scafide, Elizabeth Moore, and Treina Fabre. The research on which this analysis is based was partially supported by the U.S. Department of Transportation and the U.S. Environmental Protection Agency, neither of which necessarily agrees with its conclusions.

more dramatically. Partly as a result of these reductions, ambient air quality in metropolitan areas has improved overall. Nonetheless, air pollution remains a heated issue in American politics. In a substantial fraction of the nation's large metropolitan areas, attainment of the national air quality standards first adopted in the early 1970s is still a major challenge. Meanwhile, the U.S. Environmental Protection Agency (EPA) has recently promulgated still more ambitious standards for ozone and particulate matter. And the United States has provisionally made international commitments to reduce greenhouse gases, produced to a great degree by automobiles.[1] So the issue of reconciling transportation with clean air objectives seems certain to remain on the political and policy agendas for quite some time.

Given this prospect, an analysis of the politics of transportation pollution control efforts since 1970 seems appropriate. Not all elements of the federal regulatory strategy for transportation have contributed equally to the positive results so far achieved. This paper focuses primarily on one major source of the differences—variations in *political and implementation feasibility*—because those factors have been critically important in shaping the uneven results of the three approaches. Some federal policies have proved controversial and ultimately unacceptable to state and local governments, while others have proved difficult to implement because of strong resistance from affected interests. The paper also considers whether the regulatory policies make sense in economic terms. Although full treatment of that topic is beyond the scope of the current paper,[2] cost-effectiveness data suggest that, at least to date, political logic has been roughly consistent with cost-effectiveness considerations.[3] The politically feasible auto technology mandates have proved quite cost-effective relative to the more controversial efforts to regulate personal behavior, with some exceptions.

1. Although the United States initialed the Kyoto treaty in December 1997, the Senate must still ratify this agreement. The treaty does not become internationally binding until ratified by at least fifty-five countries accounting for at least 55 percent of the 1990 carbon dioxide emissions of the developed countries.

2. Auto emission control regulations have been strongly criticized from a cost-benefit perspective. See, for example, Crandall and others (1986: 109–16). The Environmental Protection Agency has recently issued a major assessment; see EPA Office of Air and Radiation (1997). And economists have more generally debated the wisdom of the new standards. See Lave (1997) and Crandall (1997).

3. In reporting cost-effectiveness, we narrowly consider the dollar cost of reducing a ton of pollutant, not whether that reduction is "worth" the cost in terms of ultimate social value. That question, while significant, goes well beyond what can be treated in this paper, indeed, beyond the economics of the issue.

What explains the differences in political and implementation feasibility? The first set of policies—national mandates requiring large corporations to improve product technology—has proved easier to sustain politically and far more cost-effective in reducing transportation-related emissions than other policies. Although the auto industry has frequently argued that federal "technology-forcing" policies are too aggressively paced, too costly, or technically infeasible, and has often secured deferrals of compliance deadlines, automobiles of the 1990s emit only a small fraction of the pollutants that their predecessors of the 1960s and early 1970s did and at reasonable cost. Meanwhile, with little fanfare, oil companies have totally eliminated lead from gasoline. And new fuel mixes, marketed in specifically targeted metropolitan areas, are reducing emissions of carbon monoxide and volatile organic compounds. These mandates account for the vast majority of reductions in transportation-related emissions.

By contrast, efforts to regulate personal behavior through restrictions or economic disincentives have typically provoked intense controversy and in the end been given up as politically infeasible. This is not to say that motorists have been untouched by air pollution regulations. They have paid for improved pollution control technology when purchasing vehicles and fuel (although these product characteristics are not separately priced), and they have accommodated to requirements for the periodic inspection and maintenance of their onboard, factory-installed, pollution control systems. They have been almost entirely successful, however, in preserving their freedom to use available roads as and when they please—free not only from regulatory prohibitions but also from market disincentives.

As to the third policy approach—regulation of infrastructure investments—successive iterations of federal regulations have made transportation planners pay far more attention to air quality as an objective. The 1970 and 1977 Clean Air Act Amendments were ineffective in ensuring consistency between state transportation investments and state commitments to improve air quality. With rare exceptions, transportation agencies were able to keep environmental officials from playing a significant role in determining project and spending priorities. But these circumstances have changed somewhat in the 1990s. The Clean Air Act Amendments of 1990 embody a more realistic appreciation of how state transportation decisions are made, and the requirement that they "conform" with clean air plans is backed by a serious threat of federal fiscal penalties for failure to comply. The invigorated "conformity" requirement has greatly enhanced the attention paid to air quality objectives in metropolitan transportation planning, although it has not, to date, significantly affected state transportation investment decisions.

Impacts and Extent of Transportation-Related Air Pollution

The key transportation-related air pollutants regulated under the Clean Air Act are *ground-level ozone*, formed by the sunlight-induced chemical reaction in the atmosphere of volatile organic compounds (VOC), primarily hydrocarbons, and nitrogen oxides (NO_x), both from engine emissions and fuel evaporation;[4] *carbon monoxide* (CO) from engine exhaust; *small particulate matter* (PM) from engine exhaust, tire and brake wear, and dust kicked up by auto operations; *lead* from fuels; and *sulfur dioxide* (SO_2), overwhelmingly produced by industrial processes unrelated to transportation but also by burning high-sulfur transportation fuels.

The Clean Air Act regulates these pollutants primarily because of their effects on human health.[5]

—Ozone harms lung tissues, reduces lung function, and sensitizes lungs to other irritants, creating problems (generally reversible), not only for individuals with respiratory problems such as asthma but also for otherwise healthy people engaged in moderate exercise.

— PM also causes respiratory problems, especially to children and the elderly, and can seriously aggravate the condition of people with existing pulmonary and cardiovascular diseases or asthma.

—CO reduces the delivery of oxygen through the bloodstream, affecting those with cardiovascular disease and posing hazards even to healthy individuals at higher levels of exposure.

—Inhaled lead (as well as that ingested in food, dirt, or water) accumulates in blood, bone, and soft body tissues. Not easily excreted, it can affect the kidneys, liver, nervous system, and other organs and can cause seizures and mental retardation. Fetuses and children are especially vulnerable to damage from lead.

—Nitrogen dioxide, one type of NO_x, can irritate lungs and lower resistance to respiratory infections.

---

4. Ground-level ozone is not directly emitted by transportation sources, but its precursors, VOC and NO_x, are. This form of ozone is not to be confused with the stratospheric (or "good") ozone that partially shields the earth from solar radiation.

5. Material in this section is taken from EPA Office of Air Quality Planning and Standards (1997b: 7–42).

—SO_2 affects breathing and can aggravate existing respiratory illness and cardiovascular disease.

In addition to health impacts, ozone causes damage to crops and trees. Particulate matter carries air toxics and contributes to reduced visibility in several locales, while airborne NO_x and SO_2 deposited as acid rain in bodies of water contribute to algae growth and unhealthy conditions for fish.

Regulatory Standards

Under the Clean Air Act Amendments of 1970 and subsequent versions of the law, the EPA administrator is empowered to set allowable pollution levels for specific pollutants as necessary to protect public health. These are the primary national ambient air quality standards (NAAQS). The act requires that the standards be set exclusively on the basis of their effects on human health, permitting cost-benefit considerations, among others, to come into play only in the choice of policies to achieve the health-based standards. By statute, the EPA periodically reviews (and sometimes changes) the standards according to procedures that provide for both expert advice and extensive comment by interest groups and the public.[6] The ozone and PM standards were revised most recently in 1997.[7]

On the basis of empirical data from air quality monitoring stations, the EPA identifies geographic areas that do not meet ("attain") the NAAQS.[8] "Nonattainment" areas are required to develop plans for reducing pollu-

6. The result is a complex decisionmaking process involving science, policy analysis, and politics. See Landy, Roberts, and Thomas (1994: 49–88) for a careful case history of how the ozone standard was reassessed and changed in the late 1970s.

7. In 1971 the ozone standard was originally set on an hourly basis at 0.08 parts per million (ppm), not to be exceeded more often than once a year. In 1979 this hourly standard was revised to 0.12 ppm. In 1997 the ozone standard was tightened once again to 0.08 ppm, which, however, was to be measured as an eight-hour average not to be exceeded more often than three times a year. For particulate matter, as a result of new public health data, the standard was changed in 1987 from one originally regulating total suspended particulate matter to one focused on particulate matter smaller than 10 microns in diameter (PM_{10}). As a result of new epidemiological studies, this standard was augmented in 1997 with a new standard regulating particulate matter smaller than 2.5 microns in diameter ($PM_{2.5}$). For the new ozone and particulate matter standards, see "National Ambient Air Quality Standards for Ozone; Final Rule." *Federal Register* 62 (138, July 18, 1997): 38855—96; and "National Ambient Air Quality Standards for Particulate Matter; Final Rule." 62 *Federal Register* (138, July 18, 1997): 38651–760.

8. Current nonattainment area boundaries were set on the basis of the NAAQS in effect at the time the 1990 act was enacted. The EPA will be designating nonattainment areas under the new particulate and ozone NAAQS over the next several years.

Table 7-1. *Total Vehicle Miles Traveled and Highway Vehicle Emissions, 1970–95*

(Millions of short tons, unless noted)

Category	1970		1995		Total percent reduction 1970–95 in	
	Highway vehicles	Percent of total U.S. emissions	Highway vehicles	Percent of total U.S. emissions	Highway vehicle emissions	Highway vehicle emissions per VMT
Vehicle miles traveled, VMT (millions)	1,109,724	...	2,422,775	...	...	...
Emissions of pollutants						
Carbon monoxide	88.03	68.6	54.1	60.3	38.7	71.9
Nitrogen oxides	7.39	34.2	7.3	30.6	0.9	54.6
Volatile organic compounds	12.97	42.1	5.7	27.7	56.0	79.9
Particulate matter	...	...	13.1	48.6	...	...
Fuel-related	0.44	3.4	0.3	1.1	33.9	69.7
Fugitive dust	...	...	12.8	47.5	...	...
Lead (thousands of short tons)	171.96	77.9	< 0.01	0.5	> 99.9	> 99.9

Source: Bureau of Transportation (1996: Appendix A) for data on travel; EPA Office of Air Quality Planning and Standards (1997a: table A-1, A-2, A-3, A-5, A-6) for data on emissions. Percentages were calculated from data in the tables.

tion to allowable levels by specified statutory deadlines, which have been extended in successive revisions of the Clean Air Act.

Extent of Pollution Reductions

The United States has made substantial progress in reducing emissions of air pollutants under Clean Air Act regulations. Between 1970 and 1996, lead emissions from all sources (not transportation alone) have been reduced by more than 98 percent, CO by 31 percent, and VOC by 38 percent. Aggregate NO_x emissions, however, have increased by 8 percent, and particulate emissions are up by 137 percent.[9]

Diminished emissions have helped produce improvements in ambient air quality. As implementation of the 1990 amendments began, the EPA identified ninety-eight ozone and forty-two CO nonattainment areas. By late 1997, only fifty-nine ozone and twenty-eight CO nonattainment areas remained. The number of PM nonattainment areas—primarily rural areas and small towns—has increased from seventy to seventy-three, however, as better monitoring data has been obtained.[10] Moreover, the number of ozone and PM nonattainment areas will rise again as the tighter NAAQS established in 1997 are applied.

Transportation has contributed substantially to the reduction of emissions and the consequent improvement in ambient air quality, even though auto use has increased significantly. Athough total vehicle mileage more than doubled between 1970 and 1995, emissions of all auto-related pollutants declined on an absolute basis, as table 7-1 shows. (Only auto-related NO_x emissions have remained essentially unchanged). These reductions are even more dramatic when considered on the basis of vehicle miles traveled. Even NO_x declined 50 percent on a per-mile basis. For each type of pollutant, moreover, transportation-related emissions constituted a smaller share of aggregate national emissions in 1995 than they did in 1970.

Although the extent to which transportation-related pollutants have been reduced varies among metropolitan areas, almost every locale has felt

9. Calculated from data in EPA Office of Air Quality Planning and Standards (1997a: tables A-1, A-2, A-3, A-5, A-6, pp. A-2 to A-18 and A-23 to A-29).

10. The list of 1990 nonattainment areas can be found in Hawthorn and Meyer (1992: 27–28). The 1997 list, updated as of October 9, was taken from an EPA internet site (http://www.epa.gov/oar/oaqps/greenbk) on February 12, 1998.

Table 7-2. *Percentage Change in Transportation Emissions for Selected Major Metropolitan Areas, 1985–94*

Metro area	VOC	NO_x	CO	PM_{10}
North				
New York, northern New Jersey[a]	–32.7	–7.3	–26.2	–17.9
Chicago, Gary	–39.9	–9.5	–31.2	–18.9
Pittsburgh, Beaver Valley	–46.0	–26.1	–36.9	–31.0
Indianapolis	–20.1	3.0	–1.7	–4.9
South				
Dallas, Ft. Worth	–46.4	–17.4	–34.9	–24.7
Houston, Galveston	–41.9	–15.3	–27.5	–34.1
Miami, Ft. Lauderdale	–34.9	6.3	–14.1	–7.1
Tampa, St. Petersburg	–41.7	–1.6	–23.5	–12.6
West				
Los Angeles, Anaheim, Riverside	–31.7	–8.8	–25.9	–18.3
San Francisco, Oakland, San Jose	–30.1	–15.8	–22.2	–24.6
Seattle, Tacoma	–28.3	–8.9	–23.3	–16.8
San Diego	–34.8	–15.2	–30.4	–22.1
Portland	–28.4	–5.2	–22.7	–12.6

Source: Bureau of Transportation Statistics (1995: table 8-1). Metropolitan areas are as defined by the Bureau of the Census using 1990 census data.

a. Does not include parts of two Connecticut counties included in the 1990 census definition.

the positive results. Table 7-2 shows changes in transportation-related emissions for selected major metropolitan areas in the period 1985–94.

Technology and Product Mandates: New Cars and Fuels

The first and most important approach to reducing automotive pollution has been national technology mandates on auto manufacturers and oil companies intended to make cars run cleaner. Table 7-3 summarizes the progression of federal automobile emission standards, as actually implemented, by year and pollutant. Gasoline automobiles meeting the 1994 standards were designed to emit about 97 percent fewer hydrocarbons, 96 percent less CO, 88 percent less NO_x, and 73 percent less PM than uncontrolled vehicles of the 1960s.[11]

11. Calculated from the data presented in table 7-3.

Table 7-3. *Federal Emission Standards for Passenger Cars*

(Grams per mile)

Year	Hydro-carbons (HC)	Carbon monoxide (CO)	Nitrogen oxides (gasoline)	Nitrogen oxides (diesel)	Particulates
Uncontrolled	8.20	90.0	3.4, 4.0[a]	. . .	0.3[b], 0.5[c], 1.0[d]
1968–69	5.90	50.8	. . .	. . .	. . .
1970–71	3.90	33.3	. . .	. . .	. . .
1972	3.00	28.0	. . .	. . .	. . .
1973–74	3.00	28.0	3.1	. . .	. . .
1975–76	1.50	15.0	3.1	. . .	. . .
1977–79	1.50	15.0	2.0	. . .	. . .
1980	0.41	7.0	2.0	. . .	. . .
1981	0.41	3.4	1.0	1.0	. . .
1982–84	0.41	3.4	1.0	1.0	0.60
1990	0.41	3.4	1.0	1.0	0.20
1991	0.41	3.4	1.0	1.0	0.20
1994	0.25	3.4	0.4	1.0	0.08
2004–2006[e]	0.13	1.7	0.2	0.2	0.10

Source: For years before 1980, White (1982:15); after 1980, Bureau of Transportation Statistics (1997a:189). Standards are those actually applied to cars of the indicated model year, with the exception of 2004–2006.

a. NO_x emissions from a car controlled for HC and CO at the 1970 standards.

b. Emissions from a vehicle burning leaded gasoline; emissions from a vehicle with a catalytic converter burning unleaded gasoline are under 0.01.

c. Emissions from an uncontrolled diesel automobile.

d. Emissions from a diesel automobile controlled to meet the 1980 NO_x standard.

e. To be implemented no sooner than the 2004 model year and no later than the 2006 model year, contingent on a demonstration by EPA that further controls are needed, technically feasible, and cost-effective.

New Car Emission Standards

The Clean Air Act Amendments of 1970 marked a critical turning point in U.S. efforts to deal with transportation-related air pollution. Congress required auto manufacturers to reduce auto emissions significantly by the 1975 model year. The statutory targets were to reduce CO and hydrocarbon emissions by 90 percent from earlier federal requirements, and NO_x

emissions, previously uncontrolled, by 90 percent between 1971 and 1976.[12] This technology-forcing strategy effectively required the auto manufacturers to get catalytic converters ready for mass production and 50,000 mile useful lives within four years and to install them as standard equipment on all new passenger cars.

The auto industry stoutly resisted this aggressive pace. Ultimately, despite three one-year extensions, the industry announced it would shut down production at the beginning of the 1978 model year if the law were not revised. Galvanized by this threat, Congress overcame a multiyear legislative gridlock less than three weeks before the start of the 1978 model year.

The resulting Clean Air Act Amendments of 1977 left the hydrocarbon and CO emission standards for new cars unchanged, but extended the deadlines until 1980 and 1983, respectively. It relaxed the NO_x standard, from 10 percent to 25 percent of the 1971 level, and extended the deadline to 1982. The EPA administrator was further authorized to relax the NO_x requirement selectively until 1984 for innovative technologies that promised better fuel economy.[13]

Despite interim setbacks and continuing industry pressure for extensions, the emission characteristics of new vehicles constantly—and dramatically—improved under the 1977 amendments. As vehicles manufactured in the 1960s and early 1970s were retired, emission controls became ubiquitous in the U.S. automotive fleet.

New Rules

Notwithstanding these advances, it became clear that many metropolitan areas could not meet the NAAQS under the regulatory policies of the 1977 amendments. Because Congress and the Reagan administration could not agree on how to change the legislation, however, a new law was not enacted until the Bush administration took office. Regarding auto technology, the Clean Air Act Amendments of 1990 mandated a new round of

---

12. Congress had authorized new car emission standards, which California had begun setting earlier in the decade, in the Motor Vehicle Air Pollution Control Act of 1965; the secretary of health, education, and welfare subsequently ordered automakers to meet the California standards for carbon monoxide and hydrocarbons by 1968. See Jacoby and others (1973) and Altshuler, with Womack and Pucher (1979).

13. On these initial regulatory efforts, see especially Crandall and others (1986). See also Jacoby and others (1973); Harrison (1975); Quarles (1976); Mills and White (1978); Altshuler, with Womack and Pucher (1979); and White (1982).

vehicle emission reductions (so-called Tier I controls) by the 1994 model year. In addition, it authorized even more stringent Tier II controls on a contingency basis, to be imposed in 2004 by the EPA administrator if further studies show they are needed, technically feasible, and cost-effective.[14] Moreover, the 1990 act for the first time established standards to control evaporative emissions, namely, emissions that occur after engines are shut off.

The 1990 law, like its predecessors, had authorized California, which has the nation's worst air pollution problems, to impose even stricter vehicle emission standards. California decided to require manufacturers to achieve, in stages, fleet-weighted average emissions even lower than those mandated by the federal Tier I regulations, beginning with the 1994 model year. The state further mandated that manufacturers market a small number of zero-emission vehicles (ZEVs, effectively electric-powered cars) by 1998 and achieve a 10 percent market share for these vehicles in California by 2003.[15]

The Clean Air Act Amendments of 1990 also authorized other states voluntarily to opt for the California standards; and several northeastern states, notably Massachusetts and New York, chose to do so. Subsequently, under another provision of the 1990 act, the Ozone Transport Commission, a statutory organization representing the twelve states from Maine to Virginia and the District of Columbia, was persuaded by several of its members to petition the EPA to impose these auto technology measures on the full region, including the states that had not done so individually. Combined with California, this action would have extended the California standards to about 40 percent of the total U.S. auto market.

The industry argued vehemently that the technology was not commercially ready because current battery technology gave the vehicles too little range and because recharging infrastructure was inadequate. It proposed an alternative: to market a national low-emitting vehicle (NLEV) in forty-nine states that would meet the first two levels of the California standards (tougher than what the automakers were otherwise required to do by law), if all states other than California would abandon the remaining California requirements, especially for zero-emission vehicles. For several years, the EPA unsuccessfully sought to broker an agreement between the thirteen

---

14. The EPA has reported to Congress that additional controls are required. See EPA (1998).
15. Sperling (1991).

northeastern jurisdictions and the industry. California ultimately delayed the timing of its ZEV mandate until model year 2003. But the four northeastern states that had individually adopted the California requirements—Maine, Massachusetts, New York, and Vermont—refused to accept NLEV as a substitute, and the industry refused to produce it unless they did.[16]

In early 1998, however, competition among the "Big Three" U.S. auto manufacturers and three major Japanese companies pushed them to pledge voluntarily to market NLEV vehicles in the forty-five states that had not mandated California cars.[17] Although still opposed to tighter regulatory mandates, the auto manufacturers recognize the direction that U.S. air pollution law and international treaties on global warming are pushing. They have recently begun marketing prototype electric vehicles and hybrid gasoline-electric cars and have stepped up research on other technological alternatives to gasoline engines such as fuel cells.[18]

Fuel Standards

Federal mandates on the composition of automotive fuels have been less contentious than vehicle standards. Under the 1970 act, the EPA required oil refiners to market unleaded fuel by 1975 (necessary to avoid damage to the catalytic converters appearing on new vehicles) and to reduce gradually the lead content in all gasoline. Although the EPA temporarily suspended these rules when refiners challenged them in court, the agency's litigators prevailed in 1976. The standards were then implemented without further controversy.[19]

The 1990 act totally banned lead in gasoline effective as of 1995; by 1993 the market penetration of unleaded gasoline was 99 percent. The 1990 act also required additional measures—"oxygenated" fuel in the winter months to reduce CO emissions in certain nonattainment areas, and "reformulated" gasoline in summertime to reduce hydrocarbons—in severe and extreme ozone nonattainment areas. Even though not required to do so, some other areas have also chosen to require these fuels as elements of their clean air strategies. Oxygenated and reformulated gasoline met

16. See Scott (1997).

17. Matthew L. Wald, "Big Three to Make Cleaner Cars Than Required," *New York Times*, February 5, 1998, p. A-20.

18. See Rebecca Blumenstein, "Shifting Gears: Auto Industry Reaches Surprising Consensus: It Needs New Engines," *Wall Street Journal*, January 5, 1998, p. A-1; and Keith Bradsher, "US Auto Makers Showing Interest in Fuel Efficiency," *New York Times*, January 5, 1998, p. A-1.

19. Altshuler with Womack and Pucher (1979: 184, note 12).

minor consumer resistance in a few metropolitan areas. By and large, how-ever, they have won acceptance.

Experience with Technology and Product Mandates

Despite some differences, the politics of vehicle emission control and clean fuel regulations are extremely similar. Experience with both suggest that environmental regulation can succeed when it targets a small number of large corporations and focuses on inducing significant (but not radical or technologically infeasible) changes in product technology. When the government is seeking the universal deployment of new technology, how-ever, the process may be marked by considerable sound and fury, together with hard-nosed bargaining and litigation. Delays are often unavoidable, particularly if industry can credibly claim that the product technology has not been sufficiently perfected to satisfy consumer expectations. Elected officials, however, perceived that most voters support corporate regulation to achieve clean air targets, even if by-products include small price increases and, on occasion, slight vehicle performance degradation.

Industry leaders often argue, of course, that regulations threaten jobs, collateral objectives such as energy conservation, or inflationary price in-creases. But when regulators are trying to hasten the arrival of technologies that already exist in prototype, firms cannot simply claim that the desired improvements are unachievable at a reasonable price because competitors may in short order prove them wrong. Even with more far-reaching tech-nology mandates, as soon as one or two major competitors agree that the technology is ready for the marketplace, resistance tends to crumble. Ac-tual costs have then often proved less than anticipated as production expe-rience is acquired and scale economies are secured. After all, the regulators are guaranteeing a mass market. Since the missed deadlines under the 1970 act, moreover, Congress has generally given the EPA administrator consid-erable room for bargaining over the scope, details, and timing of regulatory requirements. In this framework, government officials can generally make accommodations between legislative purposes and industry interests.

The political logic of the policies implemented to date has proved roughly consistent with cost-effectiveness considerations.[20] As table 7-4

---

20. Thorny methodological dimensions are involved in estimating the cost-effectiveness of these measures. See McConnell, Walls, and Harrington (1995). The data cited in Krupnick (1992) and in Harrington, Walls, and McConnell (1994) represent careful efforts to compare policies intended to reduce hydrocarbon emissions by auto technology and fuel measures.

Table 7-4. *Cost-Effectiveness of Technology Measures
in Reducing Hydrocarbon Emissions*
(dollars)

Technology measures	Cost per ton of HC reduced
New auto emission standards	
1969 vs. uncontrolled	56[a]
1980–81 vs. 1977-79	3,500[a]
1994 vs. 1981	6,400[a]
Onboard refueling controls	1,100[a]
California gasoline vehicles	
TLEV	3,700–21,000[b]
LEV	2,200–27,000[b]
ULEV	4,200–41,000[b]
Alternative fuel vehicles	
Methanol	30,000–60,000[b]
Compressed natural gas	12,000–22,000[b]
Electric (ZEV)	29,000–108,000[b]
Gasoline reformulations	
11 to 9 Reid vapor pressure	500[a]
Federal standard	1,900-3,900[b]
California standard	4,100-5,100[b]
Inspection and maintenance	
EPA enhanced	4,500–$6,000[b]
Remote sensing	2,600–6,000[b]

a. Krupnick (1992); costs are stated in constant 1988 dollars
b. Harrington, Walls, and McConnell (1994); costs are not standardized.
Sources provide additional information about emission reductions, cost per unit, and sources of data.

shows, the earliest automobile emission control devices were highly cost-effective. Securing additional reductions has become progressively more expensive, in large measure because the early controls had already eliminated a high proportion of the emissions that the earlier vehicles had produced. But subsequently implemented vehicle emission control improvements, including the Tier I requirements under the 1990 amendments, have remained relatively cost-effective. Similarly, improvements in vehicle refueling systems (in the design of auto gas tanks and the pumps at service stations) and reformulations of gasoline have produced relatively cost-effective emissions reductions. By contrast, the estimates in table 7-4 for California cars and, particularly, alternative fuel vehicles, including the electric vehicles stoutly resisted by the automakers, show far higher costs per ton of hydrocarbon emissions reduced. The magnitude and wide range of cost estimates reflect the experimental nature of these vehicle types. The technologies are not mature, nor are they ripe in either cost-effectiveness or political terms.[21]

Changing Behavior: Transportation Controls and Vehicle Maintenance Requirements

A second policy approach focuses on reducing emissions by inducing motorists to reduce their vehicle use, by ensuring that they maintain onboard vehicle emission control systems in good working order, or both. Efforts to curtail motor vehicle travel have almost invariably failed in the face of political resistance. Efforts to require vehicle maintenance have been more successful, although the EPA's latest effort to rachet up the rigor of inspection and maintenance regulation has encountered opposition.

Restrictive Transportation Controls

Beginning in 1971 the EPA required the states to develop transportation control plans for their air pollution control areas (normally metropolitan regions). The plans were to be incorporated into the overall State Implementation Plans for attaining and maintaining compliance with national air quality standards. Because the 1970 act required attainment of the standards by 1975, it appeared that draconian transportation controls would be required in many areas—including measures such as parking supply restrictions, high taxes or surcharges on parking, downtown access restrictions, mandatory inspection and maintenance of auto emission control devices, and retrofit of vehicles without control equipment. But these policies proved highly controversial. State officials quickly perceived that

21. As noted earlier, these considerations do not engage the question of whether the reductions in emissions produce sufficient social benefits to warrant these regulatory measures. Many economists would argue that although the cost per unit of pollution abatement has been *rising*, the benefits of an additional unit of reduction—in human health effects, for example—have been *declining* so much that further reductions are not worth the cost. See Crandall (1997).

however much the public supported clean air legislation, it was ambivalent about or hostile to virtually all measures that would directly affect its own behavior. Consequently, despite the federal mandate, most states refused to submit transportation control plans.[22]

As required by the act, the EPA therefore developed and promulgated federal transportation control plans for nineteen major metropolitan areas in the summer of 1973. These included, however, exactly the types of policies that the states had already refused to impose on their own authority.[23] Still unwilling to commit themselves to intensely unpopular policies, the vast majority of state and local officials simply refused to implement the federal requirements.[24] Even though it had sufficient legal authority, the EPA soon realized that it had little or no organizational capacity to implement them by direct federal action. Nor did it have any reason to believe that Congress would appropriate funds for a massive expansion of federal field bureaucracies to do so.

For its part, Congress, faced simultaneously by widespread public outrage at stringent transportation controls and continued strong support for the goals of the clean air act, appeased both sentiments. It enacted amendments restricting the EPA's authority to require price disincentives (such as road-use tolls and parking surcharges) or to restrict parking at all. Key legislators also made clear (in a conference report on a bill that failed for extraneous reasons) that they intended to block the EPA if it ever sought to require gasoline rationing as part of a state plan. At the same time, Congress resisted calls to relax the standards or deadlines mandated in the act. Recognizing the evident discontinuity between congressional attitudes toward the policy and toward some methods required to carry it out, the EPA for the most part abandoned efforts to enforce the federal control plans.[25]

22. The statutory language of the 1970 Clean Air Act Amendments was permissive but very broad; it did not specifically require or authorize the types of measures that the EPA ultimately sought to impose under its aegis. See Howitt (1984), Altshuler with Womack and Pucher (1979), and Meyer and Gómez-Ibáñez (1981).

23. See Altshuler with Womack and Pucher (1979), and Suhrbier and Deakin (1988) for discussions of such control measures.

24. Commencing in October 1973, moreover, these policies became inextricably linked in the public mind with long lines at service stations, sharp increases in gas prices, and the economic recession triggered by the first (and most severe) Arab oil embargo. See Howitt (1984).

25. Altshuler with Womack and Pucher (1979); Howitt (1984).

New Legislation

The 1977 act, which extended the federal deadline for achieving national air quality standards from 1975 to 1987, was generally crafted to avoid the political problems encountered under the 1970 act. It did not place restrictions on personal travel even in the most severely polluted areas, although it permitted states to adopt restrictions if they wished. To encourage state and local cooperation, the new act required bringing elected officials more directly into the air quality planning process, provided greater opportunity for public participation, and authorized more money for planning. It also empowered the federal government to withhold most federal highway grants from any state failing to submit an acceptable air quality plan to the EPA. The political incentives facing state and local officials remained essentially unchanged, however. They believed that the public was unwilling to accept significant restrictions on auto use or economic disincentives to discourage such use. As a result, while the states did routinely submit required plans this time around, very few proposed even the mildest controls on personal travel—and fewer still implemented any.[26]

For its part, the EPA sought to avoid conflict with the states on the issue of travel demand reduction. The agency concluded, however, that annual inspection and maintenance was essential to ensure that the tailpipe controls it was requiring manufacturers to install on all new cars did not malfunction in use. The EPA's determination intensified as evidence accumulated that large numbers of motorists, concerned about degradation of auto performance, were intentionally disabling emission controls or damaging them by using leaded gasoline. The EPA applied persistent pressure on individual states to adopt inspection and maintenance programs. Such programs differed politically from other transportation controls because they did not affect everyday travel behavior and, in many cases, could be combined with regular vehicle safety inspection requirements.[27] Even so, a number of resistant states adopted inspection programs only when the federal government, invoking the sanction authorized by the 1977 act, temporarily suspended much of their highway funding.

---

26. See Horowitz (1978), Deakin (1978), National Commission on Air Quality (1981), Howitt (1983), and Yuhnke (1991).

27. In several instances, however, the auto repair shops initially opposed inspection and maintenance programs because they did not want to incur the expense of acquiring testing equipment and feared that test fees would not adequately compensate them for the expected disruption of their regular business.

The 1990 Act and ISTEA

The 1990 act, which once again extended the time frame for achieving national air quality standards, adopted a new regulatory strategy: different attainment deadlines and interim measures for different regions, depending on the current severity of their air pollution problems.[28] The law left the question of whether to adopt transportation demand measures to the discretion of state and local officials, with one major exception—mandated employer trip reduction programs in the ten most severely polluted nonattainment areas. It also required more than thirty areas with serious pollution problems to adopt an "enhanced" form of inspection and maintenance.[29] Politically, the 1990 act gave state and local decisionmakers some latitude to draw up regionally acceptable pollution-reduction plans, while holding over their heads the threat of much stronger penalties than before.[30]

The new law made two types of federal sanctions available: denial of federal highway aid; and the imposition of stricter new-source offset requirements. (These are requirements that any emissions generated by new pollution-generating facilities be offset by reductions elsewhere in the same nonattainment area.) It also gave the EPA much more latitude in deciding when sanctions could be imposed. In addition, the new "conformity" provision posed a threat to the flow of federal funds if metropolitan transportation plans were not shown to be consistent with state air quality commitments. (This provision is discussed in more detail below.)

The potential impact of the 1990 act on the transportation sector was substantially increased by congressional enactment one year later of the Intermodal Surface Transportation Efficiency Act (ISTEA) of 1991. This bill authorized federal transportation appropriations for a six-year period and laid out requirements for state and regional transportation planning procedures. The two laws were far more closely synchronized than any previous pairing of air quality and transportation statutes. Thus, as the 1990 clean air amendments commanded new priority for environmental

28. The new deadlines for ultimate compliance with the ozone standard varied from three to twenty years. (The only region given twenty years to achieve full ozone compliance was Los Angeles.) That for carbon monoxide varied from five to ten years.

29. Key transportation elements of the clean air act are clearly summarized in Hawthorn and Meyer (1992).

30. To induce greater state and local commitment, the new clean air act mandated the development of the state implementation plan with participation by local elected officials, representatives of the state and local air quality agency, the metropolitan planning organization, the state department of transportation, and members of the general public.

goals in urban transportation, ISTEA provided core financial support and prescribed institutional processes to achieve them.[31] Together, they clearly made achievement of national air quality goals a powerful constraint on transportation policy and, arguably, made air quality the premier objective of the nation's surface transportation programs.

The crucial factor moving state and local transportation decisionmakers to address air quality concerns was the credibility of federal will to make use of clean air act penalties. The 1990 act appeared to strike a realistic balance between regulatory ambition and economic-technical realism, and ISTEA reinforced the sense that this time the federal government meant business. Consequently, many states at first seemed willing to contemplate policies that would force some changes in everyday travel behavior or impose higher costs on motorists. For example, a number of the ten areas required by the 1990 act to reduce automobile commuting to work sites initially proceeded with the EPA's Employee Commute Option program. And most states, where required, began planning for enhanced inspection and maintenance programs in the form prescribed by the EPA, despite outcries from service station operators and auto dealers and concern by some legislators that citizens would find the program onerous.[32] Both of these programs, however, were specific statutory mandates. Even in the early stages of implementing the 1990 act, the states showed little inclina-

---

31. For a brief summary and interpretation of ISTEA, see "The Public's Capital: A Forum on Infrastructure Issues," *Governing Magazine*, vol. 5, April 1992, pp. 65–76.

32. The EPA's enhanced inspection and maintenance regulations recognized that the "basic" test was not able to determine adequately whether the increasingly high-tech emission control systems on new vehicles were functioning properly. The EPA also sought to separate the "test" and "repair" functions of inspection and maintenance, which, typically joined in existing basic systems, created opportunities for fraud and made it difficult to detect incompetent repair-shop performance. Under enhanced inspection and maintenance, the EPA believed, more sophisticated testing equipment and a broader set of tests would more accurately determine whether vehicle pollution controls were working effectively. Independent testers, moreover, would have no stake in whether or where repairs were done and could determine when they had been done correctly. The EPA's program design proved very unpopular in states where inspection and maintenance was historically carried out by the private repair industry. Service stations and auto dealers did not want to lose what they now saw as a lucrative test business with resulting repair jobs. If they could not administer and charge fees for the tests themselves, they did not want to purchase the expensive test equipment needed to diagnose vehicles that had failed at testing stations. In addition to sympathizing with these interests, many elected officials were concerned about potential citizen complaints. They feared that because the new test-only stations would be fewer and less convenient for motorists than the existing network of service stations and repair shops, auto owners would face long waiting lines. Moreover, the new system seemed likely to send motorists "ping-ponging" back and forth between test stations and repair shops until their cars could pass the emission test. And its greater rigor would result in more expensive repair bills than the existing system.

tion to restrict transportation voluntarily. For example, a congestion pricing demonstration program authorized by ISTEA, which would have subsidized experiments with economic disincentives, found only a few jurisdictions willing to examine the idea seriously—and none willing to implement even a demonstration project.[33]

Two conflicts in 1994 seriously undermined the credibility of the federal government's commitment to enforce specific statutory mandates. The first conflict involved the employee commuting program, which encountered growing, often bitter, resistance from business groups.[34] Because the program promised meager emission benefits at best, it was difficult for the EPA to defend. As the most recalcitrant areas suffered no consequences, other areas began to rethink their willingness to comply and lobbied Congress to repeal the requirement. Congress ultimately made the program voluntary in December 1995, effectively killing it.

The second controversy involved challenges to the enhanced inspection and maintenance requirement, most notably by California. The EPA at first resisted making any policy concessions (although it did not impose sanctions on the increasing number of recalcitrant states).[35] After the 1994 elections shifted party control of Congress, however, the EPA, fearing ma-

---

33. Howitt, Anderson, and Altshuler (1994), and Anderson and Howitt (1995).

34. The EPA changed the name of this program from Employer Trip Reduction (ETR) to Employee Commute Option (ECO). The change reflected the EPA's nervousness about its potential to arouse conflict. Although several of the mandated areas (such as New York and Houston) developed ECO plans without provoking much controversy, business groups in some other regions—particularly Baltimore, Chicago, and Philadelphia—protested vociferously. They were concerned about high administrative costs, the inflexibility of federal requirements, the burden of imposing an unpopular federal mandate, and the possibility of incurring federal penalties if they failed to achieve program goals.

35. Through 1993 the EPA had taken an extremely strong stand, threatening to use "discretionary" sanctions against states failing to adopt enhanced inspection programs. (In contrast to the clean air act's "mandatory" sanctions, which took effect only after eighteen or twenty-four months notice, discretionary sanctions could be imposed immediately.) In January 1994, however, as the agency was preparing to impose sanctions on California, a major earthquake struck the Los Angeles area. With the White House reportedly reluctant to risk cutting off infrastructure funding needed for earthquake recovery in an electorally pivotal state, the EPA allowed California to adopt an inspection and maintenance program differing in major respects from what it was insisting that other states accept. The agency soon faced a raft of demands from other states, which it sought to resist, for modifications in or alternatives to the inspection program. These demands increased and intensified later in 1994, following Maine's ill-prepared launch of enhanced inspection and maintenance. Maine officials, finding themselves on the receiving end of a rash of citizen complaints and negative media coverage, quickly shut down the program. Several other states then put their plans on hold.

jor statutory changes, negotiated with several states about alternative ways to meet the 1990 act's inspection and maintenance requirements. Nonetheless, Congress provided states with even greater latitude in a provision of the National Highway System Designation Act, enacted in November 1995. Most states subject to the requirement are currently proceeding with some form of enhanced inspection and maintenance program, but few have been willing to adopt the full set of practices that the EPA prescribed in its original regulations regarding enhanced inspection and maintenance.

Some states have adopted inspection programs that assign a supplementary role to on-road emissions testing, using remote sensing technology, as well as requiring periodic inspections in testing centers. When programs of this type are implemented, roadside enforcement officers identify vehicles with malfunctioning emission control systems (roughly as speeders are identified by radar) and record license plate numbers. Owners are then cited by mail, required to submit their vehicles for confirming or disconfirming tests, and, if necessary, have repairs made. In principle, the use of remote sensing has several advantages over an inspection system that depends entirely on testing at two-year intervals as prescribed by the EPA regulations. In particular, it permits early identification of so-called "gross emitters"—autos whose emission control systems have entirely ceased to function because of defects, misuse, or tampering—rather than waiting until a periodic inspection requirement forces their owners to bring them to a test facility. Remote sensing may also be a more cost-effective technique for reducing pollution than a program that requires all vehicles to be inspected regularly.[36]

The effectiveness of this approach depends on continuous, reasonably intensive enforcement, however, thereby posing a different kind of political test. Because the EPA has not required or actively promoted remote sensing, states are adopting it voluntarily. It remains to be seen whether these states will face pressures from citizens resentful at being cited for on-road violations and forced to repair emission controls, and whether EPA will forcefully insist that the chosen method of enforcement be aggressively applied. If not, its effectiveness in reducing emissions will be significantly compromised.

---

36. See Harrington and McConnell (1993).

Experience with Behavioral Change Policies

With few exceptions, regulatory efforts under successive versions of the clean air act to limit motorists' use of their cars or to impose direct charges with the intent of reducing use have proved politically infeasible.[37] Elected officials fear voter backlash if they try to prevent or discourage motorists from using their vehicles in ways to which they have been long accustomed. A visceral political resistance to pricing policies that was clearly evident in the reaction to EPA policies under the 1970 act has, if anything, become more intense since the 1980s as a consequence of state and local "tax revolts." At the national level, therefore, Congress has rarely mandated *specific* policies of this type, the principal exception being the Employee Commute Option program in the 1990 act. At the state and local levels, many politicians have been willing to defy EPA mandates for such policies, except when confronted with a seemingly clear federal determination to invoke sanctions. But the federal government has proved unable to sustain a credible threat to impose penalties for noncompliance. Faced with strong protest against the EPA's aggressive policies under the very general statutory language of the 1970 act, Congress responded in the mid-1970s by forbidding specific forms of regulation—and clearly signaling its intent to bar others—if the EPA did not change its policies. The commuting program suffered a similar fate in 1995.

Some *voluntary* behavioral change policies (such as ride-sharing programs, enhancement of existing transit service, compressed work weeks, and telecommuting), which provide alternative means of transportation or permit individuals to forgo trips, have won political acceptance, but they generally have quite limited capacity to affect overall auto use, each yielding at best 1–3 percent reductions in vehicle miles traveled.[38]

Inspection and maintenance programs require behavioral response by individual citizens, but they do not restrict everyday behavior. Although they have evoked political resistance at times, opposition has been stronger from elements of the auto repair industry than from aggrieved citizens themselves. In turn, because of lower citizen impacts, the federal government has been willing to keep a greater degree of pressure on state and local officials in support of inspection programs than restrictive transportation

---

37. Traffic rules, highway tolls for use, and gas taxes to finance roads are less problematic because their aim is to facilitate, rather than restrict, automobile use.

38. See Apogee Research, Inc. (1994).

Table 7-5. *Cost-Effectiveness of Transportation Control Measures in Reducing Hydrocarbon Emissions*

(dollars)

Control measure	Cost per ton of HC reduced	
	1990	*1997*
Bicycle, pedestrian paths	233,000	376,000
Employer trip reduction	227,000	365,000
Major rail transit improvements	220,000	353,000
Park-and-ride lots	118,000	188,000
HOV lanes	88,000	141,000
Congestion pricing	53,000	85,000
Incident management	. . .	83,000
Parking pricing: worktrips	38,000	61,000
Traffic signal timing	23,000	. . .
Areawide ridesharing	13,000	20,000
Buy-backs of older cars	3,000	. . .
Emissions/VMT tax	near 0	near 0

Source: Apogee Research, Inc. (1994:34); see text for additional explanatory material.

Note: Estimates are based on current cost information, not always reflecting actual experience and dependent on the level of implementation and specific local assumptions. Estimates were rounded to the nearest thousand. Estimates for 1997 were not adjusted for inflation and assume that federal vehicle emission control measures are implemented so that reductions in vehicle miles traveled (VMT) have less effect on emissions produced by a cleaner fleet.

Information was unavailable to make cost-effectiveness estimates for several measures, including parking pricing, coompressed work weeks, telecommuting, and land use planning, but these measures were seen as potentially highly cost-effective.

controls. In the early 1980s Congress stayed out of the fray as the EPA invoked sanctions against states unwilling to adopt basic inspection and maintenance programs. It did intervene in 1995, forcing the EPA to soften its enhanced inspection policies, but it did not revoke the mandate.

Again the political logic is roughly consistent with cost-effectiveness considerations, with the important exception of economic incentive policies. As the data presented in table 7-4 indicate, the one mandatory behavioral change policy that has proved politically feasible—inspection and maintenance—is somewhat less cost-effective than technology controls, but not substantially so. Table 7-5 provides data about other behavioral measures.[39]

39. This data is drawn from an extended analysis of this issue in Apogee Research, Inc. (1994: 30–41).

Voluntary transportation controls (such as ride-sharing, telecommuting, and compressed work-week schedules) also seem cost-effective. Conversely, the most controversial mandatory type of behavioral restriction—employer trip reductions, such as the Employee Commute Option program—appears dramatically less cost-effective. As the data in table 7-5 reflect, moreover, policies that reduce vehicle miles traveled become less cost-effective over time if federally mandated vehicle emission control regulations are implemented. As cars become cleaner, it takes a greater reduction in vehicle miles traveled to produce equivalent emission reductions.

Measures such as congestion pricing or taxes on emissions per vehicle miles traveled are the major examples of deviation between political and cost-effectiveness considerations. Economic incentive policies have not been adopted to improve air quality, even though their cost-effectiveness for this purpose and congestion reduction has been strongly advocated by many economists. Compared to alternatives, these policies also have the possibility of yielding somewhat greater reductions in travel and associated emissions.[40] As discussed, however, elected officials and other policymakers strongly regard the imposition of direct auto-use charges on individuals as politically infeasible. Fundamentally, this is a collective benefits problem. From the perspective of any particular citizen or firm, these policies promise few perceptible positive effects, at best a hypothetical (and marginal) improvement in air quality or travel time; but they do impose significant individual costs in inconvenience or dollars. As a result, these policies have few strong political advocates other than some economists, planners, and environmental activists, and they tend to provoke intensely motivated opponents exercised by the associated costs. Knowing they will get little public credit for support from the beneficiaries, politicans shy away from the heat generated by such opposition.

Transportation Planning and Infrastructure Investments

Environmentalists have long sought a regulatory lever to discourage the financing of increased highway capacity and boost mass transit. Most environmentalists believe that highway capacity expansion, by improving access and reducing travel times to outlying regions of the metropolitan area, is a major cause of urban sprawl. In turn, they believe, low-density

40. See Apogee Research, Inc. (1994:17–21).

development increases the number and length of auto trips, decreases auto occupancy rates, and diminishes the practicality of pedestrian and transit trip making. Similarly, they argue that the main effect of road building to alleviate congestion in densely developed corridors is to induce additional travel, because there is invariably a great deal of latent travel demand in such areas, suppressed mainly by the existing congestion.[41] All things equal, they believe, additional auto travel generally means more pollution.[42] But air pollution concerns are only part of the story. Environmentalists also object to highway expansion as a threat to other key values, such as preserving open space and agricultural lands, maintaining pedestrian- and transit-friendly patterns of settlement, and conserving energy.

The National Environmental Policy Act (NEPA) of 1969, which required that federally funded projects be broadly analyzed for their impacts on the environment, gave advocacy groups a regulatory tool to challenge road-building proposals. In tandem with other environmental laws, NEPA provided leverage throughout the 1970s and 1980s to delay, and sometimes kill, specific highway projects or to secure commitments to mitigation measures such as new transit service. But NEPA requires only that environmental impacts be considered in evaluating projects; it does not provide substantive guidelines for determining which projects should proceed. Therefore, environmentalists found that it does not prevent decisionmakers from moving ahead with projects that have adverse environmental effects, as long as these effects were considered. In addition, NEPA's project-by-project focus ignores the cumulative environmental effects of multiple projects on the transportation system as a whole.

Since the early 1970s environmental advocates have thought air quality regulation had potential for a more systemic perspective. Early efforts to create strong links between air quality regulation and transportation planning, however, encountered significant institutional problems and resistance. Until the 1990 clean air amendments, neither federal law nor the practices of metropolitan transportation planning provided clean air advocates and regulators with much leverage to influence urban transportation investment policy.

41. Others argue that the causal factors shaping metropolitan growth and development are more complex than this viewpoint allows. See Transportation Research Board (1995:174-209).

42. As cars become cleaner, however, emissions per vehicle mile decline; and congestion relief may also reduce emissions per vehicle mile.

Section 109(j) of the Federal-Aid Highway Act of 1970 did require the secretary of transportation, in consultation with the EPA administrator, to issue regulations to ensure that federally assisted highway projects would be "consistent" with the air quality plan for each pollution control area. But the regulations were extremely vague on the crucial question of how consistency should be determined, and they entrusted state transportation officials rather than environmental regulators with making consistency determinations. In most areas, EPA regional offices—politically beset, understaffed, and preoccupied with other responsibilities (including the need to develop transportation control plans)—made little effort to activate Section 109(j). Where they did, the effect was minimal.[43] The 1977 clean air amendments contained stronger language, but it was only marginally more effective.[44]

Strengthened Connections

The 1990 act, reinforced by ISTEA a year later, required much tighter integration of clean air and transportation planning at the regional level. To implement a stronger conformity clause in the 1990 act, the EPA mandated a complex analytic procedure intended to ensure that transportation-related emissions in nonattainment areas would stay within the act's

43. See Garrett and Wachs (1996: footnote 52) and Howitt (1983). The EPA's particularly aggressive New England regional office, for example, was vigorously rebuffed by state transportation officials when it tried to claim a veto over Boston area transportation projects. There, as elsewhere, EPA officials had very little training or experience in the field of transportation. Nor were they tied into institutional and personal networks of transportation officials, which severely limited the agency's capacity for information gathering, constructive discussion, formulation of policy alternatives, persuasion, and tactical flexibility in seeking its goals.

44. It prohibited metropolitan planning organizations (MPOs) from adopting a "project, program, or plan" that did not "conform" to the provisions of an approved state implementation plan (SIP), and authorized the U.S. secretary of transportation to withhold most federal highway aid upon a finding of nonconformity. The Federal Highway Administration (FHWA) and Federal Transit Administration were assigned responsibility to monitor compliance with the conformity requirement, in consultation with the EPA. After extended negotiations, the FHWA and EPA operationalized the statutory requirement in extremely general terms. As a practical matter, they required only that states ensure the timely implementation of transportation control measures they elected—at their own initiative—to include in their SIPs. In no case did the secretary of transportation withhold transportation funds from a state for noncompliance with this requirement. Consequently, the "conformity" requirement of the 1977 Clean Air Act Amendments was a negligible factor in transportation investment decisions, although environmental advocates occasionally used conformity as a litigation "hook," most successfully to challenge transportation planning methods in the San Francisco Bay area. See Garrett and Wachs (1996).

limits. Backed by the potential penalty of a transportation funding cutoff, these conformity procedures provide far more powerful incentives than ever before for state-local compliance with the clean air act.

The conformity analysis is based on computer-generated forecasts of travel patterns and emissions under various scenarios of transportation system development.[45] If aggregate transportation emissions, forecast for several milestone years during a twenty-year planning period, are within the aggregate mobile source budget established in the area's state implementation plan, the area can receive federal transportation funds and proceed with its projects. [46] If emissions are projected to exceed the budget, then the area may not use its federal transportation money (except for limited types of exempt projects). Conformity generally applies to the *net* emission profiles of entire regional transportation plans or the shorter-term investment programs derived from that plan, given socioeconomic trends and specific transportation policies, such as transit fares or expressway speed limits in the area. It does not bar specific projects that individually raise pollution, so long as the aggregate levels of each pollutant fit within the mobile source budget.[47]

Conformity Effects

Conformity puts large amounts of federal grant money at stake—more than $100 million a year in some metropolitan areas.[48] To date, however, the most widespread effects of conformity have been procedural and cul-

45. The required modeling is typically done by the metropolitan planning organization or the state department of transportation, often with input from the air quality agency on procedures for estimating emissions. The methodology for determining conformity remains a work in progress. The regulatory requirement demands a degree of analytic precision from the transportation demand and emissions models that the current generation cannot fully achieve. Intensive efforts to create a new generation of models are under way. See, for example, Weiner and Ducca (1996) and Chatterjee and others (1997).

46. The conformity budget test is applied to VOC and NO_x emissions in ozone nonattainment areas and to CO and PM_{10} emissions in nonattainment areas for those pollutants. The complexities of the conformity rule have also required many areas to apply a "build–no build" test (in which the emissions generated by a particular plan or program must be less than those expected assuming that the program or plan were not implemented), to show that transportation emissions are lower than they were in 1990, or both.

47. For carbon monoxide, a project-level "hot spot" test may also be applied.

48. Many in the transportation community fear that the flow of funds will be disrupted by modeling results well within the margins of error of the models, while many environmentalists fear that transportation officials are manipulating the results. In practice, however, modeling results are neither easily distorted nor rigidly applied at the margins. See Howitt and Moore (1998), which will examine conformity experience in fifteen major metropolitan areas.

tural. With greater interaction, transportation and environmental agencies have gained more knowledge about and a greater appreciation for each others' perspectives. Although transportation officials typically view environmental protection as a constraint rather than a primary mission, most today accept the legitimacy and high priority of environmental values in transportation decisionmaking. Air quality considerations are being far more carefully considered in investment decisionmaking.

Some rapidly growing metropolitan areas have experienced conformity difficulties that may ultimately force hard choices between pollution control and transportation objectives. Atlanta and Charlotte, for example, have had federal transportation funding interrupted because of conformity problems. In conjunction with the fiscal constraint provision of ISTEA, the conformity rule has made it more difficult to justify major new highway capacity expansion. As further emission reductions are required in the years ahead, more rapidly growing nonattainment areas are likely to experience conformity as an extremely salient constraint. How the conflicts between transportation and air quality goals in such areas will be resolved—and whether the federal government will remain firm in enforcing the regulation—remains uncertain.

To date, however, the conformity rule has not generally forced metropolitan planning organizations to abandon or significantly modify major transportation projects in the planning pipeline. Nor has it led to widespread increases in financial support for rail transit projects, because conformity modeling has generally shown very small pollution reduction benefits from such extremely costly transit improvements.[49] More generally, as the data in tables 7-4 and 7-5 indicate, infrastructure policies, including high-occupancy vehicle lanes, park and ride lots, and bicycle and pedestrian facilities, appear far less cost-effective than technology policies. But these types of projects have been more widely programmed since ISTEA was enacted because the Congestion Mitigation and Air Quality program provides a dedicated source of federal funding for them.

Future Implications

Achieving national air quality standards is likely to remain a major issue for transportation in the foreseeable future, but one should not an-

49. See Howitt and Moore (1998).

ticipate dramatic changes in the way policy has been made and implemented to date.

Problems clearly still remain. According to EPA data, fifty-nine areas were out of compliance with the existing ozone standard, twenty-eight with the CO standard, and seventy-three with the particulate standard as of October 1997.[50] In July 1997, moreover, after heavy business lobbying and a fierce internal battle between the EPA and the administration's economic policymakers, the EPA won President Clinton's approval to promulgate tougher ozone and particulate standards (the latter of which it had developed pursuant to a court order). The ozone standard has been sharply criticized in cost-benefit terms, and the particulate standard is a matter of controversy.[51] But Congress let them stand, which will make the task of achieving the national ambient air quality standards tougher for many of the areas noted above, return a number of "maintenance" areas (which had previously brought air pollution under control) to nonattainment status, and bring more than 200 new counties under federal air pollution regulation for the first time. To ease the impact of meeting the new standards, the EPA plans an extended time frame for compliance, including extensive data gathering about the particulate problem.[52]

As this paper has argued, technology improvements—in the form of vehicle emission controls and fuel refinements—have in the past provided by far the greatest leverage on transportation-related air pollutants, and these have also proved the most politically feasible forms of regulation. But because emission rates for gasoline vehicles have been reduced so much already, further improvements to the gasoline-powered internal combustion engine are limited. Some analysts have therefore argued that technology improvements will be overwhelmed by aggregate increases in vehicle miles traveled, reversing the downward trajectory of aggregate transportation emissions as soon as the first decade of the twenty-first century.[53]

In addition to the regional air pollution problems addressed by the clean air act, the United States is beginning to address global warming. In

50. Taken from the EPA World Wide Web site (Http://www/epa.gov/oar/oaqps/greenbk). The ozone and carbon monoxide nonattainment areas are primarily major metropolitan regions, while the particulate nonattainment areas, with exceptions, are predominately smaller cities and rural areas.

51. See, for example, Lave (1997) and Crandall (1997).

52. Previous particulate regulations had applied to particles as small as 10 microns in diameter (PM_{10}); the new standard applies to particles as small as 2.5 microns in diameter ($PM_{2.5}$). Current ambient air monitoring equipment is not adequate to measure the prevalence of the smaller particles.

53. Noted in U.S. Department of Transportation and Environmental Protection Agency (1993:18).

December 1997 the United States initialed the Kyoto treaty agreeing to reductions of greenhouse gas emissions, primarily carbon dioxide, although Senate ratification is uncertain. If the treaty goes into effect, the United States will be obligated to reduce net emissions by 7 percent from 1990 levels, whereas current trends would see increases of 13 percent by 2000 and of 30 percent by 2010.[54] Compliance with the treaty would almost certainly require significant reductions by the transportation sector through reduced travel, increased fuel economy, or development and deployment of new vehicle propulsion technologies and energy sources.[55]

It is not at all clear at this juncture how much practical potential exists for radical departures from existing vehicle technologies for reducing automotive emissions, let alone in what time frame and at what price. These measures, however, seem the most likely way to achieve substantial future reductions of both regional pollutants and greenhouse gases.[56] Most of the available strategies for reducing transportation demand either have very limited capacity for substantially reducing vehicle miles traveled or have so far proved politically infeasible. (Transit investments, ride-sharing, and new community forms are examples of the former type of strategy; congestion pricing, gasoline tax increases, and strong land use controls are examples of the latter type.) It seems highly improbable that strong measures will be adopted when they were politically unacceptable in the past to deal with worse conditions. Moreover, because global warming is an abstract problem whose most severe effects are likely to lie in the (politically) distant future, it is difficult to conceive of Congress soon legislating strict controls on transportation to avert this threat, absent a series of dramatic natural disasters that can credibly be linked to global warming.

54. See William K. Stevens, "Meeting Reaches Accord to Reduce Greenhouse Gases," *New York Times*, December 11, 1997, p. A-1.

55. See Transportation Research Board (1997: ch. 2–3).

56. There are, however, some tensions in the technology measures appropriate for dealing with regional pollutants as opposed to greenhouse gases. Current catalytic converters transform NO_x into nitrous oxide, a greenhouse gas 300 times more potent than CO_2 in trapping heat. See Matthew L. Wald, "Autos' Converters Increase Warming as They Cut Smog," *New York Times*, May 29, 1998, p. A-1.

References

Altshuler, Alan, with James P. Womack and John R. Pucher. 1979. *The Urban Transportation System: Politics and Policy Innovation*. MIT Press.

Anderson, Joshua P., and Arnold M. Howitt. 1995. "Clean Air Act: SIPs, Sanctions, and Conformity." *Transportation Quarterly* 49 (Summer): 67–82.

Apogee Research, Inc. 1994. *Costs and Effectiveness of Transportation Control Measures (TCMs): A Review and Analysis of the Literature*. Washington, D.C.: National Association of Regional Councils. January.

Bureau of Transportation Statistics. 1995. *National Transportation Statistics, 1996*. U.S. Department of Transportation.

———. 1996. *National Transportation Statistics, 1997*. U.S. Department of Transportation.

Chatterjee, Arun, and others. 1997. "Improving Transportation Data for Mobile Source Emission Estimates." Report 394. National Cooperative Highway Research Program, Washington, D.C.

Crandall, Robert W. 1997. "The Costly Pursuit of the Impossible." *Brookings Review* 15 (Summer): 41–47.

Crandall, Robert W., and others. 1986. *Regulating the Automobile*. Brookings.

Deakin, Elizabeth A. 1978. "Air Quality Considerations in Transportation Planning." *Transportation Research Record 670*. National Research Council, Transportation Research Board, Washington, D.C.

EPA (Environmental Protection Agency). 1998. *Tier 2 Report to Congress*. EPA 420-R-98-008. Washington, D.C. September.

EPA Office of Air Quality Planning and Standards. 1997a. *National Air Pollutant Emission Trends Report, 1900–1996*. EPA 454-R-97-011. U.S. Environmental Protection Agency. December.

———. 1997b. *National Air Quality and Emissions Trends Report, 1996*. EPA 454-R-97-013. U.S. Environmental Protection Agency. October.

EPA Office of Air and Radiation. 1997. *The Benefits and Costs of the Clean Air Act, 1970–1990*. EPA 410-R-97-002. U.S. Environmental Protection Agency. October.

Garrett, Mark, and Martin Wachs. 1996. *Transportation Planning on Trial: The Clean Air Act and Travel Forecasting*. Thousand Oaks, Calif.: Sage Publications.

Harrington, Winston, and Virginia McConnell, 1993. "Cost-Effectiveness of Remote Sensing of Vehicle Emissions." Discussion paper QE93-24. Resources for the Future, Washington, D.C.

Harrington, Winston, Margaret A. Walls, and Virginia McConnell. 1994. "Shifting Gears: New Directions for Cars and Clear Air." Discussion paper 94-26-REV. Resources for the Future, Washington, D.C.

Harrison, David A., Jr. 1975. *Who Pays for Clean Air? The Cost and Benefit Distribution of Federal Automobile Emission Controls*. Cambridge, Mass.: Ballinger.

Hawthorn, Gary, and Michael D. Meyer. 1992. *A User Friendly Guide to the Transportation Provisions of the 1990 Clean Air Act Amendments*. Washington, D.C.: American Association of Highway and Transportation Officials.

Horowitz, Joel. 1978. "Integrated Planning and Management of Transportation and Air Quality." *Transportation Research Record 670.* National Research Council, Transportation Research Board.

Howitt, Arnold M. 1983. "Regulation in the Federal System: EPA and Transportation Controls." Paper delivered at the annual meeting of the American Political Science Association, Chicago. September.

————. 1984. *Managing Federalism: Studies in Intergovernmental Relations.* CQ Press.

Howitt, Arnold M., Joshua P. Anderson, and Alan Altshuler. 1994. "The New Politics of Clean Air and Transportation." Harvard University, Kennedy School of Government, Taubman Center for State and Local Government.

Howitt, Arnold M., and Elizabeth Moore. 1998. *Linking Transportation and Air Quality Planning: Implementation of the Transportation Conformity Regulations on 15 Nonattainment Areas.* Harvard University, John F. Kennedy School of Government, Taubman Center for State and Local Government.

Jacoby, Henry D., and others. 1973. *Clearing the Air: Federal Policy on Automotive Emissions Control.* Cambridge, Mass.: Ballinger.

Krupnick, Alan J. 1992. "Vehicle Emissions, Urban Smog, and Clear Air Policy." Discussion paper QE92-09. Resources for the Future, Washington, D.C.

Landy, Mark K., Marc J. Roberts, and Stephen R. Thomas. 1994. *The Environmental Protection Agency: Asking the Wrong Questions.* Expanded edition. Oxford University Press.

Lave, Lester B. 1997. "Clean Air Sense." *Brookings Review* 15 (Summer): 41–47.

McConnell, Virginia, Margaret Walls, and Winston Harrington. 1995. "Evaluating the Costs of Compliance with Mobile Source Emission Control Requirements: Retrospective Analysis." Discussion paper 95-36. Resources for the Future, Washington, D.C. August.

Meyer, John R., and José A. Gómez-Ibáñez. 1981. *Autos, Transit, and Cities.* Harvard University Press.

Mills, Edwin S., and Lawrence J. White. 1978. "Government Policies Toward Automotive Emissions Control." In *Approaches to Controlling Air Pollution,* edited by Ann F. Friedlaender. MIT Press.

National Commission on Air Quality. 1981. *To Breathe Clean Air: Report of the National Commission on Air Quality.* Washington, D.C.

Quarles, John. 1976. *Cleaning Up America: An Insider's View of the Environmental Protection Agency.* Houghton Mifflin.

Scott, Esther. 1997. "Low Emission Vehicles (Part A): The Pursuit of a Regional Program." and "Low Emission Vehicles (Part B): The Search for a National Program." C15-97-1398.0 and 1399.0. Harvard University, Kennedy School of Government Case Program.

Sperling, Daniel. 1991. "Future of the Car in an Environmentally Constrained World." Paper prepared for delivery at the World Motor Conference, Frankfurt, Germany. September.

Suhrbier, John H., and Elizabeth A. Deakin. 1988. "Environmental Considerations in a 2020 Transportation Plan: Constraints or Opportunities." In *A Look Ahead: Year 2020.* Special Report 220. National Research Council, Transportation Research Board.

Transportation Research Board, National Research Council. 1995. *Expanding Metropolitan Highways: Implications for Air Quality and Energy Use.* Special Report 245. Washington, D.C.

———. 1997. *Toward a Sustainable Future: Addressing the Long-Term Effects of Motor Vehicle Transportation on Climate and Ecology.* Special Report 251. Washington, D.C.

U.S. Department of Transportation and Environmental Protection Agency. 1993. *Clean Air Through Transportation: Challenges in Meeting National Air Quality Standards.* Washington, D.C. August.

Weiner, Edward, and Frederick Ducca. 1996. "Upgrading Travel Demand Forecasting Capabilities: U.S. DOT Travel Model Improvement Program." *TR News* (186): 2–6.

White, Lawrence J. 1982. *The Regulation of Air Pollutant Emissions from Motor Vehicles.* AEI Studies 356. American Enterprise Institute for Public Policy.

Yuhnke, Robert E. 1991. "The Amendments to Reform Transportation Planning in the Clean Air Act Amendments of 1990." *Tulane Environmental Law Journal* 5(December): 239–54.

CHARLES LAVE
LESTER LAVE

8

Fuel Economy and Auto Safety Regulation: Is the Cure Worse than the Disease?

The automobile has transformed American cities, the economy, and even social interactions. The appeal of mobility, convenience, and affordability have all contributed to an enormous demand for cars and light trucks. The sheer number of vehicles—there are now 1.1 cars and light trucks per licensed driver in the United States—has led to a prodigious use of resources: steel, other metals, and glass; petroleum, both for plastics and for fuel; and land for highways and parking. The use of these vehicles has also created important negative externalities including congestion, air pollution, and 3.5 million injuries and 42,000 deaths each year.[1]

According to one recent study, total economywide energy use associated with making a 1990 mid-size car was 114 million British thermal units (Btus), or the equivalent of 20 barrels of petroleum; the energy associated with operating the vehicle was 984 million Btus, or 170 barrels of petroleum.[2] Environmental discharges, both direct and indirect, of toxic chemicals (the Toxic Release Inventory chemicals) from the manufacture and use of the car during its lifetime were more than 273 kilograms—more than a

1. NHTSA (1997: table 2).
2. MacLean and Lave (1998).

257

quarter of a ton; and the emissions of conventional air pollutants (sulfur dioxide, carbon monoxide, nitrogen dioxide, volatile organic compounds, and particulate matter) were more than three tons. Finally, the total direct and indirect greenhouse gases emitted in the manufacture and operation of the car were 93 metric tons (expressed in terms of the amount of carbon dioxide required to produce this level of warming). Multiplying these estimates for a single car by the almost 200 million light-duty vehicles on U.S. highways gives some idea of the prodigious effect of personal transportation vehicles on the U.S. environment.

Federal laws enacted to deal with these environmental consequences generally accomplished their immediate objectives but often created new or additional problems in the process. Congress and the regulators have tended to neglect the effect of their actions on vehicle price and consumer appeal, thereby creating incentives for consumers to circumvent the goal of the regulations. Out of this evolving morass of primary problems, many of which are exacerbated by regulation, we have chosen to examine two—fuel economy standards and speed limits—and their implications for safety.

Cars and light trucks now consume about 40 percent of all the petroleum used in the United States.[3] Since the oil shortages of the mid-1970s, the United States has tried three major policies to reduce gasoline consumption: mandatory national fuel efficiency standards; mandatory national speed limits; and policies to increase mass transit ridership.

The first two policies affected gasoline consumption, but they also had implications for safety, although safety was not the intended effect. Fuel economy standards led to major changes in car design and operation, notably, a switch to more fuel-economic cars, which were smaller and so inherently less safe. The lower speed limit had only a minimal effect on fuel economy, but appeared to increase safety. Recent studies suggest that the increased safety may have had little to do with the lower speed limit, however, while consumer demand for more powerful cars is threatening to undo gains in fuel economy as well as to increase some highway risks.

The third policy, promotion of mass transit, was a total failure. To make transit more attractive, buses were air-conditioned, their weight was increased to improve the ride, and service was expanded. New rail systems were built and station amenities added. But these energy-consuming changes lured few drivers out of their cars, and energy per person served actually increased. Between 1975 and 1995, energy consumption per passenger-mile

---

3. Davis (1997: tables 2.5, 2.10).

increased by 29 percent for rail transit and by 65 percent for bus transit.[4] On a passenger-mile basis, the measured energy consumption of mass transit and cars is now equal.

Government Regulation of Vehicle Fuel Economy

Most Americans, like consumers around the world, prefer larger, more powerful cars, other things equal. Until the oil embargo in 1973, the average new car sold in the United States gained weight, size, and power each year. The oil embargo, together with popular books such as *Limits to Growth* convinced most Americans that the days of cheap, plentiful oil were gone and that the government had to do something about it.[5]

The federal government decided to intervene directly rather than allow market incentives to handle the problem. Rather than allow gasoline prices to rise, which would encourage drivers to reduce their purchases, government regulators put a cap on crude oil prices and barred refineries from raising the price of gasoline. Because price was not used to signal motorists to consume less, the embargo-induced supply reductions resulted in a gasoline shortage. Knowing that the price cap would create a market disequilibrium, because the demand for gasoline was greater than supply at the regulated price, the federal government also intervened in the market to allocate the limited supply of gasoline. The results of the price cap were long queues, rising frustration, and times when no gasoline could be purchased. When the embargo ended, federally mandated allocation ceased and gasoline prices were allowed to rise. For the next several years, however, Congress continued to regulate the price of petroleum pumped from U.S. wells that had been in production before the embargo; new wells and stripper wells (those producing less than ten barrels a day) could charge market price.

Setting the CAFE Standards

To reduce future gasoline consumption, Congress decided to force automakers to double the fuel economy of new cars. As with allocating the limited supply of gasoline, the federal government did not trust the mar-

---

4. Davis (1997: table 2.15).
5. Meadows and others (1974).

ket, in this case automakers and new car buyers, to respond appropriately to the gasoline shortages. The fuel economy regulations were enacted without regard for air pollution or safety goals, however. The optimal engine setting for fuel economy is not the optimal setting for emission reduction. More important, lighter cars use less fuel but are inherently less safe in a crash.

more NO_x

Because of the uncertainty about future oil prices, Congress did not trust market signals about oil prices to generate the desired conservation. Many economists were saying the price increases imposed by the Organization of Petroleum Exporting Countries (OPEC) would not persist because commodity cartels are inherently unstable and have a difficult time holding price above competitive levels. Furthermore, OPEC was bucking a trend of decreasing price for natural resources. A well-known study by Barnett and Morse of Resources for the Future concluded that after adjusting for inflation, the prices of virtually all raw materials had fallen during the previous century.[6] Although policymakers and auto industry executives could not know the path of future oil prices, this research suggested that the high price of petroleum would not persist and that therefore the necessary market signals would not persist. That is precisely what happened. Gasoline prices rose from about 60 cents a gallon in 1973 to about $1.70 a gallon in 1981 and then fell gradually to about $1.00 a gallon in 1985; prices have fluctuated around that level since then (in current dollars).[7]

In addition, congressional policy analysts knew it would take very large price signals to bring about significant changes in consumer behavior. Studies showed that the short-run price elasticity of gasoline was only about −0.2.[8] And a study by the National Academy of Sciences showed that because of the trade-offs between purchase cost and operating cost, the total cost of driving is approximately constant over a wide range of fuel economies.[9] Fuel-efficient vehicles are cheaper to operate, but they cost more to make because they require new technology and more expensive materials. Thus, a moderate rise in gasoline prices would not be expected to lead consumers to shift their purchases toward vehicles that were much more fuel efficient. From society's viewpoint, automakers should take advantage of the ap-

6. Barnett and Morse (1963).

7. In fact, world petroleum prices did not keep pace with inflation in the late 1970s. Only the Iran-Iraq war, which removed a considerable amount of the oil supply from world markets, succeeded in temporarily boosting oil prices above the 1975 levels. In 1998 the world appears to be awash in petroleum, with large reserves. The U.S. price for oil is only slightly above the 1974 oil price; after accounting for inflation, petroleum prices have dropped substantially.

8. Greene (1990).

9. CONAES (1980).

proximately constant total cost of driving by going to the upper end of the fuel economy range. Consumers would be expected to choose the lower end of the range in order to minimize their purchase price.

Even though consumers in 1975 wanted greater fuel economy, no one could predict how long that demand would persist. Consumer demand for fuel economy was probably motivated more from fear of gasoline lines and rationing than from fear of gasoline price increases. If the OPEC cartel collapsed or if the federal government stopped controlling the gasoline market and allowed prices to rise, the inconvenience of lines and rationing would disappear. Automakers faced not only the uncertainty of consumer demand, but also the enormous cost of responding: production of new fuel-efficient vehicles would require expensive research and development and extensive investments in modifying plants to produce the new vehicles. If the demand for fuel efficiency proved to be transitory, the automakers would be stuck with unsalable new models that not only were more expensive to build but that also had lower levels of performance and comfort compared to the 1974 models. A significant commitment to increasing fuel economy, in effect, put the company at risk of bankruptcy. Any individual automaker was unlikely to follow this risky course of action unless all automakers were following it together.

Concluding that it had to act quickly to give detailed instructions to automakers and consumers concerning future fuel economy, Congress passed the Energy Policy and Conservation Act of 1975. The act mandated a series of higher fuel economy standards to increase the fuel economy of the average new car sold from approximately 14 miles per gallon (mpg) in 1974 to 18 mpg in 1978 and 27.5 mpg in 1985 and thereafter.

The act was carefully structured to give automakers long lead times to meet specific goals. This structure promoted extensive R&D to improve fuel economy and major investments in factories to produce the new cars. Instead of requiring *every* car to meet the fuel economy standard, the act specified that the *average* new car sold by each automaker had to attain the standard. This requirement allowed each automaker to produce a variety of cars to meet the variety of consumer needs. Automakers were subject to substantial fines if they did not comply with the standard. The law gave a carrot to companies that exceeded the corporate average fuel economy (CAFE) standard by allowing them to accumulate credits that could be used to offset CAFE shortfalls in other years. The law was carefully structured to promote R&D and investment in new factories by setting out specific standards for each year for the next decade.

Were the Standards the Best Option?

Although the act increased automobile fuel economy, it is less clear whether it increased social welfare. An energy or environmental regulation is likely to increase social welfare only if there have been important market failures for it to correct. What might those market failures have been? The following arguments are frequently given to justify the CAFE standards. First, the United States is such a large purchaser of petroleum that it is in essence a monopsonist, which affects the price Americans must pay to purchase additional oil. Thus, the marginal cost of oil to the United States is greater than its price, and American consumers should face the marginal cost, not the price. Second, to keep the oil supply secure, a large proportion of U.S. security forces must be allocated to the Middle East. These defense costs should be added to the market price of oil to ensure that consumers face the correct price. Third, because the amount of petroleum is finite, Americans should account for future scarcity by paying a higher price now.[10] Fourth, many vehicles are purchased by people or organizations that do not pay for fuel, such as rental car companies. If so, the purchasers might try to minimize the costs of buying the car instead of the total costs of buying and operating it.[11] Finally car buyers do not internalize the social costs of tailpipe emissions of greenhouse gases.

These arguments all lead to the conclusion that consumers are purchasing more gasoline at current prices than is socially optimal. One solution would be to impose a tax to account for the externalities. Gasoline taxes, however, are unpopular. The CAFE standards are thus an attractive alternative for politicians who find a gasoline tax politically inexpedient or who believe that regulation is a more equitable mechanism for reducing future demand. Although the CAFE regulation is more attractive to politicians, economists are quick to note that the cost of achieving the desired

10. This argument is not so much an indictment of commodity markets as a statement that market interest rates are higher than social discount rates in valuing commodities in the future. Although social discount rates are regarded as being less than market rates, CAFE is a good illustration of the difficulties encountered when a government intervention values a commodity more highly than does the market.

11. Certainly a growing number of cars are leased rather than purchased; however, the lease price depends on the resale price for the vehicle at the end of the lease. Vehicles that are less fuel economic than resale purchasers desire will sell at lower prices and thus have higher lease prices, compared with the vehicles with characteristics that consumers desire. Thus, insofar as leasers are able to anticipate resale price, they will be acting as if they were concerned about the entire cost of the vehicle, not just its purchase price.

goal is likely to be higher with regulation than with a market approach, such as an externality tax. A market approach provides an incentive to change behavior immediately while giving maximum flexibility to all parties to achieve the desired goals.

A further difficulty is that Congress made a guess that doubling fuel economy was the right regulation. With oil prices below 1973 levels, after accounting for inflation, the CAFE standards specify fuel economy levels much higher than are demanded by consumers. A careful examination of these externalities would justify only lower CAFE standards. Although Greene and Liu make a mild case that the social benefit of CAFE exceeded its social cost, at least in the early years, other economists have disagreed.[12] Crandall and others argue that there are trade-offs among fuel economy, safety, and tailpipe emissions and that a market solution would have been preferable to this regulation.[13] Crandall and Graham estimate that downsizing cars to meet CAFE requirements caused a 14–27 percent reduction in safety.[14] Crandall reiterates the superiority of a gasoline tax, saying it could achieve the same fuel economy without as much downsizing and thus loss of safety.[15] His review of the literature finds substantial welfare losses in both CAFE and gasoline taxes, however. Kwoka noted that automakers had to change their pricing and promotion structure to meet the standard in many years.[16] As gasoline prices declined, automakers raised prices on large cars to subsidize the price of small ones.

Kleit observed that setting a standard for a corporate average rather than a standard for each type of vehicle created advantages for some automakers.[17] For example, a company like Mercedes-Benz that made only large cars had no reasonable way to achieve a 27.5 mpg level for the average car it sold in the United States. But a company like General Motors that made a full line of cars could offset its large, less fuel-efficient cars by producing many small, light cars. When GM found that it could not sell enough of the small cars for its corporate average to meet the CAFE standards, it had two alternatives. It could produce fewer large cars, or it could reduce the price of the small cars to induce consumers to buy them. Lowering the price of its small cars would pressure other automakers to lower the prices

12. Greene and Liu (1988).
13. Crandall and others (1986).
14. Crandall and Graham (1989).
15. Crandall (1992).
16. Kwoka (1983).
17. Kleit (1990).

of their small cars too. GM could afford to lower the price of its small cars by increasing the price of its large cars and using the profits to subsidize the lowered price of its small cars. But a company like Toyota that made only small cars had to cut the price of those cars, lowering its profits or even suffering net losses. Thus CAFE favored GM and Ford at the expense of Honda, Toyota, and Mercedes-Benz.

Although an academic debate has raged over the desirability of the CAFE standards, American automakers say they had no choice but to comply with the regulations and they embarked on an elaborate, costly program to raise fuel economy. They lightened cars within each size category, reduced engine size, and worked to convince buyers to select smaller cars. For example, the average weight of cars declined from 3,608 pounds in 1976 to 2,730 in 1982. During the same period, horsepower declined by almost 40 percent. Engine size declined from 298.5 cubic inches in 1976 to 176.1 in 1982 and 162.2 in 1988. The "full size" 4,000-pound car with an eight-cylinder engine all but disappeared by the early 1980s. The average interior space of cars remained essentially constant, however, varying by less than 1 percent between 1976 and the early 1990s.[18]

Initially, the CAFE standards helped automakers. From 1975 through the early 1980s, consumers desired cars with greater fuel economy than that mandated by CAFE and so the constraint was not binding. The standards forced automakers to redesign and retool to produce the cars that consumers wanted. As gasoline prices fell after 1980, however, consumers became less concerned with fuel economy and wanted larger, more powerful cars; they began to switch from subcompact cars with four-cylinder engines to larger cars with six- or even eight-cylinder engines. As a result, domestic automakers did not satisfy CAFE requirements from 1983 to 1985, drawing on the credits they had earned in earlier years to stay in compliance with the regulation. As they began to run out of credit, they persuaded the federal government to lower the CAFE standard from 27.5 mpg to 26 mpg for 1986 through 1988. Regulators raised the standard slightly, to 26.5 mpg, in 1989 and then returned to the previous standard of 27.5 mpg. Between 1983 and 1988 domestic automakers began to ration the sale of large engines and large cars that that did not meet CAFE standards. An increasing number of consumers began switching to light trucks—pickups or full-sized vans—because these vehicles were not regulated as strictly. The share of the market held by these vehicles increased from 15 percent in 1971 to 22 percent in 1980.[19]

18. Davis (1997).
19. Godek (1997).

In the 1980s automakers introduced a new kind of light truck: minivans and sport utility vehicles (SUVs). These luxurious vehicles offered consumers what they wanted—greater room, greater safety, and more powerful engines—but their fuel economy was far below the CAFE standards. By 1988 all U.S. manufacturers were having trouble attaining the CAFE standard of 20 mpg for light trucks and 27.5 mpg for cars. Because about half the new vehicles sold to consumers were light trucks, the average fuel economy of new vehicles was declining. Congress has put automakers in a bind. With gasoline selling at about $1 a gallon and consumer incomes rising, the demand for larger, more powerful vehicles is increasing, yet the CAFE standards prevent automakers from offering consumers as many of these vehicles as they desire.

Were the Fuel Efficiency Standards Necessary?

Even after accounting for the increasing market share of SUVs and other light trucks, there is no question that vehicle fuel economy has improved since 1974. Can this improvement be attributed to CAFE regulation? Some economists have argued that fuel economy increases from 1974 through the mid-1980s were simply a market response to the higher gasoline prices and threats of scarcity, with no contribution from CAFE. Nature did not run a parallel experiment without the CAFE mandates, but there are reasonable arguments that support the contribution from regulating fuel economy.

First, most consumers seemed more concerned about gasoline shortages than about moderate price increases. The long waits to get gasoline during the OPEC embargo and uncertainty about whether gasoline would be available at all convinced most consumers that a price increase was easier to accept than uncertainty about being able to get fuel. During the embargo, a common practice was to limit each customer to $2 worth of gasoline. Obviously, a car that got 30 miles to the gallon was preferred to one that got 10 mpg. Because gasoline is a small proportion of the cost of owning and operating a car, the price elasticity would be expected to be small.

Second, as noted before, commodity cartels are often unable to maintain a monopoly price for longer than a few years. Thus, automakers faced vast uncertainty in 1975. Would the price of a gallon of gasoline in 1990 be $1 or $5? If and when gasoline prices returned to low levels, consumers would eschew fuel-efficient cars in favor of larger, more powerful vehicles, thus bankrupting a company that had spent tens of billions of dollars to redesign and build cars to be fuel efficient.

Third, there was little uncertainty about government enforcement of regulation. Detroit's general experience with federal regulation was that the government was no pushover. For example, the 1970 Clean Air Act Amendments regulating the amount of air pollutants that could be emitted from automobile tailpipes was pushed through Congress over Detroit's opposition. The Environmental Protection Agency enforced these standards despite Detroit's vigorous protests and a model year (1974) where the emissions standards were achieved by making the fuel mixture so lean that drivers had a hard time starting their cars and reported that the vehicles would stall frequently, even on the freeway at speeds of 60 miles an hour. With this experience, automobile company executives were not inclined to believe that they could get the courts or public opinion to rescind the fuel economy standards or wink at violating them.

Given this set of circumstances, fuel economy regulation almost certainly had an immediate effect, forcing technology to improve fuel economy. Predicting the price of petroleum over the next few decades involved so much uncertainty that few people were willing to bet the company on any single forecast. Whatever their judgments about the future price of petroleum, believing that CAFE standards would be enforced removed the uncertainty. Because doubling the fuel economy of cars, as the regulation required, necessitated major reengineering and significant changes in production facilities, automakers had no viable alternative to getting started immediately. If a company dawdled for several years while it tried to get a better prediction about world oil markets, it was unlikely to meet the CAFE standards of the 1980s. The consequences would be large fines and media condemnation, which could result in bankruptcy.

Moreover, because consumers bought cars that had greater fuel economy than that demanded by CAFE through the early 1980s, the regulations reinforced consumer demands. As petroleum prices began to plummet after 1980, however, consumers began to purchase larger, more powerful cars, testing the ability of automakers to meet the CAFE standards. For a few years, research and development efforts enabled automakers to produce larger vehicles with more powerful engines that still achieved the standards. For example, the 0–60 miles-per-hour acceleration time was about 14 seconds from 1975 to 1982. The acceleration rate has improved since then—by 1996 it was 10.7 seconds, and cars were just managing to attain the standards. When the limits of fuel economy technology were reached, automakers encouraged consumers who wanted more size and power to switch from big cars to light trucks; that strategy allowed the automakers to satisfy those consumers while still meeting CAFE standards. Furthermore, the profit margins on light trucks were higher, particularly on the more luxurious vehicles. In addition, the demand for light trucks allowed the automakers to explore and perfect a class of vehicles that would eventually sell throughout the world, in contrast to American cars that have not enjoyed much export success. Although this light truck strategy worked for many years, the truck CAFE standards are now constraining U.S. manufacturers. According to a recent news report, GM failed to meet the light truck CAFE in five of the last eight years and Chrysler failed to meet the standard in the last four years.[20] Automakers now find themselves in the same difficulty that they faced with the car CAFE; their greatest profit margins are on the largest, most powerful vehicles. Yet, to meet CAFE standards, automakers must limit sales of those vehicles and try to persuade many buyers to choose a smaller engine and smaller models.

Another strategy for meeting CAFE is to take advantage of the credits given for selling vehicles that use alternative fuels. A truck designed to run on either gasoline or E85 (a mixture that is 85 percent ethanol and 15 percent gasoline) is evaluated only on the basis of the gasoline it uses. Thus a truck or automobile that gets 12 mpg on E85 would be treated as if it got 80 mpg in terms of CAFE computations. The credit does not depend on whether the vehicles are ever actually fueled with E85. Chrysler, Ford, and GM have all produced vehicles than run on alternative fuels.

Yet another way of coping with the CAFE standards is to build SUVs on a car chassis, rather than a truck chassis. The result is a lighter vehicle with a more comfortable ride. Some consumers prefer these smaller SUVs, but their market penetration is still small.

Contradictions among Federal Regulations

Fuel economy and low tailpipe emissions are inherently contradictory.[21] Although a higher combustion temperature that burns more of the hydrocarbons in the engine produces greater fuel economy and reduces emis-

20. Ann Job and Tom Lankard, "GM Gets Credits in Flex-Fuel Change," *Detroit News*, May 31, 1998, Autos section.

21. Crandall and others (1986).

sions of carbon monoxide and volatile organic compounds, two of the major air pollutants released through engine combustion, it also produces more nitrogen oxides, a major precursor of ozone. Automakers find the nitrogen oxides standard the most difficult one to meet. Federal tailpipe emissions standards can be met by recirculating exhaust gas and using catalysts. Unfortunately, the additional weight lowers fuel economy.

Another important contradiction is between the regulatory goal of increasing safety and that of increasing fuel economy. Although improvements in fuel economy were achieved principally through technological advances, automakers also contributed to fuel economy by reducing vehicle weights significantly.[22] Unfortunately, simple physics shows that when two vehicles collide, the lighter vehicle will suffer greater deceleration forces. A collision between two small cars of equal weights is more dangerous because small cars tend to have less structure to absorb the crash energy.

The National Highway Traffic Safety Administration (NHTSA) regulates automobile safety by setting design standards and by requiring cars to pass a crash test, which simulates a vehicle crashing into a solid barrier. Of all crashes involving fatalities, however, only 29 percent involve a single vehicle hitting a fixed object. Forty-one percent involve two or more vehicles; 19 percent involve a collision with a nonfixed object, such as a pedestrian; and 10 percent involve rollovers.[23] Thus, the NHTSA crash test is of limited relevance for most fatal crashes. A series of research studies shows that occupants of the smaller car in a two-vehicle crash are at much greater risk than the occupants of the larger vehicle. Table 8-1 shows the relative risks to drivers in head-on crashes between two vehicles; that is, the likelihood of fatality for the driver of Car A in a head-on collision with Car B. The main diagonal of the matrix shows that in head-on collisions of similar-size cars, drivers of the largest cars have about half the chance of being killed as drivers of the smallest cars (5.07 to 10.14). When cars of markedly different size crash, the driver of the smaller car is at much greater risk. For illustration of this last point, look at the northeast and southwest squares of the matrix. If Car A weighs 500–900 kilograms, the risk of fatality for the driver in a collision with Car B weighing 1,800–2,400 kilograms is 20.7. If this example is reversed, and Car A, weighing 1,800–2,400 kilograms, collides head-on with Car B, weighing 500–900 kilograms, the relative likelihood of fatality for the driver of Car A is 1.0. Thus the driver of

22. Greene (1996).
23. NHTSA (1997: table 32).

Table 8-1. *Relative Likelihood of Driver Fatality in Head-On Collisions between Cars of Different Weights*

Weight in kilograms

Car A	Car B					
	500–900	900–1,100	1,100–1,300	1,300–1,500	1,500–1,800	1,800–2,400
500–900	10.14	20.41	23.12	21.70	22.10	20.70
900–1,100	6.98	17.12	17.14	22.00	19.84	20.31
1,100–1,300	5.78	8.57	10.37	12.58	12.03	12.58
1,300–1,500	2.71	3.43	6.89	8.85	9.09	9.80
1,500–1,800	1.01	3.31	3.47	4.96	6.38	8.02
1,800–2,400	1.00	2.30	2.35	3.35	4.56	5.07

Source: Evans and Wasielewski (1987), based on FARS data for 1975–80. Relative likelihood of fatality for driver in Car A in a head-on collision with Car B. See text for explanation.

the smaller car is at 20.7 times the risk of being killed as the driver of the larger car. This ratio gets smaller as the cars become more similar in weight.

Crandall and Graham estimate that the CAFE standards decreased the weight of the average 1989 car by 500 pounds (14 percent) from what it would have been without the standards.[24] Based on data like that in table 8-1, the decreased weight implies a 14–27 percent increase in fatality risk. Greene, however, argues that the effects of the fuel economy standards on safety cannot be inferred from simple use of such data for two reasons. First, driver characteristics (particularly age and sex) are a major determinant of crashs and rollovers. Because there is strong relation between vehicle size and driver characteristics, much of the apparent correlation between weight and safety is really the effect of driver characteristics, Greene says. Second, Greene argues, for most of the period since 1975, the effect of the standards was to reduce the weight dispersion of the vehicle fleet, making car-to-car collisions more equal and hence less harmful.[25]

Crandall and Graham also observe that the increased market share for light trucks generated by the fuel economy standards has safety consequences. Although a light truck is safer for its occupants, it is more dangerous for other vehicles on the road. Because a crash between a small vehicle and a larger one entails a much greater risk for the occupants of the smaller ve-

---

24. Crandall and Graham (1989).
25. Greene (1996).

hicle, each large vehicle on the road potentially increases the number of fatalities. Recent concern has centered on dangers created by SUVs: they have substantially greater weight than the fleet average and are built higher to have greater ground clearance for off-road uses. The greater height means that the SUVs strike a normal passenger car above the frame, transferring the energy of the crash to the body of the car, rather than to its frame.

The general point is that people who drive larger cars, light trucks, and SUVs impose an externality on people riding in smaller vehicles. Even though this externality was largely created by the CAFE regulations, NHTSA has not attempted to deal with it.

Conclusions about CAFE

The 1975 legislation setting corporate average fuel economy standards has had a major effect on Americans. It spawned a new generation of cars that was more fuel efficient than older vehicles, greatly improving the fuel economy of the whole light-duty fleet. The smaller and lighter cars, however, are inherently less safe for their occupants. A large gasoline tax might have improved fuel economy more quickly and cheaply than the CAFE standards. But the inability of Congress to pass even a five-cent gasoline tax increase in the immediate aftermath of the oil crisis demonstrated clearly that higher taxes were not a politically feasible alternative. Analyses of the fuel efficiency standards often miss the major uncertainties prevailing in 1975 (and subsequent years) about the future price of petroleum. If the real price of petroleum today were $100 a barrel, as many in 1974 feared it might be, the CAFE standards would be hailed as an extraordinarily insightful law. With the actual price of petroleum at $11 a barrel, the standards seem like a vestigial organ that should have been excised in the early 1980s.

In short, the decline in gasoline prices undermined CAFE. With gasoline hovering at $1 a gallon for the past several years, most Americans are demanding larger, more powerful cars at the expense of fuel efficiency. Precisely because they constrained consumer choice, the CAFE standards led to the increased market share for light trucks. As a result fuel efficiency for the average new vehicle on the road is below the 27.5 miles per gallon required by the standards. The lesson: government policy that attempts to require manufacturers to produce a mix of vehicles that is incompatible with consumer demand will result in manufacturers and consumers finding ways around the regulations. Even though it is clear to Congress and the regulators that the intent of the law is being violated, they are unlikely to take any action that would incur consumer anger.

To resolve the conflicting signals, Congress should either forgo the efforts at fuel economy and repeal CAFE or increase gasoline prices (through taxes) to the point where consumers desire a mix of vehicles consistent with CAFE. Congress is not willing to grasp either of these nettles. Absent some crisis, a gasoline tax hike is politically unthinkable. Eliminating CAFE would have far-ranging consequences. CAFE has helped to contain U.S. demand for petroleum, thereby helping to reduce greenhouse gases. At the UN conference on global climate change, held in Kyoto, Japan, in December 1997, the United States agreed to reduce its greenhouse gas emissions. Congress is unlikely to ratify the agreement, but eliminating CAFE would be a slap at President Clinton and the other signatories.

Energy Savings, Speed Limits, and Safety Effects

At the time of the first OPEC oil embargo, most states had speed limits of 65–75 miles per hour (mph) on their interstate highways. Congress's first policy response to the oil embargo was to set a national maximum speed limit of 55 mph, which took effect in 1974. Although energy analysts warned that the fuel savings would not be large, Congress apparently felt that some kind of action was necessary, even a weak one. Subsequent analyses showed that the energy effects of the new law were indeed small; one estimate, for example, found the lower speed limit reduced fuel consumption by no more than 1 percent and perhaps by as little as two-tenths of a percent.[26] But the law was retained because of the large improvement in safety that accompanied it: highway fatalities dropped by more than 9,000, from 55,511 in 1973 to 46,402 in 1974.[27]

In later years, however, drivers began speeding up, and enforcement of the 55 mph limit became more and more difficult. By its tenth anniversary, many politicians were calling for repeal. What had begun as an uncontroversial, although misguided, attempt to save energy had become a heated political question: Should the national 55 mph speed limit be retained? The safety establishment had a ready answer: speed kills. But the absolute certainty of their answer is not borne out in the traffic literature.

---

26. Blomquist (1984).
27. National Research Council (1984: 1).

What is the relationship between speed limits and safety? We explore the safety question by looking at the data resulting from three changes in the national speed limit: the initial drop to 55 mph in 1974; the increase to 65 mph on rural interstate highways in 1987; and the abolition of the national 55 mph limit in 1996. We draw two main conclusions. First, coordination of speeds among vehicles, producing a smooth flow of traffic, seems to be more important for safety than limiting speed; that is, variance kills. Second, strict enforcement of low speed limits can create perverse consequences through its effect on allocation of highway resources and policing resources; hence, by permitting a more efficient allocation of resources, an increase in speed limits might actually contribute to an improvement in safety, as it did in 1987. Contrary to widespread predictions of highway carnage if the speed limit were allowed to rise, fatality rates actually decreased when the 55 mph national speed limit was abolished in 1996.

The 1974 Reduction in Speed Limits

How much did the 1974 reduction in the speed limits contribute to safety? With the 55 mph limit growing more and more controversial in the early 1980s, Congress decided to appoint a commission to study the issue and possibly make recommendations for change. The first task undertaken by this commission was to analyze the effects of the 55 mph limit on safety.[28] Certainly the entire drop in fatalities was not a consequence of the drop in average speeds. The commission cited two other important factors unrelated to speed. First, total fatalities always fall in recessions because travel falls, and the oil embargo set off one of the largest recessions in the postwar era. Second, the 1974 drop in travel was even greater than usual during a recession because of the sheer problem of obtaining gasoline, reinforced by newspaper pictures of trucks and cars stranded on the highways, waiting for gasoline. The commission also noted the likelihood of a disproportionate drop in a particularly dangerous form of travel, vacation driving, which typically involves long hours of driving on unfamiliar roads with high passenger loads. Finally, the commission noted reductions not only in average speeds, but also in the dispersion of speeds, which should have a positive effect on safety. The commission was unable to quantify the effect of all these factors because the necessary data had never been collected. But it did

28. National Research Council (1984).

make an informed estimate that the 55 mph speed limit was probably responsible for reducing fatalities by between 2,000 and 4,000 in 1983.

With no data available to analyze the historic effects of the 55 mph limit in the period immediately following the oil embargo, Charles Lave turned to an analysis of the contemporary effects of the national speed limit.[29] He measured the direct relationship between speeding and the fatality rate using 1981 and 1982 state cross-section data. He found no statistically discernible relation between average travel speed and the fatality rate. A change in the speed limit does cause a change in the average speed of highway vehicles, but does a change in average speed produce a change in the fatality rate? Holding other factors constant, do the states with higher speeds also have higher fatality rates? Using data from six highway types for 1981 and 1982, Lave ran twelve regressions. The dependent variable was the fatality rate on each road type. There were four explanatory variables: the average speed on that highway, expected to be positive if speed kills; variance of speeds, expected to be positive because greater dispersion of speeds among vehicles leads to more passing; hospital access, to account for the quality of medical care available in the event of a crash; and speeding citations per driver.[30]

When these regressions were run, there was no evidence for the importance of average speed. The regression coefficient of the average speed variable was statistically insignificant for all twelve equations; furthermore, it was actually negative in ten of them, in total opposition to the speed-kills theory. But the speed variance variable had the expected positive sign and was significant in half of the regressions—that is, variance kills. Lave also tried replacing average speed with three other speed measures: the percentage of cars exceeding 55 mph, the percentage exceeding 65 mph, and the

---

29. Lave (1985).

30. Lave measured both the number of hospitals per square mile and the uniformity of their distribution. The variable used was hospitals per square mile multiplied by the proportion of population living in nonmetropolitan areas. Several variants were examined, and this one proved to be superior.

The number of speeding citations per driver is a function of both driver aggressiveness and police conscientiousness. If driving behavior were relatively constant across states, but law enforcement effort varied considerably, then citations per driver would serve as measure of enforcement effort and a negative coefficient would be expected; if driver behavior varied more than enforcement effort, a positive coefficient would be expected. The results show a positive coefficient in ten of the twelve cases. Thus, it seems likely that the number of citations per driver is primarily a measure of driver behavior. Partial confirmation of this idea is seen in the negative correlation between citations and average driver age: a high proportion of young, presumably aggressive, drivers leads to a high citation rate.

Table 8-2. *Final Regression Equations on the Effects of a Change in Average Speed*

Road type	Speed variance	Citations per driver	Hospital access	R^2	N	Average speed IF entered[a]
Rural interstate						
1981	0.176 (2.3)	0.0136 (4.6)	−7.75 (3.6)	0.624	41	(−0.5)
1982	0.190 (2.6)	0.0071 (2.8)	−5.29 (3.7)	0.532	44	(−0.4)
Rural arterial						
1981	0.677 (3.5)	0.0122 (1.6)	0.92 (0.2)	0.237	46	(−1.3)
1982	0.375 (2.0)	0.0116 (1.7)	−0.42 (0.1)	0.101	47	(−0.5)
Rural collector						
1981	0.011 (0.1)	0.0041 (0.6)	−8.61 (1.6)	0.019	41	(−0.1)
1982	0.046 (0.3)	0.0139 (2.4)	−0.83 (0.2)	0.089	41	(−1.2)
Urban freeway						
1981	0.892 (1.3)	0.0634 (1.9)	−0.13 (1.1)	0.269	19	(−1.2)
1982	0.281 (0.7)	0.0410 (2.5)	−2.86 (0.5)	0.193	18	(−0.5)
Urban interstate						
1981	0.103 (1.2)	0.0101 (2.0)	0.32 (0.2)	0.139	26	(0.7)
1982	−0.011 (0.2)	0.0106 (2.8)	−0.17 (0.1)	0.167	27	(0.3)
Urban arterial						
1981	0.526 (2.4)	−0.0187 (1.9)	−1.93 (0.5)	0.177	23	(−0.6)
1982	0.304 (1.9)	−0.0068 (1.2)	−5.72 (2.2)	0.168	21	(−1.0)

Source: Lave (1985). *t*-ratios shown in parentheses; R^2 is corrected for degrees of freedom.

a. Column shows what the *t*-ratio of the average speed variable would have been if the variable had been added to the equation (its potential significance and sign).

85th percentile speed (that is, the speed at which 85 percent of cars are traveling at or below that speed). The results were no different. Once the effect of speed variance is held constant, speed itself has no direct effect on the fatality rate. (This conclusion is not contradicted by the observed drop in the number of fatalities following the imposition of the 55 mph limit, because both total travel and speed variance fell that year.) Table 8-2 shows the final regression equations. Average speed has been removed from the equations because it was insignificant, but column 7 indicates the significance and sign it would have if it were to be included. The column shows that average speed is not only insignificant, but actually has a perverse sign in ten of the twelve equations. As expected, hospital access plays its biggest role on rural interstates, those highways that are far removed from emer-

Figure 8-1. *Deviation from Average Speed vs. the Collision Rate (Solomon Curve)*

Collision rate (per 100 million vehicle miles)

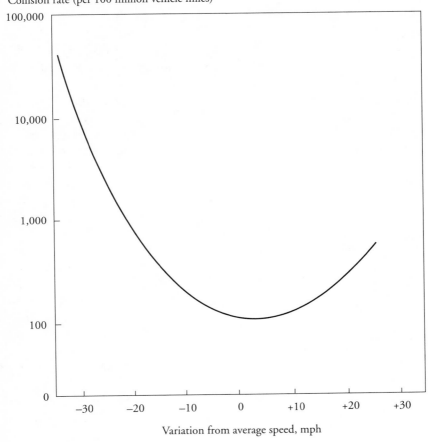

Variation from average speed, mph

Source: Solomon (1964).

gency medical services. Also as expected, the effect of speed variance is least on relatively uncongested, multilane highways—the rural and urban interstates.

These results are not unprecedented in the traffic engineering literature, although they do seem to have been forgotten. In 1964 Solomon investigated the relation between accident rates and variance in speeds and plotted the results (figure 8-1). The curve shows that it is safest to drive at the median speed and increasingly dangerous to deviate from this speed in either direction; that is, slow drivers are equally responsible for causing accidents. In 1971 Hauer provided a theoretical foundation for the Solomon curve: he derived the number of overtakings expected at various speeds (for example, if I drive at 45 mph, while the median of the pack is 60 mph, how many cars will pass me in an hour and hence have a chance to collide with me) and showed that the theoretical distribution was nearly identical to the Solomon curve.[31]

These results may be recast into more general form. Although laws are usually thought of as *limits* to people's behavior, "the crucial element is often coordination. People need to do the right things at the right time in relation to what others are doing."[32] Thus, laws are also made to establish conventions of expected conduct: motorists are required to drive to the right, not because driving on the left is evil, but because it is important that the direction of flow be commonly agreed upon. Likewise, traffic lights are best viewed as coordinating devices, allowing the flow of alternating lanes of traffic and reducing the confusion and loss of time that would occur if the intersection had no signal.

For peculiar historical reasons, speed laws evolved as limits on driver behavior, rather than as signaling devices meant to coordinate behavior. Guided by the limit rationale, police concentrate on those drivers who exceed the legal speed and tend to ignore those drivers who disrupt coordination by traveling much slower than the norm. To avoid accidents and fatalities, it is important that everyone drive at about the same speed. Thus a major consideration in setting a speed limit is to choose a limit that drivers are willing to obey. Finally, although the results of Lave's regressions show that only variance matters, these results do not necessarily imply that it is safe to raise the speed limit, because the effect of a higher limit on speed variance is unknown.

The 1987 Increase in Speed Limits

Although the speed limit commission could not provide a definitive estimate of the contemporary effects of the 55 mph speed limit, it did find enough evidence to recommend that states be allowed to raise speed limits on rural interstate highways in situations where traffic was not high, and

31. Solomon (1964); Hauer (1971).
32. Schelling (1978:121).

road geometry was favorable. In 1987 Congress granted this permission, and forty states raised speed limits on portions of their rural interstates. What was the result?

Many analyses were made. Typically they found that total fatalities had risen after the speed limit was raised. But these analyses did not control for the increase in travel; obviously, more driving would cause more fatalities. Nor did the analyses consider that easing the burden of an unpopular speed limit would permit policing resources to be reallocated to other safety activities and other roads, Finally, they did not consider that higher legal speeds on the interstates might lure some drivers away from other, more dangerous roads. Because these latter two *systemwide* effects work in a positive direction, the increased speed limits could lead to an overall improvement in highway safety, even though fatalities on the highways with higher speed limits increase.

Lave and Elias apply the systemwide perspective to the 1987 increase in speed limits.[33] They consider allocation of policing and highway resources.

THE ALLOCATION OF POLICING RESOURCES. Lave and Elias found strong evidence that the state highway patrols felt they had been forced to misallocate their labor because of the federally mandated 55 mph limit. The federal government had imposed detailed compliance requirements that necessitated strict new enforcement efforts. In response, highway patrols shifted resources from other safety activities, such as staffing drunk driving checkpoints and enforcing truck safety, to speed enforcement on the interstate highways. These highways have the densest concentration of high speed traffic, hence a patrol-hour of activity there will control the greatest number of potential speeders. By 1983, 29 percent of patrol staff hours were devoted to rural interstate highways, although these were already the safest high-speed rural highways in the nation, producing only 9 percent of fatalities.[34]

The state highway patrols protested being forced to allocate so many hours to speed patrol. Testifying before Congress, a spokesperson for the International Association of Chiefs of Police said that federal financial sanc-

---

33. Lave and Elias (1997).
34. National Research Council (1984: 227). Other rural 55 mph highways accounted for 57 percent of patrol staff hours and 72 percent of the fatalities, while urban 55 mph highways, including interstates, accounted for 13 percent of the staff hours and 18 percent of the fatalities.

tions "force the over-concentration of limited resources for the express purpose of attaining compliance [with the 55 mph limit] rather than application of resources in a manner most effectively enhancing total highway
safety. . . ."[35] After Congress allowed speed limits to rise to 65 mph on rural
highways, state highway patrols reallocated patrol resources to activities
that they believed had a greater effect on safety.

THE ALLOCATION OF HIGHWAY RESOURCES. Their design and limited access
make interstates the nation's safest roads. Higher legal speeds on the
interstates would be expected to lure traffic away from other roads, thus
reducing fatalities on those inherently more dangerous roads. To measure
this effect in the 65 mph states, Lave and Elias compared the growth of
vehicle miles traveled on specific highway types to the growth rate statewide and found that vehicle miles traveled on rural interstates grew almost
twice as fast as the overall growth in vehicle miles for these states. Vehicle
miles traveled on noninterstate highways grew 11 percent less than the
overall rate. Both results are consistent with the theory.

Did the new allocations of traffic and highway patrol resources make a
difference? What happened to fatalities?

Lave and Elias began with the simplest test. They then aggregated the
states into two groups, those that raised the speed limit to 65 mph and
those that did not, and computed each group's fatality rates: the total number of fatalities within each group, divided by its total vehicle miles traveled (table 8-3). In the states that raised their speed limits, the overall fatality
rate fell by 4.68 percent in 1987 (compared with 1986, when the limit had
been 55 mph), and then fell an additional 1.55 percent in 1988. In the
states that did not change their speed limits, fatality rates were essentially
unchanged in 1987 compared with 1986 and then fell by 2.55 percent in
1988. The 55 mph states form a quasi–control group for the 65 mph speed
limit experiment. The difference in fatality rates between the two groups of
states indicates that the 65 mph experiment reduced the fatality rate by
3.53 percent from 1986 to 1988.

Such an unexpected result demands a more thorough analysis, so Lave
and Elias disaggregated the data to model the determinants of the fatality
rate explicitly. They built on the work of Garber and Graham, who modeled the fatality rate on rural interstate highways—the local effects—using
monthly time series data for 1976 through 1988, with separate regressions

35. Tippet (1990).

Table 8-3. *Percentage Change in Statewide Fatality*

Speed limit	Change from 1986 to 1987	Change from 1987 to 1988	Change from 1986 to 1988
States with 65 mph limit	-4.68	-1.55	-6.15
States with 55 mph limit	-0.07	-2.55	-2.62

Source: Lave and Elias (1997); NHTSA (1989).

for each state.[36] Speed limit effects were measured by a dummy variable that took on the value zero before the limit was changed and the value one thereafter. The regressions showed a positive coefficient for the speed limit dummy, indicating that the increased speed limit had increased fatalities. Their results are widely cited: they confirm the conventional wisdom that speed kills; and their analysis is one of the most sophisticated in the literature.[37] By building on the Garber-Graham model and data, Lave and Elias sought to avoid any suspicion that they had selected variables and data to favor their hypothesis.

They did make one important change in the Garber-Graham model, however, expanding the scope of the dependent variable to include any systemwide effects. Garber and Graham measured the effects of the speed limit on local roads. But the resource allocation perspective implies that changes in speed limits would also have systemwide effects, so Lave and Elias used the statewide fatality rate as their dependent variable. The rest of the specification was identical.

Table 8-4 shows the results. The fit is good: the mean R^2 for the forty regressions is 0.61. The estimated coefficients of the unemployment variable are negative, as expected (increased unemployment decreases the fatality rate), and the estimated coefficients of the seat belt dummy variable are mostly negative (seat belt laws decrease the fatality rate).

The results indicate that overall highway safety improved following the change to the 65 mph limit. The preponderance of the speed limit

36. Garber and Graham (1990).
37. For each state, Garber and Graham model fatalities per month as a function of the seasonally unadjusted unemployment rate for the state, because economic conditions strongly influence both the amount and type of driving; a dummy variable for states with mandatory seat belt use laws; a linear time trend to capture secular changes in roads, cars, traffic, or the population; dummy variables for each month of the year to control for seasonality effects; the number of weekend nights in each month, because more drinking occurs on weekends, and drinking is highly associated with accidents; and a 65 mph dummy variable.

Table 8-4. *Results of Regressions on the Estimated Effect of the*
65 MPH Speed Limit in Forty States

State	65 mph speed limit dummy		Percent unemployed		Belt use dummy		R^2	Mean of fatality rate
Ala.	−0.0014	(−0.89)	−0.00054	(−2.98)	...	...	0.650	0.031
Ariz.	−0.0099	(−5.81)	−0.00243	(−8.29)	...	...	0.761	0.041
Ark.	−0.0005	(−0.24)	−0.00005	(−0.12)	...	...	0.516	0.034
Calif.	−0.0018	(−2.28)	−0.00134	(−8.11)	−0.00127	(−1.51)	0.859	0.028
Colo.	−0.0025	(−0.76)	−0.00024	(−0.60)	0.00411	(1.20)	0.724	0.027
Fla.	−0.0034	(−2.70)	−0.00093	(−3.78)	−0.00355	(−2.70)	0.747	0.033
Ga.	0.0008	(0.53)	−0.00221	(−7.59)	−0.00382	(−2.41)	0.774	0.029
Idaho	−0.0026	(−0.56)	−0.00061	(−0.93)	0.00388	(0.98)	0.569	0.036
Ill.	0.0022	(1.93)	−0.00047	(−2.46)	0.00070	(0.61)	0.808	0.026
Ind.	0.0025	(0.53)	−0.00011	(−0.63)	−0.00453	(−0.99)	0.680	0.026
Iowa	0.0047	(2.01)	−0.00060	(−1.37)	0.00005	(0.02)	0.667	0.028
Kan.	−0.0016	(−0.75)	−0.00097	(−1.69)	−0.00105	(−0.50)	0.604	0.028
Ky.	0.0025	(1.56)	0.00026	(1.22)	...	...	0.662	0.030
La.	−0.0017	(−0.57)	−0.00044	(−1.07)	−0.00065	(−0.22)	0.689	0.038
Maine	−0.0015	(−0.66)	−0.00021	(−0.37)	...	...	0.444	0.026
Mich.	0.0005	(0.61)	−0.00034	(−3.14)	−0.00030	(−0.29)	0.821	0.025
Minn.	0.0017	(1.08)	−0.00153	(−5.25)	−0.00222	(−1.36)	0.817	0.022
Miss.	−0.0703	(−1.96)	−0.01293	(−2.38)	−0.02880	(−0.74)	0.089	0.065
Mo.	0.0044	(2.14)	−0.00099	(−2.33)	0.00044	(0.18)	0.465	0.030
Mont.	−0.0094	(−1.70)	−0.00111	(−1.26)	0.00528	(0.92)	0.562	0.037
Neb.	−0.0018	(−0.80)	−0.00111	(−1.97)	...	...	0.466	0.025
Nev.	−0.0096	(−1.36)	−0.00179	(−3.51)	0.01067	(1.53)	0.534	0.041
N.H.	−0.0051	(−2.57)	−0.00053	(−1.33)	...	...	0.520	0.024
N.M.	−0.0013	(−0.45)	−0.00089	(−1.76)	0.00012	(0.04)	0.674	0.045
N.C.	−0.0026	(−2.23)	−0.00047	(−1.96)	0.00081	(0.61)	0.770	0.032
N.D.	0.0149	(0.56)	0.00829	(0.93)	−0.00624	(−0.17)	0.108	0.041
Ohio	0.0002	(0.21)	−0.00053	(−3.72)	−0.00084	(−0.72)	0.757	0.024
Okla.	−0.0109	(−0.17)	−0.00762	(−1.63)	−0.01796	(−0.28)	0.090	0.050
Ore.	0.0004	(0.26)	−0.00055	(−2.32)	0.00088	(0.57)	0.678	0.030
S.C.	−0.0033	(−1.97)	−0.00081	(−3.19)	−0.00473	(−2.85)	0.592	0.036
S.D.	0.0043	(1.23)	−0.00048	(−0.40)	...	...	0.458	0.028
Tenn.	−0.0026	(−1.68)	−0.00047	(−2.29)	0.00101	(0.66)	0.695	0.032
Texas	−0.0029	(−2.66)	−0.00131	(−5.21)	−0.00288	(−2.60)	0.859	0.030
Utah	−0.0047	(−1.90)	−0.00098	(−2.33)	0.00223	(0.91)	0.535	0.028
Vt.	−0.0000	(−0.01)	−0.00243	(−3.16)	...	...	0.429	0.028
Va.	0.0004	(0.30)	−0.00090	(−3.22)	−0.00135	(−0.90)	0.780	0.023
Wash.	−0.0015	(−0.97)	−0.00132	(−6.20)	−0.00078	(−0.53)	0.777	0.025
W.Va.	0.0001	(0.02)	−0.00019	(−0.77)	...	...	0.485	0.038
Wis.	−0.0018	(−0.81)	−0.00040	(−1.93)	0.00170	(0.78)	0.742	0.024
Wy.	0.0031	(0.86)	−0.00111	(−1.65)	−0.00264	(−0.70)	0.713	0.038

Source: Lave and Elias (1997). The dependent variable is the monthly statewide fatality rate. Separate regressions are given for each state. Each regression also includes variables for number of weekend days per month, linear time trend, and dummies for month of the year.

dummies are negative, and their unweighted average shows a 3.21 percent drop in the fatality rate. This is strikingly close to the estimated 3.53 percent decline shown in table 8-3, when Lave and Elias compared the change in aggregate fatalities between states that did and did not adopt the new speed limit. But unlike the aggregate results, the estimates in table 8-4 do not depend on comparisons across states. Rather the effect in each state is measured compared with its own time trend and variables. That is, each state is treated as a separate speed limit "experiment": all these states raised limits, but there was no uniformity in their other actions.

Figure 8-2 plots the results from the systemwide model and the Garber-Graham model. Each bar is the t-ratio of a speed limit dummy for one state. If the bar points to the right, fatalities increased after the speed limit was raised; if it points to the left, they declined. The longer the bar the greater the significance of the estimate. Figure 8-2a shows the Garber-Graham results, the local effects of the higher speed limit; most of the bars point to the right. Figure 8-2b shows the results of the new model, the systemwide effects of the higher speed limit; most of the bars point to the left. If a t-ratio of 1.5 is used as a rough dividing point, the local effects show eleven fatality increases and two decreases; the systemwide effects show four increases and eleven decreases. (Of course, the systemwide effects subsume the local effects.)[38]

DEFINING THE DEPENDENT VARIABLE. Although it seems plausible that a change in speed limits on rural interstates would have effects beyond the immediate area, it is not clear how far those affects might extend. In particular, is it appropriate to use the statewide fatality rate in the model? What bias might this create? Statewide data will capture the wider effects of a speed limit change, but they will also include a lot of extraneous events that occur on roads outside the "ripple" area. That is, use of statewide fatality rates will

---

38. Lave and Elias performed a number of tests on these results. First, they examined an alternative hypothesis. Suppose there had been a nationwide break in fatality trends starting in 1987 and that fatality rates had begun an overall drop for some reason other than the new speed limit. If this were true, the 65 mph speed limit dummy would pick up the effect of this trend break and be spuriously negative. They checked this possibility using data from the states that had not raised their speed limits and found that, to the extent any trend break was detectable, it was in the opposite direction of the alternative hypothesis.

To make more efficient use of the data, they fit a regression that combined data to estimate a single regression for the forty states that had raised speed limits. The resultant speed limit dummy showed a 5.06 percent decrease in the fatality rate ($t = 3.19$, $R^2 = 0.61$) after the speed limits were raised. They deleted seven representative states, performed a Chow test, and found that this result was robust.

Figure 8-2. *Statewide vs. Local Effect of Increase in Speed Limit to 65 Miles per Hour*

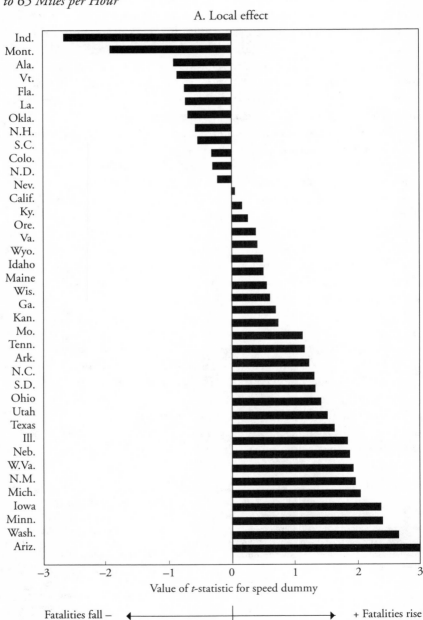

A. Local effect

Figure 8-2 *(continued)*

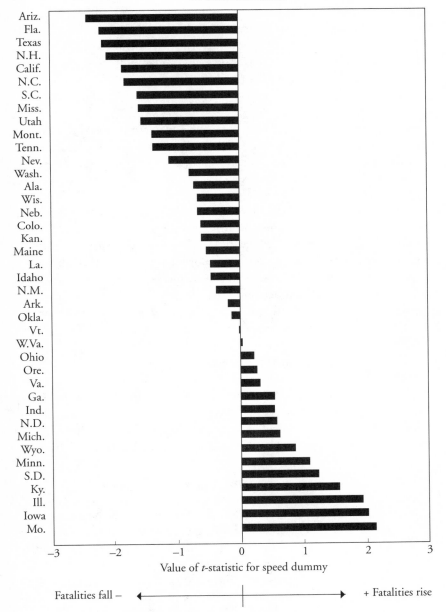

B. Statewide effect

Value of *t*-statistic for speed dummy

Fatalities fall −   ⟵—————————⟶   + Fatalities rise

Source: Lave and Elias (1997); Garber and Graham (1990).

measure the desired variable plus some amount of noise. If the noise is
random (in other words, if it is uncorrelated with the true measure), the
relationship between fatalities and higher speed limits will be harder to
measure, and so the explanatory power of the regression will go down.
Thus use of the statewide fatality rate will bias the speed limit dummy
toward insignificance. Despite this bias, it is apparent from figure 8-2 that
the statewide fatality model fits the data as well as the local effects model,
while subsuming its results.

SUMMARY. Previous evaluations of the 1987 increase in speed limits measured only the local effects of the change. From a resource allocation perspective, that is not the correct measure. Estimates of the systemwide effect
show that the new balance between local and statewide effects produced an
increase in safety: statewide fatality rates fell by between 3.2 and 5.1 percent

It appears that patrol resources and traffic had been misallocated. What
could have caused the misallocation? Consider the history of the 55 mph
speed limit. The causes of the initial fatality drop are difficult to disentangle, but whatever the reason for the original safety impact, the effects
were fading by the mid-1980s. Drivers were increasingly breaking the speed
limit, radar detectors had become a growth industry, drivers sought alternative routes, and the highway patrols found it increasingly burdensome to
allocate enough patrol officers to control speeding and maintain compliance with federal mandates.

Given these conditions, the new 65 mph speed limit freed highway
patrols to shift resources from speed enforcement on the interstates to other
safety activities and other highways; and the higher limit reallocated traffic
by making the (safer) interstate highways more attractive. Apparently, the
positive effects from improved resource allocation were more than enough
to offset any negative effects of higher speed on the interstate highways.

Effects of Abolishing the 55 MPH National Limit in 1996

In the fall of 1995 Congress considered abolishing the 55 mph national maximum speed limit and allowing the states to set their own speed
limits. The major national safety organizations responded with extensive
comments and testimony, predicting that increased speed limits would increase fatalities by between 4,000 and 6,400 fatalities a year. Apparently,
for them, the intuitive appeal of the speed-kills model still dominated any
possibility of offsetting behavior and systemwide effects. Nonetheless, Con-

gress did abolish the 55 mph national speed limit, and the data on subsequent events provide another chance to test the effects of the speed-kills model against the systemwide-effects model.

Thirty-two states, accounting for about three-quarters of total travel, raised their speed limits during 1996 (most did so by May). Nationwide traffic fatalities had risen by 1.5 percent in 1994 and by 2.0 percent in 1995.[39] In 1996, with the higher speed limits in place, total fatalities remained essentially unchanged from 1995. According to the NHTSA, they rose two-tenths of a percent; according to the National Safety Council, they fell by one-tenth of a percent.[40] Either figure is far below the additional 9.2–15 percent increase predicted by the speed-kills model. Furthermore, total travel increased in 1996, which means that the fatality rate actually fell. Preliminary data for 1997 show a continued failure of the speed-kills model: again, fatalities were level while total travel increased, thus producing a further decline in the fatality rate.

Obviously these are only preliminary results—the kind of detailed regression modeling that was done on the 1987 data must still be performed. But the results are very much in line with those obtained in the earlier analysis. Although higher speeds might lead to more deaths on the directly affected highways, it is more important to concentrate on policies that shift traffic from two-lane rural highways to interstate highways and that encourage minimum dispersion of highway speeds. The analysis indicates that shifting traffic to the interstate highways and deploying police more effectively led to a drop in state fatality rates, despite the higher speed limits.

Incidental Note on Driver Behavior

Part of the controversy over speed limits is rooted in two contrasting views of driver behavior: the "enforcement" view, and the "natural limit" view. Proponents of the enforcement view say that when choosing travel speeds, drivers give primary attention to posted limits and enforcement practices—they go as fast as they can get away with. Those who espouse the natural limit view say that when choosing travel speeds, drivers give primary attention to road geometry and traffic, not to speed limits—they travel at what they regard as the natural speed for that section of road.

Both theories predict that drivers will exceed the speed limit if it is set

---

39. National Safety Council (1997:2).
40. NHTSA (1998); National Safety Council (1997).

below the natural limit, which was probably the case with the old 55 mph limit. The critical test is what happens when the limit is raised. The enforcement view predicts that a 10 mph increase in posted speeds will cause a 10 mph increase in average observed speeds; the natural limit view does not. The data support the natural limit theory: 10 mph increases in posted speed usually resulted in 3–4 mph increases in average speed.[41] Apparently drivers were exceeding the old speed limit because it was below the natural limit, but when posted limits were raised, most drivers saw no reason to increase their speed. Traffic engineers were not surprised. Their studies had long supported the natural limit view, which is one reason why highway engineering manuals recommend setting speed limits at the 85th percentile speed of free-flowing traffic.

Summary of the Speed Limit Research

Congress instituted the 55 mph national maximum speed limit in 1974 to save energy. It didn't, but Congress kept it to save lives. Fatalities fell in 1974 for several reasons: reduced travel; the effects of the deep recession; the reduction in average speed; and probably of major importance, the reduction in speed variance among vehicles. We cannot untangle the relative contribution of these factors, because the necessary data were not collected at the time.

Whatever the original reasons, by the mid-1980s, the economy had recovered, and travel had increased. The police were finding it increasingly difficult to enforce an unpopular limit and both speed and speed variance were increasing.

Analysis of 1981–82 data show that the signaling rationale underlying speed limits (inform drivers about a reasonable common speed to follow, hence reduce variance) was more important than the control rationale. What matters most in setting a speed limit is choosing a limit that people will obey, hence reducing the variation in speed between cars.

The 1987 increase in speed limits provided an opportunity to explore another consequence of speed limits, their systemwide effects. When speed limits on rural interstate highways were raised in 1987, police were able to reallocate their resources to the activities they had argued were more important, and drivers were encouraged to move from dangerous highways to

41. National Research Council (1998:298–305).

faster, but safer interstates. The balance of these effects over the entire system was a reduction in fatalities.

A further test of the systemwide effects theory is provided by the data from the first two years of higher speed limits after the 55 mph national speed limit was abolished. The patterns in the data contradict the predictions of the speed-kills model, but are easily explained in terms of the systemwide model.

Overall Conclusions

Federal legislation and regulation of automobiles focus on the immediate concern, whether it is tailpipe emissions, safety, or fuel economy. The regulation, however, tends to take a myopic view of the issue, ignoring the possibility of system effects or behavioral changes. Congress, for example, did not intend vehicles to be less safe because it mandated a fuel efficiency standard of 27.5 mpg; it did not take into account that lighter, smaller vehicles are less safe, other factors held constant. The result has been the growth of solution-caused problems.

To be fair, it is not easy for regulators to calculate behavioral effects in advance. The transport system is complicated and highly interactive. There is no magic model that would allow Congress or the NHTSA to anticipate the systemwide implications of a new rule. Moreover, regulatory intervention will almost always produce unanticipated consequences. Drivers and passengers are not passive actors who simply do what they are told. Instead, they weigh personal considerations when deciding whether to adhere to a speed limit, buckle their seat belts, or drive faster because a vehicle has been made inherently safer; and they find ways around regulations, such as buying light trucks instead of cars to get the size and engine power that they desire. If regulations are to achieve their goal, they must be supported with other actions, such as public education on the benefits of buckling up, and higher gasoline prices to increase the desire for fuel-economic vehicles.

References

Barnett, Harold J., and Chandler Morse. 1963. *Scarcity and Growth: The Economics of Natural Resource Availability.* Johns Hopkins University Press for Resources for the Future.

Blomquist, Glenn. 1984. "The 55 M.P.H. Speed Limit and Gasoline Consumption." *Resources and Energy* 6:21–39.

CONAES (Committee on Nuclear and Alternative Energy Systems), National Research Council, National Academy of Sciences. 1980. *Energy in Transition 1985–2010: Final Report*. San Francisco: W.H. Freeman and Co.

Crandall, Robert W. 1992. "Policy Watch: Corporate Average Fuel Economy Standards." *Journal of Economic Perspectives* 6 (Spring):171–80.

Crandall, Robert W., and John D. Graham. 1989. "The Effect of Fuel Economy Standards on Automobile Safety." *Journal of Law and Economics* 32 (April): 97–118.

Crandall, Robert W., and others. 1986. *Regulating the Automobile*. Brookings.

Davis, Stacy C. 1997. *Transportation Energy Data Book: Edition 17*. ORNL-6916. Oak Ridge, Tenn.: Oak Ridge National Laboratory.

Evans, Leonard, and Wasielewski, Paul. 1987. "Serious or Fatal Driver Injury Rate Versus Car Mass in Head-on Crashes Between Cars of Similar Mass." *Accident Analysis and Prevention* 19(2): 119–131.

Garber, Steven, and John D. Graham. 1990. "The Effects of the New 65 Mile per Hour Speed Limit on Rural Highway Fatalities: A State-by-State Analysis." *Accident Analysis and Prevention* 22:137–49.

Godek, Paul E. 1997. "The Regulation of Fuel Economy and the Demand for 'Light Trucks.'" *Journal of Law and Economics* 40 (October): 495–510.

Greene, David L. 1990. "CAFE or Price: An Analysis of the Effects of Fuel Economy Regulation and Gasoline Price on New Car MPG, 1978–89." *Energy Journal* 11 (July): 37–58.

———. 1996. "Transportation and Energy." Eno Transportation Foundation, Inc., Lansdowne, Virginia.

Greene, David L., and Jin-Tan Liu. 1988. "Automobile Fuel Economy Improvements and Consumer Surplus." *Transportation Research* 22: 203–18.

Hauer, E. 1971. "Accidents, Overtaking, and Speed Control." *Accident Analysis and Prevention* 3 (January):1–12.

Kleit, Andrew W. 1990. "The Effect of Annual Changes in Automobile Fuel Economy Standards." *Journal of Regulatory Economics* 2 (June): 151–72.

Kwoka, John E. 1983. "The Limits of Market-Oriented Regulatory Techniques: The Case of Automobile Fuel Economy." *Quarterly Journal of Economics* 98 (November): 695–704.

Lave, Charles. 1985. "Speeding, Coordination, and the 55 MPH Limit." *American Economic Review* 75 (December): 1159–64.

Lave, Charles, and Patrick Elias. 1997. "Resource Allocation in Public Policy: The Effects of the 65-MPH Speed Limit." *Economic Inquiry* 35 (July): 614–20.

MacLean, Heather L., and Lester B. Lave. 1998. "Life Cycle Analysis: A Life-Cycle Model of an Automobile." *Environmental Science and Technology* 32 (July): 322–36.

Meadows, Donella H., and others. 1974. *Limits to Growth; a Report for the Club of Rome's Project on the Predicament of Mankind*. New York: Universe Books.

NHTSA (National Highway Traffic Safety Administration). 1989. "The Effects of the 65 MPH Speed Limit through 1988: A Report to Congress." U.S. Department of Transportation. October.

———. 1997. *Traffic Safety Facts, 1996*. U.S. Department of Transportation.

———. 1998. "The Effect of Increased Speed Limits in the Post-NMSL Era: Report to Congress." U.S. Department of Transportation. February.

National Research Council, U.S. Transportation Research Board. 1984. *55: A Decade of Experience,* edited by Edythe Traylor Crump. Special report 204. Washington, D.C.

_____. 1998. *Managing Speed: Review of Current Practice for Setting and Enforcing Speed Limits.* Special report 254. Washington, D.C.

National Safety Council. 1997. "Accident Facts." Chicago. October.

Schelling, Thomas C. 1978. *Micromotives and Macrobehavior.* W. W. Norton.

Solomon, David. 1964. "Accidents on Main Rural Highways Related to Speed, Driver, and Vehicle." U.S. Department of Transportation, Federal Highway Administration. July.

Tippet, Elmer. 1990. Testimony on highway safety in behalf of the International Association of Chiefs of Police, Division of State and Provincial Police, before the Surface Transportation Subcommittee, U.S. House of Representatives, March 22.

ROBERT A. LEONE

9

Technology-Forcing Public Policies and the Automobile

The Clean Air Act in the 1970s. Corporate average fuel economy standards in the 1980s. Air bags in the 1990s. These federal regulations all have two things in common: the automobile, of course; but more important, they were motivated by a shared belief that new technology could make cars cleaner, more fuel efficient, and safer without the political pain and economic disruption of limiting city driving, imposing high gasoline taxes, or enforcing unpopular changes in driver behavior.

These policy initiatives did not merely require the use of readily available technologies. Unlike the first safety regulations in the late 1960s that made mandatory previously optional items as simple as turn signals and windshield washers, these policies set regulatory standards at levels unachievable by then-existing technology. These technology-forcing mandates were often high-stakes confrontations between technical expertise and political tenacity. The Clean Air Act Amendments of 1970, for example, required a 90 percent reduction in emissions, with few means available to achieve the goal. In the Clean Air Act Amendments of 1977, Congress gave the industries two additional years to comply but raised the goal at the

The author thanks Jane Xi for her excellent assistance and Michael Thomas for his ideas and insights.

same time; Congress raised it again in the Clean Air Act Amendments of 1990. By then, regulations had also required the elimination of lead in gasoline; the reformulation of gasoline itself, and the demonstration that emissions control systems could withstand 100,000 miles of driving.[1]

As a result of these requirements, auto technology and air pollution appear to have improved substantially and at an apparently acceptable cost politically. Nevertheless, policy analysts still must ask whether technology-forcing regulation was the best alternative. Could the improvements in performance have been attained by other means at lower costs? To understand the issues involved in this question more fully, let us first look briefly at three sets of technology-forcing regulations aimed at achieving cleaner air, higher fuel economy, and greater auto safety.

Clean Air

From the public's perspective, policymakers' insistence that automakers build cleaner cars set in motion a sequence of technological advances that have dramatically reduced automotive emissions (see chapter 7). Through the accomplishment of a series of technological feats, many of which were deemed infeasible at the time they were first mandated, today's internal combustion engine emits 96 percent less pollution than its uncontrolled predecessors.[2] Although the antipollution advances in auto technology are apparent to every consumer, it is less apparent to analysts that these advances were achieved as quickly or as cost effectively as they might have been. Would tailpipe emissions fees have done the job better and faster?[3] On the one hand, such fees would discourage pollution from both new and old cars, equalizing the marginal cost of pollution control across all vehicles and thereby creating more ways to meet society's overall pollution control goals efficiently. On the other hand, establishing the proper fee and enforcing it on a fleet of more than 180 million vehicles could entail administrative costs so high that they could swamp the efficiency gains from the use of the pricing solution. Was it necessary in 1970 to impose the same standards on all types of automobiles? Would writing different standards for different pollution situations have permitted development of a

---

1. Dunn (1998: table 3-1, p. 55).
2. Scott (1997: 14).
3. See, for example, Hahn and Hester (1989) who discuss the use of pollution fees to control water pollution in Europe.

variety of pollution-reducing vehicles? Or would it simply have led to the inefficient purchase of vehicles in one jurisdiction for relocation to another jurisdiction with more costly control requirements?

Was the regulatory compliance time horizon of the 1970 clean air act so short that it virtually required the development of chemically based solutions such as catalytic converters instead of the electronic engine controls that are so effective today? Or would a slower approach have signaled a lack of political will to sustain these initiatives and lowered the priority of compliance to automotive researchers?

Fuel Economy

The public witnessed a similar phenomenon with corporate average fuel economy (CAFE) standards (see chapter 8). Legislated after the oil embargo in the early 1970s, the CAFE standards challenged automakers to improve the average gasoline mileage for new cars sold to 27.5 miles per gallon. Despite the need for a temporary relaxation of the standards in 1986, automakers eventually succeeded. By combining new lightweight materials with creative vehicle redesign and engine enhancements and by changing the relative prices of large and small cars, automakers have nearly doubled the fuel economy of the new car fleet by 55 percent since 1977. Even as the fuel economy regulations were being enacted, however, expectations of rising gasoline prices were also challenging automakers to improve fuel efficiency to satisfy the demands of their customers.

The challenge to the analyst of distinguishing between the role of price expectations and the role of regulation in achieving fuel economy is far from straightforward. Several economists who have reviewed the economic evidence have shown that expectations of rising fuel prices alone can explain much, if not all, of the gains in fuel efficiency.[4] Other analysts, however, note the uncertainty that surrounded gasoline market conditions when CAFE standards were imposed. These analysts point to a political unwillingness to decontrol gasoline prices, let alone allow them to reach levels that would reflect both energy market realities and negative externalities of gasoline use, such as air pollution and U.S. dependence on imported oil. Moreover, the distinction between the highly inelastic short-run demand for gasoline and the more elastic long-run demand was well recognized. In

---

4. See Crandall and Keeler (1987), Leone and Parkinson (1990), Crandall (1992), and Fauth (1994). For a somewhat contrary view, see Goldberg (1998).

the short run, consumers have greatly restricted options for reducing gasoline use because they have already purchased vehicles with particular fuel efficiency characteristics and because changing commuting patterns and the like in the short run is difficult. In the long run, consumers have more options. They can purchase vehicles that are more fuel efficient, for example, or even relocate their housing. One possible effect of a mandated improvement of fuel efficiency was to accelerate the movement from the short run to the long.[5] Sorting out these effects is difficult, but important, if analysts are to provide sound guidance on future public policies.

Automobile Safety

The effort to offer the driving public greater personal safety in the event of an accident illustrates not only the dilemma facing policymakers, but also the kinds of challenges confronting analysts. Although drivers and their passengers apparently wanted greater protection, many of them were unwilling both to buckle up on their own or to use the known seat belt interlock technology. Drivers rebelled at the mandatory installation of interlock systems that prevented them from starting their cars before fastening their seat belts—a common sequence even for regular seat belt users. The public outcry was so strong that Congress prohibited interlock systems and required that the buzzer reminding drivers to buckle up cannot sound for longer than eight seconds.[6]

The public, however, still wanted safer automobiles. So Congress passed technology-forcing regulations that required development of entirely new passive restraint technology that did not require driver activation—the air bag. Once again automakers came through, with innovations in crashworthy design as well as air bags. Drivers and passengers now experience vehicular deaths at half the rate they did in 1950.[7]

---

5. See, for example, Leone and Bradley (1982).

6. Gómez-Ibáñez (1997: 1).

7. Gómez-Ibáñez (1997: 14) It is useful to note that although drivers and passengers have seen their risks of a fatal crash decline by half for a given amount of driving, the increases in driving mean that this figure overstates the aggregate improvement. Similarly, auto emissions have not fallen 96 percent in the aggregate because people are now driving far more miles. Likewise, fuel economy may have increased substantially, but gasoline consumption has not fallen proportionately because people are driving more and driving more vans and light trucks that offer less fuel economy. This phenomenon is relevant to the assessment of all technology-forcing initiatives. Changes in technology that effectively lower the "price" of certain automobile attributes such as safety and fuel economy also stimulate demand, thus partially offsetting the intended effect in the aggregate.

Although few people would deny that today's vehicles are safer than those of the 1950s, analysts must still ask if these advances were cost-effective. For example, would correction of inefficient insurance practices have induced change more quickly and at lower cost than mandatory installation of air bags? Largely unregulated life insurance companies offer discounts for individuals who do not smoke, but the highly regulated auto insurance market does not offer discounts to individuals who wear seat belts. Or was safety regulation simply a less costly way to deal with the political challenge of automobile insurance regulation and the lack of consumer access to the information necessary to make informed decisions about safety? And just as with fuel efficiency, analysts are debating whether changes in driver behavior have nullified some of the benefits of mandated safety improvements in the vehicle.[8]

The Challenge to Analysts

At first glance the challenge to policy analysts is straightforward. Change in automotive technology can be created in three ways: by implementing price incentives that use market forces to bring about change; by mandating the use of existing, already developed technology; or by mandating new, technology-forcing solutions. Absent high transaction costs, limits to information, and political obstacles, the pricing alternative is especially attractive. It allows the decentralized decisions of producers and consumers to create innovative and cost-effective solutions to society's driving needs. It can make the use of known technologies widespread without a regulatory mandate and can stimulate technology change and effectively "force" the development of creative, new technologies. But transaction costs are sometimes high, information is not always widely available or fully understood, and political obstacles can be costly to overcome. It is, therefore, sometimes more desirable to mandate the use of a known technology or to set a technology-forcing standard than it is to construct and implement a market-based solution.

In the world of practical policymaking where costs and benefits are not always apparent, public support for the technology-forcing policy alternative is particularly understandable. The objective is clear, the method direct, and the outcome tangible. A price incentive often sounds like a tax,

---

8. See, for example, Peltzman (1975), Crandall (1984), Graham (1984), Garbacz (1990), Risa (1994), and Mannering and Winston (1995).

with the attendant political baggage. Known technologies have known costs and known imperfections. In contrast, the cost of a technology-forcing mandate is uncertain, its imperfections unknown. There is always the possibility that technology will create a low-cost solution. The analyst's challenge is to look beyond the public view, identify the opportunities and barriers to the successful implementation of various policies, and weigh the costs and benefits of what are likely to be less-than-perfect alternatives.

This chapter discusses general principles for evaluating technology-forcing policies, first by distinguishing between the economic rationale for mandating the use of *known* technologies and that for forcing the invention and use of *new* technology. The focus is on market imperfections and issues of dynamic efficiency that can make technology-forcing mandates an attractive policy option. The chapter then explores the political arguments for technology-forcing regulations that analysts must often rebut. The chapter applies these concepts to the specific case of electric vehicles, one of the latest areas of technology-forcing policy. The chapter then concludes with lessons generally applicable to emerging transportation technologies.

Why Have Technology Mandates?

The first question any analyst must ask is whether the benefits of government intervention justify the costs of that intervention.[9] When externalities do justify public intervention, price incentives can internalize externalities and still allow the many decisions of individual producers and consumers to assess risks, make trade-offs, and develop innovative ways to address society's ills. When price mechanisms are either politically unpalatable or excessively costly to develop or administer, the second economic choice tends to be reliance on a technology requirement.

Even in this case, it is important to distinguish between policy alternatives calling for a regulatory *performance standard* and those requiring a specific *technology standard*. A performance standard, for example, might specify that a driver must be able to survive a head-on collision at 25 miles per hour. A technology standard might mandate an air bag that achieved that same objective. The performance standard, depending on its stringency, need not force the development of new technology, but it does allow

---

9. See Blomquist and Peltzman (1981) and Crandall and others (1986).

for the possibility that someone might be able to invent something better than an air bag to achieve the desired objective.

Circumstances such as imperfect consumer information, high transaction costs, or the need to coordinate standards among manufacturers can justify technology standards. Sometimes it simply costs less to require a safety device than to educate consumers about the merits of different technologies. The transaction cost can be very high if the teaching device is an injury in an auto accident, for example. Sometimes the technology requirement is primarily to achieve the benefits of standardization as in the case of bumper heights or gasoline tank openings. Analysts are also aware that sometimes the practical consequence of setting a performance standard is to set a *de facto* technology standard because the performance requirements are based on a prototype technology (this is the case with the electric vehicle example discussed later). A performance standard based on surviving a crash at 25 miles per hour is different from a performance standard for a restraint system that protects in crashes up to 25 miles per hour. The former allows the automaker to achieve the goal with any means available. The latter starts with the presumption that a restraint system will be used to achieve this goal. The first approach might result in a radically different car design, while the second approach yields seat belts and air bags.

Mandating New Technology

Although the same reasons that justify government mandates of known technologies can also justify technology-forcing mandates, it is imperative to recognize the fundamental difference between the two types of technology regulation from the analyst's perspective. Economic debates over requiring the use of known technology are largely about issues of comparative static efficiency: what are the costs and benefits of the known technology versus known alternatives? Debates over technology-forcing policies, in contrast, are largely about issues of dynamic efficiency. They respond to the reality that the world is not static and that policy itself can create and shape the options society faces in meeting its needs.

For example, the cost of new technology typically declines as experience with both its production and use accumulates.[10] A government mandate or some other form of regulatory initiative can facilitate this "learning

10. See Abernathy (1978), Abernathy and Utterback (1978), Freeman (1982), Ghemawat (1985), and Girifalco (1991).

curve" effect. Government-mandated emissions control technology, for example, might have a projected social benefit of $500 per vehicle, but an initial cost of $1,000 per car. Based on experience with similar technologies, the analyst may be able to predict confidently that as production experience increases, the cost will fall to, say, $300, while the benefits remain unchanged. After properly accounting for the time value of money and the period in which costs exceed benefits, the analyst might conclude that society would benefit from "forcing" the initially uneconomic introduction of the technology through a regulatory mandate.

A second argument for technology-forcing policy is behavioral. From a managerial viewpoint, technology-forcing policies are the public equivalent of "stretch goals" that managers use to motivate private organizations and fuel creativity; in this case, the managers are policymakers seeking to take account of a negative externality. The ideas are the same, with similar possibilities and limitations. A manager's stretch goals do not succeed if they are so limited in their reach that they simply encourage modest, incremental improvement, but no fundamental change in thinking. Thus, a manager might ask the manufacturing division to reduce costs by 5 percent when its average annual rate of productivity improvement has been 3 percent. That is a stretch goal, but one likely achievable without a fundamental change in the ways of doing business. Worse, workers might accomplish this goal in the short run by cutting corners and sacrificing quality. Another manager might ask for a 50 percent cost reduction and so frustrate workers by the impracticality of this "stretch" that nothing good happens. Still a third manager might say, "Cut costs 25 percent" and stimulate new ways of thinking about cost control that result in radical improvements in performance. The same logic applies to technology-forcing public policies. A small stretch likely means that technological fixes will be minor, may unintentionally sacrifice benefits of existing technology, and may not force technology at all. Seat belt interlock systems are a case in point. The more substantial technological stretch to passive restraints, in contrast, led to air bags. Conversely, excessively large stretches mean that nothing is likely to be achieved. Requiring automakers to produce cars that get 80 miles per gallon and are pollution free does not make such cars either technologically or economically feasible.

Learning Curve versus Stretch Goals

The learning curve and stretch goal arguments are fundamentally different both in their focus and their intent. Learning curves focus on the economics of technological development, while stretch goals focus on human behavior and organizational dynamics.

The learning curve concept applies to an *existing* prototype technology with current costs in excess of current benefits, but expectations of cost reductions associated with learning. The product innovation already exists. The cost improvement results from *process innovations and incremental product changes* that come from experience producing the prototype product over time. Thus, when Intel forecasts the price at which it can profitably sell Pentium chips, it is using learning curve techniques. These methods do not apply, however, to the invention of the Pentium chip itself. A stretch goal, in contrast, typically seeks a *product innovation* in the first place, as when Lee Iaccoca challenged Ford engineers to build a small, sporty car for under $2,500 and they created the Mustang in the early 1960s, or when Congress challenged automakers to reduce auto emissions by 90 percent in 1970.

The Public Role in Facilitating Learning Curves

Product innovations that become profitable only with the benefits of learning curve cost reductions are common in the marketplace. Private investors regularly finance such innovation with no government intervention. Indeed, that is the process behind virtually all new consumer product innovations from VCRs to hand-held computers. When the technology is intended to respond to an externality, such as air pollution, a public role emerges, as illustrated in the previous example of the mandated pollution control device whose cost drops from $1,000 to $300 as its producers move down the learning curve. Even in the case of externalities, however, analysts have to ask whether there is a more cost-effective alternative to a technology mandate and whether the costs of intervention itself exceed the value derived from reducing the social costs of the externality. For example, a tailpipe emission fee that successfully internalized the cost of pollution might encourage private investors to pursue learning curve economies associated with pollution control devices without the need for a technology-forcing mandate. In this example, the analyst's task is to subtract the administrative costs of a price incentive from the efficiency gains and then compare that net result to the net efficiency from implementing a technology-forcing mandate.

The Public Role in Setting Stretch Goals

Technology-forcing policies based on stretch goals have the positive characteristic that they focus both corporate and consumer attention. A technology-forcing mandate not only places demands on producers, but can alert and inform the public as to the potential merits and possibilities of new technology. Would consumers have known enough to demand air bags in cars, for example, if policy entrepreneurs like Ralph Nader and regulatory initiatives had not encouraged their development? There is, of course, a "chicken and egg" character to this kind of behavioral argument, but it seems unwise to conclude that the public debate and entrepreneurial policy initiatives surrounding technology-forcing regulations do not play an important role in articulating social demands, educating consumers, and focusing the attention of producers.

Stretch goals in the public arena are also different in some fundamental ways from stretch goals in private organizations, so the analogy should not be carried too far. Regulatory and administrative practices have far more formal procedural elements than even the most bureaucratic corporation and must cope with a far broader set of competing political interests. A major characteristic of this institutional process is the possibility that a special interest might capture a regulatory proceeding, which might then extend a policy commitment to a new technology long after its economic merits have proven limited. The supersonic transport and nuclear power—both public stretch goals in their infancy—are examples outside the auto industry. The prospects of commercial supersonic aircraft seemed quite appealing when this technology was on the drawing boards. As the environmental consequences, technological challenges, and costs revealed themselves, however, the promise largely evaporated, but the political pressure to continue to fund the European joint venture did not. Similarly, the promise of nuclear power to generate electricity "too cheap to meter" disappeared as concerns about safety and environmental issues drove up both capital and operating costs. Long after these economic realities were apparent, regulatory practices and government policy continued to direct resources to nuclear power plants.

There is also a tendency when addressing public stretch goals to focus the policy debate on the extremes of the competing claims—for example, those who say it is indeed possible to build, say, an automobile that averages 80 miles per gallon and those who say it cannot be done. Although the wise observer often discounts the claims of both sides in such public debates, one material consequence of the debate is often to divert attention from more basic and ultimately far more important economic questions about the effectiveness of command and control regulatory regimes or the way research and development is organized and managed in an advanced economy.

Diminishing Returns to Stretch Goal Policies

There is also a danger that the perceived success of technology-forcing stretch goal policies will lead to their overuse. Even if technology-forcing policies worked well in the past, that is no guarantee they will work well in the future. In the past, individual technological breakthroughs added a few hundred dollars to the cost of a new car. Consumers grumbled, but paid the extra costs. The concept of diminishing returns suggests that each further technological breakthrough is likely to be more costly than the one before it. It is essential to ask whether consumers are nearing the limits of what they will pay for increasingly sophisticated automobile technology. In the past, some of the initial innovations—especially those related to emissions controls—proved relatively easy to achieve because this was a largely untapped technological arena. Today's automotive technology is sufficiently advanced that "Mr. Goodwrench" is as likely to use a computer as a socket wrench. Again, the concept of diminishing returns compels analysts to ask if technology has been pushed so far in the past thirty years that the costs of further technology-forcing policies will be unacceptable to consumers.

An Additional Real World Complexity

The static efficiency arguments for mandating known technologies can be distinguished conceptually from those dynamic efficiency arguments justifying technology-forcing policies, just as the arguments for price incentives can be distinguished from arguments for mandates. But the reality is that all these arguments are often mixed together in the policy arena. Economists may conclude that gasoline taxes are more efficient than fuel economy regulations in achieving both static and dynamic efficiency, but the public may find a more costly regulation preferable to something called a "tax." Indeed, Congress clearly and deliberately opted for technology-based fuel efficiency standards over higher gasoline taxes, even though economists argued strenuously the merits of the price incentive alternatives.[11] Economists can argue with unquestionable logic and reams of empirical data that a particular solution would be the most economically efficient, but if that solution is not politically acceptable, it is unlikely to be implemented, and policymakers are likely to turn to a technology mandate—

11. Leone and Bradley (1982).

perhaps forcing, perhaps not. Sometimes, the seemingly more heavy-handed approach of a technology-forcing mandate is necessary to focus large, bureaucratic corporations on their own self-interest. Efficient prices in perfect markets may well provide the most effective way to deal with many issues of social regulation, but just as markets are not perfect, organizations are not perfect either. Automakers long had a self-interest in fuel efficiency and auto safety that they did not exploit to their own benefit, for example, until policy entrepreneurs brought these issues to the forefront and legitimized and informed consumer demand. Ralph Nader, after all, first wrote *Unsafe at Any Speed* for public consumption and then parlayed his subsequent fame into the political strength behind technology-forcing safety regulation.

Political pressures compound the analytical challenges facing policymakers evaluating technology-forcing policies. To understand why, consider James Dunn's characterization of the views of those political interests advocating both technology mandates and technology-forcing policies:

> First, auto manufacturers have made billions by imposing heavy external costs on the American public by vehicle designs that are less safe, less fuel efficient, and more polluting than they could be. Strong public regulatory standards must be imposed to compel auto makers to develop the technologies and vehicle designs to reduce the negative externalities of their products.
>
> Second, technology-forcing regulatory standards for automobiles, backed by the threat of stiff financial penalties against auto manufacturers, should be set as high as outside experts deem feasible. The objections of the wealthy auto companies that the cost of compliance is too high should be discounted in advance.[12]

While these notions may be persuasive politically, their economic logic is clearly flawed, and dealing with these flaws poses a challenge of its own to analysts. First, despite the claims, it is not apparent that automakers have profited as greatly from their allegedly flawed designs as some advocates of social regulation claim, especially from the production of less safe or less fuel-efficient vehicles. In an efficient marketplace, automakers have a clear financial incentive to improve fuel efficiency, for example, as an indirect means of competing for consumer dollars that would otherwise go

12. Dunn (1998: 57).

to petroleum companies. Similarly, automakers have no inherent interest in unsafe vehicles. The cost of auto insurance is a major element in the cost of automobile ownership, and the production of safer vehicles, particularly vehicles less subject to damage in crashes, would permit automakers to compete for consumer dollars otherwise going to auto insurers. Domestic automakers may not have felt the profit incentive to respond to these consumer pressures when they were the more oligopolistic "Big Three," but international competition has changed that former reality. Today, the competitive pressures for an automaker to extract every dollar of profit in a highly competitive global marketplace are intense. The case that automakers, especially in a highly competitive global market, have less incentive to deal with emissions problems is more persuasive, because pollution is an obvious externality that can be costly to control. The costs are focused on the consumer, while the benefits are dispersed to society.

Even if the critics of automakers are correct, however, the conclusion that technology-forcing policies are the proper response does not follow. There are ready alternatives to technology-forcing policies, which, if not necessarily preferred, certainly require consideration. Restructuring auto insurance practices to deal efficiently with safety issues would encourage the design of safer vehicles and safer driving at the same time. A gasoline tax that reflects the social costs of petroleum and automobile use could internalize those social costs and, unlike the CAFE standards, not have the unintended effect of lowering the incremental cost of automobile use and thereby encouraging auto users to drive more miles. The air pollution issue could be addressed by various pollution pricing regimes designed to internalize this externality and perhaps encourage owners to retire older, more polluting vehicles more quickly.[13] And finally, the marginal social cost of the most feasible technology may exceed its marginal social benefits and thus not justify any intervention at all, despite the existence of an externality.

In short, the political claim of less safe, less fuel efficient or more polluting vehicles, even if true, is not a logical argument for technology-forcing regulation. The argument that automakers are wealthy has its own set of logical difficulties because it ignores questions of incidence. Whether or not automakers are wealthy, by itself, says little about who bears the actual cost of technology-forcing regulatory initiatives: Is it really shareholders in lower dividends and lower rates of capital appreciation? Or is it labor in

13. Whether the transactions costs associated with the implementation of any of these alternatives are feasible remains to be seen, but the conclusion that they ought to be considered does not.

lower wages and fewer jobs? Is it consumers in higher prices and fewer choices? Answers to these questions require thoughtful analysis, not merely convenient assertions that technological progress can make change costly only to automakers.

It is the analyst's challenge to deal with the political arguments for technology-forcing policies and to distinguish the comparative static and dynamic efficiency arguments for mandates. It is also the analyst's obligation while meeting these challenges not to lose sight of what can be sound economic and behavioral arguments for technology-forcing policies.

The Case of Electric Vehicles

The electric vehicle (EV) is perhaps the latest in a long list of technology-forcing regulatory initiatives in the auto industry and one that can illustrate the attraction and the pitfalls of technology-forcing regulation. The EV case has many familiar elements. The political attraction of the technology is seemingly obvious: a pollution-free vehicle that operates quietly without using a petroleum-based fuel. The mandate to produce EVs is not literally a technology standard, but a performance standard to build zero emission vehicles. Electric technology appears to be the most feasible near-term option for achieving the standard in the mandated time period, and it is supported by a strong lobby of environmentalists, auto industry skeptics, and electricity interests. Some of the economic pitfalls are also obvious. Advocates are quick to acknowledge that EVs are currently not economically viable, but they also maintain that experience with the technology will eventually bring the costs down.

The political impetus for EVs began in California where automobile-related air pollution problems remain very serious, despite the extraordinary advances in automobile emissions control.[14] Many options for addressing California's remaining air pollution problems are politically unpalatable or extremely expensive: these include unpopular restrictions on driving; costly public transit investments that are disruptive and require long lead times; and fundamental changes in land use that require even longer lead times. EVs, in contrast, emit no emissions at the point of use and, therefore, do not require driving restrictions. Although the electricity to power them does generate pollution at the power plant, these discharges

14. Dabels (1992).

typically occur away from urban areas (at least in California) and need not exacerbate the air pollution problems in an urban air basin. The highway infrastructure already exists to accommodate EVs, and no pervasive changes in land use are necessary.

The regulatory approach in California was straightforward. In 1992 California policymakers required that 2 percent of all new cars manufactured for sale in the state in 1998 must be zero emission vehicles; the share was required to rise to 5 percent in 2001 and to 10 percent in 2003. Effectively this was an EV mandate because no other zero emission technology was far enough along in development to have a chance of meeting the 2 percent requirement. The idea caught on in other jurisdictions with their own air quality compliance problems. Maine, Massachusetts, New York, and Vermont soon adopted the California mandates, as federal law allowed.[15]

Following costly court and political battles in several jurisdictions, the California mandates for 1998 were subsequently eliminated because of the impracticality of so aggressive a pace of technological and consumer change.[16] But the requirement that EVs represent 10 percent of the vehicles offered for sale by 2003 remained in place.[17] This goal, too, may prove unrealistic. Technical challenges aside, it would be extraordinary for any automobile—whether a new or old technology—to gain a 10 percent market share in just five years, from 1998 to 2003, given the wide variety of consumer tastes and the equally wide variety of vehicle types in the automotive marketplace. The political appeal of EVs and the mandates for 2003 notwithstanding, analysts must still ask whether EVs satisfy basic criteria for economic soundness and ought to be mandated.

Four Analytical Questions

To make this determination, analysts need to answer at least four different questions. The first deals with social benefits. Does mandating production of EVs ensure that the benefits to society (which presumably justified

---

15. Scott (1997: 1–19).
16. Scott (1997: 19–21). Because the other states had literally adopted the California mandate, the relaxation of the mandate in California led to its relaxation elsewhere. Whether other states must literally adopt the California mandate under the federal clean air act is itself a contentious legal issue.
17. Because the mandate applies to producers, not consumers, there is further legal hairsplitting on just what the base is to which the 10 percent mandate applies.

imposition of the mandate in the first place) will outweigh the costs? The second and third questions deal with the benefits to the consumer from owning and operating an EV. If EVs cost more than consumers are now willing to pay, will a policy of production mandates help make the cars less expensive by forcing them down the learning curve? Even if EVs are, or become, economically feasible, will consumers accept their driving characteristics? If not, will a policy of production mandates lead to the invention of a new vintage of EVs more acceptable to consumers? Fourth, to the extent that there is a public policy interest in developing EV technology, is a production mandate a cost-effective way of doing so?

Weighing the Social Benefits and Costs

The first question the analyst must answer is whether the technology being mandated is the right technology from society's standpoint. A cost-benefit assessment of the prototype EV technology suggests that it is not. Public advocates argue for EVs on grounds that their impact on the environment will be minimal. The evidence indicates, however, that this enthusiasm is misdirected. The current vintage of EV technology does not appear to meet a social cost-benefit test after accounting for environmental externalities for three reasons.

POLLUTION-SHIFTING TECHNOLOGY. First, current EV technology is pollution shifting rather than pollution reducing. The vehicle itself may not emit harmful emissions, but the power plant that generates its electricity does. Because the health effects caused by the physical concentration of pollutants in urban areas are different from those caused by the same volume of pollutants in less populated areas, there is a potential societal gain from pollution shifting in some areas, but not in others. To achieve these gains, it is essential to consider carefully the implications for regions downwind of the fuel-burning power plants. This is especially important in high-density corridors such as the Northeast. The existence of a net social benefit in this dimension is ambiguous, at best.

From a greenhouse gas standpoint, what matters is total emissions and not dispersal or concentration. According to one study, the United States' current reliance on coal to generate electricity means that on a per vehicle basis, EVs may actually increase greenhouse gas emissions by 5 percent compared with gasoline-powered vehicles. More favorable, but less realistic assumptions that EVs are much more fuel efficient than gasoline ve-

Table 9-1. *Estimated Changes in Pollutant Emissions Caused by Shifting from Gasoline-Powered Vehicles to Electric Vehicles*

Category	Volatile organic compounds	Carbon monoxide	Nitrogen oxides	Sodium oxides	Particulate matter
Percentage changes from shifting to EVs	−98.7	−98.7	20.4	303.9	25.3
Gross EV vehicle emissions (grams per kilometer)	0.16	2.10	0.25	0.01	0.01
Changes from gasoline-powered vehicles (grams per kilometer)	0.16	2.07	0.05	0.25	0.00
Annual change from shifting to EVs (grams)	3,158	41,454	1,020	492	35

Source: OECD (1993: tables 4.8, 4.9, and 4.11). Average annual mileage for each car is 20,000 kilometers. The OECD study considers two scenarios. The one portrayed here compares high-efficiency EVs to low-efficiency gasoline-powered vehicles. The alternative scenario further reduces the benefits and increases the costs of EVs.

hicles find that EVs reduce greenhouse gases by 45 percent.[18] Whether there is a benefit or cost in this dimension appears to be highly uncertain and must be considered in a much broader context than that of just the EVs themselves.

DIFFERENCES IN THE MIX OF POLLUTANTS. Second, EVs do not merely shift pollution from one location to another, they alter the level and mix of pollutants, as table 9-1 shows. For example, particulate emissions from power plants are greater than those emissions from gasoline-powered vehicles. Because particulate emissions have especially serious health effects, the shift in the mix of pollutants associated with EVs therefore results in costs that can offset some or all of the benefits from reductions in total emissions and emission shifting. As reported in Small and Kazimi, the benefit to the citizens of Los Angeles of reducing one ton of volatile organic compounds is $10,670, while the cost to them of adding one ton of sodium oxide is $109,900. For every ton of volatile organic compounds eliminated, EVs add 0.156 tons of sodium oxide. The cost of the higher levels of

18. OECD (1993: table 4-12).

sodium oxide (0.156 tons times $109,900 a ton) is $17,144 versus a benefit of $10,670, yielding a net social loss.[19]

INDIRECT ENVIRONMENTAL EFFECTS. Third, EVs themselves indirectly create new forms and levels of pollution. The hazard of battery disposal is one.[20] In the absence of infrastructure systems capable of producing and recycling lead in an environmentally benign manner, these hazards alone may fully offset any other perceived environmental benefits of EVs. Less commonly cited is the effect of EVs on total emissions from the driving fleet. EVs have high capital costs, but low operating costs relative to gasoline-powered vehicles (and even lower relative variable costs if public policy increases the gasoline tax as many analysts advocate.)[21] With low variable costs, EV owners will likely use their vehicles more intensively than owners will use gasoline-powered vehicles, perhaps reducing car-pooling or the use of public transit.

Whatever the mechanism, the lower variable cost will encourage use of EVs in the applications for which they are most suited. That includes commuting and implies, therefore, that EVs will likely contribute to urban congestion. Increased congestion means increased pollution from the existing fleet of gasoline-powered vehicles caught in slowed traffic. With most urban vehicles still powered by gasoline, therefore, one consequence of increased use of EVs will be to increase the emissions from the gasoline-powered fleet. Table 9-2 shows that the magnitude of this effect is unclear, hinging critically on the price elasticity of demand for driving.[22] The direction is clear, however: the impact is negative and, therefore, if properly accounted for, would further reduce the social benefits of EVs.[23]

19. Small and Kazimi (1995)

20. Lave, Hendrickson, and McMichael (1995).

21. The calculations reported here are based on an operating cost advantage for electric vehicles of approximately $0.01 per mile. In table 9-2, this differential results from an assumed gasoline price of $1.40 per gallon and an assumed electricity cost of $0.117 per kilowatt hour. If the gasoline price is dropped to $1.00 per gallon to reflect current prices and the cost per kilowatt hour is dropped to $0.08 to reflect off-peak charging and other effects of deregulation in electricity markets, the operating cost differential of EVs remains about $0.01 per mile.

22. Table 9-2 calculates the congestion effect of two alternative price elasticities of demand for driving: −0.3 and −2.0. These empirically based estimates might usefully be thought of as the short-run and long-run elasticities, respectively. The choice of elasticity notwithstanding, the conclusion holds that an operating cost differential between EVs and gasoline-powered vehicles will stimulate more intensive use of EVs. Although the added driving may be small, basic principles of queuing indicate that even small increments to already congested highway systems can yield large congestion effects.

23. If EVs achieve a critical mass and displace a sufficiently large number of gasoline-powered cars, this pollution effect is eliminated—but not the effect of added congestion on driver welfare.

Existing EV prototypes do not currently satisfy a social cost-benefit test. Although they reduce some pollutants in some locations, their systemwide environmental impact is negative. Without fundamental changes in battery technology and recycling and associated changes in power plant emissions controls, future EVs are still unlikely to pass a social cost-benefit test. Will a technology-forcing policy of product mandates help meet these formidable challenges?

None of these required developments benefit specifically from the learning curve economies associated with a technology-forcing policy mandating production of EVs. Power plant emissions are clearly an issue of their own. The pace of mandated EV production virtually compels automakers to use available lead battery technology and thereby diverts resources from fuel cell development or hybrid vehicles that use both electric and fossil fuel technology. EV production mandates might indirectly stimulate the creation of a lead battery recycling infrastructure, but more direct methods for achieving that same objective are easy to envision—for example, a mandatory battery recycling program or a battery return deposit fee collected at purchase.

Can one make a stretch goal argument for a technology-forcing policy of EV mandates? A successful stretch goal works by combining two mechanisms: organizational focus and learning. Although the intricacies of these mechanisms can be very difficult to understand, it is not difficult to appreciate that the success of a stretch goal depends critically on the choice of focus and subject for learning. A production mandate focuses on process learning, but as the preceding cost-benefit analysis demonstrated, society has little to gain and possibly much to lose from simply learning how to make existing EVs more economically. The first problem, therefore with the stretch goal argument for a technology-forcing mandate of EV production is that even if it is successful, it is aimed at the wrong target. Learning needs to be focused either on development of different low or zero emission technologies or on the recycling and power generation industries.

Consumer Cost

From a private perspective, current EVs may well be able to reap the cost reductions associated with learning and meet a consumer cost-benefit test, but even that is unlikely to happen within the mandated time frame. Current cost estimates suggest that battery-powered vehicles are likely to cost between $5,000 and $21,000 more than comparable gasoline-powered

Table 9-2. *Stylized Simulation of the Congestion Consequences of Electric Vehicles*

Scenario	Year												
	1	2	3	4	5	6	7	8	9	10	11	12	13
Base assumptions													
Percentage of new cars sold that are EVs[a]	2	2	2	5	5	10	10	10	10	10	10	10	10
Percentage of EVs in the driving fleet[b]	0.2	0.4	0.6	1.1	1.6	2.6	3.6	4.6	5.6	6.6	7.6	8.6	9.6
Scenario A													
(Demand elasticity for additional driving = –2.0)													
Percentage increase in vehicle equivalents[c]	0.12	0.23	0.35	0.64	0.93	1.50	2.08	2.66	3.24	3.82	4.39	4.97	5.55
Passenger cars per lane per mile[d]	72.3	72.4	72.5	72.9	72.9	73.3	73.7	74.1	74.6	75.0	75.4	75.8	76.2
Urban driving speed (miles per hour)[e]	30.0	29.9	29.9	29.8	29.7	29.5	29.3	29.1	28.9	28.6	28.5	28.3	28.1
Gasoline-vehicle emission index[f]	100	100	100	100	100	101	101	101	101	101	102	102	102
Scenario B													
(Demand elasticity for additional driving = –0.3)													
Percentage increase in vehicle equivalents[c]	0.02	0.03	0.05	0.10	0.14	0.23	0.31	0.40	0.49	0.57	0.66	0.75	0.83
Passenger cars per lane per mile[d]	72.2	72.3	72.3	72.3	72.3	72.4	72.5	72.5	72.6	72.6	72.7	72.7	72.8
Urban driving speed (miles per hour)[e]	30.0	30.0	30.0	30.0	30.0	29.9	29.9	29.9	29.8	29.8	29.7	29.7	29.7
Gasoline-vehicle emission index[f]	100	100	100	99	99	98	97	96	95	94	93	92

Source: Turner (1973); Transportation Research Board (1985); Gómez-Ibáñez and Fauth (1980). Gómez-Ibáñez and Fauth show three elasticities of demand for driving; this simulation uses two of them.

a. This stylized simulation assumes a base of 100 million automobiles. The life of a car is ten years, and all vehicles purchased ten years earlier are retired and replaced each year. In the first year of the simulation, 2 percent of the 10 million new vehicles are electric; this percentage increases over time, stabilizing at 10 percent in year 6.

b. For simplicity, all new vehicles replace all retiring vehicles on the first day of the year, resulting in a rising percentage of EVs over time, nearing its steady state rate of 10 percent at the end of the simulation.

c. This calculation begins with the assumption that the energy efficiency of an EV is 0.25 kilowatt hour per kilometer and the electricity price is \$.117 per kilowatt hour, yielding a variable cost of driving an EV of \$0.029 per kilometer. The assumed energy efficiency of a gasoline-powered vehicle is 9 kilometers per liter and the gasoline price is \$1.40 per gallon, yielding a variable cost of driving a gasoline-powered vehicle of \$0.041 per kilometer. Under these assumptions, EVs therefore have a variable cost of driving that is 28.9 percent lower than the cost for gasoline-powered vehicles. The demand elasticity effect is first calculated in additional kilometers driven and then divided by the average number of kilometers per vehicle to yield the "vehicle equivalent" increase in driving.

d. A typical urban driving density in the United States is seventy-two passenger cars per lane per mile. This figure rises proportionately as more vehicle-equivalent driving takes place.

e. The initial simulation conditions assume an average urban driving speed of 30 miles per hour. Congestion increases as more vehicle-equivalent driving takes place. This congestion, in turn, slows traffic.

f. The initial simulation conditions set the total emissions from gasoline-powered vehicles at 100. As EVs replace gasoline vehicles, this index number falls; as the driving speed falls, emissions from the remaining gasoline-powered vehicles increase as vehicles stay on the road longer. See Turner (1973).

cars.[24] Despite the size of this cost gap, experience with learning curves in other sectors suggests that increased production volume could narrow it substantially. To illustrate: As part of the political agreement to eliminate the 1998 EV production mandate of 2 percent of all new cars offered for sale in California, seven major automakers have committed to producing a total of 3,750 EVs between 1998 and 2000. Even at this low production volume, assuming a learning rate of 20 percent, the cost of an EV could approach the cost of a gasoline-powered vehicle by 2012.[25] A policy of production mandates, therefore, would appear to offer the prospect of narrowing the gap between the prices consumers would be asked to pay for electric and gasoline-powered vehicles. Without a social benefit argument for doing so, however, there is no need for the public to intervene to bring this cost reduction about. Private markets can and routinely do achieve this type of result without public intervention.

Consumer Learning

Virtually all observers agree that in addition to substantial reductions in cost, substantial improvements in performance—or perceptions of performance—will be necessary to make EVs privately attractive to the consuming public. From a consumer viewpoint, EVs are currently lacking: they are expensive and untested; the refueling process is unfamiliar, and few refueling sites are available; and the EV driving range is limited.

One advance that does depend directly on EV production and use is the stimulation of consumer learning from experience. Thus once the man-

---

24. Scott (1997:14).

25. Assume that a gasoline-powered vehicle costs $20,000 and a closely equivalent EV costs $30,000. By 2003, more than 3,750 EVs will have been produced for California alone. At this rate, vehicle production experience will double by 2006. At a learning rate of 20 percent, the cost would drop to $24,000. By 2012, volume will have doubled once again and the cost would be $19,200. Of course, this learning rate is hypothetical, but reasonable, based on experience in other manufacturing sectors where rates of 20 to 30 percent are common. Intuitively, a rate of 20 percent seems high, with many people expecting faster learning at early stages in a product's life cycle. The learning rate, however, applies to *cumulative* production experience. A 20 percent rate means that each time cumulative volume doubles, costs fall by 20 percent. Volume doubles quickly early in a product's life cycle and slowly as cumulative experience increases. Thus, for example, a learning rate of 20 percent for gasoline-powered vehicles would lead only to a 20 percent cost reduction after doubling the total number of cars built, counting all the cars that have been built to date. That would take many years. Over time, relative price and regulatory changes are likely to add to costs. Finally, some technological advances in EVs will improve performance, not lower cost. The conclusion remains, however, that it is reasonable to expect EVs to satisfy a *private* cost-benefit test in a decade or so.

dated EVs have come to market and are put into use, consumers may come to see EVs very differently from the way they are viewed now. For example, EVs are quiet and easy to maintain. The unfamiliar fueling pattern could be ideal for refueling at the workplace or overnight at home, with no smelly hands or side trips to the gas station. The short driving range becomes largely irrelevant once consumers view EVs as complements to a family's "fleet" of vehicles, which might contain a passenger car and a sports utility vehicle—both less attractive commuting vehicles than EVs.

Is it possible, then, that the benefits from consumer learning necessary to help consumers understand the benefits of electric vehicles justify the costs of a technology-forcing mandate even though there are serious environmental problems with the widespread use of existing EV technology? Again, the answer would appear to be "no" and for two different reasons. First, as discussed below, consumer experience derived from a policy of mandates may actually "teach" consumers the wrong things about alternatives to gasoline-powered vehicles; and second, there may be far more productive and less costly strategies for learning about new technology.

Policymakers desiring to advance the legitimate social objective of encouraging new automotive technology without costly and counterproductive mandates have a wide variety of instruments available to them that do not involve technology-forcing production mandates. These instruments facilitate learning at relatively low cost and deal with some of the market imperfections impeding development of automotive technology. Unlike mandates, however, they do not have costly indirect and unintended effects, nor do they risk focusing efforts on the wrong target. From the consumer viewpoint, the key issues relating to any new auto technology are costs, risks, and performance. The policy challenge is to overcome the cost and risk barriers of innovative new technologies so consumers can decide about performance themselves. Once again, EVs serve as a case study of ways to address cost and risk issues facing consumers.

INCENTIVES THAT REDUCE FIRST COST. Because EVs are expensive to purchase, it may be appropriate to construct a consumer incentive that focuses on this first-cost disadvantage. (Mandated production can accomplish this indirectly by exerting pressure on manufacturers to lower prices so vehicles do not simply accumulate in inventory.) Possible options include direct purchase subsidies (either as rebates or direct discounts) for vehicle or battery purchases. This approach offers simplicity but otherwise has little else to recommend it. Because the current vintage of EVs does not meet the social cost-benefit test, first-cost incentives do not merit public subsidy either directly or indirectly through mandates.

Suppliers of EVs or power companies, however, may well use their private means to reduce first costs. Just as the local cellular telephone company provides the telephone instrument below cost, an EV supplier might provide recharging units below cost. An automaker might price EVs at less than initial cost in anticipation of building market share and achieving learning curve economies over time. A power company might subsidize EVs to profit from the subsequent sale of electricity. Some of these private actions may require public facilitation but not public subsidy. For example, electric utilities may need changes in regulation to permit risk-taking on behalf of their shareholders.

It is important to recognize that incentives oriented toward the reduction of first costs—whether publicly or privately provided—do little to address uncertainty. They may even have the negative psychological effect of undermining the very market they are attempting to stimulate by sending the implicit signal that the market cannot be sustained without some form of subsidy. Thus, a consumer trying to evaluate the merits of an EV purchase sees a lower price as a result of the subsidy, but also a potential problem in the resale market, because the resale price of a subsidized product is likely to be relatively low.

To illustrate the point that it can be counterproductive to undermine first costs, suppose Honda had introduced Accords to the U.S. market by subsidizing them. Would consumers have taken the subsidy as evidence of a bargain or evidence of the potentially weak resale value of a Honda? Honda's actual strategy of rationing supply helped establish a high resale price for Accords, thus creating capital value for Honda purchasers and supporting the company's objective of changing the public's then-negative image of "made in Japan."

One first-cost incentive that differs materially from vehicle rebates and subsidies is investment in home charging units. Such infrastructure investments may overcome both psychological and economic barriers to EV purchases.

—Because gasoline-powered vehicles do not require a special device like a charging unit into which the vehicle must be plugged, the need to purchase such a unit might appear to the consumer as an "extra purchase," even if the total cost of the vehicle plus charger were comparable to the cost of the gasoline-powered vehicle alone.

—Because charging units are little more than specialized electrical outlets, investment in them outlives the EV itself, therefore solving the problem of the rapid turnover in EV technology that is likely if EVs are successful.

—Charging units have the outward appearance of being "utility-like" equipment—much like an electric meter. This fact helps reinforce the notion that EVs are, in fact, a bit more conventional than they might first appear. (This is important to consumers who often want the newest technology—so long as it is not "too new.")

Through the use of existing organizational competencies of electric utilities, economies of scale in master building permits for installing charging units, and other mechanisms, both first costs and uncertainty can be reduced. Again, some of these actions require public facilitation, but they do not require public subsidy or mandates.

INCENTIVES THAT REDUCE USAGE COSTS. The cost of driving a conventional car for a mile includes fuel and maintenance costs. A significant selling point of EVs is that the operating cost per mile is expected to be less than that of a conventional vehicle if off-peak electricity is used for recharging. The larger the expected difference in operating costs between electric and conventional vehicles, the more attractive EVs will be to operate once purchased. This point is important because not all ownership incentives encourage intensity of use, whereas incentives that lower operating costs do. If analysis shows that the congestion effects of EV use are not an issue in a particular jurisdiction, then regulatory authorization of economically rational off-peak charging rates for electricity would provide one such usage incentive.

To encourage EV usage, performance guarantee incentives could even be designed to outlive the first EV. For example, an incentive could be granted to the owner of the vehicle who might be given a lifetime per-mile fuel price incentive, in much the same way that AT&T exempted initial users of its Universal credit card from annual fees for life. Such exemptions might be transferable from one EV owner to subsequent owners, and thus, help bolster resale values. To the extent that next generation EVs prove to be less costly to maintain, such a life-of-owner arrangement could significantly reduce consumer uncertainty (and enhance the attractiveness of being one of the "pioneer" EV owners) at relatively little incremental cost beyond that of a more traditional life-of-vehicle guarantee program.

There are numerous variations on incentive schemes once a device has been created for providing them on a usage versus a lump-sum basis. For example, at the end of each month or year, the EV owner might indicate the mileage driven to date and then receive a corresponding incentive payment from an electricity supplier. Rewarding more intensive EV use—particularly if the demands on a utility's system from recharging do not exacerbate localized constraints or peak demands—is a strategy that is likely to be particularly consistent with the long-term strategic objectives of electricity suppliers. Such an approach is also especially attractive to fleet users who try to manage their capital assets intensively.

INCENTIVES THAT REDUCE OWNERSHIP RISK AND UNCERTAINTY. The future of the EV market, like the future of any new technology, is uncertain.[26] Failure to account for this uncertainty can easily lead to misdirected policies. For example, EV advocates tend to downplay the limited range of EVs by suggesting that such limitations are largely irrelevant because most drivers have relatively stable and predictable driving patterns.[27] These analyses understate the importance consumers place on various forms of "insurance protection" that their automobiles represent. Thus, many drivers pay a substantial premium for off-the-road four-wheel drive capability, but only rarely do they use this capacity.

Not all of the uncertainties, however, relate to the EVs themselves. Some relate to broader market circumstances such as the price of auto insurance or the price of the competing fuel. Management of these risks may also provide policymakers with attractive program options. For example, consumers may be concerned that electricity costs will behave differently from gasoline costs. Fuel price risk may be managed by an insurance program or pricing contract that guarantees a particular relationship between gasoline and electricity prices so that EVs would maintain a specified operating cost advantage relative to gasoline vehicles across a range of fuel price scenarios.

A second approach is to recognize that risk management is typically best done by individual consumers and not by suppliers. Thus, individual consumers not only have different risk preferences, but different means for addressing these risks by trading them off with other risks in their "risk portfolios." By providing consumers with accurate information on the risks that they face in purchasing EVs and by providing them with a menu of

26. Turrentine and Sperling (1992).
27. Turrentine and Sperling (1992). For example, a 1984 study found that 60 percent of all households drive fewer than 96 miles a day on 348 days a year. A 1982 study estimated that 57 percent of all households could function with a vehicle with only 80 miles of daily range. A 1989 study found that 77 percent of Los Angeles residents commute fewer than 40 miles roundtrip.

options for dealing with these risks, policymakers can achieve a less costly and more effective introduction of EV technology. Fuel economy labels on automobiles or mailings from a state insurance commissioner describing a consumer's auto insurance purchase options are examples of this approach.

LEASING AS A WAY TO MANAGE RISK FOR CONSUMERS. It is not easy to design a program of risk reduction for consumers without sending tacit signals that undermine the intended message. One common means of managing resale risk to automotive consumers without sending explicitly negative signals is the lease. Leasing incentives are common, even during periods of low interest rates, because of several attractive characteristics. First, they eliminate or greatly reduce the required down payment. The lease also allows the automaker to exploit its advantage in access to capital without having to dissipate much of that advantage through an ineffective interest subsidy. Most important, through the residual value clause in the lease agreement the automaker can manage resale price without sending negative signals to the consumer about the product's intrinsic value. Saab, Acura, Infiniti, Lexus, Audi, and Jaguar have aggressively exploited the incentive lease approach. Thus, an added dimension of the leasing approach is that it is currently associated in consumers' minds with luxury vehicles.

Forming subsidized lease alliances with rental fleet owners may be particularly attractive, first, because the driving patterns of rental cars often meet the technical constraints of electric cars, and, second, because rental car use is often concentrated in those high-density urban markets where the pollution reduction benefits of EVs may actually be valuable. Furthermore, by virtue of the choices of automobile types available through most rental companies, consumers could avoid the risk of mismatch between their needs and the limitations of EVs. From the consumer's perspective, the rental operator's fleet provides a portfolio of vehicle choices, thus reducing the exposure to the technical limits of EVs.

Leasing also shifts the risk of technological obsolescence from the consumer to the lessor and thus responds directly to a key objection to EVs— the risk of ownership. In addition, the characteristics of individuals who lease vehicles are consistent with the characteristics of those who might be expected to purchase EVs: younger, urban professionals with high incomes, intensive vehicle use, and a tendency to replace vehicles on a relatively short cycle.[28]

28. Turrentine and Sperling (1992).

Leasing is especially attractive from the supply side viewpoint. Their potentially long physical lives notwithstanding, EVs can be expected to become technically obsolete quickly. [29] Indeed, failure to become obsolete would mean that the technology has not evolved and that the future of EVs is bleak. If the vehicles do evolve quickly, the lessor will experience a capital loss on the contracted residual value. This obsolescence occurs only when EVs prosper, however. To stimulate sales of first-generation EVs, the parties who would actually experience benefits from the success of EVs could absorb the potential capital loss associated with rapid technological obsolescence.

FREE RENTAL CAR DAYS AS A WAY TO OVERCOME LIMITED DRIVING RANGE. It is no secret that EVs will have a relatively limited driving range compared with conventional vehicles. As such, EVs are "specialty" vehicles rather than general purpose vehicles. Studies suggest that EVs, for example, will have their strongest appeal to multicar households—those with demonstrated willingness to purchase automobiles better suited to special circumstances (for example, four-wheel drive vehicles and small sports cars). [30] In contrast, the ordinary consumer values the convenience, flexibility, and "insurance" that a general purpose conventional car provides. To make EVs more attractive to this larger cross-section of the car-buying public, an incentive program that provides a specified number of free annual rental car days with each EV purchased could be devised. Such an incentive would directly enhance the suitability of the EV to the general driving habits of many consumers and offer added peace of mind by reducing the risk and expense of needing but not having transport available for longer trips or trips that entail more time spent away from recharging facilities.

REDUCING THE RISK OF SERVICE PROBLEMS. Another area to consider in evaluating EV incentives options available to program participants is the cost and uncertainty associated with obtaining adequate and timely maintenance. Manufacturers of specialty conventional vehicles experience similar challenges and have tended to respond to that problem in three ways. First, many of them bundle service with the initial purchase price in the form of extensive vehicle warranties. Second, they have addressed the geographic challenge by offering loaner cars and customer pickup ser-

29. Excluding the battery, EVs are expected to require less overall maintenance than conventional vehicles. See Dabels (1992).

30. See, for example, Turrentine and Sperling (1992), and Beggs and Cardell (1980).

vices. Finally, they have addressed consumer concerns about competent service personnel by aggressively promoting the certification of qualified technicians.

Battery service is somewhat different from vehicle service, if only because it is the unfamiliar characteristic of the EV. Customer conservatism is strong and new technologies, even when superior, are often viewed with suspicion. Note, for example, the unquestionable superiority of electronic controls versus mechanical controls on conventional vehicles, but note also the loud complaints of consumers about the "computers" in their cars. To address this problem, GM has gone so far as to formally certify and heavily promote "Mr.Goodwrench," a sophisticated electronic technician, but with a comforting piece of old-fashioned hardware in his name. A similar program of technician certification may be required to reduce the consumer's perception of risk. Such certification may even have more credibility if undertaken by agencies independent of the service providers themselves.

In sum, it is critical to distinguish among policies that reduce a consumer's first cost, those that reduce usage costs, and those that reduce ownership uncertainty. Because of the uncertainty in the EV market, incentives designed to reduce it are very attractive, especially if they reinforce conventional decisionmaking parameters such as the resale value of vehicles. None of these initiatives to encourage learning and to facilitate the development of EVs or other alternative fuel technologies have the dramatic impact of a production mandate. And few of the initiatives require public action beyond the normal public functions of facilitating infrastructure development by removing impediments to change. To make these alternative technologies more attractive does require action in other policy areas, including electricity pricing, power plant emissions control, and possibly antitrust policies (to encourage strategic alliances). None of these actions, however, requires or even necessarily benefits from technology-forcing production mandates.

Lessons Learned

Technology-forcing policies are deceptively attractive. The public appears to like them, and they may promote valid economic goals including learning curve economies and correction of market imperfections. But because arguments against technology-forcing policies often involve analytical subtleties that challenge the conventional wisdom, it is easy for the public to have a positive predisposition to accept the simpler, optimistic view of the merits of these policies.

Electric vehicles served as a case in point. The new technology has a simple appeal, but an assessment of the indirect and unintended effects of EV technology leads to a different view of the technology's merits. All analyses of technology-forcing mandates will not lead to the same conclusions as in the EV case, but all analyses of technology-forcing policies will require analysts to ask the same fundamental questions. Do the benefits of the likely mandated technology outweigh the costs? Do technology-forcing mandates overcome real market imperfections? Do they induce learning curve benefits that private markets will not? Does the stretch goal of the technology-forcing policy focus efforts on a real bottleneck to technological development? And, most important, are there more cost-effective ways to achieve the legitimate objectives of technology-forcing mandates?

Economic efficiency can justify a technology-forcing policy under some circumstances, but it is important to recognize that the ultimate purpose of any technology-forcing policy is to learn how to eliminate a bottleneck restricting society's efforts to accomplish an important objective. That bottleneck may be economic, technological, institutional, or behavioral. It is equally important to recognize that breaking one bottleneck always creates one or more bottlenecks elsewhere in the production system. EVs demonstrate this phenomenon by revealing bottlenecks in power plant emission control, lead battery recycling, and consumer learning. The EV production mandate does nothing to address these bottlenecks. The challenge to transportation analysts is to identify the true bottlenecks to the development of new transportation technologies and then to devise ways to break those bottlenecks.

Perhaps the wisest counsel for transportation analysts is to cultivate a healthy skepticism for the claims of technology-forcing policies. Such skepticism is essential to ensuring that society's resources are devoted to their highest and best use. I do not counsel skepticism, however, on the benefits of learning to overcome the bottlenecks that impede society's advance. The challenge to the analyst is to stay focused on the opportunities for learning and not to be preoccupied with technology-forcing mandates as the sole, preferred, or even feasible avenue to that learning. As the EV case was intended to illustrate, many different instruments are available to encourage learning. These instruments will vary with the technology, of course, but the list of possibilities is by no means limited to the heavy-handed policy of costly and often counterproductive technology-forcing mandates.

Policy assessment and design is difficult for new and untested technologies, especially if public infatuation with a new technology and impatience over its implementation lends political support to unwise regulatory mandates and public subsidies. If transportation analysts are to succeed on society's behalf, they must make full use of the analytical and policy tools available. An emerging technology is not just good or bad. Not all good technologies should be mandated or subsidized, nor all technologies with a negative externality banned. Not every public effort to facilitate a new technology is a subsidy. This chapter has attempted to demonstrate that successful technological change can be promoted in many ways, some subtle, some counterintuitive. All involve learning. In isolation, these individual instruments may appear limited in impact. In combination, they can be powerful.

References

Abernathy, William J. 1978. *The Productivity Dilemma: A Roadblock to Innovation in the Automobile Industry.* Johns Hopkins University Press.

Abernathy, William J., and James M. Utterback. 1978. "Patterns of Industrial Innovation." *Technology Review* (June-July): 40–47.

Beggs, S., and N.S. Cardell. 1980. "Choice of Smallest Car by Multi-Vehicle Households and the Demand for EVs." *Transportation Research* 14 (5-6): 389–404.

Blair, Roger D., David L. Kaserman, and Richard C. Tepel. 1984. "The Impact of Improved Mileage on Gasoline Consumption." *Economic Inquiry* 22 (April): 209–17.

Blomquist, Glen C., and Sam Peltzman. 1981. "Passive Restraints: An Economist's View." In *The Scientific Basis of Health and Safety Regulation,* edited by Robert W. Crandall and Lester B. Lave. Brookings.

Bresnahan, Timothy F., and Dennis A. Yao. 1985. "The Nonpecuniary Costs of Automobile Emissions Standards." *Rand Journal of Economics* 16 (Winter): 437–55.

Crandall, Robert W. 1984. "Automobile Safety Regulation and Offsetting Behavior: Some New Empirical Estimates." *American Economic Review* 74 (May: *Papers and Proceedings*): 328–31.

———. 1992. "Policy Watch: Corporate Average Fuel Economy Standards." *Journal of Economic Perspectives* 6 (Spring): 171–80.

Crandall, Robert W., and John D. Graham. 1989. "The Effect of Fuel Economy Standards on Automobile Safety." *Journal of Law and Economics* 32 (April): 97–118.

———. 1991. "New Fuel-Economy Standards?" *The American Enterprise* (March-April): 68–69.

Crandall, Robert W., and Theodore E. Keeler. 1987. "Public Policy and the Private Auto." In *Energy: Markets and Regulation: Essays in Honor of M. A. Adelman,* edited by Richard L. Gordon, Henry D. Jacoby, and Martin B. Zimmerman. MIT Press.

Crandall, Robert W., and others. 1986. *Regulating the Automobile.* Brookings.

Dabels, John. 1992. "Environmental Requirements and the Impact Prototype Vehicle." In *The Urban Electric Vehicle: Policy Options, Technology Trends, and Market Prospects*, 311–16. Proceedings of an International Conference, Stockholm, May 25–27, 1992. Paris: Organization for Economic Cooperation and Development.

Dunn, James A, Jr. 1998. *Driving Forces: The Automobile, Its Enemies, and the Politics of Mobility.* Brookings.

Fauth, Gary. 1994. "Regulating the Automobile: Learning from Cost-Effective Analysis." *Business Economics* 29 (October): 23–28.

Freeman, Christopher. 1982. *The Economics of Industrial Innovation*, 2nd ed. MIT Press.

Garbacz, Christopher. 1990. "How Effective Is Automobile Safety Regulation?" *Applied Economics* 22 (December): 1705–14.

Ghemawat, Pankaj. 1985. "Building Strategy on the Experience Curve." *Harvard Business Review* 63 (March-April): 143–49.

Girifalco, Louis A. 1991. *Dynamics of Technological Change.* Van Nostrand Reinhold.

Goldberg, Pinelopi-Koujianou. 1998. "The Effects of the Corporate Average Fuel Efficiency Standards in the U.S." *Journal of Industrial Economics* 46 (March): 1–33.

Gómez-Ibáñez, José A. 1997. "Recission of the Passive Restraints Standard: Costs and Benefits." C16-83-562. Harvard University, Kennedy School of Government Case Program.

Gómez-Ibáñez, José A., and Gary R. Fauth. 1980. "Using Demand Elasticities from Disaggregate Model Choice Models." *Transportation* 9 (2): 105–24.

Graham, John. 1984. "Technology, Behavior, and Safety: An Empirical Study of Automobile Occupant-Protection Regulation." *Policy Sciences* 17 (October): 141–51.

Gruenspecht, Howard. 1982. "Differentiated Regulation: The Case of Auto Emissions Standards." *American Economic Review* 72 (May: *Papers and Proceedings*): 328–31.

Hahn, Robert W., and Gordon Hester. 1989. "Where Did All the Markets Go? An Analysis of EPA's Emissions Trading Program." *Yale Journal on Regulation* 6 (Winter): 109–53.

Innes, Robert. 1996. "Regulating Automobile Pollution under Certainty, Competition, and Imperfect Information." *Journal of Environmental Economics and Management* 31 (September): 219–39.

Lave, Lester B., Chris T. Hendrickson, and Francis Clay McMichael. 1995. "Environmental Implications of Electric Cars." *Science* 268 (May 19): 993.

Leone, Robert A. 1986. *Who Profits: Winners, Losers, and Government Regulation.* Basic Books.

Leone, Robert A., and Stephen Bradley. 1982. "Federal Energy Policy and Competitive Strategy in the U.S. Automobile Industry." *Annual Energy Review,* vol. 7: 61–86. U.S. Department of Energy, Energy Information Administration.

Leone, Robert A., and Thomas W. Parkinson. 1990. *Conserving Energy: Is There a Better Way?* Arlington, Va: International Automobile Manufacturers.

Mannering, Fred, and Clifford Winston. 1995. "Automobile Air Bags in the 1990s: Market Failure or Market Efficiency?" *Journal of Law and Economics* 38 (October): 265–80.

Nader, Ralph. 1965. *Unsafe at Any Speed.* Grossman.

OECD (Organization for Economic Cooperation and Development), International Energy Agency. 1993. *Electric Vehicles: Technology, Performance and Potential.* Paris.

Peltzman, Sam. 1975. "The Effects of Automobile Safety Regulation." *Journal of Political Economy* 83: 677–725.

Risa, Alf Erling. 1994. "Adverse Incentives from Improved Technology: Traffic Safety Regulation in Norway." *Southern Economic Journal* 60 (April): 844–57.

Scott, Esther. 1997. Low Emissions (Part A): The Pursuit of a Regional Program." C15-97-1398.0. Harvard University, Kennedy School Case Program.

Small, Kenneth A., and Camilla Kazimi. 1995. "On the Costs of Air Pollution from Motor Vehicles." *Journal of Transport Economics and Policy* 29 (January): 7–33.

Turrentine, Tom, and Daniel Sperling. 1992. "How Far Can the EV Go on 100 Miles?" In *The Urban Electric Vehicle: Policy Options, Technology Trends, and Market Prospects,* 259–69. Proceedings of an International Conference, Stockholm, May 25–27, 1992. Paris: Organization for Economic Cooperation and Development.

Transportation Research Board. 1985. "Highway Capacity Manual." Special report 209. National Research Council, Washington, D.C.

Turner, Roy E. 1973. "Transportation Technical Notes, Air Pollution Abstracts." Federal Highway Administration, U.S. Department of Transportation. February.

GREGORY K. INGRAM
ZHI LIU

10

Determinants of Motorization and Road Provision

The number of motor vehicles in the world is growing rapidly. Between 1980 and 1995—just fifteen
years—the global fleet of cars, trucks, and buses increased by 60 percent,
with a third of that increase in developing countries.[1] The increasing number of vehicles brings many benefits but is also associated with worsening
negative externalities including congestion and air pollution. In addition,
motor vehicles need roads, and road networks have been expanding to accommodate the rising number of vehicles. Roads are costly to build and
maintain, and they also produce externalities. For example, road network
expansion is a major determinant of development patterns, particularly in
urban areas. Opinions are divided on the desirability of increased motorization. Some commentators view the effects of the growth of motor vehicle use and road networks as inevitably adverse, while others argue that
national patterns of motor vehicle use are sustainable.[2]

The authors are grateful to Chiaki Yamamoto for research assistance and to Esra Bennathan, Kenneth Button, Marianne Fay, Reuben Gronau, Kenneth Gwilliam, David D. Li, Lant Pritchett, and
Louis Thompson for helpful comments and advice on earlier versions of this paper.
1. International Road Federation (various years).
2. For an example of the first viewpoint, see "Taming the Beast: A Survey on Living with the Car,"
The Economist, June 22, 1996), pp. 1–18. For the second viewpoint, see Prud'homme and others
(1997).

325

The analysis presented here reviews past trends in vehicle ownership and road network expansion. It examines the determinants of past growth to better understand what the future patterns of motor vehicle and road network growth are likely to be and how policy interventions can influence future growth. Because motorization raises different issues at the urban and national levels, city-level and national patterns are analyzed separately using data from a sample of cities and countries ranging across all income levels.

Motor vehicles are central to policy debates on urban transport because their increased use causes congestion, contributes to low-density development, and reduces transit use.[3] Some analysts have argued that urban development densities must be increased to reduce auto dependence and promote transit use.[4] Moreover, vehicular emissions have contributed to the degradation of the air quality in many cities, particularly in developing countries. Motor vehicle use and road provision are concerns at the national level because large investments are needed for road infrastucture and because countries want to ensure that their national transport policy reflects the comparative advantages of each transport mode (road, rail, water, and air). And at both the national and the global levels, emissions from transport are a growing source of carbon dioxide emissions. Motor vehicles produced 22 percent of global anthropogenic carbon dioxide emissions in 1990 (and their *share* of emissions is also growing); roughly 70 percent of motor vehicle carbon dioxide emissions are produced in high-income countries.[5]

In market economies most motor vehicles are privately owned, and most of the roads they use are publicly owned. Relatively little is known about how road provision varies across countries or with vehicle ownership, and few analysts have examined the provision of roads at either the national or urban level. In urbanized areas road construction has high economic costs and is politically contentious. The resettlement of households residing in the right-of-way of planned urban roads is a concern in both high-income and developing countries.

This chapter confirms the findings of many studies that income is a strong determinant of vehicle ownership at both the national and the city level and that motor vehicle ownership increases at about the same rate as income at both levels. More surprisingly, this chapter also finds that in-

3. For a summary of these arguments, see Meyer and Gómez-Ibáñez (1981).
4. See, for example, Newman and Kenworthy (1989).
5. World Resources Institute (1996: 86).

come is a major determinant of the length of roads at the national level: national paved road length has also been increasing at about the same rate as income, and total road length less rapidly than income. Because national paved road networks are expanding at about the same rate as national motor vehicle fleets, congestion on them is unlikely to be worsening. But at the urban level, road length is growing much more slowly than income— and much more slowly than the number of motor vehicles. Urban congestion is therefore rising with income over time, and the increase in urban congestion is stimulating decentralized urban growth. Breaking the ties that link income growth, rising congestion, and decentralization at the urban level will be very difficult. Restraining auto ownership in urban areas requires very high tax rates, increasing the supply of roads in urban areas is very costly, and increasing the supply of transit alternatives is not only costly but has been shown to have had little effect on congestion in the few cases where it has been studied.

This chapter outlines some basic economic hypotheses about motorization and road provision and then evaluates these hypotheses with some simple summary statistics compiled at the national and city levels in high-income and developing countries. Next it surveys more sophisticated empirical work on motorization and on road provision and summarizes this knowledge as stylized facts. It then examines the production of motor vehicle transport services—passenger and freight transport that uses vehicles and roads as inputs—and ends with a prognosis and issues that need to be addressed.

Economic Hypotheses concerning Motorization and Road Provision

Economic reasoning produces several hypotheses about the relationships among motor vehicle ownership, road provision, and the production of motor vehicle transport services. Although the vehicle fleet will grow with income, the number of cars should increase more rapidly than trucks. This is because the production of services grows faster with income than do freight volumes and the production of goods And as incomes rise, labor costs rise relative to capital costs, leading to an increase in average truck size, capacity, and load, thereby reducing the number of trucks needed to produce a given number of ton miles of freight transport.

Passenger travel for all purposes (work, shopping, social, and so forth) also grows with income, but car ownership may grow even more quickly than travel. Income growth raises the value of time, shifting demand from slower, cheaper modes of transportation to faster, costlier modes, such as the automobile. In urban areas, as demand shifts from transit to cars and transit passenger volumes decline, transit service often degrades, prompting more riders to abandon transit. Increases in the value of time also make the circuitous routing required to serve multiple passengers by car more costly, which lowers the number of passengers per car and raises the demand for cars. For both freight and passenger travel, however, the presence of potential competing modes such as railways and transit should reduce demand for both trucks and cars.

The nature of demand for roads is likely to differ at the national and urban levels. The road network at the national level primarily connects urban centers and provides access to rural areas. It links human settlements and economic activities distributed across the nation and is rarely congested. The coverage of national road networks and the total length of national roads should increase with output, allowing increased accessibility to the whole country. If other variables are held constant, urbanization's effect on the national road network is difficult to predict. Urbanization might raise the demand for nonurban roads, because the specialization of production in individual cities associated with urbanization may increase demand for roads between cities.

Urban growth should increase the demand for urban roads, although the presence of competing modes, particularly railways and transit, should temper demand and reduce the need for roads. Urban road networks are much more heavily used than rural roads, are frequently congested, and exist not only to connect locations but also to provide traffic-carrying capacity. Providing roads in urban areas is usually more costly than providing roads nationally. These higher costs may lead to a lower ratio of urban road length to population and a slower rate of urban road network expansion than at the national level.

The higher costs of urban roads may be offset by their larger benefits, however, because increasing urban road capacity can reduce congestion and travel time—benefits that become more valuable as incomes increase. In congested urban areas, more vehicles increase congestion and travel times. Because the value of travel time increases with income and is a component of travel costs, in urban areas the cost per kilometer of motor vehicle transport services increases with income and may be greater than at the national level where average speeds are higher. Income growth increases the benefits from urban roads and may stimulate additional road provision to relieve congestion and raise speeds. Such a response would tend to reduce the ratio of motor vehicles to roads in urban areas with high income levels.

The relative prices of motor vehicle services and roads are also likely to change with development because motor vehicles are traded goods (whose prices are reasonably constant around the world), and roads are nontraded goods (whose prices vary with wage levels across countries). The ratio of the prices of nontraded to traded goods rises with wage levels and income. Hence roads become more costly relative to vehicles as incomes rise (assuming minimal congestion at the national level), and the ratio of motor vehicles to national roads should rise with income as traffic volumes increase on national road networks.

Finally, road quality is also an issue. Motor vehicle speeds rise and operating costs fall as road quality improves, so arguments based on economic efficiency suggest that road quality—particularly the share of roads that are paved—should increase as the value of time (related to income) and the intensity of road use rise.

Of course, these hypotheses stem from economic principles. Because public road providers face few market incentives, however, a substantial question is whether predictions based on economic reasoning are relevant.

Summary Statistics

Summary statistics on vehicle ownership and road provision at the national and urban levels for developing and high-income countries, shown in table 10-1, provide a crude test of the hypotheses based on economic reasoning. The cross-country and cross-urban area data sets summarized in the table cover a wide range of country income levels, ranging in 1990 from $260 to $28,000 per capita in 1987 U.S. dollars at market exchange rates.[6] The national and urban samples summarized in table 10-1 do not overlap precisely in geographical terms or in time, but they provide a useful comparison of urban and national measures for developing countries and high-income countries.

6. National data on population, vehicles, and road length include urban and rural areas. Data on urban road length are from a variety of sources and are not broken down into paved and unpaved categories, as are national data. Typically a greater proportion of urban roads than of national roads are paved, so the analysis of urban roads may be more comparable to the analysis of national paved roads than to total roads.

Table 10-1. *Sample Summary Averages, 1980*

Item	Developing economies		High-income economies[a]	
	National (31 countries)	Urban (9 cities)	National (19 countries)	Urban (26 cities)
Per capita GNP in 1987 US$[b]	546	1,589	14,247	15,037
Population per sq. km.	86	14,982	125	3,989
Motor vehicles per 1,000 people	41	60	379	482
Auto share of fleet (percentage)	60	61	86	82
Kilometers of road per sq. km.	0.2	5.9	1.2	10.9
Percentage of roads paved	34	n.a.	77	n.a.
Meters of road per capita	3.7	0.5	16.5	4.5
Meters of paved road per capita	1.0	n.a.	11.2	n.a.
Motor vehicles per km. of road	12	142	31	152
Motor vehicles per paved km.	41	n.a.	41	n.a.

Source: Ingram and Liu (1998). Country-level data are from fifty countries with full data for 1970, 1980, and 1990. The city-level data are for thirty-five cities with full data for 1960 and 1980. Because it is the only common year, data for 1980 are shown here.
n.a. Not available.
a. In 1980 high-income countries had a GNP per capita over $4,800; see World Bank (1992).
b. Average weighted by population.

Relative to countries as a whole, urban areas in both developing and high-income countries obviously have much higher population densities, higher road network densities, somewhat more vehicles per thousand people, much less road length per person, and more motor vehicles per kilometer of road. Although it is used here as a rough proxy for the volume-to-capacity ratio frequently used in traffic analysis, the number of motor vehicles per kilometer of road is an imperfect measure because it does not contain information on average vehicle utilization and traffic peaking. Nonetheless, the large difference between the national and urban levels shown in table 10-1 suggests that, on average, nonurban national road systems are uncongested, whereas urban road systems are congested. Compared with high-income countries, developing countries at the national level have a lower share of cars in their vehicle fleets, a lower share of paved roads, fewer motor vehicles per kilometer of total roads, fewer meters of paved road per capita, and similar numbers of motor vehicles per kilometer of paved road.

The summary averages also show some key differences among urban areas. Cities in developing countries have much higher population densities, lower road network densities, many fewer motor vehicles per thousand people, and much less road length per person than do cities in high-income countries The result is the relatively small difference in motor vehicles per kilometer of road between developing and high-income cities.

The overall patterns evident in table 10-1 are consistent with many of the hypotheses based on simple economic reasoning sketched earlier. For example, the number of vehicles per kilometer of total road at the national level is greater in high-income than in developing countries but similar at the urban level. And autos make up a higher share of motor vehicle fleets in high-income than in developing countries. These patterns suggest that economic behavior is an important determinant of motorization and road provision across countries.

Motorization

What have analysts discovered about the determinants of motor vehicle ownership? Because vehicles are mainly privately produced and purchased, vehicle ownership is usually analyzed in the traditional economic demand framework. Knowledge about the effects on car ownership of income, prices, demographic trends, and transport policy is needed to predict the effect that specific policies might have on vehicle ownership patterns.

During the last four decades, many empirical studies have modeled and forecast the trends of motor vehicle ownership and use in various countries.[7] These studies fall into three categories, based on the type of data used. In the first category are models that analyze motorization using time-series data (trends over time in a city or country) or that attempt to extrapolate national or regional motor vehicle ownership trends to future years under the explicit assumption of a saturation level.[8] The second category uses cross-section data (data from a single point in time where variations are analyzed across households, cities, or countries). Some of these studies use aggregate data to produce long-run income elasticity estimates, while others use disaggregate household level data to explain household car

7. For a concise survey of the commonly used methodologies, see Ortúzar and Willumsen (1994: 405–13). For more thorough discussions of the econometric techniques, see Glaister (1981); Button, Pearman, and Fowkes (1982); Mogridge (1983); and Train (1986).

8. See, for example, Wildhorn and others (1974), Sweeney (1978), and Chin and Smith (1997). The time series models that extrapolate motor vehicle ownership trends assume that the number of vehicles per person has an upper limit, beyond which changes in income or other attributes will have no effect on vehicle ownership. This upper limit is termed a saturation level. For examples of these models, see Tanner (1962, 1978) and Mogridge (1967, 1989).

ownership behavior.[9] The third category of models uses panel data, which includes both cross-sectional and time-series information.[10] Studies of all three types measure the effects of economic, demographic, and geographic variables on the levels and rates of motorization, using variables such as per capita income, vehicle prices, fuel prices, population density, degree of urbanization, and availability and prices of competing transport modes.

Income Elasticities of Motor Vehicle Ownership and Use

Because most motor vehicles are purchased by individuals, households, or firms and are privately owned, per capita income is perhaps the most important economic variable that determines the level of motorization. Representative estimates of income elasticities of motor vehicle ownership and use from previous studies are summarized in table 10-2.[11] Many estimates indicate that motorization increases rapidly with income, although the elasticities vary. Some of the variation relates to income definition, but income elasticities also vary depending on the types of data and the methodologies used.[12]

Four stylized facts emerge in the estimates shown in table 10-2. First, income elasticities from time-series data are typically smaller than those from cross-section data. That is because cross-section analyses produce long-run elasticities, and long-run behavior is generally more responsive to income changes than short-run behavior. Roughly speaking, long-run income elasticities of motor vehicle (especially car) ownership are greater than 1.0,

9. For studies using aggregate data, see Beesley and Kain (1964), Silberston (1970), Wheaton (1982), and Kain and Liu (1994). Studies using disaggregate household level data include Quarmby and Bates (1970); Bates, Gunn, and Roberts (1978); Mannering and Winston (1985); Train (1986); and Hensher, Milthorpe, and Smith (1990).

10. Pindyck (1979); Button, Ngoe, and Hine (1993); Johansson and Schipper (1997); and Ingram and Liu (1997, 1998).

11. These income elasticities measure the percentage change in vehicle ownership or use when income changes by 1 percent. An elasticity greater than 1 means that vehicle ownership or use changes more rapidly than income.

12. Cross-country per capita income can be measured on the basis of market exchange rates or purchasing power parity (PPP) exchange rates. Income measured at market exchange rates may be more relevant for cross-country studies of motorization because vehicles are traded goods, and market exchange rate income measures the ability of an economy to purchase traded goods. Income at PPP exchange rates spans a narrower range than income defined at market exchange rates, because PPP-based income substantially exceeds market-rate-based income for low-income countries. Thus income elasticities estimated using income at market exchange rates tend to be smaller than those using income at PPP exchange rates. For a discussion of purchasing power parity exchange rates, see Summers and Heston (1991).

Table 10-2. Income Elasticities of Motor Vehicle Ownership and Usage

Study	Sample	Cross section	Time series	Panel data
Vehicle ownership, national level				
Silberston (1970)	38 free market countries, 1965, cars	1.14	...	...
	38 free market countries, 1965, total vehicles	1.09	...	...
	46 countries, 1965, cars	1.21	...	...
Wildhorn and others (1974)	U.S., 1950–73	...	0.88	...
Sweeney (1978)	U.S., 1950–73	...	0.82	...
Pindyck (1979)	11 Western countries, 1955–73	...	...	0.30
Wheaton (1982)	25 countries, early 1970s, cars	1.38	...	...
	25 countries, early 1970s, total vehicles	1.19	...	...
	42 countries, early 1970s, cars	1.43	...	...
Kain (1983)	23 OECD countries, 1958	1.95	...	...
	23 OECD countries, 1968	1.59	...	...
	98 noncommunist countries, 1977	1.30	...	...
Button, Ngoe, and Hine (1993)	58 developing countries, 1968–87, cars	...	...	0.53 – 1.12
	29 developing countries, 1968–87, commercial vehicles	...	...	0.84 – 1.50
Kain and Liu (1994)[a]	52 countries, 1990, cars	1.58	...	...
	52 countries, 1990, commercial vehicles	1.15	...	...
	52 countries, 1990, total vehicles	1.44	...	...
Johansson and Schipper (1997)	12 OECD countries, 1973–92	...	...	0.75 – 1.25
Ingram and Liu (1997, 1998)	50 countries, 1970, 1980, 1990, cars	1.02 – 1.21	...	1.12
	50 countries, 1970, 1980, 1990, commercial vehicles	0.64 – 0.94	...	1.12
	50 countries, 1970, 1980, 1990, total vehicles	0.90 – 1.09	...	0.98

(Table continues)

Table 10-2 (continued)

Study	Sample	Cross section	Time series	Panel data
Vehicle ownership, urban level				
Beesley and Kain (1964)	45 U.S. cities, 1960	0.73	...	...
Kain and Liu (1994)[a]	60 world cities, 1980, cars	1.02	...	...
Chin and Smith (1997)	Singapore, 1968–89	...	0.53 – 0.61	...
Ingram and Liu (1997, 1998)	35 urban areas, two points in time, cars	0.50 – 0.91	...	1.83 – 1.88
	35 urban areas, two points in time, commercial vehicles	0.37 – 0.60	...	0.53 – 0.14
	35 urban areas, two points in time, total vehicles	0.52 – 0.83	...	1.01 – 1.03
Vehicle usage, national level				
Pindyck (1979)	11 Western countries, 1955–73	...	...	0.66
Wheaton (1982)	25 countries, early 1970s, cars	0.54	...	...
	25 countries, early 1970s, total vehicles	0.53	...	...
	42 countries, early 1970s, cars	0.33	...	...
Button, Ngoe, and Hine (1993)	58 developing countries, 1968–87, cars	...	...	0.71
	29 developing countries, 1968–87, commercial vehicles	...	...	0.52
Johansson and Schipper (1997)	12 OECD countries, 1973–92	...	...	–0.1 – 0.35
Vehicle usage, household level				
Mannering and Winston (1985)	U.S., over 1,000 households, 1978–80:			
	Households with one vehicle	0.06		...
	Households with two vehicles	0.11		...
Train (1986)	California, 105 households, 1976–80	0.29		...
Hensher, Milthorpe, and Smith (1990)	Sydney, 1,172 households, 1981–82	0.05 – 0.14		...

a. Kain and Liu (1994) used per capita GDP at purchasing power parity exchange rates.

Figure 10-1. *Per Capita Income and Motor Vehicle Ownership in Fifty Countries and Thirty-Five Cities*

Motor vehicles/1,000 population

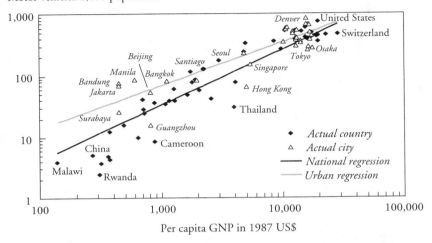

Per capita GNP in 1987 US$

Source: Ingram and Liu (1998). Both axes are in logarithms, and the slope of a line on such a diagram is the elasticity. A straight line indicates a constant elasticity.

while short-run income elasticities are less than 1.0. Second, income elasticities from urban-level data are similar to or smaller than those from country-level data, largely because there are more competing modes of transportation and greater congestion in urban areas, both of which reduce the attraction of motor vehicles. In fact, the long-run elasticities from urban-level data are closer to those from country-level data than are the short-run elasticities. Using the data sets summarized in table 10-1, figure 10-1 indicates that motor vehicle ownership increases somewhat more rapidly with income at the national level than at the urban level. Third, income elasticities are generally larger for automobiles than for commercial vehicles, supporting the economic hypothesis that the share of passenger cars in the motor vehicle fleet increases with income. Finally, income elasticities of motor vehicle use are less than unity, smaller than long-run income elasticities of motor vehicle ownership, and smaller for households with one vehicle than for those with two, indicating that motor vehicle use increases less rapidly than motor vehicle ownership. These findings also support the earlier economic hypotheses.

Table 10-3. *Price Elasticities of Motor Vehicle Ownership, Usage, and Fuel Efficiency*

Study	Vehicle ownership	Vehicle usage	Fuel efficiency	Vehicle depreciation
Vehicle price elasticities				
Pindyck (1979)	-0.78	...	...	-0.71
Gasoline price elasticities				
Wildhorn and others (1974)	-0.25	-0.36	0.17	...
Sweeney (1978)	...	...	0.72	...
Pindyck (1979)	-0.64	...	1.43	...
Wheaton (1982)	Insignificant	-0.48 – -0.55	0.09 – 0.14	...
Train (1986)	-0.11	-0.27	...	...
Hensher, Milthorpe, and Smith (1990)	...	-0.22 – -0.39	...	...
Johansson and Schipper (1997)	-0.02 – 0.00	-0.35 – -0.05	0.45 – 0.35	...
Vehicle operating cost elasticities				
Mannering and Winston (1985)				
one-car household—short-run	...	-0.23	...	...
one-car household—long-run	...	-0.28	...	...
two-car household—short-run	...	-0.06	...	...
two-car household—long-run	...	-0.10	...	...

Price Elasticities of Motor Vehicle Ownership and Use

Motor vehicle prices affect individuals' decisions to own a vehicle. The fleet comprises a variety of vehicle types, however, which makes it difficult to construct an average price index for the entire fleet. Because of this problem, only a few empirical studies include vehicle prices as an explanatory variable for vehicle ownership.[13] Increases in vehicle prices were found to reduce vehicle registrations and prolong vehicle life, which reduces vehicle depreciation rates (table 10-3).[14]

Unlike vehicle prices, gasoline prices are generally available and thus are included in many studies. Although some analysts found that increases in gasoline prices reduce vehicle ownership, others found that gasoline prices had little effect on vehicle ownership.[15] The effect on vehicle use is clear, however: an increase in gasoline prices decreases vehicle usage and increases the average fuel efficiency of the vehicle stock by encouraging the purchase of more fuel-efficient vehicles.[16] When facing higher operating costs, households with two or more cars reduce usage less than one-car households by shifting usage to their more efficient car. These results are summarized in table 10-3.

A comparison of available estimates suggests that income elasticities are greater than price elasticities in absolute terms for both motor vehicle ownership and use.[17] This finding has an important policy implication because prices are often suggested or used as an instrument to control motor vehicle ownership and use. If price elasticities are half as large as income elasticities, prices would have to grow twice as fast as incomes to stabilize vehicle ownership. In fact, prices have not increased much in real terms. Vehicle prices have increased faster than income in the 1990s, but that

13. The absence of vehicle prices in a vehicle ownership model may cause bias to the income elasticity estimates. For a treatment of the problem, see Mogridge (1967), who adjusted the income variable to "car purchasing income" by the cost of motoring before fitting the vehicle ownership equations.

14. Pindyck (1979).

15. For studies concluding that gasoline price increases reduce vehicle ownership, see Wildhorn and others (1974), Pindyck (1979), and Ingram and Liu (1998); for studies finding little effect, see Wheaton (1982) and Johansson and Schipper (1997).

16. Wildhorn and others (1974); Pindyck (1979); Wheaton (1982); and Johansson and Schipper (1997).

17. These price elasticities measure the percentage change in vehicle ownership or use when its price changes by 1 percent. A price increase usually reduces demand, so price elasticities are normally negative.

reflects mainly increases in vehicle quality. Fuel prices have varied but have not grown as fast as income and have actually declined from 1980 to 1995 after increasing in the 1970s. Per capita income has grown in both developing and high-income countries and is expected to continue to do so. In the future, average vehicle prices may decline as a result of lower production costs, or they may increase at a rate similar to that of income. If the past magnitudes of income and price elasticities hold for the future, global motorization can be expected to grow unless there are strong increases in the prices of—or the taxes and fees on—vehicles, fuels, and vehicle use.

The Role of Population Density

At both national and urban levels, population density is a crude proxy for the spatial distribution of economic activities. Everything else being equal, low overall population density should increase average trip lengths and spur motorization. In high-density cities, congestion caused by density should impose higher costs on motoring and may reduce auto ownership and use. Empirical studies find that population density is negatively related to motor vehicle ownership both at national and urban levels, but the elasticity of motor vehicle ownership with population density is much greater at the urban level (–0.4) than at the national level (–0.1).[18]

Unlike at the national level, the causal relation between population density and motorization at the urban level runs in both directions. The boundaries of countries rarely change, while most cities can expand by annexing outlying areas that have lower densities than the urban core. By increasing travel speeds, motorization can induce decentralization of both job and residential locations, which expands the urbanized area and reduces densities. The lower densities raise transit costs or reduce transit service levels, either of which further promotes car ownership and use. Hence motorization is both determined by and a determinant of urban density.

At the national level, the share of urban population is another proxy for the spatial distribution of economic activities, but its effect on vehicle ownership is ambiguous. On the one hand, urbanization may be negatively associated with motor vehicle ownership because motorized road transport is more attractive in rural than in urban areas.[19] With everything else held

18. Ingram and Liu (1997). A small, negative, but insignificant relation between vehicle ownership and population density at the national level was found in Silberston (1970).

19. Wheaton (1982) found a negative but statistically insignificant relation between the share of urban population and the level of auto ownership.

constant, rural households are more likely than are urban households to own motor vehicles.[20] On the other hand, urbanization is positively associated with per capita income.[21] Cross-country analysis indicates that the net effect of urbanization on vehicle ownership is positive.[22]

Saturation Levels for Motor Vehicle Ownership

It is often hypothesized that motor vehicle ownership in high-income countries will increase at a declining rate with per capita income growth and eventually stop increasing when a saturation level is reached. A recent study estimated ownership saturation levels for fifty countries (under a "business as usual" scenario) at 770 passenger cars and 1,180 total motor vehicles per thousand people, and for thirty-five cities at 750 passenger cars and 1,080 total motor vehicles.[23] These estimates exceed the maximum observed ownership levels in 1990 of 574 passenger cars and 755 motor vehicles per thousand people (for the United States).

These estimates are larger than earlier ones.[24] If estimated vehicle ownership saturation levels change over time, they are of little use for forecasting. In fact, that may be the case as there is little direct evidence that saturation levels are stationary or that they have a straightforward behavioral interpretation. The income elasticity of motor vehicle ownership may decline as incomes rise. Estimates that allow income elasticities to vary with country income produce declining income elasticities but do not have greater explanatory power than do constant elasticity specifications.[25]

Road Provision

What are the determinants of road provision, or the increase in road networks, at the national and city level?[26] Unlike motor vehicles, roads are

---

20. Deaton (1987).

21. For a summary of empirical evidence, see Ingram (1997).

22. Ingram and Liu (1997).

23. Ingram and Liu (1997).

24. Two of the previous estimates (or assumptions) were provided by Tanner (1962) and Mogridge (1967). Tanner predicted a saturation level of 400 cars, and Mogridge, 660, per thousand people in the United Kingdom.

25. Ingram and Liu (1998).

26. This section draws heavily from Ingram and Liu (1997, 1998).

not usually privately provided, and their provision may not be strongly conditioned by economic considerations. Nonetheless, knowledge about the recent trends in road provision and its relation to income, population, and settlement patterns is a useful guide to future road provision and an important input to transport policymaking. Although the impact of economic development on roadway networks has long been a subject of descriptive studies for several countries, cross-country empirical studies are recent.[27]

National Road Networks

The few available studies of road provision across countries are based on data that provide information on road length but not on road width or numbers of lanes. Data available for paved roads and total roads are reported by the countries and generally include urban roads, but country-level definitions sometimes vary with respect to coverage and technical classification. Data on paved roads are more comparable across countries than data on total roads because there is less ambiguity about what constitutes a paved road than what constitutes an unpaved road versus a track or trail.[28]

The size of the national road network is associated with the size of the economy, geographical area, population, income per capita, and population density. Per capita income is a major determinant of road length at the national level. Both paved and total road length increase at a constant rate with per capita income, as can be seen in figure 10-2.[29] Estimates at the national level (using the techniques employed for vehicle ownership) find no saturation level for road density with respect to per capita income.

Paved road length has an elasticity of 1.0 with respect to income (when income increases by 1 percent, paved road length increases by 1 percent),

---

27. Bennathan, Fraser, and Thompson (1992); Canning (1998); and Ingram and Liu (1997, 1998). Bennathan, Fraser and Thompson used data from 36 countries to analyze the relation of domestic rail and road freight transport demand (in ton-kilometers) to country income and land area variables. Canning analyzed several infrastructure stocks—including roads, telephones, and electric generating capacity—using a panel data set containing from 95 to 145 countries. Ingram and Liu analyzed the regularities of provision of roadway length using data from 50 countries and 35 cities spanning a wide range of income levels; their findings are summarized in this section.

28. Data are available from a number of sources, including *World Road Statistics* published annually by the International Road Federation. The problems with road definitions are discussed in Canning (1998).

29. Nonlinear specifications produced R^2 no higher than those of the simpler linear specification.

Figure 10-2. *Per Capita Income and Per Capita Road Length, Fifty Countries and Thirty-Five Cities*

Per capita road length in meters

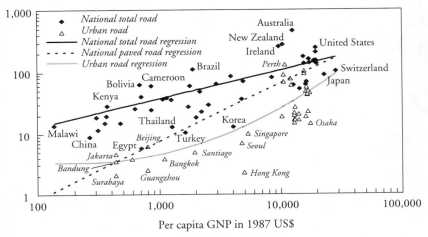

Per capita GNP in 1987 US$

Source: Ingram and Liu (1998). Both axes are in logarithms. Data points for paved roads are not shown for the sake of clarity.

while overall road length increases only about half as fast as income (table 10-4). Population is a significant determinant of national total and paved road length, whereas population density affects only total road length. The national level of urbanization, the length of the rail network,[30] and gasoline prices have little influence on the length of either paved or unpaved roads at the national level. These estimates were based mainly on the cross-sectional variation in panel data, but estimates based on first differences over time in the same panel data produced generally similar results (except for the relation of total road length with population), as shown in table 10-4.

The major implication of these findings is that at the national level, paved road length increases with per capita income at roughly the same rate as vehicle ownership. As a result, congestion does not appear to be a current or growing problem for the national road network in most countries.

---

30. Ingram and Liu (1997) find that the length of the rail network is strongly related to per capita income (elasticity of 0.5) and population density (elasticity of -0.4), results similar to those for total roads.

Table 10-4. *Estimated Effects of Population, Per Capita Income, and Population Density on Road Length*

Dependent variable	Functional specification	Coefficient estimates		
		Population	Per capita income	Population density
At the national level				
Length of total road	Cross-section	1.0 [a]	0.5 [a]	−0.3[a]
	20-year first differences	0.4	0.5	...
Length of paved road	Cross-section	1.0 [a]	1.0 [a]	0.0
	20-year first differences	1.3 [a]	0.8 [a]	...
At the urban level				
Length of road	Cross-section	0.8 [a]	varies[b]	−1.0 [a]
	First differences	0.5 [a]	0.1 [a]	−0.4 [a]

Source: Ingram and Liu (1997, 1998). All variables are in natural logarithm, and elasticities are jointly estimated.
a. Statistically significant at the 0.05 level.
b. Income elasticity increases with income level.

Paved road density (length of paved road per unit of area) has an elasticity of 1.0 with respect to both population density and income density (income per unit of area), whereas total road density has an elasticity of about 0.7 with the same two variables. Paving roads is an efficient way to increase the quality of the national road network and is less expensive than constructing new roads because existing rights-of-way are used. The percentage of roads paved increases with per capita income and population density; from 1970 to 1990 the percentage of roads paved in the fifty countries studied had an elasticity of approximately 1.0 with respect to both variables. Paving occurs most intensively in low- to middle-income countries. Developing countries with average population densities (100 people per square kilometer) and average per capita incomes ($550 a year in 1987 prices) have about a third of their roads paved, a share that rises to more than three-quarters when annual per capita incomes reach $1,000.

Urban Road Networks

Road provision at the urban level differs greatly from that at the national level. Holding income and density unchanged, urban road length

Figure 10-3. *Per Capita Income and Population Density in Thirty-Five Cities*

People/sq. km.

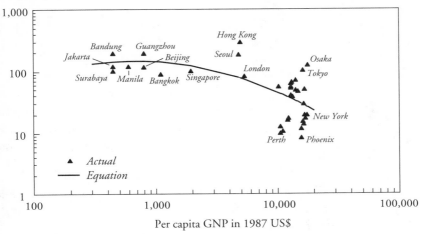

Per capita GNP in 1987 US$

Source: Ingram and Liu (1998). Both axes are in logarithms.

increases more slowly than population; its elasticity with population is 0.8 (see table 10-4). The elasticity of urban road length with per capita income is not constant, as it is at the national level, but increases with income (see figure 10-2), and the elasticity of road length with population density is much stronger at the urban level (−1.0) than at the national level (0.0 to −0.3).[31]

Urban population densities are often low when per capita income is high, but population densities vary widely in high-income cities (figure 10-3). This wide variation reflects the effect of historical paths of development on urban form. Cities that have experienced much of their population growth when auto ownership levels have been high have lower densities than other cities. In addition, high relative land prices are likely to raise population densities. The nonlinearity between urban population density and income shown in figure 10-3 contributes strongly to the nonlinear-

31. These results are based on panel data from thirty-five cities in developing and industrial countries, and the elasticities take into account the strong negative relation between per capita income and population density at the urban level.

ity between per capita roads and per capita income at the urban level in figure 10-2.

Comparisons of city data over time indicate that average population densities are falling in virtually all high-income cities as both employment and residences decentralize from the central city. Overall urban population growth occurs through expansion of the urban perimeter by annexation of surrounding municipalities with lower densities than the core city.

When city effects are controlled for in first-difference estimates, many of the relations differ from the cross-city panel estimates (unlike at the national level, where the panel and first-difference results are broadly similar). In particular, the first-difference estimates suggest that urban road length barely increases with per capita income over time; the income elasticity of urban road length is around 0.1 (see table 10-4). Using the techniques pioneered for vehicle ownership, it is possible to estimate the saturation level of urban road provision, which is 23 kilometers of road length per square kilometer of area, a level very close to the 24.9 kilometers observed in Tokyo in 1960.

These results indicate that urban road length is increasing much more slowly over time than urban vehicle ownership. A 1 percent increase in income produces a 1 percent increase in the number of urban vehicles and a 0.1 percent increase in urban road length. In fact, relatively little new road length is being constructed in built-up urban areas, presumably because the cost of new rights-of-way is high in both economic and political terms. Most increases in urban road length come from annexing areas contiguous to the city that are the sites of new urban growth and have lower land costs, more open space, and less congested roads. Hence, most new road capacity in urban areas comes from spreading development over space and not by increasing the density of roads in existing built-up areas.

Producing Motor Vehicle Transport Services

Thus far the analysis has focused on vehicles and roads, but what consumers and firms actually seek or demand are transport services—that is, the movement of goods and passengers from one point to another. How do we relate our information about vehicles and roads to these transport services that are the object of demand? Transport services are produced by combining vehicles with roads (and other factors), much as labor and land are combined to produce agricultural products or as labor and machinery are combined to produce manufactured goods.[32] Economics has long used production functions to relate inputs to outputs, and this approach is used here to analyze how economies combine vehicles and roads to produce transport services.

In the context of a typical production function, the cost-minimizing solution is for the ratio of inputs to depend on their relative prices and on technological factors that may differ across countries. The question is whether assumptions of competitive behavior and efficiency are relevant in producing motor vehicle transport services. What really matters in this framework is government provision of roadways. Vehicle owners have an incentive to be efficient, but do government road departments? To the extent that governments invest in roads based on economic approaches (such as cost-benefit analysis) or in response to economic pressures, road provision may be reasonably efficient in economic terms. As shown earlier, road provision has strong relations with economic variables.

A direct measure of the ratio of inputs for a production function approach would be actual traffic volumes (vehicle kilometers traveled) per kilometer of road network. There is surprisingly little information on aggregate traffic volumes at the national or urban level, however, and such data are often based on intermediate variables such as fuel consumption. Most traffic volume data are measured on specific streets or roads because the information is needed to analyze network use. Motor vehicles per kilometer of road has been used as an indirect measure of the ratio of inputs in the work reported here and is a proxy for the more desirable volume measure.

How good a proxy is this indirect measure? There is a strong relation between speed (or congestion) and traffic volume, which is typically summarized in a speed-volume diagram showing that speed falls (and congestion rises) as traffic volumes increase. At the urban level, the ratio of vehicles per kilometer of road has a relation with average speed similar to the speed-volume curves for segments of streets or roads (figure 10-4).

The cost of roads varies systematically across countries, reflecting differences in the price of land and of the (mostly) nontraded inputs, such as labor and most construction materials used in road construction. The price of motor vehicles should not vary across countries because they are traded goods (although countries obviously impose different taxes and fees on motor vehicles). The ratio of the prices of nontraded to traded goods typically increases with per capita income. If a network is congested, however,

---

32. This section draws heavily on Ingram and Liu (1997, 1998).

Figure 10-4. *Vehicle-Road Ratio and Average Road Speeds in Urban Areas*
Average road speed (km/hr)

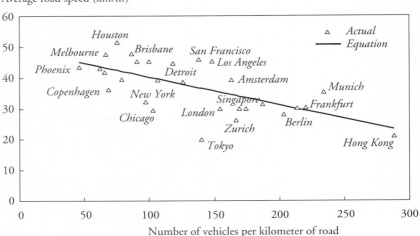

Source: Generated from data provided in Newman and Kenworthy (1989).

then increases in the number of motor vehicles per kilometer of road will
reduce speeds and increase the cost of vehicle operation. Congestion costs
increase with the value of time (which increases with per capita income)
and have the potential to offset the effect of rising road costs on the ratio of
vehicles to roads.

In most countries the national road network is not congested, so the
cost of roads relative to vehicles should rise with per capita income, and
there will be no offsetting time saving from lowering congestion. As a result, the ratio of vehicles to roads should increase at the national level. At
the urban level, the costs of congestion will increase with income, and the
benefits of reducing congestion will tend to offset the increasing cost of
roads relative to vehicles, making it difficult to predict, a priori, how the
ratio of vehicles to roads will vary with per capita income. Other variables
can be used in this production function approach, but the focus here is on
income and population density.

Motor Vehicle Services at the National Level

As shown earlier, both motorization and the provision of roads are
strongly associated with per capita income at the national level. Because

Table 10-5. *Estimated Effects of Population, Per Capita Income, and Population Density on Vehicle-Road Ratio*

Dependent variable	Functional specification	Coefficient estimates		
		Population	Per capita income	Population density
At the national level				
Vehicles/total road km.	Cross-section	0.0	0.4[a]	0.2[a]
	20-year first differences	0.3	0.4	...
Vehicles/paved road km.	Cross-section	0.0	0.0	−0.1[a]
	20-year first differences	−0.9	0.2	...
At the urban level				
Vehicles/road km.	Cross-section	0.1	varies[b]	0.6[a]
	First differences	0.5	0.9[a]	0.5

Source: Ingram and Liu (1997, 1998). All variables are in natural logarithm, and elasticities are jointly estimated.

a. Statistically significant at the 0.05 level.

b. Elasticity first rises and then falls with income.

the number of vehicles increases faster with income than does the total national road length, the number of vehicles per kilometer of total road increases with income; the income elasticity is around 0.4 (table 10-5, figure 10-5). These increases are occurring at low ratios of vehicles to roads, however, confirming that congestion on national roads is not a common problem even in high-income countries. The relation between vehicles per kilometer of total roads and income is reasonably similar in cross-section and first-difference (time-series) specifications using constant elasticities.

This result is consistent with the hypothesis that the cost of roads at the national level increases more rapidly than the cost of vehicles as incomes rise (because roads are nontraded and vehicles are traded goods). The number of vehicles per kilometer of total roads is independent of population but positively associated with population density (the elasticity is about 0.2).

The length of paved road at the national level increases with income at about the same rate as the number of vehicles, so it is not surprising that the number of vehicles per kilometer of paved road length is constant or declining with per capita income. There may be some increase in this ratio

Figure 10-5. *Per Capita Income and Vehicle-to-Road Ratio in Fifty Countries and Thirty-Five Cities*

Vehicles per kilometer of road

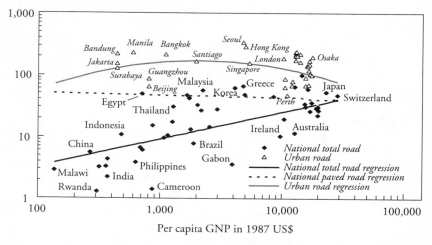

Per capita GNP in 1987 US$

Source: Ingram and Liu (1998). Data points for paved roads are not plotted for the sake of clarity. Both axes are in logarithms.

over time (the first-difference elasticity with income is 0.2, but it is not statistically different from zero in table 10-5). Population density has a mildly negative effect on the number of vehicles per kilometer of paved road, with an elasticity of –0.1, suggesting that both paved roads and alternative modes may be associated with density.

Estimates of saturation levels for the vehicle-to-road ratio do not converge for either vehicles per kilometer of total road or vehicles per kilometer of paved road. This is consistent with the view that national roads are generally uncongested.

Motor Vehicle Services at the Urban Level

Urban vehicle ownership increases regularly with income, while urban road length increases very little with income initially, and then rapidly, in a nonlinear fashion. As a result, the ratio of motor vehicles to roads in cities rises with income when incomes are low and then declines with income when incomes are high (see figure 10-5). This result, based on comparisons across cities, indicates that the high costs of congestion in high-income cities may stimulate road building. Time-series results based on first differences indicate, however, that the ratio of motor vehicles to roads is rising over time in virtually all cities, reflecting the slower increase in urban road length than in urban vehicle ownership over time. The ratio of motor vehicles to roads in urban areas is positively related to population density, with an elasticity from 0.5 to 0.6 in both cross-section and first-difference estimates. Estimates of the saturation level for motor vehicles per kilometer of road in urban areas yield a value of 550 vehicles per kilometer of road. The maximum value observed in a sample of thirty-five cities is 425 (in Paris).[33]

These results reflect the interaction of countervailing forces generated by congestion in urban areas. At the national level, where roads have little congestion, the ratio of vehicles to roads increases over time because roads become more expensive relative to vehicles as incomes rise. At the urban level, however, rising congestion creates travel delays that become more costly as incomes rise. This makes it attractive eventually to increase the supply of roads in high-income urban areas. The cheapest way to do this is by expanding the urban area—incorporating into it existing roads that are relatively uncongested—a solution that produces decentralized urban growth.

Prognosis

Analyses reviewed here indicate that income growth is the main determinant of increases in motor vehicle fleets at both the national and urban level and that the elasticity of vehicle ownership with income is constant or declining over the range of country incomes. Together, those findings suggest that there is no critical income level at which vehicle ownership suddenly begins to accelerate. Although elasticity estimates vary, a good point estimate for the elasticity of fleet growth is approximately 1.0 both with respect to per capita income (measured across countries using market exchange rates) and to population. These values mean that country motor vehicle fleets grow in proportion to total country incomes. With these values, simple projections of motor vehicle fleets can be made at global, regional, and country levels.

---

33. Ingram and Liu (1997).

Global Motor Vehicle Fleet Growth

Table 10-6 shows the share of population, gross national product (GNP), and motor vehicle fleet held in 1995 by 23 high-income countries and by 125 low- and middle-income countries; it also shows motor vehicle fleet projections for the same sets of countries.[34] The low- and middle-income countries had a modest share of global GNP and motor vehicles, but a high share of population. The simple illustrative motor vehicle fleet projection in table 10-6 is based on the assumption that GNP grows at 3 percent in high-income countries (close to actual experience in 1980–90) and 5 percent in low- and middle-income countries (an optimistic rate, based on the highest rates experienced in each region over the past fifteen years).

Based on these growth rates, the projections indicate that more than half of the world's annual increase in motor vehicles will occur in high-income countries until 2025. The motor vehicle fleet in low- and middle-income countries is not projected to exceed that in high-income countries until after 2050 Because the GNP growth rates used for low- and middle-income countries are optimistic, the time taken to achieve equivalence of fleet increments is likely to be longer than suggested by these estimates. The growth rates of incomes and fleets in low- and middle-income countries are high, but they are operating on a small base.

Barring a profound change in vehicle fuels and fuel efficiency or alterations in land use patterns that would shorten average travel distances per vehicle, emissions of carbon dioxide are likely to increase at about the same rate as vehicle fleets. More than half of vehicular carbon dioxide emissions will come from high-income countries for the foreseeable future, however. The production of other emissions (hydrocarbons, nitrogen oxides, and so forth) are likely to vary dramatically across countries because emission control technologies vary. The fleets in high-income countries typically have much lower emission rates than the essentially uncontrolled fleets in low- and middle-income countries. That is changing, however, as many low- and middle-income countries are requiring emission controls for vehicles and are beginning to control the production of heavily polluting technologies such as two-cycle gasoline engines. The adoption of emission controls by most low- and middle-income countries is overdue because

---

34. High income countries are defined by the World Bank as those having a per capita gross national product of $9,386 or more in 1995. See World Bank (1997: xxii).

Table 10-6. *Share of Global Population, GNP, and Motor Vehicle Fleet in High-Income and Low- and Middle-Income Countries, and Motor Vehicle Fleet Projections*

	Low- and middle-income countries	High-income countries	All countries
Initial global shares (percent) 1995			
Population	84	16	100
GNP	19	81	100
Motor vehicles	25	75	100
Projected motor vehicles by year (in millions)			
1995	164	487	651
2000	209	565	774
2010	340	759	1,099
2020	555	1,020	1,575
2030	905	1,370	2,275
2040	1,470	1,840	3,310
2050	2,400	2,475	4,875

Source: World Bank (1997); American Automobile Manufacturing Association (1996).

many of their large cities have the worst urban air pollution in the world, and the costs of vehicular emission controls have fallen over time.

Simple projections of motor vehicle fleet growth ignore changes in prices that may affect demand. The available evidence suggests that vehicle users react to price changes in ways that moderate the effects of price changes on vehicle ownership and use. Increases in gasoline prices encourage the purchase of vehicles that are more fuel efficient and reduce vehicle use somewhat. Increases in the price of new vehicles (for example, by means of purchase taxes on new cars) also increase the price of second-hand vehicles and extend the life of vehicles. That reduces the annual depreciation rate (a major component of the annual user cost of a capital good) and helps to offset the effect of the price increase. Thus price increases can reduce the demand for vehicle ownership and use, but demand is fairly inelastic with respect to price, partly because of the possibilities for compensating behavior. Therefore, price increases that are significantly larger than income increases will be required to produce substantial effects on vehicle ownership.

The distributional impact of taxes is often a policy concern. In low- and middle-income countries taxes on automobile ownership and use are progressive with income because it is the high-income households that own cars.[35] That is not true in high-income countries, where the vast majority of households own a car.

Vehicles and Roads at the National Level

Road infrastructure has expanded with income at the national level across countries. Paved road length has been expanding at about the same rate as the number of motor vehicles, but total (paved and unpaved) national road length has expanded only about half as fast. High-income countries now have less scope for expanding paved roads faster than total roads because a large proportion of their roads are already paved. Paving existing roads remains a cost effective way for low- and middle-income countries to improve the productivity of their road systems as motor vehicle fleets expand.

The income elasticity of road provision appears to be constant across country income levels. This constancy is so strong that saturation levels for roads at the national level cannot be estimated. Although the number of motor vehicles per unit of total national road length increases with country income levels, the ratios are so low that few national roads are congested. Moreover, simple economic reasoning suggests that it is efficient for the ratio of vehicles to roads to increase with income as long as the roads are uncongested.

Vehicles and Roads at the Urban Level

At the urban level vehicle ownership trends and determinants parallel those at the national level. Urban vehicle ownership is strongly determined by income and its elasticity with income is also approximately 1.0. This parallel does not extend to road provision. At the urban level roads expand very little with income at low-income levels, and then more rapidly at high-income levels, producing a ratio of vehicles to roads that first rises with income and then declines. Another sharp distinction is that the ratio of vehicles to roads is much higher in urban areas than in national systems, and urban road systems are frequently congested.

To reduce congestion in urban areas, either vehicle ownership and use can be reduced or road space and the efficiency of road use can be in-

---

35. Hughes (1987).

creased. Reducing ownership and use can be done by increasing prices of cars and gasoline, but as noted earlier, very large price increases are required to have much of an effect. Because the levels of auto-related negative externalities are chiefly associated with use, public policies targeting vehicle use, rather than vehicle ownership, will be more effective in addressing those externalities. The first-best price for reducing congestion would be a congestion toll because it directly prices the negative externality. The limited experience with congestion tolls suggests that they can be effective at curbing auto use. In Singapore, which has the longest experience with congestion tolls, they appear to help reduce congestion.[36]

During recent decades, urban areas have coped with congestion by spreading their activities over larger areas and adding road space by annexation. Decentralized urban development is most evident in high-income countries, such as the United States and Australia, where land costs at the periphery of urban areas are relatively low. Yet over a twenty-year period in the global sample of thirty-five cities analyzed here, average population densities declined in twenty-five cities and the urban area increased in thirty, so urban area expansion and decentralization is a common pattern of urban growth. Cities with high densities typically face high relative land prices at their peripheries, and their expansion will occur at higher densities than in cities that face low land prices. As a result, urban areas are not likely to converge to similar levels of population density and congestion. Instead, population densities and congestion in a particular city will depend on relative land prices at the urban periphery, urban income levels, and the city's historical endowment of structures and roads.

Unanswered Questions

Other than its contribution to the formation of global greenhouse gases, the most serious negative externalities from motorization—congestion and air pollution—are experienced primarily in urban areas. Further analysis of rapidly growing urban areas in developing countries is needed both to obtain more detail on the composition of motor vehicle fleets and to evaluate policy options in transport. For example, few studies of motorization include motorcycles (which are present in significant numbers in many coun-

36. For an analysis of Singapore's experience, see Hau (1992). Several other cities, including Oslo and Trondheim, have more recently instituted area license schemes like that of Singapore. Chapter 6 in this volume addresses congestion tolls.

tries), and little attention has been given to such components of the fleet as buses and trucks. In addition, the effects on urban vehicle ownership and use of available transit modes have received little attention outside high-income countries, where the effects appear to be small. Two other data weaknesses pervading studies of motorization and roads are that comparable data on prices and taxation across cities and countries and over time are elusive, and the most readily available data on roads measure only road length, whereas lane miles of road or better measures of road capacity would clearly be more appropriate.

Traffic congestion appears to have a strong impact on urban development patterns, as cities decentralize and spread their development into surrounding areas in order to increase the supply of urban roads and moderate congestion. This phenomenon deserves more attention and analysis. If firms and households move in ways that foster low-density development at the periphery of urban areas in order to reduce congestion, they may also do so in order to avoid congestion tolls. How urban development will react to congestion tolls is an open question.

The fact that road provision across countries behaves in accordance with predictions based on economic efficiency is surprising. The economic predictions are derived from behavior conditioned by economic discipline. But roads are not supplied by private firms functioning in market environments—they are typically planned and financed by governmental agencies, which often seem to be well insulated from market forces. Yet even though road agencies are not actors in a market, they do operate in a political environment that is affected by economic forces and may produce outcomes that are reasonably efficient in economic terms. Albert Hirschman has developed this point, arguing that public infrastructure is provided by the public sector in a framework of "induced decisionmaking" that tracks economic growth in a process of overbuilding and shortfalls and produces outcomes that are responsive to economic needs.[37] The pattern of road provision across countries is consistent with Hirschman's argument.

References

Bates, J.J., H.F. Gunn, and M. Roberts. 1978. "A Model of Household Car Ownership." *Traffic Engineering and Control* 19 (11/12): 486–491, 562–566.

Beesley, Michael E., and John F. Kain. 1964. "Urban Form, Car Ownership, and Public Policy: An Appraisal of Traffic in Towns." *Urban Studies* 1 (November): 174–203.

37. Hirschman (1958).

Bennathan, Esra, Julia Fraser, and Louis Thompson. 1992. "What Determines Demand for Freight Transport?" Policy Research Working Paper 998. World Bank, Infrastructure and Urban Development Department, Washington, D.C. October.

Button, Kenneth, Ndoh Ngoe, and John Hine. 1993. "Modelling Vehicle Ownership and Use in Low Income Countries." *Journal of Transport Economic and Policy* 27 (January): 51–67.

Button, Kenneth, A.D. Pearman, and A.S. Fowkes. 1982. *Car Ownership Modelling and Forecasting.* Aldershot, Hampshire, U.K.: Gower Publishing Company Ltd.

Canning, David. 1998. "A Database of World Infrastructure Stocks 1950–1995." Policy Research Working Paper 1929. World Bank, Infrastructure and Urban Development Department, Washington, D.C.

Chin, Anthony, and Peter Smith. 1997. "Automobile Ownership and Government Policy: The Economics of Singapore's Vehicle Quota Scheme." *Transportation Research* 31A (March): 129–40.

Deaton, Angus. 1987. "The Demand for Personal Travel in Developing Countries." World Bank, Infrastructure and Urban Development Department, Washington, D.C. August.

Glaister, Stephen. 1981. *Fundamentals of Transport Economics.* New York: St. Martin's Press.

Hau, Timothy D. 1992. "Congestion Charging Mechanisms for Roads: An Evaluation of Current Practice." Policy Research Working Paper 1071. World Bank, Infrastructure and Urban Development Department, Washington, D.C. December.

Hensher, David A., Frank W. Milthorpe, and Nariida C. Smith. 1990. "The Demand for Vehicle Use in the Urban Household Sector: Theory and Empirical Evidence." *Journal of Transport Economics and Policy* 24 (May): 119–37.

Hirschman, Albert O. 1958. *The Strategy of Economic Development.* Yale University Press.

Hughes, Gordon. 1987. "The Incidence of Fuel Taxes: A Comparative Study of Three Countries." In *The Theory of Taxation for Developing Countries*, edited by David Newbery and Nicholas Stern, 533–59. Oxford University Press.

Ingram, Gregory K. 1998. "Patterns of Metropolitan Development: What Have We Learned?" *Urban Studies* 35 (June): 1019–35.

Ingram, Gregory K., and Zhi Liu. 1997. "Motorization and the Provision of Roads in Countries and Cities." Policy Research Working Paper 1842. World Bank, Infrastructure and Urban Development Department, Washington, D.C.

———. 1998. "Vehicles, Roads, and Road Use: Alternate Empirical Specifications." Policy Research Working Paper 2036. World Bank, Infrastructure and Urban Development Department, Washington, D.C.

International Road Federation. Various years. *World Road Statistics.* Geneva.

Johansson, Olof, and Lee Schipper. 1997. "Measuring the Long-Run Fuel Demand of Cars: Separate Estimations of Vehicle Stock, Mean Fuel Intensity, and Mean Annual Driving Distance." *Journal of Transport Economics and Policy* 31 (September): 277–92.

Kain, John F. 1983. "Impacts of Higher Petroleum Prices on Transportation Patterns and Urban Development." In *Research in Transportation Economics*, vol. 1, edited by Theodore E. Keeler. Stamford, Conn.: JAI Press Inc.

Kain, John F., and Zhi Liu. 1994. "Efficiency and Locational Consequences of Government Transport Policies and Spending in Chile." Harvard Project on Urbanization in Chile, Harvard University.

Khan, A., and L.G. Willumsen. 1986. "Modeling Car Ownership and Use in Developing Countries." *Traffic Engineering and Control* 27 (11): 554–60.

Mannering, Fred, and Clifford Winston. 1985. "A Dynamic Empirical Analysis of Household Vehicle Ownership and Utilization." *Rand Journal of Economics* 16 (Summer): 215–36.

Meyer, John R., and José A. Gómez-Ibáñez. 1981. *Autos, Transit, and Cities.* Harvard University Press.

Mogridge, M. J. H. 1967. "The Prediction of Car Ownership." *Journal of Transport Economics and Policy* 1 (January): 52–74.

————. 1983. *The Car Market: A Study of the Statics and Dynamics of Supply-Demand Equilibrium.* London: Pion.

————. 1989. "The Prediction of Car Ownership and Use Revisited: The Beginning of the End?" *Journal of Transport Economics and Policy* 23 (January): 55–74.

Motor Vehicles Manufacturers Association of the United States. 1996. *World Motor Vehicle Data.* Detroit.

Newman, Peter W.G., and Jeffrey R. Kenworthy. 1989. *Cities and Automobile Dependence: A Sourcebook.* Brookfield, Vt.: Gower Technical Publishing Company Ltd.

Ortúzar, Juan de Dios, and Luis G. Willumsen. 1994. *Modelling Transport.* 2ᵈ ed. New York: Wiley.

Pindyck, Robert S. 1979. *The Structure of World Energy Demand.* MIT Press.

Prud'homme, Remy, and others. 1997. *Is Our Present Transport System Sustainable?* Observatoire de l'Economie et des Institutions Locales, Universite de Paris.

Quarmby, D.A., and J.J. Bates. 1970. "An Econometric Method of Car Ownership Forecasting in Discrete Areas." *MAU Note 219.* London: Department of Environment.

Silberston, Aubrey. 1970. "Automobile Use and the Standard of Living in East and West." *Journal of Transport Economics and Policy* 4 (January): 3–14.

Summers, Robert, and Alan Heston. 1991. "The Penn World Table (Mark 5): An Expanded Set of International Comparisons, 1950–1988." *Quarterly Journal of Economics* 106 (May): 327–68.

Sweeney, J. L. 1978. "Energy Policy and Automobile Use of Gasoline." Stanford University.

Tanner, J.C. 1962. "Forecasts of Future Numbers of Vehicles in Great Britain." *Roads and Road Construction* 40 (September): 263–74.

———— 1978. "Long-Term Forecasting of Vehicle Ownership and Road Traffic." *Journal of the Royal Statistical Society.* Series A, 141(3, Part 1): 14–63.

Train, Kenneth E. 1986. *Qualitative Choice Analysis: Theory, Econometrics and an Application to Automobile Demand.* MIT Press.

Wheaton, William C. 1982. "The Long-Run Structure of Transportation and Gasoline Demand." *Bell Journal of Economics* 13 (Autumn): 439–54.

Wildhorn, Sorrel, and others. 1974. *How to Save Gasoline: Public Policy Alternatives for the Automobile.* Report R-1560-NSF, prepared for the National Science Foundation. Santa Monica, Calif.: Rand

World Bank. 1992. *World Development Report 1992.* Oxford University Press.

————. 1997. *1997 World Development Indicators.* Washington, D.C.

World Resources Institute. 1996. *World Resources 1996–97.* Oxford University Press.

PART III

Transportation and Cities

JOHN F. KAIN

11

The Urban Transportation Problem: A Reexamination and Update

Transit use in North American cities has declined steadily since World War II, a result of market forces, changes in transportation technologies, and decisions by government policymakers and transit managers. Analysis suggests that the decline is rooted in long-term trends. The steady rise in auto ownership and declines in transit use since 1895 were largely efficient responses to changes in technology and rising incomes. At the same time mistakes in public policy and errors by transit operators in their choice of technologies caused not only declines in transit ridership in the last half of the twentieth century, but also larger public subsidies for transit than were necessary.

This chapter is concerned primarily with the comparative costs of alternative transit technologies, the technological and operating choices made by transit managers, and the lessons learned from these choices. Experience strongly suggests that policymakers and transit managers generally erred by using disproportionate amounts of available subsidy dollars to construct and operate costly and ineffective rail transit systems instead of improving bus service and reducing fares. I also argue that the decision to convert the largely private transit industry to public ownership and operation was a serious mistake. Subsidy dollars could have been used to pay private transit operators to provide unprofitable, but desirable, services, and the efficiency gains from private operation could have been used to buy more vehicle

359

miles of bus service and lower fares. At the same time, governments failed to charge urban motorists prices that reflect the long-run social costs of providing highway facilities and services. Although there is little indication that policymakers here or abroad are likely to correct this error in the near future, it is difficult to think of any other policy measure that would do more to improve both general mobility and the viability of public transit.

The History of Transit Technologies

Before the mid-1800s all but the very wealthiest city residents walked to work and to other destinations. As a result, nineteenth century cities were compact, with residential and nonresidential uses side by side and little or no segregation by income or race.[1] The introduction of horse- or mule-drawn street railways provided city residents with a nonwalking option. With their greater capacity and higher speeds, which reduced per-trip costs and fares, these railways quickly displaced omnibuses (an urban version of the stagecoach) that had operated in some cities. By the 1890s nearly 5,700 miles of horse-car lines were in use in American cities.[2]

The horse-car era lasted barely thirty years. In 1888 Frank Sprague developed a single-pole electric trolley system to power street railways. By 1902 there were 22,000 miles of electric street railways, while only 259 miles of horse-car lines remained in service.[3] Like the horse-cars had previously, electric street railways dramatically increased speeds and lowered costs. The result was a rapid growth both in transit use and in the size and extent of the nation's cities.

Soon after the invention of the internal combustion engine, transit operators began replacing street railway services with more flexible and less costly bus and jitney services. Route miles of motor bus services grew rapidly, from a mere 1,380 miles in 1917 to about 61,000 miles in 1930 and 98,600 miles in 1950. From its peak of 44,119 route miles (including interurban) in 1917, electric street railway operations decreased by 17 percent during the 1920s and continued to decline in subsequent decades as bus mileage grew and per capita auto ownership steadily increased. World

1. Kushner (1976).
2. Harrison (1978: 4).
3. Harrison (1978: 4).

War II provided a temporary respite, but with the cessation of hostilities, transit operators again began replacing their street railway systems with diesel and electric (trolley) buses.

By 1974 only 484 miles of surface rail services—streetcars and the more modern light rail transit (LRT)—were still operating. Proponents of urban rail systems showed little interest in LRT in the first three decades following World War II, emphasizing instead the need for costly, high-performance, heavy rail systems to "compete with the private auto." The key difference between heavy rail and LRT is the source of locomotive power. Heavy rail systems generally obtain their power from a high-voltage third rail, while LRT systems usually obtain their power from an overhead wire. The need to protect people and vehicles from the voltage in the third rail requires that the rail system be separated from other forms of transportation, and this full-grade separation is both the source of heavy rail's "high performance" and its high capital costs.

Heavy rail systems did not exhibit the boom and bust character of light rail. Heavy rail mileage grew steadily if slowly, from 313 miles in 1902 to 1,134 miles in 1928 and to a prewar high of 1,379 miles in 1937. Thereafter, heavy rail mileage slowly declined until 1954.

The Yonge Street Line in Toronto, which began operations in 1954, was the first new heavy rail line to be completed in North America after World War II. A year later, the Cleveland Transit System (CTS) began operations on its new heavy rail line, and a 1968 extension to the airport gave CTS bragging rights as the first North American transit system to provide direct downtown-to-airport rail service.[4] In 1972, in what would be the last heavy rail start without federal assistance, the San Francisco Bay Area Rapid Transit System (BART) opened the "first new regional rail transit system to be built in the United States in over 50 years."[5]

The prospects for rail improved dramatically in 1971, when Congress provided federal capital grants for new rail starts. BART was the first recipient of federal construction dollars under the new program; federal capital grants accounted for 20 percent of BART's capital funds by 1976.[6] Federal grants eventually paid for up to 80 percent of the capital costs of entirely new heavy rail systems in Atlanta, Baltimore, Los Angeles, Miami, and

---

4. Van Tassel and Grabowski (1987).
5. Metropolitan Transportation Commission (1979: 2).
6. Metropolitan Transportation Commission (1979: 34).

Washington, D.C., and additions to and modernization of existing systems in Boston, Cleveland, New York, and Philadelphia. In 1989 Pickrell estimated that the capital costs of the new systems in constant 1988 dollars varied from $1.3 billion for Baltimore's 7.6 mile system to $8.0 billion for Washington's 60.5 mile system.[7] Fueled by federal grants, new systems and additions to existing systems combined to produce a 26 percent increase in heavy rail mileage between 1968 and 1980 and an additional 58 percent between 1980 and 1996.

The experience of the new heavy rail systems was disappointing. Ridership was much lower than projected, and costs were much higher.[8] Rail enthusiasts, who had shown little interest in LRT in the immediate postwar period, now embraced it as a low-cost alternative to heavy rail. The widely acclaimed "success" of San Diego's LRT system, which began operations in July 1981, heightened interest in light rail.[9] Nine additional U.S. cities completed more than 250 miles of new LRT services in the following years, but the ridership and cost-effectiveness of these systems have also generally been disappointing.

Land Use Changes, Car Ownership, and Declines in Transit Use

As figure 11-1 reveals, total transit ridership grew steadily between 1910 and 1926; ridership peaked at 300 rides per urban resident in 1912 and then steadily declined.[10] The Depression had a disastrous effect on the transit industry, and both total ridership and ridership per urban resident reached their pre–World War II lows in 1933. Rapid growth of urban employment and population, in combination with gas and tire rationing, produced dramatic surges in ridership during the war, both in total numbers and in ridership per urban resident. Thereafter, both per capita and total ridership declined steadily until 1972, when massive government subsidies and a temporary boost from higher gas prices and shortages stimulated an

7. Pickrell (1989).

8. Pickrell (1989); Metropolitan Transportation Commission (1979).

9. Gómez-Ibáñez (1985); Kain and Liu (1995).

10. The estimates of transit ridership, particularly for the period before 1917, are very crude. Based on street railway route miles, they assume ridership per route mile was the same as in 1917. The estimate of urban population is also problematic, but it is more meaningful than total population.

Figure 11-1. *Indexes of Total and Transit Ridership per Urban Resident and Auto Ownership Per Capita, 1910–1995*

Indexes (1950 = 100)

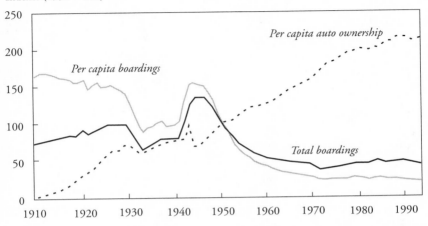

Source: Boardings are from Bureau of the Census (1975: part 2, 721); APTA (1977: table 7; 1997: table 32). After 1979 commuter rail passenger trips are subtracted from the total. Auto ownership is based on motor vehicle registration from the Bureau of the Census (1975: part 2, 715; various years). Population is from Bureau of the Census (1975: part 1, 12; various years).

increase. Slower growth in real subsidies and continued suburbanization in the 1980s led to small but persistent declines. Between 1972 and 1989 total boardings grew by 31 percent, most of it in the first eight years. This period, however, was characterized by large increases in rail operations, which have higher transfer rates. When estimates by Small and Gómez-Ibáñez are used to correct the boardings data for this spurious source of increases in ridership, the growth in total linked trips between 1972 and 1995 is less than 6 percent.[11] (Linked trips combine the components, or boardings, of a single integrated trip. For example, a single linked transit trip might consist of three boardings—a feeder bus journey, a rail journey, and a second bus ride.)

The first data on automobile ownership are for 1910 when there were 5,000 registered automobiles. By 1920 that number had increased to 76,000, and this rapid growth continued until 1929, when the Depression slowed and then World War II halted its growth. After VJ Day per capita auto

11. Small and Gómez-Ibáñez (1996).

Table 11-1. *Number of Transit Worktrips and Transit Share by Metropolitan Area, Selected Years*

Metro area	Transit worktrips (thousands)				As a percent of total worktrips			
	1960	*1970*	*1980*	*1990*	*1960*	*1970*	*1980*	*1990*
New York	2,570	2,459	1,995	2,158	43.7	37.5	29.6	26.9
Chicago	754	662	570	514	28.2	21.4	16.4	13.4
Philadelphia	489	399	294	282	26.0	18.3	12.7	10.1
Boston	n.a.	225	208	221	n.a.	15.8	12.9	10.4
San Francisco	202	204	282	291	14.5	11.2	11.3	9.1
Los Angeles	202	159	261	308	6.9	4.2	5.0	4.5
Washington	185	192	235	295	21.3	15.3	15.1	13.3
Cleveland	169	112	93	56	16.7	9.7	7.8	4.5
Detroit	165	124	65	48	11.6	7.3	3.5	2.3
Pittsburgh	153	122	104	75	18.8	14.3	11.4	7.9
33 large metro areas	6,092	5,567	5,082	5,127	14.3	9.4	7.6	5.7
All other areas	1,715	957	982	621	4.8	2.7	2.0	1.2
All U.S.	7,807	6,514	6,007	5,890	12.1	8.5	6.2	5.1

Source: Wendell Cox Consultancy, "US Employment & Public Transport Work Trips 1960–1990," January 21, 1997. www.publicpurpose.com.

ownership returned to its early rapid growth path until about 1980, when the rate appears to have slowed somewhat. The lower rate of growth in per capita auto ownership after 1980 may be due in part to a saturation phenomenon and to slower per capita income growth.

Transit primarily serves commuters in large metropolitan areas; in 1990 commuters in the seven largest metropolitan areas accounted for 69 percent of all U.S. transit trips (table 11-1). In addition, with the exception of Los Angeles, the largest metropolitan areas also have much higher transit mode splits (the share of total trips accounted for by transit modes) than smaller urban areas. The proportion of commuters in the New York metropolitan area who use transit, 26.9 percent, is more than twice that of the next metropolitan area, Chicago.

Most transit trips within large metropolitan areas are made by people who live and work in the central city. In 1980, for example, 16.1 percent of all workers who both worked and lived in the central cities of metropolitan areas used transit to reach work, compared with 8 percent of the workers who lived in the suburbs but worked in the central city and 1.6 percent of the workers who both lived and worked in the suburbs.[12] (Data for 1990 show essentially the same results.) Although the causes of these trends are many and complex, the fivefold increase in per capita income since 1900 is clearly the dominant factor.[13] For most trips, transit is cheaper than private cars, but commuting by car is usually more convenient and faster. As real wages and per capita incomes have risen, increasing numbers of households have opted for the greater convenience and time savings of cars, and transit use steadily declined.[14] Transit accounted for only 1.8 percent of total daily trips and 3.2 percent of worktrips in 1995.[15]

Rising per capita incomes also affected auto ownership and transit use in other, more indirect, ways. Households in the United States, and particularly those with children, have strong preferences for lower-density housing arrangements. Rising incomes and higher levels of auto ownership enabled growing numbers to live in single family homes and low-density neighborhoods. These trends resulted in large declines in central city populations and densities and a pronounced flattening of urban density functions.[16] (Urban economists widely use urban density functions to describe changes in gross population densities with distance from the city center.) Moreover, the difficulty of providing frequent service to low-density residential areas together with the choice of lower-density living arrangements by growing numbers of commuters further increased the relative advantage of private over public transportation for urban trips.[17]

The adverse effects on transit of the suburbanization of residences were exacerbated by accompanying changes in the geographic distribution of

12. Meyer, Kain, and Wohl (1965); Meyer and Gómez-Ibáñez (1981); Pisarski (1987).

13. Kain (1983) provides support for this proposition. His regression analyses demonstrate that per capita income alone explains more than 80 percent of the variance in per capita auto ownership for five very different samples: a time series of annual U.S. data for the period 1900–63; cross-section samples for twenty-three industrialized countries in 1958 and 1968; and a cross-section sample of the sixty-eight non-Communist countries with per capita income greater than $300 in 1977.

14. Kain (1983: 7) estimates that real time costs to commuters rose from $0.81 an hour in 1930 to $1.62 in 1947 and to $2.84 in 1978. He adds that "the effects of this rapid increase in time costs of travel—which explain much of the shift from slower to faster modes, as well as the growth of car ownership—are . . . partially embodied in the reduced form estimates of the income elasticity of demand for auto ownership." These elasticity estimates, which were obtained from the regression equations described in the previous footnote, vary between 1.0 and 2.0.

15. Federal Highway Administration (1995). Due to differences in definition, these figures are not directly comparable with data in table 11-1.

16. Kain (1968); Muth (1969); Harrison and Kain (1974); Mills (1970).

17. Beesley and Kain (1964); Kain, Fauth, and Zax (1978); Kain and Liu (1996); and Liu (1993) are examples of the dozens, if not hundreds, of empirical analyses that show the pronounced impact of net and gross population densities on the transit share of worktrips.

employment. Steady improvements in the performance, size, and operating costs of trucks and in the quality and amount of urban streets and roads contributed to this dispersion of employment throughout the urban area, while the completion of new intercity highways (notably the Interstate Highway System) and steady improvements in air transportation enabled trucks and airlines to capture ever-increasing shares of intercity passenger and freight movements. These changes produced further employment decentralization and declines in transit ridership.[18]

Central business district employment levels are especially critical to transit ridership, particularly on the new rail transit systems that were designed specifically to serve large projected increases in central city employment.[19] Although data are fragmentary and difficult to interpret, they, nonetheless, indicate that few central business districts experienced significant employment growth after World War II.[20] This conclusion will surprise many individuals who have equated the construction of new office space within central business districts of large cities with employment growth. Overly optimistic forecasts of central city employment are important contributors to the excessively optimistic forecasts of transit ridership of proposed rail systems.[21]

These trends within metropolitan areas are reinforced by differential rates of regional growth. Newer, lower-density metropolitan areas in the Sun Belt have grown much more rapidly than older, denser metropolitan areas in the Frost Belt. Southern and western metropolitan areas, which have low central city densities and even lower overall densities, experienced most of their growth during periods when incomes were high and the private auto was the principal mode of urban tripmaking. The dispersed employment patterns and low population densities that characterize southern and western metropolitan areas make it difficult for transit operators to provide competitive services. As a result, the fractions of trips by transit are much lower in these regions than they are in older and denser metropolitan areas. More rapid growth in areas with low levels of transit use and high levels of private automobile use, of course, reduces the average rates of transit use and increases the rates of auto use for the nation as a whole.

18. Meyer, Kain, and Wohl (1965); Moses and Williamson (1967).
19. Meyer, Kain, and Wohl (1965); Hendrickson (1986); Kain (1990).
20. Kain (1990); Meyer, Kain, and Wohl (1965); Meyer and Gómez-Ibáñez (1981).
21. Kain (1990).

Comparative Costs of Alternative Transit Modes

One of the longest standing controversies in urban transportation has been whether and under what circumstances rail transit is more suitable or cost-effective than buses. The debate was intense during the 1940s and 1950s when bus services were replacing many street railways. But it was not until 1965, when Meyer, Kain, and Wohl published *The Urban Transportation Problem*, that the first "objective" estimates of the comparative costs of alternative urban transportation modes became available. This analysis, which considered both operating and capital costs and allocated all capital costs to peak-hour users, estimated one-way passenger costs for peak-hour corridor volumes for between 5,000 and 50,000 passengers and for systems built in high- and medium-density metropolitan areas.[22] In contrast to previous studies, which generally considered only the line-haul portion of the typical commuter trip, Meyer, Kain, and Wohl also analyzed residential collection and downtown distribution costs. These trip segments differ greatly in terms of the technical challenges they pose and the performance and costs of the alternative modes in serving residential areas and central business districts that vary by size and density.

Urban rail systems often—but not always—perform both the line-haul function and the larger part of downtown distribution. Atlanta, Chicago, and San Diego are examples of urban rail systems that provide downtown distribution for most trips to the central area. In other cities rail systems depend on feeder buses (Cleveland, for example) or a people mover (Miami) to distribute people once they have reached the central area. Bus rapid transit systems can either operate to a downtown terminal, such as the Port Authority Terminal in New York City, or depend on feeder buses, and in the case of New York City on subways, for downtown distribution. In addition, bus rapid transit systems can and frequently do operate on central area streets, providing their own downtown distribution, as some New York City and all Houston express buses do. Even when express buses drop most users within walking distance of their destinations, the bus system may depend on varying degrees on other transit modes to complete the distribution of their passengers within the central area.

In modeling and costing central area distribution, Meyer, Kain, and Wohl examined the costs and performance of both rail and bus subways and terminals at the edges of the central business district. Downtown dis-

22. Meyer, Kain, and Wohl (1965).

tribution from these fringe rail and bus terminals was provided by local buses or special feeder bus systems, whose cost and performance depended on the size of the central area and the density of destinations. The advantage of rail and bus tunnels is that they reduce the demand for street space by transit vehicles and may reduce door-to-door travel times. Their disadvantage, of course, is their cost; they dramatically increase both capital and total costs per trip.

In determining the cost of downtown distribution by auto, Meyer, Kain, and Wohl estimated the capital and operating costs of downtown parking lots or structures and allocated these costs to peak-period commuters. Motorists parking in lots at the edge of the downtown were assumed to pay less than those parking at lots closer to their downtown destinations and to have lower mileage costs, but they were also assumed to have larger time costs. In general, recognizing the differences in trip times increases the attractiveness of private cars, express buses, and a subway with a large number of stops over systems that require feeders. Meyer, Kain, and Wohl did not include these performance differences, which tended to favor integrated buses and private cars, in their cost analyses.

The cost and trip times for residential collection and distribution depended on the size of the residential commuter shed and the destinations or origins within it, factors that Meyer, Kain, and Wohl explicitly analyzed in their cost analyses. The principal difference between rail and other modes is that rail cannot perform its own residential collection because it cannot operate on local streets. Instead it must depend on feeder buses or autos for residential collections of all users who live too far from the rail station to walk. Because express buses and private cars can operate as their own collectors, they can reduce door-to-door travel time and do away with the need for transferring, which empirical research indicates commuters strongly dislike.

The cost curves shown in figure 11-2, which are for only the line-haul portion of a typical commuter trip, illustrate how the one-way passenger trip costs of each mode vary as corridor volumes increase for a ten-mile-long line built in a high-density urban area such as Chicago and a medium-density area such as Pittsburgh. Most of the metropolitan areas in the United States that have completed rail systems since the end of World War II and those that are currently building or planning new systems have significantly lower densities than the medium-density case. Thus, the argument for heavy rail transit in these cities is even less favorable than these curves suggest.

Figure 11-2. *Line-Haul, One-Way Passenger Trip Costs for High- and Medium-Density Metropolitan Areas with Complete Two-Way Service*

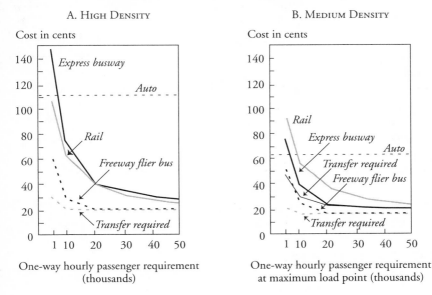

A. High Density

B. Medium Density

One-way hourly passenger requirement (thousands)

One-way hourly passenger requirement at maximum load point (thousands)

Source: Meyer, Kain, and Wohl (1965). One-way passenger trip costs are for a 10-mile route in a high-density city (Chicago) and a medium-density city (Pittsburgh). See text for a full explanation.

Meyer, Kain, and Wohl's comparative cost analyses yielded the following broad generalizations about the costs and performance of alternative high-performance systems:

—Express buses operating on exclusive busways had significantly lower costs per passenger trip than heavy rail systems in all but a few situations.

—Heavy rail had lower per trip costs than express buses on exclusive rights-of-way only when routes were very short and peak-hour volumes and net residential densities were very high.

—"Freeway fliers," that is, express buses operating on uncongested but shared, express highways, had substantially lower costs than heavy rail, buses on exclusive rights-of-way, or private autos at all peak-hour volumes and in every situation considered.

Although rail transit advocates bitterly attacked Meyer, Kain, and Wohl's findings, their results were confirmed by all but one of a small number of subsequent "objective" comparative cost analyses.[23] Studies for the Institute of Defense Analysis (IDA) and of the BART system used similar procedures and reached similar conclusions.[24] The only dissenting analysis was a 1982 study by Pushkarev, Zupan, and Cumella.

The methodologies used in the IDA and BART studies differ from Meyer, Kain, and Wohl principally in their inclusion of the value of travel time in the per trip cost of each mode. As noted above, Meyer, Kain, and Wohl made a conscious decision not to include the value of commuting time as a cost. Instead, they sought, to the extent possible, to represent trip time and other aspects of service quality as "minimum service levels" and confined per trip costs to the capital and operating costs of each system. At the same time they emphasized that the relative travel times of the several modes would affect ridership and thus the applicable volume levels or thresholds in figure 11-2. The disadvantage of their approach is that trip time is in fact a cost; failure to include it tends to bias the analysis toward high-capacity rail and exclusive busway modes. The advantage is the maintenance of a clear distinction between cost and supply considerations and the determinants of demand and system benefits.

Pushkarev, Zupan, and Cumella's *Urban Rail in America* is the only scholarly study to conclude that new rail transit systems would have lower costs than bus transit in a wide range of circumstances in U.S. urban areas.[25] The terminology and approach they used make it difficult to understand why their results differ so dramatically from those obtained in earlier scholarly studies. Fortunately, Pickrell completed a painstaking reanalysis that clarifies these issues.[26] He found that Pushkarev, Zupan, and Cumella understated both the capital and operating costs of new rail systems relative to bus systems and used somewhat optimistic ridership projections when they applied their cost estimates to particular metropolitan areas.[27] For example, they compared "actual" bus system costs with "idealized" rail system costs. When Pickrell used more realistic "best practice" costs, he found that much, if not all, of the alleged operating cost advantage of rail systems disappeared. Similarly, when he used more extensive and detailed capital cost data for new rail systems, he found that Pushkarev, Zupan, and

23. Hamer (1976).
24. Boyd, Asher, and Wetzler (1973); Keeler, Small, and Associates (1975).
25. Pushkarev, with Zupan and Cumella (1982).
26. Pickrell (1985a).
27. Pickrell (1985b).

Cumella had significantly underestimated these costs. As devastating as Pickrell's critique is, it understates the case against this study. He did not note that its cost analyses assume the competitive buses operate on congested streets and roads and, as a result, average 12 miles per hour.[28] In contrast, Meyer, Kain, and Wohl, as well as the IDA and BART studies, all assumed express buses that would operate on exclusive or congestion-controlled rights-of-way and would thus be able to attain speeds equal to or better than heavy rail.[29]

With the exception of *Urban Rail in America*, none of the comparative cost studies outlined above paid much attention to LRT. Its principal attraction, relative to heavy rail, is much lower capital costs—at least where extensive grade separation is not provided. Its disadvantage is lower speeds. Full grade separation enables heavy rail to achieve higher speeds and better reliability than do LRT systems with less grade separation or buses operating on congested roads. LRT feasibility studies all too often claim the capital cost savings obtainable from limited grade separation and at the same time assume the speed and reliability that can only be achieved in a rail system with complete grade separation.

Commuter rail is also largely absent from comparative cost studies, which focus on high-capacity, high-performance systems. Commuter rail typically connects distant suburban and exurban commuters to jobs in the central area. In nearly all instances it serves a single central area terminal and must depend on other modes to distribute its users through the central area. Its performance varies greatly depending on the amount of grade separation, the quality of the rolling stock and track, frequency, and station spacing. Nonetheless, commuter rail systems carried large numbers of suburban commuters in several U.S. cities until the end of World War II, and smaller systems, carrying far fewer commuters, still exist in several U.S. cities. After the war, rapid increases in per capita incomes, extensive highway improvements, and rising levels of car ownership caused steady declines in commuter rail usage, despite huge increases in suburban populations. Even so, there were 3,250 directional route miles (mileage in each direction) of commuter rail serving U.S. cities in 1995, which is a modest increase from 1986. Commuter rail route miles in 1995 were three times the sum of light and heavy rail mileage in the same year. In terms of

28. Pushkarev, with Zupan and Cumella (1982).
29. Kain (1988) provides a more detailed discussion of this point and other problems with the Puskarev-Zupan study.

ridership, however, commuter rail carried only 15 percent as many passengers as did heavy and light rail combined.[30] Much of the current appeal of commuter rail arises from the fact that service can often be implemented relatively quickly at a capital cost that is often substantially less than the cost of a new rail rapid transit system. The rights-of-way, often with extensive grade separation and, in many cases, the tracks, already exist, and modest commuter operations can be introduced at the cost of acquiring suitable rolling stock. Commuter rail and freight services, however, are difficult to operate on the same tracks because of their speed differences, which is one of the reasons private rail operators were so eager to discontinue their commuter services after World War II. System costs, moreover, rise dramatically as available excess capacity is used up and new capital outlays are undertaken to increase system capacity or improve performance. Despite the widespread tendency to think of commuter rail as cheap rail transit, experience throughout the world demonstrates that this notion is largely illusory. Few, if any, examples of unsubsidized commuter rail operations exist, and in most instances per trip subsidies for commuter rail operations exceed those required for even light and heavy rail transit.

Experience with Shared Bus, Carpool Facilities

Express bus systems using shared, high-performance, general-purpose freeways—what Meyer, Kain, and Wohl termed "freeway fliers"—are a cost-effective way to provide high-performance transit in medium- and low-density cities with low to moderate transit demand. Kain and others described the development and operation of highly successful bus-carpool facilities in thirteen metropolitan areas, including Houston, Los Angeles, New York, San Francisco-Oakland Bay Area, and Washington, D.C.[31] Although buses using these high-occupancy vehicle (HOV) facilities serve significant numbers of transit users, they use only a small fraction of HOV capacity (table 11-2). The 179 buses operating on northern Virginia's Shirley Highway during the morning peak hour, for example, carry 6,265 riders but use less than 10 percent of the capacity of its two reversible HOV lanes. Even if the Shirley Highway were a one-lane facility, the buses using it would still require only 19 percent of its capacity. Of the remaining twelve

---

30. APTA (1997).
31. Kain and others (1992); see also Small (1983).

Table 11-2. *Busway-HOV Peak Hour Capacity and Demand*

Facility	Year	Total person trips	Person transit trips	Cap/ PCU*	Vanpools, carpools	Buses	Demand/ capacity (percent) Buses	Total
Washington, D.C.								
Shirley Highway	1988	16,526	6,265	3,000	2,100	179	9.5	80
I-95	1988	7,153	1,470	1,500	1,474	42	4.5	103
I-66	1988	5,795	665	3,000	1,619	19	1.0	55
Los Angeles								
El Monte	1977	4,551	2,708	1,500	657	81	8.6	52
Houston								
North	1996	4,622	2,005	1,500	1,244	71	7.6	91
Katy	1996	3,120	1,190	1,500	793	39	4.2	57
Gulf	1996	3,057	830	1,500	1,048	26	2.8	73
Northwest	1996	3,688	815	1,500	1,398	17	1.8	95
Southwest	1996	3,340	520	1,500	1,346	23	2.5	92
Boston								
Southeast Expressway	1977	4,175	2,124	1,500	695	54	5.8	52
Miami								
I-95	1977	3,809	352	1,500	1,613	10	1.1	109
Portland								
Banfield Freeway	1980	3,376	657	1,500	1,292	22	2.3	88
San Francisco								
U.S. 101	1976	4,608	3,686	1,500	385	97	10.3	36

Source: Kain and others (1992: table 15-1); Stockton and others (1997).

*The shares of HOV lane peak-hour capacity (Cap) required for bus operations are calculated using the assumption that a one-lane bus-carpool facility can accomodate 1,500 passenger car equivalents (PCUs) an hour and that a bus requires 1.6 times as much capacity as the average auto. The 1,500 PCUs an hour capacity figure, selected as a level that would ensure reliable travel at 55–60 miles per hour for vehicles using these facilities, is intentionally conservative.

facilities, buses using the bus-carpool lane on San Francisco's U.S.-101 (Marin County to the Golden Gate Bridge) use the largest fraction of available capacity, and they require only 10.3 percent.[32]

None of the recently constructed light or heavy rail systems, exclusive busways, or HOV facilities uses more than a fraction of its peak-hour ca-

32. The transit ridership figures in table 2 may seem modest to readers. They are not. In recent years, Cleveland's Shaker Heights line carried 4,400 peak-hour, peak-direction passengers; the much acclaimed San Diego LRT 1,920; Buffalo, 4,672; Pittsburgh's LRT, 4,896; Portland, 3,152; and Sacramento, 2,304. See CRA (1988: H-10).

pacity to accommodate current peak-hour demand. In contrast to expensive, unused capacity on exclusive busways or light and heavy rail lines, excess capacity on bus-HOV lanes can be used by carpools, vanpools, and other high occupancy vehicles. If transit ridership increases, a larger fraction of the capacity of these facilities can be allocated to buses. The ability of bus-HOV facilities to share capacity with other users makes a big difference. On the Shirley Highway HOV lanes, for example, for roughly every three people on a bus, five people are in car- or vanpools.

Table 11-2 also indicates that even with extensive carpool use, all but two of the thirteen bus-HOV facilities listed still had spare capacity at the time the data were collected. Only two facilities had excess morning peak-hour demand: I-95 in northern Virginia, where the HOV lanes were used illegally by large numbers of vehicles with fewer than the required three occupants, and I-95 in Miami, where the HOV lane was discontinued even though it carried substantially more people than each general-purpose freeway lane.[33]

Since publication of Meyer, Kain, and Wohl in 1965, researchers have accumulated much evidence relating to the relative cost-effectiveness of investments in new rail systems and high-performance bus systems. Some of this evidence is shown in table 11-3, which presents estimates of total construction costs, costs per mile, and costs per directional lane or track mile for seven bus-HOV facilities, two exclusive busways, and eight rail systems studied by Pickrell.[34] The last three columns are the heart of this analysis. The first of them indicates that the construction cost per weekday transit trip for the El Monte busway in Los Angeles, at $8,290, is nearly twice as large as the same figure for the Shirley Highway HOV lanes. The next column, where construction costs are divided by total (transit, vanpool, and carpool) weekday trips, clearly demonstrates the advantage of being able to share costly right-of-way.[35] When both transit and carpools are included, the cost per trip on the El Monte busway is only about a third as large as when the full capital cost of the busway is charged to transit. Capital costs per rider for the Shirley Highway are only 44 percent as large when carpools and vanpools are included.

33. Kain and others (1992).
34. Pickrell (1989).
35. These calculations allocate capital cost according to person trips. Because buses use much less road space per passenger than carpools, there is an argument for allocating the capacity costs according to the share of capacity used by each. This would, of course, dramatically reduce estimated capital costs per transit trip.

Table 11-3. *Daily Person Trips and Construction Costs Per Mile and Per Round Trip for Selected Transit Modes*

Facility	Miles	Daily person trips Transit	Total	Construc- tion cost (millions of 1989 dollars) Total	Mile	Construction cost per trip Transit (1989 dollars)	Total (1989 dollars)	As a percent of LRT
Transitways								
El Monte Busway	11.0	13,221	43,000	109.6	10.00	8,290	2,549	12.8
Shirley Highway	12.0	28,140	63,486	127.2	10.60	4,520	2,004	10.1
Houston Transit- ways[a]	67.7	23,405	78,562	302.1	4.46	12,907	3,845	19.3
I-66, Virginia	9.6	3,430	31,270	180.0	18.70	52,478	5,756	...
Commuter lanes								
I-95, Virginia	6.0	5,670	27,630	5.8	1.00	1,023	210	1.1
Rte 92, California	8.0	n.a.	19,102	0.2	0.03	n.a.	10	0.1
Rte 55, California	n.a.	n.a.	45,990	0.4	0.06	n.a.	9	...
Exclusive busways								
Ottawa	12.8	200,000	200,000	403.2	31.50	2,016	2,016	10.1
Pittsburgh	10.8	47,000	47,000	178.9	16.60	3,806	3,806	19.1
New rail systems[b]								
Heavy rail	29.0	168,500	168,500	3,459.7	119.40	20,532	20,532	103.2
Light rail	12.6	23,475	23,475	467.1	37.10	19,898	19,898	100.0

Source: Kain and others (1992: table 15-2).

a. Houston data include costs of associated park & ride lots, transit centers and access ramps, and usage data.

b. Weighted averages.

The final column in table 11-3 compares the construction costs per total weekday trips of the bus-HOV systems to the average of the same statistic for four new LRT systems. This figure, shown in the last row of the table, is $19,898 per weekday trip. This measure indicates that LRT capital costs per trip were from five to ten times as much as those for the transitways.

The advantage bus-HOV facilities have in sharing capital costs is even more evident in the case of I-66, the HOV parkway between northern Virginia and the District of Columbia. Both peak-direction lanes of this four-lane parkway are used as a bus and 3+ carpool facility during the morning and evening rush hours. Bus use is quite limited, however; as table 11-2 indicates, during the morning peak hour only nineteen buses, carrying fewer than 700 passengers, use I-66. If transit had to bear the entire cost, the capital cost per daily trip would be almost $52,478. But when total daily trips, including carpools, are used in the denominator, per trip construction costs plummet to $5,756.[36]

Commuter lanes are HOV lanes created by simply designating an expressway lane as a carpool, or diamond, lane. Of the three, I-95 in northern Virginia is the most costly by far, and it is the only one with significant transit use. The I-95 diamond lanes are six-mile-long lanes (both directions) that feed the Shirley Highway HOV lanes.[37] As the construction cost data indicate, the I-95 diamond lanes are dramatically cheaper both in total cost per mile and cost per trip than the El Monte Busway, the Shirley Highway, the transitways in Houston, or I-66. The costs of constructing these lanes consisted of marking the roadway and building an emergency shoulder where none had existed before.

Efforts to estimate the capital costs of HOV facilities encounter several difficulties. The most serious arise from the fact that bus-HOV facilities are generally built within existing freeway rights-of-way and thus entail joint capital costs with the general-purpose freeway lanes. The most important of these are the costs of building or rebuilding overpasses and bridges.[38] In addition, most HOV facilities have been built as part of freeway renovation and widening projects. Space for many, if not most, operational HOV facilities was obtained, at least in part, by adopting lower design standards than those that prevailed when the facility was first built. Depending on the situation, concrete barriers replaced wide, landscaped medians, traffic lanes and shoulders were narrowed, and in some cases a shoulder was eliminated altogether. On the presumption that the earlier, more generous design standards had some justification, a cost is obviously associated with adopting lower ones. As a practical matter, the effects of these changes on capacity and safety appear to have been small, in part because many of the original designs were very conservative, and in part because lower standards have generally been accompanied by much higher traffic volumes and lower freeway operating speeds.

One approach to dealing with both joint cost problems and the more subtle issues of lower design standards is to compare the benefits from adding an actual or proposed HOV lane to the benefits from adding or subtracting a general-purpose freeway lane. In this framework, the person

36. Route I-66 has been changed to a 2+ carpool facility since the 1992 study. This change would presumably increase total auto passengers and total trips by a significant amount, thereby strengthening the point. No updates are currently available, however.

37. Kain and others (1992).

38. Meyer, Kain, and Wohl (1965) provides a useful discussion of the determinants of highway construction costs. Also see Small, Winston, and Evans (1989).

capacity of an unrestricted general-purpose traffic lane (assuming typical vehicle occupancy rates) is viewed as the opportunity cost of allocating a lane to exclusive bus and carpool use. Assuming a capacity of 1,800 autos an hour and 1.1 persons a car, the opportunity cost of a HOV lane is 1,980 persons plus any additional construction costs that may arise from using the facility as a HOV facility rather than as a general traffic lane.[39] As the peak-hour person trip volumes in table 11-2 make clear, all thirteen bus-HOV facilities easily pass this threshold.

Shared Bus-HOV Facilities vs. Exclusive Busways

It is tempting to conclude that because buses using HOV lanes are able to share excess capacity with carpools, it is always better to build shared bus-HOV facilities than exclusive busways. Experience with exclusive busways in Ottawa and Pittsburgh suggests such a conclusion would be premature, however. The exclusive busways in these two cities differ in important respects from and serve rather different markets than shared bus-HOV facilities.

Both the Ottawa and Pittsburgh busways have on-line stations and carry significant amounts of walk-on traffic. In addition, they are used by large numbers of express buses that collect their passengers at park-and-ride lots or in suburban residential areas and use the busway for a fast nonstop trip to the central area. A shared bus-HOV facility can have on-line stations (the El Monte Busway has one, for example), but they create numerous engineering, safety, and operational problems and may significantly increase capital costs. Where transit demand is sufficient to use a large fraction of an exclusive busway's capacity, there may be a good case for keeping the busway exclusive and excluding carpools.[40]

---

39. SCAG (1987) in an analysis of this sort estimates that a proposed HOV system would cost $363 million, compared with $266 million (1989 dollars) if the same highway lanes were developed as incremental general-purpose freeway lanes. These data imply that commuter lanes cost about 1.4 times as much as incremental general-purpose traffic lanes. Commuter lanes are not physically segregated from the general traffic freeway lanes and are accessed from the general traffic lanes. Barrier-separated facilities such as the Shirley Highway and the Houston transitways cost much more to construct. In contrast, Ulberg (1987) finds that bus-carpool lanes in the Seattle area would cost only about 10 percent more to construct than an additional general-purpose freeway lane, that their marginal net present value would be on the order of $520 to $630 per commuter per year (1989 dollars), and that the "marginal benefit/cost ratio" was greater than six for all cases.

40. Pittsburgh's South Busway has considerable excess capacity over much of its length, but it operates at close to capacity through the Mt. Washington Tunnel, where busways share the roadway with the new South Hills LRT line and the aging South Hills streetcar system (Kain and others, 1992).

Successful exclusive busways are likely to be short and located in built-up and fairly dense areas with relatively high levels of transit ridership. In such situations, they may both provide a superior service for existing transit riders and serve as a high-speed right-of-way for express services from suburban residential areas. It should be understood, moreover, that a well-designed, high-performance bus system might include both exclusive busways and shared bus-HOV facilities. Where an extensive network of regional expressways already exists, including several miles of shared bus-HOV facility in the system design almost certainly makes sense. Within existing built-up areas, however, with high densities and a potential for walk-on ridership, exclusive busways may be the preferred solution. This is particularly true in areas such as Pittsburgh, where underutilized or abandoned rights-of-way are too narrow for a major highway but are wide enough for an exclusive busway or a light or heavy rail line.[41] In such situations, it may be desirable to build an exclusive busway, even if allowing vanpools and carpools to use it would reduce the cost per daily user.

Table 11-3 provides cost and ridership data for Ottawa's and Pittsburgh's exclusive busways. In terms of total ridership, Ottawa's 12.8-mile, Phase I transitway system is in a league of its own. With 200,000 transit users a day, it dwarfs the bus-HOV lanes in northern Virginia and Houston. Ottawa's exclusive busways also have the lowest capital cost per transit trip, at $2,016. When construction cost per total trip (excluding commuter lanes) is used as the criterion, however, the cost per trip for the Shirley Highway HOV lanes and the Ottawa exclusive busways are nearly identical.

Even though Ottawa's exclusive busways cost about twice as much to build per mile as Pittsburgh's, Ottawa's much higher ridership makes Pittsburgh's system nearly twice as expensive per transit trip. When the comparison is limited to transit trips, the Pittsburgh busways' per trip cost is less than those of any of the shared bus-HOV facilities. When total daily trips are used in the denominator, however, the per trip costs of shared bus-HOV facilities are less. Even so, the per trip costs of Pittsburgh's exclusive busways are only about 50 percent larger than the per trip cost of the Shirley Highway and about the same as the Houston Transitways. Measured either

---

41. The fact that busways often can be designed as one-way reversible facilities with buses using parallel streets, arterials, and freeways for trips in the off-peak direction makes it even more likely that a busway would be able to use a narrow right-of-way of this kind.

way, these costs are rather small potatoes compared with the capital costs per trip of new light and heavy rail systems.[42]

Busway Operating Costs

Few would dispute the busway capital cost estimates provided above or the results of Ottawa's alternatives analysis, which indicated that the overall capital cost of a busway system would be only 68 percent as large as the cost of a comparable light rail system.[43] That analysis also found that the annual operating costs of Ottawa's all-bus system would be only 82 percent as large as the annual operating costs of the LRT-bus alternative. This result was somewhat surprising given the frequent claims about the operating cost advantages of LRT compared with buses. According to the system's general manager, the busway's lower operating costs were attributable to its closer match between demand and capacity, savings from connecting two suburban–central area bus routes rather than allowing them to deadend in the central area, and the difficulty of turning trains around before they reach the end of the line (short turning) and of making other rail system adjustments to match demand and capacity.[44] Ottawa's operating cost comparisons, which refer to the entire system including feeder bus operating costs, contrast with all-too-frequent comparisons of the operating costs of LRT services to the *average* cost of a system's or area's *entire* bus services. Such comparisons are misleading because new rail lines invariably replace the most heavily used, most cost-effective bus routes.[45]

The director of planning and business development for the Port Authority of Allegheny County (Pittsburgh) has reached similar conclusions about the relative advantages of exclusive busways and LRT. His assess-

---

42. If the share of capacity used by buses is used in place of the transit share of total trips, as it arguably should be, the cost per transit trip of these shared bus-HOV facilities would be less than the same figure for even the Ottawa exclusive busways.

43. Bonsall (1987); Kain and others (1992).

44. Bonsall (1987).

45. Gómez-Ibáñez (1985) illustrates this point by comparing San Diego's actual LRT costs to hypothetical bus costs for the routes the LRT replaced. He found the operating costs of these bus lines would be 20 percent less than LRT operating costs. Comparisons are even less favorable to LRT when capital costs are included. His estimate of capital costs for a bus alternative to San Diego's LRT was only $0.38 per revenue passenger, compared with $2.32 for the trolley. Total costs per revenue passenger of using buses to serve the routes currently being served by the LRT are thus only 38 percent as large as LRT costs per revenue passenger, $1.35 for bus versus $3.53 for LRT (all figures are in 1989 dollars).

ment is especially telling because the port authority owns and operates both exclusive busways and a modern LRT system. In assessing the county's experience, he concludes that "in nearly all areas of comparison, busways appear to offer advantages over light rail systems." He also supports the Ottawa finding that busways are cheaper to operate, saying they "cost less than half as much per passenger to operate than light rail."[46]

Rubin and Moore, provide further evidence that rail operating costs may exceed bus costs. They compare LRT (Blue Line), heavy rail (Red Line), and commuter rail operating costs in Los Angeles to systemwide bus operating costs (including both heavily and lightly traveled routes) and find that bus costs are significantly lower than those of the several rail modes.[47] Specifically, bus operating costs per passenger trip in 1992 were $1.49 for the entire system and $1.07 for the seventeen most traveled routes, compared with $3.63 for the Blue Line LRT, $4.68 for the Red Line heavy rail, and $11.41 for commuter rail. Commuter rail and LRT trips are longer than bus trips; based on operating cost per mile, buses still have the advantage, but it is somewhat smaller. When capital costs are included, the cost advantage of buses over the rail modes, of course, becomes much larger. Rubin and Moore do not provide estimates for buses using the El Monte busway, but their operating costs are virtually certain to be significantly lower than those for either heavy or light rail and much lower than for commuter rail.

At-Grade Busways in Developing Countries

Transport planners in developing countries have increasingly turned to bus lanes and low-cost, at-grade, segregated busways, a variant of the exclusive busway, to accommodate the rapid growth in transit ridership.[48] Advocates of these systems, which can handle large volumes of trips, contend that while buses on at-grade, segregated busways generally travel at slower speeds than modern metros or largely grade-separated LRT systems, door-to-door travel times are very similar.[49] Stops on segregated busways are twice as frequent as on the typical metro or LRT, and the same bus acts as the residential collector, or feeder bus, and as the line-haul bus, saving

46. Biehler (1989: 96–97).
47. Rubin and Moore (1996).
48. Kain (1991b).
49. Kain (1991b).

Figure 11-3. *Typical Physical Arrangement of a Two-Lane, At-Grade Segregated Busway in a Road 23 Meters Wide*

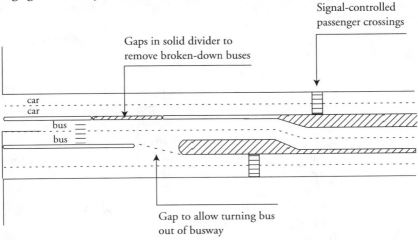

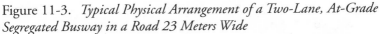

Source: HFA (1985). From the top of the drawing down, the roadway consists of two car lanes, each 3.125 meters wide, two bus lanes, each 3.5 meters wide, segregated from car lanes by solid dividers, two passenger islands, each 1.5 meters wide, and two more car lanes, each 3.125 meters wide.

travelers the inconvenience and increased travel time associated with transfers. Curitiba, Porto Alegre, Belo Horizonte, and São Paulo in Brazil have operated at-grade, segregated busways for several years and, more recently, similar busways have begun operating in several other cities including Bogota, Colombia; Lima, Peru; and Seoul, Korea. Although the design of these facilities varies somewhat, the most common type, depicted in figure 11-3, requires two traffic lanes and can be implemented in any arterial street with at least 23 meters of width. Most often located in the center of the street, the busways consist of a physically segregated exclusive bus lane in each direction and passenger platforms at intervals of about 600 meters. Stops are staggered to conserve precious street space, and passengers reach the busway at crosswalks, which usually have stop signals. Because segregated busways are put in place only when existing bus volumes are very high, they generally do not reduce the amount of road space available to other vehicles. In fact, in some cases the capacity of the general traffic lanes is actually increased.

According to Armstrong-Wright, the incremental cost of building Porto Alegre's segregated busways was about $500,000 a kilometer in 1986 dollars.[50] Curitiba has the best-known system.[51] It totals 33.6 miles and consists of five at-grade, segregated busways that link as many corridors to the central area. Total ridership on Curitiba's busways in May 1982 was more than 492,000 a day, and ridership on the individual busways ranged from 5,000 to 12,000 an hour in the peak direction. The system operates a trunk-and-feeder bus system with sixteen passenger terminals served by feeder buses. Trunk line buses also serve on-busway stops. The buses are privately owned and operated, but only buses belonging to the scheme may use the busway.[52] Passenger volumes on these systems are so much higher than those for North American systems because of the lower levels of per capita incomes and car ownership; 60 to 80 percent of all trips in these cities are by transit.

Even larger numbers use Porto Alegre's busway system. Its five segregated busways totaled 17.1 miles in length and carried 776,000 passengers a day in 1984. To provide some perspective, recall that Ottawa, with 200,000 passengers a day on its 12.8 mile busway system, had more riders than any other busway system in North America. Similarly, the highest daily ridership for any of the four new LRT systems studied by Pickrell was less than 31,000 a day. Finally, Washington's 60.5 mile, heavy rail system, the most heavily used of the new rail systems studied by Pickrell, had only 411,600 daily riders—little more than half of the ridership of Porto Alegre's busway system.

Adding a passing lane at bus stops can increase both capacity and speeds of at-grade, segregated busways and permit both along-the-line stops and express services. Local planners claim that Sao Paulo's eight-kilometer-long 9 de Julho at-grade, segregated busway, which has a passing lane at stops, can accommodate approximately 30,000 passengers in the peak hour, peak direction at the maximum load point without significant difficulty.[53] This busway is used both by Sao Paulo's municipal bus system, which operates motor and trolley buses, including double-deck units, and by several private companies that use conventional single-deck, diesel-powered buses. An estimated 40 percent of the buses using the busway operate over its

---

50. Armstrong-Wright (1986).
51. TRRL-TTC (1990: 3-7).
52. Kain (1991b).
53. Kain (1991b). This figure is about 50 percent higher than counts made by TRRL-TTC (1990) analysts during two days in October 1989.

entire length from a large at-grade terminal in the central area, adjacent to a Metro station, to a modern, well-designed transfer terminal at the end of the busway. The rest enter the busway at intermediate points or are express buses that use local streets to collect passengers in various suburbs before entering the busway at the end and traveling nonstop to the central area.

Because rail costs per passenger in industrialized countries are substantially higher than bus costs, advocates of rail transit generally resort to other arguments to justify investments in rail transit. The most common claim is that the capacity of the streets or of bus transit is insufficient to accommodate future travel. In some instances this argument focuses on corridor demands and capacity, while in others it emphasizes the demand for and capacity of central area street systems. In making these arguments, the proponents of rail transit systems ignore or are ignorant of the large passenger volumes currently being carried by bus systems in cities throughout the world; the experience of bus systems in several developing countries, discussed by Kain, is thus highly relevant.[54]

High-Performance Bus vs. New Rail Systems

As the data in table 11-3 conclusively demonstrate, the per trip capital costs of light and heavy rail systems far exceed those of exclusive busways and shared bus-HOV facilities. With one exception, this result holds whether one is comparing transit trips or total trips. In many respects the most surprising feature of these data is the similarity of the average capital costs per daily transit trip, which are just 3 percent higher for heavy rail than for light rail. Much of the interest in light rail is grounded in the idea that it is cheaper than heavy rail. These data suggest otherwise. Although the per mile construction cost of LRT may be much less than that of heavy rail, the capital cost per daily transit trip is almost the same for the eight federally funded systems studied by Pickrell.

When construction costs per trip for both light and heavy rail systems are compared with the same costs for exclusive busways and shared bus-HOV facilities, the situation is markedly different. Mean capital costs per transit trip for the four light rail systems studied by Pickrell are five times larger than the capital cost per transit trip for the Pittsburgh exclusive busways and nearly ten times larger than those for the Ottawa exclusive busways. They range from more than five (Houston Transitways) to almost

54. Kain (1991b).

ten times larger (Shirley Highway) than the costs for shared bus-HOV facilities.

Predicted and Actual Ridership and Costs for New Rail Systems

With few exceptions, academic studies of the cost-effectiveness of alternative modes of transportation have found that some form of express bus system, operating on either an exclusive right-of-way or a shared congestion-free facility, would have lower costs and higher performance than either light or heavy rail systems in nearly all, if not all, U.S. cities. Despite this finding, transit operators in the United States and elsewhere continue to plan and build costly rail systems. The tendency of policymakers to ignore the abundant evidence on the superiority of high-performance bus systems is explained by a prior commitment to rail and a willingness to "cook the numbers" until they yield the desired result.[55]

Pickrell's controversial study of new federally funded rail systems provides compelling evidence that system planners in the cities studied seriously overestimated future ridership and seriously underestimated both the operating and capital costs of the proposed rail systems.[56] As table 11-4 indicates, Pickrell found that the forecasts of total costs per passenger trip ranged from $1.53 to $3.04, while actual costs varied between $5.06 and $16.77. Actual total cost per rider as a percentage of projected total cost per rider ranged from a low of 288 percent for Washington, D.C., to a high of 969 percent for Buffalo. Other studies document similar gaps between projected and actual ridership for other new rail systems.[57]

---

55. Berryhill and Butler (1983); Hamer (1976); HFA (1989); Kain (1990, 1992); Wachs (1990).
56. Pickrell (1989).
57. See HFA (1989), which obtained similar results for new rail rapid transit systems in developing countries. The authors of the BART impact study similarly report that "BART's patronage has not reached forecast levels," and that in 1962 system planners predicted that BART would carry 259,000 one-way trips a day at full service levels of operation, adding that patronage in 1978 was 146,000 one-way trips on weekdays and that a recent forecast predicts 180,000 trips by 1981 (Metropolitan Transportation Commission, 1979: xxv). In addition, a UMTA (1988) report to Congress provides actual and predicted daily ridership for the Santa Clara LRT (11,000 actual, compared with 40,000 predicted) and San Diego's East Line (4,500 actual, compared with 6,900 predicted). The BART impact study, which also compared projected and actual capital costs, found that projected costs in 1962 were just under $1 billion, while actual expenditures to 1980 were about $1.6 billion. The authors estimated that more than half of the difference was caused by "inflation due to delays" and that another 32 percent was caused by "changes in scope" (Metropolitan Transportation Commission, 1979: 136).

Table 11-4. *Forecast and Actual Ridership and Costs for Eight Federally Funded Light and Heavy Rail Systems*

	Heavy rail systems				Light rail systems			
	Wash-ington	Atlanta	Balt-imore	Miami	Buffalo	Pitts-burgh	Port-land	Sacra-mento
Year service began	1976	1979	1983	1986	1986	1985	1986	1987
Length (miles)	60.5	26.8	7.6	21.0	6.4	10.5	15.1	18.3
Number of lines	4	2	1	2	1	1	1	2
Number of stations	60	26	9	20	14	13	24	28
Weekday rail boardings (thousands)								
Forecast	569.6	n.a.	103.0	239.9	92.0	90.5	42.5	50.0
Actual	411.6	184.5	42.6	35.4	29.2	30.6	19.7	14.4
Percent actual/ forecast	72	n.a.	41	15	32	34	46	29
Actual per mile (number)	6,803	6,884	5,605	1,686	4,563	2,914	1,305	787
Construction cost (millions of 1988 dollars)								
Forecast	4,352	1,723	804	1,008	478	699	172	165
Actual	7,968	2,720	1,289	1,341	722	622	266	188
Percent actual/ forecast	183	158	160	133	151	89	155	114
Annual operating costs (millions of 1988 dollars)								
Forecast	66.3	13.2	None	26.5	10.4	None	3.8	7.7
Actual	199.9	40.3	21.7	37.5	11.6	8.1	5.8	6.9
Percent actual/ forecast	302	305	n.a.	142	112	n.a.	153	90
Operating cost per rail passenger (1988 dollars)								
Forecast	0.12	n.a.	n.a.	0.11	0.11	n.a.	0.09	0.15
Actual	0.49	0.22	0.51	1.06	0.40	0.26	0.29	0.48
Percent actual/ forecast	417	n.a.	n.a.	959	351	n.a.	329	311
Total cost per rail rider (1988 dollars)								
Forecast	3.04	n.a.	n.a.	1.73	2.15	n.a.	1.68	1.53
Actual	8.75	5.06	13.10	16.77	10.57	7.94	5.19	6.53
Percent actual/ forecast	288	n.a.	n.a.	969	492	n.a.	309	427

Source: Kain and others (1992: table 14-4); derived from data presented in Pickrell (1989).

Although they do not in themselves directly prove anything about the relative cost-effectiveness of exclusive busways and rail systems, Pickrell's findings are relevant for at least three reasons. First, they provide strong confirmation for the widely held view that rail system planners typically use optimistic assumptions when they develop rail system costs. Second, there is substantial evidence that planners frequently "gold-plate" busways and use a variety of other assumptions that reduce the effectiveness of bus alternatives. Finally, overprediction of future ridership biases system choice toward rail because of its high fixed costs and because it allows rail advocates to rely on a variety of ad hoc arguments to justify their construction. One of the most common of these is the "inability" of central area streets to accommodate the huge projected numbers of buses.[58] The large number of buses projected to use the streets is, of course, a result of overly optimistic ridership projections.

A widely used way to show that a light or heavy rail system would be cheaper to build than a busway is to require the buses to operate in exactly the same manner as the preferred rail alternative and to "overdesign" the busway alternative. Kain discusses this use of strawmen by Houston's transit authority, METRO, in its 1987 and 1991 alternatives analyses of proposed rail systems. Assessing earlier rail proposals, Berryhill and Butler concluded that "busways failed in METRO's alternatives' analysis because they were designed to fail."[59] Wachs confirms the widely shared suspicion that these and similar forecasting errors were intentional:

> I have interviewed public officials, consultants and planners who have been involved in these transit planning cases, and I am absolutely convinced that the cost overruns and patronage overestimates were not the result of technical errors, honest mistakes, or inadequate methods. In case after case, planners, engineers, and economists have told me that they have had to "revise" their forecasts many times because they failed to satisfy their superiors. The forecasts had to be "cooked" in order to produce numbers, which were dramatic enough to gain federal support for the projects. . . .[60]

Proponents of rail rapid transit systems have used extravagant projections of future ridership to justify the large capital costs these systems entail. In fact, because new rail rapid transit systems are typically built in

58. See Kain and others (1992) for a detailed discussion of this point.
59. Kain (1992); Berryhill and Butler (1983: 107).
60. Wachs (1990, p.144).

well-developed transit corridors, where the new rail lines replace the most heavily traveled bus lines, they attract relatively few *new* riders. Building new rail transit lines in such situations may offer benefits, but a large increase in the number of new transit passengers is not among them. Any growth in ridership would have to come from reductions in door-to-door travel time, which in most instances are modest.[61] In contrast, the El Monte Busway, the Shirley Highway, and Houston's North Freeway contraflow lane (the predecessor to the North Transitway) all appear to have had much larger impacts on transit ridership than has been true for new rail systems.[62]

There are three principal reasons why these three busways generated far more growth in transit ridership than most new rail systems have. First, they provided large travel time savings relative to the situation that existed before they were implemented. The effect of new rail systems on door-to-door travel times has been far more problematic. Second, each was implemented in a rapidly growing and heavily congested corridor, while new rail lines are usually built in corridors with heavily used bus routes as these alignments maximize rail ridership. Finally, the implementation of the busway was typically accompanied by a major expansion in transit service levels and by the extension of transit service to previously unserved areas.[63]

The Effect of Public Policy

At the end of World War II, urban public transport in the United States was still predominantly a private for-profit activity, although several larger cities had publicly owned and operated transit systems. After the war ridership declined, the result of declining densities and rising car ownership and of related difficulties in serving an increasingly dispersed pattern of workplaces and residences. In all too many cases, these adverse trends were exacerbated by regulators who refused to allow operators to raise real fares or make service cuts that might have enabled them to remain profit-

---

61. These observations apply to a somewhat lesser extent to the exclusive busways in Pittsburgh and Ottawa. Although these busways have reduced operating costs and have enabled the transit authorities to provide somewhat more reliable and faster service, the measurable short-run impact on ridership appears to have been small.

62. Kain and others (1992).

63. Even so, the time savings provided by these facilities also was an important factor in increasing transit use. In the case of Houston's North Freeway contraflow lane, morning peak period ridership for February 1981 averaged about 3,200; Atherton and Eder (1982) estimate that without the contraflow lane and the same level of transit service, ridership would have been in the range 1,379 to 2,066.

able. Declining profitability led to bankruptcy in some cases and, with increasing frequency, to public acquisition of private transit systems by local governments. In 1955 only 3 percent of transit systems were publicly owned; by 1980, 55 percent were publicly owned, and they accounted for 94 percent of all transit boardings.[64] More than two-thirds of seventy-three large transit operators studied by Kain and Liu were privately owned in 1960, compared with fewer than half by 1980 and none in 1990.[65]

The Impact of Public Ownership and Subsidies

The public acquisition of private transit firms was frequently completed in conjunction with the creation of regional transit authorities, which frequently were given authority to impose dedicated taxes, most often sales or payroll taxes. Pucher notes that this practice was virtually unknown in 1970, but by 1980, 15 of the 26 largest U.S. metropolitan areas relied primarily on earmarked transit taxes to fund transit and that 21 of 101 cities surveyed by the U.S. Conference of Mayors in 1980 expected to implement such taxes by 1982.[66] The decisions to embrace public ownership, to create regional transit authorities in many large metropolitan areas, and to provide dedicated sources of tax revenues for transit led to rapid increases in both capital and operating subsidies.

Public takeovers reduced the productivity and cost-effectiveness of transit systems serving the nation's cities and metropolitan areas.[67] Cervero, for example, found that the changeover from private to public ownership and the subsequent creation of government assistance programs during the 1970s was accompanied by more than a tripling in the nationwide cost of transit service and an increase in the industry's operating deficit from just under $300 million to about $4 billion, both in nominal dollars.[68] Pickrell, similarly, in his study of the causes of U.S. transit system growth from 1972 to 1982, found that the industry's total deficit increased from $328 million in 1970 to $4.5 billion annually in constant 1982 dollars. Decomposing these increases, he found that more than 60 percent was attributable to a rapid growth in operating expenditure per vehicle mile of transit service and that

64. Tramontozzi and Chilton (1987).
65. Kain and Liu (1996).
66. Pucher (1982).
67. Anderson (1983); Cervero (1984); Lave (1991); Liu (1993); Pickrell (1985c); and Pucher (1982).
68. Cervero (1984).

increases in service (vehicle miles of service) accounted for less than 10 percent of the subsidy growth. The interaction between service growth and expense growth accounted for another 8 percent.[69] Finally, he found that demand factors, reductions in real fares and increased demand (ridership), accounted for only 14 percent and 8 percent, respectively, of the growth in real subsidies. Pucher, using a regression analysis of eighty-six U.S. bus systems in 1979, found that costs per bus were sixty-one cents higher for every additional dollar of federal subsidy and twenty-three cents higher for every additional dollar of state subsidy.[70]

Transit operating deficits are relatively recent in the United States. Lave in his analysis of sixty-two transit properties over the period 1950 through 1985 found that as late as 1964, 49 of the firms had revenue-to-operating-expense ratios above 1.0, six more had ratios between 0.95 and 1.0, and only three were below 0.91.[71] The only really low ratio was 0.70 for the San Francisco Muni system, which had been publicly owned and operated since 1912.[72] Based on further analysis of these data, Lave concluded that if transit productivity had merely remained constant from 1964 through 1985 "total operating expenses would be 40 percent lower in the later year."[73] Lave added that there is nothing inherent about transit that would account for such a decline in productivity because productivity in the private bus industry rose by 8.3 percent during the 1970–85 period.

The causes of the growing transit subsidies, both per trip and systemwide, during the past three decades are numerous and complex. Lave and other analysts emphasize "inefficiencies" that appear to be related to the shift from private to public ownership. At the same time, it cannot be denied that ridership declines and the worsening financial position of private operators also reflected an unrelenting suburbanization of jobs and residences and a determination to provide transit service to many suburban communities, even when the service could not be provided without subsidy.[74] Finally, growing levels of congestion and the gross mispricing of

---

69. Pickrell (1985c).

70. Pucher (1982).

71. Lave (1991).

72. The picture is less favorable when the depreciation is included; the unweighted ratio of commercial revenue to operating expense plus depreciation for the sixty-two systems was slightly below one (0.98) in 1964. Twenty years later in 1985, the unweighted ratio of commercial revenues to operating expense had declined precipitously to 0.34.

73. Lave (1991: 115).

74. Liu (1993); Kain (1991a).

many streets and roads made it nearly impossible for private, for-profit transit to provide the combination of fares and service demanded by the public and its representatives and still make a profit. Analyses by Lave and others strongly suggest the level of subsidy might have been much smaller, if governments had responded to this dilemma by subsidizing private firms to provide the desired combinations of fares and service.[75] Whatever the merits of these arguments, and I would contend they are considerable, the reality is that the deep subsidies provided to public providers currently make private, unsubsidized operation uneconomic except in situations where subsidized public transit providers choose not to provide service.

It cannot be overemphasized that the dramatic shift from private to public ownership and operation was the result of explicit decisions by federal, state, and local policymakers to replace private operation with public ownership and operation. As an alternative, they could have permitted continued private operation, while providing subsidies for socially desirable fare levels and services that could not be provided at a profit. In fact, some subsidies, typically indirect, were provided to existing private operators. In the end, encouraged by federal legislation and policy, nearly all local governments opted for public ownership and operation of their transit systems.

The U.S. experience with government ownership and operation of urban transit systems is by no means unique; public ownership and operation of formerly private transit systems is a worldwide phenomenon with results similar to those in this country.[76] In addition, governments throughout the world have increasingly sought to slow the seemingly endless growth of transit subsidies. Slower subsidy growth, in turn, has made publicly owned transit operators more receptive to contracting out and other forms of privatization. Great Britain, which has privatized the provision of all urban road transport services outside of London and has contracted out more than half of London's bus services, has been a leader in this area.[77]

Although privatization has made less progress in the United States, Cox and Love nonetheless estimate that approximately 10 percent of U.S. passenger transport service was competitively tendered in 1991.[78] In assessing these developments, moreover, they contend that these services cost considerably less than the comparable services provided directly by public

75. Lave (1991).
76. Armstrong-Wright and Thiriez (1987); Bly, Webster, and Pounds (1980).
77. Gómez-Ibáñez and Meyer (1990, 1993); Cox, Love, and Newton (1997).
78. Cox and Love (1993).

transport authorities. Referring to comparative analyses of seventeen urban areas, they conclude that, on average, competitive services are nearly 60 percent less costly than noncompetitive bus services. Cox and Love further report that the real costs per mile of San Diego's bus system declined by more than 20 percent from 1979 to 1993, a result they attributed to the use of competitively tendered services operated by private carriers.[79]

Returning to the U.S. experience with transit subsidies, Love and Cox estimate that in the quarter century before 1991, U.S. taxpayers put more than $100 billion in subsidies into the nation's urban transit systems.[80] In an assessment of the cost-effectiveness of these subsidies, published in 1988, Deich and Wishart found that new transit systems financed with federal aid, particularly rapid rail projects, generally reduced the efficiency of transit services by adding expensive unused capacity.[81] Transit's deficits have continued to grow; during 1991–96, local, state, and federal governments spent at least $100 billion more. Indeed, a 1996 Federal Transit Administration publication proudly announced that the $6.4 billion in grants it had obligated in fiscal 1995 was "the highest level ever achieved in the history of the program." Of this amount, 85 percent was for capital expenditures, mostly rail transit.[82]

Several authors have questioned the large sums of public monies that have been used to build new rail systems or extend existing ones and have suggested these subsidy dollars might have been better spent on improving and expanding existing bus services. Kain provides a detailed quantitative assessment of this question for Atlanta's MARTA system.[83] MARTA, which came into being with the public purchase of a private company in 1972, achieved a 39 percent increase in boardings and a 38 percent increase in linked trips during its eight years of all-bus operations. During the next thirteen years (1981–93), after it began operating its heavy rail system, the system's boardings grew by 39 percent and linked trips grew by 3 percent.

The large difference in ridership growth between MARTA's periods of all-bus and rail-bus operations is easily explained. Overwhelming econometric evidence shows that decreases in real fares and increases in vehicle

79. Cox and Love (1993); Kain and Liu (1995) provide a detailed discussion of the political and administrative arrangements that encouraged these developments.

80. Love and Cox (1991).

81. Deich and Wishart (1988).

82. Tuchi (1996: 1).

83. Kain (1997).

miles of service produce increases in transit ridership.[84] In contrast, essentially no empirical support exists for the view that rail transit *per se* increases transit ridership. During its period of all-bus operations, MARTA reduced real fares by 66 percent and increased vehicle miles of service by 57 percent. During the subsequent period as a rail-bus system, it increased real fares by 61 percent and vehicle miles of service (rail plus bus) by 1.5 percent. As a result of MARTA's policy to force-feed its rail system, its systemwide transfer rate (boardings – linked trips/linked trips) increased by 65.7 percent between its period as an all-bus operator and a rail-bus operator.[85]

Riders dislike transfers and thus a system requiring transfers to complete a high fraction of trips is less attractive than one that permits most users to reach their destinations without transferring. At the same time, a higher transfer rate can produce operating cost savings, particularly for the rail portion of the system, by concentrating demand. In the Atlanta case, the large increase in the systemwide transfer rate between 1981 and 1993 also explains the disproportion in the 39 percent increase in boardings and 3 percent increase in linked trips over the same period. Rail advocates have used the growth in boardings on Atlanta's rail system as evidence of the system's effectiveness. The fact that total (linked) transit trips grew hardly at all during the same period is never mentioned.

Kain estimated what MARTA's cumulative ridership (linked trips) would have been between 1980 and 1993 if it had spent its subsidy dollars on further bus system improvements instead of rail.[86] Of ten alternative all-bus scenarios, one of the more interesting indicates that if MARTA had simply kept real fares at their 1978 level and operated an all-bus system with the same net operating deficit as its bus-rail system, total ridership (linked trips) would have been 9 percent greater. The cumulative total cost (operating cost plus annualized capital cost) for this all-bus alternative, moreover, would have been only 31 percent as large as MARTA's expenditures for the same period. A second all-bus scenario, which assumed 1978

84. Kain and Liu (1995, 1996); Liu (1993); Gómez-Ibáñez (1985); Mayworm, Lago, and McEnroe (1980); Linsalata and Pham (1991); Schimek (1997).

85. MARTA's first full year of rail service was 1980. The period 1981–93 was used in the above comparisons to represent MARTA's period of rail operations because use of 1980 as the starting point overstates MARTA's ridership decline by including the temporary increase in ridership that resulted from high gas prices and shortages in the initial year. If the 1980–93 period is used, boardings increase by 31 percent and linked trips decline by 12 percent (Kain, 1997).

86. Kain (1997).

real fares and cumulative total expenditures that were slightly less than MARTA's actual ones, yielded a total ridership for 1980–93 that was more than twice MARTA's actual ridership. These and similar analyses provide compelling support for the view that if MARTA had continued to pursue the combination of low fares and service expansion it implemented during its first nine years of existence, instead of choosing rail, it could either have bought much larger increases in transit ridership with the same amount of money or the same ridership with less than one-third its actual expenditure.

The Impact of Mispricing Street Space

Governments made mistakes in taking over operation of formerly private transit services and in emphasizing huge capital outlays for rail transit. But their most serious error was the failure to charge users appropriate amounts for using costly-to-expand urban transport facilities in large and dense cities. Mispricing of urban streets and roads has especially pernicious effects on transit. The use of too much street and road space in congested areas by low-occupancy vehicles adversely affects transit speeds, reliability, and performance, and thereby creates something of a vicious cycle. High levels of congestion seriously degrade the performance of road-based public transit vehicles, which in turn leads to still more use of low-occupancy vehicles and still worse congestion. The introduction either of road pricing or of management schemes that mimic efficient road pricing could lead to dramatic reductions in congestion and travel times in many situations and would thereby reduce the levels of both highway and public transport investment that are required to serve a given population and employment pattern.[87]

It would be a mistake to conclude that appropriate pricing of road space and the privatization of transit services would restore transit use to levels found in U.S. metropolitan areas in the 1960s and 1970s. This is in part because higher charges for using congested streets and roads would affect far more than transit use. In the short run, motorists would make fewer trips, change their time of travel, and alter their destinations. In addition, some users who drove alone would form carpools to minimize the higher road user charges. This option might be particularly attractive to workers employed at suburban workplaces with little or no transit service. In the

87. Kain (1994).

long run, higher road user charges would eventually affect the dispersed patterns of workplaces and residences that were in part induced by congestion.

Reductions in peak-period auto use, moreover, would increase the speeds and reliability of both private cars and buses that continued to use the formerly congested roads. The largest increases in transit use from these improvements would no doubt occur in corridors that already had significant transit use. The biggest welfare gains would occur where a large fraction of the users of particular streets and roads are transit users. In the metropolitan areas of many developing countries, it is not uncommon to find that 80 percent or more of the users of heavily congested streets are bus riders. In these situations fairly modest reductions in the private car use of these streets would produce very large reductions in travel time savings for transit users and very large decreases in operating costs for transit operators. A significant part of these cost savings would, of course, be passed on to consumers in the form of lower transit fares. The impacts of congestion pricing on transit use in the United States and other industrialized countries would be less because the fraction of trips made by transit is much smaller and urban roads and streets are much less congested than they are in developing countries. This is particularly true in the case of low-density metropolitan areas with dispersed workplaces and extensive road networks. Even in these situations, however, the benefits from appropriate prices of street space could be substantial.

The usual alternative to pricing, pursued in the United States and elsewhere, has been to try to build enough highway capacity to eliminate congestion. The U.S. experience clearly demonstrates that massive highway construction programs can provide some congestion relief—but much less than might be expected. One reason is that without appropriate road pricing, the higher speeds that result will induce commuters and other motorists to make longer and more frequent trips. Analyses by the author using cross-section data on trip length and travel times in forty-one metropolitan areas indicates that a 1 percent increase in average worktrip speed leads to about a 1 percent increase in worktrip length in miles.[88]

Among the many potential benefits of congestion pricing is the possi-

88. This result is based on a series of multiple regression equations estimated by the author. Average length of a trip to work in miles is the dependent variable in this equation, and average speed, metropolitan area population, and median family income are the explanatory variables. Because all variables are transformed to natural logarithms, the regression coefficients may be interpreted as constant elasticities. This equation explains nearly 80 percent of the variance in average trip length. The coefficient for average speed, which is a constant elasticity, is approximately 1.0.

bility of reversing the ruinous past three decades of public ownership and operation of transit services. In this regard, I would strongly urge caution in accepting the frequent arguments in favor of using a significant part of the large revenues from congestion pricing to provide additional transit subsidies. Some additional subsidy might be required in the short run to pay for additional service if congestion price–induced increases in transit use were very large. Nonetheless, serious consideration should be given to implementing fare increases that, in combination, with the large reductions in operating costs that could accrue to some systems, would permit either significant reductions, or even the elimination, of public subsidies for urban public transport.

Analyses suggest, moreover, that congestion pricing and fare increases should be accompanied by efforts to privatize all or large parts of publicly owned and operated transit systems.[89] If these analyses are correct, privatization, possibly in combination with somewhat higher fares, could eliminate the need for subsidy altogether in many situations. Even if existing public transit authorities are not fully privatized, fare increases and reductions of subsidies to these firms, in combination with the elimination or reduction of barriers to entry, could permit new private operators to begin providing private unsubsidized services. This has been the experience of Mexico City, where after thirty years of massive subsidies to the metro and the public bus company, the government has raised metro and public bus fares substantially and has begun encouraging private operators to compete for a growing share of Mexico City's transit market.[90] Privatization led to a similar, and in some respects more impressive outcome, in Chile.[91]

Conclusions

Since the publication of Meyer, Kain, and Wohl in 1965, new light and heavy rail transit systems have been completed in a large number of American cities and in an even larger number of cities in other nations. In addition, high-performance express bus systems have been implemented in a growing number of cities. In a few cases, the speed and reliability of these systems has been ensured by the provision of exclusive busways. In even

89. Lave (1991).
90. Kain (1991b).
91. Kain and Liu (1994).

more cases, congestion has been controlled by the provision of shared bus-carpool facilities.

Meyer, Kain, and Wohl's assessments and predictions of land use trends have been largely borne out, although they were highly controversial at the time. Central city population and employment declines have continued; dramatic increases in the construction of office space in the central business districts of several large cities have not been accompanied by large increases in employment. In general, any gains in office employment that central business districts may have enjoyed have been more than offset by losses in manufacturing, wholesaling, and retailing employment. Not surprisingly, these land use trends have had adverse effects on transit ridership. Despite huge and growing subsidies and a 30 percent increase in total urban population, total transit ridership in 1995 was more than 16 percent lower than it was in 1965.[92]

Evidence presented in this paper strongly indicates that although the entire loss in transit ridership might not have been prevented, much higher levels of transit ridership could have been achieved with the same level of subsidy or the same ridership could have been achieved with much less subsidy. The most effective alternative policy would have been more explicit and aggressive pricing of congested and costly-to-expand road space in large and dense metropolitan areas. Further gains could have been achieved by retaining private transit operations rather than converting the largely private transit industry to public ownership and operation. Finally, with or without road pricing or private ownership and operation of transit, large sums could have been saved or larger increases in transit ridership could have been achieved if transit operators had spent a larger fraction of available revenues on bus system improvements rather than on costly and ineffective rail systems.

Even though land use patterns are slow to change, they have responded to the flawed transportation policies followed by governments in both this country and abroad during the last thirty years. Consequently, restoring viability to the transit industry will be more difficult than it would have been at the time Meyer, Kain, and Wohl was published. Nonetheless, there remains a strong, if not compelling, case to begin charging road users the full social cost of their road use, for reversing the public ownership and operation of transit services, and for stopping wasteful expenditures on ineffective rail systems.

92. This statement assumes 600,000 boardings were subtracted from the 1995 boardings number to correct for overstatement of transit trips using boardings rather than linked trips.

References

Anderson, Shirley C. 1983. "The Effect of Government Ownership and Subsidy on Performance: Evidence from the Bus Transit Industry." *Transportation Research-Part A General* 17A(3): 191–200.

APTA (American Public Transit Association). Various years. *Transit Fact Book*. Washington, D.C.

Armstrong-Wright, Alan. 1986. "Urban Transit Systems: Guidelines for Examining Options." World Bank Technical Paper 52. Washington, D.C.

Armstrong-Wright, Alan, and Sebastian Thiriez. 1987. "Bus Services: Reducing Costs, Raising Standards." World Bank Technical Paper 68. Washington, D.C.

Atherton, Terry J., and Ellyn S. Eder. 1982. "Houston North Freeway Contraflow Lane Demonstration." Cambridge Systematics, Cambridge, Mass. December.

Beesley, M.E., and John F. Kain. 1964. "Urban Form, Car Ownership, and Public Policy: An Appraisal of Traffic in Towns." *Urban Studies* 1 (November): 174–203.

Berryhill, Michael, with David Butler. 1983. "Fast Track: Where Is the MTA Taking Us?" In "Rail Transit in Houston: A Special Report." *Houston City Magazine* 7 (April): 41–44, 100–107.

Biehler, Allen D. 1989. "Exclusive Busways Versus Light Rail Transit: A Comparison of New Fixed-Guideway Systems." In *Light Rail Transit: New System Success at Affordable Prices*, 89–97. Special Report 221. Washington, D.C.: National Research Council, Transportation Research Board.

Bly, P. H., F.V. Webster, and Susan Pounds. 1980. "Effects of Subsidies on Urban Public Transport." *Transportation* 9: 311–31.

Bonsall, John A. 1987. "Transitways: The Ottawa Experience." OC Transpo, Ottawa, Canada. October.

Boyd, J., N. Asher, and E. Wetzler. 1973. *Evaluation of Rail Rapid Transit and Express Bus Service in the Urban Commuter Market*. Report prepared for the Office of Transportation Planning Analysis, Institute for Defense Analysis, U.S. Department of Transportation. Washington, D.C.

Bureau of the Census. 1975. *Historical Statistics of the United States*. Parts 1 and 2. U.S. Department of Commerce.

———. Various years. *Statistical Abstract of the United States*. U.S. Department of Commerce.

CRA (Charles River Associates). 1988. *Characteristics of Urban Transportation Demand: An Update*. rev. ed. July. DOT-T-88-18. Washington, D.C.: U.S. Department of Transportation.

Cervero, Robert. 1984. "Cost and Performance Impacts of Transit Subsidy Programs." *Transportation Research-Part A General* 18A (5/6): 407–13.

Cox, Wendell, and Jean Love. 1993. "The Competitive Future of Urban Passenger Transport." Paper presented at Third International Conference on Competition and Ownership in Public Transport, Toronto, Ontario. September.

Cox, Wendell, Jean Love, and Nick Newton. 1997. "Competition in Public Transport: International State of the Art," Paper presented to the Fifth International Conference on Competition and Ownership in Passenger Transport, Leeds, May 28.

Deich, Michael, and Jennifer Wishart. 1988. "New Directions for the Nation's Public Works." Congressional Budget Office. Washington, D.C. September.

Federal Highway Administration. 1990. *National Personal Transportation Survey.* Washington, D.C.

Gómez-Ibáñez, José A. 1985. "A Dark Side to Light Rail? The Experience of Three New Transit Systems." *Journal of the American Planning Association* 51 (Summer): 337–51.

Gómez-Ibáñez, José A, and John R. Meyer. 1990. "Privatizing and Deregulating Local Public Services: Lessons from Britain's Buses." *Journal of the American Planning Association* 56 (Winter): 9–21.

———. 1993. *Going Private: The International Experience with Transport Privatization.* Brookings.

Hamer, Andrew Marshall. 1976. *The Selling of Rail Rapid Transit: A Critical Look at Urban Transportation Planning.* Lexington, Mass.: Lexington Books.

Harrison, David, Jr. 1978. "The Impact of Transit Systems on Land Use Patterns in the Pre-Automobile Era." Discussion Paper 078-21. Harvard University, Department of City and Regional Planning.

Harrison, David, Jr., and John F. Kain 1974. "Cumulative Urban Growth and Urban Density Functions." *Journal of Urban Economics* 1 (January): 61–98.

Hendrickson, Chris. 1986. "A Note on Trends in Transit Commuting in the United States Relating to Employment in the Central Business District." *Transportation Research-A* 20A, 1: 33–37.

HFA (Halcroft, Fox, and Associates). 1989. "The Study of Mass Transit in Developing Countries." Report prepared for the U.K. Department of Transport, Transport and Road Research Laboratory, Overseas Unit.

Kain, John F. 1968. "The Distribution and Movement of Jobs and Industry." In *The Metropolitan Enigma: Inquiries into the Nature and Dimensions of America's "Urban Crisis,"* edited by James Q. Wilson, 1–39. Harvard University Press.

———. 1983. "Impacts of Higher Petroleum Prices on Transportation Patterns and Urban Development." In *Research in Transportation Economics,* edited by Theodore E. Keeler, Vol. I, 1–26. JAI Press.

———. 1988. "Choosing the Wrong Technology: Or How to Spend Billions and Reduce Transit Use." *Journal of Advanced Transportation* 21(3, Winter): 197–214.

———. 1990. "Deception in Dallas: Strategic Misrepresentation in Rail Transit Promotion and Evaluation." *Journal of the American Planning Association* 56 (Spring): 184–96.

———. 1991a. "Trends in Urban Spatial Structure, Demographic Change, Auto and Transit Use, and the Role of Pricing." Statement prepared for the United States Senate Committee on Environment and Public Works, Subcommittee on Water Resouces, Transportation, and Infrastructure (February 7). S. Hrg. 102-8, 102 Cong., 1 sess.

———. 1991b. "Urban Transportation Investments in Latin American Cities: A Progress Report." Report prepared for the Inter-American Development Bank, Washington, D.C. April 8.

———. 1992. "The Use of Straw Men in the Economic Evaluation of Rail Transport Projects." *American Economic Review* 82 (May, *Papers and Proceedings*): 487–93.

———. 1994. "The Impacts of Congestion Pricing on Transit and Carpool Demand and Supply." In Committee for the Study of Urban Transportation Congestion Pricing, Transportation Research Board, National Research Council, *Curbing Gridlock: Peak-Period Fees to Relieve Traffic Congestion. Vol. 2, Commissioned Papers.* Washington, D.C.: National Academy Press.

————. 1997. "Cost-Effective Alternatives to Atlanta's Rail Rapid Transit System." *Journal of Transport Economics and Policy* 31(1, January): 25–50.

Kain, John F., and Gary R. Fauth. 1979. "Increasing the Productivity of Urban Expressways: Combining TSM Techniques and Transit Improvements." Research Report R79-1. Harvard University, John F. Kennedy School of Government. October.

Kain, John F., Gary R. Fauth, and Jeffrey Zax. 1978. "Forecasting Auto Ownership and Mode Choice for U.S. Metropolitan Areas." Vol. 1. Final report prepared for the U.S. Department of Transportation DOT/RSPA/DPB-50/78/21. (December).

Kain, John F., and Zhi Liu. 1994. "Efficiency and Locational Consequences of Government Transport Policies and Spending in Chile." Paper prepared for the Harvard Project on Urban and Regional Development in Chile. Presented at conference in Santiago, Chile. May 11–12.

————. 1995. "Secrets of Success: How Houston and San Diego Transit Providers Achieved Large Increases in Transit Ridership." U.S. Department of Transportation, Federal Transit Administration, Washington, D.C. May.

————. 1996. "An Econometric Analysis of Transit Ridership: 1960–1990." Report prepared for the U.S. Department of Transportation, Volpe National Transport Center, Cambridge, Mass.

Kain, John F., and others. 1992. "Increasing the Productivity of the Nation's Urban Transportation Infrastructure: Measures to Increase Transit Use and Carpooling: Final Report." Report DOT-T-92-17 prepared for the U.S. Department of Transportation, Federal Transit Administration, Washington, D.C.

Keeler, Theodore, Kenneth A. Small, and Associates. 1975. *The Full Costs of Urban Transportation, Part III: Automobile Costs and Final Intermodal Cost Comparisons.* Monograph 21. Institute of Urban and Regional Development, University of California, Berkeley. July.

Lave, Charles. 1991. "Measuring the Decline in Transit Productivity in the U.S." *Transportation Planning and Technology* 15 (2/4): 115–24.

Linsalata, Jim, and Larry H. Pham. 1991. *Fare Elasticity and Its Application to Forecasting Transit Demand.* Washington, D.C.: American Public Transit Association.

Liu, Zhi. 1993. "Determinants of Public Transit Ridership: Analysis of Post World War II Trends and Evaluation of Alternative Networks." Ph.D. dissertation. Harvard University, Department of Architecture, Landscape Architecture, and Urban Planning. October.

Love, Jean, and Wendell Cox. 1991. "False Dreams and Broken Promises: The Wasteful Federal Investment in Urban Mass Transit." *Policy Analysis* 162 (October 17).

Mayworm, Patrick, Armando M. Lago, and J. Matthew McEnroe. 1980. "Patronage Impacts of Changes in Transit Fares and Services." Report prepared for the Urban Mass Transportation Administration, U.S. Department of Transportation, Washington, D.C.

Metropolitan Transportation Commission. 1979. "BART in the San Francisco Bay Area: The Final Report of the BART Impact Program." Berkeley, Calif. June.

Meyer, John R., and José A. Gómez-Ibáñez. 1981. *Autos, Transit, and Cities.* Harvard University Press.

Meyer, John R., John F. Kain, and Martin Wohl. 1965. *The Urban Transportation Problem.* Harvard University Press.

Mills, Edwin S. 1970. "Urban Density Functions." *Urban Studies* 7 (1, February): 5–20.

Moses, Leon M., and Harold F. Williamson, Jr. 1967. "The Location of Economic Activity in Cities." *American Economic Review* 57 (May: *Papers and Proceedings*): 211–22.

Muth, Richard F. 1969. *Cities and Housing: The Spatial Pattern of Urban Residential Land Use.* University of Chicago Press.

Pickrell, Don H. 1985a. "Urban Rail in America: A Review of Procedures and Recommendations from the Regional Plan Association Study." Staff Study, SS-64-U.5. U.S. Department of Transportation, Transport Systems Center, Cambridge, Mass. January.

———. 1985b. "Estimates of Rail Transit Construction Costs." U.S. Department of Transportation, Transport Systems Center, Cambridge, Mass. February.

———.1985c. "Rising Deficits and the Uses of Transit Subsidies in the United States." *Journal of Transport Economics and Policy* 19 (September): 281–98.

———. 1989. "Urban Rail Transit Projects: Forecast versus Actual Ridership and Costs." U.S. Department of Transportation, Transport Systems Center, Cambridge, Mass. October.

Pisarski, Alan E. 1987. "Commuting in America: A National Report on Commuting Patterns and Trends." Eno Foundation for Transportation, Inc, Washington, D.C.

Pucher, John. 1982. "Effects of Subsidies on Transit Costs." *Transportation Quarterly* 36 (4, October): 549–63.

Pushkarev, Boris, with Jeffrey Zupan and Robert S. Cumella. 1982. *Urban Rail in America: An Exploration of Criteria for Fixed-Guideway Transit.* Indiana University Press.

Rubin, Thomas A., and James E. Moore II. 1996. "Ten Transit Myths: Misperceptions about Rail Transit in Los Angeles and the Nation. Part 2 of a Series on the MTA." Policy Study 218. Reason Foundation, Los Angeles. November.

SCAG (Southern California Association of Governments). 1987. "HOV Facilities Plan, A High Occupancy Vehicle Lane Study." Los Angeles. September.

Schimek, Paul. 1997. "Understanding the Relatively Greater Use of Public Transit in Canada Compared to the USA." Ph.D. dissertation. Massachusetts Institute of Technology, Department of Urban Studies and Planning. June.

Small, Kenneth A. 1983. "Bus Priority and Congestion Pricing on Urban Expressways." In *Research in Transportation Economics,* edited by Theodore E. Keeler, 27–74. JAI Press.

Small, Kenneth A., and José A. Gómez-Ibáñez. 1996. "Urban Transportation." Draft paper. February.

Small, Kenneth A., Clifford Winston, and Carol A. Evans. 1989. *Road Work: A New Highway Pricing and Investment Policy.* Brookings.

Stockton, Bill, and others. 1997. *An Evaluation of High-Occupancy-Vehicle Lanes in Texas, 1996.* College Station, Texas: Texas Transportation Institute.

Tramontozzi, Paul N., and Kenneth W. Chilton. 1987. "The Federal Free Ride: The Economics and Politics of U.S. Transit Policy." Number 82. Washington University, Center for the Study of American Business, St. Louis. October.

Transportation Research Board (TRB). 1985. *Highway Capacity Manual.* Special Report 209. National Research Council, Washington, D.C.

TRRL and TTC (Transport and Road Research Laboratory and Traffic and Transport Consultants). 1990. "Study of Bus Priority Systems for Less Developed Countries: Phase 3 Report." United Kingdom, Draft (April 14).

Tucci, Jo. 1996. "1995 Grant Assistance Programs Statistical Summaries." Report FTA-TPM-10-96-1. Federal Transit Administration, Office of Resource Management and State Programs, Washington, D.C. February.

Ulberg, Cy. 1987. "An Evaluation of the Cost-Effectiveness of HOV Lanes." Report 1 WA-RD-121.1. University of Washington, Washington State Transportation Center, Seattle.

UMTA (Urban Mass Transportation Administration). 1988. "The Status of the Nation's Local Mass Transportation: Performance and Conditions: Report to Congress." U.S. Department of Transportation. June.

Van Tassel, David, and John J. Grabowski, eds. 1987. *The Encyclopedia of Cleveland History.* Indiana University Press.

Wachs, Martin. 1990. "Ethics and Advocacy in Forecasting for Public Policy." *Business & Professional Ethics Journal* 9 (Spring): 141–58.

DON PICKRELL

12 | *Transportation and Land Use*

The historical evolution of transportation, from horse-drawn carriage to trolley to car and bus, together with investment and pricing practices for supporting infrastructure have been two of the most influential forces shaping the development of metropolitan areas and the resulting geographic patterns of urban land use. By continuously raising the speed of urban travel and reducing its costs, innovations in transportation technology and investments in the resulting physical infrastructure have provided a powerful impetus for continuing decentralization of urban areas.[1] These same developments have also fostered rapid growth in the demand for transportation services within urban areas, reshaping the spatial and temporal patterns of personal travel and freight transportation at the same time as they have influenced the developing geography of urban land uses.

---

1. Of course, demographic growth, rising real incomes, and the evolving mix of economic output have also contributed to the ongoing decentralization of U.S. metropolitan areas, while more recently, contentious issues of racial segregation, fiscal redistribution, and neighborhood-level externalities have spurred continuing dispersion of urban populations and economic activity. For a discussion of the relative importance of these different factors, see Mieszkowski and Mills (1993).

Although the historical effect of transportation on land use has been pronounced, current and foreseeable technological innovations and investment levels are likely to have less influence on travel costs and speeds and thus a smaller effect on housing and business location patterns. Moreover, most published evidence exaggerates the influence of land use patterns on the volume and geographic pattern of urban travel, primarily because these studies fail to control adequately for the influence of household characteristics and other variables that affect travel demand.

Transportation Costs and Location Decisions

The central influence of transportation on metropolitan development patterns is predicted by the critical role of transportation costs in theoretical models of household and firm location decisions. According to theory, households choose to locate at a point where the costs of commuting to work exactly balance the savings in housing costs that accrue from living at a more distant location. The theory thus implies that the distance separating each household's equilibrium location from its workplace—and thus its demand for commuting travel—will increase as the cost of traveling falls. Similarly, the theory of firms' location decisions stresses the trade-offs among costs for transporting raw materials and finished products, workers' commuting costs, and spatial variation in land rents in choosing among different sites. These theories have implications for the role of transportation in urban development.

Household Location

In the basic model of residential location, households derive utility from consuming housing and other commodities, but the utility level they can attain is constrained, as usual, by their limited incomes.[2] Employment is usually assumed to be concentrated in the city center, although more complex models relax this assumption. The price per unit of housing services (dwelling space and the accompanying amenities) is assumed to decline with increasing distance from the city center, while the cost of

---

2. The classic references are Wingo (1961), Alonso (1964), and Muth (1969). Muth's treatment is impressive for its detail and thoroughness. More recently versions of the basic model developed by these authors include those in Mills (1972) and Solow (1973).

commuting to work increases as the household locates farther from its workplace. The prices of commodities other than housing are assumed to be invariant with household location. Households choose a combination of housing (denoted h) and other goods (g) to maximize a utility function of the form: $U = u(h,g)$, subject to a budget constraint given by $gP_g + hP_h(d)$ $+ T(d,Y) = Y$, where P_g denotes the composite price of nonhousing goods. $P_h(d)$, the price *per unit* of housing, is a function of distance d from the workplace, and $T(d,Y)$ denotes transportation costs for commuting to and from work; these costs depend both on commuting distance and on income Y, through the latter's effect on the value of travel time.

In the simplest version of the model, all households are assumed to consume the same quantity of housing services h, either because they have identical preferences for housing or because housing units are identical except for their locations. Under this assumption, the relevant first-order condition for a constrained maximum of utility is $- h(\partial P_h/\partial d) = \partial T/\partial d$. This condition states that at the household's equilibrium location, the change in its housing costs from moving slightly closer to or farther from the workplace (the left-hand side of the expression) would exactly offset the resulting change in commuting costs (the right-hand side).[3] This condition can also be written to show how the price the household will be willing to pay for a standard housing unit varies with distance from its centrally located place of employment : $\partial P_h/\partial d = -(\partial T/\partial d)/h$. This relationship between its bid price for housing and distance is termed the household's bid-rent function; it shows that the price the household is willing to pay for housing declines with distance from its workplace in proportion to the rate of increase in transportation costs ($\partial T/\partial d$).

If the assumptions of uniform housing preferences and identical housing units are relaxed, households will consume different quantities of housing services both because their underlying demands for housing will differ

---

3. The formal solution to this model proceeds by forming the Lagrangian function for a maximum of utility subject to the constraint on household income: $L = u(h,g) + \lambda[Y - gP_g - hP_h(d) - T(d,Y)]$; where λ is a Lagrangian multiplier. The first-order conditions for a constrained maximum of utility are that the partial derivatives of this expression with respect to consumption of housing (h), other goods (g), distance from the workplace (d), and λ be equal to zero: $\partial L/\partial h = \partial u/\partial h - \lambda P_h = 0$; $\partial L/\partial g = \partial u/\partial g - \lambda P_g = 0$; $\partial L/\partial d = \lambda[-h(\partial P_h/\partial d) - \partial T/\partial d] = 0$; and $\partial L/\partial \lambda = Y - g P_g - hP_h(d) - T(d,Y) = 0$. Solving the third of these yields the equilibrium condition for household location given above: $-h \, \partial P_h/\partial d = \partial T/\partial d$. For the development of this model and an extended discussion of its implications for the response of households' location decisions to income growth and price changes, see Muth (1969: ch. 2). A fascinating graphical development of essentially the same model and result is given in Alonso (1964: ch. 1).

and because they will respond to the decline in housing prices with distance from the city center by demanding more housing services at more distant locations. In this slightly more complex case, the household's equilibrium condition for housing consumption is $(\partial u/\partial h)/\lambda = P_h(d)$, where, as usual, λ represents the marginal utility of income.[4] Because housing prices are assumed to decline as d increases, housing consumption will increase with d under the usual assumption that the marginal utility of housing decreases with increasing consumption.[5]

Similarly, the household's equilibrium location condition becomes $-(h+\partial h/\partial P_h)(\partial P_h/\partial d) = \partial T/\partial d$, which again states that the household will locate where the savings in housing costs on the slightly larger unit that will be purchased at a more distant location is offset by the increase in commuting costs.[6] Larger households and others with preferences for more residential space will tend to seek more distant locations, because they can realize larger savings in housing costs from doing so.[7] Housing producers will respond to declining land prices at increasing distances from the city center by substituting progressively more land for capital; that is, by constructing lower density housing.

The interaction of these processes implies that the density of residential development will decline with increasing distance from concentrations of employment, most notably the city's central business district. As a consequence, higher levels of household travel demand (in the form of longer travel distances) will be associated with lower density residential development, both because of the longer distances separating low density areas from employment concentrations and because of the inherently higher travel demands of the larger households that tend to occupy the more spacious dwelling units found in lower density residential areas.

Firm Location

As with households, the theory of firm location stresses the influence of transportation costs on conventionally assumed economic behavior. The

4. This results from solving the above first-order condition for housing consumption and recalling that housing prices are a function of distance from the city center ($\partial P_h/\partial d < 0$).

5. The assumption of declining marginal utility of additional housing consumption means that $\partial^2 u/\partial h^2 < 0$, so that when the value of $P_h(d)$ declines as d increases, housing consumption must be increased to restore the condition for equilibrium housing consumption.

6. This follows from the fact that $\partial L/\partial d = \lambda[-h(\partial P_h/\partial d) - P_h(\partial h/\partial d) - \partial T/\partial d] = 0$.

7. For the household to have a stable equilibrium location, housing prices must decline with increasing distance from the workplace. All employment is often assumed to be in the city center to guarantee this condition.

critical distinction is that firms attempt to maximize profits rather than utility, and trade-offs among costs for transporting raw materials and finished products, wages, and geographic variation in land rents cause firms' profits to vary with location. Firms' costs for shipping materials and products are assumed to rise with increasing distance from centrally located freight transportation terminals, whereas workers' wages increase with the distances they must commute to their places of employment, and land rents decline with distance from the metropolitan center.

Thus firms attempt to maximize the difference between total revenues (TR) and total costs (TC), both of which may be affected by distance from the city center: $\pi(d) = TR(d) - TC(d)$.

Thus where the firm combines capital (K), land (L), labor (N), and materials (M) according to a production function $q = q(K,L,N,M)$ to produce its output, which it transports to the city center at a cost per unit $t_q d$ and sells at a price per unit P, its total revenues are $TR(d) = (P - t_q d)$ $q(K,L,N,M)$. The firm's total costs are the sum of the quantity of each input the firm uses multiplied by its unit price: $TC = vK + rL + wN + (c + t_M d)M$, where v is the unit cost of capital, r is the rental rate per unit of land, and w is the wage rate paid to workers. The term $(c + t_M d)$ is the unit price of raw materials delivered to the firm's location, which consists of the purchase price at the centrally located terminal and the cost of transporting the materials to the firm's site. For the reasons noted earlier, r and w decline with distance from the city center, so the firm's optimal input combination also varies as a function of its location.[8]

Thus the firm's profit-maximizing location will be at a distance d from the city center where the following condition holds: $qt_q + Mt_M = -[L(\partial r/\partial d) + N(\partial w/\partial d)]$.[9] This condition states that the firm will locate at a dis-

---

8. This model is similar to those developed in Moses (1958), Moses and Williamson (1967), Solow (1973), and Beckmann (1968). A slightly more elaborate version that allows for the possibility that firms can ship or sell their outputs from noncentral locations is developed by White (1976).

9. The firm's profits as a function of its location are given by

$$\pi(d) = TR(d) - TC(d) = (P - t_q d)\, q(K,L,N,M) - [vK + rL + wN + (c + t_M d)M];$$

and profits will vary with its location according to

$$\partial\pi/\partial d = (P - t_q d)[(\partial q/\partial K)(\partial K/\partial d) + (\partial q/\partial L)(\partial L/\partial d) + (\partial q/\partial N)(\partial N/\partial d) + (\partial q/\partial M)(\partial M/\partial d)]$$
$$-qt_q - [v(\partial K/\partial d) + r(\partial L/\partial d) + L(\partial r/\partial d) + w(\partial N/\partial d) + N(\partial w/\partial d) + (c + t_M d)(\partial M/\partial d) + Mt_M].$$

This can be rewritten as

$$\partial\pi/\partial d = [(P - t_q d)(\partial q/\partial K) - v](\partial K/\partial d) + [(P - t_q d)(\partial q/\partial L) - r](\partial L/\partial d)$$
$$+ [(P - t_q d)(\partial q/\partial N) - w]\,(\partial N/\partial d) + [(P - t_q d)(\partial q/\partial M)$$
$$- (c + t_M d)](\partial M/\partial d) - qt_q - L(\partial r/\partial d) - N(\partial w/\partial d) - Mt_M.$$

tance from the city center where the increase in costs of transporting its raw material inputs and its products to and from the city center is offset by savings in its production costs. These consist of savings in land costs from the lower unit land rents prevailing at more distant locations and the savings in labor costs from lower wage rates, which arise from the effect of less central locations on workers' commuting costs (an effect that is explained in the next section). The condition for the firm's profit-maximizing location can also be solved to yield the rate at which its bid-rent function declines with increasing distance from the city center: $\partial r/\partial d = -[qt_q + Mt_M - N(\partial w/\partial d)]/L$, which highlights the critical role of transportation costs for both raw materials and finished goods in affecting the land rents it will offer for different locations.

Combined Equilibrium of Households and Firms

The link between equilibrium locations of firms and households is established by the relationship between commuting costs and the geographic pattern of wage rates. For firms at different locations to attract workers, differences in wage rates they offer to equivalently skilled workers must reflect variation in potential employees' costs for commuting from their residential locations to alternative workplaces. Increases in workers' commuting costs resulting from increased separation of firm and household locations must be compensated by offers of higher wages by firms at more distant locations relative to the geographic distribution of households.

To achieve a stable equilibrium of household and firm locations and their housing and land consumption levels, the equilibrium conditions for household and firm locations derived in the previous sections must jointly hold. The requirement that spatial variation in wages exactly compensate workers for commuting cost differences means that $\partial T/\partial d = \partial w/\partial d$. This equality links the equilibrium location conditions of households—which

---

For a profit-maximizing firm, each of the first four terms will be equal to zero because each of its inputs will be utilized at a level that equates the value of its marginal product to its price, so that

$$\partial \pi/\partial d = -qt_q - L(\partial r/\partial d) - N(\partial w/\partial d) - Mt_M.$$

Setting this expression equal to zero, which is the first-order condition for a maximum of profits, yields

$$qt_q + Mt_M = -[L(\partial r/\partial d) + N(\partial w/\partial d)],$$

which is the condition given in the text.

depend on how commuting costs increase with distance ($\partial T/\partial d$)—and of firms, which respond to spatial variation in wage rates ($\partial w/\partial d$).

Using this result, the condition for the firm's equilibrium location can be written as $qt_q + Mt_M = -[L(\partial r/\partial d) + N(\partial T/\partial d)]$, which shows that it depends on the relative magnitudes of transportation costs for raw materials (t_M) and finished goods (t_q), workers' commuting costs ($\partial T/\partial d$), and the pattern of land rents ($\partial r/\partial d$).[10] Shipping costs for firms' raw material inputs and finished products are likely to exhibit similar patterns; in fact, there is some arbitrariness in distinguishing between the two because of the importance of various intermediate stages of production. Thus the effect of commuting costs on geographic variation in wages means that the combined equilibrium of firms' and households' locations will reflect the *relative* importance of variation in transportation costs for passengers and freight.[11] High costs for freight movements relative to workers' commuting costs will lead to centralized employment relative to the distribution of households and population, while high commuting costs relative to freight transportation expenses will cause employment to disperse in a pattern similar to that of households.

Effects of Changes in Transportation Costs

Transportation costs have two important components: the monetary costs associated with specific passenger trips or freight movements; and the economic value of travelers' time or the inventory costs of goods while they remain in transit. The level and geographic pattern of transportation costs within metropolitan areas are determined by a combination of prevailing technologies for transporting passengers and freight, the cumulative value and spatial configuration of investments in the capital infrastructure used to produce transportation services, and public policies governing the pric-

---

10. It is also possible that households' costs for shopping travel will be reflected in spatial variation in the sale prices of retail goods and services, so that the left side of this expression will vary with passenger as well as freight transportation costs. This possibility is incorporated in models by Christaller (1966) and Berry (1967). The equilibrium condition for household location would also be more complex if shopping travel and spatial variation in goods prices were recognized in household location models.

11. This effect will be accentuated if households' costs for shopping travel are also capitalized into variation in the sale prices of goods.

ing of the transportation infrastructure, a substantial portion of which is publicly supplied.

Transportation technologies determine the potential speed of travel and the level of resources required to produce any level of transportation services, which in turn are translated into the time and monetary components of travel costs that individuals and shippers face. The level of capital investment in the facilities used for different forms of transportation service determines the speeds at which different volumes of passenger and freight-carrying vehicles can travel, as well as users' monetary costs. For example, additional investment in higher-capacity highways and exclusive transitways allows peak traffic volumes to move at higher speeds and reduces operating costs for cars, trucks, and transit vehicles. In addition, the location of capital facilities and the configuration of the networks they compose determine the geographic extent and specific patterns of movement that these systems can accommodate. As an illustration, the radial highway networks most urban areas have constructed facilitate travel to and from downtown, while the beltways surrounding some major cities enable high-speed circumferential travel as well. Finally, the pricing policies for services provided by public infrastructure determine an important fraction of the monetary component of transportation costs. Highway or bridge tolls often represent a substantial fraction of the costs of driving, for example, whereas transit fares—including features such as transfer charges, peak-hour fare premiums, or zone surcharges—determine riders' out-of-pocket expenses for travel.

Household Location and Residential Development

Technological developments that lower per-mile transportation costs or improve travel speeds reduce the *rate* at which households' commuting costs rise with increasing distance from their members' workplaces. Because households seek to locate where the savings in land and housing costs from more distant locations offset the increase in commuting costs, the resulting decline in per-mile commuting costs induces households to seek more distant and lower-density residential locations. The collective effect of household relocations is multifaceted. Not only do the travel demands of households that relocate increase correspondingly, but over time the perimeter of urban development moves outward, while the decline in population density with distance from the metropolitan center becomes less pronounced. Investments in transportation infrastructure that supports different transportation technologies can also influence the geographic pattern of urban development, for example by concentrating it along the radial spines provided by rail transit lines or major expressways.

The simple model of household location developed previously is unrealistic in one respect: its apparent implication that the entire urban area will be reconfigured to adapt to the flattening transportation prices that result from successive innovations in technology. This feature arises from the model's failure to recognize the durability of and the costs of modifying the capital stock of structures inherited from an urban area's historical development, which limit the speed and extent to which existing patterns of household and firm locations can adjust to subsequent changes in the geographic pattern of transportation costs. A more realistic view is that urban development represents the *cumulative* effect of incremental additions to the metropolitan area at its periphery, which reflect the influence of prevailing transportation technologies. In this cumulative development process, innovations in transportation technology affect the density of development primarily within the land areas that were *added* to growing urban centers during the time each such technology represented the dominant mode of urban transportation.[12]

Firms' Locations and the Distribution of Employment

As the model of firm location indicated, firm location depends on how innovation or investment affects the relative magnitudes of passenger and freight travel costs. Many technological innovations and investments affect the speeds and costs of moving both freight and people; for example, the internal combustion engine facilitated the development of automobiles and freight trucks, while investments in urban highways improved travel speeds and reduced costs for both.

On balance, developments that lower freight transportation costs by more than commuting costs tend to preserve centralized employment, while those that reduce travel costs for people relative to those for goods contribute to dispersion of employment as well as of households. The net effect of technological innovations or capital investments in transportation is likely to vary among different industries, however—manufacturing versus service production, for example—and perhaps even among individual firms, depending on the relative importance of costs for input and product transportation compared with their workers' commuting costs.

12. See Harrison and Kain (1974).

Transportation's Influence on Urban Land Use

In the cumulative version of the urban development process, successive "rings" of development surrounding the historical metropolitan core exhibit progressively lower density in response to the falling transportation costs and increasing travel speeds produced by the progression of urban transportation technologies. Table 12-1 shows the dramatic effects of the successive improvements in passenger transportation on travel speeds, which increased approximately ten-fold during the period it spans. Equally important, the table shows the decline in the duration of trips that adapt to the flattening of transportation prices resulting from the inverse relationship between speed and travel time per unit of distance.

Residential Development

Combined with powerful economic and demographic developments, particularly rising real incomes and changes in the size and composition of households, investments in successive transportation technologies produced rapid decentralization of population within U.S. urban areas and led to pronounced declines in the density of residential development in progres-

Table 12-1. *Effects of Technological Innovations on Travel Speeds and Times*

Technology	Approximate date introduced	Typical door-to-door speed (mph)[a]	Travel time per mile (minutes)
Walking	Early	3	20
Horse-drawn omnibus	1827	4	15
Horse-drawn streetcar	1835	5	12
Cable car	1875	8	7.5
Electric streetcar	1890	10	6
Rail rapid transit	1910	15	4
Motor bus	1915	20	3
Automobile	1920	30	2

Source: Author's calculations based on Weiglin (1976).

a. Typical door-to-door speed differs from operating speed because it includes access to transit stops, waiting, transfers, and so forth; the data are for all trips using the technology not just commuting.

Figure 12-1. *Density of New Residential Development by Decade for Selected Cities, 1900–1960*

Density

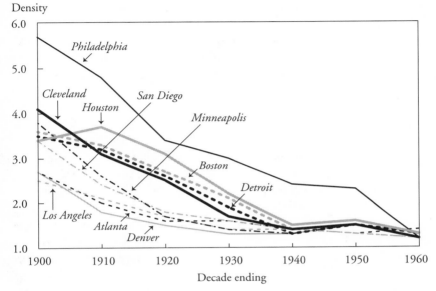

Decade ending

Source: U.S. Census of Housing: 1940, Characteristics by Type of Structure; 1950, vol. 2, by City, table A-6; 1960, vol. 2, by City, table A-6. Density is measured by the reciprocal of the share of new dwellings that are single-family detached houses. After 1960 most of the lines cluster together at about the same value, although some rise to about the 2.0 value by 1980.

sively more distant suburbs.[13] Figure 12-1 illustrates the declining density of new residential development in a sample of large U.S. urban areas over the period from 1900 to 1960. Using the fraction of new dwellings added during each decade that were single-family detached houses as an index of development density, the figure shows striking similarity in the density of new development occurring in all ten urban areas during each decade of this period.[14]

13. The classic description of this process is Warner (1962).

14. After 1960 the long-term increase in the fraction of new development that consisted of single-family dwellings was reversed in many of the urban areas included in figure 12-1. The increase in the fraction of new housing in multifamily units resulted in part from a combination of rising suburban land prices caused by development restrictions, increasing importance of higher-density "infill" development, and government-sponsored urban redevelopment programs. The measure employed in figure 12-1 consequently becomes a much less reliable indicator of the density of incremental development after 1960.

The size, historical timing, and geographic orientation of the massive investments—originally private, but over time increasingly public—in transportation infrastructure helped shape patterns of metropolitan development. An often-overlooked feature of this process is that each successive innovation in passenger transportation, including the significant advances in urban transit technology preceding the advent of the automobile, contributed in turn to metropolitan decentralization and lower development densities compared with those in preceding eras.

Employment Decentralization

Pronounced economies of scale in the earliest technologies for interregional freight transportation—barges and then railroads—led manufacturing firms to locate close to route junctions or network hubs in their efforts to minimize input costs and shipping charges for finished goods.[15] Geographic considerations such as limited depth of ports and waterways and grade restrictions on railroad routes (to avoid the costs of tunnels) accentuated the effects of scale economies by restricting the potential locations for route hubs. Within urban areas, intercity freight route networks converged on one or a few large, centrally located terminals, which provided scale economies in loading and unloading of interregional freight shipments while minimizing local collection and distribution costs.

Similar economies of scale and network design characterized the prevailing technologies of urban passenger transportation (street trolleys and later, rail rapid transit), which reduced firms' wage costs at central city locations where transit routes converged relative to outlying locations. The introduction of freight trucks—and the roughly simultaneous advent of the motor bus and the automobile—fundamentally altered the cost structure of freight and passenger movements within cities by dramatically reducing scale economies in both freight distribution and commuting. Of course, large-scale public investment in urban street and highway networks facilitated the widespread adoption of these innovations, as did the systematic underpricing of their use. Continuing advances in truck technology combined with massive public investments in interstate highways allowed freight trucking to develop into a competitive form of interregional transportation for many commodities as well as to become the dominant mode for local collection and distribution.

15. To some extent these scale economies may have been an artifact of government regulation of particular transportation industries. For example, railroad regulation by the Interstate Commerce Commission may have required network designs that increased scale economies in railroad operations.

These developments reversed the cost advantages once held by central city locations and made outlying locations—particularly those near the junctions of major urban and interstate highways—attractive to manufacturing firms. Increasing automobile ownership and continuing expansion of metropolitan highway systems also allowed firms locating in peripheral areas to reduce wage costs relative to more central locations. Changes in manufacturing technology that required more space for production facilities increased the cost advantages provided by the characteristically lower land rents available at outlying locations, while gradual evolution in the commodity structure of the U.S. economy toward nonmanufacturing outputs may also have increased the number of firms for which suburban locations afforded production and transportation cost advantages. Thus in parallel with the dispersion of households into progressively lower-density suburban areas, employment within U.S. urban areas decentralized rapidly throughout much of the twentieth century.

Moreover, the pattern of street and highway networks has exerted an important influence on the overall geographic pattern of firm locations and thus the spatial distribution of employment. Urban road networks typically consist of several major radial and one or more circumferential highway routes overlaying a grid-type street network. Although this pattern serves downtown-bound commuting effectively, it has also accommodated a more ubiquitous distribution of employment within metropolitan areas. Large concentrations of office employment—sometimes rivaling the downtown in scale—have developed in most metropolitan areas along circumferential highway routes or near major highway interchanges.

The Modern Influence of Transportation

Current and future evolution in transportation technology and investment is likely to have a much weaker influence on patterns of urban development than did the developments of the past. Recent studies of household location show that workers' commuting distances are significantly longer than predicted by the simple model of household location behavior, while several studies show that transportation costs are less important than other variables in influencing firms' location decisions.[16] This weakening role for transportation probably occurred because changes in travel costs fostered

---

16. These studies include Hamilton (1982), Hamilton (1989), Giuliano and Small (1993), and Small and Song (1992). White (1988), in contrast, finds that the model predicts observed commuting distances reasonably well.

by technological innovation and investment have been much smaller than was historically the case, while nontransportation variables that are overlooked in simple models of household and firm location are becoming increasingly influential.[17]

As table 12-1 indicated, the dramatic innovations in transportation technology that occurred between 1830 and 1920 increased typical travel speeds within metropolitan areas nearly ten times. More recent developments in transportation technology have improved travel speeds, but by much less than did earlier innovations such as the electric streetcar or the automobile. The newer developments have tended to improve the comfort, privacy, and safety of travel more than they have affected its speed. Continuing but smaller increases in travel speeds have also been translated into progressively *smaller* reductions in trip times, because of the inverse relationship between speed and travel time per unit of distance.

Continuing investments in the scope and capacity of metropolitan area transportation systems have also led to progressively smaller improvements in travel speeds and trip times, and the effects of future investments are likely to continue to diminish. Even massive investments in the capital infrastructure making up most urban transportation networks represent comparatively modest additions to the cumulative value of investments that are already in place. The extent and capacity of modern urban transportation networks already provide extremely high degrees of connectivity and redundancy, so that even significant additional investments in new or expanded facilities typically produce only small reductions in travel times or costs between a limited number of locations. As a result, their influence on households' and firms' location choices—and thus on the urban development process and the land use patterns it produces—is likely to grow progressively weaker over time.

The potential influence of even major changes in transportation costs on the future geography of urban land uses also appears to be diminishing, as other factors become increasingly influential in households' and firms' location decisions. The growing importance of multiple-worker households and the increasingly heterogeneous mixes of job and worker characteristics greatly complicate households' location decisions and may reduce the central role of commuting costs. Shorter employment durations and high fixed costs associated with moving may also reduce households' incentives to

---

17. For extended discussions of transportation's weakening influence on urban land use, see Gómez-Ibáñez (1985) and Giuliano (1995).

economize on commuting costs, and the growing importance of nonwork travel also suggests that household locations may increasingly reflect overall transportation costs rather than simply the commuting component. Finally, there is considerable evidence that urban residents also regard housing and neighborhood characteristics as extremely important considerations in their location choices, and rising incomes may lead households to assign increasing priority to these factors compared with transportation costs.

Location models' predictions that transportation has a strong influence on firm's location decisions were historically accurate but are increasingly at odds with recent evidence of transportation's more modest effects. In the case of firms' location decisions, however, this diminished influence appears to stem less from the models' omission of critical variables than from evolution in the commodity structure of the U.S. economy and innovations in nontransportation technologies. The economy's continuing shift away from heavy manufacturing toward production of high-value commodities, personal services, and more recently, information-based products reduces the number of firms facing substantial costs for shipping raw materials or finished products and thus the influence of freight transportation costs on land use patterns.[18] At the same time, dramatic innovations in information processing and telecommunications technology allow firms to produce efficiently and deliver products at low cost from a wider range of locations and to locate internal functions with varying input demands (such as for labor and space) at different places. Agglomeration economies remain important in many firms' location decisions, but developments in complementary technologies are likely to continue to reduce the influence of transportation costs on firms' location choices and on the evolving spatial distribution of employment within urban areas.

Land Use and Transportation Models

During the past four decades researchers have developed various models that attempt to replicate actual patterns of urban land use by math-

---

18. Because freight transportation demand is derived from the demand for commodities themselves, the price elasticity of demand for shipments of a commodity is proportional to the fraction of its total value that is represented by shipping costs. Thus the economy's shift toward production of higher-valued commodities contributes to the diminished influence of transportation costs on firm location decisions.

ematically representing the influence of transportation costs on the metro-politan development process. Increases in the scale and complexity of these models over time have roughly paralleled advances in computing capabilities, although the realism of the models continues to be limited by the simplicity of theories linking household and firm location decisions to transportation costs and by the difficulty of obtaining detailed historical data on land use patterns.

Types of Transportation–Land Use Models

Two broad categories of transportation and land use models have been developed; interestingly, the earliest examples of each appeared nearly simultaneously about 1960.[19] The first includes models that attempt to replicate land use patterns by simulating the process of transportation investment and urban development that produces them. The second category consists of models that represent the equilibrium between an urban area's transportation system and its land markets; these types are used to determine the optimal distribution of land uses within an urban area or flows over its transportation system. Both types of models represent the effects of transportation costs on the location decisions of households and firms at some level of geographic aggregation rather than for individual households and firms. Simulation models have been used to investigate the interactions between transportation investments and land use as well as to support development of metropolitan land use and transportation plans, while optimization-type models have generally been developed and used for research purposes.

LAND USE SIMULATION MODELS. Figure 12-2 illustrates the general structure of land use simulation models. Early versions assumed a fixed distribution of employment and used simplified representations of household location decisions to simulate the resulting distributions of residences and population within an urban area. The simplest versions allowed instantaneous adjustment of the distribution of population to changes in transportation costs between residences and travel destinations such as employment sites and shopping areas. In effect they "resimulated" the equilibrium distribution of residences and populations implied by an altered structure of

---

19. There appear to be nearly as many detailed surveys of the structure of urban land use models as there are models themselves; among the most recent and therefore most extensive are Kain (1987), Berechman and Small (1988), and Webster, Bly, and Paulley (1988).

Figure 12-2. *Typical Structure of Transportation–Land Use Simulation Models*

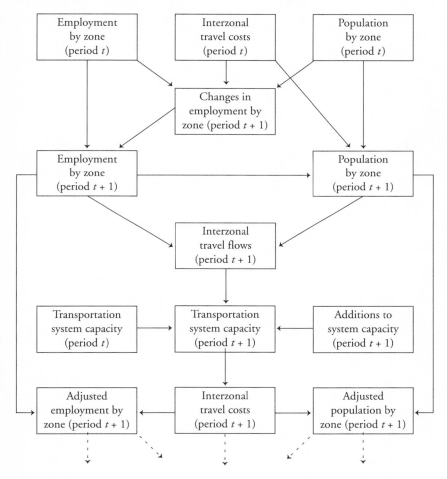

Source: Author's representation. The dashed arrows indicate that the computation process repeats itself until a solution is found.

transportation costs as if the new pattern of travel costs had prevailed throughout the area's development. Examples of this type include the pioneering models developed by Lowry and Mills; an interesting feature of Lowry's model is that only the location of "basic" employment (primarily in manufacturing industries) is fixed, while employment in "population-serving" activities such as retailing and personal services is allowed to relocate in response to changes in the spatial distribution of residences.[20]

More recent land use simulation models represent the cumulative nature of the development process by estimating changes in the distribution of population that occur in response to changes in the distribution of employment and the pattern of transportation costs. Thus the pattern of land use at the end of each time period depends on the distributions of population and employment that prevailed at its outset, as well as on the adjustments prompted by employment growth or relocation and changes in transportation costs during the period. Prominent examples include those developed by the National Bureau of Economic Research and the more recent Chicago Area Transportation/Land Use Analysis System (CATLUS) and New York Area Simulation Model.[21] Although most of these were intended primarily to analyze housing market dynamics rather than transportation and land use interactions, the last was developed to evaluate the effects of alternative investments in transportation infrastructure on urban land use and travel patterns.

Other transportation and land use models attempt to forecast the future distributions of both population and employment simultaneously by simulating changes in their distributions during each future time period in response to changes in travel times and costs. The earliest example of this type was the EMPIRIC model, developed for use in the Boston area's early travel forecasting process.[22] Probably the most widely employed land use simulation model is the Integrated Transportation Land-Use Package (ITLUP), developed by Putman, which is used by the transportation agencies of many cities to forecast future geographic distributions of population and employment as inputs to the metropolitan transportation planning process they are required by federal regulations to conduct.[23]

OPTIMIZATION MODELS. The second broad type of land use model uses simplified representations of the effect of travel costs on the location decisions of households and firms to simulate the spatial distributions of housing, employment, and travel generated by equilibrium in the urban land

20. These are described in Lowry (1964) and Mills (1967).

21. The National Bureau of Economic Research model is documented in Ingram, Kain, and Ginn (1972). Development of the CATLUS and New York models is described in Anas (1984, 1992).

22. Development of the Boston prototype of EMPIRIC is described in Hill, Brand, and Hansen (1966) and in Brand, Barber, and Jacobs (1967).

23. See Putman (1983, 1991).

market. Some use mathematical programming or assignment techniques to determine the equilibrium distribution of different land uses within an urban area that result from the configuration and performance of its transportation system. For example, one common approach is to "assign" workers who hold jobs in each geographic zone to residences in zones that offer the shortest commute (measured in miles or travel time). Other versions calculate the optimum patterns of residential locations and travel flows over an urban area's transportation network that are associated with a given distribution of employment and housing, thus allowing the costs of accommodating different distributions of jobs and population to be compared.

The linear programming formulation developed by Herbert and Stevens represents the earliest prototype of these models.[24] More elaborate versions of their basic framework have been used to simulate travel characteristics—such as length or time of commuting trips—that are predicted by the optimizing behavior incorporated in household location models, so that they can be compared to observed behavior.[25] To maximize the total value of land within the metropolitan area, allocation models typically assign specific land uses (manufacturing or housing, for example) to individual geographic zones on the basis of transportation costs between zones.[26] Finally, transportation optimization models use prevailing land use patterns to compute cost-minimizing travel flows over the urban area's network.[27]

How Useful Are These Models?

These models have provided useful evidence about the dynamics of interactions between transportation and land use patterns. Their ability to replicate urban areas' actual land use patterns with reasonable accuracy provides some confirmation that the theories of household and firm location on which they are based offer reasonable, if greatly simplified, explanations of their decision mechanisms and the factors influencing their location choices. More specifically, they suggest that changes in transportation costs fostered by technological innovation and investment policies have played an important role in determining contemporary development and land use patterns within metropolitan areas.

24. Herbert and Stevens (1960).
25. Wheaton (1974); White (1988).
26. Boyce (1980); Kim (1983); and Boyce and Lundqvist (1987).
27. Harris and Wilson (1978); Boyce (1980).

Large-scale mathematical models of transportation and land use are also increasingly employed in the planning processes conducted by local government agencies to anticipate the effects of alternative levels and forms of investment in transportation facilities.[28] These models rely on such simplified representations of household and firm location decisions, however, that they typically provide only rough guidance about likely long-term changes in urban land use patterns, in contrast to detailed land use forecasts that can guide choices among specific transportation investments. Thus while their use in the local transportation planning process is increasingly common, the forecasts the models produce are often adjusted to reflect expert judgment or political considerations.

The Effect of Land Use on Travel Behavior

In the usual model of the urban development process, technological innovation and investment in transportation infrastructure determine the spatial pattern of transportation costs. In turn, this pattern influences the demand for travel by both households and firms through its effects on their location choices, and the geographic pattern of land uses represents the cumulative outcome of households' and firms' individual location choices and land consumption decisions. Because the geographic patterns of urban land use and transportation demand are *simultaneously* determined by the evolving structure of transportation costs, land use and travel demand are likely to display some association.

But the underlying connection is far weaker than this superficial association might suggest. The static relationship between urban land use patterns and travel demand is often interpreted as evidence that land use *itself* determines the geography of travel flows; an influential early study asserted that urban travel demand is "derived" from the pattern of land uses.[29] According to the models of location and urban development discussed previously, however, the relationship between land use and travel patterns stems largely from the simultaneous influence of transportation costs on both. Insofar as land use patterns *per se* affect travel behavior, it is through their influence on travel speeds, costs, or other attributes of transportation ser-

---

28. The 1990 amendments to the federal Clean Air Act require urban areas planning transportation investments to predict their effects on future land use and travel patterns.
29. Mitchell and Rapkin (1954).

vices, and this influence is likely to be secondary to the direct effects of transportation technology and infrastructure investments on travel demand. Careful empirical studies of the effects of land use patterns on urban travel behavior confirm that their relationship is indeed much weaker than widely imagined.

Residential Density and Auto Use

The most widely noted association between urban land use and travel behavior is between residential density and various measures of automobile usage. The conventional logic is that by attracting commercial and other development, higher *residential* densities also increase the number of potential destinations—jobs and retail stores, for example—within a given radius of any trip's origin, thus reducing the length of driving trips and making some of them amenable to alternatives such as walking or riding transit. Higher residential densities are also thought to concentrate trip origins spatially, thereby reducing walking times to transit routes and contributing to the passenger volumes that make high-frequency transit operable at reasonable costs. Analysts must carefully control for the effects of household income and demographic characteristics on housing size and location choices, however, to isolate the effects of residential density.

Although empirical evidence on the relationship between residential density and various aspects of travel behavior has been widely reported, surprisingly little of it withstands even the most superficial scrutiny. For example, one widely cited recent study reports that across an international sample of thirty-two cities, automobile ownership, average trip lengths, the proportion of travel by automobiles, and gasoline consumption each decline exponentially (as illustrated in figure 12-3) with increasing residential density when these variables are measured at the metropolitan-area scale.[30] Yet none of these results explicitly recognizes the critical influence of differences in income, household size, gasoline prices, and automobile taxation. Differences in these variables can be particularly large in international comparisons of residential density, as are differences in the historical timing of different cities' development and thus in the transportation technology that influenced land use during periods of their most rapid growth. Thus the failure to include controls for their effects casts serious doubt on the strength of the reported relationships between density and auto use.

30. Newman and Kenworthy (1989a, b).

Figure 12-3. *Hypothesized Relationship of Auto Use to Residential Density*
Auto travel per capita

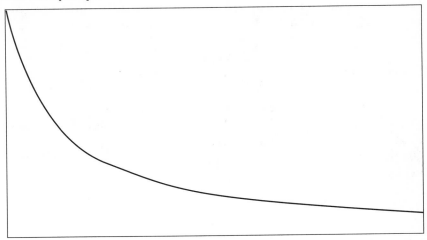

Residential density

Source: Newman and Kenworthy (1989a).

Other studies report that household auto ownership levels, auto trip frequency, and average distances driven each increase as residential densities decline.[31] Based on an analysis of transit ridership and metropolitan-wide residential density in a large sample of U.S. cities, another widely cited study argues that higher residential densities are associated with sharply higher shares of household travel by transit and higher overall transit ridership levels.[32] Yet virtually all of these reported relationships are inferred from simple regressions of some measure of automobile use or transit ridership on gross population density—regressions that have limited, if any, controls for household incomes, demographic characteristics, or other predictable influences on travel behavior. These studies also typically lack any clear discussion of how residential density might be expected to influence travel behavior and often impose arbitrary functional relationships

31. Widely cited recent studies include analyses of the relationship between residential density and annual per capita automobile travel in California suburbs, reported by Holtzclaw (1990) and Deakin and Harvey (1991).
32. Pushkarev and Zupan (1977).

between their density measures and travel behavior variables. Because they universally employ geographically aggregated, rather than household-level, data, their reported relationships are also likely to exhibit the spurious effect of geographic aggregation on the apparent strength of behavioral relationships.[33]

Only a few studies use carefully specified models of the relationships among density, other important variables such as income and household demographic characteristics, and travel behavior and examine the strength of these relationships using household-level rather than geographically aggregated data; table 12-2 summarizes their findings. They generally conclude that many of the effects of density itself on travel behavior are less certain and probably far weaker than implied by the widely publicized studies based on geographic aggregation, and that factors such as income and household size explain much of the observed association between density and travel behavior. These studies provide some evidence that even after controlling for other variables, higher residential densities may reduce automobile ownership and use, but they also show that changes in travel behavior are extremely modest at normal residential densities (2,000–5,000 people per square mile).

Most of these studies also show that reductions in auto ownership and use become significant only at densities of 10,000 people or more per square mile—densities that American suburbs are unlikely to reach. For example, results obtained by Cheslow and Neels indicate that if density in their suburban sample were to increase to the density levels found in the central areas of the nation's largest cities (25,000–40,000 people per square mile), auto travel would decrease by only 11–25 percent.[34] Similarly, Schimek reports that increasing residential density by 50 percent from its 1990 mean value within U.S. urban areas (from 3,600 to 5,400 people per square mile) would by itself reduce automobile travel by less than 3 percent once the effects of household and neighborhood characteristics are taken into account.[35] Thus the relationship of automobile ownership and use to residential density may be more nearly convex than the concave shape shown in figure 12-3, with automobile use relatively insensitive to increasing density below a threshold of about 4,000–5,000 people per square mile; sig-

33. Pas (1978).
34. Cheslow and Neels (1980).
35. Schimek (1996).

Table 12-2. *Estimated Effects of Residential Density on Travel Behavior*

Source	Variables controlled for:	Travel measure	Estimated elasticity of measure at residential density of:		
			2,000/sq. mi.	*5,000/sq. mi.*	*10,000/sq. mi.*
Oi and Shuldiner (1962)	Household size	Daily person-trips/dwelling unit	<−0.01	<−0.01	<−0.01
	Household income	Daily person-trips/dwelling unit	−0.05	−0.05	−0.05
Cheslow and Neels (1980)	Household income	Household auto ownership	−0.08	−0.08	−0.08
	Household size	Average automobile trip length	−0.04	−0.04	−0.04
	Auto ownership	Daily vehicle trips per household	−0.15	−0.15	−0.15
	Travel speeds	Proportion of trips by transit	0.11	0.29	0.57
	Transit service				
Schimek (1996)	Household income	Annual VMT per household	−0.28	−0.22	−0.22
	Household size	Household vehicle ownership	−0.11	−0.24	−0.39
	Race and ethnicity	Annual VMT per household	−0.13	−0.28	−0.43
	Urban area size				
	Geographic region				
Pickrell and Schimek (1996)	Household income	Daily VMT per capita	−0.32	−0.55	−0.89
	Household size	Proportion of all trips by auto	−0.17	−0.24	−0.45
	Race and ethnicity				
	Urban area size				
Pickrell and Schimek (1997)	Household income	Daily VMT per capita	−0.15	−0.15	−0.15
	Household size	Annual miles driven per vehicle	−0.05	−0.05	−0.05
	Race and ethnicity				
	Urban area size				

Sources: Author's calculations based on results reported in individual references. VMT = vehicle miles traveled.

nificant effects are likely to be apparent only when density reaches the extreme upper range.

These findings are confirmed by a detailed analysis of household-level data on residential density, automobile travel, and related variables from the 1990 and 1995 Nationwide Personal Transportation Surveys. This analysis estimated linear regression models of both average daily automobile miles driven per household member and the share of all household members' trips made by automobile, using as explanatory variables the household's income, the number and employment status of its members, and racial or ethnic characteristics, together with measures of the size of the urban area and geographic region where it is located.[36] Residential density is measured by the number of people per square mile residing in the household's zip code (a relatively large geographic unit) in the 1990 survey and in the household's census block (a more localized measure) in the 1995 survey.

The study first estimated the effect of variation in density on travel characteristics by including density and its squared value as explanatory variables in these regressions. An alternative specification used the component of density that was unexplained by the regression of density on household income, size, race or ethnicity, city size, and geographic region (the value of the residual term from this regression) as an explanatory variable. The results of these alternative density measures and estimation procedures were surprisingly consistent: they show that both the census block and zip code measures of gross residential density have a moderate independent influence on both daily household auto use and the proportion of trips made by automobile. Significant reductions in these measures do not occur, however, until zip code residential densities reach 4,000 people per square mile (five or six dwelling units per acre, depending on exact household size), well above the sample mean of 2,000 people per square mile. The decline in automobile usage is more pronounced above densities of 7,500 per square mile (twelve to fifteen units per acre of residential land), but these are typically found only in central city neighborhoods of the nation's largest urban areas.[37] Thus residential density does show some rela-

36. The race or ethnicity of the household is included to reflect the possibility that housing market discrimination confines minority households to higher-density neighborhoods than they might otherwise occupy and alters their travel behavior accordingly.

37. Schimek (1996) reports very similar results from further analysis of these data using a slightly modified modeling structure.

tionship to automobile travel and trip distances, even after controlling for the effects of household characteristics that affect travel demand indirectly through their influence on the density of neighborhoods. But this relationship is weak up to and well beyond typical values found in U.S. metropolitan areas.

Employment Clustering and Transit Commuting

Clustering employment into high-density zones—or on a smaller scale, into individual high-rise buildings—is often advocated as a strategy to foster the concentrations of employment that allow dedicated, high-frequency transit service to be operated at manageable costs. By increasing the number of commuters with a common destination, employment clustering also reduces the time and circuity entailed in distributing carpool members at their workplace destinations and reassembling them for the return trip. Again, however, the limited evidence on the relationship between employment density and commuting behavior suggests that the hypothesized effects actually occur only to a limited degree and only in the presence of important accompanying circumstances.

Pushkarev and Zupan provide some statistical evidence to support their assertion that employment density is a more important determinant of transit ridership than residential density.[38] They estimate that raising employment densities is likely to have three times as large an effect on the proportion of commuters who use public tansit as an equal percentage increase in residential density. Cervero found that employees commuting to the largest suburban employment centers were apt to carpool slightly more often than other suburban employees, while slightly more people used public transit when jobs were agglomerated into a single large building than when they were dispersed among more numerous small buildings.[39] Both of these effects were modest enough, however, that they could be explained by factors not included in the survey, including differences in the supply and price of on-site parking, the accessibility of transit vehicles to critical distribution points, and ease of pedestrian travel within the development.[40] Incorporating complementary land uses such as retailing, res-

38. Pushkarev and Zupan (1977).
39. Cervero (1989a).
40. Wilson (1992) reports that the pricing of parking even at outlying suburban employment centers exerts a strong effect on commuters' travel choices.

taurants, and banking within large employment centers also appeared to have at least as important an effect on automobile commuting by employees as did the large agglomerations of employment themselves.

Mixed Land Use and Trip Lengths

More than 70 percent of all housing in U.S. urban areas is suburban, and since World War II much of the residential building in the suburbs has been built within subdivisions under zoning codes that limit the land uses exclusively to housing. Even the most benign population-serving activities have been restricted to major arterial streets on the periphery of the subdivision. After several decades of advocating careful segregation of housing from nonresidential land uses, planners have recently begun to argue that permitting limited mixing of land uses within primarily residential areas would reduce the length of many trips and thus would encourage residents to substitute walking and bicycling for some automobile travel.[41] Most empirical research on the effects of mixed land use consists of simulations of differences in average trip lengths and automobile trip generation rates between traditional suburban subdivisions and mixed-use developments using conventional urban transportation planning models or paired-comparison case studies.[42] Although these studies suggest the potential for impressive reductions in local trip lengths and in automobile traffic volumes on collector and arterial streets, the models they employ are notoriously imprecise in forecasting changes in local travel patterns and their linkage to land uses.[43]

More recently, Cervero reports cross-sectional econometric evidence that households located in mixed use residential areas make fewer and shorter automobile trips than their counterparts in totally residential neighborhoods, although these differences are once again extremely modest.[44] The highly publicized study "Making the Land Use–Transportation–Air Quality Connection"(LUTRAQ), conducted for the Portland, Oregon, metropolitan area, developed an integrated system of urban transportation planning and land use allocation models in an effort to predict the com-

41. Calthorpe (1993).
42. Simulation studies include Kulash, Anglin, and Marks (1990) and McNally and Ryan (1993). Paired-comparison case studies include Ewing, Haliyur, and Page (1994) and Frank and Pivo (1994).
43. Pickrell (1989) reports that the average error in ten forecasts of transit ridership produced using such models was nearly 50 percent.
44. Cervero (1996).

bined effects of increased residential densities and land-use mixing on travel behavior. It estimated that households residing in moderately dense, mixed use developments sited near rail transit stations would make 22 percent fewer daily automobile trips than residents of more conventional suburbs, while their use of transit for commuting would rise to 20 percent, double the 10 percent share predicted for other areas. These differences, however, resulted primarily from a set of ambitious road and parking pricing measures incorporated by the land use proposals that were modeled, rather than from the higher densities or land use mixing incorporated into the planned development sites or the high levels of transit service provided.[45]

Jobs-Housing Balance and Commuting Distances

The influence on travel behavior of one specific measure of mixed land use, the balance between the numbers of jobs and dwelling units located within delimited areas of a metropolitan region, has been the focus of considerable research. The earliest study hypothesized that the "differential accumulation" between jobs and housing in an urban area—as measured by the difference between the number of jobs contained within a given radius of downtown and the number of employed residents living within that same distance—was the primary determinant of the average length of commuting trips and the fraction likely to be made by automobile.[46] More recently, Cervero and others have asserted that closer matching between the number and types of jobs and residents within relatively small districts of a larger metropolitan area would permit more employees to reside near their workplaces, which would not only shorten many commutes, but also encourage people to commute by public transit or by walking.[47] Closer "balancing" of jobs and housing, they argue, would also reduce traffic congestion by permitting more automobile commute trips to be made exclusively on local and arterial streets, rather than burdening the regional highway system.

But empirical research on these hypotheses remains largely unconvincing, primarily because the models take inadequate account of the critical

45. Cambridge Systematics, Inc. (1992). These pricing measures included a charge of $0.10 per mile for automobile travel within the region and a $3.00 parking charge for all automobile trips. Most measures of travel behavior differed insignificantly from the predicted baseline case until these measures were added to the proposed land-use plan.

46. Zahavi (1977).

47. Cervero (1989).

effect of spatial variation in housing prices and transportation costs on residential location decisions.[48] Because much of this research also uses proxy measures of employment and housing opportunities that may be related only crudely to actual local imbalances between jobs and residential capacity, the implications of these studies for the relationship between job-housing differentials and travel behavior is also unclear.[49] In any case, these various proxy measures add only marginally to the explanatory power of the regression models for average trip lengths and commuting volumes between geographic zones. Thus the empirical case that localized imbalances between employment and residential opportunities lengthen commuting distances appears to be quite weak.

Transportation and Land Use: A Reassessment

The relationship between transportation and urban land use exhibits two major paradoxes. First, while developments in transportation technology and investments in transportation infrastructure have had profound effects on urban development in the past, their future effects on urban land use patterns are likely to be much weaker. Urban planners and local political officials cite this historical influence of transportation on urban development to buttress their calls for increased use of transportation planning and investment policy as tools to shape urban land use patterns and their arguments that expanding metropolitan highway systems will encourage continued decentralization of population and employment within urban areas. Seldom do they acknowledge the diminished effects that recent and future innovations or investments in transportation are likely to exert on urban development and land use, either because they misinterpret the historical evidence or because they choose purposely to misrepresent it.

Second, while historical developments in transportation have clearly influenced today's geographic patterns of urban land use and travel demand, the influence of land use patterns themselves on travel behavior is quite modest. Critical examination shows that the relationships between

48. The importance of households' efforts to minimize commuting times in their location decisions implicitly assumed by these studies may also be overstated; see Calfee and Winston (1998).
49. For example, Cervero uses distance from the central business district as a proxy for the local density of employment and the amount of land within subregions that is zoned for residential development to approximate the resident population.

land use characteristics—such as residential and employment density, mixing of different uses, and the relative distributions of employment and population—and measures of urban travel demand are generally empirically weak and often statistically unreliable. The lack of compelling evidence of these relationships means that the *changes* in land use patterns likely to be fostered by metropolitan planning cannot be relied upon to alter the volume or geographic pattern of urban travel demand in predictable ways, despite planners' increasingly frequent assertions to the contrary.[50]

Land use planning as a means to mitigate externalities such as traffic congestion and air pollution generated by urban transportation thus seems unlikely to be an effective substitute for rationalizing investment levels and pricing policies in urban transportation. In contrast, the effects of economically optimal pricing and investment policies for transportation infrastructure on urban travel behavior and the externalities it generates seem likely to be significant, although the potential effects of these policies on urban land use patterns are extremely difficult to predict. Improving our understanding of the likely consequences of changes in infrastructure investment and pricing policies for land use and travel behavior might thus be an important step toward the design of more rational transportation systems *and* land use patterns.

References

Alonso, William. 1964. *Location and Land Use: Toward a General Theory of Land Rent.* Harvard University Press.

Anas, Alex. 1984. "Discrete Choice Theory and the General Equilibrium of Employment, Housing, and Travel Networks in Lowry-Type Models of the Urban Economy." *Environment and Planning A* 16:1489–1502.

———. 1992. *NYSIM (The New York Area Simulation Model): A Model for Cost-Benefit Analysis of Transportation Projects.* New York: Regional Planning Association.

Beckmann, Martin J. 1968. *Location Theory.* Random House.

Berechman, Joseph, and Kenneth A. Small. 1988. "Research Policy and Review 25: Modeling Land Use and Transportation: An Interpretive Review for Growth Areas." *Environment and Planning A* 20 (October):1285–1309.

50. Assertions of the ability of land-use planning to accomplish an ambitious menu of goals are now commonplace, but their confident air is illustrated by the declaration of the California Air Resources Board (1993:1) that the "form and shape that growing cities take in the next two decades will have an important impact on the future air quality of California's major metropolitan areas. A growing body of literature and research indicates that land use and transportation strategies can reduce vehicle trips and vehicle miles traveled, and thus reduce the air pollution produced by automobiles."

Berry, Brian J. L. 1967. *Geography of Market Centers and Retail Distribution*. Prentice-Hall.

Boyce, David E. 1980. "A Framework for Constructing Network Equilibrium Models of Urban Location." *Transportation Science* 14: 77–96.

Boyce, David E., and L. Lundqvist. 1987. "Network Equilibrium Models of Urban Location and Travel Choices: Alternative Formulations for the Stockholm Region." *Papers of the Regional Science Association* 61: 93–104.

Brand, Daniel, Brian Barber, and Michael Jacobs. 1967. "Techniques for Relating Transportation Improvements and Urban Development Patterns." *Highway Research Record* 207: 53–67.

Calfee, John, and Clifford Winston. 1998. "The Value of Travel Time: New Evidence and Hypotheses." *Journal of Public Economics* 69 (July): 83–102.

California Air Resources Board. 1993. "Land Use–Air Quality Linkage: How Land Use and Transportation Affect Air Quality." Sacramento. January.

Calthorpe, Peter. 1993. *The Next American Metropolis: Ecology, Community, and the American Dream*. New York: Princeton Architectural Press.

Cambridge Systematics, Inc. 1992. *The LUTRAQ Alternative/Analysis of Alternatives: Interim Report*. Portland, Ore.: Parsons Brinkerhoff.

Cervero, Robert 1986. *Suburban Gridlock*. Rutgers University, Center for Urban Policy Research.

———. 1989a. *America's Suburban Centers: The Land Use–Transportation Link*. Boston: Unwin Hyman.

———. 1989b. "Jobs-Housing Balancing and Regional Mobility." *Journal of the American Planning Association* 55 (Spring): 136–50.

———. 1996. "Mixed Uses and Commuting Behavior: Evidence from the American Housing Survey." *Transportation Research*. 30A (September): 361–78.

Cheslow, Melvyn D., and J. Kevin Neels. 1980. "Effect of Urban Development Patterns on Transportation Energy Use." *Transportation Research Record* 764: 70–78.

Christaller, Walter. 1966. *The Central Places of Southern Germany*. Translated by C. Baskin. Prentice-Hall.

Deakin, Elizabeth, and Greig Harvey. 1991. *Toward Improved Transportation Modeling Practice*. Washington, D.C.: National Association of Regional Councils.

Ewing, Reid, Padma Haliyur, and G. William Page. 1994. "Getting Around a Traditional City, a Suburban Planned Unit Development, and Everything in Between." *Transportation Research Record* 1466: 53–62.

Frank, Lawrence D., and Gerald Pivo. 1994. "Impacts of Mixed Use and Density on Utilization of Three Modes of Travel: Single-Occupant Vehicle, Transit, and Walking." *Transportation Research Record* 1466: 44–52.

Giuliano, Genevive. 1995. "Land Use Impacts of Transportation Investments: Highway and Transit." In *The Geography of Urban Transporation,* edited by Susan Hansen. New York: Guilford Press.

Giuliano, Genevive, and Kenneth A. Small. 1993. "Is the Journey to Work Explained by Urban Structure?" *Urban Studies* 30 (November): 1485–1500.

Gómez-Ibáñez, José A. 1985. "Transportation Policy as a Tool for Shaping Metropolitan Development." In *Research in Transportation Economics: A Research Annual Series,* edited by Theodore E. Keeler. Vol 2: 55–81. JAI Press.

Hamilton, Bruce. 1982. "Wasteful Commuting." *Journal of Political Economy* 90 (October): 1035–51.

———. 1989. "Wasteful Commuting Again." *Journal of Political Economy* 97 (December): 1497–1504.

Harris, Britton, and A. G. Wilson. 1978. "Equilibrium Values and Dynamics of Attractiveness Terms in Production-Constrained Spatial Interaction Models." *Environment and Planning A* 10: 371–88.

Harrison, David A. Jr., and John F. Kain 1974. "Cumulative Urban Growth and Urban Density Functions." *Journal of Urban Economics* 1 (January): 61–98.

Herbert, John D., and Benjamin H. Stevens. 1960. "A Model for the Distribution of Residential Activity in Urban Areas." *Journal of Regional Science* 2 (2): 21–36.

Hill, D. M., Daniel Brand, and Walter Hansen. 1966. "Prototype Development of Statistical Land-Use Prediction Model for the Greater Boston Region." *Highway Research Record* 114:51–70.

Holtzclaw, John. 1990. "Explaining Urban Density and Transit Impacts on Auto Use." San Francisco: Sierra Club.

Ingram, Gregory K., John F. Kain, and J. Royce Ginn. 1972. *The Detroit Prototype of the NBER Urban Simulation Model.* New York: National Bureau of Economic Research.

Kain, John F. 1987. "Computer Simulation Models of Urban Location." In *Urban Economics,* edited by Edwin S. Mills. Vol. 2 of *Handbook of Regional and Urban Economics,* 847–75. Amsterdam: North-Holland.

Kim, T. J. 1983. "A Combined Land-Use Transportation Model When Zonal Travel Demand Is Endogenously Determined." *Transportation Research* 17B: 449–62.

Kulash, Walter, J. Anglin, and D. Marks. 1990. "Traditional Neighborhood Development: Will the Traffic Work?" *Development* 21: 21–24.

Lowry, Ira S. 1964. *A Model of Metropolis.* RM-4035-RC. Santa Monica, Calif.: Rand Corporation.

McNally, Michael G., and Sherry Ryan. 1993. "Comparative Assessment of Travel Characteristics for Neotraditional Designs." *Transportation Research Record* 1407: 67–77.

Mieszkowski, Peter A., and Edwin S. Mills. 1993. "The Causes of Metropolitan Suburbanization." *Journal of Economic Perspectives* 7 (Summer): 135–47.

Mills, Edwin S. 1967. "Transportation and Patterns of Urban Development: An Aggregative Model of Resource Allocation in a Metropolitan Area." *American Economic Review* 57 (May: *Papers and Proceedings*): 197–241.

———. 1972. *Studies in the Structure of the Urban Economy.* Johns Hopkins University Press.

Mitchell, Robert B., and Chester Rapkin. 1954. *Urban Traffic: A Function of Land Use.* Columbia University Press.

Moses, Leon N. 1958. "Location and the Theory of Production." *Quarterly Journal of Economics* 72 (May): 259–72.

Moses, Leon N., and Harold F. Williamson, Jr. 1967. "The Location of Economic Activity in Cities." *American Economic Review* 57 (May): 211–22.

Muth, Richard F. 1969. *Cities and Housing: The Spatial Pattern of Urban Residential Land Use.* University of Chicago Press.

Newman, Peter W. G., and Jeffrey R. Kenworthy. 1989a. "Gasoline Consumption and

Cities: A Comparison of U. S. Cities with a Global Survey." *Journal of the American Planning Association* 55 (Winter): 24–37.

———. 1989b. *Cities and Automobile Dependence: A Sourcebook.* Brookfield, Vt.: Gower Technical.

Oi, Walter, and Paul Shuldiner. 1962. *An Analysis of Urban Travel Demands.* Northwestern University Press.

Pas, Eric I. 1978. "An Empirical Comparison of Zonal, Household, and Personal Models of Home-Based Trip Generation." *Traffic Engineering and Control* 19: 64–68.

Pickrell, Don H. 1989. *Urban Rail Transit Projects: Forecast versus Actual Ridership and Costs.* Washington, D.C.: Urban Mass Transportation Administration. October.

Pickrell, Don H., and Paul Schimek. 1996. "Analysis of the Effects of Residential Density on Travel Behavior Using the 1990 Nationwide Personal Transportation Survey." U.S. Department of Transportation, Cambridge, Mass.

———. 1997. "Growth in Motor Vehicle Ownership and Use: Evidence from the Nationwide Personal Transportation Survey." Paper presented to a Federal Highway Administration Symposium on the 1995 Nationwide Personal Transportation Survey, Bethesda, Md.

Pushkarev, Boris S., and Jeffrey M. Zupan. 1977. *Public Transportation and Land Use Policy.* Indiana University Press.

Putman, Stephen H. 1983. *Integrated Urban Models: Policy Analysis of Transportation and Land Use.* London: Pion Ltd.

———. 1991. *Integrated Urban Models 2: Policy Analysis of Transportation and Land Use.* London: Pion Ltd.

Schimek, Paul. 1996. "Household Motor Vehicle Ownership and Use: How Much Does Residential Density Matter?" *Transportation Research Record* 1552: 120–25.

Small, Kenneth A., and Shunfeng Song. 1992. "'Wasteful' Commuting: A Resolution." *Journal of Political Economy* 100 (August): 888-98.

Solow, Robert M. 1973. "On Equilibrium Models of Urban Location." In *Essays in Modern Economics,* edited by Michael Parkin with Ardino R. Nobay, 2–16. London: Longman.

Warner, Sam Bass, Jr. 1962. *Streetcar Suburbs: The Process of Growth in Boston, 1870–1900.* Harvard University Press.

Webster, F. V., P. H. Bly, and N. J. Paulley. 1988. *Urban Land Use and Transport Interaction Policies and Models.* Aldershot, U.K.: Avebury.

Weiglin, Peter C. 1976. "A Short History of Transit in the United States." In *Transit Fact Book,* 9–22. Washington, D.C.: American Public Transit Association.

Wheaton, William C. 1974. "Linear Programming and Locational Equilibrium: The Herbert Stevens Model Revisited." *Journal of Urban Economics* 1 (July): 278–87.

White, Michelle. 1976. "Firm Suburbanization and Urban Subcenters." *Journal of Urban Economics* 3 (October): 323–43.

———. 1988. "Urban Commuting Journeys Are Not 'Wasteful.'" *Journal of Political Economy* 96 (October): 1097–1110.

Wilson, Richard N. 1992. "Estimating the Travel and Parking Demand Effects of Employer-Paid Parking." *Regional Science and Urban Economics* 22 (March):133–45.

Wingo, Lowdon. 1961. *Transportation and Urban Land.* Washington, D.C.: Resources for the Future.

Zahavi, Yacov. 1977. *The UMOT Model.* Washington, D.C.: World Bank.

KATHERINE M. O'REGAN
JOHN M. QUIGLEY

13

Accessibility and Economic Opportunity

On August 11, 1965, the worst U.S. riot in four decades erupted in Los Angeles. Thirty-four people were killed, hundreds were injured, and some $35 million of property was damaged. A formal investigatory body, known as the McCone Commission after its chairman and former CIA director John A. McCone, analyzed the underlying causes of the riot and concluded that lack of jobs and inadequate transportation to jobs played a large role in creating the conditions that led to urban unrest. Spurred in part by the increasing national concern over urban riots, the American Academy of Arts and Sciences (AAAS) asked John Meyer to organize an exploration of the links between transportation and poverty. During the spring of 1968, Meyer commissioned a dozen papers on topics ranging from the impact of free public transit on urban poverty to a calculation of the social costs of urban expressways.

The resulting conference and the collected papers drew widespread attention to the relationship between accessibility and its employment consequences for low-income households. A major conclusion of the initial exploration was that "post-war changes in urban structure and urban trans-

The authors are grateful to Tracy Gordon and David Huffman for research assistance. The Transportation Center and the Fisher Center for Real Estate and Urban Economics, University of California, Berkeley, supported this research.

portation systems have conferred significant improvements and greater satisfactions on the majority, [but] they almost certainly have caused a relative deterioration in the access to opportunities, if not in the actual mobility of a significant fraction of the poor."[1] Thirty years later, the residential mobility of the poor and their access to jobs are still problems. In the face of national welfare reform, with time-limited benefits and increasingly stringent work requirements, the link between transportation and employment outcomes continues to be of critical importance.

This chapter reviews the advances that have been made during the last three decades in understanding the link between employment access and economic opportunities. We present new evidence of changes in job access for the poor and review, rather selectively, recent analyses documenting the labor market effects of urban space, including transportation systems and accessibility. Finally we present a selective review of policy initiatives aimed at increasing economic opportunity through improved transport access.

Basic Issues

Standard models of urban location suggest that commuting patterns differ systematically by household income and demographic conditions. The choice of where one lives depends not only on rents and commuting costs, but also on the associated amenities the location offers. Central city locations tend to be closer to jobs and other centralized urban amenities but are more expensive in rent and provide capital-intensive housing. Household characteristics, such as wage income, labor force attachment, family size, wealth, and life-cycle influences, all affect household location.

For example, consider the influence of income. Households with higher incomes and greater demands for space will obtain larger aggregate savings by choosing their more spacious housing at locations farther away from the central city and incurring longer and more expensive commutes. Because lower-income households demand only small amounts of space, they will obtain larger aggregate savings by choosing central locations, paying higher unit prices for space but economizing more on commuting costs.

Similarly, predictable differences in the demand for space or in the cost of commuting will affect household commuting behavior. Households with several workers and without children may have lower demands for residential space. Households with multiple workers whose skills or human capi-

1. AAAS (1968: 2).

tal endowments are similar (and that do not contain a "secondary worker" who searches for employment after the residence has been chosen) may also achieve greater savings from locating in areas with improved access to central workplaces. Households that receive only a small fraction of their incomes from wages or salaries may be more likely to choose central locations if those locations are more accessible to the income-elastic urban amenities they desire than outlying areas are.

This model implies a sorting of households across space that accommodates housing and commuting choices. As employment opportunities decentralize, so too, eventually, do household locations adjust. The benign circumstances that arise in the economic model of equilibrium described above may not be achieved costlessly, however, and the reassuring normative implications of this neoclassical model are certainly not immune to dynamic considerations. Real capital investments—in offices and industrial plants and in residences as well as transportation systems—have long lives. Workplaces locate or relocate in response to demand and production technology, and because these changes occur much faster than do changes in the stock of housing suitable to different demographic groups, the transportation system may be called upon to buffer the mismatch between where people live and where they work. That role will certainly be harder for the transportation system to play when it is itself characterized by a fixed capital stock of rail and road networks.

Therefore, although the abstract model assumes costless transitions, the reality of fixed investment means that changes in urban structure will result in real, and perhaps large, adjustment costs. Two factors reinforce the dynamic disadvantages of central city housing. First, the rapid decentralization of employment in the postwar period has improved the locational advantage of residences and housing tracts in the suburbs. Simultaneously, this trend has made central city residences less accessible to geographical areas experiencing rapid job growth. If the housing stock could adjust cheaply and quickly—so that low-income residential areas in central cities could be converted to more spacious high-income housing and so that high-income housing in the suburbs could be converted to low-income housing—the decentralization of workplaces need not disadvantage the poor. Conversion costs are high, however, and land use, environmental policies, and political opposition all restrict the production of new housing appropriate for low-income populations in the suburbs.

Second, and more important, the legacy of racial segregation and housing market discrimination greatly increases mobility problems for minority households. Absent this distortion in the housing market, land rents in central city and suburban locations could adjust fully—at least in principle—to changing patterns of metropolitan workplaces. Housing market discrimination and exclusionary zoning, however, prevent minority and poor households from following jobs to the suburbs. These limits on residential adjustment concentrate minority and poor households in central and segregated neighborhoods, decreasing their knowledge of and increasing their commuting costs to suburban jobs. Several additional factors exacerbate the situation.

Income constraints on poor households greatly limit their commuting options. For obvious reasons, poor households are less likely to have access to private automobiles and are more likely to rely on public transportation for commuting to and from work. This increases their commuting costs in both time and money for any given distance traveled. These increased commuting costs are particularly significant in the oldest metropolitan areas, those served primarily by radial, spoke-and-hub public transportation systems, and those populated more heavily by minorities.

In sum, two primary forces are responsible for the inadequate access to employment that limits the economic opportunities available to low-income and minority households: slow adjustment in real capital markets to changes in suburban locational advantage; and explicit barriers to the residential mobility of low-income or minority households. These combine to imply that centrally located minorities are at a disadvantage in the labor market.

The first empirical test of the proposition described above was published by John Kain in 1968, about the time that Meyer organized the AAAS study.[2] Kain's statistical analysis was quite straightforward and rather primitive. Using aggregate data from Chicago and Detroit postal zones, which were of very unequal areas and shapes, Kain measured the fraction of "local" employment, by industry and occupation, held by black workers. He found that the fraction of black employment in a postal zone was positively related to the fraction of black residences in that zone and negatively related to its airline distance from the central urban ghetto. The findings suggested that the distribution of black employment within the metropolitan areas was affected by the pattern of black residences; the intense residential segregation in these two cities affected the spatial distribution of employment for black workers.

2. Kain (1968). A preliminary version of the empirical analysis was published much earlier (Kain, 1964), however, and the mechanism was hinted at in Meyer, Kain, and Wohl (1965).

In addition to affecting the *location* of employment, the spatial mismatch hypothesis purports to affect labor force participation, and therefore the *level* of employment. In this vein, Kain used the results of the statistical models to conduct a striking-thought experiment—to estimate the level of black employment in each metropolitan area in the absence of residential segregation. This counterfactual was computed by assuming that black households were evenly distributed across the metropolitan area and that the distance to the black ghetto was equal (to zero) for each postal zone. The largest estimates of this redistribution were found to increase black employment by as much as 9,000 jobs in Detroit and almost 25,000 jobs in Chicago. These findings implied that the existing spatial pattern of black residences reduced black employment in these two metropolitan areas by 7 to 9 percent. This result, combined with historical evidence on the suburbanization of jobs in the two cities, supported the conclusion that constraints on residential patterns increasingly disadvantaged black households in the labor market. The postwar dispersal of jobs had reduced black employment, and the magnitude was not negligible.

The conclusions of the work contained the usual academic disclaimers. Kain indicated that the conclusions and especially the forecasts were "highly tentative" and speculative.[3] Nevertheless, given the timeliness of the topic and the pedigree of the work, the 1968 paper received widespread attention. It certainly affected the substance and conclusions of Meyer's contemporaneous report to the AAAS, as well as the subsequent Kain-Meyer essay on transportation and poverty published in *The Public Interest*.[4]

Spatial Trends in Residency and Jobs after 1970

How have the factors affecting job accessibility changed in the thirty years since Kain published the results of his study? The first factor affecting job accessibility for poor and minority households is the continuing decentralization of jobs. Between 1970 and 1990, central cities continued to lose jobs not only in the declining manufacturing sector, but also in the growing retail and service sectors.[5] This shift in employment out of central

---

3. The assumed values of the independent variables for Kain's forecasts were certainly within the range of variation of the raw data, but Kain did not present standard errors of the forecasts or other diagnostics.

4. Kain and Meyer (1970).

Table 13-1. *Centralization of Jobs and Workers, 1970 and 1990*

Workers	Percent working in central city		Percent living in central city		Central city jobs per central city worker	
	1970	*1990*	*1970*	*1990*	*1970*	*1990*
All	50.9	23.4	46.5	18.0	1.09	0.93
White	49.6	20.2	42.3	13.1	1.17	1.00
Black	60.7	36.9	79.2	37.2	0.77	0.70

Sources: Census Bureau (1973: table 26); Census Bureau (1992).

cities can be seen in table 13-1. In 1970 more than half of all jobs held by metropolitan workers and more than 60 percent of jobs held by black metropolitan workers were still located in the central city. By 1990 less than 24 percent of all metropolitan jobs were clearly identified as located in a central city.[6] Although jobs held by black workers are still more concentrated in the central city than are all jobs, less than 40 percent are now found in central cities.

There has, of course, been a concomitant decentralization of population to the suburbs. Large declines in central city residency occurred for both white and black workers from 1970 to 1990, but the much higher centralization of black workers has been maintained (see table 13-1).[7] In 1990 black workers were still three times as likely as white workers to live in a central city. As a result of the decentralization of both jobs and people, jobs per worker in the central city declined from a slight surplus in 1970 to a slight deficit in 1990. Over this entire time period, there is a much greater centralization of black workers than of jobs held by black workers. And this mismatch has widened over time.

To address the question of truly accessible jobs—by skill requirements and geography—John Kasarda examined central city employment changes

5. Kasarda (1995).
6. Changes in Census definition account for some of this decline. Geographic definitions used by the U.S. Census Bureau now classify areas as central city, noncentral city, and "other." The introduction of the last category preserves confidentiality in the Census's Public Use Micro Sample (PUMS). It includes geographic areas that may contain both central city and noncentral city areas. Here we identify as central city only geographic areas entirely within the central city, potentially understating the centralization of work places.
7. Again, changes in Census definitions may overstate this change.

in nine large cities from 1970 to 1990.[8] Kasarda classified industries by the mean years of schooling completed by job holders in 1982, distinguishing between industries in which the mean level of schooling was twelve years or less from those in which some schooling beyond high school was the norm.[9] Overall, Kasarda found that the fraction of jobs available to workers with less than a high school education was smaller, frequently a great deal smaller, than the representation of these workers in central city populations (table 13-2).

Cities in the North (and Denver) experienced a decline in the number of central city jobs requiring less than a high school diploma. Although this trend generally resulted in a loss of aggregate employment, almost all of these cities gained jobs requiring more than a high school education. For these cities, the net loss in jobs between 1970 and 1990 seriously understates the decline in central city jobs available for less skilled workers. In the South and West, job growth occurred in both categories, although here, too, the relative shift from lower educational qualifications to higher qualifications was large.

The continued decentralization of jobs (and more specifically, relevant jobs) has direct implications for the second factor we examine—commuting patterns of and commuting costs to low-income and minority workers. Table 13-3 provides commute flow information for metropolitan areas in 1970, by residence and poverty status. Among nonpoor workers, both whites and blacks, the dominant form of commuting in 1970 was within the same residential area: central-city-to-central-city, or suburb-to-suburb. For nonpoor white workers, however, the suburban-suburban commute was most frequent, whereas commutes for nonpoor black workers were primarily within the central city. If they were not working in central cities, nonpoor blacks were most likely to live and work in the suburbs, but this pattern is closely followed by central city residence and a reverse commute to the suburbs. Nonpoor blacks working in the suburbs are observed living in the suburbs with far less frequency than are poor whites.

Poor households in 1970 typically lived and worked in central cities, regardless of race, although there were racial differences in magnitudes.

---

8. Kasarda (1995). Holzer (1996) has approached this issue by comparing the number of unemployed and the number of vacant jobs in four large metropolitan areas accounting for in-commuting flows. In each of these cities, fewer jobs were available for residents in the central city than for suburban residents.

9. The average level of educational attainment is taken as an indication of the educational requirements of the industry.

Table 13-2. *Central City Jobs in Industries in which the Average Education of Employees is More than or Less than Twelve Years*
(thousands, unless noted)

City	1970	1990	Job change	Percent change
Atlanta				
Less than 12 years	179	190	+11	+6.1
More than 12 years	92	165	+73	+79.3
Baltimore				
Less than 12 years	207	110	+97	−46.9
More than 12 years	90	118	+28	+31.1
Boston				
Less than 12 years	189	128	−61	−32.3
More than 12 years	185	237	+52	+28.1
Dallas				
Less than 12 years	337	468	+131	+38.9
More than 12 years	107	334	+227	+212.1
Denver				
Less than 12 years	120	107	−13	−10.8
More than 12 years	72	120	+48	+66.7
New York				
Less than 12 years	1,552	977	−575	−37.0
More than 12 years	1,002	1,253	+251	+25.0
Philadelphia				
Less than 12 years	430	226	−204	−47.4
More than 12 years	205	231	+26	+12.7
San Francisco				
Less than 12 years	132	173	+41	+31.1
More than 12 years	135	204	+69	+51.1
St. Louis				
Less than 12 years	210	107	−103	−49.0
More than 12 years	98	79	−19	−19.4

Source: Computed from data reported in Kasarda (1995).

Poor black workers who did not work and live in the central city were somewhat more likely than poor white workers to undertake reverse commutes to the suburbs rather than to live and work in the suburbs. Conversely, poor white workers who did not both live and work in the central city were much more likely to live and work in the suburbs than to undertake reverse commutes. In fact, poor white workers were more likely to live

Table 13-3. *Workplace and Residential Location of Metropolitan Area Workers in 1970, by Race and Poverty Status*

(percent)

Work in	Nonpoverty households living in		Poverty households living in	
	Central city	Suburb	Central city	Suburb
All workers				
Central city	36.4	18.1	48.5	10.7
Suburb	8.8	36.7	9.2	31.7
White workers				
Central city	33.4	19.3	43.0	12.1
Suburb	8.1	39.1	8.1	36.8
Black workers				
Central city	62.9	7.0	64.0	6.8
Suburb	12.2	17.9	15.3	13.9

Source: Census Bureau (1973: table 26).

in the suburbs and to commute to the central city than they were to follow the commuting pattern of poor black workers. These racial differences in commuting patterns, after controlling for poverty status, are consistent with constrained residential choices.

Table 13-4 presents similar—although not directly comparable—numbers for 1990. [10] Although the magnitudes are affected by the new categories, making it hard to assess trends, the dominance of within-area commuting continued among nonpoor workers of both races in 1990. This pattern is also found among the poor, although with greater centralization. By 1990 it was no longer true that poor black workers were more likely to live in a central city and commute to the suburbs rather than live and work in the suburbs. Although suburban living had increased for poor black workers, it had also increased for poor white workers—who are now slightly more likely to live and work in the suburbs than to live and work in the central city. Given the importance of the "intermediate" category, it is hard to discern more than this.

If workers had made some residential adjustment to match the decentralization and restructuring of jobs, then commuting costs might not have

10. PUMAs (Public Use Microdata Area) that are designated as solely central city or noncentral city are classified as such. PUMAs that contain both central city and noncentral city portions of a metropolitan statistical area are classified as "intermediate."

Table 13-4. *Workplace and Residential Location of Metropolitan Area Workers in 1990, by Race and Poverty Status*

(percent)

	Nonpoverty households living in			Poverty households living in		
Work in	Central city	Inter-mediate	Suburb	Central city	Inter-mediate	Suburb
All workers						
Central city	15.9	2.7	11.1	24.6	1.4	5.6
Intermediate	2.9	30.8	9.3	4.2	36.0	5.4
Suburb	3.4	1.8	22.1	4.5	2.0	16.5
White workers						
Central city	12.3	3.0	11.5	16.3	1.8	6.0
Intermediate	2.4	34.0	10.4	2.8	43.4	6.5
Suburb	0.3	2.9	23.3	2.9	2.2	18.2
Black workers						
Central city	33.4	1.6	9.7	35.6	1.1	4.2
Intermediate	5.2	23.3	4.6	5.3	34.2	3.4
Suburb	5.4	1.6	13.3	4.8	1.2	10.3

Source: Census Bureau (1992).

increased during this twenty-year span. Table 13-5 presents data for one aspect of commuting costs—commute times—indicating that black workers (controlling for poverty status) have longer average commutes than white workers do. The average one-way commuting time for nonpoor black households in 1990 was about two and a half minutes longer than for nonpoor white households; for poor black households, the commute time was about four minutes longer than for poor white households. This is a continuation of a trend that was apparent in the 1980 Census and is con-

Table 13-5. *Average Duration of One-Way Commutes for Metropolitan Area Workers in 1990, by Race and Poverty Status*

(minutes)

Workers	Nonpoverty households	Poverty households
All	22.7	20.4
White	22.4	18.9
Black	25.1	22.7

Source: Census Bureau (1992).

Table 13-6. *Average Duration of One-Way Nonstop Commutes in 1990, by Race, Income, and Size of Metropolitan Area*
(minutes)

| | Metropolitan area population | | | | | |
| | Less than 1 million | | 1–3 million | | More than 3 million | |
Income	Black	White	Black	White	Black	White
Less than $15,000	14.3	16.7	17.1	16.7	23.9	21.7
$15,000–$24,999	19.6	17.3	23.1	18.9	26.3	16.2
$25,000–$39,999	16.2	18.2	20.4	20.1	27.0	21.8
$40,000–$54,999	15.9	19.5	19.3	20.6	25.8	24.4
More than $55,000	21.0	18.4	19.0	22.2	29.0	26.7

Source: Federal Highway Administration (1995).

sistent with continuing residential constraints for black workers, both poor and nonpoor.[11]

Table 13-6, based on Department of Transportation information for 1990, helps to disentangle the role of race, income, and location. The differences in 1990 commute times by race are related in part to the concentration of minority workers in large cities. Commute times are higher in larger metropolitan statistical areas (MSAs), and black workers are more concentrated in large MSAs. Even within large MSAs, however, and controlling for income, black workers spend more time commuting than do white workers. (Below we examine differences in mode of transit, also a contributing factor.) Note one additional difference in income-commute patterns by race. White workers' commute times within similar-sized MSAs generally increase with income, but this is less true for black workers. As income rises, blacks generally do not translate their higher earnings into residential choices requiring longer commutes. This finding suggests that there are pronounced differences in the residential consumption preferences of blacks or, more likely, in their residential options.[12]

---

11. Census Bureau (1992). Comparable data for 1970 are not available.

12. In addition to time costs, commuting patterns and options are affected by out-of-pocket costs. For travel by private automobile, these costs are large and perhaps, for low-income households, prohibitive. Over the twenty years considered, the cost of a new car increased by one-third in constant (1990) dollars, from $12,000 in 1970 to $16,000 in 1990. In terms of income, in the 1970s the cost of a new car was equivalent to twenty weeks of the median pay. By 1990, it cost twenty-five weeks of median pay. However, total operating costs, inclusive of fuel, maintenance, insurance, and so forth, have remained more stable. See Pisarski (1996).

Table 13-7. *Percent of Metropolitan Area Workers without Automobile Access in 1990, by Residential Location, Poverty Status, and Race*
(percent)

Category	All U.S.	Residential location		
		Central city	Intermediate	Suburb
Nonpoor working				
All	4.0	12.8	2.3	1.9
White	2.4	8.6	1.6	1.3
Black	13.0	21.2	8.5	6.6
Nonpoor not working				
All	9.0	21.4	7.0	5.8
White	7.6	18.2	6.6	5.9
Black	21.9	30.8	16.6	12.0
Poor working				
All	16.5	31.1	13.5	10.4
White	9.5	20.5	8.6	6.7
Black	34.4	44.9	30.0	25.5
Poor not working				
All	32.3	51.5	28.5	23.0
White	25.5	40.8	24.5	22.4
Black	53.3	62.2	50.0	43.2

Source: Census Bureau (1992).

Although changes in the spatial form of cities potentially affect all workers, low-income workers are differentially affected by their greater concentration in older cities with antiquated transportation systems (including public transit) and by their more limited abilities to adjust their housing to workplace changes. One way to adjust to spatial deconcentration of jobs is to make greater use of the most flexible form of commuting (automobiles). Auto usage increased from 81 percent of worker commutes in 1970 to 88 percent in 1990.[13] These increases are not uniform across categories of workers, however. For one thing, reliance on automobiles is lower in the largest metropolitan areas, where poor and minority households are disproportionately represented. For another, many lower-income households do not own cars and are limited to public transit.

Table 13-7 documents the dramatic differences in car ownership by

13. Pisarski (1996: appendix A).

Table 13-8. *Public Transit Usage Rates in 1970, by Workplace, Residential Location, Race, and Poverty Status*
(percent)

| | Nonpoverty households living in | | Poverty households living in | |
Work in	Central city	Suburb	Central city	Suburb
All workers				
Central city	21.3	9.6	27.5	10.8
Suburb	8.6	2.5	22.1	4.8
White workers				
Central city	20.3	9.4	19.4	9.1
Suburb	6.2	2.3	12.7	3.3
Black workers				
Central city	35.9	14.5	42.6	18.9
Suburb	20.2	9.6	37.6	12.6

Source: Census Bureau (1973).

race, employment, and poverty status. Ownership rates are much higher for workers, the nonpoor, and white households, and differences among these groups are quite large. Controlling for residential location, the working poor are four times more likely to lack access to a car as are the working nonpoor. All else equal, blacks are generally twice as likely as whites to be without a car. So, although only 11.5 percent of households nationally are without an auto, 45 percent of central city poor black workers have no access to a car. That figure rises above 60 percent for central city poor black nonworkers.

Tables 13-8 and 13-9 examine public transit use in 1970 and 1990. Even after controlling for commuting patterns, we find that blacks, whether poor or nonpoor, rely much more heavily on public transit than do poor whites. Location does play an important role, however. Within any racial and poverty category, those working or living in the central city rely more upon public transit than those outside the central city. For whites, after controlling for commuting patterns, poverty increases public transit use only for those living in the central city, and the increase is generally small. For blacks, poverty has a larger and more systematic effect on transit mode. Being both poor and black has a marked effect on public transit use, especially among central city residents.

These differences in commute mode have a large impact on the time

Table 13-9. *Public Transit Usage Rates in 1990, by Workplace, Residential Location, Race, and Poverty Status*
(percent)

	Nonpoverty households living in			Poverty households living in		
Work in	Central city	Inter-mediate	Suburb	Central city	Inter-mediate	Suburb
All workers						
Central city	21.1	9.9	10.3	28.1	12.6	11.7
Intermediate	5.6	1.5	1.4	13.6	5.5	4.3
Suburb	7.4	2.5	1.7	18.4	5.8	5.7
White workers						
Central city	15.6	8.9	9.4	17.7	8.6	7.3
Intermediate	3.2	1.0	1.0	8.8	3.5	2.3
Suburb	3.7	1.2	1.1	8.9	2.0	2.5
Black workers						
Central city	31.3	12.7	16.3	40.0	21.5	25.0
Intermediate	12.7	5.5	5.2	27.3	12.8	14.7
Suburb	16.0	6.9	6.6	32.6	8.3	13.2

Source: Census Bureau (1992).

spent commuting. Table 13-10 presents one-way commute times by residence-workplace pairs and commute mode for 1990. Within any residence-workplace pair, commuting by public transit takes considerably more time than traveling by car. The commute for workers who live and work in the central city is twice as long by public transit as it is by car, amounting to more than an hour a day. For noncentral city residents working in the central city, the public transit commute times are frequently much longer.

The role of the public transit system itself in commute times can be seen by examining commute times for nontransit users. Here, for all categories of workers, commute times are always considerably shorter for within-area commutes. For public transit users, the commute times do not vary in such a systematic way. Clearly, spatial distance is not the prime determinant of commute time.

Examining differences by poverty status, for each mode choice, nonpoor whites have longer commutes than do poor whites. This is consistent with expectations about income and residential choices. We find much smaller differences among blacks, however.

Holding poverty status constant, there remains a difference in com-

Table 13-10. *Average Duration of Commute for Metropolitan Area Workers in 1990, by Transit Mode, Workplace, Residential Location, Race, and Poverty Status*

(minutes)

	Use public transit and live in			Use other modes and live in		
Work in	Central city	Inter-mediate	Suburb	Central city	Inter-mediate	Suburb
Nonpoverty households						
All workers						
Central city	40.1	53.1	52.1	19.6	29.9	29.1
Intermediate	40.1	32.1	41.2	23.5	18.3	24.1
Suburb	42.1	38.1	37.2	25.1	28.8	20.7
White workers						
Central city	37.9	54.5	53.2	18.5	30.4	29.0
Intermediate	37.9	31.7	42.2	23.0	18.3	24.4
Suburb	39.9	37.9	36.6	24.9	29.6	20.3
Black workers						
Central city	42.4	44.2	48.6	21.9	29.4	30.0
Intermediate	40.9	32.6	40.4	25.1	19.0	25.4
Suburb	42.9	35.2	37.5	27.0	29.0	22.6
Poverty households						
All workers						
Central city	38.2	43.7	40.9	18.8	25.7	26.3
Intermediate	41.9	30.4	34.3	21.0	17.0	21.9
Suburb	41.2	34.4	34.4	24.0	25.9	19.0
White workers						
Central city	35.6	50.2	38.1	16.4	26.8	25.9
Intermediate	36.2	29.7	35.4	19.3	16.6	22.3
Suburb	31.9	35.7	26.9	23.1	26.7	18.3
Black workers						
Central city	40.0	44.4	40.9	20.3	24.2	25.8
Intermediate	45.5	31.8	36.1	21.6	17.4	21.8
Suburb	42.5	33.6	39.9	24.1	26.4	20.6

Source: Census Bureau (1992). "Other modes" include private car.

mute times across the races. Within each residence-workplace pair, blacks commuting by car travel slightly longer than do whites commuting by car. This is also true for public transit commuters in almost all categories—always for central city residents. The commute time differences suggest

Table 13-11. *Poverty Rates and Poverty Concentrations, 1970, 1980, and 1990*

(percent)

Category	1970	1980	1990
Poverty rate for all residents			
All	10.3	12.4	12.8
White	10.3	9.0	9.0
Black	34.6	29.9	29.1
Hispanic	24.4	23.6	24.7
Poverty rate for metropolitan residents			
All	10.9	11.1	11.8
White	7.7	7.4	7.5
Black	28.1	27.0	26.4
Hispanic	21.4	22.6	23.9
Percent of poor living in poor neighborhoods			
All	12.4	13.6	17.9
White	2.9	3.3	6.3
Black	26.1	28.2	33.5
Hispanic	23.6	19.2	22.1

Source: Jargowsky (1997: tables 2-2, 2-3, and 2-4). Poor neighborhoods are those with poverty rates of 40 percent or more.

that either residential or workplace options for black households are more constrained than for whites.

Finally, since publication of the AAAS report in 1968, some researchers have examined the spatial concentration and isolation of poverty households—the increasing numbers of the poor who live in neighborhoods with other poor people and are isolated from those who are not poor. For example, Jargowsky compared census data for 1970 and 1990 and found that the number of census tracts with poverty rates greater than 40 percent more than doubled and that the total number of persons living in such areas almost doubled.[14] Although the majority of poor do not live in these areas, the share who do has increased from 12 to 18 percent (table 13-11). This increase was not distributed equally among different demographic groups. Although the percent of white poor living in high poverty tracts

14. Jargowsky (1997). See also Wilson (1987).

more than doubled in this time period, it started from a low level; in 1990 only 6.3 percent of white poor lived in areas of concentrated poverty, compared with a third of the black poor.

Increased concentrations of urban poverty in particular neighborhoods changes those neighborhoods in ways that may affect the production of human capital—the quality of schools, the rates of crime, the availability of role models, and so forth. Furthermore, the lower employment levels and the dearth of informal contact with employed people in these neighborhoods undoubtedly creates obstacles for informal job search and acquisition of general labor market knowledge.

To summarize the trends apparent from the 1970 and 1990 data: the observed decentralization of jobs and the centralization of minority and poor households that caused concern in the 1960s has clearly persisted. Jobs, particularly those available for low-skill workers, are increasingly located outside central cities. The residences of minorities and poor have also decentralized, although not nearly as much as jobs, and their car ownership rate has increased. The one condition, however, that has irrefutably worsened, and that may be of increasing labor market importance, is the spatial concentration and isolation of the poor themselves.

Empirical Evidence since 1970

As the shape of urban areas has evolved, so too has the academic literature assessing its consequences on access to jobs for the poor. Kain's original work in 1968 showing a connection between inadequate transportation and unemployment was rather quickly challenged and subjected to reanalysis—using the same data, using better data, and using completely different (sometimes even contradictory) models.[15]

---

15. For example, Offner and Saks (1971) soon established that small changes in the statistical model led to large changes in the estimates of jobs lost by black workers. Others emphasized that the average access of black urban workers to urban jobs was no worse than the access of white workers or disputed the extent of suburbanization of low-skilled jobs (Fremon, 1970; Noll, 1970). Still others enriched the simple model of relative employment in a variety of ways. For example, Mooney (1969) analyzed the average ratio of employment to population in ghetto census tracts in large metropolitan areas. Masters (1975) devoted an entire monograph to the analysis of the effect of segregation on the relative incomes of black and white males. Harrison (1972, 1974) compared the earnings of black and white households residing in suburban and central city neighborhoods. Vrooman and Greenfield (1980) found that suburban black residents had substantially higher earnings than black residents of central cities. This finding was confirmed in a more credible analysis by Price and Mills (1985), who

Analyses of data from the 1980 Census provided important additional data. Leonard, for example, related average commute times for a large sample of census tracts in California's Los Angeles and Orange counties to a variety of aggregate sociodemographic characteristics, including the percentage of residents who were black or Asian, the proportion of local blue collar or manufacturing jobs, commuting modes, and several measures of accessibility. [16] He found a negative and significant relationship between the average distance to jobs in a census tract and the commute times of residents of the tract. He also found, however, a positive relationship between the percent black in a neighborhood and average commute times—a relationship that was robust to a variety of specifications of job access as well as measures of other demographic conditions. Thus, for a given distribution of surrounding jobs, black workers had longer commutes than whites. Leonard concluded that active discrimination in employment, not accessibility per se, caused blacks to search further afield, on average, to find employment.

Ihlanfeldt and Sjoquist analyzed annual earnings (net of commuting costs) of heads of households living in the central city as a function of individual demographic factors, and metropolitanwide data on employment, racial composition, and job location, all taken from the 1980 Census.[17] They found that job decentralization reduced the net incomes of both white and black male workers. For low-skilled workers, the magnitude of the estimated effect was large. For female workers the effects of job decentralization on net earnings were much smaller.

An influential book by Wilson, published in 1987, drew further attention to the isolation of the inner city poor whose access to jobs, schools, and decent neighborhoods had declined. In *The Truly Disadvantaged*, Wilson described the hopelessness of those "left behind" as the more able had left decaying neighborhoods. His rich verbal analysis points to a major scientific problem in the interpretation of those studies relating the spatial access of locations to the employment and earnings of individuals. It is certainly possible, as Wilson argued, that those with weak attachments to

---

reported about a one-third difference in the annual earnings of black and white full-time male workers. Of this, five or six percentage points (or almost 18 percent) could be attributed to central city-suburban residential patterns. All of these findings were based upon data collected in the 1950s, 1960s, and 1970s.

16. Leonard (1987).
17. Ihlanfeldt and Sjoquist (1989).

the labor force "choose" to live in less accessible neighborhoods. Indeed, because housing in more accessible neighborhoods is more expensive, those who "plan" less attachment to the labor market are better off living where job access is reduced. This statement about sample selectivity may seem callous to those who are not disabled by training in the dismal science, but it is, of course, exactly the logical implication of Wilson's argument.

Thus, sample selectivity, by itself, could provide a logical explanation for the findings previously reported—suburban black residents with higher earnings than inner city residents, ghetto residents with lower levels of labor force participation and employment. Many of the implications of sample selectivity can be overcome by the detailed measurement of household demographic factors, in an attempt "to hold constant" their effects. Nevertheless, the possibility of selectivity bias opens to some question the interpretation of much of the evidence comparing the labor market outcomes for adult workers.

If this sample selectivity issue is important, then evidence on the labor market outcomes for youth living at home is potentially quite important. It is implausible to expect that such youth have chosen their residential sites in response to the calculus described above. It is more reasonable to presume that their residential locations are given exogenously (by the "choices"—perhaps severely constrained—made by their parents). Youth take their neighborhood locations and their job access as givens and search for employment. If inadequate spatial access impairs labor market opportunity, that should be reflected in the labor market outcomes of teenagers. The effects, if any, cannot be attributed to nonrandom sampling.

Ellwood's study of the employment of Chicago youth provided the first quantitative evidence on this issue. Using 1970 census tract data, Ellwood related percentages of out-of-school youth who had jobs to three measures of access: the number of jobs within a half-hour commute by public transit; the neighborhood job-to-resident ratio; and the average commute time for neighborhood residents. In a series of multiple regressions, controlling for a variety of aggregate socioeconomic characteristics, the three proximity measures were statistically significant. Yet none explained a substantial share of the variation in youth employment rates. Ellwood interprets: "the result is not consistent with a model in which the likelihood of finding a job is sharply reduced when jobs are not located very nearby."[18]

18. Ellwood (1986: 172).

The most important determinant of youth employment rates in these models was the racial composition of the census tract. Ellwood reestimated the model to allow for fixed neighborhood effects, and the result persisted. After controlling for any neighborhood-specific effects, the effect of the racial variable was at least as important as before.

A third test of the link between access and youth employment relied upon the differences in spatial access to employment between the West and South Sides of Chicago. Ellwood used data from the 1970 Census Employment Surveys (CES) to evaluate a "natural experiment," finding essentially no improvement in the labor market outcomes for youth living in the far more accessible West Side over those living in the South Side. Finally, Ellwood used the 1970 CES to analyze the employment patterns of workers of differing races, finding that racial differences swamped all other differentials.[19]

Leonard replicated part of Ellwood's analysis using aggregate data from the 1980 Census for Los Angeles.[20] Leonard related average youth employment rates by census tract to measures of job proximity and to the aggregate socioeconomic characteristics of the tract's residents. Leonard measured job access by the number of blue collar jobs within a fifteen-minute commute as a fraction of resident adults. In common with Ellwood's study—in a very different city a decade earlier—Leonard found highly significant effects of job access on average youth employment rates, but the magnitudes were also quite small. Using aggregate census tract data, the effects of job proximity on the employment outcomes for youth were estimated to be quite small.

In contrast to these studies using aggregate data, those based upon the analysis of more recent microeconomic data on individuals and their households have found sizeable effects. Ihlanfeldt and Sjoquist have conducted a series of analyses based upon the Public Use Micro Sample (PUMS) of the 1980 Census and the National Longitudinal Sample of Youth cohorts for 1981–82. For example, they used PUMS data for at-home youth in forty-three metropolitan statistical areas to relate individual employment probabilities to the average travel times of low-wage workers who live in their neighborhoods and to a variety of individual and household characteristics.[21] They also included measures of metropolitan occupational structure

---

19. Ellwood's careful analysis has been criticized by Leonard (1986a), Kasarda (1989), and Kain (1992). None of these criticisms is really damaging.

20. Leonard (1986b).

21. Ihlanfeldt and Sjoquist (1991).

and unemployment rates. In these statistical models, average commuting time was an important predictor of youth employment; differential commuting times between black and white youth were reflected in differential employment rates.

In a related paper, the same authors estimated a more detailed empirical model using 1980 PUMS data for Philadelphia.[22] Again, measures of neighborhood commuting time proved to be important predictors of youth employment. The authors were also able to estimate a version of this model for 1980 for Chicago and for the Los Angeles metropolitan area. Their results establish the importance of access in affecting employment—in contrast to the results obtained earlier for the same urban areas by Ellwood and by Leonard using more primitive methods.

Holloway used the Ihlanfeldt and Sjoquist methodology more recently in an analysis of youth employment in fifty metropolitan statistical areas in 1980 and 1990.[23] Holloway confirmed the importance of neighborhood commute time as a predictor of male youth employment. Steven Raphael's recent analyses of Oakland introduced several more sophisticated measures of youth employment access, documenting a growing spatial disadvantage of black households in an expanding metropolitan area.[24] This analysis is also based on microdata from the 1990 Census.

In a series of recent papers, we have extended these analyses of youth employment using data from the 1990 Census and a more comprehensive definition of accessibility.[25] As several researchers have emphasized, most information about employment is disseminated informally through contacts—friends, relatives, and associates.[26] Some, perhaps most, of these contacts are residence-based.[27] Thus, the labor market access of youth living in neighborhoods of high unemployment or low labor force attachment is likely to be impaired. Individuals with whom these youth have informal contact are likely to impart less information about employment opportunities than those in other neighborhoods.

We tested the importance of these various dimensions of accessibility upon youth employment outcomes by matching the census records of individual at-home youth and their families in four New Jersey metropolitan

---

22. Ihlanfeldt and Sjoquist (1990).
23. Holloway (1996).
24. Raphael (1998 a, b).
25. O'Regan and Quigley (1996a, b, 1998).
26. See Holzer (1987), O'Regan (1993), and Fernandez and Harris (1992).
27. Granovetter (1974).

statistical areas to neighborhood information provided by census tract aggregates and also to job proximity information.[28] The access of each census tract to metropolitan employment was computed by census tract from zone-to-zone commute flows for the metropolitan areas. Other neighborhood characteristics were measured by census tract aggregates—the percent white, percent poor, percent on public assistance, percent unemployed, and the percent of adults not working.

We analyzed two outcome measures—employment and "idleness" (that is, not employed and not enrolled in school)—for white, black, and Hispanic youth aged sixteen through nineteen. For the four metropolitan areas we studied, the results were remarkably similar. First, the social access (or spatial concentration of the poor and unemployed) and job proximity of neighborhoods made a substantial difference in the employment or idleness probabilities of youth. Job proximity per se was more important in predicting employment or idleness for black youth than for Hispanics or whites. Second, each of the other measures of the demographic or social composition of neighborhoods "mattered" in the employment of youth—regardless of race. All else being equal, teenagers who live in neighborhoods with larger fractions of adults on public assistance or larger fractions of adults not working have lower probabilities of employment and higher probabilities of idleness.

Third, the combined effects of poor social access and inaccessible residential locations greatly affect minority employment. For example, the "average Newark youth" (that is, one with the average level of education and training and household characteristics) had about a 44 percent employment probability if he or she lived in the "average neighborhood" in which white youth reside. But employment probability declined to 37 percent if the youth lived in the average Hispanic neighborhood and to 33 percent if the youth lived in the average black neighborhood.

Fourth, and perhaps most crucial: the largest source of differences in the employment probabilities of white and black youth is the systematic variation in the measured human capital and household attributes of youth. Roughly two-thirds of the difference in black-white youth employment rates in the metropolitan areas studied was attributable to differences in

28. This matching was accomplished by building and analyzing a linked data set within the Census Bureau, thereby preserving the confidentiality of respondents (but also linking individual records to census tract identifiers).

education and training. The other third arose from variations in spatial proximity to jobs and from social access.[29]

The importance of these neighborhood factors helps explain why more recent empirical studies find spatial effects on labor markets. These empirical findings may not arise from improved methodology but rather from the ability to measure an increasingly important factor in urban labor markets.

Policy Insights: Past Lessons and Current Prospects

Policy interventions to address this isolation can take one of three forms: moving people to jobs (integrating the suburbs); moving jobs to people (redeveloping central cities), or improving the *movement* of central city residents to suburban jobs (improving transportation access).

The first option addresses directly both neighborhood and access concerns. Although results from one such program—the Gatreaux project, currently being replicated in ten cities—do suggest improved employment outcomes, large-scale integration of the suburbs faces serious political opposition.[30] Conversely, widespread political support for large-scale redevelopment is hindered by economic feasibility. We address here the third of these approaches, focusing on transportation interventions.

When Meyer first analyzed transportation and poverty, a variety of "demonstrations" or "experiments" were under way, seeking to address the imbalance between where people lived and where potentially they might work.[31] Several of these demonstrations were funded by the federal government in direct response to the McCone Commission report on the Los Angeles riots.

The earliest projects were community-based efforts to improve bus service. For example, one demonstration provided express bus service be-

---

29. O'Regan and Quigley (1998). Although the relative importance of transportation access versus neighborhood characteristics varied across cities, the latter effect was dominant. Overall, the independent effect of transportation access generally accounted for about six percentage points of the observed employment differences across race and ethnicity.

30. Rosenbaum and Popkin (1991); Ladd and Ludwig (1997).

31. The AAAS report describes several demonstrations initiated in 1966 and 1967 that were a substantial departure from historical practice. The federal government played a very minor role in urban transit, until 1961, when federal transit aid was first authorized; capital investment subsidies were first appropriated in 1965. It was only in 1967, however, that some began to see federal transport policy as a way to combat poverty.

tween the growing industrial parks in Nassau and Suffolk counties in New York and concentrations of low-income populations in Long Beach, Hempstead, Hicksville, and other parts of Long Island close to the central city. Similar experiments using express buses were undertaken in Boston, Los Angeles, and St. Louis, among other places.

The overwhelming consensus is that these projects of the 1960s and 1970s demonstrated only meager success, at best.[32] According to one report, many of the job openings at the suburban destinations of new express bus programs remained unfilled.[33] Minimum wage jobs with no scope for advancement remained unattractive because bus commute times could not be shortened enough to reduce the reservation wages of potential workers. Second, as indicated in the previous section, a more important obstacle to the employment of urban poor and ghetto residents was the lack of skills and education required to qualify for nonmenial suburban jobs.

A few demonstrations were successful in increasing the employment opportunities of the poor, but, ironically, these projects were not financially viable. When the unemployed obtained jobs under these experimental programs, they were likely to use their earnings to buy autos to economize on commuting times. Thus, an experiment "successful" in alleviating poverty might have few riders and a larger deficit than other routes serving stable middle-income workers. Maintaining adequate numbers of riders on such reverse commute lines then required the continual recruitment of new riders.

More recent reverse commute programs have taken a much wider range of forms. In a study of those projects specifically focused on inner-city employment, Rosenbloom confirms that transportation is not the only obstacle to employment and perhaps not even the primary one.[34] Those programs that succeeded in increasing employment did not merely improve transport access. Rather, transportation was one component in a package of employment services provided. And the transportation provided was generally transitional. Establishing a financially viable permanent transportation system was usually not an objective of the program.

These conclusions from policy demonstrations are consistent with the research findings. Job access does play a role in gaining employment, at least for youth, but none of the research suggests it is the primary determi-

---

32. Gómez-Ibáñez and Meyer (1981); Altshuler, Womack, and Pucher (1979).
33. Blake (1989).
34. Rosenbloom (1992).

nant. Individual characteristics (education, job skills) and labor market conditions (unemployment, industry mix) clearly dominate. This finding suggests that transportation policies pursued in isolation may be largely unsuccessful.

One example of a more comprehensive approach to job access is provided by the Public/Private Ventures' "Bridges to Work Program," located in several cities around the nation. Participants are given counseling and assistance with job search, and the program emphasizes creative, locally designed interventions to meet transportation needs. Another example, which has yet to be implemented, is the Clinton administration's Access to Jobs program, a response to welfare reform and to the increased pressure to place large numbers of welfare recipients in jobs.[35] Although comprehensive transportation planning is the major emphasis, the program envisions not only improved access to jobs, but also access to the related support services necessary for attaining and sustaining employment.

New Jersey has already adopted a similar approach. As part of a larger state welfare reform, which provides a collection of poverty services, the state identifies and addresses transportation needs by using a geographic information system to map welfare recipients, their prospective employers, and ancillary support services (day care centers, employment and training services, and educational institutions). This program is too new for its effectiveness to have been tested. But its basis in transport research is clear.

A policy proposal to increase automobile ownership among the poor may offer real promise. For dispersed employment, automobile ownership is the best solution for the nonpoor, and it may have large employment effects for the poor as well. For example, in a survey of lower-skilled workers in the Detroit area, Farley, Holzer, and Danziger specifically focused on job search patterns.[36] They found systematic differences in the search patterns of the unemployed who owned cars compared with the unemployed who did not. Those with cars searched for work over a wider range of areas, and this wider range affected the type, number, and character of job opportunities discovered. Differences in auto ownership also seem to have affected success in a recent program designed for noncustodial fathers of children on welfare. Participants in the program were provided job and training assistance. The Manpower Demonstration Research Corporation's

35. This new program was funded under the Job Access and Reverse Commute Grants portion of the Transportation Equity Act for the 21st Century, which was signed into law on June 9, 1998.
36. Farley, Holzer, and Danziger (1995).

analysis of attrition concluded that car ownership was an important pre-requisite to participation in the program and to successful labor market outcomes.[37]

Currently, auto ownership is lowest among the poor who are recipients of welfare. Family asset limitations under the previous welfare law made owning a functioning car difficult. Under the current welfare system, states have broad latitude to determine asset limits, and many of them have adjusted those limits so that car ownership is not precluded; other states have eliminated this restriction completely. These reforms open the door to car ownership solutions.

Some areas have gone further in encouraging car ownership among welfare recipients. Philadelphia, for example, has created a donation system, where cars donated to welfare recipients are inspected for serviceability by mechanics from a local car dealership. Perhaps the most impressive system is in Kentucky, where fleets of cars donated to welfare recipients by corporations are repaired and maintained by students at local technical schools as part of auto mechanic training courses. Other states, less supportive of car ownership, which could burden welfare recipients with high repair and insurance costs, are creating "car clubs," in which a car is shared among a group of welfare recipients. Again, the impact of these programs is unknown, and at this point the number of participants is quite limited.

Conclusion

The 1968 AAAS report organized by John Meyer focused systematic attention on the link between inadequate transportation and urban poverty. In the ensuing thirty years, data trends suggest that access to employment by poor and minority households has declined. Jobs have continued to decentralize—much faster than the suburbanization of the low-income population. Low-skill jobs in particular are now less available in central city locations. Although automobile ownership has increased overall, among the central city poor—particularly minorities—car ownership is not high, and convenient public transit options are limited. Documentation of most of these trends is available only through 1990, but there is no reason to expect that these trends have been disrupted. The causal evidence accumulated since Meyer's report reinforces those insights about the effects of ur-

37. See Brock and others (1997).

ban space upon employment outcomes and incomes. A variety of cross-sectional analyses based on aggregate census data and, more recently, on microdata on individual workers has sought to quantify the importance of these linkages. As with most social science research, more sophisticated analyses of access and employment reveal more complexities and ambiguities in their effects.

In our assessment, this literature establishes that limitations on access experienced by low-income and minority workers do affect labor market outcomes. The literature based on the behavior of adults in the labor market is equivocal in its quantitative conclusions and is, for technical reasons such as sample selectivity, more ambiguous in its interpretation. For this reason, we are more persuaded by more recent microeconomic analyses based on the behavior of youth. Our conclusion about the strength of the link between transport access and poverty is more confident than the ambivalent summary by Jencks and Mayer (1990), but their assessment was made before much of the research on teenage employment was available.

These results relating to youth probably overstate the importance of spatial access in affecting the behavior of adults. Presumably, adults have some greater level of mobility (both residential relocation and adaption of transportation options) than youth. In terms of employment mobility, it is not clear whether adjustment is easier for youth or adults; work experience increases the probability of employment, but it also increases job specificity, which could make it harder to find employment if labor market conditions change. And there may be reason to think that observations on cross-sections of individuals understate the impact of space, which could increase over time. Because they are less likely to be able to take advantage of turnover in the labor market, and advancement achieved through the progression to new, better jobs, long-time residency in neighborhoods that lack access to jobs may have a more pronounced impact on labor market outcomes. Studies that compared youth who recently moved into such a neighborhood with those who had lived in the neighborhood more than five years found that neighborhood influences appeared larger for the longer-term residents.[38] In addition, the increased employment noted in the Gatreaux project applied to both youth and adults. Our knowledge base is too limited at this point, however, to draw confident conclusions for adults.

Furthermore, other factors beyond transportation are more important in affecting the employment of low-income and minority workers. Educa-

---

38. O'Regan and Quigley (1998).

tion, training, skills, and the overall health of the economy are all more important in affecting the labor market outcomes of disadvantaged workers than is transportation or access per se. As a result many of the most important policies to improve the labor market access of disadvantaged workers may not be transportation policies at all. Policies directed toward eliminating obstacles to the construction of low-cost housing in the suburbs and enforcing equal opportunity in the housing market may be more effective than policies emphasizing the daily movement of people in urban areas.

References

Altshuler, Alan A., with James P. Womack and John R. Pucher. 1979. *The Urban Transportation System: Politics and Policy Innovation.* MIT Press.

AAAS (American Academy of Arts and Sciences). 1968. "Conference on Poverty and Transportation." PB-180-956. U.S. Department of Commerce, Clearinghouse for Federal Scientific and Technical Information, Washington, D.C.

Blake, Stephen. 1989. "Inner City Minority Transit Needs in Accessing Suburban Employment Centers: Final Report." National Association of Regional Councils, Washington, D.C. March.

Brock, Thomas, and others. 1997. "Creating New Hope: Implementation of a Program to Reduce Poverty and Reform Welfare." Manpower Demonstration Research Corporation, New York. October.

Census Bureau. 1973. *Census of Population 1970, Subject Reports.* Final Report PC(2)-9(A), Low-Income Population. U.S. Department of Commerce.

———. 1992. *Census of Population and Housing, 1990, Public Use Microdata Sample, U.S.* (machine readable data files).

Ellwood, David. 1986. "The Spatial Mismatch Hypothesis: Are There Teenage Jobs Missing in the Ghetto?" In *The Black Youth Employment Crisis,* edited by Richard B. Freeman and Harry J. Holzer, 147–85. University of Chicago Press.

Farley, Reynolds, Harry J. Holzer, and Sheldon Danziger. 1995. "Detroit Divided: Race, Location, and Skills in the Housing and Labor Markets." Unpublished paper.

Fernandez, Roberto M., and David Harris. 1992. "Social Isolation and the Underclass." In *Drugs, Crime, and Social Isolation: Barriers to Urban Opportunity,* edited by Adele V. Harrell and George E. Peterson, 257–93. Washington, D.C.: Urban Institute.

Fremon, Charlotte. 1970. *Occupational Patterns in Urban Employment Change, 1965–1967.* Report 2662. Washington, D.C.: Urban Institute. August.

Gómez-Ibáñez, José A., and John R. Meyer. 1981. *Autos, Transit, and Cities.* Harvard University Press.

Granovetter, Mark S. 1974. *Getting a Job: A Study of Contacts and Careers.* Harvard University Press.

Harrison, Bennet. 1972. "The Intrametropolitan Distribution of Minority Economic Welfare." *Journal of Regional Science* 12 (April): 23–43.

———. 1974. *Urban Economic Development: Suburbanization, Minority Opportunity, and the Conditions of the Central City.* Washington, D.C.: Urban Institute.

Holloway, Steven R. 1996. "Job Accessibility and Male Teenage Employment, 1980–1990: The Declining Significance of Space?" *Professional Geographer* 48 (November): 445–58.

Holzer, Harry J. 1987. "Informal Job Search and Black Youth Unemployment." *American Economic Review* 77 (June): 446–52.

———. 1996. *What Employers Want: Job Prospects for Less-Educated Workers.* New York: Russell Sage Foundation.

Ihlanfeldt, Keith R., and David L. Sjoquist. 1989. "The Impact of Job Decentralization on the Economic Welfare of Central City Blacks." *Journal of Urban Economics* 26 (July): 110–30.

———. 1990. "Job Accessibility and Racial Differences in Youth Employment Rates." *American Economic Review* 80 (March): 267–76.

———. 1991. "The Effect of Job Access on Black and White Youth Employment: A Cross-Sectional Analysis." *Urban Studies* 28 (April): 255–65.

Jargowsky, Paul. 1997. *Poverty and Place: Ghetto, Barrios, and the American City.* New York: Russell Sage Foundation.

Jencks, Christopher, and Susan E. Mayer. 1990. "Residential Segregation, Job Proximity, and Black Job Opportunities." In *Inner City Poverty in the United States,* edited by Laurence E. Lynn, Jr., and Michael G.H. McGeary. Washington, D.C.: National Academy Press.

Kain, John F. 1964. "The Effect of the Ghetto on the Distribution and Level of Nonwhite Employment in Urban Areas." *Proceedings, Social Statistics Section of the American Statistical Association,* 260–71. Washington, D.C.

———. 1968. "Housing Segregation, Negro Employment, and Metropolitan Decentralization." *Quarterly Journal of Economics* 82 (May): 175–97.

———. 1992. "The Spatial Mismatch Hypothesis: Three Decades Later." *Housing Policy Debate* 3 (2): 371–460.

Kain, John F., and John R. Meyer. 1970. "Transportation and Poverty." *The Public Interest* 18 (Winter): 75–87.

Kasarda, John D. 1989. "Urban Industrial Transition and the Underclass." *Annals of the American Academy of Political and Social Science* 501 (January): 26–47.

———. 1995. "Industrial Restructuring and the Changing Location of Jobs." In *Economic Trends.* Vol. 1 of *State of the Union: America in the 1990s,* edited by Reynolds Farley, 215–67. New York: Russell Sage Foundation.

Ladd, Helen F., and Jens Ludwig. 1997. "Federal Housing Assistance, Residential Relocation, and Educational Opportunities: Evidence from Baltimore." *American Economic Review* 87 (May): 272–77.

Leonard, Jonathan S. 1986a. "Comments to David Ellwood." In *The Black Youth Employment Crisis,* edited by Richard B. Freeman and Harry J. Holzer, 185–90. University of Chicago Press.

———. 1986b. "Space, Time, and Unemployment: Los Angeles 1980." Unpublished paper. University of California, Berkeley, Haas School of Business.

———. 1987. "The Interaction of Residential Segregation and Employment Discrimination." *Journal of Urban Economics* 21 (May): 323–46.

Masters, Stanley H. 1975. *Black-White Income Differentials: Empirical Studies and Policy Implications.* New York: Academic Press.

Meyer, John R., John F. Kain, and Martin Wohl. 1965. *The Urban Transportation Problem.* Harvard University Press.

Mooney, Joseph D. 1969. "Housing Segregation, Negro Employment, and Metropolitan Decentralization: An Alternative Perspective." *Quarterly Journal of Economics* 83 (May): 299–311.

Noll, Roger. 1970. "Metropolitan Employment and Population Distribution and the Conditions of the Working Poor." In *Financing the Metropolis: Public Policy in Urban Economics,* edited by John Crecine, 481–509. Vol. 4 of *Urban Affairs Annual Reviews.* Beverly Hills, Calif.: Sage Publications.

Offner, Paul, and Daniel H. Saks. 1971. "A Note on John Kain's 'Housing Segregation, Negro Employment, and Metropolitan Decentralization.'" *Quarterly Journal of Economics* 85 (February): 147–60.

O'Regan, Katherine M. 1993. "The Effect of Social Networks and Concentrated Poverty on Black and Hispanic Youth Unemployment." *Annals of Regional Science* 27 (December): 327–42.

O'Regan, Katherine M., and John M. Quigley. 1996a. "Teenage Employment and the Spatial Isolation of Minority and Poverty Households." *Journal of Human Resources* 31 (Summer): 692–702.

———. 1996b. "Spatial Effects upon Employment Outcomes: The Case of New Jersey Teenagers." *New England Economic Review* (May/June): 41–57.

———. 1998. "Where Youth Live: Economic Effects of Urban Space on Employment Prospects." *Urban Studies* 35 (June): 1187–1205.

Pisarski, Alan E. 1996. "Commuting in America II: The Second National Report on Commuting Patterns and Trends." Eno Transportation Foundation, Inc., Washington, D.C.

Price Richard, and Edwin S. Mills. 1985. "Race and Residence in Earnings Determination." *Journal of Urban Economics* 17 (January): 1–18.

Raphael, Steven. 1998a. "The Spatial Mismatch Hypothesis and Black Youth Joblessness: Evidence from the San Francisco Bay Area." *Journal of Urban Economics* 43 (January): 79–111.

———. 1998b. "Intervening Opportunities, Competing Searchers, and the Intra Metropolitan Flow of Male Teenage Labor." *Journal of Regional Science* 38 (February): 43–49.

Rosenbaum, James E., and Susan J. Popkin. 1991. "Employment and Earnings of Low Income Blacks Who Move to Middle-Class Suburbs." In *The Urban Underclass,* edited by Christopher Jencks and Paul Peterson, 342–356. Brookings.

Rosenbloom, Sandra. 1992. "Reverse Commute Transportation: Emerging Provider Roles." Report R92–06. University of Arizona, Drachman Institute for Land and Regional Development Studies, Tucson. March.

Vrooman, John, and Stuart Greenfield. 1980. "Are Blacks Making It in the Suburbs? Some New Evidence on Intrametropolitan Spatial Segmentation." *Journal of Urban Economics* 7 (March): 155–67.

Wilson, William Julius. 1987. *The Truly Disadvantaged: The Inner City, the Underclass, and Public Policy.* University of Chicago Press.

PART IV

Regulatory Issues in Transportation

STEVEN A. MORRISON
CLIFFORD WINSTON

14

Regulatory Reform of U.S. Intercity Transportation

R AILROADS ARE becoming profitable and charging
low freight rates, airlines are filling close to 70 per-
cent of their seats, most air travelers are flying at some type of discount
fare, and large trucking firms are setting industry standards for innovative
services and efficient operations. This, the U.S. intercity transportation
system of the 1990s, is decidedly *not* the intercity transportation system of
our fathers. In the 1950s system described by John R. Meyer and his colleagues, railroads provided poor service and earned a low rate of return
regardless of the state of the economy, air travel was a luxury enjoyed by
only a minority of travelers despite technological advances that had dramatically lowered its cost, and motor carrier rates were so high that many
shippers found it more economical to provide their own trucking service.[1]

Meyer and his colleagues were among the first to pinpoint the *common*
source of these problems as economic regulation—government rules on
carriers' prices, entry, and exit. Their research helped lead an intellectual

Parts of this paper draw on and extend Clifford Winston, "U.S. Industry Adjustment to Economic
Deregulation," *Journal of Economic Perspectives*, Summer 1998. The authors are grateful to Thomas
Corsi, Darius Gaskins, and Curtis Grimm for helpful comments.
1. Meyer and others (1959).

crusade to deregulate the transportation industries and other major U.S. industries as well. This paper will show that in the two decades deregulation has been in place, each transportation industry has, in fact, undergone a similar adjustment to deregulation that has enabled it to lower its costs and pass on these cost reductions in the form of lower prices and better service to customers.

The inefficiencies that Meyer and his colleagues attributed to Interstate Commerce Commission (ICC) regulation of railroads and motor carriers and Civil Aeronautics Board (CAB) regulation of airlines gradually attracted the attention of Congress and the White House. By the 1970s—a decade characterized by high inflation—policymakers were taking an active interest in mounting empirical evidence that regulation was responsible for raising airline fares and trucking rates significantly above what they would be in an unregulated environment. This evidence proved influential in congressional hearings and ultimately in congressional legislation that deregulated the airline and motor carrier industries. In fact, Martha Derthick and Paul J. Quirk argue that deregulation "would never have occurred" if economists had not generally supported it through their research.[2]

Policymakers had also become concerned about the railroad industry. Several major bankruptcies had already forced the government to "nationalize" part of it by creating Conrail, and some worried that the industry might have to be completely nationalized. Regulation was seen as inhibiting rail profitability, and policymakers were increasingly convinced that the industry needed much greater pricing and operating freedom if more bankruptcies were to be avoided.

Adherents of the Chicago theory of regulation posit another force for regulatory change. These theorists believe that regulation primarily existed to confer benefits to the regulated industry in exchange for political support for elected officials and regulatory agencies. When regulation no longer served that purpose, or when firms could become more profitable in a less regulated environment, the industries could be expected to support—or at least not actively oppose—regulatory reform.[3] This argument can be made for the railroad industry, but making it for the airline and trucking industries is more difficult because these industries opposed deregulation. At most, some trucking firms and airlines voiced support for deregulation as it drew closer.

---

2. Derthick and Quirk (1985).
3. Peltzman (1989).

Full deregulation did not occur overnight. In the beginning, cautious regulatory agencies tried a variety of experiments and partial deregulatory actions, including CAB liberalization of airline entry and discount fare experiments during the mid-1970s and ICC liberalization of trucking and railroad rates (and railroad contracting) during the late 1970s. Congress followed the regulators' lead with the Airline Deregulation Act of 1978, the Motor Carrier Reform Act of 1980, and the Staggers Rail Act of 1980. Because policymakers expected trucking and airline deregulation to stimulate competition that would generate lower prices, they did not substantially delay full deregulation of these industries once the major deregulatory initiatives were passed. Thus, airline fares, entry, and exit were completely deregulated by 1983, and trucking entry and interstate rates were, in practice, completely deregulated in 1980 (although rates still had to be filed with the ICC; *intra*state rates were not deregulated until 1994).

Policymakers were more ambivalent about railroad deregulation. They believed it would help the industry return to profitability, but they were concerned that railroads might exercise market power and charge some shippers exorbitant rates. Thus, although railroad contract rates were completely deregulated in 1980 (the thinking was that shippers can and should be able to decide for themselves whether they want to enter into negotiations with railroads over the level and terms of their rates), tariff rates for certain commodities are still subject to maximum rate "guidelines."[4] In practice, these guidelines have had little effect on prices because only a handful of rates have ever been successfully challenged.

Regulatory reform of the intercity transportation industries represents a landmark change in federal transportation policy and was the start of one of the most important experiments in economic policy of our time. The outcome of this experiment, which includes deregulation of the financial, energy, and communications industries, has attracted the attention of analysts and policymakers worldwide.

In presenting detailed empirical evidence to substantiate the benefits claimed for deregulation, we note at the outset that our assessment of transportation deregulation—and for that matter any current assessment—will

---

4. The transportation industries are still subject to safety regulation (enforced for airlines by the Federal Aviation Administration and for motor carriers and railroads by the Department of Transportation), and subject to antitrust laws. Congress established the Essential Air Services program in 1978 to assuage concerns that airline service to small communities might disappear under deregulation. Morrison and Winston (1986) point out that the subsidies provided under this program may have been unnecessary.

be incomplete. John Meyer has pointed out many times that it will take the transportation industries decades to shed the inefficiencies that were created under regulation and to develop fully efficient and innovative operating practices. The benefits generated to date are only a portion of the total gains that the United States will eventually reap from deregulation.

Theoretical and Empirical Issues

Why, in theory, have the transportation industries become more efficient as a result of deregulation? Most important, regulation limits competition among firms, which causes an industry to accumulate substantial managerial slack or "X-inefficiency"; that is, firms do not minimize the cost of producing a given level of output. And because regulation shelters an industry from new competitors, innovations in marketing, operations, and technology are limited to incumbent firms. When an industry is deregulated, unrestricted competition among incumbent firms and from new entrants forces the industry to shed its inefficiencies and to become more innovative. In addition, specific regulations can force firms to operate in an inefficient manner. For example, entry barriers prevented airlines and trucking firms from optimally developing their networks, exit barriers prevented railroads from shedding excess capacity, and price regulations prevented all transportation carriers from efficiently marketing their capacity. Finally, regulations prevented carriers from responding effectively to external disturbances such as a recession. To sum up: the transportation industries' adjustment to deregulation is shaped by increased operating freedoms and intensified competition that force them to become more technologically advanced, to adopt more efficient operating and marketing practices, and to respond more effectively to external shocks.

We substantiate these theoretical inferences empirically by first documenting the changes in entry and exit since deregulation of the transportation industries and by identifying how these changes have intensified competition in each industry. We then describe the innovations that transportation carriers have made in the deregulated environment and indicate how these innovations have helped lower industry costs. Finally, we present evidence showing that the increase in carrier competition and improved efficiency due to deregulation have substantially benefited consumers.

Because more extensive and detailed data are collected and publicly available for airlines than for trucking firms and railroads, we are able to go into greater depth in some of our assessments of the effects of airline deregulation than in some of our assessments of the effects of trucking and railroad deregulation. But the general conclusions regarding deregulation's overall effects on U.S. intercity transportation emerge strongly from our analysis.

We focus on the direct impact of deregulation on costs, prices, and service. Because transportation is an input into firms' activities, its deregulation has also affected such matters as firms' inventory policies, the scale of their operations, and the location of their businesses. For example, deregulation has facilitated the widespread use of just-in-time inventory policies, where supplies arrive just when they are needed, slashing inventory costs. Because we are not aware of empirical estimates of these "indirect" effects of deregulation, which are clearly positive, we do not account for them here.

Because intercity transportation regulation and deregulation never existed at the national level at the same time, the most accurate way to measure the economic effects of deregulating an industry is a counterfactual analysis that estimates the price, cost, and service changes that are solely attributable to deregulation and thus *would not have occurred* had an industry still been regulated. Such an analysis can be complicated. It may need to account for the business cycle, for those elements of technological change attributable to deregulation and those not, and for changes in the characteristics of products, including service quality. Some argue that an appropriate counterfactual should also allow for regulators to learn from past errors and for regulation to have improved as it hypothetically continued, although there is little evidence that regulators learn and change this way.

To sidestep such complications, a simpler approach is to perform a "time series" counterfactual by evaluating the changes in *real* costs and prices over time, thus capturing the change in regulatory environments and providing current comparisons. For example, real airline costs in 1977, the first year before legislative deregulation, can be compared with real airline costs for the most recent period during which cost data have been collected. The time series approach is especially credible here because it is applied to roughly twenty years of transportation deregulation experience during which the U.S. economy has undergone a number of contractions and expansions. Although this simpler approach does not constitute a rigorous counterfactual, the conclusions we draw from it are strongly suggestive and qualitatively consistent with the few rigorous counterfactuals that have been performed for the transportation industries using less recent data.

In our analysis, we follow common practice and identify the start of deregulation by the year in which the major deregulatory legislation was passed. But, as noted, some administrative deregulation occurred in each transportation industry before major legislation was passed, implying that some of the benefits from deregulation were actually being realized before formal deregulation occurred. Empirical evidence that is based on the "formal" starting dates therefore tends to understate the benefits from deregulation.

Entry and the Extent of Competition

Regulation restricted entry into transportation markets both by (potential) new entrants to the industry and by incumbent firms. Deregulation allowed entry by both types of firms.

Airlines

We measure changes in airline competition as a result of deregulation by calculating changes in the number of *effective* competitors. This number is the inverse of the Herfindahl index, which is the sum of the square of each airline's market share, and thus converts the number of carriers into the number of *equivalent*-sized carriers.[5]

The number of effective competitors in the airline industry has actually declined since deregulation, from 9.2 in 1977 to 8 in 1996.[6] But deregulation has not necessarily decreased airline *competition*: for it is at the

---

5. Adelman (1969) suggested interpreting an inverted Herfindahl index as a "numbers-equivalent." The index approaches zero in the competitive case with a large number of small firms and equals one in the monopoly case, so its inverse approaches infinity in the competitive case and equals one for monopoly. The inverse may be thought of as giving the number of equivalent-sized competitors that would provide a degree of competition equivalent to that actually observed in the market-share data. The index captures inequality in market shares by summing the square of each airline's market share. For example, if two airlines each have a 50 percent market share, the Herfindahl index is $0.50^2 + 0.50^2$ = 1/2. Inverting this gives 2 (effective competitors). Similarly, the index for three equal-sized airlines is $3 \times 0.33^2 = 1/3$, so inversion gives three effective competitors. But if there were three competitors, with the largest serving 2/3 of the market and the other two each serving 1/6 of the market, the Herfindahl index would be 1/2, which also translates into two effective competitors. Thus the number of effective competitors has a more intuitive interpretation than the Herfindahl index.

6. This figure was calculated by the authors based on U.S. Department of Transportation Data Bank 1A.

Figure 14-1. *Airline Competition at the Route Level*
Number of Effective Competitors

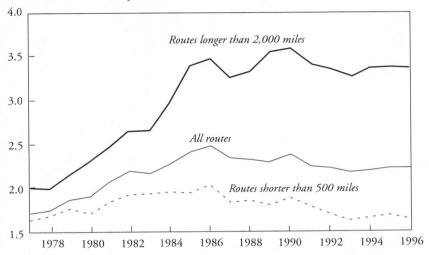

Source: Authors' calculations from data in U.S. Department of Transportation, Data Bank 1A.

route or market level that carriers compete head to head. To ascertain airline competition at the route level, we calculated the number of effective competitors on each route, then averaged over all routes, weighting by passengers. We also performed this calculation for long-distance routes (those greater than 2,000 miles) and for short-distance routes (those less than 500 miles). As figure 14-1 shows, the trend is clear over all routes. Competition increased steadily until mid-1986 and has subsequently decreased somewhat because of mergers and the liquidation of Eastern Air Lines and Pan American World Airways in 1991. Even so, airlines are clearly more competitive at the route level than they were under regulation. Competition, however, has not been uniform on short and long routes. In particular, the number of effective competitors on long-distance routes increased 70 percent between 1977 and 1996, while the number of competitors on short-distance routes increased 2 percent. The discrepancy is not surprising because CAB regulation had elevated fares substantially above costs on long routes and had held fares below costs on short routes. When the industry was deregulated, carriers were naturally attracted to those routes that had high price-cost margins under regulation.

Figure 14-2. *Average Contact by Eight Formerly Regulated Airlines with New Entrants, as Measured by Passenger Miles in City-Pair Markets, 1978–96*

Percentage

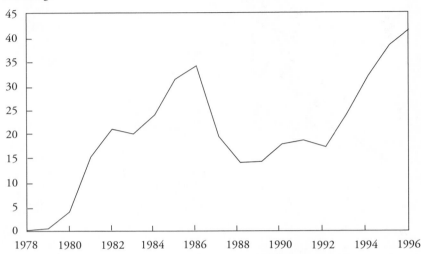

Source: Authors' calculations of the percentage of passenger miles in city-pair markets where formerly regulated airlines compete with new entrants, based on data in U.S. Department of Transportation, Data Bank 1A.

The number of effective competitors on a route is certainly an important indicator of competition among airlines, but the identity of these carriers is also important. A given route may have fewer effective competitors than a route of comparable distance and traffic density but enjoy lower fares because it is served by low-cost (low-fare) carriers. Indeed, as we shall see, the growth of new low-cost carriers, such as Southwest Airlines, has been one of the most important consequences of airline deregulation. Figure 14-2 shows the percentage of passenger miles in city-pair markets where formerly regulated carriers have competed with new entrants. Incumbents' competitive contact with new entrants steadily rose following deregulation, largely because of the growth of People Express. That competitive contact declined after Texas Air Corporation/Continental acquired the low-cost airline in 1986. Incumbents' contact with new entrants began to increase again in the early 1990s because of the growth of Southwest Airlines and other carriers. Thus, under airline deregulation, there are fewer effective competitors nationally, but carriers compete more often at the route level and with new low-cost carriers.

Trucking

Deregulation of less-than-truckload (LTL) trucking has led to changes in industry structure and competition similar to those in airlines. At the national level the number of large (Class I) LTL carriers fell from more than 600 in 1976 to around 50 in 1995.[7] Nonetheless, although figures for specific markets are difficult to obtain, competition in LTL markets has clearly become much more intense since deregulation, both because of the growth of low-cost (nonunion) regional LTL carriers such as Con-Way Transportation Services (in 1995 these carriers were growing at an annual rate of 15 to 20 percent) and because of increased competition from alternative small shipment carriers such as UPS and Federal Express. In the wake of the 1997 UPS strike, Federal Express acquired RPS to compete more effectively for small freight shipments. As shown in figure 14-3, LTL carriers' share of small shipment revenue declined from nearly 60 percent in 1980 to 35 percent in 1995.

The truckload (TL) industry has always been quite competitive, and although the number of competitors has increased since deregulation, from some 20,000 small (Class III) TL carriers in 1980 to nearly 55,000 in 1995, competition has actually intensified because of the growth of national mega-carriers (commonly referred to as advanced truckload carriers). The annual revenues of advanced truckload carriers, such as Landstar, Schneider National, and Consolidated Freightways, have grown to roughly $1 billion each, and these carriers have become so efficient that many companies are finding it more cost effective to abandon their own trucking operations and hire them. For-hire trucking services are now roughly 25 percent less expensive than private carriage, which relies primarily on (more costly) unionized labor, according to estimates from DRI/McGraw-Hill.[8] Private trucking evolved as a response to high regulated truck rates and poor service. The declining market share of these operations indicates the effects of deregulation on competition in the trucking industry.[9]

---

7. Corsi (1996a).
8. Corsi (1996b).
9. Corsi (1996b) reports that, based on revenues, private trucking's market share has declined from 47 percent in 1986 to 42 percent in 1996, and he expects for-hire TL carriers to continue to take market share from private carriers.

Figure 14-3. *Small Shipment Revenue Shares by Type of Commercial Carrier,*
1980–95
Share of total revenues

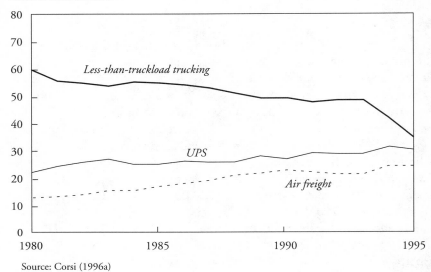

Source: Corsi (1996a)

Railroads

As in the case of airlines and LTL carriers, changes in the number of
railroads at the national level are less of an issue than changes in the intensity of competition at the market level. No large railroad has entered the
industry since deregulation, and the number of railroads at the national
level has declined as existing carriers have continued to merge. The imminent absorption of Conrail by Norfolk Southern and CSX will leave the
United States with four large (Class I) railroads—Norfolk Southern and
CSX in the East, and Burlington Northern-Santa Fe and Union Pacific-
Southern Pacific in the West. Nonetheless, since deregulation the number
of smaller low-cost (nonunion) railroads, such as Montana Rail Link, has
increased substantially; these railroads have formed small systems from track
purchased from large railroads. Railroads also must contend with competition provided by advanced truckload carriers. And competition among
incumbent railroads is much more intense. Darius Gaskins has frequently
pointed out that when he was a Berkeley economics professor, he taught

theories predicting that duopolists had considerable ability to maintain high prices. But as the CEO of Burlington Northern railroad, he learned that duopolists' prices often reflected fierce competition. Rail carriers have enhanced their competitiveness by accelerating their development of intermodal (truck-rail) service, which has increased from roughly 3 million containers in 1980 to more than 7 million containers in 1993.[10]

Innovations

The benefits from deregulating the intercity transportation industries derive from innovations in marketing, operations, and technology that have enabled carriers to become more efficient, improve service quality, introduce new services, and become more responsive to consumers' preferences.

Airlines now set fares based on revenue (yield) management, which has helped carriers increase the percentage of their seats filled by paying passengers (load factor) by offering travelers a wide range of fares from discount fares with various travel restrictions—some of the lowest discount fares are exclusively available on the Internet—to much higher fares with no travel restrictions. Freed from entry and exit regulations, airlines have accelerated their development of hub-and-spoke route networks that feed travelers from all directions into a major airport (hub) from which they take connecting flights to their destinations. Carriers use hub-and-spoke route systems to increase their load factors and, by increasing the number of feasible flight alternatives, to offer travelers much greater service frequency. For example, an additional aircraft departure from a spoke airport to a hub airport can increase the number of flight alternatives on many connecting routes. Finally, airlines have developed computer reservation systems to improve scheduling and flight reservations.

Railroads and trucking firms have negotiated thousands of price-service contracts with shippers, thus tailoring their services to shippers' production and inventory policies and making more efficient use of their own capacity. They have conducted these negotiations by themselves or through third-party logistics firms that analyze shipper distribution patterns and logistics costs and use sophisticated software to determine the lowest-cost routes and the carriers with the lowest rates. These firms also achieve cost savings for shippers by leveraging the volumes of all their clients to obtain

10. Grimm and Windle (1998).

discounts from carriers. During regulation railroad traffic was effectively prevented from moving under contract rates. Today, more than half of all rail traffic moves at a negotiated contract rate.

Improvements in network design and greater use of intermodal operations and double stack rail cars have enabled trucks and railroads to provide faster and more reliable service. And trucks and railroads have become more efficient by using computer information systems to track shipments and route their cargo. Norfolk Southern, for example, once tracked its cars and locomotives by posting a video camera at the entrance to each rail yard. Now, an electronic scanner automatically tracks each car's arrival. Truck drivers for Schneider National who once made scheduled telephone calls to headquarters to receive information now roam the highways with small satellite dishes attached to their cabs and use the data transmitted by technicians in the company's headquarters to track maintenance needs and the location of shipments.

It could be argued that many of the transportation industries' innovations have been the direct result of advances in computer technology and thus would have occurred regardless of deregulation. But the benefits from these advances were realized because deregulated firms had the incentive and operating freedom to design new networks and write computer programs to optimize operations. Under regulation, they had little financial incentive or competitive pressure to do so, and regulators did not design regulations to stimulate innovative activity.

External shocks have also spurred deregulated transportation carriers to improve the efficiency of their operations. A fundamental challenge facing the transportation industries is to match their capacity with demand. The unpredictability of demand, which arises in part because of the business cycle, could be particularly problematic for an industry that must invest in capacity long before actual demand materializes. The airline industry, for example, has made capacity commitments roughly two years in advance because of the lead times needed to acquire aircraft. The unpredictability of demand and the high income elasticity of demand for air travel created overcapacity in the early 1990s, which led to intense fare wars and huge industry losses.[11] Carriers have subsequently adjusted their operations by expanding their capacity more slowly in the face of growing demand. In addition, American and Delta Airlines have made long-term purchasing commitments to Boeing Aircraft, in return for expedited deliv-

11. Morrison and Winston (1995, 1996).

ery of planes. This puts American and Delta in a better position to tailor their capacity to demand.[12] Railroads have used contracts with shippers to align their cars and equipment with shippers' demand and reduce their vulnerability to problems caused by overcapacity.

Effects on Industry Efficiency

By stimulating competition and by giving carriers greater operating freedoms and incentives to become more innovative, deregulation has led to substantial improvements in the efficiency of intercity transportation.

As noted, airlines have made marketing and operating innovations that have significantly increased their load factor. During the decade before deregulation, load factors averaged less than 55 percent. Since deregulation they have averaged more than 60 percent, reaching nearly 70 percent in 1996. More efficient use of inputs, lower labor costs, and greater lengths of haul have enabled air carriers to lower real costs per available ton-mile more than 25 percent since deregulation (figure 14-4). Industry profits are higher under deregulation than they would have been under regulation, but the intensity of competition under deregulation has forced carriers to pass on most of their cost savings to consumers in lower fares.[13]

Trucking firms have achieved higher load factors by optimizing their routings and negotiating price-service packages with shippers to minimize their empty mileage. They have also made more efficient use of inputs and reduced their labor costs. As a result, since 1977, just before administrative deregulatory policies went into effect, LTL carriers' real operating costs have fallen 35 percent and TL carriers' costs have fallen more than 75 percent, largely because of the emergence of advanced truckload carriers (figure 14-5). Of course, deregulation should not be given total credit for all of the cost decline. For example, some of the decline in truckload carriers' operating costs occurred because these carriers largely eliminated the more costly less-than-truckload traffic from their traffic mix. Nonetheless, deregulation does deserve credit for most of the fall in costs. Despite these

---

12. Boeing has agreed not to enforce these commitments as a condition for obtaining the European Commission's approval of its merger with McDonnell-Douglas. American and Delta, however, are unlikely to change their commitments.

13. Morrison and Winston (1995) estimate that during the 1980s annual airline industry profits were $2.6 billion (1988 dollars) higher than they would have been had the industry been regulated.

Figure 14-4. *Real Cost per Available Ton-Mile for U.S. Scheduled Airlines*
1996 dollars

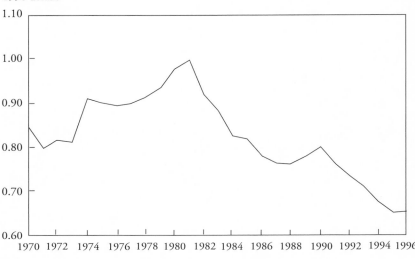

Source: Authors' calculations using data from Air Transport Association, various issues.

cost reductions, trucking profitability has fallen, on average, in both sectors. Not surprisingly, the decline has been much greater for LTL carriers, which were profitable during regulation because they faced little competition from railroads and unregulated private carriers and owner-operators, than for TL carriers, which were not especially profitable during regulation because they did face such competition.[14]

Railroads have negotiated contracts to guarantee return loads and reduce empty backhauls, made much more efficient use of labor, and abandoned one-third of their track miles since deregulation.[15] Real operating costs per ton-mile have fallen steadily, and, as of 1995, operating costs were 60 percent lower than they were when legislative deregulation began in 1980 (figure 14-6). Again, deregulation should not be given total credit for all of the cost decline. Some of it can be attributed to the long-run trend in railroads' traffic mix to include a greater proportion of low-cost bulk traffic.

14. Corsi (1996a, b).
15. Grimm and Windle (1998).

Figure 14-5. *Operating Costs of Less-Than-Truckload and Truckload Carriers, 1977–1995*
1995 dollars per vehicle mile

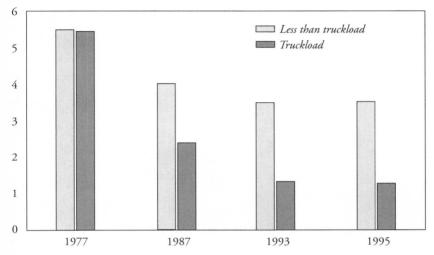

Source: Corsi 1996a, b.

Figure 14-6. *Railroad Operating Costs per Revenue Ton-Mile, 1980–1995*
(1995 dollars)

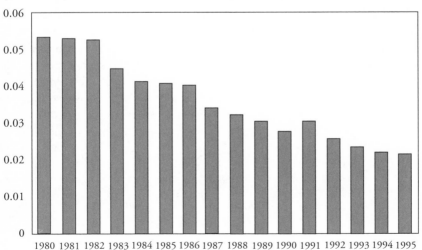

Source: Association of American Railroads (1989, 1996).

In contrast to airlines and trucking firms, but consistent with the objectives of policymakers, rail's cost efficiencies have enabled the industry to become much more profitable under deregulation than it was under regulation. During the last few years of regulation, rail's return on equity was less than 3 percent; in 1995 it was 8.5 percent. Railroads have also stopped the erosion in their market share and started to regain traffic from the trucking industry. During the early 1900s railroads carried roughly 70 percent of the nation's freight. By 1980 this figure had declined to 33 percent but has climbed to 38 percent since deregulation.[16]

Effects on Consumer Welfare

Consumers have turned out to be the primary beneficiaries of intercity transportation deregulation.

Airlines' real average fares have declined about a third since 1976, just before the CAB initiated significant regulatory reforms. To be sure, as shown in figure 14-7, real fares were falling before deregulation, suggesting that fares would have continued to fall without deregulation. But we have found in previous research that deregulation is responsible for roughly 60 percent of the decline in fares since 1976, which implies that fares are 20 percent lower than they would have been had the industry still been regulated.[17]

Although a major source of the fare decline is the general increase in airline competition, the identity of specific competitors is also important. As shown in table 14-1, fare declines have been much greater on routes served by new entrants, especially Southwest Airlines, than on routes served only by formerly regulated carriers. Further analysis shows that the competition by Southwest Airlines accounts for 31 percent of the savings from lower real fares since deregulation; competition by other new entrants, 10 percent; and competition by the established carriers, 18 percent. Improvements in carriers' operating efficiencies account for the remaining 41 percent of the savings.[18]

16. Grimm and Windle (1998), drawing on figures from the Association of American Railroads, *Railroad Facts* (various issues), Washington D.C., and others.

17. Morrison and Winston (1995). The authors used the Standard Industry Fare Level (SIFL), which was used to determine fares during regulation, to predict what regulated fares *would have been* during deregulation. The SIFL was adjusted for productivity changes induced by deregulation. The authors then compared these "regulated" fares with actual deregulated fares.

18. These results were obtained by regressing the change in real fares for all routes that were served in both the fourth quarter of 1978 and the fourth quarter of 1996 on the change in effective compe-

Figure 14-7. *Average Revenue per Passenger Mile for Domestic Airlines, Adjusted for Inflation*

1996 dollars

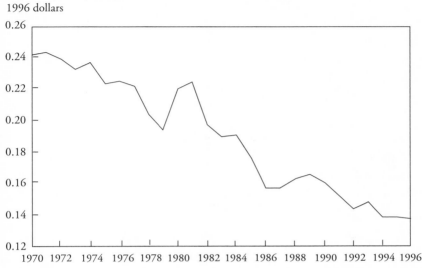

Source: Authors' calculations using data from Air Transport Association, various issues.

Deregulation has lowered average domestic air fares, but it has not lowered them uniformly across all routes. Even so, about 80 percent of airline passengers (accounting for roughly 90 percent of passenger miles) fly on routes with lower average real fares since deregulation.

Passenger welfare is not just a matter of fares. Deregulation has also affected service. Something of an amorphous concept, service covers everything from the quality of food carriers provide to the cheerfulness of flight attendants, from the frequency of flights to the number of direct flights, and so on. Not all of these services are quantifiable. But several have been analyzed with some rigor, including the frequency of service, the level of restrictions on tickets, the number of passengers who must change planes, load factors, and travel time. We have found in previous research that travelers have gained substantially from the increase in flight frequency that has largely been facilitated by the acceleration of hub-and-spoke opera-

---

tition by Southwest, the change in effective competition by other new entrants, the change in effective competition by established carriers, and the number of passengers on and the length of each route.

Table 14-1. *Average Change in Real Fares between 1978:4 and 1996:4 for All Domestic Routes Served in Both Periods*

Type of route	Fare change (using 1996:4 passenger weights) (percentage change)
Routes not served by new entrants in 1996:4 (5,983 routes)	−14.7
Routes served by new entrants in 1996:4 but not by Southwest Airlines (1,579 routes)	−30.5
Routes served by Southwest Airlines in 1996:4 but not by other new entrants (372 routes)	−47.2
Routes served by both Southwest Airlines and other new entrants in 1996:4 (360 routes)	−54.3
All routes (8,294 routes)	−32.2

Source: Authors' calculations from data in U.S. Department of Transportation, Data Bank 1A.

tions.[19] Travelers have also gained from having to make fewer connections that require changing airlines. These gains have been partially offset by more crowded flights, travel restrictions that are inconvenient for business travelers (especially the required Saturday night stay), a few more connections, and slightly longer flight times because of congestion. Accounting for fare and service quality changes, the annual net benefits to travelers from airline deregulation amount to nearly $20 billion (1996 dollars).[20]

Shippers have benefited substantially from the decline in truck rates, which have paralleled the decline in costs (figure 14-8). Since 1977 real average LTL rates have fallen more than 35 percent, and real average TL rates have fallen more than 75 percent. Eliminating higher-priced LTL traffic from their traffic mix accounts for some of the decline in TL carriers' rate, just as it accounts for some of the decline in their operating costs. Large shippers in high-density markets have undoubtedly gained more than small shippers in low-density markets, but small shippers have been able to share

19. Morrison and Winston (1995) provide a detailed discussion of the findings reported in this paragraph.
20. This figure is based on Morrison and Winston (1995). It was inflated to 1996 dollars with a gross domestic product inflator, which was also used to inflate the estimates of the benefits to truck and rail shippers to 1996 dollars.

Figure 14-8. *Average Rates of Less-Than-Truckload and Truckload Carriers, 1977–1995*

1995 dollars per vehicle mile

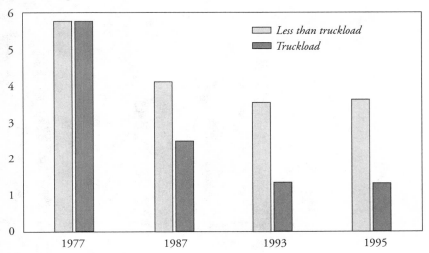

Source: Corsi 1996a, b.

in some of the benefits from lower rates through third-party logistics firms. Shippers have also gained from improvements in service time and service time reliability. Including these benefits, the annual net benefits to shippers from trucking deregulation amount to more than $18 billion (1996 dollars).[21] This figure would be even higher if it included the additional benefits to truck shippers from deregulating intrastate truck rates. Shippers have made inefficient routing and plant location decisions (such as locating just outside of state lines) in order to qualify for deregulated interstate trucking rates that were considerably lower than regulated intrastate rates. Shippers' gains from intrastate deregulation therefore include rate reductions of roughly 30 percent on their intrastate shipments and, in some

21. This figure is based on a counterfactual analysis contained in Winston and others (1990). This figure understates the benefits from motor carrier deregulation because it was based on trucking rates in 1985. As shown in figure 14-8, trucking rates have continued to decline since 1985 and much of that decline is attributable to deregulation. In addition, trucking service has continued to improve. For example, Con-Way Transportation Services has stretched two-day service—once traditionally defined as 1,000 miles—to as long as 1,600 miles.

Figure 14-9. *Railroad Freight Revenue per Ton-Mile, 1980–1995*
(1995 dollars)

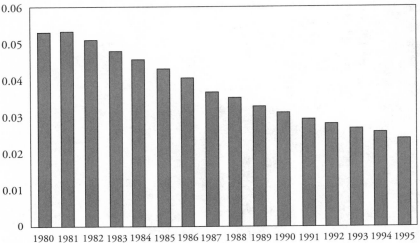

Source: Association of American Railroads (1989, 1996).

cases, the elimination of inefficiencies incurred to qualify for lower inter-state rates.[22]

Finally, shippers have benefited from the decline in railroad rates. But, in contrast to trucking rates, rail rates did not fall sharply after deregulation and then stabilize in the mid-1990s. Instead, as shown in figure 14-9, real rail rates have declined continuously. Thus far, real rail rates have fallen more than 50 percent and are likely to fall further as railroads continue to reduce their costs and pass on some of the cost savings to shippers. Some of the decline in rail rates, like the decline in rail costs, can be attributed to the long-run trend in railroads' traffic mix to include a greater proportion of lower-priced bulk traffic.

Given the nature of their technology, which involves large sunk costs in plant and equipment, railroads undoubtedly accumulated more ineffi-ciencies from regulation than did trucking firms. Not surprisingly, rail-roads are taking longer to shed these inefficiencies and the full benefits of rail deregulation will thus take longer to realize. And, as in the case of truck shippers, large rail shippers in high-density markets have been able to ne-

22. Winston and others (1990).

gotiate lower rates than small shippers in low-density markets, but small shippers have been able to increase their rate savings by obtaining lower rates through third-party logistics firms. Rail shippers have also gained from considerable improvements in service time and service time reliability. Including these benefits, the annual net benefits to shippers from rail deregulation amount to more than $11.7 billion (1996 dollars).[23]

Thus a *conservative* estimate of the annual net benefits that consumers have received from intercity transportation deregulation amounts to roughly $50 billion (1996 dollars). And these benefits have been achieved without compromising any mode's safety record, although, not surprisingly, they have come at some expense to labor.[24] From a macroeconomic perspective, these benefits are part of the substantial decline in the cost of shipping freight in the United States since deregulation, which has helped ease inflation. In 1980, shippers' freight transportation cost as a share of gross domestic product was 7.6 percent; in 1996, it was 6 percent.

Deregulation's considerable success has surprised the economics profession in some respects. The profession correctly predicted that consumers would gain from lower trucking and airline prices as a result of deregulation, but it expected rail rates to rise, or at least not to fall much, and failed to predict the large gains from improved service quality in all modes.[25] To be sure, as we have noted, not all consumers and shippers have gained from deregulation or shared equally in the benefits. But the public and some policymakers have often overstated the losses attributable to deregulation, while, in fact, the distribution of benefits generally has had a rational economic basis. For example, air travelers on all size classifications of routes have, on average, received lower fares as a result of deregulation, but the gains to air travelers on high-traffic density (large hub) routes have been much greater than those to travelers on low-traffic density (nonhub) routes. Roughly 90 percent of the difference in these gains can be explained

---

23. This figure is also based on a counterfactual analysis contained in Winston and others (1990). This figure understates the benefits from rail deregulation because it was based on rates in 1985. As shown in figure 14-9, rates have continued to decline since 1985 and much of that decline is attributable to deregulation.

24. Space precludes a full treatment of these issues here, but it should be noted that despite public concern with airline safety, the probability of dying in an airline crash has continued to decline since deregulation (see Morrison and Winston, 1995). As summarized in Winston (1993), truckers have experienced significant losses in wages, but rail and airline workers have not, while airline employment has risen, but railroad and motor carrier employment has not.

25. Winston (1993).

by the higher costs of serving travelers on low-density routes, where smaller planes have a higher cost per seat mile and fly with lower load factors.[26]

Further Adjustments to Deregulation

John R. Meyer will be remembered for his vision and his patience. Meyer identified economic phenomena that would shape consumer and firm behavior in the long run, but he also recognized that consumers and firms would need time—perhaps a long time—to adjust to these phenomena. In particular, he correctly cautioned against premature judgments about deregulation. Even after twenty years, the transportation industries have not completely adjusted to deregulation. Indeed, each industry can and will make further adjustments that will enable it to become more efficient and generate greater benefits to consumers.

Airlines are now exploring options to raise labor productivity. One is to use (lower-cost) pilots who work for their affiliates to fly the smaller (regional) jets recently introduced on short-haul routes. Unlike the trucking industry, the airline industry has not spawned new nonunion carriers to put downward pressure on labor costs, probably because the skill requirements and relative scarcity of pilots make it difficult to set up a nonunion "upstart" carrier.

Although deregulation of international markets is proceeding slowly, in our view U.S. carriers will eventually have to compete with foreign carriers allowed to enter U.S. routes to feed their international traffic. Some U.S. carriers will undoubtedly pursue mergers to compete more effectively in newly opened international markets, and a few could exit the industry entirely. But international airline deregulation will lower fares for consumers. We predict fare cuts averaging nearly 30 percent, with greater reductions in more heavily regulated Asian-U.S. markets than in European-U.S. markets.[27]

The increasing use of intermodal operations is alleviating the serious shortage of long-distance drivers that has hampered the trucking industry. Although truckers have significantly reduced their empty mileage, more progress can be made through load consolidations, especially by third-party

---

26. Morrison and Winston (1997).

27. This estimate is obtained by comparing fares for U.S.–foreign city flights with fares for U.S. domestic flights of comparable distances.

logistics firms. Competition in freight markets is likely to increase as intermodal operations continue to expand. And it is also likely that for-hire trucking firms will make further inroads in private trucking operations, which could reduce their empty trips. DRI/McGraw-Hill predicts that another 10 percent of private carriage tonnage will shift to for-hire truckers within the next ten years.[28]

Finally, although railroads have abandoned a lot of track, they can optimize their plant size by abandoning yet more unprofitable markets while building track in potentially profitable ones. Railroads can improve their fleet by taking advantage of technological innovations that have made locomotives more powerful and enabled rail cars to carry heavier loads without wearing out track. And the spread of smaller low-cost rail carriers such as Montana Rail Link should spur the industry to continue to reduce its labor costs. Finally, it is possible that more rail mergers will be proposed until only two (highly efficient) Class I railroads remain in the industry. This end-to-end restructuring, should it come to pass, would create two transcontinental railroads, but still leave two large railroads in the East and two in the West, and thus have little effect on competition.

The benefits that consumers have received to date from transportation deregulation clearly represent a lower bound on the total benefits that they are likely to reap. To be sure, policymakers and most of the public will probably have forgotten about transportation deregulation by the time these benefits fully materialize. The transportation profession, however, will always remember the intellectual source of one of the most important transportation policies that this country has ever implemented.

References

Adelman, M. A. 1969. "Comment on the 'H' Concentration Measure as a Numbers-Equivalent." *Review of Economics and Statistics* 51 (February): 99–101.
Air Transport Association. Various years. *Air Transport Annual Report.* Washington, D.C.
Association of American Railroads. 1989, 1996. *Railroad Facts.* Washington, D.C.
Corsi, Thomas M. 1996a. "Current and Alternative Federal Size and Weight Policies: Less-Than-Truckload Motor Carriers." Working paper. University of Maryland, College of Business and Management, College Park, Md.

28. Corsi (1996b).

————. 1996b. "Current and Alternative Federal Size and Weight Policies: Truckload Motor Carriers." Working paper. University of Maryland, College of Business and Management, College Park, Md.

Derthick, Martha, and Paul J. Quirk. 1985. *The Politics of Deregulation.* Brookings.

Grimm, Curtis M., and Robert Windle. 1998. "The Rationale for Deregulation." In *Regulatory Reform and Labor Markets,* edited by James Peoples. Boston: Kluwer Academic Publishers.

Meyer, John R., and others. 1959. *The Economics of Competition in the Transportation Industries.* Harvard University Press.

Morrison, Steven A., and Clifford Winston. 1986. *The Economic Effects of Airline Deregulation.* Brookings.

————. 1995. *The Evolution of the Airline Industry.* Brookings.

————. 1996. "Causes and Consequences of Airline Fare Wars." *Brookings Papers on Economic Activity: Microeconomics:* 85–131.

————. 1997. "The Fare Skies: Air Transportation and Middle America." *Brookings Review* 15 (Fall): 42–45.

Peltzman, Sam. 1989. "The Economic Theory of Regulation after a Decade of Deregulation." *Brookings Papers on Economic Activity: Microeconomics:* 1–41.

Winston, Clifford. 1993. "Economic Deregulation: Days of Reckoning for Microeconomists." *Journal of Economic Literature* 31 (September): 1263–90.

Winston, Clifford, and others. 1990. *The Economic Effects of Surface Freight Deregulation.* Brookings.

ROBERT E. GALLAMORE

15) Regulation and Innovation: Lessons from the American Railroad Industry

O n the day of the American Bicentennial, the nation's railroads were a shambles. They had given the expanding young country a century and a half of improved land transportation for cargo and passengers, but by 1976 the once powerful railways had joined heavy manufacturing industries in symbolizing the decline of "Smokestack America" and defining the economically distressed "Rust Belt" across the northeastern quadrant of the country.

From peak mileage of 254,000 in 1916, railroads had declined to 199,000 route miles in 1975. Railroad share of the U.S. intercity surface freight market had declined from 65 percent at the end of World War II to only about 35 percent, measured by ton-miles.[1] Passenger trains, once the mainstay of intercity travel and railway profits, cost railroad companies losses of hundreds of millions of dollars annually before service could be discontinued or turned over to Amtrak after its establishment in 1970. Between 1947 and 1970, the railroad industry had barely managed to stay

The author wishes to thank the many readers of earlier drafts who made useful suggestions.

1. Calculated from Transportation Association of America, *Transportation in America* (later volumes in the series published by Eno Transportation Foundation) and reported in Federal Railroad Administration (1978: 44).

493

afloat financially—substituting massive amounts of capital for labor while demand and real output stagnated.[2] Then in June 1970 the nation's largest railroad, Penn Central, declared bankruptcy and carried half a dozen other northeastern railroads with it to Chapter 11.

Within two years it was apparent that Penn Central could not be reorganized conventionally; federal planning and takeover of the northeastern properties and then establishment and subsidy of the successor Consolidated Rail Corp. (Conrail) would cost taxpayers some $8 billion over the next decade.[3] After Penn Central's collapse, granger railroads including the Chicago, Rock Island and Pacific, extending as far as Texas and New Mexico, and the Milwaukee Road, extending to the Puget Sound, fell into bankruptcy. Pundits talked of how the government might have to undertake a "Conrail West" bailout. Instead, policy leaders in the Department of Transportation and elsewhere in the Carter administration, the rail industry, and on Capitol Hill mounted a campaign to loosen the Interstate Commerce Commission's economic regulatory grip on railroads. Success came with passage of the Staggers Rail Act of 1980.

Less than a quarter century after America's railroads passed through the profound shocks of the 1970s and into the brave new world of deregulation in the early 1980s, they have achieved an industry renaissance without precedent in the nation's economic history. Freed by the Staggers Act from the straitjacket of legalistic, excruciatingly detailed regulation, railroads gradually became more savvy and nimble in the transportation marketplace. They began thinking of how to achieve a better match between their huge physical plants and work forces on the one hand and available traffic on the other. Doing so, they found ways to cut operating costs and stimulate improvement in output per employee hour. Asset utilization (a ritual of passage for capital-intensive industries) began to improve. Managements got rid of outdated organizational forms and many old operational rules-of-thumb. New technologies were deployed—in consequence of railroad companies regaining confidence in reinvestment (rather than slavishly following the "shareholder value" fads of the mid-1980s) and learning better how to use innovations to leverage post-Staggers rail economics. Newly unleashed competitive forces stimulated corporate strategies to strive for the "three Ms"—improved margin, market share, and mergers.

---

2. Meyer and Morton (1975). See also Healy (1985).

3. Author's estimate. About one-fourth of this amount was recouped in the resale of Conrail to the public in 1987—at the time, the largest initial public offering in American history.

As railroads learned how to benefit from reduced regulation and as the economy improved, traffic volumes broke loose from decades of decline and stagnation. Class I railroad ton-miles increased 27 percent in the four years 1992–96 alone.[4] Revenues began a mild upswing, and ordinary income, which was only $144 million for all the Class I railroads in 1975 (in nominal dollars), reached $3.9 billion in 1996. The railroads' new emphasis on asset utilization energized dramatic plans for restructuring physical plant and for learning how to manage smarter with computerized applications for data collection and analysis. Railroads caught the quality bug, earnestly pursuing customer satisfaction and business process reengineering initiatives. Struggling with century-old customs and regulatory legacies, the industry nonetheless negotiated significant changes in contractual agreements with labor unions and aggressively reduced employment levels.

Realizing notable success in all these areas, total factor productivity soared. Ton-miles per constant dollar of operating expense increased almost 2.5 times between 1980 and 1995, and most other indicators of railroad economic performance also improved. To illustrate the impact of deregulation and other causal factors centered on 1980, figure 15-1 compares indexes of Class I railroads' volume, constant dollar total and unit revenues, and total factor productivity for half-decades before and after passage of the Staggers Act.

The purpose of this chapter is to construct and substantiate a relationship between two economic forces, *deregulation* and *innovation*, believed to be at the center of the railroad renaissance just described. Economists and railway analysts have long suspected that government regulation of railroad industry structure, services, and rates stifled innovation and delayed technological progress. Such a causal relationship is impossible to prove statistically because of multicollinearity and the absence of a naturally occurring "laboratory experiment" in the data. At the same time, a strong before-and-after case cries out for examination, as it is apparent that railroads foundered under the final decades of Interstate Commerce Commission (ICC) regulation and have recovered remarkably since regulation was relaxed in 1980.

---

4. Class I railroads are defined by regulatory authorities as those meeting a given level of annual operating revenues. Between 1955 and 1980, Class I roads employed a little more than 85 percent of all railroad workers. The averages have now dropped to about 70 percent, because of a change in the definitional revenue threshold and "redeployment" of many former major carrier lines to new short line or regional railroads. See Kimura (1997) for a detailed analysis of the financial performance of Class I railroads since 1970.

Figure 15-1. *Indicators of Railroad Performance, Pre- and Post-Staggers Act*
1980 = 1.0

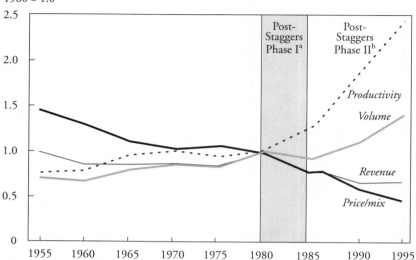

Source: Gallamore (1998a), calculated for Class I railroads using data from the Association of American Railroads (1997). Productivity is measured in ton-miles per constant dollar of operating expense; volume is measured in revenue ton-miles; revenue is measured in constant dollars, and the price/mix is measured in revenue (in constant dollars) per ton-mile. See McCullough (1993) for a recent survey of methodological issues in measuring output and pricing in the multiproduct railroad industry. McCullough follows a suggestion from Griliches (1972) to use car-miles rather than ton-miles in addressing the price/mix problem.

a. This phase was characterized by stable volume, increased productivity, lower prices, and lower revenue.

b. This phase is characterized by increased volumes, sharply increased productivity, lower prices, and stable revenue.

The remainder of this chapter attempts to draw out this theme. It begins by examining in more detail the nature of the economic, institutional, and managerial problems facing railroads before passage of the Staggers Act. The discussion establishes that the forces causing the decline of railroads were numerous, persistent, and cumulative in their effect.

Moving on to innovation, the chapter summarizes Edwin Mansfield's pathbreaking work on the economic factors affecting technology development and deployment historically—specifically his studies of the railroad industry's conversion from steam to diesel-electric locomotives in the quarter century after 1930. Using the example of Southern Railway's attempted introduction of jumbo grain cars in the 1960s, the chapter then discusses how ICC regulation could delay or thwart innovation.

Turning to the period after relaxation of regulation in 1980, the chapter relates in detail numerous ways in which deregulation has fostered railroad innovation and change. Although it is frequently reported and generally presumed to be true that the Staggers Act greatly benefited the railroads, the exact mechanisms underpinning revitalization and transformation of the industry are not well understood. This part of the chapter tries to look inside the "black box" to give one observer's view of how some of the forces released by deregulation actually manifested themselves. It is beyond the scope of this chapter to quantify or otherwise evaluate the relative importance of each of these innovations, but the discussion lays groundwork for possible future case studies. Such an undertaking might be useful in drawing conclusions on the value of stimulating research and development, standardization, technology sharing, or other policies intended to promote technological progress and productivity improvement in a fundamental industry.

An intriguing picture emerges as the chapter concludes. During its nearly two-hundred-year history, railroad technology has demonstrably progressed in surges. These stages of rapid transformation were characterized by exploitation of a widely held, paradigm-shifting vision for the future, after which progress settled back into what is now called "continuous improvement." The conclusion of the chapter argues that the regulatory era enforced a long, winding path of internal, rail-centric decisionmaking that ultimately exhausted its travelers. In sharp contrast, deregulation (slowly at first, but with gathering momentum) has enabled the industry to climb to a new vantage point. Standing at the brink of the millennium and railroading's bicentennial, the industry can envision a future in which—even more than in the past—it will draw on the ingenuity of the laboratory to meet the demands of the marketplace.

The "Railroad Problem" in the Decade before Deregulation

Penn Central's bankruptcy in the early 1970s focused public policy attention on the railroads as the warnings of academic and financial observers could not. Several blue ribbon studies were commissioned, and causes of the demise of American railroads were carefully examined and documented.[5] Among the most apparent explanations was that manifest rail

---

5. See Task Force on Railroad Productivity (1973: 1–50); U.S. Senate, Committee on Commerce (1972); U.S. Railway Association (1975: ch.1, 8); and Federal Railroad Administration (1978: 39–63).

service—general carload merchandise freight, as opposed to bulk cargo such as coal, grain, or industrial chemicals—was not competing well with truckload motor freight. With construction of the new, nonstop interstate highways, motor carriers were able to increase truck sizes and deliver manufactured goods of all kinds reliably, expediently, and with less damage than railroads could in boxcars. At the same time, bulk goods movement by rail was forced to compete with expanded barge service on the subsidized and protected inland waterways. Internally within the railroads, labor costs were too high—more than half of operating expenses. Physical plant and equipment had been allowed to deteriorate, and new investment was not expected to earn its cost of capital. Rail managements were regarded as stodgy and uninventive. And regulatory authorities in Washington had enormous power over railroad business decisions large and small; it was said that no other American industry carried a larger regulatory burden.

For generations, students of the economics of railroad transportation had described what was called "The Railroad Problem."[6] Most economists believed that over a broad range of firm sizes and individual company outputs, railroad marginal costs fell below average costs. Initial track construction costs were large, and expensive facilities and equipment had to be assembled before production could start; but once a train was running, additional cars could be handled cheaply. It was shown that "quasi-natural monopolies" or "declining cost" industries such as the railroads were not "economically efficient" in the theoretical sense; that is, the normal course of their activity would not lead to a stable, welfare-maximizing, equilibrium level of prices and production characteristic of efficient industries. To the extent that declining cost firms faced competition for additional business at eroding price levels, they could not earn a market rate of return on investment. Unless restrained by governmental authorities, moreover, they would attempt to combine into still larger firms to achieve even lower costs, eventually resulting in a single firm in the relevant market. It was assumed that the surviving firm would have power to price its product above marginal costs, achieving profits at the expense of the consumer surplus that "captive" buyers would otherwise receive. Meanwhile, railroads in com-

---

6. The "problem" took several forms historically, such as "the weak and strong road problem," price discrimination, maximum and minimum rate disputes, intermodal ownership issues, passenger service discontinuances, and finally, the northeastern bankruptcies. These provided ample grist for the mills of both activists and academicians. See, among others, Locklin (1960); Nelson (1959), part I of which is titled "Basic Factors in the Railroad Problem"; Stover (1961: 246–62); and chapter 1 of the influential monograph by railroad president John W. Barriger (1956), entitled "Basic Elements of the Railroad Problem."

petitive markets would fail altogether.[7]

Thus the railroad problem presented a Hobsonesque concoction of less-than-perfect solutions. First, regulation of mergers and rates, the traditional remedy, was intended to replace failed market mechanisms with differential rate schedules designed to sustain some customers at artificially low rates by charging higher rates to others. Second, if markets were difficult to enter or exit but not immune to rivalry, governments might sanction a workably competitive outcome under vigilant regulatory oversight—but stop short of detailed, prescriptive rate-making. Finally, the government could nationalize or subsidize the railroads and run them without expectation of profits.

Beyond these fundamental economics, the several expert studies conducted in the 1970s pointed out numerous specific factors that contributed to the decline of railroads in the post-World War II period, as summarized below.

Federal Economic Regulation

Much of railroading's failure to keep pace with changing economic circumstances has been laid at the door of the federal regulatory regime. Railroads had been the economy's most regulated industry since passage of the Act to Regulate Commerce in 1887, which established the ICC,

---

7. See Keeler (1983: 43–61 and appendix B) for the standard presentation of the "declining cost" paradigm. In the decade or two before the Staggers Act, evidence was accumulating that marginal costs were not always declining. Statistical cost function studies conducted in the 1950s and 1960s revealed few economies of scale. The findings of Meyer and others (1959) were generally more consistent with constant returns to scale than declining marginal costs. My Ph.D. dissertation (Gallamore, 1968) developed evidence (through counterfactual and control group statistical costing case studies) that large mergers in the 1960s had resulted in diseconomies, rather than the anticipated operating cost savings. By the 1970s it became necessary to recognize detailed differences in economies of *scale, density,* and *scope* in railroad cost studies. Keeler (1983: 57) concluded that "a large fraction of the nation's rail system operates subject to increasing returns to traffic density, while the more important main lines are more likely to operate at near-constant returns to traffic density." McCullough (1993) nicely summarizes econometric rail costing studies performed since the seminal work of Meyer and others (1959).

Lessons from the pre-Staggers railroad costing analyses should not be carried into the 1990s, however, without the utmost caution. As pointed out later in this chapter, lessening of regulation and managerial or technological innovation have had powerful influences on railroad economic performance—including the improved ability of managers with computerized systems and centralized facilities to operate larger firms. Especially within the last few years, under the pressure of significant volume growth running up against capacity limitations in the industry, it appears that marginal costs may be *increasing* in many instances. If broadly spread and sustained, such a trend would substantially alter the consensus understanding of the economics of railroading.

America's first independent regulatory agency. At one point there were said to be more than a trillion railroad rates on file with the ICC, and each one had to be "just and reasonable" or it was unlawful. To change a rate, discontinue a service, or issue securities, a railroad had to seek permission from the ICC in adversary proceedings, where other parties (including other railroads) could invoke a huge body of law and precedents in an attempt to stop almost any market initiative. Even though the railroads may have brought much of the elaborate governmental harassment upon themselves with their early antisocial behavior, this degree of regulation came at great cost to the economy. The Task Force on Railroad Productivity estimated in its 1973 report that "the antiquated state of the railroad industry and the waste caused by over-regulation of the intercity freight transport industry almost surely cost American consumers in excess of $10 billion per year."[8]

Competition from Other Modes

American transport policy relies on competition among the various modes of transportation as well as on intramodal competition to encourage effective performance by individual operators (companies), yet it does so in a manner almost completely abstracted from total social costs and benefits of the separate modes. Historically, government used the modes as instruments of both subsidy and regulatory policy, with little effort at consistency or even-handedness among them. Railroads benefited from government promotion in the nineteenth century, but they have been victimized by it more often than not in the twentieth century.

Automobiles able to use the new Interstate Highway System (largely completed by the 1970s) and jet aircraft decimated rail passenger and express service after 1950, until only skeletal remains of the once-great network were nationalized into Amtrak in 1970.[9] More important to freight

8. Task Force on Railroad Productivity (1973: v). The task force did not construct its own estimate, but relied on the work of Thomas Gale Moore and others. Regulatory costs stemmed from forced cross-subsidy of unprofitable services, unwillingness to permit abandonment of certain facilities, delayed approval of inflation-driven cost increases, protection of existing traffic patterns and gateways, protection of competing modes, protection of employees adversely affected by railroad restructuring, excessive use of quasi-judicial procedure, and excessive paperwork. It is impossible to say which of these factors were the most costly to railroads; all were enormously aggravating to management.

9. Railroad passenger deficits mounted in the post-World War II period to crisis proportions by the late 1960s. In an effort to relieve freight railroads of an unconscionable burden, preserve worthwhile passenger service under new circumstances, and head off large-scale subsidy to existing (unrationalized) passenger operations, the new Department of Transportation proposed legislation for what became

railroads, the interstate highways substantially improved truck transit times and operating cost performance. Larger trucks became feasible, while road taxes remained about one-third lower than required to recover the full costs large trucks imposed on the highway system.[10] Owners and operators of trip-leased "eighteen wheelers" or companies moving their own or exempt goods could escape detailed ICC regulation, while less than truckload (LTL) or irregular route truckload (TL) common carrier shipments were still subject to ICC control of "routes and rates." Owner-operators often underpaid their own labor and defaulted on financing of their equipment, but their charges were low and their market share grew dramatically in the 1960s and 1970s.

During these years railroads also faced increasing competition from barges operating on federally aided inland waterways.[11] Thus the "inherent advantages" of the railroads (as the Transportation Act of 1940 heroically labeled them) were squeezed between airline and truck service at the high end and barges at the bottom end of the rate spectrum.

Changing Demands for Freight Transport

In addition to competition from the rise of alternative modes, railroads lost market share because the composition of industrial markets was

---

Amtrak in 1970. The immediate objectives were accomplished, but a quarter century and $19 billion of subsidy later, the basic economic problem remains. Freight railroads still claim Amtrak does not pay its fair share of joint costs, but the burden on freight railroads is nothing like it was before 1970.

10. The highway safety and cost responsibility of large trucks is exceedingly controversial. The preponderance of evidence from studies sponsored over the years by the Federal Highway Administration (FHWA) is that large trucks underpay in user charges by some 33 to 40 percent. A 1997 Federal Highway Cost Allocation Study (DOT, 1997) concludes that overall equity (the relationship between highway cost responsibility and user fee payments) of combination trucks has improved since the previous allocation study in 1982. As a group, however, tractor-trailer combination trucks pay only 90 percent of their cost responsibility and the heaviest trucks underpay by the greatest amount. The 1997 study estimated that in 2000, truck combinations registered at more than 80,000 pounds would pay, on average, only about 60 percent of their cost responsibility. See also Winston, Small, and Evans (1989), who pointed out that truck damage costs would be less if roads were designed optimally for the function they are expected to perform. At the same time, however, existing highways would perform better if user charges were optimal.

11. Barges had an even better deal than the trucks; they were not required to pay any user fees at all until after passage of the Inland Waterways Revenue Act of 1978, which established an Inland Waterways Trust Fund and imposed a gradually escalating fuel tax (4 cents a gallon in 1980, rising to 10 cents a gallon by 1990 and 20 cents a gallon after 1994). See *Congressional Record*, vol. 132, no. 144, October 17, 1986, p. H 11533, and http://www.irs.ustreas.gov.

changing in ways that significantly affected demand for rail transportation. Plastics were replacing metals, making products lighter and less "rail intensive." Aluminum substituted for steel, paper and plastics for glass, composites for lumber, individually packaged products for bulk, and fresh and frozen foods for canned fruits and vegetables. Stock-keeping units of all kinds of finished consumer goods proliferated and became smaller, lighter, more valuable per pound—and more suitable to trucking than to rail. Even heavy bulk commodities were affected; for example, oil or natural gas (efficiently moved by pipeline) replaced coal for home heating.

For railroads, it was a vicious downward spiral. As traffic left the rails for other modes and excess capacity hung over the industry, railroad companies had neither need nor financial ability to invest in track and equipment improvements. To save crew and train mile costs, railroads ran longer, less frequent trains—causing service to deteriorate further and more business to flee. This led to more deferred maintenance, more derailment costs, more abandonment applications, and further traffic losses.

Labor Costs and Institutional Impediments

Many observers over the years have felt that railway labor unions and work rule restrictions were a major reason for the declining performance of railroads. Until about 1990 most trains were required to operate with "full crews" of four (sometimes even five) trainmen; the standard today for crews that perform only limited switching of cars en route is two (three if more switching is required). Trainmen were able to negotiate continuation of a daily "basis of pay" rooted in mileage traveled (originally 100 miles, later revised to 108 and then to 130 miles) rather than hours worked. Crews also received additional pay for time spent away from the home terminal and various "arbitraries" (pay for using a radio or other work rule changes management sought). Nonoperating employees attempted to protect their crafts from loss of work either to "composite" employees (those who had no specific craft) or to outside suppliers.

Obsolete Technology

Some critics believed basic railroad technology was to blame for the industry's postwar economic decline. Granting that the industry's traditional markets were changing in a way that favored motor carriers, had the basic notion of locomotive-hauled trains of steel-wheeled vehicles on steel rails become obsolete? Had the railroads failed to resupply the technology pipeline?[12] The timely and influential Task Force on Railroad Productivity, chartered by the Council of Economic Advisers and the National Commission on Productivity and chaired by John R. Meyer, took a balanced view on this question in its 1973 report.

> Generally, industries experiencing slow growth of output, long asset lives, low profits, and other obstacles to innovation tend to attract less inventive effort and hence to suffer a lower rate of innovation. . . . Gaps or lapses in railroad technology are a primary explanation of why total productivity in the rail industry has grown at a rate averaging only 1 to 2 percent per year . . . ." [13]

The task force concluded that railroad technology had developed at a remarkable pace under the circumstances, and it gave examples such as the dieselization of railroads at midcentury, and applications of computer technology to costing and car accounting. (Indeed, without these innovations, the collapse of railroads evident at the Bicentennial probably would have occurred sooner and more severely.) At the same time, the task force observed that some of the benefits of technology advancement might not be realized because of governmental barriers to deployment, meaning that deferred innovation must be counted part of the cost of excessive regulation.

Management

Throughout the postwar decline, railroad managements typically were slow to adapt to changes in their competitive environment. Critics noted the industry's dearth of product innovation and its slowness to invest in modernized plant and equipment. They blamed management (rightly so, because innovation is not only inventive activity, but also management's decision to invest scarce capital in deploying technological improvements). Keen observers such as Meyer and James Nelson pointed out that regulatory and other institutional constraints on railroad firms dulled entrepre-

---

12. Standard economic history declares that railroads were, at any time, mainly a large and specialized application of contemporary technology. See Hughes (1983: 290). Although an oversimplification, it is true that railroads massively adapted generic technologies developed elsewhere—such as steam engines, steel, electricity, diesel engines, two-way radios, and computers.

13. Task Force on Railroad Productivity (1973: 282).

neurial spirit, leading potential managerial talent to choose other careers.[14] Also, when diversification seemed the only way out, company managements typically set up holding companies to move nonrail assets out of the reach of their railroad subsidiaries.[15] This was done out of fear that railway economics would never reverse themselves, the regulatory system would continue to cause a "death of a thousand cuts," and even a fear (it seems hard to believe today) that railroad rights-of-way would be nationalized at confiscatory levels of property valuation.

Overview of Railroad Regulatory Reform

By the late 1970s, events finally had made clear that there were too many claimants on the carcass of the railroads, and not all could be satisfied. Abstract economic reasoning and quantitative estimates of the social costs of ICC-style regulation might eventually have produced reform. But the real impetus for change in the last years of the 1970s was that Conrail, after billions of dollars of public reinvestment and agonizing downsizing, was still costing taxpayers about $1 million a day in operating losses. Congress was tiring of new authorizations for Conrail and wanted a more lasting solution. The Carter administration seized on regulatory reform as a general theme, and the Federal Railroad Administration (FRA) pointed out possibilities for using deregulation in easing the burden of Conrail deficits and avoiding spread of "nationalization" to bankrupt railways in the Midwest. Conrail's chairman, Edward Jordan, became a strong supporter of the administration's approach to reform.

Pundits predicted failure of the deregulation initiative for any number of reasons: the ICC bureaucracy and its practitioners were entrenched; labor unions feared job losses; farmers and poorly located shippers and communities remained wedded to protectionism; railroad companies were sharply divided; and the general public was ill informed. Nonetheless, FRA and Department of Transportation officials put together a draft legislative proposal that eventually gained the support of influential academicians

14. See the important testimony before the Kefauver Antitrust Subcommittee in U.S. Senate, Committee on the Judiciary (1962: 24–33). See also Meyer and others (1959: 260) and McCullough (1993).

15. Examples were Union Pacific Corporation; Illinois Central Industries; Burlington Northern, Inc.; Kansas City Southern Industries; Southern Pacific Co.; Rio Grande Industries; Chicago Northwestern Corp.; Chicago Milwaukee Corp.; and CSX Corp.

and railroad experts, the White House, key congressional staff members, many large shippers, and (not without dissent) the board of the Association of American Railroads. With significant modifications, the legislation worked its way though congressional hearings, markup, and final passage—along the way taking its name in honor of retiring House Commerce Committee Chairman Harley O. Staggers. The Staggers Rail Act was signed into law by President Carter in October 1980.

This complex legislation and its effects are well summarized elsewhere.[16] The most important feature of the Staggers Act was its injunction that railroads, in the vast majority of instances, should be allowed to act as other businesses do. Thus, market forces would replace both collusive rate bureaus and ICC adversarial proceedings as the proper rate-making discipline. Contractual arrangements regarding shipment terms between railroads and their customers were explicitly allowed, subject only to confidential filing with the ICC. Minor determinations were exempted from regulation altogether, and new rules were put in place to handle the toughest cases.

Some disputes went unresolved in the Staggers Act itself and were left to the ICC, notably the issue of differential pricing under conditions of limited market competition. In a liberalized regulatory regime, railroads could segment markets and attempt to price services differentially, that is, more closely to what the traffic would bear. Using this second-best, or "Ramsey pricing," concept, railroads could earn higher margins on traffic with inelastic demand while continuing to participate in markets with more elastic demand in order to earn a contribution to common (overhead or fixed) costs. Customers who felt "captive" and who believed they were bearing an unfair share of total railroad costs fought the Ramsey pricing scheme, as their forebears had fought its precursor, ICC value-of-service rate-making, or sought alternative solutions in the marketplace.

Some of the alternative solutions shippers were able to find (by plan or circumstance) involved supply substitutes. Some power companies, for example, replaced local energy sources with nuclear energy or western subbituminous coal. In other cases after the Staggers Act so allowed, customers signed long-term contracts at favorable volume discounts. Often, simply the passage of time healed the wound, as new technology, relocation, new plant construction, or foreign competition overtook the relevance of the dispute.

---

16. In addition to countless regulatory documents and legislative testimony, see most recently Gallamore (1998a: fig. 2, p. 38). See also Winston and others (1990), Stone (1991), McCullough (1993), and Martland (1997).

In the 1990s several so-called "captive" power plants constructed new rail spurs to connections with a rival railroad. Also in the 1990s, with railroads seeking support from large customers and approval from the ICC or its successor Surface Transportation Board (STB) for proposed mergers, agreements were reached to extend rival competitive service to major producing or receiving locations over the facilities of the railroad seeking the merger.

In short, substantial efforts by complainants notwithstanding, only a handful of rates were successfully challenged under the new rules. Some shippers voiced great unhappiness with the regulatory authorities and sought changes in the law. Attempts to reverse the Staggers Act reforms failed twice, however, once in the late 1980s and again in 1996, because the act was meeting most of its goals, and rate levels were falling. Contentiousness on this point led the ICC and STB to hold extensive proceedings in an effort to determine the extent to which railroad price levels had changed since 1980. After adjusting for commodity mix, work performed, and inflation, average Class I real rail rates fell 46.4 percent between 1982 and 1996.[17] Despite claims to the contrary, this was no artifact of measurement, but rather a manifestation of markets doing a better job than the ICC's adversary, bureaucratic, regulatory procedures had been able to achieve.

The Economics of Railroad Innovation

Economists have long struggled with how to think about technological and managerial innovation occurring alongside market dynamics. Indeed, Jacob Schmookler called technological change the "terra incognita of modern economics." Specifically, the classical treatment of the basic economic inputs—land, labor, and capital—does not seem to account fully for economic change over time. Joseph Schumpeter theorized that economic growth necessarily involved a special process of "creative destruction" in which innovation overcame and set aside older skills and assets. Robert Solow won the Nobel Prize for demonstrating that new knowledge and technology were explicitly part of the formula for productivity improvement and economic growth. Fellow Nobel laureate Simon Kuznets showed how wealthy nations could, with changes in their political and social structure, employ comparative advantage in knowledge and underdeveloped economies could leverage technology transfer to stimulate economic betterment. John Jewkes catalogued the "sources of invention," and

---

17. Surface Transportation Board, Office of Economics, Environmental Analysis, and Administration, "Rail Rates Continue Multiyear Decline," February 1998.

Schmookler skillfully detailed how technological capacity grows and in turn affects economic growth. Edward Denison and John Kendrick demonstrated that knowledge and technology (apart from capital and labor) accounted for large shares of long-run growth in national income and total factor productivity. Nestor Terleckyj's researches showed that most industries underinvest in research and development. Recently, Paul Romer has illustrated the function of delicate and perishable human capital ("wetware"), along with easily replicable instructions ("software"), in supporting both productive efficiency and economic growth. To use Romer's illustration, a really great cake requires not only quality ingredients (flour, sugar, and baking powder), but also a perfect set of stored instructions (a recipe, or software), and the training and talent of a master pastry chef (wetware).[18]

In short, to fully understand economic development over time, economists had to look beyond static market considerations. This was particularly true when evaluating substitution of new for old technology in a mature industry such as railroading. Why and how do different industries accept and diffuse technological innovations? Why does it sometimes seem so easy and sometimes so difficult?

Edwin Mansfield made an important effort to answer those questions in the 1960s.[19] To understand the dynamics of new technology diffusion in an established industry, Mansfield studied the railroads' deployment of diesel-powered locomotives after their introduction by General Motors and others in the late 1920s. Although steam engines had moved railway trains since 1804, even the best of the steam locomotives had poor thermal efficiency and could not match the track adhesion characteristics of the new locomotives with their diesel prime movers and electric traction motors. The new diesel-electrics also had crewing, fueling, watering, and maintenance advantages over steam engines.

Mansfield determined that several factors affected the pace of dieselization. First, the new locomotives had to be proven to a skeptical audience; most railroaders seem to come from Missouri, and steam fans still abound. Second, suppliers of coal often included the railroads themselves—or alternatively were among the railroads' best freight customers. Not only did on-line coal resources affect the relative cost of locomotive fuel, but there was also a natural reluctance to alienate coal shippers by switching to a competing fuel. Indeed, the great coal roads like Norfolk and Western were among

---

18. Schmookler (1966: 3); Schumpeter (1942); Solow (1970); Kuznets (1973); Jewkes (1958); Denison (1974); Kendrick (1961); Terleckyj (1974); Romer (1993).
    19. Mansfield (1968a: 113 ff).

the last to dieselize, while coal-poor Southern Pacific had begun to switch to oil-burning steam locomotives before diesel-electrics were available. Third, the Great Depression clobbered both demand for rail service and companies' cash flow; new locomotives were not especially needed for capacity expansion, and funds were not readily available for investments, even those with a quick payback. Fourth, highly unionized rail labor would resist layoff of employees not required for diesel operations (such as firemen and boilermakers), so some potential cost savings might prove chimerical. Finally, World War II intervened, affecting both the relative value of alternative fuels and the pace at which railroads could physically acquire new engines of any type.

Mansfield's careful study showed that five factors explained about two-thirds of the variation in the speed of dieselization by different railroads: "profit expectation of the investment in diesel locomotives, the date when a firm began to dieselize, size of firm, the age distribution of its steam locomotives, and a firm's initial liquidity."[20] In dieselization and other studies, Mansfield showed that the rate of diffusion of innovation was akin to those laws of psychology by which the speed of a response is related to the intensity of a stimulus; a railroad's rate of deployment of diesel-electric locomotives thus was governed by the profitability to that firm of the new investment opportunity. For the rail industry as a whole (and as is the case for diffusion of new technologies in most capital-intensive industries), Mansfield found a significant threshold or "learning curve" effect; acquisition of diesels was slow to begin, then took off as railroaders became comfortable with the new technology, before tapering again as conversion opportunities were saturated. Along with the stimulus of resurgent traffic demand after the Great Depression, dieselization accelerated when managements perceived the opportunity for wholesale abandonment of a huge network of steam engine infrastructure, such as coal and water towers, turntables, and roundhouses—not to say rationalization of related steam-specialized work forces.

Regulation's role in this shift to diesel locomotives must remain some-

---

20. Mansfield (1968a: 125–26). In a study of several industries, Mansfield found faster diffusion rates not only when innovations were more profitable, but also when they required relatively small investment outlays. Diffusion rates were higher when the innovation did not replace durable equipment, when the industry was growing, and when the innovation was new. Mansfield described a "bandwagon effect" related to both industry competitive dynamics and lower risk of pioneering as diffusion progresses. Finally, he found that in railroading (as in petroleum refining and coal mining), the four largest firms would be pioneers in situations where deployment costs are high relative to firm size and where the size of the four largest firms is much greater than the average for all firms that could use the innovation. Mansfield (1968b).

what conjectural. ICC safety inspection rules and the manner in which regulation reinforced some elements of labor contracts were certainly important, as was the impact of rate regulation on the industry's profitability and appetite for entrepreneurial risk-taking. Because railroad rate regulation focused on carloads more than full trains at the time of dieselization, the effects on freight car innovation were likely greater than was the impact on locomotive technology. In sum, it would be difficult to assert that ICC regulation in the 1930s and 1940s slowed dieselization or other innovations beyond what the trauma of the Great Depression or the extraordinary conditions of World War II would have caused in any event. The same cannot be said for major innovations after the war, however, as the next section shows.

A Case Study in Regulatory Stifling of Railroad Innovation

One of the few attempts by an economist to link the existence of government regulation of freight transportation companies to their propensity to innovate was made by Aaron Gellman in 1971.[21] Gellman's two underlying hypotheses are that innovation may shift demand or average cost curves, or both, so as to yield more profitable equilibrium price and output, and that transportation managers are "profoundly influenced by the amount and character of regulation to which their industry and firm are subjected."[22] He points out that ICC minimum rate regulation was especially pernicious because its very intent was to prevent railroads from increasing market share.

Take the example of larger, more specialized freight cars, in which an innovation in car design might increase the hauling capacity of the equipment; initial purchase cost of the new car would be greater, but its use would yield lower marginal operating expenses. To exploit the innovation, a railroad might need to induce volume by lowering rates for the intended traffic. Enter minimum rate regulation: To protect competing barge operations from loss of business to railroads, the ICC could "suspend and inves-

---

21. Gellman (1971). Another was the study by MacAvoy and Sloss (1967) of railroad unit trains (solid trains of similar car types moving the same commodity exclusively), which concludes: "It was primarily the regulation of rates on a cost-saving innovation that retarded the introduction of the innovation . . ." (p. 117). Several years later, a major railroad resisted extending multiple car rates to agricultural movements from territories in which it was the principal carrier—preferring to stick with the (higher) single car rate structure inherited from the pre-Staggers era. This was a rear guard action, however, and ultimately yielded to broad competitive economics and the specific efficiencies of unit trains.

22. Gellman (1971: 169).

tigate" the lower rail rate, and then determine whether it was compensatory to the railroad or, in fact, predatory against barge companies.

This determination, to be made properly, required detailed knowledge of railroad cost curves over both the short and long run. To deal with the otherwise hopeless (one wants to say fruitless) complexity, the ICC created its "Rail Form A" costing methodology.[23] Gellman argued that although Rail Form A purported to determine out-of-pocket costs, in fact it was "an average cost concept used in many instances where a marginal cost determination would be more appropriate and would lead to better resource allocation."[24] The ICC's application of Rail Form A costs in a minimum rate case could (and did) lead to a ruling that lower rail rates designed to induce volume movements in the new freight cars were unlawful. Minimum rate regulation and use of Rail Form A by the ICC had thus dampened railroad incentives to develop and deploy innovative equipment. "The propensity to innovate on the part of both carriers and suppliers is seriously curbed by the very existence of such formulas," Gellman says.[25]

A specific example of the issues Gellman framed is the infamous case of Southern Railway's attempt in the early 1960s to use incentive pricing to introduce "Big John" aluminum grain cars.[26] This case exposed the myth that the purpose of ICC regulation was to protect commerce from rate-gouging individual railroads. It demonstrated, instead, the extent to which the ICC would go to protect existing operators and preserve existing patterns of commerce. The Big John case also clearly showed how regulation could delay innovation in an industry that sorely needed it.[27] Nor was the ruling an isolated case. In *Ingot Molds*, the ICC disallowed rail rates for

23. Meyer and others (1959) devoted an appendix of the book (pp. 274–76) to a critique of the ICC's methodology.

24. Gellman (1971: 169).

25. Gellman (1971: 174). He asserts (p. 170) that Rail Form A killed off several freight car ideas: "In an industry that is in need of technological improvement and whose performance influences so many other enterprises and industries, this situation is frustrating to shippers, carriers, and the public."

26. *Grain in Multiple-Car Shipments—River Crossings to So.*, 318 ICC 641 (1963); 325 ICC 752 (1965). The story is told in Harvard Business School Case 9-677-244, 1977, "Southern Railway System: The Big John Investment." Boston: HBS Case Services (contributions from Joel Goldhar, Robert A. Buzzell, Noel L. Perry, and John R. Meyer). The case is also summarized in Gellman (1971:175–78).

27. A colleague who was employed at the time by a competitor (and protesting) railroad explains, however, that there were also practical motives. The competitor railroad's track and bridges could not handle the heavier Big John cars, so the Southern's rates favored movement on its own line. Eventually, the competitor railroad upgraded its facilities to permit participation in the market. The point is that innovations can cause economic dislocations that public policies may wish to ease in one way or another.

shipment of heavy aluminum molds based on incremental costing concepts as violative of the National Transportation Policy established in the Transportation Act of 1940.[28] The proposed rail service, the ICC decided, would not preserve the "inherent advantages" of barge lines whose rates were based on average costs. Most transportation economists found the ICC's reasoning in these two cases shocking, and some among them began to focus their efforts on regulatory reform.

In summary, regulators traditionally failed to understand, as Gellman says, "the high correlation between anti-competitive and anti-innovative forces."[29] Innovation thrives on free competition and is thwarted by regulation. Innovation embraces risk-taking in the hope and expectation that the new will be better than the old. It seeks its reward in future profits even at the expense of forgoing current cash flow. M. A. Adelman once observed that "strong competition makes innovation a necessary condition for profit."[30] It is no less true that innovation is strongly pro-competitive because it hopes to attract profits by enabling a firm to outperform its rivals.

Experience with Railroad Innovation under Deregulation

During the debate before passage of the Staggers Act, many advocates of relaxing federal regulation of railroads argued that change was needed not so much to allow rate-making flexibility or "revenue adequacy" as to facilitate innovative structural adaptation to fundamentally changed economic circumstances. In hearings on the Carter administration reform proposal, members of the Senate Commerce Committee expressed concern that deregulation would lead to higher rail freight rates. The administration witness testified that, in fact, deregulation was likely to reduce rates. Because the legislation would permit long-term service contracts, railroads and their customers could get together to figure out win-win solutions in which, for example, rail services and equipment provision could be tailored to the customer's exact transport requirements. Costs would go down as wastes were eliminated, and facilities might improve as guaranteed volumes and long-term commitments encouraged reinvestment. This has indeed been the case, to an extent no one could have predicted.

---

28. *Ingot Molds from Pennsylvania to Steelton, KY*, 323 ICC 758 (1965).
29. Gellman (1971: 193).
30. Adelman (1967).

Most discussions of the impact of railroad deregulation skip over a matter central to my theme in this chapter, namely, the features of the Staggers Act and the economic dynamics flowing from it that opened the door to managerial innovations. Economic productivity and growth studies tend to treat education, technology, and innovation as a residual—something that happens inside a black box and that cannot be described. My intent in the following sections is to explain some of the mechanisms through which improvements actually occurred.

Cash Flow Improvement Factors

The railroad industry's financial resurgence since the Staggers Act has had a powerful impact on diffusion of technology. It is long and well established in economics that the predominant way in which new technology is diffused through an industry is by its embodiment in new capital goods, something that occurs much more rapidly when an industry is profitable and growing than when it is stagnant. The Staggers Act fed a financial recovery in railroading that not only permitted reinvestment (from current cash flows), but made it look smart (from a financial viewpoint).[31]

With billions of dollars worth of sunk, long-lived investment, it is impractical for railroads to replace old technology with new instantly. An improved type of diesel turbocharger with reliability and fuel economy advantages, for example, may not be retrofit to most existing locomotives. Instead, the advanced turbocharger appears as original equipment in new locomotives as they are delivered to the industry. The two examples below further illustrate how the railroads have realized the benefits of new technology as a by-product of incremental replacement capital spending or new investment in additional capacity. In this way I hope to demonstrate the crucial effect of railroads' improved cash flow post-Staggers on technological progress in the industry—an effect resulting in a virtuous upward spiral precisely the opposite of the vicious downward spiral railroads endured during the 1960s and 1970s.

---

31. A coincident change in federal taxation (The Economic Recovery Tax Act of 1981) also affected railroads' ability to invest in the 1980s. In place of a "betterment" standard traditionally used by the ICC, the change based railroad income taxation on ordinary capitalization and depreciation. This enabled railroad firms to deduct billions of dollars of past, undepreciated investments (the so-called "frozen base" of assets) over a period as short as five years. The change boosted industry cash flow by hundreds of millions of dollars in the 1980s. See also Kimura (1997: 212–19).

TRACK STRUCTURES. The first example of technology diffusion through embodiment in replacement or expansion investment is the use of improved steel in rails and turnouts, introduction of concrete cross-ties, and changes in maintenance techniques related to these stronger track materials. Underlying management decisions to build premium track structures are increases in rail line densities and the desire to operate heavier trains for added throughput capacity. Freight cars, long limited to 263,000 pounds gross weight on rail in interchange service, now are routinely loaded to 286,000 pounds, and occasionally to 315,000 pounds gross weight. Not only have track structure and maintenance improvements permitted higher average car weights, employment of these innovations has also almost doubled average rail service life in the last decade. Main line rail that would be scheduled for replacement after about 750 million gross ton-miles per mile of wear in the 1980s now may last for 1.7 billion gross ton-miles before being cascaded into secondary lines or yard track. Moreover, stronger and better-maintained track has contributed to greatly reduced incidence of train derailments since deregulation. Reported derailments occurred about 9 times per million train-miles in 1980, improving to 2.6 per million train-miles in 1997.[32]

The impact of deregulation in extending these rail service cycles is indirect. Heavy traffic density (stimulated by Staggers Act reforms, development of Powder River Basin coal resources, Conrail revitalization, and mergers approved in the early 1980s) made it cost-effective for railroads to invest in stronger premium steels and improved subgrade and cross-ties. Moreover, there is an incentive to build stronger track structure for a densely used line so that maintenance-of-way crews do not have to return to it for rehabilitation for a longer time. Lighter maintenance, such as grinding and profiling, can be carried out intermittently, but taking track out of service for rebuilding has a high opportunity cost when traffic is heavy. Still, market forces unleashed by deregulation are the ultimate stimulus for these innovations. Reviewing Burlington Northern's research and development and technology investment strategies in the first half of the 1980s, Steven Ditmeyer observed: "Concrete ties and wheel flange lubricators are not new concepts; it is today's competitive marketplace that provided the impetus for making these investments."[33]

---

32. Rail information provided by Samuel G. Atkinson, Jr., Union Pacific Railroad. Derailment data from Federal Railroad Administration, Office of Safety (various years).

33. Ditmeyer (1987: 8).

LOCOMOTIVES. To handle the extraordinary growth of rail traffic in the last decade, high-horsepower, fuel-efficient, microprocessor-controlled locomotives are being put into service at a rapid rate. In a period of growth and need for expanded capacity, railroads are willing to purchase more reliable (and more expensive) locomotives to avoid power shortages on heavy trains moving back to back over a single line. The newer, larger, more reliable locomotives have a higher internal return on investment if they can be kept fully employed. If traffic levels were declining, railroads would make do with older locomotives for a longer time, and the technological advances built into new models would not be as promptly available to the railroad. These advances include significantly improved fuel economy, alternating current traction motors (which achieve better adhesion and hence more tractive effort per unit of horsepower), a more comfortable ride for the crew, and improved monitoring of the locomotive's mechanical health for use in scheduling a replacement unit at the next major depot or longer-term maintenance at the locomotive's home shop.

In both the track structures and locomotive examples, investments are required for normal replacement or increased capacity, but the new technology component of purchased materials and equipment generates additional safety, reliability, and operating expense benefits. These in turn accelerate the rate of reinvestment. In some but not all instances, the collateral benefits have a strong enough prospective impact on new capital purchases that suppliers are motivated to make their own speculative investments in product research and development.

Corporate Culture and Managerial Factors

The Staggers Act changed the way railroads think about their operations, markets, and customers. Regulatory reform resulted in more aggressive railroad managements and stimulated crucial changes in railroad company culture and investment patterns aimed at these goals. The old hierarchical (or "militaristic") organizational styles common to railroads seemed increasingly out of place after 1980. Railroads began to focus on customers in earnest in the late 1980s, and most railroads adopted formal quality processes aimed at satisfying customer requirements, empowering employees, managing with better data, and developing nontraditional solutions to problems.

Among the most important of these changes was the widespread use of cross-functional teams in developing revised business processes and new information technology applications. Railroads found that by assembling subject matter experts from a variety of departments or disciplines, they could do things previously impossible; the necessary mix of skills and experience had never before been assembled and charged with team assignments and responsibilities in this way. Cross-functional teams proved particularly adept in setting requirements for computerized systems. This discovery—along with the use of powerful new graphical user interfaces, code-writing techniques, and client-server architectures—has contributed to the explosion in computer applications development since 1990. In short, the idea of focusing on customer requirements and quality processes, carried into the railroad industry by the competitive stimulus of deregulation, has turned into an ongoing capability for "working smarter." The old economic ingredients of labor, capital, and land have been joined by "know-how" in a way more powerful than Schumpeter or Solow could have imagined.

New Relationships with Customers

Perhaps the single most important change mechanism contained in the Staggers Act was its explicit sanction of long-term service contracts. Within about three years of passage of the act, contracts became the most important way for railroads and their customers to do business. The value of contracts as a share of total rail revenues grew from nothing to well over one-half in that time.[34] Today, contracts may spell out not only rate levels, but volume commitments, responsibilities for equipment provision (freight cars), transit or cycle time standards and penalties for noncompliance, the scope of ancillary services, and more. Certainly the best example of the profound way in which contracts changed railroad-shipper relationships is the story of intermodal containerization, or double-stack unit container trains, and their role in the ongoing intermodal revolution.

CONTAINERIZATION. Railroad use of intermodal containers in solid trains did not become widespread until the mid-1980s—almost exactly ten years after having been championed by the Railroad Productivity Task Force and a quarter century after marine containerization had been pioneered by Malcolm Maclean, founder of Sea-Land. Two things broke the ice: the adaptation of marine containership fastening techniques to enable stacking these containers two-high on rail flatcars; and reform of regulatory rules to permit long-term service contracts between railroads and their customers.

34. Author's estimate from uncollected contemporary ICC reports.

Double-stack container train service (DST) was put in place initially to cater to steamship companies seeking long-distance inland movement of marine containers. The level of strategic and financial commitment required for this enterprise required long-term (ten years in some cases) contracts between steamship companies such as American President Lines and Sea-Land, and railroads such as Southern Pacific, Union Pacific, and CSX. Indeed, if American President Lines were going to depend on transcontinental DST rather than transit through the Panama Canal to reach the American East Coast from the Far East, long-term partnerships based on service contracts were essential. Such contracts for trainload movements of merchandise goods were either unlawful or of doubtful legality before the Staggers Act.[35] The double-stack revolution would not have been possible, moreover, unless the international containers used by the steamship companies for transcontinental rail movements from the Pacific Coast ports could be loaded with domestic articles for return shipment to California and the Pacific Northwest. Backhauling of domestic goods in international containers was unworkable until intermodal service was exempted from ICC regulation shortly after passage of the Staggers Act. DST now eclipses piggyback (trailer on flat car, or TOFC) and has enabled railroads to win back market share from motor carriers in key long-haul traffic lanes such as Los Angeles–Chicago.[36]

INTERLINE SERVICE MANAGEMENT. A New York Central Board Chairman, Robert R. Young, once sponsored an ad campaign using the theme that "hogs can cross the country without changing cars, but you can't." He was referring to the need for transcontinental rail passengers to change to another railroad and often another station in Chicago, St. Louis, New Orleans, or elsewhere. Of course, hogs also had to be changed from the trains of one railroad to another, a laborious and time-consuming process known as freight "interlining," but that is a different story.[37]

---

35. After being appointed ICC chairman by President Carter, Darius Gaskins began administrative actions to enable limited contracting—proving that the concept could work—but a change in the law was necessary to give contracts permanent standing.

36. See Gallamore (1998b).

37. The term "interlining" is a bit colloquial and generic; it encompasses everything having to do with the connective service of two companies, from physical hand-off to compatibility of equipment to accounting for and dividing revenues for through-haul runs.

There are several strategies for reducing impedances at the "gateways" that connect two railroad lines. One is merger, and end-to-end merger applications to the STB tout the benefits of "single-line service," obviating interline connections or interchange. A second is "run-through trains," which have become a common time-saving operation since dieselization helped standardize interline locomotive operations and costing; a run-through train is one that, by agreement of two companies, operates through the traditional gateway, usually changing crews but not locomotives or freight cars. A third strategy is to by-pass congested terminals like Chicago and St. Louis and instead complete the interline connection at a nontraditional gateway such as Salem, Illinois. Run-throughs and by-pass interchange can be facilitated with automatic equipment identification technology, which permits automation of the clerical operations involved in interline accounting (such as for freight car per diem rentals and locomotive hour credits and debits).

A fourth strategy is the industry's plan for interline service management (ISM), being carried out through the Association of American Railroads. ISM is a set of protocols for full electronic data transmission among railroads so that both railroads participating in an interline move have advance billing and handling instructions for each car that is transferred from one railway line to another. The point in the present context is that ISM is the post-Staggers response to the longstanding problem of interlining. Under regulation, the issue could never be separated from ICC-approved "divisions"—that is, how much of the regulated total revenue each railroad would receive. Since deregulation, however, customer service and competition with direct door-to-door motor-carrier service across the traditional Illinois and Mississippi River rail gateways (Chicago, St. Louis, Memphis, and New Orleans) have become the key factors. The interline service management problem is by no means solved, but a model now exists, and the railroads know they need continuous improvement strategies to make their interline connections "seamless" to the customer, as competitive truckload service is.

Short Line Railroads

Another example of innovation that had been stifled by the regulatory regime before passage of the Staggers Act, but which flowered after 1980, is the proliferation of short line railroads to serve light density markets.

In the early 1970s the FRA estimated the annual avoidable losses to railroads from continued operation of about 21,000 miles of light-density lines (handling fewer than twenty-five cars per mile per year) at $57 million. The Railroad Productivity Task Force saw the operating deficit as important but was more concerned by what these excess lines represented in terms of distraction of marketing focus and lost opportunities for investment elsewhere. Noting the ICC's reluctance to grant timely abandonment authority, the task force suggested converting branch lines to independent short line companies that might be able to negotiate more lenient work rules and smaller crews, as well as customer rate adjustments. Subsidies from state governments could be tried, but the task force hinted that it might be cheaper to subsidize relocation of key shippers than continuing the operation of deficit branch lines. The task force came down clearly on the side of rationalizing little-used trackage in contrast to forcing mainline freight railroads to carry the burden of subsidizing the few remaining shippers on those lines.

After the experience of rationalizing deficit lines in the Northeast as part of the planning for Conrail, Congress changed the rules for light-density lines nationwide in the Staggers Act and even more extensively for Conrail in the Northeast Rail Services Act passed three years later. The statutory changes permitted new railroads to begin operations without a unionized work force. Legal challenges delayed the effect, but in the late 1980s the floodgates opened and Class I railroads became aggressive in selling or leasing many of their light-density lines to new operators with nonunion employees or liberalized work rules.

The deregulated environment has proved rewarding for all participants. New short lines have become well-established business operations in many cases; communities and shippers are receiving better service; some jobs have been preserved that would have disappeared; Class I railroads are receiving valuable interchange traffic from regional and short line railroads; and governments are less frequently faced with the poor choice between subsidy and discontinuance. Today, the short line and regional railroads total about 47,000 miles of track (27 percent of all rail miles), employ 29,000 people (11 percent of total rail employment), and take in about $3 billion in gross revenue (9 percent of all rail revenue). It took the bankruptcy crisis in the Northeast, an awkward transitional subsidy program, and the dismantling of nearly 100 years of regulation by independent commission, but change was achieved. Rationalization of light-density lines has played an important role in revival of the industry in the last decade.

Safety and Interoperability Standards

Safety regulation, a responsibility of the FRA, can sometimes delay or thwart investment in new technologies or more efficient operations, including those with net safety benefits. For example, cabooses were required even after end-of-train devices capable of reporting brake line pressure made them obsolete. An FRA rule that requires expensive devices for electronic locking of switches upon installation of centralized traffic control has defeated the economics of investment in centralized control in many locations—at a probable net cost to safety as well as to efficient operations. Deployment of cab signals has been discouraged by an FRA safety rule that requires more restrictive operations in the event of system failure than if the cab signals had not been installed.

Historically, to be sure, technology standardization and implementation sometimes came about through national legislation. The standard 4' 8½" track gauge (not so "standard" before the Civil War) was assured dominance by its virtual mandate in the Pacific Rail Act (1862), which authorized the first transcontinental railroad. Later in the nineteenth century, both Eli Janney's automatic coupler design (which ended dangerous link and pin coupling operations) and George Westinghouse's air brakes (which allowed longer, heavier, safer trains) were made national standards and required equipment by federal law. Today, railroads typically resist national technology mandates because they believe such requirements are likely to be suboptimal or even counterproductive. Instead, railroads would like to see federal statutes and regulations adopt a performance-based approach to safety that would evaluate actual risks and enable railroads to mitigate them in the most cost-effective way possible.

Industry standardization continues to be achieved through its trade association, the Association of American Railroads (AAR). Committees of the AAR routinely establish consensus requirements for equipment that will be exchanged among railroads in interline service. Adoption of interoperability standards benefits the industry because it increases market scope and permits economies of scale in new technology development and deployment. Also, interoperability inherently contributes to safety by helping avoid confusion in rules, equipment, or terminology as railroaders and rolling stock move around the country. An example of both benefits is the current effort to reach consensus on industry standards for a cost-effective advanced electronic system to prevent train collisions and derailments caused by a train traveling faster than it should, called positive train control. The FRA is sponsoring parallel efforts to develop consensus performance standards for positive train control and other safety rules through its participatory (labor-management-supplier-government) Railway Safety Advisory Committee.

Managing Change in Railroading

Although railroads have their specific institutional parameters and cultural peculiarities, agents of change in railroading stem from business principles similar to those in other industries. In the post-Staggers era, rail managements have adopted growth and improvement strategies such as:

—*Expense reduction,* through targeted improvements in asset utilization, operating cost performance, and employee-hour productivity;

—*Revenue growth,* through strategies to increase market share and traffic volume while maintaining or improving rate levels;

—*Earnings growth,* from improvements in margin or operating ratios, from increases in market share, and by profit-enhancing acquisition strategies;

—*Quality improvement and customer satisfaction,* with comprehensive business process reengineering aimed at meeting customer requirements cost-effectively;

—*Safety and claims improvement,* to reduce costs, improve the workplace environment, and enhance corporate reputation.

When these goals are reduced to specific priorities and performance measures, conflicts may arise. Revenue growth, for example, may be at odds with margin improvement if new traffic is taken on at lower unit profit; volume growth may strain capacity and increase unit expenses if decreasing returns to scale have set in. Top managers may understand such conflicts intellectually, but remain focused on implementing the strategy broadly and measuring progress with fairly high-level indicators, which average out sharp distinctions in a way that may trouble individual line managers. If the line manager then has to knuckle under and "meet the budget," opportunity for long-run gain can be sacrificed on the altar of cost reduction or quarterly earnings reports (whatever is the dominant corporate objective at the time). Knowing that stringent cash flow management will sometimes cut into muscle and not just fat, however, top management may relent. Such a situation can persist for years—until major shifts occur in the external or internal business environment, or both.

The Technology Dilemma under Deregulation

Competitive pressures since passage of the Staggers Act have forced railroads to manage more tightly at the same time that the lifting of regulatory impediments has enabled managements to innovate. Hence the Hobson's choice—cut research and development and defer investment in new technology to husband current cash, or stimulate development and deployment of better plant, equipment, and information systems to improve capital and labor productivity. How this dilemma plays out at individual railroads and over time has a lot to do with railroad industry economic performance in the short and long run.

Since 1980, most observers would say, the belt-tightening ethic has prevailed over research and development and direct investment in service quality improvement. The reasons are straightforward at one level, but some subtleties also need to be considered. At the simple level, opportunities to reduce costs abounded in the early years of deregulation. As long as excess capacity from the pre-Staggers era hung over the industry, "hard dollar" savings could be identified readily and brought down to the bottom line predictably. By contrast, benefits from service improvement are "soft dollars," depending on product acceptance in the marketplace and translation into future top line revenues. Research and development, by its nature uncertain, is exceptionally difficult to justify when budgets are tight. So although deregulation opened opportunities to leverage new technologies in the more competitive marketplace, development and deployment dollars came under intense scrutiny, and large, technology-intensive investments had to take the back seat.[38]

In addition to cutbacks for research and development at individual railroads, as downsizing of employment and streamlining of expenses spread through the industry, AAR's research and testing budgets were reduced significantly. Also (and among many other reasons), because railroads were now largely deregulated, Congress and the Executive Branch felt justified in reducing the FRA's research and development appropriations. These cutbacks have become a real problem because earlier FRA and AAR spending on track and train research had been key to filling the technology "pipeline" with improved products and operating methods that proved so beneficial to railroads in recent years.

---

38. For an excellent example of a management dilemma of this type, see Harvard Business School Cases 9-191-122 and 9-191-123, *Burlington Northern: The ARES Decision*, prepared by Julie H. Hertenstein and Robert S. Kaplan, HBS Case Services, Boston, February 21, 1991.

Continuous Improvement versus Paradigm Shifts

What about the more subtle aspects of the technology dilemma under deregulation mentioned above? These have to do not just with "hard" savings versus "soft" benefits, but with the nature of business decisions regarding incremental improvements versus major investments in a capital-constrained, network-based industry. Given a large array of possible technology deployments representing a wide mix of current operating expenditures and major capital projects—any subset of which would yield acceptable levels of internal return on investment—what does management do? The trade-off analysis may not be made explicitly, but most railroads would opt for incremental purchases of discrete units of technology (which can be gradually integrated into the existing asset base) over large, fixed investments (which must be implemented systemwide to realize their full worth). For example, most railroad managements faced with the need to expand traffic capacity would choose to buy new locomotives rather than, say, make an equivalent investment in a new dispatching system capable of contributing the same amount of additional network throughput capacity as the locomotives. Implicitly, railroads perceive less risk for similar rewards in choosing incremental improvement over wholesale change.

The prevailing "bias for incrementalism," to put it negatively, may help explain why railroad culture was quick to embrace the concept of quality management that became so fashionable in the late 1980s. Most consultants and advocates of "total quality management" described principles such as "continuous improvement," "manage with data," "customer focus," and "plan, do, check, adjust," all of which depend on or lend themselves to managing in increments. These principles are virtually unassailable, and, as I have contended earlier in this chapter, their adoption by railroads is one of the factors contributing to the rail renaissance under deregulation.

If there is a danger in incrementalism, however, it is that in reinforcing near-term results, it can steer managements away from attempting a wholesale shift in the reigning business paradigm. If the company's entire organization, staffing, and reward system is geared around short-term improvement, it is likely to underinvest in creating and bringing about a long-run future vision. Unless luck replaces foresight, or near-term execution is done so well that its rewards outpace changes in the external business environment, the company risks stagnation.

The case is impossible to prove one way or the other. Fortunately, as so often is the circumstance, truth is neither black nor white. Incrementalism and wholesale change coexist and both can be beneficial. For every total quality management system that highlights continuous improvement, another embraces "thinking outside the box." The wave of interest in total quality management was closely followed by a business fad for "business process reengineering," and surely companies that chose one over the other, or both, lost little ground to advocates of the contrary approach. It turned out that the most important thing was not to select one quality construct over another, but to have a change strategy of almost any variety that captured the energy of employees from top to bottom in the company.

All that said, the long train of railroad history does describe periods characterized by dramatic business, cultural, regulatory, or technological shifts, and other periods when the pace of change was gradual or even stagnant.[39] (Indeed, one of the fascinations of railroading is its four-dimensional visibility across the landscape and back through time.) Figure 15-2 illustrates this historical interpretation in a very broad and preliminary way. Examples of wholesale shifts in the prevailing business paradigm occurred at the inception of railroads in 1804, with the first full-scale commercial services a quarter century later, with building of the transcontinental railroads (when nearly every western railroad had "Pacific" in its name), with a great technological surge in the final decades of the nineteenth century, and with the introduction of diesel-electric locomotives in the 1930s. Overlaying the physical and corporate development of the industry were the paradigm shifts caused by the inception and demise of regulation. These should be understood not as single points in time, 1887 and 1980 when watershed laws were enacted, but as a phasing in and out over a number of years.

Interspersed with history-making surges and shifts, railroads experienced long periods when change was gradual or external environments brought internal improvements to a standstill. Sometimes the delay in deployment of a powerful new technology was due to its network characteristics. Examples are the Robinson track circuit-based signaling system, Janney couplers, and Westinghouse air brakes. In the latter two cases, federal legislation actually accelerated what may have been an exceptionally long diffusion process related to the cost and difficulty of wholesale change over an entire network. At other times, external circumstance delayed de-

---

39. See Mensch (1979) for an intriguing analysis of the phenomenon of technological surges in many industries over the past two centuries.

Figure 15-2. *Railroad Regulation and Innovation Timeline*

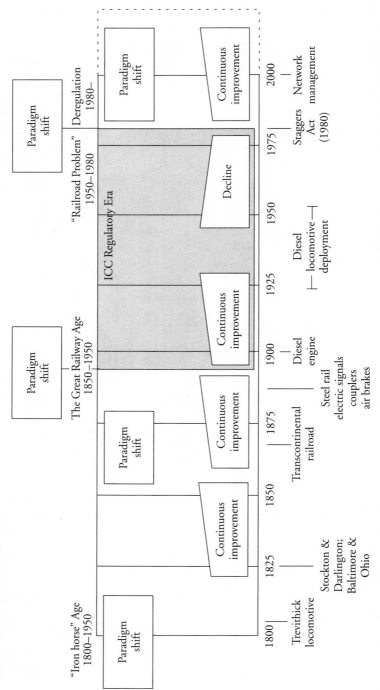

Source: Author's analysis. See Schmookler (1966: 269–78) for a comprehensive list of railroad inventions before 1950.

ployment, as with dieselization during the Great Depression and World War II. In that regard, the fifty-year span from invention of the diesel engine to completion of railroad dieselization is a cautionary tale.

Interpretation of the period since the Staggers Act is tricky because it is so recent and because all of time seems remarkably compressed late in this century. Clearly, the real impact of deregulation did not sink in until late in the 1980s, and until at least 1995 continuous improvement seems the proper characterization. In arriving at this interpretation, I fall back on the essential economic dynamics controlling railroad behavior since the Staggers Act. Rather than opening the door to rate increases, as defenders of the ICC regulatory regime claimed would occur, rail-to-rail competition and long-term contract mechanisms drove rate levels down. In time these forces pushed managements to cut costs further, husband cash flow, and develop the "three M" strategies—market share, margin improvement, and mergers—none of which can be implemented overnight and all of which remain under the sway of traditional economic and institutional restraints.

Re-Regulation?

To bring the analysis right up to date, let us look at what is clearly the hottest public policy issue confronting railroads today, the matter of customer access to competitive rail carriers. Citing inadequate service and sometimes "captivity" to their serving railroads, many important customers have organized lobbying coalitions aimed at reversing key features of the Staggers Act. Their view is that the act and subsequent regulatory interpretation has swung too far in the railroads' favor. These self-described "captive shippers" advocate injecting new rail-to-rail competition into specific market segments by requiring an existing railroad that is the sole provider to a shipping point to host a competitor on its line or to have its rate levels regulated between the shipper's location and the first junction with another railroad.

Further discussion of this "open" or "forced" access proposal (depending on one's point of view) is beyond the scope of this chapter, but the eventual outcome may have consequences for future progress in railroad technology. My hypothesis is that the result of the access, or "re-regulation," fight will come down to who makes the more persuasive argument to Congress—those who believe the future value of railroad service is best achieved by government policy favoring *rail-rail competition*, against those who believe *railroad competitiveness* is more important.

To explain, I return to the discussion of the different environmental factors resulting in continuous improvement on the one hand or a paradigm shift on the other. The Staggers Act (a paradigm shift) released competitive forces that stimulated railroad managements in many important ways, some of which most shippers liked but others found disagreeable. Railroads used their new freedom and recovering finances to focus on specific customer requirements and quality processes, to contract for volume business at lower rates, and to invest in new plant and equipment capacity. In the drive to make earnings provide an adequate return on capital, however, railroads also engaged in regional mergers and sought greater market share and margin improvements. All of this can best be described as continuous improvement under the deregulation paradigm.

But if it was rail-rail competition and continuous improvement that brought railroads to where they are today, is that the best policy for the future—or would a paradigm shift that resulted in wholesale improvements in railroad competitiveness vis-à-vis other transport modes be more beneficial to the public? This is a tough question, and the answer is not clear—but the issues need to be understood fully. The re-regulation battle is more than a series of skirmishes over profit margins between one set of big businesses and another. Instead, the intellectual and policy battle is for an understanding of how industries perform and how economic progress is achieved. In this conflict, so long as railroads are able to continue to improve their overall economic performance as they have in the last dozen years, the case for re-regulation is weak.

A Vision for Next Century's Railroads

It is plausible to argue that American railroads stand at another historical moment of truth, caused not by the rolling of the Millennium or institutional changes in Washington, but rather by the challenges of managing their vast, enormously expensive, and exposed networks. Given the explosion of computerized systems and communications technologies of all kinds, railroads that are able to develop "killer applications" aimed at enhancing network performance and customer value will be the winners in the marketplace. Examples are systems that help improve service reliability, customer satisfaction, decisionmaking intelligence, and capacity management. Success will require huge investments in technology-intensive areas where benefits, although potentially large, may be both "soft" and unrealizable for a number of years.

The vision of the future, then, is one in which the ancient efficiencies of low friction wheels on rails merge with twenty-first century "smart" systems to create an entirely new level of transportation value added for shippers. Future railroad service improvements will be based on knowledge of train and freight car position, optimized network capacity management techniques, faster transit times, and reduction of quality failures. Railroads may also finally benefit from what in the past several decades was a decided liability—production units large compared with their principal competing mode, the motor truck.

The net impact will be truly historic in its proportions—equal to the importance in the past of Janney couplers, air brakes, electric track circuits and signals, Bessemer steel rail, or diesel-electric locomotives. Indeed, the impact may be much greater than that of any single innovation since dieselization, save deregulation itself. Such a vision, nearly impossible to imagine in the years just before the Staggers Act of 1980, is no stretch at all today.

References

Adelman, M.A. 1967. "Technological and Scientific Problems in the Relations between Europe and the United States." Paper presented in Turin, Italy, November. Quoted in Gellman (1971: 192).

Association of American Railroads. 1997. *Railroad Facts*. Washington, D.C.

Barriger, John W. 1956. *Super-railroads for a Dynamic American Economy*. New York: Simmons-Boardman.

Denison, Edward. 1974. *Accounting for United States Economic Growth, 1929–1969*. Brookings.

Ditmeyer, Steven R. 1987. "Deregulation and Technological Progress in Railroading: Some Reflections from the Perspective of a Particular Carrier." *Transportation Journal* 27 (1): 5–9.

DOT (U.S. Department of Transportation), Federal Highway Administration, Federal Transit Administration, and Federal Railroad Administration. 1997. *1997 Federal Highway Cost Allocation Study*. August.

Eno Transportation Foundation. Annual. *Transportation in America*. Landsdowne, Va. (successor to Transportation Association of America volumes of the same name).

Federal Railroad Administration. 1978. *A Prospectus for Change in the Freight Railroad Industry: A Preliminary Report by the Secretary of Transportation*. U.S. Department of Transportation.

Federal Railroad Administration, Office of Safety. Various years. *Accident/Incident Bulletin*. U.S. Department of Transportation.

Gallamore, Robert E. 1968. *Railroad Mergers: Costs, Competition, and the Future Organization of the American Railroad Industry*. Ph.D. dissertation. Harvard University, Economics Department.

————. 1998a. "Perspectives and Prospects for American Railroad Infrastructure." *Infrastructure* 3 (4, Summer): 36–44.

————. 1998b. "State of the Art of Intermodal Freight Transport in the United States." In *Intermodal Freight Transport in Europe and the United States,* pp. 17–31. Lansdowne, Va: Eno Transportation Foundation.

Gellman, Aaron. 1971. "Surface Freight Transportation." In *Technological Change in Regulated Industries,* edited by William M. Capron, 166–96. Brookings.

Griliches, Zvi. 1972. "Cost Allocation in Railroad Regulation." *Bell Journal of Economics and Management Science* 3: 26–41.

Healy, Kent T. 1985. *Performance of the U.S. Railroads Since World War II: A Quarter Century of Private Operation.* New York: Vantage Press.

Hughes, Jonathan R.T. 1983. *American Economic History.* Glenview, Ill: Scott, Foresman.

Jewkes, John. 1958. *Sources of Invention.* St. Martin's Press.

Keeler, Theodore E. 1983. *Railroads, Freight, and Public Policy.* Brookings.

Kendrick, John. 1961. *Productivity Trends in the United States.* Princeton University Press.

Kimura, Kenji. 1997. *Performance of the U.S. Railroad Industry Since Deregulation.* Ph.D. dissertation. Harvard University, Urban Planning Department.

Kuznets, Simon. 1973. "Modern Economic Growth: Findings and Reflections." *American Economic Review* 63 (June): 247–58.

Locklin, D. Philip. 1960. *Economics of Transportation.* 5th ed. Homewood, Ill: Richard D. Irwin, Inc.

MacAvoy, Paul W., and James Sloss. 1967. *Regulation of Transport Innovation: The ICC and Unit Coal Trains to the East Coast.* Random House.

Mansfield, Edwin. 1968a. *The Economics of Technological Change.* W. W. Norton.

————. 1968b. *Industrial Research and Technological Innovation: An Economic Analysis.* W. W. Norton.

Martland, Carl. 1997. "Sources of Financial Improvement in the U.S. Rail Industry, 1966–1995." *Proceedings.* 39th Annual Meeting, Transportation Research Forum, Reston, Va.

McCullough, Gerard J. 1993. *Essays on the Economic Performance of U.S. Freight Railroads Under Deregulation.* Ph.D. dissertation. Massachusetts Institute of Technology Department of Civil Engineering.

Mensch, Gerhard. 1979. *Stalemate in Technology: Innovations Overcome the Depression.* Cambridge, Mass.: Ballinger.

Meyer, John R., and Alexander L. Morton. 1975. "The U.S. Railroad Industry in the Post–World War II Period: A Profile." *Explorations in Economic Research* 2 (4, Fall): 449–501.

Meyer, John R., and others. 1959. *The Economics of Competition in the Transportation Industries.* Harvard University Press.

Nelson, James C. 1959. *Railroad Transportation and Public Policy.* Brookings.

Romer, Paul. 1993. "Economic Growth." In *The Fortune Encyclopedia of Economics,* edited by David Henderson, 183–89. Warner.

Schumpeter, Joseph. 1942. *Capitalism, Socialism, and Democracy.* Harper.

Schmookler, Jacob. 1966. *Invention and Economic Growth.* Harvard University Press.

Solow, Robert. 1970. *Growth Theory—An Exposition.* Oxford University Press.

Stone, Richard D. 1991. *The Interstate Commerce Commission and the Railroad Industry: A History of Regulatory Policy.* New York: Praeger Publishers.

Stover, John F. 1961. *American Railroads.* University of Chicago Press. Midway Reprint, 1976.

Task Force on Railroad Productivity. 1973. *Improving Railroad Productivity: Final Report of the Task Force on Railroad Productivity.* A Report to the National Commission on Productivity and the Council of Economic Advisers. Washington, D.C.

Terleckyj, Nestor E. 1974. *Effects of R&D on the Productivity Growth of Industries: An Exploratory Study.* Washington, D.C.: National Planning Association.

U.S. Railway Association. 1975. *Preliminary System Plan for Restructuring Railroads in the Northeast and Midwest Region Pursuant to the Regional Rail Reorganization Act of 1973.* U.S. Government Printing Office.

U.S. Senate, Committee on Commerce. 1972. "The American Railroads: Posture, Problems, and Prospects." Prepared by Richard J. Barber and reprinted in U.S. House of Representatives, Subcommittee on Transportation and Commerce, 1977, *Congressional Symposium on Railroads—1977 and Beyond: Problems and Promises.* Committee Print 95–32.

U. S. Senate, Committee on the Judiciary. 1962. *Rail Merger Legislation, Part I,* Hearings before the Subcommittee on Antitrust and Monopoly. Washington, D.C.

Winston, Clifford, Kenneth A. Small, and Carol A. Evans. 1989. *Road Work: A New Highway Pricing and Investment Policy.* Brookings.

Winston, Clifford, and others. 1990. *The Economic Effects of Surface Freight Deregulation.* Brookings.

IAN SAVAGE

16 | The Economics of Commercial Transportation Safety

Crashes involving intercity commercial transportation carriers result in the deaths of 6,500 Americans each year, considerable destruction of equipment and merchandise, and occasional releases of hazardous materials into the atmosphere and the groundwater. Commercial transportation therefore poses the same risk to the public as the combined hazards of drownings and domestic fires. The risk is much less than that from automobiles, however; car crashes claimed approximately 37,000 lives in 1995.[1]

As shown in table 16-1, trucking accounts for about three-quarters of total commercial carrier fatalities, followed by railroads, which account for about a fifth. Commercial maritime, commercial aviation, and pipelines each account for fewer than 200 deaths in a typical year. Surprisingly, a relatively small proportion of the people killed are directly involved in the production or consumption of transportation services. Only 15 percent of the fatalities are employees of carriers, and a scant 2 percent are passengers.

---

1. National Highway Traffic Safety Administration (1996); National Safety Council (1996). The 37,000 figure excludes auto drivers killed in collisions with trucks or trains. Note that safety professionals prefer the word "crashes" to "accidents" because the latter word suggests that occurrence is due to pure fate and cannot be influenced by human decisions.

Table 16-1. *Average Annual Fatalities 1990–95*

	Trucking	Railroads	Commercial maritime	Commercial aviation	Pipelines
Employees	645[a]	44	[b]	13[a]	[b]
Passengers	n.a.	13	[b]	93	n.a.
Bystanders	0	1	n.a.	6	[b]
Trespassers or pedestrians	442	546	n.a.	n.a.	n.a.
Motor vehicle users	3,824	615	n.a.	n.a.	n.a.
Total	4,911	1,219	188	112	16

Sources: Trucking: National Highway Traffic Safety Administration (various years). Railroads: Federal Railroad Administration (various years). Maritime and Pipelines: Bureau of Transportation Statistics (various years). Aviation: National Transportation Safety Board.

n.a. Not applicable.

a. Excludes noncrash occupational fatal injuries.

b. Specific breakdown by person type is not available, but almost all fatalities are employees.

The majority of the victims are other road users and pedestrians who are involved in collisions with trucks, and trespassers and grade-crossing users who collide with trains.

Of course, unless one has knowledge of exposure, these absolute numbers give little indication of risk. Table 16-2 provides information on passenger fatalities per billion passenger miles for airlines, buses, and railroads. Because major crashes resulting in substantial loss of life are rare, the reported fatality rates are for the ten-year period from 1986 to 1995. Bus and commercial aviation have the best safety records, at about one fatality for every five billion passenger miles. Riding a train is four times as risky. To put these numbers in context, driving in the mid-1990s was ten times more risky than taking a train and forty times more risky than riding a bus or flying.[2]

Another indication of relative modal safety is fatality and injury rates for employees. Although this chapter does not focus on the labor market issues in risky occupations, employee fatality and injury rates do give some insight into relative modal safety. The maritime industry and the trucking and warehousing industries have the highest levels of employee risk.[3] These

2. For this comparison, the driving risk is calculated for the period 1990 to 1995 because automobile safety has improved considerably since the mid-1980s.

3. Bureau of Labor Statistics (1997a: table A-2; 1997b: table 1).

Table 16-2. *Passenger Fatalities per Billion Passenger Miles*

Automobiles (1990–95)	8.29
Railroad (1986–95)	0.81
Bus (1986–95)	0.23
Commercial aviation (1986–95)	0.21

Source: National Safety Council (1996).

risks are substantial: employees in these industries face more risk than if they were working in construction and about the same amount of risk as underground miners. In contrast, employees in the railroad and aviation industry face less risk, although the risks are still two or three times those in manufacturing.

Ships, planes, and pipelines operate in places where their crashes rarely affect bystanders or other third parties, although there are exceptions, such as the crash of a freight aircraft into a parking lot in Miami in 1997, and the spill of oil from the tanker *Exxon Valdez* in Alaska in 1989. In contrast, trucks and trains frequently collide with pedestrians and other road users. For the average member of the public, the annual probability of being killed in a crash involving a truck is similar to the probability of dying in a fire, while the risk of dying from a collision with a train is the same as that of being killed by the accidental discharge of a firearm. Of course, not all of these victims are innocent bystanders. Many are careless and may indeed be the "cause" of the collision.

Recent Trends in Trucking, Railroads, and Commercial Aviation

As shown in figure 16-1, fatal truck crashes per vehicle mile have declined by more than half in the past twenty years.[4] The absolute number of fatal crashes has declined somewhat, while truck miles have doubled. Much of this improvement has occurred because roads in general are safer; a fact that is also reflected in declines in the fatal crash rates for other vehicle types. Improved automotive technology, better vehicle-occupant protec-

4. National Highway Traffic Safety Administration (various years), Federal Highway Adminisration (various years).

Figure 16-1. *Fatal Crash per Vehicle Mile for Combination Trucks and Other Vehicles, 1977–96*

1977 = 100

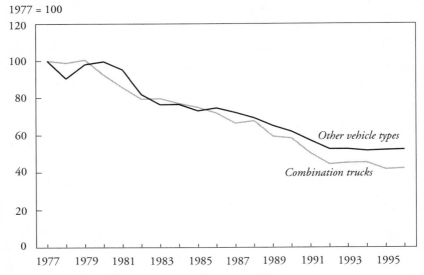

Source: National Highway Traffic Safety Administration (various years).

tion, and changing social attitudes toward the use of seat belts and drinking and driving have all contributed to safer highways. The fatal crash rate for trucks appears to have declined faster than that for other vehicle types since the mid-1980s.

Trends in railroad fatality rates since 1960 are shown in figure 16-2 for the three major types of fatalities. Employee fatalities are expressed relative to employee hours, trespassers relative to the U.S. population, and crossing fatalities relative to the number of registered motor vehicles. The casualty rate for crossings has recorded the most impressive improvement, falling rapidly since 1967. The risk is now less than a fifth of what it was in 1960. The trespasser rates also started to decline rapidly after 1967 but leveled out in 1975 at about 40 percent below the fatality rate in 1960. If anything, there may be a slight upward trend in recent years. Contrary to the popular view that trespasser victims are small children or people innocently taking a shortcut across the tracks, the reality is that most are single adult males who have consumed substantial amounts of alcohol and are using

Figure 16-2. *Railroad Fatality Rates, 1960–96*
1960 = 100

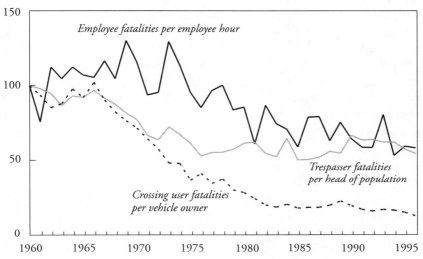

Source: Federal Railroad Administration (various years); Federal Highway Administration (various years); Bureau of the Census (various years).

the right-of-way as a place to socialize or to sleep off the effects of the alcohol.[5]

The employee casualty rates show a different picture. After many decades of improvement, the rates started to increase in the 1960s and did not resume their downward trend until 1973. Figures on the rate of collisions and derailments are more difficult to analyze because the definition of property-damage-only crashes was not adjusted for inflation until 1975. Every indication, however, is that crashes involving property damage also increased significantly in the 1960s and early 1970s and started to decline only after 1978. Since the mid-1970s the improvement in safety has been dramatic. The fatality rate is now half of what it was in 1973, and the rate of collisions and derailments is a quarter of what it was in the peak year of 1978. In part, the improvement can be explained by a change in the way

5. Pelletier (1997).

that railroads handle traffic. Starting in the late 1970s, traffic has been increasingly handled in unit trains (trains composed of permanently coupled sets of freight cars), a practice that necessitates much less switching of cars. The proportion of train miles that are represented by yard and switching miles has fallen by half, from 30 percent in the mid-1970s to close to 13 percent in 1995. Because 70 percent of collisions and 60 percent of derailments occur in yards and sidings, it is not surprising that the rate of collisions and derailments has fallen. Nonetheless, the reduction in the amount of switching does not explain all of the improvement in safety.

The fatality rate per billion passenger miles for commercial aviation since 1960 is shown in figure 16-3. The graph differentiates between large carriers, regulated under Part 121 of the federal regulations, and commuter airlines operating aircraft with thirty or fewer seats, regulated under Part 135.[6] The risk of flying a large airline has declined by more than 90 percent in the past thirty-five years. In the early years of the period the increased safety resulted from improved technology. More recently it has resulted from increased average journey length. Under economic regulation airlines priced long-distance service high to cross-subsidize short-distance trips. Since deregulation the price of long-distance travel has fallen by a greater amount than that of short-distance travel, and the average journey length has increased by 20 percent, from 825 to 990 miles. As most of the risk in air travel is in the take-off and landing stages, increased average journey length decreases the risk per passenger mile.

Perhaps the most dramatic change has been the major improvement in commuter airline safety since 1975. In that year passengers on commuter airlines were six times more likely to be killed than passengers on large airlines, whereas now the difference is only in the range of 20 to 40 percent. Again technology has been a major contributor to this improvement. The commuter segment of the industry grew rapidly after deregulation as major airlines withdrew from secondary markets. The increased traffic required the deployment of larger, safer aircraft with turboprop rather than piston engines. In 1978, 70 percent of the commuter airline fleet was powered by piston engines, and 80 percent of the passenger miles flown were in aircraft with fewer than twenty seats. By 1996 the proportions were almost exactly reversed. Seventy percent of the fleet was turboprop-powered, and 80 percent of passenger miles were on commuter aircraft with more than twenty seats.

6. In March 1997 operators of aircraft with between ten and thirty seats were made subject to the stiffer Part 121 rather than to the Part 135 regulations.

Figure 16-3. *Aviation Fatalities per Billion Passenger Miles, 1960–96*

Fatalities

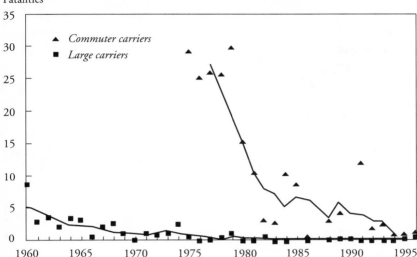

Source: National Transportation Safety Board. The symbols represent the annual rate, while the solid lines represent a five-year moving average.

The "Transportation Safety Problem"

The risk of crashes has declined by at least half in all modes of commercial transportation in the past twenty years. Yet the still substantial number of annual fatalities and the spectacular nature of many crashes keep the issue of transportation safety in the public mind. Psychologists have documented that the public is especially fearful of causes of death that claim multiple victims at a time, and the press devotes considerable coverage to these events.[7] The suggestion is that the public demands even more improvements in safety.

Safety improvements are not costless, however, although the costs incurred by carriers to prevent crashes are difficult to determine. The only relevant piece of work that I am aware of calculated that high-quality truck-

7. Lichtenstein and others (1978); Combs and Slovic (1979). Barnett (1990) calculated the ratio of front page stories in the *New York Times* to the risk for six common causes of mortality and found that reports on aviation safety appeared fifty times more frequently than any other risk.

ing firms, measured on the basis of shipper perceptions of quality measures other than safety, had costs about 6 to 7 percent higher than firms perceived to offer lower quality.[8]

The implication is that transportation safety is valued by customers but costly to provide. Economists have skills that can contribute to the consequent debate about how much safety should be provided. The interest of economists in these matters is heightened by the general feeling that optimal determination of safety cannot be left to a free-market interaction between carriers and their passengers and shippers. The most obvious manifestation of this is the long history of government regulation of safety.

The main purpose of this chapter is to review the knowledge that economists can bring to bear on the various facets of the transportation safety problem: How much safety should be provided? To what extent can the free market ensure safety? What are the major market failures? How well has existing government intervention responded to these failures? Should there be any changes in public policy?

How Much Safety?

Given the marked improvements in safety, one might well ask how much more can be provided. One of the simplest economic models, that of the social-welfare maximizing monopolist, gives the powerful result that the optimal level of safety is determined when customers' willingness to pay for a marginal increase in safety is equal to the marginal cost of supplying this safety.[9] In general, the optimal number of crashes will probably exceed the minimum technically feasible. When this occurs "society" has optimally chosen not to avert some crashes. This result is comparable to the economists' models showing that the optimal levels of congestion and pollution are also not zero.

In principle, economists can calculate this optimal level of safety from information on the value that customers place on safety, the marginal cost of preventing crashes, and the relationship between expenditures on prevention and the number of crashes. Evans and Morrison make such a calculation for a railway in Britain.[10]

---

8. Allen and Liu (1995).
9. Spence (1975).
10. Evans and Morrison (1997).

Unfortunately, few transportation markets can be characterized as monopolies. Most markets have inter- or intramodal competition. Equilibrium in these models becomes less well defined, especially if customers have different tastes for safety. Presumably nobody wants to die, but some members of society demonstrate that they are willing to bear more risk than others. For example, some people go rock climbing, ride bicycles without helmets, or engage in other pursuits that others would avoid as too risky or dangerous. On the freight side it is reasonable to suppose that shippers of expensive, delicate equipment will be more prepared to pay a premium for safer transportation than would shippers of gravel or coal.

The consequence of this variation in tastes is that a vertically differentiated market will emerge, making it optimal for several different safety levels to prevail in the market. [11] Less-safe carriers who charge a lower price may optimally coexist with safer carriers who charge a premium price. Customers will decide which carrier to patronize, and whether to consume at all, based on their tastes for safety and sensitivity to the differences in prices charged. Markets of this type clearly exist in both the maritime and trucking industry. Shippers can obtain service at almost any level of safety they want. The differentiated market also exists in aviation, where charter carriers that cater to budget-conscious travelers have poorer safety records than scheduled airlines catering to well-heeled businesspeople.

That some carriers are found to be less safe than others is considered by many lay people to be a market failure. This is not the case. In a well-functioning market, some customers decide of their own free will to patronize a less-safe carrier in preference to safer alternatives. They do so because the service is offered at a discounted price, and compared with other customers, they are less sensitive to the lower safety. This important insight is perhaps one of the most useful contributions that economists can bring to the safety debate. Society may be better served if carriers are allowed to offer a range of safety alternatives rather than being required to provide a uniform high level of safety.

The empirical literature has not attempted to characterize the equilibrium in this latter model. The reasons are threefold. First, knowledge about the distribution of customers' tastes for safety is limited. Second, the relationship between expenditures on prevention and the number of crashes is

---

11. Shaked and Sutton (1982). Entry occurs in this model until prices are driven down to marginal cost. The nature of the marginal cost functions, the number of consumers, and the distribution of their tastes determines the socially beneficial equilibrium number of carriers and hence levels of safety in the market.

poorly understood, which means that a "marginal cost of safety" function is difficult to estimate. Third, the equilibrium conditions in the vertically differentiated model are difficult to model, especially when one moves away from the social-welfare maximizing model toward the more realistic cases where a limited number of profit-maximizing carriers compete with each other.[12]

Therefore, although economists know which theoretical models should be used, they cannot make any definitive statement as to whether the observed levels of safety differ from those that would be optimally chosen by a social planner. It is embarrassing to admit that economists cannot even say whether there is currently "too much" or "too little" safety, let alone comment on the magnitudes of any deviation. All is not lost, however. Perhaps a more useful goal for the safety analyst is not predicting what the optimal levels should be, but trying to understand why a free market does not lead to an optimal determination and what can be done about it.

Market Forces and Market Failures

It would be wrong to think that a market does not operate in some fashion in the provision of safety. The mere existence of vertically differentiated service in most modes provides adequate evidence that some carriers seek to obtain a market advantage by providing a high-quality and high-safety service to customers who have a high willingness to pay for safety. Presumably, these customers must be able to recognize which carriers are providing high-safety service, and the carriers can financially justify the extra expenditures they make to prevent crashes. In general, one would imagine that since the demise of economic regulation, safety should improve in some segments of the market as some carriers elect to offer high-quality service to escape from the intense price competition at the lower end of the market.

There has been a traditional reluctance to leave the determination of safety entirely to the free market, however. This is unlike other quality attributes such as reliability, courtesy of staff, accuracy of invoicing, and cleanliness, which are generally left to be determined by the interactions between carriers and customers. Theoretical economists advance several reasons as candidates for explaining market failure in transportation safety:

---

12. See Dixit (1979) for oligopoly; Spence (1976), Dixit and Stiglitz (1977), and Koenker and Perry (1981) for monopolistic competition.

—A belief that many customers cannot observe the efforts to prevent crashes made by individual carriers;

—The possibility that carriers may be myopic, because the costs of preventing crashes occur in the present, whereas the consequences of crashes occur in the future;

—The possibility that even fully informed customers may make poor choices on safety because of the unpleasant consequences of a crash;

—The negative effects that crashes have on innocent bystanders; and

—Confusion as to which party should make the most effort to prevent crashes when other road users and trucks collide, or when trains collide with trespassers and grade-crossing users.

In the past twenty to thirty years, economic models have been developed to provide insights into the nature of market failures that may result, and the ways that public policy can contribute to their amelioration. The extent to which each market failure arises for the various modes is, of course, an open question, but the theoretical and empirical evidence for each market failure is reviewed below.

Imperfect Information

Clearly, individual customers can exercise their tastes for safety only if they can accurately assess the safety level offered by a mode and by rival carriers within that mode. This problem of imperfect information is likely to be more prevalent in passenger rather than freight transportation. Some freight shippers are so large that they have intimate contractual relationships with a small number of carriers, permitting them to make a knowledgeable appraisal of safety. Even relatively small shippers make consignments on a daily basis. The continual settling of claims for minor loss and damage provides plenty of information on safety.

In contrast the typical passenger consumes rather infrequently and does not have the necessary specialist knowledge. Consequently, passengers must form perceptions of the risks involved in traveling. Psychologists have found two systematic biases in the ways that people perceive risk.[13] The first, termed primary bias, is the tendency to overestimate infrequent causes of death, such as commercial transportation accidents, and to underestimate more frequent causes. This upward bias is compounded by a secondary bias. Hazards with an upward secondary bias are generally dramatic and sensa-

---

13. Lichtenstein and others (1978).

tional, whereas hazards with downward secondary bias tend to be unspectacular events that claim one victim at a time.

The consequences of this general tendency to believe that transportation crashes happen more frequently than they actually do can be examined in a simple model of monopoly. The general result is that the upward misperception will lead carriers to provide *less* than the optimal level of safety. This somewhat counterintuitive result emerges because customers do not fully incorporate into their demand function the "benefits" of the preventive actions taken by the carriers.[14]

The situation becomes more complicated in competitive markets where passengers not only have to have some idea of the general safety level of the mode, but also have to be able to distinguish between the safety records of individual carriers. Theoretical models show that in the extreme, if customers were unable to distinguish on the basis of safety between carriers, then no carrier would choose to supply a high-safety service because customers would not recognize the service and would be unwilling to pay a higher price to obtain it.[15] This extreme situation does not apply in practice, however. Passengers can probably identify notoriously poor carriers through press reports, but they are probably less sure about the safety rankings of more mainstream carriers. This is primarily because crashes occur rarely for individual carriers, and those crashes that do occur often are caused by a bizarre set of circumstances that makes it unclear whether passengers should infer that the carrier was at fault or instead blame the weather, an "act of God," or pure bad luck.

The situation is made worse because it is regarded as somewhat unseemly for carriers to advertise that their crash rate is better than that of their competitors. It may also be counterproductive in that highlighting an essentially negative aspect of transportation may reduce the demand for all carriers. At best carriers have to use codewords to communicate to potential customers that they are supplying a premium service. Examples are highlighting the experience of their mechanics, or indicating that they offer high quality in other attributes of service and hoping that this reputation will also be inferred concerning their safety performance. The problems in effectively communicating information to passengers probably helps explain why most mainstream passenger carriers offer similar safety to their

14. Spence (1977).
15. Akerlof (1970).

peers within their modes. For example, most of the major American airlines have statistically indistinguishable safety records.

Carrier Myopia

The most prevalent and feared market failure goes hand-in-hand with imperfect information. Some carriers that take little effort to prevent crashes can take advantage of imperfectly informed customers by masquerading as high-safety carriers, and charging a premium price. The incentives to engage in this kind of behavior are strong because the costs of prevention are borne in the present, whereas the effects of crashes occur at randomly defined points in the future. Even a carrier that becomes very careless may not suffer a visibly increased crash rate for several years. In the interim the carrier can earn excess profits, which will cease only when it incurs the costs of crashes or when its customers find out and either shun the carrier or demand a lower price.

Two types of carriers are particularly susceptible to such behavior. The first are new entrants. These carriers may take too little prevention in the present and regret it when crashes and adverse customer reaction occur in the years ahead. Although the motivation for some of this behavior might be avaricious, it is more likely to be attributable to inexperience. This is a very real concern, given the considerable new entry to the trucking, airline, and railroad industries that has occurred since economic deregulation. There is evidence that new entrant trucking firms have a worse crash record than existing carriers.[16] Investigations show that the new jet airline entrants of the early 1980s were not noticeably worse than established carriers, but that was not true of the cohort of entrants in the early 1990s.[17]

The second candidate for myopia is a more established carrier that decides to cheat. Expenditures on preventing crashes are reduced, yet prices are maintained, and the carrier hopes that its customers do not notice. This type of behavior has been studied in both the theoretical and empirical literature.[18] The usual explanation is that the carrier is close to bankruptcy and reasons that it can save on prevention costs now and declare bankruptcy to protect itself against the cost of crashes later on. A less callous

16. Corsi and Fanara (1989).
17. Savage (1999).
18. For the theoretical treatments, see Bulow and Shoven (1978), Golbe (1981), Klein and Leffler (1981), and Shapiro (1982).

explanation may be that a financially distressed carrier hopes that cost economies now can prolong its life until better times come along.

A classic example of this behavior was the railroad industry in the 1960s.
Poor management and constraints caused by regulation led many railroads
in the East and Midwest to the verge of bankruptcy. Some of these railroads responded by allowing their infrastructure to deteriorate. This is a
very insidious form of cheating because some time must pass before shippers can recognize the effects of the deterioration. Ultimately, the cheating
led to the reversal of the previous longstanding improvements in the rates
of collisions, derailments, and employee casualities. The rates started to
improve again only after deregulation was implemented and the overall
financial health of the industry began to improve.

In the airline and trucking industry, deregulation is said to have had
the reverse effect. The emergence of competition led to financial difficulties for some long-established but poorly managed carriers. Some of these
carriers ultimately exited the industry. Empirical evidence shows that financial distress leads to poorer safety performance in the trucking industry
and among small- to medium-sized airlines.[19]

Impending bankruptcy is not the only cause for cheating. Carriers may
cheat simply because they feel that they need a short-term financial boost
to improve their stock price or to make them more attractive to a potential
purchaser. An example is the Union Pacific Railroad, which in the summer
of 1997 wished to demonstrate to its stockholders that it had made cost
economies as a result of acquiring the Southern Pacific Railroad. Unfortunately, these economies led to a decline in service quality and an increase in
crashes. Fortunately, this action was soon discovered both by shippers and
the press, and the railroad had to improve its quality in the face of adverse
customer and government reaction.

Needless to say, most carriers don't behave in this fashion. Some re-
frain from cheating for moral reasons, others because of market constraints.
There is some literature, most of it dealing with the airline industry, on
whether crashes lead to a decline in demand for individual carriers or a
decline in stock prices.[20] In general, the evidence of long-lasting effects on
either demand or stock value is limited. Of course, casual empiricism could
point to specific examples of carriers with notoriously poor records having
been forced to contract or exit the market. Most of the high-profile ex-

---

19. Chow (1989); Rose (1990).
20. For a summary, see Rose (1992).

amples have been in aviation. Nevertheless, market failure caused by myopia is not only theoretically very plausible, but, according to ample empirical evidence, it occurs in all modes of transportation.

Customer Rationality

It is reasonable to suppose that shipping managers rationally compare the prices quoted by the various carriers and different modes, assess the probability that their goods will be lost or damaged in transit, and make an informed and calculated choice. Transportation passengers may not make similar rational choices, however. The unpleasant consequences of a crash may cause even fully informed passengers to downplay the probability of a crash. This cognitive dissonance was evident in 1996, for example, when many passengers continued to patronize a low-fare airline with a known poor safety record because they believed that "it will not happen to me." Calabresi explains this behavior as the "Faust attitude" whereby people are myopic when making a choice between a lower price now and increased probability of death or injury later.[21]

Whether this type of behavior would be described as a "market failure" is a matter of semantics, given that the failure is in the minds of the customers rather than in the trade between customers and carriers. Intervention in the market might therefore be justified to protect customers from themselves rather than to protect them from the carriers!

There is a related issue: in a vertically differentiated safety market, high-safety choices will be available at a premium prices, whereas low-safety choices will be available at discounted prices. Less well-off members of society may be able to afford to patronize only carriers with very poor safety records. Even though these people may make that choice in a fully informed way, society may paternalistically decide that it would prefer that these people did not travel rather than face inordinate risks.

Externalities

A well-known result in economics is that markets fail if there is no mechanism for carriers to internalize harms caused to third parties. If carriers do not pass on the costs of externality harms to customers, the prices

---

21. Calabresi (1970). Oi (1973) explains the phenomenon as consumers with a very high time preference who in retrospect regret their choices because their retrospective time preference is different.

charged will be too low, and too much transportation will be produced. The carrier will also select a lower-than-optimal level of preventive effort because it is no longer motivated to increase preventive efforts to reduce the negative externalities caused to third parties.[22]

Bilateral Crashes

Not all third parties to transportation crashes are innocent bystanders. Table 16-1 shows that more than 80 percent of all fatalities occur in collisions at rail-highway grade crossings, between trucks and automobiles, between trucks and pedestrians, and between trains and trespassers. In the law and economics literature, these types of crashes are called bilateral crashes because the probability of a crash depends on the amount of effort (or "care," as it is known in legal parlance) taken by both the carrier and the other party to prevent the crash.

The socially optimal level of care that each party should take is determined by the relative costs each party incurs in taking care and the extent to which they can influence the probability of a crash. Absent legal liability, a market failure will occur in this determination when the consequences of not taking care by one party significantly increase the harm that the other party can expect to suffer from crashes.[23]

Legal Institutions that Ameliorate Market Failures

Many of these market failures have been recognized for more than a century. Consequently, longstanding legal arrangements have developed to respond to three of them: imperfect information, externalities, and bilateral crashes.

The 1906 Carmack Amendment to the Interstate Commerce Act of 1887 made common carriers strictly liable to shippers; that is, carriers must pay shippers for the "full actual loss and injury" caused by reasons of loss, damage, or delay. The situation for passenger travel is a bit different in theory, but perhaps not in practice. Injured passengers have to show that the carrier acted negligently and that the passenger's negligence did not make the situation worse. For most crashes, however, the standard of proof

---

22. Shavell (1987).
23. Shavell (1987) provides a comprehensive analysis.

to show negligence is quite low, and carriers nearly always have to compensate innocent passengers.[24] (Awards may not reflect actual losses, however. For example, the Warsaw Convention limits the size of awards to international airline passengers.) Consequently, the carrier bears the cost of both preventing crashes and compensating for the harm caused when crashes occur. In theory, therefore, the carrier should be able to make an informed decision on the correct level of safety to supply, irrespective of the knowledge of customers.

In practice, however, there are limitations to this legal solution. Injured customers can rightly complain that legal judgments are inherently market corrections after the fact. Even so, carriers still have strong incentives to engage in myopic behavior. The theoretical economics literature also points to some less obvious limitations. Liability totally ameliorates the market failure caused by imperfect information only when customers are risk neutral, have homogeneous tastes, and are fully compensated for both pecuniary and nonpecuniary harms.[25] In practice it is unlikely that all three conditions will be met. Although freight shippers may plausibly be risk neutral, some costs, such as delays in production schedules or the costs of claim administration, cannot be legally recovered. Passengers are unlikely to be risk neutral and, in fact, are probably risk averse. Passengers or their relatives are unlikely to feel that they can be adequately compensated for their loss by legal settlements or insurance payments. Passengers therefore attach a higher disutility to the risk of crashes than would be covered by an actuarially determined amount of harm they can expect to suffer in a crash.

These observations should not be taken as a condemnation of the usefulness of liability to customers. Liability undoubtedly restrains some carriers from engaging in myopic behavior, although it obviously does not totally eliminate it. In contrast, liability does play a large role in ameliorating market failure caused by externalities. Injured bystanders have had longstanding rights to bring a claim against a carrier. The bystander must show that the carrier was negligent in causing the harm. Evidence that a plane crashed on your house or that a railroad spilled hazardous chemicals on your field would be taken as prima facie evidence of negligence, however. Compensation can be obtained for loss of property or increased out-of-pocket expenses, but certain types of losses such as loss of profits are not

24. Kenworthy (1989).
25. Spence (1977).

recoverable under law. Therefore, carriers will internalize most of the externalities caused. Of course, this does not totally mitigate the concern because psychologists have shown that bystanders who are involuntary exposed to a hazard are far less tolerant of the risk than customers or employees who are voluntarily involved.[26] The intolerance may far exceed the monetary harms that bystanders incur. For example, there was considerable public outrage over the spill from the tanker *Exxon Valdez* despite unprecedented expenditures by Exxon to clear up the spill and settle lawsuits.

Legal processes regarding liability in bilateral crashes also provide incentives to take appropriate care.[27] In most jurisdictions in the United States, the legal rule is that of comparative negligence. Courts determine the care that each party should have taken, known as "due care" in legal parlance, compare this with the actual conduct of the parties, and award damages based on the relative deviations from due care. The main complaint about this system centers primarily on the ability of the courts to determine the level of due care expected of each party. The law does provide some guidance, but it is up to the court to decide how this translates into the specific conduct expected. Carriers frequently argue that "anticorporate sentiment" biases juries to give the noncarrier party the benefit of the doubt. The main example is collisions at rail-highway grade-crossings. It is frequently argued that juries take a permissive view of the behavior of highway drivers, while finding railroads negligent for not installing flashing lights or gates, even at crossings where a cost-benefit analysis would indicate that such warning devices are not justified. This problem is caused in part by a legal failure in that railroad companies are legally responsible for safety at highway grade crossings even though decisions on providing gates and flashing lights are made by the highway authority.

Legal judgments may not be a sufficient deterrent to all of the people involved in bilateral crashes. Many automobile drivers who are involved in collisions with trucks and trains do not exercise the proper amount of skill or attention; frequently they are driving under the influence of alcohol or drugs. Many poorly educated single males still trespass on the railroad right-of-way to drink and socialize even though the law firmly places the burden of taking care on the trespasser.

---

26. Starr (1969).
27. Shavell (1987) provides a comprehensive analysis.

Public Policy Responses to Market Failure

Although legal arrangements undoubtedly reduce the magnitude of many of the market failures, they do not totally eliminate them. Consequently, a sizeable theoretical literature has developed that explains why government intervention should be deployed as a complement to existing legal processes.[28] The government has several options available to it; it may require insurance, provide information to customers, and directly regulate carriers. Each of these deals with a subset of the market failures. Table 16-3 presents a matrix showing which policy option may be applicable to each market failure.[29] An important conclusion of the literature is that these policy responses should be seen as complements to each other and not as direct substitutes.

Insurance Requirements

A common concern with a purely legal response is that myopic carriers can declare bankruptcy to avoid paying large legal judgments. Therefore, in most modes of transportation the government requires that carriers hold insurance to cover tort liability settlements. The primary benefit is that insurance companies pool risks across carriers, thus ensuring that crash victims will obtain some compensation. A secondary benefit is that insurance can reduce the incidence of myopia, especially among new entrants. By charging premiums to cover future losses, insurance companies make inexperienced new carriers very aware of future crash costs. Carriers can then decide on appropriate levels of safety by trading off between the size of insurance premiums and levels of preventive effort.

Of course, myopic behavior is still possible if, as is generally likely, insurance companies have imperfect knowledge of carriers' crash probabilities. An unscrupulous carrier can take actions, such as reducing maintenance expenditures, that adversely affect crash risk yet are hidden to the insurer.[30] Such behavior is equivalent to the cheating described earlier. The

28. See Kolstad, Ulen, and Johnson (1990); Shavell (1984a, b).
29. There is an additional market failure that has not been discussed. Many transportation markets are characterized by competition among relatively few carriers due to economies of density at the route level. Therefore relatively few safety choices will be offered to the customer, which could lead to reduced social welfare. Of course, market power will have far more dramatic effects in raising prices and restricting output, and this will probably be the motivation for an antitrust response by government.
30. Shavell (1979).

Table 16-3. *Matrix of Market Failures and Legal and Policy Responses*

Market failure	Liability	Insurance requirement	Information provision on safety Outputs	Inputs	Safety regulation
Imperfect information	X	...	X	X	X
Myopia	...	X	...	X	X
Customer rationality	...	...	...	...	X
Bystanders	X	...	...	...	X
Bilateral crashes	X	...	...	...	X

Source: Author's calculations.

only difference is that the insurance company is the ultimate victim, because injured parties receive at least some compensation from the insurance company.

Making Customers Better Informed

An obvious response to a market failure caused by imperfect information is for the government to provide appropriate data to customers. Carriers in all modes have a legal obligation to report all serious crashes to the federal government. These data are tabulated but are typically disseminated in obscure documents. There seems to be a certain squeamishness in making the information more widely available. Change is in the air, however, spurred by the development of the Internet. Since March 1997 the Federal Aviation Administration has provided safety information on airlines to the public on its World Wide Web site.

Direct Safety Regulation

Government has been involved in the direct regulation of safety for more than a century. Safety regulations for railroads were introduced in 1893, for the maritime industry in 1914 (by international convention, following the sinking of the *Titanic* two years earlier), for trucking in 1940, and for commercial aviation in 1958. Safety regulations continue to be revised and tightened. There was considerable rulemaking concerning the railroads in the early 1970s, commercial aviation in the mid-1970s, and trucking in the early 1980s.

In general the approach taken has been to set minimum training quali-fications and maximum hours of work for staff, and engineering rules on the design and maintenance of plant and equipment. To monitor and en-force these standards, government inspectors conduct semi-random inspec-tions of equipment and staff records and issue citations for violations found. The government retains the power to close down very dangerous carriers.

The underlying theory is that a perfectly informed government should be able to calculate the levels of safety that will maximize social welfare. The lowest common denominator would then be used to define the mini-mum standard. The government then translates the minimum desired safety output into minimum specification or design standards for safety inputs. Carriers that wish to provide a higher level of safety are free to deviate upward from this minimum. The advantage of expressing safety objectives in these terms is to detect carriers with poor equipment and staff before crashes occur.

The primary thrust of safety regulations is directed at the problem of myopia. Regulations act to inform new carriers of appropriate minimum standards. In some modes such as aviation, new carriers must demonstrate that they meet certain requirements before they can begin operations. Safety inspectors then serve as a deterrent to prevent established carriers from acting myopically and to detect and punish those carriers who cheat.

The Effectiveness of Public Policy in Recent Safety Performance

With the foregoing as background, let us revisit figures 16-1, 16-2, and 16-3 to determine the role of public policy relative to other factors in explaining the improvements in crash rates witnessed in all modes in recent times.

The Trucking Industry

As reported earlier, the trucking industry's crash rate has declined faster than might be explained by factors that have improved safety on the roads in general. The good record of the trucking industry might come as some-what of a surprise given the predictions that economic deregulation of the industry in 1980 would lead to declining safety. Before deregulation much of the safety regulation was embodied in the economic controls that limited entry into the industry. Consequently some observers expressed concern that new entrants might act in a myopic, fly-by-night fashion and cater to the taste of those shippers who prefer discounted prices over additional safety.

The government responded by substituting explicit safety regulation and enforcement activities for the implicit safety regulations inherent in the old system. Legislation in the early 1980s tightened vehicle standards, introduced new rules for transporting hazardous materials, and implemented a coordinated national "commercial drivers' license." The new license requirements impose uniform testing across states and prevent drivers from holding multiple licenses as a way to avoid the consequences of revocation in one jurisdiction. Many states had to raise driver-testing standards considerably. In addition, federal funding allowed increased enforcement through safety audits of carriers and semi-random inspections at the roadside.

The Railroad Industry

In response to a worsening safety record, brought about by financial problems that led some segments of the railroad industry to reduce maintenance expenditures, Congress passed the Federal Railroad Safety Act of 1970. This act was the first substantial change in railroad safety regulation in sixty years; until its passage, the railroads had very little formal regulation. The 1970 regulations introduced design standards for track for the very first time and codified existing industry standards on the design and maintenance of freight cars. The government also appointed an inspectorate force to ensure compliance with the laws.

What happened next is the subject of considerable controversy.[31] Everyone agrees that collision and derailment rates and employee injury rates have improved since the mid- and late 1970s; the disagreement is over the source of the improvement. The Federal Railroad Administration says it is a direct result of safety regulatory efforts. The industry points to the deregulation of the industry in 1980, which allowed railroads to spin off unprofitable branch lines and negotiate price with shippers. As a result, the financial health of the industry improved, and there is clear evidence that maintenance expenditures increased dramatically.[32] Unfortunately for the analyst, the increase in deregulation-induced expenditures parallels increases

31. Savage (1998).
32. Association of American Railroads (various years).

in the number of federal safety inspections and decreases in the amount of risky switching. It is probably impossible to separate these effects econometrically. Meanwhile the federal government and the railroads are at an impasse as to whether federal safety regulations have helped or hindered the industry.

One area where government intervention has clearly had a measurable effect has been grade-crossing collisions. Figure 16-2 shows an impressive decline in risk since the mid-1960s. A federal government program, enacted in 1973, to equip crossings with active warning devices such as flashing lights and gates, is in part responsible for the decline. The justification for the government funding is that some auto drivers cannot be trusted to act appropriately at crossings with only a "crossbucks" warning sign, despite a railroad-funded campaign *Operation Lifesaver* to educate the public on appropriate behavior.

Commercial Aviation

Most of the improvement in aviation safety can be attributed to new technology. The government has played a considerable role, however. A government-funded air traffic control system was developed in the late 1950s and early 1960s to respond to the increased probability of collisions as the skies became more crowded. Regulations also contributed to the dramatic improvement in commuter airline safety in the 1975–85 period. The safety regulations for the commuter industry were changed substantially in 1978 with stricter pilot qualification and training requirements, new maintenance requirements, and an upgraded list of required safety equipment.

The government has also had a role in restraining some of the myopic behavior that occurred after economic deregulation. The evidence of entry of inexperienced new jet airlines with a lower level of safety than incumbent carriers has already been discussed, as has the financial distress among some incumbent carriers that led to myopic reductions in maintenance and training. The success of some of the regulatory activities can be determined by investigating whether deregulation slowed any of the longstanding improvements in safety for large airlines.

Figure 16-4 shows five-year moving average fatality rates for midpoint years 1960 through 1994 for large air carriers. Five-year averages have been used to smooth out year-to-year variations. A logarithmic time trend is fitted to the pre-deregulation data for 1960 through 1978 and then ex-

Figure 16-4. *1960–78 Time Trend Fitted to Five-Year Moving Average of Fatality Risk per Billion Passenger Miles for Large Airline Carriers, 1960–94*

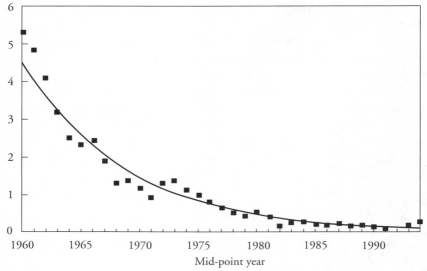

Fatalities

Mid-point year

Source: Author's calculations based on National Transportation Safety Board data.

trapolated forward. This is shown as the smooth curve. As one can see, the actual postderegulation fatality rates, indicated by the squares, continued to follow the decline from the previous decades, at least until an unusual rash of high-fatality crashes in 1994, 1995, and 1996, which were not repeated in 1997 or the first half of 1998.

Policy Recommendations

Analysts cannot definitively say whether current levels of safety are too high or too low. What is known is that safety has been improving dramatically in all modes of transportation in recent decades. Yet, there is still pressure for more and even tougher safety regulations. Underlying these possibly contradictory pieces of evidence is the well-documented fact that as a nation grows richer, its citizens demand lower mortality risks from all forms of hazards. Crash rates that were deemed acceptable in the 1950s and 1960s are quite likely to be considered unacceptable today.

How these future improvements will be achieved, and whether these improvements are justified, is somewhat speculative. Undoubtedly technological advances will continue to be very important, especially in aviation. Improved scientific understanding of how human beings function will help government and carriers take actions to combat fatigue and inattention. Changes in the nature of demand will also improve safety by allowing deployment of even larger "regional jet" aircraft in secondary markets and further reducing the need for switching of railcars. Because profit-maximizing firms are taking the lead in all of these areas, it is safe to assume that all of these safety improvements would pass a cost-benefit test.

There are also possible changes in public policy that may bring about improved safety at reduced cost to taxpayers and carriers. These include the provision of more information, greater involvement by the insurance industry, and innovative strategies in safety regulation.

A More Informed Public

In recent years the development of personal computers and the Internet has made it possible to provide up-to-date safety information directly to passengers and shippers. The longstanding requirement for carriers in all modes to report crashes puts the federal government in the ideal position to make this information available. In theory such information could attack the root cause of a major safety market failure.

Whether wide dissemination of this information will help customers make better choices and dissuade carriers from indulging in myopic behavior is an open question, however. The traditional concern is that the public is unable to draw proper inferences from data on events that occur with a low probability. This concern would seem to be a trifle patronizing. A more serious concern is that providing historical crash data does nothing to ameliorate the problem of current myopic carriers. Unscrupulous carriers who wish to cheat will, by definition, deviate from their past performance. Consequently, it is often argued that the public should be provided with information on carriers' safety inputs such as the average experience of staff and the age and condition of equipment. In this way customers can make predictions of future safety performance. This information is currently not widely available or disseminated. Some also argue that this data may be misleading because even safety professionals cannot definitively relate input measures to the expected effect on safety. Nevertheless, the information age provides the opportunity for disseminating safety information directly to the public. Future research will show whether the experiment is successful and whether a more-informed public obviates the need for some safety regulations.

A Greater Role for Insurance Companies

Currently insurance companies play a somewhat subsidiary role in correcting market failures in commercial transportation. In other markets, such as consumer-product safety and automobiles, insurance companies are in the forefront of encouraging safe practices and punishing errant parties. This difference in roles may result from extensive government regulation of carriers. Insurance companies can avoid the expense of conducting their own investigations of the safety practices of potential policyholders by relying on government agencies to specify which carriers are safe and which are not.

Insurance companies could play a large role in providing the economic incentives for small and newly formed carriers not to engage in myopic behavior. Yet premium schedules are currently of a coarse nature and, in the extreme, set on the basis of the overall risk displayed by the industry or some broad subset of it. Thus carriers do not necessarily face a premium closely related to the level of prevention they undertake. This is particularly the case in the trucking industry, where most small firms are placed into a "pool" that is then divided among the various insurance companies.

In other words, extensive direct regulation has allowed insurance companies to free-ride on the backs of the regulators. Consequently they have not been heavily involved in providing economic incentives for safe operation. It would be interesting to see what would happen if a greater responsibility for monitoring the activities of the industry were placed on insurance companies.

A New Era for Safety Regulation?

The safety regulators who appear to have had some success in reducing crash rates in most modes in recent decades are not without their critics. In general, these critics do not question the need for safety regulation. Rather, they question whether there are better and cheaper ways of regulating safety. The critics point to two major failings. The first is the mechanism by which standards are set. The second is the strategy by which federal agencies monitor and enforce these standards.

Regulators face an unenviable task in setting minimum safety regulations. Not only must they form a view on the elusive question of "how safe is safe enough?" but they must also translate this into minimum standards on the quality and quantity of staff and equipment. Because the exact specification of the production function for safety is generally unknown, even the most well-intentioned rulemaker is unlikely to get it just right.

This uncertainty about the production function for safety opens the door for parties such as labor unions, trade associations, and manufacturers of safety equipment to argue for legislation for self-interested purposes by claiming that the legislation is justified on the basis of safety. Classic examples are the activities of railroad unions to attempt to use legislation to retain the services of firemen on diesel locomotives, or to write brake inspection laws that provide work for a specific type of employee. The larger trucking firms have pushed for increased safety standards as a barrier to entry against new carriers. Such lobbying can succeed because there is always that element of doubt about whether even the most blatantly avaricious proposals might have beneficial safety effects.

A legislature may also respond to perceived safety problems in a knee-jerk fashion, implementing regulations that make the legislator look good in the eyes of constituents but that may have questionable safety effects. An excellent example is the Oil Pollution Act of 1990, which requires the use of double-hulled oil tankers. Congress was reacting very quickly to the public outrage concerning the grounding of the oil tanker *Exxon Valdez*. My research found that even under the most wildly favorable assumptions, the benefits are fifty cents for every dollar of costs, while under more reasonable assumptions the benefits are only twenty cents.[33]

In fairness it should be said that the Department of Transportation has a very good record in evaluating proposed regulations, particularly when a comparison is made with other government agencies such as the Environmental Protection Agency and the Occupational Safety and Health Administration.[34] There is a long history of the use of cost-benefit analysis to assess the desirability of various regulations in transportation, and trans-

---

33. Brown and Savage (1996).
34. Viscusi (1996).

portation has been at the forefront of estimating the social cost of crashes and the valuation of lives saved.

Designing a strategy for monitoring and enforcing standards to prevent myopic behavior is a nontrivial economic problem.[35] Because monitoring is costly, both to the government and to carriers, the government bears a heavy burden to design an effective and efficient system. My observation is that the traditional methods of conducting semi-random inspections are becoming discredited, partly because of the costs of inspection and partly because randomly written citations do not seem to modify the behavior of carriers. My own work has found substantiating evidence in the inspection of trucks at the roadside and the inspection of railroad track and cars.[36] Some government agencies have responded by using their inspectorate force more effectively. Under a very successful program in the trucking industry, inspectors audit the safety management practices of carriers, assign safety ratings, and concentrate enforcement efforts on the worst carriers.

Problems with traditional methods of regulation have given rise to a new regulatory strategy commonly referred to as performance standards. Under this strategy the desired minimum safety level is expressed in terms of the output of safety. An example might be the setting of a particular crash rate as the minimum. The government agency would then act as a risk analyst by observing crash rates and taking action against carriers who fail to meet the standard.

This strategy has three big advantages. First, the regulator does not have to infer the relationship between specifying standards for safety inputs and the consequent effect on crashes. Second, carriers are no longer constrained in their decisions on how to combine inputs to achieve the desired safety standard at minimum cost. Third, performance standards are less susceptible to politicking.

Performance standards are not a panacea in all situations. They are of limited use when crashes occur very infrequently or when the amount of exposure to crashes is small. In these situations, it would be difficult to determine whether the performance of an individual carrier is changing from year to year given the inherent variation that one would expect when observing low-probability events. For performance standards to be mean-

35. Becker (1968).
36. Moses and Savage (1997); Savage (1998).

ingful, one has to select a measure of crashes that occur relatively frequently and confine the analysis to carriers with large exposure to crashes. It is likely that small carriers in all modes would have to continue to be regulated by traditional means.

The common argument against performance standards is that they are essentially an ex post form of regulation in that deficient carriers are identified only after their crash rate has increased. The solution to this problem is to use measures of less serious crashes that occur relatively frequently to indicate the presence of conditions that might lead to a major catastrophe. There are opportunities for statistically minded researchers to help in developing measures of safety performance. Another disadvantage is that performance standards may "encourage" some carriers to try to avoid enforcement by not recording and reporting crashes. Such behavior may have a negative effect on the safety consciousness of employees who could take the failure to report a crash as an indication that a carrier's management does not place a very high priority on safety.

Trials of performance standards are now under way. The Occupational Safety and Health Administration pioneered such an approach, called the Cooperative Compliance Program, in a trial in Maine in 1993 and is extending the strategy nationwide. Under this program, larger firms undertake to achieve a certain level of safety performance through self-evaluation and development, if necessary, of a remediation plan. If they meet these criteria, they are exempted from random inspections and may even be allowed to operate under liberalized specification regulation. If they do not meet their targets, however, the traditional methods of monitoring and enforcement kick in with a vengeance. The Federal Highway Administration has a similar program for trucking firms that achieve crash rates that put them in the safest quarter of the industry for three consecutive years. It remains to be seen whether the Federal Aviation Administration or the Federal Railroad Administration will move in the same direction. Ultimately, there will be research opportunities to investigate empirically whether this new strategy is superior to traditional methods.

In conclusion the risk of commercial transportation crashes has declined considerably in recent decades. Nonetheless, opportunities for further reductions are apparent. Some will come from market-driven changes in technology, human factors, and the nature of demand. Others will come from a review of the most cost-effective methods by which public policy deals with the pervasive market failures.

References

Akerlof, George A. 1970. "The Market for 'Lemons': Quality Uncertainty and the Market Mechanism." *Quarterly Journal of Economics* 84 (August): 488–500.

Allen, W. Bruce, and Dong Liu. 1995. "Service Quality and Motor Carrier Costs: An Empirical Analysis." *Review of Economics and Statistics* 77 (August): 499–510.

Association of American Railroads, Office of Information and Public Affairs. Various years. *Railroad Facts.* Washington, D.C.

Barnett, Arnold. 1990. "Air Safety: End of the Golden Age?" *Chance: New Directions for Statistics and Computing* 3 (Spring): 8–12.

Becker, Gary S. 1968. "Crime and Punishment: An Economic Approach." *Journal of Political Economy* 76 (March/April): 169–217.

Brown, R. Scott, and Ian Savage. 1996. "The Economics of Double-Hulled Tankers." *Maritime Policy and Management* 23 (April/June): 167–75.

Bulow, Jeremy I., and John B. Shoven. 1978. "The Bankruptcy Decision." *Bell Journal of Economics* 9 (Autumn): 437–56.

Bureau of the Census. Various years. *Statistical Abstract of the United States.* U.S. Department of Commerce.

Bureau of Labor Statistics. 1997a. *Fatal Workplace Injuries in 1995: A Collection of Data and Analysis.* Report 913. U.S. Department of Labor. April.

———. 1997b. *Survey of Occupational Injuries and Illnesses in the United States by Industry, 1995.* Summary 97-7. U.S. Department of Labor. May.

Bureau of Transportation Statistics. Various years. *National Transportation Statistics.* U.S. Department of Transportation.

Calabresi, Guido. 1970. *The Costs of Accidents: A Legal and Economic Analysis.* Yale University Press.

Chow, Garland. 1989. "Deregulation, Financial Distress, and Safety in the General Freight Trucking Industry." In *Transportation Safety in an Age of Deregulation,* edited by Leon N. Moses and Ian Savage, 219–40. Oxford University Press.

Combs, Barbara, and Paul A. Slovic. 1979. "Newspaper Coverage of Causes of Death." *Journalism Quarterly* 56 (Winter): 837–43, 849.

Corsi, Thomas M., and Philip Fanara, Jr. 1989. "Effects of New Entrants on Motor Carrier Safety." In *Transportation Safety in an Age of Deregulation,* edited by Leon N. Moses and Ian Savage, 241–57. Oxford University Press.

Dixit, Avinash. 1979. "Quantity and Quality Competition." *Review of Economic Studies* 46 (October): 587–99.

Dixit, Avinash, and Joseph E. Stiglitz. 1977. "Monopolistic Competition and Optimum Product Diversity." *American Economic Review* 67 (June): 297–308.

Evans, Andrew W., and Alan D. Morrison. 1997. "Incorporating Accident Risk and Disruption in Economic Models of Public Transport." *Journal of Transport Economics and Policy* 31 (May): 117–46.

Federal Highway Administration. Various years. *Highway Statistics.* U.S. Department of Transportation.

Federal Railroad Administration, Office of Safety. Various years. *Accident/Incident Bulletin.* U.S. Department of Transportation.

Golbe, Devra L. 1981. "The Effects of Imminent Bankruptcy on Stockholder Risk Preferences and Behavior." *Bell Journal of Economics* 12 (Spring): 321–28.

Kenworthy, William E. 1989. *Transportation Safety Law Practice Manual.* Vol. 1. Stoneham, Mass.: Butterworth Legal Publishers.

Klein, Benjamin, and Keith B. Leffler. 1981. "The Role of Market Forces in Assuring Contractual Performance." *Journal of Political Economy* 89 (August): 615–41.

Koenker, Roger W., and Martin K. Perry. 1981. "Product Differentiation, Monopolistic Competition, and Public Policy." *Bell Journal of Economics* 12 (Spring): 217–31.

Kolstad, Charles D., Thomas S. Ulen, and Gary V. Johnson. 1990. "Ex Post Liability for Harm vs. Ex Ante Safety Regulation: Substitutes or Complements?" *American Economic Review* 80 (September): 888–901.

Lichtenstein, Sarah, and others. 1978. "Judged Frequency of Lethal Events." *Journal of Experimental Psychology: Human Learning and Memory* 4 (November): 551–78.

Moses, Leon N., and Ian Savage. 1997. "A Cost-Benefit Analysis of United States Motor Carrier Safety Programs." *Journal of Transport Economics and Policy* 31 (January): 51–67.

National Highway Traffic Safety Administration. Various years. *Traffic Safety Facts.* Formerly *Fatal Accident Reporting System.* U.S. Department of Transportation.

National Safety Council. 1996. *Accident Facts.* Chicago.

National Transportation Safety Board. Various years. Press release on aviation safety and fatalities usually published in January or February by the Office of Government and Public Affairs.

Oi, Walter Y. 1973. "The Economics of Product Safety." *Bell Journal of Economics and Management Science* 4 (Spring): 3–28.

Pelletier, Andrew. 1997. "Deaths among Railroad Trespassers: The Role of Alcohol in Fatal Injuries." *Journal of the American Medical Association* 277 (April 2): 1064–66.

Rose, Nancy L. 1990. "Profitability and Product Quality: Economic Determinants of Airline Safety Performance." *Journal of Political Economy* 98 (October, Part 1): 944–64.

———. 1992. "Fear of Flying? Economic Analysis of Airline Safety." *Journal of Economic Perspectives* 6 (Spring): 75–94.

Savage, Ian. 1998. *The Economics of Railroad Safety.* Norwell, Mass.: Kluwer Academic Publishers.

———. 1999. "Aviation Deregulation and Safety in the United States: The Evidence after Twenty Years." In *Taking Stock of Air Liberalization,* edited by Marc Gaudry and Robert Mayes. Norwell, Mass.: Kluwer Academic Publishers.

Shaked, Avner, and John Sutton. 1982. "Relaxing Price Competition through Product Differentiation." *Review of Economic Studies* 49 (January): 3–13.

Shapiro, Carl. 1982. "Consumer Information, Product Quality, and Seller Reputation." *Bell Journal of Economics* 13 (Spring): 20–35.

Shavell, Steven. 1979. "On Moral Hazard and Insurance." *Quarterly Journal of Economics* 93 (November): 541–62.

———. 1984a. "Liability for Harm versus Regulation of Safety." *Journal of Legal Studies* 13 (June): 357–74.

———. 1984b. "A Model of the Optimal Use of Liability and Safety Regulation." *Rand Journal of Economics* 15 (Summer): 271–80.

———. 1987. *Economic Analysis of Accident Law.* Harvard University Press.

Spence, A. Michael. 1975. "Monopoly, Quality, and Regulation." *Bell Journal of Economics* 6 (Autumn): 417–29.

———. 1976. "Product Selection, Fixed Costs, and Monopolistic Competition." *Review of Economic Studies* 43 (June): 217–35.

————. 1977. "Consumer Misperceptions, Product Failure, and Producer Liability." *Review of Economic Studies* 44 (October): 561–72.

Starr, Chauncey. 1969. "Social Benefit versus Technological Risk. *Science* 165 (September 19): 1232–38.

Viscusi, W. Kip. 1996. "Economics Foundations of the Current Regulatory Reform Efforts." *Journal of Economic Perspectives* 10 (Summer): 119–34.

Contributors

Alan Altshuler
Kennedy School of Government
Harvard University

Ronald R. Braeutigam
Department of Economics
Northwestern University

Robert E. Gallamore
Union Pacific Railroad

José A. Gómez-Ibáñez
Kennedy School of Government
Harvard University

Arnold M. Howitt
Kennedy School of Government
Harvard University

Gregory K. Ingram
Research Advisory Staff
The World Bank

John F. Kain
Green Center for the Study of
   Science and Society
University of Texas at Dallas

Charles Lave
Department of Economics
University of California, Irvine

Lester Lave
Graduate School of Industrial
   Administration
Carnegie Mellon University

Robert A. Leone
School of Management
Boston University

Zhi Liu
Transport Economist
The World Bank

563

564

Herbert Mohring
Department of Economics
University of Minnesota

Steven A. Morrison
Department of Economics
Northeastern University

Katherine M. O'Regan
School of Management
Yale University

Don Pickrell
John A. Volpe National
   Transportation Systems Center
U.S. Department of
   Transportation

John M. Quigley
Goldman School of Public Policy
University of California, Berkeley

Ian Savage
Department of Economics
Northwestern University

Kenneth A. Small
Department of Economics
University of California, Irvine

William B. Tye
The Brattle Group

Clifford Winston
Economic Studies
The Brookings Institution

Index

Who Was Traded for Lefty Grove?

Who Was Traded for Lefty Grove?

Baseball's Fun Facts
and Serious Trivia

MIKE ATTIYEH

The Johns Hopkins University Press
BALTIMORE LONDON

The Johns Hopkins University Press
2715 North Charles Street
Baltimore, Maryland 21218-4363
www.press.jhu.edu

A catalog record for this book is available from the British Library.

Library of Congress Cataloging-in-Publication Data

Attiyeh, Mike.
Who was traded for Lefty Grove? : baseball's fun facts and serious
trivia / by Mike Attiyeh.
p. cm.
Includes bibliographical references (p.) and index.
ISBN 0-8018-7039-9 (alk. paper)
1. Baseball—Miscellanea. I. Title.
GV873 .A88 2002
796.357—dc21

2001007419

This book is dedicated to my grandparents,
who have taken care of me as their own since I was one year old.
I consider myself blessed to have known their love.

Contents

Introduction

Not only do I remember the first baseball game I ever saw, I can also remember with great clarity what was going on in the rest of my life at the times when I witnessed my greatest baseball moments. I'm so enamored with The Game, I commemorate most of my life's events through the memories of baseball contests.

I first saw a Major League Baseball game when my uncle Awni turned the television channel from "S.W.A.T." to a Mets-Astros game in 1973. I was six, and not too pleased that Uncle Awni had zapped my favorite television program. But I was soon enraptured by the game—played at the Astrodome, I remember—and to this day remain grateful that my uncle knew better.

I remember the 1975 World Series as so intense that my late father lost his voice for a few days after the game. The Reds-Red Sox engagement was profound for the eight-year-old me, trying to comprehend how a little kids' game could bring so many people and generations together, and inspire so much passion. It was a moment of insight, and the beginning of a permanent love affair with The Game.

Besides Tim McCarver, Ralph Kiner, Joe Garagiola, and Bob Costas, the single person who taught me the most about The Game was my uncle Mark. We were inside his 7-11 store when I asked him, "What is a perfect game?" He answered that one—and many more questions that followed. My father also worked at the 7-11, so I spent most Saturdays and many off-days from school in the store talking baseball, reading about baseball from the magazines and newspapers on the shelf, and bouncing a rubber ball off the wall, playing imaginary games.

My uncle Abraham bought me a Joe Torre bat and a Kentucky Fried Chicken dinner just before we sat down in our house to view

Game One of the 1976 World Series. We both rooted for the Reds, although Chris Chambliss' dramatics were too much for a nine-year-old to comprehend.

In 1986, Uncle Abraham, my cousin Jimmy, and I were on the edge of our seats in my baseball shrine of a room as the Mets were rallying for three runs in the top of the ninth, tying the sixth game of the National League Championship Series at a silenced Astrodome. That game was so long that I listened to Billy Hatcher's game-tying home run during the bottom of the 14th inning on the car radio en route to my Holiday Inn job and saw the nail-biting 16th inning in front of the mobbed television set in the hotel bar.

Most amazing was how all the employees—banquet clerks, waitresses, maids, front desk clerks, bartenders, cooks, busboys, and even the strict managers—appeared to be "excused" from their duties. Work stopped; all of life seemed to revolve around that 16th-inning excitement. It was the first pennant my Mets had won since I had been consumed by The Game.

In 1990, my cousin Tom and I watched as his Reds shocked the world by sweeping the overwhelming favorite Oakland Athletics in the World Series. I still remember Tom's glee following Eric Davis' spectacular grab in center field.

But the most beautiful moment came on October 14, 1992, when Francisco Cabrera's heroic Game Seven-winning two-run single off Pittsburgh's Stan Belinda vaulted the Atlanta Braves to the pennant and drove my uncle Jimmy, my cousin Kal, and me wild with delight at the beauty and drama of The Game. As I walked from my uncle's house that chilly night amidst the fallen leaves, I realized another glorious season of baseball was nearing its end, and I thought of the paean written to The Game by the late Bart Giamatti, entitled "The Greenfields of the Mind:"

> It is designed to break your heart. The game begins in the spring, when everything else begins again, and it blossoms in the summer, filling the afternoons and evenings, and as soon as the chill rains come, it stops and leaves you to face the fall alone. You can count on it, rely on it to buffer the passage of time, to keep the memory of sunshine and high skies alive, and then just when the days are all twilight, when you need it most, it goes. . . . And summer is gone.

You can then imagine how I—and millions like me—felt betrayed in October of 1994, when for the first time in 90 years there was no World Series to speak of, or even a real spring to look forward to. To realize the owners, league officials, and union members had put aside tradition and the best interests of baseball indeed left a sour taste in the mouth—but never for The Game. I never thought for a second to take my anger out on The Game. My displeasure was directed toward the owners and the high-ranking officials of the Major League Baseball Players Association.

Obviously, I am not the only fan who feels that way: A record for attendance was set for the second time in three years in 2000. Major League Baseball drew 72,748,970 fans in 2000, and the average attendance topped 30,000 for the first time since the 1994–95 strike. Many, like myself, chose to view The Game as just that—a baseball game—overlooking some ugly aspects of the business, such as greed, commercialization, and a lack of leadership.

That forebearance was rewarded with a pair of remarkable moments during the 1995 season. Cal Ripken, Jr., on the unforgettable date of September 6, demonstrated the pure spirit of The Game by playing in his 2,131st consecutive contest. One month later, I witnessed in person the last four games of an epic five-game series between the Seattle Mariners and New York Yankees, validating my faith that the right with The Game far outweighed the wrong.

Attending a post-season game at famed Yankee Stadium is one of the most fulfilling and captivating experiences. Being around so many baseball-savvy fans endears you to the hallowed halls where so many legends once roamed. During that Yankees-Mariners series, no one complained about the length of Game Two as the drama escalated with every pitch before ending on a dramatic two-run homer by Jim Leyritz in the bottom of the 15th inning. Although my new favorite team lost, that night I remember feeling proud for The Game and inspired by the enthusiasm we all felt for it.

I then traveled nearly three thousand miles to Seattle to see the conclusion of this newly added AL Division Series, and I was not disappointed. The Mariners and Seattle had developed a new lease on baseball life as the Emerald City showed its support in droves toward the end of that 1995 campaign. It was obvious the Mariners gathered inspiration from it, winning all three home games in the most intense and dramatic fashion. As Ken Griffey, Jr. scored from first base on Edgar Martinez's game-winning, two-run double in the bottom of the 11th, I was overcome by the beauty and drama of The Game once again. If only for one night, I was in heaven and I wasn't alone.

The summer of 1998 clinched my devotion to The Game. From Kerry Wood's 20-strikeout, one-hit performance and David Wells' perfect game to the national home run fireworks put on by Mark McGwire and Sammy Sosa and the complete dominance displayed by the New York Yankees, the 1998 campaign was pretty darn good evidence The Game was back in top form.

My passion for The Game took a new turn one day in December 1988. A friend and I dropped by a tavern on our way to Staten Island, and the hour I spent in that bar and grill changed my career goals and my outlook on life. It also sparked the idea for this book. My friend introduced me to a 70-year-old man who supposedly knew everything about The Game. This guru and I began talking, and before too long he asked me the first trivia question: "Which Dodger did (Don) Larsen strike out for the final out of his perfect game?"

I had never even heard of Dale Mitchell (whose .312 average over an 11-year career was overshadowed by the penultimate plate appearance of his career). I began feeling a little defeated after I couldn't name the umpire that day either: Babe Pinelli. I quickly regained some of my confidence and pride after he couldn't name all nine players to win back-to-back MVP Awards (Barry Bonds became the 10th in 1993 and Frank Thomas became the 11th to do so in 1994). But then the old man struck back and began to school me. I was amazed at my rawness—a stunned and silenced youngster in defeat and denial. I have forgotten the venerable master's name and that of the tavern where we met, but I will always remember the slew of questions, the intriguing answers, and the guru's impressive performance. That meeting sparked my hunger for more, and it transformed my passion for The Game into the collection of fascinating stories and facts before you.

Spring Training

Who are the 11 players to win back-to-back MVP Awards? (Look at question 32 to find the answer.) How did Roger Maris benefit from having Mickey Mantle batting behind him in his pursuit of Babe Ruth's single-season home run record? (Question 157.) Who is the only player to win 150 games and collect 2,000 hits? (You'll find the answer is not Babe Ruth by checking question 227.) What was the most lopsided trade in major league history? (Question 304.) And, of course, who was traded for Lefty Grove? (Question 317.)

If you know the answers to any of these questions, then congratulations! You've just been hired as the manager of a miserable, cellar-dwelling, last-place team. Your job is to reconstruct the team. You have two full seasons to do it: Your contract calls for a two-year plan to transform this sad-sack ball club into a serious contender.

How can you do it? By not only reading *Who Was Traded for Lefty Grove?* but playing it as well. You don't have to take the job, of course: You can simply read the book and enjoy its question-and-answer format. But if you're up to this managerial challenge, here's how it works: Each chapter (season) includes 162 questions (games). In the First Season, you must answer 100 questions correctly (win 100 games) to qualify for post-season play. Every correct answer is a win and every incorrect answer is a defeat. The answer must be complete (matching answers must also be complete) and correct to obtain the win. The Second Season's win-total requirement is 96: Answering 96 questions correctly will net you a post-season berth. The "Did You Know?" facts interspersed throughout the text are merely for information and entertainment along the way and do not figure into the final score.

Included in the question format are trivia questions, matching questions, fill-in-the-blanks, true or false, fill-in-the-lineup, and multiple choice. All the facts are updated through the 2001 Major League Baseball season. To keep you on your toes, the questions are not grouped by category or design. And a good number of questions deal with many matters at once. (This is not your ordinary baseball book.)

Once you gain post-season entry, you must win (answer) four League Championship Series games (questions) to advance to the World Series. To become a world champion, you must win the best-of-seven by answering four more questions correctly.

Think you can handle it? If so, good luck, skipper, and don't forget that you will be judged on your performance when it comes time to decide whether you'll be tendered another contract. The team will grant you, the participating manager, a contract extension if you win (1) a pennant or world championship, or (2) two division titles, or (3) 170 regular-season games.

So use a piece of paper to cover the answers and keep track of your results. Compare your scores with the manager's requirement for rehiring (as decided by your general manager), also located after the completion of Season Two's postseason. Without further ado, let's throw out the first pitch and play ball!

Opening Day

The phrase "opening day" is as refreshing as a cold one on a hot summer afternoon. Just say the words and you'll likely open a floodgate of memories that will put a smile on your face and erase your worries. Opening day officially brings to an end long winters and exhibition baseball, ushering in a new wave of excitement that can only be compared with opening an unexpected gift. Although each major league season brings about unforeseen events, opening day itself is as unpredictable as an earthquake—but charged with the thrill of anticipation. Even cynics can hope that maybe, just maybe, this is their team's year. "Hey, remember what everyone thought of the 1969 Mets on opening day?" they reason.

Throughout major league history, opening day has produced many great moments, and, like the World Series and All-Star Games, may at any time produce unique and exciting additions to the baseball legend. Opening day represents the introduction of another major league season. It's a day when a Hall of Famer can falter and an eighth-place hitter can prosper, just like any other day. But it's a day with unique conditions and a distinctive atmosphere. It may not reveal much about the remainder of the season, but trying to predict the end from the beginning can be incredibly intriguing.

Here are some opening day "Did You Know?" tidbits to get you warmed up.

♦ Did you know on April 22, 1876, the Boston Red Caps defeated Philadelphia, 6-5, at Athletic Park before just over 3,000 fans in the first-ever major league game? Jim O'Rourke collected the first hit and Boston starter Joseph Borden earned the inaugural win. Starter Alonzo Knight of the hometown Athletics delivered the first pitch in NL history. The Red Caps (later renamed the Braves) scored twice in the ninth inning to win. Although other games were scheduled that day, rainouts postponed every other opener.

♦ Did you know the Cubs' leadoff hitter Karl "Tuffy" Rhodes hit three home runs off Dwight Gooden on April 4, 1994, to join George Bell as the only players in major league history to homer thrice on opening day? Bell accomplished the feat six years earlier for Toronto against Kansas City's Bret Saberhagen. Joe Torre remains the only player to homer twice on opening day for two straight years, doing so in 1965 and 1966. The Yankees' Yogi Berra, the Expos' Gary Carter, and the Mets' Todd Hundley share the record for homering on four straight opening days.

♦ Did you know the Detroit Tigers' Gerald Walker is the only player to ever record a cycle on Opening Day? On April 20, 1937, against the Cleveland Indians, Walker did so in descending order, homering, tripling, doubling, and then singling.

♦ Did you know six players had multi-homer games on opening day, 2000, establishing a new opening day record? On April 3, Shannon Stewart, Tony Batista, Jason Giambi, Gabe Kapler, Ivan Rodriguez, and Vladimir Guerrero each connected twice for their respective teams. The previous record of four was set on opening day in 1988.

♦ Did you know the Philadelphia Phillies beat the Boston Braves in the most offensive-minded opening day game in history? The Phillies won this April 19 contest to open the 1900 season in 10 innings, 19-17, after the Braves had scored nine runs in the bottom of the ninth.

♦ Did you know the Milwaukee Brewers' Sixto Lezcano is the only player in major league history to hit two career grand slams on opening day? Lezcano first accomplished the feat in 1978 as part of the team's record barrage, which included a salami in each of the team's first three games during a three-game sweep over Baltimore by a combined score of 30-11. Lezcano came through again in 1980 by clubbing a dramatic, game-winning bases-loaded homer with two out in the bottom of the ninth inning for a 9-5 win against the Red Sox.

♦ Did you know in 1986, Boston Red Sox right fielder Dwight Evans became—and remains—the only batter ever to hit the major league season's first pitch out for a homer? Evans timed Detroit's Jack Morris just perfectly.

♦ Did you know on opening day 1909 (April 15), New York Giants pitcher Leon "Red" Ames held Brooklyn hitless through 9⅓ innings before losing a heartbreaker, 3-0, in 13 innings. Unbelievably, Ames encountered a similar fate in the next two opening days as well. He threw seven hitless innings before losing 3-2 to Boston in 1910, and hurled six hitless frames before going down, 2-0, to Philadelphia in 1911.

♦ Did you know Frank Robinson homered in his first at-bat as a player-manager for the Cleveland Indians on April 8, 1975, giving him a major league record eight career opening day home runs? For Robinson, that day was special in another way: He also became the first black manager of a major league team. A quartet of great batsmen, including a currently active slugger, have seven such home runs. They are Babe Ruth, Willie Mays, Eddie Mathews, and the current Cincinnati Red, Ken Griffey, Jr. The 32-year-old Griffey has a great chance of surpassing Robinson's record.

Who Was Traded for Lefty Grove?

First Season

♦ Did you know John Olerud, Paul Molitor, and Roberto Alomar became the first teammates in one hundred years to finish first, second, and third in a league batting race as members of the 1993 Toronto Blue Jays? Olerud hit .362, Molitor hit .332, and Alomar ended at .326. The only other trio to accomplish the feat was Billy Hamilton (.380), Sam Thompson (.370), and Ed Delahanty (.368) of the 1893 Philadelphia Phillies.

♦ Did you know the 1969 Mets beat all six of the following pitchers three times each: Steve Carlton, Bob Gibson, Ferguson Jenkins, Gaylord Perry, Phil Niekro, and Don Sutton? The six pitchers combined for 117 wins that year, and all made the Hall of Fame.

1. *Can you name the solid fielding third baseman who from 1906 to 1910 completed the Chicago Cubs' Tinker-to-Evers-to-Chance infield?*

   ANSWER: Harry Steinfeldt

   Steinfeldt, a sure-handed fielder with an outstanding arm, must have felt unappreciated after shortstop Joe Tinker, second baseman Johnny Evers, and first baseman Frank Chance were immortalized in the famous poem "Baseball's Sad Lexicon."
   Steinfeldt, a .267 career hitter whom the Cubs acquired in a trade from the Cincinnati Reds right before the 1906 season, had his best campaign that year. Aside from leading all third basemen in fielding, Steinfeldt batted .327 with league-best figures of 83 RBI and 176 hits to help the Cubs win the first of three straight National League pennants. Steinfeldt also led the NL in fielding in 1907, giving the club the best defensive third baseman for the third straight season (Doc Casey led in 1905). Arguably the best defensive performer of

the bunch, Steinfeldt never received the recognition accorded the aforementioned trio. He ended his 14-year career with the Braves in 1911, and passed away three years later of a cerebral hemorrhage.

Interestingly, the Cubs' Hall of Fame trio of Tinker, Evers, and Chance never led the league in double plays. In fact, they didn't even finish second in that category during their eight full seasons together (1903–10). But that was perhaps attributed to the small number of baserunners the team's excellent pitching staff yielded. The troika turned its first double play on September 15, 1902, and played briefly as a unit in 1911 and 1912.

"Baseball's Sad Lexicon" was written by columnist Franklin Pierce Adams on July 18, 1910, as a tribute to the teamwork turned in by Tinker, Evers, and Chance. Although many renditions of the celebrated poem exist, this is the original version that appeared in the *New York Evening Mail* that day:

> These are the saddest of possible words:
> "Tinker to Evers to Chance."
> Trio of bear cubs, and fleeter than birds,
> Tinker and Evers and Chance.
> Ruthlessly pricking our gonfalon bubble,
> Making a Giant hit into a double—
> Words that are heavy with nothing but trouble:
> "Tinker to Evers to Chance."

◆ Did you know Johnny Evers, Joe Tinker, and Frank Chance were inducted, as a trio, into the Hall of Fame in 1946? Interestingly enough, 11 players were honored in 1946: the most ever elected in one year. The other eight inductees were Jesse Burkett, Jack Chesbro, Clark Griffith, Tom McCarthy, Joe McGinnity, Eddie Plank, Rube Waddell, and Ed Walsh.

2. *Three players have won Most Valuable Player Awards at different positions. Robin Yount was the last player to do so. Name the first two.*

ANSWER: Hank Greenberg and Stan Musial

Greenberg and Stan "The Man" Musial are the only other multiple-MVP Award winners to earn their hardware at different positions. Greenberg earned the MVP in 1935 at first base and won the award in 1940 as a left fielder. Musial won his 1943 and 1948 awards as an outfielder and his MVP in 1946 at first base. Yount won his 1982 MVP at shortstop and his 1989 award in center field, playing very good defense at each position without needing much of a transitional period.

♦ Did you know Stan Musial received the moniker "The Man" from Brooklyn Dodger fans for the endless torment he put Dodgers pitchers through almost every time he played in Ebbets Field? Dodger fans would stand up and say, "Uh, no, here comes that man again" or "Here's the man." Although a super gentleman, Musial was dubbed "The Man" for his ways with the bat.

3. *Joel Youngblood is the only player to get a hit for two different teams in two different cities on the same day, and he did so off two Hall of Fame pitchers. Name the distinguished pair of arms.*

ANSWER: Ferguson Jenkins and Steve Carlton

Youngblood began the afternoon of August 4, 1982, in a New York Mets uniform, playing center field in Chicago, and ended that night playing right field in a Montreal Expos uniform at Philadelphia. In between, the career .265 right-handed hitter made history.

As a Met, Youngblood drilled a game-deciding, two-run single in the third inning off the Cubs' Jenkins at Wrigley Field. After receiving news of his trade to the Expos the following frame, Youngblood bagged his belongings, caught a plane to Philadelphia, and arrived at Veterans Stadium in the third inning. Inserted in the sixth as a defensive replacement, Youngblood singled late in the game off Carlton. By the way, Youngblood was traded for left-handed reliever Tom Gorman.

♦ Did you know Max Flack and Cliff Heathcoate played for two different teams in one day after getting traded for each other on May 30, 1922? Traded between games of a doubleheader, Flack was moved to the Cardinals, and Heathcoate to the Cubs, who swept the twinbill.

4. *Under which circumstances did the paths of pitchers Joe Oeschger and Leon Cadore cross for an unforgettable and historic occurrence?*

ANSWER: Oeschger of the Braves and Cadore of Brooklyn were the starting and finishing pitchers in an amazing 26-inning marathon on May 1, 1920, that concluded in a 1-1 tie. The game was called due to darkness by umpire Barry McCormick. Although both pitchers willed themselves to the dual Herculean feat, the game obviously took its toll on them. For the next few days, Oeschger (pronounced "Esk-ker") had to brush his teeth left-handed because he couldn't raise his pitching arm. Cadore slept for the vast majority of the next 36 hours, according to fellow Society for American Baseball Research member Norman Macht.

Neither pitcher allowed a run over the last 20 innings, and Oeschger didn't yield a hit over the last nine. Oeschger was a bit more impressive than Cadore, allowing just nine hits (to 15 for Cadore) and walking four, one less than his Brooklyn counterpart. Oeschger batted 1-for-9 against Cadore, while the latter was hitless in 10 at-bats. Oeschger's 21 consecutive scoreless innings that game remain a record, breaking Art Nehf's single-game mark of 20 straight scoreless frames, set on August 1, 1918.

Oeschger went on to register a 15-13 mark with a 3.46 ERA in 1920, and captured his only 20-win campaign the following season. But he suffered through a lackluster 16-45 record over his final five years, retiring with a sub-par ledger of 82-116 and an ERA of 3.81.

Cadore went on to win 15 of 29 decisions that year with a 2.62 ERA, helping the Dodgers win the pennant. But the righthander never won as many games again, concluding his career with a 25-31 record over his final five seasons. He ended a 10-year career in 1924 with a 68-72 mark and a 3.14 ERA.

The game also took its toll on the Dodgers. A day after playing the longest game in history, the Dodgers on Sunday lost a home contest 4-3 in 13 innings to the Philadelphia Phillies. On Monday, the Dodgers returned to Boston to play the Braves and lost a 2-1, 19-inning meet. In summary, Brooklyn played 58 innings in three days, and went winless (the 26-inning game was replayed in June, and the Dodgers lost). Interestingly enough, 19 years later, on June 27, the same two teams played to a 23-inning, 2-2 tie in the same park.

♦ Did you know the May 1, 1920, marathon between Boston and Brooklyn not only included 73 putouts recorded by first basemen, but also took only three hours and 50 minutes? Braves first baseman Walter Holke accounted for a still-standing record of 42 putouts, 10 more than anyone else in history.

Braves second baseman Charlie Pick went 0-for-11; that remains the record for most hitless at-bats in a game.

♦ Did you know Jack Coombs outdueled Joe Harris in a 24-inning battle on September 24, 1906? Both rookies lasted the distance, with Coombs' Philadelphia Athletics defeating Harris' Boston Americans, 4-1. Coombs went on to a stellar career, registering 158 regular-season victories in addition to three wins in the 1910 World Series. Harris wound up losing 21 of his 23 decisions that season. Harris was released, following an 0-7 mark in 1907, with a career mark of 3-30.

5. *On April 14, 1974, within the confines of Fulton County Stadium in Atlanta, Georgia, Henry Louis Aaron broke Babe Ruth's career home run mark of 714 with a blast off Dodgers' southpaw Al Downing. Can you name the Dodgers' first baseman who offered his congratulations as Aaron rounded first? Can you also name the left fielder who watched as the ball sailed over his head? And can you name the relief pitcher in the Braves bullpen who caught the home run ball?*

ANSWER: Steve Garvey, Bill Buckner, Tom House

Garvey was the first baseman, Buckner was the left fielder, and House was the reliever who caught the ball and brought it to Aaron during the wild celebration that took place at home plate. The historic pitch Aaron clobbered off Downing was a 1-0 slider, low and down the middle. For those who have never heard broadcaster Milo Hamilton's call, you're missing out. It's my favorite call of all time. It goes like this: "Here's the pitch by Downing . . . swinging. Well hit [to] deep left-center field. This ball is gonna be . . . outta here. It's gone; it's 715. There's a new home run champion of all time, and it's Henry Aaron."

♦ Did you know Hank Aaron's name is the first alphabetically among the 15,000-plus players in major league history? Dutch Zwilling, an outfielder who played for the American League's Chicago White Sox, the Federal League's Chicago Whales, and the National League's Chicago Cubs, is the last player listed. The left-handed hitting Zwilling received 87 at-bats in his lone season with the White Sox in 1910, drove in 95 and a league-best 94 runs in his two years with the Whales, and received just 53 at-bats in his lone season with the Cubs. Zwilling's 29 career Federal League homers is tops in that circuit's brief history.

6. *In Game Four of the 1947 World Series, New York Yankees pitcher _____ had a no-hitter and a 2-1 lead with two aboard and two out in the ninth inning. Reserve Dodger third baseman _____ then doubled off the right-field wall to account for Brooklyn's only hit and its 3-2 win. Fill in the blanks.*

   ANSWER: Bill Bevens, Cookie Lavagetto

Bevens, who was wild in walking 10 Dodgers that game, issued a bases on balls to Carl Furillo (who was replaced by pinch-runner Al Gionfriddo) and an intentional pass to Pete Reiser (replaced by pinch-runner Eddie Miksis) in the ninth. Lavagetto, hitting in place of Eddie Stanky, followed by pulling a Bevens' offering, plating Gionfriddo and Miksis. The win enabled the Dodgers to even the series at two games apiece, before losing in seven thrilling contests. Lavagetto wasn't as heroic the next day, striking out as a pinch-hitter with a potential tying runner on second base and two out in the bottom of the ninth.

7. *Of the 16 pitchers to hurl a perfect game (including Don Larsen), only five have been left-handed. Name four of them.*

   ANSWER: David Wells, Kenny Rogers, Tom Browning, Sandy Koufax, and John Lee Richmond

Wells of the 1998 New York Yankees, Rogers of the 1994 Texas Rangers, Browning of the 1988 Cincinnati Reds, Koufax of the Los Angeles Dodgers in 1965, and Richmond of the Worcester Brown Stockings in 1880 are the only five southpaws to have pitched a perfect game.

Of course, Harvey Haddix, who once took a perfect game into the 13th inning before losing, was left-handed as well. On May 26, 1959, the skinny Pirate hurler set down the Braves in order for 12 straight frames at Milwaukee's County Stadium, striking out eight and fooling others with an effective changeup. In the bottom of the unlucky 13th, Haddix induced Felix Mantilla to hit an easy grounder to third baseman Don Hoak. But Hoak threw the ball away, permitting Mantilla to reach via an error and become the Braves' first baserunner of the evening. Mantilla then advanced to second as Eddie Mathews sacrificed. Tiring, Haddix intentionally walked Hank Aaron to set up a potential double-play ball against Joe Adcock. With the no-hitter still in hand, Haddix was a pitch away from advancing to the 14th. But Adcock had other ideas, drilling Haddix's second delivery over the right-center field fence to end the marathon. Although Adcock's three-run homer was changed to an RBI double, because the excited Aaron ran off the field after touching second base, the 1-0 margin was sufficient to bring an end to an unforgettable contest.

♦ Did you know Tom Browning is the only pitcher to carry a perfect game into the ninth inning after having already thrown a perfect game? Within three outs of a second gem on July 4, 1989, Browning yielded a lead-off double in the ninth to Dickie Thon of the Phillies and settled for a 2-1 victory. Browning fashioned his masterpiece a year earlier on September 16, 1988, mowing down the Dodgers, 1-0.

♦ Did you know David Cone's perfect game in 1999 was the fourth of the decade, more than any other decade? The gem also marked the first time that perfect games were pitched in consecutive years, although a pair was thrown in 1880.

8.   *Choose the slugger who reached triple digits in RBI and runs scored for 13 consecutive seasons:*

A Al Simmons
B Hank Aaron
C Babe Ruth
D Lou Gehrig
E Jimmie Foxx
F Stan Musial

ANSWER: D

Gehrig accomplished the tremendous feat from 1926 to 1938. "The Iron Horse" had seven seasons of more than 150 RBI, and eight years of more than 135 runs scored. Gehrig's 1,995 RBI ranks third all time and his 1,888 runs rank ninth.

Foxx in 1941 matched Gehrig's mark of 13 straight 100-RBI seasons, creating a still-standing, three-way tie with Gehrig and Ruth for overall triple-digit RBI campaigns. Simmons reached the 100-RBI mark in each of his first 11 seasons, and 12 of his first 13. Simmons, a .334 career hitter, scored at least 100 runs six times. Hardly brought up in heavy RBI talk is Goose Goslin, who reached the 100-RBI plateau 11 times over a 13-year stretch from 1924 to 1936. From 1923 to 1936, Goslin drove in at least 91 runs a year for all but one season.

♦ Did you know Lou Gehrig remains the only player to bat .300, club 20 homers and leg out 10 triples four straight years?

9. *This Hall of Famer came the closest to the glorified 3,000-hit club without reaching it. He is:*

A Sam Crawford
B Willie Keeler
C Frank Robinson
D Sam Rice
E Rogers Hornsby

ANSWER: D

Rice retired with 2,987 hits. According to Lee Allen and Tom Meany, co-authors of *King of the Diamonds,* Rice simply didn't know how many hits he had when he retired. Although invited to come back for those 13 safeties a few years later by Senators owner Clark Griffith, Rice refused. He never suspected that much ado would be made of reaching 3,000 hits. Rice, who had six 200-hit seasons, and retired with a .322 career batting mark, hit .293 in his last season (1934).

Crawford (2,964), Keeler (2,962), Robinson (2,943), and Hornsby (2,930) were also close, as was Al Simmons (2,927). It is clear that numbers were not considered so important back in the 1930s. If Harold Baines (2,866) returns for the 2002 season, it'll be with 3,000 hits in mind.

Robinson, however, was a most peculiar case because he was aware of the plateau's importance and was his own manager, with the ability to insert himself as often as he wanted. But over the 1975 and 1976 seasons, he gave himself a combined 185 at-bats. Just 57 hits shy, he retired as a player to focus full time on managing for the 1977 campaign. A more selfish man would have reached the milestone, but Robinson knew the importance of his decisions as a manager (especially the first African-American manager) far outweighed an individual landmark.

Keeler, one of the shortest and lightest players in major league history at five feet four inches and 140 pounds, defied all laws in establishing himself as one of the greatest batsmen of all time. Although diminutive in size, "Wee" Willie Keeler was deemed a giant by pitchers as he was able to get on base quite often by using a logical concept: "Keep a clear eye and hit 'em where they ain't." The left-handed Keeler had the uncanny ability to place the ball precisely where he wanted, a skill that rewarded him with a .341 lifetime batting average and a pair of batting titles. Aside from making a name for himself as arguably the game's best place hitter, Keeler was also a great bunter. Using an exaggerated choke on his light (29-ounce) bat, Keeler also became adept at the "Baltimore chop," slapping the ball off the packed dirt in front of the plate either high in the air or high over the infielders' heads. A master with the bat, Keeler also worked the hit-and-run as few others did, especially with teammate John McGraw running the bases. Although 86% of his hits were singles, Keeler showed some extra-base ability, reaching a dozen triples seven times and getting to the 20-double mark on five occasions. Keeler, who stole 495 bases, used his speed to produce 30 of his 33 career home runs.

Keeler, a right fielder, enjoyed his best season in 1897. That year he hit in 44 straight games—his first 44 of the season—en route to a .424 batting average (the third highest of all time) with another league-leading figure of 239 hits. His 44-game hitting streak remains the NL record, tied by Pete Rose in 1978 but never surpassed.

10. *On October 6, 1991, the Mets'* _____ *struck out 19 Phillies at Veteran's Stadium, tying the then–NL mark set by Steve Carlton (versus the Mets) and equaled by Tom Seaver (a Met).*

ANSWER: David Cone

Cone was caught by Charlie O'Brien. On May 6, 1998, Cubs' 20-year-old rookie Kerry Wood set the NL record, and equaled Roger

Clemens' major league nine-inning mark, by fanning 20 Houston Astros in a one-hit shutout at Wrigley Field. Wood relied on an amazing curveball, a great slider, and a hopping fastball to limit the Astros to an infield hit (by Ricky Gutierrez) that third baseman Kevin Orie played tentatively. The only other Astros batter to reach base was Craig Biggio, who was hit by a pitch.

On May 8, 2001, Randy Johnson tied the mark of 20 Ks over nine innings, set by Clemens (twice) and equaled by Wood. In all four instances, the record-setting pitchers did not issue a walk. (Johnson actually pitched the 10th inning of his 20-K game, but was given a share of the record because he registered his 20 whiffs over the course of nine innings.)

♦ Did you know Kerry Wood, David Cone, and Tom Seaver are the only pitchers to strike out at least 19 batters in a nine-inning day game dating back to 1900? It's an accepted theory that pitches are easier to locate in games under the sun.

♦ Did you know Hugh "One-Arm" Daily was cheated of a 20-strikeout performance on July 7, 1884, while pitching a one-hitter for the Chicago Unions of the Union Association? Daily was given credit for 19 strikeouts, because rules of that day gave the official scorer the option of ruling an error for a wild-pitched strikeout. With two outs in the fifth inning, catcher Bill Krieg dropped a third strike pitched by Daily that permitted hitter Pat Scanlon to reach first base. The official scorer could—some say should—have given Krieg an error and Daily a strikeout, but did not that day.

11. *Although George Sisler's 257 hits is the major league single-season record, _____ co-holds the NL mark of 254 hits.*

ANSWER: Bill Terry or Lefty O'Doul

Terry hit .401 in 1930; Lefty O'Doul batted .398 in 1929. Sisler set the AL mark in 1920, when he batted .407. Al Simmons, Chuck Klein, and Rogers Hornsby are the only other players to reach the 250-hit plateau outside the 1887 campaign, when walks drawn counted as hits.

Terry retired after the 1936 season with 2,193 hits in just 6,428 at-bats. The Hall of Famer was adept at driving the balls into the Polo Grounds' vast gaps, focusing more on doubles and triples than on home runs. In 1924, the rookie first baseman had to have a great bat just to crack the Hall of Fame-laden lineup of the New York Giants.

The six other Cooperstown inductees in batting order were George Kelly (first base), Frankie Frisch (second baseman), Travis Jackson (shortstop), Fred Lindstrom (third baseman), Ross Youngs (right fielder), and Hack Wilson (center fielder). In fact, it took Terry four years to become a regular as even the great Mel Ott—then a youngster—rode the bench during the 1926 and 1927 seasons. Even the manager, John McGraw, was a Hall of Famer.

♦ Did you know the hitting-rich New York Giants boasted the only starting Hall of Fame infield for two years—with a different alignment each season? The 1925 Giants sported Bill Terry at first base, George Kelly at second, Travis Jackson at shortstop, and Fred Lindstrom at third. The 1926 lineup featured Kelly (a .297 career hitter) back at his normal position of first base, Frankie Frisch at his normal spot at second, Jackson (a .291 career hitter) at short, and Lindstrom (a .291 career hitter) at third. The offense was so packed with Hall of Fame talent that Terry only came to bat 225 times in 1926, and Frisch had to divide 120 games between second, third, and short in 1925. For a small portion of the season, the 1924 Giants also had a Hall of Fame infield. Kelly played first base in 125 games, Frisch played second in 143 contests, and Jackson guarded short for 151 games. But Lindstrom played just 11 of his 34 games at third in 1924. Heinie Groh was the regular third baseman, playing that position in 145 contests.

12. *Match these players with their accomplishments:*

1	Hugh Duffy	A	owns the all-time career and single-season records for steals by a catcher
2	Rudy York	B	won baseball's second triple crown in 1894
3	Ray Schalk	C	set a single-month record with 18 homers in August of 1937—as a rookie
4	Buck Ewing	D	caught three no-hitters, excluding one broken up in the 10th

ANSWER: 1—B, 2—C, 3—D, 4—A

Duffy hit an all-time, single-season record .438 en route to winning the Triple Crown in 1894. A right-handed center fielder for the Boston Beaneaters (later renamed the Braves), Duffy also socked 18 homers with 145 RBI. Taking advantage of South Ends Grounds' cozy dimensions down each line (250 feet down the left-field line, and 255 down the right-field line), Duffy also led the NL in slugging (.694), total bases (374), hits (237), and doubles (51). Although Duffy was a beneficiary of his home park and the era's offensive dominance (as pitchers adjusted to pitching from 60 feet, six inches after the 1892 season), he hit almost 100 points better than any of his teammates in 1894. From 1890 to 1897, the five-foot-seven Duffy batted at least .300 each year and averaged 133 runs and 110 RBI. The .324 lifetime hitter went on to manage for eight years and teach a young hitter by the name of Ted Williams a thing or two about hitting before getting inducted into the Hall of Fame as a 78-year-old in 1945.

The Cubs' Sammy Sosa broke York's record by clubbing 20 home runs in June of 1998. Willie Mays held the NL mark of 17 home runs in one month (August 1965) for 33 years.

One of Schalk's three no-hitters caught was Charlie Robertson's 1922 perfect game. His other two no-hitters caught were Ed Cicotte's 1917 gem, and the one tossed by Joe Benz three years before. In 1914, Schalk caught a great performance by Jim Scott, who lost a no-hitter and the game in the 10th inning. Twelve other catchers have caught three no-hitters. In reverse chronological order, they are Charles Johnson, Alan Ashby, Jeff Torborg, Del Crandall, Yogi Berra (if you include Don Larsen's World Series perfect game), Roy Campanella, Jim Hegan, Luke Sewell, Val Picinich, Bill Carrigan, Ed McFarland, and Steve Flint. Torborg remains the only receiver with at least one no-hitter caught in each league. Lou Criger and Johnny Edwards each caught a trio of no-hitters through nine, but each had one of their games end in extra innings. Johnson, of course, is still active and can add to his total. He caught the no-hitters of Al Leiter, Kevin Brown, and A. J. Burnett.

Ewing's 53 stolen bases in 1888 and 47 thefts five years later remain the two highest marks achieved by a catcher over a single season. Ewing's 354 career steals is comfortably ahead of the pack. John Wathan's 36 thefts in 1982 broke Ray Schalk's previous 20th-century mark of 30, set in 1916. Schalk's 176 career steals remains the AL record. Jason Kendall of Pittsburgh set the 20th-century NL record with 26 thefts in 1998, eclipsing the previous mark of 25, accomplished by John Stearns 20 years earlier.

♦ Did you know Ernie Lombardi remains the only receiver to catch back-to-back no-hitters by a pitcher? Yes, Lombardi was the catcher in each of Johnny Vander Meer's consecutive no-hitters. In addition to calling great games, Lombardi combined for three hits, including a homer, and two RBI in the historic games.

13. *Can you name the only two batters to hit .400 from 1900 on and yet not win the batting title?*

ANSWER: Joe Jackson and Ty Cobb

Jackson's .408 mark fell short of Ty Cobb's .420 in 1911, and Cobb himself, with a .401 average in 1922, was second to George Sisler (.420 average) in that year. Jackson, beautiful swing and all, never won a batting title, thanks to Cobb's dominance. Jackson's .356 career mark is the highest without a batting title.

Riggs Stephenson's .336 career mark is the second highest sans batting title. Stephenson's lifetime figure of .336 is also the second highest of any player eligible but not elected to the Hall of Fame. Pete Browning's .341 career average tops that list. Browning, a three-time batting champion, collected 1,646 hits in 4,820 at-bats from 1882 to 1894. Stephenson accrued 1,515 hits in 4,508 at-bats.

♦ Did you know Joe Jackson was the only 20th-century ball player to average .380 or higher after his first 700 at-bats? Tuck Turner of the Phillies was the only other player to do it, between 1893 and 1895, but slipped and was released after the 1898 season.

14. *Match these players with their unique feats:*

1	Grover Alexander	A	hit a home run in all four divisions in one season
2	Christy Mathewson		
3	Babe Ruth	B	enjoyed four 30-win seasons in the 1900s
4	Fred Lynn		
5	Dave Kingman	C	hurled a record 16 shutouts in one season
6	Hank Aaron		
		D	career leader with 2,297 RBI
		E	won the MVP Award as a rookie, eclipsing rookie Pete Reiser's runner-up MVP finish in 1941
		F	won nine consecutive home-run titles

ANSWER: 1—C, 2—B, 3—F, 4—E, 5—A, 6—D

Alexander's mark is even more amazing considering he accomplished the feat while playing half his games in Philadelphia's Baker Bowl, a field with inviting dimensions to batters, especially left-handed sluggers. Alexander, a righthander who relied on an outstanding curve and a moving fastball, had a year for the ages in 1916, winning 33 games, with a microscopic 1.55 ERA spanning 389 innings of work.

Mathewson relied on a great screwball (which he called "fadeaway"), unbelievable control, tremendous endurance, and an intellectual mindset on the mound to record a quartet of 30-win seasons over a six-year stretch en route to 373 career victories. Mathewson also completed 434 of his starts, and earned five ERA titles, five strikeout crowns, and four victory titles.

Also in 1975, Jim Rice (Lynn's teammate) became the only other rookie to finish in the MVP voting's top three before 2001, when Seattle's Ichiro Suzuki duplicated Lynn's rookie-MVP feat. Lynn and Rice in 1975 delighted Red Sox hopefuls with a double dose of rookie stardom en route to the AL pennant. The left-handed Lynn excelled in all facets of the game. He earned a Gold Glove for his acrobatic play in center field, and took home the Rookie of the Year Award and MVP based in large part on his .331 batting average, 21 homers, 105 RBI, and league-best figures in runs, doubles, and slugging. Rice, a left fielder, clubbed 22 homers and also placed in the top five in batting, RBI, and runs scored. Alas for Boston, an inside pitch during the last week of that regular season broke Rice's left hand and shelved him for the upcoming postseason. The Red Sox swept the three-time defending champion Oakland A's in the American League Championship Series before losing a thrilling seven-gamer to the Cincinnati Reds in the World Series.

Aaron reached the 100-RBI mark 11 times, missing by five or fewer on four other occasions.

◆ Did you know Babe Ruth and Dave Kingman are the only players with at least 10 major league seasons to boast career slugging averages double their career batting averages? Babe Ruth slugged .690 and hit .342; Kingman slugged .478 and hit a measly .236.

15. *Hall of Famer Mel Ott of the New York Giants hit 19 home runs as a teenager. Can you name the player who hit the most homers as a teenager?*

ANSWER: Tony Conigliaro

Conigliaro of the Boston Red Sox hit 24 homers before he turned 20, all during his 1964 rookie season. He followed that up with a 32-homer campaign as a 20-year-old, making him the youngest home-run leader in American League history. Conigliaro had 104 homers by August 18, 1967. That's when his season came to an abrupt halt, and his career turned off the golden path it had been riding. On that day, he was beaned and almost blinded by California Angels pitcher Jack Hamilton, whose high, inside fastball broke Conigliaro's cheekbone and eye socket. Conigliaro lay motionless while the medical staff attended to him before being carted off on a stretcher to a nearby hospital. With his vision so badly damaged, Conigliaro couldn't return to the batter's box for 20 months. The sweet-swinging right-handed slugger came back to win AL Comeback Player of the Year honors in 1969 and put forth his best performance in 1970, reaching career bests with 36 home runs, 116 RBI, 89 runs scored, and 149 hits. But the detached retina he suffered from the beaning began to affect his vision, and he became depressed after a shocking trade to the Angels prior to the 1971 season. In 1975, he returned to Boston, where he played 21 games before calling it quits. After suffering a heart attack that rendered him disabled in 1982, Conigliaro died in 1990. The abrupt career change is quite simply one of the saddest turn of events associated with major league baseball.

16. *The 1996 and 1997 Colorado Rockies became the second and third teams in history to have three players hit at least 40 home runs, tying the mark set by the 1973 Atlanta Braves. Can you name the Braves' troika in 1973?*

ANSWER: Davey Johnson (43), Darrell Evans (41), and Hank Aaron (40)

Dusty Baker added 21 and Mike Lum 16 to contribute to a ferocious Atlanta lineup that led the league with 799 runs scored. But the

Braves' league-worst 4.25 ERA did them in as they finished with a 76-85 ledger, fifth in the NL West.

♦ Did you know Davey Johnson hit 42 home runs while playing second base in 1973, tying him with Rogers Hornsby's feat in 1922?

17. *Back in 1941, when Ted Williams of the Boston Red Sox became the last player to hit .400, fly outs that drove runners home were counted as at-bats, as an 0-for-1. True or False?*

ANSWER: True

A sacrifice fly in today's game is not counted as an official at-bat. After a statistical change introduced the sacrifice fly in 1908, the sacrifice fly reverted back to an at-bat, 0-for-1, in 1931. After switching back and forth in 1939 and 1940, the sacrifice fly was brought back for good in 1954. None of that, however, mattered to the "The Splendid Splinter." The focused and confident Williams entered the final day of the 1941 campaign with a .39955 batting average, a figure that would have been rounded off to .400. Given the opportunity by manager Joe Cronin to sit out the doubleheader and safeguard his mark, the tough-minded Williams refused. "The Thumper" faced the challenge and succeeded, going 6-for-8 in the twinbill for a season-ending .406 mark. No player has batted .400 since. Williams, whose .482 career on-base percentage ranks as the best of all time and whose .634 slugging percentage ranks second (behind only Babe Ruth), retired with a .344 lifetime batting mark. A keen student of the art of hitting, Williams is recognized as the foremost authority on the subject. Blessed with incredible eyesight and adept at knowing the ins and outs, Williams was said to recognize pitches faster than anyone and possessed greater knowledge of the strike zone than any other man who ever played. Williams led the AL in walks for eight consecutive full seasons. His walks to strikeouts ratio of almost three to one is incomprehensible for a man who hit 521 home runs. Williams never struck out more than 64 times and was whiffed 50 times just thrice.

♦ Did you know Ted Williams was the only distinguished major leaguer to fight in World War II and the Korean War? Williams missed almost five seasons to serve in the military. The combined four and three-quarter seasons missed cost Williams certain membership into the 3,000-hit, 600-homer,

2,000-RBI, and 2,000-run clubs. In fact, Williams could conceivably have reached the 3,500-hit, 650-homer, 2,400-RBI, and 2,400-run plateaus. Williams, a pilot, flew 39 missions over Korea. Williams was so prepared, and his skill so honed that he hit .407 in 37 games upon returning from Korea late during the 1953 season. That's like being blindfolded, spun around 10 or 15 times, and asked to make 20 straight free throws—not easy. There was nothing Williams couldn't do with a bat.

18. *What do Bernie Williams, Terry Pendleton, Tim Raines, Willie McGee, Willie Wilson, Pete Rose, and Mickey Mantle have in common?*

ANSWER: The only switch-hitters to win a batting crown

Rose leads this pack with three batting titles, in 1968, 1969, and 1973. McGee won a pair, in 1985 and 1990. Raines came out on top in 1986, Terry Pendleton was the victor in 1991, Wilson earned his in 1982, and Williams finished first in 1998.

Mantle won his crown in 1956, although his .365 average the following year is the highest for a switch-hitter in the modern era—defined in this book as post-19th century. (George Davis' mark of .373 in 1893 remains the all-time standard for ambidextrous hitters.)

In case you're wondering, Rose became the all-time hits leader among switch-hitters on July 25, 1977, passing Frankie Frisch with his 2,881st hit.

♦ Did you know Garry Templeton and Willie Wilson are the only two players in history to collect 100 hits from each side of the plate in one season? Amazingly, the feat was accomplished in consecutive seasons, with Templeton doing so in 1979 for the Cardinals, and Wilson for the Royals in 1980. Aware of the historical significance of the feat, Templeton batted almost exclusively as a right-handed batter (against right-handed pitchers) over the last week of the season to reach 100 hits from that side of the plate. Templeton had 111 hits batting from the left side.

♦ Did you know in 1998 the Yankees' Bernie Williams became the first player to win a batting title, a World Series, and the Gold Glove in the same year? Williams hit .339, played stellar center field, and was a very important member of the 125-win squad. The following year, Williams almost repeated the feat, winning another Gold Glove and World Series ring, but finishing third in the batting race. Note that there was no Gold Glove before 1958.

19. *Match these Yankee greats with their October successes:*

1	Mickey Mantle	A	played on a record 10 world champions and in a record 14 World Series
2	Joe DiMaggio		
3	Yogi Berra	B	was a part of 12 pennants and seven world championships
4	Phil Rizzuto		
5	Babe Ruth	C	appeared in 10 fall classics, seven with New York
6	Hank Bauer		
		D	won nine of the 10 fall classics he was in
		E	outfielder who took part in nine pennants and seven championships
		F	shortstop whose defensive exploits promoted the Yankees to nine pennants and seven series wins

ANSWER: 1—B, 2—D, 3—A, 4—F, 5—C, 6—E

Incredibly, DiMaggio won a world championship in each of his first four seasons, 1936–39, and five of his first six seasons. He was a winner of the first rank who demanded by example (not by mouth) the same of his teammates. He was his own worst critic, a perfectionist who was never satisfied. When once asked why he played all out every game, he responded, "Because there might be someone out there today who's never seen me play before." This remains the most inspiring statement I've ever read about The Game.

In 1950, Rizzuto did more than just play solid defense, batting .324 with 200 hits, 92 walks, and 125 runs scored to earn the AL MVP Award. Ruth appeared in the 1915, 1916, and 1918 World Series as a member of the Red Sox. Berra also holds World Series records for games (75) and hits (71), and shares the mark of 10 doubles with Frankie Frisch.

To most youngsters today, Berra is the amusing former major leaguer known for such comical phrases as "It's like déjà vu all over again" and "No one goes there anymore, it's too crowded." He's also known for his ever-so-true statement, "The game ain't over, til it's over." Even to fans, "Yogiisms" have become as much a part of Berra's mystique as his winning aura and tremendous ability to come through in the clutch or on a big stage. Almost to a man, colleagues who played in Berra's era agree that the Yankee Hall of Famer was the most dangerous batter when the game was on the line.

◆ Did you know Frankie Frisch played in a record eight World Series as a National Leaguer? Frisch, a great leader who also managed 16 seasons, appeared in four straight fall classics with the Giants from 1921 to 1924, and represented the Cardinals, the only other team he played for, in the World Series in 1928, 1930–31, and 1934. He was player-manager of that 1934 world championship team. Frisch also played on six second-place clubs.

20. *Only six teams have come back from a three-games-to-one deficit in the World Series and won. Fill in the blanks:*

	Year	Winning Club	Losing Club
	1903	Boston Pilgrims	Pittsburgh Pirates
A	1925	_____	Washington Senators
B	____	New York Yankees	Milwaukee Braves
C	1968	Detroit Tigers	_____
	1979	Pittsburgh Pirates	Baltimore Orioles
D	1985	_____	_____

ANSWER: A—Pittsburgh; B—1958; C—St. Louis; D—Kansas City, St. Louis

The Pilgrims (later renamed the Red Sox) won the inaugural 1903 World Series, winning the last four contests to take the series five games to three.

In 1968, the Cardinals appeared well on their way to a second straight world championship when the tide turned in Game Five. With a golden opportunity to add to a 3-2 lead, St. Louis watched as a base-running blunder by Lou Brock in the fifth inning aborted a rally and gave momentum to Detroit. On second base, as a result of his second double of the game and third hit of the contest, Brock dashed home on a single to left by Julian Javier. Racing against the throw from left fielder Willie Horton, the speedster appeared to have the run scored with ease. But Brock stunned witnesses by attempting to score standing up, instead of sliding, and was tagged out at the plate by surprised catcher Bill Freehan who told the media afterward that Brock would have scored with a slide. Detroit scored three times in the seventh inning—Al Kaline singled in two runs, and Norm Cash followed with an RBI safety of his own—and held Brock and St. Louis scoreless the rest of the game to stay alive. The rejuvenated Tigers then traveled to St. Louis and routed the Cardinals in Busch Stadium, 13-1 and 4-1, for a heart-breaking Series victory. Following the blunder, Brock singled twice in nine at-bats, didn't score, was picked off first base, and committed an error.

♦ Did you know the St. Louis Cardinals are the only team in history to lose more than one post-season series after taking a three-games-to-one lead? The Cards lost to the Detroit Tigers in the 1968 World Series, the Kansas City Royals in the 1985 fall classic, and the Atlanta Braves in the 1996 National League Championship Series.

♦ Did you know Pittsburgh's Jimmy Sebring hit the first World Series home run, during Game One of the 1903 fall classic? Patsy Dougherty had the first multi-homer game in series history, the very next day for the Boston Pilgrims.

21. *Can you name the man who played in more winning games than any other player in team sports history?*

ANSWER: Peter Edward Rose

Rose's teams won 1,972 of his record 3,562 regular-season games played, and came out victorious in 2,011 overall contests, including the almighty postseason. As Lyle Spatz of the Society for American Baseball Research has pointed out, Rose played the equivalent of 22 full seasons of 90 wins a year, winning 55% of his games. Baseball's all-time hits leader with 4,256, Rose also holds career records for at-bats (14,053) and singles (3,215). His total of 5,752 total bases remains a standard for switch-hitters. The three-time batting champion, 17-time All-Star, and 1973 MVP also ranks second in doubles (746) and fifth in runs scored (2,165). More importantly to Rose, he was a part of three world championship clubs: the 1975–76 Reds and the 1980 Phillies. He played in six World Series and eight National League Championship Series, batting a combined .321 with 86 hits and 28 walks in 67 post-season contests.

As his game totals attest, Rose was extremely durable, and played with aggressive abandon. The intense yet effervescent Rose played every game with a drive so obvious and an energy level so high that he inspired teammates and bewildered opponents. His relentless, no-quit style and his zest for The Game further endeared the fan-favored Rose to the public, which adopted him as an inspiration and role model. Not blessed with raw talent or height, the stocky Rose realized he had to work harder than any man on the field to make up for his shortcomings. He hustled so hard, in fact, that he made himself into one of the best players in major league history. Pitchers couldn't keep him off base. Batting from a crouch, Rose scattered line drives all over the field from each side of the plate, year after year after year. Ultimately, Rose reached the 200-hit plateau a record 10 times, as his longevity enabled him to collect at least 100 safeties for a record 23 consecutive seasons.

His playing career reached a memorable climax on September 11, 1985, at Riverfront Stadium. Rose singled off San Diego's Eric Show, surpassing Ty Cobb as the all-time hits leader with 4,192. Rose received a thunderous, five-minute standing ovation that turned the aggressive and cocky ballplayer into an emotional and humbled 44-year-old looking up at the sky and seeking his late father's approval. For his achievement, Rose received a bright red Corvette from team owner Marge Schott. Before the gambling allegations were made against him, Rose may have been the most idolized non-Yankee ever to play ball.

22. *These top-notch pitchers have combined for an unbelievable 2,036 wins. Match the five winningest pitchers with their win totals:*

1	Walter Johnson	A	511
2	Warren Spahn	B	373
3	Cy Young	C	417
4	Christy Mathewson	D	363
5	Grover Alexander		

ANSWER: 1—C, 2—D, 3—A, 4—B, 5—B

Spahn's 363 wins are the most ever by a lefthander. In 1963, Spahn surpassed Eddie Plank (327 wins) as the southpaw with the most wins. Spahn was seemingly ageless, hurling his first no-hitter at the age of 39 (in 1960) and his second gem at the age of 40 (in 1961).

♦ Did you know Alexander didn't want to retire until after his 373rd win? At the time, the retired Mathewson was credited with 372. Long after Alexander had retired, missing records were discovered and so was another Mathewson win—for a total of 373.

♦ Did you know that Walter Johnson's career win total was changed from 416 after the Society for American Baseball Research discovered an uncounted victory in 1912?

23.   *This season is regarded by many as the best campaign ever put together by a major league batter. His 59 home runs led the league, as did his 171 RBI, 177 runs scored, 144 walks, his record 457 total bases, and .846 slugging percentage. His .378 batting average was third, his 44 doubles ranked him second, and he legged out 16 triples to boot. Who was this Hall of Famer and what was the year?*

ANSWER: Babe Ruth, 1921

Ruth was voted the greatest player in history in an extensive 1969 poll of sportswriters. The season is even more awesome when compared with the numbers of just a few years earlier, during the Dead Ball Era. Catapulting Ruth's 1921 numbers into the stratosphere were their huge margins over those of the rest of the league. With players of today scaling to new heights, it's easy to forget that Ruth's 59 homers were 35 more than the runner-up. Ruth had 32 more RBI than the runner-up, he scored 45 more runs than the second-best run scorer, and he out-slugged his nearest competitor by a whopping 240 points.

The 1920s marked a new age of offense. With the end of the Dead Ball Era (in the wake of the "fixed" 1919 World Series) came tightly wound baseballs, frequent changes of baseballs (for better visibility), and the banning of the spitball. These reforms worked: attendance picked up, fans flocked to ballparks to admire long home runs (especially by the rotund Yankee slugger), and the game's image improved, healing the scar caused by the Black Sox scandal.

A teammate of Ruth's in Boston, Harry Hooper, described "The Sultan of Swat" better than anyone when talking to Lawrence Ritter, author of *The Glory of Their Times.* "Sometimes I still can't believe what I saw. This 19-year-old kid, crude, poorly educated, only lightly brushed by the social veneer we call civilization, gradually transformed into the idol of American youth and the symbol of baseball the world over—a man loved by more people and with an intensity of feeling that perhaps has never been equaled before or since."

If numbers could talk, Barry Bonds' 2001 season would make a very strong argument for the best campaign ever put together by a National League player. Bonds broke a host of major league records, including the single-season home run mark with 73, the single-season walk record with 177, and the single-season standard for slugging percentage (.863). And he almost matched Babe Ruth's 1.3791 OPS (on-base plus slugging percentage). Although Bonds accomplished these feats in an offensively inflated era, the Giants left-handed slugger put up extraordinary numbers despite pitchers' general reluctance to challenge him. Bonds' mind-boggling 2001 performance grows to mythical proportions when considering he broke Ruth's single-season walk mark despite batting in front of the league's reigning MVP. Pitchers simply wanted no piece of Bonds; they feared his maplewood bat, which struck a home run every 12 swings.

Although Bonds didn't dominate his league in 2001 the way Ruth did in 1921 (or in 1920 for that matter), Bonds still put up numbers that boggle the mind and will continue to do so, as many of us attempt to explain to a younger generation how he accomplished all this at the age of 37. Bonds made a "Barry" strong statement to those who thought he would begin to decline in 2001. With that short and choked-up swing, lightening-quick bat speed, and tremendous discipline at the plate, Bonds now appears to have a chance at Hank Aaron's career home run record: He's 188 home runs away. Let the countdown begin!

♦ Did you know Barry Bonds holds the major league record with 355 career intentional walks, a statistic kept since 1955? Bonds' intentional walk total is 62 more than the aggregate of Hank Aaron.

♦ Did you know Barry Bonds actually got off to a sluggish start in 2001, batting just .103 with a homer and one RBI seven games into the season? Then, after a conversation with his famous father, Barry erupted with a homer in each of his next six games en route to a .328 average and 73 homers.

24. *Who was the only player to play in all 44 New York Yankees–Brooklyn Dodgers World Series games?*

ANSWER: Harold "Pee Wee" Reese

Dodgers shortstop Reese's team lost six of the seven series between the two powerhouse foes. Among other things, the Dodgers captain will be remembered for smoothing Jackie Robinson's entry into major league baseball. During one particularly ugly instance of racial abuse at Crosley Field in 1947, Reese walked over and put his arm around the rookie's shoulder to demonstrate a show of unity between a white and a black player that spoke louder than words. That moment is cited as a turning point in Robinson's transition. Although the slurs and hateful treatment by fans, opponents, and teammates alike didn't abruptly cease like a flick of the lights, it at least provided a striking example of racial unity to those closed to the idea of integration in any aspect of life, in or out of baseball. It certainly widened a few eyes and began the process of changing a few hearts. Robinson was able to build on Reese's gesture and promote racial harmony and civil rights, in baseball and in America. Because of his achievements in this area, many historians agree that Robinson is the most significant athlete in American history.

♦ Did you know "Pee Wee" Reese gained his moniker from his prowess at marbles as a youngster, and not because of his size? Born Harold Henry Reese, "Pee Wee" once finished second in the *Courier-Journal* marble national championship tournament.

25. *This pitcher won 15 games and became the youngest player to hurl a World Series shutout at the age of 20. Who was this three-time Cy Young Award winner?*

ANSWER: Jim Palmer

Palmer was the only pitcher to win a World Series game in three decades. Palmer hurled a four-hit shutout in Game Two of the 1966 World Series, outdueling Sandy Koufax. Palmer also won a World Series game in each of the years 1970, 1971, and 1983. Palmer retired with an 8-3 post-season record. Palmer's Hall of Fame career nearly failed to materialize after a severe sore arm shelved him for most of the 1967 campaign and all of 1968. In fact, he was left unprotected for the expansion draft, and the Kansas City Royals, Seattle Pilots, Montreal Expos, and San Diego Padres would not take a chance on him. Palmer returned in 1969, showing his old form before again visiting the disabled list—this time for just over a month. Four days after coming back, Palmer threw a no-hitter as part of a 16-4 season with a 2.34 ERA. He recorded the first of eight 20-win campaigns the following year en route to a Hall of Fame career.

26. *Some individuals must overcome great obstacles not encountered by their teammates on their way to becoming outstanding players. Match these players with their challenges:*

1 Mordecai Brown		A	only three and a half fingers
2 Pete Gray		B	one arm missing
3 Jim Abbott		C	illiterate
4 Joe Jackson		D	only one digit on his left foot
5 Red Ruffing		E	one hand missing
6 Hugh "One Arm" Daily			

ANSWER: 1—A, 2—B, 3—E, 4—C, 5—D, 6—E

"Three Finger" Brown used his handicap to his advantage. After losing his right index finger in a childhood accident involving his uncle's corn shredder, his third and fourth fingers healed in a rather distorted fashion following an encounter with a hog. Having to use an uncommon grip, Brown developed what some said was the best curveball in the game. Nicknamed "Miner" by his teammates, for his coal mining experience, Brown won 239 games against just 130 losses.

Gray, who lost his right arm as a child in a wagon accident, became a source of inspiration for many—handicapped or not—as he reached the major leagues in 1945 as a member of the St. Louis Browns. Although he hit just .218 over 234 at-bats in his lone season, Gray went on to play in the minors through 1949. Naturally right-handed, Gray taught himself how to bat and throw with his left hand. After catching the ball, Gray would stick his glove under the stump of his right arm before drawing the ball clear with his left hand

and throwing. Gray was never quite convinced he was promoted to the majors on his own merit, although many assured him he was not a publicity stunt. But some teammates insisted that Gray's throwing, slow for obvious reasons, cost the Browns the 1945 pennant.

An uneducated farm boy from South Carolina, Jackson was mercilessly mocked, especially by the Athletics—his first team, a squad that included college-educated players such as Eddie Collins, Eddie Plank, Jack Barry, and Jack Coombs. The ridicule got so bad that Jackson contemplated retiring after the 1909 season. But Athletics manager Connie Mack traded him to the Indians, for whom he showed off his great baseball abilities, playing dazzling defense and batting .408, .395, and .373 in his first three full seasons. In August of 1915, Jackson was traded by the financially strapped Indians to the Chicago White Sox for three players and more than $30,000. Although Jackson struggled a bit for his new team over the last month and a half of the 1915 season, "Shoeless" Joe gathered himself to put up five straight .300 campaigns in Chicago, including four seasons above .340.

Ruffing lost four toes in a childhood mine accident, weakening his delivery and landing. Ruffing pursued a successful career despite his handicap.

Daily's moniker was a misnomer, for he had a left arm; what he lacked was a left hand. A pitcher for parts of six seasons, Daily went 73-87, showing flashes of brilliance. The righthander threw a no-hitter in 1883 and became the first ever to throw consecutive one-hitters the following season. As a hitter, Daily batted .157 over 562 at-bats.

♦ Did you know Hall of Famer Jim "Catfish" Hunter and nine-time All-Star Ron Santo were diabetics?

♦ Did you know Napoleon Lajoie was a teamster? Lajoie worked in a Rhode Island mill at age 10, before earning pay as a teamster and hack driver in his pre-major league days, according to J. M. Murphy of the Society for American Baseball Research. Murphy also listed Buck Ewing as a teamster, Hugh Duffy as a dye-shop worker, Ed Walsh as a coal miner, and Jack Chesbro as a worker in a mental hospital. More recently, Sammy Sosa was once a shoe-shine boy.

27. *This Jewish first baseman hit 331 homers with 1,276 RBI, despite missing a combined four and one-half years due to World War II. Who was this Hall of Famer?*

ANSWER: Hank Greenberg

Greenberg actually volunteered before the draft and was the second player drafted into the military on May 7, 1941 (Hugh Mulcahey was the first). Many thought that, aside from Jackie Robinson, Greenberg took more abuse than any other player in the game's history. Being Jewish was not much easier than being African American, and Greenberg took all sorts of verbal abuse. And like Robinson, Greenberg had to take the abuse without retaliation or he would have found himself involved in a fight every game (and been thrown out). Greenberg was often pitched around, even in routs or lopsided games, to reduce his chances of breaking any records or increasing his offensive numbers. In one of many examples, he entered the final five games of the 1938 season with 58 homers—two away from Ruth's then-record of 60. But pitchers refused to give Greenberg anything good to hit, pitching around him almost every chance they got. Alas, the strategy worked, and Greenberg had to settle for 58 home runs. When in 2001 Barry Bonds was pitched around in Houston during the final week of the season, many cried "travesty." But both the Astros and the Giants were fighting for separate division titles. In 1938, the pennant was long secured: Greenberg's treatment was a real travesty.

28. *Bobby Thomson's "Shot heard 'round the world" off the Dodgers Ralph Branca in the final game of the 1951 NL play-off gave the Giants the NL pennant and baseball followers the most dramatic moment in major league history. Let's see if you can match these pitchers with the memorable home runs they allowed:*

1	Pat Darcy	A	Babe Ruth's 60th homer in 1927
2	Mark Littell	B	Bill Mazeroski's 1960 Series-winning homer
3	Tom Zachary	C	Carlton Fisk's dramatic homer in 1975 Series
4	Ralph Terry	D	Chris Chambliss walk-off homer in 1976 AL Championship Series off the Royals

ANSWER: 1—C, 2—D, 3—A, 4—B

Thomson's three-run shot came with one out in the bottom of the ninth at the Polo Grounds, giving the Giants a 5-4 win. Ruth's total of 60 home runs in 1927 represents 13.7% of the 439 home runs hit in the American League that year. In today's game, a player would have to hit over 350 home runs to match that percentage. Mazeroski's walk-off homer in the ninth at Forbes Field gave the Pirates the 1960 World Series title. Fisk's home run over Fenway Park's Green Monster led off the bottom of the 12th, forcing a seventh game against the Reds in 1975. The image of Fisk waving the ball fair as he hopped toward first base is one of baseball history's most famous images.

Chambliss' home run over the right-center field wall led off the bottom of the ninth and turned Yankee Stadium into a madhouse, as he had to avoid hundreds of fans who stormed the field in his route toward home plate. The home runs hit by Mazeroski, Fisk, and Chambliss overshadowed other important home runs that either set up or preceded their own.

Those virtually unheralded home runs include Hal Smith's huge three-run homer that set up Mazeroski's Series-winning blast, Bernie Carbo's three-run blast that set up Fisk's dramatics, and George Brett's homer that preceded Chris Chambliss' heroics. Sent in to catch for Smokey Burgess in the top of the eighth, Smith, the reserve catcher, hit one over the left-field wall for a 9-7 Pirate lead. The Yankees tied the game at 9-9 in the top of the ninth before Mazeroski led off the bottom of the ninth. Carbo's second pinch-hit home run of the series came with two on base off Reds' reliever Rawly Eastwick in the bottom of the eighth, producing a 6-6 tie. In the 12th, Fisk earned his moment in the sun with a dramatic home run that forced Game Seven. Brett of Kansas City hit a three-run home run in the eighth to tie Game Five of the 1976 AL Championship Series at 6-6. What followed was Chambliss' series-winning homer at wild Yankee Stadium.

◆ Did you know Chris Chambliss' dramatic homer to end the 1976 AL Championship Series was one of a record nine walk-off post-season homers for the Yankees? Bernie Williams was responsible for two of them, one to finish off the Orioles in Game One of the 1996 AL Championship Series and one to finish off the Red Sox in the opener of the 1999 AL Championship

Series. Williams remains the only player with more than one post-season walk-off homer. Jim Leyritz ended a dramatic 15-inning duel with a home run to beat the Mariners in Game Two of the 1995 AL Division Series. The Yankees have had four of those nine post-season, walk-off homers in World Series action. The last came off the bat of Derek Jeter in Game Four of the 2001 World Series. Before that, Chad Curtis belted a launch that handed the Braves a defeat in Game Three of the 1999 World Series, Mickey Mantle broke the Cardinals' heart in Game Three of the 1964 World Series, and Tommy Henrich dealt the Dodgers a blow in the opener of the 1949 World Series.

♦ Did you know Todd Pratt's game-winning home run in the bottom of the 10th inning of Game Four of the 1999 NL Division Series was the fourth post-season series-clinching "walk-off" homer in history? Pratt's homer eliminated Arizona from the NL Division Series. The other three were: Mazeroski's 1960 World Series-winning homer, Chris Chambliss' 1976 AL Championship Series-winning shot, and Joe Carter's 1993 World Series-winning blast.

29. *Ty Cobb garnered the most votes in the Hall of Fame's inaugural election class of 1936, which included five legends. Can you name the other four players forever immortalized that year?*

ANSWER: Babe Ruth, Honus Wagner, Christy Mathewson, and Walter Johnson

Ty Cobb received 222 votes out of 226; Babe Ruth, 215; Honus Wagner, 215; the deceased Christy Mathewson, 205; and the great Walter Johnson, 189. Falling short of the requisite 75% of the total vote (170 votes in this case) to gain election were Nap Lajoie (146), Tris Speaker (133), Cy Young (111), Rogers Hornsby (105), and Mickey Cochrane (80). Lajoie, Speaker, and Young got in the following year, along with executives/managers Morgan Bulkeley, Ban Johnson, Connie Mack, John McGraw, and George Wright. Hornsby and Cochrane were enshrined later. The voting was a reflection of the general attitude of the time. But with the public's growing fascination with the home run, Ruth gained public and professional appeal as the better player, or at least a better slugger than Cobb. More than a few observers have noted how impressive Cobb's vote total was—especially compared with Ruth's—considering that Cobb was so despised. But Cobb appears to have been less surly to the press, particularly those writers he knew well and trusted, than he was to almost anyone else. Scores of contemporary features about Cobb and the definitive book *Cobb* (by Al Stump) portray Cobb as hostile, bigoted, vindictive, and full of anger. Only a very few people—such teammates as Matty McIntyre, who heckled, hazed, and abused Cobb as a rookie—might have expected such harsh responses from Cobb. But Cobb, it seemed, offended so many people that only three major leaguers—Mickey Cochrane, Nap Rucker, and Ray Schalk—attended his funeral.

Cobb, an intelligent man, realized he could use the media to his advantage, and did so repeatedly. Cobb often permitted trusted sportswriters access to his phone number and hotel room, even allowing them to call him early in the morning if needed. In between major league offseasons, Cobb used the media to gain better publicity and to obtain bargaining leverage with tight-fisted owners.

At age 17, Cobb manipulated one of the best and most famous sportswriters of all time, Grantland Rice, to get his first break in baseball. Despite having a lowly batting average of .237 in the South Atlantic League in 1904, Cobb had a believer. A "news-tipster" by the name of "James Jackson" frequently sent Rice reports detailing the youngster's talent, according to biographer Al Stump. The letters usually embellished Cobb's ability in the batter's box, in the field, on the base paths, and in the seats with regard to the attention he was receiving. Despite never having seen Cobb play, Rice once wrote, "This Cobb has great talent and may be one of the coming stars of baseball. Cobb hits well and has speed on the bases." And so the ploy worked: Cobb himself was "James Jackson, news-tipster." What desire and what confidence! Cobb improved, and, of course, the rest is history.

◆ Did you know that Ty Cobb's father was shot and killed by Cobb's mother? The August 1905 shooting was supposedly an accident. The mother thought that Cobb's father was an intruder because he had been on a trip and wasn't supposed to come home that day.

Years later, Cobb told biographer Al Stump, "My father had his head blown off with a shotgun when I was 18 years old—by a member of my own family. I didn't get over that. I've never gotten over that."

◆ Did you know Ty Cobb in 1906 was so affected by the harsh hazing and abuse he endured from his teammates that he spent 44 days in a sanatorium? Tigers owner Frank Navin told the press that Cobb was experiencing stomach trouble. This abuse may have helped to trigger his offensive behavior in later years.

30. *Match these promising stars with the accidents that greatly affected their careers:*

1 Pete Reiser	A	was run over by Pete Rose in the 12th inning of the 1970 All-Star game
2 Herb Score		
3 Dizzy Dean	B	was hit by Earl Averill Sr.'s line drive during an All-Star game
4 Ray Fosse		
	C	twice ran into a brick center-field wall
	D	was struck in the right eye by a Gil McDougald line drive

ANSWER: 1—C, 2—D (1957), 3—B (1937), 4—A (1970)

In their book *The 100 Greatest Baseball Players of All Time*, authors Lawrence Ritter and Donald Honig wrote, "Of all the careers aborted by injuries, Pete Reiser's may have well been the greatest." In 1941, the 22-year-old Reiser led the NL with a .343 mark, 39 doubles, 17 triples, 117 runs, and a .558 slugging percentage. Alas, it was Reiser's only injury-free season.

The 1957 line drive came on the heels of Score's first two seasons in 1955–56, during which the hard-throwing lefthander won a combined 36 games for the Indians, led the AL in strikeouts each year, and earned the 1955 AL Rookie of the Year Award. Score was never the same again. McDougald felt so badly about the accident that he had to be talked out of retirement.

Dean was headed toward a fifth straight 20-win season when Averill's drive broke his left small toe, forcing Dean to pitch differently. In doing so, Dean injured his arm and was never the same. The left-handed Averill went on to the Hall of Fame. Averill used League Park's short right-field dimensions to his advantage, compiling five 100-RBI seasons and a trio of 30-homer campaigns. A six-time All-Star, Averill also played good defense in center field and would have added to his power numbers but for a congenital spinal problem that left him temporarily paralyzed, stripping him of his powerful swing. Over a 13-year career, Averill accrued 2,019 hits, batted .318, with an on-base percentage of .395 and a slugging average of .534.

Fosse, ironically a dinner guest of Rose the night before his accident, learned the hard way that the stocky Reds catalyst only knows one way to play—no holds barred. Fosse, a promising two-time Gold Glover for the Indians with some pop in his bat, fractured his shoulder in the incident and was never quite the same. Some observers still argue Rose didn't have to collide with Fosse—a slide would have done the job. But in his book *Pete Rose: My Way* (with Roger Kahn), Rose said, "People forget that Fosse played the next game for his club. I couldn't play the next one for mine." At the time of the accident, Rose was excited because the play involved the winning run in the All-Star Game in his hometown. In the book, he added this strong statement: "Besides, nobody told me they changed [the rules] to girls' softball between third and home."

Rose, in fact, earned the nickname "Charlie Hustle" as part of a sneer for his absolute fervor. After drawing a walk against the Yankees in a 1963 exhibition game, the rookie Rose ran to first base. The Yankees' Whitey Ford then smirked and said, "Look at Charlie Hustle." The comment drew laughter from the Yankees' dugout, but Rose had the last laugh en route to a tremendous and eventful playing career. When asked if Rose, his All-Star teammate, hustles, Hank Aaron answered, "Does Pete hustle? Before the All-Star Game, he came into the clubhouse, took off his shoes, and they [his shoes] ran another mile without him."

♦ Did you know Pete Rose got the idea of running out his walks from watching Enos Slaughter of the St. Louis Cardinals? In his book *Pete Rose: My Way* (with Roger Kahn), Rose said, "I always ran to first. Never walk when you can run. . . . I know where I got the idea. Enos Slaughter of the St. Louis Cardinals used to run out his walks. I liked the way he played. Not the biggest man on the field, but hustling, driving himself every play."

31. *This player not only had as many hits on the road as he did in his home ball park, but he also had the distinction of hitting the most home runs without a home run title. Who is this man?*

ANSWER: Stan Musial

Stan "The Man" Musial hit 475 home runs. Musial was so consistent, he batted at least .300 for 16 straight seasons and evenly divided his 3,630 hits—1,815 at home and 1,815 on the road. Musial batted with an unorthodox corkscrew stance, winding himself up as he turned away with his back almost facing the mound. Writer Roger Kahn has described Musial's stance: "Curled, poised, waiting, Musial [was] suddenly a cobra coiled for a deadly strike." Musial, one of the most admired and endearing figures ever to don a major league uniform, collected more MVP votes than any other player. Of the noble Musial, Commissioner Ford Frick said, "Here stands baseball's perfect warrior. Here stands baseball's perfect knight." Those words were inscribed on Musial's bronze statue, which has stood in front of Busch Stadium since 1968.

♦ Did you know Stan Musial is the only player to be among the top 20 in career singles, doubles, triples, and homers? Musial recorded 177 triples, 725 doubles, and 2,253 singles to go with his 475 home runs.

♦ Did you know Stan Musial asked for and received a substantial pay cut in January of 1960? Claiming he was overpaid following the first sub-.310 season of his career, the 18-year veteran demanded and received a drop in salary from $100,000 to $80,000. In 1958, the honorable Musial became the first NL player to earn a $100,000 salary.

32. *Before Barry Bonds won the NL MVP in 1992 and 1993, and Frank Thomas won the AL MVP in 1993 and 1994, nine players had won back-to-back MVP Awards in consecutive seasons, coincidentally enough to field a team. Each position was represented, although not all three outfielders were spread. Fill in the MVP winners with their alignments:*

First base _____
Second base _____

Shortstop _____
Third base _____
Outfield _____ , _____ , _____
Pitcher _____
Catcher _____

ANSWER:

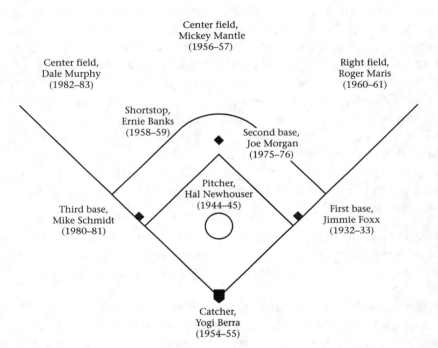

Center field,
Mickey Mantle
(1956–57)

Center field,
Dale Murphy
(1982–83)

Right field,
Roger Maris
(1960–61)

Shortstop,
Ernie Banks
(1958–59)

Second base,
Joe Morgan
(1975–76)

Pitcher,
Hal Newhouser
(1944–45)

Third base,
Mike Schmidt
(1980–81)

First base,
Jimmie Foxx
(1932–33)

Catcher,
Yogi Berra
(1954–55)

Dale Murphy was such a perfectionist that he thought he needed some extra work at the Arizona Fall League following his 1982 NL MVP season. Rather than rest on his laurels, Murphy honed his craft. His reward was the 1983 NL MVP as well. His conduct is a lesson in avoiding complacency for those willing to learn from it.

Morgan was the best player in the major leagues during the mid-1970s, displaying a great blend of power, speed, and patience. Morgan boasted an on-base percentage of at least .406 each year from 1972 to 1977, and scored at least 107 runs each season during that stretch.

The left-handed Newhouser went a combined 54-18, with a 2.01 ERA over his two years as MVP.

33. *Match these players with their achievements:*

1	Joe Morgan	A	won a major league record five straight ERA titles
2	Sandy Koufax		
3	Tony Gwynn	B	had 23 consecutive .300 seasons
4	Grover Alexander	C	became the first player to compile 25 homers and 60 stolen bases in the same year
5	Ty Cobb		
6	Amos Rusie		
		D	owns the NL record for consecutive .300 seasons
		E	won 245 games during a nine-year stretch before 1900
		F	recorded a famous save in the seventh game of the 1926 World Series against the Yankees

ANSWER: 1—C, 2—A, 3—D, 4—F, 5—B, 6—E

Morgan also became the first player in history to compile 500 career stolen bases and 200 career home runs. Koufax's five ERA titles were captured in his last five years. Cobb's 23 consecutive seasons of batting .300 are followed by the 19 of Gwynn, 17 by Honus Wagner, Stan Musial's 16, and the 15 such campaigns by both Ted Williams and Rod Carew. The personable and charismatic bat magician Gwynn retired with the conclusion of the 2001 season.

With his Cardinals clinging to a precarious 3-2 lead in the bottom of the seventh inning of the deciding game of the 1926 World Series, Alexander came through, as usual, with flying colors. "Pete," who pitched his team to complete-game victories in Games Two and Six, struck out the Yankees' Tony Lazzeri with the bases loaded. He also pitched hitless balls in the eighth and ninth innings—only Babe Ruth reached, via a walk—to register the save and secure a world title for the Cardinals. In all, Alexander went 2-0, with that one save and a 1.33 ERA in 20⅓ innings during the series. Pretty good for a guy who was waived (by the Chicago Cubs) earlier in the season.

Author Jack Kavanagh, who wrote *Ol' Pete,* debunks the myth that Alexander, an admitted alcoholic, was drunk or hung over during his most heroic moment. Alexander and his wife always blamed manager Rogers Hornsby for never dispelling the myth, even though Hornsby took measures to ensure that Alexander stay in his hotel room instead of heading to the saloon before the game. Hornsby simply thought the fable made for a good story, and so never bothered to correct it. Alexander's deceptive motion and incredible control of a curve and a sinking fastball helped him record three consecutive seasons of 30 wins from 1915 to 1917 en route to a .642 lifetime winning percentage, a career 2.56 ERA, and a NL record 90 shutouts.

◆ Did you know that Grover Cleveland Alexander and Tony Lazzeri were epileptics? Alexander, however, was not an epileptic until after serving in World War I, according to Jack Kavanagh's *Ol' Pete.* Named after the country's 22nd president by a zealous Democrat farming father in Nebraska, Alexander also suffered permanent deafness in one ear and claimed to have lost some zip after returning from the war. *Ol' Pete* reveals that Judge Kenesaw Mountain Landis and National League President Ford Frick worried about Alexander's alcohol dependency following retirement and secured funds for Alexander to keep him from being destitute and save the National League from embarrassment. Alexander, while in the minor leagues, spent 36 hours in a near-death coma after getting hit between the eyes as he ran toward second base on a double-play ball.

◆ Did you know Kid Nichols holds the record for most wins in a decade, with 297 from 1890 to 1899? Nichols retired with a 361-208 ledger to go with a 2.94 ERA and 532 complete games.

◆ Did you know Ty Cobb's lowest batting average outside his first season was .320?

34. *The 1977 Los Angeles Dodgers were the first team in history with four players hitting at least 30 home runs. Can you name each member of the Dodgers' powerful quartet?*

ANSWER: Steve Garvey (33), Reggie Smith (32), Ron Cey (30), and Dusty Baker (30)

Baker reached his 30 home runs in his very last at-bat of the season. In 1995, the Rockies became the second such team as Dante Bichette hit a league-leading 40 home runs, Larry Walker slugged 36, Vinny Castilla finished with 32 roundtrippers, and Andres Galarraga smacked 31. With newcomer Ellis Burks, the Rockies duplicated the feat in 1996 and 1997, and, with newcomer Todd Helton, in 1999. In

Coors Field, the Rockies play in perhaps the most offensively advantageous park in history. The 1997 Dodgers and 1998 Braves also achieved the milestone.

The 2000 Angels became the first AL team to accomplish the feat, as Troy Glaus hit 47 home runs, Mo Vaughn hit 36, Garret Anderson 35, and Tim Salmon 34. Right behind the Angels were the Blue Jays, whose quartet of Carlos Delgado (41), Tony Batista (41), Brad Fullmer (32), and Jose Cruz Jr. (31) made Toronto the second such AL team.

◆ Did you know the 1956 Reds were one home run shy of becoming the first team with four players to hit at least 30 home runs, and three home runs shy of becoming the first team to boast five players with at least 30 home runs? Left fielder Frank Robinson hit a team-high 38, right fielder Wally Post hit 36, first baseman Ted Kluszewski hit 35, while center fielder Gus Bell hit 29 and catcher Ed Bailey connected a career-high 28 times.

◆ Did you know Vinny Castilla is the only player in history to duplicate his Triple Crown numbers in consecutive years? Castilla of the Colorado Rockies hit 40 home runs with 113 RBI and a .304 batting average in both the 1996 and 1997 seasons.

35. *In 2001, Karl "Tuffy" Rhodes tied Sadaharu Oh's single-season, Japanese League home run record. Can you name the American player who in 1985 fell one homer short of Oh's mark?*

ANSWER: Randy Bass

Bass hit 54 home runs for the Hanshin Tigers, 21 years after Oh clubbed 55 for the Yomiuri Giants. Oh is criticized for unsportsmanlike conduct to keep the American from tying the record. Oh, acting as the opposing manager of the rival Giants, had his pitcher walk Bass in each of the four plate appearances during the season finale. (Bass held his bat upside down in disapproval during one of those walks.) Near the end of the season 16 years later, Oh again managed against the man vying for his record—this time at the helm of the Daiei Hawks—and once again had his pitcher issue a base on balls four times. The Japanese League Commissioner Hiromori Kawashima called the obviously intentional walks "completely divorced from the essence of baseball, which values the supremacy of fair play."

Rhodes, a Kintetsu Buffaloes outfielder, had a chance to beat Oh's record as he entered the 2001 finale with 55 homers, but he flied out three times and grounded out once against the Orix BlueWave.

According to *Nikkan Sports*, Oh's 55 homers in 1964 made up 7.6% of all the homers that year, whereas Rhodes' 55 made up 5.4%. Oh homered every 8.6 at-bats, whereas Rhodes went deep every 9.9 official trips to the plate. Rhodes hit 32 homers on the road (away from the Osaka Dome), whereas Oh managed just 23 away from the cozy confines of Korakuen Stadium, which measured just 90 meters down the line. Rhodes, Oh, and Bass all batted left-handed. Bass hit nine major league home runs, and Rhodes finished with 13.

Don't feel too bad for Bass. In that 1985 season, he still managed to win the Triple Crown (with .350 and 134 RBI as well) before capping off his tremendous season by leading the Tigers to the Japanese championship over the Nishitetsu Lions. Bass went on to win his second straight Triple Crown in 1986, tying Oh in that category. After an embittered contract dispute, Bass ended a six-year Japanese career with 202 home runs and a .337 career batting average. Bass became a huge media success in Japan, beloved by all.

♦ Did you know in 1999 Sadaharu Oh earned his first Japan Series title as a manager by leading the Fukuoka Daiei Hawks to their first championship since 1964?

36. *This 300-game winner shares the modern record with Christy Mathewson for 13 seasons of at least 20 wins. He also joined Cy Young as the only pitchers to hurl no-hitters after their 40th birthday, before Nolan Ryan achieved the feat as well. Can you name him?*

ANSWER: Warren Spahn

Spahn led his league in wins a record eight times and led his league in complete games on nine occasions for yet another impressive career record. In addition, Spahn led his league in shutouts four times, and compiled the lowest ERA thrice. And even though he wasn't regarded as a strikeout pitcher, Spahn led the NL in whiffs each season from 1949 to 1952. Of Mathewson's 13 seasons of 20 or more wins, 12 were consecutive. Cy Young holds the all-time record for consecutive-season wins, with 14 straight 20-win campaigns.

◆ Did you know Warren Spahn went 23-7 with a 2.60 ERA, 22 complete games, and seven shutouts at the age of 42?

37. *If you don't think Hall of Famers Ed Walsh (195-126) and Addie Joss (160-87) had a rivalry going, think again. Walsh, a White Sox great, produced baseball's lowest career ERA of 1.82 and the Cleveland Indian rival Joss provided the second lowest mark of 1.89. Do you know what happened on the next-to-last day of the season (October 2) in 1908 when these two pitchers and their pennant-hungry clubs clashed?*

ANSWER: Although by day's end Detroit emerged as the American League champions, Joss and Cleveland denied Walsh a record-tying 41st win (Yankee Jack Chesbro's 41 victories in 1904 is the modern record) by winning, 1-0. Joss retired all 27 batters for baseball history's fourth perfect game. Walsh surrendered only four hits and struck out 15. Two years later, Joss again threw a no-hitter at Chicago, becoming and remaining the only pitcher in history to no-hit the same team more than once.

◆ Did you know Addie Joss broke in the major leagues with a controversial one-hit debut? On April 26, 1902, Joss one-hit the Browns, 3-0. Jesse Burkett's disputed sixth-inning single was all the Browns could muster; even then, many argued the ball was caught by right fielder Erwin Harvey.

◆ Did you know Ed Walsh popularized the spitball? Russ Ford invented the emery ball (so named because the pitcher used an emery board to scuff the ball), Dave Danforth invented the shine ball, and Tim Keefe is credited as the first to use the changeup. A commonly held misconception about the action of spitballs is that the saliva alters the ball's course once the ball is released; in fact, the saliva allows the pitcher's fingers to slip, causing a sharper break than a dry ball can achieve.

38. *This slugger was often called the greatest batsmen of any era, winning a pair of MVP Awards and missing out on many more because of his bad relationship with the press and fans. Can you give the full name of this splendid thumper (first name Theodore), who was given five Major League Player of the Year Awards by* The Sporting News?

ANSWER: Theodore (Ted) Samuel Williams

Williams won MVP Awards in 1946 and 1949, but (you may not believe this) failed to win the award in his Triple Crown years of 1942 and 1947. In 1942, Williams lost out to Joe Gordon (who scored 53 fewer runs, hit 34 points lower than Williams in 16 more at-bats, and slugged .491 to Williams' league-leading .648). The only categories Gordon led the league in were strikeouts, double plays grounded into, and errors by a second baseman. In 1947, Williams was again robbed of an MVP Award. Joe DiMaggio won the award that year, despite scoring 28 fewer runs, hitting 28 points lower, with 12 fewer homers, 17 fewer RBI, 98 fewer walks, and a slugging of .522 to Williams' .634 mark—all in six more at-bats. DiMaggio received 202 votes and Williams got 201. One writer didn't even give Williams a 10th-place vote, which is worth one point—an obvious case of injustice and lack of fairness on the part of the scribe.

And then in 1941—Ted's .406 season—fans and sportswriters were blind to almost everything other than DiMaggio's 56-game hitting streak. Again the numbers do not compare, although the judgment this year was understandable, given the magnitude of DiMaggio's feat. But it should be pointed out that Williams even out-hit DiMaggio, .412-.408, during The Streak. Overall, Williams out-batted DiMaggio by 49 percentage points, posted a much higher slugging percentage, a much higher on-base percentage (his .551 figure remains the best ever), scored 13 more runs, hit seven more homers, and drew 69 more walks than DiMaggio. DiMaggio had eight more hits and five more RBI. You decide who was better.

Although in 1957, the case at least debatable, Williams was beaten out by Mickey Mantle for the MVP despite pacing the AL in batting, on-base, and slugging as a 39-year-old, and out-homering "The Mick" to boot in 12 fewer games. Of course, another Yankee pennant helped Mantle win the hardware. Granted, Williams was surly and cold to the media, but that shouldn't have decided the league's MVP. The talented and dedicated Williams proved to be the best batsmen year-in and year-out, and achieved his lifelong dream of being called "the best hitter who ever lived" by his peers and followers.

39. _____ *was on deck when Bobby Thomson hit the "shot heard 'round the world" off Brooklyn to give the Giants the pennant in*

1951. Don Newcombe (Dodgers) and Sal Maglie (Giants) were the starters of the third playoff game. Fill in the blank.

ANSWER: Willie Mays

Mays, the NL's Rookie of the Year that season, stood in the on-deck circle as Thomson took Ralph Branca deep over the short left-field wall for the dramatic, 5-4 win. Giants' 23-game winner Larry Jansen won the game in relief. Although Mays, who later admitted to being tense as he watched in the on-deck circle, didn't get a chance to make something happen, he would do so time and time again in the following years. After returning from a nearly two-year military stint, Mays in 1954 tore up the NL on his way to an MVP season as well as another World Series appearance.

Using all five of his tools, Mays led the senior circuit in batting (.345) and slugging (.667) with 41 home runs, 110 RBI, and 119 runs scored. Mays also displayed great speed and range, catching nearly everything hit his way in center field (448 putouts), and he showed off a strong arm, doubling off nine men. In the 1954 World Series, Mays led his underdog Giants to a surprising sweep of the juggernaut Cleveland Indians ballclub. Mays' over-the-shoulder catch in Game One of that Series displayed an abundant athleticism that left no doubt of his greatness. His performance deflated the Indians and spurred the Giants.

In 1955, Mays led the major leagues with 51 home runs, 13 triples, and 382 total bases, and threw out an astounding 23 base-runners from his center field position, becoming the majors' best all-around player. The flashy and spirited Mays won his first of four straight stolen base crowns, with a total of 40 thefts in 1956. In 1957, Mays achieved a feat no one else in the history of the game has been able to pull off. He compiled 20 or more doubles (26), triples (20), home runs (35), and stolen bases (38) in the same season. Think about that for a second! In addition to his numerous feats and spectacular plays in the following years, that 1957 achievement helped Mays establish his claim as the most well-rounded player of all time. Long after a Hall of Fame career that produced 660 home runs, 1,903 RBI, 2,062 runs scored, 3,283 hits, 338 stolen bases, and 12 Gold Gloves, Mays' legacy remains unequaled in terms of all-around abilities and the fulfillment of potential in each of his five tools. Over the course of the game's illustrious history, only a few players have hit for more power. And only a few had a higher batting average, or were faster, or may have had a stronger arm. And only God—and perhaps Tris Speaker—patrolled center field as well as Mays. But no being ever presented a baseball package as complete as the one Mays displayed for 22 years.

♦ Did you know the Dodgers' Hall of Fame catcher Roy Campanella wasn't available in that final game of the 1951 National League play-off due to a tight hamstring that also caused him to miss the previous contest? Reserve receiver Rube Walker called Ralph Branca's forgettable pitch to Bobby Thomson, which barely cleared the left-field wall, 315 feet away. Dodgers left fielder Andy Pafko hugged the wall, waiting for the ball to drop, as the drive landed over the 16-foot-high wall with but a foot to spare.

40. *Match these clubs with their nicknames or slogans:*

1	1950 Phillies	A	"The Gas House Gang"
2	1927 Yankees	B	"The Lumber Company"
3	1934 Cardinals	C	"The Whiz Kids"
4	1979 Pirates	D	"You gotta believe"
5	1973 Mets	E	"Murderers Row"

ANSWER: 1—C, 2—E, 3—A, 4—B, 5—D

Although the 1927 Yankees are noted for their intimidating lineup, their pitching wasn't bad either. In fact, their pitching staff was also the best in the major leagues. With a 3.20 ERA, the Yankees pitching was head and shoulders above the White Sox, whose 3.91 ERA was the AL's second best. The staff was led by righthander Waite Hoyt, whose 22 wins led the league; his 2.63 ERA was the second-best figure, and his .759 winning percentage was third. Righthander Urban Shocker won 18 of 24 decisions, with a 2.84 ERA (third). Southpaw Herb Pennock went 19-8 with a 3.00 ERA. The team's fourth and fifth starters, Dutch Ruether and George Pipgras, were effective as well, combining for a 23-9 ledger. Spot starter and closer Wilcy Moore was a great story, going 19-7 with 13 saves and a league-best 2.28 ERA.

Hoyt was clearly the ace of the 1927 Yankees staff as well as the consolidating arm the Yankees relied on as they won six AL pennants from 1921 to 1928. After a pair of mediocre seasons in a Red Sox uniform, Hoyt was traded to New York following the 1920 campaign. From 1921 to May 30, 1930, Hoyt posted a 157-98 record for the Yankees. He followed his stellar 1927 campaign with a performance that featured a 23-7 mark and a league-leading eight saves in 1928. After a trade to Detroit in 1930 and a trade in 1931 to the Philadelphia Athletics, for whom he won 10 of 15 decisions and helped to the World Series, Hoyt spent the last seven years of his career in the NL. Hoyt retired in 1938, with a 237-182 record, 52 saves, and three world championships en route to the Hall of Fame.

41. *Can you name the Hall of Fame outfielder who signaled his infield hit to be turned into an error, preferring that his 3,000th hit be a clean one rather than a "cheap infield" safety?*

ANSWER: Paul Waner

Waner finished his career in 1945 (three years after reaching the milestone) and ended up with 3,152 hits, 1,626 runs scored, 1,309 RBI, and a .333 career average. He also had a tremendous right-field arm. Waner, one of the best line-drive hitters in the history of the game, proved particularly adept at achieving doubles and triples. As of the end of 2001, he still ranks in the top ten all time in each category, with 605 and 191, respectively. After batting .336 with a league-best 22 triples in his 1926 rookie season, Paul was joined in the outfield the following year by his rookie brother Lloyd in center. Paul responded by winning the 1927 MVP Award in carrying the Pirates to the NL pennant. The diminutive left-handed hitter that season won his first of three batting crowns with a whopping .380 mark, while also leading the NL in RBI (131), hits (237), total bases (342), and triples (18). In 1927, the speedy Waner brothers combined for 460 hits and 247 runs (Lloyd led the league with 133) as the Pirates reached the World Series.

◆ Did you know Paul and Lloyd Waner were tagged "Big Poison" and "Little Poison" by a Brooklyn fan? Tired of seeing the same scenario, this fan stood up and shouted, "Them Waners! It's always the little poison on third and the big poison on first." This origin for the joint moniker is widely accepted by many historians. Lloyd, at five feet, nine inches, was actually only a half inch taller than Paul.

42. *Prior to Hall of Famer Tommy Lasorda, which manager engineered the Dodgers the longest?*

ANSWER: Walter Alston

Alston guided the Dodgers for 23 years, from 1954 to 1957 in Brooklyn, and from 1958 to 1976 in Los Angeles. He won seven pennants and four world championships. Lasorda resigned during the 1996 season after 21 years of managing the Dodgers.

Lasorda breathed so much life into the game of baseball and was a symbol of the proud Dodgers organization. After suffering a heart attack, he retired to reduce the chances of inducing another attack. Lasorda, who still works for the Dodgers as a senior vice president, retired with 1,599 wins (13th all time), four pennants, and two world championships. Baseball already misses Lasorda, who was as big an ambassador of The Game as was Casey Stengel.

♦ Did you know, before Rupert Murdoch took over ownership of the Dodgers in March 1998, Chuck Dressen was the last Dodgers' manager fired (in 1953)? Since March of 1998, the Dodgers have had four different managers. The Dodgers still have had only 26 managers in their NL history, compared with 55 for the Reds, 49 each for the Phillies and Cardinals, 47 for the Cubs, and 44 for the Braves. In 1977, the Rangers had four managers in a seven-day span.

43. *Casey Stengel managed the Yankees from 1949 to 1960, leading the Bronx bombers to 10 pennants and seven world championships. Which two teams interloped on the Yankees' dominance, preventing them from 12 consecutive pennants during that span?*

ANSWER: The Cleveland Indians (1954) and the Chicago White Sox (1959)

Both the 1954 Cleveland Indians squad and the 1959 Chicago White Sox clubs were managed by Hall of Famer Al Lopez. Ironically, Stengel's 1954 Yankees won 103 games, the winningest team of his illustrious career. Prior to becoming the Yankees manager, Stengel had guided just one team—the 1938 Braves (77-75)—to a winning record in his 13 previous seasons as manager. Before becoming the Yankees manager, Stengel's reputation at the helm just wasn't that good. The cab driver who in 1943 slammed the door on Stengel's leg (breaking it) was named Boston's Man of the Year by a local columnist.

44. *This brash legend correctly predicted that he and his brother would combine to win all four World Series games. Can you name this colorful character?*

ANSWER: Dizzy Dean

The beloved Dean (born Jay Hanna Dean) was the biggest braggart in a baseball uniform, and also the best, because he usually backed up his fearless claims. Joe Namath's boasts were a flash in the pan compared with Dean's numerous guarantees.

Before the 1934 World Series, the Cardinals fireballing right-hander calmly predicted he would win two games and his brother Daffy (born Paul Dee Dean) would also win a pair to finish off the Tigers. That's exactly what happened. Dizzy won the opener, 8-3, and threw a six-hit shutout in Game Seven. Daffy pitched complete-game victories in Games Three and Six, allowing just two earned runs.

A 19-year-old Dean broke in on the final day of the 1930 season, hurling a three-hit victory. A more seasoned Dean returned to the majors in 1932 to win 18 games and pace the NL in innings, shutouts, and strikeouts. After winning 20 the following year, Dizzy was joined on the team in 1934 by his brother Daffy, who was more shy and stern than his saucy sibling. The confident Dizzy predicted that his Cardinals would win the NL pennant, his younger rookie brother would "win 18 or 20 games," and added, "I'll count 20 to 25 for myself. I won 20 last season, and I know I'll pass that figure." He was right on all counts. Daffy won 19, and Dizzy earned a towering 30 victories (against only seven losses) with seven shutouts en route to garnering the NL MVP Award. No National League pitcher has won 30 games since. As he put it, "It ain't bragging if you can do it."

The Dean brothers were quite an act. Late during that 1934 season, the pair showed a preview of their World Series greatness. In the first game of a September 21 twinbill at Ebbets Field, Dizzy three-hit the Dodgers, 13-0, carrying a no-hitter into the eighth inning. Daffy followed that up with a no-hitter, yielding only a first-inning walk in the impressive doubleheader sweep. That's when Dizzy made his famous remark, "If I'd a known Paul was gonna do it, I would have pitched one too." Believe him: he was that strong-willed. Dodgers catcher Al Lopez was quoted as saying, "We were all up there with our mouths open in admiration at the stuff those two were throwing."

In 1935, Dizzy won 28 games to lead the NL again, also earning his fourth straight strikeout title. Paul, who threw even harder but without the solid curve his brother had, duplicated the 19 victories from his rookie season. Paul injured his arm in 1936 and never fully recovered, adding just 12 more wins spanning small parts of seven seasons.

In 1936, Dizzy won 24 games, led the NL with 11 saves, and pitched more than 300 innings for the third straight season. But after suffering a fractured toe in the 1937 All-Star Game, Dizzy hurt his arm trying to compensate for a tough landing, and was never the same. Traded to the Cubs in the offseason, he went 7-1 with a 1.81 ERA in helping Chicago reach the 1938 World Series, but won just nine more games after that. Dean came out of a six-year retirement in 1947 to pitch one game for the St. Louis Browns as a publicity stunt. He concluded a frequently spectacular career with four scoreless innings. Despite the shortened career, Dean's numbers were too dizzying for the Hall of Fame voters to ignore. Although he won only 150 games and pitched just six full seasons, Dean was inducted into Cooperstown in 1953.

He may not have lasted, but no one can deny that Dizzy Dean was a great player for five years. From 1932 to 1936, he won 120 games (an average of 24 wins per year), finishing no lower than second in strikeouts, no lower than second in appearances, no lower than third in innings, finishing no lower than fourth in wins, thrice leading the NL in complete games, and twice in shutouts. Oh yes, he also saved more games (29) than any other National Leaguer during that stretch, and thrice finished among the top six in ERA. Given his peak dominance, the injury-caused end to his supremacy, his career length, and final numbers, I'm convinced that on the field, Dean was the right-handed version of Sandy Koufax (but definitely not off the field, as the Dodgers lefthander was modest and soft-spoken). Koufax retired with a 165-87 mark over 12 years. Dean compiled a 150-83 ledger spanning 12 years.

♦ Did you know Dizzy Dean once shut out the Boston Braves without taking a sign from his catcher? Intent on throwing all fastballs that day, Dean let

Boston in on his strategy before the game and acted on his brash intentions by mowing the flabbergasted Braves.

♦ Did you know Joe McGinnity and Christy Mathewson make up the only pitching duo to each win 30 games for two straight years? McGinnity won 31 games and Mathewson added 30 for the Giants in 1903, and McGinnity had 35 wins, two more than Mathewson, the following season.

45. *One of the most exclusive clubs is the 500-homer and 3,000-hit resort. In 1996, Eddie Murray became the third member. Name the first two:*

A Hank Aaron and Ted Williams
B Willie Mays and Frank Robinson
C Babe Ruth and Mel Ott
D Willie Mays and Hank Aaron
E Stan Musial and Ted Williams

ANSWER: D

Murray, who retired following the 1997 season with 3,255 hits, belted his 500th home run on September 6, 1996, as an Oriole. Barry Bonds, who has 567 homers, is 687 hits away from joining the exclusive club. Rafael Palmeiro is 53 home runs and 515 hits away.

♦ Did you know Mark McGwire reached 500 home runs in fewer at-bats than anyone else? McGwire, the 16th member of that exclusive club, reached that milestone in 5,487 at-bats. McGwire has 583 home runs through 2001.

46. *Babe Ruth hit All-Star Game history's first home run. Who hit the first All-Star Game homer for the National League in the same contest?*

ANSWER: Frankie Frisch

Frisch did so later in the same game at the 1933 mid-summer classic at Comiskey Park. Ruth's two-run shot off Wild Bill Hallahan gave the AL a 3-0 lead in the third en route to a 4-2 win. Starter Lefty Gomez pitched three scoreless innings for the win, and Lefty Grove earned the save with three goose eggs of his own in the inaugural mid-summer classic. Each pitched to catcher Rick Ferrell, who caught all nine innings. Hallahan, who started for the National League, took the loss. Gomez, incidentally, also drove in the first run. John McGraw came out of retirement to manage the National League in this game.

Frisch, who played in each of the first three All-Star Games despite his advanced age (he was almost 35 when he played in the 1933 contest), batted .316 over a 19-year career that featured 1,532 runs scored and 466 doubles. "Fordham Flash," whose moniker comes from his great speed and his days at Fordham University, swiped 419 bases over his career, thrice leading the league. A great contact hitter, Frisch struck out fewer than 15 times per season, walking almost three times as often as he whiffed (728 walks to 272 strikeouts).

♦ Did you know Frankie Frisch holds the distinction of having played the most World Series games (50) without homering, yet he hit a home run in each of the two All-Star Games he played? Frisch, who hit .294 in 197 career World Series at-bats spanning a half-dozen fall classics, had four hits in seven All-Star Game at-bats.

47. *On September 9, 1965, the Dodgers' Sandy Koufax and opposing pitcher Bob Hendley of the Cubs allowed only one hit between them (an unprecedented feat) as Koufax threw major league history's eighth perfect game. The same player that connected for the game's only hit also scored the game's only run. Can you name that player?*

ANSWER: Lou Johnson

Outfielder Johnson's bloop double to right field broke up Hendley's no-hit bid with two out in the seventh. But Johnson didn't score in the seventh. He scored the only run in the home fifth by drawing a walk, moving to second on a sacrifice bunt, stealing third base, and scoring on the errant throw by catcher Chris Krug over the awaiting third baseman.

Koufax's performance was stellar, as he also struck out 14 batters in a fast-moving game that took just one hour and 43 minutes to play. With the gem, Koufax set the record with his fourth no-hitter to eclipse the previous mark set by Larry Corcoran and equaled by Cy Young and Bob Feller. Although not dominant, Hendley was stellar in completing his first start of the season, allowing the unearned run, yielding one hit and one walk, and striking out three. If Harvey Haddix's 12 perfect innings on May 26, 1959, was the best single-game pitching performance of all time, then Koufax's masterpiece is certainly the best since. And that, in my opinion, includes Kerry Wood's 20-strikeout, one-hit shutout of the Houston Astros on May 6, 1998.

♦ Did you know Bob Hendley used that 1965 performance to inspire him for his next start four days later, during which he pitched a four-hitter to beat Sandy Koufax and the Dodgers, 2-1, at Wrigley Field? Those assignments against Koufax were Hendley's only two complete games of the season, which he ended at 4-4 with a hefty 5.96 ERA.

♦ Did you know Harvey Kuenn was the last out in two of Koufax's four no-hitters? Kuenn, who was the last out in Koufax's second no-hitter (against the Giants in 1963), struck out on three pitches to end the perfect game, representing the Cubs. Koufax struck out seven of the last nine men to face him in his perfect game.

48. *Eight players have won the coveted MVP Award three times. Yankee greats Mickey Mantle, Yogi Berra, and Joe DiMaggio are three. Can you name four of the remaining five?*

ANSWER: Barry Bonds, Mike Schmidt, Roy Campanella, Stan Musial, and Jimmie Foxx

Bonds became the first four-time MVP following a spectacular 2001 campaign. He remains the only player to win three MVP Awards in a four-year span (1990, 1992, and 1993). In 1991, Bonds lost out to Terry Pendleton by a slim margin (274 to 259).

DiMaggio was the first three-time MVP, becoming so in 1947. Foxx and Musial joined DiMaggio the following year.

In 1948, Musial had one of the most commanding offensive seasons in NL history, missing the Triple Crown by one home run in the process. Musial didn't just lead his league in 10 offensive categories in 1948; he topped them by margins so great that he established himself as a man among boys that year. Musial's .702 slugging percentage towered over his nearest NL competitor by .138. His 429 total bases was 113 more than anyone else's total in the NL. Musial's .376 batting average was 43 points higher than runner-up Richie Ashburn's. His 230 hits was 40 more than any other senior circuit member. The 103 extra-base hits Musial compiled was 29 more than Del Ennis' number. His .450 on-base percentage was 27 points higher than that of Bob Elliott. Musial's 135 runs led by 18 and his 131 RBI led by a half-dozen. His 46 doubles and 18 triples also led by six. Only his 39 home runs fell short of the 40 posted by Ralph Kiner and Johnny Mize.

◆ Did you know Yogi Berra never led the league in any major offensive category? The 15-time All-Star who started out as a poor defensive catcher, ironically, twice led the league in fielding percentage. The wild-swinging Berra was consistently productive, hitting at least 20 home runs for 10 consecutive years, without ever surpassing 30. For 11 straight seasons, he tabulated at least 82 RBI, reaching as high 125. The goofy Berra reached the .300 mark thrice, hitting as high as .322.

◆ Did you know Joe DiMaggio was selected for the All-Star Game in each of his 13 years in the majors? World War II, injuries, and pride kept DiMaggio from playing more often. After the 1951 season, the proud DiMaggio retired rather than play at a level below his standards.

49. *This player edged out Ted Williams by .00016 points in 1949, preventing the Red Sox legend from a third Triple Crown. Name him:*

    A Joe DiMaggio
    B George Kell
    C Dale Mitchell
    D Bobby Doerr
    E Bob Dillinger

ANSWER: B

Hall of Famer Kell won the 1949 batting crown with a mark of .342911. It was the second closest batting race in history. On the last day of the season, Kell went 2-for-3 with a walk to edge the hitless Williams (.342756).

Aware of Williams' outcome, Kell was on deck with Eddie Lake at the plate, a man on, and one out in the ninth inning of the season finale. He didn't need to bat to win the batting championship. Manager Red Rolfe even asked if he wanted to sit down to ensure the batting title. Kell refused, despite realizing that making an out would drop him below Williams and cost him the crown. Kell later said that his mind was made up after recalling Williams' decision to not sit out the season-ending doubleheader eight years earlier, despite being assured of a .400 average. As it turned out, Kell never had to bat, as Lake grounded into a game-ending double play. Had Kell batted and made an out, his batting average would have dropped to .342256. A right-handed line-drive hitter who hardly ever struck out, Kell whiffed just 13 times in 1949. Because batter strikeout totals were first counted in 1910, only Ernie Lombardi in 1942 struck out less often (12) while winning a batting title. Kell enjoyed eight straight .300 seasons en route to a .306 lifetime batting average spanning a 15-year career. He twice led the league in hits and doubles, totaling 56 two-baggers in 1951.

As good as Kell was with his bat, he may have been even better guarding the line at third. The tough-minded Kell was a superb fielder who led AL third basemen in fielding percentage seven times and assists four times. During his last major league season, the 1957 campaign with the Orioles, Kell taught a young third baseman in Baltimore by the name of Brooks Robinson the ins and outs of playing the hot corner. Robinson became the best fielding third baseman of all time, and the two were inducted into the Hall of Fame together in 1983.

50. *Baseball's only on-field tragedy occurred on August 16, 1920, when the Yankees' _____ beaned Indians shortstop _____, killing him. On September 10, rookie and future Hall of Famer Joe Sewell filled the position for the next 13 seasons. Fill in the blanks.*

ANSWER: Carl Mays, Ray Chapman

Chapman, whose skull was fractured, got up and started to head toward first base before collapsing again. The 29-year-old Chapman was declared dead at 4:40 the next morning. There were indications that Chapman, who liked to crowd the plate, never saw the scuffed-up ball because the combination of Mays' right-handed side-arm delivery and the white shirts in the centerfield bleachers made the ball difficult to locate. Mays was exonerated, but his 208-126 (2.92 ERA) career record was not worthy of Hall of Fame induction due to suspicion of throwing the 1921 World Series. Mays was quoted years later as saying, "I won over 200 big-league games, but no one today remembers that. When they think of me, I'm the guy who killed Chapman with a fastball." Mays, who was surly to begin with, became more unpopular after the beaning.

Ray's daughter Rae died of the measles 18 months after the accident, and his wife took her own life eight months afterward. Chapman was a .278 career-hitting shortstop who scored 671 runs and swiped 233 bases over nine seasons.

◆ Did you know Tom "Shotgun" Rogers of the 1921 Yankees was also known for beaning a batter to death, killing John Dodge with a pitch during 1916 in a Southern Association game?

51. *Can you name the only player to win an MVP in the National League and American League? Known for his intense, back-down-from-nobody mindset, this right-handed slugger earned his MVP Awards five years apart.*

ANSWER: Frank Robinson

Robinson dominated AL pitchers in 1966 en route to winning the Triple Crown and his second MVP Award. Robinson led the AL with 49 home runs, 122 RBI, a .316 average, 122 runs scored, a .410 on-base percentage, and .637 slugging.

"Robby" won his first MVP with Cincinnati in 1961, but was traded following the 1965 season by Reds General Manager Bill DeWitt, who claimed Robinson was "an old 30." Robinson went on to a Hall of Fame career, and DeWitt lost his job. Aside from being the only player to be awarded the MVP in the American League as well as the National League, Robinson was the first to hit an All-Star Game homer in both circuits and the first to hit 200 home runs in both leagues.

◆ Did you know Frank Robinson won the MVP Award, the Triple Crown, the Athlete of the Year, the All-Star Game MVP Award, the World Series MVP, and the Manager of the Year Award?

52. *Can you name the first American League president?*

ANSWER: Bancroft Johnson

"Ban" Johnson was the force behind the birth of the American League as we know it and was that circuit's first president, serving from 1901 to 1927. Johnson, believing in his product and recognizing the demand, decided to recruit millionaire owners, establish a structure, and challenge the National League, clearly the nation's superior baseball circuit since its inception in 1876. Johnson officially formed the American League in 1900, with the intent of ushering in its debut the following year.

Johnson believed that his league would prosper, especially after the National League discontinued four of its franchises, a decision that left many capable players without a team and in need of a salary. Johnson also believed that he had an advantage because he had eager and deep-pocketed owners who were willing to pay a higher salary and outbid the National League for the services of some of its own well established superstars. Many underpaid players jumped at the chance, among them superstars Napoleon Lajoie and Cy Young.

Johnson was so confident in his brand new American League that he decided to directly challenge the National League by placing three teams in cities—Philadelphia, Boston, and Chicago—that already included a NL club. Johnson's confidence was rewarded as the American League outdrew the National League in each of these cities. The American League's five other original teams were Detroit, Cleveland, Washington, Baltimore, and Milwaukee. In choosing these cities, Johnson strategically placed ballclubs in cities the National League had abandoned. Milwaukee was moved to St. Louis in 1902.

Johnson and White Sox owner Charles Comiskey worked together to make the American Leauge as good, if not better, than the National League (a thought once mocked), and ultimately forced the National League to compete in a World Series in 1903. Thus was born the World Series as we recognize it today. As the American League won 14 of the first 24 World Series, Johnson earned respect for himself and his league. For his tremendous efforts, he also earned a place in the Hall of Fame.

♦ Did you know Sunday baseball was prohibited in most major league cities during the first two decades of the 1900s? Sunday baseball was one of the features that made the American Association an attractive league until its demise following the 1891 season. Alcoholic beverages and half-priced tickets (25 cents) were the other attractions used to lure the fans.

53. *In 1901, _____ won the most lopsided batting race in history, defeating Baltimore's Mike Donlin by 82 percentage points. Fill in the blank.*

ANSWER: Nap Lajoie

Lajoie hit an AL record .422 for the Philadelphia Athletics that year to garner his first of three batting titles and win the Triple Crown. Lajoie, the French Canadian who made the American League more credible by jumping from the National League's Philadelphia Phillies to the Athletics following the 1900 season, was ordered off the Athletics squad when the Phillies obtained an injunction preventing a player from going from one team to another in the same city. During the 1902 season, Athletics manager Connie Mack sold Lajoie to Cleveland, where he played through the 1914 season. Lajoie went back to the Athletics for his last two years, concluding a brilliant, 21-year major league career that featured a .339 lifetime batting average, 3,252 hits, 1,599 RBI, 1,506 runs scored, 652 doubles, 164 triples, and 396 steals.

The graceful and smooth Lajoie was as good defensively as he was with the bat, leading the league in fielding percentage seven times, and in double plays and putouts five times each. The right-handed Lajoie (pronounced Lah-Zhwa) retired with a .966 fielding percentage, a spectacular figure for his era and for a second baseman with his range. According to his contemporaries, he glided to the ball with a flair impossible to imitate. Baseball writer Arthur Daley once wrote "(Lajoie) glided with Gallic grace and effortless ease over tremendous stretches of ground. Never did he make a play seem hard. . . . He was the most graceful ballplayer who ever lived."

The demure superstar who batted .350 or higher 10 times (his opposite league peer Honus Wagner did so four times) also punished the best pitchers of the time. According to biographer J. M. Murphy, Lajoie batted over .300 against nine Hall of Famers: Joe McGinnity (23-for-45; a .511 average), Clark Griffith (36-for-88; .409), Cy Young (78-for-206; .379), Eddie Plank (49-for-136; .360), Amos Rusie (9-for-25; .360), Rube Waddell (49-for-140; .350), Kid Nichols (19-for-56;

.339), Ed Walsh (53-for-166; .319), and Jack Chesbro (40-for-129; .310). Against Walter Johnson, Lajoie was "held" to a .292 mark (40-for-137). One Hall of Famer, however, did give Lajoie trouble, limiting the aging batsmen to a .185 mark (5-for-27). That southpaw was Babe Ruth.

Interestingly, Lajoie (who played from 1896 to 1916) thought that his numbers would have been even better had he not taken on the dual role of manager from 1905 to 1909. He thought that managing affected his production on the field, and that his responsibilities carried over to the clubhouse and away from the ballpark.

54. *To help raise pension money for eligible players, Major League Baseball had two All-Star Games a season from 1959 to 1962. Which pitcher started two All-Star Games in one season?*

ANSWER: Don Drysdale

Drysdale started each game in 1959, losing the second contest. He was a powerful side-arming righthander who intimidated batters and was a workhorse on the mound. Drysdale pitched at least 211 innings for 12 consecutive years, including a span of four consecutive seasons with at least 308 innings. The six-foot five-inch Drysdale ended a 14-year career with a 209-166 ledger and a 2.95 ERA for the Dodgers.

Drysdale's most notable achievement was hurling 58 consecutive scoreless innings (six shutouts were included during that stretch) in 1968, breaking the previous mark of 56 set by the great Walter Johnson 55 years earlier. Before surpassing Johnson's mark, Drysdale almost ended the streak on May 30, hitting batter Dick Dietz with a pitch and the bases loaded. But home plate umpire Harry Wendelstedt ruled that Dietz never attempted to get out of the way, thus giving Drysdale another chance, and Drysdale retired Dietz en route to his fifth straight shutout. The streak ended nine days later.

Drysdale was a Dodgers broadcaster 20 years later, when Los Angeles righthander Orel Hershiser broke his mark with 59 consecutive scoreless innings. Hershiser also benefited from a rarely invoked rule to reverse a run scored, thanks to a runner interference judgment.

55. *In 2001, Sammy Sosa became the first player in major league history to reach the 60-homer plateau three times. Despite hitting 66 home runs in 1998, 63 homers in 1999, and 64 roundtrippers in 2001, Sosa has only won a single home run crown. Identify the year.*

ANSWER: 2000

Ironically, Sosa won his lone home run crown in 2000, when he hit 50. The Cubs' right-handed slugger fell four short of Mark McGwire in 1998, two shy of "Big Mac" the following year, and nine behind Barry Bonds' record total in 2001.

Such a result is the product of the greatest power era in the history of the game. That Sosa didn't win a home run title in any of his 60-homer campaigns speaks volumes about the almost comical frequency of the home run in this high-scoring, high-soaring period of baseball. Gone are the ooohs and aaahs that normally accompany multi-homer games and 50-homer performances. Vanished is the reverence most of us had for the numbers 60 and 61. The single-season home run record used to hold a romantic place in our baseball hearts. Now, we watch like frenzied sharks for the next dose of home-run-filled highlights that are usually accompanied with a computed distance. Some games resemble a Home Run Derby more than they do baseball. Through 1995, a total of 18 players hit at least 50 homers in a season, and just two reached 60. Those aggregates span the first 120 years of major league baseball history. In the six years since, 15 players have hit 50 or more in a season, and six of them have reached 60. And, of course, two of them have climbed to 70.

Owners and executives of major league baseball evidently decided that more offense would bring in more fans, which was especially important after losing viewers because of the 1994 strike. Following the demoralizing truth of the 1919 "Black Sox" scandal, Babe Ruth's prowess revitalized the game. And following the period of the Great Depression, more tightly wound balls were used from 1929 to 1931 to create more offense and attract more fans.

More brilliant displays worked each time to increase ballpark attendance. Of course, the latest drop in popularity was self-inflicted by the executives, although once again, baseball has seemingly survived lousy management by drawing 70,589,505 fans in 1998, almost matching that total in 1999, and reaching a record level in 2000. Many observers think both leagues have livened up the baseballs to stir this power surge and create interest among fans disgusted with the game following the strike. Teenagers may also have been the target of this ploy, as that age group has recently taken more interest in other fast-paced, high-scoring sports.

Major League Baseball representatives deny livening up the baseballs. Regardless of the reason—juiced ball, small strike zone, more tightly wound balls, diminutive and hitter-friendly ballparks, diluted pitching caused by expansion, muscled-up hitters, or any combination thereof—home runs are ruling today's game. The almighty home run has been cheapened. It may put more fannies in the seats, but at what expense? It's a short-term solution, especially when fans become jaded with annual 60-homer performances and a run at the record book every three years. Are baseball fans really ready to embrace an 80-homer campaign so soon after we made such a big deal of McGwire's and Sosa's 1998 campaign, and Bonds' 2001 season? I say move the fences back a tad, raise the mound a few inches, and bring back the strike zone outlined in the rule books— the rules most of us grew up on.

56. *This reliever once pitched 22⅓ consecutive hitless innings, a stretch that included a no-hitter. Can you name this side-armed righty?*

ANSWER: Dennis Eckersley

The side-armed Eckersley came within two outs of the overall mark set by Cy Young before his streak came to an end on June 3, 1977. Seattle's Ruppert Jones hit a fifth-inning home run to end the hot stretch.

Young accomplished the feat in 1904, in the middle of his 14th straight 20-win season. From the seventh inning of his April 25 assignment through the sixth frame of his May 11 outing, Young did not yield a single hit (in between, Young appeared in relief during an April 30 contest). Included during that amazing stretch was a perfect game on May 5 against fellow Hall of Famer Rube Waddell of the Philadelphia Athletics.

To see how impressive Young's and Eckersley's streaks were, note that Johnny Vander Meer (whose streak of 21 innings Eckersley eclipsed for second longest) retired his last batter in a June 7, 1938, start, threw a no-hitter in his June 11 start against the Bees, didn't yield a hit in his historic June 15 no-no in Ebbets Field (that park's first night game), and wasn't touched for a safety until Debs Garms of the Boston Bees singled with one out in the fourth inning of his June 19 assignment.

As a starter-turned-reliever, Eckersley had his best year as a closer in 1990, going 4-2 with 48 saves (only two blown chances), a minuscule 0.61 ERA, walking only four and striking out 73 in 73⅓ innings. Eckersley's 0.61 ERA in 1990 remains the lowest single-season mark in history, based on a minimum of 25 innings. In his 63 appearances, "The Eck" capitulated only 41 hits. And by season's end, Eckersley had issued 35 walks over his last 320 innings pitched. Eckersley, without much competition, remains the only pitcher to have saved as many as 50 games in a season and won 20 in another. In 1978, Eckersley went 20-8 with a 2.99 ERA.

♦ Did you know in 1990 Dennis Eckersley became the first reliever to total more saves (48) than hits allowed (41) in a season? In 1998, San Diego's Trevor Hoffman became the second with 53 saves and 41 hits permitted. That membership doubled to four in 1999, when Mariano Rivera (45 saves, 43 hits) and Billy Wagner (39, 35) joined the club.

♦ Did you know Cy Young remains the oldest pitcher to throw a perfect game, doing so at the age of 37 in 1904? David Cone and Dennis Martinez were each 36 when they threw their gems. Monte Ward remains the youngest, doing so at the age of 20 in 1880. By the way, Young's perfect game was the first in AL history, and the first since the mound was pushed back to 60 feet six inches.

57. *Which pitcher holds the single-game strikeout record, regardless of innings?*

ANSWER: Tom Cheney

Senator Cheney fanned 21 Orioles in 16 innings during a September 12, 1962, contest. The 2-1 complete game victor allowed 10 hits and walked four. Cheney struck out five different Orioles three times each: Russ Snyder, Jim Gentile, Dave Nicholson, Marv Breeding, and pitcher Dick Hall. The right-handed pitcher twice struck out the side, and whiffed at least two Orioles in seven different innings.

Possessing a flare for dramatics, Cheney mastered eight shutouts among his 19 career victories. Cheney, who pitched bits and pieces of eight major league seasons, never recorded a winning campaign in a career that lasted from 1957 to 1966 (minus 1958 and 1965). A St. Louis Cardinals farmhand, Cheney spent a season in Pittsburgh (earning a ring in 1960) before arriving in Washington in 1961. Despite a 7-9 mark, Cheney's 3.17 ERA in 1962 was seventh in the American League. Cheney, often injured, was never the same after an elbow injury in 1963.

58. *This Hall of Famer gets more attention for his defense, but he was not exactly a shabby offensive player. This doubles machine, nicknamed "The Grey Eagle," loved the game. When he broke his right arm as a kid, he was so anxious to play that he learned to bat and throw left-handed. Name the player.*

ANSWER: Tris Speaker

Constantly praised for his unparalleled defensive style in center, Speaker was an invaluable offensive player as well. Besides doubling more often than any other player in history (792 times), the left-handed batsmen hit .344 and slugged .500 over a 22-year career that also included 222 triples (sixth highest total ever), 1,882 runs scored (10th), 5,101 total bases (11th), and 1,529 RBI. As impressive as those numbers are on their own merits, they take on a whole new meaning when considering that Speaker played most of his career in the Dead Ball Era. And Speaker's .428 on-base percentage ranks 12th all time through 2001.

♦ Did you know Giants manager John McGraw and Pirates owner Barney Dreyfuss each had a chance to sign a young Tris Speaker? McGraw had too many outfielders and Dreyfuss didn't because "[Speaker] smoked cigarettes," according to *Total Baseball*.

59. *Arguably the best season ever put together by a pitcher was compiled in 1913. This Hall of Famer won 36 of 43 decisions for a league-best .837 winning percentage. This right-handed flame-thrower also had the league's lowest ERA (a minuscule 1.14), with*

*league highs of 29 complete games, 346 innings pitched, 243
strikeouts, and 11 shutouts. Can you name this AL hurler?*

ANSWER: Walter Johnson

Senator Walter Johnson also pitched 55⅔ consecutive scoreless
innings along the way in 1913. As if all those numbers weren't sufficiently mind-boggling, Johnson walked merely 38 batters in 47
games pitched, and earned two saves. In addition, the 25-year-old
player contributed in the batter's box as well, collecting 35 hits, including two homers, for a .261 batting average.

◆ Did you know the modern single-season major league record for the
lowest ERA belongs to Dutch Leonard, and not Bob Gibson? Gibson's distinguished mark of 1.12 in 1968 was relegated to the best among those with
more than 300 innings after historians discovered Leonard's 0.96 ERA for the
Boston Red Sox in 1914. The sparkling, microscopic mark came over 224⅔
innings. The all-time lowest ERA over a single season is Tim Keefe's 0.86 standard in 1880, when he pitched 105 innings during an 84-game schedule.

60. *After the New York Mets' horrible 1967 season, George Weiss
retired and M. Donald Grant took over as the team president. Grant
hired Gil Hodges as the manager for the 1968 season. Hodges
accomplished in his first year what former manager Wes Westrum
was able to do on just one occasion—finish out of the cellar. During
that season of rebuilding and improving, the Mets boasted three
representatives in the 1968 All-Star Game. Can you name two of
them?*

ANSWER: Tom Seaver, Jerry Koosman, and Jerry Grote

Seaver, the rookie Koosman, and catcher Grote were selected to
play in that All-Star Game at the Houston Astrodome, marking the
first time the Mets received more than the single mandatory nomina-
tion. Seaver, who saved the All-Star Game for the National League the
year before as a rookie (pitching the 15th inning in Anaheim), hurled
the seventh and eighth innings with an impressive five strikeouts
along the way. Koosman, the phenomenal lefthander with six of his
eventual seven shutouts that year behind him, repeated Seaver's performance of the previous year by retiring the last AL batter to save the

1-0 victory. Thanks to the efforts of Seaver and Koosman, the well pitched contest remains the lowest scoring mid-summer classic in history.

The Mets matured under the tutelage of Hodges—a man considered perfect for a post that required much patience—and went on to win the 1969 World Series, no longer resembling the franchise that posted a dismal record of 321-648 in its first six years.

The Mets made some key acquisitions (Tommie Agee, Al Weis, Wayne Garrett, and Donn Clendenon) and benefited greatly from Hodges' ability to squeeze the absolute most out of his players by giving a purpose to every member of the team. One of the biggest reasons for the team's success in 1969 was Hodges' successful platoon system, which became increasingly prominent down the stretch as he had 10 players sharing five positions. Ed Kranepool and Clendenon formed the first-base platoon, Ken Boswell and Weis shared the duties at second base, Garrett and Ed Charles handled the hot corner, Ron Swoboda and Art Shamsky combined to roam right field, and Jerry Grote and J. C. Martin split time behind the plate.

That year, the Mets won 100 games in the regular season, swept the Braves in the NL Championship Series and borrowed "the little engine that could" theory to upset the powerhouse Baltimore Orioles in the World Series. Seaver (25-7) finished second behind Willie McCovey in one of the closest MVP voting in history, and outfielders Agee and Cleon Jones finished among the top seven finalists. Seaver and Koosman combined to go 42-16, and finished fourth and fifth, respectively, in ERA with figures of 2.21 and 2.28.

Although not blessed with noisy bats like the Braves, the Mets cleverly used the barrage of pitchers their great farm system produced. The starting rotation received most of the recognition, but the Mets relievers were a major reason for the club's success.

It was hard to believe that the same group of guys (Tug McGraw, Ron Taylor, and Nolan Ryan) that lost 37 of 63 one-run games and 13 of 15 extra-inning contests the previous year was dominating those situations in 1969, consistently clamping the door on the opposition. The Mets went on to win 41 of 64 one-run decisions, and 10 of 16 extra-inning affairs to complete a tremendous turnaround.

The Mets' defense was just as incredible, using Buddy Harrelson's solid glove at short, Grote's great defensive skills behind the plate, and Agee's unbelievable range in center field. Hodges and Grant had a lot to be proud of as they built this "miracle team" almost from scratch. The team that cruised by Baltimore in the World Series was the result of careful design.

After winning one more pennant in 1973, the Mets suffered a decade-long decline that was partially due to lack of leadership. After Hodges died of a heart attack during spring training of 1972 (Yogi Berra took over) and owner Joan Whitney Payson also passed away in 1975, Grant traded away Seaver, Koosman, and slugger Dave Kingman. The future of the club was shaky as Payson's heirs handled the franchise for five years before selling the club to Nelson Doubleday and Fred Wilpon in January of 1980.

A renewed commitment to the club was ensured as the new co-owners hired Frank Cashen to be the general manager. Cashen succeed as the Mets compiled the second-best record of the 1980s (the Yankees were just five and one-half games better), won the 1986 World Series, and put that magical aura back in Shea Stadium. Cashen had done the same for the Baltimore Orioles franchise in the late 1960s.

♦ Did you know Fernando Valenzuela's eight shutouts as a rookie in 1981 tied the major league freshman mark, set in 1913 by Reb Russell of the White Sox? Russell also had an outstanding rookie campaign, going 22-16 with a 1.90 ERA. Left-handed like Valenzuela, Russell never reached 20 wins again, but did enjoy an 18-11 ledger in 1916 and a 15-5 mark the following year. He pitched to just two batters in 1919 before being released with a dead arm. But Russell returned as an outfielder with the Pirates in 1922, and slugged a combined .568 with 21 homers over the next two years.

61. *What do Babe Ruth, Waite Hoyt, Wally Schang, Herb Pennock, Carl Mays, and Everett Scott all have in common?*

ANSWER: They were all dealt away to the New York Yankees by Boston Red Sox owner Harry Frazee. Between the time he purchased the defending champion Red Sox in 1917 and the time he sold the franchise six years later, Frazee drove the franchise into the ground. Not only had the Red Sox been degraded to last-place status, but they had squandered away the likes of Ruth, Hoyt, Schang, Pennock, Mays, and Scott for little, if any, promising talent in return. To make matters worse, their historic rival, the Yankees, were the inheritors. The series of transactions during Frazee's tenure ignited the Yankees' success and reversed Boston's course as the most successful team over the first two decades of the 20th century. Frazee single-handedly helped the Yankees end their drought and put his own Red Sox franchise into a championship famine it has yet to recover from, nearly a century later.

Frazee sold Mays in July 1919, and Ruth five months later. He then traded Hoyt and Schang in an eight-player deal in December 1920, Scott as part of a six-player package in December 1921, and Pennock in January 1923 for three obscure players and cash. They all played a role in the Yankees' first world championship of 1923. Ruth and Pennock played big roles in the Yankees' championship drives of 1927, 1928, and 1932. Hoyt was there in 1927 and 1928.

Clearly, the Red Sox were just business to Frazee, a theatrical producer who in 1923 sold the club for $1.5 million—a $1.1 million profit. To Frazee, the players were simply a means to cover his theatrical investments.

Joe Lannin, Frazee's predecessor, made a blunder of his own in April of 1916. Lannin traded Speaker to the Cleveland Indians after his star center fielder refused to take a pay cut from $11,000 to $9,000. Speaker had reason to take umbrage at Lannin's request: In leading his Red Sox to a second title in four years, "The Grey Eagle" in 1915 posted his seventh straight .300 season and again played awesome defense. Lannin reasoned Speaker's batting average had decreased (to .322) for the third straight season. But Speaker held out, forcing Lannin to trade him to the Indians for Sad Sam Jones, Fred Thomas, and $55,000.

Speaker, determined to prove Lannin wrong, did so with conviction. The field general batted at least .344 eight times over the next 10 years, a stretch that also featured five performances of .378 or better. Speaker was so highly regarded that the Indians appointed him player-manager during the 1919 season, a post he held through 1926. In 1920, Speaker rewarded the Cleveland franchise by guiding the Indians to their first world championship. He hit a gaudy .388 with a .483 on-base percentage and a league-best 50 doubles in the process. The left-handed slugger also hit .320 with six runs scored in the team's World Series victory over Brooklyn. Speaker's seven and one-half seasons as Indians manager produced an impressive 617-520 record.

Red Ruffing was yet another Red Sox player who went on to help the Yankees add to their post-season fortunes, although no one could fault Boston owner Robert Quinn and his front office. Unlike the aforementioned players, Ruffing was by no means considered a solid producer in May 1930, when he was dealt to New York for a fellow named Cedric Durst and $50,000. In fact, his trade was cheered. But a strange thing happened to the man who lost more often than any other AL pitcher in 1928 and 1929. Wearing pinstripes suddenly improved the righthander's fortunes.

Ruffing, who was an awful 39-96 at the time of the trade, went 231-124 over the next 15 years for the Yankees. And it wasn't just the winning percentage that Ruffing improved. At the time of the trade, Ruffing had a career ERA of 4.61 with six shutouts. In 15 years with the Yankees, Ruffing posted a 3.47 ERA with 42 shutouts. During that stretch, Ruffing won seven of nine World Series decisions as the Yankees won six world championships in seven fall classic appearances. Ruffing retired after losing five of eight decisions in his final season of 1947 as a member of the White Sox.

The Yankees have also taken advantage of the Orioles, acquiring the services of Reggie Jackson (free agent), David Wells (trade), and Mike Mussina (free agent) from Baltimore, as well as the team name and city. The Yankees were originally born as the Baltimore Orioles in 1901 before moving to New York (Hilltop Park) and changing their name to the Highlanders in 1903. They became the Yankees in 1913, moving in to share the Polo Grounds with the Giants.

◆ Did you know Babe Ruth was sold to the Yankees for $100,000, and a $300,000 loan with Fenway Park used as collateral, by Red Sox owner Harry Frazee? Forced to make the move for financial reasons involving the Red Sox and his theatrical ventures, Frazee agreed to receive one-fourth of the sale price on the spot, plus $25,000 a year at 6% interest. The deal was made on December 26, 1919, although it was not announced until January 5. Had Frazee realized that Ruth could have solved his financial problems, the Red Sox owner might never have traded Ruth. The Yankees built a park designed to take advantage of Ruth's awesome power, a sight they were sure would fill the seats. Perhaps Frazee wasn't aware of Ruth's inspiring power because Fenway Park was arguably the toughest home run park in the American League. Among Ruth's 49 homers in a Red Sox uniform, only 11 were at Fenway.

62. *Which team took advantage of "Merkle's Boner" to win the NL pennant and, eventually, the 1908 World Series?*

ANSWER: The Chicago Cubs

The Chicago Cubs owe the 1908 world championship to their Hall of Fame second baseman Johnny Evers. He cleverly warned the umpires that Fred Merkle, the Giants runner at first base who was making his first start in the majors, might not touch second base if Mike McCormick was to score from third on a hit from Al Bridwell (with two out) during that infamous September 23 contest. Bridwell indeed "singled" to center and, as McCormick crossed the plate, Merkle ignored touching second base and headed toward the dugout (located in center field) to avoid the mob. Every player did so in those days to elude the fans, who usually departed the Polo Grounds by crossing the field and using the center-field exit. Even the umpires tried to time it so they would avoid the fans. Awaiting the throw from center fielder Solly Hofman, amid the rush of the fans, was Evers. But noticing Evers' intention and the departure of the umpires despite the warning by Evers, Giants pitcher Joe McGinnity intercepted the throw and darted the ball into the left-field bleachers.

Merkle's teammates, then in the clubhouse, were persuading him to run back on the field and touch second base. When Merkle returned to touch the bag, Evers was there waiting for him with another baseball to tag him out. After much arguing by Cubs player-manager Frank Chance, who dragged home plate umpire Hank O'Day from the umpire's clubhouse, Merkle was declared the third out in the bottom of the ninth inning. O'Day, who did not see the play and was later pummeled by Giants fans, had to make the call because a non-call in a very similar situation had cost the Cubs a game two weeks prior against the Pirates. It was the first time that call had ever been made.

The game was officially called because of darkness, although the clock read 5:30 in the afternoon in mid-September. In fact the game could not be continued because Giants fans had saturated the field, and a tie-breaking game was to be played, if necessary, at the end of the season to determine a pennant. As fate would have it, each team was 98-55 at regular season's end, making an October 8, pennant-deciding makeup game necessary. The Cubs won said game, 4-2, hence "Merkle's Boner." Mordecai "Three Fingers" Brown, who relieved a struggling Jack Pfiester in the first inning, outdueled Christy Mathewson with Frank Chance going 3-for-4. Among Chance's hits was a two-run double in the Cubs' four-run third inning at the Polo Grounds.

The matchup was so eagerly anticipated that 250,000 people were waiting outside the Polo Grounds, and four people died as they fell off the overcrowded "L" Section of the stadium. It's a shame Merkle is best remembered (and, in most cases, only remembered) for this gaffe. He batted at least .283 in six of his 16 major league seasons, stole at least 20 bases eight times, and reached five World Series.

♦ Did you know NL President Harry Pulliam took his own life on July 25, 1909? According to author G. H. Fleming in *The Unforgettable Season,* Pulliam voluntarily ended his life due to what his doctors said was "a severe state of depression that had been brought on by the turmoil that followed the Giants-Cubs game on September 23, 1908," otherwise known as the game of "Merkle's Boner." Pulliam had taken a leave of absence following the 1908 season. He shot himself in the right temple.

63. *Although not in the Hall of Fame, these players make a strong argument for induction. Can you correctly state each player's position in the field?*

    A Rocky Colavito
    B Maury Wills
    C Stan Hack
    D Joe Gordon
    E Mickey Vernon

    ANSWER: A—right field, B—shortstop, C—third base, D—second base, E—first base

Others deserving enshrinement or at least more consideration are catchers Gary Carter, Ted Simmons, and Bob Boone; first basemen Keith Hernandez, Gil Hodges, and Dick Allen; second baseman Lou Whitaker; third baseman Ron Santo; outfielders Jim Rice, Dwight

Evans, Dale Murphy, Vada Pinson, Lefty O'Doul, Dave Parker, Al Oliver, Pete Browning, Minnie Minoso, and Bob Johnson; starting pitchers Bob Caruthers, Bert Blyleven, Jim Kaat, Tommy John, Deacon Phillippe, Sam Leever, Jim McCormick, Tony Mullane, Jesse Tannehill, Carl Mays, Will White, Luis Tiant, Charlie Buffington, Lew Burdette, and Gus Weyhing; and closers Rich Gossage, Bruce Sutter, Jeff Reardon, and Lee Smith. And if the 10-year requirement is ever relaxed, especially for those who played in the 19th century, the careers of Tommy Bond, Larry Corcoran, and Ed Morris should be reviewed. Catcher/infielder Joe Torre might receive serious consideration based on his overall contribution as a player and manager.

Of course, some still argue that Pete Rose and outfielder Joe Jackson should be in. But neither is on the ballot to receive Hall of Fame votes because of their independent banishments from the major leagues for gambling. In fact, Rose accepted a lifetime ban following an investigation of his gambling. (In 1991, the Hall of Fame Committee voted against any banned player or official being placed on the Hall of Fame Ballot unless he was reinstated.)

Dave Winfield and Kirby Puckett were elected by the Baseball Writers Association of America (BBWAA) in January 2001, and Bill Mazeroski and negro league pitcher Hilton Smith earned the honor via the Veterans Committee two months later. The BBWAA is made up of baseball writers who have covered the game for at least 10 years. To get elected by the esteemed BBWAA, a player must receive 75% of the vote.

Before the recent restructuring of the Veterans Committee and its rules for election, 12 votes (or 75% of the votes) from the 15-member committee were required for induction into the Hall of Fame. But in the summer of 2001, the Veterans Committee as we knew it was replaced by a group that features the surviving members of the Hall of Fame, the living recipients of the Ford C. Frick Award and the J. G. Taylor Spink Award, plus a few incumbent Veterans Committee members. This new group of 90 members will meet every two years (starting in 2003) to decide on deserving players, and every four years (also starting in 2003) to select deserving managers, executives, and umpires. The Veterans Committee was formed in 1953 with the object of giving players overlooked by the BBWAA another review to determine their Hall of Fame merit.

♦ Did you know pitcher Nolan Ryan, third baseman George Brett, and shortstop-outfielder Robin Yount were elected to the Hall of Fame in January of 1999 by the BBWAA, marking the first time since the very first election in 1936 that three first-year nominees were elected by the BBWAA? Carlton Fisk, who was inducted in 2000, just missed being the fourth in 1999, falling 43 votes shy.

64. *Which of the great, Hall of Fame Yankee managers directed the team to eight pennants and seven world championships after the Miller Huggins era and before the Casey Stengel era?*

ANSWER: Joe McCarthy

McCarthy managed the Yankees from 1931 to the early part of the 1946 season, reaching the 100-win mark six times during his Yankee tenure and never losing more than 71 games. Angered at his dismissal, McCarthy went to the rival Red Sox and led them to consecutive 96-win seasons in 1948 and 1949.

If current Yankee manager Joe Torre keeps up his pace, Huggins, McCarthy, and Stengel could have company. Torre has won four World Series for the Yankees since 1996, winning a record 14 straight World Series games in the process. In fact, the Yankees are 19-7 in World Series play since 1996. Torre's .731 World Series winning percentage is among the best in history. Torre joins Stengel as the only managers to win their first four World Series.

65. *Boston's Tracy Stallard surrendered Roger Maris' record-breaking 61st home run in 1961. But do you know which Oriole pitcher capitulated Maris' 60th?*

ANSWER: Jack Fisher

Fisher also allowed a home run to Ted Williams in the Boston Hall of Famer's final career at-bat. Maris tied Babe Ruth's single-season home run record in the Yankees' 158th game, four contests after the North Dakota native hit his 59th. Maris hit the historic 61st homer into Yankee Stadium's right-field bleachers during the regular-season finale on October 1. The fourth-inning shot off Stallard proved to be the only run of that game. When fan Sal Durante returned the ball to Maris following the game, Maris told the truck driver to keep the ball and make money off it. (Durante sold the ball for $5,000. By comparison, Mark McGwire's 70th home run ball fetched $3 million.)

But the chase for the home run record for Maris wasn't as exhilarating as the pursuit put on by McGwire and Sammy Sosa 37 years later. Since Maris didn't break or tie Ruth's record by the 154th game, Commissioner Ford Frick agreed that a clear distinction should be made in the record books for homers during a 154-game season and homers during a 162-game campaign.

Frick, a biographer and former ghost writer for "The Bambino," basically stripped the chase of its deserved drama. A smarter and less egotistical man would have given the occasion the stage it deserved, if only to enhance the romance of the sport he presided over. Instead, Frick (usually a righteous being with a great track record) infected an otherwise majestic season with cynicism—so much so that only 23,154 fans witnessed Maris' 61st homer in person on that October day.

It was one of many slights that Maris had to endure that summer and fall. Instead of being able to enjoy the chase, Maris endured a nightmare of a season. He received criticism, taunts, and threats almost continuously once it became clear he and Mickey Mantle had a chance at the record. Ardent Yankee fans harassed and booed their own right fielder, preferring that Mantle break the record because he was a "true" Yankee and a genuine superstar. Maris, who found his hair falling out from all the stress, also had to contend with ignorant followers and media members who claimed he was "not worthy" of the record because he was a "fluke" and had the advantage of eight more regular-season games than Ruth. Even Yankee teammates wanted Mantle to break the record. Maris could never quite fathom why Yankee fans, teammates, and media turned on a man playing for them.

Sadly, Maris passed away on December 14, 1985, with the distinction still being made in the record books between a 154-game season and a 162-game season. In 1991, Commissioner Fay Vincent finally removed the distinction, and recognized Maris as the undisputed single-season record holder.

Upon chasing Ruth's career home run record, Hank Aaron also endured ill treatment. Aaron told me he never had the chance to enjoy "the chase," instead having to fear for his and his family's lives and being forced to deal with a slew of hate mail (he received almost one million letters in 1973 and 1974) that frequently included ugly terms. Aaron is currently serving as the senior vice president of the Atlanta Braves.

66. *Name five of the six silver sluggers who have come away with at least seven batting titles.*

ANSWER: Ty Cobb (12), Tony Gwynn (eight), Honus Wagner (eight), Rod Carew (seven), Stan Musial (seven), and Rogers Hornsby (seven)

Gwynn won a fourth straight title in 1997 to surpass Musial and Hornsby and tie Wagner for the most batting crowns in NL history.

Cobb, whose lifetime .367 batting average remains the standard, won nine straight batting titles from 1907 to 1915 and earned his 12 batting crowns over a 13-year stretch. Cobb also stole 892 bases, drove in 1,933 runs, scored 2,45 times, belted 725 doubles, and legged out 296 triples. There was nothing Cobb couldn't do. The greatest competitor ever to step on a major league field, Cobb used any tactic he could use to gain an edge. Catcher Moe Berg once said of Cobb, "To him, a ballgame wasn't a mere athletic contest. It was a knock-'em-down, crush 'em, relentless war. He was their enemy and, if they got in his way, he ran right over them."

And that competitiveness did not cease after he retired from playing in 1928. During a 1947 old-timers game at Yankee Stadium, the 60-year-old Cobb advised opposing catcher Benny Bengough to move back. Cobb told Bengough he hadn't practiced his swing in a while and didn't want to club Bengough by accident. With Bengough far back behind the plate, Cobb laid down a beautiful bunt for an easy hit, and the embarrassed catcher had no chance once he finally caught up with the ball.

◆ Did you know Rogers Hornsby led the National League in batting average, on-base percentage, and slugging each year from 1920 to 1925? In perhaps the most dominating hitting stretch in NL history, Hornsby led the senior circuit in on-base percentage plus slugging percentage (OPS) 10 times from 1920 to 1931. Aside from winning seven batting championships, Hornsby led the National League in on-base percentage and slugging nine times each. Hornsby was the epitome of a tough out.

✦ Did you know Tony Gwynn's .372 mark in 1997 enabled the San Diego Padre batsmen to become the first NL player since Rogers Hornsby (1920–25) to hit .350 or better for five straight seasons? Gwynn hit .358 in 1993, .394 in 1994, .368 in 1995, and .353 in 1996. He retired with a .338 lifetime batting average, the highest of anyone who began his career after World War II and the 17th best all time.

67. *These two speedsters each stole home seven times in a season, one shy of the single-season record set by Ty Cobb in 1912. They are:*

A Pete Reiser and Lou Brock
B Pete Reiser and Rod Carew
C George Joseph Burns and Maury Wills
D Max Carey and Rickey Henderson
E Tim Raines and Vince Coleman

ANSWER: B

Although six of Cobb's eight thefts of home were on the back end (all seven of Carew's thefts of home were straight), Cobb pilfered home a record 50 times over his career. Max Carey accomplished the feat 33 times, with Burns (a .287 career hitter) marking 28 of his 383 thefts at home. Honus Wagner was fourth, with 27. Amazingly, Brock never stole home. In case you're wondering, Jackie Robinson stole home 19 times in the majors.

68. *In one of the worst trades in the history of the sport, Nolan Ryan, Don Rose, Leroy Stanton, and Francisco Estrada were traded to California for this shortstop who wound up being traded after just a year and a half in New York. Who was this disappointing infielder who came over to the Mets on December 10, 1971?*

ANSWER: Jim Fregosi

Fregosi, a career .265 hitter, batted .233 for the Mets over a 146-game span. A little known fact is that Ryan's wife didn't like living in New York—in fact she was terrified—and begged Ryan to request a trade.

69. *Who was Carl Hubbell's catcher when the Giant lefthander struck out Babe Ruth, Lou Gehrig, Jimmie Foxx, Al Simmons, and Joe Cronin in succession during the first two innings of that memorable 1934 All-Star Game?*

ANSWER: Gabby Hartnett

Hartnett caught the left-handed Hubbell, who allowed the first two runners to reach base. After Charlie Gehringer led off the first inning with a single and Heinie Manush followed with a walk, Hubbell regrouped with his screwball to fan Ruth, Gehrig, and Foxx, ending the frame. Hubbell then struck out Simmons and Cronin to begin the second. In all, the National League's Hubbell struck out six hitters over three scoreless innings, overshadowing winner Mel Harder, who allowed just one hit over five scoreless innings in relief for the American League.

In addition to being an excellent catcher who called a great game, Hartnett was a solid batter. A .297 hitter with 236 homers spanning a 20-year career, Hartnett was easily the best NL catcher of his era and perhaps the best the National League had ever known until Johnny Bench arrived on the scene three decades later.

♦ Did you know Boston's Pedro Martinez set an All-Star strikeout record by whiffing the first four batters in the 1999 mid-summer classic? Martinez punched out Barry Larkin, Larry Walker, Sammy Sosa, and Mark McGwire to start his assignment. Martinez earned game MVP honors with five strikeouts over two perfect innings. The record for strikeouts in a single All-Star Game is six, set by Carl Hubbell, and tied by Johnny Vander Meer (1943), Larry Jansen (1950), and Ferguson Jenkins (1967).

70. *Which batter ended Carl Hubbell's record All-Star streak of five strikeouts during that 1934 mid-summer classic?*

ANSWER: Bill Dickey

The New York Yankees Hall of Fame catcher Dickey, a contact hitter, singled with two strikes and two out in the second inning to snap Hubbell's memorable string of Ks. American League pitcher Lefty Gomez then became Hubbell's sixth overall strikeout victim that day. Hubbell, or "Meal Ticket" as he was nicknamed, allowed two hits and two walks, leaving after three innings with a 4-0 lead only to see the American League rebound to win, 9-7.

Dickey could be considered the best catcher in major league baseball's first 100 years. A masterful handler of pitchers, Dickey owned a "deadly accurate" throwing arm (as the Hall of Fame citation mentions) and was incredibly durable behind the plate in his 17 years as a Yankee catcher. His AL record of catching at least 100 games 13 years in a row remains standing some 60 years later.

Asked by manager Miller Huggins to focus on batting average in a lineup laden with such power hitters as Babe Ruth, Lou Gehrig, and Joe DiMaggio, the left-handed hitting Dickey obliged by reaching the .300 mark in 10 of his first 11 full seasons en route to a .313 lifetime mark. Dickey nevertheless became a home run hitter midway through his career without sacrificing his batting average. After hitting 76 homers over his first eight years, Dickey smashed 102 home runs from 1936 to 1939 to help the Yankees win four straight world titles. Dickey batted at least .302 each season, including a high of .362 in 1936 that remains unsurpassed by a catcher. Equally impressive, Dickey struck out just 289 times, or an average of just 17 whiffs per season. Although the All-Star Game was born six years into his career, Dickey still earned a trip to 11 mid-summer classics.

In addition to helping the Yankees win eight pennants and seven World Series as a team player, Dickey served as coach on 10 more pennant-winning Yankee clubs. His biggest contribution as coach was to tutor future Hall of Famer Yogi Berra. Although always a solid hitter, Berra eventually became an excellent defensive catcher thanks in no small part to Dickey's direction.

♦ Did you know Bill Dickey did not play at any other position than catcher during his major league career? Dickey played in 1,708 games behind the plate and served as a pinch-hitter in 81 other contests. Dickey also caught in all 38 World Series games he played in, committing just two errors and collecting 19 assists. A clutch performer, Dickey batted .438 in the 1932 World Series and an even .400 in the fall classic six years later. He also drove in 24 runners in his 38 series games.

71. *Many great North American baseball players were born in countries other than the United States. Match these players of All-Star caliber with their countries of origin:*

1	Roberto Clemente	A	Holland
2	Bert Blyleven	B	Mexico
3	Jorge Orta	C	Puerto Rico
4	Juan Marichal	D	Dominican Republic
5	Tony Oliva	E	Cuba

ANSWER: 1—C, 2—A, 3—B, 4—D, 5—E

Clemente became the first Latino player to reach the magical 3,000-hit plateau. Blyleven retired after the 1992 season with 287 wins and 3,701 strikeouts. Only Tommy John, at 288, came closer to 300 wins without reaching it.

In 1963, Marichal became the first Latino to throw a no-hitter, silencing Houston on June 15. A little more than two weeks later, the 25-year-old Marichal outdueled Warren Spahn, 1-0, in 16 innings as each pitcher went the distance. The feat was even more brilliant, considering that five future Hall of Fame batsmen were penciled in the starting lineups: Willie Mays, Willie McCovey, and Orlando Cepeda for the Giants, and Hank Aaron and Eddie Mathews for the Braves. A walk-off home run by Mays off the 42-year-old Spahn finally ended the masterful pitching duel. Marichal told me in 1999 that he twice refused manager Al Dark's request for relief. His reason at the time was "I didn't want that old man lasting longer than me."

♦ Did you know Roberto Clemente's Hall of Fame plaque was altered to reflect a cultural tradition? Instead of reading "Roberto Walker Clemente," the plaque will read "Roberto Clemente Walker" to preserve Latino heritage, in which a person's mother's maiden name traditionally follows the given last name.

♦ Did you know the Reds and Dodgers battled the longest scoreless duel in major league history, lasting 19 innings on September 11, 1946? Neither team scored as the game ended in a 0-0 tie at Ebbets Field. Cincinnati's Johnny Vander Meer started and pitched 15 innings, striking out 14, according to *The Baseball Chronology*. Hal Gregg started for Brooklyn and lasted 10 innings.

72. *George Gore and Billy Hamilton each stole seven bases in a game during the 19th century. Which three players share the record for the most bases swiped (six) in a game dating back to 1900?*

A Ty Cobb
B Eddie Collins
C Tris Speaker
D Maury Willis
E Otis Nixon
F Eric Young

ANSWER: B, E, F

Collins stole a half-dozen bases twice in a 12-day span in 1912 for the AL record; Nixon performed the feat in 1991, and Young did it on June 30, 1996. In the latter game, Young also pilfered three bases in one inning, tying a mark held by many players during a wild 16-15 win over the Dodgers.

73. *With a .300 batting average being the meter stick, who got the better of the other in head-to-head encounters over the course of their careers: Walter Johnson or Ty Cobb?*

ANSWER: Ty Cobb

In 245 at-bats spanning 67 games, Cobb hit .335 against Johnson, the pitcher most often acknowledged as the best of all time. Early in the second game of a twinbill on August 2, 1907, Cobb welcomed the man who would eventually be called "Big Train" by reaching on a bunt single (his only hit in four trips to the plate against Johnson in the pitcher's major league debut). Biographer Charles C. Alexander quoted Cobb regarding his first meeting against Johnson: "I encountered the most threatening sight I ever saw on a ball field. The ball hissed with danger." Cobb's career accomplishments against Johnson were a testament to his own greatness.

In the book *The Glory of Their Times,* Cobb's teammate Sam Crawford told author Lawrence Ritter: "Walter Johnson and I were very good friends, and once in a while, Walter would sort of give me a hit or two, just for old time's sake. But when Ty came up there, Walter always bore down all the harder. There was nothing he enjoyed more than fanning Ty Cobb. Cobb could never figure out why I did so well against Walter, while he couldn't hit him with a 10-foot pole." Cobb was such a great hitter (.367 lifetime mark) and manhandled so many pitchers that hitting .335 against a pitcher (even Johnson) gave the appearance of a struggle—even to his teammate. That's how good Cobb was.

♦ Did you know Ty Cobb was 15-for-46 (.326) versus Babe Ruth? All 15 hits were singles.

74. *Who said: "My first edict if I were commissioner of baseball would be to get rid of the designated hitter, to bring back the 25-man roster, to get rid of Astroturf, maintain smaller ballparks and revamp quality old ballparks. I'd outlaw video instant replays. I'd outlaw mascots. I'd put organic foods in the stands. I would make cold, pasteurized beer mandatory from small breweries located near the ballparks—no giant multinational breweries. I would bring back warm, roasted peanuts. Just the smell of grass and those warm, roasted peanuts should be enough to make people come to the park. I would just try to reduce it to an organic game; the way it used to be."*

ANSWER: Bill Lee

Red Sox lefthander Lee was truly unique in his opinions. Lee distinguished himself time and time again with off-the-wall comments that garnered him the nickname of "Spaceman." When he first saw Fenway Park's Green Monster, he asked, "Do they leave it there during games?" Lee, who put up a 119-90 career ledger, posted three straight 17-win seasons from 1973 to 1975.

♦ Did you know it took nine balls to walk a batter from the advent of baseball in 1876 until 1879? The figure changed to eight in 1880 and then dwindled to four by 1889. In 1888, three strikes were agreed upon for an out.

♦ Did you know the infield fly rule was first tested in 1895, then modernized in 1901? And did you know in 1914, there was a rule giving the runner at least three bases if a fielder attempts to stop the ball by throwing his glove or hat at the ball?

75. *Can you name this Hall of Fame executive who ignited the idea of farm systems to develop major league talent?*

ANSWER: Branch Rickey

The future general manager Rickey joined the Cardinals as a front office executive in 1916, after playing for the cross-town Browns until 1914. He started the farm systems because the Cardinals were in financial distress—they wore used uniforms, for crying out loud—and couldn't buy players. His farm system was so big that at one point, the Cardinals organization had over 50 farm clubs. Rickey, who managed the Browns from 1913 to 1915, managed the Cardinals from 1919 to 1925. His farm system worked so well that from 1926 to 1946, the Cardinals appeared in nine World Series, winning six of them. Not bad for a team that from 1892 to 1915 went 1,434-2,191 (a .396 winning percentage), finishing as high as third only once and finishing last on six occasions.

When Rickey resigned from the Cardinals after a difference of opinion with equally stubborn owner Sam Breadon, he left for the Dodgers organization and did the same thing for them, building the spring training complex at Vero Beach and transforming the franchise into a powerhouse.

Rickey may have been the most versatile man in major league history. Beginning as a player, Rickey also managed, served as general manager, president, majority stockholder, master innovator, vice president, and consultant. He ended as a Hall of Famer. Rickey was known for his shrewd trades and decisions, innovative skills, and a keen eye for talent. But more than anything, Rickey was perhaps the best baseball mind in major league history. Now there's a man whose brain I'd love to pick over a cup of coffee!

♦ Did you know, however, that the 1964 world champion Cardinals boasted only two regulars (Ken Boyer and Tim McCarver) from its system?

76. *There are some records that will remain as a standard throughout our lifetimes, but none are more likely to stand the test of our time like this durable pitcher's feat of 1,727 consecutive innings and 202 straight games without being relieved. Which one of these five pitchers holds the mark?*

A Vic Willis
B Kid Nichols
C Joe McGinnity
D Pud Galvin
E Jack Taylor

ANSWER: E

On June 20, 1901, Taylor started his streak for the St. Louis Cardinals and kept it going until he finally got knocked out of the box on August 13, 1906, as a Chicago Cub. Taylor pitched a record 187 consecutive complete games, and finished 278 of his 286 games started, albeit in an era almost void of relief pitchers. The streak includes 15 relief appearances, which he finished. The righthander wound up his 10-year career with a 152-139 record and a 2.67 ERA. Unless relievers go on strike, Taylor's workhorse records will never be broken.

♦ Did you know Cy Young completed 749 of his 815 starts or 91.9% of his starting assignments? Young's 749 complete games and 815 starts are records as unreachable as his 511 wins. Among those who started at least 250 games, Will White (1877–86) completed 394 of 401 starts for a record 98.25 ratio. Charles "Old Hoss" Radbourn's 489 complete games among his 503 career starts from 1881 to 1891 gave him a 97.22 ratio, the second best ever. Taylor's 97.20 ratio is third best. Over one season, it'll be tough to outdo Radbourn, who completed all 73 of his starts in 1884.

♦ Did you know Ted Lyons and Robin Roberts share the mark for most consecutive complete games since the live ball era began in 1920? With 28 straight complete games, Lyons (1941–46, with interruptions because of World War II) and Roberts (1952–53) were remembered when Oakland's Rick Langford hurled 28 complete games in 1980, 20 in succession.

77. *Who was the first Japanese position player to appear in the majors?*

ANSWER: Ichiro Suzuki

In 2001, Suzuki took the major leagues by storm, sweeping the AL Rookie of the Year and MVP Awards on a record-setting Seattle Mariners squad, whose success captured international interest. The left-handed catalyst won the AL batting title (.350), led the league with 242 hits and 56 stolen bases, and finished second with 127 runs scored, emphatically proving that his gaudy numbers in Japan were indeed indicative of his talent. A right fielder with dazzling speed, a good arm, and superb batting skills, Suzuki wanted to play in the majors sooner but was bound to a Japanese League contract through 2000. His jump to the majors was as successful as any optimist could have imagined.

In Japan, Suzuki established himself as the best player of the 1990s, winning every Pacific League batting title from 1994 to 2000. The 28-year-old, who is so popular in Japan he is simply known there as Ichiro, left his native land with a .353 career batting average.

Suzuki, who won the first of three consecutive MVP Awards in 1995, helped Orix, a city stricken by a tremendous earthquake, win the title in 1996 and the pennant the following year. The BlueWave contact hitter, who in 1994 became the first Japanese player to get 200 hits (210) in a season (a great feat, considering the 130-game schedule), participated in the Mariners' 1999 spring training before deciding to give the majors a try.

78. *Of the 13 pitchers to win three games in a World Series, six have done so without starting Game One. Can you name any three of the six to achieve this improbable feat?*

ANSWER: Bill Dinneen, Jack Coombs, Red Faber, Lew Burdette, Mickey Lolich, and Randy Johnson

Dinneen was the first to achieve the feat, doing so in 1903 for the world champion Boston Pilgrims. Dinneen was 3-1, with a 2.06 ERA in the eight-game series. Of the six performances, Coombs' in 1910 was the most implausible, because his Philadelphia Athletics needed only five games to beat the Cubs. Coombs (3-0, 3.33) won Games Two, Three, and Five of that fall classic. Faber of the White Sox won Games Two, Four, and Game Six as Chicago downed the New York Giants in 1917, four games to two. Faber was 3-1 with a 2.33 ERA, winning Game Five in relief.

Burdette was the most impressive of the group, winning all three of his starts (Games Two, Five, and Seven) with a minuscule ERA of 0.67 for the Milwaukee Braves against the New York Yankees in 1957. The Detroit Tigers received what they expected in the 1968 fall classic against St. Louis, a dominating pitching performance. But the source of such surprised many observers, including the Tigers. With 31-game winner Denny McLain unable to win in three starts of his own, Mickey Lolich was extraordinary, winning Games Two, Five, and Seven. The southpaw was 3-0 with a 1.67 ERA in 27 innings.

In 2001, Johnson of the Arizona Diamondbacks won Games Two, Six, and Seven against the Yankees, striking out 19 and allowing just nine hits in 17⅓ innings. Johnson (3-0, 1.04) won the finale in relief.

79. *Lou Gehrig leads the American League with 23 career grand slams. Who has hit the most in the National League?*

A Willie McCovey
B Chuck Klein
C Mike Schmidt
D Dave Kingman
E Willie Mays

ANSWER: A

McCovey hit a NL record 18, three of which came as a pinch-hitter. McCovey hit a grand slam in a record nine straight seasons, doing so each year from 1964 to 1972. Eddie Murray hit 19, placing him second on the all-time list. Jimmie Foxx and Ted Williams are tied for fourth place with 17. Murray's 278 career RBI with the bases loaded is the record since 1975, when statisticians started keeping track. Murray's lifetime batting average with the bases loaded was .406 (95-for-234).

♦ Did you know Seattle's Ken Griffey, Jr. set a major league single-season record with 13 three-run homers in 1996?

♦ Did you know Ken Griffey, Jr. twice tied Stan Musial's single-season record of 21 home runs by a lefthander off a southpaw pitcher? Griffey tied Musial's 1949 record in 1996 and 1998. Griffey told me that he is so successful against left-handed pitchers because his left-handed father always pitched to him when he was young, getting him accustomed at an early age to a southpaw delivery. Darryl Strawberry (1988), Ted Kluszewski (1955), and Babe Ruth (1926) each hit 20.

80. *How did the 1926 World Series end?*

ANSWER: Incredibly, Game Seven ended when the Yankees' Babe Ruth was thrown out trying to steal second base, igniting a Cardinals celebration. Most notably known for the battle between Tony Lazzeri and the aging Grover Alexander, this World Series could just as easily have been won by New York.

Trailing, 3-2, in the bottom of the ninth inning, the Yankees had the top of their batting order waiting for Alexander in relief. Earle Combs, who batted a team-high .357 in the series, grounded out to third for the first out. Mark Koenig, who hit a disappointing .125 in the series batting ahead of Ruth, also grounded out to third for out number two. Then the daunting Ruth came up and drew his 11th walk of the series, as his four home runs were too intimidating to challenge. Ruth stood on first base when the struggling Bob Meusel (who batted .238 and slugged just .381 in the classic, following a .315 regular season) stepped to the plate with Lou Gehrig (.348) on-deck.

Ruth, who had already stolen a base in the seven-game set, took off and was gunned down at second by Cardinals catcher Bob O'Farrell. The National League's MVP that year made a quick and accurate throw to second, where Rogers Hornsby applied the tag on Ruth to thwart the Yankees and end the series. Fellow member of the Society for American Baseball Research Steve Steinberg points out that Yankees General Manager Ed Barrow said it was the only dumb thing he ever saw Ruth do on a field.

In that Game Seven, the Cardinals overcame a 1-0 deficit by scoring three runs in the fourth inning. After O'Farrell tied the game with a sacrifice fly, shortstop Tommy Thevenow followed with a game-deciding two-run single to right field. Thevenow, who batted .256 during the regular season, came up big in the series, hitting .417 against the Yankees (10-for-24) with four RBI. Thevenow was also huge in a Game Two victory, in which he went 3-for-4, including an inside-the-park home run. Incidentally, Ruth's 11 walks matched the total of the entire Cardinals' lineup during the series as St. Louis strategically rendered 31 bases on balls to the fearsome Yankees' order.

◆ Did you know Babe Ruth stole 123 bases out of at least 240 attempts during his illustrious career? In 1926, Ruth was successful on 11 of 20 attempts. Most major league clubs didn't keep caught stealing records until 1920.

81. *How old was Bob Feller when he struck out 15 St. Louis Browns in his major league debut in 1936?*

ANSWER: 17

Feller, a righthander with a blazing speedball regarded as the fastest of his era, struck out eight of the first nine batters he faced in that August 23 debut, including seven consecutively. He beat the St. Louis Browns, 4-1, that day. Three weeks later, he struck out 17 Athletics to tie Dizzy Dean's modern major league mark, in addition to becoming the first pitcher to strike out his age in the century. Two years later, Feller set the modern record with 18 strikeouts in a game against the Tigers. In between, Feller graduated from his Iowa high school! He had 107 victories by the time he was 23 years of age. Feller went on to win seven AL strikeout titles in addition to throwing three no-hitters and 12 one-hitters. The latter achievement remains unsurpassed.

82. *Joe Adcock, Ed Delahanty, Rocky Colavito, Mike Schmidt, Bobby Lowe, Mark Whiten, Bob Horner, Willie Mays, Pat Seerey, Chuck Klein, Lou Gehrig, and Gil Hodges have all hit four home runs in a game. Can you place them in chronological order according to when they hit their four homers? (Dates are not necessary, just the order.)*

ANSWER: Bobby Lowe (1894), Ed Delahanty (1896), Lou Gehrig (1932), Chuck Klein (1936), Pat Seerey (1948), Gil Hodges (1950), Joe Adcock (1954), Rocky Colavito (1959), Willie Mays (1961), Mike Schmidt (1976), Bob Horner (1986), and Mark Whiten (1993)

Lowe accomplished the feat in South Boston's small Congress Street Grounds, a park the Beaneaters were forced to use because a fire destroyed their South End Grounds two weeks earlier. All four of Lowe's homers were hit off the right-handed Elton "Icebox" Chamberlain (a 157-game winner). Lowe is the only lead-off hitter of the bunch.

All four of Delahanty's home runs were also hit off the same pitcher, a reflection of the days when pitchers completed their starts almost regardless of effectiveness. Since Delahanty homered four times off righthander Adonis Terry (a 197-game winner), no other hitter has homered four times off the same pitcher in the same game.

Adcock's quartet of home runs were hit off four different Dodger pitchers: Don Newcombe, Erv Palica, Pete Wojey, and Johnny Podres. Adcock's awesome power display at Ebbets Field also included a double, allowing him to set a still-standing major league record with 18 total bases in a game. Incredibly, Adcock swung the bat just five times and, according to Retrosheet (a baseball research organization), faced just seven pitches all game. Now, that's efficient.

Horner was the only player of the group to hit four homers in a losing effort during the 1900s, doing so in an 11-8 loss to Montreal on July 6, 1986. Ed Delahanty's four-homer performance on July 13, 1896, was wasted by the Phillies in a defeat to the Cubs. During his four-homer game, Mark Whiten also tied Jim Bottomley's single-game record of 12 RBI for the greatest single-game offensive performance in major league history. Whiten and Schmidt were both sixth-place hitters, the lowest placed of the dozen.

◆ Did you know Bobby Lowe, Lou Gehrig, Rocky Colavito, and Mike Schmidt accomplished their feats of hitting four home runs in a game in four consecutive at-bats? Gehrig, in fact, had two more at-bats after his fourth homer on June 3, 1932, grounding out and then flying out to the deepest part of Shibe Park in center field.

◆ Did you know three of the 12 players who hit four home runs in a game never reached the 100-homer plateau? It took Mark Whiten nine years to reach the 100-homer mark, doing so in 1998. Whiten concluded the 2000 season with 105 homers. Bobby Lowe and Ed Delahanty were considered power threats, but played in the Dead Ball Era. As for Pat Seerey, his limited 1,815 at-bats did him in. Seerey hit just eight more homers in the rest of his career.

83. *Stan Musial and* _____ *share the record of five home runs in a doubleheader, although this Padre slugger stood alone with 13 RBI in a double dip before Mark Whiten's offensive explosion on September 7, 1993 (one RBI in the first game, 12 RBI in the second game) equaled his efforts. Fill in the blank.*

ANSWER: Nate Colbert

Colbert did it on August 1, 1972, leading San Diego to a doubleheader sweep, 9-0 and 11-7, over the Atlanta Braves.

♦ Did you know then eight-year-old Nate Colbert was in attendance to witness Stan Musial's five-homer doubleheader on May 2, 1954, at Sportsman's Park? Talk about fate.

84. *Name any one of the three men who have achieved the cycle three times, and name either of the two players to accomplish the cycle in each of the current major leagues. (Hint: A member of the latter group also scored major league history's one millionth run.)*

ANSWER: Babe Herman, Bob Meusel, and John Reilly; Bob Watson and John Olerud

Herman, Meusel, Reilly each turned three cycles; Watson and Olerud are the only players with a cycle in the National League as well as the American League. Herman recorded two cycles in 1931 for Brooklyn and one for the Cubs two years later. Meusel recorded a cycle for the Yankees in 1921, 1922, and 1928. Reilly, a little-known right-handed batter who played in Cincinnati his entire major league career, achieved a pair of cycles in 1883 for the Red Stockings of the American Association and a third for the Reds of the National League in 1890.

On June 16, 2001, Olerud became the second player to achieve the cycle in each modern major league, doing so for the Seattle Mariners four years after performing the feat for the New York Mets. (Olerud's second cycle came about in an interleague game, so both his cycles were against National League clubs.) Watson achieved the cycle in 1977 for the Houston Astros and in 1979 for the Boston Red Sox. Watson, who also scored baseball's one millionth run, received one million Tootsie Rolls and a Rado watch for scoring the historic run on May 4, 1975, for the Astros in Candlestick Park.

♦ Did you know there have been 254 cycles in major league history through 2001? Of those 254, 127 have been accomplished in the National League, 107 in the American League, 18 in the American Association, one in the Federal League, one in the Players League, and none in the Union Association.

♦ Did you know Mike Lansing's cycle for the Rockies on June 18, 2000, is believed to be the fastest cycle in history? In a game against the Arizona Diamondbacks, Lansing tripled in the first inning, homered in the second, doubled in the third, and singled in the fourth frame.

♦ Did you know Mel Ott remains the youngest player to ever achieve a cycle? On May 16, 1929, Ott of the Giants was a mere 20 years and 75 days old.

85. *Which team is Japanese baseball's best and most storied, with 19 championships?*

ANSWER: The Yomiuri Giants

The Yomiuri "Tokyo" Giants have dominated their sport much like the New York Yankees have. The Giants have owned their league (first the Japanese League and then the Central League), winning the pennant or league title 35 times. (There was only one league from 1937 to 1949.) Of their 29 trips to the Japanese Series, the Giants won 19 times. Only the installation of a draft kept the Giants from further monopolizing the league.

Tetsuharu Kawakami was the cleanup hitter of the earlier Giants teams, and was in part responsible for 14 pennants during his 21-year playing career (1938–58). He hit a then-record .377 in 1951. He managed the Giants from 1961 to 1974. In those 14 years, his Giants won 11 pennants and he managed arguably the two greatest Japanese players of all time: Sadaharu Oh and Shigeo Nagashima. Nagashima came up in 1958 and Oh entered the scene in 1959.

Like all the great teams in the United States (the 1927 and 1961 Yankees, and the 1937 Homestead Grays are prime examples), the Giants had Oh batting third and Nagashima cleanup for the greatest three-four punch in Japanese history, combining for 1,312 home runs.

Oh, like Gehrig, was always under the shadow of the hitter behind him. When Oh hit his 55 home runs in 1964, Nagashima engaged the press (no pun intended) with Japan's number one sports story of the year: his marriage. And Oh also took a back seat during his 1974 Triple Crown season (his second in a row) when Nagashima announced his retirement and hit his 444th homer in his last game. The next season, Nagashima took over as manager of the club.

♦ Did you know the Seibu Lions won eight Japan Series titles from 1982 to 1992? The same franchise that played in Nishitetsu and defeated the Yomiuri Giants in three straight Japan Series from 1956 to 1958 is considered the second-best Japanese franchise. After sweeping the 1957 series, the 1958 Lions incredibly overcame a three-games-to-none deficit in the series to win its third straight title. The Lions entered the 2000 season with 11 Japan titles.

86. *Jim Bagby, Jr. ended Joe DiMaggio's hitting streak at 56 on July 17, 1941, holding the Yankee center of attraction hitless in the eighth inning. Which Indian started the game and held DiMaggio hitless for his first three plate appearances?*

ANSWER: Al Smith

A lefthander whose mediocre 99-101 record spanned 12 years, Smith retired DiMaggio twice on sharply hit grounders to third and walked him in between. Bagby induced DiMaggio into a double play with the bases loaded in the eighth inning to end the magnificent stretch before 67,468 fans at Municipal Stadium.

The game ended a thrilling ride that captured the nation's attention. Whether in New York, Oklahoma, or California, people were glued to their radios, eager to hear what DiMaggio had done. "Did he get a hit?" fans would ask strangers in the streets. "Yeah, it's up to 32," the strangers would reply, without ever having to utter the name DiMaggio. Everyone was thinking about The Streak. The graceful, elegant, and reserved superstar transcended baseball and established his place as an American icon. Revered, DiMaggio was immortalized in Ernest Hemingway's novel *The Old Man and the Sea,* and in the Paul Simon and Art Garfunkel song "Mrs. Robinson."

♦ Did you know Joe DiMaggio started another 17-game hitting streak the next day, on July 18, 1941? No American Leaguer has put together a hitting streak of even 40 games since then, although Paul Molitor of Milwaukee reached 39 in 1987.

♦ Did you know Joe's brother, Dominic DiMaggio, had a 34-game hitting streak for the Red Sox in 1949? Playing in the shadows of his brother Joe and teammate Ted Williams, Dom is truly one of the most underrated players in the history of the game. The seven-time All-Star was a superb lead-off hitter and an outstanding defensive center fielder, spending all 11 years in a Red Sox uniform, although he only batted three times in his last (1953) season. The .298 career hitter, with a .383 career on-base percentage, was one of three players in the 20th century to average more than 100 runs scored per full season. During his 10 full campaigns, Dom DiMaggio totaled more hits than anyone else and trailed only Williams in runs scored. Dominic remains one of only five outfielders in history to collect 500 putouts in a single season. His lack of recognition stems in large part from his ballpark absence of three entire years to serve in the World War II effort.

87. *Match these sluggers with their career home run totals:*

1	Mel Ott	A	573
2	Duke Snider	B	382
3	Harmon Killebrew	C	354
4	Jimmie Foxx	D	426
5	Al Simmons	E	534
6	Mickey Mantle	F	511
7	Billy Williams	G	307
8	Ron Santo	H	536
9	Lee May	I	342
10	Frank Howard	J	407

ANSWER: 1—F, 2—J, 3—A, 4—E, 5—G, 6—H, 7—D, 8—I, 9—C, 10—B

Mantle, the Yankees' handsome, gregarious, and powerful center fielder who was loved and admired by many people, probably could have reached the 600-homer plateau had it not been for his chronic injuries and alcohol dependence. Thinking he would die young of cancer like his father, two uncles, and other relatives, Mantle partied furiously, gulping alcoholic beverages in abundance until the wee hours of the morning.

The shy youngster from Commerce, Oklahoma, took some time to adjust to the big city lights and expectations. A fragile superstar who often played in pain but at first didn't quite satisfy critical and spoiled Yankee fans, Mantle finally became a fan favorite during the

1961 season as the embattled Roger Maris took aim at the home run record. Ironically, it was Mantle's flaws and his frailty that endeared him to the fans and the media. Dying of liver cancer in 1995, the 63-year-old Mantle gave fans even more reason to idolize him when he advised all to avoid being like him—he used the dying Mickey Mantle as an example of what can happen to those who are careless with what God has given them.

Of course, despite his lifestyle, Mantle put up great numbers with his enormous talents. Blessed with blinding speed (before injuries slowed him down) and the owner of a ferocious swing from either side of the plate, Mantle has done more than stand 10th on the all-time home run list (through 2001). He also collected 2,415 hits, 1,509 RBI, and 1,677 runs scored. Nicknamed the "Commerce Comet," Mantle won a trio of MVP Awards, earned a Triple Crown, played in 16 All-Star Games, and set numerous World Series records.

♦ Did you know Yankees General Manager George Weiss basically blackmailed the married Mickey Mantle into signing reduced contracts? Weiss, who hired private detectives to follow many of his players at night, had photographs of Mantle with different women in compromising situations.

88. *Match these sluggers with their career home run totals:*

1	Norm Cash	A	442
2	Dick Allen	B	370
3	Johnny Mize	C	548
4	Eddie Mathews	D	351
5	Al Kaline	E	377
6	Gil Hodges	F	359
7	Ted Williams	G	512
8	Mike Schmidt	H	399
9	Dave Kingman	I	521

ANSWER: 1—E, 2—D, 3—F, 4—G, 5—H, 6—B, 7—I, 8—C, 9—A

Like Mathews, the enthusiastic Ernie Banks also hit 512 homers. Banks, known for his zest of the game and his "let's play two" mantra, provided sad Cub fans a great joy with his 500th home run in 1970. Banks combined with Williams to form a powerful one-two punch for the Cubs. Mize was the only member of this group to hit 50 homers in a season, belting a league-leading 51 in 1947. Kaline became the first player to hit at least 300 home runs without the benefit of a 30-homer season. Harold Baines (384) is the only other player to have hit at least 300 home runs without the benefit of a single 30-homer season. Willie McCovey also hit 521 home runs.

◆ Did you know Dave Kingman and Darrell Evans are the only two eligible players to have hit 400 home runs and not be in the Hall of Fame? Kingman's 442 homers are 28th on the all-time list entering the 2002 season. Evans' total of 414 is 32nd on the list.

89. *Who is Don Denkinger?*

ANSWER: Umpire in the 1985 World Series

Denkinger is best remembered as the umpire who single-handedly changed the outcome of the 1985 World Series. Kansas City was being shut out, 1-0, by a St. Louis Cardinals team that had not blown a lead in the ninth inning all year and was three outs away from a world championship. But Denkinger gave the Royals life, opening their coffin.

Leading off the bottom of the ninth, Royals pinch-hitter Jorge Orta greeted rookie closer Todd Worrell with a slow roller toward first. First baseman Jack Clark fielded the ball and tossed it to Worrell covering the bag. Orta was clearly beaten to first. (The replay showed Orta barely on the screen the instant Worrell caught the ball while stepping on the base.) But Denkinger inexplicably ruled Orta safe, bewildering many an observer, including the Cardinals squad. The nightmarish sequence was just beginning.

The next batter, Steve Balboni, fouled off a sure out to Clark. But the first baseman lost his concentration and dropped the ball. With a second chance, Balboni singled to left for a two-on, no-out situation. After Onix Concepcion was inserted as the pinch-runner in place of the hefty Balboni, catcher Jim Sundberg tried to sacrifice the runners over, but instead forced Orta out at third. Following a passed ball, Hal McRae was intentionally walked to load the bases. With Concepcion standing on third and the slow-a-foot Sundberg occupying second, manager Dick Howser inserted John Wathan to run for McRae at first and sent Dane Iorg to the plate. Batting for Dan Quisenberry, the left-handed Iorg followed with a single to right, plating Concepcion with the tying run and Sundberg with the winning run, just ahead of the throw by Andy Van Slyke. That sent the series to a seventh game.

Demoralized more by Denkinger's call than by Clark's dropped foul and the subsequent rally, the Cardinals were hammered, 11-0, in Game Seven. Denkinger was the home plate umpire in that finale and had to eject frustrated Cardinals manager Whitey Herzog for arguing midway through the game. One batter later in that fifth inning, Denkinger had to contend with and eject the livid Joaquin Andujar for charging the plate and arguing vehemently. Andujar was so angry that he had to be restrained by his teammates, drawing a suspension that was carried out at the start of the following season.

In an interview with *The Sporting News*, Herzog claimed, "In 1982, I won a World Series because [an umpire] misses a call [a third strike instead called ball four, helping the Cardinals win Game Two] on Lonnie Smith. In 1985, I lost one because a guy misses a call at first base. It shouldn't be like that." Herzog's admission notwithstanding, don't ever tell a Cardinals fan that the calls evened out. And don't ever tell a St. Louis native that Denkinger was an otherwise solid AL umpire who called balls and strikes for three decades sans incident—including such gems as the 1978 play-off between the Yankees and Red Sox and Game Seven of the 1991 World Series between the Twins and Braves. Trust me on this one.

90. *Match these superstars with their feats:*

1 Ed Delahanty   A the youngest batting champion (at 20 years
2 Sam Crawford   old)
3 Darrell Evans   B the only player to win a batting title in the
4 Ted Williams   National and American Leagues
5 Al Kaline   C one of only four players with a home run title
                         in the National and American Leagues
                     D the oldest batting champion (at 40 years old)
                     E the first hitter with a 40-homer season in the
                         National and American Leagues

ANSWER: 1—B, 2—C, 3—E, 4—D, 5—A

In 1901, Crawford hit 16 home runs for the Reds to pace the National League and, seven years later, hit seven for the Tigers to pace the junior circuit. Buck Freeman was actually the first to win a home run title in two different leagues, hitting 25 for the Washington Nationals in 1899, and 13 four years later for the Boston Pilgrims. Fred McGriff became the third such player when he hit 36 in 1989 for the Blue Jays and 35 three years later for the Padres. McGwire is the fourth batter to do so, winning the home run title for Oakland in 1987 and 1996, and leading the National League for the Cardinals in 1998 and 1999. Evans was joined by Mark McGwire, David Justice, Ken Griffey, Jr., and Shawn Green as the only players to hit 40 homers in a season as a member of each league.

At 40, Williams hit a league-best .329 in 1958. In 1957, he impressed everyone by batting a league-best .388. In 1955, Kaline led the league with a .340 batting average, 321 total bases and 200 hits. The youngster never again led in any of those categories over the last 19 seasons of his steady, 22-year Hall of Fame career.

◆ Did you know Sam Crawford hit a record 51 career inside-the-park home runs? Tom Leach hit 48, Ty Cobb hit 47, Honus Wagner legged out 45, and Tris Speaker had 36. Of Wagner's 45 inside-the-park homers, a record five came with the bases loaded. Leach's four inside-the-park grand slams are second, and Joe Jackson's three are third.

91. *Southpaw Carl Hubbell still holds the longest winning streak by a pitcher, racking up 24 consecutive victories over the 1936 and 1937 seasons. But Hall of Famer _____ owns the record of 19 consecutive victories at the outset of a season. Fill in the blank.*

ANSWER: Rube Marquard

Marquard accomplished his feat in 1912 (the streak would have been 20 by today's standard). Marquard, who also won his last two decisions the previous year, ended the 1912 campaign with a 26-11 mark. The second best start belongs to reliever Elroy Face, who won his first 17 decisions in 1959 en route to an 18-1 campaign. Face, by the way, also won his last five decisions in 1958 for a total of 22 straight wins. Roger Clemens in 2001 began the season 20-1 en route to a 20-3 ledger and a record sixth Cy Young award.

Dave McNally (20-7) of the 1969 Baltimore Orioles and Johhny Allen (15-1) of the 1937 Cleveland Indians share the AL record with 15-0 starts. In fact, Allen's only loss in 1937 came about on the final day of that season—a heart-breaking 1-0 defeat to Detroit in which the game's lone run scored on an error.

For winning streaks during a season, Marquard and Tim Keefe (1888) share the record of 19. (Hubbell won his last 16 decisions in 1936 and first eight the following season.) Hubbell, Marquard, and Keefe each accomplished his feat for the New York Giants. The AL record for most consecutive wins during a single season is 16, shared by four pitchers: Walter Johnson and Joe Wood in 1912 (the same season as Marquard's streak), Lefty Grove in 1931, and Schoolboy Rowe three years later. (The venerable Mickey Cochrane caught Grove and Rowe during their streaks.)

McNally and Allen's joint AL standard of 17 consecutive wins over more than one season fell by the wayside in 1999 as Roger Clemens of the New York Yankees won 20 straight, dating back to the 1998 season with Toronto. For good measure, Clemens in 2001 became the first player with a pair of winning streaks that stretched to at least 16 games.

♦ Did you know "Smokey" Joe Wood and Walter Johnson dueled in one of the most hyped matchups in history during the 1912 season? On September 6 at Fenway Park, Wood outpitched "Big Train," 1-0, to extend his streak to 14 en route to 16. Johnson's 16-game win streak had ended on August 26. Wood finished that season with a spectacular 34-5 ledger, and Johnson was a stellar 33-12.

♦ Did you know Lefty Grove had his 16-game winning streak end on a misjudged fly ball in a 1-0 loss during the 1931 season? Trying to set an AL record with a 17th straight winning decision, Grove saw his streak come to an end (against the pitiful St. Louis Browns, of all teams). Engaged in a scoreless duel, young outfielder Jim Moore, who was substituting for the injured Al Simmons, misplayed a lazy fly. The temperamental Grove not only let Moore have it, but also smashed everything in sight in the clubhouse and even had a few choice words for Simmons. Grove argued it would have never happened with Simmons out there. According to Jim Kaplan, author of *Lefty Grove: American Original*, "Lefty never, ever forgave Al Simmons."

92. *A May 1981 college baseball playoff game pinned Yale against St. Johns. Both teams went scoreless as each starter spent the first 11 innings baffling his opponents; in fact St. Johns was hitless as well.*

*In the 12th inning, the Yale hurler lost his no-hitter and the game
to the Redmen and their southpaw, 1-0. Name either of the starters.*

ANSWER: Ron Darling and Frank Viola

Darling was the Yale righthander and Viola was St. Johns' star
lefthander. Both Darling and Viola went on to have solid careers in
the majors. Darling won 136 games over a 13-year career that included a 1986 world championship with the New York Mets. Viola
was just a bit more successful, earning 176 wins over a 15-year career
that included a 1988 Cy Young Award, a pair of 20-win campaigns,
and a 1987 World Series MVP with the champion Minnesota Twins.

♦ Did you know there are two World Series MVP Awards? The familiar one
endorsed by Major League Baseball and used in the *World Series Media Guide*
is the MVP trophy given out by *Sport* magazine, which began its presentation in 1955 and usually includes the gift of a Corvette. But in 1949, the New
York chapter of the BBWAA established the Babe Ruth Award, to be given to
the most valuable player in each World Series, in honor of the legend who
had passed away the previous year. Venerable historian and *Total Baseball*
contributor Bill Deane wrote "[the *Sport* MVP] has eclipsed the Babe Ruth
Award in prestige and public recognition" and pointed out that the original
honor isn't announced as promptly as the *Sport* award. From 1955 through
2000, the two World Series MVP bodies differed in their choices 14 times.
From 1949 to 1954, the following players won the only existing World Series
MVP trophy at the time (the Babe Ruth Award): Joe Page, Jerry Coleman, Phil
Rizzuto, Johnny Mize, Billy Martin, and Dusty Rhodes.

93. *Which three teams have never pitched a no-hitter?*

ANSWER: The New York Mets, the San Diego Padres, and the Colorado Rockies

The Mets, the oldest of the three aforementioned franchises,
have 21 one-hitters to their credit. Heck, even the Florida Marlins,
who entered the majors with the Rockies in 1993, have thrown three
no-hitters already.

♦ Did you know San Diego is also among just three teams without a cycle?
Florida and Tampa Bay are the other two teams.

♦ Did you know Philadelphia Athletics teammates Mickey Cochrane, Pinky Higgins, and Jimmie Fox each had a cycle in a 13-day span, from August 2 to August 14, 1933?

♦ Did you know the Mets are the only team which entered the majors prior to 1993 yet to boast an MVP Award winner? The Padres finally won their first MVP when Ken Caminiti garnered the award for his efforts in 1996, and the Mariners received their first MVP plaque in 1997 after the tremendous season put forth by Ken Griffey, Jr.

94. *Who played center field and went 4-for-4 on April 30, 1946, the day Bob Feller became the only pitcher to no-hit the Yankees in Yankee Stadium?*

ANSWER: Bob Lemon

Lemon subsequently transformed into a pitcher of Hall of Fame caliber. After making the transition from a lowly hitting infielder, Lemon became a great pitcher and actually pitched a no-hitter just two years later, on June 30. He then became an outstanding pitcher for the Cleveland Indians (joining a powerful rotation consisting of Feller, Mike Garcia, and Early Wynn), winning 20 games seven times over a nine-year stretch from 1948 to 1956. The seven-time All-Star retired with an impressive 207-128 mark.

Lemon's pitching ability was discovered, of all places, in Hawaii during World War II. Serving in the Navy, Lemon joined a service team there and was asked to pitch after injuries sidelined the team's hurlers. Lemon was great, displaying a sensational curveball. Upon his return to the majors, Indians manager Lou Boudreau was on the cusp of releasing Lemon when a few players told Boudreau of Lemon's gift on the mound. Incredibly, Lemon refused at first to pitch, unwilling to give up his dream of becoming a starting infielder. Boudreau finally convinced Lemon, and the rest is history.

95. *Name either of the two teams to go through an entire season without being shut out.*

ANSWER: The Yankees (1932) and the Reds (2000)

The Yankees went from August 3, 1931, through August 2, 1933, with nary a shutout thrown against them. The 2000 Reds rebounded from being blanked by the Mets in a one-game play-off the previous October to duplicate the Yankees' feat. Those Reds weren't blanked until May 24, 2001, ending the National League's longest such streak at 208 games.

The 1993 Phillies almost accomplished the feat before being blanked on September 30, falling seven games short of the then-NL record of 181 games, set by the 1893–95 Phillies. The 2001 Rangers were blanked in their penultimate game.

The Yankees' mark of 308 consecutive games with at least one run scored comfortably remains the major league standard. The Yankees, of course, benefited from a loaded lineup that featured Babe Ruth, Lou Gehrig, Tony Lazzeri, Bill Dickey, Earle Combs, and the often-overlooked Ben Chapman. The infielder-turned-outfielder provided speed, versatility, and outstanding defense to a team that already boasted plenty of power. The right-handed Chapman brought with him a level of multi-faceted skills that turned heads and helped the Yankees capture the 1932 world championship. Chapman led the American League in steals each year from 1931 to 1933, averaging 42 thefts as well as 109 RBI, 111 runs, 12 home runs, 10 triples, and 35 doubles over that time span. Chapman was a poor man's Bobby Bonds.

96. *This pitcher shut out the Yankees on August 3, 1933, ending New York's record string of 309 consecutive games without being blanked. Name this southpaw.*

ANSWER: Lefty Grove

Philadelphia Athletics' Grove that year registered his seventh straight 20-win season, pacing the American League with 24 victories, a .750 winning percentage, and 21 complete games. The 1933 season also marked the first time in five years he didn't win the ERA crown, although he still finished a respectable fourth. For all his greatness, however, Grove was traded that offseason to the Boston Red Sox by Athletics owner-manager Connie Mack as part of a Depression salary dump. Mack received $125,000 in return. Grove spent eight seasons with the Red Sox, for whom he recorded his 300th and final victory in 1941. Not bad for a pitcher who was once traded in the minor leagues for an outfield fence!

97. _____ *doubled for career hit number 3,000 in the final plate appearance of his 1972 season and career. Fill in the blank.*

ANSWER: Roberto Clemente

Clemente belted an 0-1 curveball off the Mets' Jon Matlack for the historic hit on September 30, a Saturday afternoon game. Although three days later Clemente entered as a defensive replacement in the ninth inning of the season finale, his 3,000th hit represented his last regular-season trip to the plate. Clemente went 4-for-17, with a homer and three walks in the ensuing National League Championship Series against the victorious Cincinnati Reds.

Clemente was killed in a plane crash on New Year's Eve three months later. On the last day of 1972, Clemente boarded a DC-7 in San Juan, Puerto Rico. It was packed with 16,000 pounds of supplies that he had helped gather for the victims of an earthquake in Nicaragua. But shortly after taking off, the pilot, whose license had been suspended, had trouble controlling the overloaded plane. A few seconds later, one of the engines caught fire and the DC-7 plunged into the Caribbean Sea off the island's coast. The 38-year-old Clemente's body was never found.

Some people choose to remember his cannon arm, which helped him garner 12 consecutive Gold Gloves, or his aggressive swing that netted nothing but line drives to the tune of four batting titles, 12 All-Star selections, and an MVP Award. He is also remembered for his hustle, his desire to win, and his drive to be recognized for the sake and pride of his people. Other associates recall how he personally touched them. Although the Pittsburgh Pirate right fielder did plenty on the field to leave behind a strong legacy, in the end it was his off-the-field contributions that touched the hearts of everyone. Clemente, a proud black Puerto Rican, worked tirelessly to help poor people and to eradicate racial bigotry. He once said, "I work with the rich and live among the poor."

Puerto Rico was silenced by the death of Clemente. The city of Pittsburgh lost a hero. Major league baseball lost a warrior. And the world lost a great humanitarian. Commissioner Bowie Kuhn aptly stated that Clemente "had about him the touch of royalty." Kuhn, normally a stoic and reserved man, delivered a heart-warming statement at Clemente's posthumous Hall of Fame induction. It included the following passage: "So very great was he as a player. So very great was he a leader. So very great was he a humanitarian in the cause of his fellow men. So very great was he an inspiration to the young and to all of us in baseball and throughout the world of sports. And so very great was his devotion to young people everywhere and particularly to the young people of his native island of Puerto Rico. Having said all those words, they are very inadequate to describe the real greatness of Roberto Walker Clemente."

♦ Did you know the DC-7 that crashed and killed Hall of Famer Roberto Clemente had been smashed into a concrete wall earlier in the month and was carrying two tons more than its weight limit? The flight engineer was an unqualified mechanic. The plane had scarcely been used in four months, co-pilot Arthur Rivera had had his license suspended for 180 days that year, and witnesses said they saw fire on the left side of the plane as it took off. Of the five who died on the plane, only pilot Jerry Hill's body was found. The plane didn't take off until 9:00 P.M. on December 31, 1972, 17 hours after its originally scheduled departure time.

♦ Did you know Roberto Clemente was a part of the first all-black starting lineup, which included a few Latinos, during the 1971 season? On September 1, the Pittsburgh Pirates fielded a lineup that included Al Oliver at first base, Rennie Stennett at second, Jackie Hernandez at short, Dave Cash at third, Willie Stargell in left, Gene Clines in center, Clemente in right, Manny Sanguillen behind the plate, and Doc Ellis on the mound. The Pirates beat the Phillies, 10-7. The 1971 Pirates team included seven African Americans, six Latinos, and one Polish American.

98. *During the early part of the 1969 season, New York columnist Dick Young once asked this Chicago Cub, "What do you think of our Mets?" The Cub replied, "Are you trying to compare the Mets to us?" Name this Cub who ate his words as the Mets won the division.*

ANSWER: Ron Santo

The third baseman hit .289 with 29 home runs and 123 RBI during the season in which his Cubs led by as many as 9½ games in August, only to see the Mets (who had been finishing an average of

41 games out of first in their first seven years) win 38 of their last 49 games.

Santo had further provoked the Mets by excessively celebrating after his Cubs won the opener of a three-game set in July. It angered the Mets' coaching staff, which called Santo's act "bush" and immature. The Mets were intent on making Santo eat his words. And he did look bewildered, mumbling something about not believing what had just happened after New York won the last two games of the three-game set in Wrigley Field to head into the All-Star break just 3½ games back.

During their season-ending 49-game stretch, the Mets played a crucial two-game series with the Cubs at Shea that began on September 8. The first game, which New York won to pull within 1½ games of Chicago, was best remembered for a black cat—that classic symbol of bad fortune—that scooted into the Cubs' dugout. The Mets swept the brief series and captured first place for keeps on September 10. The Mets won the division by a whopping eight games, despite having only one player (Ron Taylor) on the team with post-season experience.

♦ Did you know Tom Seaver pitched a memorable near-perfect game to fuel the Mets' chase of the Cubs on July 9, 1969? Perfect with one out in the ninth inning, Seaver and 59,083 Shea Stadium fans watched with disappointment as the Cubs' Jimmy Qualls (a little-used, weak-hitting outfielder) ruined the perfecto with a slap single to left-center field. Seaver stranded the rookie Qualls, preserving the 4-0, one-hit shutout. For the right-handed Qualls, that single represented one of just 31 career hits.

99. *What is Houston pitcher Ken Johnson best known for?*

ANSWER: Throwing a no-hitter game and losing it

The right-handed Johnson of the Houston Colt .45s became the first pitcher in history to throw a nine-inning, complete game no-hitter and lose, as he did by the score of 1-0 on April 23, 1964, to the Cincinnati Reds. The Colt .45s committed a pair of errors in the ninth inning, handing the six-foot four-inch control artist the loss. Johnson finished the season at 11-16, but rebounded with three straight winning campaigns after being traded to the Braves the following season.

The 1964 contest remains the only complete game no-hitter to result in a loss. The only other official no-hitter to end in a loss was the combined effort of Baltimore's Steve Barber and Stu Miller on April 30, 1967. Detroit beat them, 2-1. Although later stripped of its no-hitter label, Andy Hawkins' performance on July 1, 1990, also deserves a mention. Pitching for the Yankees against the White Sox at Comiskey Park, Hawkins held the ChiSox hitless but lost by a score of 4-0 due in great part to three Yankee errors in the bottom of the eighth inning.

100. *After being burned for ignoring Babe Ruth, Connie Mack decided to take up Jack Dunn (manager of the International League's Baltimore Orioles, who habitually sold off his top talent) on his offer and pay him a record $100,600 for an incredible southpaw. Can you name this lefthander, who won 108 games for Baltimore and didn't appear in his first major league game until he was 25 years of age?*

ANSWER: Robert Moses Grove

Grove was known as "Lefty" to many Athletics fans. After a 23-25 record for his first two seasons, Grove went on to post seven straight 20-win seasons. The Society for American Baseball Research concluded from an extensive ballot of its members in 1999 that Lefty Grove was the 10th best player of the 20th century. Needless to say, Babe Ruth came out number one, with more than double the points of runner-up Ty Cobb. Willie Mays finished third, Ted Williams fourth, with Honus Wagner rounding out the top five. Sixth was Walter Johnson, seventh was Lou Gehrig, eighth Hank Aaron, with Joe DiMaggio chosen as the ninth best player.

101. *What do Al Kaline, Lou Brock, Eddie Murray, Carl Yastrzemski, Robin Yount, Dave Winfield, Cal Ripken, Jr., and Rickey Henderson have in common?*

ANSWER: They are the only eight members of the 3,000-hit club with career averages under .300. Kaline (.297) collected 3,007 hits, Brock (.293) had 3,023 safeties, Murray (.287) retired with a total of 3,255 hits, Yastrzemski (.285) gathered 3,419 hits, Yount (.285) had

3,142 hits, Winfield (.283) got 3,110, Ripken (.276) retired with 3,184 hits, and Henderson (.280) became the latest entry with a double in his final at-bat of the 2001 season.

Brock's case was the most unusual. A leadoff hitter, Brock cost himself a .300 career average by being unable to improve on his patience at the plate. Brock struck out at least 107 times on nine different occasions, reaching figures of 99, 96, and 93 three other times. Brock, who retired in 1979, had been struck out more often than any other batter: 1,730 times in his career, or a staggering 2.27 times per walk. Dismal even by a free-swinger's standards, that figure is awful for a leadoff hitter—the complete antithesis of the slot's nature. Even the wild Reggie Jackson only walked once for every 1.89 strikeouts. All told, Brock whiffed 120 more times than he scored over his 19-year career.

◆ Did you know Lou Brock remains the only 3,000-hit member who retired with fewer than 1,000 RBI? Brock called it quits with 900 RBI.

◆ Did you know Reggie Jackson and Darrell Evans each hit under .300 a total of 19 times? Counting 90 games as a full season, Graig Nettles was next on the list with 18 such campaigns. Joe Morgan, Carl Yastrzemski, Dwight Evans, Willie McCovey, Rabbit Maranville, and Luis Aparicio hit under .300 a total of 17 times.

102. *Robin Yount, Dave Winfield, Eddie Murray, Paul Molitor, Cal Ripken, Jr., and Rickey Henderson are the most recent players to reach 3,000 hits without gaining a batting title. Can you name the other two to reach that plateau without winning a batting crown?*

ANSWER: Eddie Collins and Lou Brock

Collins (3,313 hits), of course, had to contend with the likes of Ty Cobb, and Brock had to battle with the likes of Roberto Clemente, Pete Rose, and Bill Madlock. In 1990, Murray came awfully close to winning a title. In fact, his .330 batting average for the Dodgers that season was the highest in the majors. But Murray couldn't quite nail down the NL batting crown because the Cardinals' Willie McGee was hitting .335, with enough bats to qualify, when traded in August to the American League's Athletics. Although McGee hit just .274 in his 29 games with Oakland, it didn't affect his NL batting average (league batting averages don't carry over from one to the other, although they are combined to form a major league figure). For the season, McGee combined to hit .324, six points lower than Murray.

♦ Did you know Connie Mack tried to sneak Eddie Collins into his lineup late in the 1906 season by calling him Eddie "Sullivan," to protect the prospect's college eligibility at Columbia University? On September 17, 1906, Collins made his debut as "Sullivan," going 1-for-3 against Ed Walsh. The star of Columbia's baseball team was eventually discovered and barred from playing his senior year. He did, however, complete his degree, also becoming Columbia's coach. Being called "Sullivan" also served to delay his mother's discovery of his love for baseball, as well as his career ambition for the sport. Baseball was not an accepted profession in those days, leaving many aspirers to conceal their love for the game some people thought fit only for those who could do nothing else. It wasn't until a slew of college graduates entered the major leagues that baseball received its proper share of respect as a profession.

103. *Bob Feller hurled history's only opening day no-hitter, but can you name the pitcher who hurled the earliest calendar no-no in history?*

ANSWER: Hideo Nomo

On April 4, 2001, Boston's twirling righthander no-hit Baltimore to eclipse the previous mark of April 7, shared by Ken Forsch and Jack Morris. Nomo did so after a horrible spring training performance, during which he was 0-3 with an ERA of 11.37 in four starts. In 1979, Forsch of the Astros no-hit the Braves in Houston. In 1984, Morris of the Tigers no-hit the White Sox at Chicago. Cleveland's Feller no-hit the White Sox on April 16, 1940. In 45-degree weather, Feller shut down the White Sox, 1-0, at Comiskey Park, outdueling Edgar Smith. Catcher Rollie Hemsley drove in the game's lone run with a triple. Of course, the Giants' Red Ames no-hit the Dodgers for 9⅓ innings before allowing a hit in the 10th and losing, 3-0, in 13 innings on opening day, April 15, 1909.

♦ Did you know Luke Appling of the White Sox made Bob Feller sweat out his 1940 opening day no-hitter by fouling off 15 straight pitches during one plate appearance? Appling's uncanny ability to foul off pitches was a key to his success at the plate as he waited for the pitch he wanted to hit.

◆ Did you know Bob and Ken Forsch are the only brothers to throw a no-hitter? Bob's first of two gems came against the Phillies on April 16, 1978. His second, also for the Cardinals, came on September 26, 1983, against the Expos. In between, Ken no-hit the Braves in Houston.

104. *Match these players with their unparalleled feats:*

1	Rogers Hornsby	A	had 206 singles in one year
2	Mickey Mantle	B	had a 200-hit, 100-RBI season in each league
3	Willie Keeler	C	batted .400 and reached the 40-homer plateau in the same season
4	Al Oliver	D	hit a record 18 World Series home runs

ANSWER: 1—C, 2—D, 3—A, 4—B

In 1922, Hornsby hit 42 home runs and batted .401. "Rajah" almost did it a second time three years later, averaging .403 with 39 homers. Mantle's 40 RBI and 42 runs are also fall classic standards. Mantle and Reggie Jackson share the record of 18 post-season homers, although Mantle hit his in 65 World Series contests, and Jackson compiled his in 77 post-season games. With a four-homer show in the 1999 ALDS, Jim Thome upped his total to 16 in 49 games, passing Ruth. "The Bambino" swatted 15 in just 41 World Series games. David Justice surpassed Jackson's 48 career post-season RBI and enters the 2001 postseason with a record 54. In 1898, Keeler set a still-standing record with 206 singles, to go with seven doubles, two triples, and a homer. Keeler also has the third- and fifth-highest marks. The modern mark belongs to Lloyd Waner, who collected 198 singles, 17 doubles, six triples, and two homers in his rookie season of 1927. With Ichiro Suzuki emerging onto the major league scene, both those marks are in jeopardy over the years to come.

◆ Did you know on August 20, 1974, Davey Lopes set the single-game record for total bases by a leadoff hitter (15)? Playing for the Dodgers, Lopes nailed three homers, doubled, and singled in an 18-8 rout of the Cubs.

105. *This Hall of Fame left-handed pitcher ignored traditional training methods and trained via kung fu, isometrics, and hand resistance against rice. Who was he?*

ANSWER: Steve Carlton

The unorthodox lefthander Carlton used to twist his hands in buckets full of rice to strengthen his wrists for sharper action on his slider and curveball. A six-time 20-game winner, "Lefty" in 1982 became the first man ever to win four Cy Young Awards. Carlton relied on arguably the best slider in the history of the game to win five strikeout crowns, lead the National League in victories on four occasions, and throw 55 career shutouts. His catcher in Philadelphia, Tim McCarver, said, "If Carl Hubbell will be known as having the best screwball in the history of the game and Sandy Koufax the best curveball, Steve Carlton will go down as having the best slider." Carlton's 329 victories rank ninth on the all-time list, ahead of contemporaries Nolan Ryan (324), Don Sutton (324), Phil Niekro (318), Gaylord Perry (314), and Tom Seaver (311).

In 1980, Carlton went 24-9 with a 2.34 ERA to lead the Phillies to their first world championship. His first two Cy Young seasons were in 1972 (he won the pitcher's Triple Crown that year) and 1977. Carlton's career turned following the 1968 season, when he developed that wicked slider, which broke down and in to right-handed hitters. As a result, Carlton won 17 games with a dazzling 2.17 ERA and 210 strikeouts in 1969. After earning the starting assignment for the National League in that year's All-Star Game and winning, Carlton blossomed. On September 15, 1969, at Shea Stadium, Carlton set the major league record with 19 strikeouts, breaking the old mark of 18 set by Bob Feller (1938) and equaled by Sandy Koufax (1959 and 1962) and Don Wilson (1968).

◆ Did you know Steve Carlton lost the game in which he set the single-game strikeout record with 19 Ks against the Mets on September 15, 1969? The Mets' Ron Swoboda hit a pair of two-run homers, dealing Carlton a 4-3 defeat.

106. *What is Steve Busby best known for?*

ANSWER: The right-handed hurler for the Kansas City Royals remains the only pitcher to throw a no-hitter in each of his first two full seasons. After making his debut in 1972, Busby went 16-15 in his 1973 rookie campaign, no-hitting Detroit that April. As a less erratic pitcher in 1974, Busby earned 22 victories with 198 strikeouts and an ERA almost one run lower than the previous year. On June 19, 1974,

Busby no-hit Milwaukee to make history. Busby went on to win 18 games in 1975, earning his second straight All-Star Game appearance before a shoulder injury the following year stunted what could have been a tremendous career. After repeated comeback attempts, Busby retired with a 70-54 ledger over an eight-year career that ended in 1980.

107. *Match these pitchers with the reasons for receiving their monikers:*

1 William "Candy" Cummings	A for the color of hair
2 Joe "Iron Man" McGinnity	B meaning "best" in that era's slang
3 James "Catfish" Hunter	
4 Urban "Red" Faber and Charles "Red" Ruffing	C for no other reason than publicity
	D for winning five games in six days and working in a factory

ANSWER: 1—B, 2—D, 3—C, 4—A

"Candy" also implied sweet: Cummings was admired for being a very pleasant person. Athletics owner Charlie Finley dubbed Jim Hunter "Catfish" just to spice up the image of the otherwise bland and humble farm boy from North Carolina.

108. *Choose the two batterymates who worked together for the longest period of time:*

A Red Ruffing and Bill Dickey
B Mickey Lolich and Bill Freehan
C Whitey Ford and Yogi Berra
D Steve Carlton and Tim McCarver
E Christy Mathewson and Roger Bresnahan

ANSWER: A

Dickey caught Ruffing for 14 years. Dickey called pitches for Ruffing from 1930 through 1942 and for the 1946 season, following a three-year hiatus from each other (two of which were spent in World War II). Dickey was perhaps as big a reason for Ruffing's improvement as any other factor, including leaving the Red Sox and joining the Yankees. His ERA as a Yankee was over a run lower than his ERA anywhere else.

Carlton pitched to McCarver either on the Cardinals or on the Phillies for 12 non-consecutive seasons. Carlton simply felt most comfortable with McCarver. Even with Bob Boone, a very good receiver, catching him, Carlton requested that the Phillies trade for McCarver in 1975. Carlton's ledger improved with McCarver as his own personal catcher—his "caddy," as Carlton called him. McCarver has often quipped that when the duo dies, they should be buried 60 feet six inches from each other.

Although Bresnahan only caught Mathewson for 6½ seasons (from mid-1902 through the 1908 campaign), "Big Six" acknowledged Bresnahan as his favorite catcher.

♦ Did you know that each of the pitching greats Cy Young, Grover Alexander, and Ed Walsh also had his own catcher partnership? Young and his batterymate Lou Criger worked together for 13 years (spanning three teams) and were even traded together, much like Alexander and his batterymate Bill Killefer, who worked together for 11 years. Hall of Fame pitcher Walsh and batterymate Billy Sullivan spent 11 years in close company. So close in fact that their sons (named after their respective fathers) were also batterymates in 1932 for the White Sox, making the only known father-son batterymates in history.

109. *Hank Aaron surpassed Babe Ruth's lifetime home run total (714) in 1974. Whom did Ruth surpass with his 120th dinger in 1921?*

ANSWER: Gavvy Cravath

Ruth breezed by six-time home run champion Cravath, who hit a then-awesome total of 119 during the Dead Ball Era (Cravath played from 1908 to 1920). Roger Connor had held the pre-modern record of 138 homers. Ned Williamson held the single-season home run mark of 27 (1884) until Ruth clobbered 29 in 1919. George Hall led the National League with five homers in major league baseball's first season of 1876. Charley Jones (who hit 56 career home runs) took over the reign the following year and held it until 1884. Then Harry Stovey (122) ruled as the career home run king for two years before Dan Brouthers borrowed the crown for two years of his own. Brouthers (106) relinquished the crown in 1889, when Stovey (122) retook it. Roger Conner took over the reign from Stovey and held it until Ruth assumed the mantle.

♦ Did you know Harry Davis became the first player to lead or tie for the lead in home runs for four straight years? The Dead Ball Era slugger hit a total of 38 home runs between 1904 and 1907. The three others since Davis are Frank Baker (1911–14), Babe Ruth (1926–31), and Ralph Kiner (1946–52). Ruth (1926–29) and Mark McGwire (1996–99) are the only two players to lead the majors for four straight years. Although McGwire did not lead either league in 1997, his 58 homers paced the majors.

110. *The 1927 New York Yankees are regarded by most historians as the greatest major league team ever assembled. They won 110 games, losing just 44, and left their American League counterparts in the dust. Even the richly talented Philadelphia Athletics stood no chance, finishing 19 games behind the Yankees, despite boasting a pretty impressive ledger of their own (91-63). Besting the majors by huge margins in runs, slugging percentage and home runs, and their circuit in ERA, this Yankees juggernaut boasted six Hall of Famers. Fill in the blanks in the figure to complete the alignment of the 1927 Yankees:*

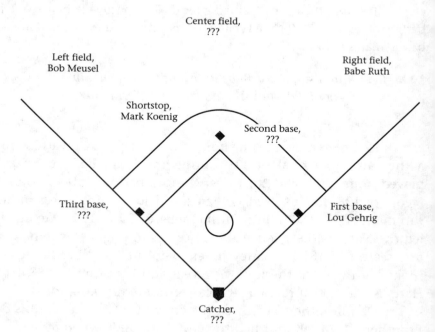

Center field,
???

Left field,
Bob Meusel

Right field,
Babe Ruth

Shortstop,
Mark Koenig

Second base,
???

Third base,
???

First base,
Lou Gehrig

Catcher,
???

ANSWER: Second baseman, Tony Lazzeri; third baseman, Joe Dugan; catcher, Pat Collins; center fielder, Earl Combs

Ruth and Gehrig were 1-2 in slugging percentage, one-base percentage plus slugging percentage (OPS), runs, home runs, and walks. Gehrig and Ruth were 1-2 in RBI and total bases. Ruth, Gehrig, Lazzeri, Combs, Waite Hoyt, and Herb Pennock were the team's six Hall of Famers.

111. *Match these players and their unprecedented feats:*

1 Johnny Mize	A hit 50 homers and stole 20 bases in the same season
2 Chuck Klein and Ty Cobb	
3 Ken Griffey, Jr.	B first two players to represent each league in the All-Star Game and World Series
4 Frank Robinson and Reggie Smith	
	C led the league in home runs and stolen bases in one year
	D 50 homers and fewer than 50 strikeouts in one year

ANSWER: 1—D, 2—C, 3—A, 4—B

In 1947, Mize led the league with 51 homers, striking out just 42 times and walking 74 times. In 1998, Griffey joined Willie Mays and Brady Anderson as the only players with 50 home runs and 20 steals in the same season. Griffey powered up for 56 homers and limbered for 20 steals. Mays had 51 homers and 24 steals in 1955, and Anderson pilfered 21 bases and slammed 50 dingers in 1996. In 2001, Shawn Green missed by a homer, and Alex Rodriguez fell two steals shy of joining that exclusive club.

♦ Did you know Braves outfielder Tommy Holmes did the unthinkable in 1945 by leading the league in homers (28) and least strikeouts (nine in 636 at-bats)? Usually a side effect of high home run totals, strikeouts weren't in Holmes' vocabulary. A contact left-handed hitter, Holmes never struck out more than 20 times in a season, and whiffed on just 122 occasions over an 11-year career. Holmes, who also led the National League in hits, doubles, and slugging in 1945, retired with a .302 batting average.

112. _____ *is not only the first player to win a Cy Young Award in both leagues, but he and his brother Jim are the only brothers to win the coveted award for pitching supremacy. Fill in the blank.*

ANSWER: Gaylord Perry

In 1972, Gaylord Perry won his first Cy Young Award for the Indians, and six years later earned his second, for the Padres. His brother, Jim Perry, earned his award for the Twins in 1970.

In 1999, both Arizona's Randy Johnson and Boston's Pedro Martinez joined Gaylord Perry as the only hurlers to win pitching's premier award as a member of each league. Johnson and Martinez each added a third Cy Young in 2000, and Johnson won his fourth award in 2001.

Johnson won his first award for Seattle in 1995, and Martinez garnered his first Cy Young trophy in 1997 for Montreal. Martinez's 1999 and 2000 seasons are easily among the best ever, especially considering today's era of high-scoring games and exaggerated home run totals.

Aside from a stellar 23-4 record and 313 strikeouts in 213⅓ innings, Martinez posted a magnificent 2.07 ERA for the pitcher's Triple Crown in 1999. His miniscule ERA was 1.37 points lower than that of runner-up David Cone (3.44). Martinez's numbers are even more compelling given that the average American League starting pitcher had an ERA of 5.03, almost three runs higher than Martinez. In 2000, Martinez's 1.74 ERA was nearly two runs better than runner-up Roger Clemens' 3.70 mark, and again nearly three runs lower than the average.

Martinez struck out 313 in 1999: no other AL pitcher was able to register 200 that year. His average of 13.23 Ks per nine innings in 1999 is the best ratio ever for a starter. In achieving these figures, Martinez accomplished something no other pitcher has ever done: he struck out at least 11 batters in eight straight games. To boot, Martinez's 37 walks in 1999 were the fewest of any pitcher with 300 strikeouts, topping Curt Schilling's 58-walk, 319-strikeout season in 1997.

The right-handed Martinez, clearly the best pitcher in the American League today, relies on a quick arm that produces a 98-mile-per-hour fastball, mixing in wicked curveballs, deceptive changeups, and a cutter with great control. The left-handed Johnson, arguably the best pitcher in the National League today, owns a fastball that reaches triple figures and a nasty slider. At six feet, 10 inches, Johnson is one of the most intimidating pitchers ever, especially on days when he's a tad wild.

♦ Did you know that Sandy Koufax (1965–66) and Greg Maddux (1992–95) are the only NL pitchers to win consecutive Cy Young Awards? Koufax won three Cy Young Awards in a four-year span at a time when only one was given out per year. Maddux, relying on a wide variety of pitches, outstanding control, and a keen knowledge of the strike zone, won four straight.

113. *What do these nine players all have in common: Babe Ruth, Johnny Mize, Mark McGwire, Dave Kingman, Darryl Strawberry, Larry Parrish, Claudell Washington, Cory Snyder, and Darnell Coles?*

ANSWER: Each has hit three homers in a game in each league. McGwire became the ninth player to do so on April 14 during his record-setting 1998 season. Strawberry joined the club two years earlier, clubbing a trio of homers for the New York Yankees. Of the group, McGwire is the only member with a pair of three-homer games in each league.

♦ Did you know in 1998, Mark McGwire was named NL Player of the Month for April, May, and September, becoming the first man to earn that honor thrice in one year? Because McGwire won that monthly award in September of the previous year as well, he also became the first to earn that plaque three months in succession (September 1997, April 1998, and May 1998). It was, of course, in September 1998 that the red-haired Cardinal slugger hit 15 home runs to shatter Roger Maris' single-season home run record en route to an unfathomable total of 70. On September 8, McGwire hit his record-breaking 62nd home run, a screaming line drive to left off the Cubs' Steve Trachsel. In a season of prodigious blasts, McGwire's 62nd was ironically his shortest, measuring 341 feet. McGwire hit three homers over the next 15 days before exploding for five more over the final weekend, including number 70 in his final at-bat of the season off Montreal's Carl Pavano.

♦ Did you know George Brett earned Player of the Week honors a record 12 times?

114. *Reggie Jackson is the only player in history to win a home run title with three different teams. Of Jackson's four home run crowns, three of them were shared. Name the three sluggers he tied with for the American League lead. (Hint: All three were Milwaukee Brewers.)*

ANSWER: George Scott, Ben Oglive, and Gorman Thomas

Jackson, who won his first home run title for Oakland in 1973, shared the lead in winning his next three crowns. As a member of the A's again, Jackson tied Scott in 1975 (with 36); as a Yankee, he tied Oglive in 1980 (with 41); and, as a member of the Angels, Jackson tied Thomas (with 39).

115. *Match the Alou brothers with their career achievements and status:*

1 Felipe	A	a 15-year right-handed hitter with a .280 average
2 Jesus	B	a 15-year left-handed hitter with a .307 average and one batting title
3 Matty	C	a 17-year right-handed batter with a .286 average, 206 homers, and 2,101 hits

ANSWER: 1—C, 2—A, 3—B

Felipe, the best player of the three Alou brothers, is also carving a reputation as a pretty good manager, too. He is the winningest manager in Expos' history, taking a 603-590 record into the 2000 season. Felipe is also the father of Moises, an All-Star outfielder, and the uncle of closer Mel Rojas.

116. *Carl Mays still holds the major league record for the best win-loss mark against another team. His gaudy 35-3 career ledger against the Philadelphia Athletics is without competition. Can you name the righthander who beat the New York Mets in 21 of 23 career decisions?*

ANSWER: Larry Jackson

Jackson used his success against the Mets to retire with a winning record (194-183). A hard thrower, Jackson threw for the Cardinals, the Cubs, and the Phillies from 1955 to 1968. Over the last seven seasons of his career, Jackson dominated the Mets, who were awful in their first seven years in the National League. Jackson was actually 15-0 against the Metropolitans through 1966, according to Zita Carno of the Society for American Baseball Research. The consistent Jackson won at least 13 games in each of his last dozen campaigns, enjoying his best season in 1964, when he went 24-11 for the eighth-place Cubs to lead the circuit in wins and innings. The four-time All-Star also won 18 games for the Cardinals in 1960.

Mays feasted on the depleted and talent-stripped Athletic teams of the mid-teens to mid-20s to win 35 of 38 career decisions, including 23 straight (a record streak of domination over another team) against Connie Mack's squad. Even without his 35-3 career mark against the Athletics, Mays was still an impressive 172-123.

The active Mike Mussina enters the 2002 season with a 17-2 career mark against the Twins, and Roger Clemens is 28-8 against the Angels.

♦ Did you know Tigers fireballer Frank Lary dominated the Yankees like no other, defeating them 13 times in 14 decisions during one incredible stretch in the late 1950s? Lary posted a flashy 7-1 mark against the Yankees in 1958, becoming the first pitcher in 42 years to beat the Bombers that often. Lary was also 5-1 against the Yankees in each of the 1956 and 1959 seasons, according to Zita Carno of the Society for American Baseball Research. In 1961, Lary won four of six decisions against one of the very best teams of all time. The three-time All-Star incredibly won 28 of 41 career decisions against the Yankees, a powerhouse of a club during that era, yet was a mediocre 100-103 against all the other teams combined. The 21-game winner in 1956 also led the American League in innings and complete games three times each.

Before Lary, Cicotte was 7-1 against the Yankees in 1916. Eight years earlier, Ed Walsh defeated the New York Yankees (then known as the Highlanders) nine times in 10 decisions.

117. *What do these four pitchers have in common: Johnny Vander Meer, Allie Reynolds, Virgil Trucks, and Nolan Ryan?*

ANSWER: Each tossed a pair of no-hitters in one season. Vander Meer's back-to-back no-hitters came in 1938. Reynolds' and Trucks' dual no-hitters came about in consecutive years, 1951 and 1952, respectively. Ryan's first two were exactly two months apart in 1973. Incredibly, Ryan came within simple execution of a third no-hitter that year. On August 29 (45 days after the second no-no) against the Yankees, Ryan allowed only a routine pop-up that dropped between two confused Angels infielders in an otherwise hitless 5-0 shutout.

In 1965, Cincinnati's Jim Maloney had a no-hitter through 10 innings on two occasions, and came away with one official gem. On June 14, Maloney kept the Mets hitless into the 11th, when

New York's Johnny Lewis ended the game with a home run off the big Reds righthander, who struck out 18. About two months later, Maloney again pitched 10 no-hit innings. But this time he won as Leo Cardenas homered in the top of the 10th for a 1-0 Reds win at Chicago (in the first game of a doubleheader). Maloney walked 10, but struck out 12. As a side note, Dean Chance pitched a five-inning perfect game on September 5, 1967, versus Boston and a 2-1 no-hitter versus Cleveland 20 days later.

♦ Did you know Virgil Trucks' no-hitters, incredibly, came in the midst of a 5-19 season? However, his no-hitters were no surprise as he had pitched four no-nos in the minors.

♦ Did you know on September 1, 1906, Dodger pitcher Harry McIntire pitched 10⅔ innings of no-hit ball versus the Pirates before losing, 1-0, in 13 innings? Why is it that mediocre pitchers seem to turn in the most spectacular performances? Consider, for example, Harvey Haddix, Don Larsen, Johnny Vander Meer, Virgil Trucks, Art Nehf, and Charles "Red" Barrett. Nehf was the Brave who, on August 1, 1918, hurled 20 shutout innings before losing, 2-0, to the Pirates in the 21st inning. Barrett was the Braves right-handed and red-headed hurler who threw a shutout on August 10, 1944, on a record-low 58 pitches. Barrett's one-hour and 15-minute gem remains the shortest night game ever.

118. *Eight teams have had two different pitchers throw a no-hitter in a single season. How many teams have had three different pitchers throw a no-hitter in one season?*

ANSWER: Zero

The eight clubs with two different pitchers throwing a no-hitter are: the 1904 Red Sox (Cy Young and Jesse Tannehill), the 1908 Indians (Addie Joss and Bob Rhoads), the 1916 Red Sox (Rube Foster and Dutch Leonard), the 1917 Browns (Ernie Koob and Bob Groom), the 1956 Dodgers (Sal Maglie and Carl Erskine), the 1960 Braves (Warren Spahn and Lew Burdette), the 1962 Red Sox (Earl Wilson and Bill Monbouquette), and the 1972 Cubs (Burt Hooten and Milt Pappas).

119. *Match the artists with their Picassos:*

1	Bobo Holloman	A	also hit two home runs in his 4-0 no-hitter
2	Rick Wise	B	pitched a no-hitter in his debut
3	Jim Bunning	C	tossed a no-hitter in each league
4	Len Barker	D	only pitcher after 1892 to hurl a no-hitter in his first major league start
5	Bumpus Jones	E	threw a perfect game

ANSWER: 1—D, 2—A, 3—C, 4—E, 5—B

The Browns' Alva Lee Holloman, better known as Bobo, no-hit the Athletics, 6-0, on May 6, 1953. The burly righthander, about to be demoted after doing a horrible job in relief, pestered manager Marty Marion and owner Bill Veeck for a starting assignment to prove his worth. Marion and Veeck agreed, rather than listen to the talkative, fun-loving pitcher endlessly complain. They gave the 28-year-old rookie a start against the weak-hitting Athletics.

On that rainy evening at Sportsman's Park, Holloman took the mound. Although his pitches were continuously belted, they were hit right at his fielders, according to Veeck in his autobiography *Veeck—as in Wreck.* And even when Holloman began to tire, according to Veeck, the righthander was given a break as a shower delayed the game, giving Holloman enough time to rest. Holloman, who was caught by Less Moss, walked five and struck out three for his first major league victory, earning a spot in the Browns' rotation.

After nine more starts, however, Holloman was waived and demoted to the minor leagues. Holloman was never given another opportunity, recording a 3-7 ledger with a 5.23 ERA in his lone major league season. He retired from playing baseball in 1954, leaving behind a minor league win-loss column of 120-79.

Wise walked only one batter in his June 23, 1971, no-hitter against a Reds lineup that featured the likes of Pete Rose, George Foster, Lee May, Johnny Bench, Tony Perez, and Hal McRae. Wise finished with six homers on the year in 1971.

Barker's gem fell on May 15, 1981, for the Indians against the five-year-old Toronto Blue Jays. A fastball pitcher, the 25-year-old Barker crossed up the Blue Jays with an abundance of curveballs, of which he had near-perfect command. Barker, who didn't reach a single three-ball count, struck out 11 batters, all from the fourth inning on.

Jones, who walked four in pitching Cincinnati over Pittsburgh by a score of 7-1 on October 15, 1892, remains the only man in major league history to have thrown a no-hitter in his first major league appearance. The righthander, however, couldn't maintain his success after the pitching distance was lengthened the following year.

♦ Did you know San Diego's Jimmy Jones threw a one-hit shutout in his major league debut against Houston on September 21, 1986? The hard-throwing righthander allowed just a third-inning triple to Bob Knepper, the opposing pitcher. Arm trouble kept Jones from reaching his potential.

♦ Did you know Oakland's Vida Blue threw a one-hit shutout against the Kansas City Royals in his second major league start on September 11, 1970, and tossed a no-hitter against the Minnesota Twins just 10 days later?

♦ Did you know Jim "Catfish" Hunter drove in three of Oakland's four runs in his perfect game on May 9, 1968, versus Minnesota? Hunter, who reached a three-ball count seven times, struck out 11 players.

120. *When asked if he liked golf, this Hall of Fame slugger replied, "Golf? When I hit a ball, I want somebody else to chase it." Name this hitting machine.*

ANSWER: Rogers Hornsby

Hornsby is regarded as the greatest right-handed hitter who ever lived. Hornsby still holds the NL record of six consecutive batting titles, from 1920 to 1925. Hornsby concluded his career with 301 home runs, 1,584 RBI, 1,579 runs scored, 2,930 hits, a .577 slugging percentage, and the second highest lifetime batting average of .358 (second to Ty Cobb's .367 career mark, of course).

He accomplished all these feats with a rather unorthodox batting stance. Standing in the far corner of the batter's box, "Rajah" strode diagonally into the pitch. So overwhelming was Hornsby as a hitter that he secured a spot on most historians' all-time team as the best second baseman ever, although he was less than solid defensively. Converted from shortstop and inserted everywhere else in the infield, Hornsby finally settled in at second base. At his peak, he was better than average with the glove, but experienced a lot of trouble chasing pop-ups. And his defense got worse as he aged. Of course, his bat more than made up for it. (In case you're wondering, Hornsby was named Rogers after his mother's maiden name, according to my colleagues at the Society for American Baseball Research. Before marrying, she was Mary Dallas Rogers.)

◆ Did you know Ken "Hawk" Harrelson retired during the 1971 season to join the Professional Golfers' Association Tour? The right-handed first baseman and outfielder was hitting .199 with five homers 52 games into the season for the Indians. Overall, the rowdy Harrelson hit 131 homers with 421 RBI over nine seasons. Harrelson, nicknamed "Hawk" for his curved nose, didn't flourish on the links. He later became a White Sox broadcaster.

121. *Jim Maloney pitched major league history's third extra-inning, complete game no-hitter. Can you name either of the first two such pitchers?*

ANSWER: George "Hooks" Wiltse and Fred Toney

Wiltse first accomplished the feat in 1908 for the New York Giants, and Cincinnati righthander Fred Toney became the second in 1917. The left-handed Wiltse was actually one strike away from a perfect game in his July 4 start that season before losing the gem to the opposing pitcher. That's right: Wiltse retired the first 26 Phillies that day before having to face hurler George McQuillan in a scoreless duel. A strike away from a perfect game through nine innings, Wiltse threw an apparent strike three. But home plate umpire Cy Riger called it "ball two," evening the count. Wiltse was so rattled by the call that he hit McQuillan with the next pitch, losing his mint performance. Nevertheless, Wiltse retired the next batter and pitched a perfect top of the 10th before the Giants scored a run in the bottom half to crown their pitcher with a 10-inning, no-hit victory.

In that May 2, 1917, contest, Toney and Cubs' lefthander James "Hippo" Vaughn each took a no-hitter into the 10th inning—an unparalleled feat. Vaughn had his no-hitter and shutout erased on a one-out, run-scoring infield single by Jim Thorpe: the same Thorpe who won the gold medal in the decathlon event during the 1912

Olympics and who made a name for himself as a two-time All-American football player. Toney kept his gem in tact, as the Reds won, 1-0. Neither of the three aforementioned pitchers won more than 141 games, although their winning percentages were good.

◆ Did you know Fred Toney also has the distinction of throwing and winning the longest no-hitter in organized baseball history? Toney pitched 17 hitless innings for the Winchester Kentucky club in the Blue Grass (Class D) League in 1909. An interesting story behind that game was that his teammates proclaimed a moratorium in their assigned duties, and refused to score any runs. Upset with their designation as Class D material, Toney's teammates didn't put forth an effort until the 17th frame. In his first year of professional baseball, Toney didn't mind starting at the low minor league level.

122. *Match these final-year teams with their new cities or franchises:*

1	1960 Washington Senators	A	Milwaukee
2	1952 Boston Braves	B	Texas
3	1954 Philadelphia Athletics	C	Minnesota
4	1969 Seattle Pilots	D	Kansas City
5	1971 Washington Senators		

ANSWER: 1—C, 2—A, 3—D, 4—A, 5—B

The 1960 Senators became the Twins, the Braves in 1953 moved to Milwaukee, the Athletics in 1955 moved to Kansas City, the 1971 Senators became the Rangers, and the Pilots became the Milwaukee Brewers. (The Braves moved again to Atlanta in 1966, and the Athletics in 1968 moved to Oakland.)

Those sorry Pilots lasted but one season, drawing just under 678,000 for the entire campaign. The team drew a pathetic 14,993 in its home opener at Sick's Stadium, and a mere 5,473 in its finale. Bud Selig purchased the Pilots for $10,800,000 and moved the team to Milwaukee just in time for the 1970 season. The city of Seattle threatened legal action, but settled for the Mariners in the 1977 expansion. In 1998, Selig's Brewers became the first team since the inception of the American League in 1901 to switch leagues, moving to the National League Central. Selig, of course, was also baseball's acting Commissioner.

◆ Did you know all four 1969 expansion teams—the Kansas City Royals, the San Diego Padres, the Montreal Expos and the Seattle Pilots—won their inaugural game on April 8? The Expos also won their home opener six days later, overcoming a 7-0 deficit to notch the first win in Canada. More early fortune fell Montreal's way as Bill Stoneman on April 17 pitched a no-hitter at Philadelphia in just his fifth career start. The wild but hard-throwing Stoneman became the franchise's first ace, pitching his second no-hitter in 1972—the first ever thrown in Canada.

123. *Alexander Cartwright is the inventor of baseball. True or False?*

ANSWER: False

Cartwright is no longer regarded as such, thanks to a New York University librarian who in July of 2001 unearthed a pair of newspaper articles that reveal "base ball" was played in Manhattan as early as the 1820s. The articles, found by George Thompson, Jr., appeared in the April 25, 1823, editions of *The National Advocate* as well as *The New-York Gazette*. This discovery favors those keen historians who have argued that the game evolved from the games of "rounders" and "crickets" and was not invented by any one person.

Before this recent revelation, most regarded Cartwright—a New York bank teller—as the creator who came up with the first set of rules in 1845. A 1938 Hall of Fame inductee, Cartwright organized the Knickerbocker Base Ball Club in Hoboken, New Jersey, in 1845. Abner Doubleday, a West Point cadet, was originally thought to have been the inventor until evidence by Cartwright's grandson, Bruce, proved otherwise.

And now it turns out that the celebrated baseball game of June 19, 1846, in Hoboken, New Jersey, was neither the first-ever game nor the first-ever organized contest. On that day, the New York Nine defeated the Knickerbockers (23-1 in four innings) at Elysian Fields. The city of Hoboken and the state of New Jersey on June 19, 1996, celebrated the 150th anniversary of "the first" organized game with a re-creation of the event. The mound was only 45 feet away, and home plate was in the shape of a diamond.

Cartwright's contribution to baseball, however, remains lofty and integral. He was responsible for the game's early progression. Besides founding the first organized baseball club, Cartwright also took the sport west to the Pacific Coast and Hawaii. Hall of Fame Vice President Jeff Idelson maintains Cartwright's election into the Hall of Fame isn't tarnished by the recent discovery. Although Idelson admitted to me that Cartwright's appellation as "The Father of Baseball" may be an overstatement now, he whole-heartedly supports Cartwright's inclusion in the Hall of Fame. "His role in helping to pioneer the game and grow its popularity undoubtedly justifies his place in Cooperstown," Idelson said before adding that Cartwright also "likely played a key role in formalizing the first published rules of the game."

◆ Did you know the Hall of Fame was placed in Cooperstown, New York, because that's where Abner Doubleday had lived? Although it was later discovered (in 1938) that Doubleday didn't invent baseball, Cooperstown remained the home of the Hall of Fame. Doubleday is not a member of the Hall of Fame.

◆ Did you know that having to touch each base in order was not a rule until 1863?

124. *The 1991 Atlanta Braves and Minnesota Twins became the first two teams ever to go from last place to first in one year. True or False?*

ANSWER: False

The 1889 Louisville Colonels finished with an abysmal 27-111 record in the American Association (a major league), and the 1890 squad did a complete turn-about with an eye-opening record of 88-44. To this day, the Colonels' one-year turnaround of 64 games remains the largest in history. Since the Twins and the Braves accomplished the feat in 1991, facing off against each other in the World Series, the Phillies turned the trick in 1993, the Giants did the same in 1997, the Padres in 1998 and the Diamondbacks in 1999. As a matter of fact, the Braves and the Giants each finished last for two years straight before making their remarkable turnarounds. You can expect to see this happen a little more frequently nowadays, because of a higher player turnover ratio and less-populated divisions.

◆ Did you know the Louisville Colonels' ERA dropped from a league-worst 4.81 to a league-best 2.58? Also, the 1890 Colonels led in batting (.279) after the 1889 team hit a league-worst .252. William "Chicken" Wolf led the league in hitting (.363) as Louisville also pilfered 138 more bases. Astoundingly, the team's seasonal fielding average also sky-rocketed from a league-worst .907 average to a league-best .933 mark. In fact, team ace Scott Stratton woke up from the dead (3-13 in 1889) to post a league best 34-14 record and a 2.32 ERA to go with 207 strikeouts.

125. *Regarded as the best-ever at his position, _____ persistently refused raises after earning a $10,000 salary early in his career. He may have very well been one of the most likeable and modest of players. This gentleman's baseball card is the most precious in the sports card business, because he demanded that the tobacco company stop printing his cards. Although he smoked, he didn't want to encourage the habit in kids. The card is very rare, hence its value. Fill in the name of the player and his position.*

ANSWER: Shortstop Honus Wagner

A 1910 Wagner card was sold for $640,500 in September 1996. Of the 150 that were made, only 50 are still around and only two mint Wagner cards exist. "The Flying Dutchman," born John Peter Wagner, hit .327 over a 21-year career with 3,418 hits, 1,735 runs, 642 doubles, 252 triples, and 722 stolen bases. Bow-legged and stocky, Wagner was a natural. Many who played against him insisted he could have been the very best at whatever position he chose. Wagner was, in fact, fooled into playing shortstop by Pirates owner Barney Dreyfuss and manager Fred Clarke after spending his childhood and minor league career playing every position except short and catcher.

♦ Did you know John Peter "Honus" Wagner was referred to as "Hannis" as early as his minor league days? "Hannis" was a moniker that later evolved into "Honus" and "Hans," according to William Hageman, author of the book *Honus*.

126. *Buck Freeman was one of the most underappreciated players in the late 1800s and early 1900s. The strong, hard-nosed, and durable right fielder played in 534 straight games and 5,341 consecutive innings from 1901 to 1905 for the Red Sox franchise. His streak of consecutive contests was exceeded soon thereafter, but it wasn't* *until 1985 that his consecutive-inning streak was surpassed. Can you name the similarly impervious man who eclipsed Freeman's standard of consecutive innings played?*

ANSWER: Cal Ripken, Jr.

Ripken played in 8,243 consecutive innings (a longer streak of which nary a historian has been able to find) before taking a seat in the late innings of a September 14, 1987, game in Toronto. It brought to an end a streak that began five years, three months, and nine days earlier on June 5 of the 1982 season. And the only reason Ripken sat out the final two innings was that Toronto, with the aid of a single-game record 10 home runs, was routing Baltimore by a score of 18-3. Ron Washington filled in for Ripken at short. (As a point of comparison, Lou Gehrig played every inning of every game just once, in 1931.)

Ripken began his record consecutive-game streak of 2,632 games, all starts, on May 30, 1982, replacing Floyd Rayford at third base. From May 30, 1982, through the 1997 season, Ripken played in 22,250 of Baltimore's 22,510 innings. In 1983, Ripken became the only player to play in every single inning of the regular season, the League Championship Series, and the World Series.

Ripken sat himself down on September 20, 1998, ending his streak as Ryan Minor started and played at third base that night. Ripken, who played the first 27 games of the streak at third, played 2,216 consecutive games at shortstop prior to returning to third base for the first of six straight games on July 15, 1996. Lou Gehrig's longest streak at first base was 885 games due to a few token appearances at short.

The left-handed Freeman slugged 82 home runs in his short, brilliant career and batted .293 overall. Freeman was such a force that he clubbed 25 home runs in 1899 for Washington with 122 RBI. Only Ned Williamson hit more homers (27) during a season prior to the advent of the live ball era in 1919.

♦ Did you know Detroit Tigers third baseman Travis Fryman was the only major leaguer to play in every inning of every game during the 1995 season, the same year Cal Ripken, Jr. broke Lou Gehrig's record for most consecutive games played?

127. *Babe Ruth's best year as a pitcher featured a 23-12 record with a league-best 1.75 ERA, 23 complete games, a league-high nine shutouts, and 170 strikeouts in 323⅔ innings. During which year did Ruth accomplish these feats for the Boston Red Sox?*

A 1916
B 1917
C 1918
D 1919

ANSWER: A

Ruth's 94-46 career record, 17 shutouts, and 2.28 ERA had many batters grateful for his switch to the outfield. From 1915 to 1917, Ruth won 65 games, more than any other southpaw. His nine shutouts in 1916 have yet to be surpassed by any American League southpaw. His 14-inning, 2-1 victory over the Brooklyn Dodgers' Sherry Smith in Game Two of the 1916 World Series remains the longest complete game in fall classic history. After allowing a first-inning, inside-the-park home run to Hy Myers, Ruth did not allow a run. That started a then-record 29⅔ scoreless-inning streak that ended two years later.

In 1919, Ruth enjoyed perhaps the most unique and underappreciated season in major league history. With his arm, Ruth went 9-5 with a 2.97 ERA while completing 12 of his 15 starts. With his bat, Ruth belted 29 homers (no one else in either league hit more than 12), drove in 114 runs, scored 103 times, batted .322, slugged .657, and even legged out a dozen triples. In summary, Ruth finished 10th in winning percentage; tied for 10th in saves; broke the major league home run record; led the American League in RBI, runs, on-base percentage, and slugging; finished second in walks drawn; fifth in doubles; sixth in triples; and eighth in batting average. No one else in the history of the game has put together a season so well-rounded, and Ruth did so while introducing to baseball-viewing America a new and impressive brand of baseball. Yet to this day, Ruth's 1919 performance seems to take a back seat to his best hitting years or his best pitching years.

♦ Did you know Babe Ruth made a great impression on the Yankees with his arm, beating them in 17 of 22 career decisions? Only Kevin Brown at 12-3 and Dickie Kerr at 14-4 have a better career record against the Bronx Bombers.

128. *Paul "Pee Wee" Wanninger is best known for:*

    A his contributions to the 1927 championship Yankee ball club
    B ending Everett Scott's 1,207 consecutive-game streak by playing for him at shortstop
    C being the shortstop Lou Gehrig pinch-hit for to start the famous 2,130 consecutive-game streak
    D A and B
    E B and C

ANSWER: E

Wanninger made quite some noise for a man who played only two seasons (playing 117 games for the Yankees in 1925 and a combined 46 games for the Red Sox and Reds in 1927). His .234 average was his weakness.

On June 1, 1925, Gehrig pinch-hit for Wanninger to start an ironman streak of 2,130 consecutive games played. In 1933, Gehrig had to correct the baseball writers who had erroneously traced the origin of the streak back to Gehrig's first start on June 2, 1925. According to *The New York World-Telegram*, Gehrig told the paper "The baseball writers have overlooked the fact that I was a pinch-hitter the day before I broke in as a regular on the Yankees. Walter Johnson was pitching for Washington and we were getting our fifth straight defeat. In the eighth inning, Miller Huggins told me to bat for Pee Wee Wanninger, whose being sent to short that spring had snapped Scott's streak. I am sorry to say that I flied out to Goose Goslin." Gehrig doubled and singled twice off Washington's George Mogridge in his first start.

Wally Pipp was the first-bagger whose headache on June 2 enabled Gehrig to step in and not relinquish first base duties until 14 years later in 1939. Pipp was a .281 lifetime hitter and a two-time home run champion with 996 RBI and 148 triples from 1913 to 1928. A fine fielder who played 11 years with the Yankees, Pipp said afterward they were "the two most expensive aspirins in history" after allowing Gehrig to play in his second consecutive game. Although

Pipp lost his starting job, Gehrig that day actually replaced Fred Merkle, who started for the ailing Pipp.

◆ Did you know the Yankees offered Lou Gehrig to the Red Sox for a fellow by the name of Phil Todt in 1925? That's right, Gehrig could have been a member of the Red Sox, but Boston made yet another poor front-office decision in choosing to stick with Todt, a tremendous fielding first baseman whose left-handed swing was made for Yankee Stadium's short right-field porch. The left-handed Gehrig wasn't a pull hitter, which probably worried the Yankees at first, given the dimensions of their park. The Yankees soon found out Gehrig's bat strength.

129. *This outfielder set a record by playing in the World Series with four different teams. However, it was his late, base-running blunder in a Game Seven that cost him a fourth world championship ring. Who is he?*

ANSWER: Lonnie Smith

Smith cost his Braves the 1991 World Series when he failed to score from first base on a hit-and-run pitch that Terry Pendleton drove to the left-center field wall in the eighth inning of the finale against host Minnesota. In lieu of looking at the third base coach, "Skates" fell prey to the decoy of Twins' rookie second baseman Chuck Knoblauch and veteran shortstop Greg Gagne, who worked the "invisible 4-6-3" to perfection. It served to slow down Smith, who was fooled into believing a ground ball had been hit to the second baseman.

The game then proceeded scoreless into extra innings, where the Twins' Jack Morris proved to be a diligent stalwart in this age of specialists by throwing a 10th goose egg under the most intense conditions. (Braves starter John Smoltz lasted 7⅓ innings.) In the bottom half of the 10th, Gene Larkin singled over the drawn-in outfield (the bases were loaded with one out) for a dramatic 1-0 win, marking the Twins' second world championship in four years.

Smith played a major role for the 1980 Phillies, the 1982 Cardinals, and the 1985 Royals. The Royals acquired him from St. Louis early in 1985 to make for a boastful October.

The 1991 World Series became the first to feature four walk-off RBI, the first to feature a scoreless seventh game through nine, and just the second to feature a 1-0 Game Seven (the 1962 finale was the first such game). The series also showcased five one-run games and plenty of bitten nails. Despite hitting the 16th grand slam in World Series history, Smith and his Braves also lost the 1992 fall classic.

◆ Did you know Lonnie Smith is among five men to play on a world championship team for three different franchises? Smith, who played for the 1980 champion Phillies, the 1982 Cardinals, and the 1985 Royals, became the third member to achieve this feat. Wally Schang was the first, winning a title with the Athletics in 1913 and 1930, the Red Sox in 1918, and the Yankees in 1923. Stuffy McInnis became the second, winning a title for the Athletics in 1910, 1911, and 1913, the Red Sox in 1918, and the Pirates seven years later. Jack Morris was the fourth player to accomplish the feat, winning with the 1984 Tigers, the 1991 Twins, and the 1992 Blue Jays. Dave Stewart followed suit in 1993 with the Blue Jays, after earning a world championship ring with the 1981 Dodgers and the 1989 Athletics.

130. *During a sensational 25-3 campaign in 1978, each of Ron Guidry's three defeats came at the hands of a pitcher named Mike from the same American League East Division. Can you name two of the three Mikes who defeated Guidry that year?*

ANSWER: Mike Caldwell, Mike Flanagan, and Mike Willis

Caldwell of Milwaukee, Flanagan of Baltimore, and Willis of Toronto were the only pitchers to defeat Guidry in 1978. Although Caldwell won 22 games that season and Flanagan 19, Willis was just 3-7 in 1978. A spot starter, Willis' complete game victory over Guidry served as the only complete game of his major league career. All three Mikes, by the way, threw left-handed.

Besides leading the majors with 25 wins, Guidry, a southpaw himself, also led the majors with a 1.74 ERA and nine shutouts in carrying the Yankees to their second straight world title. His .893 winning percentage in 1978 remains the best ever for a 20-game winner. "Louisiana Lightning" retired with a 170-91 record over 14 years and five post-season victories to his credit.

◆ Did you know Lefty Grove was defeated by Yankees' journeyman Hank Johnson four times in 1928, despite posting a stellar 24-8 overall record?

Grove was 1-6 against the Yankees that season, and 23-2 against the rest of the American League.

131. *Match these players with their heavyweight pitching achievements:*

1	Grover Alexander	A	pitched a record 38 career 1-0, complete game wins
2	Ned Garver		
3	Walter Johnson	B	registered a record 45.8% of team's wins during a season
4	Sandy Koufax		
5	Steve Carlton	C	struck out 300 batters thrice
		D	became the first pitcher in history to win the pitcher's Triple Crown three times
		E	earned 20 victories and hit .300 for a team that won just 52 games

ANSWER: 1—D, 2—E, 3—A, 4—C, 5—B

Alexander led the National League in victories, ERA, and strikeouts in 1915, 1916, and 1920. He was joined by Walter Johnson, who accomplished the feat in 1913, 1918, and 1924, and by Sandy Koufax, who earned his trio over a four-year span starting in 1963. Garver was the lone standout on a last-place 1951 St. Louis Browns team that lost 50 games more than it won. Garver went 20-12, with a 3.73 ERA. No other Browns pitcher won more than six games. The right-handed Garver even hit .305, with a homer and nine RBI in 95 at-bats. Johnson's 38 shutouts by margins of 1-0 were more than double the nearest competitor—Alexander won 17 such contests.

After coming from St. Louis in an off-season trade for Rick Wise, Carlton put on one of the best-ever pitching displays. In his first of many eventual Hall of Fame-caliber seasons with the Phillies, "Lefty" went 27-10, struck out 310 batters, fashioned a 1.97 ERA, hurled 30 complete games, and pitched 346⅓ innings—all league-best figures. Those numbers border on the astronomical when considering Carlton did so for a team that went 59-97 with him and a dismal 32-87 in games he didn't win or lose. To Carlton's benefit, however, Philadelphia had the National League's second-best defense. As for Wise, he was traded three more times, posting consecutive 16-win seasons for the Cardinals, 19-, 14-, and 11-victory campaigns for the Red Sox, and a 15-10 season for the Indians before retiring as a Padre in 1982.

♦ Did you know Walter Johnson lost a record 26 games by a 1-0 score? Pitching for the weak-hitting Washington Senators, Johnson had to fight claw, and earn his way to 417 career wins. Jim Bunning was second in this unenviable category, losing 15 games by a 1-0 score.

132. *Before finally winning the World Series in 1955, the Brooklyn Dodgers lost their first seven fall classics. Among those seven downfalls were five World Series defeats to the New York Yankees. Identify the years of those five World Series losses to their New York rivals:*

A 1942, 1946, 1949, 1952, and 1953
B 1941, 1949, 1951, 1952, and 1954
C 1941, 1947, 1949, 1952, and 1953
D 1941, 1942, 1949, 1952, and 1953

ANSWER: C

After losing to the Boston Red Sox in 1916, the Cleveland Indians in 1920, and the Yankees in 1941, 1947, 1949, 1952, and 1953 the Dodgers rejoiced in 1955. That rejoicing allowed the Dodgers to discard their yearly slogan of "Wait 'til next year," a cry that had become synonymous with disappointing Octobers in Brooklyn. Of course, the Yankees won the following October when the two teams met again. Since moving to Los Angeles, the Dodgers franchise is 5-4 in fall classic competition, including a 2-2 ledger against the Yankees

133. *The only two players to play in both the 1951 and 1962 play-offs between the Giants and Dodgers were:*

A Willie Mays and Duke Snider
B Pee Wee Reese and Orlando Cepeda
C Juan Marichal and Don Drysdale
D Maury Wills and Alvin Dark

ANSWER: A

Note, however, that Alvin Dark played shortstop for New York in 1951 and managed the 1962 New York Giants team. The play-offs were eerily similar. The Giants won each time, two games to one. On both occasions, New York won the opener and the deciding game

Each time, the Giants entered the ninth inning of the third game trailing by at least two runs and each time they came up with a four spot for the dramatic win. Spooky, isn't it?

134. *Match these great teams with their accomplishments:*

1	1975 Reds	A	began the season with a 22-2 mark
2	1974 Athletics	B	own the best 30- and 40-game starts in history: 26-4 and 35-5
3	1955 Dodgers	C	began by splitting their first 40 games before winning 41 of their next 50 contests
4	1963 Dodgers	D	had nary a .300 hitter, 100-run scorer, or 30-home run slugger as only 845,693 fans came to see this great team bat only .247
5	1984 Tigers	E	held the Yankees to only four runs and 22 hits in the World Series

ANSWER: 1—C, 2—D, 3—A, 4—E, 5—B

The Reds of 1975 became a powerhouse team soon after manager Sparky Anderson brought in reserve outfielder George Foster to play every-day left field and moved the versatile Pete Rose to third base in place of John Vukovich. The 1955 Dodgers and 1984 Tigers are also two of eight clubs in history to occupy first place from the first day of the season to the final day, without interruption. The other six clubs are the 1923 Giants, 1927 Yankees, 1990 Reds, 1997 Orioles, 1999 Indians, and the 2001 Mariners.

The 2001 Mariners overachieved perhaps more than any other club in major league history, ignoring the devastating departures of Randy Johnson (trade), Ken Griffey, Jr. (trade), and Alex Rodriguez (free agency) to win 116 regular-season games. This Mariner club turned heads with a unique brand of 21st-century baseball—not the homer-slanted, high-scoring formula other squads strove for. The Mariners won at a jaw-dropping .716 clip with a selfless and superior brand of play that featured quality starting pitching, a great bullpen, solid defense, hectic speed, and timely hitting. Ichiro Suzuki set the tables and Bret Boone, Edgar Martinez, and John Olerud cleaned them up. On the mound, Jamie Moyer, Freddy Garcia, Paul Abbott, and Aaron Sele went a combined 73-21. Locking the door on opponents' rallies was closer Kazuhiro Sasaki, who notched 45 saves.

◆ Did you know a total of 11 teams have won at least 41 games during any 50-game stretch? The 1906 Cubs had the best 50-game stretch, winning 45 games. The 1912 Giants won 43 of 50. The 1941 Yankees and the 1942 Cardinals posted 42-8 stretches. The other seven teams recorded 41-9 surges (the 1975 Reds, 1953 Dodgers, 1946 Red Sox, 1944 Cardinals, 1931 Athletics, 1914 Athletics, and the 1909 Pirates). The 110-42 Pirates had two cycles of 41-9 in 1909. Boston's 41-9 stretch in 1946 began the season, representing the best 50-game start in the 20th century. Each team won its pennant, and five of them won the World Series.

135. *Match these umpires with their notable achievements:*

1	Bill Klem	A	had 31 years of umpiring under his mask before retiring
2	Jake Beckley	B	umpired a record 37 seasons, 18 World Series, and 104 World Series games
3	Bill McGowan	C	only Hall of Fame player to later umpire
4	Doug Harvey	D	umpired for 30 seasons and a record 2,541 consecutive games

ANSWER: 1—B, 2—C, 3—D, 4—A

Because of his superior ability to recognize balls and strikes, Klem umpired exclusively behind the plate during his first 16 years as an umpire. "The Umpire of Umpires," Harvey retired after the 1992 campaign (due to bad knees), after having served 42,786 innings, making five World Series appearances, eight NL Championship Series appearances, and six All-Star Games. Harvey became the first $100,000 umpire, and in 1991 became the first $200,000 umpire. McGowan never missed an inning during his three decades.

◆ Did you know the Society for American Baseball Research concluded from its balloting for 20th-century honors that Bill Klem was the best umpire? Manager John McGraw described Klem as stern yet reasonable. Finishing second was Doug Harvey, with Al Barlick, Jocko Conlon, and Bill McGowan rounding out the top five.

136. *In what year was the Federal League born?*

ANSWER: 1913

The Federal League was born in 1913 as an independent, six-team circuit, whose talent was considered to be of minor league level. The Federal League of Baseball Clubs was organized on March 8 that year, due in large part to the efforts of founder John Powers, who brought together an ambitious group of businessmen and was named president of the league. Aware of the deep pockets and the strong grip on baseball both the National and American Leagues possessed, Powers wasn't out to compete against either major circuit, and made it a point to not go after their talent.

Following a successful six-week 1913 season, during which interest in expanding to eight teams became strong, the rash and over-confident owners replaced the careful Powers with the aggressive James Gilmore, declaring themselves a major league that would rival the National League and the American League. That change served as the league's first turning point. Gilmore persuaded Charles Weeghman, Phillip Ball, and Robert Ward—among the richest men in America—to invest in the Chicago team, the St. Louis squad, and the Brooklyn franchise, respectively. Gilmore also stated his league would not honor the reserve clause and would attempt to lure as much talent as possible to enhance his league's standing.

The Chicago Whales made the Federal League's first big acquisition that winter, landing Joe Tinker to be their player-manager for the 1914 season. "Three Fingers" Brown and George Mullin soon followed to St. Louis and Indianapolis, respectively. Al Bridwell and Howie Camnitz were also among those who skipped to the Federal League that offseason. Hal Chase left his White Sox club midway through the 1914 season to accept an offer from Buffalo. Star pitchers Eddie Plank, Chief Bender, Ed Reulbach, and Hooks Wiltse jumped to the Federal League for the 1915 season. In total, 43 players spurned major or minor league contracts to join the new league.

The Federal League even offered lucrative contracts to the likes of Walter Johnson, Ty Cobb, and Tris Speaker. Like many others, however, Johnson, Cobb, and Speaker used their Federal League offers as leverage to boost their major league salaries and succeeded. Although the three players could have asked for yet more money (Johnson even accepted a bonus from a Federal League owner, at first) and received it from any of the major leagues, they valued the integrity of the two established leagues they had spent their careers contributing to.

◆ Did you know the 1914 Federal League champion Indianapolis Hoosiers moved to Newark as the Peps in 1915, becoming the only pennant winner in major league history to move to a new city the following year? In 1913, the same club won the minor league championship of the Federal League, going by the team name of Federals. In Newark, the club finished fifth.

137. *A player cannot be considered a _____ during a given year after collecting 130 at-bats or 50 innings pitched over previous seasons.*

ANSWER: Rookie

A player also cannot be considered a rookie if he has already spent 45 or more days on the 25-man roster limit during a previous season or seasons. A player becomes a major league rookie in the very season he reaches any of the aforementioned criteria. (He then ceases to be a rookie the following year.) This is without regard to age or experience playing in leagues outside of Major League Baseball. Although Ichiro Suzuki, for example, spent the better part of a decade playing in the Japanese League, he was considered a rookie in 2001. And although Satchel Paige spent over 20 years in the negro leagues and other circuits, he was still considered a 1948 rookie when he was finally allowed to play in the majors. It would have been silly not to award Suzuki the Rookie of the Year Award, as some suggested, for (among many reasons) he was honored as AL Rookie of the Month four times.

138. *In 1964, the _____ led by 6½ games with 12 contests remaining before losing 10 straight and finishing in a second-place tie (92-70). Fill in the blank.*

ANSWER: Philadelphia Phillies

The Phillies finished one game behind the eventual World Series champion St. Louis Cardinals, who trailed by seven games with 12 to play. In between were the Reds, who were 6½ out. While the Phillies were dropping 10 straight, Cincinnati was winning nine and St.

Louis eight in a row. Only victories in Philadelphia's final two games salvaged a second-place tie.

The 6½-game lead was not the largest margin ever wasted, although it was probably the most devastating collapse, considering the few games left. The 1995 California Angels blew an 11-game lead. The 1979 Houston Astros lost a 10½-game lead. The 1978 Boston Red Sox and the 1993 San Francisco Giants allowed a 10-game advantage to slip through their hands. And on August 14, 1969, the Chicago Cubs saw a 9½-game lead disappear. In 1962, the Dodgers lost six of their last seven games as the Giants stormed back to force a best-of-three play-off series for the NL pennant.

139. *Who doubled in Enos Slaughter from first base for the late, tie-breaking run in Game Seven of the 1946 World Series?*

ANSWER: Harry Walker

Walker's run-scoring two-bagger in the bottom of the eighth inning propelled the St. Louis Cardinals to the world title over the Boston Red Sox. For Walker, his six RBI led all series participants and his .412 batting mark made people forget his lackluster regular season.

Walker's double is sometimes mistakenly referred to as a single by those attempting to explain Slaughter's "mad dash" toward the plate. After greeting Red Sox reliever Bob Klinger with a single to lead off the eighth, Slaughter remained at first with two out as Walker's turn came around. Running on the pitch, Slaughter never slowed as Walker's drive headed toward left-center field. Leon Culberson, a late replacement in center, fielded the ball and relayed it to shortstop Johnny Pesky, who didn't appear to expect Slaughter to round third base. Seemingly caught off guard, Pesky hesitated in his relay to the plate before firing. That moment of indecision allowed Slaughter to score with the series-winning run. The Red Sox rallied in the top of the ninth, as Rudy York and Bobby Doerr singled with none out, but St. Louis winner Harry Brecheen induced a foul pop up and two grounders to end the series.

Although best remembered for that lapse, Pesky enjoyed a solid, 10-year career that started in 1942. After spending the next three seasons in the military, he returned to the Red Sox in 1946 without missing a beat. In 1947, Pesky led the league in hits for the third straight campaign in which he played, also ranking in the top three in batting for the third time over that stretch. A hit-and-runs machine, Pesky also possessed a good eye, finishing in the top ten in on-base percentage six times en route to a career OBP of .394. Defensively, Pesky was better than average at short and at third.

140. *Can you name the youngest player ever to reach 3,000 hits?*

ANSWER: Ty Cobb

At the age of 34 years, eight months, and one day, Cobb reached the milestone. "Georgia Peach" hit at least .350 an amazing 16 times, including 11 straight. Hank Aaron reached the milestone at 36 years, three months, and 12 days of age. Robin Yount was the third youngest at the age of 36 years, 11 months, and 24 days. Pete Rose was 37 years and three weeks old. Cap Anson was the oldest at 45 years and three months of age when he reached that mark in 1897. Rickey Henderson in 2001 was 42 years and nine months old.

141. *Three players share the All-Star Game record of 24 appearances. They are:*

   A Stan Musial, Henry Aaron, and Carl Yastrzemski
   B Frank Robinson, Willie Mays, and Henry Aaron
   C Willie Mays, Stan Musial, and Henry Aaron
   D Pete Rose, Willie Mays, and Al Kaline

ANSWER: C

Mays, Musial, and Aaron benefited from playing in two games each year from 1959 to 1962. Aaron was selected a record 25 times and played in a record 23 consecutive mid-summer classics. Aaron and Mays played on the winning side a record 17 times. The record for All-Star Games pitched in is eight, a mark shared by Jim Bunning, Don Drysdale, Juan Marichal, and Tom Seaver.

♦ Did you know Denny McLain missed his starting assignment for the 1969 All-Star Game, arriving in the fourth inning of the mid-summer classic? McLain, who allowed a solo home run to Willie McCovey and struck out two in his lone inning of work, also left early. He apparently kept his dentist appointment made for that afternoon, which was supposed to be an off-day (the previous day's rainout moved the All-Star Game one day back). Mel Stottlemyre started in McLain's stead.

142. *The day before the 1960 season-opener, the Cleveland Indians traded home run champion Rocky Colavito to Detroit for batting champion Harvey Kuenn. Later, on August 3, 1960, these two clubs were involved in major league history's only swap of managers. Who were the managers?*

ANSWER: Jimmie Dykes and Joe Gordon

Dykes was traded to Cleveland and Gordon was dealt to Detroit. The trade did not work out for either party. Dykes was at the end of a managing career anyway, but the swap really hurt Gordon.

Gordon appeared to be a very promising manager, going 184-151 before the historic exchange. Gordon won just 121 more games over parts of three seasons before calling it quits. Gordon also had his brilliant playing career somewhat dampened by a factor beyond his control: World War II, which caused him to miss out on two prime seasons. An excellent second baseman who combined agile feet, acrobatic defense, and a powerful swing, Gordon was Ryne Sandberg before there ever was a Ryne Sandberg. The right-handed Gordon, who played for the Yankees and Indians, earned nine All-Star appearances in 11 seasons. During the course of his career, he finished among the top ten home run hitters nine times and among the top ten RBI men five times. "Flash" Gordon retired from playing after the 1950 season, with career averages of 23 homers and 89 RBI.

143. *Which pitcher holds the modern single-season record for strikeouts?*

ANSWER: Nolan Ryan

It took a 16-strikeout, 11-inning performance in the season finale, but Ryan's 383 whiffs surpassed Sandy Koufax's 1965 total of 382. Ryan's feat is unquestionably more impressive. Not only did Ryan reach his record season total in 10 fewer innings and from a lower mound, but the righthander didn't have the luxury of pitching to pitchers as he took the more difficult designated-hitter route in 1973. Ryan's 383rd strikeout came against the Twins' Rich Reese on his last pitch of the season.

In 2001, Arizona's Randy Johnson struck out 372 batters for the third-highest single-season total ever (Ryan's 367 Ks in 1974 rank fourth). "Big Unit" had a start remaining, but opted to rest for the postseason instead. In 1999, Johnson struck out 364 batters for the fifth-highest mark. In 1997, Curt Schilling struck out 319 batters to set the NL record by a righthander, surpassing the total of 313 by J. R. Richard in 1979. Only Koufax and Johnson, among NL pitchers, have struck out more batters in one season than Schilling.

◆ Did you know Nolan Ryan owns or shares more than 40 major league, AL, or NL records—a record in itself?

◆ Did you know Nolan Ryan never won the Cy Young Award? His two best seasons, 1973 and 1974, coincided with an influx of 20-game winners in the American League. In 1973, Ryan was 21-16, with a 2.87 ERA, a record 383 strikeouts, and 26 complete games. But 11 other AL pitchers reached the 20-win mark, including Jim Palmer, who took home the Cy Young Award with a 22-9 mark and an ERA of 2.40. The following year, Ryan was 22-16, with a 2.89 ERA and 367 strikeouts. But eight others won at least 20 games, including the deserving Jim "Catfish" Hunter, who led the circuit with 25 wins and a 2.49 ERA.

144. *Can you name the Indians' third baseman who twice robbed Joe DiMaggio on the night of July 17, 1941, to help end "Joltin Joe's" streak of 56 consecutive games with a hit?*

ANSWER: Ken Keltner

The Cleveland third bagger Keltner was playing, almost literally, on the line to prevent a double, and that strategy helped the Indians stop DiMaggio's streak. DiMaggio smashed two shots down the third-base bag (to almost identical spots, according to witnesses) with identical results: out by an eyelash.

Keltner robbed many a hitter during his day, gaining a reputation as an outstanding fielder. The seven-time All-Star posted a .965 career fielding percentage over a 13-year career that ended in 1950, before the inception of the Gold Glove Award. Keltner did some damage with his bat as well, three times finishing in the top ten in homers and RBI. He saved his best for 1948, helping the Tribe win the world championship with career-bests of 31 homers and 119 RBI. His three-run homer in that year's AL play-off game against the Red Sox solidified his tag as an opportune hitter, a subsequent 2-for-21 performance in his lone World Series notwithstanding.

♦ Did you know Joe DiMaggio extended his hitting streak to 56 games against the Indians in League Park the night before being denied a hit by the Indians in Municipal Stadium? On July 16, 1941, Indians starting pitcher Al Milnar posed no challenge to DiMaggio, who went 3-for-4 with three runs scored in the Yankees' 10-8 win in the more cozy ballpark.

♦ Did you know the ketchup company H. J. Heinz was about to reward Joe DiMaggio with a million-dollar advertising contract had he extended his streak to 57 games? Bill Francis of the Baseball Hall of Fame told me he learned that the deal fell through after DiMaggio's streak ended at 56, as Heinz refused to change its slogan to Heinz 56 Varieties. According to Heinz, the company had in fact more than 57 varieties, but founder Henry Heinz chose 57 because the numbers five and seven held a special significance for him and his wife.

145. *Before the 2001 season, the last world championship team to boast a 35-homer player was:*

A New York Mets
B Oakland Athletics
C Philadelphia Phillies
D Kansas City Royals
E Los Angeles Dodgers

ANSWER: D

That's right, the 1985 Royals—with Steve Balboni—were the last such team to win a world championship before the 2001 campaign. In 1985, Balboni led the squad with 36 homers and drove in 88 runs to go with a .243 batting average. Before Balboni, you must scan back to the 1980 Phillies (with Mike Schmidt) to find another such world champion. This evidence suggests that teams that don't rely on the home run are more successful, selfless, and team-oriented, and therefore maximize their opportunities. Home run hitters, for the most part, are streaky hitters who whiff more often and are all-or-nothing contributors. Consider that of the eight 60-homer performances, just three have led to a post-season appearance and two have led to a world championship: Babe Ruth's 1927 season for the Yankees and Roger Maris' 1961 campaign for the same franchise. In each case, the team was a powerhouse club that also finished high in batting average and ERA.

146. *In an attempt to return to the majors, Joe Wilhoit put together a professional baseball record 69-game hitting streak in 1919 for Wichita of the Western League. Joe never returned. Can you name the 18-year-old by the same first name who hit in 61 consecutive games for a Pacific Coast League record 14 years later?*

ANSWER: Joe DiMaggio

The San Francisco Seals outfielder DiMaggio accomplished the feat in 1933 (his first full minor league season), providing a preview of things to come. Eight years later, DiMaggio broke George Sisler's AL record 41-game hitting streak and Willie Keeler's major league mark of 44.

◆ Did you know Bill Dahlen accrued a 42-game hitting streak in 1894, three years prior to Willie Keeler's 44-game streak? A shortstop for 21 years, Dahlen followed that streak with one of 28 games.

◆ Did you know Ed Walsh, Jr., the son of the Hall of Fame pitcher, ended Joe DiMaggio's 61-game Pacific Coast League hitting streak in 1933? Walsh Jr., who was 11-24 over four years with the White Sox from 1928 to 1932, died in 1937. He suffered from rheumatic fever.

147. *Match these teams with their ups and downs:*

1 Chicago Cubs	A	shared the record for the highest winning percentage in a 162-game season before the 1998 Yankees
2 New York Yankees		
3 Pittsburgh Pirates		
4 Boston Braves	B	hold the AL record for best road mark in a season
5 Baltimore Orioles		
	C	are enduring the longest pennant drought of any team
	D	finished a record 66½ games out of first
	E	hold the NL record for best home record (56-15) in a season

ANSWER: 1—C, 2—B, 3—E, 4—D, 5—A

The Cubs have not won a pennant since 1945. According to legend, former Billy Goat Tavern owner William Sianis is responsible for the drought, placing a curse on the Cubs after his pet goat (named Sonovia) was denied entry onto the premises of Wrigley Field for Game Four of the 1945 World Series. The Cubs, who had admitted Sonovia during the entire regular season, lost Game Four, Game Five, and Game Seven, and have never returned to the World Series. The St. Louis Browns, arguably the worst franchise in baseball history, hold the AL record of 42 seasons without a pennant (from 1902 to 1943), breaking the drought with a World Series berth in 1944. The only pennant in their history was tainted as World War II had recruited many major leaguers, depleting most rosters and creating a dearth of quality talent.

The 1939 Yankees were an incredible 54-20 (.730) on the road, holding off a challenge from the 2001 Mariners (.728). The most impressive road record in the National League belongs to the 1906 Cubs, who were a gaudy 60-15 away from home. As a matter of fact, it was these Cubs who finished 66½ games ahead of the Boston Braves in 1906. The 1902 Pirates played .789 ball at home.

The 1969 Orioles finished with a 109-53 record, tying the 1961 Yankees mark (.673). The 1998 Yankees were 114-48 (.704), a percentage since passed by those 2001 Mariners (.716). Although the Mariners matched the 116 regular-season wins by the 1906 Chicago Cubs, they did so in a 162-game schedule. The 1906 Cubs did so in a 154-game schedule.

♦ Did you know the 1906 Chicago Cubs were shocked in the World Series by the White Sox, after posting 116 regular-season wins? The Cubs were defeated in six games after compiling a magnificent ledger of 116-36 (with two ties) for a record winning percentage of .763. Before the Seattle Mariners in 2001 tied the Cubs' mark of 116 wins with a winning percentage of .716, the American League's best winning percentage belonged to the 1954 Indians (111-43). Those Indians, who won at a .721 clip, were also stunned in the World Series—in fact, they were swept. The 2001 Mariners, of course, entered the postseason as favorites before their AL Championship Series defeat.

148. *Place these Commissioners in chronological order of service: Fay Vincent, William Eckert, Happy Chandler, Kenesaw Landis, Bowie Kuhn, Bartlett Giamatti, Ford Frick, Peter Ueberroth.*

ANSWER: Landis (November 12, 1920–November 25, 1944), Chandler (April 25, 1945–July 15, 1951), Frick (September 20, 1951–November 16, 1965), Eckert (November 17, 1965–December 20, 1968), Kuhn (February 4, 1969–September 30, 1984), Ueberroth (October 1, 1984–March 31, 1989), Giamatti (April 1, 1989–September 1, 1989), and Vincent (September 13, 1989–September 7, 1992)

Bud Selig spent almost six years (September 9, 1992–July 8, 1998) as interim commissioner, and officially took over the post on July 9, 1998. That does not sit well with baseball purists, who argue that baseball needs an objective commissioner who gets paid by both the owners and players (not just the owners, who might make him their "puppet").

Selig was a key figure in the tragedy known as the 1994 strike. In what is believed to be an attempt to bolster his own team (his Milwaukee Brewers are a small-market team), Selig cancelled the remainder of what looked like a very promising conclusion to the 1994 regular season. He also cancelled the postseason, including the sacred World Series, and voiced his desire to use replacement players.

He is partly to blame for the downfall in attendance in the ensuing three seasons: Before his actions, 1994 Major League Baseball was clearly on track for its highest attendance figures in history. Many fans took the cancellations as a dismissal of their significance as well as that of baseball, and some fans have lost all interest in the sacred game. I think that any other commissioner would have salvaged the 1994 season. Even William Eckert would have found a way to reach an accord—at least until after the season!

The 1994 strike was counter to The Game's best interest. When Major League Baseball action abruptly ceased following the scheduled games on August 11, it hit many of us like a ton of bricks that Selig and Players Association chief Donald Fehr were far more concerned about the business of baseball than they were about The Game.

The 1994 campaign was shaping up to be the most exciting many of us had ever witnessed. When the negotiations between Selig and Fehr reached an impasse, Matt Williams and Ken Griffey, Jr. had 43 and 40 home runs, respectively, in their quest of the single-season, home run record—then held by Roger Maris. Tony Gwynn was hitting .394 in his quest to become the majors' first .400 hitter since Ted Williams in 1941. (Gwynn told me he was in such a groove he genuinely thought he could have reached the mark.) Frank Thomas and Albert Belle were among the top three in homers, RBI, and batting average; each was pursuing the goal of becoming the first player since Carl Yastrzemski in 1967 to earn a Triple Crown. A record average of 31,612 fans per game attended major league contests that year.

I've since forgiven Selig and Fehr—interviewing them played a role in that pardon, as did the 1998 season—but I ask "what if?" pretty often for a baseball nut who has supposedly reached closure. The strike was a shame no matter how you look at it.

♦ Did you know that Ford Frick, the same man who held down the post of commissioner and the NL presidency, previously served as a sportswriter and sportscaster? Frick devoted his entire life to baseball, starting out as a sportswriter and, later, a New York broadcaster before becoming the director of the National League Service Bureau in 1934. Nine months later, he was elected as NL president, a position he held for 17 years. On September 20, 1951, he became baseball's third commissioner. Frick, who also helped found the Hall of Fame, is celebrated with an annual award that bears his name: the Ford C. Frick Award. It is presented to a broadcaster for "major contributions to baseball," according to the Hall of Fame. The award has been presented annually since 1978, and honorees include such venerable and distinguished figures as Mel Allen, Red Barber, Russ Hodges, Ernie Harwell, Vin Scully, Curt Gowdy, Jack Buck, the late Harry Caray, Joe Garagiola, and Lindsey Nelson.

149. *Name the only team to sweep the League Championship Series and the World Series during the same postseason.*

ANSWER: The 1976 Reds

The Reds obliterated the Phillies in three games and the Yankees in four. Cincinnati's "Big Red Machine" outscored the Phillies and the Yankees by a combined 41-19 margin, out-homering them 7-2. The Reds were almost unbeatable, with a lineup that consisted of Hall of Famer Johnny Bench behind the plate, the consistent Tony Perez at first base, two-time MVP Joe Morgan at second, the defensively solid Dave Concepcion at short, superstar Pete Rose at third, the fearsome George Foster in left field, Cesar Geronimo patrolling center field, and the underrated Ken Griffey, Sr. performing quite well in right. Venerable historian Bill James calls this collection of talent "possibly the greatest starting lineup of all time." How good were they? Of the combined 104 games (including postseason) that these eight players started together in 1975 or 1976, the Reds won 83 and lost just 21. That's a startling winning percentage of .798.

150. *Who made the following statement? "In the absence of a hearing and therefore in the absence of evidence to the contrary, I am confronted by the factual record of Mr. Dowd. On the basis of that, yes, I have concluded he bet on baseball. The Matter of Mr. Rose is now closed. Let no one think it did not hurt baseball. That hurt will pass, however, as the great glory of the game asserts itself and a resilient institution goes forward. Let it also be clear that no individual is superior to the game."*

ANSWER: A. Bartlett Giamatti

Commissioner Giamatti made the statement on August 24, 1989, after banning Pete Rose for gambling on baseball. Giamatti went on to add, "The banishment for life of Pete Rose from baseball is a sad end of a sorry episode. One of the game's greatest players has engaged in a variety of acts which have stained the game, and he must now live with the consequences of those acts. There is absolutely no deal for reinstatement." Giamatti passed away eight days later.

To this day, Rose has fans, media, and players who defend him, refusing to allow the gambling issue to cloud their perception of "Charlie Hustle," the man whose accomplishments may be an inspiration in their lives. But Major League Baseball would never have banned Rose unless it was absolutely sure he bet on baseball. What motive would Major League Baseball have in embarrassing one of its own greats? After all, banning Pete Rose, one of the game's most beloved characters, was not exactly a good public relations move.

Rose, who signed an agreement in 1989 from Giamatti in which he accepted a lifetime ban, admits now that he is a compulsive gambler. But he still denies this is a serious problem and denies he ever bet on baseball, despite the evidence. That's why Mr. Rose, in my opinion, will never get elected into the Hall of Fame. And it's a shame because, outside of the gambling circle, Rose is a very approachable and wonderful character, with a refreshing knowledge of the game's history. His enthusiasm remains strong for The Game. Get him to talk about baseball (don't bring up gambling, of course) and he's remarkably pleasant to listen to. He clearly appeals to the common man—anyone who can appreciate an unflagging work ethic.

♦ Did you know the Baseball Hall of Fame is the the only one of the four major sports shrines that judges players on their off-the-field behavior as well as on-field performance? Gambling rules have accompanied Major League Baseball throughout its history, and were underscored following the Black Sox scandal of 1919. And of the 14 men permanently banned by baseball for gambling, nary a one has been reinstated.

151. *Match these players with their achievements:*

1	Bo Jackson and Willie Mays	A	the first teammates to reach 30-30 in the same season
2	Jose Canseco, Barry Bonds, and Alex Rodriguez	B	the first repeaters of the 30-30 club
3	Rickey Henderson and Eric Davis	C	the first two players to homer and steal a base in one All-Star Game
4	Bobby Bonds and Willie Mays	D	the only two players to reach 20 homers and 80 steals in one year
5	Darryl Strawberry and Howard Johnson	E	the only players to reach 40 homers and 40 steals in one season

ANSWER: 1—C, 2—E, 3—D, 4—B, 5—A

Canseco (1988) and Bonds (1996) each had 42 home runs and 40 steals eight years apart, and Rodriguez had 46 thefts to go with his

42 home runs in 1998. Since HoJo and Strawberry reached 30-30 for the Mets in 1987, only Colorado's Ellis Burks and Dante Bichette have accomplished the feat (in 1996). In 1998, Toronto's Shawn Green and Jose Canseco almost joined that group. Canseco hit 46 homers, but fell one steal shy. Henderson was the first to achieve 20-80, with 24 homers and 80 steals in 1985. Both Henderson and Davis did so the following year.

Playing center field for the Reds, the lean, six-foot-three Davis showed a glimpse of his awesome talent and potential with 27 homers and 80 steals in 1986. Most impressively, those numbers came in limited action (415 at-bats), as the right-handed speedster didn't become a full-time starter until June 15. Alas for Davis, a slew of injuries (as well as cancer a decade later) often sidelined him and prevented him from reaching his full potential. In June 1997, Davis underwent surgery to remove a colorectal cancer tumor. Unbelievably, Davis returned to the field (for the Orioles) in less than three months, earning a score of awards celebrating his valiant fight against the disease—most notably, the Roberto Clemente Award and the Hutch Award. (The Hutch Award honors players who display the "fighting spirit and competitive desire" of Fred Hutchinson, the Reds manager who fought cancer while guiding his Cincinnati ballclub in 1964, knowing he would die that year.) The valiant Davis retired following the 2001 season with 282 home runs, 349 steals, and a .269 batting average.

◆ Did you know Reds manager Fred Hutchinson concealed his cancer from the Cincinnati players for most of the 1964 season? After being informed of the throat disease by his cancer surgeon—his brother—the previous winter, Hutchinson managed Cincinnati for 99 games before taking himself out and entering a hospital in late July. With the players' knowledge of his terminal condition, he returned a week later, and managed 10 more games before leaving for the final time. He lost his fight in mid-November. Forgotten was Hutchinson's career as a pitcher for the Tigers. The righthander, after missing five seasons due to World War II, returned in 1946 and enjoyed five straight winning seasons, earning at least 13 victories each year. He retired from pitching, with a 95-71 career ledger. As a manager, "Hutch" won 830 games and took his Reds to the 1961 World Series.

152. *Who said it?*

1 "Hitting against Sandy Koufax is like drinking coffee with a fork"

2 "I don't want to replace Babe Ruth, I just want them to remember me"

3 "Blind people come to the park just to listen to him [Tom Seaver] pitch"

4 "Trying to sneak a fastball past Hank Aaron is like trying to sneak the sun past a rooster"

A Reggie Jackson
B Willie Stargell
C Hank Aaron
D Curt Simmons

ANSWER: 1—B, 2—C, 3—A, 4—D

In the July 1981 issue of *Sports Illustrated,* Frank Deford paid Seaver a great compliment: "Even at his fastest, Seaver always had the image of a thinking artist rather than a hurler." Those who saw Seaver pitch would agree.

Seaver was the Ted Williams of pitching, a student of the mechanics on the mound. The six-foot-one righthander had an exceptional combination of power and precision on the mound in addition to excellent durability and consistency. So perfect was his form that he didn't suffer any arm trouble until his third decade in the majors. The owner of a devastating fastball and a wicked slider, the intelligent Seaver defied all stereotypes of power pitchers, who are not known for impeccable form and pinpoint control. Those who saw him pitch will always remember how Seaver's right knee dragged the mound on the follow-through, the result of his "drop-and-drive" delivery. Seaver used that right knee to put up some great numbers on the mound.

Among his accomplishments were five 20-win campaigns, a major league record nine straight seasons of 200 or more strikeouts, and a trio of Cy Young Awards. He also led the league in strikeouts five times, and paced his circuit in wins and ERA three times apiece. Seaver's achievements were all the more remarkable considering the low run support he received in New York. Like "The Big Train" Walter Johnson, Seaver succeeded despite his teams and not because of them. With more offensive support, Seaver could have perhaps challenged Christy Mathewson and Grover Alexander (373 wins each) for the third highest victory total in history.

◆ Did you know Tom Seaver was turned away in his attempt to become the first pitcher to win four Cy Young Awards despite a league-best 14-2 ledger during the 1981 strike-shortened season? Aside from leading the National League in wins and winning percentage for the Reds, Seaver was denied the award in favor of Dodgers rookie Fernando Valenzuela. The left-handed screwballer became a national sensation with a no-look, pirouette delivery that caught the nation's attention and gave birth to "Fernandomania." After an amazing start, the southpaw began tiring near the end of the season, and labored to a 13-7 record, and an ERA (2.48) barely lower than Seaver's 2.54. Of course, Valenzuela did throw seven more shutouts, five more complete games, with 93 more strikeouts than Seaver.

153. *Match these players with their deeds:*

1	Lew Burdette	A	Hall of Fame catcher who is credited with inventing shin guards
2	Don Newcombe		
3	Vida Blue	B	matched Harvey Haddix with 12 shutout innings before Haddix lost the perfect game and the contest in the 13th
4	Chad Kreuter		
5	Roger Bresnahan		
		C	youngest MVP ever at 22
		D	caught Nolan Ryan's 5,000th strikeout
		E	surrendered Dick Sisler's 10th-inning, pennant-winning three-run homer in the 1950 season finale

ANSWER: 1—B, 2—E, 3—C, 4—D, 5—A

Burdette, the crafty and confident righthander, completed a 12-hit shutout without issuing a walk and striking out just two Pirates in that unforgettable duel. Burdette was a winner. The post-season stalwart won 203 of 347 career regular-season decisions, twice reaching the 20-win plateau and twice attaining 19 victories. Ryan's 5,000th strikeout on August 22, 1989, was a 96-mile-per-hour fastball past Rickey Henderson. It came just four years after Ryan's 4,000th strikeout, a curve eluding the Mets' Danny Heep. Newcombe's Dodger teammate Ralph Branca lost the pennant in a similar fashion the following season.

Blue's standard as the youngest to ever win an MVP Award was threatened by 21-year-old Alex Rodriguez of the Seattle Mariners in 1996. Rodriguez finished a close runner-up to Juan Gonzalez of the Texas Rangers, despite a record-breaking season that netted him Player of the Year recognition by a slew of organizations. Johnny Bench of the Reds was also 22 in 1970, but was just one month shy of his 23rd birthday. Hal Newhouser (1944), Jeff Burroughs (1974), Fred Lynn (1975), and Cal Ripken, Jr. (1983) were all 23 years of age when they won their first MVP.

The innovative Bresnahan was also, reportedly, the first to explore a batting helmet, coming up with the idea during a stay in the hospital stemming from a beaning. But no one saw his vision then, and batting helmets had to wait until the 1970s.

♦ Did you know Jack Clements of Philadelphia from the Union Association became the first catcher to wear a chest protector in 1884? A few give Charles Bennett of Detroit in 1886 the credit for first wearing a chest protector, but most historians side with Clements. James Alexander from Harvard University was the first to wear a catcher's mask, doing so on April 12, 1877. Incidentally, the mask was invented by Harvard graduate Frederick Winthrop Thayer. Clint Courtney of the St. Louis Browns was the first catcher to wear glasses (in 1953). Courtney was also the first to wear the "big mitt," a 50% larger catcher's glove (designed by Paul Richards), to receive knuckleball pitcher Hoyt Wilhelm. These pioneers were severely ridiculed when they first introduced their innovations.

♦ Did you know Toronto's Charlie O'Brien became the first to use a hockey-style catcher's mask, doing so on September 13, 1996, for the Toronto Blue Jays? The mask looks like a hockey goaltender's mask, protecting a lot more of the head than the regular-style catcher's mask and also providing a bigger opening from the front. At 50 ounces, it is 10 ounces heavier than the normal catcher's mask and costs about $1,200. It took Major League Baseball four months to approve the mask.

154. *Who was the first batter to collect double figures in hits in the League Championship Series as well as World Series during the same postseason?*

ANSWER: Marty Barrett

Boston Red Sox second baseman Barrett gathered 11 hits versus the California Angels in the 1986 AL Championship Series and 13 safeties against the New York Mets in the World Series for a then-record 24 hits in a single postseason. Barrett tied the World Series hit mark set by Bobby Richardson in 1964 and equaled by Lou Brock four years later.

Will Clark holds the League Championship Series record of 13 hits, doing so in just five games in 1989. Taking advantage of a three-tier post-season format in 1995, Atlanta's Marquis Grissom combined for a new record of 25 hits, then in 1996 duplicated Barrett's feat of 10 or more hits in the League Championship Series and World Series. In the 1993 AL Championship Series, Tim Raines of the White Sox and Devon White of the Blue Jays each went 12-for-27 at the plate, eclipsing Barrett's mark.

155. *Match these Triple Crowners with their circumstances:*

1 Ty Cobb
2 Heinie Zimmerman
3 Frank Robinson
4 Paul Hines
5 Tip O'Neil

A died in 1935 not knowing he was a Triple Crown winner
B is the only "Quadruple" Crown winner, also leading his league in stolen bases
C won an American Association Triple Crown in 1887 (also leading in runs, hits, doubles, triples, total bases, and slugging)
D was one of only two AL players to bat .300 the year he won the Triple Crown
E is no longer considered a Triple Crown winner by some sources

ANSWER: 1—B (1909), 2—E (1912), 3—D (1966), 4—A (1878), 5—C

In 1909, Cobb led the American League with nine homers, 107 RBI, a .377 batting average, and 76 steals. In fact, Cobb led the majors in all four of those figures. Now, that's domination. Because *The Baseball Encyclopedia* didn't want to retract the statement, Zimmerman is still credited with a Triple Crown, despite new evidence that his RBI total was 99, three fewer than Honus Wagner's 102. The Baseball Records Committee met in 1968 and ascertained that Hines did indeed win the batting title for the Triple Crown.

♦ Did you know that Paul Hines and Heinie Zimmerman are the only Triple Crown winners not to reach the Hall of Fame?

♦ Did you know Heinie Zimmerman was forced to move from second base to third base for his 1912 Triple Crown season, because of Jim Doyle's death? A position change usually diminishes a player's offensive production, but Zimmerman responded with a career year. He batted .372 with 14 homers. Doyle died on February 1, 1912, following an appendicitis operation. In 1911, Doyle played third base and batted .282, and Zimmerman played at second to form an unusual keystone combination with shortstop Joe Tinker. Johnny Evers was limited to 155 at-bats in 1911 because of a nervous breakdown. (In 1912, Evers rebounded with a .341 batting average.)

156. *The record for the most intentional walks drawn in one season (45) is held by:*

A Willie McCovey
B Frank Howard
C Mickey Mantle
D Henry Aaron
E Harmon Killebrew

ANSWER: A

John Olerud (1993) and Ted Williams (1957) share the AL mark of 33. Sammy Sosa in 2001 set the record for most intentional walks by a right-handed batter with 37. In 1987, Tim Raines set the single-season record of 26 intentional passes drawn by a switch-hitter.

157. *Do you know how many intentional walks Roger Maris drew in his record-breaking 1961 campaign?*

ANSWER: Zero

Pitchers had little choice but to pitch to Maris, with Mickey Mantle batting behind him in the cleanup spot. With Mantle on deck, Maris batted .293 with 54 homers in 475 at-bats according to the Society for American Baseball Research. Without Mantle backing him up, Maris was held to a porous .174 mark and seven home runs in 115 at-bats. The latter stats include early-season figures when Maris batted seventh in the batting order. Imagine how many home runs Mantle would have hit had he batted third and Maris fourth! Mantle was walked a league-high 126 times that year. Incidentally, Maris drew four intentional walks in a 12-inning game the following season. AL pitchers had learned their lesson.

Alex Rodriguez of the Mariners is the only other player in history with at least 40 homers and zero intentional walks. In 1998, A-Rod hit 42 without a free pass. Hitting behind him was a fellow by the name of George Kenneth Griffey, Jr.

♦ Did you know Roger Maris didn't homer in his record-breaking 1961 campaign until April 26? Maris also failed to hit a grand slam that season.

158. *Hughie Jennings holds the unenviable career record of being hit by a pitch 287 times. Don Baylor holds the modern record of being hit by a pitch 267 times. Whose modern mark of 243 did Baylor surpass?*

ANSWER: Ron Hunt

Hunt held that mark, although he only played 12 years, from 1963 to 1974. Hunt, a .273 career-hitting second baseman for five NL teams, set a still-standing single-season record of being hit by a pitch a whopping 50 times for Montreal in 1971. Hunt, who batted close to the plate almost without regard for his body, never hit more than 10 homers in a season and retired with just 39.

The menacing Baylor, who also batted close to the plate, was a different kind of hitter, retiring with 338 home runs and 1,276 RBI. Baylor's 35 hits by pitches in 1986 remain the AL record. Like Hunt, Baylor played his entire career in one league.

Jennings was hit by a pitch at least 46 times on three separate occasions in his colorful career. The Hall of Famer, who also managed the Tigers from 1907 to 1920, batted .311 over parts of 17 seasons (1891–1918) and reached base 39% of the time. This hyper and lovable character often annoyed opponents as manager of the Tigers with his earsplitting, trademark shouts of "ee-yah" from the third-base's coaching box.

159. *The Mets' Todd Hundley hit 41 home runs in 1996, all while catching, to break Roy Campanella's 43-year record for most homers strictly as a catcher. But can you name the only catcher to lead the league in home runs?*

ANSWER: Johnny Bench

Bench did it twice, leading the National League with 45 home runs in 1970 and 40 home runs in 1972. In 1970, Bench hit 38 as a catcher with six coming as an outfielder and one as a pinch-hitter. In becoming the first catcher to reach the 40-homer plateau in 1953, Campanella hit 40 while catching and one while pinch-hitting.

◆ Did you know Roy Campanella's .500 career slugging percentage is the best among catchers? The Mets' Mike Piazza, however, is not that far off from qualifying as the best. He takes a .579 career slugging average, spanning 4,638 at-bats, into the 2002 season. Piazza's certain to reach his 5,000th at-bat then.

160. *Match these players with their record-setting feats:*

1 Ralph Kiner	A was the first player in history to belt home runs in his first two major league at-bats
2 Ivan Rodriguez	
3 Bob Nieman	B led or tied for the home run lead in seven straight years
4 Hack Wilson	
	C holds the single-season record with 191 RBI
	D set the AL single-season record for homers by a catcher with 35

ANSWER: 1—B, 2—D, 3—A, 4—C

Remarkably, Kiner's seven straight home run titles came during his first seven years. Kiner hit 369 home runs spanning a 10-year career that came to an end due to back problems. In 1999, Rodriguez set the mark for catchers with 35 to eclipse the previous mark of 34 by Terry Steinbach, achieved three years earlier. Steinbach, who hit a total of 35 roundtrippers in 1996, surpassed the 33 Carlton Fisk hit for the White Sox in 1985. Fisk had a total of 37 that season.

On July 6, 2000, Keith McDonald of the Cardinals became the second and only player besides Nieman to homer in his first two at-bats. Bert Campaneris, Mark Quinn, and Charlie Reilly are the only other players to hit two homers in their first major league game. Campaneris of the Kansas Athletics did so on July 23, 1967, Quinn accomplished the feat for the Kansas City Royals on September 14, 1999, and Reilly achieved the feat in the American Association in 1889. Nieman and Campaneris combined for 204 home runs over a composite of 31 years.

After 69 years, Major League Baseball in 1999 officially changed Wilson's RBI total from 190 to 191, after overwhelming evidence was brought forth supporting the claim.

◆ Did you know it was the Society for American Baseball Research (SABR) that discovered the hidden RBI during Hack Wilson's record-breaking 1930 campaign? For 69 years, Wilson's record was recognized as 190 RBI. But evidence to the contrary brought forth by SABR began the process that culminated in Major League Baseball historian Jerome Holtzman's decision to change the record. Based on evidence showing that an RBI single during the second game of an August 28 doubleheader was never counted, SABR made the case to have the record identified as 191. Accounts of said game in newspapers such as *The Chicago Daily News, The Chicago Tribune, The Cincinnati Enquirer, The New York Times,* and *The Washington Post* corroborate the discovery.

161. *Match these players with their unique feats:*

1	Jim Rice	A the first designated hitter with 100 RBI
2	Bubbles Hargrave	B the only player to lead the league in
3	Rusty Staub	triples, homers, and RBI in the same
4	Maury Wills	season
5	Mike Piazza	C played in a season-record 165 regular
6	Ted Williams	season games
		D one of only two catchers to win the
		batting crown
		E reached base a record 16 straight plate
		appearances
		F holds the record for catchers with 201
		hits in a season

ANSWER: 1—B, 2—D, 3—A, 4—C, 5—F, 6—E

Ernie Lombardi was the other catcher to win a batting title. In fact, he won it twice (in 1938 and 1942). Hargrave's title came in 1926 based on his .353 average. Ted Simmons's mark of 193 hits by a full-time catcher (130 or more games) stood for 22 years until Piazza surpassed the mark in 1997. Yogi Berra still holds the season mark of 192 hits while exclusively catching.

During the 1997 season, Frank Thomas of the White Sox reached base in 15 consecutive trips to the plate, falling one short of the major league record. Barry Bonds and John Olerud share the NL mark of reaching base in consecutive plate appearances with 15, a streak they each reached in September of 1998. Bonds broke Pedro Guerrero's stretch of 14.

♦ Did you know the Los Angeles Dodgers' Mike Piazza in 1997 tied Bill Dickey's single-season record for batting average by a full-time catcher with a .362 mark? Dickey set the mark in 1936 for the Yankees while playing 112 games and catching 107 of them. Like Dickey, Piazza also finished third in batting. But Piazza appeared in 152 games, catching 139 of them. Piazza is bound to challenge a lot more catching standards, after hitting at least .300 in each of his first nine full seasons. Among those catchers with at least 1,000 games caught, Piazza owns the highest career batting average, with a .325 mark entering the 2002 season.

162. *Match the players from "Who's on First?" with their position:*

1	First baseman	A	Because
2	Second baseman	B	Why
3	Third baseman	C	I Don't Know
4	Shortstop	D	What
5	Left fielder	E	Today
6	Center fielder	F	Who
7	Pitcher	G	I Don't Give a Darn
8	Catcher	H	Tomorrow

ANSWER: 1—F, 2—D, 3—C, 4—G, 5—B, 6—A, 7—H, 8—E

For some reason, actors Bud Abbott and Lou Costello never identified the right fielder during their famous skit, featuring a befuddled Costello asking Abbott about players with "very peculiar" names on their new baseball team. Of all the routines the lanky Abbott and the rotund Costello performed together throughout the 1930s, 1940s, and 1950s, this one stands out as their most popular. The comedians' "Who's on First?" routine can be heard in a special room at the Baseball Hall of Fame in Cooperstown. It never ceases being funny.

FIRST POSTSEASON

Best-of-Seven League Championship Series

For those who earned 100 regular-season victories, I welcome you to the first postseason. You must raise the level of your intensity and hone your skills to meet the grueling demands of a world championship. Play ball!

Game One Question:

Whose record of 18 consecutive scoreless innings in League Championship Series action did Steve Avery break by extending his mark to 22⅓ consecutive shutout innings in 1992 League Championship Series play?

ANSWER: Ken Holtzman

Holtzman pitched brilliantly for Oakland, yielding only one run in 20 innings (to win both starts) in 1973 and 1974 combined. In working Game Three of the 1973 AL Championship Series, Holtzman threw a marvelous 11-inning, complete game three-hitter, in which Baltimore's Mike Cuellar had a three-hitter before capitulating a dramatic, game-ending home run to Bert Campaneris leading off the bottom of the 11th. Not having been scored upon from the second inning, Holtzman threw a five-hit shutout in Game Two of the 1974 AL Championship Series versus Baltimore.

Named the 1991 NL Championship Series MVP, Avery scorched the Pirates for two wins while holding them scoreless over his 16⅓ innings. The streak came to an end after six scoreless innings during a victory in Game Two of the 1992 NL Championship Series versus the same Pirates.

♦ Did you know Ken Holtzman earned a combined 59 regular-season victories during Oakland's run of three straight world championships from 1972 to 1974? The southpaw, traded west for Rick Monday, rebounded from a 9-15 season with the Cubs in 1971 to notch campaigns of 19, 21, and 19 victories for the A's. Holtzman added six post-season wins to that total, with a 2.30 ERA.

Game Two Question:

> *Can you name the only co-MVPs in League Championship Series history?*

> ANSWER: Randy Myers and Ron Dibble

Cincinnati Reds relievers Myers and Dibble shared the League Championship Series MVP for the National League in 1990 against the Pittsburgh Pirates. Myers saved three games and pitched 5⅔ scoreless innings. Dibble was even more dominant in saving a game, pitching five hitless innings, and striking out 10. Their combined totals: four saves, 10⅔ innings, no runs, 17 strikeouts, four walks, and only two hits allowed.

Incredibly, this duo maintained its high octane level of success in the subsequent World Series versus the mighty Oakland Athletics. Myers and Dibble combined for one save, one win, five hits allowed, one walk, and seven strikeouts in 7⅔ innings pitched for another combined 0.00 ERA performance. Whew!

However, Jose Rijo won the MVP honors in that classic, with two wins and a 0.59 ERA as the Reds shockingly swept an Oakland ballclub that most fans expected to do the sweeping. Cincinnati proved the adage that good pitching prevails, silencing the Athletics' bats and limiting them to nine runs, a .200 batting average, and a powerless .304 slugging mark.

Game Three Question:

> *Can you name the only pitcher to start a record four playoff games in one year prior to the new eight-team post-season format?*

> ANSWER: Fernando Valenzuela

Valenzuela took advantage of the 1981 strike-shortened season to show off his screwball to millions of spectators and set a playoff record. During the NL Western Division playoff (best-of-five) to determine the division's representative in the NL Championship Series, Valenzuela started Game One (eight innings, one run, six hits, no decision) and Game Four (complete game, four-hit, 2-1 victory) as Los Angeles came back from a two-games-to-none deficit to win in five games versus Houston.

During the NL Championship Series versus Montreal, Valenzuela started and lost Game Two (six innings, three runs, seven hits) and won Game Five (8⅔ innings, one run, three hits), thanks to Rick Monday's dramatic home run off Steve Rogers in the top of the ninth inning for a 2-1 pennant clincher. Bob Welch saved the game as the Dodgers overcame a two games-to-one deficit. Interestingly, the rookie southpaw started only one game in the 1981 World Series (a Game Three victory). But Valenzuela's complete game awakened the Dodgers as they, again, overcame a two-none deficit in games to win the next four. The Rookie of the Year and Cy Young Award winner was upstaged by Ron Cey, Pedro Guerrero, and Steve Yeager, the World Series' tri-MVPs (baseball history's only tri-award winners of any kind). Burt Hooton garnered the NL Championship Series MVP with two wins and no earned runs in 14⅔ innings.

Game Four Question:

In what year did Dusty Baker earn NL Championship Series MVP honors?

ANSWER: 1977

Baker became the first-ever League Championship Series MVP in 1977 (the award's first year in the National League) by slugging .857 with two home runs (a grand slam included) and eight RBI in the four-game Dodger triumph over Philadelphia.

In 1978, the Dodgers again defeated the Phillies in four games, with Steve Garvey winning the NL Championship Series MVP. Garvey slugged over 1.000 and hit .389 with four home runs (tying the mark set by Bob Robertson in 1971 and tied by Jeff Leonard in 1987 and Jim Thome in 1998), one double, one triple, and seven RBI.

Game Five Question (if necessary):

Willie Stargell was the oldest player to receive a post-season award at the age of 39. Can you name the oldest player to garner an AL Championship Series MVP?

ANSWER: Graig Nettles

Nettles was 37 years, one month, and 25 days old when he won the 1981 AL Championship Series MVP. Nettles hit .500 with a three-run double in Game One (a 3-1 Yankee win), a three-run homer in Game Two (a 13-3 Yankee win), and another three-run double in Game Three (which they also won, 4-0, to win the pennant).

Stargell, ever a clutch performer since teammate Roberto Clemente's death, was 39 years of age when he won the 1979 NL Championship Series and World Series MVPs. Stargell hit .455 with two home runs (including an 11th-inning three-run homer to give the Pirates a 5-2 victory in Game One) and six RBI in the NL Championship Series sweep over Cincinnati. The Hall of Fame first baseman hit .400 in the World Series with three homers, four doubles, seven runs scored, and seven RBI versus Baltimore.

When Orel Hershiser won the 1995 AL Championship Series MVP, he fell 24 days short of Nettles' mark at 37 years, one month, and one day old. Hershiser was 2-0 with a 1.29 ERA against the Mariners. "Bull Dog" struck out 15 and walked three in 14 innings.

♦ Did you know Orel Hershiser is the only player to win a League Championship Series MVP Award for a NL team and an AL team? With the Dodgers in 1988, Hershiser was 1-0 with a save and a 1.09 ERA in 24⅔ innings against the Mets. Hershiser even had one RBI and a run scored.

Game Six Question (if necessary):

Which Kansas City Royal won the first AL Championship Series MVP in 1980?

ANSWER: Frank White

Second baseman White hit .545 with three RBI, three runs scored, and great defense to collect the 1980 AL Championship Series trophy. His homer in the top of the fifth inning of Game Three gave Kansas City a 1-0 lead before the Yankees scored twice in the sixth to precede George Brett's three-run shot off Rich Gossage in the seventh. The three-game sweep of New York came after League Championship Series defeats to the Yankees in 1976, 1977, and 1978. The first-time pennant winners lost to the Phillies in the 1980 World Series, four games to two.

Game Seven Question (if necessary):

From 1988 to 1990, Oakland landed three straight AL Championship Series MVPs. Can you name this trio in chronological order?

ANSWER: Dennis Eckersley, Rickey Henderson, and Dave Stewart

Eckersley saved all four games in helping Oakland sweep Boston for the 1988 honor, allowing just one hit over six scoreless innings. Henderson was a terror in the 1989 AL Championship Series to lead Oakland past Toronto in five games. He batted .400, stole a League Championship Series record eight bases, hit two home runs, scored eight times, and drove in five. And Stewart won the 1990 AL Championship Series MVP with two wins (the last against Boston's Roger Clemens) and a 1.13 ERA.

In sweeping Boston again, Stewart became the first pitcher to win his team's pennant-clinching game for the third straight year. Stewart did it a record fourth time in 1993 for Toronto. Including his 1992 AL Championship Series Game Five victory and his two victories in the 1993 AL Championship Series for Toronto, Stewart is an unmatched 8-0 (2.03 ERA) in League Championship Series play.

◆ Did you know Dave Stewart's Game Four win in the 1990 AL Championship Series marked his eighth straight overall victory against Roger Clemens?

If you have won four League Championship Series Games, you advance to the first World Series.

Best-of-Seven World Series

The following questions are for managers who won four League Championship Series Games.

Game One Question:

Can you name the unheralded Pirates second baseman and shortstop who erupted in the 1979 World Series, combining for 22 hits, five doubles, one triple, 10 runs scored, and eight RBI?

ANSWER: Phil Garner, Tim Foli

Second baseman Garner hit .500 (12-for-24) with four doubles and five RBI, and shortstop Foli hit .333 (10-for-30) with six runs scored. That performance made up for the five errors (Foli had three) they committed versus Baltimore. The keystone combination also excelled in the NL Championship Series versus the Reds. Garner batted .417 with a homer, and Foli hit .333 with three RBI.

Game Two Question:

Reggie Jackson is the last player to win two World Series MVP Awards since the inception of the award in 1955. Can you name the two other players to earn the World Series MVP twice?

ANSWER: Sandy Koufax and Bob Gibson

Koufax became the first, winning the award in 1963 and 1965. Bob Gibson won his two World Series MVP Awards in 1964 and 1967.

In the Dodgers' 1963 sweep of the Yankees, Koufax won the award on the basis of a 2-0 record (defeating New York ace Whitey

Ford each time), 1.50 ERA, and 23 strikeouts in 18 innings. Two years later, Koufax was 2-1 (his loss in Game Two was abetted by three Dodger errors leading to four of the five runs being unearned) with two shutouts (a four-hitter in Game Five and a three-hitter, after two days' rest, in Game Seven). Koufax had a minuscule 0.38 ERA and 29 strikeouts versus Minnesota in the 1965 World Series.

Gibson recorded a 2-1 mark with 31 strikeouts to earn the 1964 World Series MVP versus the Yankees. His 10-inning six-hitter in Game Five (batterymate Tim McCarver hit a three-run homer in the top of the 10th inning for a 5-2 win) and complete game in Game Seven were big. Gibson was outstanding in the 1967 World Series. He pitched a complete game 2-1 victory in Game One, a five-hit shutout in Game Four, and a three-hit complete game victory in Game Seven. In total, Gibson was 3-0 with an ERA of 1.00, 26 strikeouts, and only 14 hits allowed in 27 innings pitched.

In 1973 with Oakland, Jackson led the A's to a seven-game World Series win over the Mets. Jackson hit .310 with five extra-base hits and six RBI, including a key two-run homer in Game Seven. In the 1977 fall classic, Jackson (later dubbed "Mr. October" for his implausible performance under pressure) hit .450 with a record five home runs, eight RBI, and 10 runs scored. His record-tying three home runs in Game Six finished off the Dodgers.

♦ Did you know Reggie Jackson is the only player to hit a home run in four consecutive World Series games? Jackson homered off the Dodgers' Rick Rhoden in the sixth inning of Game Four (1977), homered off Don Sutton in the eighth inning of Game Five, hit the three consecutive blasts in Game Six, and then homered in the seventh inning off Tommy John in Game One of the 1978 World Series.

♦ Did you know Bob Gibson (7-2, 1.89 ERA in fall classic play) won seven straight World Series decisions (1964, 1967, 1968) book-ended by a 1964 Game Two loss and a 1968 Game Seven defeat?

Game Three Question:

> *Can you name either of the two hitters with the highest lifetime World Series batting average (with a minimum of 50 at-bats)?*

ANSWER: Johnny "Pepper" Martin and Paul Molitor

Martin and Molitor each hit .418, with 23 hits in 55 World Series at-bats. Martin did it over his three World Series with the St. Louis Cardinals. The outfielder was used as a pinch-runner once in the 1928 series and had nary an at-bat. In the 1931 fall classic, Martin went 12-for-24. In the 1934 fall classic, Martin went 11-for-31. Martin's seven doubles, seven stolen bases, and .636 slugging percentage all remain in the top 10 on lifetime World Series lists. St. Louis was swept by the Yankees in 1928, but defeated the Athletics and Tigers (in seven games each time) in 1931 and 1934, respectively. Molitor was 11-for-31 for Milwaukee in his first World Series in 1982, and 12-for-24 in the 1993 World Series for Toronto.

Lou Brock, whose 14 stolen bases tie him with Eddie Collins for the World Series career mark, hit .391 over three World Series and 87 at-bats. Brock, also a Cardinals outfielder, went 9-for-30 (.300) in the 1964 fall classic, 12-for-29 (.414) in 1967, and 13-for-28 (.464) in the 1968 thriller versus the victorious Tigers. Brock's .655 slugging percentage is fifth.

Lou Gehrig has the highest lifetime World Series batting average with a minimum of 100 at-bats. Gehrig had 43 hits in 119 at-bats for a .361 mark. Gehrig's eight doubles, three triples, 10 home runs, 30 runs scored, 35 RBI, and a .731 slugging percentage are all among the top six in their respective categories.

Bobby Brown still owns the highest batting mark (.439) among those with at least 40 at-bats, getting 18 hits in 41 at-bats. Among the active players with 50 or more at-bats, Marquis Grissom owns the highest mark at .390 (30 hits in 77 at-bats), as of the end of 2001.

Game Four Question:

Which of the following pitchers didn't *win three games in a single World Series?*

A Harry Brecheen
B Red Faber
C Joe Wood
D Babe Adams
E Lefty Grove

ANSWER: E

Grove didn't receive a decision in his two 1929 World Series relief appearances and won two of the three decisions in each of the following two fall classics (1930, 1931).

Brecheen won his three during the 1946 World Series victory over the Red Sox. The Cardinals hurler (132-92, 2.92 during career) threw complete games in Game Two and Game Six, and won Game Seven in relief. The lefty with a 4-1 overall World Series record (he went 0-1 in the 1943 series defeat to the Yankees and 1-0 in the 1944 series victory over the Browns) recorded a minuscule ERA of 0.45 in 20 innings of work.

Faber also won a game in relief to help himself to a 3-1 mark in his only World Series appearance (1917). Despite not starting the first game, Faber (a 253-211 career pitcher) won Game Two, Game Five (in relief), and the finale, Game Six. Faber (2.33 series ERA) lost Game Four to the classic's defeated Giants.

"Smokey" Joe Wood also went 3-1, winning the finale in relief in his lone World Series appearance and pushing his Red Sox to the world championship over the Giants in 1912. As a rookie, Babe Adams won three games for Pittsburgh in the 1909 series win over Detroit, limiting the Tigers to 18 hits over 27 innings.

◆ Did you know in 1997, Livan Hernandez became the sixth rookie pitcher to win a pair of games in a World Series? Hernandez became the first since the Yankees' Spec Shea accomplished the feat in 1947. Babe Adams in 1909 became the first—and remains the only—freshman to win three. Dickie Kerr of the Black Sox, Paul Dean of the 1934 Cardinals, and John Beazley of the 1942 Cardinals also performed the feat in between.

◆ Did you know Ray Kremer is the only pitcher besides Harry Brecheen and Randy Johnson to win Games Six and Seven of the same World Series? After dropping a 4-3 decision in Game Three of the 1925 fall classic against the Washington Senators, Pittsburgh's Kremer bounced back with a six-hit, 3-2 victory in Game Six to tie the series. With Washington ahead by a 6-3 score in the deciding game (two days later because of rain), Kremer entered the game in the fifth inning. He allowed just one run over four innings, as the Pirates rallied for a 9-7 victory to culminate a comeback from a three games-to-one deficit. Kremer, a two-time 20-game winner who won 143 games against just 85 losses with a 3.76 career ERA, lost his only other World Series decision, a defeat to the New York Yankees in 1927.

Game Five Question (if necessary):

Who holds the World Series record for the most triples in a single series?

ANSWER: Tommy Leach

Leach hit four triples (two in Game One, one in Game Four, and one in Game Five) for the Pirates in the 1903 World Series loss to Boston (five games to three games). Leach hit .273 in that series and blew a chance for more triples in the 1909 World Series, which saw him hit .320 with four doubles.

Tris Speaker (two triples in 1912 for Boston, one in 1915 for Boston, and one for Cleveland in 1920-all winners) and Billy Johnson (one in 1943 for the Yankees and three in 1947 for the Yankees) later tied Leach's career record. Johnson was the Yankees' third baseman in 1943 and from 1946 to 1950.

Game Six Question (if necessary):

Seattle Mariners catcher Dan Wilson in 2000 snapped the longest hitless streak in post-season history by finally ending an 0-for-42 slump. Whose mark of post-season futility did Wilson break?

ANSWER: Marv Owen

The previous dubious record was an 0-for-31 skid by Detroit's Owen, bridging the 1934–35 World Series. The Tiger third baseman failed in his last 12 at-bats of the 1934 World Series and his first 19 at-bats of the 1935 fall classic. Overall, Owen (a .275 career hitter) was 3-for-49 in World Series action. Wilson is 8-for-88 (.091) overall in post-season play through 2001.

During the 1992 postseason, Toronto's Kelly Gruber went hitless in 23 consecutive at-bats, surpassing Dal Maxvill's and Dave Winfield's mark of 22 straight at-bats without a hit in a single postseason. Gruber went hitless in his last 15 at-bats of the 1992 AL Championship Series and his first eight at-bats of the 1992 World Series.

Winfield went hitless in his last six at-bats of the 1981 AL Championship Series and his first 16 at-bats of the 1981 World Series. With his "Mr. May" debacle in the 1981 fall classic, Winfield added a 5-for-22 performance in the 1992 series for a .137 collective World Series scar.

♦ Did you know Seattle Mariners catcher Dan Wilson went hitless in 16 at-bats during the 1995 AL Championship Series, tying the League Championship Series record of futility? Wilson's 0-for-16 performance matched the sub-par efforts of Gene Alley of the 1972 Pittsburgh Pirates and Aurelio Rodriguez of the 1972 Detroit Tigers.

Game Seven Question (if necessary):

Name the Game Seven winning pitchers of three of the following World Series: 1947, 1952, 1973, and 1975.

ANSWER: In 1947, the Yankees' Joe Page won the game in relief over Brooklyn, as did Yankee Allie Reynolds in 1952. Oakland's Ken Holtzman won the game over the Mets in 1973. In 1975, Cincinnati's Clay Carroll won the game in relief over Boston.

Allie Reynolds (who won seven of his nine World Series decisions and saved four others) was sometimes used in an emergency relief role by Casey Stengel; Reynolds proved Stengel a genius by winning Game Seven in relief after starting Game One and Game Four of the 1952 World Series. Reynolds also started Game One of the 1953 World Series and won Game Six (the finale) in relief. His diversity (182-107, with 49 saves during his career) put Brooklyn away each year.

Allow me to congratulate you on your world championship if you answered four questions correctly!

Second Season

♦ Did you know Babe Ruth is the only major leaguer to ever amass at least 2,000 hits, 2,000 RBI, 2,000 walks, and 2,000 runs scored? Ruth accrued 2,873 hits, 2,213 RBI, 2,062 walks, and 2,174 runs scored in his famed 22-year career.

♦ Did you know Greg Maddux set a record with 18 straight road wins, bridging the 1994 and 1995 seasons? Maddux (who lost his first road decision in 1996) put together an incredible stretch of 20 road starts from July 2, 1994, through the 1995 season, during which he posted an 18-0 ledger with a minuscule 0.99 ERA (17 earned runs in 154⅔ innings). His ERA of 1.63 in 1995 was 2.55 better than the National League average, almost matching his own mark from the previous season. The previous standard of 16 consecutive road wins was shared by Richard Dotson, Denny McLain, and Cal McLish. Yes, that is the one and only Calvin Coolidge Julius Caesar Tuskahoma (Buster) McLish.

163. *Match these relievers with their accomplishments:*

1	Randy Myers	A	saved at least 30 games 10 times
2	Trevor Hoffman	B	saved 304 wins
3	Bobby Thigpen	C	saved 347 wins
4	Jeff Montgomery	D	holds the mark of four straight 40-save seasons
5	Lee Smith	E	is the youngest to reach 200 saves

ANSWER: 1—C, 2—D, 3—E, 4—B, 5—A

In 2001, Hoffman surpassed Dennis Eckersley (1990–92) and Lee Smith (1991–93) with his fourth straight campaign of at least 40 saves. Hoffman also surpassed Eckersley and John Wetteland with a fifth overall season of at least 40 saves, and became the first with seven straight years of at least 30 saves. Wetteland reached the 300-save mark in 2000, matching Smith to the day as the youngest ever to reach that plateau (33 years, eight months, and 21 days of age); he also needed fewer games (553) than any pitcher other than Eckersley, who did it in 499 appearances.

♦ Did you know Jeff Reardon's record of 11 consecutive 20-save seasons came to an end with eight saves in 1993? From 1982 to 1992, Reardon averaged 31 saves. Lee Smith surpassed Reardon with 13 straight 20-save seasons.

♦ Did you know Dennis Eckersley is the only pitcher with 200 saves and 100 complete games? The last of his 100 complete games came in 1986 with the Cubs. Eckersley didn't earn his fourth save until 1987.

164. *Match these teams and their record achievements:*

1	1959 Pirates	A	stole a 20th-century record 347 bases
2	1949 Red Sox	B	turned a NL record 215 double plays
3	1911 Giants	C	drew a record 835 bases on balls
4	1966 Pirates	D	won an incredible 42 one-run games
5	1978 Giants	E	won 19 extra-inning games

ANSWER: 1—E, 2—C, 3—A, 4—B, 5—D

From this group of clubs, only the 1911 Giants reached the World Series, losing in six games to the Athletics. The 1966 Pirates came within two twin killings of matching the mark set 17 years earlier by the Athletics, who only played 154 games—eight fewer than Pittsburgh. Giants relievers Gary Lavelle and Randy Moffitt combined for 21 and 26 saves in 1978. Starters Bob Knepper, Vida Blue, and Ed Halicki each placed among the top 10 NL ERA leaders.

♦ Did you know the 1941 Yankees hit a home run in 25 consecutive games, a record later tied by the 1994 Detroit Tigers and 1998 Atlanta Braves? The Yankees won 18 games and hit 40 home runs during their stretch. The Tigers won 15 contests and hit 46 roundtrippers during theirs. The Braves won a sizzling 20 games, smacking 45 homers.

165. *The 1942 St. Louis Cardinals were clearly the best team of the 1940s. Branch Rickey's profound and talented farm was a huge reason, resulting in Cardinal pennants in 1942, 1943, 1944, and 1946. Other teams struggled to compensate for the players lost to military service, but the Cardinals welcomed the challenge. In fact, they unveiled baseball's "natural," Stan Musial, in this era. In 1942, St. Louis overcame a 10½-game deficit to Brooklyn in mid-August by winning 43 of its final 51 games and edging a Dodgers team that had won 104 contests. Manager Billy Southworth's Cardinals won 106 games, losing only 48 for a still-franchise record .688 ball. Without the benefit of a 15-homer or 100-RBI slugger, this resilient squad still led the league in runs (755) and pitching (2.55 ERA). Then, in a World Series upset that almost ranks with the 1914, 1960, 1969, 1988, and 1990 fall classics, the Cardinals dominated the Yankees in five games. Complete the 1942 Cardinals alignment:*

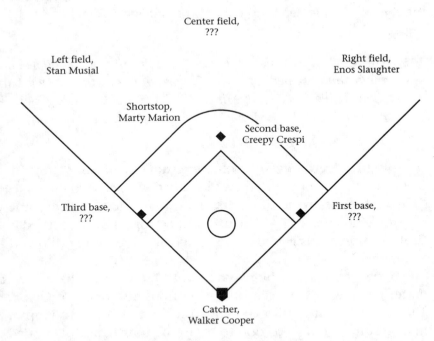

Center field,
???

Left field,
Stan Musial

Right field,
Enos Slaughter

Shortstop,
Marty Marion

Second base,
Creepy Crespi

Third base,
???

First base,
???

Catcher,
Walker Cooper

ANSWER: Center field, Terry Moore; First base, Johnny Hopp; Third base, Whitey Kurowski

Slaughter led the National League in hits, triples, and total bases and paced the Cardinals with a .318 batting average and 98 RBI. Slaughter and Musial (.315) finished second and third in batting. Musial finished fourth in slugging as a rookie. Pitchers Mort Cooper (Walker's brother) and John Beazley combined for a 43-13 record and a 1.93 ERA.

The Cardinals' 106 wins preceded totals of 105 in each of the next two campaigns, making them the second of four teams in history with three straight 100-win seasons. The first to accomplish the feat was the 1929–31 A's squad with win totals of 104, 102, and 107. The 1969–71 Orioles and the 1997–99 Braves are the other two juggernauts.

♦ Did you know Stan Musial reached the World Series during each of his first four full seasons (1942, 1943, 1944, and 1946)? In 1941, Musial appeared in 12 games and he spent the 1945 campaign serving the country in the military during World War II. The Cards split the 1942 and 1943 fall classics with the Yankees, before defeating the Browns and Red Sox in 1944 and 1946, respectively.

166. *Dale Mitchell was the last batter, Babe Pinelli was the home plate umpire, and catcher Yogi Berra jumped into the arms of Don Larsen following his strikeout of Mitchell. Which Brooklyn Dodger pitcher opposed Larsen in the latter's 1956 World Series perfect game?*

ANSWER: Sal Maglie

Maglie threw a five-hit complete game in a losing effort for the Dodgers, striking out five and walking two in the 2-0, Game-Five loss. "The Barber" scattered nine hits in a Game-One complete game victory for a 2.65 series ERA. The two other Dodgers Larsen retired in the ninth inning of his gem, besides Mitchell, were Carl Furillo and Roy Campanella.

From various play-by-play accounts, I reconstruct here how each batter fared against Larsen on the glorious afternoon of October 8, 1956. Lead-off hitter Jim Gilliam struck out to begin the top of the first, grounded out to second to begin the fourth, and grounded out to short leading off the seventh. Number two hitter, "Pee Wee" Reese struck out looking in the first, grounded out to second in the fourth, and flied out to deep center in the seventh. Batting third, Duke

Snider lined to right in the first, struck out looking in the fourth, and flied to left in the seventh. Clean-up hitter Jackie Robinson came the closest to a hit by leading off the second with a hard drive that caromed off Yankee third baseman Andy Carey and was scooped up by shortstop Gil McDougald, who threw the speedy Robinson out at first by a hair. In his other turns, Robinson led off the fifth with a deep fly to right, and led off the eighth with a comebacker to Larsen. Gil Hodges struck out in the second, lined out to the outstretched Mickey Mantle in deep left-center in the fifth, and lined out to third in the eighth. Sandy Amoros popped up to Yankee second baseman Billy Martin in the second, grounded out to him in the fifth, and flied out to rather deep center in the eighth.

Furillo, the right fielder who batted fifth in the 1955 World Series, and Campanella, the Hall of Fame catcher who batted fourth in that same classic, batted seventh and eighth, respectively, due to injuries and age. Furillo flied out to right in the third, Campanella struck out in the third, and Maglie lined out to center to end the frame for the Dodgers. Furillo popped up to Martin in short right to open the sixth, as Campanella followed with a pop up to Martin in short center, and Maglie ended the inning with a whiff. In the ninth, Furillo flied to right on a 1-2 count for the first out. Campanella made the second out—a grounder to Martin (who registered four assists and three putouts in the game). And hitting for Maglie, the left-handed Mitchell took the first pitch wide for ball one. The second pitch was a strike one called by Pinelli, behind the plate. Mitchell swung and missed at the third delivery for a 1-2 count. After fouling off Larsen's 96th pitch the other way, Mitchell was mesmerized by a "strike three" call to end the game. Larsen struck out seven Dodgers and reached a three-ball count to Reese only in the first.

♦ Did you know Babe Pinelli's called third strike on Dale Mitchell in Don Larsen's perfect game was the last call of his career? He immediately retired following a 22-year umpiring tenure. That might explain why he was so quick to call Larsen's last pitch—apparently outside—a strike. The next time you have a chance, check out the highlight. Including his playing career, Pinelli spent a total of 30 years in the majors. The right-handed third baseman batted .276 (twice exceeding .300) over a career that covered 774 games, mostly for the Cincinnati Reds, and ended in 1927.

167. *Match these men with their major league roles:*

1 Clarence Owens   A   is blamed for keeping Blacks out of Major
2 Bobby Valentine   League Baseball until 1947
3 Cap Anson   B   home plate umpire with whom pitcher Babe
4 Buzzie Bavasi   Ruth had a scuffle that resulted in Ruth's and
                                 his catcher Pinch Thomas' ejection
                      C   Angels general manager who couldn't re-sign
                                   Nolan Ryan after the 1979 season
                      D   center fielder behind Nolan Ryan in his first
                                   no-hitter with California

ANSWER: 1—B, 2—D, 3—A, 4—C

In that June 23, 1917, game, Ruth walked the first Senators batter, Ray Morgan. Disliking Owens' ball-four call, Ruth engaged in a vigorous disagreement with Owen and even threw a punch after his ejection. Righthander Ernie Shore relieved Ruth for Boston. Shore, on the mound when Morgan was caught stealing, proceeded to retire the next 26 batters en route to what was then counted as a perfect game. Ruth was fined $100 and had his suspension lifted after nine days.

A highly touted prospect out of the Dodgers organization, Valentine was traded to the Angels following the 1972 season. The highly energetic infielder-turned-outfielder broke his right leg crashing into a center-field wall in 1973, and was never the same again. A passionate man, Valentine became a manager in 1985 and today is regarded as one of the very best in his profession.

Anson, the game's most popular player during the late 1800s, is said to have objected to the presence of blacks on the field, hence the ban. On August 10, 1883, the player-manager of the Chicago White Stockings vehemently protested the presence of Moses Walker in an exhibition against Walker's minor league club. Walker, a black catcher for Toledo, was playing right field that day. Anson threw a fit, and threatened to not play. But of course, the blame on the ban of blacks goes much deeper. After all, Anson was just a player. Plenty of league officials are to blame as well.

Ryan made it known that the only way he would ever return to the Angels organization was if Bavasi was no longer the team's general manager. Ryan didn't respect Bavasi. Incidentally, Buzzie's son,

Peter, was a respected former general manager with various major league clubs (the Blue Jays, Indians, and Padres).

168. *Al Simmons and Charlie Gehringer held the AL record of five straight 200-hit seasons until it was broken by:*

A Wade Boggs
B Nap Lajoie
C Ty Cobb
D George Sisler
E Tony Oliva

ANSWER: A

Boggs accomplished the feat for seven straight years, 1983–89. Boggs retired following the 1999 season with 3,010 career hits, good for 22nd place on the all-time list. Like Boggs, Gehringer also had seven overall 200-hit campaigns, and Simmons boasted a half-dozen such seasons. Simmons accrued 253 hits in his second major league season, 1925. Boggs reached a high of 240 hits in 1985. Gehringer reached a high of 227 hits, including 60 doubles, in 1936.

♦ Did you know Charlie Gehringer, a second baseman known for his hitting, led in assists an AL-record seven times? The owner of 2,839 hits, 574 doubles, and a .320 career average, the smooth Gehringer also led the American League in fielding percentage seven times. Gehringer was known as "The Mechanical Man" for his consistent play.

169. *Lou Brock won a record nine straight stolen base titles. True or False?*

ANSWER: False

Luis Aparicio rendered that exploit, leading the league in thefts from 1956 to 1964. Brock came within six steals of nine straight stolen-base crowns. Brock, who led the National League in swipes from 1966 to 1969 and from 1971 to 1974, finished with 51 steals in 1970, six behind Bobby Tolan. Rickey Henderson won a record 12 overall titles; Max Carey is second with 10 stolen base crowns. Tim Raines, one of the very best leadoff hitters ever, won a stolen base crown in each of his first four full seasons, but has not led a league in steals since 1984. But make no mistake about it, Henderson is the best lead-off hitter of all time (in case you're wondering, Ty Cobb batted third and fourth during most of his career). The all-time leader in runs scored (2,248), stolen bases (1,395), and walks (2,141), Henderson also reached the 3,000-hit plateau in 2001.

With 290 home runs entering the 2002 season (at press time, he said he was not yet ready to retire), Henderson is one of the most multifaceted players ever. Consistently one of the best players in the majors over a prolonged stretch, Henderson is certainly the most distracting. His bold baserunning allows him to take over games single-handedly, driving pitchers and catchers crazy. And for all the talk (sometimes justified) of his lackadaisical play in the field, Henderson enters the 2002 season with the third most putouts of any outfielder in the game's history—as a left fielder, no less.

◆ Did you know Rickey Henderson's total of 12 stolen base titles ties him for most career crowns of a single major statistical category? Babe Ruth won 12 home run titles, Ty Cobb won 12 batting championships, Ted Williams led the American League in on-base percentage a dozen times, and Walter Johnson led in strikeouts on 12 occasions. Nolan Ryan came close with 11 strikeout crowns.

170. *In Game One of the 1996 World Series, Atlanta's Andruw Jones became the 21st player to hit a home run in his first World Series at-bat. In his next turn, Jones connected again to become just the second player to homer in his first two World Series at-bats. Name the only other player to do so.*

ANSWER: Gene Tenace

Tenace of the Oakland A's twice went deep in Game One of the 1972 fall classic, en route to a Series MVP performance. Tenace homered off Cincinnati Reds starter Gary Nolan in the second and fifth inning. The catcher slugged .913 in the series with four homers and nine RBI. Interestingly, Tenace didn't homer in any of the other eight post-season series he played in. Of course, that didn't keep Mr. Tenace from other World Series records, such as the standard-tying 11 walks he drew the following October against the New York Mets.

In duplicating Tenace's home run feat, the 19-year-old Jones also became the youngest player to start a World Series game as well as homer (surpassing Mickey Mantle by a few months). Jones homered in the second inning off Yankees starter Andy Pettitte and the next frame off Brian Boehringer. For the series, which his Braves lost in six games, Jones slugged .750 and drove in six runs. Jones' achievement takes on a remarkable meaning when considering he started that 1996 year in Single A. There's no substitute for pure talent.

◆ Did you know in 1999, the Mets' Edgardo Alfonzo became the first player in major league history to hit a grand slam in his first post-season game?

171. *The awful 1962 Mets (40 wins and a record 120 losses) had a losing record against every other NL team except this rival. Name the club the Mets split 18 games with.*

ANSWER: The Chicago Cubs

The Cubs' 59-103 record earned them ninth place. That Mets squad, the worst team of the past eight decades, batted a major league-worst .240, had a major league-worst 5.04 ERA, and owned the league's worst fielding percentage (.967) by far to finish 60½ games out of first place. The winless Mets quickly fell 9½ games out of first place just nine contests into the season—by contrast, the Pirates won 10 games right out of the gate—and never recovered.

◆ Did you know the Mets ended their woeful 1962 season by hitting into a triple play? Well, sort of. It happened during the eighth inning of their final game of the season, on September 30. Sammy Drake was on second base after a pinch-single and Richie Ashburn was on first following a safety of his own. True to form, the Mets' Joe Pignatano hit a broken bat blooper behind second, which Cubs' second baseman Ken Hubbs caught with a leaping backhand stab on the grass (as the Mets' media guide describes it), catching both runners by surprise. Hubbs threw it to first baseman Ernie Banks for the second out. Banks darted a pass to shortstop Andre Rogers at second to complete the triple play. Interestingly, for Ashburn, that play marked the last of his Hall of Fame career. Drake and Pignatano remained in the contest for the ninth inning, but also never played another game. That's why the Mets call that triple play the one that ended three careers.

172. *Before the New York Giants embarked on one of the most incredible comebacks ever and forced a three-game playoff with the Brooklyn*

Dodgers (which the Giants won) in 1951, the Giants trailed by as much as _____ on August 12. Fill in the blank.

A 12 games
B 13½ games
C 11 games
D 13 games

ANSWER: B

When factoring in games remaining, the Giants' comeback may be the most remarkable in history. But in terms of overcoming a deficit, it ranks behind the 1914 Boston Braves and the 1978 Yankees, and just ahead of the 1995 Mariners. In 1914, "The Miracle Braves" overcame a 15-game deficit on July 15 to win the pennant and world championship. The Yankees were 14 games behind the Red Sox on July 19, 1978, before turning it around (winning 52 of their last 73) and capturing their third consecutive AL East Division title and pennant, and second straight World Series title. In 1995, Seattle overcame a 13-game deficit on August 2, and were 12½ games out as late as August 20, before getting hot and winning the AL West Division title for the franchise's first-ever post-season berth, saving Major League Baseball in Seattle. An argument could thus be made that the Mariners enjoyed the greatest comeback on record. The 1930 Cardinals erased a 12-game deficit to the Dodgers in early August, and wound up edging the Cubs for the pennant, thanks to a 21-4 September.

As for the Yankees and the collapse of the Red Sox in 1978, it was during that season the Bronx Bombers dealt Boston its most humiliating and demoralizing head-to-head defeat. En route to overcoming a deficit of 14 games and ousting the Red Sox in a one-game playoff, the Yankees came into Fenway in early August for an important four-game series, down by four games. New York proceeded to destroy Boston by scores of 15-3, 13-2, 7-0, and 7-4 in a sweep that will forever be regarded as the "Boston Massacre."

◆ Did you know Yankees shortstop Bucky Dent used Mickey Rivers' bat to hit his dramatic three-run homer in the 1978 American League East one-game play-off? After fouling off a pitch from Red Sox righthander Mike Torrez, Dent was handed his teammate's bat and assured through the batboy that Rivers said, "there are lots of hits in it. [You'll] get a home run." Suddenly,

Dent wasn't carrying a .243 season batting average with four homers and 37 RBI: He was waving a fateful, magical wand. With it, Dent connected off Torrez, lofting a lazy fly ball to left that carried and carried before barely clearing Fenway Park's Green Monster for a homer that erased the deficit and vaulted New York into a 3-2 lead. The Yankees scored one more run— Rivers crossed the plate—in that seventh inning and one in the eighth on a Reggie Jackson homer to dead center, en route to a 5-4 triumph.

173. *Who was the youngest ball player ever to be elected into the Hall of Fame?*

ANSWER: Sandy Koufax

Koufax was elected on January 19, 1972, at the age of 36 years and one month. He was inducted on August 7 of that year. Before Koufax, Lou Gehrig had been the youngest when inducted at the age of 36 years and five months on December 7, 1939 (the same date as his election, because there was no formal induction during the summer of 1940).

Koufax retired at the youthful age of 30 to avoid jeopardizing his arthritic elbow. Unlike many athletes who hang on too long or deem their athletic careers more valuable than the rest of their lives, Koufax proved his mental fortitude and maturity by hanging up his spikes, stating that his elbow was a body part he intended to use well after his baseball career. "I've got a lot of years to live after baseball and I would like to live them with the complete use of my body," said Koufax, who was born Sanford Braun but took on the last name of his stepfather.

That announcement ended, arguably, the most dominating six-year stretch by any pitcher of the live-ball era. From 1961 to 1966, Koufax was nothing short of spectacular, compiling a record of 129-47 with a composite ERA of 2.19. During that time, Koufax led the National League in ERA during each of his last five seasons, paced the circuit in strikeouts four times, in wins and shutouts thrice apiece, in complete games twice, and in innings pitched on a pair of occasions. He also won the pitcher's Triple Crown in 1963, 1965, and 1966.

Only Jim Brown, Michael Jordan, Rocky Marciano, and Gene Tunney can say they retired while still dominating their sport. But none of them can say, like Koufax can, that their last season was their best. In 1966, Koufax won a career-high 27 games (against nine losses), had a career-best 1.73 ERA, struck out 317 batters in 323 innings, and tied a career-high by going the distance 27 times.

♦ Did you know Hank Greenberg is the only other Hall of Fame player besides Sandy Koufax to lead his league in any statistical category during his final season? Greenberg led the American League with a 104 walks in 1947, a year after leading the junior circuit in homers and RBI.

174. *Match these managers with their roles:*

1	John McGraw	A	became the first player-manager
2	Casey Stengel	B	managed his teams to 37 World Series game victories
3	Cap Anson	C	won seven of his nine World Series, winning 30 of 43 games (.698)
4	Frank Selee	D	finished at .500 or better in 29 of his 34 seasons with 10 pennants and three world championships
5	Joe McCarthy	E	had a .598 career winning percentage

ANSWER: 1—D, 2—B, 3—A, 4—E, 5—C

McGraw, who relied on the hit-and-run and yet disdained the sacrifice bunt, was probably the most effective manager that any team has ever had, never ceasing to inspire and motivate his players by using psychology. This Hall of Famer was as complex as they came. His players noted that he always took the pressure off of them by diverting the opposition to himself. His wild tactics included tantrums, profanities, and controversies directed at his Giants' opponents. "Little Napoleon" managed like he played—aggressively and with a rebellious attitude. He was the Ty Cobb of managing, minus the slew of crimes.

Anson managed the Cubs to five pennants and four second-place finishes. Selee, whose winning percentage over 16 seasons is the fourth best of all time, led the Boston Beaneaters to five pennants in the 1890s. In 1999, Selee became only the 15th manager to gain entry into the Hall of Fame.

♦ Did you know John McGraw's .466 career on-base percentage remains the third-highest mark? Only Ted Williams (.482) and Babe Ruth (.474) rank higher. Although overshadowed by his managerial accomplishments, McGraw was quite a player as well. A left-handed-hitting third baseman, the fiery McGraw batted .334 over parts of 16 seasons, stealing 436 bases in the process. He also scored over 100 runs five times, including figures of 156, 143, and 140. In 1899, he posted a .547 on-base percentage, still the best NL mark and the second-highest figure in the game's history. Aside from perhaps Joe Torre, McGraw was the best player ever to become a great manager.

♦ Did you know John McGraw lost his 23-year-old wife in August of 1899 to complications following surgery for appendicitis? He buried her on August 31 in Baltimore.

175. *Jose* _____ *held the record of 25 pinch-hits in a single season before Colorado infielder John Vander Wal collected 28 hits in the pinch during the 1995 season. Fill in the blank.*

ANSWER: Morales

Morales corralled his record with the Montreal Expos in 1976, retiring with 123 career pinch-hits. As a pinch-hitter, Vander Wal was 28-for-92 (.389) with four homers, 17 RBI, seven doubles, and one triple in 1995. Vander Wal is a starter these days. Another single-season pinch-hit mark fell by the wayside in 2000, as Dave Hansen hit seven homers in the pinch to break the record of Brooklyn's Johnny Frederick, who hit six in 1932. Pittsburgh rookie Craig Wilson matched Hansen's year-old mark in 2001.

♦ Did you know Hall of Famers Babe Ruth, Hank Aaron, Ty Cobb, Honus Wagner, and Carl Yastrzemski each struggled miserably as pinch-hitters? With a mere 13 hits in 67 pinch-hit at-bats, Ruth batted just .194 in that role. Aaron hit .198 as a pinch-hitter (17-for-86), Cobb was a .217 career hitter in the pinch (15-for-69), Wagner mustered only five pinch hits (in 31 at-bats for a .161 mark), and Yastrzemski just eight (in 52 at-bats for a .154 figure).

176. *Eddie Murray broke Mickey Mantle's record for most games with a homer from each side of the plate. Do you how many times Murray achieved this amazing feat?*

A nine times
B five times

C 11 times

D 10 times

ANSWER: C

Murray surpassed Mantle's 10 switch-hitting homer games, yet another category in which Murray outdid the legendary Mantle. Chili Davis and Ken Caminiti have each performed the feat 10 times, tying Mantle's standard; Caminiti's 10 represent a NL record. Caminiti became the first to do so three times in a season during the 1995 campaign, achieving the feat over an incredible four-game span. Caminiti then broke his own record in 1996 with four such games.

◆ Did you know on September 17, 1995, San Diego's Ken Caminiti homered from each side of the plate for the second consecutive game to join Eddie Murray as the only two players in history to accomplish the feat? (Murray did so on May 8 and 9, 1987.) Then Caminiti homered as a righty and lefty on September 19 (his third time in four games).

◆ Did you know on April 23, 2000, Yankees teammates Bernie Williams and Jorge Posada became the first pair of players to hit switch-hit home runs in the same game?

177. *No player holds both career and single-season records for any major category. True or False?*

ANSWER: False

Nolan Ryan and Rickey Henderson both hold such records. Ryan (the single-season record holder) fanned Montreal's Brad Mills for strikeout number 3,509 on April 27, 1983, surpassing Walter Johnson for the all-time record. Ryan, who had to regain the career strikeout lead in 1984, finished with an untouchable 5,714 strikeouts.

Henderson (the single-season record holder) broke Lou Brock's all-time stolen base record on May 1, 1991, with theft number 939—and he did so in six fewer seasons. Henderson's record-breaking steal was a theft of third base off the Yankees' battery of Tim Leary and catcher Matt Nokes. Jose Canseco was batting with a 1-0 count. Henderson showed no modesty whatsoever in proclaiming—in Brock's presence—"Lou Brock was certainly a great base stealer, but today I am the greatest of all time." Baseball fans across America forgave

Henderson for his lack of diplomacy and focused on his tremendous accomplishments, cheering him through a record-setting 2001 campaign. Henderson has 1,395 stolen bases entering the 2002 season.

◆ Did you know the pitcher that Rickey Henderson has pilfered the most bases against is Jack Morris (18) and the catcher he has caught off guard most often is Jim Sundberg (55)?

178. *Match these solid-hitting pitchers with their record exploits:*

1	Jim Tobin	A	is the only pitcher to lead the league in home runs
2	Tony Cloninger	B	batted .300 eight times
3	Babe Ruth	C	collected 114 career pinch-hits
4	Red Lucas	D	hit three home runs in a game
5	Wes Ferrell	E	belted two grand slams and nine RBI in one game
6	Red Ruffing	F	hit 37 career home runs as a pitcher and one as an outfielder

ANSWER: 1—D, 2—E, 3—A, 4—C, 5—F, 6—B

Tobin hit three home runs for the Boston Braves on May 3, 1942, a day after homering in the pinch. The only other pitcher to homer thrice in a game was Guy Hecker, who on August 15, 1886, did so for Louisville of the American Association.

Cloninger performed his incredible feat on July 3, 1966, against the Giants, also making him the first player (regardless of position) in the history of the National League to belt two grand slams in one game. The single-game feat gave him a whopping 18 RBI over four appearances that included yet another two-homer performance.

Ferrell also holds the pitcher's record with nine home runs during the 1931 season. Bob Lemon and Warren Spahn (NL career leader) each hit 35 home runs as a pitcher, Red Ruffing hit 34 as a pitcher and Earl Wilson hit 33. Interestingly, Wes Ferrell hit 10 more career homers than his brother Rick, the .281-hitting catcher with 4,852 more at-bats.

Ruth hit 29 homers for the Red Sox in 1919 (although 23 of them came as an outfielder), outdistancing every other American Leaguer by a whopping 19 roundtrippers. Ruth never again pitched more than two games in a season after 1919. In 490 career at-bats as a pitcher, Ruth reached via a hit 149 times for a .304 batting average, with 15 homers and 73 RBI, according to the Dead Ball Era Committee of the Society for American Baseball Research.

◆ Did you know Cy Young holds the record among pitchers with 618 career hits? Walter Johnson (who had 542 hits) and Red Ruffing (520 hits) were the only other pitchers with at least 400. George Uhle still holds the single-season record by a pitcher with 52 hits. In that 1923 season, Uhle hit .321.

◆ Did you know Walter Johnson remains the only pitcher in history to win 20 games and bat .400 in the same season? In 1925, Johnson posted a 20-7 ledger on the mound and hit a pitcher record .433 (42-for-97), with two homers. Incidentally, no other pitcher is even close to Johnson's single-season batting mark. Red Ruffing's .364 mark (40-for-110) in 1930 remains the second best.

179. *Among pitchers with 3,500 innings pitched, the following hurlers own the best ERAs. Match them:*

1	Walter Johnson	A	2.28
2	Will White	B	2.13
3	Eddie Plank	C	2.17
4	Christy Mathewson	D	2.34
5	Jim McCormick	E	2.43

ANSWER: 1—C (5,923⅔ innings), 2—A (3,542⅔ innings), 3—D (4,505⅓ innings), 4—B (4,782 innings), 5—E (4,275⅔ innings)

Johnson's 2.17 career ERA is even more remarkable if you consider that all six of the lower career marks were achieved entirely within the Dead Ball Era, whereas Johnson hurled the last eight years of his career in the live ball era. Johnson recorded an ERA of under 2.00 in 11 of his first 13 seasons, adding to the list of reasons why he is considered the best pitcher ever. But there is plenty of other evidence for this statement. Using a blinding sidearm fastball during the days of contact baseball, Johnson struck out 3,508 batters; he won 417 games for a primarily second-division team with a poor offense; and he dominated hitters more than any of his contemporaries were able to do. A peer of Johnson's, "Smokey" Joe Wood once told author Roger Angell, "If he'd had the team behind him that I had, he'd have set every kind of (pitching) record in baseball. You have to remember that Walter Johnson pitched for a second-division team almost all through his career."

Jim McCormick is not to be confused with Mike (no relation). Winning 265 of 478 decisions, Jim McCormick (a right-handed pitcher from 1878 through 1887) is the most successful European-born major leaguer. McCormick was born in Glasgow, Scotland.

Mordecai Brown (2.06 ERA), Eddie Cicotte (2.37), and Doc White (2.38) pitched fewer than 3,500 innings but more than 3,000.

♦ Did you know Walter Johnson hurled three shutouts in a four-day span against the same team late in the 1908 season? Johnson, in his second year, blanked the New York Highlanders on September 4, September 5, and (following an off-day) in the first game of a September 7 doubleheader.

180. *This workhorse still holds the AL single-season record of 464 innings pitched. In the same season, he set other career-best figures of 40 victories, 42 completed games, 11 shutouts, and 269 strikeouts. Name this player.*

ANSWER: Ed Walsh

The 1908 season of the right-handed White Sox spitballer Walsh stands as one of the best ever. Walsh's 40 wins for a team that registered 88 represents the second-highest percentage (45.5%) by any pitcher. No pitcher has won as many games since. Walsh hurled 422⅓ innings the previous year, working at least 368 innings in three of the four seasons from 1909 to 1912. From 1907 to 1912, Walsh averaged 374⅔ innings, leading the American League in appearances five times during that stretch. The heavy load took a toll on Walsh's arm: He won just 13 games thereafter. The Hall of Famer retired with a 195-126 ledger.

♦ Did you know research has verified "only" 36 wins by Walsh in 1908? The extra four wins will not be removed from his record until their rightful owners are discovered.

181. *The only player to win the Rookie of the Year Award, the MVP Award, and the Cy Young Award is _____. Fill in the blank.*

ANSWER: Don Newcombe

Brooklyn's Newcombe won the Rookie of the Year Award in 1949 and both the MVP and Cy Young Awards in 1956. The three-time 20-game winner retired following the 1960 season with a 149-90 record over 10 years.

◆ Did you know Tom Seaver, Rick Sutcliffe, Dwight Gooden, and Fernando Valenzuela are the only four of 27 pitchers that have won the Rookie of the Year to win 150 games? Stan Bahnsen came close, winning 146 games.

182. *Is Reggie Jackson the only player to win a World Series MVP with two different teams?*

ANSWER: Yes

Jackson won the honor in 1973 with the Oakland A's and with the New York Yankees in his showcase 1977 fall classic. Appearing in five fall classics, "Mr. October" hit .357, 10 homers, with 24 RBI and a record .755 slugging average.

◆ Did you know "Mr. October" was held to a .227 batting average, six home runs, and 20 RBI in 163 at-bats over 11 AL Championship Series? Reggie Jackson also struck out 41 times and had just 13 extra-base hits among his 37 AL Championship Series hits.

183. *How did the Giants-Dodger rivalry begin?*

ANSWER: It actually began in the winter before the 1934 season as player/manager Bill Terry told a slew of writers how confident he was that his Giants would win the pennant. When asked about Brooklyn—after he had stated that Chicago, Pittsburgh, and St. Louis would give his Giants some trouble—Terry replied, "Brooklyn? Gee, I haven't heard a peep out of there. Are they still in the National League?" As fortune had it, the Giants and Cardinals were tied for first place with just two games remaining in the regular season. The Cardinals faced the Reds, and guess who the Giants played? Yes, the Dodgers.

Although the games were played at the Polo Grounds, thousands of Dodger fans showed up with banners that read: "YEP, WE'RE STILL IN THE LEAGUE." They harassed and ridiculed the Giants on their own home field. The Dodgers won both games, and the Cardinals won their games as well, giving St. Louis the pennant.

Some trace the origins of the heated Giants-Dodgers battle of wills to the Giants-Athletics World Series in 1913. Giants manager John McGraw blamed his friend and first base coach Wilbert Robinson for a questionable "green light" in Game Five. Robinson, in turn, blamed McGraw and ridiculed his moves; McGraw retaliated by terminating his coach. Robinson immediately found work, managing the Dodgers in 1914. With Robinson, the Dodgers won the NL pennant in 1916 and 1920. Meanwhile, Robinson and McGraw refused to talk to each other until 1930. The acrimonious fallout was ironic—the two men had been so close that McGraw actually refused a trade in 1899 to the more powerful Brooklyn club to stay in Baltimore, where he and Robinson co-owned a saloon.

Since the Dodgers joined the National League in 1890, the two rivals have played rough with each other, wrestling like competitive and unyielding brothers on every pitch, every base, and every run. After all these years, the two franchises maintain their intense rivalry, each pulling out all the stops to beat the other—even in meaningless season finales. In 112 years of head-to-head competition, the Giants have won 1,088 games to the Dodgers' 1,064: Just 24 games separate the two clubs.

184. *Whose season record of 38 consecutive stolen bases without being caught did Vince Coleman break?*

ANSWER: Davey Lopes

Coleman surpassed Lopes' 1975 mark in 1989. Coleman swiped 50 consecutive bases (bridging the 1988 and 1989 season) before being thrown out on his 45th attempt in 1989 by Montreal's Nelson Santovenia. Coleman, who set the rookie record with 110 thefts in 1985, was an immediate terror on the base paths, pilfering at least 100 bases in each of his first three seasons. He won the stolen base crown in each of his first six campaigns en route to a career total of 752, good for sixth all-time. Coleman, who looked like a good bet to enter the 21st century as the all-time leading steals king after swiping 549 bases over his first six years, was successful on 80.9% of his 929 career attempts.

In 1995, Tim Raines ran his AL record of consecutive thefts to 40 (dating back to 1993) before being caught by Toronto's Randy Knorr on September 2. Interestingly, Brady Anderson of Baltimore had his AL mark of 36 straight swipes stopped earlier in the 1995 campaign. Minnesota's Paul Molitor also pilfered 36 straight before getting caught on his first attempt of the 1996 season. Lopes retired with 557 steals out of 671 attempts for an astounding 83% success ratio.

185. *On the subject of incredible exploits, can you name the only pitcher to start both ends of a doubleheader and hurl a shutout in each game?*

ANSWER: Ed Reulbach

The Chicago Cubs' Reulbach shut out the Brooklyn Dodgers, 5-0 and 3-0, on September 26, 1908. Reulbach, the poor-sighted right-hander who required his catchers to wear white-painted gloves, was asked to pitch the second game as well due to a depleted pitching staff. Reulbach went on to a 24-7 campaign, leading the National League in winning percentage for the third straight season. Over a 13-year career, Reulbach earned 182 wins out of 288 decisions, with a 2.28 ERA.

On June 19, 1927, Jack Scott (35 years old) became the oldest and the last pitcher to hurl two complete games in one day. Scott's Phillies beat Cincinnati, 3-1, then lost (3-0) in the second game.

186. *The four Hall of Fame sluggers listed below have amassed the greatest number of total bases in history. Match the slugger with his total:*

1	Stan Musial	A	6,856
2	Hank Aaron	B	6,134
3	Ty Cobb	C	6,066
4	Willie Mays	D	5,863

ANSWER: 1—B, 2—A, 3—D, 4—C

In Aaron's incredibly revealing book *I Had a Hammer,* contributing author Lonnie Wheeler said that having the most total bases in history was Aaron's most significant accomplishment. Wheeler wrote, "There have been hitters with higher batting averages than Hank Aaron, with higher slugging percentages, higher home run ratios; there have been hitters who struck out less often, who walked more, who hit the ball farther; a few may even have been feared more by pitchers and managers. But when every player has hit every ball he ever hit and run as far as those hits would take him—that is, when all the total bases have been paced off—and the dust has cleared, Hank Aaron is exactly 12.3068 miles in front of the next guy." According to Wheeler, being the all-time leader in total bases and RBI was "more significant than home runs in the deeper baseball scheme, but just [doesn't] market as well: Total Base King Hank Aaron." Babe Ruth's 5,793 total bases and Pete Rose's aggregate of 5,752 are fifth and sixth, respectively.

♦ Did you know the Hank Aaron Award made its debut in 1999, honoring the hitter in each league with the most combined hits, home runs, and RBI? The award was created to celebrate the greatness of the all-time home run, RBI, and total-base leader. Cleveland's Manny Ramirez and Chicago's Sammy Sosa each won his circuit's inaugural award.

187. *Who was the first pitcher to win three games in one World Series? (Clue: the righthander won his third game by Game Four.)*

ANSWER: Deacon Phillippe

Phillippe won the only three games for the Pittsburgh Pirates in the inaugural 1903 World Series, which the Boston Pilgrims won five games to three. The right-handed Phillippe also lost the last two games in the series. Phillippe compiled a career 189-107 record with a 2.59 ERA. Bill Dinneen also won three games, including the finale, for the Pilgrims that series.

188. *Name the only slugger to slam 35 home runs and garner 200 hits for three consecutive seasons.*

A Hank Aaron
B Jim Rice
C George Foster

D Rogers Hornsby

E Hack Wilson

ANSWER: B

Lou Gehrig almost accomplished the feat, missing by a single homer in 1932 after reaching each of those figures in 1930 and 1931. Rice's 1978 season (with 46 roundtrippers and 213 safeties) still represents the last time a player led the league in home runs and hits during the same season. Among the players today whom I think have a chance of duplicating Rice's three-year feat are Alex Rodriguez, Todd Helton, Vladimir Guerrero, Lance Berkman, Nomar Garciaparra, and Carlos Delgado.

♦ Did you know Ted Williams never had 200 hits in a season? As flabbergasting as this appears, there's a perfectly logical explanation: Williams had an eagle eye and drew over 2,000 walks.

♦ Did you know in 2001, Alex Rodriguez joined Babe Ruth, Jimmie Foxx, and Hack Wilson as the only four players in history to compile 50 homers and 200 hits in the same season?

189. *Jackie Robinson paved the way for African Americans in Major League Baseball and became the first black MVP with a great 1949 season for the Brooklyn Dodgers. Who was the first African-American AL MVP?*

ANSWER: Elston Howard

Yankee catcher Howard received the honor in 1963. His production included 28 homers and 85 RBI with the bat, and a Gold Glove for his defensive excellence. And just like Robinson's 1949 Dodgers, Howard led the Yankees to the pennant. Howard, who also won a Gold Glove the following season, was elected as an All-Star nine times in a 14-year career that also earned him 10 trips to the World Series. Howard twice finished in the top ten in batting, three times reaching the 20-homer plateau.

190. *Can you name the first Japanese player to play in the major leagues?*

ANSWER: Masanori Murakami

Murakami became the first Japanese man to play in the majors on September 1, 1964, pitching a scoreless inning of relief for the San Francisco Giants against the New York Mets at Shea Stadium with 50,000 fans looking on. The southpaw reliever, who traveled with two other players from Japan to the Giants' farm teams in Fresno and Magic Valley in 1964, was 20 years of age at the time of his major league debut. He earned the promotion by impressing the Giants with an 11-7 minor league record. For the Giants, the well mannered Murakami was 1-0 with a save, a 1.80 ERA, and 15 strikeouts over 15 innings.

When the Giants decided to sign him for the 1965 season, the Japanese League refused to allow it, stating that Murakami's stint in the U.S. major leagues was only a trial and that he didn't want to go back to the United States anyway. Commissioner Ford Frick threatened to break off the Major League Baseball-Japanese Baseball relationship, but then Murakami chose his own destiny and played one more year in San Francisco, where he performed well again: 4-1, eight saves, 3.75 ERA, and 85 Ks in 74⅓ innings. In 1966, Murakami was offered $40,000 from the Nankai Hawks (double the amount the Giants were offering) and the lefthander took it—only to fall short of his potential in Japan.

Hideo Nomo was the second Japanese to play in the majors, starting his career in Japan, winning Japan's Rookie of the Year and Cy Young Award in 1990, and leading the Pacific League in wins and strikeouts each season from 1990 through 1993. Nomo retired from the Japanese League after the 1994 season and signed a $2 million bonus with the Dodgers on February 13, 1995. In 1995, Nomo won the NL Rookie of the Year Award. And in 1996, he won 16 games and threw a no-hitter in Coors Field—a tremendous feat, considering the park's overwhelming advantage to hitters. In 2001, Nomo came back from a few off-years to post 13 victories and throw another no-hitter. There's no doubt Nomo's success set a trend that many more Japanese players will follow. Ichiro Suzuki credited Nomo's success for his desire to make the trip.

♦ Did you know Hideo Nomo pitched the first and only no-hitter at Coors Field as well as Camden Yards? Incredibly, Nomo didn't throw a shutout in between the two no-hitters, which were five seasons apart. Nomo is the second pitcher since 1900 to throw the first no-hitter at two different major league parks. The other pitcher, according to the Elias Sports Bureau, was Cy Young, who achieved his feat at Boston's Huntington Avenue Baseball Grounds and New York's Hilltop Park.

♦ Did you know on June 18, 1997, pitchers Hideo Nomo of the Dodgers and the Angels' Shigetoshi Hasegawa made history when they became the first Japanese-born players to appear in the same major league game? Nomo started and took a no-decision in Los Angeles' 7-5 win. Hasegawa made his appearance in relief.

♦ Did you know on May 7, 1999, pitchers Hideki Irabu of the Yankees and Mac Suzuki of the Mariners made history when they became the first Japanese-born pitchers to start against each other? Irabu and the Yankees clobbered Suzuki and the Mariners, 10-1.

♦ Did you know on April 13, 2001, Seattle's Ichiro Suzuki and the Angels' Shigetoshi Hasegawa faced off to mark the first time a Japanese-born hitter batted against a Japanese-born pitcher in the U.S. major leagues? Ichiro reached on an infield hit.

191. *Besides Bob Gibson, only one other pitcher has won two Seventh Games of a World Series. True or False?*

ANSWER: False

Gibson alone possesses that distinction, defeating the Yankees in the finale of the 1964 classic and the Red Sox in Game Seven of the 1967 series. In the 1964 finale, Gibson scattered nine hits in a 7-5 complete game victory over the Yankees. Three years later, Gibson three-hit the Red Sox for a clinching, 7-2 win. An intimidating force on the mound, Gibson was best when the stage was biggest.

♦ Did you know Bob Gibson enjoyed a dominating stretch during the 1968 season, in which he allowed just two runs in 95 innings? Gibson allowed 38 earned runs over 304⅔ innings that season for a minuscule 1.12 ERA.

♦ Did you know Bob Gibson suffered from asthma, pneumonia, and rickets as a child? Gibson was also a very skinny kid at one point.

192. *At the age of 31, this shortstop led the Indians to the 1948 world championship, also winning the AL MVP Award (.355, 18 homers, 106 RBI, 116 runs) as the team's player-manager. Name him.*

ANSWER: Lou Boudreau

Boudreau often led by example as he did in the 1948 AL play-off game versus the Red Sox, going 4-for-4 with two homers and three runs scored in the 8-3 triumph. The Hall of Famer accomplished the feat six years after being appointed as baseball's youngest player-manager. Boudreau wasn't only good with the bat; he also led AL shortstops in fielding eight times. A .295 career right-handed batter, Boudreau finished in the top ten in MVP balloting eight times.

◆ Did you know Detroit's Mickey Cochrane was the only other player-manager to be named MVP? Cochrane achieved this feat during his 1934 pennant-winning season at Detroit.

◆ Did you know Rogers Hornsby remains the only player to win the Triple Crown as a player-manager? Hornsby replaced Branch Rickey as manager on May 30, 1925, guiding the team to a 64-51 record in his 115 games at the helm. "Rajah" batted .403, with 39 homers and 143 RBI. Hornsby also amassed 381 total bases, 203 hits, 133 runs scored, and 41 doubles. Hornsby's .756 slugging percentage stood as the highest in NL history for 76 years; Barry Bonds eclipsed it in 2001.

193. *Match these strikeout artists with their Picassos:*

1	Nolan Ryan	A six 300-strikeout seasons
2	Walter Johnson	B second on the all-time list with 4,136 strikeouts
3	Tom Seaver	C struck out at least 200 batters in each of his first three years
4	Dwight Gooden	D struck out a record 10 straight batters in one game
5	Steve Carlton	E his 3,508 strikeouts stood as a major league record until 1983

ANSWER: 1—A, 2—E, 3—D, 4—C, 5—B

Walter Johnson still holds the record of eight straight strikeout titles, and 12 overall.

On April 22, 1970, Seaver struck out 19 Padres to match the then-record for a nine-inning game, including the last 10 to preserve a 2-1, two-hitter. After receiving his 1969 Cy Young Award in a ceremony before the game, Seaver dominated the Padres lineup by recording more than two-thirds of his outs via strikeout. The hard throwing Seaver walked two, allowing a home run to Al Ferrara in the second inning, and a single to Dave Campbell two innings later. Seaver allowed nary a baserunner over the last five frames. Jose Garcia was the only Padre who didn't fan on that afternoon. In the ninth Seaver fanned Van Kelly, Cito Gaston, and Ferrara.

In 1984, Gooden broke Herb Score's modern rookie record by fanning 276 batters in just 218 innings. Tagged "Dr. K," Gooden was simply dominating in his early years. In a stretch of 50 starts from 1984 to 1986, Gooden was an incredible 37-5, with a microscopic ERA of 1.38.

Carlton remains the left-handed strikeout king as well as the NL strikeout king.

♦ Did you know Nolan Ryan holds the dubious record of 10 grand slams yielded? He allowed two slams in his final month of play to catapult Jerry Reuss, Milt Pappas, and Ned Garver for the "top" spot. Lee Smith and Frank Viola have since tied Reuss, Pappas, and Garver with nine.

194. *Can you name the two teams involved in the last tripleheader, played on October 2, 1920?*

ANSWER: The Cincinnati Reds and the Pittsburgh Pirates

The Cincinnati Reds were asked by league officials to comply with the request of the Pittsburgh Pirates (who badly wanted to finish in second place) and play a tripleheader (three games) on the final day of the season to make up for their missed games. The Reds obliged and went on to beat the Pirates in the first two games by scores of 13-7 and 7-3, separating Pittsburgh from the second-place money share. The Pirates were awarded a victory in the last game ahead by a 6-0 score when the game was called because of darkness after six innings.

Tripleheaders were more common in the 19th century, when extensive long-distance travel was rare. Tripleheaders, obviously, had a way of making an impact. On September 7, 1896, the first-place Baltimore Orioles (of the National League) swept a tripleheader from the Louisville Colonels as well as a doubleheader the next afternoon for five victories in two days. Louisville finished 53 games behind the pennant-winning Baltimore club.

♦ Did you know Cleveland in 2000 hosted the second three-team double-header in major league history? Made necessary because of a rescheduling conflict, the Indians lost, 4-3, to the Minnesota Twins after defeating the White Sox, 9-2, earlier in the day. These games marked the first three-team doubleheader since September 13, 1951, when the Cardinals beat the New York Giants 6-4 and then lost to the Boston Braves, 2-0, at Sportsman's Park.

♦ Did you know the New York Yankees and Mets played a historic double-header on July 8, 2000, marking the first time two teams played two games in one day at two different ballparks in 97 years? Having to make up for an earlier postponement, the schedule makers decided to create the home-and-home, day-night doubleheader. The Yankees won each game by a 4-2 score, the first at Shea Stadium and the second in Yankee Stadium. On September 7, 1903, the New York Giants and Brooklyn Superbas (Dodgers) split their same-day, home-and-home doubleheader, with each team winning on the "road." The Giants won, 6-4, at Washington Park and the Dodgers recorded a 3-0 shutout at the Polo Grounds.

♦ Did you know on April 15, 1998, Shea Stadium became the first stadium in the 20th century to host four different teams on the same day? Aside from hosting a Mets-Cubs night game, Shea Stadium hosted an Angels-Yankees contest earlier in the day. The Yankees were forced to play at Shea after a 500-pound beam fell in Yankee Stadium.

195. *Match these men with their "claims to fame" in baseball:*

1	Marty Schwab	A	*Chicago Sun Times* writer credited with inventing the "save" in 1959 for unheralded relievers
2	Jerome Holtzman	B	invented the sinker pitch
3	Tom Rice	C	*Brooklyn Eagle* writer who first filled the league's need for scoreboards and announcers
4	Nat Hudson	D	San Francisco Giants' groundskeeper who practically flooded the infield whenever the Dodgers' Maury Wills played in Candlestick Park during the 1962 season
5	George Hildebrand	E	invented the spitball

ANSWER: 1—D, 2—A, 3—C, 4—B, 5—E

Schwab realized that a wet path would slow down speedsters like Wills as the Giants won the three-game pennant play-off against the Dodgers to earn a 1962 World Series berth. For his efforts, Schwab was given a full World Series share.

Holtzman, who was officially appointed as Major League Baseball's historian in 1999, came up with the formula for the "save" with pitchers like Roy Face in mind. His formula evolved into the official statistic in 1969, although the criterion was altered six years to make it easier to achieve. Billy Singer, who started 40 games in 1969 recorded the first "official" save in a rare relief appearance on April 7 that year for the Dodgers. Of course, historians have since delved into the archives of the game's glorious past to count up all the saves.

Hildebrand, who eventually became an umpire in 1912, invented the spitball in the minor leagues during the 1902 season.

◆ Did you know Hall of Famer Tommy McCarthy is credited by some historians as the creator of the hit-and-run play as well as field signals? The right-fielding McCarthy, who served as a team leader for the explosive Boston Beaneaters from 1892 to 1895, starred alongside center fielder Hugh Duffy in Boston's outfield to form the talented duo dubbed "The Heavenly Twins." McCarthy put together four .300 campaigns as well as three seasons of at least 95 RBI. Although he batted .292 with 468 stolen bases spanning just over 5,000 at-bats, his 13-year career is one of inconsistent play, containing more than a few sub-par seasons of low batting averages and insufficient participation. A player with superb fielding skills and a knack for reaching base during his prime, the alert McCarthy is enshrined in Cooperstown mainly for his heady and creative ability to confuse defenses and set up strategic plans. His innovations are still used in baseball. According to James D. Smith III of the Society for American Baseball Research, McCarthy's innovations were a big reason for his 1946 election. Smith wrote, "the message was clear: the Hall of Fame is not simply the 'Hall of Stats.'"

196. *The Pirates' Rennie Stennett and the Dodgers' Wilbert Robinson share the record of seven hits in a nine-inning game. Which Cleveland Indian collected a record nine hits in an extra-inning game?*

ANSWER: Johnny Burnett

Burnett's big game (seven singles and two doubles) came versus the Philadelphia Athletics on July 10, 1932, in an 18-inning duel. Robinson, by the way, also had 11 RBI in his big game. Cesar Gutierrez and Rocky Colavito each had seven-hit games, on June 21, 1970 (12 innings), and June 24, 1962 (22 innings), respectively. On April 20, 1994, Tim Raines tied Gutierrez's record of reaching base seven times in a nine-inning game without being out.

Stennett's 7-for-7 performance on September 16, 1975, included a double and single in the opening inning, a single in the third, a double and single in the fifth, a single in the seventh, and a triple in the eighth frame. Stennett, who totaled 11 bases, scored five times and drove in a pair, also had a hit against each Reuschel brother, the starter Rick and the reliever Paul.

On June 10, 1892, Robinson also went 7-for-7, adding a whopping 11 RBI for good measure in Brooklyn's 25-7 romp of the St. Louis Browns. Robinson's single-game RBI mark stood until September 16, 1924, when the Cardinals' Jim Bottomley drove in a dozen runs in a 17-3 triumph against the very Dodgers Robinson managed. In that 1924 game, Bottomley homered twice, singled thrice, and doubled once.

197. *The 1985 World Series (Kansas City beat St. Louis), the 1987 World Series (Minnesota beat St. Louis) and the 1993 World Series (Toronto beat Philadelphia) were only the second, third, and fourth fall classics, respectively, to be played entirely on artificial turf. Which was the first?*

ANSWER: The 1980 World Series

The 1980 World Series, which pinned the Philadelphia Phillies against the Kansas City Royals, was the first not played on grass. The Phillies won the classic in six games, earning a victory in all three contests at Veterans Stadium.

The key plays in the series came in Game Five. As the Royals stood three outs away from a third straight victory after dropping the first two games in Philly, the pendulum swung. Trailing by a run in the top of the ninth at Royals Stadium, the resilient Phillies fought hard with their backs against the wall. Series MVP Mike Schmidt led off with a single, pinch-hitter Del Unser doubled him in to tie the game, and—two outs later—Manny Trillo singled in Unser for a 4-3 lead. In the bottom half, reliever Tug McGraw, working his third full inning, gave manager Dallas Green some more gray hair by loading the bases before escaping with a victory for the club and himself.

In Game Six, Schmidt pushed his series RBI total to seven with a two-run single, Steve Carlton pitched seven brilliant innings for his second win, and McGraw threw two scoreless innings to nail down his second save as well as the franchise's first world championship.

198. *Milwaukee's Rollie Fingers (1981), Detroit's Willie Hernandez (1984), and Oakland's Dennis Eckersley (1992) became the second, third, and fourth relief pitchers to win the MVP. Can you name the first?*

ANSWER: Jim Konstanty

The Philadelphia Phillies' Konstanty was awarded the MVP for his 16 wins and 22 saves in the pennant-winning 1950 season. Konstanty, who fashioned a 2.66 ERA over 74 appearances, was the first player wearing glasses to win the award. Konstanty didn't start a game during the entire 1950 regular season, but was given the starting assignment for the 1950 World Series opener.

In 1981, Fingers won six of nine decisions, saved 28, and registered a minuscule 1.04 ERA. Hernandez was 9-3 with 32 saves and a 1.92 ERA in 1984. Eckersley won seven of eight decisions and saved 51 games with a 1.91 ERA.

199. *Hall of Famers Willie Stargell and Mike Schmidt are the only players to be named MVP of the regular season, the League Championship Series, and the World Series in one year. True or False?*

ANSWER: False

Schmidt failed to win the MVP in the championship series against Houston in 1980. In 1979, however, Willie Stargell did so, although in a most unusual manner. Stargell shared the regular season MVP Award with the Cardinals' Keith Hernandez.

◆ Did you know Willie Stargell and Keith Hernandez's tie in 1979 resulted in the only dual award in MVP history? Each first baseman received 216 points.

200. *Denny McLain in 1968 won 31 games—a figure no pitcher has yet to approach—to unanimously sweep the Cy Young and MVP Awards. McLain won 24 the following year. With whom did McLain share the Cy Young Award in 1969?*

ANSWER: Mike Cuellar

McLain shared the honor with Baltimore's Cuellar in 1969, resulting in the only tie in the award's history. McLain followed his 31-6 season (1.96 ERA) in 1968 with a formidable 24-9 record and a 2.80 ERA in 1969. He also led the league in innings (325) for the second straight year, and posted a league-best nine shutouts. The 1969 season represented McLain's third (and last) season of at least 20 wins as a string of bad decisions and poor conduct that led to suspensions and felony charges curtailed a potential Hall of Fame career. A winner of 131 games and the owner of 29 shutouts, McLain left the game at the young age of 28. Chances are excellent that McLain will remain the last 30-game winner for quite a while, given the five-man rotations used throughout the majors. McLain remains one of only four pitchers since 1900 to win 30 in a season and not be enshrined in the Hall of Fame: Jack Coombs, Jim Bagby, Sr., and Joe Wood are the other three.

The Orioles left-handed Cuellar went 23-11 with a 2.38 ERA in 291 innings, in addition to 18 complete games and five shutouts. For Cuellar, the 1969 season marked the first of three straight 20-win seasons and four overall. The consistent southpaw retired with a 185-130 ledger, a 3.14 ERA, and two World Series wins in three fall classics.

♦ Did you know Denny McLain and Bill Freehan are the only batterymates ever to place 1-2 in the MVP balloting? Tigers righthander McLain received 280 points in 1968, with catcher Freehan getting 161. Outfielding teammate Willie Horton finished fourth.

201. *Fred Snodgrass' misplay of a lazy fly ball in the bottom of the 10th inning had an immense effect on the outcome of the 1912 World Series. As a result, the _____ rallied for two runs in said frame to win the seventh and deciding game (excluding the tie) by a 3-2 score over Snodgrass' New York Giants. Fill in the blank.*

ANSWER: Boston Red Sox

Although Snodgrass' error was dubbed the "$30,000 Muff" (the winner's share), notorious teammate Fred Merkle let Tris Speaker's one-out foul pop drop. Speaker hit a game-tying single three pitches later. Hitting .179 in the series, Larry Gardner (who hit his team's only home run of the series in Game Six) followed with the game-winning sacrifice fly, a fly ball that should have been the fourth out of the inning. Christy Mathewson lost his second decision of the series (despite a 1.57 ERA). Joe Wood won the game in relief. Although the excellent-fielding Snodgrass made a great catch on the very next play and helped the Giants reach three straight World Series, he never lived down the "$30,000 Muff."

202. *The most controversial out in World Series history occurred during Game Three of the 1925 fall classic, as Washington's Sam Rice allegedly caught Earl Smith's long drive to right field. Many swore they saw the ball handed to Rice by a fan after Rice fell over the fence. Although the Senators won the game, 4-3, the "miss-call" didn't affect the final result of the World Series as the Pittsburgh Pirates pulled the classic out in seven games with a 9-7 win in Game Seven. Can you name the Game Seven loser?*

ANSWER: Walter Johnson

Johnson lost Game Seven, despite winning his first two decisions in the series. Ironically, Johnson went 0-2 before winning Game Seven in the 1924 series.

A big reason Washington blew its three-games-to-one lead in the 1925 fall classic was its porous defense. The Senators committed nine errors, eight of which were made by shortstop Roger Peckinpaugh. Ironically, Peckinpaugh entered the series on a high after receiving word he was named AL MVP for the concluded regular season, in which he batted .294 and provided solid leadership. The same shortstop who batted .417 in helping the Senators win the previous October was the goat whose two errors in Game Seven in 1925 accounted for four unearned runs in a 9-7 defeat. His eighth-inning error in Game Two also made a difference in that loss.

However, the Senators can't complain after winning the 1924 World Series via a comedy of errors by the New York Giants. Tied at

3-3 in the bottom of the 12th inning of Game Seven, the Senators took advantage of quite a few miscues and breaks to win the first title in franchise history. With one out, the Senators' Muddy Ruel hit a foul pop that seemed like a sure second out. But Giants catcher Hank Gowdy tripped over his face mask and missed the foul pop. Given a second chance, Ruel doubled down the left-field line. Allowed to bat, Johnson hit a grounder to short, where Travis Jackson misplayed the ball for an error as Ruel held at second. Earl McNeely followed that up with a grounder to third that took a bad hop and skipped over Giants third baseman Fred Lindstrom's head, scoring Ruel for the series-winning run. Johnson, who came on in relief to open the ninth and pitched four scoreless innings, was the beneficiary in that 1924 series finale. In that series' opener, Johnson went the distance in a 12-inning, 4-3 defeat.

203. *Nolan Ryan pitched a record seven no-hitters to seven different catchers. Those seven catchers were Alan Ashby, Tom Egan, Art Kusnyer, Ellie Rodriguez, Jeff Russell, Mike Stanley, and Jeff Torborg. Arrange them in order of Ryan's seven no-hitters.*

ANSWER: Torborg, Kusnyer, Egan, Rodriguez, Ashby, Russell, and Stanley

Ryan's first no-hitter came with Torborg on May 15, 1973, a 3-0 win at Kansas City. The Angel fire-baller defeated Royals hurler Dal Canton with the help of 12 strikeouts and three walks issued. The second gem came on July 15, 1973, with Kusnyer, a 6-0 win at Detroit. Ryan defeated Jim Perry in addition to striking out 17, including eight straight, and walking four. It was in this gem that Tigers first baseman Norm Cash walked to the plate in the ninth inning carrying a piano leg (umpire Ron Luciano made Cash walk back to get a bat, with which he popped out to end the game). On September 28, 1974, Ryan put together his third no-no, a 4-0 win versus the Twins in Anaheim. Ryan's batterymate Egan helped "The Express" whiff 15, despite eight walks issued. Ryan's fourth and last no-hitter as an Angel came with Rodriguez on June 1, 1975. Ryan defeated Baltimore pitcher Ross Grimsley, 1-0, in Anaheim with nine Ks and four walks to his credit. On September 26, 1981, Ryan set a record with his fifth no-hitter, in the Astrodome. With Ashby, Ryan defeated

Ted Power and the Dodgers 5-0, whiffing 11 and issuing three bases on balls. On June 11 nine years later, Ryan came through with his sixth no-hitter—this time as a member of the Texas Rangers. Ryan shut out the mighty Athletics, 5-0, in Oakland, defeating Scott Sanderson to become the first to throw a no-no for three teams. Russell called the game as well as all 14 strikeouts and two walks.

Ryan's seventh no-hitter was a Picasso if there ever was one. On May 1, 1991, in Arlington Stadium, the 44-year-old Ryan bemused the Toronto Blue Jays, 3-0, on the strength of 16 whiffs and just two walks. Stanley was Ryan's catcher, and Jimmy Key was the Toronto loser. Interestingly enough, Ryan's last three no-hit victims were post-season participants.

204. *Who is the only pitcher to lead the majors in strikeouts, winning percentage, and ERA in the same year more than once?*

ANSWER: Lefty Grove

Grove, of the Philadelphia Athletics, rendered these exploits in 1929, 1930, and 1931. Grove posted ERA figures of 2.81, 2.54, and 2.06 during that stretch, a span noted for its offensive dominance. During that span, Grove was a combined 79-15, with 70 complete games and eight shutouts.

205. *This pitcher was assigned a record 16 opening day starts. Who is he?*

A Steve Carlton
B Tom Seaver
C Warren Spahn
D Phil Niekro
E Cy Young

ANSWER: B

Jack Morris started 14 to tie Walter Johnson for the second best total, although Morris' 14 were in consecutive seasons, spanning his days with Detroit, Minnesota, Toronto, and Cleveland. Seaver and Robin Roberts started 12 consecutive opening days.

◆ Did you know Hall of Famer Phil Niekro holds the dubious mark for the worst record on opening day, with an 0-7 ledger? Only Steve Carlton (3-9) lost more often on opening day. According to Lyle Spatz of the Society for American Baseball Research, Cy Young and Robin Roberts each went 5-7 on opening day.

206. *Match these players with their pilfering feats:*

1	Babe Ruth	A	stole 15 bases for the lowest league-leading figure in history
2	Dom DiMaggio	B	this noble catcher was stolen on 13 times in one game, a 20th-century record
3	Craig Biggio	C	stole home 10 times during his career
4	Branch Rickey	D	joined Tris Speaker as the only players with 50 doubles and 50 steals in one season

ANSWER: 1—C, 2—A, 3—D, 4—B

Lou Gehrig edged Ruth in this department at least, stealing home a remarkable 15 times, all on the back end of a double steal. Dom DiMaggio led the league in thefts in 1950. Biggio accomplished his feat in 1998, or 86 years after Speaker had. Speaker remains the all-time doubles king with 792 two-baggers.

Rickey, catching for the Yankees, watched as Senator after Senator stole a base in a 16-5 Washington victory on June 28, 1907. Rickey played but 119 games and managed for parts of 10 seasons. He later became a Hall of Fame executive for the Cardinals and Dodgers, carving his niche in the history of baseball. Of all his ideas, inventions, and decisions, none were as important as bringing in Jackie Robinson to Major League Baseball. He told Jackie that in order for integration to work, he needed him "to have the courage NOT to fight back." The principled Robinson, who was court-martialed (and acquitted) for refusing to sit in the back of an Army bus years earlier, put the needs of an entire race ahead of his own. Robinson's discipline paved the way for many and stood as an epitome of character.

The first brawl between a black and white star didn't occur until 1959, when the Reds' Frank Robinson and the Braves' Eddie Mathews engaged in a fist fight, after Robinson slid hard and with spikes high into the Braves' white third baseman.

♦ Did you know on May 11, 1897, catcher Duke Farrell set a still-standing record by throwing out eight men attempting to steal? A receiver for the NL's Washington Senators, Farrell that day threw out eight of the nine vying to pilfer a base. Farrell, a switch-hitting catcher, also displayed some talent in the batter's box, winning a home run title and sharing an RBI crown in 1891 for the pennant-winning Boston Reds of the American Association. Bill Bergen (Dodgers) and Wally Schang (Athletics) each threw out six runners in a game in 1909 and 1915, respectively, to share the modern mark.

◆ Did you know Earl Webb, whose 67 doubles in 1931 for the Boston Red Sox remain the single-season record, never hit more than 30 two-baggers in any other season? Webb, who broke George Henry Burns' mark of 64 doubles set five years earlier, retired with 155 career two-baggers.

207. *Four black players integrated the 1949 All-Star Game. They were Jackie Robinson, Larry Doby, _____, and _____. Fill in the blanks.*

ANSWER: Don Newcombe and Roy Campanella

Doby and the rest of the AL team beat Robinson, Newcombe, Campanella and the others on the NL team, 11-7, at Ebbets Field. Newcombe took the loss, allowing two runs in the fourth inning. Joe DiMaggio, a late addition to the roster after an injury-plagued first half, and Eddie Joost combined to drive in five runs for the American League, overcoming NL homers by Stan Musial and Ralph Kiner.

208. *Fans were not allowed to vote and decide on players for the All-Star Game from 1958 to 1969. True or False?*

ANSWER: True

The fan vote was taken away and given to the managers after Cincinnati Reds fans abused their privilege in 1957, stuffing the ballot box with mostly Reds players. The ballot stuffing resulted in seven of the Reds' eight position players being chosen to start that year's All-Star Game at Busch Stadium. Only George Crowe at first base for the Reds was not voted in, losing out to the Cardinals' Stan Musial.

The voting abuse prompted Commissioner Ford Frick to pull two of the Reds, Gus Bell and Wally Post, from the starting lineup in favor of a couple of guys named Willie Mays and Hank Aaron, although manager Walter Alston later brought back Bell. Frick thus gave the vote to managers, coaches, and players from 1958 to 1969. Assistant Secretary to Major League Baseball Jack Lang told me Commissioner Bowie Kuhn reinstated the fan vote in 1970, because "he felt the fans wanted the vote. He felt the fans were for whom the game was played to begin with."

209. *The originator of the All-Star Game was:*

    A Ford Frick
    B Kenesaw Landis
    C Arch Ward
    D Ban Johnson

ANSWER: C

That's why the award given to the All-Star Game MVP is called the Arch Ward Memorial Award. Ward convinced baseball officials of the idea. The trophy was first awarded in 1962 (twice) and has been given out each year thereafter.

♦ Did you know the inaugural All-Star was sponsored by *The Chicago Tribune* as a World's Fair feature? In 1933, *The Sporting News* wrote, "There is no doubt that such an All-Star Game played in the middle of the season is a great stimulus for baseball and ought to be encouraged. It creates fresh enthusiasm at a time when interest may begin to lag."

210. *Which pitcher owns the All-Star Game record with three wins?*

ANSWER: Lefty Gomez

Gomez took on the best competition and silenced them. The Yankees southpaw allowed two hits over three scoreless innings in the inaugural 1933 game for his first win. After getting roughed up the following July, he earned his second win in 1935 by yielding just three hits over six splendid innings (one run). Gomez won his third mid-summer classic in 1937, with three more outstanding innings. His loss in 1938 was no fault of his, as he permitted only one unearned run in three more quiet frames.

Overall, Gomez enjoyed a stellar career that spanned parts of 14 seasons, during which he won 189 of 291 decisions. The Hall of Famer put together four 20-win seasons, including a 26-victory campaign in 1934, en route to seven All-Star selections and a pair of pitcher's Triple Crowns. Gomez was instrumental in the Yankees' five world championships during the 1930s. Gomez, a colorful and magnetic personality off the mound, also possessed the demeanor and grit necessary to work with men on base. In a tough contest on August 1, 1941, Gomez issued 11 bases on balls and allowed 15 St. Louis Browns to reach base, including three in the ninth. Keeping his composure, Gomez escaped jam after jam, preserving a most unique shutout.

◆ Did you know Lefty Gomez, Spud Chandler, and Al Benton are the only pitchers to hurl more than three innings in a single All-Star Game? Gomez's six-inning stint in 1935 is the longest in history. Chandler (four innings pitched) and Benton (five innings in relief) combined to beat the 1942 NL squad. Afterward, a rule prohibited starting pitchers from pitching more than three innings, and required three innings of work for a starter's victory. Today, a starter needs just two innings to become eligible for the win.

211. *This Hall of Famer was sent a crushing blow during the prime of his career when he was diagnosed with acute sinusitis, leaving him with double vision. This forced him to sit out a year. But he made a remarkable and courageous comeback. Can you name this focused man and hitter?*

ANSWER: George Sisler

Sisler had just hit a remarkable .420 in 1922, giving him 1,498 hits through his first eight seasons (a .361 clip) before learning of his acute sinusitis. Fighting blindness, Sisler sat out the 1923 season in hopes of restoring his vision. Sisler got his wish as he came back to hit .320 (albeit with reduced power) over his next seven years, before retiring following the 1930 season because of his increasing eye problems. Sisler retired with a .340 lifetime average and an amazing 2,812 hits over a 15-year career. Without a doubt, Sisler's career is one of the best ever aborted. Even with eye trouble, Sisler still managed to hit .327, .331, .326, and .309 in his final four years. Sisler, a great fielding first baseman as well, retired with 375 stolen bases and four stolen base titles.

◆ Did you know Ted Williams and Rogers Hornsby took eye care to the limit to assure themselves of their most valuable assets? It's no coincidence that "Terrible Ted" and "Rajah" became two of the very best hitters of all time as a result. They were so enamored with the art of hitting that they never read in a car, bus, train (or airplane, in Williams' case), or any other moving vehicle. To protect his eyes, Hornsby never smoked, drank, or even attended movies. He also made it a point to sleep 12 hours a day. Williams went to the extreme of not chewing gum, as it caused his pupils to move up and down. Williams was so obsessed with hitting that his sole goal in life was to have people say, "There goes Ted Williams, the greatest hitter who ever lived." Hornsby was equally driven. As a manager, Hornsby expected his players to be equally fanatical in safeguarding their playing assets, not realizing that few others shared his commitment. Hornsby lent credibility to the theory that Hall of Fame players have little tolerance and patience as managers.

212. *Do you know what righthander Clement Labine did to Hall of Famer Stan Musial?*

ANSWER: The 13-year reliever (Labine only started 38 of his 513 games) retired Musial an eye-boggling 49 straight times. It's an amazing accomplishment, considering Musial retired with a .331 lifetime batting average, a .417 on-base percentage, and a .559 slugging average. Labine, the sinkerballing righthander, earned two All-Star appearances for the Dodgers, twice leading the National League in saves (1956 and 1957) and going 13-5 with a league-leading 60 appearances for the 1955 world champion club.

The great reliever, however, will forever be remembered in Dodgers lore for a pair of superb high-pressured starts. In the second game of the 1951 NL play-off, the rookie Labine blanked the Giants, 10-0, to force the unforgettable third game. Following Don Larsen's perfect game in Game Five of the 1956 World Series, Labine turned in a masterpiece of his own with a 10-inning, 1-0 shutout to force a seventh game. The Dodgers lost each series.

213. *Match these relievers with their accomplishments:*

1	Rollie Fingers	A	made 1,050 relief appearances
2	Kent Tekulve	B	heads the all-time list with 1,131 games pitched and 1,127 relief appearances
3	Mike Marshall	C	pitched in a season-high 106 games
4	Jesse Orosco	D	retired as the all-time leader with 341 saves

ANSWER: 1—D, 2—A, 3—C, 4—B

Fingers' mark of 709 games finished by a reliever was surpassed by Lee Smith, who retired after the 1997 season with 802. In 1999, Orosco broke Dennis Eckersley's one-year-old record of 1,071 games pitched. (In the last game of Eckersley's career, "The Eck" came out of the bullpen to break Hoyt Wilhelm's mark of 1,070 appearances.) Orosco also surpassed Tekulve's mark for relief appearances.

While making 106 appearances—all in relief—during that unbelievable 1974 campaign, Marshall pitched a relief-record 208 innings, winning 15 games and saving 21 others. He also holds the AL single-season record, with 90 appearances for the Twins in 1979. Although Marshall never again approached 200 innings, his 1974 workload didn't spell doom for his right arm, as you might have guessed. Marshall pitched at least 99 innings thrice more following the 1974 season. The workhorse nearly averaged 100 innings per season over his 14-year career.

In 1997, Smith became the fourth pitcher to have appeared in 1,000 games, ending with 1,022. Only Orosco (1998), Eckersley, Wilhelm, and Tekulve (who never made a start) are ahead of Smith, who passed Rich Gossage with his 1,003rd appearance.

♦ Did you know in 2000, relievers Mike Myers and Buddy Groom became the first two pitchers to appear in 70 games for a fifth straight season? Myers was the first to accomplish the feat, in a Rockies uniform on September 12. Groom followed, in an Orioles uniform on October 1. Curiously, the two were traded for each other late in 1995, the year before they began their streaks.

214. *The 1971 World Series-bound Baltimore Orioles owned a quartet of 20-game winners: Jim Palmer, Dave McNally, Mike Cuellar, and Pat Dobson. However, this AL squad, a half-century earlier, also had four 20-game winners, but in a second place finish. Name the AL team.*

ANSWER: The 1920 White Sox

The White Sox's 96-58 record fell short of the Indians' 98-56 total. Chicago was blessed with the performances of Red Faber (23-13), Lefty Williams (22-14), Dickie Kerr (21-9), and Eddie Cicotte (21-10). Catching the quartet was Hall of Fame catcher Ray Schalk.

Interestingly, Palmer, McNally, Cuellar, and Dobson all won their 20th game during a six-day span, from September 21 to September 26. McNally, the first Bird to reach 20 wins, ended the season with a 21-5 record. Cuellar (20-9) and Dobson (20-8) followed suit, with Palmer (20-9) trailing. Ellie Hendricks and Andy Etchebarren did a fine job of catching the Orioles' quartet.

Baltimore's 1971 pitching staff was the result of a work in progress. In 1968, McNally was the lone 20-game winner for the Orioles. A year later, McNally and Cuellar reached 20 wins. In 1970, McNally, Cuellar, and Palmer reached that circle before Dobson joined to form a unique quartet in 1971. The feat may never be duplicated again, because the vast majority of teams now employ a five-man rotation.

◆ Did you know the 1998 Atlanta Braves and the 1902 Pittsburgh Pirates are the only teams in history to boast five 16-game winners? Tom Glavine, who won his second Cy Young Award in 1998, led the staff with 20 wins. Greg Maddux won 18, Kevin Millwood and John Smoltz recorded 17 apiece, and Denny Neagle brought up the rear with 16 victories. The 1902 Pirates had three 20-game winners and two 16-game winners for a dominating squad that won 103 of its 139 games. Jack Chesbro led the way with 28 wins; Deacon Phillippe and Jesse Tannehill each won 20. Sam Leever and Ed Doheny added 16 wins apiece.

215. *Match these players with their All-Star performances:*

1	Stan Musial	A	won the All-Star Game MVP twice
2	Willie Mays, Steve Garvey, Gary Carter, and Cal Ripken	B	hit a record six home runs in All-Star competition
3	Pie Traynor	C	hit two home runs in an All-Star Game
4	Arky Vaughan, Ted Williams, Al Rosen, Gary Carter, and Willie McCovey	D	drove in a record 12 runs in All-Star competition
5	Ted Williams	E	stole home

ANSWER: 1—B, 2—A, 3—E, 4—C, 5—D

Mays won the All-Star Game MVP in 1963 and 1968; Garvey earned the award in 1974 and 1978; Carter in 1981 and 1984; and Ripken, Jr., in 1991 and 10 years later. In 1974, Garvey was actually elected to the All-Star Game as a write-in candidate, making his MVP performance in that mid-summer classic even more unlikely. Four years later, Garvey became the first player to receive four million All-Star votes. Overall, Garvey batted .393 in 10 All-Star Games, slugging .955 (a record among those with 20 at-bats). Charlie Gehringer's .500 batting average (10-for-20) in six games is the highest among those with at least 20 at-bats. Dave Winfield's seven doubles are also a record.

Traynor's real name was Harold Joseph Traynor. "Pie" was a moniker given him for his fondness of the dessert. Other interesting tidbits about Traynor are that he walked to the ballpark and didn't own a car while playing in the major leagues.

◆ Did you know in 1937, Joe Medwick became the first player in All-Star Game history to collect four hits in a mid-summer classic? With a 4-for-5 performance in the opener of the 1934 World Series, Medwick remains the only player to gather four hits in an All-Star Game and a World Series contest.

◆ Did you know in 2000, Derek Jeter became the first Yankee to ever win All-Star Game MVP honors? Jeter went 3-for-3 with two RBI in the American League's 6-3 victory.

216. *In which year did Yankee manager Joe McCarthy bench all six of his players to quiet down objections that he padded his All-Star lineup with his own players?*

ANSWER: 1943

In the 1943 All-Star Game—the first mid-summer classic played at night—McCarthy avoided using his players while still leading the American League to a 5-3 victory at Shibe Park in Philadelphia. To quiet down accusations of blatant favoritism, McCarthy didn't deploy a single Yankee to the field that evening, as pitchers Tiny Bonham and Spud Chandler, catcher Bill Dickey, second baseman Joe Gordon, and outfielders Charlie Keller and John Lindell all watched. To this day, the 1943 All-Star Game remains the only mid-summer classic in which a Yankee did not play.

Bobby Doerr hit a three-run homer and Dutch Leonard earned the victory in that game. In a losing effort, Pittsburgh's Vince Di-

Maggio went 3-for-3 with a home run, a triple, and a single, after entering the game as a pinch-hitter in the fourth inning.

There may have been reason for the 1943 accusations of favoritism, given that McCarthy had selected a still-standing record nine players from the same team (the Yankees, of course) four years earlier. Of the nine Yankees, McCarthy started six of them, with five playing the entire game in the American League's 3-1 victory at Yankee Stadium. (Even Jimmie Foxx and Luke Appling went unused.) The nine Yankees selected were Dickey (started), Gordon (started), Joe Di-Maggio (started), Lefty Gomez, Red Ruffing (started), Frank Crosetti, John Murphy, Red Rolfe (started), and George Selkirk (started). And that's not including Lou Gehrig, who served as an honorary member of the American League after having retired three weeks earlier.

Although Joe DiMaggio hit a solo homer, it was a Cleveland Indian who proved to be the hero of the 1939 game. Bob Feller, who relieved Tommy Bridges with one out and the bases loaded in the sixth, immediately induced Arky Vaughan into an inning-ending double play before pitching three more scoreless innings for the impressive save.

217. *Match these all-time greats with their predecessors or successors:*

1	Joe Jackson	A	replaced Bobby Thomson in the outfield
2	Babe Ruth	B	was succeeded by Bibb Falk
3	Hugh Duffy	C	succeeded Football Hall of Famer George Halas
4	Mickey Mantle	D	succeeded Joe DiMaggio
5	Ted Williams	E	replaced evangelist Billy Sunday in the outfield
6	Willie Mays	F	was succeeded by Carl Yastrzemski

ANSWER: 1—B, 2—C, 3—E, 4—D, 5—F, 6—A

Falk did an admirable job in succeeding "Shoeless" Jackson, playing left field with great intensity and hitting line drives with "alarming" consistency, according to accounts of the time. The left-handed Falk batted .314 over a 12-year career that included six seasons of at least 82 RBI and another half-dozen campaigns of at least 30 doubles. Playing for the White Sox and subsequently the Indians, Falk struck out only 279 times and averaged nearly 18 outfield assists between 1924 and 1929.

In 1888, Duffy stepped into Sunday's right-field spot on the roster of the Chicago White Stockings (renamed the Cubs), embarking on a Hall of Fame career with heavy hitting and great defense. Sunday spent the following three seasons in Pittsburgh, where he concluded an eight-year career with a .248 lifetime batting average and 246 stolen bases. Sunday went on to become the famous evangelist who ignited the Prohibitionist movement. Sunday, in fact, preached the sermon at Addie Joss' funeral.

The 1951 World Series featured three Hall of Fame center fielders: DiMaggio, Mantle, and Mays. While DiMaggio was playing in his last, Mantle and Mays were appearing in their first World Series.

♦ Did you know Joe DiMaggio can plausibly be faulted for Mantle's chronic knee injuries? During Game One of the 1951 World Series, DiMaggio waited until the very last second to call off Mantle, the rookie right fielder, for a drive DiMaggio had all along. Mantle was forced to put on the brakes and, in doing so, caught his leg in a water drainage ditch, tearing his knee and sidelining him for the series. The knee hampered Mantle throughout his career, and most certainly diminished what some say was the best pure baseball potential to ever wear spikes. Besides having prodigious power from each side of the plate, Mantle possessed blazing speed. Most observers point out that DiMaggio (who retired after the series) should have called Mantle off long before he did: he failed to do so because he wanted to look good making the catch just in time. Over his career, DiMaggio hardly ever called for a ball. It wasn't the first time DiMaggio hurt a fellow outfielder. On July 28, 1936, in Detroit, the rookie left-fielding DiMaggio and the veteran center-fielding Myril Hoag collided and struck heads at full speed while giving chase to a line drive. Although Hoag rose to his feet after the collision, he collapsed two days later with a blood clot and slipped into a brief coma. Three holes had to be drilled in Hoag's skull to relieve the pressure on his brain and save his life. Meanwhile, DiMaggio took over center field for good on the first day of August.

218. *In 1966, the Orioles allowed only two runs on 17 hits in the four-game World Series sweep over the Dodgers. Which World Series champions won four games to one and yielded no earned runs?*

ANSWER: The 1905 Giants

That year, the Giants threw four shutouts at the Philadelphia Athletics, largely behind the spectacular and magnificent performance given by their ace Christy Mathewson. "Big Six" hurled three shutouts and allowed a combined 14 hits, walking just one and striking out a whopping 18. The Giants kept their series ERA at 0.00 despite a 3-0 loss in Game Two. All three runs were unearned. In fact, only seven earned runs were scored throughout the series.

♦ Did you know the Christy Mathewson-Eddie Plank matchup in Game One of the 1905 fall classic was the first Hall of Fame confrontation in World Series history? The Giants' Mathewson won, 3-0, hurling a four-hitter. Two more Hall of Famers faced off the following game, with the Athletics' Chief Bender throwing a four-hit shutout of his own against Joe McGinnity. The score: 3-0.

219. *Can you name the only pitcher to hit a grand slam in World Series history?*

ANSWER: Dave McNally

Baltimore's McNally belted the bases-loaded slam off Cincinnati reliever Wayne Granger in the third game of the 1970 World Series. It helped McNally's cause, as he won by a 9-3 score to give the Birds a commanding three-games-to-none lead en route to a five-game victory. McNally's grand slam is among 17 in fall classic history.

In 1970, Baltimore was running on all cylinders, taking out its frustration from the previous October on its AL opponents. After winning 108 regular-season games by virtue of the league's best offense, best pitching, and second-best defense, the Orioles swept the Minnesota Twins (98-64) convincingly in the AL Championship Series. Baltimore played flawless ball, outscoring Minnesota by a 27-10 margin. In the fall classic, Baltimore finally redeemed its disappointing 1969 Series loss to the New York Mets by discarding a Reds team that had earned 102 victories in the regular season.

♦ Did you know Dave McNally and Bob Gibson are the only two pitchers to hit two home runs in World Series competition? And, incredibly, they each accomplished the feat over consecutive years. McNally's grand slam during the 1970 World Series was preceded by a two-run homer in the 1969 classic against the New York Mets' Jerry Koosman. Gibson's first fall classic homer came in 1967 against Boston's Jim Lonborg during a triumphant Game Seven. His second bomb, also on the road, came against Detroit's Joe Sparma during a victorious Game Four outing in 1968. Alas, for Gibson and the Cardinals, they lost the final three games in 1968.

220. *Of the four most prolific home run hitters in the history of professional baseball, regardless of era or league, which man hit the most roundtrippers per 550 at-bats: Hank Aaron, Josh Gibson, Sadaharu Oh, or Babe Ruth?*

ANSWER: Sadaharu Oh

Oh hit an average of 49 home runs per 550 at-bats. Gibson averaged 48, Ruth averaged 45, and Aaron 34. Many argue that Oh's total of 868 home runs is misleading and overrated. After all, he didn't face major league pitchers, they say, and had the luxury of hitting over fences shorter than 300 feet away. However, Oh never came to bat as often as 500 times in a season. He also drew about one walk per game, faced a lot more junkball pitchers, and played in a 130-game schedule. Among Oh's great achievements are 13 straight RBI crowns (for a Japanese record total of 2,170), 13 home run titles in a row (15 overall), nine MVPs, five batting titles, and nine Diamond Gloves (Japan's version of the Gold Gloves). Now, that's dominance!

♦ Did you know Henry Aaron out-slugged Sadaharu Oh, 10-9, in a 1974 orchestrated home run contest in Tokyo? Aaron still had two more swings left in his turn, but opted not to take them.

221. *Besides showcasing Bill Wambsganss' unassisted triple play, Game Five of the 1920 World Series also featured the first-ever World Series grand slam. Who hit it?*

ANSWER: Elmer Smith

Indians right fielder Smith's grand slam in Game Five (along with a .692 slugging percentage and six RBI) helped Cleveland defeat Brooklyn five games to two. And aside from witnessing post-season history's only triple play, Game-Five winner Jim Bagby hit a three-run homer to become the first pitcher to hit a home run in World Series play.

♦ Did you know that four World Series were played in the best-of-nine format? They were the inaugural 1903 classic (in which the Boston Pilgrims beat the Pittsburgh Pirates five games to three), the "fixed" series in 1919 (in which the Cincinnati Reds beat the Chicago White Sox five games to three), the aforementioned 1920 World Series, and the 1921 classic (featuring the New York Giants beating the New York Yankees in eight games).

222. *Which pitcher held the single-season strikeout record before Sandy Koufax whiffed 382 National League batters in 1965?*

ANSWER: Rube Waddell

Philadelphia Athletic Waddell whiffed 349 plate foes in 1904. Waddell led the American League in strikeouts for six straight seasons (1902–07). The southpaw, who retired with a 191-145 record in 1910, won his first of seven strikeout crowns for Pittsburgh of the National League in 1900.

Waddell was very talented but unfocused, frequently missing games because of his preoccupation with alcohol, marbles (of all things), and fire engines. Waddell, perhaps the most eccentric major leaguer in history, frequently arrived at the ballpark late or just in time to take the mound after being dragged from another bottle of alcohol or a game of marbles. At times, he would actually get dressed en route to the mound in front of the audience. And once on the mound, he was not sure to stay there. Fixated on fire engines, Waddell would throw down his ball and glove in mid-delivery to chase after whistling fire trucks. He was also such a notorious spendthrift that his team's owner and manager, Connie Mack, began to pay him in one-dollar bills, hoping to make the pitcher's money last longer and to avoid constant requests for loans.

With more discipline, the immensely talented southpaw might have been the best pitcher of all time. A victim of retardation and/or emotional immaturity, Waddell's sole ambition was to have a good time. A grand fisherman, he also wrestled alligators, played rugby, and acted.

♦ Did you know Rube Waddell was born on a Friday the 13th (October 1876) and died on April Fool's Day of 1914?

223. *Bobby Thomson's "shot heard 'round the world" is synonymous with this broadcaster's famous chant: "There's a long drive. It's gonna be I believe! . . . The Giants win the pennant! The Giants win the pennant! The Giants win the pennant! The Giants win the pennant! Bobby Thomson hit it into the lower deck of the left-field stands. . . . The Giants win the pennant. And they're going crazy; they're going crazy. Yeaaahoo! . . . I don't believe it! I don't believe it. I cannot believe it!" Name this memorable voice.*

ANSWER: Russ Hodges

Hodges worked the first three and last three innings on the radio and the middle three on television. Hall of Fame announcer Ernie Harwell worked the ninth inning on television and said, "It's gone," allowing the picture to speak for itself—a great strategy in itself, but one overlooked by Hodges as he made his dramatic call. Both Hodges and Harwell are in the Hall of Fame for their broadcasting contributions.

224. *In one of the most impressive pitching displays ever, this fire-baller took it upon himself to dominate his league in 1931 with a 31-4 record, a masterful 2.06 ERA, 27 complete games, 175 strikeouts, and four shutouts—all league-leading figures. This tough competitor even came out of the bullpen to earn five saves. Who was he?*

ANSWER: Lefty Grove

The Athletics' Grove was arguably the best left-handed pitcher of all time. A winner of four victory titles and seven consecutive strikeout crowns, Grove remains the only modern southpaw to reach the 30-win plateau. The determined ace of Connie Mack's squad, Grove fashioned a spectacular ERA in 1931 despite the era's offensive splurge. Grove excelled during that period of offensive dominance, faring far better than his peers in what was perhaps the era least favorable to pitching prior to the mid-1990s. Despite pitching in hitter's parks, to boot, throughout his career, Grove led his league in ERA a staggering nine times over a 14-year stretch within his 17-year career, or better than once every two seasons.

To this day, Grove's nine ERA titles are three more than any other pitcher has earned in the history of the major leagues. Roger Clemens' six ERA titles are second on the list, ahead of the five earned by Hall of Famers Walter Johnson, Christy Mathewson, and Sandy Koufax. Grover Alexander won four ERA titles.

225. *The New York Giants and the Detroit Tigers have the dubious distinction of losing three World Series in consecutive years. True or False?*

ANSWER: True

The Giants won the NL pennant in 1911, 1912, and 1913, only to lose to the Philadelphia Athletics, the Boston Red Sox, and the Athletics again in the World Series for those years. The Tigers of 1907, 1908, and 1909 lost in the World Series to the Chicago Cubs the first two years and the Pirates in 1909.

That 1908 world championship for the Cubs remains the franchise's last, a title drought 10 years longer than that of the cursed Boston Red Sox. Almost a century later, the Cubs are still seeking their third World Series victory after winning consecutive fall classics in 1907 and 1908. Following a sweep of the Tigers in 1907, the Cubs dominated the men from Detroit the next October. Chicago won the first three games by a combined margin of 24-10, due in no small part to the offense provided by player-manager Frank Chance, second baseman Johnny Evers, right fielder Frank Schulte, and center fielder Solly Hofman. The Cubs closed the series out in Game Five, as Orval Overall pitched a three-hit shutout to match Mordecai Brown's two series victories. The Cubs hope to add to their slender championship chapter as they forge into the 21st century, with Sammy Sosa leading the way.

♦ Did you know Mordecai Brown remains the only pitcher to throw a shutout in three straight World Series? Brown blanked the White Sox in Game Four of the 1906 Series, the Tigers in Game Five of the 1907 classic, and the Tigers again the following October in Game Four.

226. *Match these women of courage with their feats:*

1	Helen Callaghan	A	was the only woman to ever bat in a major league game on July 31, 1935
2	Kitty Burke		

3	Pam Postema	B	"Queen of Baseball" who signed with the semi-pro Providence Independents in 1918
4	Jackie Mitchell		
5	Elizabeth Murphy	C	Triple-A umpire who worked the majors during spring training one year
6	Margaret Gisolo		
		D	first professional female baseball player in the 20th century
		E	batting champion and the mother of major leaguer Casey Candaele
		F	14-year-old superstar in Indiana in whose favor Judge Kenesaw Landis ruled in 1928, saying that the American Legion rules did not prohibit the participation of women

ANSWER: 1—E, 2—A, 3—C, 4—D, 5—B, 6—F

Callaghan, who was immortalized in the film *A League of Their Own*, stole 354 bases in 388 games. Her light-hitting son hit .249 with 36 stolen bases, playing for the Expos and Astros during a seven-year major league career. Nightclub singer Burke was a Reds fan who asked Babe Herman if she could bat for him in the bottom of the eighth inning after she exchanged comments with the Cardinals' Ducky Medwick. (She was only 20 feet away from Herman: The over-sold game had 8,000 fans within the Crosley Field foul grounds.) Burke grounded Daffy Dean's delivery right back to Dean, who personally tagged her. Her at-bat doesn't count in the history books as it didn't count in that game.

Postema sued Major League Baseball for discrimination, and wound up settling out of court, according to Major League Baseball's public relations department. But according to venerable umpire Doug Harvey, in an interview with *Up-Close* host Roy Firestone, Postema had an attitude and refused advice, claiming sufficient knowledge to present her case. Bernice Gera was the first woman to umpire in professional baseball in 1972, lasting just one game before quitting. The abrupt retirement was surprising, because it took her six years of battling in court to get the opportunity to umpire. Following her only game on June 24, 1972, Gera quit, agitated after an argument with one of the other managers. In 1904, Amanda Clement was the first woman to umpire a men's baseball game, doing so in Hayward, Iowa.

Mitchell signed her contract with a class AA minor league team. Taught to pitch by Dazzy Vance, the left-handed Mitchell once struck out nine men in a row during an amateur game. Her biggest moment came about when she struck out Babe Ruth and Lou Gehrig consecutively during a 1931 exhibition match, at the age of 17. (Ruth and Gehrig were summoned to glisten Mitchell's legend.) Judge Landis disallowed the contract that Chattanooga manager Joe Engel signed her to, claiming that baseball was too strenuous for women. The banning of women from organized baseball, which became official on June 21, 1952, prohibited women from signing professional baseball contracts with men's clubs.

Beginning on June 12, 1974, girls were permitted to play in Little League, although some other leagues for minors (such as Senior Baseball) still ban girls from experiencing the joy of The Game. Today, women are allowed to play professional baseball, but are still not allowed to play in the major leagues. President and founder of the Women's Baseball League Justine Warren told me, "I would obviously like that changed, but there are more pressing issues. There are leagues besides Little Leagues that girls can't play in. And even in the Little Leagues, girls can't play beyond the age of 14."

♦ Did you know the Bloomer Girls (a women's league that toured the country) produced Hall of Famer Rogers Hornsby and the great "Smoky" Joe Wood? The Bloomer Girls circuit, which lasted from the 1890s until 1934, on occasion filled roster spots with men. To gain experience, youngsters Hornsby, Wood, and a few others donned wigs to blend in with female starters, making for co-ed teams in the early 1900s. And Hall of Famers Jimmie Foxx, Max Carey, and Dave Bancroft were once managers of the All-American Girls Professional Baseball League. The founder was Phillip K. Wrigley.

♦ Did you know that in 1989, first baseman Julie Croteau became the first woman to play NCAA men's varsity baseball at St. Mary's College in Maryland? The left-handed thrower and hitter hit .222 as an 18-year-old freshman. Six years later, she became the first female assistant coach in men's collegiate division I baseball at the University of Massachusetts—Amherst. As a 12th grader, in 1988, she sued Osborne Park High School in Manassas, Virginia, for not allowing girls to play baseball. She lost the case, but clearly made her point at St. Mary's. The glove she used at St. Mary's is in the Baseball Hall of Fame.

227. *Who is the only player ever to register 150 wins as a pitcher and accrue 2,000 hits? (Hint: It's not Babe Ruth.)*

ANSWER: John Montgomery Ward (better known as Monte Ward)

A right-handed pitcher, Ward enjoyed seasons of 22-13, 47-17, 40-23, and 19-13. Relying on guile and a great curveball, this five-foot nine-inch, 165-pound hurler also pitched baseball history's second perfect game in 1880. He won 108 games before his 21st birthday. But injuries forced the 24-year-old to leave behind a record of 158-102 and a masterful ERA of 2.10, the fourth-lowest career mark. Not yet ready to retire and abandon the camaraderie he so enjoyed, Ward taught himself how to hit (both ways), and honed his fielding skills.

In 1885, he became an every-day player, playing until 1894. Ward compiled lifetime marks of .278, 26 homers, 2,122 hits, 686 RBI, at least 540 stolen bases (stolen bases were sometimes not counted back then), and 1,408 runs scored primarily as a shortstop. Ward, who in the 1890s led the Giants to their first championship, was elected into the Hall of Fame in 1964.

But Ward was much more than a versatile player. A player, manager, labor organizer, and team owner, Ward was quite simply the most significant baseball man in the 19th century. A multifaceted man and a strong leader, Ward was integral in establishing the first players' union in baseball history as well as instituting a rival major league (the Players League) at one point. Never satisfied, the ambitious Ward hit the books hard and earned two degrees—one in law and one in political science—at Columbia University, graduating with honors. Ward subsequently became a full-time lawyer and opened his own practice, at times representing major leaguers.

♦ Did you know Monte Ward introduced the intentional walk to baseball?

228. *Match these stars and their backgrounds:*

1 Keith Hernandez	A	a 19th-round draft pick
2 Robin Ventura	B	a 42nd-round draft pick
3 Don Mattingly	C	drafted 10th overall

4 Mark McGwire   D set a college record 58-game hitting streak at Oklahoma State, earning NCAA Player of the Year honors and the Golden Spikes Award

ANSWER: 1—B, 2—D, 3—A, 4—C

Although it's no surprise McGwire was selected in the first round of the 1984 draft, it's amusing to read the list of those chosen ahead of "Big Mac": Shawn Abner (first), Billy Swift, Drew Hall, Corey Snyder, Pat Pacillo, Eric Pappas, Mike Dunne, Jay Bell, and Alan Cockrell. As a sophomore pitcher/infielder at the University of Southern California, McGwire allowed fewer runs than teammate Randy Johnson and hit 19 home runs to break the school record of 17. As a junior, McGwire hit 32 home runs to shatter his own mark. Out of high school, McGwire was only recruited by USC and was drafted in the eighth round by the Expos. McGwire was eager to sign, but Montreal only offered $8,500.

♦ Did you know Dave Winfield had a 19-4 career collegiate record as a pitcher for the University of Minnesota? Winfield had an ERA of 2.24, with 229 strikeouts in 30 games pitched. A member of the All Big-Ten each year from 1971 to 1973, Winfield was 13-1, and batted over .400 during his senior year.

229. *Who was the first player in history to draw an intentional walk with the bases loaded?*

ANSWER: Nap Lajoie

Cleveland's Lajoie was given the honor in 1901, the year he also won the 20th century's first Triple Crown. Interestingly, only two others have since received an intentional walk with the bases loaded: Bill "Swish" Nicholson in 1944 and Barry Bonds in 1998.

230. *Babe Ruth's purported "called shot" off the Cubs' Charlie Root in Game Three of the 1932 World Series was provoked by unmerciful Cubs players and fans who were taunting the slugger. The taunting in one of the most heated fall classics in history came about because Ruth took umbrage upon learning that a former teammate was denied World Series shares after almost single-handedly leading* *the Cubs to their pennant. Can you name this former teammate whom Ruth spoke up for?*

ANSWER: Mark Koenig

Shortstop Koenig helped the Cubs overcome six games in the standings with 33 contests left after replacing the injured Billy Jurges. Following a promotion from the Pacific Coast League on August 5, Koenig batted .353 and slugged .510 the rest of the way. Although not the equal of the slick fielding Jurges at short, Koenig sparked the club's offense in out-hitting Jurges by 100 percentage points and out-slugging him by 162.

After the Yankees won the first two games of the classic in New York, the series shifted to Chicago, where the Wrigley Field occupants unleashed a barrage of taunts at Ruth. The slurs continued even after Ruth's three-run homer in the first inning. As Ruth faced an 0-2 count with no one aboard in the fifth frame, he made a gesture with his index finger. (From this gesture stems the controversy and the legend.) Whatever his intention, Ruth blasted Root's 0-2 curveball into the center-field bleachers to unlock a 4-4 tie and silence his hecklers. Lou Gehrig followed with his second home run as well, giving the Yankees a 6-4 lead en route to a 7-5 triumph and a commanding three games-to-none advantage in the series, which New York wrapped up the next afternoon.

The right-handed Root was adamant that Ruth never called his famous home run. Root was resolute "The Bambino" was signaling with his finger that he had one strike left. The at-bat remains legendary to this day.

◆ Did you know Cubs shortstop Billy Jurges was shot by a showgirl named Violet Valli on July 6, 1932, forcing Chicago to sign Mark Koenig? Jurges, shot twice, was back in a month and, inexplicably, did not press charges.

231. *Giants reserve Bill Bathe's homer in the 1989 World Series made him only the second player ever to homer in his first career series at-bat as a pinch-hitter. Who was the first?*

ANSWER: Dusty Rhodes

Rhodes, also a Giant, hit a three-run, pinch-hit homer in the bottom of the 10th inning off Indians starter Bob Lemon to give New York a 5-2 win over Cleveland in Game One of the 1954 World Series. Rhodes' walk-off homer on the first pitch traveled all of 260 feet, clearing the right-field wall with two on and one out in the oddly shaped Polo Grounds. Rhodes, who was hitting in place of Monte Irvin, went 4-for-6 with two homers and seven RBI in the sweep of the Indians, including a 3-for-3 performance in the pinch. It was a great feat for a player with a .212 career pinch-hitting average.

Ironically, that game's greatest play featured a ball hit almost 200 feet longer, yet resulting in an out. Tied at 2-2 in the eighth inning, the Indians' Vic Wertz greeted southpaw reliever Don Liddle with a drive to the deepest part of the field. That's when Willie Mays made his famous over-the-shoulder catch some 460 feet away from home plate to keep the Indians from scoring.

Wertz entered the at-bat having singled twice, doubled, tripled, and driven in a pair of runs in four plate appearances. Although best remembered for his long drive, Wertz established himself as a four-time All-Star who hit 266 homers and eclipsed the 100-RBI plateau five times.

Marv Grissom, who pitched 2⅔ scoreless innings, won the game in relief of Sal Maglie and Liddle for New York. *Total Baseball* claims that when manager Leo Durocher walked up to Liddle and asked for the ball, having signaled Grissom to relieve, Liddle told Durocher, "Well, I got my guy." Now that is a classic line.

232. *Among the 17 sweeps in World Series history, the Yankees have been involved in 11 of them, winning eight. Can you name the three teams to sweep the Yankees in the fall classic?*

ANSWER: The Cincinnati Reds (1976), the New York Giants (1922), and the Los Angeles Dodgers (1963)

In the 1922 fall classic, the Yankees actually tied the Giants, 3-3, in Game Two. In getting outscored by an 18-11 margin (a figure that includes the tie), those Yankees lost a pair of one-run games and a 5-3 decision in the finale. In the 1963 classic, the Yankees were outscored 12-4. In the 1976 World Series, New York was dominated, getting outscored by a 22-8 margin.

233. *Who holds the record for most hits (238) in a season by a Yankee:*

    A Lou Gehrig
    B Babe Ruth
    C Joe DiMaggio
    D Don Mattingly

ANSWER: D

Mattingly set the record in 1986. A classy gentleman, he retired with a .307 batting average, 222 home runs, and 1,099 RBI over a 14-year career. Mattingly, whose beautiful left-handed swing became affected by back problems, also retired with nine Gold Gloves at first base and the second-best fielding percentage (.99582) of all time at that position. Alas, he never had a chance to play in the World Series, beginning in 1982 (a year after the Yankees' 1981 pennant) and ending in 1995 (a year before the franchise's 23rd title). Mattingly was the 10th captain in Yankee history. He also became the 15th Yankee to have his number (#23) retired by the organization.

234. *The only player to hit four home runs in a game and leg out three triples in another is:*

    A Willie Mays
    B Lou Gehrig
    C Rocky Colavito
    D Frank Robinson

ANSWER: A

Mays hit four homers in a 1961 game and had three triples in an 11-inning game the previous year. In his four-homer game on April 30, 1961, Mays did so in five at-bats, also driving in eight runners during a 14-4 rout at Milwaukee. A total of 10 homers were hit in that game, including two by Braves center fielder Hank Aaron. Mays, who led the league in triples thrice, led the senior circuit in both categories in 1955, with 51 homers and 13 triples. Mays, in fact, is one of only five players to lead his league in triples and home runs during the same season. The others are Harry Lumley (nine homers, 18 triples; 1904), Jim Bottomley (31 homes, 20 triples; 1928), Mickey Mantle (37 homers, 11 triples; 1955), and Jim Rice (46 homers, 15 triples; 1978).

♦ Did you know Willie Mays used Joey Amalfitano's bat to produce his four-homer game on April 30, 1961? Amalfitano, a light-hitting infielder, homered just nine times in 1,715 at-bats over a 10-year career. Mays wasn't the only major leaguer to belt four homers in a game using a teammate's bat. On July 31, 1954, Joe Adcock used the lumber of Charlie White, a catcher whose brief and unimpressive career spanned 123 at-bats and featured a grand total of one home run.

235. *Can you name the only player to appear in as many as 243 games before his 20th birthday?*

ANSWER: Robin Yount

Yount's major league debut came at the age of 18. (Mel Ott came close to Yount's youthful record: He played in 241 games as a teenager, making his debut at the age of 17.) Yount was too impressive to keep away from the big-league club in Milwaukee, the Brewers' front office correctly decided. Unbelievably, Yount went on to become the best Brewer ever, although he didn't hit .300 until his ninth major league season. From 1974 (his 344-at-bat rookie year) through the 1981 campaign, Yount had 1,153 hits in 4,212 at-bats for a mark of .274, hardly the mark of the man inducted into the Hall of Fame in 1999. But he rebounded by twice winning the MVP, and by collecting 1,989 hits over his last 12 years.

♦ Did you know Robin Yount collected his 1,000th, 2,000th, and 3,000th hits against the Cleveland Indians?

♦ Did you know Robin Yount's brother, Larry, had the shortest career in major league history? Larry Yount, a right-handed pitcher for the Houston Astros, was warming up on September 15, 1971, about to make his debut, when he injured his arm and couldn't pitch. He never returned to the majors.

236. *Match these relievers with their records:*

1	Greg Minton	A	lost 16 games in relief in one season
2	Gene Garber	B	posted an 18-1 ledger in relief one year
3	Mike Marshall	C	pitched 269⅓ consecutive innings without
4	ElRoy Face		serving up a home run
		D	appeared in 13 straight games as a reliever

ANSWER: 1—C, 2—A, 3—D, 4—B

Minton, the successful sinkerballer whose streak came to an end when the Mets' John Stearns homered during the 1982 season, told me (laughing) he "drilled (Stearns) right in the ribs next time up." Face's .947 winning percentage in 1959 remains the best ever among pitchers with at least 13 wins. The Yankees' Tom Zachary went 12-0 in 1929 for the best undefeated season. Most recently, Dennis Lamp completed an 11-0 campaign in 1985 for the Blue Jays, who also had Tom Filer going 7-0 that year. Garber went 6-16 with a 4.33 ERA for the Braves in 1979, a year after he boasted an ERA less than half that (2.15) and combined with starter Larry McWilliams to stop Pete Rose's 44-game hitting streak on August 1. Yet in 1979, Garber managed to duplicate his 25-save performance of the previous year en route to a career total of 218.

◆ Did you know Terry Felton holds the unenviable single-season mark of recording the most losses (13) without a win? Felton, pitching for the Twins in 1982, was shelled for an ERA of 4.99 that year. Russ Miller and Steve Gerkin each had an 0-12 season, in 1928 and 1945, respectively. Felton, by the way, retired with an 0-16 ledger, the worst lifetime mark for a winless pitcher.

237. *Match these pitchers with their performances:*

1	Ron Davis	A	threw a rain-shortened, five-inning perfect game in 1983
2	Bill Campbell		
3	Tom Seaver	B	was the first Cy Young winner not to win 20 games
4	David Palmer		
5	John Hiller	C	tied an AL record by striking out eight straight batters in one game
		D	share the AL record 17 wins as a reliever

ANSWER: 1—C, 2—D, 3—B, 4—A, 5—D

Davis tied the mark set by Nolan Ryan, who twice accomplished the feat, and was later joined by Roger Clemens. Within a span of two years, Hiller (1974) and Campbell (1976) each surpassed the mark of 16 relief wins, set by Dick Radatz in 1964. In 1973, Seaver went 19-10 with league-best figures of 18 complete games, 251 strikeouts, and an ERA of 2.08.

Did you know pitchers Hod Eller, Moe Drabowsky, and Todd Worrell share the record for most consecutive strikeouts in a post-season game (six)? All three accomplished the feat in World Series competition. For Cincinnati, Eller struck out six straight White Sox batters in Game Five of the 1919 World Series. Drabowsky of the Orioles accomplished the feat in relief en route to an inspiring 11-strikeout performance during Game One of the 1966 World Series against the Dodgers. In 1985, St. Louis' Worrell tied the mark in a Game Five loss to Kansas City.

238. *On June 8, 1950, the Boston Red Sox defeated the St. Louis Browns for the most lopsided win of the 20th century. Can you identify the score?*

    A 29-4
    B 25-4
    C 25-0
    D 29-0

ANSWER: A

The Red Sox won by a vast 25-run margin, one day after a 20-4 rout of the same team. The 29 runs set a 20th-century record, as did the 51 hits over two games. The Red Sox also set major league records for most long hits (17; nine doubles, one triple, and seven homers); most total bases (60); and most runs over two games. The mark for runs scored in a game was tied five seasons later on April 23, 1955, when the Chicago White Sox belted the Kansas City Athletics by 29-6.

Incidentally, the Red Sox also hold the mark for the most lopsided victory in post-season history. In Game Four of the 1999 Division Series, the Red Sox blew out the Cleveland Indians by 23-7, setting a slew of other post-season records in the process. Among them are most runs, hits (24), most total bases (44), and most extra-base hits (12).

♦ Did you know first baseman Walt Dropo started for the winning team in each 29-run outburst? In the Red Sox's 29-4 victory over the Browns in 1950, Dropo had two homers, two singles, five runs scored, and a whopping seven RBI. In the White Sox's 29-6 rout five years later, Dropo homered once, singled twice, scored thrice, and drove in three.

239. *Of the 14 relievers who have saved as many as 300 games in their career, seven have saved 100 in each league. Name five.*

ANSWER: Lee Smith, Jeff Reardon, Randy Myers, Rollie Fingers, Rich Gossage, Doug Jones, and John Wetteland

The all-time saves leader, Smith retired 22 saves short of 500 (saving 347 in the National League). John Franco, who has spent his entire career in the National League and owns that circuit's career save record, became the first lefthander to reach the 300-save mark in 1996 and enters the 2002 season with 422, the second-best career total. Dennis Eckersley, who owns the AL record with 324 saves, retired with 390.

Reardon retired prior to the 1995 season with 367 saves (192 in the American League). Fifth on the all-time list, Myers has 347 saves (104 in the American League). Fingers recorded 233 of his 341 saves in the American League. Wetteland is seventh on the list with 330 saves, 224 of which have come in the American League. Rick Aguilera (318) joined Wetteland as a 300-save member in 2000. San Diego's Trevor Hoffman (314) became the club's newest member in 2001. Tom Henke, abruptly retired prior to the 1996 season with 311 saves. Gossage retired with 310 saves (182 in the American League). A pair of pitchers cracked the 300-save plateau in 1999 as Kansas City's Jeff Montgomery retired with 304 saves, and Oakland's Jones had 303 (including 103 in the National League). Bruce Sutter saved exactly 300, all in the National League, a senior circuit figure eclipsed only by Franco, Smith, and Hoffman. Tampa Bay's Roberto Hernandez enters the 2002 season with 294 saves.

♦ Did you know Dennis Eckersley was voted the best reliever in the history of the Rolaids Relief Man award during a 20th-anniversary survey of media and club representatives in 1996? "Eck" received 51.1% of the votes, Lee Smith received 22.2%, Rich Gossage got 13.3%, Rollie Fingers had 8.9%, and Bruce Sutter finished with 6.7%. John Franco was voted as the best left-handed reliever since the award's inception in 1976. Eckersley was also voted, among other things, as having the best control, best able to get ahead in the count, and as putting together the best relief season (1990). Gossage was voted as having the best fastball and as being the most dominating. Smith was voted as the most durable, Gregg Olson was rewarded for his curveball, Sutter was honored for the best specialty pitch (the split-fingered fastball, which he revolutionized), and Doug Jones was tabbed to have the best changeup. But most voters decided that Fingers was the man to put on the mound if just one out was needed to win the World Series. I'm sure Mariano Rivera and Trevor Hoffman would earn some of those honors should the survey be conducted today.

240. *Tris Speaker, Rogers Hornsby, and Gabby Street were confirmed as members of the Ku Klux Klan, according to published reports. True or False?*

ANSWER: True

Several historians, most notably Fred Lieb, have uncovered an appalling connection between these recognized major leaguers and the KKK.

Ty Cobb, by the way, was never proven to be a member of the KKK, although he openly abhorred Blacks. A southerner, Cobb had at least five run-ins with Blacks, several of which resulted in lawsuits and his incarceration. Included among the incidents were a pair of episodes that nearly resulted in death or murder. In fact, because a warrant had been issued for his arrest in the State of Ohio for a case involving a black night-elevator operator, Cobb was considered a fugitive and had to go through extreme measures just to play in the 1909 World Series against the Pirates. He had to be secretly driven (by his uncle) from Detroit to Pittsburgh during that fall classic to avoid arrest. His uncle drove toward Canada to skirt Ohio. So obvious was Cobb's disdain for Blacks that he, jealous of Babe Ruth's accomplishments in the early 1920s, insisted that Ruth was black and, therefore, shouldn't be allowed to play.

♦ Did you know that San Diego Padre pitching teammates Dave Dravecky, Eric Show, and Mark Thurmond were reportedly members of the John Birch Society?

241. *October 17, 1989, was to be the date of Game Three of the 1989 World Series between the Oakland Athletics and host San Francisco Giants. Alas, a massive earthquake registering 6.9 on the Richter scale occurred just prior to the scheduled start, devastating the Bay Area, killing many residents, and causing major destruction. The*

autumn classic was postponed for 10 days. Can you name the
scheduled starting pitchers for that dreadful day of October 17?

ANSWER: Bob Welch (Oakland) and Don Robinson (San Francisco)

The series came to an end as the Athletics swept the Giants in dominating fashion. As it turned out, series MVP Dave Stewart and Mike Moore started and won all four games for Oakland. Stewart sported a 1.69 series ERA over 16 innings, and Moore proudly displayed a 2.08 ERA over 13 innings. Scott Garrelts lost both his starts for the Giants, each time failing to go more than four innings.

The series was arguably the most lopsided in fall classic history, with Oakland winning all four games by a collective score of 32-14. The Athletics, who never trailed in the series, also showed up the Giants in batting average (.301-.209) and ERA (3.50-8.21). San Francisco never even had the tying run on in any of its final at-bats.

242. *The Yankees' total of 26 World Series titles is well recognized. But*
which two franchises are tied with nine championships apiece?

ANSWER: The Cardinals and the Athletics

Of the Athletics' nine world championships, five have taken place in Philadelphia and four in Oakland. The Dodgers (five in Los Angeles and one in Brooklyn) are next with six. The Red Sox, Pirates, Reds, and Giants (all in New York) can each boast of five championships.

♦ Did you know no World Series trophy was given to the winner until 1967, when the St. Louis Cardinals captured the title? The official name of the trophy is "The Commissioner's Trophy."

243. *The first-ever all-California World Series was in 1974. Can you*
name the two teams involved? These clubs also faced off in the
1988 fall classic.

ANSWER: The Oakland A's won the 1974 series, 4-1, over the Los Angeles Dodgers to become the only team other than the Yankees to win three straight World Series titles. The Dodgers won by the same margin 14 years later.

♦ Did you know the Oakland A's were actually outscored in World Series competition during their run of three straight titles from 1972 to 1974? The Reds, Mets, and the Dodgers combined to outscore the A's by a 56-53 margin. Nine one-run victories helped, and demonstrated how great a bullpen Oakland had.

244. *Match these sluggers with their World Series power exploits:*

1	Lenny Dykstra	A	hit six total World Series home runs
2	Babe Ruth	B	twice hit four roundtrippers in a series
3	Willie Aikens	C	twice hit three home runs in a game
4	Roger Maris	D	hit four homers in one fall classic
5	Duke Snider		

ANSWER: 1—A, 2—C, 3—D, 4—A, 5—B

Ruth hit a total of 15 World Series homers, including three in Game Four of the 1926 World Series and a trio in Game Four of the 1928 fall classic. Each three-homer performance came against the Cardinals, and each in Sportsman's Park. Dykstra hit four dingers for the Phillies in the 1993 series against Toronto, and two for the Mets in the 1986 classic against Boston. Maris played in seven World Series. Aikens hit four homers for the Royals in the 1980 fall classic against the Phillies. Snider still holds the NL record for World Series home runs (11) and RBI (26).

245. *Can you name the Hall of Fame outfielder who was "robbed" of 87 hits and 3,000-hit recognition?*

ANSWER: Sam Crawford

Crawford, whose stellar career spanned 2,517 games from 1899 through 1917, rightfully deserves to have 3,048 hits. But the statisticians of that time ignored the 87 safeties Crawford garnered with Grand Rapids—a club from the same Western League that Ban Johnson presided over.

When Johnson's American League made its debut in 1901, the National Commission ruled that any player from the Western League who entered either major circuit would be credited with all hits and statistics from the Western League. But instead, the .309 lifetime hitter with a record of 312 triples never had his stats updated. The only change came decades later when some statisticians dropped his hit aggregate from 2,964 to 2,961. Of course, Crawford could have reached the milestone had such plateaus been given their due attention in his day. Crawford was healthy enough to enjoy a few great seasons in the Pacific Coast League following his major league days. Batting behind Cobb in Detroit's lineup, the left-handed Crawford won three RBI titles, driving in a total of 1,525 runners. The big and hard-hitting slugger also played alongside Cobb in the outfield, serving as the team's right fielder. You would think that baseball would be kinder to a man who tolerated the detested Cobb for over a decade.

♦ Did you know only three players have ever legged out 30 or more triples in a season, but none since 1912? Dave Orr in 1886 and Heinie Reitz eight years later each hit 31 triples. Owen Wilson's 36 three-baggers in 1912 established a new standard; Kiki Cuyler has since come the closest with 26 in 1925.

246. *Reggie Jackson became the second player in World Series history to slug three home runs in a game, doing so against the Dodgers in the sixth contest of the 1977 fall classic. "Mr. October" hit his blasts in consecutive at-bats, each on the first pitch. Can you name the three different pitchers off whom Reggie made his fame?*

ANSWER: Burt Hooton, Elias Sosa, and Charlie Hough

Jackson's two-run blast off Hooten came in the fourth inning. Jackson followed that with a two-run homer of Sosa in the fifth, and a solo shot off Hough in the eighth frame of an 8-4 Yankee triumph.

The following fall, Jackson had another great World Series against the same Dodgers, although he was best remembered in that 1978 series for a duel against rookie Bob Welch. Down 4-3 with runners on first and second and two out in the ninth inning, the Yankees had Jackson at the plate going against the right-handed Welch. With a full count following a few foul balls, Welch prepared to deliver the ninth pitch of the at-bat, focusing as Jackson adjusted his glasses. Welch then hurled a high, inside fastball that Jackson swung through, giving the Dodgers a two-games-to-none lead. Jackson, however, rebounded to bat .391 in the classic with a pair of homers and eight RBI as the Yankees won the next four games for their second straight world championship.

247. *When Mickey Mantle and Roger Maris combined for 115 home runs during that historic 1961 season, whose record of homers by a team duo did they break?*

ANSWER: Babe Ruth and Lou Gehrig

The 107 home runs belted by the duo of Ruth (60) and Gehrig (47) in 1927 stood for 34 years. In 2001, Barry Bonds and Rich Aurilia snuck in between the two Yankee pairs with a combined 110. Ruth (163) and Gehrig (184) still hold the all-time record of 347 RBI of a team duo set in 1927.

♦ Did you know right fielder Roger Maris was one of 11 former Kansas City Athletics on the Yankees' 1961 championship team? After a third-place finish in 1959, Yankees General Manager George Weiss figuratively stole Maris from Athletics owner Arnold Johnson, a former colleague. Weiss sent out-fielder Hank Bauer, righthander Don Larsen, and first basemen Norm Siebern and Marv Throneberry to Kansas City for Maris, first baseman Kent Hadley, and shortstop Joe Demaestri. (Aside from Maris, only the young Siebern had anything left in the tank, earning three All-Star appearances.) Maris (61 homers and 142 RBI) and right-handed starter Ralph Terry (16-3) headlined a list of former Athletics that also included third baseman Clete Boyer, left fielder Bob Cerv, southpaw Bud Daley, righthanders Art Ditmar, Ryne Duren and Duke Maas, utility players Hector Lopez and Deron Johnson, and Demaestri.

The Yankees' front office, from the late 1950s to the early 1960s, often dealt with the Athletics, whose owner, Johnson, previously presided over a Yankee farm team and still possessed a bit of stock in the Yankees. Many competitors found this unfair. Hank Greenberg, the Hall of Fame slugger who served as general manager of the Indians and White Sox in the 1950s, echoed the sentiments of many when he said, "It must be great to have your own farm system in the same league."

♦ Did you know General Manager Frank Lane traded Roger Maris, Rocky Colavito, Norm Cash, and Red Schoendienst, and almost traded Stan "The Man" Musial? "Trader Frank" (or "Frantic Frank"), as he was labeled, may have been the most destructive general manager in the game's history. For his wild and pell-mell trading style, Lane was disliked by Cardinal fans and Indian fans alike. From December of 1955 through the 1956 season, Lane sent more than 40 Cardinals packing via trades, including Schoendienst on

June 14, 1956. Schoendienst went on to enjoy two more .300 campaigns and his first hits crown. None of the four players Lane received in the nine-player deal lasted more than a year in St. Louis. There was more to come.

During the same stretch, the hasty and careless Lane had the audacity to attempt to trade Musial. Owner Gussie Busch saved the day by blocking the deal. Cardinal fans remain thankful, as Stan "The Man" went on to enjoy three more typical Musial years, a span that featured his seventh batting title and second RBI crown. With Cleveland, Lane single-handedly crippled the franchise, trading Maris, Colavito, and Cash, among others. Lane sent the 23-year-old Maris to Kansas City on June 15, 1958, for Vic Power and Woodie Held. From Kansas City, Maris was dealt to the Yankees, for whom he won consecutive MVPs and set a season record with 61 homers in 1961. On April 12, 1960, Lane traded Cash to Detroit for Steve Demeter. Cash never even got a chance to play a game for the Indians after arriving in an off-season deal. Cash went on to hit 373 more home runs. Demeter retired with the very two career hits he had when he came to Cleveland. The death of the franchise, if you ask many unforgiving Tribe fans, occurred five days later, when Lane traded fan favorite Colavito to the Tigers for defending batting champ Harvey Kuenn. Colavito, the defending home run champion, hit 173 homers over the next five seasons before returning to Cleveland. By that time, Indian fans had lost interest in the club, as attendance figures show. Kuenn lasted just one season in Cleveland.

In 1961, each of the three aforementioned Indians went on to enjoy a spectacular season for other AL clubs. The trio combined to slug 147 homers and drive in 414 runs, converging on a Triple Crown. Cash batted .361 to lead the league, while Maris paced the American League in homers and RBI. Colavito had his best season as well, with a .290 mark, 45 homers, and 140 RBI. Indian fans still blame the franchise's downfall and inability to win another World Series on "Colavito's Curse."

248. *Match these pitchers with their roles:*

1	Pud Galvin	A	lost a modern record 29 games in one season
2	Whitey Ford	B	his .717 winning percentage is the best in history for 100-game winners
3	Spud Chandler	C	registered a NL record 10 seasons of at least 200 strikeouts
4	Vic Willis	D	is second to Cy Young with 308 career losses
5	Tom Seaver	E	his .690 winning percentage (236-106) is the best of all time among 200-game winners

ANSWER: 1—D, 2—E, 3—B, 4—A, 5—C

Galvin also earned 360 victories over a stellar 14-year career that ended in 1892. The righthander never led the league in wins or losses. Although Willis' 29 defeats (against just 12 wins) for the Braves in 1905 represent the ebb of success from 1900 on, the 249-game winner doesn't own the dubious all-time record. Many have lost more than Willis, including John Coleman, a lefthander who was beaten 48 times in 1883 as a member of the Phillies franchise. Coleman also won just 12 games.

Gooden was not too far behind Chandler with a 132-53 record (.714) before his 1992 record (10-13), his 1993 record (12-15), and his 1994 record (3-4) bought him down. Gooden was suspended for the 1995 season by Major League Baseball for violating his substance abuse aftercare program. That made for an unbelievable story as Gooden returned to the diamond in 1996. An emotionally stable Gooden went 11-7 with a no-hitter (against the Seattle Mariners on May 14) to help the New York Yankees win a world championship. Gooden retired in the spring of 2001 with a career record of 194-112 and an impressive .634 winning percentage. So ended a career that seemed headed for immortality, but achieved so much less. Oh, those vices.

♦ Did you know Bob Caruthers owns the best winning percentage among 200-game winners not in the Hall of Fame? The 19th-century righthander retired with a most impressive 218-99 record for a winning percentage of .688. Caruthers, who won the American Association ERA title in each of his first four seasons, had a pair of 40-win campaigns and five seasons of at least 29 wins. He pitched nine years and played a 10th as an outfielder.

249. *Eight players from the Chicago White Sox team were banned by Major League Baseball for "fixing" the 1919 World Series, hence the term "Black Sox." Can you name at least five of the expulsed members?*

ANSWER: Joe Jackson, Ed Cicotte, Lefty Williams, Buck Weaver, Oscar Felsch, Chick Gandil, Swede Risberg, and Fred McMullin

Left fielder Jackson, starting pitchers Cicotte and Williams, third baseman Weaver, center fielder Felsch, first baseman Gandil, shortstop Risberg, and third baseman McMullin were barred for life from professional baseball at the end of the 1920 campaign for "throwing" the 1919 World Series versus Cincinnati. Jackson, Cicotte, and Williams each signed a written confession, all three of which were stolen from the district attorney's office before a trial to determine if a crime had been committed. Contrary to popular belief, the jury that judged the eight members of the White Sox was not set in place to determine if the eight members fixed the series, for such an act—although corrupt—was not criminal. So when the players were acquitted, they were acquitted of committing crimes, not of throwing the series.

Although not proven to have stumbled between the lines, Jackson and Weaver were banned because they had prior knowledge of the fix and did not report the forbidden activity. Thus, many fans complain that Jackson and Weaver were banned without much cause. But the fact remains: Both players failed to report the fix, which is also intolerable by the regulations of Major League Baseball. Weaver even attended the crooked meetings before deciding against them; Jackson signed a confession in which he admitted to taking the money and agreeing to throw the series.

That Jackson batted .375, hit the series' lone homer, and committed no errors in the field is irrelevant, as harsh as it may seem. That Weaver batted .324 is equally unimportant in reviewing his banishment. But just for the sake of argument, there are indications that Jackson could have been involved in the on-field fix as well. These indications are neither evidence nor proof. They do suggest that Jackson might have given less than optimal effort. Although he hit .545 (6-for-11) in the three games his team won, he hit "just" .286 (6-for-21) in Chicago's five losses. Even discounting the 0-for-4 effort in Game One, it is difficult to ignore that he went hitless in nine consecutive at-bats, spanning from the third inning of Game Four through the fourth inning of Game Six. But that still proves nothing. The following, however, are some questionable scenarios that would raise a few eyebrows and issues in today's scrutiny-driven sports society.

In the second inning of Game Two, Jackson held at third base on a second-out grounder to shortstop by Gandil, with the weak-hitting Risberg (who batted .080 in the World Series, and just .256 with 38 RBI in the regular season) coming up. After getting four hits in his previous five at-bats, the slugging Jackson (batting clean-up) surprised many by unsuccessfully trying to sacrifice a pair of runners over with none out in the third inning of Game Three. He popped his bunt attempt up to first base, killing a rally. In the sixth inning of said game, both Jackson and Felsch reached first and were caught stealing on consecutive turns. It was Jackson's first caught stealing since 1916. In the first inning of Game Seven, Jackson again made a base-running blunder as he got himself caught in a rundown following an RBI single, but was saved from being tagged out thanks to a Reds error. And according to *The World Series,* an invaluable reference that provides play-by-play accounts of every World Series game, two Reds hitters (including pitcher Dutch Ruether) tripled in Jackson's area, supposedly the region "where triples went to die." Years later, White Sox pitcher Dickie Kerr voiced his disapproval, having observed his outfielders playing out of position during the series. Again, these are not proven instances of Jackson cheating. These are merely possibilities that Jackson may have given less than his best effort.

Commissioner Kenesaw Mountain Landis, who took office after baseball banned the eight players, chose not to reinstate them, explaining that "regardless of the verdict of juries, no player that throws a ballgame; no player that undertakes or promises to throw a ballgame; no player that sits in a conference with a bunch of crooked players and gamblers where the ways and means of throwing games are planned and discussed and does not promptly tell his club about it, will ever play professional baseball." Landis was well aware of the importance of the banishment of Jackson and Weaver. By doing this, Landis ensured that those "throwing" games couldn't trust a soul, thus giving them even less incentive to participate in such activity. It was a brilliant decision that helped stunt the rampant dishonesty in baseball of that day. By enforcing the rules and laws of the game, Landis rescued the national pastime after the "Black Sox" scandal. Of course, Babe Ruth helped a great deal with his bat, drawing fans with prodigious home runs and an outlandish personality.

An indication that Jackson was hitting his prime at the time of his banishment can be seen in his 1920 numbers: a .382 batting average, and career-best figures in homers (12) and RBI (121), to go with 42 doubles and 20 triples. What might have been! I, for one, forgive Jackson, but do not believe he belongs in the Hall of Fame.

250. *Todd Hollandsworth became the fifth consecutive Dodger to win the NL Rookie of the Year Award in 1996. Hideo Nomo won the award in 1995, Raul Mondesi captured the honor in 1994, Mike Piazza earned the 1993 freshman award, and Eric Karros garnered the hardware in 1992. The Dodgers have earned 16 Rookies of the Year since the inception of the award in 1947 (the first of two years where a combined selection took place). Amazingly, the Dodgers also had four consecutive winners from 1979 to 1982. Can you name them in order?*

ANSWER: Rick Sutcliffe, Steve Howe, Fernando Valenzuela, and Steve Sax

Each won the "Jackie Robinson" Rookie of the Year Award, named after the first winner of the award. Incidentally, Piazza wasn't chosen until the 62nd round of the 1988 draft by the Dodgers' organization and that was as a favor to Tom Lasorda, whose boyhood friend Vince Piazza is Mike's father. Piazza need not worry about money, as his father is worth over $150 million. Vince, who was part of a group that tried without success to move the San Francisco Giants to Tampa Bay in 1992, owns more than 20 auto dealerships and a construction company.

◆ Did you know the Pittsburgh Pirates have never had a Rookie of the Year?

251. *Only two teams in major league history have had four players with at least 200 hits. The 1929 Philadelphia Phillies were the first. Do you know the other?*

ANSWER: The 1937 Detroit Tigers

The Tigers had Gee Walker (213), Charlie Gehringer (209), Pete Fox (208), and Hank Greenberg (200) on board in 1937. The 1929 Phillies were led by Lefty O'Doul (254), Chuck Klein (219), Fresco Thompson (202), and Pinky Whitney (200).

◆ Did you know Pete Fox's six doubles in the 1934 World Series remains the single-series record? The Tigers right fielder went 8-for-28 with two RBI in the series. Fox had three more doubles the following October as he hit .385 and slugged .577 to help the Tigers win their first world championship.

252. *On May 28, 1986, Joe Cowley of the Chicago White Sox struck out the first seven Texas Rangers to come to the plate, setting a record. However, that mark didn't last long as a rookie lefthander for the Houston Astros whiffed the first eight batters of a game later the same year. Name that southpaw.*

ANSWER: Jim Deshaies

Deshaies proceeded to strike out 10 Dodgers in a two-hit shutout on September 23, less than four months after Cowley's performance. Deshaies went 12-5 that season in helping the Astros win the National League West Division. Cowley, by the way, wasted his great start, losing 6-3. The righthander finished the year at 11-11, with 132 Ks in 162⅓ innings.

253. *Match the elite sluggers with their super feats:*

1	Harry Heilmann	A	hit a career-high .393 in 1923
2	Lou Gehrig	B	1934 Triple Crown winner
3	Ty Cobb	C	the first player to win the current MVP Award for two teams in the same league
4	Babe Ruth	D	led the American League in slugging eight times
5	Jimmie Foxx	E	hit over .390 four times

ANSWER: 1—E, 2—B, 3—D, 4—A, 5—C

Perhaps the most underrated of the great hitters, Heilmann won four batting titles during the 1920s, each with a figure of at least .393 for the Tigers. The right-handed gap batsmen batted at least .309 with 89 RBI each year from 1919 to 1930 en route to Hall of Fame recognition. Heilmann retired after the 1931 season with a .342 career average (14th highest ever) and 1,539 RBI. The outfielder reached the 40-double plateau eight times, reached 100 RBI eight times, and batted at least .344 eight times.

Gehrig was not given the MVP in 1934, joining Ted Williams and Chuck Klein as the only other Triple Crown winners not to win the MVP since its inception in 1931. Gehrig lost to player-manager Mickey Cochrane in 1934, despite a huge advantage in batting average (.363-.320), homers (49-2), RBI (165-76), and slugging percentage (.706-.412). Cochrane's managerial skill, however, was obviously an advantage (leading the Tigers to a 101-53 record and a seven-game victory over Gehrig's Yankees for the pennant). Klein was beaten in the competition for the 1933 MVP by Carl Hubbell, who enjoyed a magnificent season (23-12, 1.66, 22 complete games, five shutouts, 156 strikeouts, 309 innings pitched, and five saves). "Meal Ticket," trailing only Dizzy Dean in the strikeout category in his pursuit of the pitcher's Triple Crown, led the Giants to the pennant and world championship.

Cobb, although remembered for choking up on the bat with a separated grip and strategically placing hits between fielders, also displayed pop in his lumber. His swift legs enabled him to compile enough extra bases for six straight slugging titles from 1907 to 1912.

Ruth didn't have any trouble getting accustomed to the dimensions of brand new Yankee Stadium in 1923. Ruth that year also achieved personal bests of 205 hits, 45 doubles, and a staggering .545 on-base percentage (third highest ever) in the inaugural season of the park aptly dubbed "The House that Ruth Built." Fittingly, Ruth christened Yankee Stadium with a game-deciding, three-run homer in the opener before 74,200. Foxx won the MVP Award in 1932 and 1933 for the Athletics, and in 1938 for the Red Sox.

♦ Did you know Babe Ruth and Ty Cobb, two of the greatest players in the history of the game, married the same woman? Cobb married 17-year-old Claire Hodgson in 1908. After a divorce some 13 years later, Hodgson married Ruth in 1929. Cobb was, as you might gather, so abusive and neglectful of Claire that she and the kids called him "Mr. Cobb" throughout their marriage. She later wrote a book entitled *The Babe and I,* in which she called Cobb "the greatest" and Ruth her favorite.

254. *Match these great hitters with their deeds:*

1 Cap Anson
2 Louis "Pete" Browning
3 Jake Beckley
4 Jesse Burkett

A known as the original Louisville Slugger, he became the first player to order a bat shipment from John Hillerich

B perhaps the best bunter in history, he hit .400 twice

C came up with the idea of spring training and was the first to implement a pitching rotation

> D not only did this Hall of Framer hit
> 244 triples and 2,931 hits, but he
> also invented the hidden-ball trick

ANSWER: 1—C, 2—A, 3—D, 4—B

In an extensive ballot conducted by the Society for American Baseball Research, Anson was chosen as the best player of the 19th century. King Kelly finished second, Cy Young was third (he split time between centuries), Ed Delahanty fourth, and Buck Ewing finished fifth. Rounding out the top 10 were Dan Brouthers, Charlie Radbourn, Roger Connor, Billy Hamilton, and "Wee" Willie Keeler.

Burkett's two .400 campaigns were eventually surpassed by Ty Cobb and Rogers Hornsby. Burkett was such a great bunter that he once bragged he could bunt .300. In fact, Burkett's frequent bunting attempts were a major reason for the 1901 ruling that made foul balls (and bunt fouls with two strikes) count as strikes. The fast Burkett used his batsmenship and his legs to beat out many bunts en route to a half-dozen 200-hit seasons.

John Hillerich specialized in wagon tongues, bed posts, butter churns, and wooden bowling bowls until 1881, when Browning asked Hillerich's nephew Bud—a fellow amateur player—to make him some bats, commencing a tradition now entering its 122nd year. Bud became the founder of J. F. Hillerich & Son and, in 1911, joined with sales manager Frank Bradsby. In 1916, the company name changed to its current name of Hillerich & Bradsby. Current President and CEO John Hillerich III, whose company now grosses over $100 million a year, said the company's aluminum bat sales recently eclipsed the Louisville Slugger sales for the first time in the venerable company's history. It's safe to say the Triple-A Louisville Red Birds—the team Hillerich partially owns—use Louisville Sluggers.

♦ Did you know over 40,000 trees (average age of 50 years) are cut annually for baseball bats? A player averages 72 bats per season, according to Hillerich & Bradsby. By the way, Honus Wagner was the first to autograph his bats, doing so in 1905.

♦ Did you know Babe Ruth, before the start of the 1919 season, was the first player to order a bat with a knob on the end of the handle? With that Louisville Slugger-made bat, Ruth set the first of his four single-season home run records in 1919.

255. *The 1949–51 Philadelphia Athletics became the only team in history to turn 200 double plays for three years in succession. Hank Majeski was the third baseman and Pete Suder was the second bagger. Can you come up with the names of the first baseman and shortstop?*

ANSWER: Ferris Fain (first baseman) and Eddie Joost (shortstop)

Fain's nine-year career produced two batting titles and established him as one of the best defensive first basemen of all time, following in the footsteps of Hal Chase and raising the bar for successors such as Keith Hernandez. Well before Hernandez opened eyes in the 1980s by fielding bunts on the third-base side of the mound and darting throws to third, Fain had used that daring style with success.

During the 1949 season, Fain was involved in a record 194 double plays. He saw action in 192 twin-kills in 1950. Although the team turned a still-standing record of 217 double plays in 1949 and followed that up with 208 in 1950, the 1951 group may have been the best fielding unit (with 204 double plays). The club's overall .978 mark tied for the league's best, and each member posted his highest fielding average during that three-year span. Fain posted a fielding percentage of .990, Suder led all second basemen with a .987 mark, and Joost (who led all shortstops in double plays and total chances per game) and Majeski each had a .974 percentage. Certainly, the 1951 Athletics infield deserves some consideration when discussing the best infield ensemble ever.

The 1999 Mets infield of John Olerud, Edgardo Alfonzo, Rey Ordonez, and Robin Ventura is the latest unit to make its mark, making the fewest errors ever. The 1998 Orioles unit of Rafael Palmeiro, Roberto Alomar, Mike Bordick, and Cal Ripken, Jr. combined to make just 35 errors—only eight more than the Mets' core. The 1982 Cardinals squad with Keith Hernandez, Tommy Herr, Ozzie Smith, and Ken Oberkfell has to rank up there as well. But no discussion about the best infield ever can take place without mention of perhaps the most suffocating one: the Orioles from the late 1960s through the mid-1970s. At its peak, Baltimore's infield defense consisted of Boog Powell, Davey Johnson, Mark Belanger, and Brooks Robinson. Other well-oiled infields include the 1980 Phillies (Pete Rose, Manny Trillo,

Larry Bowa, and Mike Schmidt), 1950 Dodgers (Gil Hodges, Jackie Robinson, Pee Wee Reese, and Billy Cox) and, of course, the famous 1906 Cubs infield, better known as (Joe) Tinker to (Johnny) Evers to (Frank) Chance. Third baseman Harry Steinfeldt was no slouch either, leading all hot corner men in fielding. Although that 1906 team made 194 errors—a sign of the times—the total was 34 fewer than any other team, and accompanied by what was easily the best fielding percentage of the circuit.

◆ Did you know the Baltimore Orioles franchise is the only one to boast as many as three Gold Glovers in its infield more than once, accomplishing the feat a staggering four times? The 1971 Orioles squad was the first to achieve the feat, with third baseman Brooks Robinson, shortstop Mark Belanger, and second baseman Davey Johnson receiving the honor. With newcomer Bobby Grich replacing Johnson at second and joining Robinson and Belanger, the Orioles repeated the act from 1973 to 1975.

256. *This 1960 Rookie of the Year winner holds the major league record of 10 home runs in a six-game span. He is:*

A Willie McCovey
B Orlando Cepeda
C Frank Howard
D Frank Robinson

ANSWER: C

Howard, an intimidating slugger, hit 23 home runs with 77 RBI as a rookie for the Dodgers. He continued to play through 1973. The six-foot eight-inch, 250-pound giant was better known for his days with the lowly Washington Senators, for whom he played seven years, leading the league in home runs twice and RBI once. Howard combined for 136 homers from 1968 to 1970, a stretch noted in baseball's annals for pitching advantage because of the higher mound. During the 1968 season, Howard hit 10 home runs from May 12 through May 18, doing so in just 20 at-bats. Howard also set the record for homering eight times over a five-game stretch (since tied by Manny Ramirez of Cleveland and Barry Bonds of San Francisco), accomplishing the feat twice during the 1968 season.

Howard's AL homering streak of six straight games was broken by Don Mattingly in 1987.

Mattingly went on to tie Dale Long's 1956 major league record of home runs in eight consecutive games, hitting 10 during that torrid span. (Seattle's Ken Griffey, Jr. later matched the feat in 1993.) Also in 1987, Mattingly broke Ernie Banks' and Jim Gentile's single-season record of five grand slams by hitting six.

♦ Did you know Don Mattingly's record six grand slams in 1987 also represented his career total? That's right. Mattingly didn't hit any home runs with the bases loaded outside of the 1987 campaign.

♦ Did you know Barry Bonds enjoyed two streaks of six straight games with a homer in 2001? No one else has done that over a career, never mind a season.

257. *Match these winners with their awards:*

1	Bob Turley	A	1960 NL MVP
2	Lou Gehrig	B	1958 Cy Young
3	Dick Groat	C	1936 AL MVP
4	Joe Black	D	1937 AL MVP
5	Charlie Gehringer	E	1952 NL Rookie of the Year

ANSWER: 1—B, 2—C, 3—A, 4—E, 5—D

The Cy Young Memorial Award marked its beginning in 1956 after former commissioner Ford Frick stongly urged that an award be established to give pitchers their belated due. From 1956 to 1966, only one selection was made. Frick named the award after the winningest pitcher in history.

♦ Did you know Ford Frick suggested the award bear the name of Cy Young and not Walter Johnson, Christy Mathewson, or Grover Cleveland Alexander, because Young excelled in both the National League and the American League? Because initially the award was intended to honor the best pitchers from both leagues (not each circuit, as it currently does), Young was chosen.

258. *Before the 1910 season, automobile tycoon Hugh Chalmers (president and general manager of the Chalmers Motor Company) thought of a promotional gimmick with which to honor the hitter* *with the major league's highest batting average. The prize, however, was not just the usual medal or trophy, but a very luxurious automobile: a Chalmers "30." Because of a scandal and poor stat-keeping by Major League Baseball, Mr. Chalmers presented two Chalmers "30" automobiles to avoid controversy. Can you name these two eventual Hall of Famers who received the luxury cars in 1910?*

ANSWER: Ty Cobb and Nap Lajoie

To this day, baseball references all over this great land cannot agree on who won the batting title of the 1910 AL season. Cobb entered the final day of that season (October 9) leading Lajoie by a very comfortable margin, .383 to .376. It was so comfortable in fact, that Cobb decided to rest on his laurels and not play, while Lajoie faced a doubleheader. Cobb, however, was so despised that St. Louis Browns manager Jack O'Conner (the opponent of Lajoie's Indians) ordered his rookie third baseman Red Corriden to play very deep at third as to allow Lajoie to beat out seven bunt hits. Lajoie also stroked a "misjudged" triple in center field for a fixed eight-for-eight double-header. The gift twin-bill that Lajoie received gave him a .384 total season average, which seemed to wrap up the batting title and the automobile.

But AL President Ban Johnson weighed in and declared Cobb the winner because of a "discrepancy" in the official records. The current official records of that season read that Cobb hit .385 (196-for-509) and won the batting title, and that Lajoie hit .384 (227-for-591). Although neither Lajoie nor Corriden was found guilty of fixing the game, O'Conner was fired by the Browns as the team's manager for his act of irreverence toward the game.

◆ Did you know that *The Sporting News* historian Paul MacFarlane un-covered discrepancies, through extensive research, that prove Lajoie did in-deed win the 1910 batting title and that Cobb should have a .366 career average and 4,190 career hits? In 1981, MacFarlane discovered that Cobb was awarded a "phantom" two-for-three game, had two hitless at-bats not counted during the 1910 season (which would drop his 1910 average to .382), and that a one-for-eight extra-inning game was omitted from Cobb's 1906 records (which would have left him at .316, not .320). Even Lajoie's records were somewhat inaccurate: His 1910 average should have been .383 (due to a discovered hitless at-bat)—still good enough to beat Cobb for the batting title. The real tragedy is that 1981 Commissioner Bowie Kuhn refused to correct the mistakes, stating that Ban Johnson's decision on the matter should not be overturned. It is no wonder that every reference or baseball encyclopedia has different accounts of the 1910 AL batting champion. It remains baseball's most famous statistical ambiguity, until Bud Selig or a subsequent commissioner finds the courage to rectify the mistake.

259. *Prior to the advent of the MVP balloting in 1931, there existed nary an award to acknowledge the league's best or most valuable player. True or False?*

ANSWER: False

From 1911 through 1914, the Chalmers Award was presented to honor each league's best player, rewarding them with a Chalmers automobile. After the awkward ordeal of the previous season, Mr. Chalmers in 1911 decided to allow a writer from each major league city (eight in each circuit) to vote on the best player in each league. The Tigers' Ty Cobb and the Cubs' Frank "Wildfire" Schulte were the first winners. Tris Speaker and Larry Doyle won the Chalmers Award in 1912. Walter Johnson and Jake Daubert won in 1913, and Eddie Collins and Johnny Evers won the last presentation of the award in 1914.

After a seven-year hiatus, the American League presented a League Award to the Browns' George Sisler in 1922 for being the most valuable player ("the most important and useful player to his club and to the league at large in point of deportment and value of services rendered"). Once again, eight baseball writers (one from each AL city) were chosen to select the best representatives. These judges contended with rules that made both past winners and player-managers such as Sisler (from 1924 to 1926), Speaker, and Cobb ineligible for the award. These ridiculous criteria brought an end to the League Award presentations in the American League after 1928. They also explain why Babe Ruth was only given one award (in 1923) during the decade he dominated.

The National League adopted the MVP concept in 1924 and honored Brooklyn pitcher Dazzy Vance. It did not impose those impractical AL criteria that created so many objections; thus Rogers Hornsby was allowed to earn two League Awards. The National League also awarded $1,000 to the winner. After the 1929 season, however, the National League also decided to halt its award presentation: Its greedy owners decided that the winners were using the award for leverage in contract negotiations.

In 1930, *The Sporting News* and *The Associated Press* each made an unofficial selection to substitute for the leagues' defunct honors. Bill Terry of the Giants and Joe Cronin of the Senators came away winners of those polls. After that, the Baseball Writers Association of America (BBWAA) took over the responsibilities of naming the Most Valuable Player in each league. During the winter meetings following the 1930 season, the BBWAA decided to elect a committee responsible for choosing the writers who would select each league's MVP.

♦ Did you know Walter Johnson was the only player to earn a Chalmers Award as well as a League Award? "Big Train" added to his 1913 Chalmers with a 1924 League Award as a member of the American League's Senators. After a few off-years (by his own standards), Johnson won the pitcher's Triple Crown in 1924 to carry his Senators to their first world championship.

♦ Did you know Mickey Cochrane and Lou Gehrig were the only two players to earn a League Award as well as the modern MVP Award? After earning the League Award in 1928 with the Athletics, Cochrane six years later earned the AL MVP for the Tigers. Gehrig earned his League Award in 1927 and his MVP trophy, as voted on by the BBWAA, in 1936. The aging Ruth never won a modern MVP Award to complement his 1923 League Award.

260. *Can you name all four infielders who comprised the longest unity of any infield in history?*

ANSWER: First baseman Steve Garvey, second baseman Davey Lopes, shortstop Bill Russell, and third baseman Ron Cey played together for a little over eight and a half years. The quartet played its first game as an infield unit for the Dodgers on June 13, 1973. They didn't separate until after the 1981 season, when Lopes was traded to Oakland in the offseason.

♦ Did you know Steve Garvey actually came up as a third baseman? Garvey played suspect defense at the hot corner from 1969 to 1972, moving over to first base as Ron Cey entered the scene.

261. *Five Hall of Fame-destined pitchers won their 300th game during the 1980s. They were _____ (1982), Steve Carlton (1983), Tom Seaver (1985), _____ (1985), and _____ (1986). Fill in the blanks.*

ANSWER: Gaylord Perry, Phil Niekro, Don Sutton

Perry, Seaver, Carlton, Niekro, and Sutton were inducted into the Hall of Fame in 1989, 1992, 1994, 1997, and 1998, respectively. Sutton finally received the necessary votes after being passed up in his first three years of eligibility. Many Hall of Fame voters argued that he was never dominant. But Sutton simply won more games than Niekro (324 vs. 318), had a better winning percentage (.559 vs. .537), had a lower ERA (3.26 vs. 3.35), struck out more batters (3,574 vs. 3,342), and issued fewer walks (1,340 vs. 1,809) than the knuckleballer. But then again, Niekro failed four times before getting in, so perhaps Sutton's delay makes sense. Another Hall of Famer, Nolan Ryan, became the 21st 300-game winner during the 1991 campaign.

Enlightening research by Herm Krabbenhoft of the Society for American Baseball Research revealed that Seaver fared the best of the aforementioned half-dozen pitchers in head-to-head competition. Seaver was 27-14 with five no-decisions against Carlton (11-3), Sutton (7-4), Niekro (6-5), Perry (3-2-0), and Ryan (0-0). Carlton fared the worst, going 12-22 with seven no-decisions. Carlton was 3-12 against Seaver (receiving an extra loss in a matchup that handed Seaver a no-decision).

♦ Did you know Niekro and Hoyt Wilhelm are the only pure knuckleballers in the Hall of Fame? Hall of Famer Jesse Haines, who won 210 games for the Cincinnati Reds, made the knuckleball an important part of his repertoire midway through a 19-year career.

262. *Match these outstanding performers with the team that originally drafted them:*

1	Nolan Ryan	A	Cincinnati Reds
2	Frank Robinson	B	Philadelphia Athletics
3	Mickey Cochrane	C	Kansas City Athletics

4 Reggie Jackson   D New York Mets
5 Steve Garvey   E Los Angeles Dodgers

ANSWER: 1—D, 2—A, 3—B, 4—C, 5—E

Garvey, a right-handed line-drive hitter with huge forearms, was a part of perhaps the single best draft by any team. In 1968, the Dodgers drafted a total of 15 players who went on to play in the major leagues. Among them were Garvey, Bill Buckner, Ron Cey, Davey Lopes, Geoff Zahn, Joe Ferguson, Bobby Valentine, and Tom Paciorek. The right-handed Garvey ended a 19-year career in 1987 with a .294 lifetime batting average, 272 home runs, 1,308 RBI, 440 doubles, and a hit shy of 2,600. Garvey reached the 200-hit mark six times from 1974 to 1980, falling eight safeties short in 1977. Garvey batted .356 in 22 NL Championship Series games, and .319 in 28 World Series games. Aside from being a clutch hitter who played on five pennant winners, Garvey also set a few defensive records, won four Gold Gloves, and played in more consecutive games than any man in NL history.

♦ Did you know Roberto Clemente was left unprotected by the Brooklyn Dodgers in the 1954 draft, enabling the Pirates to purchase the outfielder's contract for a mere $4,000? As a rule, any "bonus baby" (a player who was signed to a bonus of $4,000 or more) had to be on the major league roster or the team would be forced to leave him unprotected in the winter draft (where opposing teams were allowed to draft from any minor league club). Because the Dodgers were involved in a pennant race in 1954 and had Carl Furillo playing right field, they decided against wasting Clemente's enormous talents on the bench. The Dodgers vice president Buzzie Bavasi decided to take a risk and allow Clemente to hone his skills playing for their minor league (International League) team in Montreal. Bavasi's decision was made despite Al Campanis' warning. Bavasi ardently hoped no one would notice Clemente. The managers knew that Clemente's talents were obvious and went to extreme measures to hide his skills. They benched the future Hall of Famer at times, upon learning of scouts' presence in the stands. They even tried to keep his statistics modest as they pulled him from games against mediocre pitchers. The Dodgers must have thought they did a great job of camouflaging Clemente as he was kept unexposed, and batted just .257. But Pirates' scout Clyde Sukeforth had seen enough of him in practice and in the batting cage. Clemente was a player with all five tools: great hitting skills, great power, great speed, great defense, and an exceptional throwing arm. The last-place Pirates shocked the Dodgers by selecting the 20-year-old Clemente with the first overall pick in the draft on November 22, 1954. At $4,000, the Pirates had the "steal" of the century. Clemente began his career with Pittsburgh in 1955, hitting .255 in 124 games. That marked the last time his bat was described as modest.

263. _____ was the last National Leaguer to win the Triple Crown in 1937. Fill in the blank.

ANSWER: Joe Medwick

The Hall of Fame left fielder was nicknamed "Muscles" for his physique and "Ducky" for his bow-legged walk. He hit 31 home runs, drove in 154 runners, and batted .374 for the 1937 Cardinals. The owner of a .324 lifetime batting average, Medwick also hit 205 home runs and drove in 1,383 runners over a 17-year career. A beaning at the hands of former teammate Bob Bowman in the middle of the 1940 season caused the beginning of the end of Medwick's stardom, although "Ducky" did help the 1941 Brooklyn Dodgers to their first pennant in 21 years.

Gary Sheffield of the Padres was a Triple Crown candidate until the final week of the 1992 season. The third baseman led the league with a .330 mark, hit 33 home runs (two behind teammate Fred McGriff), and drove in 100 runs (nine behind MVP Barry Bonds). Alas, Sheffield was forced to miss the last four games due to a broken finger.

♦ Did you know Medwick and Bowman got into a verbal argument within the confines of an elevator the night before the June 18, 1940, beaning? Bowman, a teammate of Medwick's just six days earlier, warned the recently traded "Ducky" and his companion, Dodgers manager Leo Durocher, that they had not heard the last of him. Bowman followed up on his threat by striking Medwick with a fastball to the temple, sending the All-Star left fielder to the hospital. Bowman was escorted from the park by policemen. Although Medwick's power numbers didn't drop until after the 1941 season, his slugging dropped off severely thereafter. Medwick made quite a few enemies, as his harsh demeanor and offensive disposition made him perhaps the least-liked major leaguer since Ty Cobb and Jesse Burkett.

264. *Can you name the eight-time 20-game winner who never led the league in wins, ERA, or strikeouts? This crafty lefthander is remembered for taking so long in between pitches (talking to himself and walking around the mound) that he made batters over-anxious.*

ANSWER: Eddie Plank

Many hitters of his era considered the Hall of Fame pitcher annoying. Plank, who became the first southpaw to reach 300 victories en route to a career total of 327, was a model of consistency. Relying on a good fastball and a sidearm breaking ball he called his "crossfire," Plank won at least 14 games in each of his first 16 seasons, enjoying a dozen campaigns of at least 17 victories.

In an Athletics rotation that at various times included Rube Waddell, Chief Bender, and Jack Coombs, Plank wasn't always the clear-cut ace of his team and was never quite the best AL pitcher during his splendid 17-year career. Although nearly occulted by AL peers Cy Young, Walter Johnson, Ed Walsh, Addie Joss, Jack Chesbro, and later, "Smokey" Joe Wood, Plank kept triumphing year after year. Never winning a pitcher's Triple Crown category didn't dampen Plank's career ledger, which included 133 more victories than losses, a 2.35 ERA, and 2,246 strikeouts in an era marked by contact baseball.

Unchallenged is Plank's firm stance as the best lefthander over the first 75 years of baseball history. His 69 career shutouts and 412 complete games still stand as records for southpaws. Many hitters would rather have faced some of the aforementioned pitchers than be foreced to wait until Plank was ready to deliver. Well before lefthanded great Warren Spahn stated "hitting is timing, and pitching is upsetting timing," Plank embodied this philosophy.

He unnerved batters by taking his time between deliveries. Aside from circling the mound, Plank frequently encouraged himself by talking to the baseball, constantly adjusted his uniform and endlessly shook signs from his catcher. Batters were restless by the time Plank made his delivery, thus explaining why he averaged just 2.1 walks every nine innings over his career. His good control helped as well.

Plank helped the Athletics win six pennants. Although Plank won just two of seven World Series decisions, he can't be blamed. He registered an ERA of 1.32 in fall classic competition spanning 54⅔ innings, during which he struck out 32 batters and walked 11. His Athletics were shut out in four of his five losses. The Giants' Christy Mathewson and Joe McGinnity each blanked Plank in the 1905 World Series by scores of 3-0 and 1-0, respectively. Eight years later, Plank was again blanked by Mathewson, against whom he exacted revenge by winning the series-clincher, 3-1, in Game Five. Bill James of the Braves also blanked Plank, 1-0, in Game Two of the 1914 World Series.

◆ Did you know 327-game winner Eddie Plank never played baseball before entering Gettysburg University, and was 25 years old before his first major league action in 1901? Plank went straight from college baseball to the Athletics after graduating from Gettysburg.

265. *Match these relative unknowns with their firsts:*

1 Neal Ball	A	hit the first night game home run on July 10, 1935
2 Babe Herman		
3 Hugh Daily	B	won baseball history's first Triple Crown in 1878
4 Paul Hines		
5 George Bradley	C	shortstop who turned modern baseball's first unassisted triple play in 1909
	D	hurled the first no-hitter in major league history
	E	the first one-handed pitcher to hurl a no-hitter

ANSWER: 1—C, 2—A, 3—E, 4—B, 5—D

Daily's 1883 NL no-hitter for Cleveland came versus Philadelphia. Daily, who lost his left hand as a child while playing with a pistol, threw sidearm with his back foot planted. Jim Abbot, the left-handed pitcher who threw a no-hitter 110 years later, was without a right hand. Not only did Hines win baseball's first Triple Crown; he also turned the first unassisted triple play in 1878. Bradley, pitching for the St. Louis Brown Stockings, no-hit the Hartford Dark Blues, 2-0 on July 15, 1876. Bradley went on to an excellent 45-19 campaign. The righthander retired with 138 wins following the 1884 season.

◆ Did you know the first professional no-hitter wasn't thrown until 1875, the fifth and last year of the National Association? Joe Borden, pitching for

Philadelphia of the National Association, no-hit the Chicago White Stockings on July 28, 4-0, before joining the Boston Red Caps (now known as the Braves) of the newly formed National League the following year. The right-hander in 1876 had a mark of 11-12 and an ERA of 2.89 in his lone major league season. The Baseball Records Committee does not recognize the National Association as a major league.

266. *Match these dominant teams with their powerhouse years:*

1	New York Yankees	A	four championships from 1936 to 1939
2	Oakland Athletics	B	three championships from 1972 to 1974
3	St. Louis Cardinals	C	three pennants and two championships from 1929 to 1931
4	New York Giants	D	four pennants and three championships from 1942 to 1946
5	Philadelphia Athletics	E	four pennants and two championships from 1921 to 1924

ANSWER: 1—A, 2—B, 3—D, 4—E, 5—C

The Yankees won an amazing 16 of 19 World Series games from 1936 to 1939. In fact, Rob Neyer and Eddie Epstein, co-authors of *Baseball Dynasties,* both voted this sustained high-performance team the best ever. Of course, the Yankees began another impressive run 10 years later by winning the first of five consecutive world titles.

Until the 1997–99 Atlanta Braves, the 1942–44 Cardinals were the only NL club to win 100 games for three straight years. The Cardinals were 106-48 in 1942, 105-49 in 1943, and 105-49 in 1944.

♦ Did you know the dominance of the 1936–39 Yankees so discouraged the rest of the American League that in December following the Yankees' fourth straight title, AL owners passed a rule prohibiting a league champion from trading or purchasing players? According to *The Sporting News,* the champion could not make such a transaction until a new champion was crowned. The rule lasted all of one year or until the Yankees' streak ended, depending on how you look at it.

267. *This alleged fastest-ever baseball player was said to circle the bases in twelve seconds. Some were so boggled by his awe-inspiring speed that they joked this outfielder could hit a line drive up the middle and have the ball hit his back as he rounded second base. Others cracked that he could turn off the light switch and hop into bed before the room turned dark. Who is this cool character?*

ANSWER: James Bell

Negro leaguer "Cool Papa" Bell was inducted into the Hall of Fame in 1974.

Seventeen other players who were disallowed from playing in the major leagues (either completely or until late in their career) were voted into baseball's shrine on the basis of their performance in the Negro National Leagues (NNL). Satchel Paige became the first NNL inductee in 1971; Josh Gibson and Buck Leonard were elected in 1972. Monte Irvin (who went on to play eight years in the majors, batting .293 with an RBI title) was honored in 1973. Judy Johnson was inducted in 1975, Oscar Charleston was enshrined in 1976, and pitcher Martin Dihigo as well as shortstop John Henry Lloyd were honored in 1977.

When the Committee on Negro Baseball Leagues was closed and the power of selecting former negro leaguers was put in the hands of the Veterans Committee, three years went by before manager Rube Foster was recognized in 1981. Third baseman Ray Dandridge was inducted six years later. The Veterans Committee picked up its pace in 1995 and has since selected a negro leaguer each year. In order beginning with 1995, the Veterans Committee has selected the versatile Leon Day, southpaw Bill Foster, shortstop Willie Wells, two-way player "Bullet" Joe Rogan, fireballer "Smokey" Joe Williams, center fielder Turkey Stearnes, and right-handed hurler Hilton Smith.

268. *Why was Negro National League Hall of Famer James Bell nicknamed "Cool Papa?"*

ANSWER: The switch-hitting outfielder was given that moniker, because—as a pitcher—he was once found sleeping right before a big game versus Rube Foster's American Giants. Bell played with "Smokey" Joe Williams for the 1926 Homestead Grays, who won a record 43 straight games (mostly versus white semi-pro teams). Bell registered a record 1,335 hits in the NNL. Bell was timed from home to first in 3.1 seconds, and all the way around in 12.0 seconds. Bell played on the two best teams in NNL history: The Crawfords and Grays.

269. *Not only were the 1915 Red Sox one of the best teams of all time, but the 1915 world champions were one of the most interesting. The Red Sox hit only 14 home runs (the second lowest total of the three major leagues that year), had the fewest stolen bases (118) of all three major leagues, and had no unquestionable infield or catching regular. However, the 1915 Red Sox had the best and deepest pitching staff (2.39 ERA), a richly talented outfield, and one of the best defenses in the majors. Oh, yes. That season the Red Sox also unveiled a rookie by the name of George Herman Ruth, who turned out to be Boston's third winningest pitcher (18-8, 2.44) and best home run hitter (four roundtrippers in 92 at-bats). Another future hitter, "Smokey" Joe Wood (15-5) led the American League with a 1.49 ERA. Complete the 1915 Red Sox alignment:*

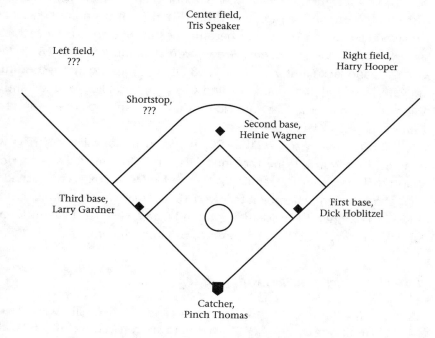

Center field,
Tris Speaker

Left field,
???

Right field,
Harry Hooper

Shortstop,
???

Second base,
Heinie Wagner

Third base,
Larry Gardner

First base,
Dick Hoblitzel

Catcher,
Pinch Thomas

ANSWER: Shortstop—Everett Scott; left field—Duffy Lewis

Ernie Shore (19-8, 1.64), Rube Foster (19-8, 2.11), and Dutch Leonard (15-7, 2.36) were the other three starters who made up this relentless quintet. The 1915 Red Sox are one of only nine teams in history with five 15-game winners. Carl Mays led the American League with seven saves as this Red Sox staff even carried future Hall of Famer Herb Pennock. The outfield trio of Speaker (21 assists), Hooper (23 assists), and Lewis combined for 69 assists.

♦ Did you know the 1930 Senators preceded the 1998 Atlanta Braves as the last team to boast five 15-game winners? The second-place Senators were led by Lloyd Brown's 16 wins and 15 wins apiece for Bump Hadley, General Crowder, Sad Sam Jones, and Firpo Mayberry.

The first club to achieve this feat was the first-place 1902 Pirates squad. Led by Jack Chesbro's 28 wins, the Pirates received 20-win performances from Jesse Tannehill and Deacon Phillippe, and 16-win campaigns from Ed Doheny and Sam Leever to become the first of only two teams with five 16-game winners. The 1904 Cubs were paced by Jack Weimer's 20 wins, Button Briggs' 19 wins, the 17 wins by Carl Lundgren and Bob Wicker, and the 15 victories by sophomore Mordecai Brown. That Cubs team finished second. The world champion 1907 Cubs became the fourth team to achieve the feat as Orval Overall won 23 games, Brown won 20, Lundgren won 18, Ed Reulbach 17, and Jack Pfiester 15. The 1908 Pirates (finishing in a second-place tie with New York, one game behind Chicago) had Nick Maddox and Vic Willis win 23 games apiece, and Howie Camnitz win 16 as Leever and Lefty Leifield gained 15 victories apiece.

Christy Mathewson led the 1905 world champion Giants with 31 wins as Red Ames won 22, Joe McGinnity 21, and Dummy Taylor and Hooks Wiltse each garnered 15 victories. After the 1915 Red Sox accomplished the feat, another world champion followed 10 years later. The 1925 Pirates had a 19-game winner in Lee Meadows; three 17-game winners in Remy Kremer, Johnny Morrison, and Emil Yde; and a 15-game winner in Vic Aldridge.

270. *Match these catchers with their roles:*

1	Jim O'Rourke	A this player and Goose Goslin were the only
2	Hank Gowdy	hitters with six consecutive hits in World
3	Thurman Munson	Series competition before 1990

4 Chief Myers

B was a New York Giant catcher throughout three pennant years
C was the first player to enlist in World War I and only player to see action in both world wars
D became the oldest (age 54) to catch a game, and the oldest to play a full contest

ANSWER: 1—D, 2—C, 3—A, 4—B

In 1904, O'Rourke asked his manager John McGraw if he could play in one final game, although he retired 11 years earlier. A versatile player who excelled as an outfielder and played every position on the field throughout his Hall of Fame career, O'Rourke squatted for one game in 1904, during which he made one error in five chances and went 1-for-4 at the plate. Dubbed "Orator Jim" for his eloquence, the .314 career hitter drove in 1,203 runs over a career that began in 1872.

In the 1990 fall classic versus Oakland, the Reds' Billy Hatcher connected for seven straight hits (and five consecutive extra-base hits, for another record) en route to yet another series mark of a .750 average (9-for-12).

Did you know Goose Goslin remains the only player to hit three World Series home runs in consecutive years? Goslin belted three homers for the Washington Senators in their victorious 1924 World Series against the New York Giants, and again slugged a trio of roundtrippers in 1925 against the Pittsburgh Pirates. Goslin helped the Senators win their only three pennants. After being dealt away during the 1930 season, Goslin returned in 1933 to help the Senators win their third AL flag, hitting one home run in that World Series. Goslin was again traded following the 1933 campaign, helping the Detroit Tigers win consecutive pennants in 1934–35 as he drove in 100 and 109 runs those years.

271. *Match these sluggers with their roles:*

1 Joe DiMaggio
2 Jimmie Foxx
3 Brooks Robinson

A holds the modern-day record of six walks drawn in a nine-inning game
B stole home in two World Series games

4 Bob Meusel   C became the first player to receive a
                            $100,000 per-year contract
                         D hit into four triple plays over his career

ANSWER: 1—C, 2—A, 3—D, 4—B

In 1999, Houston's Jeff Bagwell tied the mark set by Foxx in 1938 for walks in a game, although Bagwell accomplished his feat in 16 innings. Billy Rogell, Mel Ott, Eddie Stanky, and Jose Canseco share the major league record of walking in seven straight plate appearances, according to *The Sporting News Complete Baseball Record Book.*

◆ Did you know Max Bishop twice walked eight times in a doubleheader

◆ Did you know the Boston Red Sox signed Ted Williams to a $125,000 contract for the 1950 season, one year after Joe DiMaggio's $100,00 signing? In 1972, Hank Aaron became the first major leaguer to earn $200,000 a season.

◆ Did you know Hall of Famer Frank "Home Run" Baker, working as a scout, signed a 16-year-old youngster in 1924 by the name of Jimmie Foxx?

272. *Who succeeded Lou Gehrig at first base on May 2, 1939, to end his mammoth record streak of 2,130 consecutive games played?*

ANSWER: Babe Dahlgren

Dahlgren succeeded (not replaced) Gehrig at first base by hitting .235 with 15 home runs and 89 RBI in 1939. The dominant Yankees led by Joe DiMaggio, won the World Series anyway, although first base at Yankee Stadium has never been the same. The right-handed Dahlgren slugged just .383 over a 12-year career that produced 82 home runs.

After being diagnosed with his incurable illness, Gehrig on July 4, 1939, delivered his famous and courageous speech on Lou Gehrig Appreciation Day at Yankee Stadium as close to 62,000 fans listened. It has since become baseball's version of the Gettysburg Address:

> Fans, for the past two weeks you have been reading about the bad break I got. Yet, today I consider myself the luckiest man on the face of this earth. I have been in ballparks for 17 years and have never received anything but kindness and encouragement from you fans.

Look at these grand men. Which of you wouldn't consider it the highlight of his career just to associate with them for even one day? Sure I'm lucky. Who wouldn't consider it an honor to have known Jacob Ruppert? Also, the builder of baseball's greatest empire, Ed Barrow? To have spent six years with that wonderful little fellow, Miller Huggins? Then to have spent the next nine years with that outstanding leader, that smart student of psychology, the best manager in baseball today, Joe McCarthy? Sure I'm lucky. When the New York Giants, a team you would give your right arm to beat, and vice versa, sends you a gift—that's something. When everybody down to the groundskeepers and those boys in white coats remember you with trophies—that's something. When you have a wonderful mother-in-law who takes sides with you in squabbles with her own daughter— that's something. When you have a father and a mother who work all their lives so you can have an education and build your body—it's a blessing. When you have a wife who has been a tower of strength and shown more courage than you dreamed existed—that's the finest I know. So I close in saying that I may have had a tough break, but I have an awful lot to live for.

On June 2, 1941, two years after his gallant and memorable speech, Gehrig died of amyotrophic lateral sclerosis, now known as Gehrig's Disease. It was an unforeseen ending to the life of a stalwart whom legendary sportswriter Jim Murray once described as "a symbol of indestructibility—a Gibraltar in cleats."

273. *Match these players with their roles:*

1 Ray Chapman	A struck out the side on nine pitches in each league
2 Joe Nuxhall	
3 "Smokey" Joe Wood	B became the youngest manager ever at age 23
4 Nolan Ryan	
5 Roger Peckinpaugh	C won 34 games in a season and, nine years later, hit .366 with 60 RBI
	D became the youngest player to play a major league game
	E had a record 67 sacrifices in a season

ANSWER: 1—E, 2—D, 3—C, 4—A, 5—B

Eddie Collins holds the career record of 511 sacrifices; Jake Daubert (a .303 career hitter) holds the AL record of 392. Other impressive totals include Stuffy McInnis' 383, Willie Keeler's 340, and Ray Chapman's 340. According to the Society for American Baseball Research, Rogers Hornsby is the only player with at least 200 sacrifice hits (216) and 300 home runs (301).

Nuxhall was a mere 15 years, 10 months, and 11 days old when he made his debut on June 10, 1944. The southpaw returned to high school and didn't come back to the majors for another eight years. He concluded a 16-year career, mostly for the Reds, with a 135-117 record. Although Nuxhall was the youngest to play (and pitch) in the majors, Jim Derrington was the youngest to start (at 16 years old). The left-handed Derrington started for the White Sox on September 30 of the 1956 season. Although he started six games in his brief career, he never won a game.

◆ Did you know Chuck Finley of the Anaheim Angels has struck out four batters in an inning three times, whereas no one else in history has accomplished the feat more than once? Coincidentally, Finley's first two four-K feats came about in 1999, with his third in 2000. The feat has been done 39 times in major league history. On August 17, 1999, Montreal's Steve Kline became the 14th pitcher to strike out the only four batters in one inning.

274. *Match these clubs with their history:*

1 1929 Boston Braves	A	set a modern major league record with 13 straight wins to start a season
2 1980 Oakland A's		
3 1982 Atlanta Braves		
4 1944–45 Philadelphia Phillies	B	played a record nine consecutive doubleheaders
	C	hurled 94 complete games—the most since the 162-game season was introduced
	D	were actually known as the "Blue Jays"

ANSWER: 1—B, 2—C, 3—A, 4—D

Postponed games due to rain caused the Braves to play 18 games from September 4 through September 15. The Braves set a standard for futility by losing 10 games in five days. The Milwaukee Brewers also started off at 13-0 just five years after the Atlanta Braves did so, but finished in third place, despite a 91-71 record. The all-time rec ord, however, for most wins to start a season belongs to the Union Association's St. Louis Maroons, who won their first 20 in 1884 en route to a 94-19 ledger. Philadelphia was renamed the Phillies for the 1946 season, after a two-year experiment. Interestingly, the Phillies played the Toronto Blue Jays in the 1993 World Series, losing in six games.

✦ Did you know in 2001 the Seattle Mariners set the major league record with 20 wins during the month of April, breaking the Atlanta Braves' four-year-old mark of 19? The Mariners raced out to a 20-5 ledger en route to a historic season. The 1997 Braves broke the mark of 18, shared at one time by six different clubs: the 1971 and 1973 Giants, the 1981 and 1989 Athletics, the 1984 Tigers, and the 1987 Brewers. Also in 1997, the Cubs set the NL futility mark with 19 losses in April. The 1988 Orioles lost a record 22 games in April.

275. *In which year did the World Series commence on September 5?*

ANSWER: 1918

The 1918 regular season ended on Labor Day and the fall classic began a mere three days later, due to wartime regulations. The Boston Red Sox (75-51) beat the Chicago Cubs (84-45) four games to two in that World Series. In early July of that year, United States President Woodrow Wilson issued his "work or fight" order, demanding that each military-aged male join the military or seek employment in an essential industry. Although AL President Ban Johnson was all for ending the season in July for the sake of the country, Major League Baseball was exempted through early September. So Major League Baseball ended its regular season a month early. That explains the low offensive totals across the board: No player reached the 80-RBI mark or the 90-run plateau.

276. *In which year did Ty Cobb and his Detroit Tigers face off against Honus Wagner and his Pittsburgh Pirates for their only World Series encounter?*

ANSWER: 1909

Honus and his Pirates prevailed to win their first world championship in a series that witnessed a best-of-seven format reach its limit for the first time. (The eight games played in 1903 were in a best-of-nine series.) Unlike the other early great World Series, this one was not marred by errors or lapses of concentration as the Pirates rookie Babe Adams (a late-comer in the season) proved his 12-3 record was no fluke by winning Games One, Five, and Seven.

The Pirates' player-manager Fred Clarke hit two homers, drove in another series high of seven runners, and drew five walks. Wagner hit .333 with six runs batted in and six stolen bases off Tiger catchers (who yielded a record 18 stolen bases). Meanwhile, the season's Triple Crown winner Ty Cobb only hit .231 on a team that also included batsmen Sam Crawford and Jim Delahanty and pitchers George Mullin, Wild Bill Donovan, and Ed Summers. Surprisingly, Tommy Leach of the Pirates had series-best figures of a .360 batting average, nine hits, eight runs, and four doubles to help spell doom for the Tigers—who lost their third straight World Series.

The Pirates were 110-42 during their impressive regular season. The most often-recited fable of that series was when Cobb supposedly called out from first base to the shortstop Wagner, yelling, "Watch out, Krauthead, I'm coming down." The tale has it that Wagner (a gentle giant of a man at 200 solid pounds) knocked Cobb's teeth loose when he tagged out the Tiger outfielder attempting to steal. But it never happened: The story was a fabrication by the media. In *Cobb,* the biography written by Al Stump, Cobb and Wagner deny the remark. In *Honus,* author William Hageman proves the remark never occurred by illustrating that Cobb was not thrown out at second base all series, and that in his one successful steal of second there was no tag as the ball was thrown wide. Hageman even included the following quote from Cobb about Wagner. "Spike Honus Wagner? It would have taken quite a foolhardy man . . . he could block off a baserunner with his huge bearlike body in a manner that made the boys very careful when they slid in his vicinity." Cobb was ferocious, but he was also realistic and smart.

♦ Did you know Fred Clarke is the only man with 1,500 career wins as a manager and 1,500 career hits as a player? Clarke won 1,602 games for a .576 winning percentage during a 19-year managing career that featured four first-place finishes in Pittsburgh and the 1909 world championship. The left fielder accumulated 2,675 hits while batting .312 over 21 years.

277. *Playing for Roswell, New Mexico, in 1954, Joe Bauman set a minor league single-season record of 72 home runs in addition to 224 RBI, a .400 batting average, a .916 slugging percentage, a .545 on-base percentage, and 188 runs scored. Bauman:*

A played only 13 games for the New York Giants in 1956
B played eight years for the Boston Braves
C batted only 218 times for the Cincinnati Reds
D never played in the majors

ANSWER: D

Bauman reached as high as the Triple A level, batting just once for the Milwaukee ballclub of the American Association in 1948, the same year he averaged .275 with but 10 homers in 98 games for the Hartford team (Single A) of the Eastern League. According to Bob Rives of the Society for American Baseball Research, Bauman played semi-pro ball while sitting out the 1949, 1950, and 1951 seasons due to a contract dispute with the Braves organization, which signed the left-handed hitter following his stint with the Navy.

Bauman's fortunes took a turn for the better when a Longhorn League owner bought his contract in early 1952. The six-foot five-inch slugger responded with a pair of monster years for the Class C Artesia club, combining for 103 home runs with 298 RBI over the 1952 and 1953 seasons. Instead of seeking the major leagues, Bauman arranged a move to Roswell, staying in the Longhorn League, which featured teams in Texas and New Mexico. Given a salary comparable with the majors ($1,000 per month) at that time, Bauman was content to play for Roswell, where he became a celebrity in hitting 72 homers and was able to buy a nearby Texaco gas station, which he renamed Joe Bauman's Texaco Service. Bauman's powerful swing was perfectly suited for Roswell's Park Field, which provided cozy dimensions with a center-field fence just 385 feet away.

Bauman's one-time professional home run standard of 72 eclipsed the mark of 69 set by Minneapolis' Joe Hauser of the American Association in 1933 and equaled by Amarillo's Bob Crues of West Texas-New Mexico 15 years later. Overall, Bauman belted 337 homers and totaled 1,057 RBI in a professional career that spanned just 1,019 games. Bauman's 1954 Triple Crown season featured one of four home run titles for America's most famous gas pumper.

◆ Did you know the professional baseball record for most homers in a game belongs to Nig Clark, who slugged eight roundtrippers on June 15, 1902? Playing for Corsicana of the Texas League, Clark took advantage of the small park to deposit eight balls out of the yard in a 51-3 lambasting of Texarkana. The score was so lopsided, some telegraph operators thought it was a mistake and instead reported the score as 5-3.

◆ Did you know on May 9, 1999, Florida State's Marshall McDougall set two NCAA records by hitting six consecutive homers and collecting 16 RBI in a 26-2 rout of Maryland? McDougall, who went 7-for-7 in the game, broke the NCAA single-game home run mark set by Henry Rochelle of Campbell. Rochelle, who hit five against Radford in 1985, also went 8-for-8 in a 38-0 win over Radford, while driving in 10 runs and scoring eight. The RBI record belonged to Louisville's Jim LaFountain, who drove in 14 against Western Kentucky in 1976.

◆ Did you know pitcher John Gillespie of Bridgeport hit four homers in a 1923 minor league game? A right-handed pitcher and batter, Gillespie pitched for the Cincinnati Reds the previous year, going 3-3 with a 4.52 ERA. He hit .133 in 15 at-bats for the Reds.

278. *This ballhawk revolutionized center field positioning by playing so shallow that he was routinely involved in infield double plays, and yet still managed to record 6,787 putouts (second on the all-time list). Who is this integral member of perhaps the best defensive outfield ever?*

ANSWER: Tris Speaker

Speaker played alongside right fielder Harry Hooper and left fielder Duffy Lewis on the Boston Red Sox from 1910 to 1915. In those six years, the trio combined for 455 assists. Speaker, whose incredible range and tremendous knowledge of opposing batters afforded him the luxury of playing shallow, was regularly part of 4-8-3 double plays (in lieu of the usual 4-6-3 twin-killings). He often took the flip from the second baseman and threw to first base. The all-time outfield assists leader with 450 and double plays with 135, he shares the AL single-season assist record of 35, set by Sam Mertes in 1902.

The graceful Speaker accomplished the feat in 1909 and 1912. "The Grey Eagle," however, doesn't hold the 20th-century record.

That figure of 44 belongs to Chuck Klein of the Philadelphia Phillies. In 1930, Klein registered 44 assists, with a big chunk of them coming via the 9-3 route. Because the Baker Bowl (his team's home stadium) had such a shallow right field (281 feet from home plate), the Hall of Famer used to take away routine singles with his close positioning and good arm. The all-time single-season record of 45 outfield assists belongs to Buffalo's Hardy Richardson, who accomplished the feat in 1881.

♦ Did you know the Phillies' Johnny Callison is the only player ever to lead his league in outfield assists for more than two straight years? Callison, a rifle-armed right fielder, accomplished the feat each year from 1962 to 1965. Callison was also solid with the bat, enjoying consecutive 30-homer, 100-RBI seasons in 1964 and 1965. Callison is best known for a walk-off home run that earned the National League a victory in the 1964 All-Star Game, and earned him the classic's first-ever game MVP Award.

♦ Did you know Roberto Clemente's practice of throwing the javelin built his legendary arm strength? According to Bruce Markusen, author of *Roberto Clemente: The Great One,* Clemente could throw the javelin 190 feet and was thought of as a candidate to represent Puerto Rico in the 1952 Olympic Games in Helsinki. Markusen added, "he may not have known it at the time, but the footwork, release and general dynamics employed in throwing the javelin coincided with the skills needed to throw a baseball properly."

279. *Can you name the only three Hall of Fame pitchers with losing records?*

ANSWER: Rollie Fingers (114-118), Satchel Paige (28-31), and William "Candy" Cummings (21-22)

Paige had not been allowed to pitch in the major leagues until after his 42nd birthday and was inducted based upon his production in the Negro National Leagues. Cummings, who contributed to baseball by inventing the curveball, won 128 games in the National Association (1872–75) before burning out in the majors.

280. *Only three teams since the start of divisional play have registered their league's best record without winning a single post-season game that year. The 1975 A's and the 1980 Yankees were the first two. Choose the last one:*

A the 2000 Braves
B the 2000 White Sox
C the 1999 Astros
D the 1998 Rangers

ANSWER: B

After winning 95 games in the regular season to garner the AL Central Division flag, the White Sox fell flat on their faces in the Division Series, losing three straight to the surprising Seattle Mariners. The White Sox led the AL in scoring and boasted the circuit's fourth lowest ERA in the regular season, but were held to seven runs and 17 hits in the short series. Designated hitter Frank Thomas and right fielder Magglio Ordonez combined for 269 RBI in the regular season, but were silenced by Mariners pitching.

281. *Can you name the 1916 club that registered a major league record 26 straight victories despite a fourth-place finish?*

ANSWER: The New York Giants

The Giants earned all 26 of those wins at home. Earlier in the season, they won 17 in a row—all on the road. This streaky team, which finished at 86-66, played to a 1-1 tie (vs. Pittsburgh on September 18) 11 games into its 26-game winning streak. However, the 1935 Cubs and the 1880 Chicago White Stockings share the record of 21 straight wins without a tie. The Cubs in 1935 did so to overtake the Cardinals for the NL pennant. The AL record is 19 consecutive wins, held by the 1906 White Sox and the 1947 Yankees. Each club won the World Series. The 1906 ChiSox put together a 93-58 record en route to their first title, and the 1947 Bronx Bombers went 97-57 to win for the 11th time.

♦ Did you know the 1988 Boston Red Sox won a major league record 24 consecutive home games (without a tie)? Boston, which won the AL East Division with an 89-73 mark, surpassed the league mark of 22 straight home victories, set by the 1931 Philadelphia Athletics. The Red Sox were 53-28 at Fenway Park in 1988.

♦ Did you know in 1987, the independent Salt Lake City Trappers equaled the longest winning streak in professional baseball history by notching 27 straight victories? Incredibly, the Trappers did so without a single major league draftee.

282. *The 1959 White Sox (Nellie Fox, Luis Aparicio, Early Wynn) and the 1966 Baltimore Orioles (Frank Robinson, Brooks Robinson, Boog Powell) are the only two AL teams with teammates finishing first, second, and third in the MVP voting. Pick the sole NL team so honored:*

A 1942 Cardinals
B 1960 Pirates
C 1976 Reds
D 1941 Dodgers

ANSWER: D

Dolph Camilli won the award, with Pete Reiser finishing second and pitcher Whit Wyatt placing third. Reiser was a rookie. In 1966, the Twins followed the Orioles' top-placed trio with three straight representatives of their own, placing fourth-sixth: Harmon Killebrew, Jim Kaat, and Tony Oliva.

283. *Match these rookies with their feats and records:*

1	Wally Berger and Frank Robinson	A	drove in a rookie record 145 runs
2	Joe Jackson	B	held the rookie mark of 38 homers before Mark McGwire's 49 in 1987
3	Harvey Kuenn	C	his rookie record of 233 hits stood for 90 years
4	Mike Piazza	D	1953 Rookie of the Year Award winner
5	Ted Williams	E	hit a rookie record 35 home runs for his position

ANSWER: 1—B, 2—C, 3—D, 4—E, 5—A

Berger set the mark for the Braves in 1930, and Robinson tied it 26 years later. "Shoeless" Jackson's rookie hits standard was finally surpassed in 2001 by Seattle's Ichiro Suzuki. Piazza is establishing himself as arguably the best-hitting catcher of all time, carrying a .325 career batting average, 314 homers, and 975 RBI into the 2002 season. Even as a fresh-faced youngster, Williams was confident in his hitting. And he didn't waste time showing his veteran teammates and AL colleagues why, putting his picture-perfect swing on display in 1939 to the tune of a .327 batting average, 31 homers, and those 145 RBI.

In 2001, Albert Pujols set the NL rookie mark with 130 RBI, just a year removed from Single A. He joined Williams as the only two rookies with a batting average of at least .300, an on-base percentage of at least .400, and a slugging figure of at least .600. The right-handed slugger more than met the Cardinals' expectations, and carried the club's offensive load when Mark McGwire was injured for a good portion of the season.

♦ Did you know Mark McGwire, who entered the final day of the 1987 campaign with 49 homers, sat out the final game of said season to witness the birth of his son Matthew? Rather than try to become the first rookie to hit 50 home runs, McGwire prophetically stated he would have other chances to hit 50 roundtrippers, but only one chance to see his son Matthew being born. Now there's a man with his priorities in order.

284. *Many don't know the first All-Star Game was actually played on July 24, 1911. The interleague contest was a benefit for the widow of Addie Joss, who died of a rare form of tubercular meningitis on April 14. The game drew 15,000 spectators and raised $12,914.60 for Mrs. Lillian Joss. This All-Star Game, held at Cleveland's League Park, matched the Cleveland Naps against the best AL players. Hall of Famers Ty Cobb, Tris Speaker, Eddie Collins, Frank Baker, Sam Crawford, Walter Johnson, and Bobby Wallace played for the American League. Can you name the two Hall of Famers representing Cleveland?*

ANSWER: First baseman Nap Lajoie and pitcher Cy Young (in his last season) were the two inductees who represented the Naps. Also representing Cleveland was Joe Jackson.

♦ Did you know Cleveland altered its team moniker from Naps (in honor of the player-manager Nap Lajoie) to Indians, in honor of Louis Sockalexis? Sockalexis was the first American Indian major leaguer, playing for Cleveland from 1897 to 1899? The change was made in 1914, after Lajoie's release.

285. *This team won 25 of its final 31 games in the 1914 season to dethrone the New York Giants (winners of the previous three NL pennants) by 10 games and earn the moniker "The Miracle _____." Fill in the blank.*

ANSWER: (Boston) Braves

The Braves' achievement was even more remarkable, considering that they occupied last place and were 15 games behind the Giants on July 15. The Braves, who finished in last place from 1909 to 1912, swept the powerhouse Philadelphia Athletics in the 1914 World Series. Boston overcame a 4-18 start by winning 68 of its final 87 games to finish at 94-59. The Giants (84-70) finished second. Hall of Famers Johnny Evers and Rabbit Maranville played up the middle while sturdy Hank Gowdy did the catching. In the series, Gowdy hit .545 with three doubles, a triple, and a home run. That .545 average stood as the fall classic standard until Babe Ruth hit .625 in 1928.

286. *Match these sluggers with the number of home run titles they won:*

1	Babe Ruth	A	4
2	Barry Bonds	B	12
3	Harmon Killebrew	C	3
4	Jim Rice	D	6
5	Mickey Mantle	E	1
6	Roger Maris	F	2

ANSWER: 1—B, 2—F, 3—D, 4—C, 5—A, 6—E

Maris' only home run title came in 1961, when he hit 61. Maris never hit more than 33 dingers after that campaign, as a hand injury curtailed his power. From 1962 to 1964, Maris had totals of 33, 23, and 26 homers en route to a career sum of 275. The two-time MVP and RBI champ was traded to St. Louis following the 1966 season, playing a role in the Cardinals' 1967 world championship and 1968 NL pennant. Maris batted .385 with seven RBI in the 1967 World Series.

♦ Did you know in 2000, Ken Griffey, Jr. joined Babe Ruth, Hank Aaron, and Harmon Killebrew as the only players to reach the 40-homer mark seven times? In his first year in the National League, Griffey hit precisely 40 home runs for his seventh season of at least 40 dingers over the last eight campaigns. Ruth reached 40 homers 11 times; Aaron and Killebrew accomplished the feat on eight occasions.

287. *Match these batters with their batting preferences:*

1	Eddie Waitkus	A	right-handed
2	Maury Wills	B	left-handed
3	Alex Johnson	C	switch-hitter
4	Earle Combs		
5	Mickey Cochrane		
6	Nellie Fox		
7	Enos Slaughter		
8	Al Rosen		

ANSWER: 1—B, 2—C, 3—A, 4—B, 5—B, 6—B, 7—B, 8—A

Johnson batted .288 over a 13-year career, which included a batting title for California in 1970. The unheralded Combs batted .325 spanning a dozen major league campaigns for the Yankees, thrice leading the American League in triples and once in hits. He retired prematurely in 1935 following a shoulder separation, one year after fracturing his skull crashing into a wall.

♦ Did you know in 2001 Houston's Lance Berkman became the first switch-hitter ever with as many as 30 homers and 50 doubles in the same season? The Astros' natural hitting machine from Rice University concluded the season with 34 homers and 55 doubles. He also batted .331 with 126 RBI.

288. *Match these pitchers with their pitching preferences:*

1	Lynwood "Schoolboy" Rowe	A	right-handed
2	Eddie Plank	B	left-handed
3	Herb Pennock		
4	Herb Score		
5	Eddie Lopat		
6	Al Downing		
7	Hal Newhouser		
8	Ralph Terry		
9	Fred Toney		
10	Tommy Bridges		

ANSWER: 1—A, 2—B, 3—B, 4—B, 5—B, 6—B, 7—B, 8—A, 9—A, 10—A

Lopat won 166 of 278 career decisions spanning 12 years. Lopat had the great fortune of spending the majority of his career with the Yankees, for whom he led the American League in winning percentage and ERA in 1953. He also won four of five World Series decisions in earning five straight world championship rings. Downing retired with a 123-107 ledger. The 1967 All-Star enjoyed his best season in 1971, when he went 20-9 with a 2.68 ERA. Bridges, a three-time 20-game winner, earned 194 victories over a 16-year career spent entirely in a Tigers uniform. He came within an out of a perfect game in 1932 and helped lead the Tigers to the world championship three years later. Bridges went 21-10 in the 1935 regular season and won both his decisions in that victorious fall classic.

289. *Which Yankee runner was doubled off first base when Brooklyn's Sandy Amoros made a tremendous catch on Yogi Berra's line drive down the left-field line in Game Seven of the 1955 World Series?*

ANSWER: Gil McDougald

McDougald was doubled off first base in that sixth inning, stunting yet another Yankee rally that afternoon. Behind the complete-game effort of southpaw Johnny Podres, some solid defense, and a pair of RBI from Gil Hodges, the Dodgers won, 2-0, for their first world championship.

Brooklyn was winless in seven World Series appearances prior to 1955. As a matter of fact, the Dodgers lost to the Yankees in the World Series the following season for the franchise's eighth defeat in nine attempts at Brooklyn. The Dodgers' fortunes have changed a bit in Los Angeles, winning five of nine World Series results. The 12 World Series losses for the Dodgers (6-12) match the 12 of the Yankees (26-12) and are just higher than the Giants' total (a combined 5-11 in New York and San Francisco). The Cubs have lost eight.

290. *Match the pitchers or batters who yielded or hit these home runs of magnitude:*

1	Warren Spahn	A	hit the first home run ever at Shea Stadium
2	Vic Raschi	B	served up Willie Mays' first career homer
3	Willie Stargell	C	hit Wrigley Field's first night game home run
4	Lenny Dykstra	D	yielded Hank Aaron's first career homer

ANSWER: 1—B, 2—D, 3—A, 4—C

Mays' first home run on May 28, 1951, was also his first major league hit, after 12 hitless at-bats to start his career. Spahn joked that he could have lowered Mays' confidence had he not allowed the home run. "I'll never forgive myself," Spahn said. "We might have gotten rid of Willie forever if I'd only struck him out." Mays went on to make Spahn his favorite home run target, hitting 17 more off the Hall of Fame southpaw. Aaron had also doubled off Raschi eight days earlier for his first hit.

Stargell was a power hitter (475 home runs) who possessed a flair for the prodigious home run. With the trademark pinwheeling of his bat before each pitch, the burly, six-foot four-inch slugger hit the first two home runs completely out of Dodger Stadium as well as smashing an estimated 535-foot shot in Montreal's Olympic Stadium. At one time, Stargell held the mark for the longest home runs in six different parks. Stargell's power then was almost like McGwire's force today. Stargell might have hit another 50 home runs had he not played his home games (through the midpoint of the 1970 season) at cavernous Forbes Field, a Death Valley for left-handed hitters. Yet Stargell belted seven of the 18 home runs to clear the right-field roof at Forbes Field.

♦ Did you know Chicago's Ross Barnes hit the first home run in major league history on May 2, 1876? Coming to the National League from a stellar career in the National Association, Barnes hit an inside-the-park homer off Cincinnati's Cherokee Fisher in a game during which he also tripled, singled, scored four times, and swiped two bases. It was the only homer of the year for Barnes, who went on to lead the league with a .429 mark in helping his club to the pennant. Barnes' .429 batting average stands as the second best in major league history, behind Hugh Duffy's .438. Mack Jones of the Expos hit the first home run in Canada, doing so on April 14, 1969, off St. Louis' Nelson Briles. Steve Finley of the Padres hit the first home run in Mexico on August 16, 1996, off the Mets' Robert Person. The Cubs' Shane Andrews hit the first homer outside of North America, clubbing a shot at the Tokyo Dome in Japan. The March 29, 2000, roundtripper came off the Mets' Dennis Cook. In the 2001 major league season-opener at Hiram Bithorn Stadium, Toronto's Shannon Stewart hit the first major league home run in Puerto Rico.

291. *Who was Eddie Gaedel?*

ANSWER: Gaedel was the three-foot-seven midget that innovative St. Louis Browns owner Bill Veeck sent to bat on August 19, 1951. Signed for a day and sent to pinch-hit for rookie right fielder Frank Saucier, leading off the bottom of the first inning in the second game of a doubleheader against the Tigers, the 65-pound Gaedel walked to the plate wearing number ⅛. After a protest by Tigers manager Red Rolfe and many questions by home plate umpire Ed Hurley, Browns manager Zach Taylor produced Gaedel's contract, validating his appearance at the plate. Gaedel, whose strike zone was rendered even more minute by his batting crouch, promptly walked on four high pitches as Detroit starter Bob Cain threw in bemusement. After Gaedel reached first base amidst an ovation, Jim Delsing pinch-ran for him, although he didn't score in the 6-2 Browns defeat.

The next day, AL President Will Harridge refused to approve Gaedel's contract with the Browns, claiming it was not in baseball's best interest. For Gaedel, that was his lone plate appearance. Before the game, Veeck had to strenuously talk Gaedel out of swinging at any pitches. Gaedel, who was paid $100 for his appearance, was seen repeatedly practicing his swing before the game. He badly wanted to swing when at bat but remembered his owner's demand.

292. *Which Phillies outfielder threw the Dodgers' Cal Abrams out at home plate in the ninth inning of the 1950 regular season finale to force extra innings, where Dick Sisler's dramatic home run sent the Whiz Kids to the fall classic?*

ANSWER: Richie Ashburn

The brilliant center fielder made the throw that nailed Abrams in the bottom of the ninth at Ebbets Field. In the top of the 10th, Sisler slugged a three-run homer off Brooklyn's Don Newcombe to give the Phillies a pennant-winning, 4-1 triumph. Philadelphia ace Robin Roberts, working on short rest, started and earned his 20th win.

In the World Series against the Yankees, the Phillies played the Yankees tough, losing (in order) 1-0, 2-1, 3-2, and 5-2. Game Two was decided in the top of the 10th as Joe DiMaggio homered off Roberts, who lost a tremendous pitching duel to the victorious Allie Reynolds.

Game Three was decided by a walk-off single off the bat of Jerry Coleman in the ninth.

♦ Did you know the 32 seasons (from 1918 to 1949) that the Phillies went without a 20-game winner is the dubious standard? Robin Roberts' 20 wins in 1950 represented the first such result for the Phillies since Grover Alexander won a whopping 30 in 1917. According to Dave Zeman of the Society for American Baseball Research, the second-longest drought belongs to a pair of teams looking to avoid the Phillies' fate. Both the Angels and Indians enter the 2002 season unable to boast a 20-game winner since 1974. Nolan Ryan (Angels) and Gaylord Perry (Indians) are those team's last 20-game winners.

293. *This man was waived by the New York Giants in 1955 and traded for money the following May to the Brooklyn Dodgers, for whom he went 13-5 with a 2.87 ERA in leading them into the 1956 World Series. Who was he?*

ANSWER: Sal Maglie

The career 119-62 pitcher was waived by the Giants earlier during the 1955 season and picked up by the Indians later that campaign. After being used just twice over the first month of the 1956 season, Dodgers General Manager Buzzie Bavasi bought Maglie's contract, shocking Dodger players and fans alike.

Initially, Maglie was absolutely detested in Brooklyn after excelling against the beloved Dodgers for so many years as a member of the rival Giants. Players hated him because he consistently threw high and tight, almost shaving batters' chins, to keep them from crowding the plate (hence his nickname "The Barber"). But Dodger players and Brooklyn fans quickly learned Maglie was the kind of player you loved if he represented your team, because he did anything to win. Maglie won two huge games in the final week of the regular season, including a no-hitter over the Phillies as the Dodgers beat out the Milwaukee Braves by one game. Maglie also won the opening game of the World Series against the Yankees. The righthander, who finished second in the MVP balloting that year for his late brilliance, won just 11 more games over the next two seasons before retiring.

294. *Rogers Hornsby, Nap Lajoie, and Harry Heilmann are the only right-handed hitters to have batted .400 in the 1900s. True or False?*

ANSWER: True

Hornsby thrice reached .400. That hat trick included a performance of .424 in 1924, the 20th-century standard and the highest mark by any batter—righty or lefty—since Willie Keeler's .424 mark in 1897. Hornsby missed a fourth .400 season by three percentage points. Using a quick and potent swing, Heilmann averaged .403 in 1923, winning his second of four batting titles. Heilmann batted .393 or higher three other times. Lajoie batted .422 in 1901 (an AL standard) en route to a .339 career average.

Left-handed hitters like Keeler almost always have greater success because there are three times as many right-handed pitchers as there are southpaws. Batters generally perform better against their "opposites": hurlers who throw from the other side, because the ball tails into their zone instead of away from it. This is why left-handed pitchers are a commodity.

295. *Match these players with their unique roles:*

1	Dale Alexander	A	committed a record three errors in one inning during a World Series
2	Don Demeter	B	registered an AL record 13 shutouts in one season
3	Jack Coombs	C	posted seven wins and four saves in World Series play
4	Allie Reynolds	D	became the only player to win an AL batting title while playing for two teams in a season
5	Willie Davis	E	played the outfield 266 consecutive games without an error, a mark since passed by Darren Lewis

ANSWER: 1—D, 2—E, 3—B, 4—C, 5—A

Alexander won the 1932 batting title while playing for Detroit and Boston. In 1990, Willie McGee became the only player to win a batting title in one league despite spending the last month in the other league. McGee hit .335 for St. Louis and ended in Oakland.

Davis made three successive miscues during the fifth inning, leading to three unearned runs in Game Two of the 1966 World Series.

296. *The Philadelphia Athletics took advantage of some shoddy defense to win Game Four of the 1929 World Series, overcoming an 8-0 deficit by scoring 10 runs in the seventh inning. Can you name the Cubs' Hall of Fame outfielder who misplayed two fly balls in that inning, allowing the Athletics to take a three-games-to-one lead in the series?*

ANSWER: Hack Wilson

Wilson lost Bing Miller's fly in the sun and, trying to make up for the mistake, misplayed Mule Haas' line drive into an inside-the-park, three-run homer. The eight-run deficit remains the largest overcome in series and post-season history, and the 10-run seventh stands as a series record for an inning (since tied by the Tigers in Game Six, 1968).

The ferocious slugger went 8-for-17, but failed to hit a homer or drive in a run during the 1929 World Series, which the Cubs lost in five games. Although down on himself after the series, Wilson rebounded to enjoy an incredible campaign in 1930. In that season, Wilson used every ounce of his rock-hard, five-foot six-inch, 200-pound frame to smash 56 homers and drive in 191 runs. The two-time RBI champ and four-time home run leader fell victim to alcohol abuse and retired following the 1934 season with 244 home runs, 1,063 runs batted in, and a .307 batting mark.

297. *Match these one-time Yankee players with their achievements:*

1	Bob Meusel	A the first lefthander in NL history to homer 50
2	Johnny Mize	times in a season
3	Babe Ruth	B made as much as $80,000 a year
4	Yogi Berra	C handled a record 950 consecutive chances
		without making an error
		D the only teammate of Babe Ruth to out-homer
		the "Sultan of Swat" in a season during the
		1920s

ANSWER: 1—D, 2—A, 3—B, 4—C

Ruth negotiated that salary for the 1930 and 1931 seasons. When chided for making more money than U.S. President Herbert Hoover ($75,000), Ruth supposedly replied, "Why not? I had a better year." Ruth, a keen negotiator aware of his overall value, earned much more than Lou Gehrig. The financially modest Gehrig, who won the 1927 MVP, earned one-tenth what Ruth made.

Meusel led the Yankees and the league with 33 homers and 138 RBI in 1925, while the ill-disciplined Ruth (who was dealing with bad health and unruly behavior) mustered just 25 homers and 66 RBI. Berra played 148 consecutive games without an error, a standard since passed twice, by also-Yankee Rick Cerone (159 games), and the Florida Marlins' Charles Johnson (172 games). Mize stood as the lone left-handed National Leaguer to club 50 homers in a season until joined in 2001 by both Barry Bonds and Luis Gonzalez.

♦ Did you know Babe Ruth was suspended by the American League a record five times during the 1922 season for insubordinate behavior, and lasted as a Yankee caption for just six games?

♦ Did you know Babe Ruth once held up salary negotiations because he insisted on a $52,000 salary, for he had always wanted to make $1,000 a week? After his remarkable season of 1921, Ruth asked Yankee general manger Ed Barrow for a $50,000 salary. Barrow refused, but the owner Jake Ruppert had no option but to give in to Ruth's even-higher demand of $52,000. After earning a $52,000 salary for the five years through 1926, Ruth asked for a $200,000, two-year deal before settling for a three-year contract for $70,000 per year. In 1927, Ruth passed Commissioner Kenesaw Landis and Ty Cobb on baseball's salary list. Ruth responded admirably by averaging 53 home runs, 153 RBI, 147 runs scored, and a healthy .341 batting mark over that period.

298. *Who was the only major league commissioner to be "let go" before Fay Vincent was forced out of office in 1992?*

ANSWER: William Eckert

Ironically, the retired Air Force general was fired because he failed to provide leadership and had a poor public image. Eckert, hired in 1965 only because the owners couldn't collectively decide on the other candidates, wasn't familiar with the major league structure and it showed. In late 1968, the owners terminated Eckert's contract, before hiring Wall Street attorney Bowie Kuhn, who introduced his divisional play concept.

299. *Can you name the last playing-manager in the National League to lead his team to the pennant?*

ANSWER: Leo Durocher

Durocher guided the Brooklyn Dodgers to a 100-54 regular-season mark and the 1941 World Series, appearing in 18 games with a .286 batting average and six RBI as a middle infielder and pinch-hitter.

Any chance the Dodgers had of winning that World Series was lost as catcher Mickey Owen dropped the apparent game-ending third strike, allowing the Yankees to come back and win Game Four for a commanding three-games-to-one series lead. With the Dodgers on the cusp of tying the series at two games, Owen dropped reliever Hugh Casey's full-count pitch—perhaps a spitter. Batter Tommy Henrich raced to first base, igniting a four-run rally from scratch as the Yankees won, 7-4, en route to a five-game classic victory. After Henrich reached first, Joe DiMaggio singled and Charlie Keller pulled a two-run double off the right-field wall. After a walk to Bill Dickey, Joe Gordon also came through with a two-run double. A solid fielder and a four-time All-Star, Owen will always be remembered for the dropped third strike.

300. *Which pitcher came within two outs of duplicating Johnny Vander Meer's Herculean feat of throwing back-to-back no-hitters?*

ANSWER: Ewell Blackwell

Blackwell, who hurled his first no-hitter (6-0 over the Boston Braves) for the Reds on June 18, 1947, came within two outs of another when the Dodgers' Eddie Stanky broke it up with one out in the ninth four days later. Blackwell finished with a 4-0, two-hitter. On September 7, 1923, Howard Ehmke of the Red Sox almost matched Vander Meer's feat when he no-hit the Athletics (although he lucked out when Philadelphia pitcher William "Slim" Harris was called out for failing to touch first base after hitting Ehmke's delivery off the vall) and held his opponent to one hit on September 11. A controversial call erased his second no-hit bid.

Did you know Nolan Ryan came within two innings of duplicating Johnny Vander Meer's Herculean feat of back-to-back no-hitters on July 19, 1973? After hurling his second no-hitter of the year four days earlier, Ryan yielded a soft single to center to Baltimore shortstop Mark Belanger en route to a 10-inning, one-hitter. The hit led off the eighth.

301. *Can you name the Yankee second baseman whom Willie McCovey lined out to, ending the 1962 World Series as the tying run was on third and the winning run stood on second base?*

ANSWER: Bobby Richardson

Richardson caught the line drive in San Francisco's bottom half of the ninth to preserve the Game Seven 1-0 victory and the Yankees' 20th world championship. Many in attendance claim that McCovey's line drive was the hardest-hit ball they've ever seen—but it went right to Richardson. The second baseman later admitted to moving to that particular spot to avoid a few pebbles he had spotted.

The truly acute observer will notice that Yankee right fielder Roger Maris actually saved the day. Before McCovey stepped to the plate, Willie Mays doubled into the right-field corner with Matty Alou aboard at first. Maris, always a great fielder, got to the ball in a hurry and threw a perfect relay to keep Alou from scoring.

302. *Of the following keystone (second base and shortstop duo) tandems in major league history, which one holds the record for the fewest errors in a season (based on full-time activity)?*

A   Mark Belanger and Davey Johnson; 1972
B   Larry Bowa and Manny Trillo; 1979
C   Joe Tinker and Johnny Evers; 1908
D   Cal Ripken, Jr. and Billy Ripken; 1990
E   Rey Ordonez and Edgardo Alfonzo; 1999

ANSWER: E

Ordonez and Alfonzo combined for just nine errors, breaking the mark of 11 set by the Ripken brothers nine years earlier. Ordonez made just four errors, none after June 13, and Alfonzo committed five, none on grounders (also a record). In 1990, Cal made three miscues (a record that Cleveland's Omar Vizquel tied in 2000) and brother Billy had eight.

Due to the poor defensive conditions (poor gloves) in the early 1900s, even Evers and Tinker could only keep their combined error aggregate to 64 in 1908. In December of 1995, the Orioles signed free agent Roberto Alomar to form one of the best keystone combinations ever. But alas, Ripken moved back to third base in the 1997 season after 15 years at short. So Alomar signed with the Indians after the 1998 season, and spent the summer of 1999 alongside shortstop Vizquel to form an even better tandem.

The only long-term keystone combinations to be enshrined are Brooklyn shortstop "Pee Wee" Reese and second baseman Jackie Robinson (who played up the middle together from 1947 to 1952), Boston's Joe Cronin and Bobby Doerr (1938–41), the Cubs' Joe Tinker and Johnny Evers (1903–12), and the White Sox's Luis Aparicio and Nellie Fox (1956–62).

Hall of Fame second baseman Frankie Frisch played with a few Cooperstown-bound shortstops with the Giants and Cardinals, but none for longer than two years. Frisch teamed with Dave Bancroft for the Giants in 1922 and 1923. "The Fordham Flash" teamed with Travis Jackson for New York in 1924 and 1926 before being traded to St. Louis, where he teamed with Rabbit Maranville in 1928. Over the last five years of his career, Frisch teamed with a shortstop who later was inducted into the Hall of Fame, but only for his managerial excellence: Leo Durocher. Monte Irvin and Larry Doby made up a double play combination for the Newark Eagles in the Negro National Leagues.

♦ Did you know Nellie Fox and Luis Aparicio of the 1959 White Sox became the first mid-infield duo to win a Gold Glove in the same season?

♦ Did you know Billy Ripken, one of 33 different second basemen his brother Cal played alongside as a shortstop during The Streak, was given special permission to miss an American Association playoff game from the Buffalo Bisons so he could attend his sibling's ceremonial record-breaking game on September 6, 1995? The mesmerizing night was unforgettable: 46,272 fans packed Camden Yards and millions of others were transfixed in front of their television sets as Cal took eight curtain calls (totaling 22 minɪtes and 15 seconds) when the game became official after the top of the ɪfth inning. Cal modestly requested no ceremony, but received the grandest ɔf receptions for taking so much pride in a sport that so many young partici-ɔants forget is a privilege. A downtown building in Baltimore wore a huge ʀipken painting with the following message: "Death, Taxes and Cal Ripken, ʀ." Among the thousands of signs displayed were ones that read "Cal: ¯hanks for saving baseball" and "We consider ourselves the luckiest fans on ᴛhe face of this earth." In his speech after the game, Cal stated his dedication ᴛemmed from his "love for the game, motivation for the team and desire to ᴛompete at the very highest level."

³03. *When Nolan Ryan notched his seventh no-hitter on May 1, 1991,*
versus Toronto in Arlington Stadium, a little known fact was that
Ryan became the oldest pitcher (at age 44, breaking his own record
of a year earlier) to strike out 16 batters in a game. Prior to Ryan,
who was the oldest pitcher to whiff 16 in a game?

A Walter Johnson
B Rube Waddell
C Warren Spahn
D Steve Carlton
E Lefty Grove

ANSWER: B

Waddell struck out 16 in a game during the 1908 season, at the ᴀge of 32. Waddell, who whiffed most of his 2,316 opponents for the ⁺hiladelphia Athletics, enjoyed his 16-K game against Connie Mack's ᴀthletics, pitching for the St. Louis Browns on July 29.

Did you know Walter Johnson holds the major league record of losing 65 ᴀames by shutout? Nolan Ryan is second with 63 and Phil Niekro is third ᴠith 59.

³04. *Can you identify the player(s)-for-player(s) Reds-Giants deal*
considered by many historians as the most lopsided in baseball
history? (Remember, Boston's Harry Frazee traded Babe Ruth for
money.)

ANSWER: On December 15 of the year 1900, the Cincinnati Reds ᴛaded a rookie righthander by the name of Christopher Mathewson to the New York Giants for two-year holdout Amos Rusie. With all 245 wins behind him, Rusie ended his Hall of Fame career after only three appearances for the Reds in 1901. Mathewson was a steal (almost literally) for the Giants, as he had 373 victories ahead of him. Mathewson lost all three decisions for the Giants in 1900 before being released and then drafted by the Reds.

Cincinnati owner John Brush, who was looking into buying the Giants from the unpopular Andrew Freedman in a deal that would benefit both franchises, arranged it so his Reds would trade Mathewson back to the Giants, as he wanted a pitcher with plenty of potential when he took over the New York franchise. Brush made the deal, knowing he'd be with the Giants after selling his Reds promptly afterward. Although the trade took place in mid-December of 1900, Brush didn't officially sell his Reds and buy the Giants until August of 1902. Manager Buck Ewing, Mathewson, and Brush all left the Reds for the Giants.

The trades that netted Lou Brock, Nolan Ryan, Joe Morgan, Jeff Bagwell, Sammy Sosa, Pedro Martinez, David Cone, Steve Carlton, Mark McGwire, and Roger Maris were also one-sided deals pulled off by the Cardinals, Angels, Reds, Astros, Cubs, Expos, Mets, Phillies, Cardinals, and Yankees, respectively.

Although each of those teams benefited greatly without giving up much, no trade paid off as quick a dividend as the acquisition of Brock. Batting a lowly .251 with an on-base mark of .300, two homers, and just 10 steals 52 games into the 1964 season, Brock was traded from the Cubs to the Cardinals for Ernie Broglio (a former 21-game winner who won 18 in 1963 but just seven more after the trade). Brock flourished for the Cardinals, whose more spacious Busch Stadium allowed the left-handed hitter to squeeze the ball into the gaps and use his blazing speed to pile up doubles and triples. In just 103 games as a Cardinal that year, Brock batted a scorching .348 with 146 hits, 21 doubles, nine triples, 12 homers, 33 steals, 81 runs scored, and a surprising .527 slugging percentage to surge St. Louis to a NL pennant. In a hard-fought World Series against the Yankees, Brock batted .300 with five RBI, including a key home run in the team's triumphant seventh game. Brock played 15 more seasons in St. Louis, electrifying Busch Stadium audiences with his dazzling speed, daring baserunning, and unexpected power.

On August 31, 1990, the Red Sox traded Bagwell (a Boston native who idolized the Red Sox) to the Astros for the comical reliever Larry Anderson. The White Sox traded Sosa along with Ken Patterson to the cross-town Cubs for George Bell on May 30, 1992. On November 19, 1993, the Expos acquired Martinez from the Dodgers for Delino DeShields. In March of 1987, the Mets lured the Royals into trading David Cone and a minor leaguer for Ed Hearn, Rick Anderson, and Mauro Gozzo. McGwire was dealt by the Athletics (a small-market team that could no longer afford his salary) to St. Louis on July 31, 1997, for T. J. Mathews and two minor leaguers. The other deals are mentioned elsewhere in this book.

♦ Did you know the pitching distance was moved back to 60-feet six-inches (the present distance) from the 55-foot measure, because of Amos Rusie's domination of opposing batters? Before the change in 1893, the six-foot one-inch righthander struck out 341, 337, and 288 batters in the previous three seasons with ERAs under 2.89.

305. *A total of 24 rookie pitchers, through 2001, have thrown a no-hitter. Two of them took it a step further and hurled a perfect game. A college kid named John Lee Richmond was the first. The other is:*

A Monte Ward
B Addie Joss
C Charlie Robertson
D Ernie Shore

ANSWER: C

Robertson threw a 2-0 perfect game against Detroit on April 30, 1922. Ironically enough, this ChiSox righthander never had a winning season and finished 49-80 over an eight-year career.

Richmond was a senior at Brown University in 1880 when he pitched the first perfect game in major league history for the Worcester Brown Stockings. Richmond's gem on June 12 came five days before Monte Ward's perfect game. Aside from winning his only decision the previous year, Richmond also never enjoyed a winning record throughout a brief career that featured 75 wins and 100 defeats. Of those who have thrown a no-hitter as a rookie, only Christy Mathewson (1901) went on to a Hall of Fame career.

306. *Match these players with their feats:*

1	Todd Helton	A	led all major leaguers in hits during the 1990s
2	Claudell Washington	B	became the first player to win the Rookie of the Year Award and MVP in consecutive seasons
3	Mark Grace		
4	Robin Yount	C	became the first player to amass 100 extra-base hits in consecutive seasons
5	Cal Ripken, Jr.		
		D	led all major leaguers with 1,731 hits during the 1980s
		E	was struck out 39 times by the "Ryan Express"

ANSWER: 1—C, 2—E, 3—A, 4—D, 5—B

Grace collected 1,754 hits from 1990 to 1999, just seven more than Rafael Palmeiro, 26 more than Craig Biggio, and 41 more than Tony Gwynn. Gwynn, however, batted .344 during the decade, 15 points higher than anyone else. In the 1970s, Pete Rose beat out everyone with 2,045 hits. In the 1960s, Roberto Clemente led the way with 1,877 hits. In the 1950s, Richie Ashburn collected 1,875 hits. In the 1940s, Lou Boudreau gathered 1,578 hits. During the 1930s, Paul Waner had a decade-best 1,959 hits. In the 1920s, Rogers Hornsby set a record with 2,085 hits in a decade. Ty Cobb dominated the teens with 1,949 safeties. Honus Wagner's 1,847 hits were the most from 1900 to 1909. Ripken earned 1982's top rookie honor, and took home the AL MVP Award in 1983. Helton improved on his 103 extra-base hits in 2000 with 105 in 2001.

◆ Did you know Will Clark led the small trail with six home runs off Nolan Ryan as Mike Schmidt hit five? Clark's home run off Ryan on April 8, 1986, was the very first pitch the intense left-handed slugger ever saw in the majors.

◆ Did you know the record for most homers hit off a pitcher in a single season is six, shared by George Kelly, Ted Williams, and Ted Kluszewski? The Giants' Kelly set the mark off the Cubs' Vic Aldridge in 1923. Williams tied the mark 18 years later by belting the White Sox's Johnny Rigney for a half dozen dingers. Cincinnati's Kluszewski simply owned Max Surkont of the Pirates in 1954.

307. *Cal Ripken, Jr. (2,632); Lou Gehrig (2,130); Everett Scott (1,307); and Steve Garvey (1,207) own the four-longest streaks of consecutive games played. Match these players with the next four longest streaks of consecutive games played:*

1	Billy Williams	A	895 games
2	Stan Musial	B	829 games
3	Eddie Yost	C	1,117 games
4	Joe Sewell	D	1,103 games

ANSWER: 1—C, 2—A, 3—B, 4—D

Gehrig played despite enduring 17 fractures, which healed while he extended his streak. Among the fractures was a broken toe and a broken thumb. Williams, who also drove in 1,475 runs during an 18-year career, never led his league in home runs or RBI, but was as consistent at the plate as he was reliable on the field. The smooth-swinging left-handed hitter hit at least 20 homers with 84 RBI every year from 1961 to 1973. He also won a batting title in 1972. Gus Suhr and Nellie Fox own the ninth and 10th longest streaks in history, playing in 822 and 798 straight contests, respectively.

♦ Did you know Earl Averill had his consecutive-game streak end at 673 during the 1935 season when he was hurt while lighting firecrackers?

308. *Who said, "I do not feel I am a piece of property to be bought and sold irrespective of my wishes"?*

ANSWER: Curt Flood

Flood was the player most responsible for ending the reserve clause and putting the wheels in motion for free agency. Those words were written in a letter to Commissioner Bowie Kuhn after Flood turned down a trade from the St. Louis Cardinals to the Philadelphia Phillies on October 7, 1969. Flood even refused a $100,000 offer from the Phillies, choosing to stand up for a cause he believed in and opting to challenge the reserve clause (which bound a player to a team indefinitely) in federal court.

He filed a suit on January 16, 1970, charging Major League Baseball with violation of the antitrust laws. After two appeals, the suit reached the Supreme Court. On June 19, 1972, in the case of *Flood vs. Kuhn*, the Supreme Court ruled in favor of Major League Baseball (by a 5-3 vote), stating that antitrust laws do not apply to baseball.

In 1971, between the appeals and the verdict, Flood attempted a comeback with the Washington Senators after sitting out the 1970 season. The seven-time Gold Glover, three-time All-Star, and .293 career hitter retired, however, after just 13 games despite a $110,000 salary. The embattled Flood was more concerned about the principle of freedom of action than he was about the money involved. When asked later why he retired, Flood said, "If you did what I did to baseball, you are a hated, ugly, detestable person." However, with Players Union leader Marvin Miller's help, the reserve clause was seriously reconsidered and then rendered nearly obsolete because of a new bargaining tool: arbitration.

In 1974, Jim "Catfish" Hunter was awarded free-agency on a technicality. And when pitchers Andy Messersmith and Dave McNally were declared baseball's first legal free agents by the federal courts in 1975, the reserve clause became a thing of the past. In a landmark decision, players were no longer bound to their team once their contracts expired.

An accomplished artist, Flood moved to France to paint. He returned for one year as a broadcaster for the Oakland A's in 1978. Flood passed away on January 20, 1997, of cancer. Sadly, a good percentage of today's players don't know who Flood is, failing to realize his important contribution to their professional well-being.

◆ Did you know Twins reliever Dock Woodson won baseball's first arbitration, getting awarded a $29,000 salary on February 11, 1974? Illustrating the financial progression of the game, Atlanta's Andruw Jones in February of 2001 won a record $8.2 million arbitration case.

◆ Did you know U.S. President Bill Clinton signed into law the Curt Flood Act in 1998, which provides for a limited repeal of baseball's antitrust exemption? This act essentially means that players can now sue Major League Baseball over labor matters, whereas they had no such right before. In May of 1922, the U.S. Supreme Court ruled that baseball was a sport and not a business, and therefore, exempt from antitrust laws.

309. *Match these Negro National League (NNL) superstars with their heroics:*

1 Rube Foster	A this powerful slugging catcher was considered the "Babe Ruth of the Negro Leagues"
2 Josh Gibson	
3 Judy Johnson	
4 "Smokey" Joe Williams	B the "Lou Gehrig of the Negro Leagues"
5 Oscar Charleston	
6 Buck Leonard	C is recognized as the best all-around NNL player
	D only Satchel Paige can compare in terms of pitching supremacy in NNL history
	E known as "The Father of Black Baseball" for organizing it
	F the best defensive third bagger

ANSWER: 1—E, 2—A, 3—F, 4—D, 5—C, 6—B

During a schedule that included games in the NNL, Mexican Leagues, and exhibitions, Gibson hit 75 overall homers in 1931, 69 in 1934, and 84 during an extended 1936 schedule (170 games). In 16 NNL seasons, Gibson won nine home run titles and four batting crowns. Leonard challenged Gibson for the home run title a few times. Gibson (batting third) and Leonard (batting cleanup) formed an awesome power tandem for the Homestead Grays, receiving the moniker of "The Thunder Twins." They were often compared to Ruth and Gehrig, who also batted third and fourth, respectively. Leonard, who retired at the age of 48 (five years after the Grays folded in 1950), played in a record 13 East-West All-Star Games, according to Larry Lester of the Society for American Baseball Research.

Charleston possessed power, speed, and range in center field, playing in the mold of a future Hall of Famer by the name of Willie Mays. Williams didn't make the Hall of Fame until 1999, probably because he retired in 1932—too soon to have an impact on the racial barrier fight. There's no other explanation for the lengthy delay in inducting a pitcher who was so dominant that he once fanned 27 Kansas City Monarch batters and surrendered just one hit in a 12-inning, 1-0 masterpiece as a 45-year-old for the Grays.

Foster is best known as "The Father of Black Baseball" for his efforts to publicize black baseball and eventually the founding of the Negro Leagues. Foster was a star pitcher in 1902, before becoming the manager (in 1910) of a team that challenged any squad—white or black—because there was no black league at the time. His first attempt to form the NNL in 1910 was to no avail: The league collapsed before a single contest was played. But he later made a second try and the first Negro League game was played in 1922. Rube (whose first name was really Andrew) remained the NNL president until his death in 1930.

Foster was well known for his tremendous dedication to broadening the game of baseball for Blacks and to breaking the color barrier, which was finally broken 17 years after his death. Foster's accomplishments were the single biggest impetus for integration. The Jackie Robinsons, Willie Mays, Henry Aarons, and Roy Campanellas would have never been allowed to showcase their brilliant talents without Foster's crucial groundwork.

♦ Did you know Joe Williams was called "Cyclone" (à la Cy Young) long before being given the moniker "Smokey" for his blazing fastball?

♦ Did you know Oscar Charleston was the scout who chose Jackie Robinson when the color barrier fell?

♦ Did you know Buck Leonard was approached by Cleveland Indians owner Bill Veeck about playing major league ball, but refused? Leonard, then 40 years of age, reasoned that he didn't want a sunset performance to hurt the chances of a younger black player who might otherwise be considered.

310. *Which pitcher saved the life of a 61-year-old fan who had suffered a heart attack just before a July 17, 1978, game?*

ANSWER: Doc Medich

The Texas Rangers pitcher, who was a medical student, provided the fan with heart massage therapy until the medical unit arrived at Memorial Stadium in Baltimore. Following an 11-year career that featured a 124-105 record, including a 19-win campaign in 1974, Medich retired after the 1982 season to practice sports medicine. Medich began attending medical school in 1972, a day after making his major league debut for the Yankees.

11. *Can you name the only player to win the batting title, home run title, and RBI title at least three times each?*

ANSWER: Ted Williams

Williams won six batting titles (1941–42, 1947–48, and 1957–8), four home run crowns (1941–42, 1947, and 1949) and led the AL 1 RBI four times (1939, 1942, 1947, and 1949). Babe Ruth and Lou ehrig each won just one batting title. Ty Cobb paced the league just nce in home runs, and Honus Wagner never led the league in omers.

Did you know Babe Ruth, Ted Williams, and Lou Gehrig are the only three layers to rank in the top 20 in career home runs, RBI, and batting average?

12. *Who was known as "Ol' Aches and Pains" and how did this Hall of Famer acquire this moniker?*

ANSWER: Luke Appling, the shortstop who played his entire 20-ear career with the Chicago White Sox, was tagged "Ol' Aches and ains" by his team's trainer, who was convinced his charge was a ypochondriac. After a rough start, Appling made a name for himself s a great hitting shortstop. Appling hit over .300 in his third full eason, enjoying the first of 14 such campaigns. Three years later, he went 4-for-4 in the 1936 season finale to become the first AL short-top and the first Chicago White Sox player to capture the batting rown, doing so with an impressive mark of .388. In 1943, Appling won his second batting title. He spent most of the next two years in he military.

Despite leading the league in errors for five straight years (an AL ecord that still stands), and committing a whopping 643 miscues in ,218 career games at short, Appling continued reaching more balls han anyone else. He set a major league record by leading the league n assists seven times, a standard since passed. The .310 lifetime hit-er, recognized almost as much for his imagined ailments as for his onsistent production at the plate, retired following the 1950 season.

Did you know the Chicago Cubs and the Cincinnati Reds played an entire ine-inning game with just one baseball? It happened on June 29 of the 916 season. It had happened before, but has never happened since.

313. *Which team established a major league record by having its first three batters of the game homer in succession?*

A the New York Mets
B the Oakland A's
C the San Diego Padres
D the Boston Red Sox

ANSWER: C

On April 13, 1987, the Padres accomplished the feat as Marvel Wynne led off the bottom of the first with a home run, and Tony Gwynn and John Kruk followed with homers of their own off Giants pitcher Roger Mason. It was interesting because none of the batters were known as home run hitters. Wynne hit 40 over an eight-year career, Gwynn hit 135 over his 20 seasons, and Kruk averaged 10 a campaign over his 10-year career. And yet Mason was not a gopher ball pitcher: He gave up less than a home run per nine innings.

314. *Match these players with their clutch feats:*

1 Willie Mays	A hit 16 extra-inning home runs
2 Ralph Kiner	B hit 18 extra-inning home runs
3 Babe Ruth and Frank Robinson	C hit a record 22 extra-inning
4 Jack Clark	homers
	D homered in a record three
	straight All-Star Games

ANSWER: 1—C, 2—D, 3—A, 4—B

Mays hit half of his 22 extra-inning homers in the 10th and four in the 12th inning. Hank Aaron, Jimmie Foxx, and Mickey Mantle hit 14 extra-inning home runs apiece. In 1995, Ron Gant of the Reds hit four extra-inning home runs to tie Mays' NL single-season record. Charlie Maxwell hit a major league record five extra-inning homers for the 1960 Detroit Tigers.

Five players share the mark of two extra-inning homers in the same game, but clearly the most interesting performance from that group belongs to Art Shamsky. The Reds outfielder entered the August 12, 1966, contest in the top of the eighth inning as a defensive replacement. In the bottom half, Shamsky hit a two-run homer to put the Reds ahead, 8-7. In the 10th, Shamsky hit a solo shot to tie

he game at 9-9. An inning later, he belted a two-run homer to tie the
game again at 11-11. The Pirates scored thrice in the 13th to win a
wild, 14-11 game that featured a then-major league record-tying 11
home runs. Mike Young was the last to accomplish the feat in 1987.
Vern Stephens (1943), Willie Kirkland (1963), and Ralph Garr (1971)
were the other three to homer twice in extra innings.

Did you know Willie Mays homered in each inning from the first to the
6th? No other player has done this, according to David Vincent of the
Society for American Baseball Research. Dante Bichette, Jack Clark, Howard
Johnson, Craig Nettles, Andy Pafko, and Carl Yastrzemski all homered in
each frame from the first to the 14th.

Did you know Roy Face yielded a record 21 extra-inning home runs? The
next closest competitor was Hoyt Wilhelm with 14.

15. *Which of these players holds the unorthodox standard for hitting
the most home runs in a season—all in one ballpark?*

A Fred Pfeffer
B Gavvy Cravath
C Mel Ott
D Cliff Lee

ANSWER: A

Pfeffer of the Chicago White Stockings hit all 25 of his home
runs in 1884 at cozy Lake Front Park, according to historian David
Vincent of the Society for American Baseball Research. Pfeffer that
year also drove in 101 runners—another career-best figure—in helping the Cap Anson-managed club to a 62-50 ledger.

Cravath of the Phillies also took advantage of his home park
(Baker Bowl), as he marked his territory among the best home run
hitters of the Dead Ball Era. Between 1913 and 1919—a span of seven
seasons, during which he led the National League in home runs six
times—the right-handed Cravath hit just 16 home runs in road
parks. As a matter of fact, he twice won a home run title without
going deep on the road.

Although Babe Ruth is often said to have taken advantage of the
short right-field porch in Yankee Stadium, in fact he didn't. In the 12
years Ruth called Yankee Stadium home, from 1923 to 1934, "The

Sultan of Swat" hit 259 home runs at home and 252 on the road
That's slightly greater than half a home run more per season. In his
first 10 years with the Yankees, he actually hit seven more home run
on the road. The right-field fence was deceptively short. Although
the right-field porch down the line was 295 feet away, right-cente
was a monstrous 429 feet away. In 1927, Ruth hit a record 32 of his 6
home runs on the road. The record for road homers wasn't tied until
1998, by Mark McGwire, and wasn't surpassed until 2001, courtesy c
Barry Bonds' 36 homers away from Pac Bell Park.

♦ Did you know Gavvy Cravath became a judge following his major leagu
career?

316. *Almost everyone knows Babe Ruth's uniform number was 3, Hank*
Aaron's was 44, and Ted Williams' was 9. See if you can match
these players with their uniform numbers:

1	Don Drysdale	A	19
2	Ralph Branca	B	53
3	Roy Campanella	C	39
4	Satchel Paige	D	13
5	Bob Feller	E	26

ANSWER: 1—B, 2—D, 3—C, 4—E, 5—A

For the superstitious many, it's no surprise that #13 Branca had
the least successful career of the group. But then again, he did make
three All-Star teams and win 20 more games than he lost (88-68).

Feller, the six-time 20-game winner, earned 266 victories and
struck out 2,581 batters over a career interrupted by military servic
that cost him almost four prime major league seasons. Feller, how
ever, told me in July of 1999 he doesn't look back and wonder "wha
if," because it was his decision, and he was proud to serve his country
How proud? He enlisted in the Navy the day after Pearl Harbor wa
bombed and insisted on serving, despite a draft deferment he wa
allowed because he was his family's only means of support (his fathe
was dying of cancer). Feller came back with eight battle stars and fiv
campaign ribbons. Now, that's a true hero. The wonderful basebal
organization the Society for American Baseball Research awarded Fel
ler with its inaugural SABR's Hero of Baseball Award.

Did you know the Yankees began the tradition of retiring numbers when they retired Lou Gehrig's number 4 in 1939 and Babe Ruth's number 3 in 1948?

17. *Fill in the blanks for four of the following five blockbuster trades:*

  A on June 15, 1977, the Mets traded Tom Seaver to the Reds for Pat Zachry, Steve Henderson, Dan Norman, and _____

  B on December 12, 1933, the Athletics traded Lefty Grove, Max Bishop, and _____ to the Red Sox for Bob Kline, Rabbit Warstler, and $125,000

  C on December 5, 1990, the Blue Jays traded Fred McGriff and Tony Fernandez to the Padres for Joe Carter and _____

  D on August 31, 1992, the Athletics traded Jose Canseco to the Rangers for Ruben Sierra, pitchers _____ and Jeff Russell, and an undisclosed amount of money

  E on November 29, 1971, the Reds acquired Hall of Famer Joe Morgan, _____, Cesar Geronimo, Denis Menke, and Ed Armbrister from the Houston Astros, who received Lee May, Tommy Helms, and Jimmy Stewart

ANSWER: A—Doug Flynn; B—Rube Walberg; C—Roberto Alomar; D—Bobby Witt; E—Jack Billingham

But the distinction of the biggest blockbuster has to belong to the deal pulled off between the Pittsburgh Pirates and Louisville Colonels on December 6, 1899. It involved 18 players, four of whom were Hall of Famers: player-manager Fred Clarke, Honus Wagner, Rube Waddell, and Jack Chesbro. Clarke, Wagner, Waddell, Deacon Phillippe, Tommy Leach, Patsy Flaherty, Mike Kelley, Icebox Chamberlain, Walt Woods, Chief Zimmer, Conny Doyle, Tacks Latimer, and Claude Ritchey were traded to Pittsburgh. In return, Louisville received Chesbro in addition to Paddy Fox, John O'Brien, Art Madison, and $25,000.

Here's where this deal gets interesting. Right before the trade, Louisville owner Barney Dreyfuss also became 50% owner of the Pittsburgh ballclub (multiple-team ownership was permitted in those days), a move that preceded a merger between the two clubs as part of the league's effort to shed four teams, reducing the NL to eight franchises. Frederick Ivor-Campbell of the Society for American Base-

ball Research told me he's convinced "Dreyfuss knew his Louisvil
club was slated for liquidation."

Chesbro was subsequently returned to Pittsburgh, making th
multi-part transaction even more lopsided. Fox, O'Brien, and Mad
son never played again. Officially, *The Baseball Encyclopedia* explain
"Sale of the chief assets of the Louisville franchise (went) to Pitt
burgh after Louisville was dropped by the National League." Othe
wise, this deal would challenge the Christy Mathewson-Amos Rus
exchange as the most lopsided trade ever.

318. *Match these minor league superstars with their achievements:*

1	Tom Drees	A	was the best two-way performer in mino league history
2	Ron Necciai	B	once struck out 27 batters within a no-hitter
3	Roy Sanner	C	had three no-hitters, including back-to-back gems
4	William Thomas	D	threw a 15-inning no-hitter
5	Tom Walker	E	still holds minor league records for wins, losses, and appearances

ANSWER: 1—C, 2—B, 3—A, 4—E, 5—D

Drees, a southpaw, accomplished the feat for Vancouver (Ch
cago White Sox's AAA affiliate) during the 1989 season.

Necciai, a 19-year-old ace for Bristol of the Appalachian Leagu
(Class D), came through with that masterful performance on May 1:
1952, against Welch, facing just four batters over the minimum. C
the 27 strikeouts registered by the flame-thrower, four came in th
ninth, courtesy of a passed ball third strike. Necciai was a 1952 Pitt:
burgh Pirates #1 draft pick who also had single-game strikeout tota
of 24, 20, and, on three separate occasions 19 in the minors. H
didn't fare nearly as well after a promotion to the majors later in th
season. With the big club, he went 1-6 with a 7.08 ERA. Necciai als
set minor league records with five strikeouts in an inning, and 1
consecutive whiffs.

Pitcher and outfielder Sanner posted a career 138-72 record witl
a 3.61 ERA on the mound and a .327 batting average with 220 homer
and 1,071 RBI in the batter's box. While with Houma in the Evan

geline League, he also won the pitchers' Triple Crown (in 1948), going 21-2 on the mound with a 2.58 ERA and 251 Ks.

Thomas pitched from 1926 to 1952, earning 383 wins, losing 347, and pitching in 1,016 games. The right-handed curveball specialist, who didn't have a major league fastball, also holds the records for innings pitched (5,995), runs allowed (3,098), and hits allowed (6,721). According to Bob Hoie of the Society for American Baseball Research, Thomas was jailed for the 1930 season, suspended from 1947 to 1949 on gambling charges he never admitted to, and died in an Oakland flophouse under another pitcher's name.

On August 4, 1971, Walker threw the second-longest no-hitter in minor league history for the Dallas-Fort Worth Spurs.

319. *Surprisingly enough, three Hall of Famers emerged from the 1919 White Sox team. Can you name two of them?*

ANSWER: Eddie Collins, Ray Schalk, and Red Faber

Second baseman Collins, catcher Schalk, and pitcher Faber were each inducted into Cooperstown's shrine, despite playing for the infamous Black Sox. They were not among the accused.

Collins (inducted in 1939) hit .319 in 1919 and .333 for his career. The left-handed batter (and right-handed thrower) hit only .226 in the World Series, averaging .328 over his six fall classics. A .253 career hitter, Schalk hit .282 in 1919 and .304 in the series, averaging .286 in his two World Series. Schalk was inducted in 1935. The 1964 Hall of Fame inductee, Faber was 11-9 during the 1919 season before a sore arm ended his campaign prematurely and didn't allow the righthander to compete in the World Series. The pitcher, who retired with a 254-213 career record, posted a 3-1 mark in the 1917 fall classic versus the defeated Giants.

◆ Did you know Lefty Williams' three defeats for the White Sox during the 1919 World Series has since only been tied by the Yankees' George Frazier during the 1981 World Series? A 35-43 career pitcher, Frazier posted a 1.61 ERA during the 1981 regular season and pitched 5⅔ scoreless innings of relief for a 1-0 record during the 1981 AL Championship Series to earn the Yankees' confidence. Frazier, who went on to pitch two scoreless innings during the 1987 World Series for the champion Twins, went 0-3 with an ERA of 17.18 in the 1981 fall classic. The reliever squandered a lead in Game

Three (with the Yankees ahead two games to none), a three-run lead in Game Four, and let the bottom fall out of a tie score in Game Six.

320. *Match the players with their final seasons:*

1	Denny McLain	A	1947
2	Lefty O'Doul	B	1911
3	Babe Ruth	C	1928
4	Grover Alexander	D	1934
5	Ty Cobb	E	1930
6	Dizzy Dean	F	1955
7	Christy Mathewson	G	1972
8	Jimmie Foxx	H	1945
9	Ralph Kiner	I	1935
10	Cy Young	J	1916

ANSWER: 1—G, 2—D, 3—I, 4—E, 5—C, 6—A, 7—J, 8—H, 9—F, 10—B

Foxx retired after the 1945 season with the Philadelphia Phillies. With his retirement ended one of the best careers in history, but also a career that could have been so much more. It's no secret that a drinking problem curtailed Foxx's full potential. Not knowing how to cope with daily life and dearly missing the game he loved, Foxx drank even more after he retired. Sadly, the extremely friendly Foxx gave away money recklessly and lost his remaining assets to bad investments.

◆ Did you know Jimmie Foxx and his wife both died from choking accidents in separate incidents? Although Foxx is listed as having passed away from a heart attack, his daughter Candace told the Society for American Baseball Research that both parents in fact choked to death.

321. *Despite being a member of the 3,000-hit club, Carl Yastrzemski retired without a 200-hit season. True or False?*

ANSWER: True

Yastrzemski, Cap Anson, Dave Winfield, Eddie Murray, and Rickey Henderson are the only men in history with 3,000 hits and nary a 200-hit season. Eddie Collins, Willie Mays, Al Kaline, and Robin Yount each had only one 200-hit season.

♦ Did you know some baseball sources don't credit Cap Anson with 3,000 hits, although Major League Baseball officially lists him with 3,081? Regarded by Major League Basball as the first to reach 3,000 hits, Anson is denied that record by some sources because he played during a time when walks were counted as hits. Baseball spokesman Rich Levin told me Major League Baseball goes "by the rule of the time, and so should everyone." Fair enough. So when Rickey Henderson reached the 3,000-hit mark in October of 2001, he became the 25th member, not the 24th. By the way, some credit Anson with over 3,400 hits, but that figure includes his five years in the National Association, a circuit the Baseball Records Committee does not recognize as a major league.

322. *How long are major leaguers required to play before being eligible for the Hall of Fame, and how long do they have to wait after retiring before becoming eligible?*

ANSWER: Ten years; five years

The only exception to the 10-year rule was Addie Joss, who played nine years (1902–1910). The Special Veterans Committee finally decided to bend the rule a bit in 1978 and deem the right-hander's accomplishments worthy of the Hall of Fame. After all, Joss died on the eve of his 10th season. Two days after his 31st birthday, Joss was struck by a rare form of tubercular meningitis.

323. *Who is the only pitcher to throw a no-hitter in four consecutive years?*

ANSWER: Sandy Koufax

Koufax recorded a no-no each year from 1962 through 1965. This Hall of Fame southpaw no-hit the Mets on June 30, 1962; the Giants on May 11, 1963; the Phillies on June 4, 1964; and the Cubs on September 9, 1965. The left-handed Koufax struck out 13 Mets at home for his first gem, a 5-0 decision. Against San Francisco, Koufax outdueled Juan Marichal, walking just two Giants in an 8-0 rout. Koufax's third no-hitter was his first on the road and second straight against a division leader. Koufax concluded his incredible string with a perfect game against the Cubs' Bob Hendley.

324. *How did Commissioner Kenesaw Mountain Landis get his name?*

ANSWER: Landis received his name as a result of his father Dr. Abraham Landis' promise to God while battling in the Civil War. Injured during the Battle of Kenesaw Mountain in 1864, Dr. Abraham Landis swore that he would name his first-born after the Georgia battle site if he recovered from the amputation of his leg. On November 20, 1866, in Ohio, the baby who would become the first major league commissioner was born. The rest is history.

SECOND POSTSEASON

Best-of-Seven League Championship Series

For those who notched 96 regular-season wins, I welcome you to the second postseason. This is where the elite separate themselves from the contenders, and earn their glory. Play ball!

Game One Question:

Which pinch-runner scored the Reds' winning run in Game Five of the 1972 NL Championship Series?

ANSWER: George Foster

Upon 23-year-old Foster (in his second full season) was bestowed the honor of scoring the series' winning run in his only series appearance. The bottom of the ninth began with the Pirates ahead, 3-2, and only three outs away from their second consecutive pennant. Pittsburgh reliever Dave Giusti was set to face Johnny Bench, Tony Perez, and Dennis Menke. However, the Reds were not about to allow the Pirates to celebrate in front of the 41,887 Reds fans in Riverfront Stadium. Bench promptly took Giusti deep for a dramatic game-tying home run. Perez and Menke each singled to relieve Giusti of his duties, as Pirate manager Bill Virdon sent in Bob Moose. Perez was replaced on the base paths with the speedster Foster (who later stole a career-high 17 bases in 1976). Two outs later with Foster on third, Moose uncorked a wild pitch to pinch-hitter Hal McRae, scoring Foster to start the celebration for the Reds. The Pirates (96-59) and the Reds (95-59) had baseball's two best records.

♦ Did you know that no team played over 156 games during the 1972 regular season due to the 13-day strike at the outset of the season?

Game Two Question:

> *Mike Scott and Jeffrey Leonard each won a NL Championship Series*
> *MVP Award despite a losing effort by his team. Can you name the*
> *only AL player to win a League Championship Series MVP in a*
> *losing effort?*

ANSWER: Fred Lynn

Lynn batted .611 (11-for-18) with five RBI for California, which lost to Milwaukee (three games to two games) in 1982. Scott was dominant in his 1986 NL Championship Series appearances, throwing a five-hit shutout in Game One and a three-hitter in Game Four for a 2-0 record, an 0.50 ERA, and 19 strikeouts versus the Mets. Leonard of the Giants hit .417 with a home run in four consecutive games—a League Championship Series record—versus the victorious Cardinals in 1987.

Game Three Question:

> *In Game Two of the 1969 AL Championship Series, Baltimore's*
> *Dave McNally pitched a masterful 11-inning shutout. Can you*
> *name the losing starting pitcher who matched McNally zero for zero*
> *until the bottom of the 11th frame?*

ANSWER: Dave Boswell

The Twins' Boswell threw 10 scoreless innings before running into some trouble in the 11th. After allowing two runners on, Boswell gave way to left-handed reliever Ron Perranoski with two out. Curt Motton, the Orioles' right-handed pinch-hitter, greeted Perranoski with a line drive single just over the glove of Twins second baseman Rod Carew, plating Powell with the winning run.

McNally, who struck out 11, earned the win, yielding just three hits and five walks. Boswell was charged with the tough loss, allowing seven hits and seven bases on balls. It remains arguably the best pitching duel in League Championship Series history, and one of the very best in post-season play. The Orioles went on to sweep the Twins the next day.

Game Four Question:

Can you name the winning pitcher in three of the following League Championship Series' deciding games? (Each won the game in relief):

A 1992 NL Championship Series
B 1984 NL Championship Series
C 1982 AL Championship Series
D 1980 NL Championship Series
E 1977 AL Championship Series
F 1976 AL Championship Series

ANSWER: A—Jeff Reardon of Atlanta won Game Seven in relief over Pittsburgh, B—San Diego's Craig Lefferts won Game Five in relief over Chicago, C—Bob McClure won Game Five in relief for Milwaukee over California, D—Dick Ruthven won Game Five in relief for Philadelphia versus Houston, E—Sparky Lyle won Gave Five in relief for New York versus Kansas City, F—Dick Tidrow won Gave Five in relief for New York versus Kansas City

Game Five Question (if necessary):

Can you name the only two players to win a pair of League Championship Series MVP Awards besides Orel Hershiser?

ANSWER: Steve Garvey and Dave Stewart

Steve Garvey duplicated his 1978 feat by hitting .400 with seven RBI in the 1984 NL Championship Series. Garvey added a dramatic flare to the series by unlocking a 5-5 tie with a game-winning two-run homer in the bottom of the ninth inning of Game Four, tying the series. Dave Stewart went 2-0 with a 1.13 ERA in 1990 versus Toronto for his first League Championship Series MVP trophy and 2-0 with a 2.03 ERA for Toronto versus Chicago in 1993 for his record third post-season MVP dating back to the 1989 World Series.

Game Six Question (if necessary):

On October 14, 1992, the Braves captured the hearts of millions as Francisco Cabrera's two-out, two-run single made Atlanta the first team in post-season history to erase a deficit and win the series on the final pitch of the game. Can you name the Pirates pitcher off whom Cabrera singled?

ANSWER: Stan Belinda

Belinda surrendered the pinch-hit, walk-off single that plated David Justice and Sid Bream for the dramatic 3-2 win. The Braves looked hopeless as they trailed 2-0 to open the inning. But a lead-of double, an error, and bad positioning made the comeback viable With Terry Pendleton on second base, Pittsburgh second bagger José Lind booted Justice's hard grounder for a first-and-third, no-out situation. Pirates starter Doug Drabek (0-3 in the series) followed by walking Bream to load the bases, prompting manager Jim Leyland's request for Belinda, also a righthander. After Gant's sacrifice fly pulled Atlanta within 2-1, the Braves reloaded the bases on a questionable ball four to Damon Berryhill. Brian Hunter followed by popping out to Lind for what should have been the third out and the pennant. But it was not meant to be.

Pinch-hitting for winner Jeff Reardon, the right-handed Cabrera (best known for his success against fire-baller Rob Dibble) lined a two-ball, one-strike breaking ball past shortstop Jay Bell to left field. That's where Barry Bonds fielded the sharp drive before throwing home, just a hair late in his attempt to nail Bream.

Testimony subsequently revealed that the Pirates suffered a breakdown as Cabrera stepped into the batter's box. The most disturbing for Pirate fans was Bonds' refusal to heed center fielder Andy Van Slyke's motion to play a bit more shallow against Cabrera. Because the play at the plate against the slow-afoot Bream couldn't possibly have been any closer, it stands to reason that Bonds' rejection of his center fielder's gesture cost the Pirates at the very least a chance to extend the game into extra innings. And the Pirates coaching can be blamed for not moving Bell closer to the hole between third and short, knowing Cabrera's quick-bat ability and Belinda's curveball intentions.

♦ Did you know Toronto became the second team in post-season history to erase a deficit and win a series all on the final pitch of the game, as Joe Carter erased a 6-5 deficit with a Game-Six-winning three-run homer off Philadelphia's Mitch Williams in the 1993 World Series? It marked just the second time in the history of the fall classic that a World Series ended on a home run, joining the 1960 series, which ended on Bill Mazeroski's homer to lead off the ninth. The Seattle Mariners became the third team to erase a deficit on the final pitch of a series in 1995. Trailing, 5-4, in the bottom of the 11th inning, Seattle had runners on the corners when Edgar Martinez lined a series-winning double off New York's Jack McDowell to win the inaugural AL Division Series. Ken Griffey, Jr. put on a running clinic as he scored from first, to cap perhaps the greatest post-season series ever.

♦ Did you know six of World Series history's 12 "walk-off" home runs have come over the past 13 years? The Yankees' Derek Jeter became the newest addition to this list by ending Game Four of the 2001 World Series with a blast off Arizona in the 10th inning.

In reverse order, Chad Curtis ended Game Three of the 1999 World Series against Atlanta. Toronto's Joe Carter ended the 1993 series with a Game Six shot. Minnesota's Kirby Puckett forced a Game Seven in 1991. Oakland's Mark McGwire ended Game Three of the 1988 classic, after Kirk Gibson had given the Dodgers a dramatic Game One triumph. Of course, in 1975, Boston's Carlton Fisk forced a Game Seven. The Yankees' Mickey Mantle brought to an end Game Three 11 years earlier. Bill Mazeroski dramatically gave the Pirates a Game Seven win in 1960. Eddie Mathews of the Braves ended Game Four of the 1957 World Series. The Giants' Dusty Rhodes disappointed the Indians in the opener of the 1954 series. The first to do so was the Yankees' Tommy Henrich in Game One of the 1949 classic.

Game Seven Question (if necessary):

Can you name the winning pitchers of the deciding games of three of the following League Championship Series?

A 1972 NL Championship Series
B 1972 AL Championship Series
C 1985 AL Championship Series
D 1987 NL Championship Series

ANSWER: A—Cincinnati's Clay Carroll won Game Five in relief, B—Oakland's Johnny (Blue Moon) Odom won Game Five, C—Kansas City's Charlie Leibrandt won Game Seven in relief, D—St. Louis' Danny Cox won Game Seven.

The losing teams were Pittsburgh, Detroit, Toronto, and San Francisco, respectively.

If you have won four League Championship Series Games, you advance to the World Series.

SECOND WORLD SERIES

Best-of-Seven World Series

The following questions are for managers who won four League Championship Series Games.

Game One Question:

Can you name the first two designated hitters (DH) in World Series play?

ANSWER: Dan Driessen and Lou Piniella

In 1976, Cincinnati's Dan Driessen and the Yankees' Lou Piniella represented their teams in the first designated-hitting World Series. From 1976 to 1985, a DH was used by both clubs in even years (1976, 1978, 1980, 1982, and 1984). From 1986 on, the DH has been used only in AL parks; the NL lineup has been used in NL parks.

Driessen, sometimes used as a first baseman, outfielder, or pinch-hitter during the regular season (54-for-219 at the plate) went 5-for-14 with a homer in the World Series. Piniella, officially the first DH to bat in the series, doubled in the second inning of Game One in Cincinnati. He went 1-for-4 in the series as a DH and 2-for-5 as a right fielder. The Yankees' other DH was Carlos May (0-for-7 as a DH and 0-for-2 as a pinch-hitter).

♦ Did you know Ron Blomberg's and Orlando Cepeda's bats are enshrined in the Hall of Fame as the first DHs in 1973's first AL game? Officially, Blomberg was the first-ever DH, because he batted first. The left-handed-hitting Yankee went 1-for-3 with an RBI in a loss to Boston. Cepeda went 0-for-6. On June 12, 1999, Glenallen Hill of the Giants became the first NL designated hitter, going 0-for-3 in the first interleague game.

Game Two Question:

Can you name the pitcher who won the World Series MVP in the award's first year?

ANSWER: Johnny Padres

Rebounding from a 9-10 regular season (3.95), the southpaw Padres hurled complete game victories in Game Three and Game Seven (a shutout) to hand the Brooklyn Dodgers the 1955 world championship. The 148-116 career pitcher totaled four career World Series wins in five decisions.

Game Three Question:

Everyone remembers Don Larsen's perfect game in the 1956 World Series. But do you know who took home the World Series MVP honors that year?

ANSWER: Don Larsen

Larsen himself earned the award despite an imperfect Game Two assignment, in which he lasted but 1⅔ innings during a 13-8 defeat. In that start, Larsen walked four batters, allowed one hit and was victimized by a second-inning error before giving way to Johnny Kucks. Because of Joe Collins' miscue at first base, all six Dodger runs that inning were ruled unearned. Lefthander Tommy Byrne relieved the ineffective Kucks and allowed a three-run homer to Duke Snider, capping the inning and tying the game at 6-6. So even with the wild outing in Game Two, Larsen's two-game total read 1-0, (0.00 ERA), 10⅔ innings, and one hit allowed. In case you're wondering, Gil Hodges had that singular hit, leading off the second inning with a single in Game Two.

Game Four Question:

Terry Pendleton, a member of the 1985 and 1987 NL champion Cardinals (as well as the 1991, 1992, and 1995 Braves) was a member of five losing World Series teams. Whom did he tie for playing in the most fall classics without winning?

ANSWER: Fred Merkle

Merkle played for the NL champion Giants from 1911 to 1913, the 1916 Dodgers, and 1918 Cubs (hitting .239 in the five series) without winning any of the five World Series. Harold "Pee Wee" Reese and Elston Howard share the record of being on six World Series losers regardless of championships won. Mickey Mantle, Carl Furillo, and Gil Hodges have each been on five World Series losers.

◆ Did you know in 1999, the Atlanta Braves lost their eighth straight World Series game to tie a dubious fall classic record for most consecutive losses? The Braves lost the last four games of the 1996 World Series to the Yankees and were swept by the same franchise three years later. The Phillies lost the last four games of the 1915 World Series and were swept in 1950. The Yankees lost the last three games of the 1921 World Series, were swept the following October, and dropped the opener of the 1923 fall classic—all to the Giants.

Game Five Question (if necessary):

Can you name the only player whose only career home run was hit in the World Series?

ANSWER: Mickey Lolich

Tigers pitcher and 1968 World Series MVP Lolich not only won three games, but the .110 career hitter (90-for-821) hit his only career home run off Nelson Briles of St. Louis in the third inning of Game Two. Lolich collected three hits in the series with two RBI (the other coming on a bases loaded walk). The Game Seven winner sported a 1.67 series ERA.

◆ Did you know Oakland pitcher Ken Holtzman homered and doubled three times in the 1973 and 1974 World Series after not batting at all during the regular seasons for those two years? Holtzman amassed his 10 total bases in just seven at-bats during those two series, for a .571 series batting average and a 1.429 series slugging mark.

Game Six Question (if necessary):

Can you name the only player in World Series history to start at three different positions in three consecutive games?

ANSWER: Joe Carter

Toronto's Carter started at first base in Game One of the 1992 World Series, started in left field in Game Two, and started in right field in Game Three. Tony Kubek and Willie McCovey are the only others to start at three different positions during a World Series. Kubek started at third base, left field, and center field during the 1957 World Series, and McCovey started at first base, right field, and left field during the 1962 series.

Game Seven Question (if necessary):

Match these October heroes with their World Series records:

1 Christy Mathewson
2 Lefty Gomez
3 Whitey Ford
4 Harry Brecheen

A his 6-0 career record is the best ever
B his 146 innings pitched is by far the most ever pitched
C his 0.83 career ERA is the best among those who have hurled at least 26 innings
D is the only pitcher to hurl four shutouts in fall classic play

ANSWER: 1—D, 2—A, 3—B, 4—C

Ford's 146 innings spanned a record 22 games (all starts) and 11 series from 1950 to 1964. Ford's 10 World Series victories and eight defeats are both records, as is his total of 94 strikeouts in fall classic play. John Smoltz, however, holds the overall post-season mark of 12 wins, surpassing the 10 put up by Ford and Dave Stewart. With a loss in Game Four of the 1999 World Series, Smoltz dropped to 12-4 lifetime in post-season play. The Yankees' El Duque Hernandez (9-2) was 8-0 in post-season play before suffering a World Series defeat in 2000. His brother Livan Hernandez is 5-0 in post-season play, tying Herb Pennock and Jack Coombs for the next best post-season marks, trailing only Gomez's 6-0 ledger. Of course, the marks of the Hernandez brothers includes the Division Series and the League Championship Series.

Brecheen also owns the second-lowest career World Series ERA, if the requirement is broadened to a minimum of 20 innings. Brecheen, the Cardinals' lefthander, appeared in three World Series and posted a minuscule ERA of 0.83 in 32⅔ innings over the 1943, 1944, and 1946 fall classics. The reliable hurler (132-92, with a 12-year ERA of 2.92) went 3-0 in the 1946 World Series against the Boston Red Sox.

♦ Did you know the Reds' righthander Jack Billingham has the lowest lifetime World Series ERA of 0.36 in 25⅓ innings? The right-handed Billingham played with five teams in his 13-year career, almost half of which were with Cincinnati. Billingham's only earned run came in his nine-inning stint against Boston in 1975. Against Oakland in 1972 (13⅔ innings) and the Yankees (two innings) in 1976, the 145-113 career pitcher didn't allow a run. Ironically, Billingham's League Championship Series ERA is 4.32.

♦ Did you know the Yankees' Mariano Rivera owns the lowest career post-season ERA, with a mark of 0.91? New York's smooth closer has allowed only eight earned runs in 79 post-season innings. Right behind Rivera are Sandy Koufax (0.95), Christy Mathewson (1.15), and Eddie Plank (1.32).

Allow me to congratulate you on your world championship,
if you answered four questions correctly!

Your two-year contract is over. The team must decide your future. The club will grant you a contract extension if you won (1) a pennant or world championship, or (2) two division titles, or (3) 170 regular-season games.

Try managing again to test your learning abilities!

Sign here _____

Barnstorming Tour

In the olden days when players sought means to supplement their income, they traveled on planned barnstorming tours with a group of fellow major leaguers and played exhibition baseball in warm spots throughout the country. With the conclusion of this book's second—and last—season, I invite you to attend a barnstorming tour of your own. Here are a few more Did You Know? tidbits to enlighten and keep you entertained until the next seasons' are ready. Enjoy!

♦ Did you know Major League Baseball celebrated its 125th year anniversary in 1994, even though that year was only its 118th year? According to Major League Baseball's public relations office, the anniversary was technically the 125th year of professional baseball since the Cincinnati Red Stockings (the first professional team, which later joined the National League in its inaugural 1876 season) began playing in 1869.

♦ Did you know the Colorado Rockies lost all 13 games they played versus the Atlanta Braves in 1993, becoming the only NL team in the 20th century to be swept of a full season series during an uninterrupted campaign? Although it was an aborted season, the Expos swept the Padres of their scheduled 12-game season series in 1994. The feat occurred on five occasions in the American League in the 20th century: Baltimore swept Kansas City (12 games) in 1970, Baltimore swept Oakland (11 games) in 1978, Kansas City swept Baltimore (12 games) in 1988, Oakland swept New York (12 games) in 1990, and Cleveland swept Detroit (12 games) in 1996. And there were five season sweeps in the 19th century. Although they did it in shortened seasons, the Cleveland Indians became the first team to sweep another for two consecutive years when they beat the Oakland Athletics six times in 1994 and seven times in 1995. A combined four series were wiped away by the strike.

◆ Did you know Frank Thomas is the only player in major league history to hit .300 or better with at least 20 home runs, 100 RBI, 100 runs scored, and 100 walks in each of his first seven full seasons? Thomas, who came up to bat just 191 times in 1990, was very impressive during that stretch. From 1991 to 1997, Thomas averaged .330 with 36 homers, 118 RBI, 107 runs scored, and 119 walks. Ted Williams accomplished the feat six years in a row, but with three years in between spent in the military. Williams did it in 1941, 1942 (and after fighting in World War II from 1943 to 45), 1946, 1947, 1948, and 1949. Lou Gehrig met those demands for four years in succession on two occasions, from 1929 to 1932 and from 1934 to 1937.

◆ Did you know in 2001, Jeff Bagwell became the first player in history with at least 30 home runs, 100 RBI, 100 runs, and 100 walks in six consecutive seasons? From 1996 to 2001, the consistent Bagwell averaged 39 home runs, 126 RBI, 127 runs, and 122 walks.

◆ Did you know the Cubs opened the 1994 season with a 20th-century NL record of 12 consecutive home losses, falling five short of the major league record set by the 1913 Yankees?

◆ Did you know the only time Major League Baseball used replacement players came about on May 18, 1912, when the Tigers club went on a one-game strike to protest AL President Ban Johnson's indefinite suspension of Ty Cobb for hitting a fan? Tired of the fan's brutal heckling, Cobb went into the stands on May 15, punched Claude Lueker at least a dozen times, according to certain accounts, and even spiked him. Cobb didn't realize Lueker was handicapped, sans hands, until it was pointed out to him. At which point, witnesses quoted Cobb as saying, "I don't care if he has no feet."

To avoid a forfeit and fine, Detroit manager Hugh Jennings recruited local college players (they were in Philadelphia) to play for the Tigers, who were lambasted, 24-2, by the Athletics. A fellow by the name of Al Travers gave up all 24 runs on 26 hits, walking seven. When Johnson reduced Cobb's suspension to 10 games, the original Tigers returned.

◆ Did you know baseball trivia helped Americans during World War II? According to Warren Spahn, Americans used baseball trivia questions to distinguish Americans from Germans who were disguised as Americans during the battle of the Bulge. Trivia questions such as "Who's the second baseman for the Bums?" were used for passwords. The courageous Spahn was a World War II hero and Battle of the Bulge combatant, earning a Purple Heart, three battle stars, and a citation for bravery. Spahn told me of his experiences and memories of World War II, during which he was wounded.

Acknowledgments

I owe an immense debt of gratitude to many organizations that patiently supplied answers to my endless (and sometimes irritating) questions. Three groups, in particular, stand out in responding with zest and quality to my drive for rich detail. I don't know where I'd be as a baseball researcher without the Society for American Baseball Research, a wonderful organization for baseball history enthusiasts like myself. Many special thanks to Mark Alvarez, Frederick Ivor-Campbell, Lyle Spatz, David Vincent, and John Zajc from that venerable brotherhood of baseball historians. The information I obtained from the National Baseball Hall of Fame was as invaluable as Jeff Idelson is to that shrine. Idelson proved time and time again why he is the single most helpful executive/spokesperson in the sports information business. Thanks, Jeff. The Major League Baseball's Media Relations Department (especially Dominick Balsamo, Matt Gould, Richard Levin, and Blakely Ricco) supported my efforts throughout and supplied help in many areas.

The following sources were also helpful: all 30 Major League Baseball teams, many major league players, the Office of the Commissioner, the Major League Baseball Players Association, Negro League Hall of Fame, Dan Latham, Michael Westbay, Vera Clemente, Josh Gibson, Jr., John Dowd, Jack Lang, Elias Sports Bureau, "The Sporting News," "SportsTicker," Baseball Weekly, Little League Baseball, Bill Deane, David Smith, ESPN, Chuck Brodsky, Justine Warren, Sue Lukasik, Jerome Holtzman, Frank Russo, Paul Lanning, Glenn Argenbright, and John Reyes.

I thank the esteemed Chris Bernucca, whose advice and ample writing skills over the years have given me a platform from which I can aspire. Chris, I still hear you when I write or edit. I would be remiss if I didn't mention Joe Carnecelli, John Mastro, Chris Mattia,

Felix Modestin, Anthony Mormile, John Palmeri, John Pezzullo, Joe Rizzo, and Daren Smith as well. To my colleague Neil Scott, I thank you (and Anna) for everything.

No appreciation would be complete without thanking all of my close-knit family. Nobody believed in me and instilled confidence in me as did my cousin Suzie, who easily garners my Most Valuable Person award. She stands out in her support of my endeavors. Suzie, thanks from the bottom of my heart. And I'll always cherish the baseball memories that I share with my wonderful wealth of uncles and score of cousins (especially Jimmy, Tom, and Ray).

Bibliography

Aaron, Hank, and Lonnie Wheeler. *I Had a Hammer*. New York: HarperCollins, 1991.

Allen, Lee, and Tom Meany. *King of the Diamonds*. New York: G. P. Putnam's Sons, 1965.

The Baseball Encyclopedia. New York: Macmillan, 1969, 1993.

Baseball's First Stars. Cleveland: Society for American Baseball Research, 1996.

Baseball Research Journal. Cooperstown, N.Y.: Society for American Baseball Research, 1985.

Baseball Research Journal. Cleveland: Society for American Baseball Research, 1991–2001.

Bouton, Jim. *Ball Four*. New York: World Publishing, 1970.

Charlton, James. *The Baseball Chronology*. New York: Macmillan, 1991.

Cohen, Richard, and David Neft. *The World Series*. New York: St. Martin's, 1976, 1990.

Epstein, Eddie, and Rob Neyer. *Baseball Dynasties*. New York: W. W. Norton, 2000.

Fleming, G. H. *The Unforgettable Season*. New York: Simon & Schuster, 1981.

Giamatti, Bart. *A Great and Glorious Game: Baseball Writings of A. Bartlett Giamatti*. Chapel Hill: Algonquin Books of Chapel Hill, 1998.

Hageman, William. *Honus: The Life and Times of a Baseball Hero*. Champaign, Ill.: Sagamore, 1996.

Hill, Art. *I Don't Care If I Never Come Back*. New York: Simon & Schuster, 1980.

Honig, Donald, and Lawrence Ritter. *The 100 Greatest Baseball Players of All Time*. New York: Crown, 1981.

James, Bill. *The Bill James' Historical Baseball Abstract*. New York: Villard Books, 1986.

Kahn, Roger, and Pete Rose. *Pete Rose: My Way*. New York: Macmillan, 1989.

Kaplan, Jim. *Lefty Grove: American Original*. Cleveland: Society for American Baseball Research, 2000.

Kavanagh, Jack. *Walter Johnson: A Life*. South Bend, Ind.: Diamond Communications, 1996.

Kavanagh, Jack, and Norman Macht. *Uncle Robbie*. Cleveland: Society for American Baseball Research, 1999.

Lansche, Jerry. *Stan The Man Musial*. Dallas: Taylor Publishing, 1994.

Linn, Ed, and Bill Veeck. *Veeck—as in Wreck*. New York: G. P. Putnam's Sons, 1962.

Longert, Scott. *Addie Joss: King of the Pitchers*. Cleveland: Society for American Baseball Research, 1998.

Markusen, Bruce. *Roberto Clemente: The Great One*. Champaign, Ill.: Sports Publishing, 1998.

The National Pastime. Cleveland: Society for American Baseball Research, 1984, 1988, 1990, 1992, 1995–99.

Nikkan Sports. September 25, 2001, p. 2.

Palacios, Oscar. *Diamond Diagrams*. Skokie, Ill.: STATS Publishing, 1997.

Riley, James. *The Biographical Encyclopedia of the Negro Leagues*. New York: Carroll & Graf, 1994.

Robinson, Ray. *Iron Horse*. New York: Harper Perennial, 1990.

Roy Firestone's Up Close. ESPN, 1993.

The Sporting News Complete Baseball Record Book. St. Louis: Times Mirror Magazine, 2000.

Sports Illustrated. Frank Deford, July 1981.

Stump, Al. *Cobb*. Chapel Hill: Algonquin Books of Chapel Hill, 1994.

Thompson, Joe. *Growing Up with "Shoeless" Joe*. Virginia: JTI Publishing, 1997.

Total Baseball. New York: Total Sports, 1988, 1999.

About the Author

Mike Attiyeh, an active member of the Society for American Baseball Research, is a published baseball historian whose works have appeared in such publications as *Baseball Digest, Pirate Report,* and *Birch Brook Press* and on numerous web sites. Attiyeh, who has appeared as an expert guest analyst on sports radio talk shows throughout the United States, is best known nationally for breaking the story of Tony Gwynn's blood clot in 1997.

In 1999, Attiyeh provided the majority of the content for "This Day in Baseball History," a segment in the Oakland Athletics' official pre-game radio show. He has interviewed and written about a score of athletes, and was a semi-finalist in the 1998 National Trivia Contest, held by the Society for American Baseball Research. He attended Piscataway High School and Rutgers University.

A former sports news director for *Today's* "Sports" and "Sports Extra," and a former editor for ESPN's "SportsTicker," Attiyeh currently lives in Elk Grove, California. He plans to devote his future to writing about baseball.